Big Data Analytics in Bioinformatics and Healthcare

Baoying Wang
Waynesburg University, USA

Ruowang Li
Pennsylvania State University, USA

William Perrizo
North Dakota State University, USA

A volume in the Advances in Bioinformatics and
Biomedical Engineering (ABBE) Book Series

Medical Information Science
RᴇFERENCE
An Imprint of IGI Global

Managing Director:	Lindsay Johnston
Managing Editor:	Austin DeMarco
Director of Intellectual Property & Contracts:	Jan Travers
Acquisitions Editor:	Kayla Wolfe
Production Editor:	Christina Henning
Development Editor:	Erin O'Dea
Typesetter:	Cody Page
Cover Design:	Jason Mull

Published in the United States of America by
Medical Information Science Reference (an imprint of IGI Global)
701 E. Chocolate Avenue
Hershey PA, USA 17033
Tel: 717-533-8845
Fax: 717-533-8661
E-mail: cust@igi-global.com
Web site: http://www.igi-global.com

Library of Congress Cataloging-in-Publication Data

Big data analytics in bioinformatics and healthcare / Baoying Wang, Ruowang Li, and William Perrizo, editors.
    p. ; cm.
  Includes bibliographical references and index.
  Summary: "This book merges the fields of biology, technology, and medicine in order to present a comprehensive study on the emerging information processing applications necessary in the field of electronic medical record management"--Provided by publisher.
  ISBN 978-1-4666-6611-5 (hardcover) -- ISBN 978-1-4666-6612-2 (ebook) -- ISBN 978-1-4666-6614-6 (print & perpetual access)
  I. Wang, Baoying, 1964- , editor. II. Li, Ruowang, 1988- , editor. III. Perrizo, W. (William), editor.
  [DNLM: 1. Computational Biology--methods. 2. Biomedical Research--methods. 3. Data Mining--methods. 4. Electronic Health Records. QU 26.5]
  R858
  610.285--dc23
                          2014032346

This book is published in the IGI Global book series Advances in Bioinformatics and Biomedical Engineering (ABBE) (ISSN: 2327-7033; eISSN: 2327-7041)

British Cataloguing in Publication Data
A Cataloguing in Publication record for this book is available from the British Library.

All work contributed to this book is new, previously-unpublished material. The views expressed in this book are those of the authors, but not necessarily of the publisher.

For electronic access to this publication, please contact: eresources@igi-global.com.

Advances in Bioinformatics and Biomedical Engineering (ABBE) Book Series

Ahmad Taher Azar
Benha University, Egypt

ISSN: 2327-7033
EISSN: 2327-7041

Mission

The fields of biology and medicine are constantly changing as research evolves and novel engineering applications and methods of data analysis are developed. Continued research in the areas of bioinformatics and biomedical engineering is essential to continuing to advance the available knowledge and tools available to medical and healthcare professionals.

The **Advances in Bioinformatics and Biomedical Engineering (ABBE) Book Series** publishes research on all areas of bioinformatics and bioengineering including the development and testing of new computational methods, the management and analysis of biological data, and the implementation of novel engineering applications in all areas of medicine and biology. Through showcasing the latest in bioinformatics and biomedical engineering research, ABBE aims to be an essential resource for healthcare and medical professionals.

Coverage

- Rehabilitation Engineering
- Genetics
- DNA Sequencing
- Biomechanical Engineering
- Structural Biology
- Gene Regulation
- Computational Biology
- Orthopedic Bioengineering
- Protein Engineering
- Health Monitoring Systems

IGI Global is currently accepting manuscripts for publication within this series. To submit a proposal for a volume in this series, please contact our Acquisition Editors at Acquisitions@igi-global.com or visit: http://www.igi-global.com/publish/.

Titles in this Series

For a list of additional titles in this series, please visit: www.igi-global.com

Emerging Theory and Practice in Neuroprosthetics
Ganesh R. Naik (University of Technology Sydney (UTS), Australia) and Yina Guo (Taiyuan University of Science and Technology, China)
Medical Information Science Reference • copyright 2014 • 377pp • H/C (ISBN: 9781466660946) • US $265.00 (our price)

Technological Advancements in Biomedicine for Healthcare Applications
Jinglong Wu (Okayama University, Japan)
Medical Information Science Reference • copyright 2013 • 382pp • H/C (ISBN: 9781466621961) • US $245.00 (our price)

Biomedical Engineering and Cognitive Neuroscience for Healthcare Interdisciplinary Applications
Jinglong Wu (Okayama University, Japan)
Medical Information Science Reference • copyright 2013 • 472pp • H/C (ISBN: 9781466621138) • US $245.00 (our price)

Pharmacoinformatics and Drug Discovery Technologies Theories and Applications
Tagelsir Mohamed Gasmelseid (King Faisal University, Kingdom of Saudi Arabia)
Medical Information Science Reference • copyright 2012 • 442pp • H/C (ISBN: 9781466603097) • US $245.00 (our price)

Machine Learning in Computer-Aided Diagnosis Medical Imaging Intelligence and Analysis
Kenji Suzuki (University of Chicago, USA)
Medical Information Science Reference • copyright 2012 • 524pp • H/C (ISBN: 9781466600591) • US $245.00 (our price)

Systemic Approaches in Bioinformatics and Computational Systems Biology Recent Advances
Paola Lecca (The Microsoft Research – University of Trento, Centre for Computational and Systems Biology, Italy) Dan Tulpan (National Research Council of Canada, Canada) and Kanagasabai Rajaraman (Institute for Infocomm Research, Singapore)
Medical Information Science Reference • copyright 2012 • 471pp • H/C (ISBN: 9781613504352) • US $265.00 (our price)

Intravascular Imaging Current Applications and Research Developments
Vasilios D. Tsakanikas (University of Ioannina, Greece) Lampros K. Michalis (University of Ioannina, Greece) Dimitrios I. Fotiadis (University of Ioannina, Greece) Katerina K. Naka (University of Ioannina, Greece, and Michaelideion Cardiology Center, Greece) and Christos V. Bourantas (University of Ioannina, Greece)
Medical Information Science Reference • copyright 2012 • 478pp • H/C (ISBN: 9781613500958) • US $245.00 (our price)

IGI GLOBAL
DISSEMINATOR OF KNOWLEDGE
www.igi-global.com

701 E. Chocolate Ave., Hershey, PA 17033
Order online at www.igi-global.com or call 717-533-8845 x100
To place a standing order for titles released in this series, contact: cust@igi-global.com
Mon-Fri 8:00 am - 5:00 pm (est) or fax 24 hours a day 717-533-8661

Table of Contents

Section 1
Big Data Analysis Methods and Applications

Chapter 1

Yan Guo, Vanderbilt University, USA
Shilin Zhao, Vanderbilt University, USA
Margot Bjoring, Vanderbilt University, USA
Leng Han, MD Anderson Cancer Center, USA

Chapter 2

Boya Xie, East Carolina University, USA
Qin Ding, East Carolina University, USA
Di Wu, Drexel University, USA

Chapter 3

Zhecheng Zhu, National Healthcare Group, Singapore
Heng Bee Hoon, National Healthcare Group, Singapore
Kiok-Liang Teow, National Healthcare Group, Singapore

Chapter 4

Anamika Basu, Gurudas College, India
Anasua Sarkar, SMIEEE Government College of Engineering and Leather Technology,
India

Section 2
Reviews and Perspectives on Big Data Analysis

Detailed Table of Contents

Section 1
Big Data Analysis Methods and Applications

Chapter 1

Yan Guo, Vanderbilt University, USA
Shilin Zhao, Vanderbilt University, USA
Margot Bjoring, Vanderbilt University, USA
Leng Han, MD Anderson Cancer Center, USA

In recent years, RNA sequencing (RNAseq) technology has experienced a rapid rise in popularity. Often seen as a competitor of and the ultimate successor to microarray technology given its more accurate and quantitative gene expression measurement, RNAseq also offers a wealth of additional information that is often overlooked, and given the massive accumulation of RNAseq data available in public data repositories over the past few years, these data are ripe for discovery. Abundant opportunities exist for researchers to conduct in-depth, non-traditional analyses that take advantage of these secondary uses and for bioinformaticians to develop tools to make these data more accessible. This is discussed in this chapter.

Chapter 2

Boya Xie, East Carolina University, USA
Qin Ding, East Carolina University, USA
Di Wu, Drexel University, USA

Driven by the rapidly advancing techniques and increasing interests in biology and medicine, about 2,000 to 4,000 references are added daily to MEDLINE, the US national biomedical bibliographic database. Even for a specific research topic, extracting useful and comprehensive information out of the huge literature data pool is challenging. Text mining techniques become extremely useful when dealing with the abundant biomedical information and they have been applied to various areas in the realm of biomedical research. Instead of providing a brief overview of all text mining techniques and every major biomedical text mining application, this chapter explores in-depth the microRNA profiling area and related text mining tools. As an illustrative example, one rule-based text mining system developed by the authors is discussed in detail. This chapter also includes the discussion of the challenges and potential research areas in biomedical text mining.

Data visualization techniques are widely applied in all kinds of organizations, turning tables of numbers into visualizations for discovery, information communication, and knowledge sharing. Data visualization solutions can be found everywhere in healthcare systems from hospital operations monitoring and patient profiling to demand projection and capacity planning. In this chapter, interactive data visualization techniques are discussed and their applications to various aspects of healthcare systems are explored. Compared to static data visualization techniques, interactive ones allow users to explore the data and find the insights themselves. Four case studies are given to illustrate how interactive data visualization techniques are applied in healthcare: summary and overview, information selection and filtering, patient flow visualization, and geographical and longitudinal analyses. These case studies show that interactive data visualization techniques expand the boundary of data visualization as a pure presentation tool and bring certain analytical capability to support better healthcare decision making.

The inference of gene networks from gene expression data is known as "reverse engineering." Elucidating genetic networks from high-throughput microarray data in seed maturation and embryo formation in plants is crucial for storage and production of cereals for human beings. Delayed seed maturation and abnormal embryo formation during storage of cereal crops degrade the quality and quantity of food grains. In this chapter, the authors perform comparative gene analysis of results of different microarray experiments in different stages of embryogenesis in Arabidopsis thaliana, and to reconstruct Gene Networks (GNs) related to various stages of plant seed maturation using reverse engineering technique. They also biologically validate the results for developing embryogenesis network on Arabidopsis thaliana with GO and pathway enrichment analysis. The biological analysis shows that different genes are over-expressed during embryogenesis related with several KEGG metabolic pathways. The large-scale microarray datasets of Arabidopsis thaliana for these genes involved in embryogenesis have been analysed in seed biology. The chapter also reveals new insight into the gene functional modules obtained from the Arabidopsis gene correlation networks in this dataset.

Chapter 5

    Marjan Trutschl, Louisiana State University – Shreveport, USA & Louisiana State University Health – Shreveport, USA

    Phillip C. S. R. Kilgore, Louisiana State University – Shreveport, USA

    Rona S. Scott, Louisiana State University Health – Shreveport, USA

    Christine E. Birdwell, Louisiana State University Health – Shreveport, USA

    Urška Cvek, Louisiana State University – Shreveport, USA & Louisiana State University Health – Shreveport, USA

Biological sequence motifs are short nucleotide or amino acid sequences that are biologically significant and are attractive to scientists because they are usually highly conserved and result in structural and regulatory implications. In this chapter, the authors show practical applications of these data, followed by a review of the algorithms, techniques, and tools. They address the nature of motifs and elucidate on several methods for de novo motif discovery, covering the algorithms based on Gibbs sampling, expectation maximization, Bayesian inference, covariance models, and discriminative learning. The authors present the tools and their requirements to weigh their individual benefits and challenges. Since interpretation of a large set of results can pose significant challenges, they discuss several methods for handling data that span from visualization to integration into pipelines and curated databases. Additionally, the authors show practical applications of these data with examples.

Chapter 6

    Paulo Fazendeiro, Instituto de Telecomunicações (IT), Portugal

    José Valente de Oliveira, University of Algarve, Portugal

Microarray generated gene expression data are characterized by their volume and by the intrinsic background noise. The main task of revealing patterns in gene expression data is typically carried out using clustering analysis, with soft clustering leading the more promising candidate methods. In this chapter, Fuzzy C-Means with a variable Focal Point (FCMFP) is exploited as the first stage in gene expression data analysis. FCMFP is inspired by the observation that the visual perception of a group of similar objects is (highly) dependent on the observer position. This metaphor is used to provide a new analysis insight, with different levels of granularity, over a gene expression dataset.

Chapter 7

    Y-H. Taguchi, Chuo University, Japan

    Mitsuo Iwadate, Chuo University, Japan

    Hideaki Umeyama, Chuo University, Japan

    Yoshiki Murakami, Osaka City University, Japan

    Akira Okamoto, Aichi University of Education, Japan

Feature Extraction (FE) is a difficult task when the number of features is much larger than the number of samples, although that is a typical situation when biological (big) data is analyzed. This is especially true when FE is stable, independent of the samples considered (stable FE), and is often required. However, the stability of FE has not been considered seriously. In this chapter, the authors demonstrate that Principal

Component Analysis (PCA)-based unsupervised FE functions as stable FE. Three bioinformatics applications of PCA-based unsupervised FE—detection of aberrant DNA methylation associated with diseases, biomarker identification using circulating microRNA, and proteomic analysis of bacterial culturing processes—are discussed.

Section 2
Reviews and Perspectives on Big Data Analysis

Chapter 8

Issam El Naqa, McGill University, Canada

More than half of cancer patients receive ionizing radiation as part of their treatment and it is the main modality at advanced stages of disease. Treatment outcomes in radiotherapy are determined by complex interactions between cancer genetics, treatment regimens, and patient-related variables. A typical radiotherapy treatment scenario can generate a large pool of data, "Big data," that is comprised of patient demographics, dosimetry, imaging features, and biological markers. Radiotherapy data constitutes a unique interface between physical and biological data interactions. In this chapter, the authors review recent advances and discuss current challenges to interrogate big data in radiotherapy using top-bottom and bottom-top approaches. They describe the specific nature of big data in radiotherapy and discuss issues related to bioinformatics tools for data aggregation, sharing, and confidentiality. The authors also highlight the potential opportunities in this field for big data research from bioinformaticians as well as clinical decision-makers' perspectives.

Chapter 9

Philip Groth, Bayer Pharma AG, Germany
Gerhard Reuter, Bayer Business Services GmbH, Germany
Sebastian Thieme, Humboldt-University of Berlin, Germany

A new trend for data analysis in the life sciences is Cloud computing, enabling the analysis of large datasets in short time. This chapter introduces Big Data challenges in the genomic era and how Cloud computing can be one feasible approach for solving them. Technical and security issues are discussed and a case study where Clouds are successfully applied to resolve computational bottlenecks in the analysis of genomic data is presented. It is an intentional outcome of this chapter that Cloud computing is not essential for analyzing Big Data. Rather, it is argued that for the optimized utilization of IT, it is required to choose the best architecture for each use case, either by security requirements, financial goals, optimized runtime through parallelization, or the ability for easier collaboration and data sharing with business partners on shared resources.

Chapter 10

Ravi Mathur, North Carolina State University, USA
Alison Motsinger-Reif, North Carolina State University, USA

As the scale of genetic, genomic, metabolomics, and proteomic data increases with advancing technology, new approaches leveraging domain expert knowledge, and other sources of functional annotation have been developed to aid in the analysis and interpretation of such data. Pathway and network analysis approaches have become popular in association analysis – connecting genetic markers or measures of gene product with phenotypes or diseases of interest. These approaches aim to leverage big data to better understand the complex etiologies of these traits. Findings from such analyses can help reveal interesting biological traits and/or help identify potential biomarkers of disease. In the current chapter, the authors review broad categories of pathway analyses and review advantages and disadvantages of each. They discuss both the analytical methods to detect phenotype-associated pathways and review the key resources in the field of human genetics that are available to investigators wanting to perform such analyses.

Chapter 11

    Amandeep Kaur Kahlon, CSIR-Central Institute of Medicinal and Aromatic Plants (CIMAP), India
    Ashok Sharma, CSIR-Central Institute of Medicinal and Aromatic Plants (CIMAP), India

The major concern in this chapter is to understand the need of system biology in prediction models in studying tuberculosis infection in the big data era. The overall complexity of biological phenomenon, such as biochemical, biophysical, and other molecular processes, within pathogen as well as their interaction with host is studied through system biology approaches. First, consideration is given to the necessity of prediction models integrating system biology approaches and later on for their replacement and refinement using high throughput data. Various ongoing projects, consortium, databases, and research groups involved in tuberculosis eradication are also discussed. This chapter provides a brief account of TB predictive models and their importance in system biology to study tuberculosis and host-pathogen interactions. This chapter also addresses big data resources and applications, data management, limitations, challenges, solutions, and future directions.

Chapter 12

    Ratna Prabha, Indian Council of Agricultural Research, India
    Anil Rai, Indian Council of Agricultural Research, India
    D. P. Singh, Indian Council of Agricultural Research, India

With the advent of sophisticated and high-end molecular biological technologies, microbial research has observed tremendous boom. It has now become one of the most prominent sources for the generation of "big data." This is made possible due to huge data coming from the experimental platforms like whole genome sequencing projects, microarray technologies, mapping of Single Nucleotide Polymorphisms (SNP), proteomics, metabolomics, and phenomics programs. For analysis, interpretation, comparison, storage, archival, and utilization of this wealth of information, bioinformatics has emerged as a massive platform to solve the problems of data management in microbial research. In present chapter, the authors present an account of "big data" resources spread across the microbial domain of research, the efforts that are being made to generate "big data," computational resources facilitating analysis and interpretation, and future needs for huge biological data storage, interpretation, and management.

Chapter 13

Kristel Van Steen, University of Liége, Belgium & University of Liege, Belgium
Nuria Malats, Spanish National Cancer Research Centre (CNIO), Spain

The identification of causal or predictive variants/genes/mechanisms for disease-associated traits is characterized by "complex" networks of molecular phenotypes. Present technology and computer power allow building and processing large collections of these data types. However, the super-rapid data generation is counterweighted by a slow-pace for data integration methods development. Most currently available integrative analytic tools pertain to pairing omics data and focus on between-data source relationships, making strong assumptions about within-data source architectures. A limited number of initiatives exist aiming to find the most optimal ways to analyze multiple, possibly related, omics databases, and fully acknowledge the specific characteristics of each data type. A thorough understanding of the underlying assumptions of integrative methods is needed to draw sound conclusions afterwards. In this chapter, the authors discuss how the field of "integromics" has evolved and give pointers towards essential research developments in this context.

Chapter 14

Jami Jackson, North Carolina State University, USA
Alison Motsinger-Reif, North Carolina State University, USA

Rapid progress in genotyping technologies, including the scaling up of assay technologies to genome-wide levels and next generation sequencing, has motivated a burst in methods development and application to detect genotype-phenotype associations in a wide array of diseases and other phenotypes. In this chapter, the authors review the study design and genotyping options that are used in association mapping, along with the appropriate methods to perform mapping within these study designs. The authors discuss both candidate gene and genome-wide studies, focused on DNA level variation. Quality control, genotyping technologies, and single-SNP and multiple-SNP analyses have facilitated the successes in identifying numerous loci influence disease risk. However, variants identified have generally explained only a small fraction of the heritable component of disease risk. The authors discuss emerging trends and future directions in performing analysis for rare variants to detect these variants that predict these traits with more complex etiologies.

Chapter 15

Hans Binder, University of Leipzig, Germany
Lydia Hopp, University of Leipzig, Germany
Kathrin Lembcke, University of Leipzig, Germany
Henry Wirth, University of Leipzig, Germany

Application of new high-throughput technologies in molecular medicine collects massive data for hundreds to thousands of persons in large cohort studies by characterizing the phenotype of each individual on a personalized basis. The chapter aims at increasing our understanding of disease genesis and progression and to improve diagnosis and treatment. New methods are needed to handle such "big data." Machine learning enables one to recognize and to visualize complex data patterns and to make decisions potentially relevant for diagnosis and treatment. The authors address these tasks by applying the method of self-organizing maps and present worked examples from different disease entities of the colon ranging from inflammation to cancer.

Section 3
Issues and Concerns in the Big Data Era

Chapter 16
    Matthew K. Knabel, Fernandez & Associates, LLP, USA
    Katherine Doering, Fernandez & Associates, LLP, USA & JD Candidate, University of
        Nebraska, USA
    Dennis S. Fernandez, Fernandez & Associates, LLP, USA

Since the completion of the Human Genome Project, biologists have shifted their efforts from understanding biology to modifying it. Synthetic biology is a rapidly growing interdisciplinary field that includes developing and manufacturing synthetic nucleotide sequences, systems, genomes, and medical devices. Gaining patent protection represents an imperative and significant tool for business development in synthetic biology. Without IP protection, investors most likely will not commit necessary resources for progress. While there have been many important breakthroughs in biotechnology, recent case law rulings and legislative statutes have created obstacles for inventors to gain patent protection of novel synthetic biology inventions. These issues cause hesitation in license agreements and postpone creation of synthetic biology start-up companies. Nevertheless, inventors still can gain patent protection in many branches of synthetic biology. This chapter examines the issues, controversies, and problems associated with patent protection in synthetic biology. It then gives solutions, recommendations, and future directions for the field.

Chapter 17
    Jane Moon, University of Melbourne, Australia
    Mary P. Galea, University of Melbourne, Australia
    Megan Bohensky, Royal Melbourne Hospital, Australia

Clinical data linkage amongst patients with Spinal Cord Injury (SCI) is a challenge, as the Australian Health System is fragmented and there is lack of coordination between multiple data custodians at the state and federal levels, private and public hospitals, and acute and allied health sectors. This is particularly problematic in chronic conditions such as SCI, where multiple data custodians collect data on patients over long periods of time. The author presents findings based on interviews with a range of data custodians for SCI categorized as clinical, statutory, and financial data custodians. It is found that data are kept in different silos, which are not coordinated, hence duplication exists and patient information that exists on many different databases is inconsistently updated. This chapter describes the importance of Clinical Data Linkage for healthcare in predicting disease trajectories for SCI and discusses how administrative and clinical data are collected and stored and some of the challenges in linking these datasets.

Andrea Darrel, University of Southern Queensland, Australia
Margee Hume, University of Southern Queensland, Australia
Timothy Hardie, Lakehead University, Canada
Jeffery Soar, University of Southern Queensland, Australia

The benefits of big data analytics in the healthcare sector are assumed to be substantial, and early proponents have been very enthusiastic (Chen, Chiang, & Storey, 2012), but little research has been carried out to confirm just what those benefits are, and to whom they accrue (Bollier, 2010). This chapter presents an overview of existing literature that demonstrates quantifiable, measurable benefits of big data analytics, confirmed by researchers across a variety of healthcare disciplines. The chapter examines aspects of clinical operations in healthcare including Cost Effectiveness Research (CER), Clinical Decision Support Systems (CDS), Remote Patient Monitoring (RPM), Personalized Medicine (PM), as well as several public health initiatives. This examination is in the context of searching for the benefits described resulting from the deployment of big data analytics. Results indicate the principle benefits are delivered in terms of improved outcomes for patients and lower costs for healthcare providers.

Preface

Mining biological, biomedical, and health data is an emerging area at the intersection between biology and data mining. There has been an exponential increase of data generation in the last 10 years due to the maturation of sequencing technology and other technologies in bioinformatics and healthcare informatics. It is no coincidence that this revolution has coincided with the completion of the Human Genome Project, but other technological breakthroughs and advances have been critical as well. The bioinformatics fields are in an important stage of new breakthroughs on dealing with dramatically increased information in terms of number, size, and complexity. A new term, "Big Data," is used to refer to such large, and often diverse, complex, longitudinal, and/or distributed data sets. Big data is usually too large and complex to be processed using traditional data processing applications. It is not so much that the data cannot be processed using traditional tools but that it cannot be processed in reasonable time without new and much faster processing tools. There is and will continue to be much research in this area. As Dr. Shah (2012) stated, "Data-centric approaches that compute on massive amounts of data (often called "Big Data") to discover patterns and to make clinically relevant predictions will gain adoption. Research that bridges the latest multimodal measurement technologies with large amounts of electronic healthcare data is increasing; and is where new breakthroughs will occur."

The biological and biomedical research fields are at a revolutionary stage with the use of large, diverse, distributed, and heterogeneous data sets. These "big data" repositories will lead to critical data-intensive decision making and decision support, including biological prediction and clinical decision making and decision support, at a level never before seen. This book can be used as a research reference or handbook offering novel methods for analyzing large-scale data sets. We wish to provide inter-disciplinary research resources in data mining and bioinformatics in this fast-growing area.

In the near future, even higher throughput technologies will only exacerbate the data overload problem and further heighten the need for new techniques and tools that can intelligently and automatically transform the data into useful information and knowledge. One of the central tenets of all information theories is that "the higher the data volume, the lower the information (and knowledge) level." This can be referred to as the Data Overload, Information Underload problem. This problem exists in most fields, not just in Biology. It has been pointed out by experts in almost all fields that involve voluminous data. The crux of the problem is volume. Data processing tools, which convert voluminous raw data to succinct pieces of information (summaries, relationships, patterns, and other "answers"), are needed which can find (data mine) pertinent, accurate information from the raw data and do it in a reasonable amount of time. So the problem is, as it has always been, *scalability* of data analytics. Scalability is always cited as one of the main, if not the main, challenge in nearly every major address given by prominent information scientists over the past 50 years. It was the principle motivation for the development of the computer in the first place. Everyone seems to agree on this point.

Scalability comes in at least two varieties, cardinality scalability (too many instances) and dimensionality scalability (too many attributes). The scalability problems can be cast in terms of table terminology as *too many rows* and *too many columns*.

An important solution for the *curse of cardinality* has been to select a representative subset of records (instances or rows), then to analyze or mine that subset. The tacit assumption is that the information (relationships, patterns, summaries, etc.) found in the subset applies to the full data set as well. Whereas, that tacit, statistical assumption can be justified in many cases, it is very difficult to justify in others (e.g., in exception mining). A random subset will almost always miss exceptions, since exceptions are, in some sense, of measure zero. Put another way, if the probability is high that sub-sampling will include an exception, then it may be incorrect to call it an exception in the first place.

An important solution for the *curse of dimensionality* is also to select a pertinent subset of features (columns or attributes). This process is often referred to as *feature selection*. For the most part, except for domain knowledge related and analytical dimension reduction, the curse of dimensionality is a fact more than a problem. That is, it is difficult to solve it without at least some loss of information. Thus, the problem is to limit the loss of information while dealing with the problem.

Each chapter in this volume addresses each of these problems in its own way.

Data mining or knowledge discovery in biological databases aims to discover useful patterns from large data volumes. A data mining system is considered linearly row scalable if, when the number of rows is increased by, for example, 10 times, it takes no more than 10 times as long to execute the same data mining process. A data mining system is considered linearly column scalable if the data mining execution time increases linearly with the number of columns or attributes or dimensions.

Data mining, in its most restricted form, can be broken down into three general methodologies for extracting information and knowledge from data. These interrelated methodologies are Association Mining, Classification, and Clustering. Many of the techniques in this book fall in one of these three categories directly, and others attempt to accomplish the same information extraction results in novel and interesting ways.

Association Mining, in short, is a matter of discovering strong association relationships among the subsets of the data. Often these subsets are subsets of columns in the schema. If these associations are unidirectional, the process is called Association Rule Mining or antecedent-consequent relationship mining. If the relationships are undirected, this is called Correlation Mining.

Classification is a matter of discovering signatures for the individual values in a specified column or attribute (called the *class label attribute*, which can be composite), from values of the other attributes, which are called the *feature attributes*, in a table, usually called the *training table*. Classification of numeric tables is usually referred to as prediction. Expert systems that use collections of expert opinions collected over time to evaluate new situations are of this data mining type.

Clustering is a matter of using some notion of instance similarity to group together training table rows so that within a group (a cluster) there is high similarity and across groups there is low similarity. In Biological Data Mining, it is very common to use clustering to accomplish classification (class discovery). That is, when some portion of the data is already classified, the entire data set can be clustered based on some similarity notion. Then unclassified samples can be assigned *likely* classes based upon the preponderance within its cluster. In Biology this is called *putative annotation*. The so-called BLAST technologies fall in this category.

For this book, *Big Data Analytics in Bioinformatics and Healthcare*, we have collected cutting-edge research topics and methodologies on managing, analyzing, visualizing, and extracting information from large, diverse, complex, longitudinal, and/or distributed biological and biomedical data sets. Throughout this book you will see, either explicitly or indirectly, the general concepts of association mining, classification or prediction, and clustering. This book, as a collection of research papers, will provide research resources to researchers, practitioners, students, and others in mining massive and complex bioinformatics data sets. This research is important for data-intensive application in the biological and medical fields.

This book encompasses the following three distinct sections: 1) Big Data Analysis Methods and Applications; 2) Reviews and Perspectives on Big Data Analysis; 3) Issues and Concerns in the Big Data Era. The following paragraphs summarize each section and provide an overview for each chapter.

In the first section on Big Data Analysis Methods and Applications, a wide array of new and exciting methods for analyzing big data are presented with special emphasis toward bioinformatics and healthcare. The selected chapters give an, albeit incomplete but well represented, selection of ongoing research questions in the field. First, Yan Guo, Shilin Zhao, Margot Bjoring, and Leng Han open the section with the important topic of RNAseq data analysis. The authors utilized their biological expertise to pinpoint data mining opportunities in RNAseq data analysis, including analysis techniques, tools, and challenges. Then Boya Xie, Qin Ding, and Di Wu discuss an issue faced by many researchers, but especially by researchers in these fields, that of finding the relevant literatures from the various and ever growing databases. These contributors develop a rule-based text mining system, miRCancer, to specifically search for literature in the microRNA profiling area. Although the techniques are specifically focused on searching the literature in microRNA profiling, the novel techniques are very generally applicable and should be of interest to a wide audience in bioinformatics and healthcare data analysis. Next, Zhecheng Zhu, Heng Bee Hoon, and Kiok-Liang Teow discuss the emerging trend of utilizing interactive visualization methods in healthcare systems and the several advantages it has over static visualizations, that is, more flexibility and user-control. A picture is worth a thousand words, it is said. Interactively, moving among pertinent pictures at the user's discretion must then be even more worthwhile. The chapter focuses on these types of results and information presentation techniques and styles. The chapter contains four case studies where interactive data visualization is applied to various aspects of healthcare systems. This is followed by a report by Anasua Sarkar and Anamika Basu, which focuses on the construction of Gene Networks (GNs) from large-scale gene expression data sets. These authors use clustering and correlation methods to reconstruct GNs from microarray data generated from different stages of embryogenesis in *Arabidopsis thaliana*. Networks are data structures that can hold a wealth of information very succinctly. The results discussed in this chapter should be applicable to a wide variety of other application areas in bioinformatics and heathcare informatics as well. The next chapter of section one is devoted to detection and employment of biological sequence motifs. In this chapter, Marjan Trutschl, Phillip Kilgore, Urska Cvek, Rona Scott, and Christine Birdwell demonstrate a set of tools for detecting, curating, and visualizing sequence and amino acid motifs. Biological sequence motifs are highly conserved across species, thus they are important in many regulatory processes and have structural implications. The next chapter by Paulo Fazendeiro and José Valente de Oliveira presents a new clustering method, fuzzy C-means with a variable focal point, to analyze gene expression data. The FCMFP algorithm is formulated based on the observation that the visual perception of a group of similar objects is dependent on the observer's position or perspective. The flexibility provided by the fuzzy approach to the well-established C-means clustering methods provides for customized perspectives depending upon the observer's preferences. The final chapter of the first section of this book is by Y-H. Taguchi, Akira Okamoto, Yoshiki Murakami, Mitsuo Iwadate, and Hideaki Umeyama. In it, the authors explore a principal component analysis technique based on unsupervised feature extraction methods to identify diseases or biological process associated features in problems, such as detection of aberrant methylation associated with esophageal squamous cell carcinoma, biomarker identification using circulating microRNA, and proteomic analysis of bacterial culturing processes. Principal component analysis has long been known to tease out the important dimensions of raw data, but the application and interpretation is domain specific. This chapter offers specifics on how to do principal component analysis in this specific area.

The middle section of the book is devoted to a very current review of big data analysis from a variety of perspectives. First, Issam El Naqa provides an in-depth review of recent advances in and current challenges to the analysis of big data in radiotherapy. This chapter describes the characteristics of big data in radiotherapy and the future of the emerging field of systems radiobiology for outcomes modeling. This review and perspective is followed by an analysis of genomic data in a cloud computing environment by Philip Groth, Gerhard Reuter, and Sebastian Thieme. They not only discusses how the use of the, so called, cloud can alleviate the burden of storing and analyzing large amount of genomics data but also caution that the challenges, such as infrastructure capability, data protection regulation, risks, and costs, still remains. They make the case that for the ever-increasing pace of data generation in the biology and healthcare sector, cloud computing is becoming an important platform for data analysis in these fields. In a real sense, cloud computing is similar to the much older and time honored "client server" computing model, but it is different as well, in that everything that the cloud provides is larger, more accessible, and more flexible. One could think of cloud computing as providing a complete and unlimited set of services to users who might only have a limited local platform, such as a smart phone or a tablet. All data issues and software needs are provided in the cloud in a time and space independent manner. The next chapter by Ravi Mathur and Alison Motsinger-Reif is more specific. In it, you will find a review of the way in which leveraging biological pathway knowledge can aid in the analysis of large-scale genomic data. This is a prime example of using novel techniques to extract important information from massive raw data stores. Next, Amandeep Kahlon and Ashok Sharma explore computational systems biology perspectives with regard to tuberculosis and in particular the related big data challenges and goals. Once again, though there is a specifically focused perspective in this chapter, tuberculosis, the ideas and solutions discussed have wide application. In the next chapter in section two, Ratna Prabha, Anil Rai, and Dhananjaya Singh give a similar but different account of how "big data" has reshaped their respective research fields by enabling researchers to uncover unprecedented amount of information using new data generation and analysis methods. This is yet another example of how specific techniques developed for specific purposes almost always have wider applicability and usefulness. Data on human complex diseases can come from many sources and be of many complex types. In the next chapter, Kristel Van Steen and Núria Malats discuss integration of other sources of data in addition to domain knowledge to build more predictive models for human complex disease data. The case is made that domain-specific knowledge can offer significant additional insights about data compared to computation alone. This chapter reinforces the very important fact, which is often overlooked by the casual user, that most computation-based systems should be used for decision support, not decision making. It is rare that a computational system is capable of independent decision making, especially in the bioinformatics and healthcare fields. Associations are relationships that hold much information for disease analysis. In the next chapter, Jami Jackson and Alison Motsinger-Reif review candidate gene and genome-wide genotype and disease associations. Not only is there information in data but there is also information in relationships. Association data mining deals with this fact and is the focus of this chapter. The final chapter in this middle section is devoted to personalized disease phenotypes from massive OMIC data. In it, Hans Binder, Henry Wirth, Lydia Hopp, and Kathrin Lembcke use self-organizing maps to analyze massive molecular medical data and present worked-out examples from different diseases of the colon ranging from inflammation to cancer. This final chapter of the section treats a further step toward the ultimate goal of identifying disease-associated genes, of tailoring disease treatment to the individual. It considers the very important topic of personalized medicine. Self-organizing maps offer both a high degree of information extraction as well as a succinct visualization of the extracted information.

The final section of the book treats some additional bioinformatics and healthcare issues that have emerged in the big data era equally as important as the fundamental data organization and information extraction issues. It addresses topics such as intellectual property and the benefits and concerns of utilizing big data in these sectors. Intellectual property management is critical if the current pace of progress is to continue. There are so many new ideas being developed and in need of IP protection that this is a big data area in its own right. Toward that end, Matthew Knabel, Katherine Doering, and Dennis Fernandez examine controversies and problems associated with intellectual property protection in the area of synthetic biology. Intellectual property protection is critically important in this area, but so is exposure and sharing so that the area can grow and problems can be solved. This trade-off and other issues make the topic very important in today's world of bioinformatics and healthcare informatics. In the next chapter, Jane Moon, Mary Galea, and Megan Bohensky study clinical data linkages in spinal cord injuries. Even though they are somewhat narrowly focused on data collected in Australia, the issues and results are not. The same issues exist and solutions apply throughout the world. In addition, the solutions can generalize to other types of injuries as well. Finally, in the last chapter of this last section, Andrea Darrel, Margee Hume, Timothy Hardie, and Jeffery Soar discuss the utilization of biological big data by government consortiums in the healthcare sector. These impacts have been overwhelmingly positive. Government involvement has been a very important stimulus and focusing element in this area.

Analysis of big data in the bioinformatics and healthcare sectors has been instrumental in the development of products and solutions for at least the past decade. It has allowed researchers and healthcare providers to have information that was formerly inaccessible. An important trend driving this success is the fact that the cost of data generation continues to decrease. For example, it used to cost $1 billion to sequence a human genome, but currently it costs less than $1000. With such affordable pricing, it is likely that we will soon routinely have our DNA sequences information as part of our medical record. Meanwhile, various hospital-led initiatives have already begun to record patients' health information in centralized databases as part of patients' Electronic Medical Records (EMRs). Analysis of big data in these areas is essential for the advancement of the science of healthcare. The diverse and comprehensive coverage of topics on big data analysis in this publication will help researchers, practitioners, and students to better understand the research, methodologies, and discoveries in these all-important fields. We hope this book will be informative to the readers and contribute to the continued growth of big data analysis in bioinformatics and healthcare.

Baoying Wang
Waynesburg University, USA

Ruowang Li
Pennsylvania State University, USA

William Perrizo
North Dakota State University, USA

REFERENCE

Shah, N. H. (2012). Translational bioinformatics embraces big data. *Yearbook of Medical Informatics,* 7(1), 130–134. PMID:22890354

Section 1
Big Data Analysis Methods and Applications

Chapter 1
Advanced Datamining Using RNAseq Data

Yan Guo
Vanderbilt University, USA

Margot Bjoring
Vanderbilt University, USA

Shilin Zhao
Vanderbilt University, USA

Leng Han
MD Anderson Cancer Center, USA

ABSTRACT

In recent years, RNA sequencing (RNAseq) technology has experienced a rapid rise in popularity. Often seen as a competitor of and the ultimate successor to microarray technology given its more accurate and quantitative gene expression measurement, RNAseq also offers a wealth of additional information that is often overlooked, and given the massive accumulation of RNAseq data available in public data repositories over the past few years, these data are ripe for discovery. Abundant opportunities exist for researchers to conduct in-depth, non-traditional analyses that take advantage of these secondary uses and for bioinformaticians to develop tools to make these data more accessible. This is discussed in this chapter.

INTRODUCTION

One major drawback of next-generation sequencing (NGS) technology is the imperfect capture technology, which produces a variety of genomic sequences as byproducts in addition to the specific region targeted. Rather than ignore these byproducts, we can turn them into useful information; for example, in DNA sequencing, people have used these byproduct reads to study mitochondria (Guo, Li, Li, Shyr, & Samuels, 2013; Picardi & Pesole, 2012), viruses (Samuels et al., 2013), and non-capture region SNPs (Guo et al., 2012). These

and similar ideas can also be applied to RNAseq data (Z. Wang, Gerstein, & Snyder, 2009).

To this point, RNAseq technology has largely been used as a strict replacement for microarrays, its scope limited to gene expression analysis and occasionally the detection of structural variants. While RNAseq is fully capable of filling this role, its extensive inventory of sequencing byproducts make it important and fruitful for researchers to move beyond the past constraints of microarrays and embrace the full potential of RNAseq data. These additional opportunities offered by RNAseq data fall into five major categories (Figure 1):

DOI: 10.4018/978-1-4666-6611-5.ch001

Figure 1. Additional areas of research offered by RNAseq technology beyond gene expression analysis

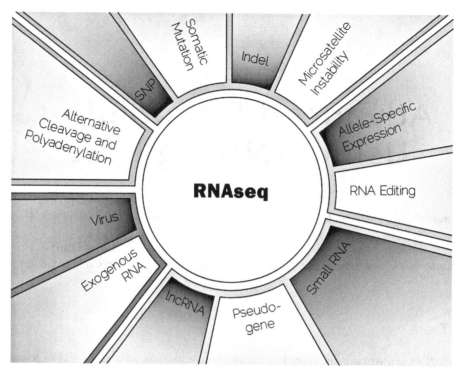

1. **Mutations:** The mutations identified by RNAseq data can include single nucleotide polymorphisms (SNPs), somatic mutations, insertions and deletions (indels), and microsatellite instability. Because RNAseq by definition contains only the expressed portions of the DNA, the variations contained in these data sets may be enriched for functional relevance.

2. **RNA Editing and Allele-Specific Expression:** RNAseq data can be used to identify both RNA editing, a post-transcriptional mechanism that diversifies the transcriptome by changing nucleotides at the RNA level, and allele-specific expression, or a difference in the expression levels of the two alleles in a gene.

3. **Non-Coding RNA:** There are three types of RNAseq which result for different species of RNA: mRNAseq, miRNAseq, and total RNAseq. Total RNAseq is naturally the most inclusive of RNA species, but even in

   mRNAseq and miRNAseq, other species of RNA are present, including long non-coding RNA, transfer RNA, and small nucleolar RNA.

4. **Exogenous RNA:** RNAseq data sets will contain some exogenous RNA content such as viruses and exogenous miRNA. Viruses such as the human papillomavirus have known oncogenic effects, and RNAseq can be used to identify exogenous sequences and determine insertion points.

5. **Alternative Cleavage and Polyadenylation:** Alternative cleavage and polyadenylation (APA) is common in mRNA with the great majority of genes having multiple cleavage and polyadenylation sites. While challenging, RNAseq can and has been used to identify APA.

This chapter will discuss in detail these five datamining opportunities including the techniques, tools, challenges, and potential rewards each of them present with the goal of enabling investigators to make fuller use of their data set or of those publically available and to encourage experimentation with novel techniques that move outside the box of gene expression.

BACKGROUND

With a central role in all aspects of modern life, information technology continues to expand our capacity to collect greater and greater volumes of information. In the field of biomedical research, the emergence of next-generation sequencing (NGS) technologies has redefined big data, enabling researchers to produce a tremendous volume of genomic data at relatively low costs.

High-throughput gene expression profiling was dominated by microarray technology for over a decade until the introduction of RNA sequencing (RNAseq) technology, an NGS technology that sequences cDNA libraries prepared from specimen RNA. Compared to microarray technology, the RNAseq provides several advantages. First, unlike microarray, RNAseq is not limited to a set of previously defined genes; it is capable of detecting all genes with all isoforms regardless of novelty. Second, with RNAseq we can examine the genome at the resolution of a single nucleotide, whereas the resolution of microarray stays at gene or exon level. With the maturation of NGS technologies, the price of RNAseq has become comparable to that of microarrays. The competitive price and ability to capture additional transcriptomic data make RNAseq an attractive alternative to microarray for expression profiling: a central focus for biomedical research today.

Despite the many benefits of RNAseq technology, it is important to recognize the significant bioinformatic challenges it presents as well. The data sets generated by RNAseq define big data, with the raw data of a single sample requiring 5 to 10 GB of storage after compression and the processing and analysis stages requiring stor-

age several times that amount. In comparison, the storage for microarray is almost negligible, making the cost of storage for an RNAseq study a significant consideration. And the rich transcriptomic information contained within an RNAseq data set brings complexity in the analysis phase, with several unique characteristics contributing to these challenges. First, the value for a non-expressed gene in RNAseq data is zero: zero reads aligned to the corresponding DNA sequence. In microarray, background intensity for non-expressed genes allows for log transformation of intensity data; due to the large number of zeros in RNAseq data (often more than 50%), however, log transformation is not practical. In addition, the typical range of RNAseq data is 0 to 50,000 counts, compared to microarray counts of 2 to 15 after robust multi-array (RMA) normalization; the huge range of RNAseq data can produce falsely inflated fold-changes. Finally, many sequencing and alignment artifacts can skew RNAseq data.

Still, many studies have provided analytical evidence to support the inevitable replacement of microarray by RNAseq (Asmann et al., 2009; Cloonan et al., 2008; Guo, Li, Ye, & Shyr, 2013; Guo, Sheng, Li, Ye, et al., 2013; Marioni, Mason, Mane, Stephens, & Gilad, 2008; Z. Wang et al., 2009), and with RNAseq becoming the technology of choice for gene expression research, it becomes increasingly important to identify secondary data mining opportunities within the existing data sets. Many of the methods presented herein can be performed more efficiently and to higher resolution using sequencing techniques targeted toward those data: for mutation identification, for example, DNA sequencing is the preferred technology, and a study screening for mutations would be wise to use this method. As researchers strive to make the most of a limited budget, however, multiple types of sequencing can become cost-prohibitive. The methods that follow are intended to allow researchers to stretch the utility of their RNAseq data sets into new avenues of investigation that will give them a more comprehensive understanding of their data.

ADDITIONAL DATAMINING IN RNASEQ DATA

Mutations

Although DNA sequencing has become the technology of choice for mutation identification, RNAseq contains much of the same information. In fact, RNAseq data may be enriched for functional variants because they contain only transcribed sequences. This potential benefit comes at the cost of very low coverage of non-expressed genes, however, making the inference of mutation status for these genes practically impossible. The major challenge in mutation identification through RNAseq data is a bioinformatic one due to high false-positive rates, and because of this, mutation identification through RNAseq data should emphasize specificity over sensitivity.

Tools for identifying mutations in DNA sequencing data, especially single-nucleotide polymorphisms (SNPs) and somatic mutations, are reliable and well-established; GATK (DePristo et al., 2011), Varscan (Koboldt et al., 2012), and MuTect (Cibulskis et al., 2013) are all regularly used with confidence to identify high-quality SNPs from DNA-seq data. For mutation identification in RNAseq data, however, far fewer tools exist, and they face the challenge of high false-positive rates for variations resulting from three major factors: cycle bias, splicing locations, and errors from reverse transcription to cDNA (Figure 2).

Cycle bias is the disproportionate prevalence of one of two alleles in a heterozygous position at the beginnings or ends of the reads (Guo, Ye, Sheng, Clark, & Samuels, 2013). Cycle bias is a systematic error introduced during sequencing, and it can be easily accounted for by removing any mutations that occur disproportionately at the beginnings or ends of reads during the quality control process.

Splicing locations in RNA can introduce error when aligned against the DNA reference sequence, and while these alignment errors do not affect gene expression analysis, which only counts the number of reads aligned to a given gene, errors in alignment at splicing locations can introduce large numbers of false positive SNPs and somatic mutations. These false positives are not as simple to identify and filter as those resulting from cycle bias. It is good practice to flag any SNPs and somatic mutations occurring near a splicing site for additional quality control checks. In theory, alignment against the transcriptome instead of the

Figure 2. Tips for detecting somatic mutation from RNAseq data

| Germline | ~ATTCTGAGT~ |
| Tumor tissue | ~ATTCGGAGT~ |

Pay attention to	Solution
cycle bias	Remove mutations near beginning or end of reads
splicing junction	Remove mutations near junction
errors from reverse transcription to cDNA	Apply strong filters

DNA reference sequence may eliminate alignment errors at splicing locations, and this is an interesting avenue for further investigation.

One additional source of false positives comes from errors in the reverse transcription of mRNA to cDNA, and unlike the previous sources of error, this one is random and difficult to detect. For this reason, SNPs and somatic mutations identified by RNAseq should always be validated via wet lab or other method.

Bioinformatic tools to detect SNPs and somatic mutations are still in their infancy, and they vary in their ability to address the above sources of false positives. RNAmapper (Miller, Obholzer, Shah, Megason, & Moens, 2013) for somatic mutations and SNVQ (Duitama, Srivastava, & Mandoiu, 2012) for SNPs were two of the first tools to tackle the challenges of mutation calling in RNAseq data, but neither address the problem of cycle bias. The recently developed RSMC (Guo, Sheng, Li, Samuels, & Shyr, 2013) and SNPiR (Piskol, Ramaswami, & Li, 2013) both filter for cycle bias and remove SNPs near splicing locations. This is an area of continuous development, and the understanding of the sources of false positives in RNAseq data and how to account for them is growing rapidly. In the near future, the use of RNAseq data to identify somatic mutations and SNPs will be a routine process similar to what is available for DNA-seq. Even now, RNAseq data has proved useful as a method of validation for mutations detected from DNA sequencing data.

Moving past point mutations, RNAseq has the ability to detect insertions and deletions (indels) as well as microsatellite instability, a type of genetic hypermutability in which repeated sequences of DNA can shorten or lengthen due to a deficiency in DNA mismatch repair. Indels face the same problem as SNPs and somatic mutations, in that RNAseq data yield many false positives. Still, there are several tools capable of detecting indels – TopHat2 (Kim et al., 2013), FX (Hong et al., 2012), and OSA (Hu, Ge, Newman, & Liu, 2012) – and there are a number of examples of this use in the literature. Similarly, the detection of microsatellite instability with RNAseq data, while not ideal, has been shown to be possible in several cancer studies (Yoon et al., 2013; Zheng et al., 2013).

In summary, the detection of mutation using RNAseq data is possible, but most ideal scenario for detecting mutation remains the use of DNAseq. With more thorough quality control and additional validation methods, however, RNAseq provides an avenue for studying mutations when use of DNAseq is not possible or practical.

RNA Editing and Allele-Specific Expression

RNA-editing is a relatively rare process in which specific nucleotides are changed directly within an RNA molecule after transcription, and it serves an important role in the diversification of the transcriptome. Editing can occur through insertion, deletion, or base substitution and in mRNA may alter the amino acid sequence and thus the encoded protein. Identification of RNA editing sites is a complex but accurate process usually relying on sequencing of both the transcriptome and the DNA of a sample and the application of stringent quality control criteria to exclude likely false positives such as splice junctions, homolog regions, and known SNPs and somatic mutations. Because this method requires both RNAseq and DNA-seq, it is a costly venture, and Ramaswami *et al.* developed an alternative method that relies solely on RNAseq data (Ramaswami et al., 2013).

Like the traditional method, Ramaswami's approach filters out common SNPs from public databases but goes on to further extract rare SNPs under the assumption that rare SNPs will vary from sample to sample while true RNA editing sites will be highly conserved. Because of this assumption, the larger the number of samples included, the greater the accuracy of RNA editing identification. This approach was consolidated into the tool REDItools by Picardi & Pesole (2013) which offers functionality for both RNAseq to DNA-seq comparison and RNAseq only.

Allele-specific expression (ASE) is another trait detectable by RNAseq in which one of two alleles in a gene shows greater expression than the other. Because the two possible causes of allele-specific expression are cis-acting variants and parent-of-origin regulation, gene expression analysis and polymorphism identification are both used in its detection. AlleleSeq (Rozowsky et al., 2011) and asSeq (W. Sun, 2012) are two tools developed for the purpose of allele-specific expression detection, and although their specifics differ, the fundamental approach is the same. The tools assign reads to alleles to measure allele-specific expression with the major limitation of examining these expression patterns only for genes with SNP sites.

Because this technique relies on SNP identification, it is subject to the same false-positive issues discussed for mutations, and in addition, allele-specific expression can be confounded by reference allele preferential bias. This bias is introduced during alignment when the alignment algorithm penalizes a mismatch from the reference genome. The presence of a non-reference allele in the read is counted as a mismatch, meaning that the read is more likely to be discarded due to error than a read containing the reference allele. This bias can introduce false positives into an analysis of allele-specific expression (Degner et al., 2009; Guo, Samuels, et al., 2013; Guo, Ye, et al., 2013; Heap et al., 2010; Stevenson, Coolon, & Wittkopp, 2013).

Both RNA editing and allele-specific expression have potential links to biological functionality. RNA editing has been linked to RNA degradation (Agranat, Raitskin, Sperling, & Sperling, 2008), and allele-specific expression is of interest due to the possibility of *cis*-acting genetic variants (Bray, Buckland, Owen, & O'Donovan, 2003) or parent of origin regulation (Gregg et al., 2010). RNAseq data provides the perfect opportunity to profile both RNA editing and allele specific expression.

Non-Coding RNA

RNAseq technology encompasses three main varieties differentiated by the selection of RNA species prior to cDNA synthesis: mRNAseq, miRNAseq, and total RNAseq. Total RNAseq is the most inclusive of RNA species, removing only ribosomal RNA (rRNA) although even the removal of that species is not complete due to the relative abundance of rRNA. Because of its inclusiveness, the sequencing demand is greater, and therefore it is not the preferred method for studies mainly focused on mRNA or miRNA. Certain species of non-coding RNA are still present in the more selective RNAseq varieties, however, due to less than 100% efficiency in the capture processes, and they can prove interesting and even functional in analysis (Figure 3).

mRNAseq selects for the poly-A tail that distinguishes messenger RNA, and because some long non-coding RNAs display this tail, an mRNAseq library typically contains them as well. Long non-coding RNAs (lncRNA) are RNA molecules defined to be longer than 200 nucleotides which do not encode a protein. There are tens of thousands of lncRNAs, many of which look very similar to mRNA, including the polyadenylation that causes their inclusion in mRNAseq data sets, and although they are non-protein coding, recent research has shown evidence of functionality in areas such as sub-cellular structural organization and embryonic stem cell differentiation.

The rise in the popularity and affordability of RNAseq technology is responsible for the growing interest in and understanding of lncRNA as researchers explore the presence of this stowaway in their mRNA data sets. While lncRNA can be studied with microarray, RNAseq is the superior technology for this purpose with greater sensitivity and the ability to detect novel lncRNAs. Cabili et al. (2011) were pioneers of lncRNA research, describing the defining characteristics of lncRNA, and the Encyclopedia of DNA Elements (ENCODE) (Djebali et al., 2012) project made a

Figure 3. Types of ncRNAs that can be detected through RNAseq data

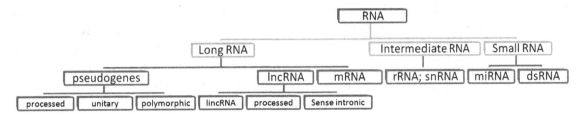

huge contribution, identifying 13,333 lncRNA and categorizing them into four classes: 1) antisense, 2) large intergenic non-coding RNAs (lincRNA), 3) sense intronic, and 4) processed transcripts. The ENCODE project also examined lncRNA expression and identified tissue-specific patterns in their expression.

Similar to the selection process in mRNAseq, miRNAseq selects for small RNAs (usually < 200 nucleotides and often in the range of 20 to 40) to enrich the data set for microRNA (Cole et al., 2009; Kawaji et al., 2008; Lee, Shibata, Malhotra, & Dutta, 2009; Liao et al., 2010; Martens-Uzunova, Olvedy, & Jenster, 2012; Thompson & Parker, 2009), capturing in the process transfer RNA (tRNA), small nuclear RNA (snRNA), small nucleolar RNA (snoRNA), and a variety of other small species as well. Investigation into small RNAs has focused mainly on miRNA, but with miRNAs composing only about 25% of the total small RNAs, there is clear reason to expand into the other species captured in miRNAseq. tRNA is especially prevalent in miRNAseq data sets, captured as a 33bp fragment after cleavage of the full length of 73 to 94 nucleotides, and recent studies have begun to explore its functions in a variety of contexts.

Yet another unintended but potentially interesting product of RNAseq is the presence of pseudogenes. These regions display homology to known genes but have become dysfunctional through an accumulation of mutations and can no longer encode a protein. Long regarded as completely nonfunctional, pseudogenes have begun to attract interest thanks to their availability in

RNAseq data, and evidence is accumulating that pseudogene expression may have functionality in some areas (Tam et al., 2008; Watanabe et al., 2008). Several pipelines (Chaudhuri et al., 2011; Kalyana-Sundaram et al., 2012; Tonner, Srinivasasainagendra, Zhang, & Zhi, 2012) have been developed to pull pseudogenes from RNA-seq data sets with the main challenge being their strong homology with functional counterparts; reads must map uniquely to the pseudogene for positive identification, and in pseudogene-gene pairs with high sequence similarity, mapping reads to the pseudogene may be difficult.

Noncoding RNA has been a focus of biomedical research during recent years. More and more researchers are starting to realize that the answers to some diseases may lie outside the coding regions. The National Human Genome Research Institute (NHGRI) launched the ENCODE consortium to study the non-coding part of the genome, and the consortium claims that 80% of the human genome is associated with some kind of biochemical function through the regulation of the expression of coding genes (Bernstein et al., 2012). RNAseq data provides us with the opportunity to study non-coding RNA at an unprecedented level.

Exogenous RNA

The purity of a library is never 100%, and an RNAseq library may contain reads that originated outside the sample genome in the form of viral genomes integrated into the host DNA or exogenous miRNA. The opportunity to study viral genomes is an important one as the oncogenic function of some viruses, notably the human papillomavirus (HPV), hepatitis B virus (HBV), and Epstein-Barr virus (EBV), has long been recognized with 15 to 20% of all cancers caused by viruses.

Most viruses lack genes with clear oncogenic function, instead causing oncogenesis by inserting their genome near or within tumor suppressor genes or oncogenes within the host genome, disrupting regulatory processes and promoting growth and uncontrolled division. Viral genomes captured in RNAseq provide an opportunity to study the patterns of viral integration which can in turn further understanding of cancer-related mechanisms by revealing novel oncogenes or tumor suppressors.

Two studies in particular demonstrate the possibilities of studying viral oncogenesis through RNAseq technology with large-scale analyses of TCGA data. Khoury et al. (2013) showed that it was possible to detect virus integration sites; focusing on HPV and HBV, they detected integration sites in a variety of cancers and identified host genes that frequently show viral integration. Another study investigated the effect of HPV on host mRNA expression and found a broad impact on the transcriptome with almost 2,000 genes showing at least a 2-fold up- or down-regulation (Tang, Alaei-Mahabadi, Samuelsson, Lindh, & Larsson, 2013).

The greatest challenge associated with virus detection with any technology, including RNAseq, is the rapid mutation rate of viruses (10^{-6} to 10^{-8} mutations per base per generation for DNA viruses and 10^{-3} to 10^{-5} mutations per base per generation for RNA viruses) (Drake, Charlesworth, Charlesworth, & Crow, 1998). A variety of tools have been developed for virus detection from sequencing data (e.g., PathSeq (Kostic et al., 2011), ViralFusionSeq (Li et al., 2013), and VirusFinder (Q. Wang, Jia, & Zhao, 2013)), and a common solution for the mutation problem is an increase in the number of mismatches allowed when aligning against the virus reference genome. Although many of these tools are designed with exome sequencing or whole genome sequencing in mind, most can be adapted to RNAseq as well.

Another source of exogenous RNA comes in the form of miRNA from bacteria and fungi, and these small exogenous RNAs can be detected in miRNAseq (K. Wang et al., 2012). This line of investigation requires careful experiment design and thoughtful analysis, but a couple of studies have shown evidence for not only the presence of exogenous miRNA but also potential functions, adding a new dimension to miRNAseq analysis (Chen, Zen, & Zhang, 2013; Dickinson et al., 2013).

Another interesting type of exogenous RNA is food-originating miRNA. The phrase, "You are what you eat," has been proven true by multiple studies. For example, one study showed that subjects' bloodstreams contained approximately 30 different miRNA from commonly eaten plants. In another study, it was shown that Chinese subjects had more rice miRNA and Caucasian subjects had more corn miRNA in the plasma extracted from blood (K. Wang et al., 2012).

RNAseq data provides the extra opportunities to study the exogenous RNAs described above. Studying viruses using RNAseq data will allow us to verify infection status and establish new virus disease association, and although no study has yet been conducted for testing the association between food miRNA and disease, it would be an interesting project to take on.

Alternative Cleavage and Polyadenylation

Protein-coding genes, along with many long noncoding RNAs as discussed above, are cleaved and polyadenylated on the 3′ end, and the clear majority of these genes, possibly as many as 70 to 75%, have multiple cleavage and polyadenylation sites. This results in widespread alternative cleavage and polyadenylation (APA) throughout the genome. APA impacts the cellular transcriptome and proteome by regulating mRNA metabolism via alternative 3′-UTRs and affecting the gene isoforms, and it exists widely in lncRNAs. APA is also dynamic under different biological conditions, such as tissue specificity, cell growth and development, and even in cancer (Tian & Manley, 2013).

Only a small fraction of reads in a typical RNAseq run will span cleavage sites, limiting the sample size available for study. The massive amount of publically available RNAseq data, however, helps to overcome that problem, making RNAseq a popular technology to study this phenomenon. Several studies have successfully used RNAseq technology to study the prevalence of APA and identify novel cleavage and polyadenylation sites (Hoque et al., 2013; Y. Sun, Fu, Li, & Xu, 2012). In addition, there are a few modifications to the standard RNAseq protocol that can assist as well: 3′-end-enriched RNAseq, including 3′ end RNA-seq, poly (A) site sequencing (PAS-seq), Poly(A)-seq, Sequencing APA sites (SAPAS), 3′-seq, A-seq, Poly (A) position profiling by sequencing (3P-seq), and 3′region extraction and deep sequencing (3′READS) provide greater coverage of cleavage sites but may suffer from false-positive calls of poly(A) sites derived from internal priming of oligo(dT) primers (Y. Sun et al., 2012). Direct RNA sequencing (DRS) does not reverse-transcribe to cDNA, thus eliminating the biases and errors resulting from that step (Ozsolak et al., 2010).

In summary, alternative cleavage and polyadenylation are the least utilized data mining opportunity provided by RNAseq data. No official software packages have been release for this purpose. But alternative cleavage and polyadenylation can be detected by following the methods described in the studies mentioned in the previous paragraph.

FUTURE RESEARCH DIRECTIONS

The major advantage of high-throughput technology compared to microarray technology is its ability to screen the whole transcript genome instead of a set of known transcripts. In the process of sequencing at nucleotide resolution, many types of information are captured, allowing researchers to mine their data for novel findings. Five different types of datamining opportunities are described here, and there are potentially unknown opportunities still eluding us. As sequencing technology becomes more advanced in terms of coverage depth and accuracy and the bioinformatic methods of handling these data become more robust, more opportunities are sure to be discovered.

CONCLUSION

The rising use of RNAseq technology is creating an invaluable resource for investigators in the form of massive amounts of publically available data. In most cases, the surface has only been scratched on these data with the focus firmly on gene expression analysis, and deep datamining efforts have great potential to provide new insights into the mechanisms of diseases. RNAseq technology should not be subjected to the same limitations imposed by microarrays, and this chapter aims to educate researchers on the full range of possibilities open to them. Table 1 contains the tools discussed in this chapter.

In particular, five avenues of research have begun to gather momentum. RNAseq has proven itself to be a capable platform for mutation identification including SNPs, somatic mutations, indels, and microsatellite instability, and with bioinformatic tools capable of automating these analyses a current focus of development, mutation identification is becoming a simple and valuable secondary analysis to any RNAseq-based gene expression study. Mechanisms such as RNA editing and allele-specific expression show the presence of influences outside what would be expected from a strict progression of DNA to RNA to protein, and with careful analysis, RNAseq makes both of these mechanisms accessible. Every RNAseq data set provides a broad sampling of RNA species,

Table 1. Tools that are useful in RNAseq data mining

Data Mining Type		Tools/Pubmed ID	URL
Mutation	SNP	SNVQ	http://dna.engr.uconn.edu/?page_id=110
		SNPiR	http://lilab.stanford.edu/SNPiR/
	Somatic Mutation	RNAmapper	http://www.rnamapper.org/
		RSMC	https://github.com/shengqh/rsmc
	Indel	TopHat2	http://tophat.cbcb.umd.edu/
		FX	http://fx.gmi.ac.kr/
		OSA	http://omicsoft.com/osa/
RNA Editing		REDItools	https://code.google.com/p/reditools/
Allele-Specific Expression	Detection	AlleleSeq	http://alleleseq.gersteinlab.org/
		asSeq	http://www.bios.unc.edu/~wsun/software.htm
Non-coding RNA	small RNAs	20498841	http://www.ncbi.nlm.nih.gov/pubmed/20498841
		18404147	http://www.ncbi.nlm.nih.gov/pubmed/18404147
		18404146	http://www.ncbi.nlm.nih.gov/pubmed/18404146
		22726445	http://www.ncbi.nlm.nih.gov/pubmed/22726445
		22908858	http://www.ncbi.nlm.nih.gov/pubmed/22908858
		21816880	http://www.ncbi.nlm.nih.gov/pubmed/21816880
	lincRNA	24476892	http://www.ncbi.nlm.nih.gov/pubmed/24476892
		21890647	http://www.ncbi.nlm.nih.gov/pubmed/21890647
	Pesudogenes	22726445	http://www.ncbi.nlm.nih.gov/pubmed/22726445
		22908858	http://www.ncbi.nlm.nih.gov/pubmed/22908858
		21816880	http://www.ncbi.nlm.nih.gov/pubmed/21816880
Exogenous RNA	Virus	PathSeq	http://www.broadinstitute.org/software/pathseq/
		ViralFusionSeq	http://sourceforge.net/projects/viralfusionseq/
		VirusFinder	http://bioinfo.mc.vanderbilt.edu/VirusFinder/
	Bacteria	24213764	http://www.ncbi.nlm.nih.gov/pubmed/24213764
		24213763	http://www.ncbi.nlm.nih.gov/pubmed/24213763
Alternative Cleavage and Polyadenylation		21145465	http://www.ncbi.nlm.nih.gov/pubmed/21145465
		23099521	http://www.ncbi.nlm.nih.gov/pubmed/23099521
		23241633	http://www.ncbi.nlm.nih.gov/pubmed/23241633

the investigation of which may offer insights into the hidden effects of non-coding and so-called "non-functional" varieties of RNA. Some RNA may even originate outside the sample genome in the form of integrated viral sequences or other exogenous RNA and may hold important clues as to the mechanisms of viral oncogenesis. Finally, RNAseq offers an opportunity to study alternative cleavage in mRNA.

These suggestions for data mining opportunities are by no means comprehensive. Understanding of the full potential of the knowledge contained within an RNAseq data set is still in its infancy, and more novel uses will undoubtedly emerge in the coming years. The authors' hope is that the information presented here will encourage a spirit of experimentation, moving beyond the constraints of gene expression, while instilling an understanding of the analytic challenges accompanying these methods and an attention to potential errors and biases that will foster high-quality, reproducible research.

REFERENCES

Agranat, L., Raitskin, O., Sperling, J., & Sperling, R. (2008). The editing enzyme ADAR1 and the mRNA surveillance protein hUpf1 interact in the cell nucleus. *Proceedings of the National Academy of Sciences of the United States of America*, *105*(13), 5028–5033. doi:10.1073/pnas.0710576105 PMID:18362360

Asmann, Y. W., Klee, E. W., Thompson, E. A., Perez, E. A., Middha, S., & Oberg, A. L. et al. (2009). 3' tag digital gene expression profiling of human brain and universal reference RNA using Illumina Genome Analyzer. *BMC Genomics*, *10*(1), 531. doi:10.1186/1471-2164-10-531 PMID:19917133

Bernstein, B. E., Birney, E., Dunham, I., Green, E. D., Gunter, C., & Snyder, M. (2012). An integrated encyclopedia of DNA elements in the human genome. *Nature*, *489*(7414), 57–74. doi:10.1038/nature11247 PMID:22955616

Bray, N. J., Buckland, P. R., Owen, M. J., & O'Donovan, M. C. (2003). Cis-acting variation in the expression of a high proportion of genes in human brain. *Human Genetics*, *113*(2), 149–153. doi:10.1007/s00439-003-0956-y PMID:12728311

Cabili, M. N., Trapnell, C., Goff, L., Koziol, M., Tazon-Vega, B., Regev, A., & Rinn, J. L. (2011). Integrative annotation of human large intergenic noncoding RNAs reveals global properties and specific subclasses. *Genes & Development*, *25*(18), 1915–1927. doi:10.1101/gad.17446611 PMID:21890647

Chaudhuri, R. R., Yu, L., Kanji, A., Perkins, T. T., Gardner, P. P., & Choudhary, J. et al. (2011). Quantitative RNA-seq analysis of the Campylobacter jejuni transcriptome. *Microbiology*, *157*(Pt 10), 2922–2932. doi:10.1099/mic.0.050278-0 PMID:21816880

Chen, X., Zen, K., & Zhang, C. Y. (2013). Reply to Lack of detectable oral bioavailability of plant microRNAs after feeding in mice. *Nature Biotechnology*, *31*(11), 967–969. doi:10.1038/nbt.2741 PMID:24213764

Cibulskis, K., Lawrence, M. S., Carter, S. L., Sivachenko, A., Jaffe, D., & Sougnez, C. et al. (2013). Sensitive detection of somatic point mutations in impure and heterogeneous cancer samples. *Nature Biotechnology*, *31*(3), 213–219. doi:10.1038/nbt.2514 PMID:23396013

Cloonan, N., Forrest, A. R., Kolle, G., Gardiner, B. B., Faulkner, G. J., & Brown, M. K. et al. (2008). Stem cell transcriptome profiling via massive-scale mRNA sequencing. *Nature Methods*, *5*(7), 613–619. doi:10.1038/nmeth.1223 PMID:18516046

Cole, C., Sobala, A., Lu, C., Thatcher, S. R., Bowman, A., & Brown, J. W. et al. (2009). Filtering of deep sequencing data reveals the existence of abundant Dicer-dependent small RNAs derived from tRNAs. *RNA (New York, N.Y.)*, *15*(12), 2147–2160. doi:10.1261/rna.1738409 PMID:19850906

Degner, J. F., Marioni, J. C., Pai, A. A., Pickrell, J. K., Nkadori, E., Gilad, Y., & Pritchard, J. K. (2009). Effect of read-mapping biases on detecting allele-specific expression from RNA-sequencing data. *Bioinformatics (Oxford, England)*, *25*(24), 3207–3212. doi:10.1093/bioinformatics/btp579 PMID:19808877

DePristo, M. A., Banks, E., Poplin, R., Garimella, K. V., Maguire, J. R., & Hartl, C. et al. (2011). A framework for variation discovery and genotyping using next-generation DNA sequencing data. *Nature Genetics*, *43*(5), 491–498. doi:10.1038/ng.806 PMID:21478889

Dickinson, B., Zhang, Y., Petrick, J. S., Heck, G., Ivashuta, S., & Marshall, W. S. (2013). Lack of detectable oral bioavailability of plant microR-NAs after feeding in mice. *Nature Biotechnology*, *31*(11), 965–967. doi:10.1038/nbt.2737 PMID:24213763

Djebali, S., Davis, C. A., Merkel, A., Dobin, A., Lassmann, T., & Mortazavi, A. et al. (2012). Landscape of transcription in human cells. *Nature*, *489*(7414), 101–108. doi:10.1038/nature11233 PMID:22955620

Drake, J. W., Charlesworth, B., Charlesworth, D., & Crow, J. F. (1998). Rates of spontaneous mutation. *Genetics*, *148*(4), 1667–1686. PMID:9560386

Duitama, J., Srivastava, P., & Mandoiu, I. (2012). Towards accurate detection and genotyping of expressed variants from whole transcriptome sequencing data. *BMC Genomics*, *13*(Suppl 2), S6. doi:10.1186/1471-2164-13-S2-S6 PMID:22537301

Gregg, C., Zhang, J., Weissbourd, B., Luo, S., Schroth, G. P., Haig, D., & Dulac, C. (2010). High-resolution analysis of parent-of-origin allelic expression in the mouse brain. *Science*, *329*(5992), 643–648. doi:10.1126/science.1190830 PMID:20616232

Guo, Y., Li, C. I., Ye, F., & Shyr, Y. (2013). Evaluation of read count based RNAseq analysis methods. *BMC Genomics*, *14*(Suppl 8), S2. doi:10.1186/1471-2164-14-S8-S2 PMID:24564449

Guo, Y., Li, J., Li, C. I., Shyr, Y., & Samuels, D. C. (2013). MitoSeek: Extracting mitochondria information and performing high-throughput mitochondria sequencing analysis. *Bioinformatics (Oxford, England)*, *29*(9), 1210–1211. doi:10.1093/bioinformatics/btt118 PMID:23471301

Guo, Y., Long, J., He, J., Li, C. I., Cai, Q., & Shu, X. O. et al. (2012). Exome sequencing generates high quality data in non-target regions. *BMC Genomics*, *13*(1), 194. doi:10.1186/1471-2164-13-194 PMID:22607156

Guo, Y., Samuels, D. C., Li, J., Clark, T., Li, C. I., & Shyr, Y. (2013). Evaluation of allele frequency estimation using pooled sequencing data simulation. *TheScientificWorldJournal*, *895496*. doi:10.1155/2013/895496 PMID:23476151

Guo, Y., Sheng, Q., Li, C., Samuels, D. C., & Shyr, Y. (2013). *RNA Somatic Mutation Caller (RSMC): Identifying somatic mutation using RNAseq data*. Retrieved from https://github.com/shengqh/rsmc/wiki

Guo, Y., Sheng, Q., Li, J., Ye, F., Samuels, D. C., & Shyr, Y. (2013). Large Scale Comparison of Gene Expression Levels by Microarrays and RNAseq Using TCGA Data. *PLoS ONE*, *8*(8), e71462. doi:10.1371/journal.pone.0071462 PMID:23977046

Guo, Y., Ye, F., Sheng, Q., Clark, T., & Samuels, D. C. (2013). Three-stage quality control strategies for DNA re-sequencing data. *Briefings in Bioinformatics*. doi:10.1093/bib/bbt069 PMID:24067931

Heap, G. A., Yang, J. H., Downes, K., Healy, B. C., Hunt, K. A., & Bockett, N. et al. (2010). Genome-wide analysis of allelic expression imbalance in human primary cells by high-throughput transcriptome resequencing. *Human Molecular Genetics*, *19*(1), 122–134. doi:10.1093/hmg/ddp473 PMID:19825846

Hong, D., Rhie, A., Park, S. S., Lee, J., Ju, Y. S., & Kim, S. et al. (2012). FX: An RNA-Seq analysis tool on the cloud. *Bioinformatics (Oxford, England)*, *28*(5), 721–723. doi:10.1093/bioinformatics/bts023 PMID:22257667

Hoque, M., Ji, Z., Zheng, D., Luo, W., Li, W., & You, B. et al. (2013). Analysis of alternative cleavage and polyadenylation by 3' region extraction and deep sequencing. *Nature Methods*, *10*(2), 133–139. doi:10.1038/nmeth.2288 PMID:23241633

Hu, J., Ge, H., Newman, M., & Liu, K. (2012). OSA: A fast and accurate alignment tool for RNA-Seq. *Bioinformatics (Oxford, England)*, *28*(14), 1933–1934. doi:10.1093/bioinformatics/bts294 PMID:22592379

Kalyana-Sundaram, S., Kumar-Sinha, C., Shankar, S., Robinson, D. R., Wu, Y. M., & Cao, X. et al. (2012). Expressed pseudogenes in the transcriptional landscape of human cancers. *Cell*, *149*(7), 1622–1634. doi:10.1016/j.cell.2012.04.041 PMID:22726445

Kawaji, H., Nakamura, M., Takahashi, Y., Sandelin, A., Katayama, S., & Fukuda, S. et al. (2008). Hidden layers of human small RNAs. *BMC Genomics*, *9*(1), 157. doi:10.1186/1471-2164-9-157 PMID:18402656

Khoury, J. D., Tannir, N. M., Williams, M. D., Chen, Y., Yao, H., & Zhang, J. et al. (2013). Landscape of DNA Virus Associations across Human Malignant Cancers: Analysis of 3,775 Cases Using RNA-Seq. *Journal of Virology*, *87*(16), 8916–8926. doi:10.1128/JVI.00340-13 PMID:23740984

Kim, D., Pertea, G., Trapnell, C., Pimentel, H., Kelley, R., & Salzberg, S. L. (2013). TopHat2: Accurate alignment of transcriptomes in the presence of insertions, deletions and gene fusions. *Genome Biology*, *14*(4), R36. doi:10.1186/gb-2013-14-4-r36 PMID:23618408

Koboldt, D. C., Zhang, Q., Larson, D. E., Shen, D., McLellan, M. D., & Lin, L. et al. (2012). VarScan 2: Somatic mutation and copy number alteration discovery in cancer by exome sequencing. *Genome Research*, *22*(3), 568–576. doi:10.1101/gr.129684.111 PMID:22300766

Kostic, A. D., Ojesina, A. I., Pedamallu, C. S., Jung, J., Verhaak, R. G., Getz, G., & Meyerson, M. (2011). PathSeq: Software to identify or discover microbes by deep sequencing of human tissue. *Nature Biotechnology*, *29*(5), 393–396. doi:10.1038/nbt.1868 PMID:21552235

Lee, Y. S., Shibata, Y., Malhotra, A., & Dutta, A. (2009). A novel class of small RNAs: tRNA-derived RNA fragments (tRFs). *Genes & Development*, *23*(22), 2639–2649. doi:10.1101/gad.1837609 PMID:19933153

Li, J. W., Wan, R., Yu, C. S., Co, N. N., Wong, N., & Chan, T. F. (2013). ViralFusionSeq: Accurately discover viral integration events and reconstruct fusion transcripts at single-base resolution. *Bioinformatics (Oxford, England)*, *29*(5), 649–651. doi:10.1093/bioinformatics/btt011 PMID:23314323

Liao, J. Y., Ma, L. M., Guo, Y. H., Zhang, Y. C., Zhou, H., & Shao, P. et al. (2010). Deep sequencing of human nuclear and cytoplasmic small RNAs reveals an unexpectedly complex subcellular distribution of miRNAs and tRNA 3' trailers. *PLoS ONE*, *5*(5), e10563. doi:10.1371/journal.pone.0010563 PMID:20498841

Marioni, J. C., Mason, C. E., Mane, S. M., Stephens, M., & Gilad, Y. (2008). RNA-seq: An assessment of technical reproducibility and comparison with gene expression arrays. *Genome Research*, *18*(9), 1509–1517. doi:10.1101/gr.079558.108 PMID:18550803

Martens-Uzunova, E. S., Olvedy, M., & Jenster, G. (2012). Beyond microRNA – Novel RNAs derived from small non-coding RNA and their implication in cancer. *Cancer Letters*, (0). doi:10.1016/j.canlet.2012.11.058 PMID:23376637

Miller, A. C., Obholzer, N. D., Shah, A. N., Megason, S. G., & Moens, C. B. (2013). RNA-seq-based mapping and candidate identification of mutations from forward genetic screens. *Genome Research*, *23*(4), 679–686. doi:10.1101/gr.147322.112 PMID:23299976

Ozsolak, F., Kapranov, P., Foissac, S., Kim, S. W., Fishilevich, E., & Monaghan, A. P. et al. (2010). Comprehensive polyadenylation site maps in yeast and human reveal pervasive alternative polyadenylation. *Cell*, *143*(6), 1018–1029. doi:10.1016/j.cell.2010.11.020 PMID:21145465

Picardi, E., & Pesole, G. (2012). Mitochondrial genomes gleaned from human whole-exome sequencing. *Nature Methods*, *9*(6), 523–524. doi:10.1038/nmeth.2029 PMID:22669646

Picardi, E., & Pesole, G. (2013). REDItools: High-throughput RNA editing detection made easy. *Bioinformatics (Oxford, England)*, *29*(14), 1813–1814. doi:10.1093/bioinformatics/btt287 PMID:23742983

Piskol, R., Ramaswami, G., & Li, J. B. (2013). Reliable Identification of Genomic Variants from RNA-Seq Data. *American Journal of Human Genetics*, *93*(4), 641–651. doi:10.1016/j.ajhg.2013.08.008 PMID:24075185

Ramaswami, G., Zhang, R., Piskol, R., Keegan, L. P., Deng, P., O'Connell, M. A., & Li, J. B. (2013). Identifying RNA editing sites using RNA sequencing data alone. *Nature Methods*, *10*(2), 128–132. doi:10.1038/nmeth.2330 PMID:23291724

Rozowsky, J., Abyzov, A., Wang, J., Alves, P., Raha, D., & Harmanci, A. et al. (2011). AlleleSeq: Analysis of allele-specific expression and binding in a network framework. *Molecular Systems Biology*, *7*(1), 522. doi:10.1038/msb.2011.54 PMID:21811232

Samuels, D. C., Han, L., Li, J., Quanghu, S., Clark, T. A., Shyr, Y., & Guo, Y. (2013). Finding the lost treasures in exome sequencing data. *Trends in Genetics*, *29*(10), 593–599. doi:10.1016/j.tig.2013.07.006 PMID:23972387

Stevenson, K. R., Coolon, J. D., & Wittkopp, P. J. (2013). Sources of bias in measures of allele-specific expression derived from RNA-seq data aligned to a single reference genome. *BMC Genomics*, *14*(1), 536. doi:10.1186/1471-2164-14-536 PMID:23919664

Sun, W. (2012). A statistical framework for eQTL mapping using RNA-seq data. *Biometrics*, *68*(1), 1–11. doi:10.1111/j.1541-0420.2011.01654.x PMID:21838806

Sun, Y., Fu, Y., Li, Y., & Xu, A. (2012). Genome-wide alternative polyadenylation in animals: Insights from high-throughput technologies. *Journal of Molecular Cell Biology*, *4*(6), 352–361. doi:10.1093/jmcb/mjs041 PMID:23099521

Tam, O. H., Aravin, A. A., Stein, P., Girard, A., Murchison, E. P., & Cheloufi, S. et al. (2008). Pseudogene-derived small interfering RNAs regulate gene expression in mouse oocytes. *Nature*, *453*(7194), 534–538. doi:10.1038/nature06904 PMID:18404147

Tang, K. W., Alaei-Mahabadi, B., Samuelsson, T., Lindh, M., & Larsson, E. (2013). The landscape of viral expression and host gene fusion and adaptation in human cancer. *Nature Communications*, *4*, 2513. doi:10.1038/ncomms3513 PMID:24085110

Thompson, D. M., & Parker, R. (2009). Stressing out over tRNA cleavage. *Cell*, *138*(2), 215–219. doi:10.1016/j.cell.2009.07.001 PMID:19632169

Tian, B., & Manley, J. L. (2013). Alternative cleavage and polyadenylation: The long and short of it. *Trends in Biochemical Sciences*, *38*(6), 312–320. doi:10.1016/j.tibs.2013.03.005 PMID:23632313

Tonner, P., Srinivasasainagendra, V., Zhang, S., & Zhi, D. (2012). Detecting transcription of ribosomal protein pseudogenes in diverse human tissues from RNA-seq data. *BMC Genomics*, *13*(1), 412. doi:10.1186/1471-2164-13-412 PMID:22908858

Wang, K., Li, H., Yuan, Y., Etheridge, A., Zhou, Y., & Huang, D. et al. (2012). The complex exogenous RNA spectra in human plasma: An interface with human gut biota? *PLoS ONE*, *7*(12), e51009. doi:10.1371/journal.pone.0051009 PMID:23251414

Wang, Q., Jia, P., & Zhao, Z. (2013). VirusFinder: Software for efficient and accurate detection of viruses and their integration sites in host genomes through next generation sequencing data. *PLoS ONE*, *8*(5), e64465. doi:10.1371/journal.pone.0064465 PMID:23717618

Wang, Z., Gerstein, M., & Snyder, M. (2009). RNA-Seq: A revolutionary tool for transcriptomics. *Nature Reviews. Genetics*, *10*(1), 57–63. doi:10.1038/nrg2484 PMID:19015660

Watanabe, T., Totoki, Y., Toyoda, A., Kaneda, M., Kuramochi-Miyagawa, S., & Obata, Y. et al. (2008). Endogenous siRNAs from naturally formed dsRNAs regulate transcripts in mouse oocytes. *Nature*, *453*(7194), 539–543. doi:10.1038/nature06908 PMID:18404146

Yoon, K., Lee, S., Han, T. S., Moon, S. Y., Yun, S. M., & Kong, S. H. et al. (2013). Comprehensive genome- and transcriptome-wide analyses of mutations associated with microsatellite instability in Korean gastric cancers. *Genome Research*, *23*(7), 1109–1117. doi:10.1101/gr.145706.112 PMID:23737375

Zheng, X., Pan, C., Diao, Y., You, Y., Yang, C., & Hu, Z. (2013). Development of microsatellite markers by transcriptome sequencing in two species of Amorphophallus (Araceae). *BMC Genomics*, *14*(1), 490. doi:10.1186/1471-2164-14-490 PMID:23870214

ADDITIONAL READING

Agranat, L., Raitskin, O., Sperling, J., & Sperling, R. (2008). The editing enzyme ADAR1 and the mRNA surveillance protein hUpf1 interact in the cell nucleus. *Proceedings of the National Academy of Sciences of the United States of America*, *105*(13), 5028–5033. doi:10.1073/pnas.0710576105 PMID:18362360

Asmann, Y. W., Klee, E. W., Thompson, E. A., Perez, E. A., Middha, S., & Oberg, A. L. et al. (2009). 3' tag digital gene expression profiling of human brain and universal reference RNA using Illumina Genome Analyzer. *BMC Genomics*, *10*(1), 531. doi:10.1186/1471-2164-10-531 PMID:19917133

Bernstein, B. E., Birney, E., Dunham, I., Green, E. D., Gunter, C., & Snyder, M. (2012). An integrated encyclopedia of DNA elements in the human genome. *Nature*, *489*(7414), 57–74. doi:10.1038/nature11247 PMID:22955616

Bray, N. J., Buckland, P. R., Owen, M. J., & O'Donovan, M. C. (2003). Cis-acting variation in the expression of a high proportion of genes in human brain. *Human Genetics*, *113*(2), 149–153. doi:10.1007/s00439-003-0956-y PMID:12728311

Cabili, M. N., Trapnell, C., Goff, L., Koziol, M., Tazon-Vega, B., Regev, A., & Rinn, J. L. (2011). Integrative annotation of human large intergenic noncoding RNAs reveals global properties and specific subclasses. *Genes & Development*, *25*(18), 1915–1927. doi:10.1101/gad.17446611 PMID:21890647

Chaudhuri, R. R., Yu, L., Kanji, A., Perkins, T. T., Gardner, P. P., & Choudhary, J. et al. (2011). Quantitative RNA-seq analysis of the Campylobacter jejuni transcriptome. *Microbiology*, *157*(Pt 10), 2922–2932. doi:10.1099/mic.0.050278-0 PMID:21816880

Chen, X., Zen, K., & Zhang, C. Y. (2013). Reply to Lack of detectable oral bioavailability of plant microRNAs after feeding in mice. *Nature Biotechnology*, *31*(11), 967–969. doi:10.1038/nbt.2741 PMID:24213764

Cibulskis, K., Lawrence, M. S., Carter, S. L., Sivachenko, A., Jaffe, D., & Sougnez, C. et al. (2013). Sensitive detection of somatic point mutations in impure and heterogeneous cancer samples. *Nature Biotechnology*, *31*(3), 213–219. doi:10.1038/nbt.2514 PMID:23396013

Cloonan, N., Forrest, A. R., Kolle, G., Gardiner, B. B., Faulkner, G. J., & Brown, M. K. et al. (2008). Stem cell transcriptome profiling via massive-scale mRNA sequencing. *Nature Methods*, *5*(7), 613–619. doi:10.1038/nmeth.1223 PMID:18516046

Cole, C., Sobala, A., Lu, C., Thatcher, S. R., Bowman, A., & Brown, J. W. et al. (2009). Filtering of deep sequencing data reveals the existence of abundant Dicer-dependent small RNAs derived from tRNAs. *RNA (New York, N.Y.)*, *15*(12), 2147–2160. doi:10.1261/rna.1738409 PMID:19850906

Degner, J. F., Marioni, J. C., Pai, A. A., Pickrell, J. K., Nkadori, E., Gilad, Y., & Pritchard, J. K. (2009). Effect of read-mapping biases on detecting allele-specific expression from RNA-sequencing data. *Bioinformatics (Oxford, England)*, *25*(24), 3207–3212. doi:10.1093/bioinformatics/btp579 PMID:19808877

DePristo, M. A., Banks, E., Poplin, R., Garimella, K. V., Maguire, J. R., & Hartl, C. et al. (2011). A framework for variation discovery and genotyping using next-generation DNA sequencing data. *Nature Genetics*, *43*(5), 491–498. doi:10.1038/ng.806 PMID:21478889

Dickinson, B., Zhang, Y., Petrick, J. S., Heck, G., Ivashuta, S., & Marshall, W. S. (2013). Lack of detectable oral bioavailability of plant microRNAs after feeding in mice. *Nature Biotechnology*, *31*(11), 965–967. doi:10.1038/nbt.2737 PMID:24213763

Djebali, S., Davis, C. A., Merkel, A., Dobin, A., Lassmann, T., & Mortazavi, A. et al. (2012). Landscape of transcription in human cells. *Nature*, *489*(7414), 101–108. doi:10.1038/nature11233 PMID:22955620

Drake, J. W., Charlesworth, B., Charlesworth, D., & Crow, J. F. (1998). Rates of spontaneous mutation. *Genetics*, *148*(4), 1667–1686. PMID:9560386

Duitama, J., Srivastava, P., & Mandoiu, I. (2012). Towards accurate detection and genotyping of expressed variants from whole transcriptome sequencing data. *BMC Genomics*, *13*(Suppl 2), S6. doi:10.1186/1471-2164-13-S2-S6 PMID:22537301

Gregg, C., Zhang, J., Weissbourd, B., Luo, S., Schroth, G. P., Haig, D., & Dulac, C. (2010). High-resolution analysis of parent-of-origin allelic expression in the mouse brain. *Science*, *329*(5992), 643–648. doi:10.1126/science.1190830 PMID:20616232

Guo, Y., Li, C. I., Ye, F., & Shyr, Y. (2013). Evaluation of read count based RNAseq analysis methods. *BMC Genomics*, *14*(Suppl 8), S2. doi:10.1186/1471-2164-14-S8-S2 PMID:24564449

Guo, Y., Li, J., Li, C. I., Shyr, Y., & Samuels, D. C. (2013). MitoSeek: Extracting mitochondria information and performing high-throughput mitochondria sequencing analysis. *Bioinformatics (Oxford, England), 29*(9), 1210–1211. doi:10.1093/bioinformatics/btt118 PMID:23471301

Guo, Y., Long, J., He, J., Li, C. I., Cai, Q., & Shu, X. O. et al. (2012). Exome sequencing generates high quality data in non-target regions. *BMC Genomics, 13*(1), 194. doi:10.1186/1471-2164-13-194 PMID:22607156

Guo, Y., Samuels, D. C., Li, J., Clark, T., Li, C. I., & Shyr, Y. (2013). Evaluation of allele frequency estimation using pooled sequencing data simulation. *TheScientificWorldJournal, 895496.* doi:10.1155/2013/895496 PMID:23476151

Guo, Y., Sheng, Q., Li, C., Samuels, D. C., & Shyr, Y. (2013). RNA Somatic Mutation Caller (RSMC): identifying somatic mutation using RNAseq data. from https://github.com/shengqh/rsmc/wiki

Guo, Y., Sheng, Q., Li, J., Ye, F., Samuels, D. C., & Shyr, Y. (2013). Large Scale Comparison of Gene Expression Levels by Microarrays and RNAseq Using TCGA Data. *PLoS ONE, 8*(8), e71462. doi:10.1371/journal.pone.0071462 PMID:23977046

Guo, Y., Ye, F., Sheng, Q., Clark, T., & Samuels, D. C. (2013). Three-stage quality control strategies for DNA re-sequencing data. *Briefings in Bioinformatics.* doi:10.1093/bib/bbt069 PMID:24067931

Heap, G. A., Yang, J. H., Downes, K., Healy, B. C., Hunt, K. A., & Bockett, N. et al. (2010). Genome-wide analysis of allelic expression imbalance in human primary cells by high-throughput transcriptome resequencing. *Human Molecular Genetics, 19*(1), 122–134. doi:10.1093/hmg/ddp473 PMID:19825846

Hong, D., Rhie, A., Park, S. S., Lee, J., Ju, Y. S., & Kim, S. et al. (2012). FX: An RNA-Seq analysis tool on the cloud. *Bioinformatics (Oxford, England), 28*(5), 721–723. doi:10.1093/bioinformatics/bts023 PMID:22257667

Hoque, M., Ji, Z., Zheng, D., Luo, W., Li, W., & You, B. et al. (2013). Analysis of alternative cleavage and polyadenylation by 3' region extraction and deep sequencing. *Nature Methods, 10*(2), 133–139. doi:10.1038/nmeth.2288 PMID:23241633

Hu, J., Ge, H., Newman, M., & Liu, K. (2012). OSA: A fast and accurate alignment tool for RNA-Seq. *Bioinformatics (Oxford, England), 28*(14), 1933–1934. doi:10.1093/bioinformatics/bts294 PMID:22592379

Kalyana-Sundaram, S., Kumar-Sinha, C., Shankar, S., Robinson, D. R., Wu, Y. M., & Cao, X. et al. (2012). Expressed pseudogenes in the transcriptional landscape of human cancers. *Cell, 149*(7), 1622–1634. doi:10.1016/j.cell.2012.04.041 PMID:22726445

Kawaji, H., Nakamura, M., Takahashi, Y., Sandelin, A., Katayama, S., & Fukuda, S. et al. (2008). Hidden layers of human small RNAs. *BMC Genomics, 9*(1), 157. doi:10.1186/1471-2164-9-157 PMID:18402656

Khoury, J. D., Tannir, N. M., Williams, M. D., Chen, Y., Yao, H., & Zhang, J. et al. (2013). Landscape of DNA Virus Associations across Human Malignant Cancers: Analysis of 3,775 Cases Using RNA-Seq. *Journal of Virology, 87*(16), 8916–8926. doi:10.1128/JVI.00340-13 PMID:23740984

Kim, D., Pertea, G., Trapnell, C., Pimentel, H., Kelley, R., & Salzberg, S. L. (2013). TopHat2: Accurate alignment of transcriptomes in the presence of insertions, deletions and gene fusions. *Genome Biology, 14*(4), R36. doi:10.1186/gb-2013-14-4-r36 PMID:23618408

Koboldt, D. C., Zhang, Q., Larson, D. E., Shen, D., McLellan, M. D., & Lin, L. et al. (2012). VarScan 2: Somatic mutation and copy number alteration discovery in cancer by exome sequencing. *Genome Research*, *22*(3), 568–576. doi:10.1101/gr.129684.111 PMID:22300766

Kostic, A. D., Ojesina, A. I., Pedamallu, C. S., Jung, J., Verhaak, R. G., Getz, G., & Meyerson, M. (2011). PathSeq: Software to identify or discover microbes by deep sequencing of human tissue. *Nature Biotechnology*, *29*(5), 393–396. doi:10.1038/nbt.1868 PMID:21552235

Lee, Y. S., Shibata, Y., Malhotra, A., & Dutta, A. (2009). A novel class of small RNAs: tRNA-derived RNA fragments (tRFs). *Genes & Development*, *23*(22), 2639–2649. doi:10.1101/gad.1837609 PMID:19933153

Li, J. W., Wan, R., Yu, C. S., Co, N. N., Wong, N., & Chan, T. F. (2013). ViralFusionSeq: Accurately discover viral integration events and reconstruct fusion transcripts at single-base resolution. *Bioinformatics (Oxford, England)*, *29*(5), 649–651. doi:10.1093/bioinformatics/btt011 PMID:23314323

Liao, J. Y., Ma, L. M., Guo, Y. H., Zhang, Y. C., Zhou, H., & Shao, P. et al. (2010). Deep sequencing of human nuclear and cytoplasmic small RNAs reveals an unexpectedly complex subcellular distribution of miRNAs and tRNA 3' trailers. *PLoS ONE*, *5*(5), e10563. doi:10.1371/journal.pone.0010563 PMID:20498841

Marioni, J. C., Mason, C. E., Mane, S. M., Stephens, M., & Gilad, Y. (2008). RNA-seq: An assessment of technical reproducibility and comparison with gene expression arrays. *Genome Research*, *18*(9), 1509–1517. doi:10.1101/gr.079558.108 PMID:18550803

Martens-Uzunova, Elena S., Olvedy, Michael, & Jenster, Guido. Beyond microRNA – Novel RNAs derived from small non-coding RNA and their implication in cancer. *Cancer Letters*(0). doi: 10.1016/j.canlet.2012.11.058

Miller, A. C., Obholzer, N. D., Shah, A. N., Megason, S. G., & Moens, C. B. (2013). RNA-seq-based mapping and candidate identification of mutations from forward genetic screens. *Genome Research*, *23*(4), 679–686. doi:10.1101/gr.147322.112 PMID:23299976

Ozsolak, F., Kapranov, P., Foissac, S., Kim, S. W., Fishilevich, E., & Monaghan, A. P. et al. (2010). Comprehensive polyadenylation site maps in yeast and human reveal pervasive alternative polyadenylation. *Cell*, *143*(6), 1018–1029. doi:10.1016/j.cell.2010.11.020 PMID:21145465

Picardi, E., & Pesole, G. (2012). Mitochondrial genomes gleaned from human whole-exome sequencing. *Nature Methods*, *9*(6), 523–524. doi:10.1038/nmeth.2029 PMID:22669646

Picardi, E., & Pesole, G. (2013). REDItools: High-throughput RNA editing detection made easy. *Bioinformatics (Oxford, England)*, *29*(14), 1813–1814. doi:10.1093/bioinformatics/btt287 PMID:23742983

Piskol, R., Ramaswami, G., & Li, J. B. (2013). Reliable Identification of Genomic Variants from RNA-Seq Data. *American Journal of Human Genetics*, *93*(4), 641–651. doi:10.1016/j.ajhg.2013.08.008 PMID:24075185

Ramaswami, G., Zhang, R., Piskol, R., Keegan, L. P., Deng, P., O'Connell, M. A., & Li, J. B. (2013). Identifying RNA editing sites using RNA sequencing data alone. *Nature Methods*, *10*(2), 128–132. doi:10.1038/nmeth.2330 PMID:23291724

Rozowsky, J., Abyzov, A., Wang, J., Alves, P., Raha, D., & Harmanci, A. et al. (2011). AlleleSeq: Analysis of allele-specific expression and binding in a network framework. *Molecular Systems Biology*, *7*(1), 522. doi:10.1038/msb.2011.54 PMID:21811232

Samuels, D. C., Han, L., Li, J., Quanghu, S., Clark, T. A., Shyr, Y., & Guo, Y. (2013). Finding the lost treasures in exome sequencing data. *Trends in Genetics*, *29*(10), 593–599. doi:10.1016/j.tig.2013.07.006 PMID:23972387

Stevenson, K. R., Coolon, J. D., & Wittkopp, P. J. (2013). Sources of bias in measures of allele-specific expression derived from RNA-seq data aligned to a single reference genome. *BMC Genomics*, *14*(1), 536. doi:10.1186/1471-2164-14-536 PMID:23919664

Sun, W. (2012). A statistical framework for eQTL mapping using RNA-seq data. *Biometrics*, *68*(1), 1–11. doi:10.1111/j.1541-0420.2011.01654.x PMID:21838806

Sun, Y., Fu, Y., Li, Y., & Xu, A. (2012a). Genome-wide alternative polyadenylation in animals: Insights from high-throughput technologies. *Journal of Molecular Cell Biology*, *4*(6), 352–361. doi:10.1093/jmcb/mjs041 PMID:23099521

Sun, Y., Fu, Y., Li, Y., & Xu, A. (2012b). Genome-wide alternative polyadenylation in animals: Insights from high-throughput technologies. *Journal of Molecular Cell Biology*, *4*(6), 352–361. doi:10.1093/jmcb/mjs041 PMID:23099521

Tam, O. H., Aravin, A. A., Stein, P., Girard, A., Murchison, E. P., & Cheloufi, S. et al. (2008). Pseudogene-derived small interfering RNAs regulate gene expression in mouse oocytes. *Nature*, *453*(7194), 534–538. doi:10.1038/nature06904 PMID:18404147

Tang, K. W., Alaei-Mahabadi, B., Samuelsson, T., Lindh, M., & Larsson, E. (2013). The landscape of viral expression and host gene fusion and adaptation in human cancer. *Nature Communications*, *4*, 2513. doi:10.1038/ncomms3513 PMID:24085110

Thompson, D. M., & Parker, R. (2009). Stressing out over tRNA cleavage. *Cell*, *138*(2), 215–219. doi:10.1016/j.cell.2009.07.001 PMID:19632169

Tian, B., & Manley, J. L. (2013). Alternative cleavage and polyadenylation: The long and short of it. *Trends in Biochemical Sciences*, *38*(6), 312–320. doi:10.1016/j.tibs.2013.03.005 PMID:23632313

Tonner, P., Srinivasasainagendra, V., Zhang, S., & Zhi, D. (2012). Detecting transcription of ribosomal protein pseudogenes in diverse human tissues from RNA-seq data. *BMC Genomics*, *13*(1), 412. doi:10.1186/1471-2164-13-412 PMID:22908858

Wang, K., Li, H., Yuan, Y., Etheridge, A., Zhou, Y., & Huang, D. et al. (2012). The complex exogenous RNA spectra in human plasma: An interface with human gut biota? *PLoS ONE*, *7*(12), e51009. doi:10.1371/journal.pone.0051009 PMID:23251414

Wang, Q., Jia, P., & Zhao, Z. (2013). VirusFinder: Software for efficient and accurate detection of viruses and their integration sites in host genomes through next generation sequencing data. *PLoS ONE*, *8*(5), e64465. doi:10.1371/journal.pone.0064465 PMID:23717618

Wang, Z., Gerstein, M., & Snyder, M. (2009). RNA-Seq: A revolutionary tool for transcriptomics. *Nature Reviews. Genetics*, *10*(1), 57–63. doi:10.1038/nrg2484 PMID:19015660

Watanabe, T., Totoki, Y., Toyoda, A., Kaneda, M., Kuramochi-Miyagawa, S., & Obata, Y. et al. (2008). Endogenous siRNAs from naturally formed dsRNAs regulate transcripts in mouse oocytes. *Nature*, *453*(7194), 539–543. doi:10.1038/nature06908 PMID:18404146

Yoon, K., Lee, S., Han, T. S., Moon, S. Y., Yun, S. M., & Kong, S. H. et al. (2013). Comprehensive genome- and transcriptome-wide analyses of mutations associated with microsatellite instability in Korean gastric cancers. *Genome Research*, *23*(7), 1109–1117. doi:10.1101/gr.145706.112 PMID:23737375

Zheng, X., Pan, C., Diao, Y., You, Y., Yang, C., & Hu, Z. (2013). Development of microsatellite markers by transcriptome sequencing in two species of Amorphophallus (Araceae). *BMC Genomics*, *14*(1), 490. doi:10.1186/1471-2164-14-490 PMID:23870214

KEY TERMS AND DEFINITIONS

Allele Specific Expression: Allele specific expression is the preferential expression of one of the two alleles in a diploid genome.

Gene Expression: Gene expression is the process by which information from a gene is used in the synthesis of a functional gene product.

MicroRNA (miRNA): miRNA is a small non-coding RNA usually containing 22 nucleotides. It functions in transcriptional and post-transcriptional regulation of gene expression.

Next-Generation Sequencing (NGS): Also referred to as high-throughput sequencing, NGS is a technology which generates the precise order of nucleotides within a genomic sequence.

Non-Coding RNA (ncRNA): Non-coding RNA are RNAs that are not translated into proteins.

Polyadenylation: Polyadenylation is the addition of a poly A tail to the primary transcript RNA.

RNA Editing: RNA editing is a molecular process through which some cells can make discrete changes to specific nucleotide sequences within an RNA molecule after it has been generated by RNA polymerase.

RNAseq: RNAseq is a utilization of NGS technology used to sequence cDNA fragments reversed transcribed from RNA.

Single Nucleotide Polymorphism (SNP): A SNP is a DNA sequence variation occurring when a single nucleotide in the genome differs between members of a biological species. SNPs are germline mutations, inherited from a parent.

Somatic Mutation: A somatic mutation is a variation in the DNA sequence that is not inherited from a parent.

Chapter 2
Text Mining on Big and Complex Biomedical Literature

Boya Xie
East Carolina University, USA

Qin Ding
East Carolina University, USA

Di Wu
Drexel University, USA

ABSTRACT

Driven by the rapidly advancing techniques and increasing interests in biology and medicine, about 2,000 to 4,000 references are added daily to MEDLINE, the US national biomedical bibliographic database. Even for a specific research topic, extracting useful and comprehensive information out of the huge literature data pool is challenging. Text mining techniques become extremely useful when dealing with the abundant biomedical information and they have been applied to various areas in the realm of biomedical research. Instead of providing a brief overview of all text mining techniques and every major biomedical text mining application, this chapter explores in-depth the microRNA profiling area and related text mining tools. As an illustrative example, one rule-based text mining system developed by the authors is discussed in detail. This chapter also includes the discussion of the challenges and potential research areas in biomedical text mining.

INTRODUCTION

Text mining is a process that automatically derives quality information from text, also known as text analysis or data analytics. It was first introduced with labor-intensive manual approaches in the mid-1980s. Later, it has evolved to use intelligent approaches and algorithms to derive useful and quality information from text. Techniques involved in text mining come from multiple disciplines, such as information retrieval, data mining, machine learning, natural language processing, etc. With the big, complex, and fast-changing text data, it is challenging yet rewarding to perform text mining to extract useful and reliable information, which will greatly benefit researchers in various fields.

DOI: 10.4018/978-1-4666-6611-5.ch002

Biomedicine has been one of these fields where text-mining is utilized extensively. Some of the text mining applications in biomedical research include gene ontology, signal transduction pathway and gene mining, yeast metabolites extracting, disease specific mutation-gene pair identification, protein interactions, and microRNA profiling. From the application perspective, text-mining could be categorized as the following five major classes: Gene-centric, protein-centric, microRNA-centric, disease related, and pathway mining. From the text analysis objective perspective, text-mining could be categorized as: name entity recognition (NER), association extraction, and event extraction. A brief introduction of all these categories is presented in the background section. Because microRNA (miRNA) is used as the example throughout this chapter, the background information of miRNA as well as a comprehensive review of miRNA-centric text-mining applications is also provided in the background section.

MiRNA is a small sequence of nucleotides that plays an important role in many biological processes. Abundant research has been carried out to study miRNA functionalities, emphasizing on its profile in diseases. This chapter takes mining for miRNA profile in human cancer as an example, walks through steps that construct a typical text-mining system: data preparation, information extraction, and result validation. Questions such as where and at what granularity to gather source text, how to clean data for miRNA specific literature are discussed in the data preparation section. Information extraction section covers miRNA, cancer, and expression term recognition, followed by the discussion of co-occurrence-based, rule-based and machine learning dependent approaches that discover miRNA-cancer relationships. Result validation and system evaluation methods are briefly described. This chapter concludes with a discussion of challenges and future research directions in miRNA-centric text mining. Potential biomedical areas that may deal with big data as well as possible approaches are presented at the end of this chapter.

BACKGROUND

The knowledge and techniques in biomedicine have been advanced drastically. Collaboration among computer science, physics, mathematics, and engineering has enabled biomedical researchers to explore solutions to many of the world's most concerned health problems. Biomedicine research topics span from molecules to macro environment. Text mining has been applied to many of these data intensive areas. The most studied areas in biomedicine text-mining are discussed as follows.

Categorize by Applied Area

Gene-centric mining is the most popular area where research is carried out to study what is gene and how it works. The double helix molecule deoxyribonucleic acid (DNA) brings instructions for development and functioning for all living organisms. The entire DNA does not carry information at each section, and regions that are informative are called genes. Understanding gene greatly helps to explain many biological processes. Gene-centric mining consists of gene name recognition (R. McDonald & Pereira, 2005; Sasaki, Tsuruoka, McNaught, & Ananiadou, 2008), gene relationship mining (Chen & Sharp, 2004; Y. Liu et al., 2005), gene-disease association mining (Al-Mubaid & Singh, 2010; Bauer-Mehren, Rautschka, Sanz, & Furlong, 2010; Ozgur, Vu, Erkan, & Radev, 2008), gene-drug relationship mining (Garten, Tatonetti, & Altman, 2010), and gene annotation (Aerts et al., 2008; Haeussler, Gerner, & Bergman, 2011). After the completion of the Human Genome Project in 2003, the genome research direction has shifted from identifying genes towards understanding the human genome functionalities in both health and disease. The Gene Ontology project (Ashburner et al., 2000) provides a unified representation of gene and gene product attributes that becomes a standard reference for many other systems annotating genes and gene products.

Protein-related mining has protein as the primary learning focus. As gene is the carrier of biology instructions, protein is the large molecule performing these instructions. Protein and gene are closely related to each other; therefore, protein-related mining is similar to gene-centric ones which include: protein name recognition (Torii, Hu, Wu, & Liu, 2009; Yamamoto, Kudo, Konagaya, & Matsumoto, 2004), mining for interactions between proteins (Kim, Kwon, Shin, & Wilbur, 2012; Krallinger et al., 2012), and protein annotation (Couto et al., 2006; Veuthey et al., 2013). Since protein is the product of gene, oftentimes protein and gene text-mining are integrated together.

MicroRNA-centric mining is a relatively new area for biomedical text-mining as microRNA (miRNA) was not introduced until recent decade. Nonetheless, it has been shown that miRNA plays an important role in biological processes as gene regulator. Corresponding text-mining studies have been carried out to discover miRNA-gene associations (Murray, Choe, Woods, Ryan, & Liu, 2010; Vergoulis et al., 2012). Research has also been extended to areas such as miRNA association with signaling pathway (Shirdel, Xie, Mak, & Jurisica, 2011), miRNA annotation (H. Liu et al., 2012), and miRNA-cancer relationship mining (Dong et al., 2013; Xie, Ding, Han, & Wu, 2013).

Disease related mining has two major objectives: discover etiology of diseases and collect information to suggest disease treatments. Text-mining has been carried out to understand the cause of disease from different perspectives, such as chemical and gene/protein interactions with diseases (Wiegers, Davis, Cohen, Hirschman, & Mattingly, 2009), and miRNA relation with diseases (Jiang et al., 2009). The etiology information is usually mined from publications of lab experiments. On the contrary, disease treatments are mostly collected from clinical documentations, such as clinic discharge summary. The kinds of information gathered to help with decision-making for disease treatments include but are not limited to:

symptoms and treatments (Yang, Spasic, Keane, & Nenadic, 2009), disease-disease relationships (Holzinger, Simonic, & Yildirim, 2012), and drug-disease connections (Frijters et al., 2010).

Pathway mining provides highly structured information about known biomolecular interactions and reaction networks. The collected data are normally presented graphically to display the intuitive view of the networks. Besides the visualization component, pathway mining is distinct from other mining applications in the way that pathways are typically not presented in literature; instead, the mining process discovers individual interactions and combines them into networks. Pathway mining is important for system biology. It helps connecting studies from different areas together. Studies have shown that molecules tend to interact as a group effect rather than individually. Some examples of pathway mining systems are: PathText (Kemper et al., 2010), Daniel's system (D. McDonald et al., 2005), and Jan's methods (Czarnecki, Nobeli, Smith, & Shepherd, 2012).

All the aforementioned application areas do not have clear boundary lines with each other. For instance, pathway mining relies on mining of gene and protein relationships. As a result, biomedical text mining sometimes is also categorized by the mining tasks.

Categorize by Mining Task

Name Entity Recognition (NER) is common to most text mining applications, which identifies research target object names from unstructured text. Depending on the characteristics of the targeting entities, different approaches are used. Generally, the approaches fall into three categories: dictionary based, rule based, and statistically based. Some hybrid systems combining these techniques have shown promising performance, such as the system described in (Sasaki et al, 2008). There are several challenges NER systems are frequently facing. First of all, synonymies are used in writing, especially when referring to biology entities without single standard naming. For instance, "MMAC1" and "PTEN" both refer to the same tumor suppressive gene; similarly, "osteoarthritis" and "degenerative arthritis" both mean the same degenerative joint disease. Secondly, even for objects that have standard name conventions, the names sometimes are written in their short form for convenience. Studies have been carried out to deal with abbreviations and acronyms, such as Acromine (Okazaki, N., Ananiadou, S., & Tsujii, J., 2010). Last but not least, scientists discover new knowledge constantly, and new names are being created all the time. Therefore the techniques detecting these names need to be able to keep up.

Association Extraction aims to detect binary relationships among biology entities. The types of identified relationships may include any type of biomedical association in the literature. The most widely studied topics in biomedical information extraction include Protein-Protein Interaction (PPI), gene and diseases relation (Chun et al., 2006), and the association between patients' symptoms and the tests or treatments they may undergo (Uzuner, South, Shen, & DuVall, 2011). Association extraction faces many of the same challenges as NER does. The approaches to solving the relation extraction problem have evolved from simple co-occurrence statistics, rule-based or classification based approaches alone to sophisticated systems utilizing syntactic analysis and dependency parsing.

Event Extraction differs from association extraction in that event extraction not only answers the question whether two objects are related, but also how they are related. The event is usually described by a verb. For example, in the sentence "miR-122 suppresses breast cancer," the verb "suppresses" states how miR-122 and breast cancer are related. Besides these binary events, nested event and multiple binary events connected into a chained event can also exist. The complexity and ambiguity in biomedical event extraction requires in-depth analysis of sentence semantics. Natural

language processing techniques has been broadly applied in event extraction. To mention some of these methods: lemmatization (Liu, Christiansen, Baumgartner, & Verspoor, 2012), semantic classification (Cohen, Christiansen, Baumgartner, Verspoor, & Hunter, 2011), Link Grammar (Pyysalo, Salakoshi, Aubin, & Nazarenko, 2006; Sleator & Temperley, 1991), and so on.

Clearly, because of the explosion of biomedical discovery and the amount of published biomedical literature, researchers need the computational assistance to cope with information overload. In this chapter, we will take microRNA, a specific biological subfield as an example to explain how text mining aids biomedical researchers in making more efficient use of the existing literature.

MicroRNA Basics

MicroRNAs, by definition, are endogenous, non-coding 21 to 23 nucleotide small RNA molecules that regulate gene expression by binding to the 3'-untranslated region of target messenger RNAs (mRNA), leading to their translational inhibition or degradation. The mechanism of regulating gene expression by small RNAs was first observed in petunia in early 1990s. When an exogenous RNA sequence was introduced into petunia, instead of being translated into protein, it 'silenced' endogenous homologous gene's expression. This gene-silencing phenomenon was then characterized in *Caenorhabditis elegans* by Andrew Fire and Craig Mello in 1998, which they termed 'RNA interference' (RNAi). The discovery of RNAi brought Andrew and Craig Nobel Prize in Physiology or Medicine in 2006. RNAi was originally recognized as a defensive response to foreign nucleic acids from virus's infection by preventing the synthesis of protein necessary for viral replication. It also protects the eukaryotic genome from endogenous transposable elements and it was later demonstrated that RNAi is required for normal development. Endogenous small RNAs, such as

Let-7 and Lin-4, were initially identified in *C. elegans* and the term 'microRNA' (miRNA) was then introduced in a series of subsequent studies in early 2000s.

miRNAs play an important role in many biological processes by binding to mRNAs, thus regulating gene expressions. Besides biological methods that validate miRNA targets, such as Northern blot analysis and real-time PCR, computational algorithms have been utilized for predicting miRNA targets based on the following two rules. The primary rule for mRNA targeting is the perfect base pairing of the 'seed region', which is located at the miRNA nucleotides 2 to 8. Perfect and contiguous Watson-Crick base pairing at this limited region associates miRNA with target mRNA (Filipowicz, Bhattacharyya, & Sonenberg, 2008). The second rule requires a mismatch to be present in the central region of the miRNA-mRNA duplex. The bulge generated by the mismatch precludes the Ago-2 mediated endonucleolytic cleavage of mRNA (Filipowicz et al., 2008). Some base pairing at the other half side of miRNAs, especially the 13-16 nucleotides would stabilize the binding between miRNA and mRNA as well (Grimson et al., 2007). Although computational predictions can efficiently identify miRNA targets, the results are not absolutely accurate because of exceptions to these rules. Experimental steps are suggested to confirm the predicted results (Kuhn et al., 2008).

Computational predictions indicate that mammalian miRNAs can regulate at least 30% of all protein coding genes (Filipowicz et al., 2008). Therefore, it is no surprise that miRNA based regulations are involved in many cellular process. miRNA plays diverse roles in cell differentiation, proliferation (Stefani & Slack, 2008), metabolism (Wang et al., 2011), and signal transduction (McCoy, 2011). Dysregulation of miRNA has been documented in developmental defects and diseases, which indicates that miRNAs may also play a role as diagnostic or prognostic biomarker. For instance, miR-1, a muscle-enriched miRNA

has increased expression level in both experiential acute myocardial infarction animal models as well as patients with acute myocardial infarction (Fichtlscherer, Zeiher, & Dimmeler, 2011). miR-423-5P increases circulating level in the plasma samples from patients with heart failure (Tutarel et al., 2013). Extensive studies have documented profound alteration of miRNA expression in all major human cancers. For example, miR-15a and miR-16 are severely down-regulated in 70% of patients with chronic lymphocytic leukemia. B-cell lymphoma 2 (BLC2), an anti-apoptotic factor was found to be the target gene of miR-15 and miR-16. Loss of miR-15 and miR-16 is responsible for the overexpression of BLC2 in chronic lymphocytic leukemia specimens (Ofir, Hacohen, & Ginsberg, 2011). Alternatively, some miRNAs are overexpressed in cancer specimens. These miRNAs are defined as oncomiR and the most characterized oncomiR is miR-21. miR-21 acts as an oncogene by regulating the tumor-suppressor genes PTEN an PDCD, and the up-regulation of miRNA has been found in over 15 different cancers (Koturbash, Zemp, Pogribny, & Kovalchuk, 2011). A number of miRNAs can work as both oncogene and tumor suppressor. For example, miR-220 is up-regulated in pancreatic and thyroid cancer, but significantly down-regulated in lung cancer (Boissonneault, Plante, Rivest, & Provost, 2009). The tumor type-selective miRNA dysregulation may be useful for diagnostic and prognostic purpose. miRNA expression profile can help distinguish tumor histopathological subtypes, determine the stage of carcinogenic process, determine tumor's aggressiveness, modulate drug resistance, and predict overall survival and recurrent rates (Koturbash et al., 2011).

Review of miRNA-Centric Mining Systems

Despite the fact that miRNA has many functionalities, the initial known profiles are limited. As a result, the need for miRNA-centric text-mining was not as high as gene or protein related ones. The earlier demands for miRNA information collection were met by manual curations. Manually-curated miRNA-centric systems include: TarBase (version 1-5) (Papadopoulos, Reczko, Simossis, Sethupathy, & Hatzigeorgiou, 2009; Sethupathy, Corda, & Hatzigeorgiou, 2006), Argonaute (Shahi et al., 2006), miR2Disease (Jiang et al., 2009), dbDEMC (Z. Yang et al., 2010), PhenomiR (Ruepp et al., 2010), miRRecords (Xiao et al., 2009), miRTarBase (Hsu et al., 2011), and TUMIR (Dong et al., 2013). As the miRNA research area expands and the volume of literature increases, it becomes more and more difficult to manually process even a specific field in miRNA research. The opportunity for automatic text-mining on miRNA related documentations leads to the creation of computer aided systems, such as: miRSel (Ozgur et al., 2008), miRWalk (Dweep, Sticht, Pandey, & Gretz, 2011), TarBase 6 (Vergoulis et al., 2012), and miRCancer (Xie, Ding, Han, & Wu, 2013). Three manually-curated systems and three automatic/semi-automatic mined systems are reviewed in the order of the published year.

- *TarBase* developed by DIANA lab is the pioneer database hosting experimentally validated miRNA targets. It was first released in 2005 with more than 550 manually curated miRNA targets from human, mouse, fruit fly, worm, and zebra fish. Since then TarBase has been updated and improved through 6 release versions where the first 5 versions are manually-curated. The latest version *TarBase 6.0* published in 2011 introduced an auto-text-mining pipeline into the curation process. As TarBase 6.0 aims to continue providing full accuracy as previous versions, the computer aided text-mining module is only used to assist manual curation rather than replacing human work. This newly added module applied strategies such as NER, association identification, scoring and en-

hanced text presentation. The benefit from text-mining module is tremendous as it has increased the miRNA targets collection to over 65,000.

- *Argonaute* is a manually curated database of mammalian miRNAs and miRNA annotations that was published in 2006. It was first published with 839 miRNAs from human, mouse, and rat, and reported 312 miRNA-target relationships. Argonaute was later transformed into *miRWalk* with emphasize on its miRNA targets prediction module. The validated targets module of miRWalk is an automated text-mining system which performs NER on abstracts from PubMed and records mammalian miRNA relationships with various biology objects, such as genes and disease. The miRWalk text-mining module currently hosts 2044 miRNAs from human, mouse and rat, and reports 67,598 miRNA-target relationships. It is automatically updated quarterly. MiRWalk claims that it provides high recall rate of over 90.07%, but the precision is not provided.

- *PhenomiR* database collected miRNA expression in diseases and biological processes by experienced biocurators. It was initially published in 2010 with 11,029 experimental miRNA expressions of 347 miRNAs. With the latest update in February 2011, PhenomiR records 675 miRNAs with 12,192 expressions in 145 types of diseases. PhenomiR not only provides expressions, comprehensive experiment information such as cohort information and study design is collected as well.

- *MiRCancer* was first published in 2013. It collects miRNA profiles in cancers by automatic text-mining approach and manual validation. The text-mining utilizes NER and rule-based information extraction. The database was recently updated in December 2014 with 2,821 miRNA-cancer relationships involving 173 types of cancers curated from 1,861 publications. The system provides 78.5% recall rate based on a test carried out over 200 selected papers. The manual validation guarantees 100% precision.

Computational mining systems have advantages in recall rate and efficiency over manual curations. The number of miRNA targets discovered by the above six systems are compared in Figure 1. It clearly shows that when a computational component is added to a manual mining system, the ability to discover potential miRNA targets of a system is drastically improved (e.g., TarBase vs. TarBase 6.0, and Argonaute vs. miRWalk). Since the study object is different between PhenomiR and miRCancer, their throughputs are not comparable. Besides recall rate, precision is another important measurement for a mining system. Manually mined system usually provides close to 100% precision while the same precision is extremely difficult for computational methods. The measurements are further discussed in the "Validation and Evaluation" section later.

MIRNA-CANCER RELATIONSHIP TEXT MINING

Despite the fact that miRNA has only been introduced two decades ago, over 5,000 miRNA related articles have been published every year since 2011, with about 25,000 to date in MEDLINE. MiRNA does not only function as general gene regulator, it also associates tightly with human cancers. Cancer is one of the leading causes of death worldwide. Experiments have shown that miRNA could be potentially used for cancer diagnosis and treatment. MiRNA profiling in human cancers has attracted great scientific and business interests. Mining for miRNA-cancer relationships will be used to illustrate how to apply text-mining techniques on complex biomedical literature.

Similar to many other text-mining applications, a typical miRNA profiling mining system has three steps: data preparation, information extraction, and validation. Data preparation gets a set of relevant data from a single or multiple resources, cleans noises, and normalizes the raw data to an acceptable format to be processed. Information extraction utilizes manual or computational tech-

Figure 1. Manual vs computational throughput comparison

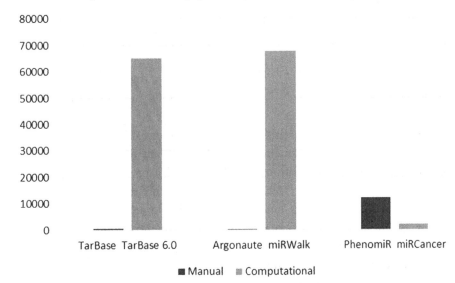

niques to gather structured information from free text. Before the extracted information is stored to a database or presented as a summarized knowledge, it needs to be validated for accuracy.

Data Preparation

Where to Get Literature?

Reviewed by (Cohen & Hersh, 2005) and (Rebholz-Schuhmann, Oellrich, & Hoehndorf, 2012), there are some scientific and commercial biomedical literature resource providers such as Thomson Reuters, National Library of Medicine (NLM), and Elsevier. These collections of biomedical literature are made available electronically and are indexed for easy search through web interfaces, for example, Thomson Reuters Web of Knowledge and PubMed. The most frequently consulted collection is MEDLINE, which is the main component of PubMed. MEDLINE contains over 19 million references with a concentration on biomedicine. A large number of journals are selected by MEDLINE and it is freely available online. Another major database accessible through PubMed is PubMed Central (PMC). It was launched in 2000, archiving 2.9 million full-text biomedical and life sciences articles. Unlike PMC, MEDLINE only provides abstracts and links to the original journal. The full text availability depends on the journal provider. This leads to the second question:

At What Granularity an Article Should Be Used?

The input source data to be mined could be full-text documents or abstracts. The entire document certainly provides completeness of information, but the completeness does not come for free. Parsing full-text is also time-consuming and almost impossible if manual text-mining is applied. Secondly, full-text is harder to be accessed, many of which are not freely available. Having a collection of articles from different publishers

may require multiple subscriptions. This not only increases the cost of a project, it also creates technical hurdle for auto-collection of literature. Additionally, full-text has more variety in format: word, pdf, scanned image, etc. It is more difficult for a system to understand all of these formats. Finally, the more texts there are, the more noises are introduced. For example, a co-occurrence system mining for protein-protein associations could easily be confused by hypothesized associations, or co-occurred pairs from experiment design descriptions. On the other hand, abstracts are much easier to be processed, freely available almost everywhere, usually in a single plain text format, and contain much less distraction information. Most importantly, in biomedical literature, results are usually presented with details to the gene, protein, molecular level in the abstract which is desired. Abstracts have been chosen as the input for many text-mining systems. However, there are some situations where full-text is preferred or cannot be avoided. When comprehensiveness is vital to the system, full-text should be used. When research details such as experiment methods and results with quantitative measures are needed in addition to results, full-text cannot be avoided because these kinds of information are more likely to be presented in the text body rather than in the abstract.

How to Retrieve Relevant Literature?

Once the data source and granularity are decided, as a common practice to text-mining, a set of relevant text is separated from the source to be further processed. The most intuitive way to gather relevant literature is to utilize the search functionality provided by the source database. The online literature databases usually provide keyword, title, and author searches. These queries are performed by indexing and string matching. PubMed provides a distinctive automatic MeSH® term and subheading mapping that includes more specific and diversified medical terminologies during search. In addition to keyword mapping, other documentation classification and clustering techniques could be used to reduce the source literature collection as well. (Bleik, Mishra, Huan, & Song, 2013; Romero, Iglesias, Borrajo, & Marey, 2011; Yanpeng, Honfei, & Zhihao, 2007) discussed approaches for biomedical text classification, such as graph kernels, K-nearest neighbor, naïve Bayes classifier, support vector machine, concept expansion and Meta-classification. Indexing and classification greatly reduce the noise from free text. Texts are then further normalized to their canonical form by 1) eliminating encodings, i.e., removing XML, HTML tags; and 2) using existing tag information, and separating text into different categories, i.e., subject, background, result, and methods. Normalization is optional but always helpful.

A naïve Bayes classifier could be easily implemented to classify miRNA related texts. Naïve Bayes classification is supervised probabilistic learning method. It requires a set of terms t_i, and estimation of the probabilities of the terms in a document of a certain class c, $P(t_i|c)$. $P(c)$ is the probability of a document that falls into class c. The probability of a document d belonging to class c is estimated as $P(c|d) = P(c)\prod P(t_i|c)$. In this search for miRNA documentation example, terms like "mir," "miRNA," "microRNA," "noncoding RNA," "RNAi," and so on, are used for estimation. The selection of terms are not limited to terms referring to miRNA itself; words appearing frequently in miRNA related researches should also be included. The probabilities are estimated from a set of manually classified documents, referred as the training set. The accuracy of the classifier is estimated by applying the classifier on another independent manually processed set of documents, referred as the test set.

Depending on the mining goal and desired recall and accuracy rate, more complex techniques are used in text classification. Support vector machine is one of the popular classification approaches. If the classification is the final

step that provides the search result, sophisticated approaches with high precision are recommended. On the other hand, for the purpose of data preparation, simple approaches such as string mapping, which guarantee great recall rate, are preferred.

How to Prepare Data for miRNA-Cancer Mining?

MEDLINE is chosen as the source database. Abstracts are used to extract the miRNA profiles in human cancers. In order to reduce the source to only miRNA-cancer related articles, a set of miRNA connected documents are first selected from PubMed utilizing PubMed search interface. For example, the query "(((mir) OR mirna) OR microrna) OR micro-rna" in PubMed is translated as mapping the literature with MeSH term "micrornas" and the queried words. PubMed allows user to save the query results into different file formats. In this example, XML format is selected for the benefit of the XML tags. A simple string matching and replacing process normalizes the query results according to these PubMed predefined XML tags. These abstracts together with the article titles are further scanned against two manually-curated dictionaries, one for cancer names, and the other for miRNA expression terms. Abstracts with all three components: miRNA terms, cancer names, and expression terms are saved for further information extraction. The construction of the two dictionaries is discussed in the "Name Entity Recognition" section later.

Information Extraction

Information extraction serves as a tool for biomedical scientists which enables timely access to desired information and provides summary of research. The kinds of information extracted should always align with biologists' interests as they are the major target users as well as the source data providers. In the past decade, miRNA becomes one of the most popular research topics because of its important role in crucial biological processes. Besides manual collection, miRNA-centric text mining algorithms can be categorized into one of the three major types: co-occurrence, rule-based, and machine learning based. In this section, we will discuss these three types of methods and their applications in miRNA profiling mining. First and foremost, before diving into mining strategies, there is one question to be answered.

How to Identify miRNA and Cancer in Free Text?

Automatically identifying miRNA and cancer name in unstructured text is one of the many kinds of Name Entity Recognition (NER) tasks. In the introduction section, different NER methods were reviewed. Comparing to other common entities of interest, such as gene, protein, pathway, and drug names, miRNA names have been formalized early enough so that they are comparably unified. A rule-based NER system is not difficult to implement based on miRNA name formation rules. A standard miRNA name consists of three parts: prefix, a number, and suffix. Most miRNAs are named with the "miR" prefix, except for a few miRNAs discovered in early years: bantam, let-7 family, lin-4, and lsy-6. Sometimes miRNA names also have additional species prefix, such as hsa- and mmu- in the front. Following the prefix is a sequentially assigned unique number. It has been shown that miRNAs are highly conserved between species and organisms (Lee, Rison, & Strauss, 2007); therefore identical miRNA sequences have the same number regardless of species. For instance, mmu-miR-223-3p and hsa-miR-223-3p have the same sequence but one is found in mouse while the other is from human. Additional suffixes are used for pairpin precursor and hairpin loci information. There are three type of suffixes in miRNA names: 1) single letter 'a' and 'b' for related miRNA sequences that only have small base changes, e.g. hsa-miR-216a and hsa-miR-216b; 2) single digits such as '-1' and

'-2' for identical miRNAs with different hairpin loci in a given organism, e.g. hsa-miR-16-1 and hsa-miR-16-2; 3) '-3p', '-5p' and '*' for miRNA sequences expressed from different arms of hairpin precursor, e.g., hsa-miR-223-5p. The complete list of miRNA suffixes is shown in Table 2 In addition to miRNAs' own naming variations, miRNA names are written in different short forms, such as "miR-123, -46, -23." Please refer to Table 1 for a list of prefix variations and Table 3 for names in short forms. A successful NER system has to tolerate all these variations. Regular expression could be used with string comparison to perform the rule-based recognition. For example, we can define miRNA name rule as regular expression "(miR|mirna|microrna|micro-rna)-\d+[a-z]?-\d+p?," and map this expression to the text "We found that miR-195-5p expression was significantly decreased in the 40 breast cancer specimens....." The string "miR-195-5p" will be identified as a miRNA name.

In addition to rule-based miRNA name recognition, dictionary-based recognition also works very well in NER. There are several miRNA databases: miRBase (Kozomara & Griffiths, 2014) which collects 30,424 mature miRNAs in 206 species, and miRNEST (Szczesniak, Deorowicz, Gapski,

Table 1. MiRNA name variations with prefix

miR, miR-, miRNA, miRNA-, microRNA, microRNA-, micro RNA, micro-RNA-, let-, miRNA-let-, miR-let-, lin-, lsy-, has-, mmu-, and etc.

Table 2. MiRNA name variations with suffix

Situation	Example
Related sequence with base change	has-miR-216a and hsa-miR-216b
Identical sequence with different hairpin loci	has-miR-16-1 and has-miR-16-2
Sequence from 3'arms	has-miR-223-3p
Sequence from 5'arms	has-miR-223-5p
Minor sequence	has-miR-100*

Table 3. MiRNA name variations with shortform

Short Form	Formal Form
miR-123, -46, -23	miR-123, miR-46, miR-23
miR-200a, b, c	miR-200a, miR-200b, miR-200c
miR-21/137	miR-21, miR-137
miR-99a/100	miR-99a, miR-100
miR-99a/b	miR-99a, miR-99b
miR-15a/16-1	miR-15a, miR-16-1
miR-221/-222	miR-221, miR-222
miR-23b/-27b	miR-23b, miR-27b
miR-let-7a/let-7b	let-7a, let-7b
miR-221&222	miR-221, miR-222

Kaczynski, & Makalowska, 2012) which records 39,122 miRNAs from 544 species. These databases could serve as the dictionary for name identification; however, rule-based recognition is recommended for miRNA names as they have unified format. On the other hand, cancer name would be a good example for dictionary-based NER.

Unlike miRNA names, cancer names are not structured, each with multiple synonymies, yet not many of them have been mentioned in literature. Researchers tend to carry out projects on cancers concerning large population rather than rarely occurred cancers. There are less than 200 kinds of cancers that have been mentioned in miRNA related articles. Manually collecting these names into a dictionary is feasible. Although it may not be an easy process, it is an effective way to capture the synonymies. For example, "bladder cancer," "urinary bladder cancer," and "bladder urothelial carcinoma" refer to the same disease. The dictionary should consist of all the synonymies for each cancer. Furthermore, acronyms sometimes are used to refer to cancers in documents. In the even more complicated situation, different cancers may share the same acronym in separate articles. "BC" has been seen in different literature referring to breast cancer and bladder cancer. In this kind of situation, the dictionary-based NER should not only be able to search a text against the dictionary, but also be able to identify the correct cancer term to which an acronym is referring in the context. There are a few acronyms dictionaries that are available and helpful: ACROMED (Pustejovsky, Castano, Cochran, Kotecki, & Morrell, 2001), ADAM (Zhou, Torvik, & Smalheiser, 2006), and Acromine (Okazaki, N., Ananiadou, S., & Tsujii, J., 2010), all of which are constructed from MEDLINE. Table 4 shows a sample of the cancer dictionary that the miRCancer system (Xie, Ding, Han & Wu, 2013) used for cancer NER. During the process of cancer NER, the dictionary is first loaded into memory. Each input text is then scanned for the synonymies and short forms. The ICD-O-3 code is used for internal system reference and one unified name is chosen as the output name.

Table 4. Sample cancer dictionary

ICD-O-3 Code	Cancer Name	Synonymies	Short Forms
C16.9, M8000/3	Gastric cancer	Gastric cancer, stomach cancer, gastric carcinoma	GC
M8170/3	Hepatocellular carcinoma	Hepatocellular carcinoma, hepatocellular cancer, hepatocarcinoma, hepatoma cancer, hepatoma	HCCS, HCC
M9801/3	Acute leukemia	Acute leukemia, blast cell leukemia, b-cell leukemia	
M9861/3	Acute myeloid leukemia	Acute myeloid leukemia, acute myelogenous leukemia, acute myelocytic leukemia, acute myelogeneous leukemia	AML
C50.9, M8000/3	Breast cancer	Breast cancer	BC
C50.9, M8010/3	Breast carcinoma	Breast carcinoma	BC
C50.9, M8140/3	Breast adenocarcinoma	Breast adenocarcinoma	
…	…	…	…

Extracting miRNA-cancer association and miRNA expression profile in cancers are different tasks, as the later one involves a third component in the miRNA-cancer relationship, which is the expression. Profile miRNA abnormal expression in cancers is shown to be important in carcinogenic and anticancerogenic studies. Therefore, expression NER is also necessary in a miRNA-cancer profiling system. There are two kinds of miRNA expressions that biologists are usually interested in: over-expression and under-expression. A dictionary of the various forms of these two kinds of expressions can be constructed by reviewing a small set of literature. Table 5 displays a list of expression terms which is very inclusive and may recognize some incorrect text as expression term. Because the expression will be further confirmed by additional rule-based algorithms, it is possible to have expression NER less precise than miRNA and cancer NER.

How to Extract miRNA-Cancer Relationships with Co-Occurrence Method?

Co-occurrence-based text-mining is one of the simplest methods to implement and a widely used approach. It discovers terms frequently appearing together thus inferring the association

Table 5. miRNA expression dictionary

Upregulate Terms
Over express*, overexpress*, over-express*, highly express*, high express*, Forced expression, enhanced expression, Up regulat*, upregulat*, up-regulat*, positive regulat*, Increase*, promote, oncogenic.
Downregulate Terms
Under express*, underexpress*, under-express*, lower express*, lower-express*, down regulat*, downregulat*, down-regulat*, negative regulat*, decrease*, inhibit, repress*, suppress*.

*: could be any 1 or more characters, like: s, es, ing, ion, ed, or, and etc.

between them. Unfortunately, co-occurrence-based systems are lack of precision, as they are usually integrated with other more sophisticated approaches or act as the preprocessing before manual text mining. One co-occurred process on miRNA, cancer, and expression terms could filter out unrelated inputs, and reduce the noise in the source. The co-occurrence could be evaluated on either the abstract level or sentence level. Evaluation at the abstract level means that as long as one miRNA term, one cancer term and one expression term are present in an abstract, regardless of whether they are mentioned in the same sentence, the text is considered as a candidate. Evaluation at the sentence level keeps the text only when all three kinds of terms are present in one sentence. Which level of evaluation should be used depends on the design of previous NER process and the remaining system. Generally, the more precise the NER and post processes are, the more inclusiveness the co-occurrence evaluation could be. For instance, if one plans to perform manual text mining after the co-occurred evaluation, evaluation at sentence level is preferred. However, if a rule-based technique as discussed below is integrated in the system, evaluation at the entire text could avoid removal of true results.

How to Extract miRNA-Cancer Relationships with Rule-Based Method?

Rule-based text-mining mimics the process of how human being comprehends text. Most rule-based strategies involve skills from NLP which tags words for part-of-speech (POS) and analyzes the linguistic patterns between interesting terms. Comparing to co-occurrence systems, rule-based systems usually provide higher precision with lower recall rate. In order to discover relationships between biomedical terms, oftentimes domain specific rules are constructed manually by experts. To illustrate, the miRNA, cancer, and expression terms identified by the previous NER process is further POS tagged. One single miRNA term (e.g. miR-205) or a group of miRNA names (e.g. miR-16, miR-200a, b, c, and miR-425) are tagged as MIR-PHRASE. Similarly, a single cancer term (e.g. leukemia) or a set of cancer names (e.g. bladder, kidney and gastric cancers) are tagged as CANCER-PHRASE. Expression verbs, such as: suppress, enhance, and increase, are tagged as EXP-V. According to the expression terms POS, they are tagged differently as: EXP-ADJ, EXP-ADV, EXP-N, and so on. Moreover, other words that will be used in rule construction should also be tagged. The tagging does not necessarily follow regular POS analysis strictly, and it could be modified to suit the need in biomedical text. For instance, phrases such as "is found to be" and "are confirmed to be" are good indications of result assertion. They can be tagged as BE-PHRASE. The tagging is done by manually creating regular expression rules according to analysis of literature. String mapping is then performed against these rules. Most languages have library for regular expression operations. The C# Regex class has matches() function which does regular expression match. In Java, the String class provides methods such as replaceAll() and replaceFirst(). Similarly, Python has "re" operations.

After POS tagging, text are separated into sentences for ruled-pattern match. A rule could be as simple as "MIR-PHRASE EXP-V CANCER-PHRASE," or as complex as "EXP-ADJ MIR-PHRASE BE-PHRASE EXP-V IN CANCER-PHRASE COMPARE-PHRASE NORMAL-PHRASE." A text such as "increased expression of microRNA-21 is shown to be up-regulate in gastric carcinoma compare with corresponding non-cancerous tissues" will be matched with the second sample rule after proper tagging. Since rules have different complexity, they appear to show different confidence in identifying accurate relationships. Applying expert knowledge or deriving from pilot data evaluation, rules could be categorized into different tiers. The higher the tier, the more restrictive and precise a rule is. miRCancer uses 75 rules that divided into 4 tiers. Tier 1 rules are complete sentences with miRNA, cancer, and expression components. Tier 2 rules have the 3 essential components, but instead of forming a full sentence, they are only able to construct a phrase. Tier 2 rules are in the form of "MIR-PHRASE AS EXP-N-PHRASE OF CANCER-PHRASE," and "EXP-ADJ MIR-PHRASE IN CANCER-PHRASE." Example sentences matching these two rules could be: "miR-34b and miR-129-3p as the known inhibitor of gastric cancers," "increased miR-499-5p levels in highly invasive CRC cell lines." Tier 3 and 4 rules are similar to tier 1 and 2 respectively, but instead of including the specific cancer names, a word or phrase referring to the general cancer is used. For this kind of rules, the specific cancer term should be inferred from other part of the text.

When matching a sentence with rules, different mechanism may be applied. 1) Sequentially match each rule: once a match is found, stop the process. Rules are required to be ordered from higher precision to lower ones. This approach provides quick response which is suitable for online real time matching. 2) Concurrently match to all rules, and summarize the result. All rules are treated indifferently. While this approach takes more processing time than the sequential approach, it potentially generates better precision. It is suitable for offline matching systems. 3) A hybrid approach that concurrently matches rules within a tier, and sequentially process between tiers. This means that each single sentence is compared with all rules within tier 1 first. Then a summarized decision is made if there is any match within tier 1, otherwise tier 2 rules are used for matching. Similarly, this process could continue until the last tier of rules. When concurrent/parallel matching is carried out, there are chances that a sentence is matched with multiple rules which might lead to different conclusions. In this situation, a result is usually summarized from multiple matched rules by voting. The voting could be un-weighted or weighted. Un-weighted voting refers to counting the number of matched rules for each different conclusion, and the majority vote wins. If rules are categorized in different precision tiers and a voting weight is assigned to each rule, then weighted vote happens. Figure 2 shows the flowchart of the information extraction process from miRCancer that process one abstract. 75 manually constructed rules are preloaded into

memory. These rules are separated as 4 tiers and are processed from tier 1 to 4.

Matching a sentence with rules does not generate the structured data of miRNA profile in cancer. Matched rules have to be interpreted. For this purpose, the earlier NER and tagging process keeps a record of which miRNA, cancer or expres-

Figure 2. Flowchart of information extraction by rules

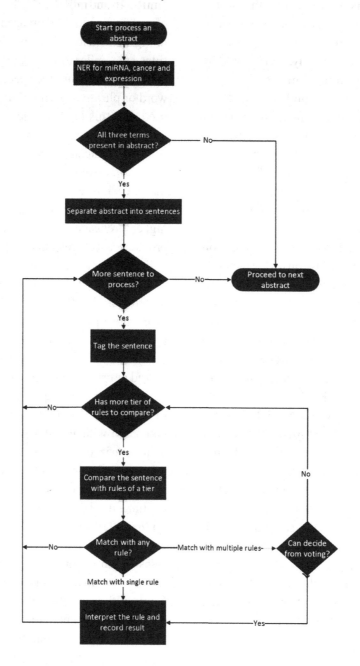

sion that a normalized tag is representing. Attach numbers to each tag to differentiate between tags and note down each indexed tag matching partner text is one way of doing this. Take the rule MIR-PHRASE EXP-V CANCER-PHRASE as an example. A sentence matching with this rule will have tags arranged like MIR-PHRASE-0 EXP-V-3 CANCER-PHRASE-1. Every miRNAs included in MIR-PHRASE-0 will pair up with each cancer name in CANCER-PHRASE-1, and the miRNAs will have an expression profile indicated by the term in EXP-V-3. The interpretation is not always as straightforward as this example. There are several challenges that the interpretation process should handle: 1) how to translate a rule with multiple expression terms. Two expression terms indicating suppressive profile could be put together to describe an oncogenic function of a miRNA. For instance, "co-suppression of miR-221/222 cluster suppresses human glioma cell growth." More interestingly, expression terms with opposite meaning can appear in one sentence as well, such as "mechanistically the down-regulation of miR-16, miR-126 and let-7d promotes PDAC." The "down-regulation" and "promotes" together declare that the mentioned miRNAs suppress pancreatic ductal adenocarcinoma. In miRCancer, the multiple expression terms are handled case by case for each rule. The interpretation method for each rule is defined by human during the rule construction process. 2) When multiple miRNAs and/or multiple cancers are represented by one tag, during interpretation, they have to be separated and translated into one miRNA to one cancer relations. 3) How to handle rules with incomplete components, such as the aforementioned tier 3 and 4 rules. The interpretation accuracy is affected by the location where the missing component is inferred. The possible place to find the missing component could be the literature title, neighboring sentences, within the same paragraph, and even the entire text. When multiple candidate terms are found, whether to construct relationships for each term or choose the

most likely term has to be decided. For miRNA-cancer related literature, in most cases, there is only one cancer name mentioned in the entire abstract including the title. miRCancer uses this only-mentioned cancer name as the implied cancer to complete interpretation. 4) Last but not least, negation terms need to be taken into consideration during interpretation.

How to Extract miRNA-Cancer Relationships with Machine Learning?

Machine learning uses computer power to construct a system by learning from abundant data. As tens of thousands articles have been published on miRNA, discovery of miRNA-cancer relationships from textual content is possible through machine learning. There are several categories in machine learning: supervised, unsupervised, and semi-supervised learning. One of the most popular supervised approaches that have been successfully applied on various biomedicine text mining field is support vector machines (SVM). SVM was first introduced by Vapnik (1979). It generally is used for classification and regression analysis based on pattern recognition. The miRNA-cancer relation identification could be modeled as a classification question which puts miRNA-cancer relationships into three classes: suppress, promote, and unidentified. The input to the SVM should be tokenized sentences. In this case, the previously POS tagged sentences could be used with the modification on all expression tags. In order to classify the relations based on expression terms, each expression should be tagged with either "suppress" or "promote." Manually annotated training sets, both positive and negative, should be provided to the SVM system to learn the sentence patterns. Negative training set should be constructed by sentences containing both miRNA and cancer terms. Positive training set should cover as many kinds of sentence structures as possible, and substrings containing necessary components are preferred over long sentences. After the system is trained, unclassified text could be processed for miRNA-cancer relations. The system needs to be evaluated for accuracy and recall rate; thus another set of annotated sets of data is required for testing.

The quality and quantity of the training set greatly affect the system performance. Oftentimes, it is difficult and time-consuming to create a training set with good coverage. For this reason, machine learning approaches have limited application in biomedicine comparing to co-occurrence and rule-based systems. Yet we see great potential in it as biomedicine data become more complex in structure and larger in size.

Validation and Evaluation

Every computer aided text-mining system, regardless of which approach it utilizes, there is always imperfection; thus, systems are usually evaluated with three measurements: precision, recall, and F-score. The evaluation mostly is carried out with a manually processed test set of literature. Depending on the target audience of the mining results, some systems aim to achieve higher precision while compromising recall rate, while others provide better recall rate but with lower precision. Generally the mining results will be most useful to biomedical scientists if the precision is guaranteed. The comprehensiveness of a system is less interested by biomedical users. This is one of the major reasons that many manually-curated systems are available even though the manual literature curation is a time-consuming process. Despite that automatic validation is available, to achieve 100% precision, manual validation sometimes is inevitable. Yet manually validating a single sentence with highly likelihood of containing useful information is much more efficient than blindly reading the entire literature. For systems such as the one presented in the previous rule-based mining section, weighted rules could provide the confidence score of a result relationship. In a well-designed rule system, results with certain confidence may be skipped for manual validation.

Only output with confidence lower than a threshold will then need human intervention.

Besides the precision and recall rate, system response time may also be measured for systems carrying out the mining on the fly. A system designed for frequent query should have a response time of no more than a few minutes. If the mining process takes long time such as hours to generate a result, channels other than viewing the result on a web page should be provided. It is unlikely for a user to open a web page and wait for hours to get the results. Offering desktop application rather than online mining tool, or sending result via email may be preferred. Systems that perform mining offline and save results to databases can be measured for data retrieval time. The underline database should be designed to facilitate efficient query. Some systems provide graphic representation for mined relationships. If the graph is generated dynamically, the rendering time could be measured. Moreover, whenever manual process is involved, either during text-mining or validation stage, how easy a system can be updated should be considered for evaluation as well. Biomedicine is undergoing a rapid change. Articles are published more frequently than before, thus text-mining systems need to be updated to reflect the current research results.

FUTURE DIRECTIONS

Biomedical text mining serves as a tool for biomedical researchers. The rapid advancing miRNA experimental methods and new focus open many demands and opportunities for text mining. While existing systems provide reasonable results and performance, new computational methods are proposed and developed to generate better accuracy and recall rate. Application on miRNA-centric mining is a new research area comparing to gene and protein related mining. There are more mature mining systems on gene, protein, and other biomedical subjects. These approaches have great potential to be customized for miRNA studies. Also, miRNA research might also inspire new text-mining strategies.

As the volume of biomedical literature is expanding, developing completely automatic text extracting system with perfect or high accuracy keeps being an open problem. To our knowledge, about half of the miRNA-centric text-mining systems are manually-curated, while others require human intervention. The number of manual work increases as the amount of published documentation increases. It becomes more difficult to update these systems where manual work is involved. Eventually the cost to keep these systems updated will surpass the value they are providing. New strategies are urged to substitute these manual processes.

After all, the purpose for biomedical text-mining applications is to facilitate biomedical researchers to solve problems more efficiently and possibly lower the cost. Systems closely following the trend of biomedical research directions will better serve this purpose and thus be more beneficial. Although documenting miRNA-gene, miRNA-disease, or miRNA-cancer one-to-one relations is an important job, studies have shown that miRNAs tend to function as a group together. Research direction has shifted from discovering one-to-one relations to signal pathways. The miRNA network integration with gene and protein pathways is expected to be much more complex than individual miRNA function dynamics. Mining for miRNA network could be the top challenge going forward.

We are living in an exciting era for biomedicine which is becoming more data intensive. Researches are gradually transforming from hypothesis-driven to data-driven as more data are generated by experiments as well as computational predictions. "Big Data" refers to collection of large size of data that is difficult to be handled by common database management systems. For text-mining on big data, the challenges consist of issues regarding access

to big source data, processing data in reasonable time, storing, querying and visualizing results. Some other bioinformatics fields have been forced to deal with big data problems, such as DNA sequencing. Big data are not widely spreading into biomedical text-mining yet. Mining healthcare reports probably is one of the only areas that has large amount of data which can be categorized as big data. Other collection of publications still can be easily handled by regular systems. For example, for over 23 million documented publications in PubMed, the total file size for all abstracts is only about 0.3 terabytes. Even the size for the full text collection is estimated to be a few terabytes. A database such as Microsoft SQL server (version 2005 to 2012) (Microsoft) that has database size limit of 524,258 terabytes and file size limit of 16 terabytes could easily handle all PubMed collections. Freely available database such as MySQL has no database size limit but file size limit of 2 gigabytes to 4 terabytes depending on the operating system (MySQL). Therefore, increasing the hardware capability is always a solution to storage. Other software solutions are also available, such as distributed systems and data warehouse. In general, the efficiency to manipulate big data could be improved by parallel processing approaches. A list of big data techniques are reviewed in 2011 McKinsey report (Manyika et al., 2011).

CONCLUSION

In this chapter, we present an overview of various techniques and tools used in biomedical text mining, in particular, in the microRNA profiling area. We used one rule-based text mining system, miRCancer, as an example to illustrate various steps and issues in biomedical text mining. miRCancer was developed to extract microRNA-cancer relationships from literature on PubMed. Discussions of the challenges and potential research areas in biomedical text mining have also been presented. There will be great demand to develop highly efficient and accurate text mining tools and techniques to deal with big data in biomedical field.

REFERENCES

Aerts, S., Haeussler, M., van Vooren, S., Griffith, O. L., Hulpiau, P., & Jones, S. J. et al. (2008). Text-mining assisted regulatory annotation. *Genome Biology*, *9*(2), R31. doi:10.1186/gb-2008-9-2-r31 PMID:18271954

Al-Mubaid, H., & Singh, R. K. (2010). A text-mining technique for extracting gene-disease associations from the biomedical literature. *International Journal of Bioinformatics Research and Applications*, *6*(3), 270–286. doi:10.1504/IJBRA.2010.034075 PMID:20615835

Ashburner, M., Ball, C. A., Blake, J. A., Botstein, D., Butler, H., & Cherry, J. M. et al. (2000). Gene ontology: Tool for the unification of biology. The Gene Ontology Consortium. *Nature Genetics*, *25*(1), 25–29. doi:10.1038/75556 PMID:10802651

Bauer-Mehren, A., Rautschka, M., Sanz, F., & Furlong, L. I. (2010). DisGeNET: A Cytoscape plugin to visualize, integrate, search and analyze gene-disease networks. *Bioinformatics (Oxford, England)*, *26*(22), 2924–2926. doi:10.1093/bioinformatics/btq538 PMID:20861032

Bleik, S., Mishra, M., Huan, J., & Song, M. (2013). Text Categorization of Biomedical Data Sets Using Graph Kernels and a Controlled Vocabulary. *IEEE/ACM Transactions on Computational Biology and Bioinformatics*, *10*(5), 1211–1217. doi:10.1109/TCBB.2013.16 PMID:24384709

Boissonneault, V., Plante, I., Rivest, S., & Provost, P. (2009). MicroRNA-298 and microRNA-328 regulate expression of mouse beta-amyloid precursor protein-converting enzyme 1. *The Journal of Biological Chemistry*, *284*(4), 1971–1981. doi:10.1074/jbc.M807530200 PMID:18986979

Carthew, R. W., & Sontheimer, E. J. (2009). Origins and Mechanisms of miRNAs and siRNAs. *Cell*, *136*(4), 642–655. doi:10.1016/j.cell.2009.01.035 PMID:19239886

Chen, H., & Sharp, B. M. (2004). Content-rich biological network constructed by mining PubMed abstracts. *BMC Bioinformatics*, *5*(1), 147. doi:10.1186/1471-2105-5-147 PMID:15473905

Chun, H. W., Tsuruoka, Y., Kim, J. D., Shiba, R., Nagata, N., Hishiki, T., & Tsujii, J. (2006). Extraction of gene-disease relations from Medline using domain dictionaries and machine learning. *Pacific Symposium on Biocomputing*, 4-15. doi:10.1142/9789812701626_0002

Cohan, K. B., Christianse, T., Baumgartner, W. A., Jr., Verspoor, K., & Hunter, L. E. (2011). Fast and simple semantic class assignment for biomedical text. In *Proceedings of Workshop on Biomedical Natural Language Processing*, (pp. 38-45). Academic Press.

Cohen, A. M., & Hersh, W. R. (2005). A survey of current work in biomedical text mining. *Briefings in Bioinformatics*, *6*(1), 57–71. doi:10.1093/bib/6.1.57 PMID:15826357

Couto, F. M., Silva, M. J., Lee, V., Dimmer, E., Camon, E., & Apweiler, R. et al. (2006). GO-Annotator: Linking protein GO annotations to evidence text. *Journal of Biomedical Discovery and Collaboration*, *1*(1), 19. doi:10.1186/1747-5333-1-19 PMID:17181854

Czarnecki, J., Nobeli, I., Smith, A. M., & Shepherd, A. J. (2012). A text-mining system for extracting metabolic reactions from full-text articles. *BMC Bioinformatics*, *13*(1), 172. doi:10.1186/1471-2105-13-172 PMID:22823282

Doms, A., & Schroeder, M. (2005). GoPubMed: exploring PubMed with the Gene Ontology. *Nucleic Acids Research, 33*(Web Server issue), W783-786. doi: 10.1093/nar/gki470

Dong, L., Luo, M., Wang, F., Zhang, J., Li, T., & Yu, J. (2013). TUMIR: An experimentally supported database of microRNA deregulation in various cancers. *Journal of Clinical Bioinformatics*, *3*(1), 7. doi:10.1186/2043-9113-3-7 PMID:23594715

Dweep, H., Sticht, C., Pandey, P., & Gretz, N. (2011). miRWalk--database: Prediction of possible miRNA binding sites by "walking" the genes of three genomes. *Journal of Biomedical Informatics*, *44*(5), 839–847. doi:10.1016/j.jbi.2011.05.002 PMID:21605702

Fichtlscherer, S., Zeiher, A. M., Dimmeler, S., & Sessa, W. C. (2011). Circulating microRNAs: Biomarkers or mediators of cardiovascular diseases? *Arteriosclerosis, Thrombosis, and Vascular Biology*, *31*(11), 2383–2390. doi:10.1161/ATVBAHA.111.226696 PMID:22011751

Filipowicz, W., Bhattacharyya, S. N., & Sonenberg, N. (2008). Mechanisms of post-transcriptional regulation by microRNAs: Are the answers in sight? *Nature Reviews. Genetics*, *9*(2), 102–114. doi:10.1038/nrg2290 PMID:18197166

Frijters, R., van Vugt, M., Smeets, R., van Schaik, R., de Vlieg, J., & Alkema, W. (2010). Literature mining for the discovery of hidden connections between drugs, genes and diseases. *PLoS Computational Biology*, *6*(9), e1000943. doi:10.1371/journal.pcbi.1000943 PMID:20885778

Garten, Y., Tatonetti, N. P., & Altman, R. B. (2010). Improving the prediction of pharmacogenes using text-derived drug-gene relationships. In *Proceedings of Pacific Symposium on Biocomputing*, (pp. 305-314). Academic Press.

Grimson, A., Farh, K. K., Johnston, W. K., Garrett-Engele, P., Lim, L. P., & Bartel, D. P. (2007). MicroRNA targeting specificity in mammals: Determinants beyond seed pairing. *Molecular Cell*, *27*(1), 91–105. doi:10.1016/j.molcel.2007.06.017 PMID:17612493

Haeussler, M., Gerner, M., & Bergman, C. M. (2011). Annotating genes and genomes with DNA sequences extracted from biomedical articles. *Bioinformatics (Oxford, England)*, *27*(7), 980–986. doi:10.1093/bioinformatics/btr043 PMID:21325301

Holzinger, A., Simonic, K. M., & Yildirim, P. (2012). Disease-disease relationships for rheumatic diseases: Web-based biomedical textmining and knowledge discovery to assist medical decision making. In *Proceedings of International Conference on Computer Software and Applications (COMPSAC)*, (pp. 573-580). Izmir: IEEE. doi:10.1109/COMPSAC.2012.77

Hsu, S. D., Lin, F. M., Wu, W. Y., Liang, C., Huang, W. C., & Chan, W. L. et al. (2011). miRTarBase: A database curates experimentally validated microRNA-target interactions. *Nucleic Acids Research, 39*(Database issue), D163–D169. doi:10.1093/nar/gkq1107 PMID:21071411

Jiang, Q., Wang, Y., Hao, Y., Juan, L., Teng, M., & Zhang, X. et al. (2009). miR2Disease: A manually curated database for microRNA deregulation in human disease. *Nucleic Acids Research, 37*(Database issue), D98–D104. doi:10.1093/nar/gkn714 PMID:18927107

Kemper, B., Matsuzaki, T., Matsuoka, Y., Tsuruoka, Y., Kitano, H., Ananiadou, S., & Tsujii, J. (2010). PathText: A text mining integrator for biological pathway visualizations. *Bioinformatics (Oxford, England)*, *26*(12), i374–i381. doi:10.1093/bioinformatics/btq221 PMID:20529930

Kim, S., Kwon, D., Shin, S. Y., & Wilbur, W. J. (2012). PIE the search: Searching PubMed literature for protein interaction information. *Bioinformatics (Oxford, England)*, *28*(4), 597–598. doi:10.1093/bioinformatics/btr702 PMID:22199390

Koturbash, I., Zemp, F. J., Pogribny, I., & Kovalchuk, O. (2011). Small molecules with big effects: The role of the microRNAome in cancer and carcinogenesis. *Mutation Research*, *722*(2), 94–105. doi:10.1016/j.mrgentox.2010.05.006 PMID:20472093

Kozomara, A., & Griffiths, S. J. (2014). miRBase: Annotating high confidence microRNAs using deep sequencing data. *Nucleic Acids Research*, *42*(D1), D68–D73. doi:10.1093/nar/gkt1181 PMID:24275495

Krallinger, M., Leitner, F., Vazquez, M., Salgado, D., Marcelle, C., & Tyers, M. et al. (2012). How to link ontologies and protein-protein interactions to literature: Text-mining approaches and the BioCreative experience. *Database (Oxford)*, *2012*(0), bas017. doi:10.1093/database/bas017 PMID:22438567

Kuhn, D. E., Martin, M. M., Feldman, D. S., Terry, A. V. Jr, Nuovo, G. J., & Elton, T. S. (2008). Experimental Validation of miRNA Targets. *Methods (San Diego, Calif.)*, *44*(1), 47–54. doi:10.1016/j.ymeth.2007.09.005 PMID:18158132

Lee, C. T., Risom, T., & Strauss, W. M. (2007). Evolutionary conservation of microRNA regulatory circuits: An examination of microRNA gene complexity and conserved microRNA-target interactions through metazoan phylogeny. *DNA and Cell Biology*, *26*(4), 209–218. doi:10.1089/dna.2006.0545 PMID:17465887

Liu, H., Christiansen, T., Baumgartner, W. A. Jr, & Verspoor, K. (2012). BioLemmatizer: A lemmatization tool for morphological processing of biomedical text. *Journal of Biomedical Semantics*, *3*(1), 3. doi:10.1186/2041-1480-3-3 PMID:22464129

Liu, H., Jin, T., Liao, R., Wan, L., Xu, B., Zhou, S., & Guan, J. (2012). miRFANs: An integrated database for Arabidopsis thaliana microRNA function annotations. *BMC Plant Biology*, *12*(1), 68. doi:10.1186/1471-2229-12-68 PMID:22583976

Liu, Y., Navathe, S. B., Civera, J., Dasigi, V., Ram, A., Ciliax, B. J., & Dingledine, R. (2005). Text mining biomedical literature for discovering gene-to-gene relationships: A comparative study of algorithms. *IEEE/ACM Transactions on Computational Biology and Bioinformatics*, *2*(1), 62–76. doi:10.1109/TCBB.2005.14 PMID:17044165

Manyika, J., Chui, M., Bughin, J., Brown, B., Dobbs, R., Roxburgh, C., & Byers, A. H. (2011). *Big data: The next frontier for innovation, competition, and productivity*. Retrieved from http://www.mckinsey.com/insights/business_technology/big_data_the_next_frontier_for_innovation

McCoy, C. E. (2011). The role of miRNAs in cytokine signaling. *Frontiers in Bioscience (Landmark Edition)*, *16*(1), 2161–2171. doi:10.2741/3845 PMID:21622168

McDonald, D., Su, H., Xu, J., Tseng, C.-J., Chen, H., & Leroy, G. (2005). Gene Pathway Text Mining and Visualization. In H. Chen, S. Fuller, C. Friedman, & W. Hersh (Eds.), *Medical Informatics* (Vol. 8, pp. 519–546). Springer. doi:10.1007/0-387-25739-X_18

McDonald, R., & Pereira, F. (2005). Identifying gene and protein mentions in text using conditional random fields. *BMC Bioinformatics*, *6*(Suppl 1), S6. doi:10.1186/1471-2105-6-S1-S6 PMID:15960840

Microsoft. (n.d.). *Maximum capacity specifications for SQL server*. Retrieved from http://technet.microsoft.com/en-us/library/ms143432(v=sql.110).aspx

Murray, B. S., Choe, S. E., Woods, M., Ryan, T. E., & Liu, W. (2010). An in silico analysis of microRNAs: Mining the miRNAome. *Molecular BioSystems*, *6*(10), 1853–1862. doi:10.1039/c003961f PMID:20539892

MySQL. D.10.3. limits on table size. (n.d.). Retrieved from http://dev.mysql.com/doc/refman/5.7/en/table-size-limit.html

Ofir, M., Hacohen, D., & Ginsberg, D. (2011). MiR-15 and miR-16 are direct transcriptional targets of E2F1 that limit E2F-induced proliferation by targeting cyclin E. *Molecular Cancer Research*, *9*(4), 440–447. doi:10.1158/1541-7786. MCR-10-0344 PMID:21454377

Okazaki, N., & Ananiadou, S. (2006). Building an abbreviation dictionary using a term recognition approach. *Bioinformatics (Oxford, England)*, *22*(24), 3089–3095. doi:10.1093/bioinformatics/btl534 PMID:17050571

Okazaki, N., Ananiadou, S., & Tsujii, J. (2010). Building a high-quality sense inventory for improved abbreviation disambiguation. *Bioinformatics (Oxford, England)*, *26*(9), 1246–1253. doi:10.1093/bioinformatics/btq129 PMID:20360059

Ozgur, A., Vu, T., Erkan, G., & Radev, D. R. (2008). Identifying gene-disease associations using centrality on a literature mined gene-interaction network. *Bioinformatics (Oxford, England)*, *24*(13), i277–i285. doi:10.1093/bioinformatics/btn182 PMID:18586725

Papadopoulos, G. L., Reczko, M., Simossis, V. A., Sethupathy, P., & Hatzigeorgiou, A. G. (2009). The database of experimentally supported targets: A functional update of TarBase. *Nucleic Acids Research*, *37*(Database issue), D155–D158. doi:10.1093/nar/gkn809 PMID:18957447

Pustejovsky, J., Castano, J., Cochran, B., Kotecki, M., & Morrell, M. (2001). Automatic extraction of acronym-meaning pairs from MEDLINE databases. *Studies in Health Technology and Informatics*, *84*(Pt 1), 371–375. PMID:11604766

Pyysalo, S., Salakoshi, T., Aubin, S., & Nazarenko, A. (2006). Lexical adaptation of link grammar to the biomedical sublanguage: A comparative evaluation of three approaches. *BMC Bioinformatics*, *7*(Suppl 3), S2. doi:10.1186/1471-2105-7-S3-S2 PMID:17134475

Rebholz-Schuhmann, D., Oellrich, A., & Hoehndorf, R. (2012). Text-mining solutions for biomedical research: Enabling integrative biology. *Nature Reviews. Genetics*, *13*(12), 829–839. doi:10.1038/nrg3337 PMID:23150036

Romero, R., Iglesias, E. L., Borrajo, L., & Marey, C. M. R. (2011). Using Dictionaries for Biomedical Text Classification. In M. Rocha, J. C. Rodríguez, F. Fdez-Riverola, & A. Valencia (Eds.), *Proceedings of International Conference on Practical Applications of Computational Biology & Bioinformatics* (PACBB 2011), (pp. 365-372). Springer. doi:10.1007/978-3-642-19914-1_47

Ruepp, A., Kowarsch, A., Schmidl, D., Buggenthin, F., Brauner, B., & Dunger, I. et al. (2010). PhenomiR: A knowledgebase for microRNA expression in diseases and biological processes. *Genome Biology*, *11*(1), R6. doi:10.1186/gb-2010-11-1-r6 PMID:20089154

Sasaki, Y., Tsuruoka, Y., McNaught, J., & Ananiadou, S. (2008). How to make the most of NE dictionaries in statistical NER. *BMC Bioinformatics*, *9*(Suppl 11), S5. doi:10.1186/1471-2105-9-S11-S5 PMID:19025691

Sethupathy, P., Corda, B., & Hatzigeorgiou, A. G. (2006). TarBase: A comprehensive database of experimentally supported animal microRNA targets. *RNA (New York, N.Y.)*, *12*(2), 192–197. doi:10.1261/rna.2239606 PMID:16373484

Shahi, P., Loukianiouk, S., Bohne-Lang, A., Kenzelmann, M., Kuffer, S., & Maertens, S. et al. (2006). Argonaute--a database for gene regulation by mammalian microRNAs. *Nucleic Acids Research*, *34*(Database issue), D115–D118. doi:10.1093/nar/gkj093 PMID:16381827

Shirdel, E. A., Xie, W., Mak, T. W., & Jurisica, I. (2011). NAViGaTing the micronome--using multiple microRNA prediction databases to identify signalling pathway-associated microRNAs. *PLoS ONE*, *6*(2), e17429. doi:10.1371/journal.pone.0017429 PMID:21364759

Sleater, D. D., & Temperley, D. (1991). Parsing English with a link grammar. *Tech Rep CMU-CS-91-196*

Stefani, G., & Slack, F. J. (2008). Small noncoding RNAs in animal development. *Nature Reviews. Molecular Cell Biology*, *9*(3), 219–230. doi:10.1038/nrm2347 PMID:18270516

Szczesniak, M. W., Deorowicz, S., Gapski, J., Kaczynski, L., & Makalowska, I. (2012). miRNEST database: An integrative approach in microRNA search and annotation. *Nucleic Acids Research*, *40*(Database issue), D198–D204. doi:10.1093/nar/gkr1159 PMID:22135287

Torii, M., Hu, Z., Wu, C. H., & Liu, H. (2009). BioTagger-GM: A gene/protein name recognition system. *Journal of the American Medical Informatics Association*, *16*(2), 247–255. doi:10.1197/jamia.M2844 PMID:19074302

Tutarel, O., Dangwal, S., Bretthauer, J., Westhoff-Bleck, M., Roentgen, P., & Anker, S. D. et al. (2013). Circulating miR-423_5p fails as a biomarker for systemic ventricular function in adults after atrial repair for transposition of the great arteries. *International Journal of Cardiology*, *167*(1), 63–66. doi:10.1016/j.ijcard.2011.11.082 PMID:22188991

Uzuner, O., South, B. R., Shen, S., & DuVall, S. L. (2011). 2010 i2b2/VA challenge on concepts, assertions, and relations in clinical text. *Journal of the American Medical Informatics Association*, *18*(5), 552–556. doi:10.1136/amiajnl-2011-000203 PMID:21685143

Vergoulis, T., Vlachos, I. S., Alexiou, P., Georgakilas, G., Maragkakis, M., & Reczko, M. et al. (2012). TarBase 6.0: Capturing the exponential growth of miRNA targets with experimental support. *Nucleic Acids Research*, *40*(Database issue), D222–D229. doi:10.1093/nar/gkr1161 PMID:22135297

Veuthey, A. L., Bridge, A., Gobeill, J., Ruch, P., McEntyre, J. R., Bougueleret, L., & Xenarios, I. (2013). Application of text-mining for updating protein post-translational modification annotation in UniProtKB. *BMC Bioinformatics*, *14*(1), 104. doi:10.1186/1471-2105-14-104 PMID:23517090

Wang, T., Li, M., Guan, J., Li, P., Wang, H., & Guo, Y. et al. (2011). MicroRNAs miR-27a and miR-143 Regulate Porcine Adipocyte Lipid Metabolism. *International Journal of Molecular Sciences*, *12*(11), 7950–7959. doi:10.3390/ijms12117950 PMID:22174642

Wiegers, T. C., Davis, A. P., Cohen, K. B., Hirschman, L., & Mattingly, C. J. (2009). Text mining and manual curation of chemical-gene-disease networks for the comparative toxicogenomics database (CTD). *BMC Bioinformatics*, *10*(1), 326. doi:10.1186/1471-2105-10-326 PMID:19814812

Xiao, F., Zuo, Z., Cai, G., Kang, S., Gao, X., & Li, T. (2009). miRecords: An integrated resource for microRNA-target interactions. *Nucleic Acids Research*, *37*(Database issue), D105–D110. doi:10.1093/nar/gkn851 PMID:18996891

Xie, B., Ding, Q., Han, H., & Wu, D. (2013). miRCancer: A microRNA-cancer association database constructed by text mining on literature. *Bioinformatics (Oxford, England)*, *29*(5), 638–644. doi:10.1093/bioinformatics/btt014 PMID:23325619

Yamamoto, K., Kudo, T., Konagaya, A., & Matsumoto, Y. (2004). Use of morphological analysis in protein name recognition. *Journal of Biomedical Informatics*, *37*(6), 471–482. doi:10.1016/j.jbi.2004.08.001 PMID:15542020

Yang, H., Spasic, I., Keane, J. A., & Nenadic, G. (2009). A text mining approach to the prediction of disease status from clinical discharge summaries. *Journal of the American Medical Informatics Association*, *16*(4), 596–600. doi:10.1197/jamia.M3096 PMID:19390098

Yang, Z., Ren, F., Liu, C., He, S., Sun, G., & Gao, Q. et al. (2010). dbDEMC: A database of differentially expressed miRNAs in human cancers. *BMC Genomics*, *11*(Suppl 4), 55. doi:10.1186/1471-2164-11-S4-S5 PMID:21143814

Yanpeng, L., Honfei, L., & Zhihao, Y. (2007). Two Approaches for Biomedical Text Classification. In *Proceedings of International Conference on Bioinformatics and Biomedical Engineering*, (pp. 310-313). IEEE.

Zhou, W., Torvik, V. I., & Smalheiser, N. R. (2006). ADAM: Another database of abbreviations in MEDLINE. *Bioinformatics (Oxford, England)*, *22*(22), 2813–2818. doi:10.1093/bioinformatics/btl480 PMID:16982707

ADDITIONAL READING

Ananiadou, S., & McNaught, J. (Eds.). (2006). *Text Mining for Biology and Biomedicine*. Artech House.

Ananiadou, S., Thompson, P., & Nawaz, R. (2013). *Mining events from the literature for bioinformatics applications*. ACM SIGWEB Newsletter.

Bhattacharya, A., Ziebarth, J. D., & Cui, Y. (2013). Somamir: A database for somatic mutations impacting microRNA function in cancer. *Nucleic Acids Research*, *41*(D1), D977–D982. doi:10.1093/nar/gks1138 PMID:23180788

Canese, K., & Weis, S. (2002). PubMed: the bibliographic database. In *The NCBI Handbook* (2nd edition). Retrieved from: http://www.ncbi.nlm.nih.gov/books/NBK153385/

Chen, H., & Sharp, B. M. (2004). Content-rich biological network constructed by mining PubMed abstracts. *BMC Bioinformatics*, *5*(1), 147. doi:10.1186/1471-2105-5-147 PMID:15473905

Cheng, D., Knox, C., Young, N., Stothard, P., Damaraju, S., & Wishart, D. S. (2008). PolySearch: A web-based text mining system for extracting relationships between human diseases, genes, mutations, drugs and metabolites. *Nucleic Acids Research*, *36*(Web Server), W399–W405. doi:10.1093/nar/gkn296 PMID:18487273

Cohen, K. B., & Hunter, L. (2008). Getting started in text mining. *PLoS Computational Biology*, *4*(1), e20. doi:10.1371/journal.pcbi.0040020 PMID:18225946

Davis, A. P., Wiegers, T. C., Johnson, R. J., Lay, J. M., Lennon-Hopkins, K., & Saraceni-Richards, C. et al. (2013). Text mining effectively scores and ranks the literature for improving chemical-gene-disease curation at the comparative toxicogenomics database. *PLoS ONE*, *8*(4), e58201. doi:10.1371/journal.pone.0058201 PMID:23613709

Erhardt, R. A.-A., Schneider, R., & Blaschke, C. (2006). Status of text-mining techniques applied to biomedical text. *Drug Discovery Today*, *11*(7-8), 315–325. doi:10.1016/j.drudis.2006.02.011 PMID:16580973

Feldman, R., & Sanger, J. (2007). *The text mining handbook: advanced approaches in analyzing unstructured data*. Cambridge University Press.

Friedman, C., Kra, P., Yu, H., Krauthammer, M., & Rzhetsky, A. (2001). GENIES: A Natural Language Processing System for the Extraction of Molecular Pathways from Journal Articles. *Bioinformatics (Oxford, England)*, *17*(Suppl 1), S74–S82. doi:10.1093/bioinformatics/17.suppl_1.S74 PMID:11472995

Hill, T., & Lewicki, P. (2007). Text mining (big data, unstructured data). In Hill, T. & Lewicki, P., *Statistics: methods and applications*. Tulsa, OK: StatSoft. http://www.statsoft.com/textbook/

Hunter, L., & Cohen, K. B. (2006). Biomedical Language Processing: Perspective What's Beyond PubMed? *Molecular Cell*, *21*(5), 589–594. doi:10.1016/j.molcel.2006.02.012 PMID:16507357

Korkontzelos, I., & Ananiadou, S. (2014). Term Extraction. In Oxford Handbook of Computational Linguistics (2nd Edition)

Manning, C. D., Raghavan, P. & SchÜtze, H. (2008). Introduction to information retrieval. Cambridge: Cambridge University Press. Retrieved from http://www-nlp.stanford.edu/IR-book/

National Centre for Text Mining. (2013). Retrieved from: http://www.nactem.ac.uk/index.php

Neveol, A., Wilbur, W. J., & Lu, Z. (2012). Improving links between literature and biological data with text mining: A case study with GEO, PDB and MEDLINE. *Database*, *2012*(0), bas026. doi:10.1093/database/bas026 PMID:22685160

Nobata, C., Dobson, P. D., Iqbal, S. A., Mendes, P., Tsujii, J., Kell, D. B., & Ananiadou, S. (2010). Mining metabolites: Extracting the yeast metabolome from the literature. *Metabolomics*, *7*(1), 94–101. doi:10.1007/s11306-010-0251-6 PMID:21687783

Novichkova, S., Egorov, S., & Daraselia, N. (2003). A Natural Language Processing Engine for MEDLINE Abstracts. *Bioinformatics (Oxford, England)*, *19*(13), 1699–1706. doi:10.1093/bioinformatics/btg207 PMID:12967967

Rodriguez-Esteban, R. (2009). Biomedical text mining and its applications. *PLoS Computational Biology*, *5*(12), e1000597. doi:10.1371/journal.pcbi.1000597 PMID:20041219

Shatkay, H., & Feldman, R. (2003). Mining the Biomedical Literature in the Genomic Era: An Overview. *Journal of Computational Biology*, *10*(6), 821–855. doi:10.1089/106652703322756104 PMID:14980013

Simpson, M. S., & Demner-Fushman, D. (2012). Biomedical text mining: a survey of recent progress. In Simpson, M.S. & Fushman, D.D., Mining text data (465-517). US: Springer. doi:10.1007/978-1-4614-3223-4_14

Xie, B., Hochberg, R., Ding, Q., & Wu, D. (2010). Mirsat & mircdb: an integrated microRNA sequence analysis tool and a cancer-associated microRNA database. In *Proceedings of International Conference on Bioinformatics and Computational Biology*, Honolulu, Hawaii, 159-164.

Zhu, F., Patumcharoenpol, P., Zhang, C., Yang, Y., Chan, J., & Meechai, A. et al. (2013). Biomedical text mining and its applications in cancer research. *Journal of Biomedical Informatics*, *46*(2), 200–211. doi:10.1016/j.jbi.2012.10.007 PMID:23159498

Zweigenbaum, P., Demner-Fushman, D., Yu, H., & Cohen, K. B. (2007). Frontiers of biomedical text mining: Current progress. *Briefings in Bioinformatics*, *8*(5), 358–375. doi:10.1093/bib/bbm045 PMID:17977867

KEY TERMS AND DEFINITIONS

Association Extraction: Association Extraction is the process to detect relationships among biology entities.

Biomedical Text Mining: Biomedical text mining is to extract useful patterns from biomedical literature using text mining techniques.

Cancer: Cancer is a term used for diseases in which abnormal cells divide without control and are able to invade other tissues.

Event Extraction: Event Extraction is the process to discover whether two objects are related and in which way they are related.

miRNA: MiRNA is a small sequence of nucleotides that plays an important role in many biological processes.

Name Entity Recognition (NER): Name Entity Recognition is the process to identify research target object names from unstructured text.

Text Mining: Text Mining is the discovery by computer of new, previously unknown information, by automatically extracting information from different written resources.

Chapter 3
Interactive Data Visualization Techniques Applied to Healthcare Decision Making

Zhecheng Zhu
National Healthcare Group, Singapore

Heng Bee Hoon
National Healthcare Group, Singapore

Kiok-Liang Teow
National Healthcare Group, Singapore

ABSTRACT

Data visualization techniques are widely applied in all kinds of organizations, turning tables of numbers into visualizations for discovery, information communication, and knowledge sharing. Data visualization solutions can be found everywhere in healthcare systems from hospital operations monitoring and patient profiling to demand projection and capacity planning. In this chapter, interactive data visualization techniques are discussed and their applications to various aspects of healthcare systems are explored. Compared to static data visualization techniques, interactive ones allow users to explore the data and find the insights themselves. Four case studies are given to illustrate how interactive data visualization techniques are applied in healthcare: summary and overview, information selection and filtering, patient flow visualization, and geographical and longitudinal analyses. These case studies show that interactive data visualization techniques expand the boundary of data visualization as a pure presentation tool and bring certain analytical capability to support better healthcare decision making.

1. INTRODUCTION

Data visualization is a collection of techniques translating data from its numeric format to graphic presentation for easy understanding and visual impact. Data visualization is not a new concept and has been widely applied to all kinds of organizations including healthcare institutions for decades. Data visualization is used everywhere within a modern hospital ranging from monitor system tracking detailed operational parameters in real time manner to annual executive reports

DOI: 10.4018/978-1-4666-6611-5.ch003

summarizing aggregated performance indicators of whole organization. With more healthcare institutions moving toward big data analytics, healthcare decision makers have easier accesses to all types of patient, operations-related raw data with finer detail and in real time manner. While big data opens possibilities of yielding useful information through extremely rich raw data, it comes with many new technical and even ethical challenges:

- **Size of Big Data:** One of the most obvious challenges is management of big data. How to acquire data? How to store data? How long data is kept? How to integrate big data with current IT system? All these questions need to be answered before big data can be effectively used to generate useful information.

- **Complexity of Big Data:** Besides its sheer volume, another challenge of big data is increasing complexity. Big data system acquires data from multiple sources. Data feeds cover not only tabular fields which are relatively easier for analysis, but also various formats such as images, audio and videos, posts and tweets. Complex business process behind data further increases difficulty of big data analysis.

- **Privacy and Security:** While big data enables capability of accessing data at the finest granularity, it also creates another challenge regarding privacy and security. One important consideration when developing big data system is to maintain security, protect people's privacy and prevent any data misusage.

Healthcare decision makers are facing all three above mentioned challenges when seeking useful information and insights from massive amount of raw data. Data volume accumulated over past years is huge and is growing at an even faster rate. New sources of information are collected and existing sources of information are collected at finer granularity. Meanwhile, information variety increases significantly due to multiple categories of information co-existing in same system, e.g., resource utilization data such as bed utilization, operating theater utilization, consultation room utilization, workload data such as emergency department attendance, inpatient admission, outpatient attendance, patient health related data such as diagnosis, lab tests, screening, medication, chronic conditions, patient demographics data such as age, gender, race, ethnic groups, finance related data such as bill size, patient's socio-economics status, subsidy level, insurance information. Additionally, complex business processes in healthcare system add another layer of complexity for data analysis. For instance, patient pathway analysis needs detailed information tracking each patient's footprint within a single visit and permutations of pathways are enormous. Disease progression analysis needs to monitor patients' health related behaviors longitudinally and geographically. Lastly, the availability of detailed patient information including socio-economics status poses another challenge of data anonymization and access level control when conducting data analysis.

Healthcare decision makers rely heavily on visualization tools to understand data better and reveal useful insights. While it is a common practice to apply bar chart, pie chart or scatter plot in data visualization, these traditional static techniques may not be sufficient to deliver all information hidden in the raw data effectively in the era of big data. Interactive data visualization techniques open possibility of conveying information in a more flexible and customized way. Compared to traditional approach of information presentation through static charts, interactive data visualization techniques demonstrate the following advantages:

- **Multiple Data Sources:** Interactive data visualization techniques enable user to switch among multiple data sources. Within a single chart, it is possible to present the relationship of multiple dimensions of variables in various chart formats.

- **Adjustable Granularity:** Working with big data, interactive data visualization techniques can present both detailed micro information and aggregated macro information within a single chart. Decision makers can study a specific problem by zooming in/out to a desirable granularity.
- **Animated Transition:** Interactive data visualization techniques are effective in describing multiple states and how they transit from one to another in a complex system. It adds extra visual impact by animating the transition between states.

The aim of this chapter is to explore the possibility of applying interactive visualization techniques to healthcare decision making by sharing four case studies. These case studies illustrate functions and versatilities of interactive data visualization techniques and how they simplify and accelerate the information sharing process.

This chapter covers a literature review focused on data visualization techniques, available data visualization tools and generic methodology of how data visualization techniques are applied. Then we use case studies to illustrate how interactive visualization techniques are applied to various aspects of healthcare systems supporting decision making.

2. LITERATURE REVIEW

Presenting various types of data in graphical forms for more effective information communication is the focus of data visualization (Cairo, 2013). The history of data visualization can be traced back to 2nd century AD (Few & Perceptual, 2007). Most development of data visualization came along with the development of statistical graphics in the 19th century (Tufte, 2001). William Playfair, the founder of statistical graphics, invented fun-

damental diagrams including line chart, bar chart and pie chart (Heyde et al., 2013). Almost all types of modern forms of data visualization tools were invented during that period: scatterplot, histogram, contour plot, time series plot and geographical map (Friendly & Daniel, 2008; Friendly, 2008), etc. With the surging development of computer and web technologies, interactive data visualization surfaced and is evolving rapidly. It gains more popularity as it provides more flexibility and visual impact over traditional static counterpart (Ward, Grinstein, Keim, & more, 2010).

In the era of big data, visualization especially interactive visualization techniques are even more important than ever due to the challenge of deriving timely and useful insights from the huge volume of data available (Liebowitz, 2013; Manyika et al., 2011; Provost & Fawcett, 2013). Key benefits of interactive data visualization include better decision making, fast information sharing and self-service capability to end users (LeFever, 2013).

Generally speaking, the functions of interactive data visualization covers the following areas (Conceptual Fundamentals, 2014):

- **Overview:** Summarize basic information or statistics of whole data set.
- **Navigate:** Organize data suitable for easy navigation and selection.
- **Zoom:** Zoom in or out a specific subset of whole dataset for better resolution.
- **Filter:** Focus on the interesting part of dataset by hiding the uninteresting one.
- **Details:** Keep details and show them when needed.
- **Relate:** Study the relationship among multiple variables.
- **History:** Allow repetition of the same action on different datasets.
- **Extract:** Export report or graphics to other formats.

One data visualization solution could cover one or more above mentioned functions. While there are no golden rules to measure the effectiveness of an interactive data visualization solution, a good solution usually meets the following criteria (Yau, 2013):

- **Adaptive and Interactive:** A good solution is customized to meet different scenarios and provides user friendly interface for inputs and outputs.
- **Integrated and Intuitive:** A good solution handles multiple data sources and complex business logics at backend, presents final results in a straight forward way.
- **Easy Access or Sharing:** A good solution is easily deployed and shared through all relevant parties.

Besides the above mentioned criteria for an efficient data visualization solution, several pitfalls or misuses should be avoided during developing data visualization solutions. For instance, avoid 3D charts if possible as it may add unnecessary complexity to the whole presentation. Do not abuse animation such as flying texts as they may cause distraction of audience's attention. Using proper scale of axes as inconsistent scale may cause misinterpretation. Data visualization solutions should be carefully developed and deployed as an improperly developed chart could easily lead to biased or even misleading conclusions (Data Visualization, 2014).

There are numerous data visualization tools in the current market. Microsoft Excel (Microsoft Excel, 2014) is extensively used for data analysis and visualization and PowerPivot (PowerPivot, 2014) is a powerful add-on enhancing Excel's capabilities significantly. Most statistics packages such as SAS (SAS, 2014), SPSS (SPSS, 2014), STATA (Stata, 2014) and R (R project, 2014) have comprehensive built-in data visualization functions.

Many specialized tools focused on interactive visualization have emerged in recent years. Some commercial packages include Tableau (Tableau, 2014), SiSense Prism (Sisense, 2014), Spotfire (Spotfire, 2014), FusionCharts (Fusioncharts, 2014). All of them provide flexible and user friendly solution for interactive data visualization. Besides above mentioned commercial software or packages, there are many free/open source alternatives, providing same quality of solutions and flexible options of sharing and deployment. Many open source tools are built upon standard web techniques such as HTML, Javascript, SVG and CSS. For instance, D3.js (D3.js, 2014) is a Javascript library for data visualization. It provides a framework to realize sophisticated and highly interactive data visualization solutions and supports almost all kinds of charts from traditional bar chart, scatter plot to heatmap, treemap, geographical information system (GIS) maps. D3.js accepts generic data formats such as csv, tsv or json as inputs and publishes the results in format of HTML pages, which can be accessed by web browsers without additional requirements. Such flexibility makes it possible to deploy the results developed by D3.js anywhere without incurring extra costs. Other than above mentioned packages or library, there are also online data visualization API provided by big companies such as Google Charts (Google Charts, 2014) and Many Eyes (Many Eyes, 2014). Both websites provide one stop solution from data import to eventual publication and provide various types of visualizations.

Table 1 lists the comparison of data visualization tools from different perspectives including input source, result publication, animated transition, user interface and licensing. It is observed that most tools are able to read data from flat files such csv, tsv, json, xml or provide connection to different databases. Most recent tools such as D3.js and Google charts are flexible to publish results locally or as web services. Relying on the latest web technologies such as HTML5, tools

Table 1. Comparison of data visualization tools

Data Visualization Tool	Input Source	Result Publication	Animated Transition	User Interface	Licensing
D3.js	flat files, database	local, server	Yes	Script	Open source
FusionCharts	flat files, database	local, server	Yes	Graphical	Commercial
Microsoft Excel/ PowerPivot	Excel spreadsheet	local	No	Graphical	Commercial
R	flat files, database	local	No	Script	Open source
SAS	flat files, database	local	No	Script	Commercial
SiSense Prism	flat files, database	local, server	Yes	Graphical	Commercial
Spotfire	flat files, database	local, server	Yes	Graphical	Commercial
SPSS	flat files, database	local	No	Graphical	Commercial
STATA	flat files, database	local	No	Script	Commercial
Tableau	flat files, database	local, server	Yes	Graphical	Commercial
Google Charts	flat files, database	local, server	Yes	Script	Free
Many Eyes	flat files	server	No	Graphical	Free

likes D3.js and Google charts can apply animated transition for extra visual impact. In terms of user interface, some tools are script based which may need some programming background while others provide user friendly graphical interface. In this chapter, D3.js is selected as the major visualization tools as it has a rich library of various chart types, flexible publication modes and open source.

Turning raw data into visual format is a multi-step procedure including data preparation, visualization pattern selection, visualization development, solution deployment and maintenance. Each step is described briefly as below:

1. **Data Preparation:** Pre-processing raw data is usually the first step of data visualization. Basic pre-processing procedures include data formatting, missing values handling,

outliers handling, value normalization and value categorization. Sampling is needed when the amount of raw data is too huge. Variable filtering is sometimes needed to remove irrelevant variables or merge redundant variables. Data aggregation is needed if purpose of visualization is to have an overview of whole dataset. Regression or clustering is also needed in certain circumstance. For interactive data visualization, multiple data sets need to be prepared and organized in a hierarchical way corresponding to the flow of visualization sequence.

2. **Visualization Pattern Selection:** The second step is to select suitable chart type to represent the processed data. Many chart types are available, each suitable for different purposes. For instance, line chart is

suitable to track trend over time or compare multiple items over the same period. Bar chart is suitable to compare values of different categories. Scatter plot is suitable to study the relationship/correlation of two variables. Bubble plot presents a third dimension of variables on top of a regular scatter plot. Pie chart is able to visually present the percentage of a component within the whole set. Gantt chart is a variation of bar chart used to present sequence and dependence of multiple activities. GIS map is very useful to visually present geographical distribution of data sets. For interactive data visualization, it is common to combine multiple chart types into final visualization solution. They can be presented simultaneously to reflect different aspects of a system snapshot, or sequentially to illustrate different levels or states when system resolution or status changes. For instance, a choropleth map can be used to show aggregated distribution of subjects in whole region. While zooming in to a specific area, a scatter plot on the map can be used to show detailed location of each subject.

3. **Visualization Development:** The third step is to translate the data set to the selected visualization pattern. One difference between static chart and interactive chart is that interactive chart allows the users to control and explore the data themselves. Several considerations are listed to develop an efficient interactive data visualization solution: Data is organized in hierarchical structure for easy collapse and expansion. User interface is provided for easy navigation among different levels of data structure. Dtailed visualization development depends on the software or package used, with drag and drop being sufficient in some software while programming may needed in others.

4. **Solution Deployment and Maintenance:** The final step is to share the visualization solution with stakeholders or deploy it

across whole organization. This step could be software dependent. Solutions developed using certain software can be accessed by its corresponding viewer, usually free. Some softwares are able to publish the solution as a web service to be accessed by any web browser. Maintenance is also needed to keep the solution up-to-date. It can be achieved either by manually updating with the latest data periodically or continuously updating with real time inputs.

3. CASE STUDIES

In this section, case studies are given to illustrate how interactive data visualization techniques are applied to various aspects of healthcare systems.

3.1. Summary and Overview

An interactive chart can be used as an effective tool when presenting massive volume of highly aggregated information to senior management. When such information is presented conventionally, a large set of static charts are usually needed to produce all information from different perspectives and levels. One possible problem is how to organize multiple static charts to tell a complete story in the best way. An interactive chart can overcome such problem by integrating all static charts. Instant switching among different perspectives and levels is achievable through pre-designed control panel. Additionally, animated transition can also be made available when switching among perspectives to highlight change and trend among multiple states.

Figure 1 illustrates an example of interactive charts applied to an overview of patient profile of different risk groups and how these patients using hospital resources within one calendar year in a hospital. It is composed of two parts: control panel on the top and display area below. Different risk groups can be selected from the control panel and

Figure 1. Example of interactive charts for overview and summary

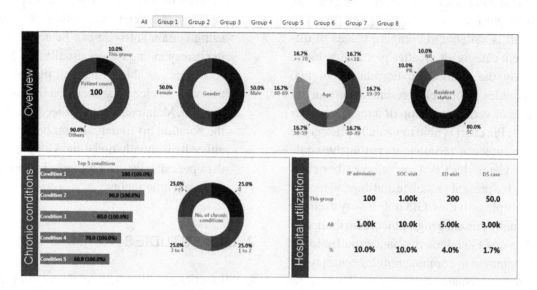

the corresponding information of the specific risk groups can be instantly refreshed in the display areas. There are three sections in the display areas, showing three classes of information.

- The overview section shows the overall workload and patient demographics including gender, age and resident status of the selected risk group. Donut charts are applied to visually illustrate the percentage distribution in each category.
- The second section shows the profiling of chronic conditions of the selected risk groups. Bar chart is applied to list the top 5 prevalent chronic conditions and their absolute volume and prevalence among the selected risk group. Donut chart is applied to illustrate the distribution of number of chronic conditions per patient in the selected risk group.
- The third section shows how the select risk groups are using hospital resources. Results are presented in table format. For types of hospital resources are summarized in the table: inpatient, outpatient, A&E and day surgery. The first row reports the ab-

solute volume of the selected risk group, the second row reports the overall volume of the whole hospital and the third row reports the percentage.

Above example shows how multiple pieces of information are integrated into one interactive chart. Compared to traditional static charts, the single interactive chart is more organized and conveys massive information more effectively. It is suitable to act as an information hub and provides a bird-eye view of all the crucial information for the decision makers.

3.2. Information Selection and Filtering

There are two common tasks when presenting data to decision makers: one is to zoom in a smaller set of data from a larger data source for further details, the other is to study the correlation of any two factors selected from a number of factors. Figure 2 illustrates how to combine these two types of analysis within one interactive chart, and an example of comparing several key performance indicators across several outpatient clinics and over

Figure 2. Example of interactive charts for dynamic information selection and filtering

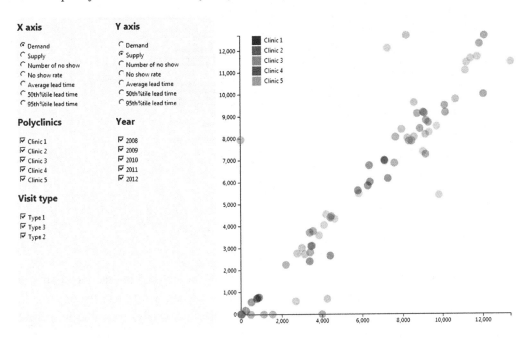

a few years. The interactive chart composed of two parts: the control panel at the left side and the display area at the right side. There are seven key performance indicators listed in the control panel: demand, supply, number of no-show, no-show rate, average lead time, 50th%tile waiting time, 95th%tile waiting time. Any two indicators can be selected from the radio boxes as either one of X or Y axis. Information filtering can be achieved by three sets of check boxes: clinic, year and visit type. Specific information can be highlighted by checking one or more check boxes. A scatter plot is represented in the display area. X and Y axes are corresponding to the indicators selected, with the axes scale automatically matching the scales of the selected indicators. Selected figures are plotted on the scatter plot. When hovering over the specific point, a textbox of tooltip will be shown for extra piece of information. The interactive charts can be used to examine the correlation between any indicators and filter out the information the decision makers are only interested in.

3.3. Patient Flow Visualization

Understanding and analyzing patient flow is an important but challenging task to any hospital service provider due to the uniqueness and complexity of patient flows. There are various approaches to study patient flow, e.g., value stream mapping in lean context and discrete event simulation. These approaches have their own pros and cons. For instance, discrete event simulation is able to deal with the uncertainties in the system and test different what-if scenarios. However, dedicated software is needed to conduct discrete event simulation and sometimes interpretation is needed to translate simulation results to useful findings. Interactive charts can be used to visualize patient flow for better understanding and communication. Figure 3 illustrates how interactive charts are applied to visualize the patient flow in an outpatient clinic with appointment system. It is composed of two parts: on the left is the control panel including a series of drop down boxes, where the specific

Figure 3. Example of interactive charts for patient flow visualization

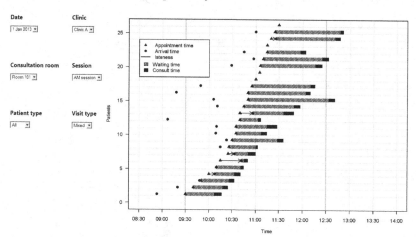

date, clinic, consultation room, session, patient type, visit type can be selected. On the right is the display area, where detailed patient flow of the selected session is presented. Gantt chart is applied to visualize the patient flow of the selected session. Each row represents one patient movement. Square represents the appointment time, dot represents the arrival time. Several observations can be made from the Gantt chart:

- Variations exist in patients' arrival time. Patients either come earlier or later than their appointment times. Some patients do not show up.
- Appointment slots are not evenly spread over the whole session, e.g., more slots are packed from 10:30 am to 11:00 am causing congestion and long waiting time.
- The first time slot is arranged at 9:30 am but the first consultation started at 10:09 am, which was 39 minutes late. It has a significant impact on both patient waiting time and clinic overtime.
- Irregular calling sequence existed in the session, where a later appointment slot was called before the patient in an earlier slot. It increases the variation in waiting time.

With the help of interactive charts, decision makers can easily evaluate the existing appointment schedules, analyze possible problems causing long waiting time and detect any bottlenecks in the current system.

3.4. Geographical and Longitudinal Analysis

There are two types of geo-studies prevalent in healthcare system: the first is distribution analysis by geographical areas and the second is longitudinal patient data analysis. The combination of geographic information system (GIS) and interactive data visualization techniques opens possibility of presenting data both geographically and longitudinally. It can be used to answer questions which cannot be answered by either technique alone. For instance, how has the catchment of a hospital shifted over the past five years? How will patients move when a new hospital is up?

Figure 4 illustrates an example of presenting longitudinal data within an interactive chart. It shows the workload distribution of five clinics from 2008 to 2012. The cross symbols represent the locations of the existing clinics. The dots represent the corresponding workload for each

Figure 4. Example of interactive maps with longitudinal data

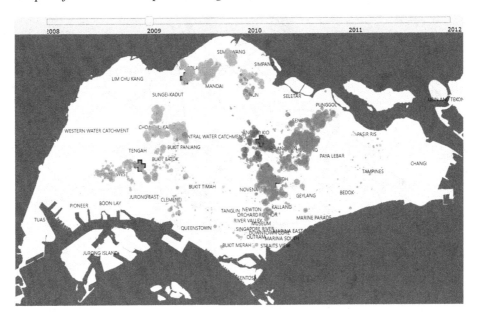

clinic. The dot size represents the density of workload in the specific location, with larger dots depicting higher workload. When the slide bar is shifted from one year to another year, an animated transition is triggered to illustrate how workload is redistributed among the existing dental clinics. Compared to the static map of each year, the interactive map integrates several static maps into one. Additionally, it establishes connections among discrete years through animated transition.

Figure 5 illustrates an example of an interactive map with adjustable granularity. It shows the same content as Figure 4 with Google Map as the base layer overlaid by a layer of locations of clinics as small cross symbols. Powered by Google Map API, the interactive map can be zoomed in/out to the desirable level. For instance, when the decision makers are only interested in the distribution of public and private clinics in a certain area, the interactive map can be zoomed in that area for more details.

4. CONCLUSION AND FUTURE RESEARCH DIRECTIONS

This chapter focuses on interactive data visualization techniques and their applications in healthcare systems. Compared to conventional static data visualization techniques, interactive data visualization techniques allow the user to explore the entire data set by instant slice and dice, and to switch among multiple data sources within a single chart. Adjustable granularity of interactive data visualization allows for both detailed micro information and aggregated macro information within a single chart. Animated transition adds extra visual impact that describes how the system transits from one state to another. There are many data visualization tools ranging from commercial to open source. Some tools has friendly user interface to realize most functions through drag and drop. Other tools need scripting for most functions. Interactive visualization solutions developed by some tools are

Figure 5. Example of interactive maps with adjustable granularity

only accessible through the corresponding readers. Although there are differences among various data visualization tools, the generic procedure of turning raw data into visualization is the same. It includes data preparation, visualization pattern selection, visualization development and solution deployment and maintenance. Four relevant case studies are given to illustrate how interactive data visualization techniques are applied to various aspects of healthcare systems. The first is the overview of patient profiling of different risk groups and how they are using hospital resources within one calendar year in a hospital. The second is an interactive chart comparing several key performance indicators across several outpatient clinics and over a few years. The third is an interactive chart visualizing patient flow in an outpatient clinic with appointment system. The fourth presents geographical and longitudinal data within an interactive chart. All four case studies illustrate that interactive data visualization techniques help better decision making and fast knowledge sharing.

The future research direction could be focused on the integration of interactive visualization techniques with other techniques to support a wider range of decision making.

- **Real Time Decision Making:** By connecting interactive visualization solution to real time data sources such as transaction database, healthcare service providers may have a bird-eye view of real time status update of key performance indicators such as bed utilization, operating theater schedule, waiting time in emergency room, queue size of consultation room. With all the real time information presented graphically, decisions and responses can be made promptly.

- **Predictive Analytical Visualization:** By combining interactive visualization solution with predictive models, healthcare service providers are equipped with a powerful tool helping them predict the future trend visually. For instance, simulation of disease progress in the next few years, patient choice transition towards a newly established hospital. Such a tool will help decision makers in both tactical and strategic planning.

REFERENCES

Cairo, A. (2013). *The functional art: an introduction to information graphics and visualization.* Academic Press.

Conceptual Fundamentals. (2014). *Conceptual Fundamentals of Effective Data Visualization Systems.* Retrieved January 9, 2014, from http://www.panopticon.com/White-Papers D3.js

Data Visualization. (2014). *Data Visualization: 7 Considerations for Visualization Deployment.* Retrieved January 10, 2014, from http://www.sas.com/en_us/whitepapers/iia-data-visualization-7-considerations-for-deployment-106892.html

Few, S., & Perceptual, E. (2007). Data Visualization: Past, Present, and Future. Academic Press.

Friendly, M. (2008). A Brief History of Data Visualization. In *Handbook of Data Visualization* (pp. 15–56). Springer. doi:10.1007/978-3-540-33037-0_2

Friendly, M., & Daniel, J. D. (2008). *Milestones in the history of thematic cartography, statistical graphics, and data visualization. Seeing Science.* Today American Association for the Advancement of Science.

Fusioncharts. (2014). *FusionCharts - JavaScript Charts for the Grown-Ups.* Retrieved January 12, 2014, from http://www.fusioncharts.com/

Google Charts. (2014). *Google Charts – Google Developers.* Retrieved January 13, 2014, from https://developers.google.com/chart/

Heyde, C. C., Crepel, P., Fienberg, S. E., Seneta, E., Gani, J. (2013). *Statisticians of the Centuries* (2001 edition.). New York: Springer.

LeFever, L. (2013). *The art of explanation: making your ideas, products, and services easier to understand.* Hoboken, NJ: John Wiley & Sons.

Liebowitz, J. (2013). *Big data and business analytics.* Boca Raton, FL: CRC Press. doi:10.1201/b14700

Many Eyes. (2014). *Many Eyes.* Retrieved January 13, 2014, from http://www-958.ibm.com/software/analytics/manyeyes/

Manyika, J., Chui, M., Brown, B., Bughin, J., Dobbs, R., Roxburgh, C., & Byers, A. (2011). *Big data: The next frontier for innovation, competition, and productivity.* Retrieved from http://www.mckinsey.com/Insights/MGI/Research/Technology_and_Innovation/Big_data_The_next_frontier_for_innovation

Microsoft Excel. (2014). *Microsoft Excel.* Retrieved January 12, 2014, from http://office.microsoft.com/en-us/excel/

PowerPivot. (2014). *PowerPivot | Microsoft BI.* Retrieved January 12, 2014, from http://www.microsoft.com/en-us/bi/powerpivot.aspx

Provost, F., & Fawcett, T. (2013). Data Science and its Relationship to Big Data and Data-Driven Decision Making. *Big Data, 1*(1), 51–59. doi:10.1089/big.2013.1508

R Project. (2014). *The R Project for Statistical Computing.* Retrieved January 12, 2014, from http://www.r-project.org/

SAS. (2014). *Business Analytics and Business Intelligence Software | SAS.* Retrieved January 12, 2014, from http://www.sas.com/en_us/home.html

Sisense. (2014). *Business Intelligence Software - SiSense Prism.* Retrieved January 12, 2014, from http://www.sisense.com/

Spotfire. (2014). *TIBCO Spotfire - Business Intelligence Analytics Software & Data Visualization.* Retrieved January 12, 2014, from http://spotfire.tibco.com/

SPSS. (2014). *IBM SPSS software*. Retrieved January 12, 2014, from http://www-01.ibm.com/software/analytics/spss/

Stata. (2014). *Stata | Data Analysis and Statistical Software*. Retrieved January 27, 2014, from http://www.stata.com/

Tableau. (2014). *Business Intelligence and Analytics | Tableau Software*. Retrieved January 12, 2014, from http://www.tableausoftware.com/

Tufte, E. R. (2001). *The Visual Display of Quantitative Information* (2nd ed.). Cheshire, CT: Graphics Pr.

Ward, M. O., Grinstein, G., Keim, D. (2010). *Interactive Data Visualization: Foundations, Techniques, and Applications*. Natick, MA: A K Peters/CRC Press.

Yau, N. (2013). *Data points visualization that means something*. Hoboken, NJ: Wiley.

ADDITIONAL READING

Berman, J. J. (2013). *Principles of big data: preparing, sharing, and analyzing complex information*. Amsterdam: Elsevier : Morgan Kaufmann. [etc.]

Cairo, A. (2013). *The functional art: an introduction to information graphics and visualization*.

Dailey, D., Frost, J., & Strazzullo, D. (2012). *Building web applications with SVG*. Redmond, Wash.: Microsoft Press.

Dewar, M. (2012). *Getting Started with D3* [creating data-driven documents]. Beijing: O'Reilly. [u.a.]

Eisenberg, J. D. (2002). *SVG essentials Includes index*. Sebastopol, CA: O'Reilly.

Few, S. (2009). *Now you see it: simple visualization techniques for quantitative analysis*. Oakland, Calif.: Analytics Press.

Foreman, J. W. (2014). *Data smart: using data science to transform information into insight*.

Herman, D. (2013). *Effective JavaScript: 68 specific ways to harness the power of JavaScript*. Upper Saddle River, N.J: Addison-Wesley.

Hurwitz, J. (2013). *Big data for dummies*. Hoboken, N.J.: John Wiley & Sons, Inc.

Iliinsky, N. P. N., & Steele, J. (2010). *Beautiful visualization: [looking at data through the eyes of experts]*. Beijing [u.a.: O'Reilly. Krishnan, K. (2013). *Data warehousing in the age of big data*.

Lankow, J., Ritchie, J., & Crooks. (2012). *Infographics: the power of visual storytelling*. Hoboken, NJ: Wiley.

LeFever, L. (2013). *The art of explanation: making your ideas, products, and services easier to understand*. Hoboken, N.J.: John Wiley & Sons.

Liebowitz, J. (2013). *Big Data and Business Analytics*. CRC Press. doi:10.1201/b14700

Mayer-Schoenberger, V., & Cukier, K. (2013). *Big data: a revolution that will transform how we live, work, and think*. Boston: Houghton Mifflin Harcourt.

Mikowski, M. S., & Powell, J. C. (2013). *Single page web applications: JavaScript end-to-end*.

Miller, T. W. (2013). *Modeling techniques in predictive analytics business problems and solutions with R*. Upper Saddle River, N.J.: Pearson Education.

Minelli, M., Chambers, M., & Dhiraj, A. (2013). *Big data, big analytics: emerging business intelligence and analytic trends for today's businesses*. Hoboken, N.J: John Wiley. doi:10.1002/9781118562260

Murray, S. (2013). *Interactive data visualization for the web* [an introduction to designing with D3]. Sebastopol, CA: O'Reilly.

Provost, F., & Fawcett, T. (2013). *Data science for business* [what you need to know about data mining and data-analytic thinking]. Beijing: O'Reilly. [etc.]

Qi Zhu, N. (2013). *Data visualization with D3.js cookbook: over 70 recipes to create dynamic data-driven visualization with D3.js*. Birmingham, England: Packt Publishing.

Resig, J., & Bibeault, B. (2013). *Secrets of the JavaScript ninja*. Shelter Island, NY: Manning.

Schutt, R., & O'Neil, C. (2013). *Doing data science*. Sebastopol, CA: O'Reilly.

Siegel, E. (2013). *Predictive analytics: the power to predict who will click, buy, lie, or die*. Hoboken, N.J.: Wiley.

Simon, P. (2013). *Too big to ignore: the business case for big data*.

Teller, S. (2013). *Data Visualization with d3.js: mold yur data into beautiful visualizations with d3.js*. Birmingham: Packt Publishing Ltd.

KEY TERMS AND DEFINITIONS

Data Visualization: A collection of techniques translating data from its numeric format to graphic presentation for easy understanding and visual impact.

Geographic Information System (GIS): A system focused on analyzing and presenting data on a map.

Healthcare Decision Making: A process to improve the performance of a healthcare system.

Interactive Data Visualization: An extension of data visualization by allowing users to explore the data and find the insights themselves.

Longitudinal Analysis: Study the trend of several observations over a long period.

Patient Flow Analysis: Analyze patients' movement in a healthcare facility such as outpatient clinics.

Patient Profiling: Describe the characteristic of a specific group of patient including demographics and disease conditions.

Chapter 4
Large–Scale Regulatory Network Analysis from Microarray Data:
Application to Seed Biology

Anamika Basu
Gurudas College, India

Anasua Sarkar
SMIEEE Government College of Engineering and Leather Technology, India

ABSTRACT

The inference of gene networks from gene expression data is known as "reverse engineering." Elucidating genetic networks from high-throughput microarray data in seed maturation and embryo formation in plants is crucial for storage and production of cereals for human beings. Delayed seed maturation and abnormal embryo formation during storage of cereal crops degrade the quality and quantity of food grains. In this chapter, the authors perform comparative gene analysis of results of different microarray experiments in different stages of embryogenesis in Arabidopsis thaliana, and to reconstruct Gene Networks (GNs) related to various stages of plant seed maturation using reverse engineering technique. They also biologically validate the results for developing embryogenesis network on Arabidopsis thaliana with GO and pathway enrichment analysis. The biological analysis shows that different genes are over-expressed during embryogenesis related with several KEGG metabolic pathways. The large-scale microarray datasets of Arabidopsis thaliana for these genes involved in embryogenesis have been analysed in seed biology. The chapter also reveals new insight into the gene functional modules obtained from the Arabidopsis gene correlation networks in this dataset.

INTRODUCTION

Recent advances in microarray technologies have made it possible to routinely measure the expression levels of tens or even hundreds of thousands of genes simultaneously. Such high-throughput experimental data have initiated much recent research on large-scale gene expression data analysis. Various data mining techniques (e.g., clustering and classification) have been employed to uncover the biological functions of genes from microarray data. Recently, these techniques have included a

DOI: 10.4018/978-1-4666-6611-5.ch004

reverse engineering approach to extracting gene regulatory networks from microarray data in order to reveal the structure of the transcriptional gene regulation processes.

The general purpose of gene regulatory network analysis is to extract pronounced gene regulatory features (e.g., activation and inhibition) by examining gene expression patterns. Changes of expression levels of genes across different samples provide information that allows reverse engineering techniques to construct the network of regulatory relations among those genes. Many studies have shown that these learned networks have the potential to help researchers propose and evaluate new hypotheses in basic research of genetic regulatory process. From various issues like noise, incompleteness, multiple cluster belongingness etc., several different trends evolve in research fields over networks. To explore different approaches with or without using prior biological knowledge, we have compared several existing approaches to find out the probable transcriptional gene network for seed maturation in *Arabidopsis thaliana.*

For multicellular organisms for systemic and better understanding of their gene regulation involved in a specific developmental stage of life cycle, Gene Network [GN] is the best way. In plant after fertilization under suitable environmental condition embryogenesis occurs. Not only for new plant generation but also for the food habit of world population, construction of a GN for seed maturation and embryogenesis of our food crops e.g. rice, maize is necessary. Here we use model plant *Arabidopsis thaliana* to identify the gene regulators for different stages of embryogenesis. For construction of GRN for different species with huge microarray datasets for seed development and maturation we use that reverse engineering as a powerful method.

BACKGROUND

Network Analysis on Microarray Data

The network and co-expression analysis of microarray data finds out probable transcriptional gene interactions and co-regulation. Network analyses typically work with the gene–gene co-expression matrix, based on the correlation between each pair of genes in the dataset. Hypothetically the amount of co-expression between two genes is associated with an increasing probability that these two genes interact. Thus, the co-expression matrix infers the networks of interactions (Pavlopoulos, 2008).

A network is the same as a mathematical concept of a graph, denoted as a pair G= {V, E}, where V is a set of vertices (nodes) and E is a set of links (edges) that connect pairs of nodes. When constructing a network, one needs to know how biological elements are related among themselves to represent nodes and edges. For example, an edge in a gene interaction network can be placed between two genes if they are functionally associated. This results in a gene interaction network. In a metabolic network, nodes correspond to metabolites and enzymes and directed edges are metabolic reactions to combine all metabolic pathways possible within a cell. Gene regulatory interactions builds a transcriptional regulatory network. Quality of data is the most limiting factor for the network analyses, because of noisy and incomplete biological data covering a significant part in public databases.

There are a number of tools available for visualizing and analysing the biological network from a microarray data set (Pavlopoulos, 2008),(Thomas, S., 2010). Table 1 shows a comparison of available tools online for analysing biological networks.

Several different methods have been used to construct networks from microarray data. Pearson

Table 1. *Available tools for analysing biological networks*

Name	Platform	Network Visualization	Compatibility	Features	Strength
Medusa (Hooper, S.D., 2005)	Java applet, open source	Fruchterman-Reingold algorithm, 2D representation, Weighted non-directed graphs	Own file format, non-compatible	Strong interactive, Supports text search for nodes	Multi-edge connections, PPIN optimized for STRING
Cityscape (Shannon, P., 2003)	Standalone Java application	2D representation of large scale networks Directed, undirected, weighted graphs, Various layouts and mapping of expression data	Supports various file formats - SIF, GML, XGMML, BioPAX, PSI-MI, SBML, OBO etc. Go and KEGG annotations, mRNA expression profile importing possible	Interactive, zoom –in and –out, network manager for multiple networks, network filtering, subset network analysing, statistical analysis, clustering of nodes	Manipulate multiple network, many free user-developed plugins, specialized analysis of connected components
BioLayout Express3D (Freeman, T.C., 2007)	Java 1.5	2D, 3D networks visualization and clustering, Fruchterman-Rheingold layout algorithm	Simple file format, compatible with Cytoscape	MCL algorithm integrated	Different analytical approaches
ProViz (Iragne, F., 2005)	Open source	2D, pseudo-3D display, Tulip drawing package, GEM force based graph layout algorithm, circular and hierarchical layouts	Supports Tulip, PSI-MI and IntAct formats	Specific vocabulary on interactions, subgraphs filtering and clustering	PPIN, with several plugins
Pajek (Batagelj, V., 1998)	Open source	2D, pseudo-3D large scale networks, great variety of layouts, separate data into layers, multi-relational networks, temporal networks, dynamic graphs	Own input file format, network exported to EPS, SVG, X3D and VRML formats	Highly interactive, clusterings, detect components, neighborhoods, cores	Various layout algorithms and pattern identification within networks
Pathway Studio (Nikitin, A., 2003)	Server- and client-side versions, Java	With ResNet mammalian and plant databases, supports KEGG		Network, pathway analysis from PubMed, expressions and proteomics data	Compare node degree with ResNet database
Ingenuity Pathway Analysis (IPA) (Kramer, A., 2013)	Licensed, Java	Core-analysis on PPIN, includes third-party interaction data like BIND, DIP, MINT, MIPS, BIOGRID and COGNIA.		IPA-metabolomics analysis, Comparative analysis for choosing biological states on experimental conditions	Substructure analysis, network descriptors like connectivity, distances, centrality, clusterings etc.

correlation, spectral decomposition, principal component analysis, Bayesian network, mutual information, dependence network, simulated annealing and K-Nearest neighbours are some of the approaches (Pavlopoulos, 2008),(Thomas, S., 2010). Approaches may differ in the prior biological knowledge of the networks.

Embryogenesis

Embryogenesis is the process where a multicellular organism forms from a single cell. In *Arabidopsis thaliana*, embryogenesis is a continuous process and it can be divided into three major phases, described as early, mid, and late. In this section, we review all these phases starting from the early phase of embryogenesis.

The early phase is one for the pattern formation and the morphogenesis. This phase defines the axes of the plant body plan and forms the organ systems. Three basic steps during embryogenesis are: i) cell growth, ii) cell differentiation and iii) morphogenesis. The embryo grows up to certain limit, and then differentiates into cells which are different from their mother cell by their structure and function. Thus different morphological structures like stem, root or flower are formed, so that a total plant can be formed. Embryo morphogenesis begins with the single-celled zygote which, in *A. thaliana*, undergoes a series of cell division and cell

elongation processes giving rise to preglobular, globular, heart, torpedo, linear cotyledon, bent-cotyledon, and mature green stage embryos.

In preglobular stage in Figure 1 embryo proper contents 4-8 cells and the length of embryo proper becomes 20-25μm. (Pilot et al., 2010) found that early embryo development is supported by stored products from mother until the preglobular stage (consisting of 16 to 32 cells).So gene expression profile for preglobular stage is important because from this stage independent development of embryo seems to be started in Arabidopsis embryogenesis.

METHODS

Data

For *Arabidopsis thaliana* in NCBI GEO Dataset for Expression data from Arabidopsis seed compartments at the pre-globular stage, Affymetrix ATH1 Arabidopsis array for 14 samples (embryo proper, micropylar endosperm, peripheral endosperm, chalazal endosperm, general seed coat, chalazal seed coat, whole seeds, 2 biological replicates each) data are available in *Series GSE12402*.

This SubSeries is part of SuperSeries: GSE12404 Expression data from Arabidopsis Seed Compartments at 5 discrete stages of devel-

Figure 1. Stages of embryogenesis and parts of preglobular stage

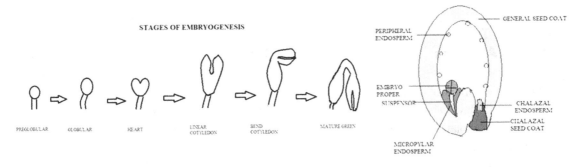

opment with 22810 data entries in GSE12404.By using FunNet, an integrative tool (Prifti, E., 2008) microarray was analysed.

Network Analysis

The 22810 arrays from NCBI GEO database were downloaded and analysed by Bioconductor for Correlation network formation and MCL clustering on the dataset. We also choose only 7551 entries with valid proteins from metadata for our network generation from this data set with 14 samples. The Pearson correlation coefficients for all gene pairs over the 14 samples were calculated.

In network analysis, the Node degree value defines the number of links connected by a node. Similarly, Network density is defined as a ratio of the observed number of edges to all possible edges among the network nodes. The clustering coefficient (C_n) of a given node n is calculated using the equation below. Let there are n nodes with k $(k \geq 2)$ directly connected neighbours, then

$$C_n = \frac{e(k)*2}{k*(k-1)}$$

Where $e(k)$ is the obtained number of edges among the k neighbours. $<C_n>$ represents the average clustering coefficient of the network over all nodes which have at least two neighbours. The clustering coefficient (C_k) with respect to k node degree is the average over all nodes each of which has exact k neighbours.

GO/Pathway Term Enrichment Analysis

The GO terms for Arabidopsis loci were downloaded from http://david.abcc.ncifcrf.gov/using David functional annotation tool. The GO terms for genes in result modules were then obtained from The Arabidopsis Information Resource

(TAIR) (Rhee, SY, 2003). GO term enrichment analysis was carried out by using David (Huang, DW, 2009). Fold enrichment value and % of target genes among total gene set are shown comparatively for all MCL result modules. If a GO term in a module shows a p value less than 0.05, then the GO term is determined to be significantly enriched in this module.

For some modules, more than 28 GO terms were significantly over-represented. To simplify our functional annotation of the module, these GO terms were consolidated to obtain a small set of representative major GO terms. Firstly, the GO terms that were too general (e.g. macromolecule metabolism) were manually discarded. We chose significant GO term for each module based on their minimum p-value shown in GO analysis. Thus, the retrieved major GO terms are associated with non-overlapping gene sets.

The pathway information for Arabidopsis genes was obtained from KEGG pathway obtained from David functional annotation tool (Huang, DW, 2009). The criteria to detect the significantly enriched pathway terms in a module depend on the availability of significant KEGG pathways for genes within the module.

RESULTS

We perform the pair-wise Pearson correlation analysis between every two genes in the chosen dataset using Cytoscape. The high quality of the gene expression data and chosen experimental conditions according to different stages in embryogenesis allow us to capture the true co-expression relationship between two genes. We choose Pearson Correlation Coefficient cut off (Pcccutoff) = -0.95 & 0.95for the analysis over the chosen dataset. The analysis results in a gene correlation network with 7564 nodes and 184 edges.

Network Topology (Correlation Network)

Figure 2 and 3 displays a layout of largest 2 modules from the correlation network developed over the gene expression dataset using the Cytoscape software using Expression Correlation package(website: http://apps.cytoscape.org/apps/expressioncorrelation). The network comprises of 7564 nodes and 184 edges generated from Pearson correlation coefficient network analysis. Within this correlation network, nodes are directly or indirectly connected. The major module in the network has 39 nodes. The smallest module contains only two nodes, and 4 such modules were found.

There are 7494 connected components in this network. On average, each node in the correlation network has 0.049 neighbours, but the distribution of the node degrees is highly skewed. Interestingly, we found that the top 382 nodes (genes) in terms of their degrees connected to each other. Each

of these 382 genes has at least 889 co-expression links (edges). We then examined the node degree distribution and network connectivity distribution over this network as shown in Figure 4. Therefore the hub genes in modules did not reach out to the entire Arabidopsis gene correlation network. They were rather densely connected only to a fraction of the network. A module is a subnetwork which is densely connected within itself but sparsely connected with rest network. Therefore these 39 genes and genes in other modules will contain larger superset of valid functional modules. It was later confirmed by network clustering results.

Network Clustering Analysis

We used the MCL algorithm to partition correlation network into gene modules. MCL is an efficient graph clustering algorithm based on the simulation of random walks within a graph. MCL has been applied to detect modules in yeast

Figure 2. Module 1 (largest module detected) in correlation network on the chosen dataset

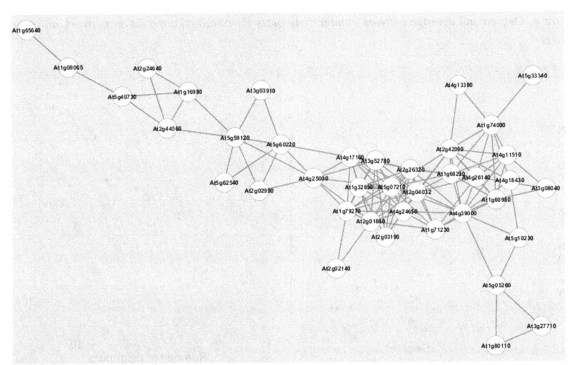

Figure 3. Module 2 (second largest module detected) in correlation network on the chosen dataset

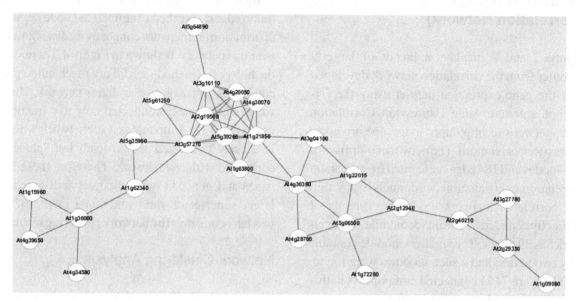

protein interaction networks (Pu, S., 2007) and protein family networks (Enright, AJ, 2002). A recent study, which evaluated four clustering algorithms for protein interaction networks, showed the superior performance of MCL in the identification of protein complexes (Brohee, S, 2006). The algorithm is very efficient and took only 4 minutes to perform clustering on the correlation network using Cluster Maker plugin in Cytoscape.

Figure 4. Degree and average network connectivity plots for obtained correlation network on chosen dataset

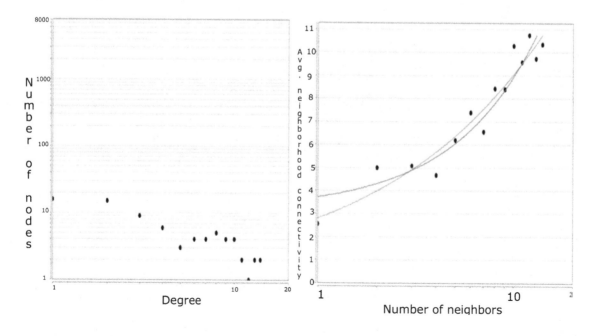

A higher value for the Inflation parameter I in MCL algorithm produces more modules in smaller size. Since a module is a densely connected sub-network and the connections between modules are sparse, clustering on a network with the intrinsic modular structure should produce a small compact mass fraction in one module. We have seen this in the clusters generated from MCL algorithm in Figures 6, 7, 8 with 7501 connected components in total network. For example, when I was set to 2.0, clustering on CN (correlation network) captured 100% of the network area with only 137 edges, reflecting the presence of modular structure in MCL clusters. Recently Brohee and vanHelden experimented MCL algorithm to identify protein complexes from yeast protein interaction networks, with inflation parameter I = 1.8 as the optimal value for I based on the analysis of 42 artificial biological networks (Brohee, S, 2006).

With the inflation value set to 2.0, MCL detected 14 modules from the CN. The five largest modules are taken for further functional analysis. The modularity value for this MCL analysis is 0.407. The module size distribution is also highly skewed. The largest module had 30 nodes with clustering coeefficient 0.353. The clustering coefficient and neighbourhood connectivity for this network has been shown in Figure 5. The higher values in neighbourhood connectivity indicate a better compact module in the solution. The network density is 0.080 and network heterogeneity is 1.229. These result values indicate the significance of the generated biologically more important functional modules form the correlation network for this big expression dataset.

Module Annotation

Module 1

All the clusters produced in MCL clustering results are taken to be relevant modules for the functional analysis. In cluster 1 (module 1), there are 16 genes. Among them six genes are related with plant-type cell wall modification(GO:0009827) where through the series of events lead to chemical

Figure 5. Clustering coefficient and neighborhood connectivity plot for largest module in MCL solutions

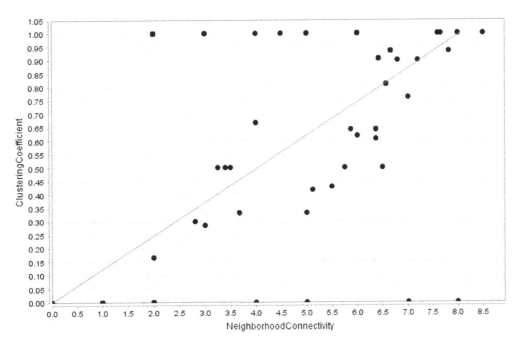

Figure 6. Module 1 obtained by MCL algorithm on chosen dataset and the names of genes from TAIR

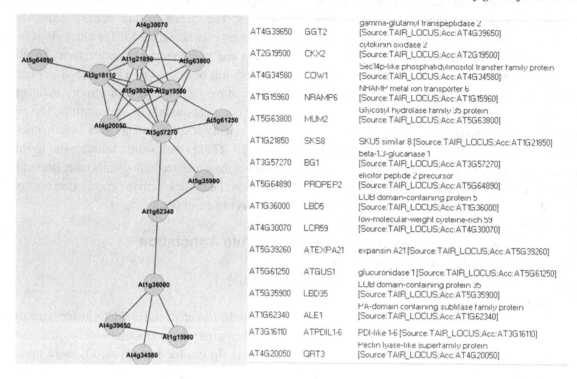

Figure 7. Module2 obtained by MCL algorithm on chosen dataset and the names and GO annotations of all genes in the module from TAIR

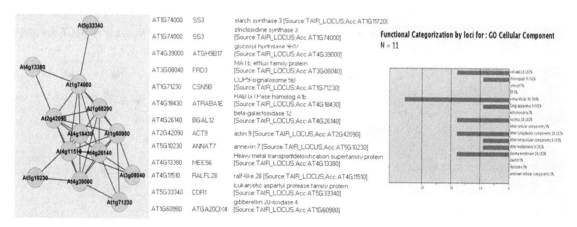

and structural alterations of an existing cellulose and pectin-containing cell wall, that can result in loosening, increased extensibility or disassembly. The other two genes are involved in plant pathogen interaction.

From the gene network we can see that ATEX-PA21 (AT5G39260) has interaction with CKX2, cytokinin oxidase 2.Cytokinins are hormones that regulate cell division and development. It was already proved that cytokinins control the exit of cells from the root meristem. Because cytokinins

Figure 8. Module3 obtained by MCL algorithm on chosen dataset and the names and GO annotations of all genes in the module from TAIR

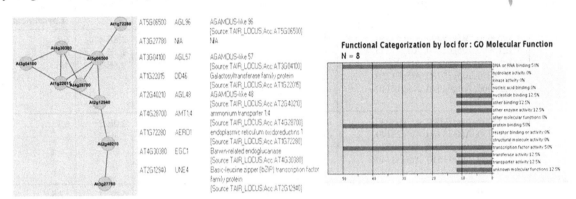

are negative regulators of root growth and lateral root formation. Thus, cytokinins have central, but opposite, regulatory functions in root and shoot meristems (Werner et al, 2003).

Both ATEXPA21 and CKX2 are related with MUM2 (AT5G63800), Glycosyl hydrolase family 35 protein in the same gene network. This gene is involved in the chemical reactions and pathways resulting in the formation of mucilage that occur as part of seed coat development. Mucilage is normally synthesized during seed coat development. The expressed proteins are present in cell wall. MUM2 is involved in modifying mucilage to allow it to expand upon hydration (Dean et al, 2007). Beta-galactosidase activity of this protein is related with the hydrolyzing O-glycosyl compounds as present in the galactosyl side-chain structure of pectin. This type of hydrolase activity, for hydrolyzing O-glycosyl compounds, also present in AT3G57270 (BG1). Pectins are a family of plant cell wall heteropolysaccharides, containing a backbone of α-1, 4-linked D-galacturonic acid. In the plant cell wall, the major carbohydrates are cellulose, hemicellulose and pectin. The cellulose microfibrils are linked via hemicellulosic tethers to form the cellulose-hemicellulose network, which is embedded in the pectin matrix. Expansins have no hydrolytic activity (glucosidase) and therefore, it has been suggested to work by breaking hydrogen bonds between cellulose fibres or between cel-

lulose and other polysaccharides (xyloglucans), using a non-enzymatic mechanism

AT1G21850 SKU5 similar 8 (sks8); FUNCTIONS IN: oxidoreductase activity, copper ion binding. The SKU5 gene belongs to a 19-member gene family designated SKS (SKU5 Similar).In 2002 Sedbrook et al suggested that SKU5 affects two directional growth processes, possibly by participating in cell wall expansion.

QRT3 (AT4G20050) has the ability for catalysis of the random hydrolysis of (1->4)-alpha-D-galactosiduronic linkages in pectate and other galacturonans. Thus this gene and ATEXPA21, both are present in a gene network, are involved in plant type cell wall modification process.

The novel classes of plant pathogenesis-related (PR) proteins include proteinase inhibitors (PR-6 family), plant defensins (PR-12 family), thionins (PR-13 family) and lipid transfer proteins (PR-14 family). PDF3.2. (AT4G30070), low molecular weight cysteine, rich protein, belongs to the plant defensin (PDF) family. This gene is specifically expressed in central cell and plant embyo during preglobular stage of embryogenesis.Pep1 is a 23-amino acid peptide that enhances resistance to a root pathogen, Pythiumirregulare. Pep1 and its homologs (Pep2 to Pep7) are endogenous amplifiers of innate immunity of Arabidopsis thaliana that induce the transcription of defense-related genes and bind to PEPR1, a plasma membrane

Table 2. Results for GO annotation using David

Cluster No	Gene IDs	Term	%	P Values	Fold Enrichment
1	At4g39650, At2g19500, At4g34580, At1g15960, At5g63800, At1g21850, At3g57270, At5g64890, At1g36000, At4g30070, At5g39260, At5g61250, At5g35900, At1g62340, At3g16110, At4g20050	extracellular region(GO:0005576) signal signal peptide	43.8 37.5 37.5	2.8E-4 1.1E-3 9.8E-3	6.1 6.6 3.5
2	At1g74000, At4g39000, At3g08040, At1g71230, At4g18430, At4g26140, At2g42090, At1g68290, At5g10230, At4g13380, At4g11510, At5g33340, At1g60980	hydrolase extracellular region	33.3 33.3	2.0E-2 2.8E-2	6.1 5.0
3	At5g06500, At3g27780, At3g04100, At1g22015, At2g40210, At4g28700, At1g72280, At4g30380, At2g12940	sequence-specific DNA binding(GO:0043565) regulation of transcription, DNA-dependent(GO:0006355) regulation of RNA metabolic process(GO:0051252)	50 50 50	6.4E-4 7.9E-3 8.0E-3	17.5 7.3 7.3
4	At1g16980, At2g44560, At5g59120, At4g25000, At2g24640, At5g62540, At3g03910, At5g60220, At2g02990	Primary metabolic process	88.9	5.5E-2	1.7
5	At4g17160, At2g04032, At4g24650, At3g52780, At5g07210, At2g03190, At2g26320, At1g32850	nucleus	37.5	9.7E-2	4.8

leucine-rich repeat (LRR) receptor kinase. In 2010 Yamaguchi et al., identified a plasma membrane LRR receptor kinase, designated PEPR2 that has 76% amino acidsimilarity to PEPR1, Both PEPR1 and PEPR2 were transcriptionally induced by wounding, treatment with methyl jasmonate, Pep peptides, and pathogen-associated molecular patterns. Expression of PROPEP2 (AT5G64890) is strongly and rapidly induced by AtPeps, in response to bacterial, oomycete, and fungal pathogens, and microbe-associated molecular patterns (MAMPs). WRKY factors are the major regulators of MAMP-induced PROPEP2 expression (Logemann et al, 2013).

Module 2

In cluster 2, 13 genes are present in a network.

From TAIR results of molecular function analysis for cluster 2 genes are shown in Figure 7.The result of functional categorization analy-

sis for GO Cellular Component in TAIR of 11 genes in Module 2 shows that 36.364% genes i.e.RALFL28 (AT4G11510), Beta-galactosidase 12 (AT4G26140), Glycosyl hydrolase 9B17 (AT4G39000) and Constitutive disease resistance 1 (AT5G33340) are present in extracellular region(GO:0005576), that means the space external to the outermost structure of a cell.

ATRABA1E (AT4G18430) RAB GTPase homolog A1E (RABA1e) involves in protein transport and small GTPase mediated signal transduction by binding GTP. In this gene network RALF28 (AT4G11510) is closely located with ATRABA1E. The transcript of second gene consists of a single exon and is characterized by a conserved C-terminal motif and N-terminal signal peptide and this gene is specifically expressed in preglobular stage of embryo. This class of protein is believed to play an essential role in the physiology of Arabidopsis and has signal transducer activity that means this protein conveys a signal or a physical entity or change in state across a cell to trigger a change in cell function or state in order to trigger a response. ATGA20OX4 (AT1G60980) is present at the rim of the developing embryo. BGAL12 (AT4G26140) has hydrolase activity for hydrolyzing O-glycosyl compounds.

Module 3

The result of functional categorization analysis for GO Molecular Function in TAIR of 8 genes in Module 3 shows that 50% genes i.e. AT2G12940 (UNE4), AT2G40210 (AGL48), AT3G04100 (AGL57) and AT5G06500 (AGL96)have sequence-specific DNA binding transcription factor activity(GO:0003700) i.e. these genes interact selectively and non-covalently with specific DNA sequences in order to modulate transcription.

Analyzing the promoter region of gene AERO1 (AT1G72280) by AGRIS (The Arabidopsis Gene Regulatory Information Server) two binding sites for bZIP transcription binding sites has been identified as shown in the following figure:

Both AT2G12940 (UNE4) UNFERTILIZED EMBRYO SAC 4, which expresses Basic-leucine zipper (bZIP) transcription factor family protein and AERO1(AT1G72280) endoplasmic reticulum oxidoreductins 1 genes are present in this gene network.Since the promoter region of second has two binding sites for bZIP transcription factors then module 3 can be hypothesized as a gene regulatory network containing 9 genes. According to AceView, functionally, the gene AERO1 has been proposed to participate in a process (protein thiol-disulfide exchange). Proteins are expected to have molecular functions (electron carrier activity, FAD

Figure 9. The promoter region analysis of gene AERO1 (AT1G72280) by AGRIS

Summary of properties of promoter region At1g72280

Promoter ID	Gene Description	Chromosome Location	Promoter Sequence	Promoter Type	Promoter Source	Regulatory Network
At1g72280	disulfide bond formation protein	Chr1:27218167 - 27219350	Get Sequence	Predicted	TAIR	...

View this promoter in genome browser	Current list of binding sites and references

Binding Sites in upstream region of At1g72280

ColorKey for Binding Sites

Documented binding sites in a specific promoter	Bindingsites in a specific TF or TF family and bindingsite motifs predicted in promoters

BS Name	BS Genome Start	BS Genome End	Binding Site Sequence	Binding Site Family/TF
AtMYC2 BS in RD22	27218586	27218591	cacatg	BHLH
Bellringer/replumless/pennywise BS1 IN AG	27218172	27218179	aaattaaa	Homeobox
ATB2/AtbZIP53/AtbZIP44/GBF5 BS in ProDH	27218889	27218894	actcat	bZIP
ATB2/AtbZIP53/AtbZIP44/GBF5 BS in ProDH	27218728	27218733	actcat	bZIP

binding, oxidoreductase activity, acting on sulfur group of donors, disulfide as acceptor, protein binding) and to localize in various compartments (endoplasmic reticulum, endoplasmic reticulum membrane).The oxidation and isomerization of disulfide bonds is necessary for the growth of all organisms. Similarly, UNE4 gene has been proposed to participate in processes (double fertilization forming a zygote and endosperm, regulation of transcription, DNA-dependent).

Module 4

The result of functional categorization analysis for GO Molecular Function in TAIR of 8 genes in Module 4 (Figure 10) shows that 62.5% genes are present under GO:0016787 hydrolase activity i.e. catalysis of the hydrolysis of various bonds, e.g. C-O, C-N, C-C, phosphoric anhydride bonds, etc. Hydrolase is the systematic name for any enzyme of EC class 3. The genes, which are present

under this GO classification, are Ribonuclease1 (AT2G02990), Ubiquitin Carboxyl-Terminal Hydrolase 19 (AT2G24640), Glycosyl Hydrolase 9B11 (AT2G44560), Alpha-Amylase-Like (AT4G25000) and Subtilase4.13 (AT5G59120). The last gene which present at the center of the network participate in processes e.g. negative regulation of enzyme activity, proteolysis with molecular functions of identical protein binding, peptidase activity, serine-type endopeptidase activity, subtilase activity.

Module 5

The result of functional categorization analysis for GO Cellular Component in TAIR of 8 genes in Module 5 shows that 50% genes i.e. AT2G26320, AT5G07210, and AT2G03190 (SKP1-like protein 16) and AT1G32850 (Putative ubiquitin carboxyl-terminal hydrolase 11) are present in nucleus (GO: 0005634). Nucleus is a membrane-bounded organ-

Figure 10. Module4 obtained by MCL algorithm on chosen dataset and the names of genes from TAIR

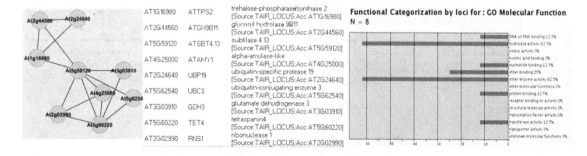

Figure 11. Module 5 obtained by MCL algorithm on chosen dataset and the names of genes from TAIR

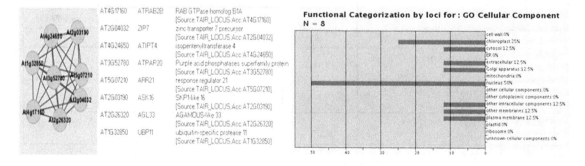

Table 3. Results for pathway analysis by David

Cluster No	ID	Gene Name	Species	KEGG_PATHWAY
1	AT2G19500	Cytokinin dehydrogenase 2	Arabidopsis thaliana	ath00908:Zeatin biosynthesis
2	AT4G39000 Arabidopsis thaliana	Endoglucanase 23	Arabidopsis thaliana	ath00500:Starch and sucrose metabolism, ath00500:Starch and sucrose metabolism
	AT1G74000	Strictosidine synthase 3	Arabidopsis thaliana	ath00901:Indole alkaloid biosynthesis pathway ath01063:Biosynthesis of alkaloids derived from shikimate pathway
3	AT4G25000	AT4G25000	Arabidopsis thaliana	ath00500:Starch and sucrose metabolism ath00500:Starch and sucrose metabolism
	AT1G16980	Probable alpha,alpha-trehalose-phosphate synthase [UDP-forming] 2	Arabidopsis thaliana	ath00500:Starch and sucrose metabolism,
	AT3G03910	Probable glutamate dehydrogenase 3	Arabidopsis thaliana	ath00250:Alanine, aspartate and glutamate metabolism, ath00330:Arginine and proline metabolism, ath00910:Nitrogen metabolism, ath01064:Biosynthesis of alkaloids derived from ornithine, lysine and nicotinic acid
	AT5G62540	Ubiquitin-conjugating enzyme E2 3	Arabidopsis thaliana	ath04120:Ubiquitin mediated proteolysis
4	AT4G24650	IPT4; adenylateisopentenyltransferase 4	Arabidopsis thaliana	ath00908:Zeatin biosynthesis, ath01070:Biosynthesis of plant hormones
	AT2G03190	SKP1-like protein 16	Arabidopsis thaliana	ath04120:Ubiquitin mediated proteolysis

elle of eukaryotic cells in which chromosomes are housed and replicated. In most cells, the nucleus contains all of the cell's chromosomes except the organellar chromosomes, and is the site of RNA synthesis and processing.

KEGG Pathway Enrichment Analysis on Modules

The results of KEGG pathway analysis from David functional annotation tool for our chosen modules are shown in the following:

1. **For Module 1:**
   a. AT2G19500 *CKX2; cytokinin oxidase 2* [EC:1.5.99.12] involves in Zeatin biosynthesis (ath00908) pathway. Zeatin is a member of the cytokinin family, a class of phytohormones involved in various processes of growth and development in plants.
   b. [EC:1.5.99.12] Catalyses the oxidation of cytokinins. This enzyme plays a part in regulating rice-grain production, with lower levels of the enzyme resulting in enhanced grain production.

2. **For Module 2:**
   a. AT4G39000 *GH9B17; glycosyl hydrolase 9B17* [EC: 3.2.1.4] is an example of hydrolase, specifically glycosylase. This enzyme hydrolyses O- and S-glycosyl compounds. Cellulose will also hydrolyse 1, 4-linkages in beta-D-glucans also containing 1, 3-linkages.
   b. AT1G74000 *SS3; strictosidine synthase 3* is present in indole alkaloid biosynthesis pathway present. (ath00901).

3. **For Module 4:**
   a. AT4G25000 *AMY1; alpha-amylase 1* [KO: K01176] [EC: 3.2.1.1] is present in Starch and sucrose metabolism - Arabidopsis thaliana (thale cress) ath00500.
   b. [EC: 3.2.1.1] Acts on starch, glycogen and related polysaccharides and oligosaccharides in a random manner; reducing groups are liberated in the alpha-configuration. The term "alpha" relates to the initial anomeric configuration of the free sugar group released and not to the configuration of the linkage hydrolysed.
   c. AT1G16980 *TPS2; trehalose-phosphatase/synthase 2* [EC: 3.1.3.12, 2.4.1.15], is present in Starch and sucrose metabolism - Arabidopsis thaliana (thale cress) (ath00500).It has two types of activities–
      i. As EC: 3.1.3.12 i.e. hydrolases, acting on ester bonds. They act as phosphoric-monoester hydrolases.
      ii. As EC 2.4.1.15 transferases, specifically hexosyltransferases.
   d. AT3G03910 *GDH3; glutamate dehydrogenase 3*[EC: 1.4.1.3] is present in Alanine, aspartate and glutamate metabolism - Arabidopsis thaliana (thale cress).
   e. [EC: 1.4.1.3] is present in enzyme class oxidoreductases, acting on the CH-NH2 group of donors. It is with NAD+ or NADP+ as acceptor. This enzyme is also present in other pathways e.g. Alanine, aspartate and glutamate metabolism, Arginine and proline metabolism, D-Glutamine and D-glutamate metabolism and Nitrogen metabolism.
   f. AT5G62540 *UBC3; ubiquitin-conjugating enzyme E2 3* [EC: 6.3.2.19], involves in Ubiquitin mediated proteolysis (ath04120). Protein ubiquitination plays an important role in eukaryotic cellular processes. It mainly functions as a signal for 26S proteasome dependent protein degradation.
   g. [EC: 6.3.2.19] are ligases; forms carbon-nitrogen bonds; i.e. they are acid-D-amino-acid ligases (peptide synthases). Ubiquitin is coupled to protein by a peptide bond between the C-terminal glycine of ubiquitin and epsilon-amino groups of lysine residues in the protein. An intermediate in the reaction contains one ubiquitin residue bound as a thioester to the enzyme, and a residue of ubiquitin adenylate non-covalently bound to the enzyme.

4. **For Module 5:**
   a. AT4G24650 *IPT4; adenylate isopentenyltransferase 4* (cytokinin synthase) involves in Zeatin biosynthesis (ath00908) pathway. Zeatin is a member of the cytokinin family, a class of phytohormones involved in various processes of growth and development in plants.
   b. AT2G03190 *S-phase kinase-associated protein 1* like protein 16, involves in Ubiquitin mediated proteolysis (ath04120). Protein ubiquitination

plays an important role in eukaryotic cellular processes. It mainly functions as a signal for 26S proteasome dependent protein degradation.

DISCUSSION

We have analysed the GSE12404 microarray dataset, using different network tools. FunNet provides network analysis based on GO and KEGG annotations of the genes in the networks. Functional genomics analysis has been performed using Bio-Analytic Resource (BAR). Classification Superviewer clusters genes among the network using a ranking method for functional classification. MapMan method also performs functional annotations over the network.

From the expression data in GSE12404 we analyzed the expressed genes for different parts of seeds of Arabidopsis as well as serial sections of whole seeds collected from seeds containing pre-globular embryo propers of 2 to 8 cells.

Gene At3g11120 expressed in all parts e.g. embryo proper, micropylar endosperm, peripheral endosperm, chalazal endosperm, general seed coat, chalazal seed coat and in whole seeds in very high amounts (62657 and 66708.9, 132715 and 128592, 74699.8 and 64336.7, 88198.6 and 105265, 47933 and 44409.6, 62986.1 and 45235.6, 54677.9 and 54436 respectively). This gene transcribes to ribosomal protein L41, which is a structural constituent of ribosome. Since independent development of embryo starts after preglobular stage, as stated earlier, the huge amount of ribosomal protein production can be correlated with increase in protein production rate required in latter stages. Similarly a water stress-induced protein, expressed from gene At1g54410, is present in peripheral endosperm, chalazal endosperm.

21484 genes are analyzed by FunNet. FunNet relies on genomic annotations provided by the Gene Ontology Consortium (GO) and the Kyoto Encyclopedia of Genes and Genomes (KEGG).

In KEGG pathway analysis for all spot Ids present in microarray dataset total 27 KEGG pathways

Figure 12. KEGG Pathway analysis over total dataset using FunNet

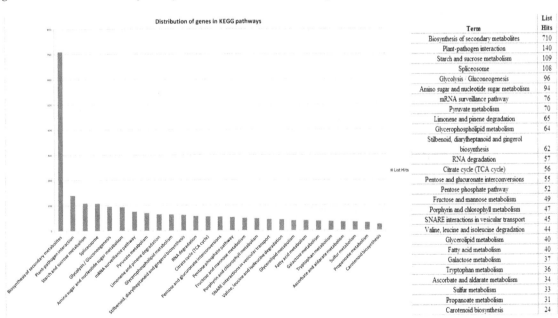

Term	List Hits
Biosynthesis of secondary metabolites	710
Plant-pathogen interaction	140
Starch and sucrose metabolism	109
Spliceosome	108
Glycolysis / Gluconeogenesis	96
Amino sugar and nucleotide sugar metabolism	94
mRNA surveillance pathway	76
Pyruvate metabolism	70
Limonene and pinene degradation	65
Glycerophospholipid metabolism	64
Stilbenoid, diarylheptanoid and gingerol biosynthesis	62
RNA degradation	57
Citrate cycle (TCA cycle)	56
Pentose and glucuronate interconversions	55
Pentose phosphate pathway	52
Fructose and mannose metabolism	49
Porphyrin and chlorophyll metabolism	47
SNARE interactions in vesicular transport	45
Valine, leucine and isoleucine degradation	44
Glycerolipid metabolism	40
Fatty acid metabolism	40
Galactose metabolism	37
Tryptophan metabolism	36
Ascorbate and aldarate metabolism	34
Sulfur metabolism	33
Propanoate metabolism	31
Carotenoid biosynthesis	24

have been identified. Among 27 pathways, 10 pathways come under carbohydrate metabolism, 3 pathways for lipid metabolism,3 pathways for Genetic Information Processing, 2 pathways for amino acid metabolism and one pathway for other classes e.g..biosynthesis of other secondary metabolites, environmental adaptation, energy me-

tabolism, metabolism of cofactors and vitamins, metabolism of terpenoids and polyketides etc. No. of significant genes distributed as follows:

We use the Bio-Analytic Resource - the BAR an user-friendly web-based tools for working with functional genomics for GSE12404.

Figure 13. No. of significant genes in KEGG pathway analysis over total dataset using FunNet

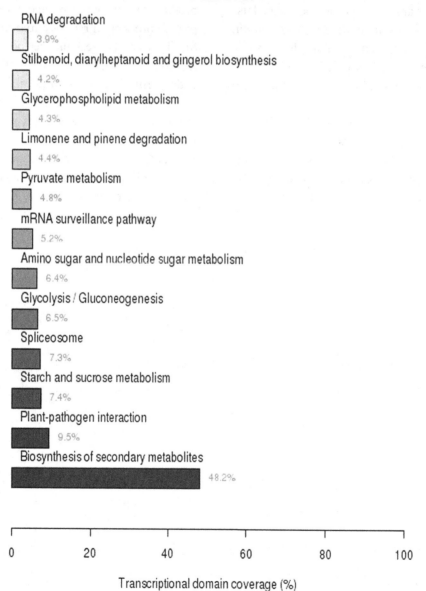

Classification SuperViewer (Povert 2003) generates an overview of functional classification of a list of AGI IDs based on the GO database. Also, a ranking score is calculated for each functional class, which may be better than absolute numbers. The input set is bootstrapped 100 times to provide some idea as to over- or under-representation reliability. Classification is based on ATH_GO_GOSLIM.20120925.txt. 21543 gene IDs entered (21365 of these have been classified). Sum is greater than number entered as genes can show homology to more than 1 functional class. Results for GO annotation are shown in Table 4.

It can be concluded that according to GO annotation database 12083 genes are related with cellular processes, whereas 11312 genes are related with metabolic processes.5404 genes have other than DNA, RNA, protein or receptor binding activity. Similarly 2765, 2712 and 1265 genes have hydrolase, transferase and kinase activity respectively. But 3270 genes have other enzyme activity except earlier three classes. Considering the cellular component analysis, nucleus the important cell organelle where the highest number of genes i.e. 7616 are expressed in the microarray.3400 genes are expressed in chloroplast.

Table 4. GO Annotation results over total dataset as obtained from classification superviewer absolute values (± bootstrap StdDev, p-value)

Biological Process			
12083	*67.9*	**0.000e+00**	other cellular processes (nr. in set: 14016)
11312	*70.2*	**4.289e-307**	other metabolic processes (nr. in set: 13242)
6064	*71.4*	**8.759e-187**	unknown biological processes (nr. in set: 9390)
4270	*61.3*	**2.219e-25**	protein metabolism (nr. in set: 5290)
3882	*60.6*	**3.417e-272**	response to stress (nr. in set: 4099)
3594	*56.4*	**9.354e-318**	response to abiotic or biotic stimulus (nr. in set: 3712)
3570	*60.1*	**6.105e-261**	developmental processes (nr. in set: 3752)
3331	*47.4*	**6.990e-251**	other biological processes (nr. in set: 3489)
3305	*54*	**1.296e-208**	transport (nr. in set: 3518)
3231	*52*	**1.399e-303**	cell organization and biogenesis (nr. in set: 3316)
2280	*42.9*	**6.358e-53**	transcription,DNA-dependent (nr. in set: 2625)
1872	*43.7*	**2.492e-109**	signal transduction (nr. in set: 2000)
881	*30.6*	**5.096e-63**	DNA or RNA metabolism (nr. in set: 923)
594	*23.2*	**2.487e-12**	electron transport or energy pathways (nr. in set: 692)
Molecular Function			
5565	*73.1*	**1.011e-244**	unknown molecular functions (nr. in set: 8910)
5409	*59.8*	**2.584e-25**	other binding (nr. in set: 6765)
3270	*43.4*	**2.110e-114**	other enzyme activity (nr. in set: 3660)
3118	*52.9*	**1.397e-159**	nucleotide binding (nr. in set: 3380)
2765	*50.7*	**7.703e-90**	hydrolase activity (nr. in set: 3109)
2712	*46.2*	**7.256e-131**	transferase activity (nr. in set: 2952)
2341	*38.9*	**4.820e-18**	DNA or RNA binding (nr. in set: 3376)
2264	*45.5*	**1.074e-94**	protein binding (nr. in set: 2492)

continued on following page

Table 4. Continued

1450	*31.1*	**1.690e-30**	transcription factor activity (nr. in set: 1680)
1265	*31.9*	**1.116e-71**	kinase activity (nr. in set: 1354)
1155	*32.3*	**1.272e-42**	transporter activity (nr. in set: 1283)
1022	*35.5*	**4.749e-19**	other molecular functions (nr. in set: 1195)
789	*25.6*	**1.970e-118**	nucleic acid binding (nr. in set: 1599)
458	*21.3*	**7.003e-07**	structural molecule activity (nr. in set: 548)
150	*11.8*	**2.819e-04**	receptor binding or activity (nr. in set: 175)
Cellular Component			
7616	*75.2*	**1.549e-47**	nucleus (nr. in set: 9463)
5436	*66.2*	**9.117e-180**	other cytoplasmic components (nr. in set: 6147)
4543	*56.7*	**8.162e-132**	other intracellular components (nr. in set: 5174)
4085	*62.9*	**0.000e+00**	unknown cellular components (nr. in set: 7533)
3400	*52.2*	**5.894e-71**	chloroplast (nr. in set: 3950)
3291	*59.3*	**7.563e-81**	other membranes (nr. in set: 3781)
2969	*48.7*	**3.526e-133**	plasma membrane (nr. in set: 3254)
2446	*43.2*	**1.525e-21**	mitochondria (nr. in set: 3551)
2009	*39.7*	**1.522e-07**	extracellular (nr. in set: 2807)
1559	*35.5*	**2.553e-83**	cytosol (nr. in set: 1678)
1246	*33.3*	**6.702e-49**	plastid (nr. in set: 1377)
982	*29.5*	**5.141e-46**	other cellular components (nr. in set: 1069)
835	*28.9*	**7.627e-37**	Golgi apparatus (nr. in set: 914)
564	*24.3*	**2.474e-28**	cell wall (nr. in set: 611)
516	*21.6*	**3.210e-18**	ER (nr. in set: 577)
384	*19.4*	**4.226e-03**	ribosome (nr. in set: 483)

Results for analysis by using MapMan database as shown in Table 5.

According to MapMan database, 417, 2503 and 3175 genes expressed in microarray analysis are related to DNA, RNA and protein respectively. A major amount of genes i.e. 6719 are not assigned in this database.

Functional classifications were done from GO as of September 27 2012, were downloaded from TAIR at ftp://ftp.arabidopsis.org/home/tair/Ontologies/Gene_Ontology (file ATH_GO_GOS-LIM.20120925.txt). The MapMan data as of June 4 2013 were downloaded from MapMan at http://mapman.gabipd.org/web/guest/mapmanstore (file Ath_AGI_LOCUS_TAIR10_Aug2012.txt).

FUTURE RESEARCH DIRECTIONS

By using genes present in each module we want to construct relevant gene regulatory network for Arabidopsis seed of preglobular stage. To do so location of every genes in each module in chromosomal region must be determined and thus significantly collocated genes can be identified. Genes present in one module, containing particular cis-promoter motifs would be identified to understand the regulatory of transcription factors in coexpressed gene network. This type of network construction can be extended for crop seeds e.g. as rice, wheat to increase seed mass of crops, which is very important for our livelihood.

Figure 14. Summary of GO Annotation results shown above

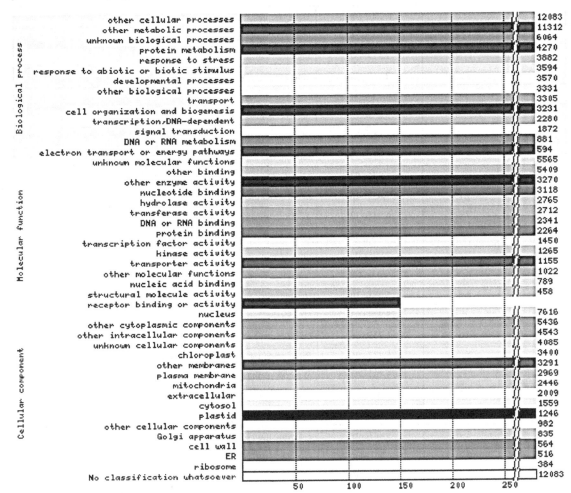

Table 5. GO annotation results over total dataset as obtained from MapMan, absolute values (± bootstrap StdDev, p-value)

6719	*63.3*	**9.243e-89**	not assigned (nr. in set: 11802)
3175	*43.8*	**5.997e-04**	protein (nr. in set: 4838)
2503	*49*	**2.992e-117**	RNA (nr. in set: 3046)
1300	*32.7*	**2.499e-57**	misc (nr. in set: 1589)
1192	*32.6*	**3.050e-88**	signalling (nr. in set: 1363)
910	*30.7*	**5.911e-77**	transport (nr. in set: 1021)
834	*25.9*	**3.682e-04**	stress (nr. in set: 1228)
726	*24.3*	**7.536e-54**	cell (nr. in set: 830)
665	*22.7*	**5.803e-38**	development (nr. in set: 788)
485	*19.9*	**1.947e-39**	cell wall (nr. in set: 548)
476	*21.2*	**3.481e-37**	hormone metabolism (nr. in set: 541)

continued on following page

Table 5. Continued

417	17.6	0.000e+00	DNA (nr. in set: 3122)
399	18.4	3.030e-36	secondary metabolism (nr. in set: 444)
388	21.4	7.814e-37	lipid metabolism (nr. in set: 429)
230	15.2	2.107e-19	amino acid metabolism (nr. in set: 260)
190	14	8.238e-19	redox (nr. in set: 210)
158	12.6	3.859e-13	nucleotide metabolism (nr. in set: 180)
148	12.5	3.612e-03	PS (nr. in set: 206)
120	8.8	8.492e-19	minor CHO metabolism (nr. in set: 124)
110	10.5	5.086e-03	mitochondrial electron transport/ATP synthesis (nr. in set: 151)
98	9.7	7.851e-16	major CHO metabolism (nr. in set: 101)
76	7.8	6.938e-12	TCA/org transformation (nr. in set: 79)
74	7.8	1.255e-08	Co-factor and vitamin metabolism (nr. in set: 81)
68	9.1	7.995e-06	glycolysis (nr. in set: 79)
57	6.6	0.063	metal handling (nr. in set: 83)
48	6.8	5.054e-10	tetrapyrrole synthesis (nr. in set: 48)
33	6	5.940e-03	C1-metabolism (nr. in set: 40)
30	5.6	1.735e-05	OPP (nr. in set: 31)
27	5.4	5.972e-05	Biodegradation of Xenobiotics (nr. in set: 28)
24	5	9.504e-04	N-metabolism (nr. in set: 26)
13	3.7	0.015	fermentation (nr. in set: 14)
13	3.7	0.079	polyamine metabolism (nr. in set: 16)
13	3.4	3.047e-03	S-assimilation (nr. in set: 13)
10	3.2	0.154	gluconeogenesis/glyoxylate cycle (nr. in set: 13)
1	0.7	1.248e-204	micro RNA, natural antisense etc. (nr. in set: 460)

The transcriptional regulatory network analysis is an important approach from microarray analysis. Our present study focuses on the modules relevant for gene regulatory network in embryogenetic preglobular stage of Arabidopsis. However, this analysis can further be extend to find out binding domains for transcription factors relevant in these stages.

CONCLUSION

The high dimensionality nature and limited sample size of the currently available gene expression data make large scale regulatory network learning from such data a difficult problem both theoretically and computationally. We overcome this problem using new computational approaches over large-scale microarray data sets. In this study, we experiment with a network-based approach to identify gene functional modules from large gene expression datasets of Arabidopsis thaliana relevant to seed biology. The study reveals new insight into the topological properties of correlation network obtained over expressions of relevant genes. The Markov clustering method is experimented to automatically detect modular structures in gene networks. The study also reveals new insight into the organization of relevant gene functional modules and regulation networks.

Figure 15. Summary of GO annotation results from MapMan shown above

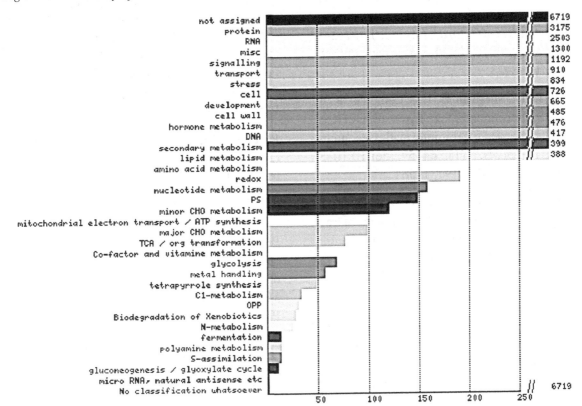

REFERENCES

Batagelj, V., & Mrvar, A. (1998). Pajek – Program for Large Network Analysis. *Connections*, *21*, 47–57.

Brohee, S., & van Helden, J. (2006). Evaluation of clustering algorithms for protein-protein interaction networks. *BMC Bioinformatics*, *7*(1), 488. doi:10.1186/1471-2105-7-488 PMID:17087821

Dean, G. H., Zheng, H., Tewari, J., Huang, J., Young, D. S., & Hwang, Y. T. et al. (2007). The *Arabidopsis MUM2* Gene Encodes a β-Galactosidase Required for the Production of Seed Coat Mucilage with Correct Hydration Properties. *The Plant Cell*, *19*(12), 4007–4021. doi:10.1105/tpc.107.050609 PMID:18165329

Enright, A. J. (2002). An efficient algorithm for large-scale detection of protein families. *Nucleic Acids Research*, *30*(7), 1575–1584. doi:10.1093/nar/30.7.1575 PMID:11917018

Freeman, T. C., Goldovsky, L., Brosch, M., van Dongen, S., Maziere, P., & Grocock, R. J. et al. (2007). Construction, visualisation, and clustering of transcription networks from microarray expression data. *PLoS Computational Biology*, *3*(10), 2032–2042. doi:10.1371/journal.pcbi.0030206 PMID:17967053

George, C. T., Ghosh, D., & Feingold, E. (2012). Comprehensive literature review and statistical considerations for microarray meta-analysis. *Nucleic Acids Research*, *40*(9), 3785–3799. doi:10.1093/nar/gkr1265 PMID:22262733

Hooper, S. D., & Bork, P. (2005). Medusa: A simple tool for interaction graph analysis. *Bioinformatics (Oxford, England), 21*(24), 4432–4433. doi:10.1093/bioinformatics/bti696 PMID:16188923

Huang, D. W., Sherman, B. T., & Lempicki, R. A. (2009). Systematic and integrative analysis of large gene lists using DAVID bioinformatics resources. *Nature Protocols, 4*(1), 44–57. doi:10.1038/nprot.2008.211 PMID:19131956

Iragne, F., Nikolski, M., Mathieu, B., Auber, D., & Sherman, D. (2005). ProViz: Protein interaction visualization and exploration. *Bioinformatics (Oxford, England), 21*(2), 272–274. doi:10.1093/bioinformatics/bth494 PMID:15347570

Krämer, A., Green, J., Pollard, J., & Tugendreich, S. (2013). Causal Analysis Approaches in Ingenuity Pathway Analysis (IPA). *Bioinformatics (Oxford, England).*

Logemann, E., Birkenbihl, R. P., Rawat, V., Schneeberger, K., Schmelzer, E., & Somssich, I. E. (2013). Functional dissection of the PROPEP2 and PROPEP3 promoters reveals the importance of WRKY factors in mediating microbe-associated molecular pattern-induced expression. *The New Phytologist, 198*(4), 1165–1177. doi:10.1111/nph.12233 PMID:23496690

Nikitin, A., Egorov, S., Daraselia, N., & Mazo, I. (2003). Pathway studio–the analysis and navigation of molecular networks. *Bioinformatics (Oxford, England), 19*(16), 2155–2157. doi:10.1093/bioinformatics/btg290 PMID:14594725

Palaniswamy, S. K., James, S., Sun, H., Lamb, R. S., Davuluri, R. V., & Grotewold, E. (2006). AGRIS and AtRegNet: A platform to link cis-regulatory elements and transcription factors into regulatory networks. *Plant Physiology, 140*(3), 818–829. doi:10.1104/pp.105.072280 PMID:16524982

Pillot, M., Baroux, C., Vazquez, M. A., Autran, D., Leblanc, O., & Vielle-Calzada, J. P. et al. (2010). Embryo and Endosperm Inherit Distinct Chromatin and Transcriptional States from the Female Gametes *Arabidopsis. The Plant Cell, 22*(2), 307–320. doi:10.1105/tpc.109.071647 PMID:20139161

Prifti, E., Zucker, J.-D., Clement, K., & Henegar, C. (2008). FunNet: An integrative tool for exploring transcriptional interactions. *Bioinformatics (Oxford, England), 24*(22), 2636–2638. doi:10.1093/bioinformatics/btn492 PMID:18799481

Provart, N. & Zhu, T. (2003). A Browser-based Functional Classification SuperViewer for Arabidopsis Genomics. In *Currents in Computational Molecular Biology*, (pp. 271-272). Academic Press.

Pu, S., Vlasblom, J., Emili, A., Greenblatt, J., & Wodak, S. J. (2007). Identifying functional modules in the physical interactome of *Saccharomyces cerevisiae. Proteomics, 7*(6), 944–960. doi:10.1002/pmic.200600636 PMID:17370254

Reimand, J., Arak, T., & Vilo, J. (2011). g:Profiler -- a web server for functional interpretation of gene lists (2011 update). *Nucleic Acids Research, 39*(suppl), W307–W315. doi:10.1093/nar/gkr378 PMID:21646343

Rhee, S. Y., Beavis, W., Berardini, T. Z., Chen, G., Dixon, D., & Doyle, A. (2003). The Arabidopsis Information Resource (TAIR): A model organism database providing a centralized, curated gateway to Arabidopsis biology, research materials and community. *Nucleic Acids Research, 31*(1), 224–228. doi:10.1093/nar/gkg076 PMID:12519987

Sarajlić, A., & Pržulj, N. (2014). Survey of Network-Based Approaches to Research of Cardiovascular Diseases. *BioMed Research International*, 10.

Shannon, P., Markiel, A., Ozier, O., Baliga, N. S., Wang, J. T., & Ramage, D. et al. (2003). Cytoscape: A software environment for integrated models of biomolecular interaction networks. *Genome Research*, *13*(11), 2498–2504. doi:10.1101/gr.1239303 PMID:14597658

Tarca, A. L., Romero, R., & Draghici, S. (2006). Analysis of microarray experiments of gene expression profiling. *American Journal of Obstetrics and Gynecology*, *195*(2), 373–388. doi:10.1016/j.ajog.2006.07.001 PMID:16890548

Thierry-Mieg, D., & Thierry-Mieg, J. (2006). AceView: A comprehensive cDNA-supported gene and transcripts annotation. *Genome Biology*, *7*(Suppl 1), S12–S14. doi:10.1186/gb-2006-7-s1-s12 PMID:16925834

Thomas, S., & Bonchev, D. (2010). A survey of current software for network analysis in molecular biology. *Human Genomics*, *4*(5), 353–360. doi:10.1186/1479-7364-4-5-353 PMID:20650822

Werner, T., Motyka, V., Laucou, V., Smets, R., Onckelen, H. V., & Schmülling, T. (2003). Cytokinin-Deficient Transgenic Arabidopsis Plants Show Multiple Developmental Alterations Indicating Opposite Functions of Cytokinins in the Regulation of Shoot and Root Meristem Activity. *The Plant Cell*, *15*(11), 2532–2550. doi:10.1105/tpc.014928 PMID:14555694

Yamaguchi, Y., Huffaker, A., Bryan, A. C., Tax, F. E., & Ryan, C. A. (2010). PEPR2 Is a Second Receptor for the Pep1 and Pep2 Peptides and Contributes to Defense Responses in *Arabidopsis*. *The Plant Cell*, *22*(2), 508–522. doi:10.1105/tpc.109.068874 PMID:20179141

ADDITIONAL READING

Barabasi, A. L., & Oltvai, Z. N. (2004). Network biology: Understanding the cell's functional organization. *Nature Reviews. Genetics*, *5*(2), 101–113. doi:10.1038/nrg1272 PMID:14735121

Barrett, T., Troup, D. B., Wilhite, S. E., Ledoux, P., Rudnev, D., & Evangelista, C. et al. (2007). NCBI GEO: Mining tens of millions of expression profiles–database and tools update. *Nucleic Acids Research*, *35*(Database issue), 760–765. http://www.hubmed.org/display.cgi?uids=17099226. doi:10.1093/nar/gkl887 PMID:17099226

Carlson, M. R. J., Zhang, B., Fang, Z. X., Mischel, P. S., Horvath, S., & Nelson, S. F. (2006). Gene connectivity, function, and sequence conservation: Predictions from modular yeast co-expression networks. *BMC Genomics*, *7*(1), 15. doi:10.1186/1471-2164-7-40 PMID:16515682

Carter, S., Brechbühler, C., Griffin, M., & Bond, A. T. (2004). Gene co-expression network topology provides a framework for molecular characterization of cellular state. *Bioinformatics (Oxford, England)*, *20*(14), 2242–2050. doi:10.1093/bioinformatics/bth234 PMID:15130938

Childs, K. L., Davidson, R. M., & Buell, C. R. (2011). Gene Coexpression Network Analysis as a Source of Functional Annotation for Rice Genes. *PLoS ONE*, *6*(7), e22196. doi:10.1371/journal.pone.0022196 PMID:21799793

Elo, L., Järvenpää, H., Oresic, M., Lahesmaa, R., & Aittokallio, T. (2007). Systematic construction of gene coexpression networks with applications to human T helper cell differentiation process. *Bioinformatics (Oxford, England)*, *23*(16), 2096–2103. doi:10.1093/bioinformatics/btm309 PMID:17553854

Faith, J. J., Hayete, B., Thaden, J. T., Mogno, I., Wierzbowski, J., & Cottarel, G. et al. (2007). Large-scale mapping and validation of Escherichia coli transcriptional regulation from a compendium of expression profiles. *PLoS Biology*, *5*(1), e8. doi:10.1371/journal.pbio.0050008 PMID:17214507

Freeman, T. C., Goldovsky, L., Brosch, M., Van Dongen, S., Maziere, P., & Grocock, R. J. et al. (2007). Construction, visualisation, and clustering of transcription networks from Microarray expression data. *PLoS Computational Biology*, *3*(10), 2032–2042. doi:10.1371/journal.pcbi.0030206 PMID:17967053

Ghazalpour, A., Doss, S., Zhang, B., Wang, S., Plaisier, C., & Castellanos, R. et al. (2006). Integrating genetic and network analysis to characterize genes related to mouse weight. *PLOS Genetics*, *2*(8), e130. doi:10.1371/journal.pgen.0020130 PMID:16934000

Girvan, M., & Newman, M. E. J. (2002). Community structure in social and biological networks. *Proceedings of the National Academy of Sciences of the United States of America*, *99*(12), 7821–7826. doi:10.1073/pnas.122653799 PMID:12060727

Lee, H. K., Hsu, A. K., Sajdak, J., Qin, J., & Pavlidis, P. (2004). Coexpression analysis of human genes across many microarray data sets. *Genome Research*, *14*(6), 1085–1094. doi:10.1101/gr.1910904 PMID:15173114

Ma, S., Gong, Q., & Bohnert, H. J. (2007). An Arabidopsis gene network based on the graphical Gaussian model. *Genome Research*, *17*(11), 1614–1625. doi:10.1101/gr.6911207 PMID:17921353

Maere, S., Heymans, K., & Kuiper, M. (2005). BiNGO: A Cytoscape plugin to assess overrepresentation of Gene Ontology categories in Biological Networks. *Bioinformatics (Oxford, England)*, *21*(16), 3448–3449. doi:10.1093/bioinformatics/bti551 PMID:15972284

Mao, L., Van Hemert, J. L., Dash, S., & Dickerson, J. A. (2009). Arabidopsis gene co-expression network and its functional modules. *BMC Bioinformatics*, *10*(1), 346. doi:10.1186/1471-2105-10-346 PMID:19845953

Mueller, L. A., Zhang, P., & Rhee, S. Y. (2003). AraCyc: A Biochemical Pathway Database for Arabidopsis. *Plant Physiology*, *132*(2), 453–460. doi:10.1104/pp.102.017236 PMID:12805578

Obayashi, T., & Kinoshita, K. (2010). Coexpression landscape in ATTED-II: Usage of gene list and gene network for various types of pathways. *Journal of Plant Research*, *123*(3), 311–319. doi:10.1007/s10265-010-0333-6 PMID:20383554

Oldham, M. C., Horvath, S., & Geschwind, D. H. (2006). Conservation and evolution of gene coexpression networks in human and chimpanzee brains. *Proceedings of the National Academy of Sciences of the United States of America*, *103*(47), 17973–17978. doi:10.1073/pnas.0605938103 PMID:17101986

Ruan, J., & Zhang, W. Systems Biology and Computational Proteomics. Vol. 4532. Berlin-Heidelberg: Springer; 2007. Identification and Evaluation of Functional Modules in Gene Co-expression Networks; pp. 57–76.

Schena, M., Shalon, D., Davis, R. W., & Brown, P. O. (1995). Quantitative monitoring of gene expression patterns with a complementary DNA microarray. *Science*, *270*(5235), 467–470. doi:10.1126/science.270.5235.467 PMID:7569999

Wang, Z., Gerstein, M., & Snyder, M. (2009). RNA-Seq: A revolutionary tool for transcriptomics. *Nature Reviews. Genetics*, *10*(1), 57–63. doi:10.1038/nrg2484 PMID:19015660

Wurtele Eve Syrkin. (2003). Li J, Diao L, Zhang H, Foster C M, Fatland B, Dickerson J, Brown A, Cox Z, Cook D, Lee E-K, Hofmann H. MetNet: Software to build and model the biogenetic lattice of *Arabidopsis. Comparative and Functional Genomics*, *4*, 239–245. PMID:18629120

Zhang Shihua, J. G. (2007). Z X-S, C L. Discovering functions and revealing mechanisms at molecular level from biological networks. *Proteomics*, *7*(16), 2856–2869. doi:10.1002/pmic.200700095 PMID:17703505

KEY TERMS AND DEFINITIONS

Correlation Network: This is a type of network that can be used for finding clusters (modules) of highly correlated genes.

Gene Annotation: Gene annotation is the process of attaching biological information to gene sequences.

Gene Regulatory Network: A gene regulatory network or genetic regulatory network (GRN) is a collection of DNA segments in a cell which interact with each other indirectly (through their RNA and protein expression products) and with other substances in the cell, to control the expression levels of mRNA and proteins.

Plant Embryogenesis: Plant embryogenesis is the process that produces a plant embryo from a fertilized ovule by asymmetric cell division and the differentiation of undifferentiated cells into tissues and organs.

Preglobular Stage of Embryogenesis: Preglobular stage is a stage of embryogenesis which occurs just before the globular stage, where embryo develops radial patterning through a series of cell divisions, with the outer layer of cells differentiating into the 'protoderm.'

Promoter Region of Gene: A promoter is a region of DNA that initiates transcription of a particular gene.

Transcription Factor Binding Site: Transcription binding sites are a type of binding site found in DNA where DNA-binding proteins (i.e. transcription factors can bind).

Chapter 5
Detection and Employment of Biological Sequence Motifs

Marjan Trutschl
*Louisiana State University – Shreveport, USA &
Louisiana State University Health – Shreveport,
USA*

Rona S. Scott
*Louisiana State University Health – Shreveport,
USA*

Phillip C. S. R. Kilgore
Louisiana State University – Shreveport, USA

Christine E. Birdwell
*Louisiana State University Health – Shreveport,
USA*

Urška Cvek
Louisiana State University – Shreveport, USA & Louisiana State University Health – Shreveport, USA

ABSTRACT

Biological sequence motifs are short nucleotide or amino acid sequences that are biologically significant and are attractive to scientists because they are usually highly conserved and result in structural and regulatory implications. In this chapter, the authors show practical applications of these data, followed by a review of the algorithms, techniques, and tools. They address the nature of motifs and elucidate on several methods for de novo motif discovery, covering the algorithms based on Gibbs sampling, expectation maximization, Bayesian inference, covariance models, and discriminative learning. The authors present the tools and their requirements to weigh their individual benefits and challenges. Since interpretation of a large set of results can pose significant challenges, they discuss several methods for handling data that span from visualization to integration into pipelines and curated databases. Additionally, the authors show practical applications of these data with examples.

INTRODUCTION

A topic of increasing interest to geneticists and biochemists is the detection and utilization of biologically-significant short sequence sections called *motifs*. Motifs are short nucleotide or amino acid sequences that are intriguing because they are usually highly conserved and have structural or regulatory implications for many biological processes. Motifs are constituents of cellular macromolecules such as nucleic acids, proteins, lipids and carbohydrates. Due to the vast number of motifs, our description of motifs primarily focuses on motifs involved in gene expression and found on deoxyribonucleic acid (DNA), ribonucleic acids (RNA) and proteins.

DOI: 10.4018/978-1-4666-6611-5.ch005

Motifs found in DNA are generally protein binding sites that regulate transcription, replication, and convey spatial organization to the human genome. RNA motifs can serve as regulatory elements for RNA processing and stability of RNA transcripts. Protein motifs are often involved in protein-protein interactions and binding to DNA and RNA for regulation of transcription, translation and DNA replication.

Reliable motif identification can lend itself to streamlining the process of discovering protein function as well as factors involved in gene regulation. To exemplify, a basic research scientist may use motifs found in the promoter region of a gene of interest to predict the context in which the cell turns on the gene. Life scientists may use the identification of RNA motifs to predict alternative splicing or regulatory RNA transcripts. Motif identification is not just useful for basic science researchers; it can also be used by clinicians to pinpoint mutations that are leading to the observed phenotype. Motifs can also be used by industry to predict drug target sites on proteins or nucleic acids. Scientists are seeking automated and reliable methods for discovering motifs that would help them guide their discoveries and generate new hypotheses.

BACKGROUND

The concept of motifs and their relationship to regulation of the cellular environment can be traced back to the late 1950s. Although regulatory elements had been shown to exist in DNA as early as 1951 (McClintock, 1951), it was the work of Jacques Monod and Francois Jacob regarding the regulation of lactose metabolism in *Escherichia coli* that lead to the first generalized theory concerning regulatory elements. Via the *lac* repressor, a protein which moderates the translation of the proteins used in lactose synthesis, Jacob et al. were able to develop a framework accounting for transcriptional regulation (Jacob, Perrin, Sanchez, and Monod, 1960). This seminal work only considered repressor elements and was primitive in comparison to modern views regarding transcriptional regulation; however, it is notable in that it presents the concept of an *operator*, a segment of DNA to which regulatory elements may bind.

At about the same time, a number of motifs were being identified within gene promoter regions. Promoters are DNA sequences which regulate the initiation of transcription of nearby genes. The 1970s saw the discovery of two conserved motifs that recruit the general transcriptional factors and RNA polymerase (Hurwitz, 1960; Stephens, 1960) to promoters: the TATA box "TATAA" (Rifton, Goldberg, Karp, & Hogness, 1978) and the Pribnow box "TATAAT" (Pribnow, 1975). The former is called the Goldberg-Hogness Box in eukaryotes, and the latter is known as the -10 sequence in bacterial promoters. Additional promoter motifs have since been identified and underscore the regulatory complexity between prokaryotes and eukaryotes. Bacterial promoters usually have three unique motifs while eukaryotic promoters can have up to seven (Clancy, 2008).

Over the years, annotation of transcription binding elements has elucidated consensus sequences that regulate binding of these factors to DNA. For instance, the constitutively expressed Sp1, a zinc finger transcription factor was found to bind the GC box motif: 5'(G/T)GGGCGG(G/A)(G/A)(C/T) 3'. The general consensus sequence for NF-kB, an inducible transcription factor involved in activation of many genes under different stimuli, is the kB site: 5' GGGR(C/A/T)TYYCC 3'. These are only 2 examples of the many proteins recruited to promoter motif sequences and involved in activation or repression of transcription (Levine & Tjian, 2003). The transcription factor binding sequences (TFBS) used by many transcription factors have been identified and are available on open sourced sites, such as the JASPAR database and the Encyclopedia of DNA Elements (ENCODE) project's factorbook, that can be readily accessed by the scientific community (Sandelin, Alkema, Engröm, Wasserman, & Lenhard, 2004; Wang, Zhuang, Iyer, Lin, et al., 2012).

Sequence motifs are not restricted to DNA and provide regulatory functions on RNA and proteins as well. RNA sequence motifs play key roles in splicing and generation of alternatively spliced transcripts. Typical splicing consensus motifs are 1) the splicing donor site (GT); the splicing acceptor site (AG) preceded by a pyrimidine rich sequence, and 3) a branch site sequence. These sequences with the consensus at the intron/exon boundary define the intronic sequences to be removed by splicing (Levine & Tjian, 2003). Protein sequence motifs are also conserved amino acid sequences involved in protein-protein interactions. One example comes from a set of oncogenic proteins encoded by the small DNA tumor viruses (human papilloma virus E7, SV40 large T antigen, and adenovirus E1A) that carries a common LXCXE motif known to disrupt the interaction of the cellular factors E2F and retinoblastoma protein to stimulate cell cycle progression (Dahiya, Gavin, Luo, & Dean, 2000). The Prosite database maintains a collection of protein domains and protein families and functional annotation for protein motifs (Sigrist, et al., 2013).

Some sequence motifs provide structural elements to DNA, RNA and protein products. These structural motifs influence secondary and tertiary structure. On DNA, g-quadruplexes are sequences with high guanine content which can form a four stranded structure and, depending on genomic context can result in the activation or repression of transcription. DNA motifs can also be modified by the addition of a methyl group to the 5 position of cytosine when it is paired with a guanine (CpG). CpG methylation can affect the binding of transcription factors to DNA. As well, the DNA structure can be altered by methyl binding proteins that recognize these methylated CpG residues to compact chromatin and form higher order structure that restricts access to transcription machinery. Tracts of GC rich regions called

CpG islands can be found in over 60 percent of human promoters. Hypermethylation of CpG islands at tumor suppressor genes is noted in many cancers and is one mechanism that leads to transcriptional silencing of tumor suppressor genes (Lao & Grady, 2011).

In the case of RNA, some structural motifs may have functional significance; for instance, stem-loops are responsible for ρ-independent termination in prokaryotes and are a notable feature of tRNAs, while a pseudoknot is critical to the activity of the *Homo sapiens* telomerase RNA component (TERC) and highly conserved in vertebrate TERCs (Chen & Greider, 2005). Furthermore, the 5' untranslated region of some viral messenger RNAs lack a cap have a secondary structure termed internal ribosome entry site (IRES), which attracts ribosomes to initiate translation in eukaryotic cells. Several prevalent nucleic acid secondary structure motifs include pseudoknots, stem-loops, and tetraloops.

Common secondary structure motifs in proteins include the β-hairpin, β-α-β, β-meander, greek key, and Ψ-loop motifs. Many transcription factors and other DNA binding proteins possess a zinc finger motif required for recognition and binding to DNA which can lead to transcriptional regulation. Motifs can also affect protein modifications such as phosphorylation, the biological activity such as the formation of an enzymatic domain, and protein-protein interactions. Thus, structural motifs can yield information assisting in high-order structure prediction, and might also imply functional predictions in some cases.

The identification of motifs in DNA, RNA and protein has been greatly aided by advances in sequencing technology. Ten years since the introduction of the Sanger method, the first automated DNA sequencer was introduced by Applied Biosystems in 1987. Automated DNA sequencing generated the entire genome sequence from various model organisms including our own human genome. Importantly, computational advances such as assembly of randomly sequenced DNA fragments, known as a shotgun sequencing approach, expedited these massive sequencing efforts (Fleischmann, Adams, White, Clayton, & others, 1995). By 1998, the first genome of a multicellular organism, *Caenorhabditis elegans*, had been sequenced, and an assembly for *H. sapiens* was released in 2003 following the completion of the Human Genome Project. As of January 2014, assemblies for over 11,000 taxa are available on NCBI Genome (hosted by the National Center for Biotechnology Information). The list is likely to grow with the availability of next-generation sequencing technologies which can sequence an entire genome within days and at a fraction of the cost of the traditional Sanger sequencing approach. The compilation of a large number of whole genome sequences has aided in identifying conserved motifs across multiple organisms as well, and will likely continue to add to our knowledge of common regulatory elements. A compendium of evolutionarily conserved DNA elements can be found as part of the NIH's Comparative Genomics Developments program (Ovcharenko & others 2004; Loots & Ovcharenko 2007).

Besides furthering the data available for computational analysis of motif discovery, the advances in sequencing have also led to advances in experimental methods for motif identification. A relatively new and popular approach to identifying protein binding motifs on DNA is chromatin immunoprecipitation-sequencing (ChIP-seq). In this approach proteins are crosslinked to the DNA and then the DNA is sheared into approximately 200 to 500 base pair fragments by sonication or enzymatic digestion. Antibodies are used to pull down the protein of interest bound to DNA. After reversing the crosslinks, a library of DNA fragments that the protein of interest binds is available for high throughput sequencing. Computational methods can be utilized after sequencing to narrow down the consensus sequence. This method among others has been employed by the ENCODE project to compile a database of transcription factor binding consensus sequences across multiple cell types.

Additionally, several notable repositories for biological data were either initiated or became widely available in this period. In 1988, the European Molecular Biology Laboratory established EMBnet, an international sequence database network (European Molecular Biology Laboratory, 2014). The NCBI assumed responsibility over GenBank (a DNA sequence database) in October 1992 (National Center for Biotechnology Information, 2004). The 2000s saw the emergence of several new databases, including the Ensembl Project (European Bioinformatics Institute & Wellcome Trust Sanger Institute, 2013) and the nematode repository WormBase in 2000, (California Institute of Technology, Washington University of St. Louis & The Wellcome Trust Sanger Institute, 2013), the UniProt Knowledgebase (UniProt Consortium, 2014) in 2002, and NCBI's RefSeq database (Pruitt, Tatusova, & Maglott, 2005) in 2005.

The availability of genomic information coupled with the increased availability of computational power that transpired throughout this period has led to addressing biological questions using computational analysis. New methods of evaluating biological data have matured in the past 30 years, and the desire to incorporate the processing of staggeringly large amounts of data into the life scientist's workflow is becoming increasingly viable. Of notable interest is the prediction of motifs, the process by which biologically significant subsequences of nucleic acids or proteins are ascertained.

MOTIF PREDICTION ALGORITHMS

Challenges

One of the chief issues surrounding motif prediction is the broadness of the term itself. The most basic definition describes it as being a sequence of biological significance; yet, significance could (in principle) cover a broad class of use cases.

As we have learned, motifs can imply functional or structural significance. These two options are neither mutually exclusive nor necessarily related. However, it is not always the case that a motif must fall into either one of these classifications; consider a highly-conserved and strongly-represented sequence in non-coding DNA. Consider the issues of satellite DNA: if the distribution of bases differs significantly in these regions compared to bulk DNA, then it might be proper to say that these regions are also significant, depending on the problem. Thus, the question of what it means for a subsequence to be biologically significant comes into play.

One conclusion that can be drawn is that significance is a product of context. If the task at hand is to identify promoter regions nearby a gene, then those regions which likely harbor promoters are significant. Yet, if we are instead trying to identify introns (regions of RNA transcripts that are excised prior to translation), we find that predicting promoters does little to fulfill that goal. Neither may come to play if we are trying to find regions of DNA that lend themselves to methylation. Thus, there must be some way to apply specificity to a general motif-prediction algorithm to reduce both type I and II errors.

A secondary issue is that of scalability. This has become more of an issue in recent times thanks to the availability of entire genomes and the annotations that come with them. There is some intuitive sense that a larger amount of input will lead to an increased running time and memory usage for most applications, but the question is the degree of growth as one varies the size of the input. Current algorithms are noted to have high running times, and the computational complexities of many are difficult to characterize because they are nondeterministic. Furthermore, it may be difficult to ascertain the combined effect of a set of parameters on performance in some cases. Performance and scalability are concerns almost as important as accuracy in some cases, for these parameters can easily affect feasibility.

Advances in parallel computing may offer some remedy to the problem at a cost. It is a viable option to look at, since it has become more affordable with the advent of mutli-core processors in the public PC market, cluster computing, and general purpose computing on graphics processing units (GPGPU). However, parallel computing is not a panacea for problems related to scalability and comes with tradeoffs. One can measure scalability by applying Amdahl's law (1) to the algorithm in question, where P is the percentage of time spent in parallel and N is the number of tasks contributing to the problem:

$$S_a\left(P,\ N\right) = \frac{1}{\left(1-P\right)+\ P\ /\ N} \tag{1}$$

Ideally, a parallel process would have *linear speedup*, or speedup proportional to N. While linear speedup is extremely difficult to obtain in practice (as it implies 100% coverage), very high values of P yield very close approximations. If one takes the limit of S_a as $N \to \infty$, it becomes apparent that the maximum speedup of any given algorithm can be predicted by its serial portion $(1-P)$. Unfortunately, some algorithms do not lend themselves well to parallelization specifically because of low coverage. For coverage of 50%, we find that speedup is limited to 2, and for lesser values, not much above unity speedup is achieved. However, it must be noted that the above is the speedup of a processes with an infinite number of threads, and that speedup below $P=100\%$ is an asymptote.

Thus, the situation can be even worse in practice; for $S_a(50\%, 2)$, speedup is *below* unity at 2/3. What this demonstrates is that parallelism can only increase performance dramatically for some algorithms. Some algorithms may require frequent synchronization as a result of waiting on a shared resource, which drives coverage down. In this case, an otherwise superior algorithm may be discarded in favor of an algorithm which is more easily parallelized.

Bayesian Inference

One of the oldest classification methods applied to sequence and pattern mining is Bayesian Inference. Bayesian inference has been applied to molecular biology and sequence mining as early as 1953 (Metropolis, Rosenbluth, Rosenbluth, Teller, & Teller, 1953), and continues to be a commonly used method of classification. It naturally leverages Bayes' theorem (or Bayes' rule) in order to permit updating the probability estimate for a hypothesis in the face of new evidence. For reference, Bayes' rule is provided by (2):

$$P(H \mid X) = \frac{P(X|H)P(H)}{P(X)} \qquad (2)$$

Let X be the initial collection of observed data points: $X \equiv \{x_1, \ldots, x_n\}$, x be an element of X, θ be the parameter of the distribution of x, and α be the hyperparameter of the prior distribution $\grave{e} \sim P(\grave{e} \mid \acute{a})$. By using Bayes' theorem, one may construct the posterior distribution of the parameters derived from the likelihood $P(X \mid \grave{e})$ and the prior, which in turn is proportional to the integrand of the marginal likelihood (3). The predictive posterior distribution (4) of a new data point $\overset{\vee}{x}$ can be derived by marginalizing over initial posterior distribution.

$$P(\grave{e}|X,\acute{a}) = \frac{P(X|\grave{e})P(\grave{e}|\acute{a})}{P(X|\acute{a})} \propto P(X|\grave{e})P(\grave{e}|\acute{a}) \qquad (3)$$

$$P(\overset{\vee}{x}|X,\acute{a}) = \int_{\grave{e}} P\left(\overset{\vee}{x}|\grave{e}\right) P(\grave{e}|X,\acute{a})d\grave{e} \qquad (4)$$

Using the above, it is possible to develop what is known as the naïve Bayesian classifier (Naïve Bayes). Now consider that each x can be assigned to one of m classes in: $C \equiv \{c_1, \ldots, c_n\}$.

The goal of Naïve Bayes (and indeed any classifier) is to assign a value of C given x. The way in which Naïve Bayes is to find the class that maximizes conditional probability given the initial data X (5):

$$P(c_i|X) \geq P(c_j|X) : \forall c_{\{i,j\}} \in C) \qquad (5)$$

$$P(c_i|X) = \frac{P(X|c_i)P(c_i)}{P(X)} \qquad (6)$$

The astute observer will realize that Bayes' rule is directly applicable here, so Naïve Bayes seeks to maximize the maximum posteriori hypothesis (6). $P(X)$ (in any circumstance) will remain constant, so this means that satisfying (5) essentially boils down to finding the C_i which maximizes the term $P(X|c_i)P(c_i)$. If one assumes equal probability for each class (i.e., $P(c_1) = P(c_2)\ldots P(c_m)$), then that can further be reduced to maximizing $P(X|c_i)$.

Prior distributions for each class are usually derived through a process called *training*. A set of samples T (the training set) is used as a basis for predicting the distributions for each class. This is usually a set such that $S \subset X$, but however it is constructed, it should be representative of the population at hand. If there are t samples in the training set and t_i of those samples belong to class c_i, then the prior distribution can be calculated as in (7):

$$P(c_i) = \frac{t_i}{t} \qquad (7)$$

In principle, Bayesian classifiers should have minimal error when compared to other classifiers; this is not necessarily so in practice. One of the critical assumptions that Naïve Bayes makes is that of class conditional independence (that is, that the attribute values are conditionally independent of one another). Thus, it can become less accurate if dependencies exist between any two attributes. An alternative classifier using Bayesian inference is the Bayesian belief network, and it is designed to address this particular issue.

As an example, let's consider a physician screening a patient for HIV. It is now known that AIDS is ultimately caused by the human immunodeficiency virus (HIV), but the symptoms of AIDS may not manifest themselves until long after infection. We know the following about the early stages of HIV infection:

- HIV is most commonly transmitted through the sharing of bodily fluids such as blood or semen. Common vectors include high-risk sexual activity with an infected partner and the recreational use of intravenous drugs.
- Some patients display flu-like symptoms (acute retroviral syndrome) within weeks of infection.
- HIV has a capsid protein (p24) which serves as an antigen.

The first (and perhaps most obvious) observation that can be made here is that the presence of flu-like symptoms is not a strong indicator of HIV infection, as many other causes (including contracting an influenza virus) may be responsible for these symptoms, and not all infected individuals display them. Likewise, it is also not the case that the vectors for HIV are a sufficient basis to conclude an HIV infection. In fact, no single positive result on any of these tests is sufficient to conclude HIV infection.

However, it should be noted that (unlike the other observations regarding early HIV infection), the common vectors have a causal relationship with HIV infection. Because the other observations are symptoms, one expects that they should have higher probability given HIV infection. However, the vectors themselves are expected to modify HIV infection. Thus, we can transitively reason that the probability of these symptoms occurring due to HIV given the vector is higher.

The above is an example of where class conditional independence fails to accurately model a system. The resulting reasoning results in a *belief network*, a directed acyclic graph of joint probability distributions (Figure 1). Each edge (or arc) in the graph represents an ancestor-descendent relationship between two nodes in question. The set of direct ancestors for a node *X* is expressed with *Parents(X)*, and the set of its direct descendents *Children(X)*. In this case, we can draw several conclusions from the belief network:

Figure 1. A Bayesian belief network modeling regarding causality of early HIV symptoms

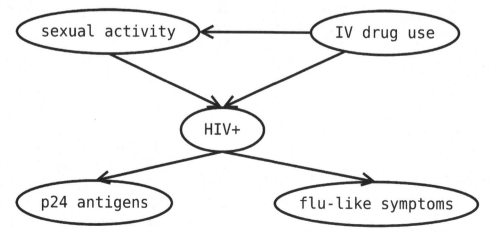

- Sexual activity influences HIV⁺
- IV drug use influences sexual activity, thereby transitively influencing HIV⁺
- Both HIV⁺ and Flu⁺ influence flu-like symptoms.

In order to do this, it is necessary to assign probabilities for each attribute in the belief network. Each node is associated of a conditional probability table (CPT) denoting the probabilities that various combinations of the parent attributes will yield the attribute in question. Basal attributes have no parents, so these tables are nullary. We note that there are two parents HIV⁺ (H): sexual activity (S) and IV drug use (D). The prior probabilities of acquiring HIV from either one of these two events are thought to be:

$$P(S) = 0.00751 \text{ and } P(D) = 0.0067$$

respectively (Center for Disease Control, 2013). The probability of developing acute retroviral syndrome during HIV infection is 89% (Schacker, Collier, Hughes, Shea, & Corey, 1996), compared to about 2.2% of ILI symptoms during moderate flu activity (Department of Health Services, Wisconsin, 2014).

As sexual activity also has a parent (IV drug use), a CPT is also needed for it. High-risk sexual activity is more prevalent in the face of intravenous drug use (Tyndall, et al., 2002), while incidence of this activity is lower otherwise (Center for Disease

Table 1. A CPT for flu-like symptoms. The statistically independent nature of infection method and illness mean that the conditional probabilities in all circumstances are simply the prior probability of acute retroviral syndrome. Other transmission vectors are considered negligible for simplicity.

	S,D	S,~D	~S,D	~S,~D
H	0.23	0.0075	0.0067	~0.0
~H	0.77	~0.99	~0.99	~1.0

Control, 2013). For the purposes of simplifying the population of this CDT (Table 2), we combine statistics for both genders, and consider only lack of condom use; however, in the literature, there are other risk factors which are normally considered.

Assessing the joint probability can be done by using the chain rule (8). Thus, the joint probability of individual having attributes HIV⁺ (H), flu-like symptoms (F), sexual activity (S), IV drug use, and is:

$$P(H, F, S, D) = 0.89 * 0.0067 * 0.65 \approx 0.0039.$$

However, we are interested in whether or not the person in question is HIV⁺, so we want to calculate $P(H \mid F, S, F)$.

Note that HIV⁺ has parents for which the state is not known: we do not know whether or not p24 antigens are present. Modern combined assays have extremely high sensitivity (effectively 100%), and average specificity of 99%. Thus, the conditional probability by known attributes K by factoring in the m nuisance variables $u \in U \mid U \equiv X - A$ in our network (9):

$$P\left(a_1, \ldots, a_n\right) = \prod_{i=1}^{n} P\left(a_i \mid Parents\left(a_i\right)\right) \qquad (8)$$

$$P\left(H \mid k_1, \ldots, k_n\right) =$$

$$\frac{\sum_{U_1 \ldots U_m \in \{T,F\}} P\left(H = T, U_1, \ldots, U_m, k_1, \ldots, k_n\right)}{\sum_{K_1 \ldots K_n, U_1 \ldots U_m \in \{T,F\}} P\left(H = T, U_1, \ldots, U_m, K_1, \ldots, K_n\right)}$$

$$(9)$$

Table 2. A CPT for high-risk sexual activity. IV drug use leads to much higher incidence of high-risk sexual activity.

	D	~D
S	0.65	0.39
~S	0.35	0.61

The denominator is the union of all instances where H is true; in our example, that value is $D \approx 0.16913$. We can therefore calculate that $P(H|F, S, D) \approx 0.79$, and this indicates that such a patient in question should probably undergo more rigorous HIV testing. Note that the resulting probabilities of the belief network are only as accurate as the belief network itself; if the underlying beliefs are incorrect, or the network is incomplete (as we have intentionally made this one), then it stands to reason that the belief network will yield inaccurate estimates.

The above Bayesian approaches are sometimes used in text classification algorithms; for instance, Naïve Bayes has long been used in email filters that detect unsolicited bulk messages. One of the most common forms of Bayesian inference found in motif predictors is achieved through the application of Monte Carlo integration, a numerical method for approximating a complex integral through random sampling. Given a function f and a volume V, one can approximate V with a set of n randomly selected points called X (10, 11):

$$\langle f \rangle = \frac{1}{n} \sum_{i=1}^{n} f(x_i) \qquad (10)$$

$$\int f dV \approx V \langle f \rangle \pm \sqrt{\frac{\langle f^2 \rangle - f}{n}} \qquad (11)$$

Monte Carlo integration is a non-deterministic method for integration (as opposed to deterministic methods such as the trapezoid rule) and can be used for an approximate integral if a simpler function is known. As an example, consider the problem of approximating π, whose value can be easily determined if from the area of a circle in terms other than π; however, this is not the case. It turns out that we do have a collision test for the circle in Cartesian coordinates which is relatively straightforward: $x^2 + y^2 \leq r^2$. With sufficiently large n, Monte Carlo integration will yield a reasonable approximation of π.

Markov chain Monte Carlo (MCMC) methods augment Monte Carlo integration by going one step further. The sampling distribution is designed in such a way that the previous samples affect what the next sample will be by using a stochastic process called a Markov chain. A Markov chain is a stochastic process where the conditional probability distribution of future states depends only upon the process's present state, rather than those that preceded it (this is sometimes called the Markov property). As we shall see, MCMC is the basis of an important sampling algorithm called Gibbs Sampling.

These concepts serve as a foundation for future elucidation on sequence mining algorithms. While classifiers that do not depend on Bayesian inference do exist, it provides a toolset by which the properties of sub-populations can be considered. In the following sections, its influence will be seen in the designs for several of the classifiers discussed. *MotEvo* (Arnold, Erb, Pachkov, Molina, & Nimwegen, 2012) is an example of a mostly Bayesian motif discovery tool which utilizes the methods we have described above.

MotEvo works by tracking evolutionary conservation and inferring binding sites for transcription factors by working backwards. Input consists of a collection of multiple sequence alignments (MSAs; optionally, sequences for a single species), a collection of position-specific weight matrices, and a phylogenetic tree relating the species in question. With one species designated as the reference species, it calculates highly-conserved regions that are likely to be transcription factor binding sites (TFBSes). This method depends strongly on the fact that TFBSes are likely to be conserved since transcription factors (TFs) are often necessary for mRNA synthesis. It also has the peculiar ability to classify a single position as belonging to multiple TFs.

MotEvo is able to make a few assumptions due to pruning done at initialization time. Let S

be a matrix in a set $\{S\}$ such that s is a row in S, $s_{[i,l]}$ denotes a segment of s that starts at position $(i+1)$ and of length l, and $S_{[i,l]}$ denote the submatrix of S including only columns $(i+1)$ through $(i+l)$. Let w also be a weight matrix in a set $\{w\}$ such that w_a^i is the probability of nucleotide a at position i. Then the probability of a sequence given the weight matrix is given by (12), where $|w|$ denotes the number of columns in w. It is possible to compare this probability to some background model b, yielding (13). Given the full phylogenetic tree T, those species whose corresponding sequences have a WM score of less than or equal to zero are removed, thus keeping only the species which are in consensus (the subtree T'). The probability ratio (14) can then be used to determine the probability of observing the MSA.

$$P\left(s|w\right) = \prod_{j=1}^{|w|} w_{s_j}^j \qquad (12)$$

$$wm\left(s|w,b\right) = \log \frac{P\left(s|w\right)}{P\left(s|b\right)} \qquad (13)$$

$$\frac{P\left(S|w,T'\right)}{P(S|b,T')} = \prod_{i=1}^{l} \frac{P\left(S_i|w^i,T'\right)}{P\left(S_i|b,T'\right)} \qquad (14)$$

This algorithm takes into account the fact that (even now) the specificity of most TFs is still unknown for most model organisms, so it is reasonable to postulate that some TFs which are not represented by $\{w\}$. Thus, MotEvo presents the concept of unknown functional elements (UFEs), the probability for which is given as (15). Additionally, prior probabilities (16) are needed to leverage Bayes' rule, and this can be calculated given the probability π_w for a weight matrix w_m to start and for which there are n_w sites. Posterior probability

ratios can then be calculated recursively (17) using a forward/backward algorithm taken from hidden Markov model theory. This can all finally be brought together to calculate the posterior probability that a binding site occurs for w (18).

$$P_{ufe}\left(S_k|T\right) = \int P(S_k|w^k,T)P\left(w^k\right)dw^k \qquad (15)$$

$$P\left(w\right) = \prod_{w\in\{w\}} \left(\eth_w\right)^{n_w} \qquad (16)$$

$$F_n = \sum_{w\in\{w\}} \eth_w \frac{P(S_{[n-l_w,\,l_w]}|w,T)}{P(S_{[n-l_w,\,l_w]}|b,T)} F_{n-l_w} \qquad (17)$$

$$P\left(w.n|S,\{w\},T\right) = \frac{F_n \dfrac{P(S_{[n,lw]}|w,T)}{P(S_{[n,lw]}|w,T)} \eth_w R_{n-l_w+1}}{F_L} \qquad (18)$$

The rest of the details of the classifier can be read in (Arnold, Erb, Pachkov, Molina, & Nimwegen, 2012). In the following sections, this will turn out to be a recurring theme; though not all motif discovery tools leverage Bayes' rule, it is nonetheless a reasonable and workable approach towards the problem of motif prediction.

Expectation Maximization

Expectation maximization (EM) is an iterative method which attempts to produce maximal parameter estimates for statistical models dependent on unobserved latent variables, and first appeared as a generalized solution in 1977, with specialized instances of it published before this time (Dempster, Laird, & Rubin, 1977). EM usually seeks to find the parameters yielding the maximum likelihood or maximum *a posteriori* probability of a statistical model (Figure 2).

Let X be a set of observed data, Z be a set of latent variables, θ be a vector of unknown parameters, and $L(\theta \mid X, Z) = P(X, Z \mid \theta)$ denote the likelihood function of a statistical model in question. Then the maximum likelihood estimate (MLE) of the model is given by (19), the sum of the likelihood of each element of Z. EM attempts to maximize the log-likelihood of θ (20; the E-step) iteratively adjusting the value of θ at time step t, which we denote as θ_t (21; the M-step). This process generates progressively better estimates of θ, leading to better estimates of Z and therefore a refined model.

$$P\left(X|\theta\right) = \sum_{z \in Z} P(X, Z | \theta) \qquad (19)$$

$$Q\left(\theta|\theta_t\right) = E_{Y|X,\theta_t}[\ \log P(X, Z|\theta)\ ] \qquad (20)$$

$$\theta_{t+1} = \underset{\theta}{\mathrm{argmax}}\, Q(\theta \mid \theta_t) \qquad (21)$$

As (14) is recursive in definition, we need a set of initial values for the base case $t=0$. It is sufficiently to randomly initialize θ_0, since successive iterations will converge towards the best parameters as a result of (13). As for Z, it stands to reason that it should be a discrete domain, and it has a cardinality equivalent to X because there is exactly one latent variable for each observation.

An early example of motif prediction software which leverages EM is the *Multiple Em for Motif Elicitation* (MEME) tool. MEME uses a two-component finite mixture model consisting of the subsequences of fixed width (called the "motif" component) and a "background" component consisting of all other positions in the sequences. An adaptation of EM for finite mixture models called MM is used to fit the model to the data set; this yields the relative frequency of motif occurrences that can be used to derive the threshold for a Bayes-optimal classifier. The resulting classifier can then be used to find motifs in other databases (Bailey & Elkan, 1994).

The MM algorithm is designed to deal with the mixed nature of the model, and thus, and thus the mixing parameter pair λ is added, and θ becomes

Figure 2. Expectation maximization is an iterative algorithm for parameter estimation

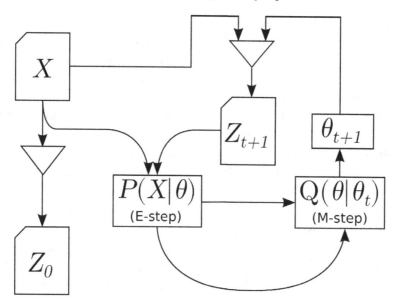

a matrix of letter frequencies. There are separate parameters for each model component, we shall call the parameter vector of ith component at time t $\theta_{t(i)}$. The resulting likelihood function is $L(\theta, \lambda \mid X, Z) = p(X, Z \mid \theta, \lambda)$.

Thus, the E- and M- steps are transformed to (22) and (23, 24) respectively.

$$Q\left(\theta, \lambda \mid \theta_t, \lambda_t\right) = \sum_{i=1}^{n}\sum_{j=1}^{2} Z_{ij}^t \log p(X_i \mid \theta_{tj}) + \sum_{i=1}^{n}\sum_{j=1}^{2} Z_{ij}^t \log \lambda_{t(j)}$$
(22)

$$\theta_{t+1(j)} = \underset{\hat{e}}{\operatorname{argmax}} \sum_{i=1}^{n} Z_{ij}^t \log p(X\_i \mid \theta_{t(j)})$$
(23)

$$\lambda_{t+1(j)} = \sum_{i=1}^{n} \frac{Z_{ij}^t}{n}$$
(24)

Let us contrast this to MotEvo, which we called an evolutionary consensus algorithm. MEME and MotEvo are similar as they both utilize some variant of the EM algorithm (although EM is not the basis for MotEvo, but rather a mechanism to refine the pre-supplied weight matrices). However, MotEvo provides only a mechanism to detect those TFBSes that were discovered as a result of alignment. The classifier that MEME generates can be used to discover novel motifs not initially, and is therefore a tool for *de novo* motif discovery.

While MEME is an example of leveraging EM for motif discovery, it is by no means not the only one, and this approach is still the subject of active research. As with Bayesian inference, we shall see that EM forms a critical component that supplements other algorithms to afford motif discovery.

Gibbs Sampling

Gibbs sampling is a Markov chain Monte Carlo algorithm used to obtain approximated sequences of observations from a multivariate probability distribution. The algorithm first appeared in 1984 (Geman & Geman, 1984) and is named after an important statistical mechanics distribution proposed by its namesake, Josiah W. Gibbs. The Gibbs sampler is a special case of the Metropolis-Hasting algorithm, and it is particularly useful whenever the joint distribution is difficult to calculate, but the conditional distribution is much more easily sampled from. We first discuss the simplest form of Gibbs sampling, the single-site sampler.

Suppose that we wish to draw k samples in sequence from an initial sample:

$$X^0 = \left(\theta_1^0, \cdots, \theta_n^0\right).$$

Let (25) be the conditional distribution for the parameter $X_j^t \in X^t$ such that $t \in \{1,\ldots,k\}$ and $j \in \{1,\ldots,n\}$. Note that the sample at each time-step t is calculated stepwise from its elements, forming the Markov chain: $\{X\} = \{X^1,\ldots,X^k\}$.

An interesting consequence of Gibbs sampling is that the final conditional probabilities are proportional to the joint probability (26); the stationary distribution becomes the joint distribution, and this can be used to calculate a normalization factor that is used (in conjunction with the conditional probability) to define joint probability.

$$X_j^t \sim P(X_j \mid X_{-j}^{t-1}) = P(X_j \mid \theta_1^{t-1}, \ldots \theta_{j-1}^{t-1}, \theta_{j+1}^{t-1}, \theta_n^{t-1})$$
(25)

$$X^t = \left(X_1^t, \ldots, X_n^t\right)$$
(26)

$$P(x_j | \theta_1, \ldots \theta_{j-1}, \theta_{j+1}, \ldots, \theta_n) = \frac{P(\theta_1, \ldots, \theta_n)}{P(\theta_1, \ldots, \theta_{j-1}, \theta_{j+1}, \theta_n)} \tag{27}$$

The initialization of X^0 can be achieved by several means. The simplest way to do this is through random initialization, but parameter estimation algorithms (like EM) are useful to yield initialization samples closer to the target distribution. It is also trivial to show that successive time-steps are not truly independent of one another and that they have some degree of autocorrelation; during a *burn-in period*, the first m samples are discarded, and thereafter, the average the next of n samples is taken. There are other ways to reduce autocorrelation by slightly changing how the Markov chain is generated, such as the block and collapsed Gibbs samplers.

Block Gibbs samplers work much like single-site samplers, except that groups of parameters are used in the conditional distribution calculation. Thus, during each time-step, we calculate conditional distribution of block B_j given the remaining parameters (28). Blocks may be populated by other methods, provided that no parameters are missing and that no new parameters are introduced (29). The sample at time-step t is analogous to the conditional probability for each block. Thus, the single-site Gibbs sampler becomes a special case of the block sampler, where there are a number of one-parameter blocks for each parameter. The *Markov blanket* of a block B_i is the set of all blocks for which there exists at least one parameter in common (31). As a result, conditional independence is maintained between parameter blocks and autocorrelation is reduced, permitting faster convergence towards the chain's stationary distribution.

$$X_j^t \sim P(X_{B_j} | X_{-B_j}^{t-1}) \tag{28}$$

$$X \equiv \bigcup_{i=1}^{d} B_i, B_i \subset X \tag{29}$$

$$X^t = \left(X_{B_1}^t, \ldots, X_{B_d}^t \right) \tag{30}$$

$$MB(B_i) = \bigcup_{i=1}^{d} (j | B_j \cap B_i \neq \varnothing) \tag{31}$$

The collapsed sampler approaches this problem by reducing the number of parameters (collapsing the Markov chain input) by choosing a set of parameters for which there is little autocorrelation, it is likely that the resulting Markov chain will stabilize quickly. Let α and θ be parameters for some distribution $P(X | á, è)$ such that $è \sim P(è | á)$; then the former distribution can be collapsed to $P(X | á)$ by integrating $P(X | á, è)$ with respect to θ; thus, θ is said to have been marginalized or integrated out (32). By removing θ, accuracy is improved because only a subspace will be sampled.

$$P(X | \alpha) = \int P(X | \alpha, \theta) \, P(\theta | \alpha) \, d\theta \tag{32}$$

It is no surprise that Gibbs sampling lends itself particularly well to belief networks; recall that conditional probabilities are trivial to calculate since they are available via CPTs. In the Geman brothers' use case, this was leveraged to facilitate image restoration; by a decade since its discovery, it had been applied to finding common protein binding sites in unaligned DNA sequences (Liu, 1994). In Liu's classifier, a motif was permitted to be a 22-nucleotide sequence, meaning that X was a 4×22 matrix. The bases were considered independent of one another. Sampling X, as a result, would have meant sampling 22 four-dimensional Dirichlet distributions; however, Liu uses collapsed Gibbs to mitigate this problem.

An important contribution made in Liu's classifier is the concept of the "shift mode." If the starting positions of the true sites Z are known, let Z^0 denote true mode of Z, such that all elements of Z^0 are offset by some small offset δ (33). Thus, Z represents the "shift mode" of the distribution, as it differs from the true mode by a constant offset. The result is that it is possible to avoid global changes for random components. The probability can then be calculated by the ratio of the true and shift modes (34). The result is a Gibbs sampler that converges quickly for all of the 20 starting sites in the data.

$$Z = Z^0 + \delta = \left(z_1^0 + \delta, \dots, z_n^0 + \delta \right) \tag{33}$$

$$P = \frac{\pi\left(Z^0\right)}{\pi\left(Z\right)} \tag{34}$$

Since Liu's classifier was published, the Gibbs sampler is a cornerstone for several modern motif prediction algorithms. *Gibbs Motif Sampler* (Thompson, Rouchka, & Lawrence, 2003) offers a recursive sampling option and relaxes the requirement of Liu that motif order remains the same throughout sequences. *PhyloGibbs* (Siddharthan, Siggia, & van Nimwegen, 2005) is a tool which (like MotEvo) takes into phylogenic relationships into consideration during discovery.

Meanwhile, *GibbsST* (Shida, 2006) (Shida, 2006) utilizes simulated tempering to afford resistance against the local optimum problem.

Phylogenetic Approach

A classical and intuitive approach to motif discovery reasons that regions strongly conserved between lineages may have important functional or structural implications, and that these regions must be motifs by definition (Figure 3). We have seen many motifs for which this notion carries some weight; transcription factor binding sites are often highly-conserved because their role in regulating the intracellular environment. It stands to reason that selection pressure has maintained these sequences because the lack thereof would inhibit viability; thus, they are propagated to the carrier's offspring, and survive into the next generation.

We have already seen two methods that leverage the above hypothesis (MotEvo and Liu's algorithm). However, there are several other approaches that are worth mentioning. One of the first published methods is the MACAW tool (Schuler, Altschul, & Lipman, 1991). The *GLAM* family of tools (Frifth, Hansen, Spouge, & Weng, 2003) is perhaps the most well know. GLAM was designed to overcome inflexibility with local MSA tools. Prior tools expected that the user might know the width of the aligned motif, and were incapable of predicted it. Furthermore, information regarding

Figure 3. An excerpt from a ClustalW MSA for HOXA1. Sequence alignment can highlight highly conserved regions with biological significance.

homeobox A1

```
TCGCTGGCCGCGCCGCCTCCAGTCTACTACCCCGCGGCGTC   H. sapiens
----GGACCTGCCCAGCCCGAGCCTACCCCTCGGACC----   P. paniscus
----GGACCTGCTCGGCGCGAGCTTACCCCTCTGACC----   M. musculus
----GGACCTGCTCAGCGCGAGCCTACCCCTCCGACC----   B. taurus
      * .**      *  .  *  *  **   *** . *  * *.    Conserved
```

* - Fully Conserved   : - Strongly Conserved   . - Weakly Conserved

the statistical significance of the alignment was usually missing from the output.

An important divergence that GLAM makes from previous attempts is its function that scores the quality of the alignment. At this time, information content was the metric of choice for scoring; however, it is less suitable for scoring an alignment with a variable width because the score can never decrease as the width of the alignment increases. Instead, a Bayesian scoring scheme is utilized based on the prior probability distribution of nucleotides at a given position for an alignment of length n and counts c (35). The Dirichlet function is chosen as the prior distribution because bias based on one to a few nucleotides is thought to be more common (36); Z is a normalization constant, and $\acute{a}_i$ is the pseudocount. Given N sequences and A sequences to be aligned, the final scoring function is reduced to (37) via pseudocount estimation.

$$S = \sum_{k=1}^{n} \ln\left[\frac{\int_{\{q_i\}} P\left(\{q_i\}\right) \times \prod_i q_i^{c_{ki}}}{\prod_i p_i^{c_{ki}}} \right] \qquad (35)$$

$$P\left(\{q_i\}\right) = \frac{1}{Z}\prod_i q_i^{\acute{a}_i - 1} \qquad (36)$$

$$S = \sum_{k=1}^{n} \ln\left[\left(\frac{``(A)}{\prod_i ``(\alpha_i)} \times \frac{\prod_i ``(c_{ki} + \alpha_i)}{``(N+A)} \right) / \prod_i p_i^{c_{ki}} \right] \qquad (37)$$

GLAM uses the Gibbs sampler technique of Lawrence et al. (Lawrence, Boguski, Liu, Neuwald, & Wooten, 1993) with a modification that permits the inference of the alignment width. The initial sample is randomized; however, with each successive step, one sequence is selected and random and alters which segment of the sequence

is included with a probability of $P = e^s$. Choices which increase alignment score therefore favorable, and the algorithm is permitted to escape local maxima.

As implied above, GLAM has served as the basis for several new tools (hence, the "GLAM family"). A-GLAM (K., Mariño-Ramírez, Sheetlin, Landsman, & Spouge, 2005) introduces an anchored alignment relative to each promoter's TSS, and an enumerative approach that finds common 8-mer DNA words of a fixed length is combined with alignment. Because of this, A-GLAM does not assume a fixed distribution for position, but instead learns it from the input. The result is that some statistically significant motifs that are otherwise inaccessible to GLAM are sometimes located.

A more recent descendent, *GLAM2* (Frith, Saunders, Kobe, & Bailey, 2008), differs significantly from the original algorithm. Notable changes include collapsing the model parameters, introducing stochastic traceback, and using simulated annealing (rather than EM) for parameter optimization. The scoring scheme is also changed slightly, as a Dirichlet mixture is used for the prior distribution instead of a Dirichlet distribution (38). GLAM2 also supports insertions (r) and deletions (d), which have probabilities given by the Beta distributions (39, 40).

$$P(\vec{c}) = S = \sum_{k=1}^{n} \ln\left[\frac{\int_{\{q_i\}} P\left(\{q_i\}\right) \times \prod_i q_i^{c_{ki}}}{\prod_i p_i^{c_{ki}} \prod_i P(d_k) \prod_i P(r_k)} \right] \qquad (38)$$

$$P(d) = \int_0^1 \phi^d (1-\phi) P(\phi) d\phi \qquad (39)$$

$$P(r) = \int_0^1 \psi^d (1-\psi) P(\psi) d\psi \qquad (40)$$

The phylogenetic approach is appealing because it meshes well with the literature, particularly since it follows that important motifs should be conserved. The drawback is that many alignments must be performed, since these algorithms seek to optimize alignment score; this process can be prohibitive when working with large data sets. However, this may be acceptable because of the high likelihood of yielding motifs with high significance.

Covariance Models

So far, we have discussed motif discovery software that works on the basis of primary structure or sequence. This is perfectly suitable for some tasks, such as mining binding site motifs; however, some biological questions are best answered from the perspective of higher-order structure. The presence and configuration of some secondary structure features are contribute to catalytic function in some biopolymers (as described in the introduction). Knowing about secondary structure also aids in RNA multiple sequence alignment.

Covariance models (CM) are well suited for inference of conserved structural motifs from sequences, and occur in the literature as early as 1994 with *COVE* (Eddy & Durbin, 1994). Eddy and Durbin had initially developed the algorithm to pursue questions related to transfer RNAs (tRNAs) and tRNA-related sequences; they were interested in conserved secondary structure, but they did not actually have secondary structure information to draw from. Prior to the utilization of Covariance models, the best means of consensus RNA secondary structure prediction was comparative sequence analysis, which is time consuming.

An ordered tree is sufficient to describe the secondary structure of RNA (Figure 4), and it captures pairwise interactions of each of the nucleobases in the molecule (some tertiary features, such as non-pairwise interactions or non-nested pairs are lost in this model). Each vertex may either be a bifurcation node (where the tree splits), or a pairwise node. The pairwise node is a pair (L, R) such that either component may be a nucleotide or nil; a pairwise node with one nil component is called a *singlet*. A modified preorder traversal (wherein L is emitted when the node is first visited and R is emitted when the node is revisited) yields the primary structure of the RNA in question.

However, the above representation of RNAs does come at the cost of inflexibility, as it is difficult to account for events such as insertion, deletion, and mismatches. The covariance model (CM) is instead a generalization of a hidden Markov model (HMM). Like the HMM, a CM is stateful and has emission probabilities; however, while HMMs model stochastic regular grammars, CMs are sufficient to model stochastic context-free grammars. Indeed, an HMM is a special case of a CM that forbids pairwise or bifurcation nodes.

Let $Q = (q_1, \ldots, q_n)$ be a vector of states (where q_1 is the initial state), Σ be an alphabet, σ be an element of Σ, δ be a matrix of state transition probabilities of the form $P(q_i \mid q_j, \sigma)$, S be a vector of symbol emission probabilities of the form $P(s_i \mid q_{j(1)}, q_{j(2)})$, and F be a set of final states such that $F \subset Q$. A CM is a quintuple $M \equiv (Q, \Sigma, \delta, q_1, F)$.

It is simplest to describe the states in terms of nonterminals, and a CM defines three important state types: the state (P), a bifurcation (B), and delete (D) states. A P state is a pair of symbols (41) and that takes the form $P \rightarrow q_{(1)} Y q_{(2)}$ (where Y is some nonterminal). There are special cases where either $q_{(1)}$ or $q_{(2)}$ are equivalent to the null string ε; these are called left-emitting (L) and right-emitting (R) states respectively. In the case where both components are null, this is the end (E) state, which always has an emission and transition probability of 1. The B state is similarly a pair of nested CMs (42), takes the form $B \rightarrow q_{1(l)} q_{1(r)}$, and again has emission and transition probabilities of 1. Finally, a D state takes the form of $D \rightarrow Y$; while it has a constant emission probability of 1, its transition probability is given by the corresponding entry δ, since it is permissible (and probably expected) that a D state is not a final state.

Figure 4. a) tRNA-Phe's secondary structure. b) The same structure represented in tree form.

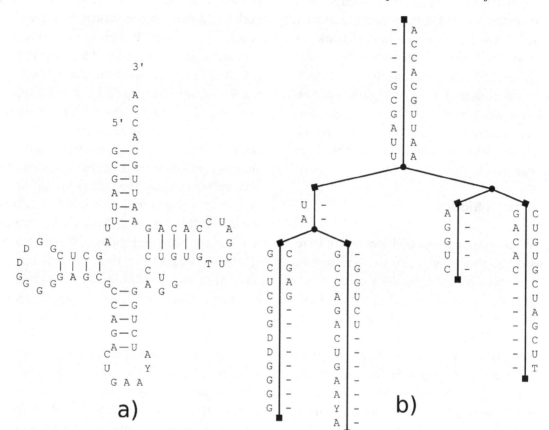

a)

b)

$$q_i = \left(q_{i(1)}, q_{i(2)}\right) : q_{i(1)} \bigcup q_{i(2)} \in \pounds \qquad (41)$$

$$q_b = \left(m_l, m_r\right) : m_l \bigcup m_r \in M \qquad (42)$$

CM training presents two problems (the combination of which has no practical rigorous solution): structure determination and parameter optimization. Both EM and Gibbs sampling can address parameter optimization, since the transition and emission probabilities are essentially hidden parameters that can be optimized locally. Structure determination is a much more difficult problem, because it is necessary to determine the set of states and transitions for an optimal CM. Eddy and Durbin use an iterative dynamic programming algorithm for this: initially, a random

alignment is generated; from that, a covariance model is constructed and then used to perform successive alignment until maximum mutual information is achieved. Let x be an non-empty element of Σ, f_x be the independent frequency of x, and $f_{x,y}$ be the joint frequency of a symbol pair (x, y). The mutual information is given by (43).

$$I\left(x; y\right) = \sum_{x,y \in (\pounds - \epsilon)} f_{x,y} \log_2 \left(\frac{f_{x,y}}{f_X f_y}\right) \qquad (43)$$

COVE's most readily apparent bottleneck is the alignment process. The dynamic programming method used by COVE utilizes a 3-dimensional matrix for its search space, meaning that resource complexity is $O(N^3)$ and runtime complexity is $O(N^4)$ given a sequence length of N. This makes

COVE intractable for large alignments due to unreachable memory demands. S.R. Eddy later refined the algorithm in 2002 with a package called *Infernal* (Nawrocki & Eddy, 2013); one of its key differences is that alignment is performed using a variant of the Myers/Miller algorithm, which has a significantly reduced resource and runtime complexities of Infernal to $O(N^2 \log N)$ and $O(|Q|^2 N^3)$ respectively. It should also be noted that in cases where optimal solutions are not necessary, approximated solutions are available. *RAGA* performs alignment using a genetic algorithm, which can provide a reasonable approximation of an optimal alignment with $O(N)$ resource complexity (Notredame, O'Brien, & Higgins, 1997). *RNASA* shows that simulated annealing is another reasonable approximate alignment that has $O(N^2)$ resource complexity (Kim, Cole, & Pramanik, 1996).

Another software package called CMfinder focuses on improving the accuracy of CM modeling (Yao, Weinberg, & Ruzzo, 2006). While scalability and runtime were important design considerations in CMfinder, the authors prioritized the generation of models that are directly usable in homology searches from a small training set. CMfinder reduces complexity by removing candidates that do not provide a stable secondary structure. These candidates are filtered out using a ranking process directed by the free energy of each candidate motif, which is then scaled by the motif length. The top-ranking candidate motifs are split into candidate regions, and between one and ten alignments are used to initialize an EM algorithm used to parameterize the CM. The CM is somewhat simplified in that a sequence is considered to be a mixture of candidate motifs; therefore, a finite-mixture model is used to describe the distribution of the regions that follow the background region.

The methods discussed here are best used when consensus high-order structure is desired, particularly for RNAs. The primary contributor

to computational complexity in CM-based motif elicitation algorithms are usually the alignment processes, as we have seen. However, this may be mitigated through via utilization of parallelism in the sequence alignment process. For more information on advances relating to this subject, please read (Rognes, 2001) and (Church, Goscinski, Holt, Inouye, Ghoting, Makarychev & Reumann, M., 2011).

Discriminative Learning

Most of the methods we have previously discussed are *generative* methods; these algorithms attempt to facilitate learning by deducing joint probabilities. Via Bayes' rule, conditional probability can then be extrapolated. However, generative tools can lead to a diminished specificity of motifs, since the resulting motifs are over-represented on a genome-wide scope. These methods can be contrasted with *discriminative* algorithms that attempt to learn conditional probability.

Discriminative motif prediction is a comparatively new approach; the *DME* algorithm (Smith, Sumazin, & Zhang, 2004) represents an early example of such an algorithm. As with many other algorithms, a likelihood model for motif over-representation compared to a set of background sequences is employed. Let $F = \{s_i \mid 1 \leq i \leq n\}$ be a multiset of strings with length w, such that the subset $F_1 \subseteq F$ includes binding-site observations from a product-multinomial model: $M = (M_1,\ldots, M_w)$ and the set of non-occuring binding sites $F_0 = F - F_1$. Then, letting the set of nucleotides be: $\Sigma = \{A, G, C, T\}$ and the predicate that indicates that a base j occurs at position i be $J(s_i = j)$, the probability that a string s is generated by the motif M is given by (44), and the likelihood of M given F_1 is given by (45). Similarly, given the base composition f where $j \in \Sigma$, the probability that an element of F_0 is generated by M is a multinominal distribution (46), and the corresponding likelihood is given by (47).

$$P(s|M) = \prod_{i=1}^{w}\prod_{j\in £} M_{ij}^{J(s_i=j)} \qquad (44)$$

$$L_{F_1}(M) = \prod_{s\in F_1} P(s \mid M) \qquad (45)$$

$$(s|f) = \prod_{i=1}^{w}\prod_{j\in £} f_j^{J(s_i=j)} \qquad (46)$$

$$L_{F_0}(f) = \prod_{s\in F_0} P(s \mid f) \qquad (47)$$

DME learns by maximizing the quality of the model. Instead of using information content as a measure of quality compared to some background set B, an objective function (48) is maximized instead. An initial search phase (in which a collection of models are built from a finite set of "column types") identifies the model which has the greatest quality (according to the objective function), and that single model $M^{(i)}$ is retained. A local binary search algorithm then finds similar matrices with a shrinking neighborhood of $M^{(i)}$. by successfully halving the g-neighborhood until the optimal motif is equal to $M^{(i)}$. The g-neighborhood of a matrix M consists of the subset of all column vectors X such that $M_i' \in N_g(M_i)$ (49).

$$I(M) = \sum_{s_i\in F}(z_{F,i}\log P(s_i|M) - \sum_{s_i\in B} z_{B,i}\log P(s_i \mid M) \qquad (48)$$

$$N_g(M_i) = \{X \mid d(M_i,X) \in \{0,2g\}, \forall_j, \mid M_{ij}-X_j \mid \in \{0,g\}\} \qquad (49)$$

DEME is a similar discriminative learning algorithm (Redhead & Bailey, 2007) that uses the Sharan-Segal algorithm (a binary classifier which labels sequences as either 1 [positive] versus 0 [negative]). The probability of such a classification for some sequence X is the sum of the log probabilities in the dataset D given parameters θ such that $D_i = (X_i, C_i)$ (50). DEME has much in common with other generative learning tools; some traditional motif discovery tools assume that exactly one instance of a motif will be found in a sequence (the OOPS model). DEME uses a slight variation of OOPS that permits a small fraction of these sequences to have zero motif instances (*Noisy OOPS* or NOOPS). DEME also uses the Dirichlet distribution for priors, as many generative tools do.

$$F(D,\ddot{e}) = \sum_{(X,C)\in D} \log P(C \mid X,\ddot{e}) \qquad (50)$$

Another discriminative tool, *Dispom* (Keilwagen, et al., 2011), has a notable characteristic in that it does not assume a fixed position distribution and that explicitly permits zero or one motif instance occurrences (ZOOPS). Let x be a string of length L over an alphabet: $\Sigma = \{A, G, C, T\}$, and x^{RC} be its reverse complement. Then, for any motif model M with motif length w, any start position distribution S, and any flanking sequence model F, the likelihood of x given parameters λ is provided by (51). Let u_1 denote the condition that x does not contain a binding site (BS) and u_2 denote the start position of the binding site in the sequence; the probability of u_2 is provided by (52), where $P^S(u_2|\ddot{e})$ denotes the probability according to S. If no BS exists in x, then it stands to reason that x is generated by the flanking sequence model; otherwise, it is thought that it is produced by the motif model and that F generates the surrounding regions (53).

$$P(x|\lambda) = \sum_{(u_1,u_2)} P(u_1|\lambda)\cdot P(u_2|u_1,\lambda)\cdot P(x \mid u_1,u_2,\lambda) \qquad (51)$$

$$P\left(u_2 | u_1, \lambda\right) = \begin{cases} 1, \; u_1 = 0 \\ P^S\left(u_2 | \lambda\right), \; u_1 = 1 \end{cases} \qquad (52)$$

$$P\left(x | u_2, u_1, \lambda\right) = \begin{cases} P^F\left(x | \lambda\right), \; u_1 = 0 \\ P^F\left(x_{1,\ldots,u_2} | \lambda\right) P^M\left(x_{u_2,\ldots,u_2+w}\right) \\ P^F\left(x_{u_2+w,\ldots,L} | \lambda\right), \; u_1 = 1 \end{cases}$$

$$(53)$$

As a discriminative algorithm, Dispom uses the maximum supervised posterior (MSP, as opposed to the MAP used in generative algorithms) estimator for parameter inference (54). Here, let c be a class label: $c \in C$, $C = \{0,1\}$ and $á$ hyperparameters of $ë$; $P(x | c = 0, \lambda)$ is provided by the ZOOPS model and: $P(x | c = 1, \lambda)$ is based off of a homogeneous Markov model of order 0. The goal, then, is to find parameters that maximize (54). The motif model can be made simpler by modifying contiguous regions on the borders of the model (insignificant regions), possibly trimming the model length by 20%; these modifications can include shifting, truncation, or expansion of the insignificant region.

$$\hat{\lambda} = \underset{\lambda}{\arg\max}$$

$$\left[\sum_{n=1}^{N} \log \left(\frac{P\left(C_n | \lambda\right) P\left(c_n | c_n, \lambda\right)}{\sum_{\tilde{c} \in C} P\left(\tilde{c} | \lambda\right) P(c_n | \tilde{c}, \lambda)} \right) \right] + \log Q(\lambda | \alpha)$$

$$(54)$$

Discriminative algorithms carry the advantage that they generally have greater classifier performance than generative methods, but that comes at the cost of flexibility. Discriminative models tend to forego the parameters necessary to optimize joint density, and (as a result) they directly solve classification tasks. However, generative models tend to reach their asymptotic error more quickly, so for smaller training sets, they may show better performance than discriminative models. This sort

of tradeoff should be considered when deciding whether or not a discriminative method should be employed.

Data Interpretation

The question of how to make sense of the output generated by motif discovery tools is a challenge that is as great (if not greater) than the process of mining the motifs themselves; after all, the data is of little value if nothing can be elucidated from it. Thus, the topics of visualization and data presentation become appropriate topics in context. There are a variety of ways to approach this issue depending on the level of detail needed to answer the topic at hand.

One of the earliest successful attempts to visualize sequence motifs was the *sequence logo visualization* (Scheider & Stephens, 1990). This is essentially a stacked bar graph with relative position on the x axis and information content on the vertical. The characters representing the sequence are proportionally scaled according to frequency. In some positions, a motif may be represented by two or more characters; in that case, the characters are sorted by occurrence frequency such that the most frequent character appears at the top of the stack. The sequence logo succinctly combines several aspects of the motif into a single diagram, including general consensus, order of residue predominance, relative residue frequency, and information content for a given position (Figure 5).

Although sequence logos work well for a small set of motifs, it becomes clear that this approach does not scale well with larger collections of motifs. An observer wants to quickly locate a significant motif from a large set of candidates and receive extended information about it; learning about the abundance of the motif, where it was found, or what other motifs are similar to it is not easily facilitated by sequence logos.

One example of such a tool is *MHC MotifViewer* (Rapin, Hoor, Lund, & Nielsen, 2010).

Figure 5. A sequence logo of the common region in HOXA1 (Figure 3) as rendered by WebLogo

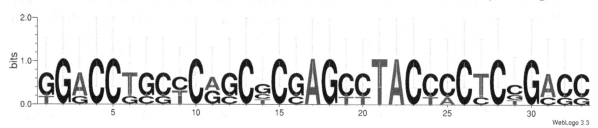

MHC MotifViewer catalogs protein binding motifs for the major histocompatibility complex (MHC) across several vertebrate species. Because MHC molecules present a distinct set of antigenic peptides to the immune system, it is difficult to perform epitope discovery in this instance. However, the problem of epitope discovery can be more easily reduced by finding MHCs with similar binding specificity. MHC MotifViewer presents a listing of

peptide binding motifs sorted by MHC alleles (Figure 6); each allele group contain the best-binding 1% of 1 million randomly-selected peptides, and position-specific scoring matrices are calculated for them. The user is initially presented with the sequence logos in the group. By clicking on the sequence logo, options to view pseudosequence and BLAST matrices become available.

Figure 6. Using MHC MotifViewer to browse MHC-binding motifs for human HLA-A Alleles MotifViz

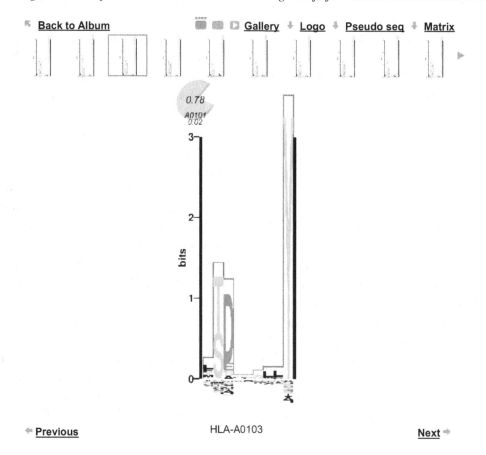

In order to automate the motif discovery process to encompass an entire range of processes from discovery to presentation, we need to create a pipeline. A pipeline is meant to streamline the workflow that biologists must deal with. In pipelines, a user presents input and specifies a limited number of parameters that control processes such as discovery, filtering, and visualization. These *jobs* are usually submitted in batch; when the pipeline finishes execution, the user is notified and can review the results. Pipelines are appealing because they can serve to standardize the computational aspect of experiments and focus on simplicity.

(Fu, Frith, Haverty, & Weng, 2004) is a web-based pipeline that performs *ab initio* motif discovery with the user's choice of either, Clover, Rover, or Motifish. A simple motif scoring algorithm called Possum is used to compare motifs by calculating a log-likelihood ratio score for the motif at each location. This allows a report to be generated that not only presents motifs discovered by the pipeline, but also allows the user to quickly identify the distribution of the motifs within the source sequence and their representation (Figure 7). RSAT peak-motifs (Thomas-Chollier, et al., 2012) is a similar pipeline designed for ChIP-seq peak sequences. It provides a pre-filtering step, a custom motif algorithm supporting high-order background models, and direct comparison with motif databases such as JASPAR (Sandelin, Alkema, Engröm, Wasserman, & Lenhard, 2004) or a custom motif collection. The results can be exported as custom UCSC browser tracks, which may optionally include visualization of the peaks themselves.

A genome-wide approach is offered by Motif-Browser (Trutschl, Kilgore, Cvek, & Scott, 2014). MotifBrowser allows the submission of entire assemblies to the pipeline (possibly consisting of thousands of genes) and uses an aggregate classifier based off of Dispom to facilitate task-level parallelism. Each classifier (or *job*) divides the input into a series of randomly sampled subsets of the input genome called rounds using a method called bootstrap aggregation. Each round is run with its own instance of Dispom, with the caveat being that the subset cannot be expected to have the same distribution of motifs as the genome; however, this is mitigated through using a voting scheme to aggregate individual classifier results.

The reports generated by MotifBrowser allow users multiple avenues of investigation. Motifs may be browsed by order of representation or by the genes or chromosomes they are associated with. The summary for a particular motif lists the genes in which it occurs, while gene summary pages list the relative positions within the genes. Because this interface allows for the quick transition between motif and gene views, links to relevant genomic databases (such as Ensembl or Entrez) are made available for further investigation (Figure 8). There are alternate methods to query the report via as a context-free query language or by uploading a file listing relevant gene identifiers.

FUTURE RESEARCH DIRECTIONS

As we move forward, motif discovery becomes more and more complex; not just in finding and characterizing the motifs themselves but also in how they interact with one another. Additionally, motifs can be found not just as a linear sequence, but in the structural context of the macromolecule. Furthermore, the advent of whole genome sequencing is becoming more viable for more labs to achieve and the databases containing the data for many genomes are freely available. With these advances in motif complexity and number as well as the increase in sheer data volume; computational methods must also continue to advance. It is critical for there to be efficient and economical methods of mining the available data for motifs of interest in a timely manner that is widely accessible. Motifs can play a regulatory role in at all levels of biological function and as such advances in motif identification will have far reaching effects.

Figure 7. Extended information for CLOVER Output via MotifViz

CLOVER Results

Gene Regulation Hub

Color key: Broad-complex Broad-complex AP2alpha S8 Ubx SQUA SRF RXR-VDR Bsap Brachyury
TBP Irf-1 CF2-II Yin-Yang GATA-3 GATA-2 GATA-1 Tal1beta-E47S Myc-Max Max E4BP4 SU
░ = protein-coding

Over/Under-represented Motifs:

Motif	Overall Raw Score	P(userbgseq)
SRF	-5.01	0
RXR-VDR	-2.06	0
Brachyury	-2.94	0
SU	-1.09	0
GATA-1	-0.0993	0
GATA-3	-0.821	0
Yin-Yang	0.568	0.001
Max	-0.94	0.001
Myc-Max	-1.77	0.001
TBP	-2.12	0.002
GATA-2	-0.819	0.004
Tal1beta-E47S	-0.0676	0.005
CF2-II	-1.36	0.006
Bsap	1.1	0.007
Ubx	-1.32	0.993
SQUA	-1.02	0.996
E4BP4	-4.17	0.999
Broad-complex	-0.645	1
Broad-complex	0.292	1
S8	-1.52	1
Irf-1	-2.79	1
AP2alpha	0.214	1

Overview of Motif Distribution: (bar height = score)

For most of the methods we described, there is still plenty of room for improvement in the realms of accuracy and statistical significance. Although novel fundamental algorithms are occasionally introduced from time to time, the question of how to improve the accuracy of motif discovery tools has become much more prevalent. Newer projects (such as A-GLAM and Dispom) focus on inferring symbol distribution from the input (rather than assuming a fixed distribution). This approach is still relatively new in motif discovery tools, and it is likely that this will remain an active topic of research for several years to come.

A problem surrounding motif discovery tools is the difficulty in systematic assessing of their general fitness for a variety of tasks. Motifs are often short, but the sequences from which they are inferred may be longer than any candidate motif by two or three orders of magnitude, and there is usually substantial statistical noise in the source.

Figure 8. Using MotifBrowser to motif hits found in PHACTR4. This page was reached by searching for genes containing GCCCAGGCTGG, so instances of that motif are highlighted.

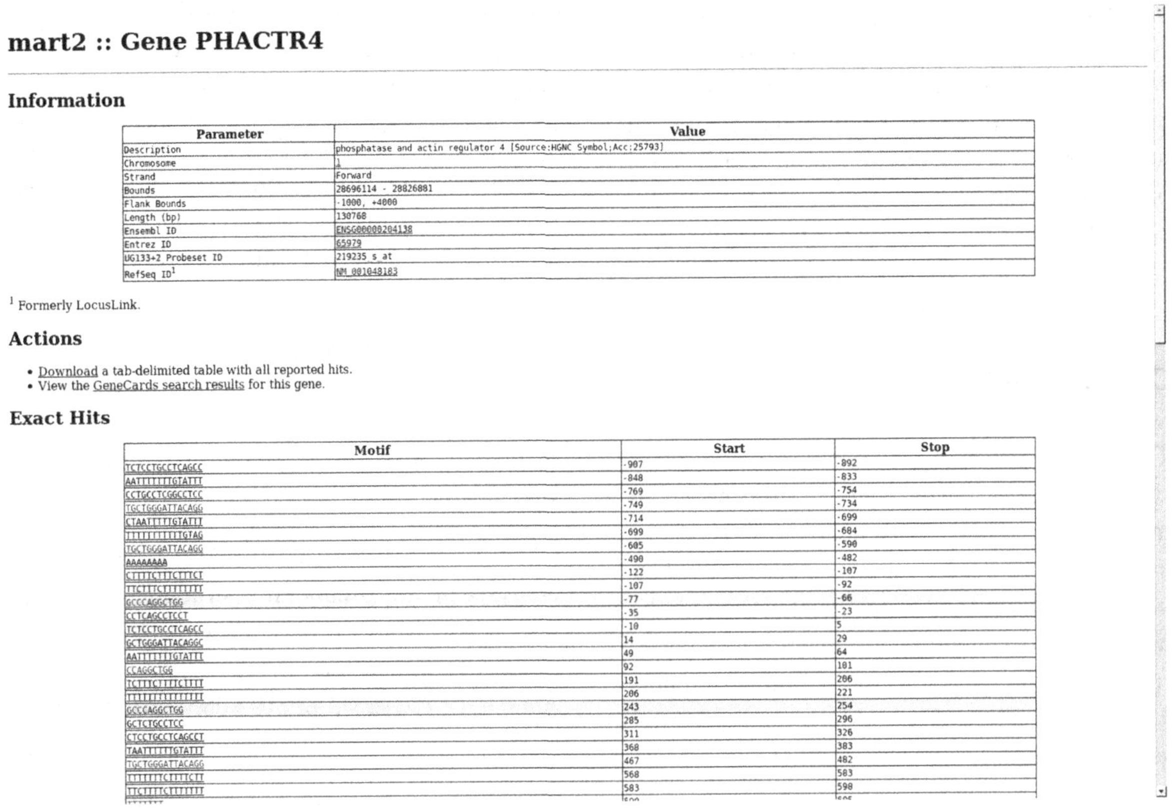

mart2 :: Gene PHACTR4

Information

Parameter	Value
Description	phosphatase and actin regulator 4 [Source:HGNC Symbol;Acc:25793]
Chromosome	1
Strand	Forward
Bounds	28696114 - 28826881
Flank Bounds	-1000, +4000
Length (bp)	130768
Ensembl ID	ENSG00000204138
Entrez ID	65979
UG133+2 Probeset ID	219235_s_at
RefSeq ID[1]	NM_001048183

[1] Formerly LocusLink.

Actions

- Download a tab-delimited table with all reported hits.
- View the GeneCards search results for this gene.

Exact Hits

Motif	Start	Stop
TCTCCTGCCTCAGCC	-907	-892
AATTTTTTTGTATTT	-848	-833
CCTGCCTCGGCCTCC	-769	-754
TGCTGGGATTACAGG	-749	-734
CTAATTTTTGTATTT	-714	-699
TTTTTTTTTTGTAG	-699	-684
TGCTGGGATTACAGG	-605	-590
AAAAAAAA	-490	-482
CTTTCTTTCTTTCT	-122	-107
TTCTTTCTTTTTTT	-107	-92
GCCCAGGCTGG	-77	-66
CCTCAGCCTCCT	-35	-23
TCTCCTGCCTCAGCC	-10	5
GCTGGGATTACAGGC	14	29
AATTTTTTTGTATTT	49	64
CCAGGCTGG	92	101
TCTTTCTTTTCTTTT	191	206
TTTTTTTTTTTTTT	206	221
GGCCAGGCTGG	243	254
GCTCTGCCTCC	285	296
CTCCTGCCTCAGCCT	311	326
TAATTTTTTGTATTT	368	383
TGCTGGGATTACAGG	467	482
TTTTTTTCTTTCTT	568	583
TTCTTTCTTTTTTT	583	598

Nonetheless, comprehensive assessment of tools available now is a relatively rare occurrence; most tools are assessed with a small number of input data sets where the motifs are known ahead of time. While this is a reasonable first step towards demonstrating classifier efficacy, a more exhaustive approach gives us a better idea of the relative performance of motif discovery tools since they may only work well when the data has a given set of attributes. It is possible that the small selection of data coincidentally happens to have these attributes (which the experimenter may be unaware of), so additional verification can demonstrate the actual strengths and weaknesses of the tool in question.

The increased availability of parallel computing will play a role in the development of new algorithms. Algorithms that were previously intractable due to running time or memory consumption may be possible to run on a computation cluster, where the workload may be distributed across several computers (compute nodes). The analogy is much like that of building a puzzle. A large puzzle may take a single person a comparatively long time to build; however, soliciting the help of a friend means that the puzzle could potentially be built in slightly more than half the time it would otherwise take. But like the puzzle-building analogy, parallelism implies some overhead, since it is occasionally necessary for compute nodes to share resources or depend on answers to subproblems calculated by other nodes. Leveraging parallel computing sometimes means choosing a suboptimal algorithm, since the most optimal ones may require constant synchronization.

We are now faced with the emergence of new technologies that not only provide much more voluminous input sets, but entirely new kinds of sequence data, such as bisulfite assays for genome methylation and chromatin immunoprecipitation (ChIP) assays for histone modification. Meanwhile, ontological databases and pathway analysis offer the possibility of leveraging data integration to answer questions regarding causality at the level of molecular interaction. Thus, scalable and accurate tools for both discovery and visualization are becoming increasingly important.

CONCLUSION

This chapter presented and demonstrated a series of tools for detection of sequence and amino acid motifs. The methods for de novo motif discovery can result in very large data sets that can be examined, summarized and supplemented through the use of curated databases. Visualization techniques further aid the analyst as motif finding remains a complex challenge for biologists and computer scientists alike.

REFERENCES

Arnold, P., Erb, I., Pachkov, M., Molina, N., & Nimwegen, E. (2012). MotEvo: Integrated Bayesian probabilistic methods for inferring regulatory sites and motifs on multiple alignments of DNA sequences. *Bioinformatics (Oxford, England)*, *28*(4), 487–494. doi:10.1093/bioinformatics/btr695 PMID:22334039

Bailey, T., & Elkan, C. (1994). Fitting a mixture model by expectation maximization to discovery motifs in biopolymers. In *Proc. 2nd. Intl. Conf. on Intell. Sys. for Mol. Bio.*, (pp. 28-36). Academic Press.

California Institute of Technology, Washington University of St. Louis & The Wellcome Trust Sanger Institute. (2013). *Mission Statement*. Retrieved Jan. 10, 2014, from WormBase: Nematode Information Resource: https://www.wormbase.org/about#0--10

Center for Disease Control. (2013, July 11). *CDC - Transmission Risk*. Retrieved Jan. 14, 2014, from CDC - HIV and the Law: http://www.cdc.gov/hiv/policies/law/risk.html

Center for Disease Control. (2013, August 16). *HIV, STD, & Teen Pregnancy Prevention*. Retrieved Jan. 17, 2014, from CDC - Sexual Risk Behavior: http://www.cdc.gov/HealthyYouth/sexualbehaviors/

Chen, J., & Greider, C. W. (2005). Functional analysis of the pseudoknot structure in human telomerase RNA. *Proceedings of the National Academy of Sciences of the United States of America*, *102*(23), 8080–8085. doi:10.1073/pnas.0502259102 PMID:15849264

Clancy, S. (2008). DNA Transcription. *Nature Education*, *1*(1), 41.

Dahiya, A., Gavin, M., Luo, R., & Dean, D. (2000). Role of the LXCXE Binding Site in Rb Function. *Molecular and Cellular Biology*, *20*(18), 6799–6805. doi:10.1128/MCB.20.18.6799-6805.2000 PMID:10958676

Dempster, A. P., Laird, N. M., & Rubin, D. B. (1977). Maximum Likelihood from Incomplete Data via the EM Algorithm. *Journal of the Royal Statistical Society. Series A (General)*, *39*(1), 1–38.

Department of Health Services. (2014). *Respiratory virus surveillance report for the week ending January 4, 2014*. Department of Health Services.

Eddy, S., & Durbin, R. (1994). RNA sequence analysis using covariance models. *Nucleic Acids Research*, 22(11), 2079–2088. doi:10.1093/nar/22.11.2079 PMID:8029015

European Bioinformatics Institute & Wellcome Trust Sanger Institute. (2013, December). *About the Ensembl Project*. Retrieved Jan. 10, 2014, from Ensembl Genome Browser: http://useast.ensembl.org/info/about/index.html

European Molecular Biology Laboratory. (2014). *EMBL History*. Retrieved Jan. 10, 2014, from EMBL Heidelberg - The European Molecular Biology Laboratory: http://www.embl.de/aboutus/general_information/history/

Fleischmann, R., & Adams, M., White, O., Clayton. (1995). Whole genome random sequencing and assembly of Hoemophilus influenzae. *Rd. Sci.*, 269(5223), 496–512. PMID:7542800

Frifth, M., Hansen, U., Spouge, J., & Weng, Z. (2003). Finding functional sequence elements by multiple local alignment. *Nucleic Acids Research*, 32(1), 189–200. doi:10.1093/nar/gkh169 PMID:14704356

Frifth, M., Saunders, N., Kobe, B., & Bailey, T. (2008). Discoverying Sequence Motifs with Arbitrary Insertions and Deletions. *PLoS Computational Biology*, 4(5), e1000071. doi:10.1371/journal.pcbi.1000071 PMID:18437229

Fu, Y., Frith, M. C., Haverty, P. M., & Weng, Z. (2004). MotifViz: An analysis and visualization tool for motif discovery. *Nucleic Acids Research*, 32(suppl 2), 420–423. doi:10.1093/nar/gkh426 PMID:15215422

Geman, S., & Geman, D. (1984). Stochastic Relaxation, Gibbs Distributions, and the Bayesian Restoration of Images. *IEEE Transactions on Pattern Analysis and Machine Intelligence*, 6(6), 721–741. doi:10.1109/TPAMI.1984.4767596 PMID:22499653

Grunberg-Manago, M., Ortiz, P. J., & Ochoa, S. (1956). Enzymic synthesis of polynucleotides I. polynucleotide phosphorylase of Azotobacter vinelandii. *Biochimica et Biophysica Acta*, 20, 269–285. doi:10.1016/0006-3002(56)90286-4 PMID:13315374

Jacob, F., Perrin, D., Sanchez, C., & Monod, J. (1960). L'opéeron: Groupe de gènes à expression coordonnée par un opérateur. *Compt. Rend.*, 1727-1729.

Keilwagen, J., Grau, J., Paonov, I. A., Posch, S., Strickert, M., & Große, I. (2011). Dispom: A discriminitive de-novo discovery tool based on the JStacs library. *PLOS Comput. Bio.*, 7(2).

Kim, J., Cole, J., & Pramanik, S. (1996). Alignment of possible secondary structures in multiple RNA sequences using simulated annealing. *Computer Applications in the Biosciences*, 12(4), 259–267. PMID:8902352

Lawrence, C. A., Boguski, M., Liu, J., Neuwald, A., & Wooten, J. (1993). Detecting subtle sequence signals: A Gibbs sampling strategy for multiple alignment. *Science*, 262(5131), 208–214. doi:10.1126/science.8211139 PMID:8211139

Levine, M., & Tjian, R. (2003). Transcription regulation and animal diversity. *Nature*, 424(6945), 147–151. doi:10.1038/nature01763 PMID:12853946

Liu, J. S. (1994). The Collapsed Gibbs Sampler in Bayesian Computations with Applications to a Gene Regulation Problem. *Journal of the American Statistical Association*, 89(427), 958–966. doi:10.1080/01621459.1994.10476829

Mariño-Ramírez, L., Sheetlin, S., Landsman, D., & Spouge, J. (2005). Alignments anchored on genomic landmarks can aid in the identification of regulatory elements. *Bioinformatics, 21*(suppl 1), i440-i448.

Metropolis, N., Rosenbluth, A. W., Rosenbluth, M. N., Teller, A. H., & Teller, E. (1953). Equation of state calculations by fast computing machines. *The Journal of Chemical Physics*, 1807–1813.

National Center for Biotechnology Information. (2004, May 21). *Programs and Activities*. Retrieved Jan. 10, 2014, from National Center for Biotechnology Information: http://www.ncbi.nlm. nih.gov/About/glance/programs.html

Nawrocki, E. P., & Eddy, S. (2013). Infernal 1.1: 100-fold faster RNA homology searches. *Bioinformatics (Oxford, England)*, 29(22), 2933–2935. doi:10.1093/bioinformatics/btt509 PMID:24008419

Notredame, C., O'Brien, E., & Higgins, D. (1997). RAGA: RNA sequence alignment by genetic algorithm. *Nucleic Acids Research*, 25(22), 4570–4580. doi:10.1093/nar/25.22.4570 PMID:9358168

Pribnow, D. (1975). Nucleotide sequence of an RNA polymerase binding site at an early T7 promoter. *Proceedings of the National Academy of Sciences of the United States of America*, 72(3), 785–788. doi:10.1073/pnas.72.3.784 PMID:1093168

Pruitt, K. D., Tatusova, T., & Maglott, D. R. (2005, January 1). NCBI Reference Sequence (RefSeq): A curated non-redundant sequence database of genomes, transcripts and proteins. *Nucleic Acids Research*, 33, D501–D504. doi:10.1093/nar/ gki025 PMID:15608248

Rapin, N., Hoor, I., Lund, O., & Nielsen, M. (2010). The MHC Motif Viewer: A Visualization Tool for the MHC Binding Motifs. *Current Protocols in Immunology*, 18(17). doi:10.1002/0471142735. im1817s88 PMID:20143317

Redhead, E., & Bailey, T. (2007). Discriminative motif discovery in DNA and protein sequences using the DEME algorithm. *BMC Bioinformatics*, 8(1), 385–404. doi:10.1186/1471-2105-8-385 PMID:17937785

Rifton, L. P., Goldberg, M. L., Karp, R. W., & Hogness, D. (1978). The organization of the histone genes in Drosiphila melanogaster. *Cold Spring Harbor Symposia on Quantitative Biology*, 42(2), 1047–1051. PMID:98262

Sandelin, A., Alkema, W., Engröm, P., Wasserman, W. W., & Lenhard, B. (2004). JASPAR: An open-access database for eukaryotic transcription factory binding profiles. *Nucleic Acids Research*, 32(suppl 1), 91–94. doi:10.1093/nar/gkh012

Schacker, T., Collier, A., Hughes, J., Shea, T., & Corey, L. (1996). Clinical and epidemiologic features of primary HIV infection. *Annals of Internal Medicine*, 125(4), 257–264. doi:10.7326/0003-4819-125-4-199608150-00001 PMID:8678387

Scheider, T. D., & Stephens, R. M. (1990). Sequence Logos: A New Way to Display Consensus Sequences. *Nucleic Acids Research*, 18(20), 6097–6100. doi:10.1093/nar/18.20.6097 PMID:2172928

Schuler, G., Altschul, S., & Lipman, D. (1991). A workbench for multiple alignment construction and analysis. *Proteins*, 9(3), 180–190. doi:10.1002/ prot.340090304 PMID:2006136

Shida, K. (2006). GibbsST: A Gibbs sampling method for motif discovery with enhanced resistance to local optima. *BMC Bioinformatics*, 7(1), 486–504. doi:10.1186/1471-2105-7-486 PMID:17083740

Siddharthan, R., Siggia, E., & van Nimwegen, E. (2005). PhyloGibbs: A Gibbs Sampling Motif Finder That Incorporates Phylogeny. *PLoS Computational Biology*, 1(7), e67. doi:10.1371/journal. pcbi.0010067 PMID:16477324

Sigrist, C., de Castro, E., Cerutti, L., Cuche, B., Hulo, N., & Bridge, A. et al. (2013). New and continuing developments at PROSITE. *Nucleic Acids Research*, 41(D1), D344–D337. doi:10.1093/nar/ gks1067 PMID:23161676

Smith, A., Sumazin, P., & Zhang, M. (2004). Identifying tissue-selective transcription factor binding sites in vertebrate promoters. *Proceedings of the National Academy of Sciences of the United States of America*, *102*(5), 1560–1565. doi:10.1073/pnas.0406123102 PMID:15668401

Thomas-Chollier, M., Herrmann, C., Defrance, M., Sand, O., Thieffry, D., & Helden, J. (2012). RSAT peak-motifs: Motif-analysis in full-size ChIP-seq datasets. *Nucleic Acids Research*, *40*(4), e31. doi:10.1093/nar/gkr1104 PMID:22156162

Thompson, W., Rouchka, E., & Lawrence, C. (2003). Gibbs Recursive Sampler: Finding transcription factor binding sites. *Nucleic Acids Research*, *31*(13), 3580–3585. doi:10.1093/nar/gkg608 PMID:12824370

Trutschl, M., Kilgore, P., Cvek, U., & Scott, R. (2014). Scalable Genome-Wide Discovery and Presentation of Motifs. In *Proceedings of 6th Int. Conf. on Bioinf. and Bio. Comp.* Las Vegas, NV: International Society for Computers and their Applications.

Tyndall, M. W., Patrick, D., Spittal, P., Li, K., O'Shaughnessy, M. V., & Schechter, T. (2002). Risky sexual behaviours among injection drugs users with high HIV prevalence: Implications for STD control. *Sexually Transmitted Infections*, *78*(suppl. 1), i170–i175. doi:10.1136/sti.78.suppl_1.i170 PMID:12083439

UniProt Consortium. (2014). *About UniProt*. Retrieved Jan. 10, 2014, from UniProtKB: http://www.uniprot.org/help/about

Watkins, K., Metzger, B. A., Woody, G., & McLellan, A. T. (1992). High-Risk Sexual Behaviors of Intravenous Drug Users In- and Out-of-Treatment: Implications for the Spread of HIV Infection. *The American Journal of Drug and Alcohol Abuse*, *18*(4), 389–398. doi:10.3109/00952999209051037 PMID:1449121

Yao, Z., Weinberg, Z., & Ruzzo, W. L. (2006). CMfinder - a covariance model based RNA motif finding algorithm. *Bioinformatics (Oxford, England)*, *22*(4), 445–452. doi:10.1093/bioinformatics/btk008 PMID:16357030

ADDITIONAL READING

Bailey, T. L. (2008). Discovering sequence motifs. *Methods in Molecular Biology (Clifton, N.J.)*, *452*, 231–251. doi:10.1007/978-1-60327-159-2_12 PMID:18566768

Cerveny, L., Straskova, A., Dankova, V., Hartlova, A., Ceckova, M., Staud, F., & Stulik, J. (2013). Tetratricopeptide repeat motifs in the world of bacterial pathogens: Role in virulence mechanisms. *Infection and Immunity*, *81*(3), 629–635. doi:10.1128/IAI.01035-12 PMID:23264049

Church, P. C., Goscinski, A., Holt, K., Inouye, M., Ghoting, A., Makarychev, K., & Reumann, M. (2011). Design of multiple sequence alignment algorithms on parallel, distributed memory supercomputers. Conf. Proc. IEEE Eng. Med. Biol. Soc., 924-927. Boston: Institute of Electrical and Electronics Engineers. doi:10.1109/IEMBS.2011.6090208

Ding, Y., Tang, Y., Kwok, C. K., Zhang, Y., Bevilacqua, P. C., & Assmann, S. M. (2013). In vivo genome-wide profiling of RNA secondary structure reveals novel regulatory features. *Nature*, *505*(7485), 696–700. doi:10.1038/nature12756 PMID:24270811

ENCODE Project Consortium, Bernstein, B.E., Birney, E., Dunham, I., Green, E.D., Gunter, C., & Snyder, M. (2012). An integrated encyclopedia of DNA elements in the human genome. *Nature*. *489(7414)*, 57-74.

Girgis, H. Z., & Ovcharenko, I. (2012). Predicting tissue specific cis-regulatory modules in the human genome using pairs of co-occuring motifs. *BMC Bioinformatics, 13*(1), 25–42. doi:10.1186/1471-2105-13-25 PMID:22313678

Grunstein, M. (1997). Histone acetylation in chromatin structure and transcription. *Nature, 389*(6649), 349–352. doi:10.1038/38664 PMID:9311776

Han, J., & Kamber, M. (2001). *Data Mining: Concepts and Techniques*. San Francisco: Morgan Kaufmann.

Johnson, L. M., Du, J., Hale, C. J., Bischof, S., Feng, S., & Chodavarapu, R. K. et al. (2014). SRA- and SET-domain-containing proteins link RNA polymerase V occupancy to DNA methylation. *Nature, 507*(7490), 124–128. doi:10.1038/nature12931 PMID:24463519

Jones, N. C., & Pevzner, P. A. (2004). *Finding Regulatory Motifs in DNA Sequences. An Introduction to Bioinformatics Algorithms (Computational Molecular Biology)*. MIT Press.

Kim, S. Y., & Kim, Y. (2006). Genome-wide prediction of transcriptional regulatory elements of human promoters using gene expression and promoter analysis data. *BMC Bioinformatics, 7*(1), 330–342. doi:10.1186/1471-2105-7-330 PMID:16817975

Lickwar, C. R., Mueller, F., Hanlon, S. E., McNally, J. G., & Lieb, J. D. (2012). Genome-wide protein–DNA binding dynamics suggest a molecular clutch for transcription factor function. *Nature, 484*(7393), 251–255. doi:10.1038/nature10985 PMID:22498630

Loots, G. G., & Ovcharenko, I. (2007). ECRbase: Database of Evolutionary Conserved Regions, Promoters, and Transcription Factory Binding Sites in Vertebrate Genomes. *Bioinformatics (Oxford, England), 23*(1), 122–124. doi:10.1093/bioinformatics/btl546 PMID:17090579

Matys, V., Kel-Margoulis, O.V., Fricke, E., Liebich, I., Land, S., Barre-Dirrie et al. (2006). TRANSFAC and its module TRANSCompel: transcriptional gene regulation in eukaryotes. *Nucl. Acids Res. 1(34, Database issue)*, D108-110.

McDonel, P., Jans, J., Peterson, B. K., & Meyer, B. J. (2006). Clustered DNA motifs mark X chromosomes for repression by a dosage compensation complex. *Nature, 444*(7119), 614–618. doi:10.1038/nature05338 PMID:17122774

Ovcharenko, I. & Nobrega, M.A. (2005). Identifying synonymous regulatory elements in vertebrate genomes. *Nucl. Acids Res. 33(Web Server Issue)*, W403-W407.

Ovcharenko, I., Nobrega, M.A., Loots, G.G., & Stubbs, L. (2004). ECR Browser: a tool for visualizing and accessing data from comparisons of multiple vertebrate genomes. *Nucl. Acids Res. 32(Web Server Issue)*, W280-W286.

Portales-Casamar, E., Thongjuea, S., Kwon, A. T., Arenillas, D., Zhao, X., & Valen, E. et al. (2010). JASPAR 2010: The greatly expanded open-access database of transcription factor binding profiles. *Nucleic Acids Research, 38*(Database issue), D105–D110. doi:10.1093/nar/gkp950 PMID:19906716

Ray, D., Kazan, H., Cook, K. B., Weirauch, M. T., Najafabadi, H. S., & Li, X. et al. (2013). A compendium of RNA-binding motifs for decoding gene regulation. *Nature, 499*(7457), 172–177. doi:10.1038/nature12311 PMID:23846655

Rhee, H. S., & Pugh, B. J. (2011). Comprehensive Genome-wide Protein-DNA Interactions Detected at Single-Nucleotide Resolution. *Cell, 147*(6), 1408–1419. doi:10.1016/j.cell.2011.11.013 PMID:22153082

Rognes, T. (2001). ParAlign: A parallel sequence alignment algorithm for rapid and sensitive database searches. *Nucleic Acids Research, 29*(7), 647–1652. doi:10.1093/nar/29.7.1647 PMID:11266569

Ryan, C. J., Cimermančič, P., Szpiech, Z. A., Sali, A., Hernandez, R. D., & Krogan, N. J. (2013). High-resolution network biology: Connecting sequence with function. *Nature Reviews. Genetics*, *14*(12), 865–879. doi:10.1038/nrg3574 PMID:24197012

Sigrist, C. J., de Castro, E., Cerutti, L., Cuche, B. A., Hulo, N., & Bridge, A. et al. (2013). New and continuing developments at PROSITE. *Nucleic Acids Research*, *41*(Database issue), D344–D347. doi:10.1093/nar/gks1067 PMID:23161676

Spence, R. (2007). *Information Visualization: Design for Interaction* (2nd ed.). Harlow, Essex: Pearson Education Limited.

Stormo, G. D. (2000). DNA binding sites: Representation and discovery. *Bioinformatics (Oxford, England)*, *16*(1), 16–23. doi:10.1093/bioinformatics/16.1.16 PMID:10812473

Thompson, W., Palumbo, M. J., Wasserman, W. W., Liu, J. S., & Lawrence, C. E. (2004). Decoding human regulatory circuits. *Genome Research*, *14*(10a10A), 1967–1974. doi:10.1101/gr.2589004 PMID:15466295

Tompa, M., Li, N., Bailey, T. L., Church, G. M., De Moor, B., & Eskin, E. et al. (2005). Assessing computational tools for the discovery of transcription factor binding sites. *Nature Biotechnology*, *23*(1), 137–144. doi:10.1038/nbt1053 PMID:15637633

Wang, J., Zhuang, J., Iyer, S., Lin, X. Y., Whitfield, T. W., & Greven, M. C. et al. (2012). Sequence features and chromatin structure around the genomic regions bound by 119 human transcription factors. *Genetical Research*, *22*(9), 1798–1812. doi:10.1101/gr.139105.112 PMID:22955990

Yang, L., Zhou, T., Dror, I., Mathelier, A., Wasserman, W. W., Gordân, R., & Rohs, R. (2014). TFBSshape: A motif database for DNA shape features of transcription factor binding sites. *Nucleic Acids Research*, *42*(1), D148–D155. doi:10.1093/nar/gkt1087 PMID:24214955

Zaki, M. J. (2000). Sequence Mining in Categorical Domains: Incorporating Constraints. In *Proc. 9th Intl. Conf. on Inf. and Knowl. Manag.*, 422-429. doi:10.1145/354756.354849

Zambelli, F., Pesole, G., & Pavesi, G. (2013). Motif discovery and transcription factor binding sites before and after the next-generation sequencing era. *Briefings in Bioinformatics*, *14*(2), 225–237. doi:10.1093/bib/bbs016 PMID:22517426

Zvelebil, M., & Baum, J. O. (2007). *Understanding Bioinformatics*. New York: Garland Science.

KEY TERMS AND DEFINITIONS

Algorithm: A list of well-defined steps for evaluating a calculation.

Classifier: An algorithm which infers the classification of a new, unlabeled record (usually on the basis of a training set).

Covariance Model: A generalization of the hidden Markov model that serves as a minimal automaton for a subset of stochastic context-free grammars.

Gibbs Sampler: A special case of the Markov Chain Monte Carlo algorithm for obtaining a sequence of samples from a multivariate probability distribution when sampling is difficult.

Markov Chain Monte Carlo: A class of algorithms for sampling from probability distributions based on the construction of a Markov chain with the desired probability distribution at equilibrium.

Motif: A short nucleotide or amino acid sequence with some biological significance.

Promoter: A DNA sequence that regulates the initiation of transcription of nearby genes.

Sequence Alignment: The process of combining two or more sequences to discover common positional elements between them. The alignment of two sequences is called a pairwise sequence alignment (PSAs), while those with more than two are called multiple sequence alignments (MSAs).

Transcription Factor: A regulatory element (such as a protein) that binds to a transcription factor binding site (TFBS) to control gene transcription.

Transcription: The process by which a segment of DNA is copied into an equivalent RNA polymer via enzymes such as RNA polymerase.

Chapter 6
Observer–Biased Analysis of Gene Expression Profiles

Paulo Fazendeiro
Instituto de Telecomunicações (IT), Portugal

José Valente de Oliveira
University of Algarve, Portugal

ABSTRACT

Microarray generated gene expression data are characterized by their volume and by the intrinsic background noise. The main task of revealing patterns in gene expression data is typically carried out using clustering analysis, with soft clustering leading the more promising candidate methods. In this chapter, Fuzzy C-Means with a variable Focal Point (FCMFP) is exploited as the first stage in gene expression data analysis. FCMFP is inspired by the observation that the visual perception of a group of similar objects is (highly) dependent on the observer position. This metaphor is used to provide a new analysis insight, with different levels of granularity, over a gene expression dataset.

INTRODUCTION

A gene usually corresponds to a sequence used in the production of a specific protein or ribonucleic acid (RNA) molecule. It is a region of deoxyribonucleic acid (DNA) that controls a hereditary characteristic. A gene carries biological information in a form that must be copied and transmitted from each cell to all its progeny. Each gene has a fixed location on its chromosome and helps to specify a trait. Defective genes may cause diseases hence they need to be identified. Despite some evidences pointing that microarray technology is slowly being phased out in favor of several next-generation sequencing methods (Ozsolak & Milos, 2011; Wang, Gerstein, & Snyder, 2009) DNA microarrays are commonly being used in first-tier clinical testing (Riggs, 2014) and still are essential tools for various genomic studies, e.g. (Belfield, 2014; Sanmann, 2013; Nylund, 2013). This technique is providing a wealth of data on global patterns of gene expression. Currently, efforts are being made to describe and understand the global view of these patterns, *i.e.*, trying to uncover the hidden structures in gene expression data.

Gene expression refers to transcription levels of genes. The expression level refers to the amount of messenger RNA (mRNA) in a gene, which is the

DOI: 10.4018/978-1-4666-6611-5.ch006

transcription of an activated gene that is later translated into a protein. A wide range of approaches are being use to measure gene expression levels. These methods, which fall under the category of microarrays technology, include cDNA microarray (Schena et al., 1996a; Schena et al., 1996b) and oligonucleotide microarray (Fodor et al., 1993; Lipshutz et al., 2000). Gene expression profiling can also be performed using serial analysis of gene expression (SAGE) (Velculescu et al., 1997) and reverse transcription-polymerase chain reaction (RT-PCR) (Somogyi et al., 1995).

The analysis of microarrays generated data remains a quite challenging task. According to (Simon, 2008) gene expression profiling offers both a great opportunity for new kinds of investigation and great risk of error because it provides a high-dimensional read-out for each specimen assayed. The datasets are typically large with large background noise, cf. (Chu et al., 1998). The yeast cell cycle dataset analysed in this chapter is one relevant example of such datasets.

Clustering is usually the first step in gene expression data analysis (Jiang, Tang & Zhang, 2004). Apart from gene expression, clustering plays a major role in data mining applications such as information retrieval and text mining, web analysis, scientific data exploration, spatial database applications, CRM and marketing, image processing and recognition systems, medical diagnostics and computational biology, just to mention a few (de Oliveira & Pedrycz, 2007; Soowhan, Lee & Pedrycz, 2009; Ming, Kiong & Soong, 2011; Zhang & Lu, 2010; Chaira, 2011).

In the past, various techniques have been used for gene expression microarray data analysis such as K-means (Tavazoie et al., 1999; Richards et al., 2008), hierarchical clustering (Eisen et al., 1998; Lein et al., 2007; Finak et al., 2008), self-organizing maps (Tamayo et al., 1999; Ghouila et al. 2009), graph-theoretic approaches (Amir & Zohar, 1999; Huttenhower et al., 2007), and fuzzy c-means (FCM) (Futschik & Carlisle, 2005;

Dembélé & Kastner; 2003). A recent review of these and other techniques can be found in (Pirim et al. 2012).

Most of the clustering methods used in gene expression analysis fall in the category of the hard clustering methods. One gene belongs to exactly one cluster. These methods implicitly assume that the clusters are well separated, which is hardly the case in gene expression data, with several biological studies reporting no clear boundaries between clusters. Moreover, hard clustering methods appear to detect clusters even in gene expression randomised data, cf. (Futschik, & Carlisle, 2005). By allowing one gene to belong, with different degree of membership, to more than one cluster, soft clustering allows to identify meaningful, biologically relevant, clusters. In this chapter we further exploited soft clustering for gene expression analysis by applying the fuzzy C-means with a variable focal point (FCMFP) algorithm (Fazendeiro & de Oliveira, 2014; Fazendeiro & de Oliveira, 2008) to the analysis of gene expression data of yeast cell cycle.

FCMFP is inspired in the following everyday live observation: The position at which the observer is located relatively to a set of objects determines how the observer perceives these objects. Suppose that the observer is located far away from the objects. In this case, and due to the observation distance objects tend to be undistinguishable, that is, objects tend to be seen as a single cluster. As the observer gets closer and closer to the objects the differences between them tend to become clearer and clearer. The initial single cluster tends to split in a number of clusters which is becoming higher and higher and eventually becomes equal to the number of objects. The authors have integrated this metaphor into the popular FCM algorithm. This is accomplished by incorporating a focal point and a zoom factor into the original FCM objective function. The focal point represents the point where the observer is located relatively to the objects to be clustered. The zoom factor acts in the same way a zoom lens does, that is, it approximates or moves away the observed objects (Fazendeiro & de Oliveira, 2014).

In this chapter, FCMFP is used to offer a wider perspective, with different levels of granularity, on the gene expression dataset. The produced results are validated by a cluster validity measure. A subset of yeast gene expression is used to compare the performance of the algorithm with the results available in the literature. The obtained number of clusters for this datasets is consistent with those found in the literature, the quality of the cluster partition being, in general, better. FCMFP is also used to identify the valid number of clusters existent within a 2951 genes yeast cell cycle gene expression dataset, for which there is no consensual best number of clusters.

The remaining of the chapter is organized as follows. In the next section a brief review on partitional fuzzy clustering is provided. Next a formalization of the FCMFP algorithm, as well as the necessary details to its implementation, is presented. Afterwards in the illustrative results we compare the performance of the FCMFP algorithm with existent results and emphasize its capability to produce solutions with a different granularuty level. The last section ends the chapter by summarizing the main conclusions.

BACKGROUND

Clustering Analysis

Informally, clustering can be viewed as the process of grouping a collection of objects into groups (clusters) in such a way that items which are grouped under the same cluster have a high level of similarity, usually measured in terms of a distance function, while items in different groups have a high level of dissimilarity (de Oliveira & Pedrycz, 2007). Clustering is thus an unsupervised learning process that aims at identifying the otherwise unlabelled structure of data for which the

definition of a distance measure plays a key role in the evaluation of different clustering solutions of gene expression profiles (Priness et al., 2007).

Clustering algorithms can be broadly classified in two types: i) hierarchical clustering, and ii) objective function based clustering, or partitional clustering. The later type can be further categorized into soft (fuzzy) and hard (crisp) clustering.

Partitional clustering algorithms minimize an objective function. The crisp clustering method assigns each data item to a unique cluster, that with the smallest distance between the datum and the cluster centroid. On the other hand, soft clustering methods allow overlapping clusters by assigning membership values of a data item to one or more clusters; a small distance value between the data item and the cluster centroid corresponds to a higher degree of membership of the datum to the cluster.

Fuzzy C-Means

Fuzzy C-means algorithm (FCM) is probably the most popular and widely used soft clustering algorithm. It allows for overlapping clusters by letting items to belong to different clusters with a variable degree of membership.

The large noise component in microarray data, as the result of biological and experimental factors, makes FCM particularly interesting for gene expression data analysis (Futschik & Carlisle, 2005; Dembélé & Kastner; 2003). The activity of genes can show large variations under minor changes in the experimental conditions. Numerous steps in the experimental procedure contribute to additional noise and bias. Though filtering the expression data may improve the quality of the results created by hard clustering, the noise still remains a problem (Futschik & Carlisle, 2005). To this end FCM may be a valuable alternative due to the robustness obtained by overlapping clusters. A single gene is usually involved in multiple functions. This behaviour is better handled by FCM as it allows genes to belong to different clusters with different degree of membership. Moreover unlike hard partition clustering algorithms, which lack a mechanism to show sub-structures in clusters, FCM allows for the assessment of the degree of cohesion within a single cluster using the degrees of membership.

Formally, FCM minimizes the objective function J_m (1) for a specified number of cluster c and a given set of observations

$$X = \left\{ x_1, x_2, \ldots, x_n \right\} \in \mathbb{R}^d :$$

$$J_m = \sum_{i=1}^{c} \sum_{j=1}^{n} u_{ij}^m \left\| x_j - v_i \right\|^2 \qquad (1)$$

where u_{ij} represents the membership of observation x_j ($j=1,..,n$) in the i-th cluster ($i=1,..,c$), v_i refers to the centroid of the i-th cluster, ||.|| stands for a norm distance in $\mathbb{R}^d$, $m>1$ being the so-called fuzziness parameter. An increase in m leads to an increase of fuzziness in the degree of membership values of each datum allowing items to belong to as many classes as needed.

The most popular and effective method to minimize the constrained objective function (1) consists in resourcing to a technique known as alternate optimization. This means that one set of parameters is considered fixed while the other is being optimized. Next, from iteration to iteration, the two sets of parameters exchange roles. In this case the two sets of parameters are the prototypes $V = [v_i]$ ($i=1,..,c$) and the partition matrix U, $U = [u_{ij}]c \times n$. Thus, for a fuzzy partition given by (U, V), FCM tries to optimize $J(U, V:X)$ through an iterative process where in each iteration, the centroid of the i-th cluster is updated by:

$$v_i = \frac{\sum_{j=1}^{n} u_{ij}^m x_j}{\sum_{j=1}^{n} u_{ij}^m}. \qquad (2)$$

As can be seen from the equation above the centroids are computed as weighted averages of the data items using the degree of membership u_{ij} as weights. Unlike crisp c-means where the value of u_{ij} is either zero or one, leading the centroids to be the arithmetic mean of the items assigned to the clusters (as the non-members will be zero), FCM uses the degree of membership. Higher degree of membership highly affects the value of the centroid while low degree of membership leaves an insignificant effect on the centroid.

The elements of the partition matrix, u_{ij}, i.e. the membership degrees are computed as follows, considering $I_j = \{i \,|x_j\text{-}v_i = 0\}$:

$$u_{ij} = \begin{cases} \dfrac{1}{\sum\limits_{k=1}^{c} \left(\dfrac{\left\| x_j - v_i \right\|}{\left\| x_j - v_k \right\|} \right)^{\frac{2}{m-1}}}, & I_j = \phi \\[4ex] \dfrac{1}{\mid I_j \mid}, & I_j \neq \phi, \; i \in I_j \\[3ex] 0, & I_j \neq \phi, \; i \in I_j \end{cases} \qquad (3)$$

Subjected to the following constraints:

$$u_{ij} \in \left[0, 1\right], \quad \sum_{j=1}^{n} u_{ij} > 0, \quad \sum_{i=1}^{c} u_{ij} = 1 \qquad (4)$$

Conditions (4) induce a fuzzy partition in the strict sense; assure that every datum has a similar global weight on the data set, and guarantee that none of the c clusters is empty, thus implying a cluster partition with no less than c clusters.

In general FCM gives information on the intra-cluster variation by stating the degree to which an item belongs to a cluster. It is also noise robust making it a good choice for noisy data like microarray gene expression (Futschik & Carlisle, 2005). However, specifying the number of clusters remains a problem. Moreover the specification of the fuzziness coefficient, *m*, which affects the performance of the algorithm, represents an additional drawback.

FUZZY CLUSTERING WITH A FOCAL POINT

This section presents a method to provide different views over the data. The proposed algorithm provides an efficient sampling process from which it is selected the more promising clustering results according to the used validity index. The proposed method is inspired by the following observer metaphor. The visual perception of a group of objects depends on the observer position. It is evident that as an observer gets away from a group of objects the tendency is to perceive these objects as a single entity. On the other hand, as the observer approaches the objects a clearer view of the existing grouping starts to emerge. The closer an observer gets to the objects the greater the number of groups will appear. In the extreme case, each object becomes itself a singleton group.

Fuzzy C-Means with a Variable Focal Point (FCMFP)

The FCMFP clustering algorithm is a derivative of Fuzzy C-means that attempts to mimic the way human beings perceive clusters of objects (Fazendeiro & de Oliveira, 2014). It is evident that as an observer goes far away from a group of objects there is a tendency to perceive them as a single entity. On the other hand, as the observer starts to move closer to the objects a clear view of the existing grouping starts to emerge. Zooming in (and out) through the Milk Way or through a city in Google earth shows exactly the described effect. Thus, the closer an observer gets to the objects the greater the number of groups that will appear. In the extreme case each object becomes a cluster.

The FCMFP algorithm is based on the above-mentioned metaphor and aims at integrating the human way of visualization of objects into the clustering process. This is accomplished by incorporating into the objective function of FCM both a Focal Point *P* and a zoom factor δ. The Focal Point is the point at which the observer is located relatively to the data to be clustered. Typically, but not necessarily, *P* is set to the data barycentre (Fazendeiro & de Oliveira, 2008). The zoom factor is used to adjust the distance of the focal point to the data. This allows the observation of the data from a given direction at variable distance. Thus, δ the can be conceptualized as a weight affecting the distance between *P* and the dataset. For increasingly large values of δ, more prototypes are attracted, resulting in fewer prototypes that contain a larger number of items. On the other hand, as δ decreases the higher becomes the number of clusters. If the number of clusters is fixed to be equal to the number of items, for $\delta = 0$ the corresponding effect will be that of an observer that is so close to the data that each object is regarded as a cluster. FCMFP results from a constrained nonlinear optimization problem which likewise FCM doesn't have a closed analytical solution. Thus alternate optimization is also used.

More formally, FCMFP results from an optimization problem that minimizes the function J_{FP} (5) for a given focal point *P* and zoom factor δ, with reasonably high initial number of cluster *c* (typically $c \cong \sqrt{n}$):

$$J_{FP} = \sum_{i=1}^{c}\sum_{j=1}^{n} u_{ij}^{m} \left\| x_j - v_i \right\|^2 + \delta \sum_{i=1}^{c} \left\| v_i - P \right\|^2 , \delta \geq 0$$

$$(5)$$

where, as before, v_i is the *i*-th centroid, u_{ij} refers to the degree of membership of observation *j* in cluster *i*, ||.|| denotes a norm distance in R^d, *P* is the focal point, $\delta \geq 0$ is the zoom factor, *m* being the fuzziness parameter.

For a fuzzy partition given by (U, V), FCMFP tries to optimize $J_{FP}(U, V: X)$ through an iterative process where the centroids are updated based on the following equation:

$$v_i = \frac{\sum_{j=1}^{n} u_{ij}^m x_j + \delta P}{\sum_{j=1}^{n} u_{ij}^m + \delta}. \quad (6)$$

As can be seen from the equation above the centroids are computed as weighted averages of the data items using the degree of membership as weights with the bias just introduced i.e. the focal point multiplied by the zoom factor. Curiously enough, the membership vales have the same updating expression (3) as for the FCM algorithm, what makes the proposed algorithm computationally comparable with FCM. Actually both algorithms share the same asymptotic time complexity i.e. $O(ndc^2)$, being n the data set size, d its dimensionality and c the number of clusters. However, with a proper implementation, the asymptotic runtime can be made linear with respect to the number of clusters if one drops the storage of the membership matrix and combines the two updates into a single update of the cluster centers (Kolen, 2002). For the interested reader a proof of convergence of the FCMFP algorithm can be found in (Fazendeiro & de Oliveira, 2014) as well as an operational specification of the algorithm.

From (6) it is also interesting and straightforward to verify that FCMFP holds FCM as a particular case, for $\delta=0$. It should be also clear that like FCM, FCMFP allows members to belong to various clusters with a varying degree of membership. In this regard it shares the benefits of FCM (like noise robustness).

On the Number of Clusters

Determining the "correct" number of clusters always has been a very challenging task, especially in interesting, large real-world datasets such as the yeast cell cycle gene expression dataset.

With the FCMFP algorithm the underlying assumption is that there is no such thing as the "correct" number of clusters as it depends on the location of the observer (Fazendeiro, & de Oliveira, 2014). An inherent problem with exploratory clustering is *ab initio* knowledge of the number of clusters (Kerr et al., 2008). FCMFP can be used to come up with a set of valid alternatives depending on the distance at which the data is observed.

In this respect, one can think of an iterated FCMFP, hereafter referred as FCMFPiter. In the beginning, the focal point, the zoom factor, and the number of clusters c is initialized (typically $c \cong \sqrt{n}$). In the iterated version, FCMFP itself is run for each iteration. Additionally, in each iteration, FCMFPiter removes irrelevant centroids, i.e., centroids that are within a given neighbourhood of the focal point. After centroids removal, FCMFPiter increases the zoom factor, δ. At each iteration, the set of relevant clusters is evaluated against a cluster validity measures such as the Xie Beni index (Xie & Beni, 1991) or the Partition Coefficient (Bezdek, 1973). In this way the FCMFPiter evaluates the quality of the current number of clusters providing an insight into the granularity of the data. It provides a range of valid structural alternatives that correspond to the clusters identified at different level of details. From this perspective, FCMFPiter has similarities to hierarchical clustering in the sense of showing the granularity in a range of scale. But, unlike hierarchical clustering, items can move between adjacent clusters preventing premature commitment of a point to a cluster.

Centroid Projection

FCMFP does not constrain at all the location of the focal point P, giving the user complete freedom to simulate the observation point of the data. This even allows setting up the focal point in a space with a dimension that is different from the data space dimension. For instance, if the data is defined in a subset of R^2, P can be set as a point of R^3, or any other dimension greater than 2, for that matter.

However, useful effects are obtained when P is defined as a point of R^{d+1}, being d the data set dimension. In order to accomplish this "look from outside" effect the focal point, as well as the centroids, are elevated into the higher dimensional space. Obviously, data remains in its original space.

Higher dimension centroids are achieved simply by adding an extra dimension to the original ones. Initially, the value of this extra coordinate is set to zero. During the optimization process, the value of this coordinate will eventually change. For evaluation purposes, the centroids are later projected into the original space using a linear projection. This last step of the algorithm, prototype projection, can be straightforwardly achieved by computing the intersection of the lines defined by the focal point P and each v_i cluster, with the original data space. This process is illustrated in Figure 1.

Box 1 presents a specification of the FCMFP algorithm for the case where the focal point is placed in a higher dimensional space.

Cluster Quality

Cluster validity measures are used to assess the quality of the identified clusters. The existing validity measures can be seen in two broad categories based on what is taken into consideration.

The first category takes only intra cluster separation, *i.e.*, the compactness of the clusters created. Examples in this category are the partition coefficient (PC) (Bezdek, 1973) and partition entropy (Bezdek, 1981). PC takes the intra-cluster as a way of showing the quality of a cluster created. It divides the membership values by the number of items. The bigger the value of PC the better the cluster is. It is computed as follows:

Figure 1. Dataset is defined in R while the focal point P belongs to R^2, v^*_1 and v^*_2 are obtained by linearly projecting v_1 and v_2, respectively, into the original space

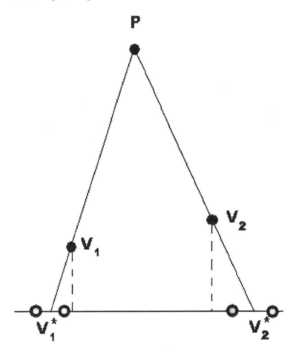

Box 1. Fuzzy c-means with focal point in a higher dimensional space algorithm

Let $X = \{x_1, x_2, ..., x_n\} \subset R^d$ be a finite set of unlabeled data.

Initialize the clusters' prototypes $V \in R^{d \times c}$.
Set C_{max}, $m > 1$, $P \in R^w (w \geq d)$ and $\delta \geq 0$.
Extend X and V into R^w by introducing $(w - d)$ null coordinates per element.
Repeat the following steps until a termination criterion has been met.
    Step 1: For i = 1,2,...,C_{max} and j = 1,2,...,n, update the partition matrix, U, according to (3).
    Step 2: For i = 1,2,...,C_{max}, update the prototypes, V, according to (6).
Project the prototypes into the original feature space R^d.

$$PC = \frac{\sum_{i=1}^{c}\sum_{j=1}^{n}u_{ij}^2}{n} \qquad (7)$$

The second class of measures take both intra and inter clusters separation indexes, Xie Beni index being a popular representative of this class (Xie & Beni, 1991). Xie Beni index is minimized when the appropriate number of clusters is reached. It is based on the principle that there has to be less coupling among clusters and there has to be high cohesion within a cluster. It is given by the following formula:

$$XB = \frac{\sum_{i=1}^{c}\sum_{j=1}^{n}u_{ij}^{m}\left\|x_j - v_i\right\|^2}{n\min_{i\neq k}\left\|v_i - v_k\right\|^2} \qquad (8)$$

This index is highly effective and widely used in practical applications reason why it was chosen to evaluate the validity of the clusters created by FCMFP in the reported experiments. We considered the tendency for increasing its value with the increase in the number of clusters, sometimes referred as one of its inherent limitations, as a desirable feature for this particular problem since it guides the analysis towards a manageable level of granularity.

ILLUSTRATIVE RESULTS

The experimental results obtained with the application of FCMFP to the yeast cell cycle dataset are presented and discussed below. The difficulty in identifying the correct number of clusters has led to a variety of results reported by different researchers for this dataset (Fodor et al., 1993; Lipshutz et al., 2000; Tavazoie et al., 1999; Futschik & Carlisle, 2005). The following sections present and discuss the results obtained for each dataset.

A Subset of Yeast Cell Cycle Data

In this section a subset of the yeast gene expression dataset is used. This subset contains 384 genes that were manually classified into five classes namely: early G1, late G1, S, G2 and M phases based on peak expression levels. The expression levels were measured at 17 time instants with a period of 10 minutes with a purpose of identifying the cell cycle controlled genes in yeast (Sugar & James, 2003; Futschik & Kasabov, 2002; Yeung et al., 2001; Cho & Yoo, 2006). The used data subset is available from (Dembélé & Kastner; 2003). Having applied FCMFPiter on this data subset, c=4, i.e. a four clusters partition, was observed to be the best alternative based on the cluster validity index used. The quality of the alternatives provided by FCMFP, as assessed by the Xie Beni index, are shown in Figure 2. From this figure we can see that a number of clusters in the two to five range can be seen as valid structural alternatives, four being the best alternative.

Figure 3 depicts the expression levels of the genes classified in each one of the five classes together with a side-by-side representation of the corresponding five clusters identified by the FCMFP algorithm.

As can be seen in Figure 3, there were observed some misclassification errors (the algorithm presented a mean accuracy level of 92%) mainly in S and G2 stages. Nevertheless it is whortwhile to mention that, from a strictly mathematical point of view, the FCMFP results in a more cohesive representation of each cluster, as is clearly seen in Figures (3.h), (3.k) and (3.l) when compared against Figures (3.c), (3.d) and (3.e) respectively.

From an analysis of the Xie Beni index (see Figure 2) it follows that a number of clusters between c = 2 to c = 5 results in a reasonable structural alternative. Figure 4 shows in separate rows the average expression level profiles of the clusters composing each one of these structural alternatives. For this data subset, five is usually the number of clusters reported in the literature,

Figure 2. Values of the XB index and the number of clusters for different values of Delta. The best XB values are associated with four clusters solutions (c=4).

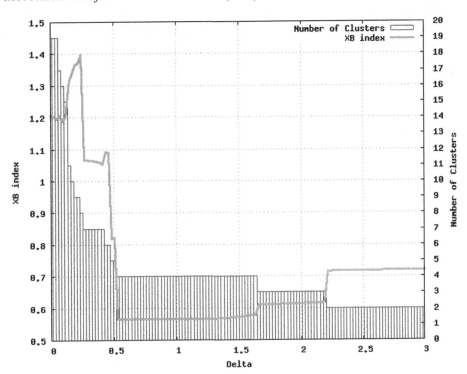

e.g., (Jonnalagadda & Srinivasan, 2009; Futschik & Kasabov, 2002). The profiles presented in the first row of Figure 4 are in close agreement with these works.

The additional solutions proposed by FCMFP are consistent with the following approximate merging: 4 clusters set composed of {early G1; late G1; S; (G2, M)}, 3 clusters set composed of {early G1; late G1; (S, G2, M)} and 2 clusters set composed of {(early G1, late G1); (S, G2, M)}.

These clusters were obtained using $m=1.17$, an extra dimension of the focal point, and a zoom factor increment of 0.024, at each iteration. These values were chosen based on the findings of (Futschik & Carlisle, 2005; Dembélé & Kastner; 2003) and after conducting a series of preliminary experiments.

The Yeast Gene Expression Dataset

FCMFP was applied to a yeast cell cycle gene expression dataset with 3000 genes collected from the yeast gene expression data that contained 6178 genes monitored at 17 time points over a span of 160 minutes (Futschik & Carlisle, 2005). While some studies (Tavazoie et al., 1999; Dembélé & Kastner; 2003) have excluded the data corresponding to the time points ninety and hundred minutes as they displayed irregularities in their expression values they were not excluded in this study. However, genes with more than 25% of the measurements missing were excluded from the dataset resulting in a reduction of 49 genes leaving it with 2951. For comparison purposes and similarly to (Futschik & Carlisle, 2005), data

Figure 3. Expression levels of the different phases and corresponding results of FCMFP. Gene expression levels over 17 time instants for: (a) Early G1 stage of the yeast cell cycle; (b) Late G1 stage of the yeast cell cycle; (c) S Phase of the yeast cell cycle; (d) G2 Phase of the yeast cell cycle and (e) M phase of the yeast cell cycle. On the left are the results of manual classification; on the right are the corresponding clusters identified by FCMFP.

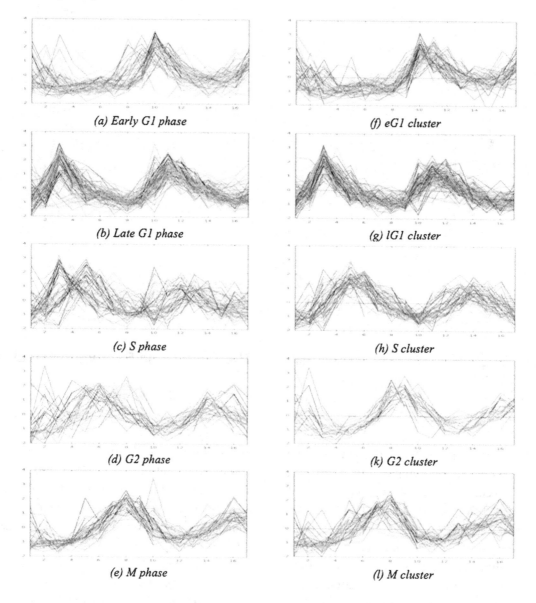

(a) Early G1 phase   (f) eG1 cluster

(b) Late G1 phase   (g) lG1 cluster

(c) S phase   (h) S cluster

(d) G2 phase   (k) G2 cluster

(e) M phase   (l) M cluster

was zero-mean standardized to one standard deviation before clustering. No filtering was made. This prevents losing of relevant genes and allows us to assess FCMFP robustness to noise. For this dataset, c=20 has been highly favoured in various studies (Lukashin & Fuchs, 2001; Liew, Yan, & Wu, 2003; Kim et al. 2006) as the number of clusters. It was also indicated in (Tavazoie et al., 1999) that it has 30 clusters without data corresponding to time instants 90 and 100. Sixteen clusters were also reported in (Lipshutz et al., 2000) using simulated annealing and with time

Figure 4. Different FCMFP structural alternatives. Each row of the table represents a solution with a different number of clusters. The plots show the average expression levels of the clusters assigned to each cluster. The filled curves represent the maximum and minimum expression levels attained by the clustered genes.

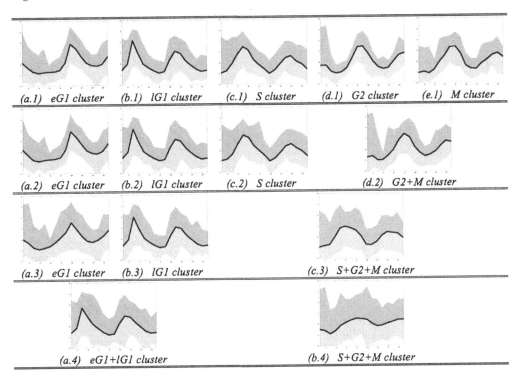

instant 90 and 100 removed. From these figures, it is clear that there is no consensus on the number of clusters for this dataset.

FCMFP came up with a set of valid alternatives for the number of clusters depending on the value of the zoom factor. These alternatives could be seen as dependent on the observer's position relatively to the data, i.e., depending on the desirable level of granularity. The quality of the valid alternatives, as measured by the Xie Beni index, can be seen in Figure 5. Again, the lower the index the better the results, the sharp discontinuity points can be seen as markers of putative valid structural alternatives; c=4 being the best one according to this criterion. The resulting assignment of the genes to these 4 clusters is shown in Figure 6.

Figure 5 further shows that there are various valid alternatives for the number of clusters: for instance four, eight, twelve, sixteen and twenty can

all be conceived as such. For a number of clusters greater than twenty, the XB index becomes quite high, indicating that his point could be seen as a cut point beyond which the results begin to deteriorate. This could be one of the reasons why the value twenty has been highly favoured by several researchers.

It is indicated in (Lukashin & Fuchs, 2001) that by using simulated annealing for a number of clusters greater than 20 empty clusters start to emerge. This phenomenon was also observed in the various experiments conducted in this study. Even though c=20 was suggested to be the best number of clusters by (Futschik & Carlisle, 2005) and (Lukashin & Fuchs, 2001), no further information was given on the quality of clusters below or above 20 especially in terms of cluster validity measurements. According to FCMFP the c values in the range of 2 to 8 have shown superior

Figure 5. XB index values as function of the number of clusters, c, as provided by FCMFP. Valid alternatives, i. e., valid c are those which have a sharp value downwards, c=4 being the best alternative, according to this index.

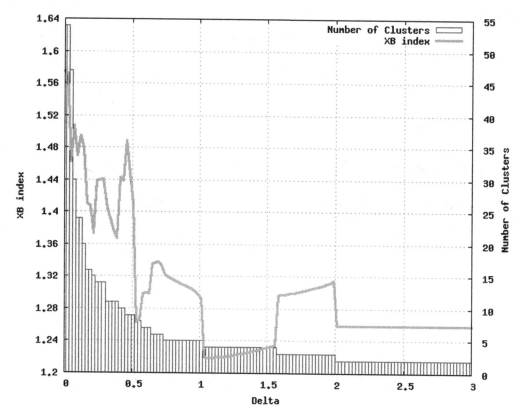

Figure 6. Four clusters generated by FCMFP and the expression levels of the genes assigned to them

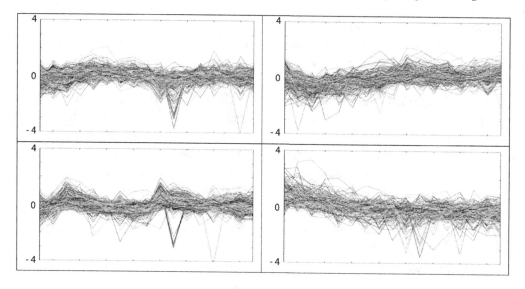

results, the best being $c=4$. This could be due to the influence of the five developmental stages of yeast cell cycle, *i.e.*, early G1, late G1, S, G2 and M phases based on peak expression levels.

As can be seen in Figure 5, a decrease in the zoom factor leads to a decrease in the attractive power of the focal point resulting in more and more clusters getting created and eventually converging to the number of data observations. This situation can be seen as the observer getting closer to the items being observed. The converse is also true, i.e., an increase in the zoom factor leads to an increase in the attractive power of the focal point resulting in fewer and fewer relevant clusters. The XB index value shows variable results depending on the quality of the alternatives. With the help of this XB line one can identify the better structural alternative, i.e., the number of clusters that correspond to lower peaks on the XB line. The lower the values on the XB line the better the quality of the corresponding number of clusters. The best alternatives according to the validity index thus corresponds to $c=4$.

It was indicated that as the number of cluster c increases sub-clusters start to emerge eventually resulting in empty clusters. The resulting sub-clusters are highly coupled as they share the overall expression pattern. On the other hand, a small c results in major structures present in the data. This behaviour was used in determining the global cluster structure by (Futschik & Carlisle, 2005). As the objective in these clustering problems is to reduce coupling and increase cohesion, one can set a cut-off point where the degree of coupling starts to be higher. As c increases genes start to belong to as many centroids as posspossible leading to a higher degree of coupling and empty clusters also start to emerge. It was found that $c=20$ is a cut-off point beyond which there was high rate of coupling and emergence of empty clusters. This result is again consistent with the results found repeatedly running FCM (Futschik & Carlisle, 2005), using simulated annealing (Lukashin &

Fuchs, 2001), and merging clusters (Liew, Yan, & Wu, 2003). This indicates that FCMFP has replicated previously published results on top of identifying the set of valid alternatives for the number of clusters. Figure 7 shows the 20 clusters generated by FCMFP and the genes assigned to them. If c is too large there is a high tendency to have similar items assigned to different clusters.

The influence of the fuzziness parameter, m, was also investigated. This was done by changing the value of m and observing the number of genes predominantly assigned to a cluster and the degree of the resulting coupling. If a cluster loosed some or all of the genes assigned to it as a result of a change in m then the cluster can be seen as a weak cluster. It was observed that an increase in m resulted in a flexibility for a gene to belong to as many clusters as possible thereby resulting in a higher degree of coupling. In our study we tested different values of m in the interval $(1; 1.25]$. The 1.25 figure corresponds to the lower bound found in (Futschik & Carlisle, 2005) for the value of m for preventing the identification of clusters in randomized data when using standard FCM.

With FCMFP, a user can choose among the valid alternatives taking into account the desirable level of granularity. The user may be interested in only an overview on the data structure or on a deeper, more detailed view.

FUTURE RESEARCH DIRECTIONS

The materialization of the information granulation in the framework of fuzzy sets presents appealing features regarding the human understandability of the produced granules. Not only the objects on the boundaries of several classes are no longer forced to fully belong to one of them, but also the partition of the dataset into fuzzy regions of interest can be transposed quite easily to propositions on meaningful linguistic labels, thus facilitating the empirical semantic validation of the model. In this

Figure 7. Solution comprising 20 clusters as generated by FCMFP

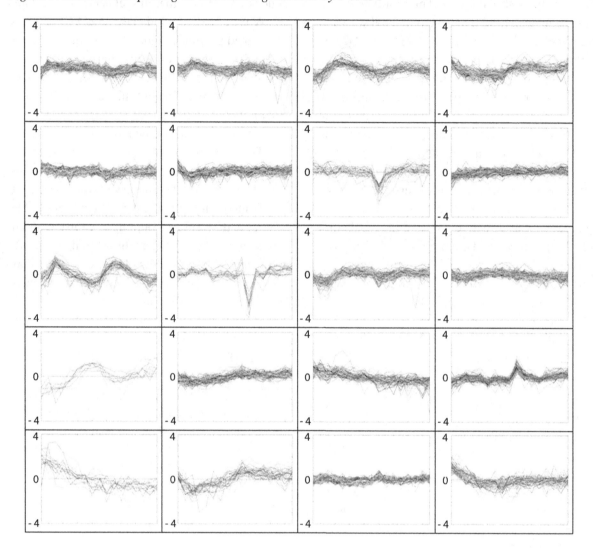

context, fuzzy clustering can be conceived as a privileged collection of techniques to search for structure in data and present it as fuzzy information granules.

In classical objective function based partitional (fuzzy) clustering the dataset is partitioned into C (fuzzy) subsets. From the algorithmic point of view this parameter has a major effect conditioning both the level of the granularity for the data analysis task and the capability of the algorithm to accurately reflect the underlying structure of the data. From the conceptual perspective it is

worthwhile to note that the number of clusters that we are able to visually identify is very dependent of the distance from where we are looking at the objects and also from the direction that we are taking when approaching the objects. To the best of our knowledge the actual clustering proposals, being those partitional or even hierarchical, do not take into account these two aspects into consideration. This is precisely the rationale behind our approach. We tried to capture the essence of the observation point by introducing as a new element, in FCM in particular, but with direct translation into objective function based partitional clustering in general, the interest to consider the distance from the clusters towards a pre-specified focal point.

As a matter of fact, the role of the parameter δ is interesting since it establishes the bridge between our focal point analogy and the observer's position, presenting a very comfortable way of systematically testing the algorithm without changing the focal point. Immediately a less compelling, more interesting, setup can be envisioned: if we drop the focal point analogy, and retake the observation point metaphor, we can let the observation point travel along any trajectory that we find interesting (not only a straight line as implied in this work).

Finally, there is a need to investigate how any objective function based partitional clustering algorithm which takes into account the observation point is related, or not, with the hierarchical approach. It is well known that due to the pairwise combinatorial nature of the process the hierarchical algorithms tend to be computationally inefficient with the growth of the number of data elements and that bad decisions made at an early stage of the algorithm will be propagated and amplified up to the end since the intermediate clusters are not revisited for further improvement (the points cannot move from one cluster to another). We believe that, at least to a certain extent, our approach can avoid these drawbacks and when properly designed can exhibit an agglomerative nature comparable with the hierarchical approach.

CONCLUSION

In this chapter, clustering of yeast cell cycle gene expression data collected using DNA microarrays was addressed. As found in the specialized literature, soft clustering is recognized as a promising data analysis tool due to the very nature of gene expression data where, typically, there exists no well-separated clusters with clear boundaries.

However, most of the currently available studies on gene expression data resort to some kind of hard clustering techniques. In this study we further exploit soft clustering techniques in gene expression analysis. A recent algorithm known as fuzzy C-means with a variable focal point (FCMFP) was presented as a helpful tool able to yield an insight into the global structure of this type of data at different levels of granularity.

FCMFP is inspired by the observation that the visual perception of a group of similar objects is (highly) dependent on the observer's position. The position at which the observer is located relatively to a set of objects determines how the observer perceives these objects. If the observer is located sufficiently apart from the objects these tend to be undistinguishable, that is, objects tend to be seen as a single cluster. As the observer gets closer to objects differences between them tend to emerge, and the initial single cluster tends to split into more and more clusters.

Besides identifying the optimal values for clusters, according to specific validity indexes, FCMFP also provides other valid alternatives for the number of clusters. To this end FCMFP shares the advantages that hierarchical clustering enjoys while avoiding its limitations in terms of computational efficiency and flexibility. The FCMFP analysis of yeast cell cycle dataset has resulted in a wide range of alternatives. Although the validity index mostly favoured smaller values of c (four being consistently the XB index optimizer) a closer look was also given to the alternatives produced by FCMFP which are found in the literature, specially the case with $c=20$.

High throughput biological data need to be processed, analyzed, and interpreted to address problems in life sciences. In an area where there are great dangers of producing misleading claims due to the orders of magnitude gap between the number of measured variables and the number of cases (Simon, 2009), the FCMFP's flexibility, proposing to the analyst a set of validated stable clusterings, can be a definitive advantage.

ACKNOWLEDGMENT

This work was partly supported by Fundação para a Ciência e Tecnologia (FCT) under the project PEst-OE/EEI/LA0008/2013. The authors wish to thank Tiago Bernardo for the cross validation of the experimental results.

REFERENCES

Amir, B.-D., & Zohar, Y. (1999). Clustering gene expression patterns. In *Proceedings of the third annual international conference on Computational molecular biology*. ACM.

Belfield, E. et al. (2014). *Microarray-based optimization to detect genomic deletion mutations*. Genomics Data.

Bezdek, J. (1973). Cluster validity with fuzzy sets. *J. Cybernet*, *3*(3), 58–73. doi:10.1080/01969727308546047

Bezdek, J. (1981). *Pattern Recognition with Fuzzy Objective Function Algorithms*. New York: Plenum. doi:10.1007/978-1-4757-0450-1

Cho, S., & Yoo, S. (2006). Fuzzy Bayesian validation for cluster analysis of yeast cell-cycle data. *Pattern Recognition*, *39*(12), 2405–2414. doi:10.1016/j.patcog.2005.12.007

Chu, S., DeRisi, J., Eisen, M., Mulholland, J., Botstein, D., Brown, P., & Herskowitz, I. (1998). The transcriptional program of sporulation in budding yeast. *Science*, *282*(5389), 699–705. doi:10.1126/science.282.5389.699 PMID:9784122

de Oliveira, J. V., & Pedrycz, W. (Eds.). (2007). *Advances in Fuzzy Clustering and its Applications*. John Wiley & Sons Ltd. doi:10.1002/9780470061190

Dembélé, D., & Kastner, P. (2003). Fuzzy C-Means for Clustering Microarray Data. *Bioinformatics (Oxford, England)*, *19*(8), 973–980. doi:10.1093/bioinformatics/btg119 PMID:12761060

Eisen, M., Spellman, P., Brown, P., & Botstein, D. (1998). Cluster analysis and display of genome-wide expression patterns. *Proceedings of the National Academy of Sciences of the United States of America*, *95*(25), 14863–14868. doi:10.1073/pnas.95.25.14863 PMID:9843981

Fazendeiro, P., & de Oliveira, J. V. (2008). A fuzzy clustering algorithm with a variable focal point. In *Proceedings of IEEE International Conference on Fuzzy Systems*, (pp. 1049-1056). IEEE. doi:10.1109/FUZZY.2008.4630499

Fazendeiro, P., & de Oliveira, J. V. (2014). Observer Biased Fuzzy Clustering. *IEEE Transactions on Fuzzy Systems*, 1. doi:10.1109/TFUZZ.2014.2306434

Finak, G., Bertos, N., Pepin, F., Sadekova, S., Souleimanova, M., & Zhao, H. et al. (2008). Stromal gene expression predicts clinical outcome in breast cancer. *Nature Medicine*, *14*(5), 518–527. doi:10.1038/nm1764 PMID:18438415

Fodor, S., Rava, R. P., Huang, X. C., Pease, A. C., Holmes, C. P., & Adams, C. L. (1993). Multiplexed biochemical assays with biological chips. *Nature*, *364*(6437), 555–556. doi:10.1038/364555a0 PMID:7687751

Futschik, M., & Carlisle, B. (2005). Noise-robust Soft Clustering of Gene Expression Time-course Data. *Journal of Bioinformatics and Computational Biology*, *3*(04), 965–988. doi:10.1142/S0219720005001375 PMID:16078370

Futschik, M., & Kasabov, N. (2002). Fuzzy clustering of gene expression data. In *Proceedings of the 2002 IEEE International Conference on Fuzzy Systems*, (pp. 414-419). IEEE.

Ghouila, A., Yahia, S. B., Malouche, D., Jmel, H., Laouini, D., Guerfali, F. Z., & Abdelhak, S. (2009). Application of multi-SOM clustering approach to macrophage gene expression analysis. *Infection, Genetics and Evolution*, *9*(3), 328–336. doi:10.1016/j.meegid.2008.09.009 PMID:18992849

Huttenhower, C. et al. (2007). Nearest neighbor networks: Clustering expression data based on gene neighborhoods. *BMC Bioinformatics*, *8*(250), 1–13. PMID:17626636

Jiang, D., Tang, C., & Zhang, A. (2004). Cluster analysis for gene expression data: A survey. *IEEE Transactions on Knowledge and Data Engineering*, *16*(11), 1370–1386. doi:10.1109/TKDE.2004.68

Jonnalagadda, S., & Srinivasan, R. (2009). NIFTI: An evolutionary approach for finding number of clusters in microarray data. *BMC Bioinformatics*, *10*(1), 40. doi:10.1186/1471-2105-10-40 PMID:19178750

Kerr, G., Ruskin, H. J., Crane, M., & Doolan, P. (2008). Techniques for clustering gene expression data. *Computers in Biology and Medicine*, *38*(3), 283–293. doi:10.1016/j.compbiomed.2007.11.001 PMID:18061589

Kim, D.-W., Lee, K.-Y., Lee, K., & Lee, D. (2006). Towards clustering of incomplete microarray data without the use of imputation. *Bioinformatics (Oxford, England)*, *23*(1), 107–113. doi:10.1093/bioinformatics/btl555 PMID:17077099

Kolen, J., & Hutcheson, T. (2002). Reducing the time complexity of the fuzzy c-means algorithm. *IEEE Transactions on Fuzzy Systems*, *10*(2), 263–267. doi:10.1109/91.995126

Lein, E., Hawrylycz, M. J., Ao, N., Ayres, M., Bensinger, A., & Bernard, A. et al. (2007). Genome-wide atlas of gene expression in the adult mouse brain. *Nature*, *445*(7124), 168–176. doi:10.1038/nature05453 PMID:17151600

Liew, A., Yan, H., & Wu, S. (2003). A novel OPTOC-based clustering algorithm for gene expression data analysis. In *Information, Communications and Signal Processing, 2003 and Fourth Pacific Rim Conference on Multimedia: Proceedings of the 2003 Joint Conference of the Fourth International Conference on*, (vol. 3, pp. 1427-1431). Academic Press.

Lipshutz, R., Fodor, S. P. A., Gingeras, T. R., & Lockhart, D. J. (2000). High density synthesis oligonucleotide arrays. *Nature Genetics*, *21*(Supplement), 20–24. doi:10.1038/4447 PMID:9915496

Looney, C. (2002). Interactive clustering and merging with a new fuzzy expected value. *Pattern Recognition*, *35*(11), 2413–2423. doi:10.1016/S0031-3203(01)00213-8

Lukashin, A., & Fuchs, R. (2001). Analysis of temporal gene expression profiles: clustering by simulated annealing and determining the optimal number of clusters. *Bioinformatics*. doi:/17.5.405.10.1093/bioinformatics

Nylund, L., Satokari, R., Nikkilä, J., Rajilić-Stojanović, M., Kalliomäki, M., & Isolauri, E. et al. (2013). Microarray analysis reveals marked intestinal microbiota aberrancy in infants having eczema compared to healthy children in at-risk for atopic disease. *BMC Microbiology*, *13*(1), 12. doi:10.1186/1471-2180-13-12 PMID:23339708

Ozsolak, F., & Milos, P. M. (2011). RNA sequencing: Advances, challenges and opportunities. *Nature Reviews. Genetics*, *12*(2), 87–98. doi:10.1038/nrg2934 PMID:21191423

Pirim, H., Ekşioğlu, B., Perkins, A. D., & Yüceer, Ç. (2012). Clustering of high throughput gene expression data. *Computers & Operations Research*, *39*(12), 3046–3061. doi:10.1016/j.cor.2012.03.008 PMID:23144527

Priness, I., Maimon, O., & Ben-Gal, I. (2007). Evaluation of gene-expression clustering via mutual information distance measure. *BMC Bioinformatics*, *8*(1), 111. doi:10.1186/1471-2105-8-111 PMID:17397530

Richards, A. et al. (2008). A comparison of four clustering methods for brain expression microarray data. *BMC Bioinformatics*, *9*(490), 1–17. PMID:19032745

Riggs, E., Wain, K. E., Riethmaier, D., Smith-Packard, B., Faucett, W. A., & Hoppman, N. et al. (2014). Chromosomal microarray impacts clinical management. *Clinical Genetics*, *85*(2), 147–153. doi:10.1111/cge.12107 PMID:23347240

Sanmann, J. N., Pickering, D. L., Stevens, J. M., & Sanger, W. G. (2013). Microarray Studies in Pediatric T-Cell Acute Lymphoblastic Leukemia/Lymphoma: A Report of Four Cases. *Cancer Genetics*, *206*(5), 213. doi:10.1016/j.cancergen.2013.05.010

Schena, M. et al. (1996a). Genome analysis with gene expression microarray. *Bioessaya*, *18*(5), 427–431. doi:10.1002/bies.950180513 PMID:8639166

Schena, M., Shalon, D., Heller, R., Chai, A., Brown, P. O., & Davis, R. W. (1996b). Parallel human genome analysis: Microarray-based expression monitoring of 1000 genes. *Proceedings of the National Academy of Sciences of the United States of America*, *93*(20), 10614–10616. doi:10.1073/pnas.93.20.10614 PMID:8855227

Simon, R. (2008). Microarray-based expression profiling and informatics. *Current Opinion in Biotechnology*, *19*(1), 26–29. doi:10.1016/j.copbio.2007.10.008 PMID:18053704

Simon, R. (2009). Analysis of DNA microarray expression data. *Best Practice & Research. Clinical Haematology*, *22*(2), 271–282. doi:10.1016/j.beha.2009.07.001 PMID:19698933

Somogyi, R., & Wen, X. et al. (1995). Developmental kinetics of GAD familym RNAs parallel neurogenesis in the rat spinal cord. *The Journal of Neuroscience*, *15*, 2575–2591. PMID:7722616

Soowhan, H., Lee, I., & Pedrycz, W. (2009). Modified fuzzy c-means and Bayesian equalizer for nonlinear blind channel. *Applied Soft Computing*, *9*(3), 1090–1096. doi:10.1016/j.asoc.2009.02.006

Sugar, C., & James, G. (2003). Finding the number of clusters in a data set, an information theoretic approach. *Journal of the American Statistical Association*, *98*(463), 750–763. doi:10.1198/016214503000000666

Tamayo, P., Slonim, D., Mesirov, J., Zhu, Q., Kitareewan, S., & Dmitrovsky, E. et al. (1999). Interpreting patterns of gene expression with self-organizing maps: Methods and application to hematopoietic differentiation. *Proceedings of the National Academy of Sciences of the United States of America*, *96*(6), 2907–2912. doi:10.1073/pnas.96.6.2907 PMID:10077610

Tavazoie, S., Hughes, J., Campbell, M., Cho, R., & Church, G. (1999). Systematic determination of genetic network architecture. *Nature Genetics*, *22*(3), 281–285. doi:10.1038/10343 PMID:10391217

Velculescu, V., Zhang, L., Zhou, W., Vogelstein, J., Basrai, M. A., & Bassett, D. E. Jr et al. (1997). Characterization of the yeast transcriptome. *Cell*, *88*(2), 243–251. doi:10.1016/S0092-8674(00)81845-0 PMID:9008165

Wang, Z., Gerstein, M., & Snyder, M. (2009). RNA-Seq: A revolutionary tool for transcriptomics. *Nature Reviews. Genetics*, *10*(1), 57–63. doi:10.1038/nrg2484 PMID:19015660

Wolberg, W. (1991). *Wisconsin Breast Cancer Database*. University of Wisconsin Hospitals Madison. Retrieved from http://archive.ics.uci.edu/ml/machine-learning-databases/breast-cancer-wisconsin/breast-cancer-wisconsin.names

Xie, X., & Beni, G. (1991). A validity measure for fuzzy clustering. *IEEE Transactions on* Pattern Analysis and Machine Intelligence, *13*, 841–847.

Yang, X., Cao, A., & Song, Q. (2006). A New Cluster Validity for Data Clustering. *Neural Processing Letters, 23*(3), 325–344. doi:10.1007/s11063-006-9005-x

Yeung, K., Fraley, C., Murua, A., Raftery, A., & Ruzzo, W. (2001). Model-based clustering and data transformations for gene expression data. *Bioinformatics (Oxford, England), 17*(10), 977–987. doi:10.1093/bioinformatics/17.10.977 PMID:11673243

ADDITIONAL READING

Anderson, D., Bezdek, J., Popescu, M., & Keller, J. (2010). Comparing Fuzzy, Probabilistic, and Possibilistic Partitions. *IEEE Transactions on Fuzzy Systems, 18*(5), 906–919. doi:10.1109/TFUZZ.2010.2052258

Bazaraa, M., Sherali, H., & Shetty, C. (2006). *Nonlinear Programming - Theory and Algorithms* (3rd ed.). New York: Wiley-Interscience. doi:10.1002/0471787779

Dubois, D., & Prade, H. (1994). Fuzzy sets - a convenient fiction for modeling vagueness and possibility. *IEEE Transactions on Fuzzy Systems, 2*(1), 16–21. doi:10.1109/91.273117

Estivill-Castro, V. (2002). Why so many clustering algorithms – a position paper. *ACM SIGKDD Explorations Newsletter, 4*(1), 65–75. doi:10.1145/568574.568575

Futschik, M., & Kasabov, N. (2002). Fuzzy clustering of gene expression data, *in Proc. of the 2002 IEEE International Conference on Fuzzy Systems (FUZZ-IEEE'02)*, pp. 414-419.

Gao, J., & Hitchcock, D. (2010). James-Stein Shrinkage to Improve K-means Cluster Analysis. *Computational Statistics & Data Analysis, 54*(9), 2113–2127. doi:10.1016/j.csda.2010.03.018

Hathaway, R., & Hu, Y. (2009). Density-Weighted Fuzzy c-Means Clustering. *IEEE Transactions on Fuzzy Systems, 17*(1), 243–252. doi:10.1109/TFUZZ.2008.2009458

Havens, T., Bezdek, J., Leckie, C., Hall, L., & Palaniswami, M. (2012). Fuzzy c-Means Algorithms for Very Large Data. *IEEE Transactions on Fuzzy Systems, 20*(6), 1130–1146. doi:10.1109/TFUZZ.2012.2201485

Huang, H.-C., Chuang, Y.-Y. & Chen, C.-S. (2012). Multiple Kernel Fuzzy Clustering, *IEEE Transactions on Fuzzy Systems*, Vol. 20, No. 1, pp. 120. Gruber, M. (1998). *Improving Efficiency by Shrinkage: The James-Stein and Ridge Regression Estimators*, CRC.

Jain, A., & Dubes, R. (1988). *Algorithms for clustering data*. Upper Saddle River, NJ: Prenticel Hall.

Jain, A., Murty, M., & Flynn, P. (1999). Data clustering: A review. *ACM Computing Surveys, 31*(3), 264–323. doi:10.1145/331499.331504

Jonnalagadda, S., & Srinivasan, R. (2009). NIFTI: An evolutionary approach for finding number of clusters in microarray data. *BMC Bioinformatics, 10*(1), 40. doi:10.1186/1471-2105-10-40 PMID:19178750

Pedrycz, W. (2005). *Knowledge-Based Clustering: From Data to Information Granules*. New York: Wiley. doi:10.1002/0471708607

Pedrycz, W., Loia, V., & Senatore, S. (2010). Fuzzy Clustering With Viewpoints. *IEEE Transactions on Fuzzy Systems, 18*(2), 274–284.

Wu, J., Xiong, H., Liu, C., & Chen, J. (2012). A Generalization of Distance Functions for Fuzzy c-Means Clustering With Centroids of Arithmetic Means. *IEEE Transactions on Fuzzy Systems*, 20(3), 557–571. doi:10.1109/TFUZZ.2011.2179659

Xu, R., & Wunsch, D. II. (2005). Survey of Clustering Algorithms. *IEEE Transactions on Neural Networks*, 16(3), 645–678. doi:10.1109/TNN.2005.845141 PMID:15940994

KEY TERMS AND DEFINITIONS

Cluster Validity: When there is no prior knowledge about the structure of the data a natural question arises: what is the right number of clusters for a particular data set? This question is known in the literature as the cluster validity problem and distinct validity measures have been proposed in order to find an answer. For partitional fuzzy clustering it is advisable that the validity indices account both for the data set (e.g. their variance) and the resulting membership degrees. An example of such class of validity indices is the Xie-Beni index, also known as the compactness and separation index, computed as the ratio of the compactness of the fuzzy partition of a data set to its separation.

Clustering: Process of searching for a finite and discrete set of data structures (categories or clusters) within a finite, otherwise unlabelled, usually multi-variate data set. In the literature it is common to find that the goal of clustering is the partition of the data set into groups so that data in one group are similar to each other and are as different as possible from data in other groups.

Dissimilarity Measures: Dissimilarity is a dyadic relation, nonnegative defined, symmetric on its two arguments and attains its minimum (zero) when the two arguments are identical. If this relation also satisfies the triangular inequal-ity property (subadditivity) it is called distance function or metric. For continuous features, each metric induces a particular topology on the data set and consequently a different view of the data (a different geometry of the clusters). In cluster analysis some common choices for distance functions include the Hamming (city block) distance inducing diamond shaped clusters, the Euclidean distance inducing (hyper) spherical clusters and the Tchebyshev distance-inducing (hyper) box shaped clusters.

Fuzzy Clustering: The fuzzy logic approach to clustering differs from the conventional set theory approach mainly because a generic datum may belong to more than one cluster with a different degree of membership (usually a value between 0, non-membership, and 1, full degree of inclusion). Hence the data points near the core (prototype) of a given cluster exhibit a higher degree of membership than those lying farther away (near its border). With this framework it is possible to capture the uncertainty, vagueness and flexibility inherent to the data set and to the concepts being formed.

Gene Expression Analysis: Gene expression is the biological process by which the genotype of an organism, i.e. its genetic information and identity, gives rise to the phenotype - the physical manifestation of that information. The influence on the phenotype involves the synthesis of structural proteins or enzymes responsible for catalyzing all reactions from various metabolic pathways. As such, given the importance that gene expression has on the functioning of organisms, its analysis is one of the key tools used in drug development, in applied life science research and in the optimization of bioprocesses.

Human Observer Analogy: The visual perception of groups of similar objects is highly dependent on the observer position. Based on this metaphor, it is possible to construct a generalization of partitional clustering aiming at the inclusion into the clustering process of both distance and direction of the point of observation towards the data set. This may be done by incorporating a new term in the objective function, accounting for the distance between the clusters' prototypes and the point of observation.

Partitional Clustering: The objective function based partitional clustering algorithms attempts to directly decompose the data set into a collection of disjoint clusters. This partition is builded during an iterative optimization process repeated until its associated cost function reaches a minimum (global or local). The cost function, also designed performance index or objective function, is a mathematical criterion expressing some desired features (emphasizing local or global structure of the data) of the resulting partition.

Chapter 7
Heuristic Principal Component Analysis–Based Unsupervised Feature Extraction and Its Application to Bioinformatics

Y-H. Taguchi
Chuo University, Japan

Hideaki Umeyama
Chuo University, Japan

Mitsuo Iwadate
Chuo University, Japan

Yoshiki Murakami
Osaka City University, Japan

Akira Okamoto
Aichi University of Education, Japan

ABSTRACT

Feature Extraction (FE) is a difficult task when the number of features is much larger than the number of samples, although that is a typical situation when biological (big) data is analyzed. This is especially true when FE is stable, independent of the samples considered (stable FE), and is often required. However, the stability of FE has not been considered seriously. In this chapter, the authors demonstrate that Principal Component Analysis (PCA)-based unsupervised FE functions as stable FE. Three bioinformatics applications of PCA-based unsupervised FE–detection of aberrant DNA methylation associated with diseases, biomarker identification using circulating microRNA, and proteomic analysis of bacterial culturing processes–are discussed.

INTRODUCTION

Feature extraction (FE) is a task that reduces the number of features (independent variables) for predicting/estimating (a dependent variable). For example, when performing face recognition as a computational task, the specific parts of facial photos, e.g., eye lines, colors of irises, or shapes of jaws, should be considered. Alternatively, to predict tomorrow's stock prices computationally, certain factors, e.g., today's prices, economical indices, or weather, should be taken into account. The problem is that increased numbers of features considered does not always result in better

DOI: 10.4018/978-1-4666-6611-5.ch007

performance. To perform better face recognition, considering hairstyle as a key feature is not useful, since it can vary. For stock price prediction, what your wife or husband cooks this morning is not useful as an important factor. However, neglecting the shape of the nose in face recognition or ignorance of this week's unemployment rate for stock price prediction may reduce performance of the task. Thus, clearly, there should be minimum number of critical features to achieve the best performance. The current problem is how to determine the specific set of such features.

The era of big data has added additional difficulty to this problem: a small number of samples (cases) versus too many features observed. For example, in facial recognition, it is not difficult to obtain many features from a facial photo that often consists of several millions of pixels, each of which has more than a million color grades. However, it is not a realistic requirement to collect a million facial photos, especially from a cost point of view, if payment is required for research use of individual photos. For stock market prediction, the situation appears better, because stock prices, even measured per second over months, can be collected and recorded. However, the use of many sample (case) numbers does not always resolve the "many features vs. small cases" difficulty, since these records are not always independent of each other. Stock price varies periodically over time, e.g., daily, weekly, or even seasonally. Thus, huge amounts of data are often simply replicates. What is required are samples taken under different economic situations. For example, if the market is lively, data should be obtained from when the market is bad. However, this kind of data is only available after the economic crash, thus stock price prediction based only on measurements taken under good economic situations naturally fails to predict price reduction (and money is therefore lost). Thus, "many features vs small samples" problems must be resolved to compete with massive data flowing into "prediction" systems.

In this chapter, we would like to propose an alternative solution to the difficulty of FE when the number of samples is much lower than the number of features. There have been many proposals to overcome this problem, e.g., stepwise feature extraction (Prasad, 2008), regression with regularization (Girosi, 1995) and Bayesian work frame (Chu, 2006). Despite these efforts, FE problems with small sample size and large number of features have not been solved completely.

Recently, unsupervised FE (De Backer, 1998) has gained the interest of many researchers. Unsupervised FE is robust and thus, it is expected to provide more stable FEs, i.e., unsupervised FEs have weaker sample dependence than other methods with optimization procedures in all senses.

Although many kinds of implementations of unsupervised FE are possible, we employed one of the simplest, principal component analysis (PCA) based FE (Murakami, 2012; Taguchi, 2013) in this chapter. Since PCA is a linear method, it is expected to have greater robustness than other more complicated methods such as those with kernel tricks (Scholkopf, 2001) or Bayesian statistics. Linear methods, such as PCA, are also expected to be less computationally challenging. Finally, it is easier to interpret the obtained results, since it is a linear combination of the original features. In contrast to these advantages, linear methods including PCA usually have poorer performances than other more complicated methods (Cao, 2003). In this chapter, we also discuss how these difficulties can be overcome when applying PCA to FEs.

The applications considered in this chapter are the detection of aberrant DNA methylation associated with diseases (Ishida, 2014; Kinoshita 2014), biomarker identification of circulating microRNA (miRNA) (Murakami, 2012; Taguchi, 2013) and proteomic analysis of bacterial culture (Taguchi, 2012). In the *background* section, we introduce FE methods and compare them to our methods. Then, we illustrate details of our proposed method and an illustrative (artificial) example. Each application of PCA based FE is described separately, and then *feature research directions, additional readings section*, and *conclusion* are discussed.

BACKGROUND

As mentioned in the *introduction*, the purpose of this chapter is to propose a new methodology to resolve difficulties within FE when many features are available, but a small number of samples (cases) are provided ("many features vs small cases" difficulty). These difficulties are two-fold: combinatorial divergence of many features and bias of small sample numbers. Combinatorial divergence of many features occurs because the possible number of feature combinations becomes divergent exponentially as the number of considered features increase. For example, if ten features are selected from one hundred available features, the total number of possible combinations is over one billion. If the number of features considered or available features increase, this already huge number further increases exponentially. Thus, small numbers of samples cannot distinctly evaluate or rank these combinations. Therefore, there is no effective way to judge which combination is best. In addition, small numbers of samples inevitably result in bias that prevents selecting the best combinations within innumerous possibilities. Finally, FE is highly sample dependent, i.e., distinct sample sets indicates which combinations are best.

Considering these two difficulties, it is apparent that the stability of FE resolves this difficulty to some extent. If FE can select features stably, not all possible combinations can be evaluated every time new sample data is provided and bias caused by a small number of samples is reduced. As can be seen later, our proposed methodology can resolve these problems by maintaining the stability of FE.

In the following section, we briefly discuss a few conventional FEs. Further information can be obtained in another well-written review article by Gyon (2003). There have been several efforts to overcome difficulties of using FE when small numbers of samples with many features are available (Table 1). The standard and simplest method is stepwise FE (Prasad, 2008) (Figure 1(a)), where FE usually starts from a small number of pre-selected features. Then, using some criterion, either the addition of a new feature or elimination of a selected feature is employed. If neither of them passes the criterion, then iteration is terminated. There are no unique definite criterion that exist for stepwise FE. However, variables such as residuals of linear regression cannot be used for this criterion since residuals are monotonic and decrease the function of the number of features. Optimal numbers of employed features are always diverse. Thus, variables used for the criterion must include a penalty term for the addition of features. One of the most frequently used criterion is Akaike Information Criterion (AIC) (Bozdogan, 1987). AIC is the sum between the number of features and negative likelihood, and decreases as the number of features increases. Likelihood generally describes the "goodness" of prediction, i.e., "smallness" of the difference between prediction and true answer. Larger likelihood means better prediction. Thus, AIC can balance between the "goodness" of prediction and the number of features. When too many features are considered, the AIC becomes larger. Since AIC is not a monotonic decreasing function of the number of features, optimal (minimum) AIC can determine the optimal number of features. The most critical drawback of stepwise FE is convergence. If the number of possible features is huge, the occasional selection of optimal combination of features is difficult. Stepwise FE is even often captured at local minimum, which is far from the true optimal combination of features. Because of the local optimization nature of stepwise FE, once it is captured at local minimum, there is no way to escape it. This forces the use of stepwise FE from a huge number of initial conditions (a trial

Table 1. Summary of three conventional FEs

Method	Description	Advantages	Disadvantages
Stepwise	Adding and removing features iteratively until no improvements are achieved	Simple, thus easy to understand and to implement	Time consuming, thus hard to converge
Regulation	Try to minimize the number of features by restricting the sum of coefficients attributed to features	Rapid to converge. Greater opportunity to reach solution	Results are strongly dependent upon how to restrict sum of coefficients. Optimal restriction must be evaluated by other criterion (e.g., cross validation)
Bayesian	Optimizing model parameters such that likelihood is maximized	Once the model is assigned, results can be obtained automatically. Additional evaluation (e.g., confidence interval) can be easily driven from the obtained probabilities	Requires massive computation because of huge size of parameter search. The results are completely model dependent

Figure 1. Schematic diagrams that illustrate conventional FE (a) STEPWISE FE (b) FE with regulation (c) Bayesian

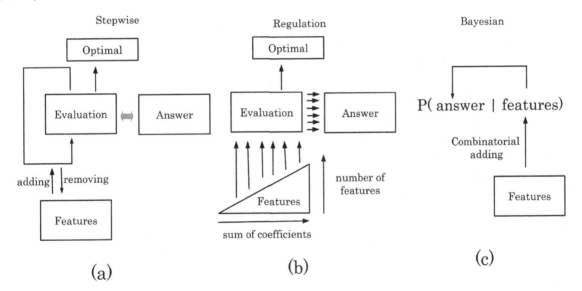

of starting combinations of features) that result in a heavy time-consuming process.

Another useful concept often used for optimal FE is regulation (Girosi, 1995). As denoted above, since residuals and likelihood are monotonic decreasing functions of the number of features, an additional penalty term is required. Regulation (Figure 1(b)) limits the number of features by the addition of "total amount" of coefficients of employed features. The most frequently used regulatory procedure is lasso (Tibshirani, 1996)

that is a shrinkage and selection method for linear regression. Lasso tries to minimize the sum of residuals by restricting the sum of absolute values of coefficients of features to less than the constant. Because of the singular property of absolute function at zero, this forces some coefficients to be zero, causing a limited number of non-zero coefficients, which automatically results in FE. As the upper limit of sum of absolute values of coefficients increases (decreases), the number of features with non-zero coefficients increases (decreases). Although regression with regulation terms often works very well, one drawback of this method is the decision of upper limit of sum of absolute values of coefficients, since there are no universal criteria for the optimal decision of this value.

Recent and more popular criterion have been obtained by Bayesian statistics (Chu, 2006). The Bayesian method (Figure 1(c)) tries to maximize conditional probability $P(y|x)$, where y and x are dependent and independent variables, respectively. If some x are causally independent of y, elimination of x simply increases conditional probability. This means no additional criterion are required to obtain the optimal combination of features, although some arbitrariness on the decision of the functional form of $P(y|x)$ still exists. An obvious drawback of the Bayesian work frame is the divergence of search space. Ideally, we must search among all combinations of y and x, and the number of combinations between y and x will increase exponentially. Since situations with a huge number of features (independent variables) are considered, the Bayesian work frame inevitably results in heavy computationally challenging problems. Thus, although the Bayesian work frame is free from the difficulties of FE, it is not useful for real problems.

In contrast to these optimization-based methods, unsupervised FE (De Backer, 1998) does not use labeling information for FE. Instead of minimizing the discrepancy between predictions and true answers, unsupervised FE attempts to find a "simpler pattern" hidden in the data set. Although there are no unique definitions of simpler patterns, this often means a smaller number of clusters or smaller number of dimensions to which objects are embedded. Elimination of useless (non-informative) features often provides a simpler pattern than when considering all features. If the obtained simpler pattern reflects the true answer, it is employed and FE is regarded to be successful. A clear drawback of unsupervised FE is that there are no guarantees to obtaining meaningful

simpler patterns coincident with true answers, in contrast to the optimal based methods that always provide answers independent of their usefulness. If unsupervised FE fails to provide simpler patterns, the unsupervised FE should be discarded. Thus, the important question is whether unsupervised FE works for a specific problem or not.

Classically, "unsupervised FE" often means "dimensionality reduction" (Jimenez-Rodriguez, 2007). In dimensionality reduction, new feature vectors are constructed from given features directly (linear transformation) or indirectly (non-linear transformation). Although many studies have followed this policy, there is a disadvantage, as every time new features are constructed, all features must be measured in advance. Thus, although dimensionality reduction technique can provide a smaller number (low dimensional) of features, the effort to measure huge numbers of features is not reduced. Unsupervised FE in our context differs from the conventional procedure. Similar to the supervised FE mentioned above, unsupervised FE in our context reduces the number of features that must be measured. Thus, we believe, in this context, this is the real meaning of unsupervised FE. To our knowledge, no previous studies have investigated this context of unsupervised FE.

In the following, we demonstrate that PCA based unsupervised FE works in at least three examples.

INTRODUCTION OF PCA BASED UNSUPERVISED FE AND ITS APPLICATIONS

Illustrative Examples of PCA Based Unsupervised FE

Before describing the application of PCA based unsupervised FE to biological examples, we would like to illustrate briefly how PCA works as an unsupervised FE. For simplicity, assume the following situation. There are M samples, each of which has N features attributed to it. Then suppose the ith feature associated with the jth sample takes the value of x_{ij}. M samples can be classified as follows. $M/2$ samples ($j=1,...,M/2$) belong to the first class and the other $M/2$ samples ($j=M/2+1,...,M$) belong to the second class. In addition, only $N' < N$ features have distinct values between the two classes and the other $N-N'$ features do not have any distinct values between the two classes. To demonstrate this situation, x_{ij}s are assumed to have the following values.

$N(1,1/2)$ ($i \leq N' < N$, $1 \leq j \leq M/2$)

$x_{ij} \in N(0,1/2)$ ($i \leq N' < N$, $M/2 < j \leq M$)

$N(\varepsilon_{ij},1/2)$ ($N' < i \leq N$),

where $N(\mu,\sigma)$ is normal distribution with mean μ and standard deviation σ, and ε_{ij} is a random number that obeys probability

$P(\varepsilon_{ij} =0)=P(\varepsilon_{ij}=1)=1/2$.

Figure 2(a) shows two dimensional embedding using PCA, of $M(=20)$ samples with $N(=100)$ features within which only the first $N'(=10)$ features have distinct values between the two classes. Figure 2(b) is the overlap plot of 100 independent trials. It is obvious that M samples are divided into two classes. The problem is how to select only features that have distinct values between the two classes, i.e., $i \leq N'$, using PCA based unsupervised FE. Figure 2(c) shows the two dimensional embedding of N features and Figure 2(d) is the overlap plot of 100 independent trials. Ten features having distinct values between two classes ($i \leq N'$) are clearly located at the left hand side. The mean probability that 10 features are included in the top most 10 left hand side features in Figure 2 (d) is 0.7. Although we did not use label information to obtain Figures 2(c) and (d), PCA-based unsupervised FE clearly has ability to select features having distinct values

between two classes ($i \leq N'$). The reason why PCA based unsupervised FE can select features having distinct values between two features ($i \leq N'$) can be understood from Figure 2(e) that shows the contribution of each sample to the first principal component (PC1). Since PC1 clearly has distinct values between two classes, features having distinct values between two classes ($i \leq N'$) have more projections to PC1, thus are located at the left hand side (Figure 2(f) is the overlap plots of 100 independent trials).

Using features with distinct values between two classes can provide clearer clustering. Figure 2(g) shows the two dimensional embedding of M samples using only features with distinct values between two classes ($i \leq N'$) and Figure 2(h) shows the overlap plot of 100 independent trials. Even using the top 10 left hand side features in Figure 2(c), better clustering can be obtained than in Figure 2(a) (Figure 2 (i), Figure 2(j) shows the overlap plot of 100 independent trials), although only 70% of selected features are taken from features $i \leq N'$.

All of these demonstrations show how well PCA based unsupervised FE can work and the great potential PCA based unsupervised FE has for selecting features with distinct values between two classes, without using labeling information. That is,

1. Even if features having distinct values between two classes are a minority ($N' << N$), PCA can identify distinctions between two classes (Figure 2 (a) and (b)).
2. PCA based unsupervised FE can extract features with distinct values between two classes (Figure 1(c) and (d)).
3. Principal component that extracts features with distinct values between two classes can be selected by investigating contributions of each sample to the PC (Figure 1(e) and (f)).
4. Using only features having distinct values between two classes, clustering can be better

Figure 2. (a) Two dimensional embedding of 20 samples using PCA. Black squares and red crosses belong to same classes. (b) Overlap plot of 100 independent trials of (a). (c) Two dimensional embedding of N features using PCA. Blue triangles are features distinct between two classes while green grosses are not. (d) Overlap plot of 100 independent trials of (c). (e) Contribution of each sample to the first principal component. (f) Boxplot of 100 independent trials of (e). (g) Two dimensional embedding of 20 samples using PCA with employing only features having distinct values between two classes. (h) Overlap plot of 100 independent trials of (g). (i) Two dimensional embedding of 20 samples using PCA with top 10 left hand side features in (c). (j) Overlap plot of 100 independent trials of (i).

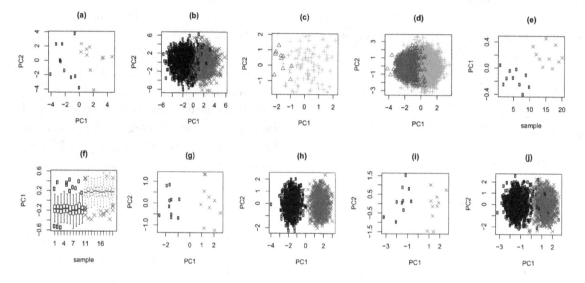

or at least not worse than clustering using all features (Figure 2(g), (h), (i) and (j)).

In this illustrative example, we assumed that the two classes obeyed two distinct normal distribution $N(\mu_1, \sigma_1)$ and $N(\mu_2, \sigma_2)$, where the marginal condition, $|\mu_1 - \mu_2| = \sigma_1 + \sigma_2$, represents discrimination. Thus, the ability of unsupervised FE can vary dependent upon whether the discrimination is easier ($|\mu_1 - \mu_2| > \sigma_1 + \sigma_2$) or harder ($|\mu_1 - \mu_2| < \sigma_1 + \sigma2$).

In the following, we would like to demonstrate how these above mentioned work using real examples.

Biological Example 1: DNA Methylation

DNA methylation is an epigenetic phenomenon and is believed to affect gene expression. For example, methylation in the promoter region can suppress the expression of genes associated with the promoter. Although many reports describe the association of aberrant DNA methylation with disease (Baylin, 2001), there were several limitations within these studies. For example, there are too many sites with aberrant DNA methylation associated with each disease. There can be more than 1000 methylation sites with aberrant DNA methylation associated with each disease. This often prevents the further study of genes associated with aberrant DNA methylation. Genes with stronger aberrant methylation were often selected and considered for further analyses, although it is not clear whether stronger aberrant methylation affects diseases to a greater extent. Thus, the problem is to select small (limited) numbers of genes that are critical to each disease from among those with promoters that are aberrantly methylated associated with each disease. To our knowledge, there is no effective method to perform this task currently.

In contrast to the selection of aberrant DNA methylation sites based on pre-defined criterion of thresholds, e.g., significance or the amount of fold change, PCA based unsupervised FE is based on more data oriented criterion, because only PC used for FE need be specified. *A priori* criteria were not set up for the evaluation of features that represent aberrant DNA methylation. Thus, our PCA based unsupervised FE can potentially select limited numbers of critical genes among those with promoters that are aberrantly methylated and associated with each disease.

The first example of applying PCA based unsupervised FE to aberrant DNA methylation is to specify genes whose promoters are aberrantly methylated associated with autoimmune diseases (Ballestar, 2011). Autoimmune diseases are complex diseases whose causes are rarely well understood, although internal abnormality of the immune systems may play critical roles in disease pathogenesis. Aberrant DNA methylation is also a potential candidate mechanism involved in the pathogenesis of autoimmune disease, because with monozygotic (MZ) twins, one might be healthy and the other develop autoimmune disease despite sharing the same genome. Javierre (2010) tried to identify genes whose promoters were commonly and aberrantly methylated in three autoimmune diseases: systemic lupus erythematosus (SLE), rheumatoid arthritis (RA) and dermatomyositis (DM). However, aberrant DNA methylation was only observed in SLE but not DM or RA. The data set they used was as follows. First, they found MZ twins that consisted of pairs of healthy controls and patients. They added two healthy age-gender matched controls to the twins. These four consisted of a unit and they collected five units for each of the three diseases. Thus, four individuals (patient or healthy control) × 5 units × 3 diseases = 60 samples. Promoter methylation of each sample was measured using microarray that had 1350 probes corresponding to promoters of potential cancer-related genes. Thus, this demonstrates the problem of FE where 1350 features are analyzed in 60 samples. Thus, can PCA-based unsupervised FE identify undiscovered genes whose promoters are commonly and aberrantly methylated in three autoimmune diseases from this data set (Ishida, 2014)?

Figure 3 illustrates a schematic of PCA-based unsupervised FE applied to the extraction of aberrant DNA methylation for autoimmune disease. First, PCA was applied to all 60 samples and probes were embedded to a 2D space. The first principal component (PC1) has almost equal contribution from each sample although the proportion of PC1 contribution is greater than 90%. Thus, we ignored PC1 while PC2 had distinct contributions from male and female samples, but contributions were not distinct between healthy controls and patients. Thus, PC2 was not interesting and we tried to suppress PC2. After the investigation, we found that the gender-dependent component PC2 expressed the differential promoter methylation of genes on chromosome X. Since females and males have different numbers of X chromosomes, it is well known that promoter methylation on chromosome X is gender dependent such that two genders have the same gene expression of genes on chromosome X. By excluding genes on X chromosome from the analysis, we successfully suppressed gender dependent PC2.

Next, we applied PCA to 20 samples in each disease separately. Again, for all three diseases, PC1 did not have a disease specific contribution from samples despite its large contribution. In contrast to PC1, PC2 (or PC3) exhibited a distinct contribution for all three diseases between patients and healthy controls, but its manner differed from disease to disease. Thus, we will discuss the distinct contributions from healthy controls and each individual disease to PC2.

For SLE, the distinct contribution from healthy controls and patients of each disease to PC2 is relatively simple. In 20 samples, for all 5 units that consist of sick and healthy MZ twins and two healthy

Figure 3. Schematic of PCA-based unsupervised FE applied to the extraction of aberrant DNA methylation for autoimmune disease

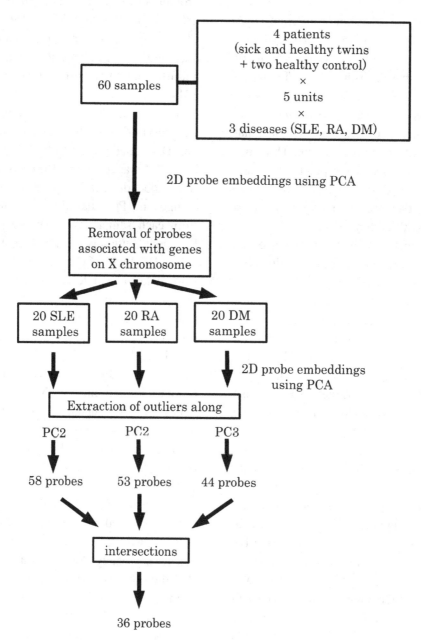

controls, magnitude correlations between sick MZ twins and three healthy controls (healthy twins and additional two age-gender matched controls) were consistent. This might explain why Javierre (2010) observed aberrant promoter methylation for SLE when they simply applied a *t*-test to detect the difference of promoter methylation between patients and healthy controls. Extracting outliers along PC2, we selected 58 probes. Because we used PC2 to detect distinctions between healthy controls and patients, it is not guaranteed that a raw promoter methylation profile will be distinct between healthy controls and patients. This point is checked by *t*-test between 58 selected probes and the remaining probes. For all five units, 58 probes were significantly more hypomethylated in sick MZ twins than in healthy twins (P < 10^{-11}). Thus, PCA-based unsupervised FE successfully extracted aberrant methylated probes associated with SLE.

The case of RA was more complicated. PC1 did not have a distinct contribution between healthy controls and patients as described above while PC2 did. Although this point was similar to SLE, the magnitude of correlations between contributions of three healthy controls and that of patients to PC2 were not consistent among the units. Two additional healthy controls had larger or smaller contributions than sick twins and were dependent upon units. In addition, among five pairs of MZ twins, the contributions of the third pair to PC2 were not distinct between healthy and RA twins. Despite these difficulties, 53 probes selected by PCA-based unsupervised FE using PC2 exhibited significant differences (hypomethylation in patients) between healthy and sick twins excluding the third pair (P< 10^{-12}, by *t*-test). This also demonstrated the difficulties in finding aberrantly methylated promoter regions using simple statistical tests. Comparisons between sick twins and healthy controls, including healthy twins, may provide a different set of aberrantly methylated promoter regions because PC2 does not reflect consistent differences between sick twins and healthy controls. This might also explain why Javierre (2010) failed to identify aberrantly methylated promoter regions for RA.

Finally, a DM case was considered. This was even harder than RA to analyze. While PC1 did not have any distinct contributions between patients and healthy controls as mentioned above, PC2 exhibited a distinction between genders but not between healthy controls and patients. Although PC3 represented a distinction between healthy and sick twins, it did not exhibit a consistent magnitude correlation between sick twins and healthy controls including healthy twins. In addition, the

magnitude correlation between healthy and sick twins was also consistent but opposite between males and females; hyper (hypo) methylated in male (female) DM twins. Despite these difficulties, 44 probes selected by PCA-based unsupervised FE using PC3 exhibited significant differences between healthy and sick twins (P< 10^{-10}, by *t*-test).

Although we successfully identified promoters with aberrant methylation associated with autoimmune diseases, the feasibility of selected probes was not sufficient. There may be more suitable methods that identify a different selection of probes. To confirm feasibility, we counted the number of probes in the intersection among the 58, 53 and 44 probes selected for SLE, RA and DM, respectively. Then 36 probes were commonly selected. Because there are 1350 probes in a microarray, the *P*-value for this accidentally occurring was less than 10^{-96}. As all three diseases are autoimmune diseases, it was plausible that probes with aberrant methylation associated with diseases were coincident. Thus, the feasibility of our analysis was high.

We also compared our results with those obtained by an independent data set. For SLE, we used the study by Jeffries (2011), where female genome methylation of T-cells from 11 SLE and 12 normal controls were measured. Because no single PCs exhibited distinct contributions between normal controls and patients, combination of PC2 and PC3 was used for probe selection. This combination exhibited distinct methylation between patients and normal controls and the selected probes significantly overlapped with probes selected in the present study. Thus, the methodology used in this study is also valid for independent data sets. For RA, we used results from the study by Liu (2013) that measured peripheral blood lymphocyte genome methylation from 335 patients and 354 normal controls. The probes selected in this study significantly overlapped with probes selected by PCA-based FE with PC2 that exhibited significant differences between patients and normal controls. Thus, the methodology used in this study was again valid for independent data sets.

To further confirm the feasibility of selected probes in this study, we checked the disease association of genes associated with the selected probes using the Gendoo server (Nakazato, 2009) (Table 2). As can be seen, most selected genes were associated with autoimmune diseases or immune related compounds, although not all of the associated *P*-values were significant. This

also confirmed the feasibility and superiority of our methodology.

Another example of the application of PCA based unsupervised FE to problems related to DNA methylation was the detection of genotype specific DNA methylation in esophageal squamous cell carcinoma (ESCC) (Kinoshita, 2014). ESCC is a lethal cancer disease whose 5-year survival rate is less than 20%. Yang (2010) investigated DNA methylation and genotypes using single nucleotide

Table 2. Disease association of genes selected by PCA based unsupervised FE

Gene Name	Disease	P-Value	Compounds	P-Value
AIM2	----		Interferon-gamma	4.00E-10
CARD15	Autoimmune Diseases	0.02		
	Immune System Diseases	1.00E-04		
	Arthritis, Juvenile Rheumatoid	8.00E-04		
CD82	Arthritis, Rheumatoid	0.13		
CSF1R	Arthritis, Rheumatoid	0.14		
CSF3	Autoimmune Diseases	0.08		
CSF3R	Multiple Sclerosis	0.05		
DHCR24	----			
ERCC3	----			
GRB7	----		Immunoglobulins	0.03
HGF	Autoimmune Diseases	0.28		
	Immune System Diseases	0.19		
	Arthritis, Rheumatoid	0.69		
HOXB2	----		Immune Sera	9.00E-03
IFNGR2	SLE	0.09		
	Multiple Sclerosis	0.09		
LCN2	SLE	0.31		
	Multiple Sclerosis	0.32		
LMO2	Severe Combined Immunodeficiency	1.00E-73		
LTB4R	Arthritis, Rheumatoid	2.00E-04		
MMP14	Arthritis, Rheumatoid	0.08		
MMP8	Arthritis, Rheumatoid	3.00E-05		
	Multiple Sclerosis	0.09		
MPL	SLE	0.02		
PADI4	Arthritis, Rheumatoid	4.00E-89		

continued on following page

Table 2. Continued

Gene Name	Disease	P-Value	Compounds	P-Value
	Multiple Sclerosis	7.00E-09		
	SLE	0.01		
	Autoimmune Diseases	0.01		
PECAM1	Multiple Sclerosis	0.12		
	Autoimmune Diseases	0.13		
PI3	Arthritis, Rheumatoid	0.11		
RARA	----		Immunoglobulin M	0.03
			Interferon-gamma	0.2
S100A2	----		Receptors, Immunologic	3.00E-05
			Interferon-gamma	0.1
SEPT9	----	----		
SLC22A18	----	----		
SPI1	Immunologic Deficiency Syndromes	5.00E-03		
	Immune System Diseases	0.02		
	Autoimmune Diseases	0.31		
SPP1	SLE	4.00E-05		
	Arthritis, Rheumatoid	5.00E-03		
	Multiple Sclerosis, Chronic Progressive	0.02		
STAT5A	Autoimmune Diseases	0.21		
SYK	Arthus Reaction	5.00E-07		
	Autoimmune Diseases	8.00E-03		
	Arthritis, Rheumatoid	0.02		
	Immunologic Deficiency Syndromes	0.04		
	SLE	0.12		
TIE1	Arthritis, Rheumatoid	0.03		
TM7SF3	----	----		
TRIP6	----	----		
VAMP8	Multiple Sclerosis	0.01		

SLE, systemic lupus erythematosus.

polymorphism (SNP) arrays that made use of two restriction enzymes, *Nsp* and *Sty*. Although each array included only about 200,000 probes that were much lower than the estimated total number of potential methylation sites (>500,000), they could detect SNP abundance and SNP specific DNA methylation simultaneously when combined with bisulfite treatment. They collected blood (non-mutated genome), tumor (mutated genome) and normal tissue adjusting to tumor (in between) samples from 30 patients.

Figure 4 illustrates how genes were selected using PCA-based FE. First, PCA was applied to genotype and DNA methylation separately for *Sty*

Figure 4. Schematic of how genes were selected using PCA-based FE applied to ESCC

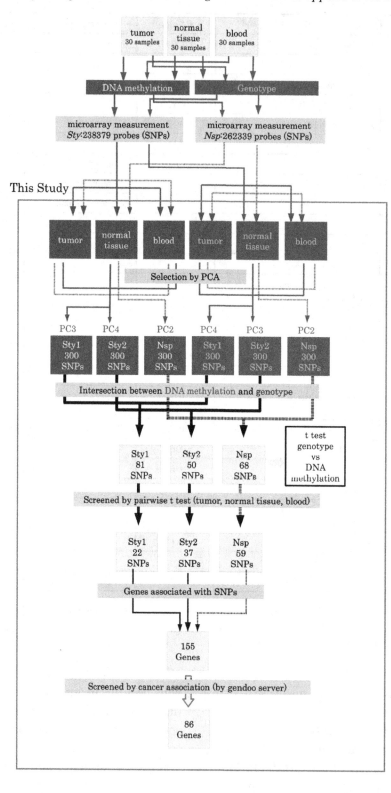

and *Nsp*. Then, PC3 and PC4 (PC2) reflected distinctions between blood, normal tissues and tumors for *Nsp* (*Sty*) array. Then, 300 outliers (probes or SNPs) along PC3 and PC4 (PC2) were extracted for *Sty* (*Nsp*) arrays of genotype/DNA methylation measurements. Next, intersection between outliers from genotype and DNA methylation was selected. For *Sty*, PC3 (PC4) from DNA methylation measurements was compared with PC4 (PC3) from genotype measurements. This set of SNPs was named Sty1(Sty2). For *Nsp*, PC2 from DNA methylation measurements was compared with PC2 from genotype measurements. This set of SNPs was named Nsp. The number of SNPs included in Sty1, Sty2 and Nsp SNP sets was 81, 50 and 68. Comparison between genotype and DNA methylation, demonstrated these selected SNPs were hypomethylated. Applying three pairwise *t*-tests (normal tissue vs tumor, blood vs tumor, and blood vs normal tissue), 22, 37 and 59 SNPs were significantly abundant in tumors compared with blood and normal tissues. Thus, we could successfully identify SNPs that were abundant and hypomethylated in tumors. Because this was a detection of SNP specific methylated SNPs, we called this "genotype-specific DNA methylation."

To determine whether the selection of these SNPs was biologically meaningful, 155 genes associated with the SNPs were tested by Gendoo server (Nakazato, 2009) that reports disease association of genes based on a text mining database. Interestingly, 86 of 155 genes were reported to be associated with cancers by the Gendoo server. Especially, nine genes (*CCND1, CKAP4, CRABP1, FGF3, MYEOV, PKP4, RPL14, SMAD3,* and *ZNF639*) were associated with "Esophageal Neoplasms" and "Carcinoma, Squamous cell." This is coincident with the fact that the cancer considered in this study was ESCC. This demonstrated the biological significance of SNPs selected by PCA-based unsupervised FE.

Finally, we compared performance of PCA based unsupervised FE with other methods. Since this problem is a three classes problem, no other methods were proposed since any other methods require ranking information between three classes (blood, tumor and normal tissue), while ranking was automatically decided when PCs used for selecting outliers were selected for PCA-based unsupervised FE. However, owing to PCA-based unsupervised FE, we identified that an abundance of SNPs associated with genes with genotype-specific DNA hypomethylation were ordered from blood, through normal tissue to tumor. Thus, we assigned these ranks when applying the other three classes of FE to the present problem. The methods employed were Pearson and Spearman correlation based FE, partial least square (PLS) based FE, stepwise FE and lasso. In correlation based FE, 300 SNPs whose abundance correlated with the ranking of three classes (tumor, normal tissue and blood) were selected. For PLS based FE, 300 SNPs with more contributions to PLS were selected. In stepwise FE, 3 class linear discriminant analysis (LDA) was applied by adding and removing SNPs until 300 SNPs were selected. In lasso, multivariate liner regression was performed with regularization terms and regularization constants were chosen such that 300 SNPs remained. Among these, stepwise FE did not converge and lasso could not be performed because of too many (>200,000) SNPs. Although PLS and two correlation based FE worked, the number of SNPs selected for Sty and SNPs were 14 and 49 (Pearson), 18 and 39 (Spearman), and 13 and 7 (PLS), which is lower than for PCA-based unsupervised FE (81, 50 and 69 for Sty1, Sty2 and Nsp 300 SNPs sets, respectively). Thus, we concluded that PCA-based unsupervised FE outperformed other FEs despite the need for three class ranking that was not required by PCA-based unsupervised FE.

In summary, we have applied PCA based unsupervised FE to two distinct examples where genes with aberrant promoter methylation associated with disease are sought. In the first example, we identified genes with promoters that are commonly and aberrantly methylated, for three autoimmune diseases, SLE, RA, and DM. In the second example, we identified genotype-specific promoter aberrant methylation associated with ESCC. To our knowledge, these two examples are the first demonstration of successful application of PCA based unsupervised FE.

Biological Example 2: Biomarkers

The next example of applying PCA-based unsupervised FE to biological problems was its use in two studies of disease biomarker identification, using circulating microRNAs (miRNAs) (Murakami, 2012; Taguchi, 2013). Identification of disease biomarkers is always an important problem for diagnosis since effective biomarkers enables us to free medical doctors from diagnosis. By simply measuring the amount of biomarkers present, some diseases can easily be identified. One problem of biomarkers is their measurement. If it is not easy to measure the particular biomarker, such as by surgery, the usefulness of the biomarker is drastically decreased since doctors must be recruited for both diagnosis and surgery. Thus, biomarkers are more useful if they can be measured non-invasively.

From this point of view, circulating biomarkers have attracted much interest (Almufti, 2014). Circulating biomarkers can be measured from various body fluids, such as blood, urine, and saliva. The advantages of circulating biomarkers are twofold; since fluid circulates through the body, it can reflect the various stages of the whole body and since it is easily obtained, it is non-invasive. However, one important disadvantage is that it might be too non-specific, in terms of disease and tissue involved. Reduced specificity makes it difficult to identify disease-circulating biomarkers. Circulating miRNAs might be promising circulating biomarker candidates (Kosaka, 2013) although miRNA alone can suppress gene expression at the post-transcriptional level. In this section, we apply PCA-based unsupervised FE to identify circulating miRNA disease biomarkers.

Thus, the problem is to identify circulating miRNAs that reflect disease status. Since it is not expected that each miRNA reflect a specific disease status, combinatorial selections must be performed. Thus, this task is a typical FE since it selects a set of miRNAs. Because disease specificity of each miRNA is not expected to be strong, an effective set of miRNAs with slight specificity to disease must be identified. This is a difficult task because to be a suitable target by our PCA based unsupervised FE it does not require labeling information.

The first example is hepatitis, an inflammatory disorder of the liver (Murakami, 2012). Although acute hepatitis is undoubtedly severe, chronic hepatitis often results in hepatic cancer through liver cirrhosis. Currently, there is no effective therapy for progressive chronic hepatitis excluding exceptional antiviral therapies. Hepatocellular carcinoma is a severe hepatic cancer that often redevelops, although the 5-year survival rate is as high as 50–60%. Thus, frequent diagnosis using non-invasive diagnosis is very important. We recently developed a non-invasive biomarker for multiple chronic hepatitis, chronic hepatitis C (CHC), chronic hepatitis B (CHB), and non-alcoholic steatohepatitis (NASH), using circulating miRNAs isolated from exosome purified blood (Murakami, 2012). Many reports studied miRNAs in progressing/suppressing liver diseases and identified multiple miRNAs as biomarkers. PCA-based unsupervised FE was applied to this problem. We collected total RNA from exosomes in blood from 64 CHC, 4 CHB, 12 NASH patients and 24 healthy controls. The amount of miRNA in each sample was measured by microarray. PCA-based unsupervised FE was applied to obtain miRNA profiles. First, 64 CHC samples and 24 normal controls were analyzed together. Nine miRNAs were selected and successfully discriminated between normal controls and CHC, with an accuracy of 96.59% using PCA-based LDA evaluated by leaving out one cross validation. Since microarray includes more than 800 miRNAs, successful discrimination using only nine selected miRNAs was remarkable. PCA-based LDA is the LDA using PCs up to some numbers. However, when all samples (64 CHC, 4 CHB, 12 NASH and 24 healthy controls) were analyzed together using twelve selected miRNAs, four classes (CHC, CHB, NASH and normal controls) were discriminated (87.50% samples were discriminated successfully). Furthermore, other pairwise discriminations between distinct diseases, i.e., CHC vs CHB, CHC vs NASH, and CHB vs NASH, achieved accuracies of 98.35, 97.37 and 87.50%, respectively, using less than 10 miRNAs. Finally, these were validated using an independent set that consisted of 31 CHC, 16 CHB, and 8 NASH patients. Using the same miRNAs selected for the original samples, CHC

vs CHB, CHC vs NASH, and CHB vs NASH, achieved accuracies of 74.47, 87.18 and 79.19%, respectively. Although performances in the independent sets were poorer than in the original set, they were still informative. This demonstrated the usefulness and robustness (stability) of PCA-based unsupervised FE when applied to the identification of circulating biomarkers. Figure 5(a) illustrates these processes.

The performance of PCA-based unsupervised FE was used not only for discrimination between diseases but also for the diagnosis of disease progression. There are two clinical measures of chronic hepatitis progression: inflammation and fibrosis. Inflammation is caused by cell injury as a result of immune system responses to virus infection (CHB and CHC) or by accumulation of fat

Figure 5. (a) Diagrams that illustrate FE applied to liver diseases; (b) Diagrams that illustrate FE applied to 14 diseases

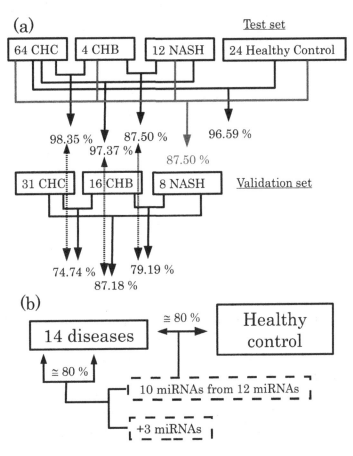

(NASH). Fibrosis is caused by cell replacement by cell regeneration that gives rise to cirrhosis. Thus, inflammation and fibrosis are important measures of chronic hepatitis progression. However, it is not easy to diagnose these two diseases, because direct observation of liver tissue is required. If a non-invasive biomarker could differentially diagnose these two disorders, it would be useful. PCA-based unsupervised FE was applied to the discrimination of inflammation (A0, A1, A2 and A3 stages) and fibrosis grades (F0, F1, F2 and F3 stages) in CHC. Three pairwise discriminations of inflammation (A1 vs A0+A2+A3, A2 vs. A0+A1+A3, A3 vs A0+A1+A2) achieved accuracies of 71.88, 75.00, and 82.81%, respectively. Similarly, three pairwise discriminations of inflammation (F1 vs. F0+F2+F3, F2 vs. F0+F1+F3, F3 vs. F0+F1+F2) achieved accuracies of 64.62, 70.31, and 73.44%, respectively. This also demonstrated the usefulness of PCA-based unsupervised FE.

Although the previous examples were limited to chronic hepatitis, many other diseases can be discriminated using circulating miRNAs in the blood. Keller (2011) tried to discriminate 14 diseases (lung cancer, pancreatitis, other pancreatic tumors and diseases, ovarian cancer, chronic obstructive pulmonary disease, ductal pancreatic cancer, gastric cancer, sarcoidosis, prostate cancer, acute myocardial infarction, periodontitis, multiple sclerosis, melanoma and Wilms' tumor) from healthy controls using circulating miRNAs in serum. Although Keller (2011) successfully discriminated 14 diseases from normal controls, they failed to list specific miRNAs used for the discrimination. From the point of clinical application, definitive and limited numbers of miRNAs used for discrimination is better. Thus, we tried to discriminate 14 diseases from normal controls using ten specific miRNAs based on their data set. First, we applied PCA-based unsupervised FE for 14 pairs that consisted of one disease and normal controls. Achieved accuracies ranged from 0.713 to 0.892. Thus, we could successfully identify 10 disease-specific circulating miRNAs

that discriminated patients of each of the 14 diseases from normal controls. To test stability of the selected biomarkers, we applied a cross validation study of FE. We randomly selected 90% of samples and selected 10 miRNAs using PCA-based unsupervised FE. Repeating this procedure 100 times, we estimated the stability of selected biomarkers. Since there are 14 diseases, in total 140 miRNAs were selected for each trial. Among 140 miRNAs, 129 miRNAs were selected for all 100 trials. Thus, miRNAs selected by PCA-based unsupervised FE are highly stable. To compare stability of PCA-based unsupervised FE with other methods, we tested the stability of multiple FE methods. FE methods tested were *t*-test based FE (Keller, 2011), significance analysis of microarrays (SAM) (Tusher, 2001), gene selection based on a mixture of marginal distributions (gsMMD) (Qiu, 2008), ensemble recursive feature elimination (RFE) (Abeel, 2005), and unsupervised feature filtering (UFF) (Varshavsky, 2007). Among them, the only method that was competitive with PCA-based unsupervised FE was UFF, where 111 of 140 miRNAs were selected for all 100 trials. The performance of the other methods were 30 (SAM), 5 (upregulation by gsMMD), 1 (downregulation by gsMMD), 1 (RFE) and 0 (ensemble RFE), respectively. Since UFF was the only unsupervised method other than PCA-based unsupervised FE, the use of unsupervised procedures was essential to achieve good stability of FE.

We followed the study of Keller (2011) to discriminate between each disease and healthy controls. We have found that PCA-based unsupervised FE combined with PCA-based LDA using 10 selected miRNAs discriminated between diseases with accuracies typically of 0.8.

Finally, we validated the biological feasibility of our selected set of miRNAs using DIANA-mirPath (Papadopoulos, 2009) that evaluates a set of miRNAs based on the Kyoto Encyclopedia of Genes and Genomes (KEGG) pathway analysis of miRNA target genes. For all 14 diseases, reported KEGG pathways by DIANA-mirPath were also related to corresponding diseases. Thus, from a biological point of view, PCA-based unsupervised FE successfully selected plausible sets of miRNAs as circulating biomarkers.

Although these analyses demonstrated the usefulness of PCA-based unsupervised FE for the selection of circulating biomarkers, there was an additional interesting finding: the possibility of a universal disease biomarker. As mentioned above, 140 miRNAs were potentially selected to discriminate between 14 diseases and normal controls. However, these 140 miRNAs were taken from only 12 miRNAs: hsa-miR-425, hsa-miR-15b, hsa-miR-185, hsa-miR-92a, hsa-miR-140-3p, hsa-miR-320a, hsa-miR-486-5p, hsa-miR-16, hsa-miR-191, hsa-miR-106b, hsa-miR-19b, and hsa-miR-30d. Even after extending to the discrimination between diseases, i.e., compared with the possible number of selected miRNAs, $140 \times 14 = 1960$, the method selected the above 12 miRNAs plus three additional miRNAs, miR-130, miR-22, miR-720. Figure 5(b) illustrates these processes. This suggests that miRNAs selected by PCA-based unsupervised FE can serve as universal disease biomarkers independent of the disease analyzed. Since the miRNAs selected from the study by Keller et al (2011) and normal controls were shared, we also evaluated the performance of the 12 miRNAs for seven other diseases (Alzheimer disease (AD) (Leidinger, 2013), carcinoma (Maclellan, 2012), coronary artery disease (CAD) (GEO ID: GSE49823), nasopharyngeal carcinoma (NPC) (GEO ID: GSE43329), hepatocellular carcinoma (HCC) (Shen, 2013), breast cancer (BC) (Chan, 2013) and acute myeloid leukemia (AML) (Rommer, 2013), using an independent data set. Combining 12 miRNAs with support vector machine (SVM) resulted in accuracies ranging from 0.72 to 0.94. These performances were also competitive with the fully supervised method (lasso). Considering the 12 miRNAs were selected from a distinct disease in an independent set, this performance was impressive. These results demonstrated that PCA-based unsupervised FE

can achieve very high performance not possible by other methods (i.e., the proposal of universal disease biomarker) (Taguchi, 2014).

In summary, we applied PCA based unsupervised FE for the identification of two distinct circulating miRNA biomarkers. In the first example, we successfully discriminated between multiple liver diseases. This is a difficult task because both diseases are classified as hepatitis. In the second disease model, we also successfully identified specific (stable) circulating miRNA biomarkers that could discriminate between 14 diseases and normal controls. To our knowledge, this is the first study to demonstrate disease discrimination by the stable identification of circulating miRNAs.

Biological Example 3: Proteome

The last biological application to be tested by PCA-based unsupervised FE is the proteome of bacteria under different culture conditions (Taguchi, 2012). After the development of antibiotics, bacterial infectious diseases were eradicated. Recently, antibiotic-resistance has become a new problem to be solved. Because of the frequent appearance of antibiotic-resistant bacteria, alternative and new antibiotics have been developed. However, the frequency of antibiotic-resistance has outperformed the frequency of the development of new antibiotics. It is now believed that most antibiotics will become ineffective in the near future because of the appearance of antibiotic-resistant bacteria. Why antibiotic-resistance can appear so frequently and quickly might be because of the unplanned overuse of antimicrobial agents and horizontal gene transfer among bacterial species, including harmful bacterial strains. In health-care or animal husbandry facilities, the overuse of antimicrobial agents allows bacterial flora drug-sensitive to become drug-resistant by selection of resistant bacteria in the guts of humans or animals. Moreover, bacteria possess horizontal gene transfer systems such as gene transformation, conjugation of plasmids, bacterial phages, and transposons.

Drug-resistant genes often transfer to other bacteria, even beyond the barrier of bacterial species, and function as drug-resistant phenotypes. Thus, if antibiotics can be developed that target only specific virulent bacteria, drug-resistance will become less frequent. However, to develop such a drug, detailed information regarding the bacterial metabolic systems is required.

To understand bacterial metabolic systems in detail, we employed proteomic analysis of bacterial growth conditions. Culturing processes are also very important for the infectious process, since bacteria must effectively increase their population to cause infectious diseases. How culturing processes differ dependent upon external culture conditions will enable us to understand the metabolic status during bacterial growth. For this process, we applied PCA-based unsupervised feature extraction.

Thus, the problem is to identify proteins that characterize the bacterial culturing process without pre-defined criterion. Proteins may monotonically decrease/increase as culturing time increases or may be expressed/suppressed only at a specific time point. Some proteins may be expressed either intra- or extracellularly or both. We aimed to collect all proteins with characteristic behavior regardless of their class. To our knowledge, no methods other than unsupervised FE can fulfill this kind of requirement.

The samples were prepared as follows. A bacterial strain, *Streptococcus pyogenes*, was cultured under two distinct incubation conditions: stable and shaking. *S. pyogenes* occasionally causes life-threatening disease, streptococcal toxic shock syndrome, although it is sometimes part of the typical normal bacteria flora. The estimated annual number of *S. pyogenes* infection cases is greater than 700 million, although not all infections are life threatening. The total proteome was measured at four time points from initial to final growth stages. Incubation was repeated 3 times. Thus, in total, two incubation conditions × four time points × three biological replicates = 24 samples

available. Prior to proteome measurement, each sample was divided into two parts, the complete cellular fraction (wc) and the supernatant fraction (snt) using centrifugation. Thus, in total, there were 48 proteome profiles.

PCA was applied to the 48 proteome profiles and they were embedded into a two dimensional space. Three clear clusters were observed, i.e., wc cluster, early snt cluster and late snt cluster. In addition, while snt under shaking incubation conditions were equally divided into the early and late snt clusters, four snts under stable incubation were divided into an early snt cluster and three that belonged to the late cluster. This suggests that incubation processes under stable incubation conditions progress faster than that under shaking incubation conditions. This observation was reasonable since oxidizing stress under shaking incubation conditions is more severe than under stable incubation conditions, which may result in a delayed growth process.

Because more than 400 proteins were observed by proteomic analyses, we tried to select a smaller number of proteins that contributed to the formation of the three cluster formation observed. PCA-based unsupervised FE was applied and 23 proteins were selected. Only using the 23 selected proteins, we obtained almost identical two dimensional embeddings of 48 proteome profiles, i.e., three clusters formation. Thus, 23 proteins were essential to form the three clusters observed and PCA-based unsupervised FE successfully extracted the important proteins. After removing 23 proteins, the 48 proteome profiles were again clustered into three clusters with a different shape by PCA, and PCA-based unsupervised FE was applied again. Then, we obtained 30 proteins where the same three clusters in two dimensional embeddings were formed by PCA. Thus, PCA-based unsupervised FE was successful. Figure 6 illustrates this process.

In summary, we identified critical and limited numbers of proteins that contribute to forming three clusters, regardless of how the expression

Figure 6. Diagrams that illustrate FE applied to proteome analysis

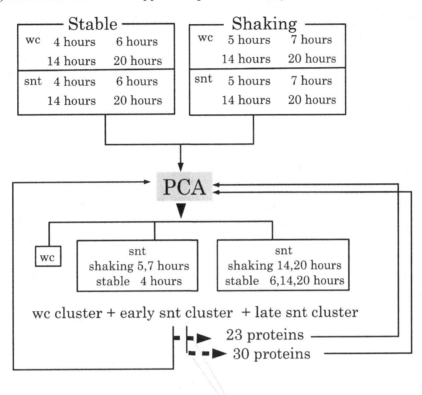

Feature Extractions

of these proteins were dependent upon time or fraction. To our knowledge, no other methods can achieve this kind of FE.

FUTURE RESEARCH DIRECTIONS

PCA based unsupervised FE seems to be a promising methodology, although what type of conditions are required for PCA based unsupervised FE to work well are unclear. If it can be understood, PCA based unsupervised FE will be a very useful method.

To achieve this, this methodology should be applied to other applications. For example, even restricted to bioinformatic approaches, there are several possibilities to apply PCA based unsupervised FE. For example, metabolome is an alternative expression to which PCA based unsupervised FE has never been applied. Since the

metabolome is tightly related to protein/mRNA expression through metabolic pathways, integrative analysis between proteome, transcriptome and metabolome using PCA based unsupervised FE might be promising.

In addition to expression analysis, there remain other epigenetic properties to which PCA based unsupervised FE has never been applied, for example, histone modification.

Furthermore, since PCA based unsupervised FE is not specially implemented to biological problems, it can be applied to any problems when stable (sample-independent) FE is especially required, even if the performances are slightly reduced. For example, motion detection needs to process massive data sets since it includes time course development. Successful PCA based unsupervised FE should have robust (thus stable) FE, and might be useful to detect motion because it reduces the effort required to record movies. Finally, all previous examples to which FE has been applied are potential targets of PCA based unsupervised FE.

CONCLUSION

In this chapter, we introduced PCA based unsupervised FE and applied it to three biological examples: detections of aberrant DNA methylation associated with diseases, biomarker identification using circulating microRNA and bacterial proteome analysis.

In the first example, the main finding is that minor PCs can have potential roles for FE. This is because we have to select a small number of features. Naturally, major PCs cannot represent these minority features. One may wonder whether minor PCs simply reflect noise. To avoid this situation, multiple information sources should be considered. When aberrant promoter methylation associated with autoimmune disease is considered, the multiple information sources are multiple autoimmune diseases. When genotype-specific DNA aberrant methylation associated with ESCC is considered, genotype and DNA methylation are considered together. Since it is not likely that simple noises are identically associated with distinct observations, this kind of integrated analysis prevents us from selecting the wrong PCs for FE.

In the second example, we found that even if each feature (circulating miRNA) does not exhibit disease specific expression, combinatorial selections of features can exhibit disease specificity. In this case, unsupervised (labeling free) FE was very useful, since we could not select features based on disease specificity.

In the third example, we selected limited numbers of features (proteins) that contributed to cluster formation. Again, no labeling information was used for FE because we did not know what kind of difference contributed to the cluster

formation. This is why we successfully selected proteins that exhibited three clusters.

For all three examples, PCA based unsupervised FE worked very well. Further applications of PCA-based unsupervised FE in biological examples should be tested.

REFERENCES

Abeel, T., Helleputte, T., Van de Peer, Y., Dupont, P., & Saeys, Y. (2010). Robust biomarker identification for cancer diagnosis with ensemble feature selection methods. *Bioinformatics (Oxford, England)*, 26(3), 392–398. doi:10.1093/bioinformatics/btp630 PMID:19942583

Almufti, R., Wilbaux, M., Oza, A., Henin, E., Freyer, G., & Tod, M. et al. (2014). A critical review of the analytical approaches for circulating tumor biomarker kinetics during treatment. *Annals of Oncology*, 25(1), 41–56. doi:10.1093/annonc/mdt382 PMID:24356619

Ballestar, E. (Ed.). (2011). *Epigenetic contributions in autoimmune disease*. Heidelberg, Germany: Springer. doi:10.1007/978-1-4419-8216-2

Baylin, S. B., Esteller, M., Rountree, M. R., Bachman, K. E., Schuebel, K., & Herman, J. G. (2001). Aberrant patterns of DNA methylation, chromatin formation and gene expression in cancer. *Human Molecular Genetics*, 10(7), 687–692. doi:10.1093/hmg/10.7.687 PMID:11257100

Bozdogan, H. (1987). Model selection and Akaike's Information Criterion (AIC): The general theory and its analytical extensions. *Psychometrika*, 52(3), 345–370. doi:10.1007/BF02294361

Cao, L. J., Chua, K. S., Chong, W. K., Lee, H. P., & Gu, Q. M. (2003). A comparison of PCA, KPCA and ICA for dimensionality reduction in support vector machine. *Neurocomputing*, 55(1&2), 321–336.

Chan, M., Liaw, C. S., Ji, S. M., Tan, H. H., Wong, C. Y., & Thike, A. A. et al. (2013). Identification of circulating microRNA signatures for breast cancer detection. *Clinical Cancer Research*, *19*(16), 4477–4487. doi:10.1158/1078-0432. CCR-12-3401 PMID:23797906

Chu, S., Keerthi, S., Ong, C. J., & Ghahramani, Z. (2006). Bayesian Support Vector Machines for Feature Ranking and Selection. In I. Guyon & A. Elisseeff (Eds.), *Feature Extraction: Studies in Fuzziness and Soft Computing* (Vol. 207, pp. 403–418). Berlin: Springer. doi:10.1007/978-3-540-35488-8_19

De Backer, S., Naud, A., & Scheunders, P. (1998). Non-linear dimensionality reduction techniques for unsupervised feature extraction. *Pattern Recognition Letters*, *19*(8), 711–720. doi:10.1016/S0167-8655(98)00049-X

Diaz-Uriarte, R., & Alvarez de Andres, S. (2006). Gene selection and classification of microarray data using random forest. *BMC Bioinformatics*, *7*(1), 3. doi:10.1186/1471-2105-7-3 PMID:16398926

Girosi, F., Jones, M., & Poggio, T. (1995). Regularization Theory and Neural Networks Architectures. *Neural Computation*, *7*(2), 219–269. doi:10.1162/neco.1995.7.2.219

Gyon, I., & Elisseeff, A. (2003). An Introduction to Variable and Feature Selection. *Journal of Machine Learning Research*, *3*, 1157–1182.

Ishida, S., Umeyama, H., Iwadate, M., & Taguchi, Y.-h. (2014). Bioinformatic Screening of Autoimmune Disease Genes and Protein Structure Prediction with FAMS for Drug Discovery. *Protein Pept Lett.* 21(8), 828-39. doi: 10.2174/09298665113209990052 PMID: 23855671

Javierre, B. M., Fernandez, A. F., Richter, J., Al-Shahrour, F., Martin-Subero, J. I., & Rodriguez-Ubreva, J. et al. (2010). Changes in the pattern of DNA methylation associate with twin discordance in systemic lupus erythematosus. *Genome Research*, *20*(2), 170–179. doi:10.1101/gr.100289.109 PMID:20028698

Jeffries, M. A., Dozmorov, M., Tang, Y., Merrill, J. T., Wren, J. D., & Sawalha, A. H. (2011). Genomewide DNA methylation patterns in CD4+ T cells from patients with systemic lupus erythematosus. *Epigenetics*, *6*(5), 593–601. doi:10.4161/epi.6.5.15374 PMID:21436623

Jimenez-Rodriguez, L. O., Arzuaga-Cruz, E., & Velez-Reyes, M. (2007). Unsupervised Linear Feature-Extraction Methods and Their Effects in the Classification of High-Dimensional Data. *Geoscience and Remote Sensing*, *45*(2), 469–483. doi:10.1109/TGRS.2006.885412

Keller, A., Leidinger, P., Bauer, A., Elsharawy, A., Haas, J., & Backes, C. et al. (2011). Toward the blood-borne miRNome of human diseases. *Nature Methods*, *8*(10), 841–843. doi:10.1038/nmeth.1682 PMID:21892151

Kinoshita, R., Iwadate, M., Umeyama, H., & Taguchi, Y.h. (2014). Genes associated with genotype-specific DNA methylation in squamous cell carcinoma as candidate drug targets. *BMC Systems Biology*, *8*(S1), S4. doi:10.1186/1752-0509-8-S1-S4 PMID:24565165

Kosaka, N. (Ed.). (2013). *Circulating microRNAs*. Heidelberg, Germany: Springer. doi:10.1007/978-1-62703-453-1

Leidinger, P., Backes, C., Deutscher, S., Schmitt, K., Mueller, S. C., & Frese, K. et al. (2013). A blood based 12-miRNA signature of Alzheimer disease patients. *Genome Biology*, *14*(7), R78. doi:10.1186/gb-2013-14-7-r78 PMID:23895045

Liu, Y., Aryee, M. J., Padyukov, L., Fallin, M. D., Hesselberg, E., & Runarsson, A. et al. (2013). Epigenome-wide association data implicate DNA methylation as an intermediary of genetic risk in rheumatoid arthritis. *Nature Biotechnology*, *31*(2), 142–147. doi:10.1038/nbt.2487 PMID:23334450

Maclellan, S. A., Lawson, J., Baik, J., Guillaud, M., Poh, C. F., & Garnis, C. (2012). Differential expression of miRNAs in the serum of patients with high-risk oral lesions. *Cancer Med*, *1*(2), 268–274. doi:10.1002/cam4.17 PMID:23342275

Murakami, Y., Toyoda, H., Tanahashi, T., Tanaka, J., Kumada, T., & Yoshioka, Y. et al. (2012). Comprehensive miRNA expression analysis in peripheral blood can diagnose liver disease. *PLoS ONE*, *7*(10), e48366. doi:10.1371/journal.pone.0048366 PMID:23152743

Nakazato, T., Bono, H., Matsuda, H., & Takagi, T. (2009). Gendoo: functional profiling of gene and disease features using MeSH vocabulary. *Nucleic Acids Res*, 37(Web Server), W166–169.

Papadopoulos, G. L., Alexiou, P., Maragkakis, M., Reczko, M., & Hatzigeorgiou, A. G. (2009). DIANAmirPath: Integrating human and mouse microRNAs in pathways. *Bioinformatics (Oxford, England)*, *25*(15), 1991–1993. doi:10.1093/bioinformatics/btp299 PMID:19435746

Prasad, S., & Bruce, L. M. (2008). Overcoming the Small Sample Size Problem in Hyperspectral Classification and Detection Tasks. In *Geoscience and Remote Sensing Symposium: Vol.5. IGARSS 2008* (pp. V381-V384) IEEE International. doi:10.1109/IGARSS.2008.4780108

Qiu, W., He, W., Wang, X., & Lazarus, R. (2008). A marginal mixture model for selecting differentially expressed genes across two types of tissue samples. *The International Journal of Biostatistics*, *4*(1), 20. doi:10.2202/1557-4679.1093 PMID:20231912

Rommer, A., Steinleitner, K., Hackl, H., Schneckenleithner, C., Engelmann, M., & Scheideler, M. et al. (2013). Overexpression of primary microRNA 221/222 in acute myeloid leukemia. *BMC Cancer*, *13*(1), 364. doi:10.1186/1471-2407-13-364 PMID:23895238

Scholkopf, B. (2001). In T. K. Leen, T. G. Dietterich, & V. Tresp (Eds.), *The kernel trick for distances* (pp. 301–307). Advances in neural information processing systems. MIT Press.

Shen, J., Wang, A., Wang, Q., Gurvich, I., Siegel, A. B., Remotti, H., & Santella, R. M. (2013). Exploration of Genome-wide Circulating MicroRNA in Hepatocellular Carcinoma (HCC): MiR-483-5p as a Potential Biomarker. *Cancer Epidemiology, Biomarkers & Prevention*, *22*(12), 2364–2373. doi:10.1158/1055-9965.EPI-13-0237 PMID:24127413

Taguchi, Y.-h., & Murakami, Y. (2014). Universal disease biomarker: Can a fixed set of blood microRNAs diagnose multiple diseases? *BMC Research Notes*, *7*, 581. doi:10.1186/1756-0500-7-581

Taguchi, Y.-, & Murakami, Y. (2013). Principal component analysis based feature extraction approach to identify circulating microRNA biomarkers. *PLoS ONE*, *8*(6), e66714. doi:10.1371/journal.pone.0066714 PMID:23874370

Taguchi, Y.-h., & Okamoto, A. (2012). Principal Component Analysis for Bacterial Proteomic Analysis. In T. Shibata, H. Kashima, J. Sese, & S. Ahmad. (Eds.), *Pattern Recognition in Bioinformatics: 7th IAPR International Conference, PRIB 2012* (pp. 441–452). Berlin: Springer. doi:10.1007/978-3-642-34123-6_13

Tibshirani, R. (1996). Regression shrinkage and selection via the lasso. *Journal of the Royal Statistical Society. Series B. Methodological*, *58*(1), 267–288.

Tusher, V. G., Tibshirani, R., & Chu, G. (2001). Significance analysis of microarrays applied to the ionizing radiation response. *Proceedings of the National Academy of Sciences of the United States of America, 98*(9), 5116–5121. doi:10.1073/pnas.091062498 PMID:11309499

Varshavsky, R., Gottlieb, A., Horn, D., & Linial, M. (2007). Unsupervised feature selection under perturbations: Meeting the challenges of biological data. *Bioinformatics (Oxford, England), 23*(24), 3343–3349. doi:10.1093/bioinformatics/btm528 PMID:17989091

Wang, Y., Tetko, I. V., Hall, M. A., Frank, E., Facius, A., Mayer, K. F., & Mewes, H. W. (2005). Gene selection from microarray data for cancer classification–a machine learning approach. *Computational Biology and Chemistry, 29*(1), 37–46. doi:10.1016/j.compbiolchem.2004.11.001 PMID:15680584

Yang, H. H., Hu, N., Wang, C., Ding, T., Dunn, B. K., & Goldstein, A. M. et al. (2010). Influence of genetic background and tissue types on global DNA methylation patterns. *PLoS ONE, 5*(2), e9355. doi:10.1371/journal.pone.0009355 PMID:20186319

ADDITIONAL READING

Bishop, C. M. (2006). *Pattern Recognition and Machine Learning.* New York: Springer.

Broemeling, L. D. (2011). *Advanced Bayesian Methods for Medical test Accuracy.* Boca Raton, FL: CRC Press. doi:10.1201/b11055

Chen, M., & Hofestädt, R. (2014). *Approaches in Integrative Bioinformatics.* Heidelberg: Springer. doi:10.1007/978-3-642-41281-3

Cho, W. C. S. (Ed.). (2011). *MicroRNAs in Cancer Translational Research.* Heidelberg: Springer. doi:10.1007/978-94-007-0298-1

Etheridge, A., Lee, I., Hood, L., Galas, D., & Wang, K. (2011). Extracellular microRNA: A new source of biomarkers. *Mutation Research, 717*(1-2), 85–90. doi:10.1016/j.mrfmmm.2011.03.004 PMID:21402084

Hamelryck, T., Mardia, K., & Ferkinghoff-Borg, J. (Eds.). (2012). *Bayesian Methods in Structural Bioinformatics.* Heidelberg: Springer. doi:10.1007/978-3-642-27225-7

Hastie, T., Tibshrani, R., & Friedman, J. (2009). *The elements of Statistical Learning: Data Mining, Inference and Prediction.* New York: Springer. doi:10.1007/978-0-387-84858-7

Hollander, M., Wolfe, D. A., & Chicken, E. (2013). *Nonparametric statistical methods.* New Jersey: Willy.

Karpf, A. R. (Ed.). (2013). *Epigenetic Alternations in Oncogenesis.* New York: Springer. doi:10.1007/978-1-4419-9967-2

Kim, D., Shin, H., Sohn, K. A., Verma, A., Ritchie, M. D., & Kim, J. H. (2014). Incorporating inter-relationships between different levels of genomic data into cancer clinical outcome prediction. *Methods (San Diego, Calif.), 67*(3), 344–353. doi:10.1016/j.ymeth.2014.02.003 PMID:24561168

Kosaka, N., Iguchi, H., & Ochiya, T. (2010). Circulating microRNA in body fluid: A new potential biomarker for cancer diagnosis and prognosis. *Cancer Science, 101*(10), 2087–2092. doi:10.1111/j.1349-7006.2010.01650.x PMID:20624164

Lopez-Serra, P., & Esteller, M. (2012). DNA methylation-associated silencing of tumor-suppressor microRNAs in cancer. *Oncogene, 31*(13), 1609–1622. doi:10.1038/onc.2011.354 PMID:21860412

Mallick, B., & Ghosh, Z. (Eds.). (2012). *Regulatory RNAs.* Heidelberg: Springer. doi:10.1007/978-3-642-22517-8

Mamitsuka, H., DeLisi, C., & Kanehisa, M. (Eds.). (2013). *Data Mining for Systems Biology: Methods and Protocols*. New York: Humana Press. doi:10.1007/978-1-62703-107-3

Mathivanan, S., Ji, H., & Simpson, R. J. (2010). Exosomes: Extracellular organelles important in intercellular communication. *Journal of Proteomics*, *3*(10), 1907–1920. doi:10.1016/j.jprot.2010.06.006 PMID:20601276

Monticelli, S. (Ed.). (2010). *MicroRNAs and the Immune System*. New York: Humana Press. doi:10.1007/978-1-60761-811-9

Novianti, P. W., Roes, K. C., & Eijkemans, M. J. (2014). Evaluation of gene expression classification studies: Factors associated with classification performance. *PLoS ONE*, *9*(4), e96063. doi:10.1371/journal.pone.0096063 PMID:24770439

Rangwala, H., & Karypis, G. (2010). *Introduction to Protein Structure Prediction: Methods and Algorithms*. New Jersey: Willy. doi:10.1002/9780470882207

Rodriguez-Ezpeleta, N., Hackenberg, M., & Aransay, A. M. (Eds.). (2012). *Bioinformatics for High Throughput Sequencing*. Heidelberg: Springer. doi:10.1007/978-1-4614-0782-9

Shen, B. (Ed.). (2013). *Bioinformatics for Diagnosis, Prognosis and Treatment of Complex Diseases*. Heidelberg: Springer. doi:10.1007/978-94-007-7975-4

Wan, J. (Ed.). (2013). Introduction to Genetics: DNA Methylation, Histone Modification and Gene Regulation. Hong Kong: iConcept press.

Witten, I. H., & Frank, E. (2005). *Data Mining*. San Francisco: Elsevier.

Wu, W. (Ed.). (2011). *MicroRNA and Cancer*. New York: Humana Press. doi:10.1007/978-1-60761-863-8

Yousef, M., & Allmer, J. (Eds.). (2014). miRNomics. New York: Humana Press.

Zen, K., & Zhang, C. Y. (2012). Circulating microRNAs: A novel class of biomarkers to diagnose and monitor human cancers. *Medicinal Research Reviews*, *32*(2), 326–348. doi:10.1002/med.20215 PMID:22383180

KEY TERMS AND DEFINITIONS

Circulating Biomarker: Biomarker that discriminates diseases and are circulating within body. Typical example is blood.

Feature Extraction (FE): FE is the method to select limited number of (useful) variables among given many variables.

Linear Discriminant Analysis (LDA): LDA is linear method that constructs combinatorial features that discriminate something, e.g., patient vs healthy control.

Principal Component Analysis (PCA): PCA is the linear method that embeds high dimensional structure onto the lower dimensional space.

Promoter or DNA Methylation: Methylation takes place along genome sequences. It is generally known to be the most significant epigenetic effects that regulate gene expression. Promoter methylation is supposed to suppress gene expression.

Proteome: Omics of proteins, i.e., a set of proteins expressed in whole bodies, cells, or environments.

Supervised and Unsupervised Learning: These are terminologies of machine or statistical learning theory. Supervised learning is to learn something, (e.g., pattern recognition, with regard to "teacher" signals). On the other hand, unsupervised learning is performed without any "correct" answers.

Section 2
Reviews and Perspectives on Big Data Analysis

Chapter 8
The Role of Big Data in Radiation Oncology:
Challenges and Potentials

Issam El Naqa
McGill University, Canada

ABSTRACT

More than half of cancer patients receive ionizing radiation as part of their treatment and it is the main modality at advanced stages of disease. Treatment outcomes in radiotherapy are determined by complex interactions between cancer genetics, treatment regimens, and patient-related variables. A typical radiotherapy treatment scenario can generate a large pool of data, "Big data," that is comprised of patient demographics, dosimetry, imaging features, and biological markers. Radiotherapy data constitutes a unique interface between physical and biological data interactions. In this chapter, the authors review recent advances and discuss current challenges to interrogate big data in radiotherapy using top-bottom and bottom-top approaches. They describe the specific nature of big data in radiotherapy and discuss issues related to bioinformatics tools for data aggregation, sharing, and confidentiality. The authors also highlight the potential opportunities in this field for big data research from bioinformaticians as well as clinical decision-makers' perspectives.

INTRODUCTION

Cancer is a leading cause of mortality in the United States and worldwide. It remains the second most common cause of death in the United States, accounting for nearly 1 of every 4 deaths. It is projected that a total of 1,665,540 new cancer cases and 585,720 cancer deaths are to occur in the United States in 2014 (Siegel, Ma, Zou, & Jemal, 2014). Radiation therapy (radiotherapy) is

one of three major treatment modalities of cancer beside surgery and chemotherapy and it remains the main option at locally advanced stages of the disease. More than half of all cancer patients receive radiotherapy as a part of their treatment. Despite radiotherapy proven benefits, it comes with a Damocles' sword of benefits and risks to the exposed patient. A key goal of modern radiation oncology research is to predict, at the time of radiation treatment planning, the probability

DOI: 10.4018/978-1-4666-6611-5.ch008

of tumour response benefits and normal tissue risks for the type of treatment being considered. Although recent years have witnessed tremendous technological advances in radiotherapy treatment planning, image-guidance and delivery, efforts to individualize radiotherapy treatment doses based on *in vitro* assays of various biological endpoints has not been clinically successful (IAEA, 2002; C. M. West, 1995). Conversely, several groups have shown that dose-volume factors play an important role in determining treatment outcomes (Bentzen et al., 2010; Blanco et al., 2005; J. Bradley, Deasy, Bentzen, & El-Naqa, 2004; J. O. Deasy & El Naqa, 2008; I. El Naqa et al., 2006; Hope et al., 2005; Jackson et al., 2010; Marks, 2002a; Tucker et al., 2004), but these methods may suffer from limited predictive power when applied prospectively. The lack of progress or major breakthroughs in radiotherapy outcomes over the past two decades demands fundamentally new insights into the methodologies used to better exploit the power of this unique non-invasive high-energy source, as well as it requires a new vision to guide the analysis of radiotherapy response and the design of new therapeutic strategies.

Outcomes in radiotherapy are usually characterized by tumour control probability (TCP) and the surrounding normal tissues complications (NTCP) (Steel, 2002; Webb, 2001). Traditionally, these outcomes are modeled using information about the dose distribution and the fractionation scheme (Moissenko, Deasy, & Van Dyk, 2005). However, it is recognized that radiation response may also be affected by multiple clinical prognostic factors (Marks, 2002b) and more recently, inherited genetic variations have been suggested as playing an important role in radiation sensitivity (J. Alsner, C. N. Andreassen, & J. Overgaard, 2008; C. M. L. West, Elliott, & Burnet, 2007). Moreover, evolution in imaging and biotechnology have provided new extraordinary opportunities for visualizing tumours *in vivo* and for applying new molecular techniques for biomarkers discovery of radiotherapy response, respectively (Bentzen,

2008; Jain, 2007; Nagaraj, 2009; C. M. L. West et al., 2007). However, biological assays, which can be performed on either tumour or normal tissues, may not be the only determinant of tumour control or risk of radiotherapy adverse reactions. Therefore, recent approaches have utilized data driven models using advanced informatics tools in which dose-volume metrics are mixed with other patient or disease-based prognostic factors in order to improve outcomes prediction (Issam El Naqa, 2012). Accurate prediction of treatment outcomes would provide clinicians with better tools for informed decision-making about expected benefits versus anticipated risks.

In this chapter, we will provide an overview of recent advances in radiotherapy informatics and discuss current challenges to interrogate big data as it appears in radiotherapy using top-bottom and bottom top-approaches. We will describe the specific nature of big data in radiotherapy, and the role of the emerging field of systems radiobiology for outcomes modeling. We will provide examples based on our and others experiences. Finally, we will discuss issues related to bioinformatics tools for data aggregation, sharing, and confidentiality.

BACKGROUND

Radiotherapy of Cancer

Radiotherapy is targeted localized treatment using ablative high-energy radiation beams to kill cancer cells. More than half of all cancer patients, particularly patients with solid tumours such as in the brain, lung, breast, head and neck, and the pelvic area receive radiotherapy as part of their curative or palliative treatment. A typical radiotherapy planning process would involve the acquisition of patient image data (typically fully 3-D computed tomography (CT) scans and other diagnostic imaging modalities such as positron emission tomography (PET) or magnetic resonance imaging (MRI)). Then, the physician would outline the tumor and important normal organ structures on a computer, based on the CT scan. Treatment radiation dose distributions are simulated with prescribed doses (energy per unit mass, Gray (Gy)). The treatment itself could be delivered externally using linear accelerators (Linacs) or internally using sealed radioisotopes (Brachytherapy) (Halperin, Perez, & Brady, 2008).

Radiotherapy Response

The biology of radiation effect has been classically defined by "The Four R's" (*r*epair of sublethal cellular damage, *r*eassortment/redistribution of cells into radiosensitive phases of the cell-cycle between dose fractions, *r*eoxygenation over a course of therapy, and cellular *r*epopulation/division over a course of therapy) (Hall & Giaccia, 2006). It is believed that radiation-induced cellular lethality is primarily caused by DNA damage in the targeted cells. Two types of cell death have been linked to radiation effect: apoptosis and post-mitotic cell death. However, tumour cell radiosensitivity is controlled via many factors (known and unknown) related to tumor DNA repair efficiency (e.g., homologous recombination or nonhomologous endjoining), cell cycle control, oxygen concentration, and the radiation dose rate (Hall & Giaccia, 2006; Joiner & Kogel, 2009; Lehnert, 2008). A rather simplistic understanding of these experimentally observed irradiation effects using *in vitro* assays constituted the basis for developing analytical or sometimes referred to as mechanistic models of radiotherapy response. These models have been applied widely for predicting TCP and NTCP and designing radiotherapy clinical trials over the past century. However, due to the inherent complexity and heterogeneity of radiation physics and biological processes, these traditional modeling methods have fallen short of providing sufficient predictive power when applied prospectively to personalize treatment regimens. Therefore, more modern approaches are investigating more advanced informatics and

systems engineering techniques that would be able to integrate physical and biological information to adapt intra-radiotherapy changes and optimize post-radiotherapy treatment outcomes using *top-bottom* approaches based on complex systems analyses or *bottom-top* approaches based on first principles as further discussed below.

Top-Bottom Approaches for Modeling Radiotherapy Response

These are typically phenomenological models and depend on parameters available from the collected clinical, dosimetric and/or biological data (J. O. Deasy & El Naqa, 2008). In the context of data-driven and multi-variable modeling of outcomes, the observed treatment outcome (e.g., TCP or NTCP) is considered as the result of functional mapping of several input variables (I. El Naqa et al., 2006). Mathematically, this is expressed as $f(\mathbf{x}; \mathbf{w}^*): X \rightarrow Y$ where $x_i \in \infty^N$ is composed of the input metrics (dose-volume metrics, patient disease-specific prognostic factors, or biological markers). The expression $y_i \in Y$ is the corresponding observed treatment outcome. The variable $\mathbf{w}^*$ includes the optimal parameters of the model $f(g)$ obtained by learning a certain objective functional. Learning is defined in this context of outcome modeling as estimating dependencies from data (Hastie, Tibshirani, & Friedman, 2001). There are two common types of learning: supervised and unsupervised. Supervised learning is used when the endpoints of the treatments such as tumour control or toxicity grades are known; these endpoints are provided by experienced oncologists following Radiation Therapy Oncology Group (RTOG) or National Cancer Institute (NCI) criteria and it is the most commonly used learning method in outcomes modeling. Nevertheless, unsupervised methods such as principle component analysis (PCA) are also used to reduce the learning problem dimensionality and to aid in the visualization of multivariate data and the selection of the optimal learning method parameters.

The selection of the functional form of the model $f(g)$ is closely related to the prior knowledge of the problem. In mechanistic models, the shape of the functional form is selected based on the clinical or biological process at hand, however, in data-driven models; the objective is usually to find a functional form that best fits the data (I. El Naqa, J. Bradley, P. E. Lindsay, A. Hope, & J. O. Deasy, 2009). A depiction of this top-bottom approach is shown in Figure 1. A detailed review of this methodology is presented in our previous work (I. El Naqa, 2013). Below we will highlight this approach using logistic regression and artificial intelligence methods.

Logistic Regression

In radiation outcomes modeling, the response will usually follow an S-shaped curve. This suggests that models with sigmoidal shapes are the most appropriate to use (Blanco et al., 2005; J. Bradley et al., 2004; J. D. Bradley et al., 2007;

Hope et al., 2005; Huang, Bradley, et al., 2011; Huang, Hope, et al., 2011; Marks, 2002b; Tucker et al., 2004). A commonly used sigmoidal form is the logistic regression model, which also has nice numerical stability properties. The results of this type of approach are not expressed in a closed form as in the case of analytical models but instead, the model parameters are chosen in a stepwise fashion to define the abscissa of the regression model $f(g)$. However, it is the user's responsibility to determine whether interaction terms or higher order variables should be added. A solution to ameliorate this problem could be offered by applying artificial intelligence methods.

Artificial Intelligence Methods

Artificial intelligence techniques (e.g., neural networks, decision trees, support vector machines), which are able to emulate human intelligence by learning the surrounding environment from the given input data, have also been utilized because

Figure 1. Top-bottom modeling approach of radiotherapy response in which heterogeneous variables are combined to improve patient's outcomes. The process could be thought of as a feedback learning system. (Spencer et al., JBB, 2009)

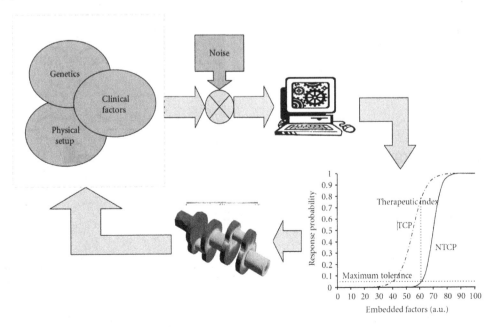

of their ability to detect nonlinear complex patterns in the data. In particular, neural networks were extensively investigated to model post-radiation treatment outcomes for cases of lung injury (Munley et al., 1999; Su et al., 2005) and biochemical failure and rectal bleeding in prostate cancer (Gulliford, Webb, Rowbottom, Corne, & Dearnaley, 2004; Tomatis et al., 2012). A rather more robust approach of machine learning methods is support vector machines (SVMs), which are universal constructive learning procedures based on the statistical learning theory (Vapnik, 1998). For discrimination between patients who are at low risk versus patients who are at high risk of radiation therapy, the main idea of SVM would be to separate these two classes with 'hyper-planes' that maximize the margin between them in the nonlinear feature space defined by an implicit kernel mapping. Examples of applying these methods are discussed in our previous work (Issam El Naqa, 2012; I. El Naqa, J. D. Bradley, P. E. Lindsay, A. J. Hope, & J. O. Deasy, 2009; I. El Naqa et al., 2010).

Bottom-Top Approaches for Modeling Radiotherapy Response

These approaches utilize first principles of radiation physics and biology to model cellular damage temporally and spatially. Typically, they would apply advanced numerical methods such as Monte-Carlo (MC) techniques to estimate the molecular spectrum of damage in clustered and not-clustered DNA lesions (Gbp^{-1} Gy^{-1}) (Nikjoo, Uehara, Emfietzoglou, & Cucinotta, 2006). The temporal and spatial evolution of the effects from ionizing radiation can be divided into three phases: physical, chemical, and biological following the multiscale representation in time and space shown in Figure 2. Different available MC codes aim to emulate these phases to varying extents. A detailed review of many current MC particle track codes and their potential use for radiobiological outcome modeling is provided in our previous work (I. El Naqa, Pater, & Seuntjens, 2012).

Figure 2. Bottom-Top outcome modeling approach representation showing multiscale modeling of tissue (Tumour) radiation response along the time and space axes (El Naqa et al., PMB, 2012)

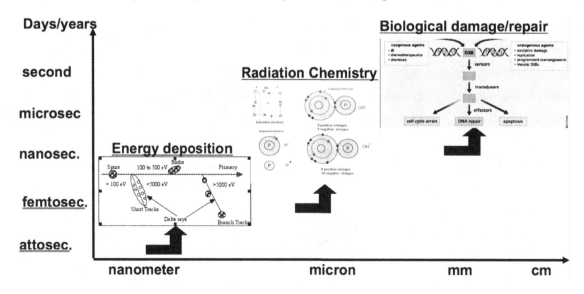

BIG DATA IN RADIOTHERAPY

Constituents of Big Data in Radiotherapy

Big data in radiotherapy could be divided based on its nature into four categories: Clinical, dosimetric, imaging, and biological. These four categories of radiotherapy big data are described in the following.

Clinical Data

Clinical data in radiotherapy typically refers to cancer diagnostic information (site, histology, stage, grade, etc) and patient-related characteristics (age, gender, co-morbidities, etc). In some instances, other treatment modalities information (surgery, chemotherapy, hormonal treatment, etc) would be also classified under this category. The mining of such data could be challenging particularly if the data was in unstructured storage format, however, this lends new opportunities for applying natural language processing (NLP) techniques to assist in the organization of such data (Shivade et al., 2013).

Dosimetric Data

This type of data is related to the treatment planning process in radiotherapy, which involves simulated radiation dose distributions using computed tomography imaging; specifically, dose-volume metrics derived from dose-volume histograms (DVHs) graphs are frequently extracted to summarize this data. Dose-volume metrics have been extensively studied in the radiation oncology literature for outcomes modeling (Blanco et al., 2005; J. Bradley et al., 2004; Hope et al., 2006; Hope et al., 2005; Levegrun et al., 2001; Marks, 2002b). Typical metrics extracted from the DVH include the volume receiving certain dose (Vx), minimum dose to x% volume (Dx), mean, maximum and minimum dose, etc. More

details are in our review chapter (J. O. Deasy & El Naqa, 2008). Moreover, we have developed a dedicated software tool called 'DREES'' for automatically deriving these metrics and modeling of radiotherapy response (I. El Naqa et al., 2006).

Radiomics (Imaging Features)

kV x-ray computed tomography (kV-CT) has been historically considered the standard modality for treatment planning in radiotherapy because of its ability to provide electron density information for target and normal structure definitions as well as heterogeneous dose calculations (Khan, 2007; Webb, 2001). However, additional information from other imaging modalities could be used to improve treatment monitoring and prognosis in different cancer types. For example, physiological information (tumour metabolism, proliferation, necrosis, hypoxic regions, etc.) can be collected directly from nuclear imaging modalities such as SPECT and PET or indirectly from MRI (Condeelis & Weissleder, 2010; Willmann, van Bruggen, Dinkelborg, & Gambhir, 2008). The complementary nature of these different imaging modalities has led to efforts toward combining their information to achieve better treatment outcomes. For instance, PET/CT has been utilized for staging, planning, and assessment of response to radiation therapy (Bussink, Kaanders, van der Graaf, & Oyen, 2011; Zaidi & El Naqa, 2010). Similarly, MRI has been applied in tumour delineation and for assessing toxicities in head and neck cancers (Newbold et al., 2006; Piet et al., 2008). Moreover, quantitative information from hybrid-imaging modalities could be related to biological and clinical endpoints; this is a new emerging field referred to as 'radiomics' (Kumar et al., 2012; P. Lambin et al., 2012). In our previous work, we demonstrated the potential of this new field to monitor and predict response to radiotherapy in head and neck (I. El Naqa, Grigsby, et al., 2009), cervix (I. El Naqa, Grigsby, et al., 2009; Kidd, El

Naqa, Siegel, Dehdashti, & Grigsby, 2012), and lung (Vaidya et al., 2012) cancers, in turn allowing for adapting and individualizing treatment.

Biological Markers

A biomarker is defined as "a characteristic that is objectively measured and evaluated as an indicator of normal biological processes, pathological processes, or pharmacological responses to a therapeutic intervention (Group, 2001)." Biomarkers can be categorized based on the biochemical source of the marker into exogenous or endogenous biomarkers.

Exogenous biomarkers are based on introducing a foreign substance into the patient's body such as those used in molecular imaging as discussed above. Conversely, endogenous biomarkers can further be classified as (1) 'expression biomarkers,' measuring changes in gene expression or protein levels or (2) 'genetic biomarkers,' based on variations, for tumours or normal tissues, in their underlying DNA genetic code. Biomarker measurements are typically based on tissue or fluid specimens, which are analyzed using molecular biology laboratory techniques (I. El Naqa, Craft, Oh, & Deasy, 2011).

Expression Biomarkers

Expression biomarkers are the result of gene expression changes in tissues or bodily fluids due to the disease or normal tissues' response to treatment (Mayeux, 2004). These biomarkers can be further divided into single-parameter (e.g., prostate-specific antigen (PSA) levels in blood serum) versus bio-arrays. These can be based on disease pathophysiology or pharmacogenetics studies or they can be extracted from several methods, such as high-throughput gene expression (aka genomics or transcriptomics) (Nuyten & van de Vijver, 2008; Ogawa, Murayama, & Mori, 2007; Svensson et al., 2006), resulting protein expressions (aka proteomics) (Alaiya, Al-Mohanna, &

Linder, 2005; Wouters, 2008), or metabolites (aka metabolomics) (Spratlin, Serkova, & Eckhardt, 2009; Tyburski et al., 2008). We will discuss examples from high-throughput gene expression (genomics) using RNA microarrays and protein expression (proteomics) analysis using mass spectroscopy.

An RNA microarray is a multiplex technology that allows analyzing thousands of gene expressions from multiple samples at the same time, in which short nucleotides in the array hybridize to the sample, which is subsequently quantified by fluorescence (Schena, Shalon, Davis, & Brown, 1995). Klopp *et al.* used microarray profiling to identify a set of 58-genes using pretreatment biopsy samples that were differentially expressed between cervix cancer patients with and without recurrence (Klopp et al., 2008). Another interesting set of RNA markers include microRNAs (miRNAs), which are a family of small non-coding RNA molecules (~22 nucleotides), each of which can suppress the expression of hundreds of protein-coding gene ('targets'). Specific miRNAs can control related groups of pathways. MicroRNAs thereby comprising a particularly powerful part of the cellular gene expression control system and are particularly attractive as potential biomarkers. We have developed a machine learning algorithm for detecting miRNA targets (X. Wang & El Naqa, 2008) and showed that miR-200 miRNA clusters could be used as prognostic marker in advanced ovarian cancer (Hu et al., 2009). In another example of the value of miRNAs as biomarkers, several miRNA (miR-137, miR-32, miR-155, let-7a) expression levels have been correlated with poor survival and relapse in non-small lung cancer (Yu et al., 2008).

Mass spectroscopy is an analytical technique for the determination of the molecular composition of a sample (Sparkman, 2000). This tool is the main vehicle for large scale protein profiling also known as proteomics (Twyman, 2004). Allal et al. applied proteomics to study radioresistance in rectal cancer. The study identified tropomodulin, heat shock protein 42, beta-tubulin, annexin V, and calsenilin as radioresistive biomarkers, and keratin type I, notch 2 protein homolog and DNA repair protein RAD51L3 as radiosensitive biomarkers (Allal et al., 2004). Zhu *et al.* applied proteomics to study tumour response in cervical cancer. They found that increased expression of S100A9 and galectin-7, and decreased expression of NMP-238 and HSP-70 were associated with significantly increased local response to concurrent chemoradiotherapy in cervical cancer (Zhu et al., 2009). In our previous work, we demonstrated the feasibility of applying bioinformatics methods for proteomics analysis of limited data in radiation-induced lung injury post- radiotherapy in lung cancer patients (J. H. Oh, Craft, Townsend, et al., 2011).

Genetic Variant Markers

The inherent genetic variability of the human genome is an emerging resource for studying disposition to cancer and the variability of patient response to therapeutic agents. These variations in the DNA sequences of humans, in particular single-nucleotide polymorphisms (SNPs) have been shown to elucidate complex disease onset and response in cancer (Erichsen & Chanock, 2004). Methods based on the candidate gene approach and high-throughput genome-wide association studies (GWAS) are currently heavily investigated to analyze the functional effect of SNPs in predicting response to radiotherapy (Jan Alsner, Christian Nicolaj Andreassen, & Jens Overgaard, 2008; Andreassen & Alsner, 2009; C. M. L. West et al., 2007). There are several ongoing SNPs genotyping initiatives in radiation oncology, including the pan-European GENEPI project (Baumann, Hölscher, & Begg, 2003), the British RAPPER project (Burnet, Elliott, Dunning, & West, 2006), the Japanese RadGenomics project (Iwakawa et al., 2006), and the US Gene-PARE project (Ho et al., 2006). An international consortium has been also established to coordinate and lead efforts in this area (C. West & Rosenstein, 2010).

Examples of this effort include the identification of SNPs related to radiation toxicity in prostate cancer treatment (S. L. Kerns et al., 2010; Sarah L. Kerns et al.).

Systems Radiobiology

In order to integrate heterogeneous big data within radiotherapy, engineering-inspired system approaches can have great potential to achieve this goal. Systems biology has emerged as a new field in life sciences to apply systematic study of complex interactions to biological systems (Alon, 2007) but its application to radiation oncology, despite this noted potential, has been unfortunately limited to date (Issam El Naqa, 2012; Feinendegen, Hahnfeldt, Schadt, Stumpf, & Voit, 2008). Recently, Eschrich *et al.* presented a systems biology approach for identifying biomarkers related to radiosensitivity in different cancer cell lines using linear regression to correlate gene expression with survival fraction measurements (Eschrich et al., 2009). However, such a linear regression model may lack the ability to account for higher order interactions among the different genes and neglect the expected hierarchal relationships in signaling transduction of highly complex radiation response. It has been noted in the literature that modeling of molecular interactions could be represented using graphs of network connections as in power lines grids. In this case, radiobiological data can be represented as a graph (network) where the nodes represent genes or proteins and the edges may represent similarities or interactions between these nodes. We have utilized such approach based on Bayesian networks for modeling dosimetric radiation pneumonitis relationships (Jung Hun Oh & El Naqa, 2009) and more recently in predicting local control from biological and dosimetric data as presented in the example of Figure 3 (J. H. Oh, Craft, Al Lozi, et al., 2011).

In the more general realm of informatics, this systems approach could be represented as a part of a feedback treatment planning system as was

Figure 3. A systems-based radiobiology approach. Top: A Bayesian network with probability tables for combined biomarker proteins and physical variables for modelling local tumour control in lung cancer. Bottom: The binning boundaries for each variable. (Oh et al., PMB, 2011)

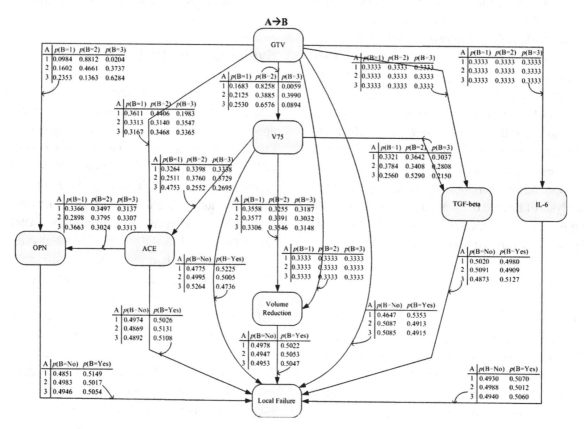

shown in Figure 1. In which, informatics understanding of heterogeneous variable interactions could be used as an adaptive learning process to improve outcomes modeling and the personalization of radiotherapy regimens.

Radiotherapy Warehouses and Database

The recent progress in imaging and biotechnology techniques has provided new opportunities to reshape our understanding of radiation physics and biology and potentially improving the quality of care for radiation oncology patients (Bentzen, 2008). However, this is also accompanied with new challenges of archiving, visualizing and analyzing tremendous heterogeneous datasets of clinical characteristics, dosimetry, imaging and molecular data in a clinical setting.

The group at John Hopkins developed a web-based infrastructure for integrating outcomes with treatment planning information called oncospace (McNutt, 2013). Moreover, the group at Maastricht has developed in collaboration with Siemens a data warehouse with automated tools for feature extraction to integrate different medical data sources for radiotherapy clinical trials. They tested the performance of this warehouse against a manual collection process for non-small cell lung cancer and rectal cancer, using 27 patients per disease. They found that the average time per case to collect the data manually was almost double that of using the warehouse tools (Roelofs et al., 2013). At our institution, we developed a clinical protocol for generating a big data protocol for lung cancer patients who receive radiotherapy we denoted as the "Lung Cancer Jamboree." The protocol aims to collect imaging scans and blood samples at five different time points: (1) pre-treatment, (2) mid-treatment, (3) end-treatment, (4) at 3-months follow-up, and (5) at 6-months follow-up. The patients are assessed for onset of radiation-induced lung injury according to the NCI Common Terminology Criteria for Adverse Events (CTCAE) v4.0 as designated clinical endpoint for outcome modeling. The different data types in this protocol including clinical data, imaging, and biological markers are collected and analyzed as represented in the schematics of Figure 4.

Multi-institutional groups in the USA and elsewhere such as the Radiation Therapy Oncology Group (RTOG) had assembled bioinformatics groups to facilitate the development of personalized predictive models for radiation therapy guidance. The data is collected from specific characteristics of patients and treatments and is integrated with clinical trial databases, which include clinical, dosimetric, as well as biological information through its biospecimen resource. Similarly, European groups have launched an initiative called the Euregional Computer Assisted Theragnostics project (EuroCAT) in the Meuse-Rhine region to address the same problem with specific goals of developing a shared database

Figure 4. Description showing the lung jamboree protocol for investigating radiation-induced lung injury (pneumonitis/fibrosis) by using a big data approach of clinical, dosimetric, imaging, and biomarkers. The top image shows the protocol longitudinal schema and the bottom one shows sample imaging and biomarkers data.

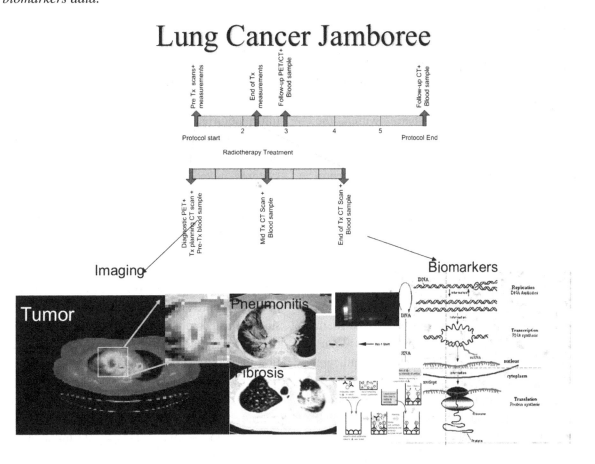

among participating European institutions that would include medical characteristics of cancer patients and identify suitable candidates for multi-institutional clinical trials.

ISSUES AND RECOMMENDATIONS

Data Sharing

Data sharing remains an issue for technical and non-technical issues (Sullivan et al., 2011). Therefore, the Quantitative Analyses of Normal Tissue Effects in the Clinic (QUANTEC) consortium has suggested that cooperative groups adopt a policy of anonymizing clinical trials data and making theses data publicly accessible after a reasonable delay. This delay would enable publication of all the investigator-driven, planned studies while encouraging the establishment of key databanks of linked treatment planning, imaging, and outcomes data (Joseph O. Deasy et al., 2010). An alternative approach is to apply rapid learning as suggested by the group at Maastricht. In which, innovative information technologies are developed that support semantic interoperability and enable distributed learning and data sharing without the need for the data to leave the hospital (Philippe Lambin et al., 2013). An example of multi-institutional data sharing is developed by the group and the Policlinico Universitario Agostino Gemelli in Rome, Italy (Gemelli) (Roelofs et al., 2014).

Imaging Transfer and Retrieval Technologies

DICOM (Digital Imaging and Communications in Medicine) version 3.0 is currently the main standard adopted by radiotherapy vendors as part of the adherence to the "Integrating the Healthcare Enterprise" in Radiation Oncology (IHE-RO). A supplement has been added to incorporate specific structures or objects related to radiotherapy called DICOM-RT, which includes organ contours and radiation dosimetry information. CT images used for simulation and patient setup are typically stored in vendors' local databases using DICOR-RT formats. Additional diagnostic imaging data is stored in picture archiving and communication system (PACS), which provides tools to manage the storage and distribution of images. The use of compression techniques is necessary to accommodate the continuously evolving size of stored images including 4D multi-slice CT, PET, and different MRI pulse sequences (Strintzis, 1998). Despite the fact that storage cost has dropped over the years, the question of using lossy compression methods has been re-opened given the exponential increase in image use in oncology(Koff & Shulman, 2006). A rather interesting technology for retrieval of medical images is the use of content-based image retrieval (CBIR) technologies, which offer computerized solutions that aim to query images for diagnostic or therapeutic information based on the content or extracted features of the images rather than their textual annotation (Issam El Naqa & Yang, 2014).

Information Technology

Information technologies, whether it was hardware (e.g., disk space, memory, processors, networking, etc) or software (e.g., database management systems, indexing, compression, querying, visualization, etc), are at the heart of any successful utilization of big data for outcome modeling in radiotherapy. The field of radiation oncology is founded on using advanced treatment delivery and imaging technologies, however, its informatics infrastructure has been limited to meet clinical needs of record and verification. The presence of such infrastructure could be utilized as a starting step towards building a big data platform in radiation oncology as described in the oncospace or the EuroCat examples mentioned above. However, additional information may need to be accessed from radiology (radiomics) and/or pathology (genomics/proteomics). This would indicate the need for a comprehensive approach with multiple collaborative partners at the medical institution to play an active role in sharing resources or access to resources using standards such as Health Level Seven (HL7).

Web Resources for Radiobiology

As of today, there are no dedicated web resources for big data studies in radiation oncology. Nevertheless, radiotherapy biological markers studies can still benefit from existing bioinformatics resources for pharmacogenomic studies that contain databases and tools for genomic, proteomic, and functional analysis as reviewed by Yan (Yan, 2005). For example, the National Center for Biotechnology Information (NCBI) site hosts databases such as GenBank, dbSNP, Online Mendelian Inheritance in Man (OMIM), and genetic search tools such as BLAST. In addition, the Protein Data Bank (PDB) and the program CPHmodels are useful for protein structure three-dimensional modeling. The Human Genome Variation Database (HGVbase) contains information on physical and functional relationships between sequence variations and neighboring genes. Pattern analysis using PROSITE and Pfam databases can help correlate sequence structures to functional motifs such as phosphorylation (Yan, 2005). Biological pathways construction and analysis is an emerging field in computational biology that aims to bridge the gap between biomarkers findings in clinical studies with underlying biological processes. Several public databases and tools are being established for annotating and storing known pathways such as KEGG and Reactome projects or commercial ones such as the IPA or MetaCore (Viswanathan, Seto, Patil, Nudelman, & Sealfon, 2008). Statistical tools are used to properly map data from gene/protein differential experiments into the different pathways such as mixed effect models (L. Wang, Zhang, Wolfinger, & Chen, 2008) or enrichment analysis (Subramanian et al., 2005).

Protecting the Confidentiality and Privacy of Clinical Phenotype Data

Issues of confidentiality and patient privacy are important to any clinical research including big data. This can emerge in single institutional or multi-institutional studies nationally or internationally. Confidentially requirement also applies in scenarios using cloud online storage systems or when sharing data across borders (e.g., teleconferencing, telemedicine, etc) whether for consultation, quality assurance, or research purpose. In the case of big data research, QUANTEC offered a solution to radiotherapy digital data (treatment planning, imaging, and outcomes data) accessibility by asking cooperative groups to adopt a policy of anonymizing clinical trials data and making the data publicly accessible after a reasonable delay (Joseph O. Deasy et al., 2010). With regard to blood or tissue samples, no recommendations were made, however, by extending the same notion, gene or protein expression assay measurements could be made available under the same umbrella, while raw specimens data could be accessed from the biospecimens resource. For example, in the RTOG biospecimen standard operating procedure (SOP), it is highlighted that biospecimens received by the RTOG Biospecimen Resource are de-identified of all patient health identifiers when enrolled in an approved RTOG study. Each patient being enrolled by an institution has to qualify and consent to be part of a particular study before being assigned a case and study ID by the RTOG Statistical Center. No information containing specific patient health identifiers is maintained by the Resource Freezerworks database, which is primarily an inventory and tracking system. In addition, information related to medical identifiers and any code lists could be removed completely from the dataset after a certain period say 10 years or so. Moreover, it has been argued that current measures by Health Insurance Portability and Accountability Act (HIPPA) of 18 data Elements may not be sufficient and techniques based on research in privacy-preserving data mining, disclosure risk assessment data de-identification, obfuscation, and protection may need to be adopted to achieve better protection of confidentiality (Krishna, Kelleher, & Stahlberg, 2007).

FUTURE RESEARCH DIRECTIONS

The ability to maintain high fidelity big data for radiotherapy studies remains a major challenge despite the high volume of clinical generated data on almost daily basis. As discussed above there have been several ongoing institutional and multi-institutional initiatives such as the RTOG, radiogenomics consortium, and EuroCAT to develop such infrastructure, however, there is plenty of work to be done to overcome, data sharing hurdles, patient confidentiality issues lack of signaling pathways databases of radiation response, development of cost-effective multi-center communication systems that allows transmission, storage, and query of large datasets such images, dosimetry, and biomarkers information. The use of NLP techniques is a promising approach in organizing unstructured clinical data. Dosimetry and imaging data can benefit from existing infrastructure for Picture Archiving and Communications Systems (PACS) or other medical image databases. Methods based on the new emerging field of systems radiobiology will continue to grow on a rapid pace, but they could also benefit immensely from the development of specialized radiation response signalling pathways databases analogous to the currently existing pharmacogenomics databases. Data sharing among different institutions is major hurdle, which seems could be solved through cooperative groups or distributed databases by developing in a cost-effective manner the necessary informatics and communication infrastructure using open-access resources through partnership with industry.

CONCLUSION

Recent evolution in radiotherapy imaging and biotechnology has generated enormous amount of big data that spans clinical, dosimetric, imaging, and biological markers. This data provided new opportunities for re-shaping our understanding of radiotherapy response and outcomes modeling. However, the complexity of this data and the variability of tumour and normal tissue responses would render the utilization of advanced informatics and datamining methods as indispensible tools for better delineation of radiation complex interaction mechanisms and basically a cornerstone to "making data dream come true"(Nature Editorial, 2004). However, it also posed new challenges for data aggregation, sharing, confidentiality and analysis. Moreover, radiotherapy data constitutes a unique interface between physics and biology that can benefit from the general advances in biomedical informatics research such as systems biology and available web resources while still requires the development of its own technologies to address specific issues related to this interface. Successful application and development of advanced data communication and bioinformatics tools for radiation oncology big data is essential to better predicting radiotherapy response to accompany other aforementioned technologies and usher significant progress towards the goal of personalized treatment planning and improving the quality of life for radiotherapy cancer patients.

REFERENCES

Alaiya, A., Al-Mohanna, M., & Linder, S. (2005). Clinical cancer proteomics: Promises and pitfalls. *Journal of Proteome Research*, 4(4), 1213–1222. doi:10.1021/pr050149f PMID:16083271

Allal, A. S., Kähne, T., Reverdin, A. K., Lippert, H., Schlegel, W., & Reymond, M.-A. (2004). Radioresistance-related proteins in rectal cancer. *Proteomics*, *4*(8), 2261–2269. doi:10.1002/pmic.200300854 PMID:15274120

Alon, U. (2007). *An introduction to systems biology: design principles of biological circuits.* Boca Raton, FL: Chapman & Hall/CRC.

Alsner, J., Andreassen, C. N., & Overgaard, J. (2008). Genetic markers for prediction of normal tissue toxicity after radiotherapy. *Seminars in Radiation Oncology*, *18*(2), 126–135. doi:10.1016/j.semradonc.2007.10.004 PMID:18314067

Alsner, J., Andreassen, C. N., & Overgaard, J. (2008). Genetic Markers for Prediction of Normal Tissue Toxicity After Radiotherapy. *Seminars in Radiation Oncology*, *18*(2), 126–135. doi:10.1016/j.semradonc.2007.10.004 PMID:18314067

Andreassen, C. N., & Alsner, J. (2009). Genetic variants and normal tissue toxicity after radiotherapy: A systematic review. *Radiotherapy and Oncology*, *92*(3), 299–309. doi:10.1016/j.radonc.2009.06.015 PMID:19683821

Baumann, M., Hölscher, T., & Begg, A. C. (2003). Towards genetic prediction of radiation responses: ESTRO's GENEPI project. *Radiotherapy and Oncology*, *69*(2), 121–125. doi:10.1016/j.radonc.2003.08.006 PMID:14643948

Bentzen, S. M. (2008). From cellular to high-throughput predictive assays in radiation oncology: Challenges and opportunities. *Seminars in Radiation Oncology*, *18*(2), 75–88. doi:10.1016/j.semradonc.2007.10.003 PMID:18314062

Bentzen, S. M., Constine, L. S., Deasy, J. O., Eisbruch, A., Jackson, A., & Marks, L. B. et al. (2010). Quantitative Analyses of Normal Tissue Effects in the Clinic (QUANTEC): An introduction to the scientific issues. *International Journal of Radiation Oncology, Biology, Physics*, *76*(3Suppl), S3–S9. doi:10.1016/j.ijrobp.2009.09.040 PMID:20171515

Blanco, A. I., Chao, K. S., El Naqa, I., Franklin, G. E., Zakarian, K., Vicic, M., & Deasy, J. O. (2005). Dose-volume modeling of salivary function in patients with head-and-neck cancer receiving radiotherapy. *International Journal of Radiation Oncology, Biology, Physics*, *62*(4), 1055–1069. doi:10.1016/j.ijrobp.2004.12.076 PMID:15990009

Bradley, J., Deasy, J. O., Bentzen, S., & El-Naqa, I. (2004). Dosimetric correlates for acute esophagitis in patients treated with radiotherapy for lung carcinoma. [pii]. *International Journal of Radiation Oncology, Biology, Physics*, *58*(4), 1106–1113. doi:10.1016/j.ijrobp.2003.09.080 PMID:15001251

Bradley, J. D., Hope, A., El Naqa, I., Apte, A., Lindsay, P. E., Bosch, W.,... Deasy, J. O. (2007). A nomogram to predict radiation pneumonitis, derived from a combined analysis of RTOG 9311 and institutional data. *Int J Radiat Oncol Biol Phys*, *69*(4), 985-992. doi: 10.1016/j.ijrobp.2007.04.077

Burnet, N. G., Elliott, R. M., Dunning, A., & West, C. M. L. (2006). Radiosensitivity, Radiogenomics and RAPPER. *Clinical Oncology*, *18*(7), 525–528. doi:10.1016/j.clon.2006.05.007 PMID:16969982

Bussink, J., Kaanders, J. H. A. M., van der Graaf, W. T. A., & Oyen, W. J. G. (2011). PET-CT for radiotherapy treatment planning and response monitoring in solid tumors. *Nat Rev Clin Oncol, 8*(4), 233–242. doi:10.1038/nrclinonc.2010.218 PMID:21263464

Condeelis, J., & Weissleder, R. (2010). In vivo imaging in cancer. *Cold Spring Harb Perspect Biol, 2*(12), a003848. doi: 10.1101/cshperspect.a003848

Deasy, J. O., Bentzen, S. r. M., Jackson, A., Ten Haken, R. K., Yorke, E. D., Constine, L. S.,... Marks, L. B. (2010). Improving Normal Tissue Complication Probability Models: The Need to Adopt a ‚ÄúData-Pooling‚Äù Culture. *International Journal of Radiation Oncology*Biology*Physics, 76*(3, Supplement), S151-S154. doi:10.1016/j.ijrobp.2009.06.094

Deasy, J. O., & El Naqa, I. (2008). Image-based modeling of normal tissue complication probability for radiation therapy. *Cancer Treatment and Research, 139*, 215–256. doi:10.1007/978-0-387-36744-6_11 PMID:18236719

Editorial, N. (2004). Making data dreams come true. *Nature, 428*(6980), 239–239. doi:10.1038/428239b PMID:15029154

El Naqa, I. (2012). Machine learning methods for predicting tumor response in lung cancer. *Wiley Interdisciplinary Reviews: Data Mining and Knowledge Discovery, 2*(2), 173–181. doi:10.1002/widm.1047

El Naqa, I. (2013). Outcomes Modeling. In G. Starkschall & C. Siochi (Eds.), *Informatics in Radiation Oncology* (pp. 257–275). Boca Raton, FL: CRC Press, Taylor and Francis.

El Naqa, I., Bradley, J., Lindsay, P. E., Hope, A., & Deasy, J. O. (2009). Predicting Radiotherapy Outcomes using Statistical Learning Techniques. *Physics in Medicine and Biology, 54*(18), S9–S30. doi:10.1088/0031-9155/54/18/S02 PMID:19687564

El Naqa, I., Bradley, J. D., Lindsay, P. E., Blanco, A. I., Vicic, M., Hope, A. J., & Deasy, J. O. (2006). Multi-variable modeling of radiotherapy outcomes including dose-volume and clinical factors. *International Journal of Radiation Oncology, Biology, Physics, 64*(4), 1275–1286. doi:10.1016/j.ijrobp.2005.11.022 PMID:16504765

El Naqa, I., Bradley, J. D., Lindsay, P. E., Hope, A. J., & Deasy, J. O. (2009). Predicting radiotherapy outcomes using statistical learning techniques. *Phys Med Biol, 54*(18), S9-S30. doi:10.1088/0031-9155/54/18/S02

El Naqa, I., Craft, J., Oh, J., & Deasy, J. (2011). Biomarkers for Early Radiation Response for Adaptive Radiation Therapy. In X. A. Li (Ed.), *Adaptive Radiation Therapy* (pp. 53–68). Boca Baton, FL: Taylor & Francis.

El Naqa, I., Deasy, J. O., Mu, Y., Huang, E., Hope, A. J., & Lindsay, P. E. et al. (2010). Datamining approaches for modeling tumor control probability. *Acta Oncologica (Stockholm, Sweden), 49*(8), 1363–1373. doi:10.3109/02841861003649224 PMID:20192878

El Naqa, I., Grigsby, P., Apte, A., Kidd, E., Donnelly, E., & Khullar, D. et al. (2009). Exploring feature-based approaches in PET images for predicting cancer treatment outcomes. *Pattern Recognition, 42*(6), 1162–1171. doi:10.1016/j.patcog.2008.08.011 PMID:20161266

El Naqa, I., Pater, P., & Seuntjens, J. (2012). Monte Carlo role in radiobiological modelling of radiotherapy outcomes. *Physics in Medicine and Biology, 57*(11), R75–R97. doi:10.1088/0031-9155/57/11/R75 PMID:22571871

El Naqa, I., Suneja, G., Lindsay, P. E., Hope, A. J., Alaly, J. R., & Vicic, M. et al. (2006). Dose response explorer: An integrated open-source tool for exploring and modelling radiotherapy dose-volume outcome relationships. *Physics in Medicine and Biology, 51*(22), 5719–5735. doi:10.1088/0031-9155/51/22/001 PMID:17068361

El Naqa, I., & Yang, Y. (2014). The Role of Content-Based Image Retrieval in Mammography CAD. In K. Suzuki (Ed.), *Computational Intelligence in Biomedical Imaging* (pp. 33–53). Springer New York. doi:10.1007/978-1-4614-7245-2_2

Erichsen, H. C., & Chanock, S. J. (2004). SNPs in cancer research and treatment. *British Journal of Cancer*, *90*(4), 747–751. doi:10.1038/sj.bjc.6601574 PMID:14970847

Eschrich, S., Zhang, H., Zhao, H., Boulware, D., Lee, J.-H., Bloom, G., & Torres-Roca, J. F. (2009). Systems Biology Modeling of the Radiation Sensitivity Network: A Biomarker Discovery Platform. *International Journal of Radiation Oncology*Biology*Physics, 75*(2), 497-505.

Feinendegen, L., Hahnfeldt, P., Schadt, E. E., Stumpf, M., & Voit, E. O. (2008). Systems biology and its potential role in radiobiology. *Radiation and Environmental Biophysics*, *47*(1), 5–23. doi:10.1007/s00411-007-0146-8 PMID:18087710

Group, B. D. W. (2001). Biomarkers and surrogate endpoints: preferred definitions and conceptual framework. *Clin Pharmacol Ther, 69*(3), 89-95. doi: 10.1067/mcp.2001.113989

Gulliford, S. L., Webb, S., Rowbottom, C. G., Corne, D. W., & Dearnaley, D. P. (2004). Use of artificial neural networks to predict biological outcomes for patients receiving radical radiotherapy of the prostate. *Radiotherapy and Oncology*, *71*(1), 3–12. doi:10.1016/j.radonc.2003.03.001 PMID:15066290

Hall, E. J., & Giaccia, A. J. (2006). *Radiobiology for the radiologist* (6th ed.). Philadelphia: Lippincott Williams & Wilkins.

Halperin, E. C., Perez, C. A., & Brady, L. W. (2008). *Perez and Brady's principles and practice of radiation oncology* (5th ed.). Philadelphia: Wolters Kluwer Health/Lippincott Williams & Wilkins.

Hastie, T., Tibshirani, R., & Friedman, J. H. (2001). *The elements of statistical learning: data mining, inference, and prediction: with 200 full-color illustrations*. New York: Springer.

Ho, A. Y., Atencio, D. P., Peters, S., Stock, R. G., Formenti, S. C., Cesaretti, J. A.,... Rosenstein, B. S. (2006). Genetic Predictors of Adverse Radiotherapy Effects: The Gene-PARE project. *International Journal of Radiation Oncology*Biology*Physics, 65*(3), 646-655.

Hope, A. J., Lindsay, P. E., El Naqa, I., Alaly, J. R., Vicic, M., Bradley, J. D., & Deasy, J. O. (2006). Modeling radiation pneumonitis risk with clinical, dosimetric, and spatial parameters. *Int J Radiat Oncol Biol Phys, 65*(1), 112-124. doi: 10.1016/j.ijrobp.2005.11.046

Hope, A. J., Lindsay, P. E., El Naqa, I., Bradley, J. D., Vicic, M., & Deasy, J. O. (2005). *Clinical, Dosimetric, and Location-Related Factors to Predict Local Control in Non-Small Cell Lung Cancer*. Paper presented at the ASTRO 47th Annual Meeting. Denver, CO. doi:10.1016/j.ijrobp.2005.07.394

Hu, X., Macdonald, D. M., Huettner, P. C., Feng, Z., El Naqa, I. M., Schwarz, J. K.,... Wang, X. (2009). A miR-200 microRNA cluster as prognostic marker in advanced ovarian cancer. *Gynecol Oncol, 114*(3), 457-464. doi: 10.1016/j.ygyno.2009.05.022

Huang, E. X., Bradley, J. D., Naqa, I. E., Hope, A. J., Lindsay, P. E., Bosch, W. R.,... Deasy, J. O. (2011). Modeling the Risk of Radiation-Induced Acute Esophagitis for Combined Washington University and RTOG Trial 93-11 Lung Cancer Patients. *Int J Radiat Oncol Biol Phys*. doi: 10.1016/j.ijrobp.2011.02.052

Huang, E. X., Hope, A. J., Lindsay, P. E., Trovo, M., El Naqa, I., Deasy, J. O., & Bradley, J. D. (2011). Heart irradiation as a risk factor for radiation pneumonitis. *Acta Oncologica (Stockholm, Sweden)*, *50*(1), 51–60. doi:10.3109/0284186X.2010.521192 PMID:20874426

IAEA. (2002). *Predictive assays and their role in selection of radiation as the therapeutic modality.* IAEA.

Iwakawa, M., Noda, S., Yamada, S., Yamamoto, N., Miyazawa, Y., & Yamazaki, H. et al. (2006). Analysis of non-genetic risk factors for adverse skin reactions to radiotherapy among 284 Breast Cancer patients. *Breast Cancer (Tokyo, Japan), 13*(3), 300–307. doi:10.2325/jbcs.13.300 PMID:16929125

Jackson, A., Marks, L. B., Bentzen, S. M., Eisbruch, A., Yorke, E. D., Ten Haken, R. K.,... Deasy, J. O. (2010). The lessons of QUANTEC: recommendations for reporting and gathering data on dose-volume dependencies of treatment outcome. *Int J Radiat Oncol Biol Phys, 76*(3 Suppl), S155-160. doi: 10.1016/j.ijrobp.2009.08.074

Jain, K. K. (2007). Cancer biomarkers: Current issues and future directions. *Current Opinion in Molecular Therapeutics, 9*(6), 563–571. PMID:18041667

Joiner, M., & Kogel, A. d. (2009). *Basic clinical radiobiology* (4th ed.). London: Hodder Arnold.

Kerns, S. L., Ostrer, H., Stock, R., Li, W., Moore, J., Pearlman, A.,... Rosenstein, B. S. (2010). Genome-wide association study to identify single nucleotide polymorphisms (SNPs) associated with the development of erectile dysfunction in African-American men after radiotherapy for prostate cancer. *Int J Radiat Oncol Biol Phys, 78*(5), 1292-1300. doi: 10.1016/j.ijrobp.2010.07.036

Kerns, S. L., Stock, R., Stone, N., Buckstein, M., Shao, Y., Campbell, C.,... Rosenstein, B. S. (n.d.). A 2-Stage Genome-Wide Association Study to Identify Single Nucleotide Polymorphisms Associated With Development of Erectile Dysfunction Following Radiation†Therapy for Prostate Cancer. *International Journal of Radiation Oncology*Biology*Physics,* (0).

Khan, F. M. (2007). *Treatment planning in radiation oncology* (2nd ed.). Philadelphia: Lippincott Williams & Wilkins.

Kidd, E. A., El Naqa, I., Siegel, B. A., Dehdashti, F., & Grigsby, P. W. (2012). FDG-PET-based prognostic nomograms for locally advanced cervical cancer. *Gynecol Oncol, 127*(1), 136-140. doi: 10.1016/j.ygyno.2012.06.027

Klopp, A. H., Jhingran, A., Ramdas, L., Story, M. D., Broadus, R. R., & Lu, K. H. et al. (2008). Gene expression changes in cervical squamous cell carcinoma after initiation of chemoradiation and correlation with clinical outcome. *International Journal of Radiation Oncology, Biology, Physics, 71*(1), 226–236. doi:10.1016/j.ijrobp.2007.10.068 PMID:18406887

Koff, D. A., & Shulman, H. (2006). An overview of digital compression of medical images: Can we use lossy image compression in radiology? *Canadian Association of Radiologists Journal, 57*(4), 211–217. PMID:17128888

Krishna, R., Kelleher, K., & Stahlberg, E. (2007). Patient confidentiality in the research use of clinical medical databases. *American Journal of Public Health, 97*(4), 654–658. doi:10.2105/AJPH.2006.090902 PMID:17329644

Kumar, V., Gu, Y., Basu, S., Berglund, A., Eschrich, S. A., Schabath, M. B.,... Gillies, R. J. (2012). Radiomics: the process and the challenges. *Magn Reson Imaging, 30*(9), 1234-1248. doi: 10.1016/j.mri.2012.06.010

Lambin, P., Rios-Velazquez, E., Leijenaar, R., Carvalho, S., van Stiphout, R. G., Granton, P.,... Aerts, H. J. (2012). Radiomics: extracting more information from medical images using advanced feature analysis. *Eur J Cancer, 48*(4), 441-446. doi: 10.1016/j.ejca.2011.11.036

Lambin, P., Roelofs, E., Reymen, B., Velazquez, E. R., Buijsen, J., & Zegers, C. M. L. et al. (2013). ‚ÄòRapid Learning health care in oncology‚Äô‚Äì An approach towards decision support systems enabling customised radiotherapy‚Äô. *Radiotherapy and Oncology, 109*(1), 159–164. doi:10.1016/j.radonc.2013.07.007 PMID:23993399

Lehnert, S. (2008). *Biomolecular action of ionizing radiation*. New York: Taylor & Francis.

Levegrun, S., Jackson, A., Zelefsky, M. J., Skwarchuk, M. W., Venkatraman, E. S., & Schlegel, W. et al. (2001). Fitting tumor control probability models to biopsy outcome after three-dimensional conformal radiation therapy of prostate cancer: Pitfalls in deducing radiobiologic parameters for tumors from clinical data. *International Journal of Radiation Oncology, Biology, Physics, 51*(4), 1064–1080. doi:10.1016/S0360-3016(01)01731-X PMID:11704332

Lu, J. J., & Brady, L. W. (2011). *Decision making in radiation oncology*. Heidelberg, Germany: Springer.

Marks, L. B. (2002). Dosimetric predictors of radiation-induced lung injury. *International Journal of Radiation Oncology, Biology, Physics, 54*(2), 313–316. doi:10.1016/S0360-3016(02)02928-0 PMID:12243802

Mayeux, R. (2004). Biomarkers: Potential uses and limitations. *NeuroRx, 1*(2), 182–188. doi:10.1602/neurorx.1.2.182 PMID:15717018

McNutt, T. (2013). *Analytic database for personalized and evidence-based radiation oncology*. Paper presented at the ICCR. Melbourne, Australia.

Moissenko, V., Deasy, J. O., & Van Dyk, J. (2005). Radiobiological Modeling for Treatment Planning. In J. Van Dyk (Ed.), *The Modern Technology of Radiation Oncology: A Compendium for Medical Physicists and Radiation Oncologists* (Vol. 2, pp. 185–220). Madison, WI: Medical Physics Publishing.

Munley, M. T., Lo, J. Y., Sibley, G. S., Bentel, G. C., Anscher, M. S., & Marks, L. B. (1999). A neural network to predict symptomatic lung injury. *Physics in Medicine and Biology, 44*(9), 2241–2249. doi:10.1088/0031-9155/44/9/311 PMID:10495118

Nagaraj, N. S. (2009). Evolving 'omics' technologies for diagnostics of head and neck cancer. *Brief Funct Genomic Proteomic, 8*(1), 49-59. doi:10.1093/bfgp/elp004

Newbold, K., Partridge, M., Cook, G., Sohaib, S. A., Charles-Edwards, E., & Rhys-Evans, P. et al. (2006). Advanced imaging applied to radiotherapy planning in head and neck cancer: A clinical review. *The British Journal of Radiology, 79*(943), 554–561. doi:10.1259/bjr/48822193 PMID:16823059

Nikjoo, H., Uehara, S., Emfietzoglou, D., & Cucinotta, F. A. (2006). Track-structure codes in radiation research. *Radiation Measurements, 41*(9-10), 1052–1074. doi:10.1016/j.radmeas.2006.02.001

Nuyten, D. S., & van de Vijver, M. J. (2008). Using microarray analysis as a prognostic and predictive tool in oncology: Focus on breast cancer and normal tissue toxicity. *Seminars in Radiation Oncology, 18*(2), 105–114. doi:10.1016/j.semradonc.2007.10.007 PMID:18314065

Ogawa, K., Murayama, S., & Mori, M. (2007). Predicting the tumor response to radiotherapy using microarray analysis [Review]. *Oncology Reports, 18*(5), 1243–1248. PMID:17914580

Oh, J. H., Craft, J., Al Lozi, R., Vaidya, M., Meng, Y., Deasy, J. O.,... El Naqa, I. (2011). A Bayesian network approach for modeling local failure in lung cancer. *Phys Med Biol, 56*(6), 1635-1651. doi: 10.1088/0031-9155/56/6/008

Oh, J. H., Craft, J. M., Townsend, R. R., Deasy, J. O., Bradley, J. D., & El Naqa, I. (2011). A Bioinformatics Approach for Biomarker Identification in Radiation-Induced Lung Inflammation from Limited Proteomics Data. *Journal of Proteome Research, 10*(3), 1406–1415. doi:10.1021/pr101226q PMID:21226504

Oh, J. H., & El Naqa, I. (2009). *Bayesian network learning for detecting reliable interactions of dose-volume related parameters in radiation pneumonitis*. Paper presented at the International Conference on Machine Learning and Applications (ICMLA). Miami, FL. doi:10.1109/ICMLA.2009.122

Piet, D., Frederik De, K., Vincent, V., Sigrid, S., Robert, H., & Sandra, N. (2008). Diffusion-Weighted Magnetic Resonance Imaging to Evaluate Major Salivary Gland Function Before and After Radiotherapy. *International Journal of Radiation Oncology, Biology, Physics*.

Roelofs, E., Dekker, A., Meldolesi, E., van Stiphout, R. G. P. M., Valentini, V., & Lambin, P. (2014). International data-sharing for radiotherapy research: An open-source based infrastructure for multicentric clinical data mining. *Radiotherapy and Oncology, 110*(2), 370–374. doi:10.1016/j.radonc.2013.11.001 PMID:24309199

Roelofs, E., Persoon, L., Nijsten, S., Wiessler, W., Dekker, A., & Lambin, P. (2013). Benefits of a clinical data warehouse with data mining tools to collect data for a radiotherapy trial. *Radiotherapy and Oncology, 108*(1), 174–179. doi:10.1016/j.radonc.2012.09.019 PMID:23394741

Schena, M., Shalon, D., Davis, R. W., & Brown, P. O. (1995). Quantitative Monitoring of Gene Expression Patterns with a Complementary DNA Microarray. *Science, 270*(5235), 467–470. doi:10.1126/science.270.5235.467 PMID:7569999

Shivade, C., Raghavan, P., Fosler-Lussier, E., Embi, P. J., Elhadad, N., Johnson, S. B., & Lai, A. M. (2013). A review of approaches to identifying patient phenotype cohorts using electronic health records. *Journal of the American Medical Informatics Association*. doi:10.1136/amiajnl-2013-001935 PMID:24201027

Siegel, R., Ma, J., Zou, Z., & Jemal, A. (2014). Cancer statistics, 2014. *CA: a Cancer Journal for Clinicians, 64*(1), 9–29. doi:10.3322/caac.21208 PMID:24399786

Siegel, R., Naishadham, D., & Jemal, A. (2013). Cancer statistics, 2013. *CA: a Cancer Journal for Clinicians, 63*(1), 11–30. doi:10.3322/caac.21166 PMID:23335087

Sparkman, O. D. (2000). *Mass spectrometry desk reference* (1st ed.). Pittsburgh, Pa.: Global View Pub.

Spratlin, J. L., Serkova, N. J., & Eckhardt, S. G. (2009). Clinical applications of metabolomics in oncology: a review. *Clin Cancer Res, 15*(2), 431-440. doi: 10.1158/1078-0432.CCR-08-1059

Steel, G. G. (2002). Basic clinical radiobiology (3rd ed.). London: Oxford University Press.

Strintzis, M. G. (1998). A review of compression methods for medical images in PACS. *International Journal of Medical Informatics, 52*(1-3), 159–165. doi:10.1016/S1386-5056(98)00135-X PMID:9848413

Su, M., Miftena, M., Whiddon, C., Sun, X., Light, K., & Marks, L. (2005). An artificial neural network for predicting the incidence of radiation pneumonitis. *Medical Physics, 32*(2), 318–325. doi:10.1118/1.1835611 PMID:15789575

Subramanian, A., Tamayo, P., Mootha, V. K., Mukherjee, S., Ebert, B. L., & Gillette, M. A. et al. (2005). Gene set enrichment analysis: A knowledge-based approach for interpreting genome-wide expression profiles. *Proceedings of the National Academy of Sciences of the United States of America, 102*(43), 15545–15550. doi:10.1073/pnas.0506580102 PMID:16199517

Sullivan, R., Peppercorn, J., Sikora, K., Zalcberg, J., Meropol, N. J., & Amir, E. et al. (2011). Delivering affordable cancer care in high-income countries. *The Lancet Oncology, 12*(10), 933–980. doi:10.1016/S1470-2045(11)70141-3 PMID:21958503

Svensson, J. P., Stalpers, L. J., Esveldt-van Lange, R. E., Franken, N. A., Haveman, J., Klein, B.,... Giphart-Gassler, M. (2006). Analysis of gene expression using gene sets discriminates cancer patients with and without late radiation toxicity. *PLoS Med, 3*(10), e422. doi: 10.1371/journal.pmed.0030422

Tomatis, S., Rancati, T., Fiorino, C., Vavassori, V., Fellin, G., & Cagna, E. et al. (2012). Late rectal bleeding after 3D-CRT for prostate cancer: Development of a neural-network-based predictive model. *Physics in Medicine and Biology, 57*(5), 1399–1412. doi:10.1088/0031-9155/57/5/1399 PMID:22349550

Tucker, S. L., Cheung, R., Dong, L., Liu, H. H., Thames, H. D., & Huang, E. H. et al. (2004). Dose-volume response analyses of late rectal bleeding after radiotherapy for prostate cancer. *International Journal of Radiation Oncology, Biology, Physics, 59*(2), 353–365. doi:10.1016/j.ijrobp.2003.12.033 PMID:15145148

Twyman, R. M. (2004). *Principles of proteomics*. New York: BIOS Scientific Publishers.

Tyburski, J. B., Patterson, A. D., Krausz, K. W., Slavik, J., Fornace, A. J., Jr., Gonzalez, F. J., & Idle, J. R. (2008). Radiation metabolomics. 1. Identification of minimally invasive urine biomarkers for gamma-radiation exposure in mice. *Radiat Res, 170*(1), 1-14. doi:10.1667/RR1265.1

Vaidya, M., Creach, K. M., Frye, J., Dehdashti, F., Bradley, J. D., & El Naqa, I. (2012). Combined PET/CT image characteristics for radiotherapy tumor response in lung cancer. *Radiother Oncol, 102*(2), 239-245. doi: 10.1016/j.radonc.2011.10.014

Vapnik, V. (1998). *Statistical Learning Theory*. New York: Wiley.

Viswanathan, G. A., Seto, J., Patil, S., Nudelman, G., & Sealfon, S. C. (2008). Getting Started in Biological Pathway Construction and Analysis. *PLoS Computational Biology, 4*(2), e16. doi:10.1371/journal.pcbi.0040016 PMID:18463709

Wang, L., Zhang, B., Wolfinger, R. D., & Chen, X. (2008). An Integrated Approach for the Analysis of Biological Pathways using Mixed Models. *PLOS Genetics, 4*(7), e1000115. doi:10.1371/journal.pgen.1000115 PMID:18852846

Wang, X., & El Naqa, I. M. (2008). Prediction of both conserved and nonconserved microRNA targets in animals. *Bioinformatics, 24*(3), 325-332. doi: 10.1093/bioinformatics/btm595

Webb, S. (2001). *The physics of three-dimensional radiation therapy: conformal radiotherapy, radiosurgery, and treatment planning*. Bristol, UK: Institute of Physics Pub.

West, C., & Rosenstein, B. S. (2010). Establishment of a Radiogenomics Consortium. *International Journal of Radiation Oncology*Biology*Physics, 76*(5), 1295-1296. doi:10.1016/j.ijrobp.2009.12.017

West, C. M. (1995). Invited review: Intrinsic radiosensitivity as a predictor of patient response to radiotherapy. *The British Journal of Radiology*, *68*(812), 827–837. doi:10.1259/0007-1285-68-812-827 PMID:7551778

West, C. M. L., Elliott, R. M., & Burnet, N. G. (2007). The Genomics Revolution and Radiotherapy. *Clinical Oncology*, *19*(6), 470–480. doi:10.1016/j.clon.2007.02.016 PMID:17419040

Willmann, J. K., van Bruggen, N., Dinkelborg, L. M., & Gambhir, S. S. (2008). Molecular imaging in drug development. *Nat Rev Drug Discov*, *7*(7), 591-607. doi: 10.1038/nrd2290

Wouters, B. G. (2008). Proteomics: Methodologies and Applications in Oncology. *Seminars in Radiation Oncology*, *18*(2), 115–125. doi:10.1016/j.semradonc.2007.10.008 PMID:18314066

Yan, Q. (2005). Biomedical informatics methods in pharmacogenomics. *Methods in Molecular Medicine*, *108*, 459–486. PMID:16028700

Yu, S. L., Chen, H. Y., Chang, G. C., Chen, C. Y., Chen, H. W., & Singh, S. et al. (2008). MicroRNA signature predicts survival and relapse in lung cancer. *Cancer Cell*, *13*(1), 48–57. doi:10.1016/j.ccr.2007.12.008 PMID:18167339

Zaidi, H., & El Naqa, I. (2010). PET-guided delineation of radiation therapy treatment volumes: A survey of image segmentation techniques. *European Journal of Nuclear Medicine and Molecular Imaging*, *37*(11), 2165–2187. doi:10.1007/s00259-010-1423-3 PMID:20336455

Zhu, H., Pei, H.-, Zeng, S., Chen, J., Shen, L.-, & Zhong, M.- et al. (2009). Profiling Protein Markers Associated with the Sensitivity to Concurrent Chemoradiotherapy in Human Cervical Carcinoma. *Journal of Proteome Research*, *8*(8), 3969–3976. doi:10.1021/pr900287a PMID:19507834

ADDITIONAL READING

Akerkar, R. (2014). *Big data computing*. Boca Raton: CRC Press.

Alam, M., Muley, A., Joshi, A., & Kadaru, C. (2014). *Oracle NoSQL database: real-time big data management for the enterprise*. New York: McGraw-Hill Education.

Bentzen, S. M. (2008). *Radiation oncology advances*. New York: Springer. doi:10.1007/978-0-387-36744-6

Berman, J. J. (2013). *Principles of big data: preparing, sharing, and analyzing complex information*. Amsterdam: Elsevier, Morgan Kaufmann.

Big data: 29th British National Conference on Databases, BNCOD 2013, Oxford, UK, July 8-10, 2013. Proceedings. (2013). (1st edition. ed.). New York: Springer.

Brady, L. W., & Yaeger, T. E. (2013). *Encyclopedia of radiation oncology*. Heidelberg: Springer. doi:10.1007/978-3-540-85516-3

Cox, J. D., & Ang, K. K. (2010). *Radiation oncology: rationale, technique, results* (9th ed.). Philadelphia: Mosby.

Cross-border challenges in informatics with a focus on disease surveillance and utilising big-data: proceedings of the efmi special topic conference, 27-29 april 2014, budapest, hungary. (2014). Washington, DC: IOS Press.

Davis, K., & Patterson, D. (2012). *Ethics of big data*. Sebastopol, CA: O'Reilly.

Halperin, E. C., Perez, C. A., & Brady, L. W. (2008). *Perez and Brady's principles and practice of radiation oncology* (5th ed.). Philadelphia: Wolters Kluwer Health/Lippincott Williams & Wilkins.

Hansen, E. K., & Roach, M. (2010). *Handbook of evidence-based radiation oncology* (2nd ed.). New York: Springer. doi:10.1007/978-0-387-92988-0

Holzinger, A. (2014). *Biomedical informatics: discovering knowledge in big data*. New York: Springer. doi:10.1007/978-3-319-04528-3

Jorgensen, A. (2014). Microsoft big data solutions (1st edition. ed.). Indianapolis, IN: John Wiley and Sons.

Kagadis, G. C., & Langer, S. G. (2012). *Informatics in medical imaging*. Boca Raton, FL: CRC Press.

Kosaka, M., & Shirahada, K. (2014). *Progressive trends in knowledge and system-based science for service innovation*. Hershey: Business Science Reference.

Kudyba, S. (2014). *Big data, mining, and analytics: components of strategic decision making*. Boca Raton: Taylor & Francis. doi:10.1201/b16666

Kutz, J. N. (2013). Data-driven modeling & scientific computation: methods for complex systems & big data (First edition. ed.). Oxford: Oxford University Press.

Lane, J. I. (2015). *Privacy, big data, and the public good: frameworks for engagement*. New York, NY: Cambridge University Press.

Leszczynski, D. (2013). *Radiation proteomics: the effects of ionizing and non-ionizing radiation on cells and tissues*. New York: Springer. doi:10.1007/978-94-007-5896-4

Li, A. (2011). *Adaptive Radiation Therapy*. CRC Press.

Lu, J. J., & Brady, L. W. (2011). *Decision making in radiation oncology*. Heidelberg: Springer.

Mehta, M. P., Paliwal, B., & Bentzen, S. M. (2005). *Physical, chemical, and biological targeting in radiation oncology*. Madison, WI: Medical Physics Pub.

Ratner, B., Ratner, B., & Ratner, B. (2012). *Statistical and machine-learning data mining: techniques for better predictive modeling and analysis of big data* (2nd ed.). Boca Raton, FL: Taylor & Francis.

Schlegel, W., Bortfeld, T., & Grosu, A. (2006). *New technologies in radiation oncology*. Berlin, London: Springer. doi:10.1007/3-540-29999-8

Starkschall, G., & Siochi, R. A. C. (2014). *Informatics in radiation oncology*. Boca Raton: CRC Press.

Van Dyk, J. (2013). The modern technology of radiation oncology, vol. 3: a compendium for medical physicists and radiation oncologists. Madison, WI: Medical Physics Pub., Inc.

KEY TERMS AND DEFINITIONS

Genomics: Study of high throughput gene expression and variants. Normal tissues complications: side effects due to irradiation.

Proteomics: Study of high throughput protein expression.

Radiation Oncology: Treatment of cancer patients with high-energy radiation beams.

Radiomics: Extraction of large number of imaging features.

Systems Radiobiology: The use of engineering inspired network analysis techniques to model radiation response.

Tumour Control Probability: The probability that no spreading cancer cells remain after irradiation.

Chapter 9
Analysis of Genomic Data in a Cloud Computing Environment

Philip Groth
Bayer Pharma AG, Germany

Gerhard Reuter
Bayer Business Services GmbH, Germany

Sebastian Thieme
Humboldt-University of Berlin, Germany

ABSTRACT

A new trend for data analysis in the life sciences is Cloud computing, enabling the analysis of large datasets in short time. This chapter introduces Big Data challenges in the genomic era and how Cloud computing can be one feasible approach for solving them. Technical and security issues are discussed and a case study where Clouds are successfully applied to resolve computational bottlenecks in the analysis of genomic data is presented. It is an intentional outcome of this chapter that Cloud computing is not essential for analyzing Big Data. Rather, it is argued that for the optimized utilization of IT, it is required to choose the best architecture for each use case, either by security requirements, financial goals, optimized runtime through parallelization, or the ability for easier collaboration and data sharing with business partners on shared resources.

INTRODUCTION

Big Data Challenges

In 2009, the total global amount of stored data was estimated to have reached 800 Exabyte (EB) (Association, 2010) and was increased by approximately 13 EB throughout the following year (Agrawal et al., 2012). It was recently estimated that the amount new data generated in 2013 alone has reached 900 EB, implying that the vast majority of data stored today have been generated in just the past two years (IBM). Of this, the global amount of healthcare data was estimated to have exceeded 150 EB in 2011 (IBM). There is a simple explanation for this strong increase: Data nowadays are generated anywhere and anytime in a mainly automated manner and storing them is relatively cheap (e.g. commercial data storage is offered for less than USD 0.01 per Gigabyte

DOI: 10.4018/978-1-4666-6611-5.ch009

and month) (AWS). The notion of 'Big Data' to describe this phenomenon that large amounts of data are generated within a specific domain or of a specific class has already been described in the mid-nineties of the last century when the term itself was first coined by John Mashey of Silicon Graphics (sgi) and since then been widely adopted (Lohr, 2013; Mashey, 1998).

Most types of Big Data have many characteristics in common, e.g. a typical life cycle. They are generated, copied and moved, processed and analyzed, versioned, archived and sometimes deleted. Each step brings up systematic issues, all of them involving IT. Handling of Big Data starts with the process of generation. To generate data and to keep them usable, it is important to document their existence. By whom, how, when and under what circumstances were they created? The lack of such attributes will reduce or even disable the usability of data. Already, this is not trivial; as such annotation should be stored in a searchable manner. A popular tool to handle Big Data, especially for data annotation, tracing and versioning is 'iRods' (www.irods.org), which is employed, for example by the CERN (for data from high energy physics experiments) and the Wellcome Trust Sanger Institute (WTSI) (for DNA sequencing data).

Assuming the data have been adequately annotated, they are oftentimes placed within the Internet for immediate global availability, creating the challenge to interested users of acquiring a local copy. Classical transfer methods based on FTP or HTTP were not designed to transfer large files (i.e. in the range of gigabytes or more). Tools like Aspera™ (using a proprietary protocol named FASP) or torrent-seeding based methods (cghub.ucsc.edu) remedy this issue to some extent but are not yet widely spread.

Finally, due to their size, Big Data are quite often stored on distributed architectures, bringing up another issue. Software meant to process Big Data must take into account partial failures of the underlying hardware (e.g. a single disk error) and communication latencies. Many popular software products are in the process of redesign to adapt to this change. To speed up the analysis of Big Data, they are processed in a parallel manner in such distributed environments. This can be done with tools like Hadoop™ (Apache, 2012), utilizing a proprietary file system to distribute data across the network and a so-called 'master-slave approach' to assign sub-tasks to interlinked compute nodes. Hadoop™ is a framework developed by Apache and used amongst others by Facebook™ and Yahoo™.

Genomic Data is Big Data

With the decoding of the human genome and the associated substantial progress in the development of laboratory and bioinformatics methods (Chen, Wang, & Shi, 2011; Kearney & Horsley, 2005; Wang, Gerstein, & Snyder, 2009) the data of known biological interrelationships has also increased dramatically. Such data comprise, for example, the complete information on an individual's genome, such as nucleotide variations, chromosomal aberrations or other structural changes within the genome, more generically known as mutations. The smallest mutation within a genome is the exchange of a single nucleotide within the DNA, the so-called 'building block of life' (see (Alberts et al., 2007; Strachan & Read, 2005) for more information). If such a mutation is shared by at least 1% of a defined population and not disease-causing per se it is called 'single nucleotide polymorphism' (SNP) (Barreiro, Laval, Quach, Patin, & Quintana-Murci, 2008; Risch, 2000). In 2005, it was estimated that there are approximately 10 million SNPs to account for variation in the human population (Botstein & Risch, 2003). But data from the 1,000 Genomes Project (Abecasis et al., 2010) have revealed that there are many more SNPs within the human genome. By 2011, more than 40 million SNPs had been identified (Eberle et al., 2011). Each SNP specifies a genotype, describing differences within the genomic sequence between individuals (de Paula Careta & Paneto, 2012). This enormous amount of variability on an individual level has created a major challenge towards data analysis and organization in order to generate new knowledge of scientific or commercial value.

Due to this increasing amount of available data the term 'Big Data' is now also commonly applied in the genomics field. In this context, Big Data refers to large sets of genomic data from patients, originating from different sources and having been generated by a plethora of high-throughput technologies, the most prominent of which are microarrays and sequencing. One of the most widely adapted uses for microarray technology today is the simultaneous measurement of abundance of mRNA representing the expression of genes in a sample (see (Brown et al., 2000; Kerr, Martin, & Churchill, 2000; Lashkari et al., 1997; Müller & Röder, 2004) for more details on the use of microarrays in gene expression analysis). Another application is the DNA microarray, an example being the array-based comparative genome hybridization (aCGH) (Pinkel et al., 1998). The aCGH is a type of microarray used to detect genomic aberrations like copy number variations (CNVs) (Pinkel et al., 1998), denoting a change in the copy number (CN) of a genomic segment caused by evolutionary events like deletions, amplifications, or translocations of chromosomal segments (Graux et al., 2004; Greenman et al., 2010; Theisen, 2008).

SNPs can be exploited for genotyping, as well as calculating CNVs by way of applying the Affymetrix Genome-Wide Human SNP Array 6.0 technology (SNP6 array) (McCarroll et al., 2008). This is a high-density microarray, containing as probes 900,000 known SNP loci in the Human Genome. In addition, 950,000 non-polymorphic CN probes of different length (up to 1,000 bp) are fixed on the chip. Due to the high resolution of this array, it is suitable to create a more detailed picture of the complex karyotypes occurring for example in cancer (Edgren et al., 2011).

The rise of DNA sequencing (DNA-seq) was given by the idea to interrupt DNA synthesis with the introduction of a so-called dideoxy nucleotide (ddNTP) at a specific nucleotide. This led to the term 'chain-termination method' and is the basic idea of Sanger sequencing (Sanger & Coulson, 1975). Sanger sequencing played a key role in the description of the Human Genome and therefore for the development of sequencing methods we know today. But with an output of 400,000 bases per machine per day the Sanger sequencing is limited in throughput (Liu et al., 2012; Wang et al., 2009).

To overcome this limitation, a new generation of DNA sequencing methods was developed, enabling a massive parallelization of sequencing and giving rise to the era of 'next-generation sequencing' (NGS). The first methods were based on Sanger sequencing technology and therefore expensive and not precise enough for unambiguous mapping of sequences or distinguishing between isoforms (Wang et al., 2009) (further reading (Brenner et al., 2000; Reinartz et al., 2002; Velculescu, Zhang, Vogelstein, & Kinzler, 1995)). Still, their development initiated the development of further high-throughput sequencing methods, e.g. by Illumina (illumina), Roche NimbleGen (NimbleGen), Complete Genomics (Genomics), Applied Biosystems (LTC-AB) and many others. Besides DNA, RNA can also be sequenced. Sequencing of RNA has been made possible by adapting DNA-seq methods. The RNA-sequencing (RNA-seq) method enables quantification of the total transcript of a cell (transcriptome) under specific conditions or at a specific stage of development (Chen et al., 2011; Kearney & Horsley, 2005; Wang et al., 2009).

The advancement of methods continues, e.g. with nanopore sequencing (Clarke et al., 2009; Kasianowicz, Brandin, Branton, & Deamer, 1996), where only a pore with a diameter of around 1 nm is used to sequence DNA. The idea is that a voltage is applied across the nanopore and the flux of the ions through the nanopore is measured. Moving a DNA molecule through this nanopore changes the ion flux for each nucleotide in a characteristic manner. Tracking the changes in the flux for an entire DNA strand enables determination of the order of the respective nucleotides in the sequence (Clarke et al., 2009). This latest advancement shows that novel technologies and methods for sequencing and microarray techniques improving speed, precision and resolution emerge constantly, with the additional result that the amount of output data is increased further. This is also the starting point for large sequencing projects like the 1,000 Genomes Project, which uses Illumina sequencers. With this project, yet another consortium adds Big Data to the public domain, having increased its sequencing data repositories from 50 Gigabyte (GB) in 2005 to 2.5 TB in 2008. In March 2013, a repository size of 464 TB was reached (Community). The advent of new technologies with the capability to produce even higher data density (see Figure 1) and further, even bigger sequencing projects is near. For example, the 'Genome England Project' has been funded by the NIH in 2013 with approximately 150 million USD in order to sequence 100,000 patients with

rare diseases using whole-genome sequencing (WGS). The size of a typical output file of raw sequencing reads (so-called BAM file) is around 300 to 500 GB per sample, initiating yet another discussion of efficient compression and storage, which is beyond the scope of this chapter.

The raw output of sequencers is of course data to be processed by computational pipelines in order to extract biologically meaningful outcome, e.g. mapping the resulting sequences to the correct position in the genome or analyzing the mapped genomic sequences for aberrations against a reference genome. Such sequencing analysis pipelines (see Figure 2 for an example) typically comprise a number of computationally intensive steps to transform raw data from a sequencer into human-readable data. Similarly, data from microarray experiments are processed in comparable pipelines, e.g. to compare gene expression differences between a diseased tissue sample and a healthy reference in a patient population or to predict disease-causing chromosomal aberrations, such as fusion genes. All of these pipelines have in common their highly modular (i.e. several algorithms work in sequence and data get passed

Figure 1. Depicts improvements in the rate of DNA sequencing over the past 30 years and into the future. From slab gels to capillary sequencing and second-generation sequencing technologies, there has been a more than a million-fold improvement in the rate of sequence generation over this time scale. (Reproduced from M. Stratton (Stratton, Campbell, & Futreal, 2009))

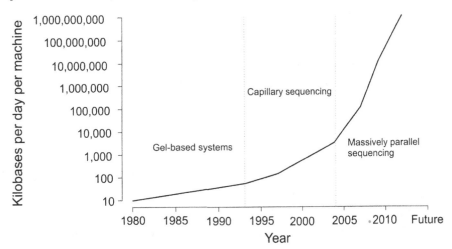

Figure 2. This typical WES pipeline consists of 11 steps. For each input file, a quality control is performed (1). FASTQ files are aligned to the reference genome (2) and converted into standard text files containing sequence and alignment data (3). Text files are converted to BAM files (4), sorted (5) and indexed (6). In the variant processing step, each nucleotide position is considered in terms of frequency and quality (7). In the variant calling step, actual somatic/germ line mutation calling is done. This step requires pileup files from both cancer and healthy samples, generating VCF files (8). In the variant filtering, false positive indels are filtered with the help of UCSC repeat masker information. Also, substitutions are filtered with regards to nearly 'non-properly-alignable' genes like olfactory receptor genes (9). Processing of VCF files through Ensembl Variant Effect Predictor generates rich variant effect annotation (10). Resulting files can be uploaded for further analysis (11).

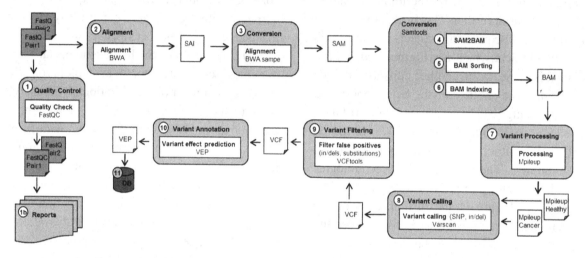

from one step to the next in different formats) and scientific (i.e. each algorithm is published and will either be improved by a community effort or surpassed by another one) nature. Finally, these pipelines almost always are meant to process data of many individuals.

Genomic data files are too large in terms of size and complexity to process them with 'traditional' applications, such as word processing or text editors. Therefore, new methods and technologies to share, store, search through, analyze and visualize these kinds of data are needed. This obvious need for analyzing Big Data in large and complex algorithmic pipelines thus poses a challenge towards an IT infrastructure. Even the advent of multi-core high-performance compute clusters and in-memory technologies are challenged by the fact that many pipelines still take several thousand CPU hours per sample to com-

plete. At the same time, such high performance infrastructures oftentimes are not in full use at all times. This can for example be attributed to the sequencing process, where one 'run' takes several days or weeks to complete by which time a large amount of data is ready for further processing. It is therefore feasible to take a look at alternative architectures, in which an infrastructure that is challenged by peak loads can be supplemented by offsite computing power, e.g. as offered by Cloud computing service providers.

BACKGROUND

Calculating Genotypes and CNVs

Structural or quantitative changes within the genome are so-called genomic aberrations; specifically, if these changes occur within a chromosome, they are called chromosomal aberrations. These changes can e.g. be detected by examining CNVs across the genome (Johansson, Mertens, & Mitelman, 1996). Such kinds of genomic aberrations also occur frequently during cancer development and are often unbalanced, meaning that there is a quantitative change in genetic material caused by a mutation event, e.g. a deletion or amplification (Johansson et al., 1996). If the total amount of genetic material does not change during a mutation event, the mutation is considered balanced (Mitelman, Johansson, & Mertens, 2007). The two genotypes for a given SNP position, which are represented by the two alleles A and B can be measured e.g. by the representative probes on a SNP6 array consisting of six technical replicates, three replicates for allele A and three replicates for allele B. The fluorophore-signal emitted from the probe-target hybridization describing one SNP allele is directly proportional to the allelic CN and sensitive enough to show differences within the allelic CN. The resulting intensity values for each allele over a set of normal samples can be clustered according to the three wild-type genotype classes AA, AB, and BB (Greenman et al., 2010).

The amount of DNA within different cells is typically very similar, especially across healthy tissues where we expect a diploid genome (Greenman et al., 2010). In contrast to normal cells, cancer cells exhibit aneuploidy (i.e. a triploid or quadraploid genome) much more often than their healthy counterparts (Rajagopalan & Lengauer, 2004).

In contrast to other tools detecting CNVs, the tool 'Predicting Integral Copy Number In Cancer' (PICNIC) (Greenman et al., 2010) calculates the copy number (CN) from SNP6 arrays to overcome the challenges deriving from aneuploidy in cancer samples. PICNIC consists of two main steps. In the first step the entire data set is corrected across all arrays of the experiment and then the probe intensity values are normalized by using Bayesian statistics. In the second step, the data will be segmented and genotyped to identify the most likely copy number segmentation by using a Hidden-Markov Model (Greenman et al., 2010). The transition region of segments with CNVs is defined as a change in the CN of two neighboring genomic segments within a chromosome. It is often referred to as a copy number breakpoint or in this context simply as a breakpoint (Ritz, Paris, Ittmann, Collins, & Raphael, 2011).

Copy Number Variation and Fusion Genes

Genomic aberrations can be more complex than CNVs. Consider, as an example for this complexity, two genes at different breakpoints, originally coding for two different proteins, which can merge to a fusion gene or chimeric gene. The resulting merged sequence contains the entire or partial information of both genes, which may lead to a protein with novel functions (Long, 2000). A fusion causes the change of the physical genomic position of one gene and therefore loses the regulatory elements of this gene. This might change the expression of the involved gene (Huang, Shah, & Li, 2012). The fusion gene TMPRSS2-ERG is a well-described prostate cancer marker gene, deriving from a 3 million bp deletion. Due to the fusion event, the ERG gene is regulated by the TMPRSS2 promoter, leading to overexpression of ERG (Tomlins et al., 2005; Yu et al., 2010). However, most of the occurring fusion genes are non-functional (loss of function of one or both genes), but may still have an influence on the cell behavior.

The detection of such fusion genes has been identified as a worthwhile effort, especially in cancer genomics approaches (Thieme & Groth, 2013). Fusion gene prediction is a computationally intensive effort requiring the knowledge of breakpoint positions throughout the genome. Ritz et al. (2011) (Ritz et al., 2011) developed the algorithm 'Neighborhood Breakpoint Conservation' (NBC), which uses the CNV information from aCGH (Suzuki, Tenjin, Shibuya, & Tanaka, 1997) data to calculate common breakpoints or pairs of common breakpoints in a given sample on the basis of Bayesian statistics. The NBC combines the calculated probabilities of pairs of common breakpoints to detect fusion genes with positional variability (Figure 3). The advantage of predicting fusion genes on the basis of breakpoints calculated by this method is the ability to find both functional and silent fusion genes.

We have recently published a related method, the Genomic Fusion Detection (GFD) algorithm (Thieme & Groth, 2013). Our algorithm consists of three main steps and one preprocessing step shown in Figure 4. In the preprocessing step the SNP6 data will be processed with PICNIC to get the copy number segmentation of the data. The algorithm takes as input the segment information calculated by PICNIC (Figure 4A). This segment information is used to predict possible fusion genes. The input data are processed within three steps. In the first step, breakpoints are determined within the predicted segmentations, artifacts are deleted and genes, which are close to a breakpoint are identified (Figure 4B). Secondly, gene pairs fulfilling certain required constraints (Figure 4C) are detected. In the last step, each result for a sample is compared to the results of all processed samples to find possible common fusion events and reduce false-positive predictions (Figure 4D). The GFD algorithm is based on the ideas of Ritz et al. (Ritz et al., 2011), extending them, however, by several key features.

In the early 1980s, Thomas and Christoph Cremer have observed and validated the existence of so-called 'chromosome territories' in healthy mammalian cells, i.e. that chromosomes seem to have a tissue-specific location within the nucleus. Roix et al. (Roix, McQueen, Munson, Parada, & Misteli, 2003) have shown that translocation-prone genes are located in close spatial proximity: The fusion of the MYC gene (located on chromosome

Figure 3. The workflow of 'Neighborhood Breakpoint Conservation' (NBC) consists of three steps. First, all possible copy number profiles are computed, from which the breakpoints can be derived from. Next the probability of a breakpoint between two probes is calculated, wherefore all possible copy number profiles of a single individual are considered. In the last step, the calculated probabilities of the break-points of each individual are combined to find recurrent breakpoints over all individuals. The outputs are common breakpoints or pairs of common breakpoints over different samples. (Reproduced from Ritz et al. (Ritz et al., 2011))

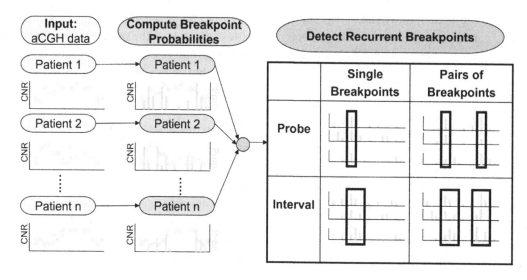

Figure 4. (A) Preprocessing step: apply PICNIC for normalization and segmentation of the data. (B) determine breakpoints within the predicted segmentation, delete artefacts and find genes, which are close to a breakpoint. (C) find gene combinations, which fulfil certain constraints. (D) compare the results of all processed samples to find common fusion events.

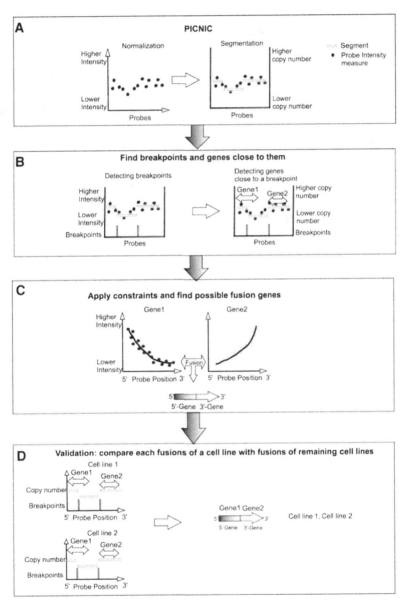

8) with the IGH gene (located on chromosome 14) causing Burkitt Lymphoma becomes clearer, considering that these two chromosomes are direct neighbors in the nucleus in B-cells of the human immune system. Thus, there seems to be a correlation between the probability for inter-chromosomal fusion genes and the distance of the involved partners. Similar observations have been reported by others (Meaburn, Misteli, & Soutoglou, 2007). With the usage of the HI-C method (van Berkum et al., 2010), an extension of the 3C method (Chromosome Confirmation

Capture), the proximities between chromosomes can be measured for each cell type. We propose to enhance the GFD algorithm by taking into account that chromosomes are not randomly positioned in the nucleus. Adding this insight to our algorithm will improve the prediction probability of fusion genes.

MAIN FOCUS OF THE CHAPTER

Cloud Computing

Attempting to find an existing definition of Cloud computing will return many results of varying usefulness, some of which are summarized in Figure 5. The overlap within all these answers is too small for being useful as a universal definition.

Therefore, we have compiled some success stories, (i.e. where the use of Cloud computing has added value to the task at hand), in order to extract some common principles of Cloud computing. Although these will not lead to any better

or more universal definition of Cloud computing, they may help create an understanding for some of the emerging central ideas (by way of simplification, we will refer to 'the Cloud' as synonym for 'Cloud Computing' of any type in this chapter):

- The New York Times™ used 100 Amazon Web Services (AWS) Elastic Compute Cloud (EC2) instances to translate 11 million articles into pdf-files within 24 hours to make them available in their online-archive (Gottfrid, 2007).
- DreamWorks™ Studios bought about 20% of the CPU hours that were needed to calculate animations in the movie Kung Fu Panda 2 from AWS (Wittmann, 2012).

Such Cloud-based models are known as 'Platform as a Service' (PaaS), whereas the next two examples shall illustrate another service model within the Cloud, which is called 'Software as a service' (SaaS):

Figure 5. Variety of definitions for cloud computing

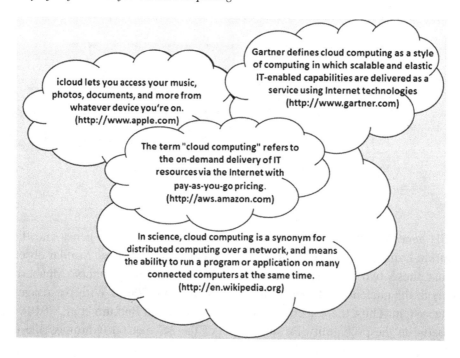

- Hundreds of Millions of Internet users are sharing their files by using portals like YouTube™ or Dropbox™. The users' files become available globally by transfer to the Cloud.
- Instead of installing and updating software and data locally, Cloud products like Google Earth™, Google Maps™ or Microsoft Office™ offer single point of entries to present the latest software and data versions to all users, regardless of the local position or hardware.

These examples clearly illustrate two of the main benefits of the Cloud for genomic data:

1. If there is a need for a large amount of computational power on short notice or for a short period of time, utilizing the Cloud is a good idea. The alternative would be to invest in a compute infrastructure, which might take a lot of time and effort to set up and may not be needed as soon as the actual one-time computation has finished. In many business cases processing of genomic data is a spontaneous and a short term task.
2. Cloud Computing offers a simple way to make software and data available anywhere, anytime on nearly any device. Collaboration on genomic data among different companies becomes easier than storing data in an internal corporate network.

In addition, Cloud providers offer further service models besides SaaS and PaaS, i.e. customers can buy infrastructure (IaaS) or networks (NaaS) as a service. Taking into account that any kind of mixtures among these services are also possible, it is obvious that the Cloud can represent nearly any business case and why finding a universal definition is not trivial. In summary, the Cloud has versatile characteristics, but a very simple basic idea: It is a one-stop shop for globally available computational resources of any kind (hardware,

network, software, storage, etc.). From the customer's perspective this creates some interesting opportunities:

- Instead of adding new hardware for a short term project, it may be rented from the Cloud. The Cloud provider takes care of basic services like secure data centers, buildings, physical access-control, power supply, cooling, backup locations, etc. This is especially helpful for small and medium enterprises (SMEs) or startup companies, which can avoid the hurdle of building up an internal IT at enormous upfront costs by utilizing Cloud services.
- Instead of buying software and licenses, anyone can rent exactly what is currently needed and will only pay for the actual use.
- Data stored in the Cloud can be made available globally as well as to a limited, exactly defined group of users.

In a detailed reflection on these principles, Table 1 summarizes some of the pros and cons of Clouds, which are deemed worthwhile considering before utilizing the Cloud as computational resource.

As shown in Table 1, one of the drawbacks in utilizing the Cloud is the perceived risk of data leakage or theft; a risk that can be possibly mitigated by employing a so called 'private' Cloud. Cloud computing is based on the Client-Server model which means that the setup of servers and software products must be done first and then clients have to be connected by a network to these new resources. Although next-generation Internet protocols like IPv6 will reduce some of the complexity to achieve this in the future, today's network designs utilize private IP addresses within a company's internal network just as Cloud providers do within their networks. Hence for connecting a Private Cloud to a company network, a virtual private network (VPN) tunnel or a dedicated leased line is needed. The advantage

Table 1. Compilation of pros and cons while utilizing the cloud for genomic data

Pros	Cons
Reduced investments in owned hardware	Dependency on a chosen Cloud provider; switching of services can be complex
Increased flexibility in computational resources	Dependency on network availability to the Cloud
Improved scalability of services, including software licenses and scope of infrastructure, Adopted to the amount and complexity of genomic data analyzes	Possible legal issues when sensitive data are stored in an unknown location especially for business critical genomic data
Global availability of software and hardware; data access is not restricted to a local network, collaboration with partners on genomic pipelines made easier	Adjustment of internal processes and regulations can be difficult e.g. the requirements of the Federal data protection act for personal data
More efficient integration of distributed sites to the same infrastructure	Internal (political) restrictions on outsourcing IT infrastructure and services
Update of resources is done on a regular basis; services rarely become outdated. The interconnectivity to the internet allows easy updates of Genomic analyzes tools and services	Perceived increased risk of data leakage especially critical for personalised genomic data
Increased competences in IT organizations; cloud knowledge is a sought-after skill	Reduced competences in IT organizations; infrastructures are set-up elsewhere

of a leased line consists of an available service level agreement (SLA) that guarantees availability and failure protection to some extent, whereas a native VPN Tunnel provides no such guarantees. However, this only addresses one of the drawbacks raised above, while leaving untouched all the others. In any case, this example shows that none of the drawbacks mentioned must become a show stopper for moving into the Cloud but all of them should be considered with priorities weighted to the task at hand and the organization as a whole.

After the initial decision has been made to use the Cloud for some purpose, finding a suitable Cloud provider is an immediate next step. The checklist below is intended to support this decision, by highlighting some of the aspects that are most likely of importance:

- Easy to get started: Creating account and providing a means for payment should suffice
- Wizard-based allocation and management of resources, such that no advanced knowledge of programming or technologies are required

- Integrated security features (e. g. access lists), which are documented in detail, easy to understand and to maintain
- Provision of a bulky Application Programming Interface (API) to automate processes
- Comprehensive listing of competitive prices, ideally supplemented by volume discounts
- Transparent and detailed accounting of charges
- Building blocks principle for combining hardware and software components
- Variety of pre-configured operating systems, application software and public data sets of general interest
- Global coverage (Laws may force the customer to keep data in a dedicated region)
- Tiered storage architecture with fast access storage and inexpensive long term archiving

Another very helpful tool that can be utilized to support the decision for a specific Cloud computing provider is for example, the 'Magic Quadrant

Analysis' conducted annually by an IT consulting company for infrastructure as a service providers (Leong, Toombs, Gill, Petri, & Haynes, 2013). In their 2012 survey of the top 15 providers of IaaS, they focus on the two evaluation criteria 'ability to execute' and 'completeness of vision', distinguishing between four types of technology providers: Leaders (strong vision, and strong position to execute in their market), Visionaries (strong vision, weaker execution), Niche Players (focus on a segment or are unfocussed and outperformed), and Challengers (execute well or dominate a market segment, but do not have a clear vision) (Cohen, 2012). According to their analysis, the far most advanced, almost lonely, IaaS 'Leader' is Amazon Web Services (AWS). As for other large companies commonly associated with advanced IT technologies, Microsoft for example is seen as a strong 'Visionary', whereas IBM or HP are rather perceived as 'Niche Players' in that market. AWS services are recommended, among others, for cloud-native applications, batch computing, e-business hosting, general business applications, and test and development. But probably the strongest reason why AWS is such a far advanced market share leader is this: AWS alone has more than five times the compute capacity in use than the aggregate total of the other fourteen providers (as of March 2014)!

The final step to move into the Cloud involves choosing a suitable connection model, that is to employ a private Cloud as described above, a public Cloud without the detour through a VPN, or to utilize 'Hybrid Clouds', i.e. a combination of private and public Clouds. This decision depends on the answer to the question where the clients are located. If the clients consist only of internal users and no access from third parties (outside of the company) is needed, a private cloud would offer the best look-and-feel to the users, because the Cloud can be set up identical to internal servers. On the other hand, this requires integrating these servers transparently into the company's common management tools (e.g. host name resolution,

security-scanning, patching, monitoring). In contrast, a public Cloud would probably offer more benefits and flexibility for a shared approach in which both internal and external users are involved.

Whatever the final choice may be, a staged solution is proposed here as a useful setup (Figure 6). For utilizing a public Cloud it is recommended to install a single entry server as a stepping stone into a larger cluster of Cloud instances. For more convenience this might be a server with a graphical user interface (GUI) and pre-installed software that can be used to connect to the other Cloud servers (e.g. via Putty). The main advantage for a single-point-of-entry server is that it reduces the number of public IP addresses for all Cloud Servers, as these are rare and expensive. Furthermore, security is increased because such a single connection component can be easily monitored. Figure 6 shows a design proposal for handling Big Data within such a set up. The Windows™ based entry server has a public IP address allowing access from the Internet, while all other Cloud instance use private IP addressing scheme. Communication from the Internet is restricted to the RDP protocol, which has a built-in encryption, but is additionally wrapped in a VPN tunnel to enable secure data transfer. Secure access lists only allow access from dedicated sources, so that the Cloud itself is protected against any access from untrusted locations. The Network File System (NFS) server is the central repository for storing data and any number of compute instances (here: 'R-servers') can be started or stopped on demand using APIs provided by the Cloud provider or custom-made programs. All internal communication is done by a secure shell (SSH) connection fitted with a private access key to ensure encryption. Additionally, some Cloud providers offer low-cost storage which can be an attractive extension of this model to store large amounts of data for an extended period of time.

Regardless of this proposed productive set up, some companies rather start exploring the usefulness of Clouds by first moving servers

Figure 6. Private cloud design for genomic data

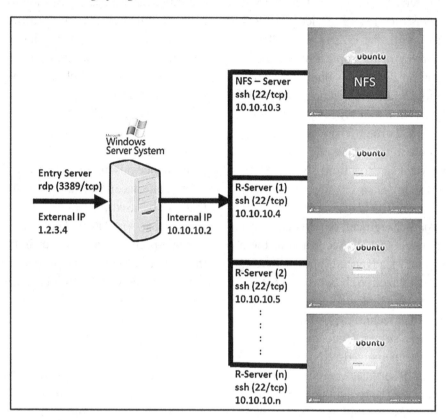

for prototype development or test environments. Another possibility to gain some first-hand experience without many risks is to try out some new software products (depending on the licensing model which is not always suitable for Cloud use) or to test a migration scenario to a newer software release. The opportunities in the realm of Cloud computing are growing rapidly. As an example, so-called 'Community Clouds' are now emerging and can be used e.g. to share requirements towards an infrastructure. The variety of available services is steadily increasing in order to cover as many business cases as possible and to become even more attractive to future customers. At the same time, as possibilities generate demand, new opportunities for Cloud use are arriving. To leverage one such opportunity would be to merge the high computational and storage demands of genomic data with capabilities of the Cloud. In an environment where in-house IT capabilities to

deal with genomic data are already available, such a move to the Cloud needs to outperform those capabilities in at least one of the existing main key performance indicators (KPI) of IT services (Availability, Security, Cost) and should not perform worse on any of those. An in-house ramp up towards such capabilities should be considered by the same criteria in comparison to Cloud services. Of course, this involves legal considerations as moving genomic data into the Cloud may not be allowed in some cases. This will be elaborated further in the next section.

Challenges with Genomic Data in the Cloud

Capability of Infrastructure

As elaborated above, genomic data poses great challenges towards the IT infrastructure. Processing requires many fast CPUs with large allocated memory. These demands are closely related to the need of complex statistical methods and to the large amount of data to be analyzed. Therefore, it is important that the Cloud provider offers high end services with a reasonable amount of memory. Certainly, such service is generating costs while it is in use. It therefore makes sense to accommodate oneself with self-made scripts or, in case of AWS, the provided API for starting and stopping servers according to current need and degree of utilization.

Additionally, it is important to have a cost-effective storage, because of the large size of a typical genomic data set. AWS has a multi-layered concept with fast and expensive disk drives, but also slower and cheaper S3 storage and finally Glacier™, an economic solution for long term storage. Glacier™ is a low cost 'offline' storage solution, which is feasible for storing files for which a retrieval time of several hours is acceptable. The price for storing data with Glacier™ is approximately 90% less than for the same amount of S3 storage. S3 and Glacier™ can also be accessed through third party tools like Cloudberry Explorer™ (www.cloudberrylab.com) but also by using the native API provided by AWS.

Availability of Bandwidth

Currently, one of the most limiting factors for efficient Cloud usage is the bandwidth between the local network and the Cloud. In order to transfer genomic data, a dedicated link (with a respective SLA) or invest into a higher bandwidth network will help avoiding delays but another important aspect is the connection tool. To this regard, one of the major benefits of using the leading AWS Cloud service is the availability of adapted solutions from other vendors fitting exactly these needs. Aspera™ (www.asperasoft.com) for example extents the AWS network with solutions to exchange Big Data across networks in an encrypted manner and with high speed. Traditional protocols like FTP, sFTP or FTPs were not designed to meet the challenges of transporting Big Data over WAN links. Technically, the usage of the User Datagram Protocol (UDP; with an add-on session handling) performs much better, than the classical Transmission Control Protocol (TCP), which includes a lot of overhead in handshaking and session reliability measures. Another exciting solution is the Fast Data Transfer (FDT) used for Big Data transfer at CERN (monalisa.cern.ch/FDT). The beauty in this approach lies in its capability of reading and writing at disk speed over wide area networks utilizing TCP and its platform-agnostic design. Some repositories of genomic data enforce their own protocols for data transfer. The University of California, Santa Cruz (UCSC) is using a torrent-based method for distribution of files among the user community. This method has proven to be a very efficient way for fast file transfer in the last years, also due to Cloud usage for storing and processing genomic data.

Data Protection

In context of Cloud computing, IT security and data protection are topics oftentimes accompanied by the thought-terminating cliché: 'If my data are no longer on my local campus, it is not secure and therefore a Cloud solution is out of the question'. Such train of thought is unfortunately still used as a killer argument to stop any further discussion. There are most certainly more intelligent approaches to analyze the security challenges of Clouds. One widely spread approach is to classify data and run a risk analysis. When dealing with genomic data which typically derive from patients, legal aspects regarding national and international data privacy legislation need to be taken into account as well.

Every piece of data has an ownership. The owner is the responsible person to deal with these topics of data classification and risk assessment. The latter typically requires support by IT experts, but data owners nevertheless must be aware of the potential risks and should also be aware of the amount of risk they are willing to take, as there is no absolutely risk-free storage of data. Table 2 shall give insight into typical risk classes and associated questions. Clearly, the individual assessment is closely related to the type of data and the data owners' risk perception.

Table 2 can then be used to derive the likelihood of an incident which then can be mapped against its estimated monetary or reputational damage. Ideally, both are specifically measurable and quantifiable. It is advisable here to also compare and quantify the risks of the Cloud against the on-premise IT solution. As an example, sending a sensitive data package by mail can be compared to an in-house data sharing site that is also accessible from outside the firewall and to the risk of hosting the same data package in a Cloud solution with access for both parties. In this particular case it is likely that the internal sharing site and the Cloud solution are equally secure and therefore should rather be compared from a commercial perspective, but the by far least secure mail option is actually most prominently used for convenience. Sensitizing data owners to these topics will help them find the right type of Cloud (private, public, etc.) and the best type of service (e.g. PaaS, IaaS,

SaaS) for their data. A Cloud solution is neither secure nor insecure by default; only the effort to make any given Cloud environment as secure as needed based on the data classification may vary.

All Cloud providers are aware that data protection is one of the key decision drivers for or against Cloud usage. Therefore, they are keen on improving their services and many offer a variety of security features. It is obvious that the Scale of Economy does not just apply to the computational resources but also to the security. Large Cloud providers can attract and employ security specialists for their environments which may be challenging for smaller companies. Also, such Cloud providers are capable to offer disaster recovery, because they have many distributed sites. Further Cloud-specific risk advantages and disadvantages are summarized in Table 3.

In light of all of these security considerations, there is an understandable desire of Cloud customers to quantify each applicable risk, including a probability of incidence measure where possible. These are put forward for example as audit or 'social hacking' requests which are typically frowned-upon by Cloud providers. Here, the customers' needs to validate the Cloud environment conflicts with the need of other customers to have

Table 2. Compilation of typical data risk classes and questions

Risk Class	Typical Questions
Access	Who may have access to my data (physical/logical)? Which processes use the data? What type of access shall be granted (read, modify, grant further permissions, etc.)?
Leakage	What is the business impact (e.g. to patents, share values, loss of market, PR damage) if the data is leaked?
Encryption	Must the data be stored using encryption? What type of encryption? Who will have access to the keys and where are these stored?
Backup	How many copies will exist and where are these stored? Is it necessary to have a copy in a remote location (disaster recovery)?
Fraud	What is the impact if someone changes the data for fraud reasons? How can fraud be discovered?
Termination	How to make sure that all data is completely erased (no further copies, no way of re-engineering by experts after deletion)?
Legal	Does any law prevent storing the data in a given place (tax laws, personal data, etc.)?

Table 3. Special risk-related cloud-specific advantages and disadvantages

Advantages	Disadvantages
Possibility of making snapshots for cloning does also offer a simple and secure way to ensure that nobody has made changes (e.g. checksum).	Shared resources lead to the risk of isolation failures, where software or data are visible to other customers residing on the same physical hardware.
Snapshots can be used in case or in suspicion of hacking to clone the servers and preform a fast forensic analysis.	Erasing of data may not mean a physical destroy of a unit, when other customers are using the same physical disks. Re-engineering might lead to restoration of data that should have been destroyed.
	Management GUIs are often based on Web-browsers, with their known security issues.

their data secured from anyone's access, including 'social' hackers. Leading Cloud providers solve this challenge by undergoing regular inspections and (ISO-) certifications by independent third parties.

Apart from assessing the level of certification, Cloud customers can also proactively protect their data. Encryption is such a crucial and commonly discussed measure especially in the context of Cloud computing. TrueCrypt™ (www.truecrypt. org) is an encryption tool universally accepted among IT security experts. The code is open source, allowing users to proof the code before usage. But TrueCrypt™ (as any other tool) is neither secure nor insecure by default. It must be used correctly to maximize security. Losing the encryption key, for example or using 'weak' passwords may enable successful data theft. But even a brute force attack against an excellent password may be successful if there is enough time or a lucky strike. Therefore, additional measures like firewalls or access control lists are useful for further reducing the risk of data theft, but certain elements of risk always remain. The risks can just be reduced to a value matching the risk class of the data.

Storage of data almost always raises legal challenges towards the data owner. National or international data protection laws or comparable rules (e.g. 'Safe-Harbor' principle) deal with the storage and protection of personal data. Among others, such regulations may impose restrictions

on the physical location and the transfer of these types of data. In all but a few cases, genomic data must be treated as personal data in need of special protection under these regulations. Oftentimes, these data derive from patients (e.g. in case of cancer studies) who need to be transparently informed e.g. on the physical location, intent for and purpose of their data. In clinical practice, this is achieved by so-called 'Informed Consent' forms, detailing this information to patients in a clear and understandable manner. If this has been achieved, such personal data can be stored and analyzed in the Cloud, provided the Cloud contractor is capable of adhering to the highest data protection standards. Such standards commonly include but must not be limited to: Data security certification by ISO 27001, ISO 27003 or ISO 27005 (and/or adherence to 'Safe Harbor' principles where applicable), signature of standard contractual clauses on data privacy that (in the European Union) comply with EU regulation 95/46/EC, and the ability to name the compute centers where the data are stored and processed. Especially in the case of genomic data, it is strongly advised here that any contract with a Cloud provider should cover these issues. Outsourcing of IT services delegates many responsibilities, but the accountability stays with the data owner.

Amazon Web Service offers all possibilities to run any business case in the Cloud. We would highly recommend reading the online documentations at AWS websites. Understanding the built-in security functionalities (e.g. 2-factor authentication for the Management GUI) helps the customer to secure their Cloud environment accordingly to their business needs.

Costs

One of the main drivers for moving services into the Cloud (or most other outsourcing activities for that matter) is to drive down the costs for internal IT. It is therefore important to elucidate beforehand the cost structures and pricing models of the different Cloud providers in order to find the suitable model. It has been elaborated earlier that one scenario for utilizing the Cloud may be to absorb peak loads of computational jobs with very high demand on CPU, memory, and storage. For such a repetitive, but non-constant demand, cost reduction can be realized by stopping Cloud servers whenever there is no workload. If Cloud servers are running permanently (7 days x 24 hours), it can be argued that the total cost of an in-house virtualized server is not essentially higher than a Cloud based alternative with same sizing parameters. Stern discipline or the usage of automation (e.g. via API) is needed to get the best out of the Cloud.

FUTURE RESEARCH DIRECTION: UTILIZING CLOUD COMPUTING TO ANALYZE SNP6 ARRAYS

Study Aim

The high amount of genomic data produced by the use of new high throughput technologies like RNA-sequencing (Chen et al., 2011; Wang et al., 2009) or high resolution microarrays (Pinkel & Albertson, 2005) yields the development of new bioinformatics tools for analyzing these data (McPherson et al., 2011). A main challenge is that many tools for e.g. genomic analysis in most cases are neither able to parallelize the different

computational steps on a cluster nor to parallelize these steps on a single computer with more than one CPU. Hence, the analysis of large datasets often requires a lot of time and money for computational resources. We address this issue by using AWS EC2 services (Fusaro, Patil, Gafni, Wall, & Tonellato, 2011), the common programming language R and by enabling a flexible and non-task bound parallelization of different jobs on an AWS EC2 environment.

Materials and Methods

In our study we focus on a software tool called PICNIC (Greenman et al., 2010). This tool is able to predict the CNV from SNP6 arrays (McCarroll et al., 2008) produced from an Affymetrix genome wide SNP6.0 array by using a Bayesian Hidden Markov Model (HMM). For segments with a constant CN we identify genes at the edges of the segment and compare the SNP measures among each other to calculate probabilities for fusion genes.

Applying PICNIC on SNP6 array data is computationally intensive. The average resources needed for the processing of one sample are about 10 GB Random-Access Memory (RAM) and 3 hours Central Processing Unit (CPU) time of an AWS EC2 High-Memory Quadruple Extra Large (m2.4xlarge). For a large dataset consisting of 1,000 samples, such an analysis would take around 125 days. One way to speed up the analysis of large datasets is parallelization, applied e.g. on AWS EC2 cloud computing instances. The calculation of a large dataset on one AWS EC2 High-Memory Quadruple Extra Large compute node (8 CPU's and 68.4 GB RAM) would then take 21 days instead of 125 days at a cost of USD 1,095. However, 21 days for 1,000 samples is not acceptable, because often there are more than 1,000 samples to process, taking more time under this condition. Due to the flexibility of AWS, the computing resources can be adjusted on-demand. Hence, if 21 days are too long, it is possible to run PICNIC on e.g. 20 of

Table 4. Study pipeline

Method	Input	Output	CPU time/CEL
PICNIC	SNP6.0 array	CN + genotype segment	~180 minutes (constant)
Fusion Calculation	Segments with CN	probability of fusion	3-120 minutes (variable)

such compute nodes and therefore 120 samples in parallel, which reduce the runtime further to 24 hours at the same costs.

The CPU time usage of our pipeline's second step (Fusion Calculation) has no predictable processing time. Depending on the output of the PICNIC step the CPU usage may vary between 3 minutes and 2 hours (Table 4).

Technical Setup (In This Use Case)

The administrative entry point from a local workstation to the AWS EC2 infrastructure is a server with a secure remote desktop connection from within the local security area. The parallelization takes place on a master server. The master server can be accessed from the entry point via ssh and serves as an NFS share with a large disc space. The master server interacts with several cloud compute nodes, on which the PICNIC processes are executed in parallel. For the central processing of the incoming results from the compute nodes, the master server is set up with approximately 17GB RAM (High-memory extra-large). The communication with the AWS EC2 compute nodes as well as the parallelization itself is implemented in R (Version 2.12.1), using the R package snow (Simple Network Of Workstation, Version 0.3-10) (Rossini, Tierney, & Li, 2003). The R program establishes a queue for the distribution of a PICNIC process with data on available compute nodes, accessible by IP-address.

Parallelization

Efficient usage of the compute nodes is achieved by using the functions of the snow package. The function *clusterApplyLB* balances the work load if the data to be processed are larger than the number of compute nodes. At first the master sends one task to each node and controls the process with a built-in communication protocol. As soon as one computing node has finished its task, the master sends the next task to this node, until the whole task list is completed.

Usage:

- clusterApplyLB(cl, x, f)
- Arguments:
- cl cluster object containing the compute nodes
- x array with arguments for the function f
- f function to be run on the compute nodes

This dynamic method fits perfectly to the requirements of the second step in our study pipeline. Although the CPU usage per input file is variable, the load-balancing algorithm leads to an excellent utilization of the allocated computing resources (Figure 7). The main disadvantage is that the execution of a job is nondeterministic and the increasing communication with the compute nodes will reduce the overall performance of the parallelization (Table 5).

Looking at the first step of our pipeline with the constant CPU usage of the PICNIC step, we wanted to avoid the overhead of the communication (Figure 8).

This can be solved by utilizing *do.call*. This function is able to construct and execute a function call from a simple vector function '*c*'. The function expects a list of arguments, which are passed to it by *clusterApply*. The data to be processed can be split according to the number of available compute

Figure 7. The advantage of function clusterApplyLB Shown for a task list with 8 tasks distributed to 3 compute nodes

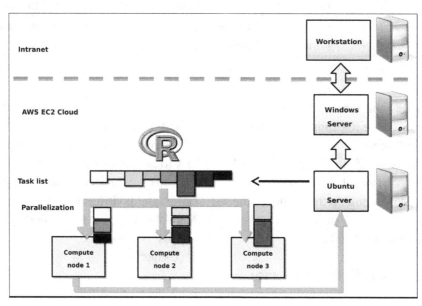

Table 5. Parallelization methods

	clusterApplyLB	splitList and clusterApply
use case	tasks with variable CPU usage	tasks with constant CPU usage
communication protocol	noisy protocol, which is reducing the overall performance	minimized communication
deterministic	no – tasks are run at the next available CPU	yes – tasks are assigned to a dedicated CPU

nodes (function call *length(cl)*, where cl is the cluster object), using *splitList*. Each job contains a list of elements of approximately similar length.

Usage:

- x=splitList (cmd, length(cl))
- do.call("c,"clusterApply(cl, x,f))

Arguments:

- cmd vector with the complete task list
- cl cluster object containing the compute nodes
- x array with arguments for the function f
- f function to be run at the compute nodes

CONCLUSION

In this chapter, it was established that by matter of size and complexity, genomic data is Big Data. New technologies and processes are therefore necessary for analysis, storage and risk assessment. It is intended to support researchers and IT consultants to come up with better-informed decisions on the most suitable IT infrastructure for genomic data analysis. It is an intentional outcome of this chapter that there is no one-fits-all solution, regardless whether the IT infrastructure is internal, outsourced, or Cloud based. Rather, it is argued here that the specific application should be taken into account and that there are certain

Figure 8. In this example the 8 tasks have an almost constant runtime. Using do.call distributes the workload at first and creates task-lists for all compute nodes

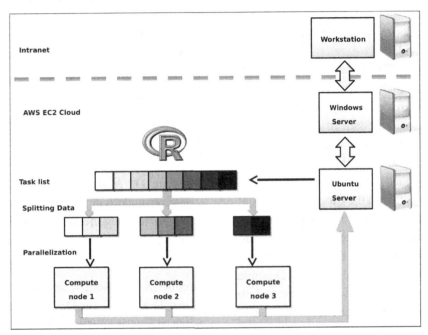

scenarios where Clouds emerge as the most suitable infrastructure:

- Clouds are suitable for applications with high demand towards CPU, memory and storage
- Clouds are suitable for long term storage of raw data in large scale (several TB)
- Clouds are suitable for de-centralized data processing

This last point concerns a novel emerging trend in the genomics field, especially in the Big Data era: As the size and amount of data sets increase, it will soon no longer be feasible to download and centralize data in order to process them. Rather, data will be processed where they reside. It is predicted here that there will be 'Data Clouds' in the near future, established by the data-generating institutions or consortia where computational power can be leased and where additional internal data and algorithms can be 'attached', e.g. by the transfer of virtual machines (VM) into that Cloud

and only results will be reported back. From this trend, a number of consequences follow. It becomes clear that the need to benefit from the wealth of public data will make 'Cloud knowledge' a highly valuable skill for IT experts. Therefore, it can be beneficial for an IT organization to identify use cases suitable for the Cloud in order to make some members of staff 'Cloud ready'. Such use cases can best be found if they match one of the three demand types named above. Furthermore, such a use case must always take into account the prerequisites for Cloud use detailed above in order to identify the proper infrastructure:

1. Capability of the Infrastructure wrt. CPU, memory and storage
2. Bandwidth of the network between local IT and Cloud
3. Data protection regulations (internal regulations as well as laws, e.g. Data Privacy)
4. Risk assessment of both, infrastructure and data
5. Costs

There are further considerations, e.g. suitability and reliability of the Cloud service provider. Here, an analytical approach e.g. as pursued by Leong et al. is a recommended method for gaining a ranked list of Cloud providers.

In the use case study presented in this chapter, R programs were parallelized on AWS EC2 Clouds, utilizing the Cloud for massively parallel processing of large scale genomic data. In addition, different options for parallelization were demonstrated to enable consideration of the advantages and disadvantages of each parallelization approach.

The main advantage of the Cloud environment utilized in this use case study lies in the independence from pre-configured AMIs or fixed IT environments. With AWS, such fixed environments are typically bound to certain regions, for example the *bioconductor-cloud-ami* which is located on *US-East-1 region*. With the introduced approach, users have full control over packages and location of their data. Identification and pursuit of such a use case is a promising first step for the analysis of genomic data in a Cloud environment.

ACKNOWLEDGMENT

The authors would like to acknowledge the support of the following people: Dan Akers, Andreas Friese, Ulf Hengstmann, Jens Hohmann, Heinz Rakel, Felix Reichel, Florian Reuter, Thomas Schilling, and Karsten Tittmann

REFERENCES

Abecasis, G. R., Altshuler, D., Auton, A., Brooks, L. D., Durbin, R. M., Gibbs, R. A., & McVean, G. A. (2010). A map of human genome variation from population-scale sequencing. *Nature*, *467*(7319), 1061–1073. doi:10.1038/nature09534 PMID:20981092

Association, T. G. (2010). Risk Management: Research on Risk Managemant, Assessment and Prevention. *Geneva Association Information Newsletter, 47*. Retrieved January, 2014, from http://aws.amazon.com/glacier/pricing/

Barreiro, L. B., Laval, G., Quach, H., Patin, E., & Quintana-Murci, L. (2008). Natural selection has driven population differentiation in modern humans. *Nature Genetics*, *40*(3), 340–345. doi:10.1038/ng.78 PMID:18246066

Botstein, D., & Risch, N. (2003). Discovering genotypes underlying human phenotypes: Past successes for mendelian disease, future approaches for complex disease. *Nature Genetics*, *33*(3sSuppl), 228–237. doi:10.1038/ng1090 PMID:12610532

Brenner, S., Johnson, M., Bridgham, J., Golda, G., Lloyd, D. H., Johnson, D., & Corcoran, K. (2000). Gene expression analysis by massively parallel signature sequencing (MPSS) on microbead arrays. *Nature Biotechnology*, *18*(6), 630–634. doi:10.1038/76469 PMID:10835600

Brown, M. P., Grundy, W. N., Lin, D., Cristianini, N., Sugnet, C. W., Furey, T. S., & Haussler, D. (2000). Knowledge-based analysis of microarray gene expression data by using support vector machines. *Proceedings of the National Academy of Sciences of the United States of America*, *97*(1), 262–267. doi:10.1073/pnas.97.1.262 PMID:10618406

Chen, G., Wang, C., & Shi, T. (2011). Overview of available methods for diverse RNA-Seq data analyses. *Sci China Life Sci*, *54*(12), 1121–1128. doi:10.1007/s11427-011-4255-x PMID:22227904

Clarke, J., Wu, H. C., Jayasinghe, L., Patel, A., Reid, S., & Bayley, H. (2009). Continuous base identification for single-molecule nanopore DNA sequencing. *Nature Nanotechnology*, *4*(4), 265–270. doi:10.1038/nnano.2009.12 PMID:19350039

Cohen, R. (2012). *Gartner Announces 2012 Magic Quadrant for Cloud Infrastructure as a Service.* Retrieved from http://www.forbes.com/sites/reuvencohen/2012/10/22/gartner-announces-2012-magic-quadrant-for-cloud-infrastructure-as-a-service/

Community, G. (2014). *1000 Genomes Statistics.* Retrieved from http://www.1000genomes.org/category/statistics

de Paula Careta, F., & Paneto, G. G. (2012). Recent patents on High-Throughput Single Nucleotide Polymorphism (SNP) genotyping methods. *Recent Patents on DNA & Gene Sequences, 6*(2), 122–126. doi:10.2174/187221512801327370 PMID:22670603

Eberle, M. A., Stone, J., Galver, L., Hansen, M., Tsan, C., & Seagale, D. (2011). A new whole-genome genotyping array of almost 4.5 million SNPs based on data from the 1000 Genomes Project. In *Proceedings of 12th International Congress of Human Genetics (ICHG).* ICHG.

Edgren, H., Murumagi, A., Kangaspeska, S., Nicorici, D., Hongisto, V., Kleivi, K., & Kallioniemi, O. (2011). Identification of fusion genes in breast cancer by paired-end RNA-sequencing. *Genome Biology, 12*(1), R6. doi:10.1186/gb-2011-12-1-r6 PMID:21247443

Fusaro, V. A., Patil, P., Gafni, E., Wall, D. P., & Tonellato, P. J. (2011). Biomedical cloud computing with Amazon Web Services. *PLoS Computational Biology, 7*(8), e1002147. doi:10.1371/journal.pcbi.1002147 PMID:21901085

Gottfrid, D. (2007). *Self-Service, Prorated Supercomputing Fun!* Retrieved January, 2014, from http://open.blogs.nytimes.com/2007/11/01/self-service-prorated-super-computing-fun/?_php=true&_type=blogs&_r=0

Graux, C., Cools, J., Melotte, C., Quentmeier, H., Ferrando, A., Levine, R., & Hagemeijer, A. (2004). Fusion of NUP214 to ABL1 on amplified episomes in T-cell acute lymphoblastic leukemia. *Nature Genetics, 36*(10), 1084–1089. doi:10.1038/ng1425 PMID:15361874

Greenman, C. D., Bignell, G., Butler, A., Edkins, S., Hinton, J., Beare, D., & Stratton, M. R. (2010). PICNIC: An algorithm to predict absolute allelic copy number variation with microarray cancer data. *Biostatistics (Oxford, England), 11*(1), 164–175. doi:10.1093/biostatistics/kxp045 PMID:19837654

Huang, N., Shah, P. K., & Li, C. (2012). Lessons from a decade of integrating cancer copy number alterations with gene expression profiles. *Briefings in Bioinformatics, 13*(3), 305–316. doi:10.1093/bib/bbr056 PMID:21949216

IBM. (n.d.a). *The Four V's of Big Data.* Retrieved January, 2013, from http://www.ibmbigdatahub.com/infographic/four-vs-big-data

IBM. (n.d.b). *What is big data?* Retrieved January, 2013, from http://www-01.ibm.com/software/data/bigdata/what-is-big-data.html

Illumina. (n.d.). Retrieved from http://www.illumina.com/

Johansson, B., Mertens, F., & Mitelman, F. (1996). Primary vs. secondary neoplasia-associated chromosomal abnormalities-balanced rearrangements vs. genomic imbalances? *Genes, Chromosomes & Cancer, 16*(3), 155–163. doi:10.1002/(SICI)1098-2264(199607)16:3<155::AID-GCC1>3.0.CO;2-Y PMID:8814447

Kasianowicz, J. J., Brandin, E., Branton, D., & Deamer, D. W. (1996). Characterization of individual polynucleotide molecules using a membrane channel. *Proceedings of the National Academy of Sciences of the United States of America, 93*(24), 13770–13773. doi:10.1073/pnas.93.24.13770 PMID:8943010

Kearney, L., & Horsley, S. W. (2005). Molecular cytogenetics in haematological malignancy: Current technology and future prospects. *Chromosoma*, *114*(4), 286–294. doi:10.1007/s00412-005-0002-z PMID:16003502

Kerr, M. K., Martin, M., & Churchill, G. A. (2000). Analysis of variance for gene expression microarray data. [Comparative Study]. *Journal of Computational Biology*, *7*(6), 819–837. doi:10.1089/10665270050514954 PMID:11382364

Lashkari, D. A., DeRisi, J. L., McCusker, J. H., Namath, A. F., Gentile, C., Hwang, S. Y., & Davis, R. W. (1997). Yeast microarrays for genome wide parallel genetic and gene expression analysis. *Proceedings of the National Academy of Sciences of the United States of America*, *94*(24), 13057–13062. doi:10.1073/pnas.94.24.13057 PMID:9371799

Leong, L., Toombs, D., Gill, B., Petri, G., & Haynes, T. (2013). *Magic Quadrant for Cloud Infrastructure as a Service*. Retrieved from http://www.gartner.com/technology/reprints.do?id=1-1IMDMZ5&ct=130819&st=sb

Liu, L., Li, Y., Li, S., Hu, N., He, Y., Pong, R., & Law, M. (2012). Comparison of next-generation sequencing systems. *Journal of Biomedicine & Biotechnology*, *251364*. doi:10.1155/2012/251364 PMID:22829749

Lohr, S. (2013). *The Origins of 'Big Data': An Etymological Detective Story*. Retrieved January, 2014, from http://bits.blogs.nytimes.com/2013/02/01/the-origins-of-big-data-an-etymological-detective-story

Long, M. (2000). A new function evolved from gene fusion. *Genome Research*, *10*(11), 1655–1657. doi:10.1101/gr.165700 PMID:11076848

LTC-AB. (n.d.). Retrieved from http://www.lifetechnologies.com/de/de/home/brands/applied-biosystems.html

Mashey, J. R. (1998). *Big Data... and the Next Wave of InfraStress*. Paper presented at the SGI. New York, NY.

McCarroll, S. A., Kuruvilla, F. G., Korn, J. M., Cawley, S., Nemesh, J., Wysoker, A., & Altshuler, D. (2008). Integrated detection and population-genetic analysis of SNPs and copy number variation. *Nature Genetics*, *40*(10), 1166–1174. doi:10.1038/ng.238 PMID:18776908

McPherson, A., Hormozdiari, F., Zayed, A., Giuliany, R., Ha, G., Sun, M. G., & Shah, S. P. (2011). deFuse: An algorithm for gene fusion discovery in tumor RNA-Seq data. *PLoS Computational Biology*, *7*(5), e1001138. doi:10.1371/journal.pcbi.1001138 PMID:21625565

Meaburn, K. J., Misteli, T., & Soutoglou, E. (2007). Spatial genome organization in the formation of chromosomal translocations. [Review]. *Seminars in Cancer Biology*, *17*(1), 80–90. doi:10.1016/j.semcancer.2006.10.008 PMID:17137790

Mitelman, F., Johansson, B., & Mertens, F. (2007). The impact of translocations and gene fusions on cancer causation. *Nature Reviews. Cancer*, *7*(4), 233–245. doi:10.1038/nrc2091 PMID:17361217

Müller, H., & Röder, T. (2004). *Der Experimentator Microarrays* (Vol. 1). München: Spektrum Akademischer Verlag, Elsevier GmbH.

Pinkel, D., & Albertson, D. G. (2005). Comparative genomic hybridization. *Annual Review of Genomics and Human Genetics*, *6*(1), 331–354. doi:10.1146/annurev.genom.6.080604.162140 PMID:16124865

Pinkel, D., Segraves, R., Sudar, D., Clark, S., Poole, I., Kowbel, D., & Albertson, D. G. (1998). High resolution analysis of DNA copy number variation using comparative genomic hybridization to microarrays. *Nature Genetics*, *20*(2), 207–211. doi:10.1038/2524 PMID:9771718

Rajagopalan, H., & Lengauer, C. (2004). Aneuploidy and cancer. *Nature, 432*(7015), 338–341. doi:10.1038/nature03099 PMID:15549096

Reinartz, J., Bruyns, E., Lin, J. Z., Burcham, T., Brenner, S., Bowen, B., & Woychik, R. (2002). Massively parallel signature sequencing (MPSS) as a tool for in-depth quantitative gene expression profiling in all organisms. [Review]. *Briefings in Functional Genomics & Proteomics, 1*(1), 95–104. doi:10.1093/bfgp/1.1.95 PMID:15251069

Risch, N. J. (2000). Searching for genetic determinants in the new millennium. *Nature, 405*(6788), 847–856. doi:10.1038/35015718 PMID:10866211

Ritz, A., Paris, P. L., Ittmann, M. M., Collins, C., & Raphael, B. J. (2011). Detection of recurrent rearrangement breakpoints from copy number data. *BMC Bioinformatics, 12*(1), 114. doi:10.1186/1471-2105-12-114 PMID:21510904

Roix, J. J., McQueen, P. G., Munson, P. J., Parada, L. A., & Misteli, T. (2003). Spatial proximity of translocation-prone gene loci in human lymphomas. [Comparative Study]. *Nature Genetics, 34*(3), 287–291. doi:10.1038/ng1177 PMID:12808455

Rossini, A., Tierney, L., & Li, N. (2003). *Simple Parallel Statistical Computing in R.* The Berkeley Electronic Press.

Sanger, F., & Coulson, A. R. (1975). A rapid method for determining sequences in DNA by primed synthesis with DNA polymerase. *Journal of Molecular Biology, 94*(3), 441–448. doi:10.1016/0022-2836(75)90213-2 PMID:1100841

Strachan, T., & Read, A. P. (2005). *Molekulare Humangenetik.* Academic Press.

Stratton, M. R., Campbell, P. J., & Futreal, P. A. (2009). The cancer genome. *Nature, 458*(7239), 719–724. doi:10.1038/nature07943 PMID:19360079

Suzuki, S., Tenjin, T., Shibuya, T., & Tanaka, S. (1997). Chromosome 17 copy numbers and incidence of p 53 gene deletion in gastric cancer cells. Dual color fluorescence in situ hybridization analysis. *Nippon Ika Daigaku Zasshi, 64*(1), 22–29. PMID:9119949

Theisen, A. (2008). Microarray-based Comparative Genomic Hybridization (aCGH). *Nature Education, 1.*

Thieme, S., & Groth, P. (2013). Genome Fusion Detection: A novel method to detect fusion genes from SNP-array data. *Bioinformatics (Oxford, England), 29*(6), 671–677. doi:10.1093/bioinformatics/btt028 PMID:23341502

Tomlins, S. A., Rhodes, D. R., Perner, S., Dhanasekaran, S. M., Mehra, R., Sun, X. W., & Chinnaiyan, A. M. (2005). Recurrent fusion of TMPRSS2 and ETS transcription factor genes in prostate cancer. *Science, 310*(5748), 644–648. doi:10.1126/science.1117679 PMID:16254181

van Berkum, N. L., Lieberman-Aiden, E., Williams, L., Imakaev, M., Gnirke, A., Mirny, L. A., & Lander, E. S. (2010). Hi-C: A method to study the three-dimensional architecture of genomes. *Journal of Visualized Experiments,* (39). doi:10.3791/1869 PMID:20461051

Velculescu, V. E., Zhang, L., Vogelstein, B., & Kinzler, K. W. (1995). Serial analysis of gene expression. *Science, 270*(5235), 484–487. doi:10.1126/science.270.5235.484 PMID:7570003

Wang, Z., Gerstein, M., & Snyder, M. (2009). RNA-Seq: A revolutionary tool for transcriptomics. [Review]. *Nature Reviews. Genetics, 10*(1), 57–63. doi:10.1038/nrg2484 PMID:19015660

Wittmann, A. (2012). *When To Pick Up Cloud As A Tool.* Retrieved January, 2014, from http://www.informationweek.com/it-leadership/when-to-pick-up-cloud-as-a-tool/d/d-id/1103313

Yu, J., Mani, R. S., Cao, Q., Brenner, C. J., Cao, X., Wang, X., & Chinnaiyan, A. M. (2010). An integrated network of androgen receptor, polycomb, and TMPRSS2-ERG gene fusions in prostate cancer progression. *Cancer Cell, 17*(5), 443–454. doi:10.1016/j.ccr.2010.03.018 PMID:20478527

ADDITIONAL READING

Alberts, B., Johnson, A., Lewis, J., Raff, M., Roberts, K., & Walter, P. (2007). Molecular Biology of the Cell (M. Anderson & S. Granum Eds. Vol. 5): Garland Science, Taylor & Francis Group, LLC.

Brenner, S., Johnson, M., Bridgham, J., Golda, G., Lloyd, D. H., Johnson, D., & Corcoran, K. (2000). Gene expression analysis by massively parallel signature sequencing (MPSS) on microbead arrays. *Nature Biotechnology, 18*(6), 630–634. doi:10.1038/76469 PMID:10835600

Brown, M. P., Grundy, W. N., Lin, D., Cristianini, N., Sugnet, C. W., Furey, T. S., & Haussler, D. (2000). Knowledge-based analysis of microarray gene expression data by using support vector machines. *Proceedings of the National Academy of Sciences of the United States of America, 97*(1), 262–267. doi:10.1073/pnas.97.1.262 PMID:10618406

Kerr, M. K., Martin, M., & Churchill, G. A. (2000). Analysis of variance for gene expression microarray data. *Journal of Computational Biology, 7*(6), 819–837. doi:10.1089/10665270050514954 PMID:11382364

Lashkari, D. A., DeRisi, J. L., McCusker, J. H., Namath, A. F., Gentile, C., Hwang, S. Y., & Davis, R. W. (1997). Yeast microarrays for genome wide parallel genetic and gene expression analysis. *Proceedings of the National Academy of Sciences of the United States of America, 94*(24), 13057–13062. doi:10.1073/pnas.94.24.13057 PMID:9371799

Müller, H., & Röder, T. (2004). *Der Experimentator Microarrays* (Vol. 1). München: Spektrum Akademischer Verlag, Elsevier GmbH.

Reinartz, J., Bruyns, E., Lin, J. Z., Burcham, T., Brenner, S., Bowen, B., & Woychik, R. (2002). Massively parallel signature sequencing (MPSS) as a tool for in-depth quantitative gene expression profiling in all organisms. *Briefings in Functional Genomics & Proteomics, 1*(1), 95–104. doi:10.1093/bfgp/1.1.95 PMID:15251069

Strachan, T., & Read, A. P. (2005). Molekulare Humangenetik.

Velculescu, V. E., Zhang, L., Vogelstein, B., & Kinzler, K. W. (1995). Serial analysis of gene expression. *Science, 270*(5235), 484–487. doi:10.1126/science.270.5235.484 PMID:7570003

KEY TERMS AND DEFINITIONS

Cloud Computing: Is defined as a computational resource or infrastructure of any kind (Software, Hardware, Network) which is available over the Internet, sold on demand and typically managed by a third-party provider. An important feature is the pay as you go concept.

Cloud Provider: A company, which offers Cloud Computing, taking over the responsibility for a well described part of the customer's value chain, e.g. providing compute nodes (hardware).

Fusion Gene: Merged genomic sequence containing the entire or partial information of at least two spatially separate genes. The merger can lead to a protein with novel functions or non-function and may increase susceptibility to diseases like cancer.

Genomic Data: Is the data generated through research on genes or entire genomes and their function.

Microarray: Describes a wide set of technologies for molecular characterization of RNA and DNA. Microarrays typically consist of thousands or millions of microscopic spots (probes) of known short RNA or DNA sequences of interest, chemically fixed on a solid surface like glass used to measure the abundance of most of the messenger-RNA (mRNA) or DNA within a sample.

Parallelization: Efficient usage of computational resources by running algorithmic pipelines or part of these at the same time on different CPUs or compute nodes in order to reduce the overall runtime.

Personal Data: Any information concerning the personal circumstances of an identified or identifiable individual. Such data, especially when containing information about the health of an individual, are protected by specific data privacy laws in many countries.

PICNIC: Algorithm, published by a group of scientists and freely available from the Wellcome Trust Sanger Institute to detect allelic copy number variation with SNP6 array for cancer samples.

Risk Analysis: A process to identify threats: their possible impact und the probability of occurrence. This type of analysis is needed, when dealing with personal data in a Cloud.

APPENDIX

Table 6. Abbreviations and their meanings

Abbreviation	Meaning
aCGH	Array Comparative Genomic Hybridization is a molecular technique to compare a given genome against a reference genome and to identify the differences.
API	Application Programming Interface is a specification for the interaction of software components.
AWS	Amazons Web Services is a collection of web services offered by Amazon (e.g. S3, EC2) (see EC2).
BAM	Dedicated file format for genomic data. Can be used as input for IGV (Integrated Genomics Viewer) and tools like SAMTOOLS (see http://samtools.sourceforge.net).
bp	Base Pairs are the building blocks of the DNA (see DNA). Hydrogen bonds make Adenine molecules connect to Thymine. Guanine builds a pair with Cytosine.
cDNA	Complementary DNA (see DNA) is a special labeled DNA used for microarrays, e.g. to identify SNP (see SNP).
CERN	European Organization for Nuclear Research doing high-energy physics research and more.
CN	Copy Number – The number of molecules of a particular type on or in a cell or as part of a cell. Usually applied to specific genes.
CNV	Copy Number Variation is a counter for alterations within the genomic code. Deletions or duplications are leading to an abnormal number of genes (see CN)
CPU	Central Processing Unit is the main part of a computer performing the basic arithmetical operations.
ddNTP	Dideoxynucleotidetriphosphate is a molecule that is used during DNA sequencing (see DNA-seq). This molecule is missing a phosphodiester bond so that the "normal" chain building stops for further analysis at this point.
DNA	Deoxyribonucleic acid encodes the genetic information in cells and viruses.
DNA-seq	DNA-sequencing is a procedure to determine the exact order of bases within a DNA molecule.
EB	Exabyte: 10^{18}bytes, which is one billion Gigabytes (see TB and GB).
EC2	Amazon Elastic Compute Cloud is a part of Amazons Web Services (AWS) to rent virtual computers (see AWS).
EU	European Union is a political and economic union of states located in Europe.
FASP	Fast and Secure Protocol is an IT protocol that optimizes data transfer between computer systems; therefore much faster than FTP (see FTP).
FASTQ	Text based format to describe a biological sequence and its quality values. Developed by WTSI (see WTSI).
FDT	Fast Data Transfer is a Java based application for fast file transfers developed by CERN (see CERN).
FTP	File Transfer Protocol is a standard IT protocol for transferring data between computer systems.
FTPs	File Transfer Protocol over SSL adds encryption to the FTP protocol (see FTP).
GB	Gigabyte: 10^9 bytes (see EB and TB)
GFD	Genomic Fusion Detection is a method to predict fusion genes on a genomic level based on SNP6 array data (see SNP6 array).
GUI	Graphical User Interface. Displays icons and other visual indicators to enable user interaction with a computer program.
HTTP	Hypertext Transfer Protocol is a standard IT protocol used by Internet browsers to fetch and display information.
IaaS	Infrastructure as a Service is a service model offered by Cloud Providers.
IP	Internet Protocol is the communication protocol developed for the Internet. TCP and UDP are based on IP (see TCP and UDP).
IPv6	Internet Protocol version 6 is the latest revision of the Internet Protocol. It was developed to solve the address exhaustion of the former version (IPv4) (see IP).
ISO	International Organization for Standardization defines worldwide industrial standards.

continued on following page

Table 6. Continued

Abbreviation	Meaning
IT	Information Technology
KPI	Key Performance Indicator is used to measure the success of predefined activities.
mRNA	Messenger RNA (see RNA) – special type of RNA, which is used to translate genomic information and steers the protein synthesis.
NaaS	Network as a Service is a service model offered by Cloud Provider.
NBC	Neighborhood Breakpoint Conservation is an algorithm for identifying rearrangement breakpoints that are highly conserved at the same locus in multiple individuals.
NFS	Network File System is a protocol that allows a user to access files over a network.
NGS	Next generation sequencing summarizes the technologies for faster and cheaper DNA sequencing (see DNA-seq).
NO-SQL	'not only SQL' – non relational databases that are used to store big data with a better performance than native SQL databases (see SQL).
PaaS	Platform as a Service is a service model offered by Cloud Providers.
PICNIC	Predicting Intergral Copy Number In Cancer
RDP	Remote Desktop Protocol is a proprietary protocol developed by Microsoft to connect remotely to a Windows computer system using a GUI (see GUI).
RNA	Ribonucleic acid – a molecule that is used to code, encode and regulate gene expression.
RNA-seq	RNA-sequencing is a procedure to determine the exact order of bases within an RNA molecule.
SAGE	Serial analysis of gene expression is a technique to collect the mRNA at a dedicated point in time.
sFTP	SSH File Transfer Protocol is an encrypted file transfer protocol using ssh (see ssh).
SME	Small and medium enterprises are companies whose personnel numbers fall below certain limits.
SNP	Single Nucleotide Polymorphism is a variation within the genome, where single information varies between the members of the same species.
SNP6 array	Detection tool for SNPs (see SNP).
TB	Terabyte: 10^{12} bytes, which is one thousand Gigabytes (see EB and GB).
TCP	Transmission Control Protocol is based on the Internet Protocol and adds session reliability as the main benefit (see IP).
sgi	Silicon Graphics is a company specialized on graphical hardware production, founded in 1981.
SLA	Service Level Agreement is a formal definition of a service as part of a contract.
SQL	Structured Query Language is the *de facto* standard for creating and modifying relational databases.
SSH	Secure Shell is an encrypted network protocol running on Windows and Unix. SSH is based on TCP (see TCP).
TCGA	The Cancer Genome Atlas – a catalogue of genomic mutations, which are treated responsible for cancer.
Torrent	Files-Sharing concept designed to distribute huge data through a network.
UCSC	University of California/Santa Crux
UCSC-browser	On-line genome browser hosted by the University of California.
UDP	User Datagram Protocol is based on the Internet Protocol and has no session reliability by default, but it's much faster than TCP (see TCP and IP).
VCF	Variant Call Format is used as a standard to describe gene sequence variations.
VM	Virtual Machine is a software-based fictitious computer, realized on a physical hardware that can run many independent VMs at the same time.

continued on following page

Table 6. Continued

Abbreviation	Meaning
VPN (-tunnel)	Virtual Private Network is an extension of a private (company) network using a public network (e.g. Internet). A VPN tunnel is used to connect both and encrypt all traffic.
WAN	World Area Network is a public or private network covering a large area and linking across boundaries.
WTSI	Wellcome Trust Sanger Institute is an institute located near Cambridge (England) doing genetic researches (see www.sanger.ac.uk).
WGS	Whole Genome Sequencing is a process to determine the complete DNA sequence at a single time (see DNA seq).

Chapter 10
Pathway Analysis and Its Applications

Ravi Mathur
North Carolina State University, USA

Alison Motsinger-Reif
North Carolina State University, USA

ABSTRACT

As the scale of genetic, genomic, metabolomics, and proteomic data increases with advancing technology, new approaches leveraging domain expert knowledge, and other sources of functional annotation have been developed to aid in the analysis and interpretation of such data. Pathway and network analysis approaches have become popular in association analysis – connecting genetic markers or measures of gene product with phenotypes or diseases of interest. These approaches aim to leverage big data to better understand the complex etiologies of these traits. Findings from such analyses can help reveal interesting biological traits and/or help identify potential biomarkers of disease. In the current chapter, the authors review broad categories of pathway analyses and review advantages and disadvantages of each. They discuss both the analytical methods to detect phenotype-associated pathways and review the key resources in the field of human genetics that are available to investigators wanting to perform such analyses.

INTRODUCTION

Recent technological developments in high-throughput genetic, genomic, and metabolomics profiling techniques has greatly expanded the potential for more systems level analysis. As such data becomes more readily available experimentally, and the scale of the data increases, this creates exciting new challenges in analyzing this "big data." Handling and summarizing such high dimensional data in an efficient and interpretable way is crucial to making good use of this data. While there are a number of different strategies for handling big "-omics" data, pathway and network analysis approaches are becoming standard approaches for discovering and summarizing the underlying relationships in the data. The pathway and network approaches rely on either external knowledge bases or strong correlation structure in the data to collapse the data from thousands or millions of variables, to hundreds or thousands of pathways/networks for analysis. The results

DOI: 10.4018/978-1-4666-6611-5.ch010

of such analyses are valuable to the process of discovering the underlying mechanism of disease or a phenotype of interest, including the events leading up to initiation, progression, and treatment of a disease.

As stated by the National Human Genome Research Institute (NHGRI), "A biological pathway is a series of actions among molecules in a cell that leads to a certain product or a change in a cell" (www.genome.org). Such a pathway can describe the function of molecules in a cell (regulatory pathway) or the change in chemical elements throughout the cell (metabolomics pathway) or a description of the initiation of a disease (disease pathway). It is now understood that biological pathways in the cell interact with one another to carry on the actions of the cell. Therefore, a group of interacting pathways comprise a biological network. There is a wealth of knowledge on such interactions that have been curated in pathway/knowledge bases that can be leveraged in statistical analysis of specific datasets. Many pathway based analysis approaches have been developed to use these databases to aid in gene function prediction, discover new associations with the trait of interest, and even to better classify patients or sample. Other approaches, more typically referred to as network approaches, focus on quantifying the connections between the gene, proteins, or metabolites to better understand the connections between the molecules that result in the phenotype/disease. A biological pathway and network can be displayed and analyzed in a graph form with vertices and edges. In such a form a vertex represents each element contained in the pathway or network and an edge represents an interaction (activation, repression, methylation, series of chemical reactions, etc.) between those elements. Figure 1 shows a graph representation of the Glycolysis Pathway, which displays many of the properties (scale-free degree distribution, high clustering coefficient, and characteristic path length) displayed in a variety of biological pathways. In the current chapter, we review many

of the major categories of pathway and network analysis tools.

Most of the pathway analysis tools developed rely on a knowledge base that defines gene sets or pathways that are statistically tested to be influential in the dataset as opposed to random chance. While the fundamental statistical approaches of the methods are largely independent of the database, in practicality many of the knowledge based and analysis approaches have been developed in tandem. Therefore the software implementations that are popularly used rely heavily on specific databases. The analysis of pathway starts by the data collection, thus we begin the chapter with a short discussion of the data collection technologies that are frequently used in human genetics. Many of these resources are also available for model organisms, but we focus on tools with direct relevance for research directly studying human health. While many of the approaches were originally developed to gene expression (particularly microarray) data, extensions of the approaches are now frequently used with deoxyribose nucleic acid (DNA) level variation, and with biochemical/metabolomics data. Due to the reliance on knowledge bases, we continue with a discussion of the most commonly used resources in human genetics. Then we will discuss the major classes/categories of gene set and pathway analysis tools, and discuss details of some of the most commonly used methods. Many of the implementation challenges will be discussed, with an emphasis on analyzing big data where often the number of samples is much lower than the number of variables or features. The chapter will conclude by discussing future research avenues and overall lessons learned from these methods so far.

BACKGROUND

Pathway analysis consists of the statistical analysis of a series of steps, all of which influence each other. The basic workflow of any pathway/network

Figure 1. Graph Representation of Glycolysis Pathway. Each vertex in the graph corresponds to an element (gene, SNP, metabolic process, etc.) and each edge corresponds to interactions between those elements. This representation was created in the Cytoscape software utilizing the KEGGscape plug-in. (http://www.cytoscape.org/)

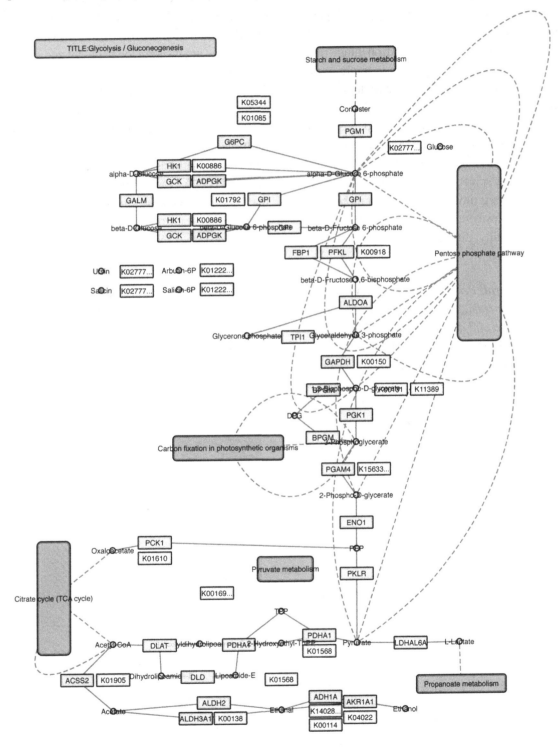

analysis is displayed in Figure 2. Pathway analysis starts by generating data from the "-omic" elements of interest. This data generation most commonly includes expression profiling (most commonly by gene expression or RNA-Sequencing experiments), Single Nucleotide Polymorphism (SNP) arrays and metabolomics collection platforms, but is rapidly expanding to include methylation chips, copy number aberration technologies, etc. Based on the elements collected in the dataset the appropriate database is selected based on the information content of the database. Next, specific pathways included in the database are selected. This selection can be those pathways the investigator is most interested in or more commonly, all pathways contained in the database can be tested. Finally, differences in the elements of

selected pathways in experimental groups (such as cases and controls) or with a quantitative trait of interest. Details of these analysis differ by the overall hypothesis tested, and the details of the methods used. Using categories established by (Ramanan, Shen, Moore, & Saykin, 2012), we discuss analysis major pathway and network analysis tools classified into three generations. These "generations" are guideline to help think about the approaches, but are not hard classifications - many techniques use elements that define multiple "generations," thus the overlap. The first generation methods include over-representation analysis (ORA) tools, the second generation is the Function Class Scoring (FCS) methods, and the third generation is the Pathway Topology (PT) approaches. With the high-dimensionality

Figure 2. Overall Process of Pathway Analysis. The process starts with data generation, which are most commonly expression, SNP arrays and metabolomics. From the raw output of these technologies the data is cleaned and analyzed for quality control standards. Based on the variables contained in this data and the technology utilized, a database that contains information on these variables is selected. Next the pathway(s) and information that the investigator would like is extracted. Finally, the data is analyzed by the pathway or network analysis approach that best fits the overall hypothesis of an investigator's experiment. The methods have overlap of whether they are considered ORA, FCS or PT methods, thus the overlap in the Venn diagram.

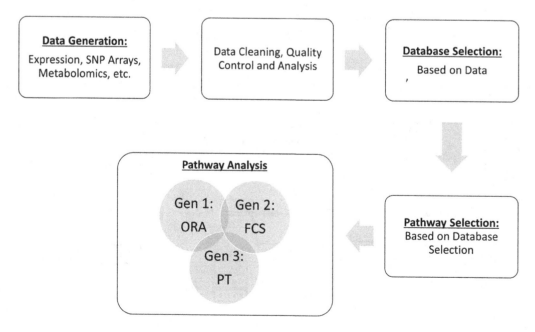

of sequencing and profiling technologies the dataset has many more variables or features than the number of samples. In analyzing such data, addition considerations to minimize over fitting have to be performed.

DATA GENERATION TECHNOLOGIES

Any pathway or network analysis begins with collecting data within an experiment with a particular trait or disease of interest, including elements that are hypothesized to influence that phenotype. With high-throughput technologies it is now accessible to assay as many as millions of elements, with sample sizes rarely on the same order of magnitude. Thus the "curse of dimensionality" is a serious problem, therefore the data that is analyzed has many more variables or features than the number of samples. In analyzing such data, additional considerations have to be taken to conduct proper analyses. The major technologies that are used in human genetics/genomics, proteomics, and metabolomics will be briefly described. As technologies are constantly advancing, the completeness of this list is constantly changing. Additionally, as each technology has very specific characteristics that must be considered in quality control and analysis, we point towards references that detail these issues with more direct guidance.

Gene Expression

Gene expression technologies quantify the amount of gene-product that a particular gene is producing. High-throughput technologies to quantify expression for the whole genome can be classified into hybridization-based techniques and sequencing-based techniques. Hybridization-based techniques include DNA microarrays (Zakharkin, 2005) and genomic tiling microarrays. Both of these techniques rely on the hybridization (bond of complement DNA segments) of fluorescently labeled cDNA. Microarrays have been in common use for over a decade, and a number of issues with batch effects, quality control and normalization approaches, etc. are well studied. Excellent reviews of best practices in collection, quality control, and standard analysis of microarray data have been produced by the MicroArray Quality Control (MAQC) project (M. Consortium et al., 2006; Shi et al., 2010).

Sequencing-based techniques include serial analysis of gene expression (SAGE) (Velculescu, Zhang, Vogelstein, & Kinzler, 1995), cap analysis of gene expression (CAGE) (Kodzius et al., 2006), massively parallel signature sequencing (MPSS) (Brenner et al., 2000) and RNA-Sequencing (RNA-Seq) (Wang, Gerstein, & Snyder, 2009b). Sequencing-based techniques have the benefits of reduced background noise and more accurate and reproducible quantification of the expression. RNA-Sequencing is currently considered the most advanced and reliable technique, therefore is growing in use as the technology becomes for accessible and affordable (Chu & Corey, 2012).

RNA-Seq utilizes next-generation sequencing technology to sequence a population of RNA extracted from a population. RNA-Seq starts by converting extracted RNA into a cDNA library, which is sequenced to provide the genomic sequences of thousands of small segments from the population (referred to as reads). The reads are either aligned to a known reference genome or assembled de novo (if reference genome is not known). This step results in a mapping of the whole genome. From this mapping, the number of reads that map to each gene in the genome are counted, and normalization for gene size is performed. The resultant count of each gene is a relative value for the expression of that particular gene. (Wang, Gerstein, & Snyder, 2009a). As RNA-Seq is more commonly used, best practices in quality control and processing is an emerging and important area of bioinformatics research. A recent review of emerging best practices and tools available can be found in (DeLuca et al., 2012).

Gene expression data (particularly microarrays) was the data type that directly inspired many of the pathway and network analysis approaches discussed below, and methods with the longest track record of development (both methodologically and the software implementations that correspond to them) are readily compatible.

Single Nucleotide Polymorphism (SNP) Arrays

A single nucleotide polymorphism (SNP) refers to a specific position in the genome where two or more different nucleotides are known to appear in a specific population. Since humans are diploid, each individual's DNA has two copies, one received from the mother and another received from the father. These allele can either be dominant or recessive. Therefore, SNP's are typically analyzed in terms of their genotype, though allelic encoding assuming an additive model is also frequent.

SNP arrays are a high-throughput technologies that analyzes thousands of SNP's in the genome. The two common companies that produce SNP arrays are Affymetrix (www.affymetrix.com) and Illumina (www.illumina.com). Both companies utilize similar technologies, which rely on the fact that complement DNA segment hybridize to each other. The most recent arrays analyze around one million SNP's on one array, which is the number of variables in the dataset. For both companies the abundance of each allele for each SNP is analyzed by a different probe (short single stranded fragment of DNA). For Affymetrix arrays the probes (about 25 base pairs in length) are fluorescently labeled and targeted by its perfect complement. The fluorescence of each probe is measured by shining a laser on the array. For Illumina, each probe (about 50 base pairs in length) is attached to a bead and targeted complementary nucleotides hybridize and emit a light. For both technologies, the emitted light from the fluorescence is measured as the raw probe intensity. Affymetrix normalizes the raw probe intensities between several arrays,

where Illumina normalizes amongst each array. Affymetrix processes the normalized probe intensities by the Birdseed algorithm (Korn et al., 2008) to receive the genotypes for each SNP. Illumina utilizes a clustering algorithm based on a transformed ratio of the probe intensities to receive the genotypes for each SNP. (LaFramboise, 2009)

SNP arrays are utilized to genotype organisms' DNA, analyze DNA copy number variation (number of copies of genomic segments) and loss-of-heterozygosity (when one copy of a genomic area is lost by the parent). An advantage of SNP array data is the ability to utilize linkage disequilibrium information. Linkage disequilibrium is when alleles at different loci are present together in one individual at a rate higher than expected. Linkage disequilibrium is interpreted as the correlation between SNPs. Linkage disequilibrium allows SNP chip technologies to effectively capture a large amount of variation across the genome through this correlation, so that association analysis can find loci with common variants that are associated with the disease or trait of interest without having to assay causal or directly functional variants.

The use of SNP data for pathway and network analysis is a relatively new extension of the pathway approaches that were designed for gene expression data. Typically, for methods that have been extended to analyze SNP data, variants are grouped within gene (using different sources of genomic annotation including linkage disequilibrium), and measures of overall variation and or association with the trait of interest are used in the pathway analysis.

Metabolomics Technologies

Metabolomics is the study and analysis of many metabolites in a sample. A metabolite is a result of interactions of the genome with the environment over time. Recent studies have shown that several metabolites are in fact part of many regulatory processes in different organisms; therefore they are getting increasingly more attention. Several different technologies are used to profile metabolites, including Nuclear Magnetic Resonance (NMR), and Gas Chromatography (GC), Liquid Chromatography (LC), Capillary Electrophoresis (CE), Supercritical Fluid Chromatography (CFC), Matrix-assisted laser desorption/ionization (MALDI), and Direct Influsion (DI) all coupled with Mass Spectrometry (MS). (Putri, Yamamoto, Tsugawa, & Fukusaki, 2013) Mass Spectrometry is a technique which generates a range of masses for atoms or molecules that are contained in a sample. The mass is measured by ionizing the compounds and measuring the mass-to-charge ratio. Chromatography is a technique that separates molecules contained in a mixture. Techniques coupled with MS are most popular and results in the highest throughput. The difference in each of the above techniques is in how the compounds are ionized.

Metabolomic assay techniques are relatively high-throughput, although not to the same degree as expression and SNP technologies. Metabolite data usually have hundreds of metabolites analyzed as opposed to a million for expression and SNP data. This is due to the many variants (different weights, polarity, and solubility) chemical can be found making the detection and quantification difficult. Therefore, a certain amount of bias is included towards any metabolomics analysis, since the researcher often targets specific metabolites. The annotation level associated with metabolomics data is also rapidly evolving (Dunn, Broadhurst, Atherton, Goodacre, & Griffin, 2011).

Data Analysis Prior to Pathway Analysis

Typically, prior to pathway/network analysis, initial analysis is performed to find associations with individual elements (genes, variants, etc.) with the disease or trait of interest. After appropriate quality control, traditional statistical tests are typically performed for individual elements. For example, in a gene expression experiment comparing cases and controls, a t-test comparing the distributions of individuals in the two groups for each gene in the genome is performed, and a p-value and measure of effect size (i.e. fold change, etc.) is recorded. In big data application, multiple testing issues become a concern, and appropriate control (such as false discovery rate) corrections are often used to find significant elements. For the ORA and FCS analysis approaches discussed below, the results of these association tests are used to then look for over-representation of elements from the same pathway in most significant findings. What is meant by "pathway" will be defined by which knowledge bases (or combination of knowledge bases) that are used for analysis, as discussed below.

DATABASES

For knowledge base-driven pathway analysis several databases have compiled information about genes and interaction elements. The diversity and number of databases is constantly growing, and we review only a small subset of the tools available here. The databases we will review include Gene Ontology (GO) (Reference Genome Group of the Gene Ontology, 2009), Molecular Signature Database (MSigDB) (http://www.broadinstitute.org/gsea/msigdb/index.jsp), Kyoto Encyclopedia of Genes and Genomes (KEGG) (Kanehisa et al., 2014), and MetaCyc (Caspi et al., 2014). These databases are summarized along with a URL to access the database is shown in Table 1. Each of these databases is constructed using a mix of highly curated (often manually) annotations and predicted pathway information from computational algorithms. The most used databases were initially driven using large teams of curators that pull out connections from the literature. All these databases make it clear what the source of the pathway information used is, and final stages of interpretation of pathway analysis results should take into account this information. Covering all details of these databases is beyond the scope of

Table 1. A Summary of common databases utilized in pathway analysis including the url to access these databases

Database	Summary	Access
GO	Annotate of the function, role and location of genes and gene products.	http://www.geneontology.org/
KEGG	System, genomic, and chemical elements displays as pathway maps, where an overall picture of the interaction between elements.	http://www.genome.jp/kegg/
MetaCyc	Experimentally curated metabolic pathways along with enzyme kinetic information.	http://www.metacyc.org/
MSigDB	Contains discovered genes sets including SNP level information.	http://www.broadinstitute.org/gsea/msigdb/index.jsp

this chapter, but we review some of the commonly used ones here. Before implementing any combination of pathway analysis approaches, investigators should be well informed about the databases they are referencing, and choose the most applicable for their specific domain application.

Gene Ontology (GO)

As one of the oldest and most curated, GO has created a uniform structured vocabulary to annotate the function, role and location of genes and gene products in many different organisms. Currently over 26,000 GO terms have been defined which reference the molecular function, biological process and/or cellular component that genes and their gene products are active. GO annotation is highly hierarchical; such that each of these terms are hierarchically structured within the function/process, etc. The network nature of GO is comprised of the relationships, where genes may be the same (or orthologs as defined by the Reference Genome Project), a part of each other, and/or regulate each other. The determination of homologous elements is conducted by the PANTHER system. (Mi et al., 2010; Thomas et al., 2003) Their method of discovering new information is both in depth and breadth, therefore creating a comprehensive database. Another advantage of the GO database is that its information is linked to other databases including SwisProt (Bairoch & Apweiler, 2000), GenBank (Benson

et al., 2000), EMBL (Baker et al., 2000), DDBJ (Tateno, Miyazaki, Ota, Sugawara, & Gojobori, 2000), PIR (Barker et al., 2000), MIPS (Mewes et al., 2000), and Pfam (Bateman et al., 2000).

Kyoto Encyclopedia of Genes and Genomes (KEGG)

KEGG is a reference knowledgebase, which contains system, genomic, and chemical information applicable to different organisms. The key element of the database pertaining to pathway analysis is the pathway maps, where an overall picture of the interaction between elements is displayed. Such information is generally presented (not organism specific) and the KEGG Ontology information is used to specify the information for an organism. KEGG's Metabolism overview maps display interaction information of chemicals, which in conjunction with KEGG Modules and KEGG Reaction provide an overall view of metabolic networks. KEGG Medicos includes information of the interaction between drugs, extracted both from FDA and Japanese sources. While originally an open-source effort, the current funding model to get access to the files comprising this database requires a fee.

MetaCyc

MetaCyc is a database of experimentally curated metabolic pathways in conjunction with enzyme kinetic information. In the database 1,800 pathways are included from different organisms. The pathway classes defined in MetaCyc include:

- **Activation:** A chemical modification to an active compound, which increases the activity of that compound.
- **Inactivation:** A chemical modification to an active compound, which decreases the activity of that compound.
- **Interconversion:** A chemical that is converted into another form, which results in either an increase or decrease in the activity of that compound.
- **Metabolic Clusters:** A collection of compounds that are not directly connected but collectively describe a specific phenomenon.
- **Biosynthesis:** The process by which an active compound is synthesized.
- **Degradation/Utilization/Assimilation:** The process by which a compound is broken down into smaller, simpler compounds.

The activation, inactivation and interconversion are defined in one class. Other classes include Generation of Precursor Metabolites and Energy and Detoxification. Recent advances in the database include bioenergy pathways, development of techniques to genetically engineer pathways and combining pathways. Furthermore, this database has the ability to combine pathways, which are referred to as a super or conspecific or chimeric pathways. Often the pathways, which are combined, are defined in different organisms, although they describe the same or similar phenomenon. The combination of these pathways results in an overview of the metabolic phenomenon that is being combined. BioCyc is a pathway/genome database created by the same organization as MetaCyc. In this database 1,700 pathways are contained for different organisms. Three tiers of pathways are included in this database, those that have been extensively studied and curated for over

one year, and those that have been curated for less than one year and those that are computationally created. The pathways that are computationally created are from the utilization of the Pathway Tools software. (Caspi et al., 2014)

Molecular Signatures Database (MSigDB)

MSigDB is a database of discovered genes sets from several sources. It contains 10,295 gene sets, which are classified into the following collections.

- **Positional:** These correspond to specific chromosomes, therefore are best used to detect chromosomal deletions.
- **Curated:** These have been collected from online databases, literature, and experts. It contains subclasses referring to specific pathways and databases.
- **Motif:** Genes that have a cis-regulatory motif conserved across human, mouse, rat and dog genomes.
- **Computational:** These have been discovered by computational mining of microarray data, mainly in the cancer field.
- **GO:** These have been named by GO and classified by them into a specific category.
- **Oncogenic:** These are implicated in pathways that are dis-regulated in cancer.
- **Immunologic:** These were literature curated to be influential in the immune system.

All of these databases contain vital information, which assist pathway analysis software to identify influential pathways and genes in the dataset of interest. These databases have ontology information, where one can access whether the information contained in their dataset has been found by other researchers or in another organism. The pathways included in these databases can be used as gene sets for the hypothesis testing performed using the pathway and network analysis approaches discussed below. Alternatively, any of the approaches discussed below could be used with custom gene sets (that an investigator builds based on prior information), though the implementation of this is not as straightforward as using the tools that are built around these well-curated databases.

PATHWAY AND NETWORK ANALYSIS METHODOLOGIES

Pathway analysis is the process of discovering meaningful relationships between cellular elements, often in context of the disease or trait of interest. The definition of the cellular elements of interest depends on the data that is being analyzed. For expression data, genes are the cellular elements. For SNP array data, the SNP can be mapped to a particular gene or the SNP positions themselves can be used as the cellular elements. For metabolite data, the chemicals analyzed are the cellular elements. The appeal of pathway analysis concerns is the summary information, which results from it. Although conducting pathway analysis, the "curse of dimensionality" still has to be dealt with. The "curse of dimensionality" is when the number of variables in the dataset is much larger than the number of samples. With such a challenge discovering patterns above the high level of noise is of great importance and appropriate statistical methods have to be taken to overcome such a challenge. Furthermore, pathway analysis has the ability to consider the interactions between cellular elements, which are critical to the functionality of the cell. Thus influential interactions in the dataset can potentially be identified.

Once the data has been collected and the proper quality control is conducted, the researcher must select pathways (often defined in the knowledge based discussed above), which needs to carefully reflect the overall goals of the study, the types of data and information that was used to build the resource. Relevant information can include pathways from other organisms, the current knowledge about the disease or mechanism under study, etc.

This information can be tailored towards the goals of the study. Although an exhaustive search can utilize all pathways in a particular database or knowledgebase information, there are statistical and computational concerns with this being really feasible. For example Figure 3 displays the Glycolysis pathway (extracted from KEGG's manual drawn database). This representation is visually different from the graph representation seen in Figure 1, although they convey similar information.

The evolution of pathway analysis methods has given rise to two different processes within the broad class of pathway/network analysis, pathway/network generation and association analysis of the pathway/network with particular disease/experimental states or phenotypes of interest. Another classification of pathway analysis methods is into three generations, Over-Representation Analysis (ORA, which is the 1st generation), Functional Class Scoring (FCS, which is the 2nd generation), and Pathway-Topology (PT, which is the 3rd generation). ORA and FCS methods are also often referred to as gene set analysis, since they test for (Khatri, Sirota, & Butte, 2012). ORA and FCS methods conduct the main task of analysis of the network, while PT methods infer and generate networks. These tasks often can be conducted in serial of each other, when both inference and analysis of the network is desired (Khatri et al., 2012). The advantages, disadvantages and common utilization of each approach is summarized in Table 2. While many specific methodologies do not necessarily fall cleanly into these categories, the overall goals and approaches of a number can be generally contextualized into these categories.

The ORA methods identify influential (those that are over-represented) cellular elements from the pathways identified. The common procedure includes three steps: 1) picking/calculating a threshold measure, 2) counting the representation of input genes (within a defined pathway), and 3) conducting a statistical test. First all elements that have input measurements that do not meet a

Figure 3. Glycolysis pathway drawn manually by kegg (Kanehisa et al., 2014)

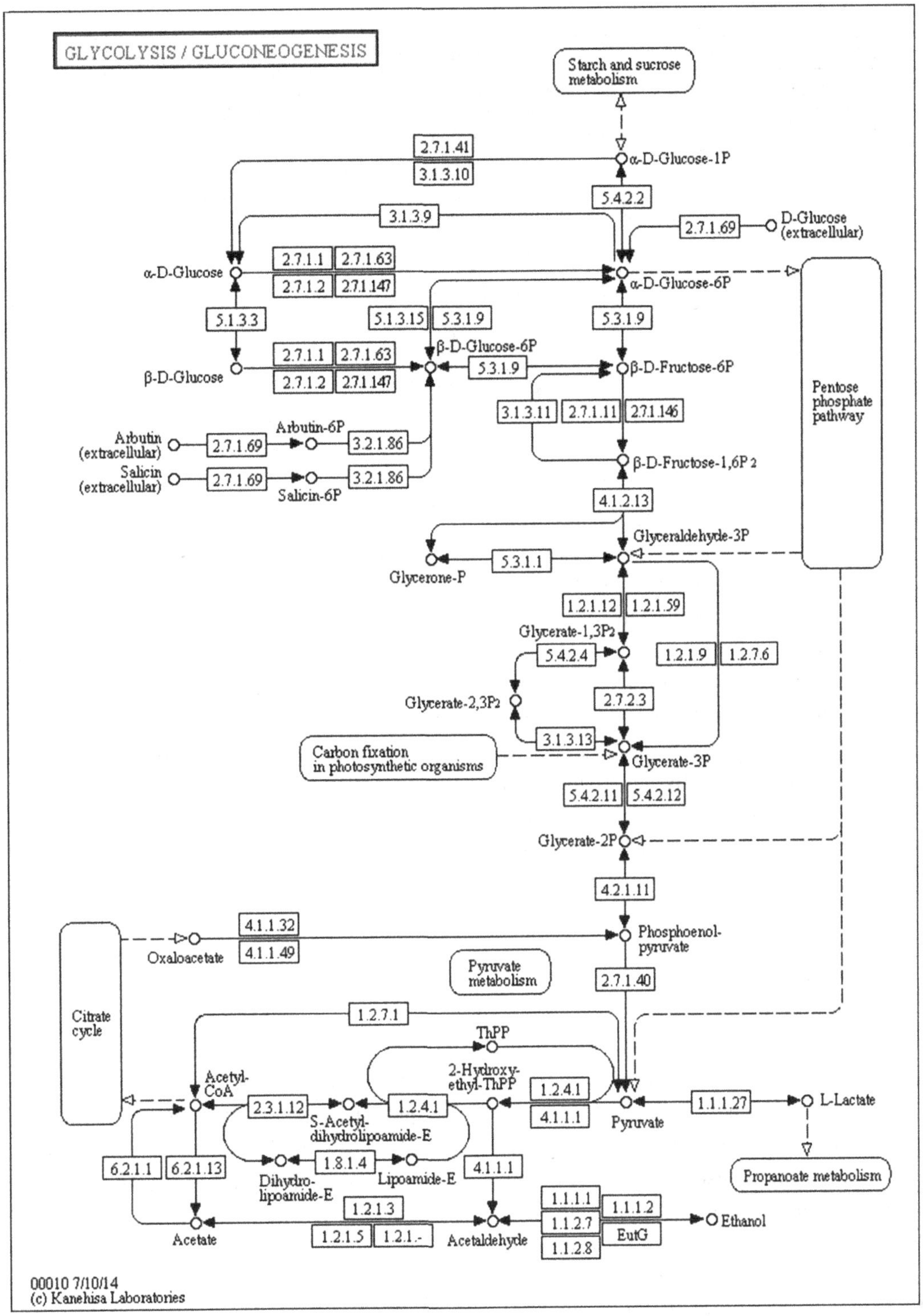

Table 2. Advantages, disadvantages and most common utilization of ora, fcs and pt pathway analysis methods

Method	Advantages	Disadvantages	Utilization
ORA	• Simple to Implement • Robust Statistics	• Statistics do not consider measurement • Arbitrary threshold • No Interactions Considered	Overall characterization of pathways displayed in the data.
FCS	• Robust Statistics • Interactions considered • Statistics consider measurement • No threshold required	• No interactions between pathways • Measurement only considered in calculation gene-level statistic.	More in depth characterization of the pathways representative in the data.
PT	• Interactions considered • Pathway topology can be inferred	• Bias towards data • Little information about the interactions is known • Topology depends on cell and environmental conditions and all scenarios are difficult to collect.	Inferring the topology of the pathway, while also characterizing the statistical significance.

specified threshold are discarded. For example a common threshold for expression data is over/under expressed by more or less than a specific value. A similar threshold utilized for expression data is to utilize false discovery rate instead of over/under expression. For the genes that meet the threshold, the numbers of genes represented in each of the analyzed pathways are counted. Finally a statistical test is conducted to assess if the observed count is statistically significant from the count randomly expected. Common statistical tests include those based on the hyper geometric, chi-squared, and binomial distribution. These statistical tests have different ways of representing the null hypothesis, which is discussed in more detail in the "Implementation Considerations" section below. The main limitations with ORA methods are that the statistical significance is measured without consideration of the element's measurement. Therefore, each genes in the statistical test is treated equally. This statistical model may not be accurate since the measurement is often an indication of the activity of the element. Thus each element should be represented according to their measurement and not equally. Another limitation for ORA methods is the arbitrary threshold of the first step. Since elements not meeting this threshold are disregarded in further analyses, a more robust

method of elimination should be utilized. A third limitation for ORA methods is that no interactions between elements are considered. Therefore, each element is analyzed independent of the others. Due to this assumption of ORA analyses, researchers refer to these methods as gene set analysis, since a set of elements is identified and their relationships are not considered. Lastly ORA methods typically assume that each pathway analyzed are independent of each other. Since all processes in the cell are interconnected (and certainly the pathways and gene sets as defined in the knowledge bases are interconnected), this assumption is not realistic. (Khatri et al., 2012) These limitations prompted the development of the second generation of pathway analysis tools.

FCS methods are those methods that analyze the network connections directly from the data analyzed. FCS methods utilize statistical techniques that detect both large and small changes to the individual elements, which significantly affect particular pathways. The dynamics of large changes in individual elements causes a direct change in the pathway. For small changes, collections of these changes are coordinated to affect the pathway. The general methods for FCS methods includes, calculating gene-level statistics, pathway-level statistics and finally accessing the significance of the pathway-level statistics. Gene-level statistics depend on the measurements from the dataset being analyzed. For example, expression data can be represented as differential expression. Other common gene-level statistics (independent of the data) include correlation, ANOVA (analysis of variance), Q-statistic, signal-to-noise ratio, a t-statistic, and a z-statistic. (Khatri et al., 2012; Ramanan et al., 2012) Such a gene-level statistic is calculated for each element in the dataset. From this gene-level statistic a pathway-level statistic is calculated for each pathway analyzed. For this calculation, only the elements contained in the specific pathway are included. The common statistics utilized include the Kolmogorov-Smirnov statistic, the sum, mean, or median of the gene-level statistic, the Wilcoxon Rank Sum statistic, and the maxmean statistic. For all of these statistical tests the different null hypotheses discussed in the "Implementation Considerations" sections has to be considered. The advantage of such pathway-level statistics is that relationships between elements can be accounted for. Thus the FCS methods overcome this limitation of ORA methods. Lastly the significance of the pathway-level statistics is calculated. Such calculation can be conducted using a competitive or self-contained null hypothesis. In the competitive null hypothesis the element labels of the pathways are permuted, thus comparing the discovered element set to other random sets, which are not in the pathway under analysis. In the self-contained null hypothesis the class labels are permuted, thus comparing the discovered element set to other random sets, which are contained in the pathway under analysis. A further discussion of these different null hypotheses is in the "Implementation Considerations" section below. This significance is calculated for all pathway-level statistics. FCS methods improve on the ORA methods by not implementing an arbitrary threshold, utilizing the element measurements in calculating pathway significance, and accounts for element interactions in the model. Although these techniques still have

limitations since the different pathways analyzed are treated independently, and some techniques only utilize the change in the measurement while calculating the gene-level statistic and disregard this information in further analysis. (Khatri et al., 2012)

PT methods generate the network and utilize ORA or FCS methods to analyze it. PT methods utilize the interactions represented in the pathway in the calculation of pathway significance. Therefore, the topology of the pathway under study is considered, which improves the pathway analysis. Furthermore, methods have been developed to infer the topology structure based on the dataset presented. The most popular methods of inferring a network are Relevance Networks and Gaussian Graphical Models (GGM). Relevance networks utilize the correlation coefficient between variables. If this correlation is above a set threshold, than a dependence exists between them, which is displayed by an edge is drawn in the network. The disadvantage of such methodology is that direct dependence as opposed to indirect dependence cannot be distinguished. Gaussian Graphical Models overcome this limitation by utilizing the partial correlation coefficient. The partial correlation is the correlation between two variables conditioned on the other variables in the dataset. Therefore two variables are independent of each other if the partial correlation between them is zero. The partial correlation is estimated based on the correlation matrix, which is estimated by a standardized unbiased covariance matrix. The presentation of the mathematics of this method is presented in Schafer and Strimmer (Schafer, 2005). The disadvantages of Gaussian graphical models are that the theory is best applied when the number of samples is greater than the number of variables. This is not the case in biological and genetic data, where the number of variable is far greater than the number of samples. This limitation can be overcome by reducing the dimensions of the data; only analyzing second order partial correlations and by regularized Gaussian graphical models. The regularized Gaussian graphical model is often most efficient, where regularization and moderation is introduced into the data by full Bayesian or empirical Bayes methods. More discussion on these Gaussian graphical models can be found in Schafer and Strimmer (Schafer, 2005). A limitation of PT methods is that the analysis is biased on the dataset analyzed and can be difficult to generalize. Although with the advent of personalized medicine and Bayesian statistical techniques, specific models are becoming very popular. Another limitation of PT methods is that strong interactions between pathways is not typically known, thus validating the interactions discovered can be tricky. Lastly, the topology of the pathway often depends on the cell and environmental conditions and obtaining data in all scenarios is impossible. (Khatri et al., 2012)

Implementation Considerations

In implementing the various pathway/gene set analysis techniques, there are two important statistical concerns that are true across all the methods. First, there are two different structures for the null hypothesis actually being tested. Second, as with any set of statistical tests where more than a single test is performed, concerns with multiple testing and potential inflated Type I (false positive) error rates must be addressed with some form of multiple testing correction.

Regarding the first concern, statistical analysis performed can be conducted using either self-contained or competitive hypothesis tests. These statistical tests provide one value (for example a score or p-value) for each pathway or gene set that summarizes the probability of the observed element changes from the given dataset by chance. The self-contained test is used when the overall null hypothesis is when "no genes in the gene set are differentially expressed." The competitive test is used when the null hypothesis is "the genes in the gene set are not more differentially expressed

than other genes in the dataset." The results from a competitive test are very sensitive to the number of elements included in the dataset (number of variables or features). Furthermore, if a large number of elements are changed than the test this will result in no gene sets that are differentially expressed. The results of the competitive test often provides a lower number of genes sets that are significant compared to the self-contained test. While these hypotheses at a superficial level may seem similar, they are actually quite different. The self-contained test corresponds to a more "-omic" wide test, where the competitive null hypothesis corresponds to more of a candidate pathway/gene-set hypothesis.

Due to conducting statistical tests multiple times for each pathway and these pathways can overlap, statistical multiple testing procedures have to be implemented. The methods to correct for multiple testing include controlling the false discovery rate, Bonferroni correction and resampling or permutation testing. Controlling the false discovery rate takes advantage of the property that pathways overlap. A Bonferroni correction takes the desired significance value and divides this by the total number of tests that are conducted. The resultant significance value is utilized for each test. This is a very conservative technique, but it is effective in all situations. Resampling or permutation testing is when the statistical test is repeated thousands of times with the sample labels or variables permuted to get an empirical estimate of the test statistics that would be expected by chance. For a self-contained test the sample phenotype labels are permuted, where under a competitive test, the variables are permuted. This quantifies the probability of observing the pattern by chance. The advantage of permutation testing is that correlations between variables is taken into account, and can lead to more valid estimates of overall error rates when implemented correctly. The disadvantage of permutation testing is that it is extremely computational intensive.

SOLUTIONS AND RECOMMENDATIONS

As with the database resources, there are a large and constantly growing number of pathway and network analysis tools. In this chapter, we review some of the commonly used tools. Methods which perform pathway/gene set analysis include GSEA (Subramanian et al., 2005), and SAFE (Barry, Nobel, & Wright, 2005). Pathway-topology methods, which create/infer networks include Genome-Wide Regulatory Network (GWRN) (Cowper-Sal lari, Cole, Karagas, Lupien, & Moore, 2011), Weighted Gene Co-Expression (Zhang & Horvath, 2005), ARACNE (Margolin, Nemenman, et al., 2006; Margolin, Wang, et al., 2006), Impact Factor (Khatri, Draghici, Tarca, Hassan, & Romero, 2007), and netGSA (Shojaie & Michailidis, 2009). A summary of each of these methods along with the URL to access the software is listed in Table 3, and the methods are briefly reviewed below.

Gene Set Enrichment Analysis (GSEA)

GSEA (Subramanian et al., 2005) is a method that is in between being classified as an ORA method and FCS method, which is due to the flexibility of its implementation. The input to this system is a set of elements (this can be a set of elements from a pathway) that the researcher hypothesizes is influential in the trait of disease studies in their data. The set of elements in the dataset are ranked based on their measure. For expression data this ranking is often the differential expression of the gene. The objective of GSEA is to detect where in the ranked list the specified element set is located. From this information an enrichment score is calculated, which measures the maximum distance from the middle of the ranked list the specified set is located. From the enrichment score, a p value is calculated by permuting the phenotype labels (self-contained null hypothesis). To correct for multiple hypothesis testing GSEA controls the false positives by computing the false discovery rate (FDR). The elements that are found to be significant are hypothesized to affect the inputted gene set based on the dataset presented. GSEA is a strong method, which utilizes both database information and accounting for correlation structure in the dataset. Although this correlation structure is ignored in calculating significance from a dataset with small number of samples. Subramanian et al. (2005) applied this method to several different cancer expression datasets, including

Table 3. Pathway analysis methods including a summary of the method and how to access software

Method	Summary	Access
GO	Genome annotation, for different organisms including interaction information.	http://www.geneontology.org/
GSEA	Detection of gene sets based on ranking.	http://www.broadinstitute.org/gsea/index.jsp
SAFE	Calculation of local and global statistics.	Bioconductor Package
IF	Detects changes in the pathway based on the data and calculates an impact factor.	http://vortex.cs.wayne.edu/projects.htm
GWRN	Developed for SNP arrays utilizing LD information, which has the ability to infer pathways based on LD.	R Package and GUI
Weighted Gene Co-Expression	Infer network based on co-expression networks.	http://labs.genetics.ucla.edu/horvath/htdocs/CoexpressionNetwork/
netGSA	Latent variable model to infer network and mixed linear model to conduct analysis.	http://dept.stat.lsa.umich.edu/~shojaie/research.html

lymphoblastoid cell lines (detecting a difference in males and females), NCI-60 collection from the National Cancer Institute (detecting difference between p53$^+$ and p53$^-$), acute leukemias (detecting a different in acute lymphoid leukemia and acute myeloid leukemia), and a comparison of lung cancer studies. In all of these applications, biologically influential genes sets were identified, thus displaying the accuracy of the GSEA method. The leukemia application also detects chromosomal aberrations in addition to gene sets, thus GSEA is flexible in its detection capability.

Significance Analysis of Function and Expression (SAFE)

SAFE (Barry et al., 2005) is a framework originally developed for expression data, although it can be extended for use in SNP arrays and Metabolomics. It is an example of a FCS methods, where it primarily analyses given pathways. The method starts by calculating a gene (or element) specific statistic (also referred as the local statistic), which is most often the t-statistic. For the application towards expression data this statistic is measuring the association between the expression measurement and the dataset response variable. Given local statistics for each element in the dataset, a global statistic is calculated. This statistic identifies deviations in the local statistics. SAFE has implemented the Wilcoxon rank sum (a nonparametric statistical model used to compare means of two populations) and Kolmogorov-Smirnov statistic (a nonparametric statistical model that is used to detect if two continuous populations are equal), thus testing the presence of discovered relationships over the noise. To determine the significance of the global statistic the response variable is permuted (self-contained null hypothesis test) and a p-value is calculated. SAFE is a great software that utilizes well-known statistical methods that are robust. Therefore accurate measures of significant pathways are obtained. SAFE is freely available online through the R Bioconductor package. SAFE

is limited to the analysis of networks and is not dynamic towards changing topology of the network. Berry et al. (2005) displayed the versatility of this techniques on a human lung carcinoma expression dataset. The technique was used to detect influential pathways between normal and cancerous samples, comparing multiple cancer subtypes and conducting survival analysis. To adapt the SAFE system for these analyses, the local statistic was specific to that kind of inference. For all of these analyses, the Wilcoxon rank sum statistics was used as the global statistic. The significance of the global statistic was measured by permuting the response variable ten thousand times (self-contained null hypothesis test) and correcting for multiple testing by false discovery rate and family-wise error rate. To conduct the comparison between normal and cancerous samples the absolute value of the Welch t-statistic was utilized as the local statistic. To conduct the comparison between the cancer subtypes (adenocarcinomas, pulmonary carcinoids, small-cell lung carcinomas, and squamous cell lung carcinoma) the analysis of variance (ANOVA) F-statistic was used as the local statistic. To conduct the survival analysis a cox proportional hazard model is utilized as the local statistic. In all studies influential pathway functionality was identified utilizing the GO and Pfam (protein family) databases. This study shows the ability for the pathway analysis using SAFE to be adaptable towards the response variable of interest and the specific questions that are asked.

Genome-Wide Regulatory Networks (GWRN)

GWRN is a technique to infer and analyze networks. The technique has been developed toward SNP data, although can be extended to other datasets. In a GWRN a node represents the genomic element that is represented by the SNP. Many other techniques map a SNP to its closest gene, although with the new the Encyclopedia of DNA Elements (ENCODE) (E. P. Consortium et al.,

2012) information available, interaction information for individual positions of SNP may be known. An edge in a GWRN is defined as an interaction between the elements. Such a representation is as described above. For SNP data, several positions of linkage disequilibrium has been identified by the HapMap consortium (Altshuler et al., 2010). Therefore the weights on an edge can be represented by the linkage disequilibrium of the pair of elements. Furthermore, the Encyclopedia of DNA Elements (ENCODE) has identified several long range physical and cistromic interactions, which can define an edge. This technique relies heavily on the information contained in the database used, where the network will be scarce when information about the dataset is not known. (Cowper-Sal lari et al., 2011)

Weighted Gene Co-Expression

Weighted Gene Co-Expression (Zhang & Horvath, 2005) is a method that creates and infers the network based on the dataset inputted. Its implementation is targeted towards expression analysis, although it can be extended towards other data. This analysis utilizes gene co-expression networks to represent the pathway. A gene co-expression network arises from interactions of genes in the network. As mentioned earlier, each node in the network represents a gene and an edge between genes represents a relationship between them. Gene co-expression networks rely heavily on the adjacency matrix of the network (matrix describing which nodes are connected in the network). To find the adjacency matrix of the network a similarity measure is defined (often correlation) between the input elements. The weight of each network connection is defined as the transformation of the similarities based on the adjacency function (often the sigmoid or power function). Optimizing the parameters in the adjacency function can optimize the adjacency matrix. Utilizing the power adjacency function implements soft thresholding since the degree of connection is expressed in the

adjacency function and not just binary (a connection is present or not). Therefore the correlation of expression values between pairs of genes is defined. Once the network is defined, the genes are analyzed in terms of modules, extracted from hierarchical clustering of the genes. Hierarchical clustering is a technique that separates inputted elements into subgroups that have measurements, which are similar. The separation is conducted in a tree-like (dendrogram graph), hierarchical manner. For this application, a distance measure of distTOM is utilized, which is a measure of dissimilarity calculated by the topological overlap between pair of nodes to determine the relative interconnectedness of the nodes. From the hierarchical clustering, clusters (or modules) are identified by cutting the dendrogram at a specific height. The information in the modules are compared to network characteristics and external information to infer its biological meaning. To infer the most influential relationships, the created network is analyzed by graph characteristics, statistics and ORA methods. Zhang and Horvath (2005) applied this technique on a brain cancer microarray dataset. This dataset was first reduced to eight thousand genes (dimensionality reduction procedure) with the highest variance (between cancer and cancer-free patients). After optimizing both the power and step adjacency functions, six biological significant modules were identified. The biological significance represents specific gene ontologies, and modules that are highly conserved. Furthermore the intramodular gene connectivity (distribution of the edges within a module) of the network was found to be correlated to cancer prognosis. This intramodular connectivity was modeled to be scale-free, where certain genes in the networks are hubs, which have high degree. This distinction was more apparent with the use of soft thresholding (power adjacency function) as opposed to hard thresholding (step adjacency function). Therefore Weighted Gene Co-Expression pathway analysis provides influential modules that display characteristics of real networks in their scale-free distribution. Furthermore, inference for the influence of the modules provides insight into the disease characteristics.

Algorithm for the Reconstruction of Accurate Cellular Networks (ARACNE)

ARACNE (Margolin, Nemenman, et al., 2006; Margolin, Wang, et al., 2006) is an analysis tool and associated software package which also creates and infers a network based on the data inputted. ARACNE starts by completely connecting (graph where all pairs of nodes are adjacent) gene triplets. The pairwise mutual information is calculated for each triplet. Mutual information is a measure of the dependence of a pair of elements. Next all triplets that have mutual information above a specified threshold are selected. This specific threshold is arbitrary and can often be difficult to justify. The selected triplets are further analyzed by the data processing inequality (DPI) method, where if two genes interact through another gene then the minimum of the pairwise mutual information is selected. Therefore the edge is retained only if no other path exists between the two genes. In this process an edge is always removed from the triplet. This type of design is relatively conservative, although it decreases false positively identified relationships. By decreasing the false positives it becomes a risk that the number of false negatives identified may increase. Thus relationships that are influential may be disregarded. The main advantage of this technique is that it can build up reliable network based on the input dataset. Furthermore the idea of triplet analysis can be extended to higher-order sets, thus improving the overall performance of the identified network. Margolin et al. (2006) applied this method on an expression dataset containing 340 B lymphocytes from normal, tumor-related and experimentally manipulated individuals. The ARACNE software was used to generate the B cell specific regulatory network. Analyzing the presence of c-MYC and

its neighbors validated the network. C-MYC is a proto-oncogene, which has been shown to be a hub gene in B cell regulatory networks. The ARACNE system performed admirably, since a statistically significant number of genes adjacent to c-MYC were biologically verified. Furthermore, second layer connections to c-MYC were not significant over the noise. Therefore, ARACNE is accurate in finding direct interactions, but may not find all secondary interactions of the overall network.

Impact Factor (IF)

Impact Factor (IF) (Khatri et al., 2007) is a systems biology technique which detects changes that the elements cause on the pathway. This change is quantified by the perturbation factor, which is dependent on both the change in measurement, and the effects of elements adjacent to the element under analysis. Often the changes detected are those that propagate throughout the pathway analyzed. From the perturbation factor a linear additive model is utilized to calculate the impact factor for each pathway. The linear additive model is a sum of the effect of obtaining pathway statistics randomly and the effect of the impact of the dataset. The impact factor is a relative measure of the influence of the pathway. IF is a simple method to implement and is freely available. IF is a more in depth and robust method for finding elements most represented in pathway (ORA type analysis). The concerns of this system include that it is limited to the pathway extracted from the database, which cannot be dynamically altered by the analysis process. Secondly the linear additive model to calculate the impact factor is very complex and for all cases may not be solvable. Kari et al. (2007) displayed IF's performance on a cervical microarray dataset. The dataset was preprocessed by applying a t-test (corrected p-value using FDR) to select the most significant genes (significance value of 0.05). This resulted in 960 genes, which were analyzed by the IF system. The system was compared to an ORA method using a hyper geometric distribution and GSEA. The results of the ORA method and IF were consistent (identifying the cytokine-cytokine receptor interaction, complement and coagulation cascades and leukocyte transendothelial migration pathways), although GSEA did not find any significant pathways. This can be explained by the authors inputted the whole 19,886 genes into the GSEA system while only inputting the 960 significant genes into the ORA and IF analysis. Furthermore, IF detects more pathways (vascular endothelial growth factor signaling, toll-like receptor signaling and ECM-receptor interaction pathways) than ORA, all of which can be verified by biological information.

Network Based Gene Set Analysis (netGSA)

netGSA (Shojaie & Michailidis, 2009) contains methods to both infer a gene network and conduct analysis for over representation analysis. The inference of the network is based on a latent variable model, which is dynamic since the weights of the model are tuned to best fit the inputted dataset. A latent variable model is similar to a linear model, although latent variables are utilized to represent the baseline element measure. The effect of the latent variable model is expressed in the influence matrix, where the expression of each element is modeled in terms of the latent variables. With this latent variable model the element measures are represented and directly tune the weights of the model. Once an optimized network is established, netGSA employs a mixed linear model to identify most influential pathways and elements within these pathways. This mixed linear model includes both random effects, the latent variables and error terms. The parameters of the model are estimated by restricted maximum likelihood. The main limitation of the netGSA system is that elements that are not included in a pathway cannot be inferred to be added to the pathway. Since netGSA only analyses the elements contained in the pathway based on the knowledgebase, new information cannot be inferred to add into the pathway. Shojaie and Michailidis (2009) display the performance of netGSA on the benchmark data of Ideker et al. (2001), which analyses expression and protein data in yeast. To apply the netGSA system the Galactose Utilization pathway identified by Ideker et al. was used as input to define the influence matrix. The results from netGSA was compared to GSEA, where both techniques found the Galactose Utilization pathway to be significant, although netGSA constructed four additional pathways which were significant. This application shows the ability for netGSA to discover pathways which are overlooked by other techniques.

Expansion to Other "-omics" Data

The methods discussed here were all developed for gene expression data, and most applications have been limited to this type of data, with some exceptions. Weighted gene co-expression analysis is the exception, where ready extension to SNPs (with an additive encoding for the number of minor alleles), allows for easy application to SNP data. SAFE is also being readily used for SNP data analysis.

There are growing applications and extensions of the approaches discussed here to other "omics" data. There are an emerging number of applications of such approaches to data with copy number variation, methylation data, etc. As these new applications are becoming more common, it will be important to really understand the consequences of using these new technologies to the existing approaches. At the level of the annotation databases, new technologies will have different and often more gaps in annotation, that need to be understood and considered in the choice of database(s) used for gene set generation for the pathway analysis approaches. Also, differences in the details of the different data (distributional assumptions, missing data structures, etc.) that may superficially not seem important need to be carefully considered before using methods that were originally understood in the microarray experiment setting. For example, while RNAseq and microarrays both measure gene expression, the differences in technology produce data with different underlying statistical distributions that need to be considered.

An Example Application

As these approaches mature, there are a number of new examples with pathway and network analysis that could have direct relevance to health care. As an example, Zhu et al. (2013) conducted pathway analysis utilizing metabolomics data in studying major depressive disorder (MDD). The researchers conducted a clinical trial to study the response of selective serotonin (5-HT) reuptake inhibitors for patients with major depressive disorder. Of great interest in this study is the effect of the drug on the methoxyindole and kynurenine subgraphs of the tryptophan pathway. Metabolomic profiling was conducted by liquid chromatography electro-chemical array for serum samples extracted from major depressive disorder patients with and without dosages of sertraline. Pathway analysis was conducted by ORA methods, where a paired t-test was used to detect metabolite changes between the weeks the patients were monitored. Correlation between the metabolites was calculated by the Pearson correlation coefficient. All p values were corrected using false discovery rate. This study asked questions about the pathways in the disease state itself, and evaluated changes in these pathways in response to therapy. The analysis revealed metabolomics signatures between the different weeks of monitoring and another set for placebo between the different weeks of monitoring. Many of these same signatures were found in comparing sertraline and placebo, indicating that that pathway structure might be shared for all individuals with MDD. While the results are preliminary, if these results replicate across other

studies, it is clear how such pathway approaches could impact healthcare. Pathway signature shared across disease class could aid in diagnosis of disease states, and if signatures of response are found, could aid in understanding or predicting response to treatment. The result in this study also shows that the structure of the pathways themselves in different treatment conditions can be different, which is an important limitation of current database/annotation structures.

FUTURE RESEARCH DIRECTIONS

Pathway analysis methods development has made several key advancements with further annotation of genomes and more in depth analysis of network(s). While these advances have been rapid, there are a few key challenges in the next steps. First, given how difficult/complex biological pathways actually are, there has been little use of simulated data to actually fairly compare methods. Very few studies rely on simulation tools, which are an important component of rigorous statistical methods development. Few simulation tools have been developed which create artificial data based on an artificial networks. Such simulated data can be used to fairly compare the performance between methods, and properly evaluate the tradeoffs between power and false positive rates. Such information can provide situations where one method is more appropriate than another for a range of realistic scenarios, thus improving the overall analysis and inference made from pathway analysis methods. Di Camillo et al. (2009) developed one such data simulator, where networks are created and expression data is simulated from the created network. In this implementation the networks contain properties of pathways discovered in biological systems such as a scale-free degree distribution, high clustering coefficient, and a small average distance between nodes. The expression data is specified by representing the change in expression in terms of the expression of the gene regulators and the type of relationship (enhancer or repressor) between the genes. By solving the system of differential equations gene expression values are found which represent the relationships represented in the pathway. The advantage of this simulator is that network and expression measurements are created which represent properties observed in nature, while still having the ability to compare methods, since the researcher will know the relationships that should arise from the pathway analysis. There are only a few network simulators that create completely artificial data, which is best for comparison of methods. Many other simulators produce benchmark dataset, which are often a perturbation of common pathways and those dataset that have been heavily studied. Although for these networks and datasets the results can only be compared to results discovered by earlier studies. If new information is discovered, no strategy is available in verifying this information – as continued evaluation of a few datasets will inevitably result in false finding and bias methods development towards approaches that over fit these benchmark datasets. Furthermore, in working with real data the relationship becomes more complicated, thus the probability for new information discovery is high. Simulators for not only expression data, but also SNP array and metabolomics should be developed and utilized.

Second, there is a divide between the methods that discover the topology of networks and those that analyze the network. There are limits in how the gene set methods that test for differences in pathways and the methods that detect topology can be used. Another limitation in the advancements of pathway analysis methods is the ability to add new elements and genes into the existing knowledgebase. To experimentally test all interactions of a new element is unrealistic, thus computational methods can be used to find the influential interactions. This can be conducted by completely connecting the discovered element to a specific pathway and utilize pathway-topology techniques to find the weight or influence of each connection. A more computationally efficient method may be to search the possible connections and only connect those that are necessary based on the weight. Possible methods to conduct this search is an evolutionary algorithm (O'Neill & Ryan, 2001) or Bayesian techniques (Christensen, 2011). A last limitation in pathway analysis techniques is that availability and use of time series data. This would greatly enhance the pathways by analyzing the change of the pathway over both location and time.

Third, it is clear that our understanding of genomic annotation is really only scratching the surface of the complex relationships in biology. (E. P. Consortium et al., 2012) Fundamentally, analysis tools that rely on knowledgebase (incorporating crucially expert knowledge) will only be as good as the knowledgebase that they use. Efforts like ENCODE have revealed that many of the simplifying assumptions that have been made (particularly about "junk" DNA) are not true. We are also learning more and more about changes in the pathway and network structures in different tissues, across time, in response to drug/chemical exposure, etc. that are currently not included in the knowledge bases. As the level of detail in the knowledgebase increases, methods development will need to "keep up" and incorporate the added complexity.

CONCLUSION

This chapter has surveyed the three generations of pathway analysis methods along with highlighting their strengths and weaknesses, as well as provided a brief overview of a few of the knowledge bases available to use with these methods.. Pathway analysis has become an important tool in genetic and genomics to help detect and interpret complex associations that are related to disease or other outcomes of interest. Pathway analysis has been applied to gene expression, SNP array and metabolomics data, and all of these techniques can be applied to this type of data. The implementations of the methods are relatively flexible to test a range of questions about pathways information. Development of better annotation in the knowledge bases, and innovative methods development now allow for interesting approaches to associate global changes in biological pathways and networks in a range of "-omics" data types.

List of *Primary* Abbreviations

DNA: Deoxyribose Nucleic Acid
FCS: Functional Class Scoring
GO: Gene Ontology
GSEA: Gene Set Enrichment Analysis
GWRN: Genome-Wide Regulatory Network
IF: Impact Factor
KEGG: Kyoto Encyclopedia of Genes and Genomes
MetaCyc: Metabolic Cycles
MSigDB: Molecular Signature Database
ORA: Over-Representation Analysis
PT: Pathway Topology
RNA: Ribose Nucleic Acid
SNP: Single Nucleotide Polymorphism

REFERENCES

Altshuler, D. M., Gibbs, R. A., Peltonen, L., Dermitzakis, E., Schaffner, S. F., & Yu, F. L. et al. (2010). Integrating common and rare genetic variation in diverse human populations. *Nature*, *467*(7311), 52–58. doi:10.1038/nature09298 PMID:20811451

Bairoch, A., & Apweiler, R. (2000). The SWISS-PROT protein sequence database and its supplement TrEMBL in 2000. *Nucleic Acids Research*, *28*(1), 45–48. doi:10.1093/nar/28.1.45 PMID:10592178

Baker, W., van den Broek, A., Camon, E., Hingamp, P., Sterk, P., Stoesser, G., & Tuli, M. A. (2000). The EMBL Nucleotide Sequence Database. *Nucleic Acids Research*, *28*(1), 19–23. doi:10.1093/nar/28.1.19 PMID:10592171

Barker, W. C., Garavelli, J. S., Huang, H. Z., McGarvey, P. B., Orcutt, B. C., & Srinivasarao, G. Y. et al. (2000). The Protein Information Resource (PIR). *Nucleic Acids Research*, *28*(1), 41–44. doi:10.1093/nar/28.1.41 PMID:10592177

Barry, W. T., Nobel, A. B., & Wright, F. A. (2005). Significance analysis of functional categories in gene expression studies: A structured permutation approach. *Bioinformatics (Oxford, England)*, *21*(9), 1943–1949. doi:10.1093/bioinformatics/bti260 PMID:15647293

Bateman, A., Birney, E., Durbin, R., Eddy, S. R., Howe, K. L., & Sonnhammer, E. L. L. (2000). The Pfam protein families database. *Nucleic Acids Research*, *28*(1), 263–266. doi:10.1093/nar/28.1.263 PMID:10592242

Benson, D. A., Karsch-Mizrachi, I., Lipman, D. J., Ostell, J., Rapp, B. A., & Wheeler, D. L. (2000). GenBank. *Nucleic Acids Research*, *28*(1), 15–18. doi:10.1093/nar/28.1.15 PMID:10592170

Brenner, S., Johnson, M., Bridgham, J., Golda, G., Lloyd, D. H., & Johnson, D. et al. (2000). Gene expression analysis by massively parallel signature sequencing (MPSS) on microbead arrays. *Nature Biotechnology*, *18*(6), 630–634. doi:10.1038/76469 PMID:10835600

Caspi, R., Altman, T., Billington, R., Dreher, K., Foerster, H., & Fulcher, C. A. et al. (2014). The MetaCyc database of metabolic pathways and enzymes and the BioCyc collection of Pathway/Genome Databases. *Nucleic Acids Research*, *42*(1), D459–D471. doi:10.1093/nar/gkt1103 PMID:24225315

Christensen, R. (2011). *Bayesian ideas and data analysis: an introduction for scientists and statisticians.* Boca Raton, FL: CRC Press.

Chu, Y., & Corey, D. R. (2012). RNA sequencing: Platform selection, experimental design, and data interpretation. *Nucleic Acid Ther, 22*(4), 271–274. doi:10.1089/nat.2012.0367 PMID:22830413

Consortium, M. (2006). The MicroArray Quality Control (MAQC) project shows inter- and intraplatform reproducibility of gene expression measurements. *Nature Biotechnology, 24*(9), 1151–1161. doi:10.1038/nbt1239 PMID:16964229

Consortium, Encode Project, Bernstein, B. E., Birney, E., Dunham, I., Green, E. D., Gunter, C., & Snyder, M. (2012). An integrated encyclopedia of DNA elements in the human genome. *Nature, 489*(7414), 57-74. doi: 10.1038/nature11247

Cowper-Sal lari, R., Cole, M. D., Karagas, M. R., Lupien, M., & Moore, J. H. (2011). Layers of epistasis: genome-wide regulatory networks and network approaches to genome-wide association studies. *Wiley Interdiscip Rev Syst Biol Med, 3*(5), 513-526. doi: 10.1002/wsbm.132

DeLuca, D. S., Levin, J. Z., Sivachenko, A., Fennell, T., Nazaire, M. D., & Williams, C. et al. (2012). RNA-SeQC: RNA-seq metrics for quality control and process optimization. *Bioinformatics (Oxford, England), 28*(11), 1530–1532. doi:10.1093/bioinformatics/bts196 PMID:22539670

Di Camillo, B., Toffolo, G., & Cobelli, C. (2009). A gene network simulator to assess reverse engineering algorithms. *Annals of the New York Academy of Sciences, 1158*(1), 125–142. doi:10.1111/j.1749-6632.2008.03756.x PMID:19348638

Dunn, W. B., Broadhurst, D. I., Atherton, H. J., Goodacre, R., & Griffin, J. L. (2011). Systems level studies of mammalian metabolomes: The roles of mass spectrometry and nuclear magnetic resonance spectroscopy. *Chemical Society Reviews, 40*(1), 387–426. doi:10.1039/b906712b PMID:20717559

Ideker, T., Thorsson, V., Ranish, J. A., Christmas, R., Buhler, J., & Eng, J. K. et al. (2001). Integrated genomic and proteomic analyses of a systematically perturbed metabolic network. *Science, 292*(5518), 929–934. doi:10.1126/science.292.5518.929 PMID:11340206

Kanehisa, M., Goto, S., Sato, Y., Kawashima, M., Furumichi, M., & Tanabe, M. (2014). Data, information, knowledge and principle: Back to metabolism in KEGG. *Nucleic Acids Research, 42*(1), D199–D205. doi:10.1093/nar/gkt1076 PMID:24214961

Khatri, P., Draghici, S., Tarca, A. L., Hassan, S. S., & Romero, R. (2007). A system biology approach for the steady-state analysis of gene signaling networks. *Progress in Pattern Recognition, Image Analysis and Applications. Proceedings, 4756,* 32–41.

Khatri, P., Sirota, M., & Butte, A. J. (2012). Ten Years of Pathway Analysis: Current Approaches and Outstanding Challenges. *PLoS Comput Biol, 8*(2). doi: 10.1371/journal.pcbi.1002375

Kodzius, R., Kojima, M., Nishiyori, H., Nakamura, M., Fukuda, S., & Tagami, M. et al. (2006). CAGE: Cap analysis of gene expression. *Nature Methods, 3*(3), 211–222. doi:10.1038/nmeth0306-211 PMID:16489339

Korn, J. M., Kuruvilla, F. G., McCarroll, S. A., Wysoker, A., Nemesh, J., & Cawley, S. et al. (2008). Integrated genotype calling and association analysis of SNPs, common copy number polymorphisms and rare CNVs. *Nature Genetics, 40*(10), 1253–1260. doi:10.1038/ng.237 PMID:18776909

LaFramboise, T. (2009). Single nucleotide polymorphism arrays: A decade of biological, computational and technological advances. *Nucleic Acids Research, 37*(13), 4181–4193. doi:10.1093/nar/gkp552 PMID:19570852

Margolin, A. A., Nemenman, I., Basso, K., Wiggins, C., Stolovitzky, G., Dalla Favera, R., & Califano, A. (2006). ARACNE: An algorithm for the reconstruction of gene regulatory networks in a mammalian cellular context. *BMC Bioinformatics, 7*. doi: Artn S7

Margolin, A. A., Wang, K., Lim, W. K., Kustagi, M., Nemenman, I., & Califano, A. (2006). Reverse engineering cellular networks. *Nature Protocols, 1*(2), 663–672. doi:10.1038/nprot.2006.106 PMID:17406294

Mewes, H. W., Frishman, D., Gruber, C., Geier, B., Haase, D., & Kaps, A. et al. (2000). MIPS: A database for genomes and protein sequences. *Nucleic Acids Research, 28*(1), 37–40. doi:10.1093/nar/28.1.37 PMID:10592176

Mi, H., Dong, Q., Muruganujan, A., Gaudet, P., Lewis, S., & Thomas, P. D. (2010). PANTHER version 7: Improved phylogenetic trees, orthologs and collaboration with the Gene Ontology Consortium. *Nucleic Acids Research, 38*(Database issue), D204–D210. doi:10.1093/nar/gkp1019 PMID:20015972

O'Neill, M., & Ryan, C. (2001). Grammatical evolution. *IEEE Transactions on Evolutionary Computation, 5*(4), 349–358. doi:10.1109/4235.942529

Putri, S. P., Yamamoto, S., Tsugawa, H., & Fukusaki, E. (2013). Current metabolomics: Technological advances. *Journal of Bioscience and Bioengineering, 116*(1), 9–16. doi:10.1016/j.jbiosc.2013.01.004 PMID:23466298

Ramanan, V. K., Shen, L., Moore, J. H., & Saykin, A. J. (2012). Pathway analysis of genomic data: Concepts, methods, and prospects for future development. *Trends in Genetics, 28*(7), 323–332. doi:10.1016/j.tig.2012.03.004 PMID:22480918

Reference Genome Group of the Gene Ontology. (2009). The Gene Ontology's Reference Genome Project: A unified framework for functional annotation across species. *PLoS Computational Biology, 5*(7), e1000431. doi:10.1371/journal.pcbi.1000431 PMID:19578431

Schafer, J., & Strimmer, K. (2005). *Learning Large-Scale Graphical Gaussian Models from Genomic Data.* Paper presented at the AIP Conference. New York, NY. doi:10.1063/1.1985393

Shi, L., Campbell, G., Jones, W. D., Campagne, F., Wen, Z., & Walker, S. J. et al. (2010). The MicroArray Quality Control (MAQC)-II study of common practices for the development and validation of microarray-based predictive models. *Nature Biotechnology, 28*(8), 827–838. doi:10.1038/nbt.1665 PMID:20676074

Shojaie, A., & Michailidis, G. (2009). Analysis of Gene Sets Based on the Underlying Regulatory Network. *Journal of Computational Biology, 16*(3), 407–426. doi:10.1089/cmb.2008.0081 PMID:19254181

Subramanian, A., Tamayo, P., Mootha, V. K., Mukherjee, S., Ebert, B. L., & Gillette, M. A. et al. (2005). Gene set enrichment analysis: A knowledge-based approach for interpreting genome-wide expression profiles. *Proceedings of the National Academy of Sciences of the United States of America, 102*(43), 15545–15550. doi:10.1073/pnas.0506580102 PMID:16199517

Tateno, Y., Miyazaki, S., Ota, M., Sugawara, H., & Gojobori, T. (2000). DNA Data Bank of Japan (DDBJ) in collaboration with mass sequencing teams. *Nucleic Acids Research, 28*(1), 24–26. doi:10.1093/nar/28.1.24 PMID:10592172

Thomas, P. D., Campbell, M. J., Kejariwal, A., Mi, H., Karlak, B., & Daverman, R. et al. (2003). PANTHER: A library of protein families and subfamilies indexed by function. *Genome Research, 13*(9), 2129–2141. doi:10.1101/gr.772403 PMID:12952881

Velculescu, V. E., Zhang, L., Vogelstein, B., & Kinzler, K. W. (1995). Serial Analysis of Gene-Expression. *Science, 270*(5235), 484–487. doi:10.1126/science.270.5235.484 PMID:7570003

Wang, Z., Gerstein, M., & Snyder, M. (2009a). RNA-Seq: A revolutionary tool for transcriptomics. *Nature Reviews. Genetics, 10*(1), 57–63. doi:10.1038/nrg2484 PMID:19015660

Wang, Z., Gerstein, M., & Snyder, M. (2009b). RNA-Seq: A revolutionary tool for transcriptomics. *Nature Reviews Genetics, 10*(1), 57-63. doi: 10.1038/nrg2484

Zhang, B., & Horvath, S. (2005). A general framework for weighted gene co-expression network analysis. *Statistical Applications in Genetics and Molecular Biology, 4.*

Zhu, H. J., Bogdanov, M. B., Boyle, S. H., Matson, W., Sharma, S., Matson, S.,... Network, Pharmacometabolomics Res. (2013). Pharmacometabolomics of Response to Sertraline and to Placebo in Major Depressive Disorder - Possible Role for Methoxyindole Pathway. *Plos One, 8*(7).

ADDITIONAL READING

Gibson, G., & Muse, S. V. (2009). *A primer of genome science* (3rd ed.). Sunderland, Mass.: Sinauer Associates.

Mitrea, C., Taghavi, Z., Bokanizad, B., Hanoudi, S., Tagett, R., & Donato, M. et al. (2013). Methods and approaches in the topology-based analysis of biological pathways. *Frontiers in Physics, 4*, 278. doi:10.3389/fphys.2013.00278 PMID:24133454

Tang, B. H., Hsu, P. Y., Huang, T. H. M., & Jin, V. X. (2013). Cancer omics: From regulatory networks to clinical outcomes. *Cancer Letters, 340*(2), 277–283. doi:10.1016/j.canlet.2012.11.033 PMID:23201140

Tomar, N., & De, R. K. (2013). Comparing methods for metabolic network analysis and an application to metabolic engineering. *Gene, 521*(1), 1–14. doi:10.1016/j.gene.2013.03.017 PMID:23537990

Torkamani, A., & Schork, N. J. (2009). Pathway and network analysis with high-density allelic association data. *Methods in Molecular Biology (Clifton, N.J.), 563*, 289–301. doi:10.1007/978-1-60761-175-2_16 PMID:19597792

West, D. B. (2001). *Introduction to graph theory* (2nd ed.). Upper Saddle River, N.J.: Prentice Hall.

KEY TERMS AND DEFINITIONS

Database: An assembly of data and information.

Gene Expression: Relative amount of protein being produced by a gene.

Metabolite: A change that results from a chemical modification within the cell.

Network: A set of vertices, edges and relations, which define the relationship between the vertices.

Pathway Analysis: The process of detecting the underlying interactions between the variables in data.

Single Nucleotide Polymorphism (SNP): When a specific locus or position in the genome has multiple alleles represented in the population.

Chapter 11
Computational Systems Biology Perspective on Tuberculosis in Big Data Era:
Challenges and Future Goals

Amandeep Kaur Kahlon
CSIR-Central Institute of Medicinal and Aromatic Plants (CIMAP), India

Ashok Sharma
CSIR-Central Institute of Medicinal and Aromatic Plants (CIMAP), India

ABSTRACT

The major concern in this chapter is to understand the need of system biology in prediction models in studying tuberculosis infection in the big data era. The overall complexity of biological phenomenon, such as biochemical, biophysical, and other molecular processes, within pathogen as well as their interaction with host is studied through system biology approaches. First, consideration is given to the necessity of prediction models integrating system biology approaches and later on for their replacement and refinement using high throughput data. Various ongoing projects, consortium, databases, and research groups involved in tuberculosis eradication are also discussed. This chapter provides a brief account of TB predictive models and their importance in system biology to study tuberculosis and host-pathogen interactions. This chapter also addresses big data resources and applications, data management, limitations, challenges, solutions, and future directions.

INTRODUCTION

Tuberculosis is caused by *Mycobacterium tuberculosis,* which results in morbidity and death worldwide. This remains a major global health problem (Nachega et al, 2003). According to global tuberculosis report 2013 of WHO (www.who.int/tb/publications/global_report/en/), one-third of the world's population is infected with *M. tuberculosis*. New tuberculosis cases (approx. 8-10 million TB cases) occur annually worldwide. Hence, the development of new therapeutic agents against mycobacterial infectious diseases is important. TB is the second highest cause of death from

DOI: 10.4018/978-1-4666-6611-5.ch011

infectious diseases after HIV/AIDS. Tuberculosis is the biggest killer of people infected with HIV. In 2012, 8.6 million people fell ill with TB and 1.3 million died from TB.

Multidrug-resistant (MDR) and extensively drug-resistant (XDR) tuberculosis have emerged as serious concerns throughout the world (Nachega et al, 2003). *Mycobacterium tuberculosis* dormancy models for *in vivo* experiments are already in use (Sikri et al, 2013) but the availability of big data for system biology has led to development of computational models for tuberculosis study. Knowledge about system biology is very important to integrate data from different levels and sources (Calvert, 2013). This helps in developing computational predictive models to study specific aspects in TB (Marcotte et al, 2001). The mathematical models are essentially representing current knowledge of respective systems. Data management strategies are important in systems biology studies (Wruck et al, 2012). The speed at which new data is generated is difficult to handle and analyze statistically (Marx, 2013). Our world is saturated in data and was implausible just a decade ago. These data sets are too big to handle with typical database and tools. However, they provide opportunities for new discoveries and innovation. In fact, the U.S. government announced $200 million to focus on big data projects in the year 2012. The White House office of science and technology policy and a number of key federal departments and agencies will be part of this big data research and development. The data is useless without the ability to understand and draw inference from it. However, there are computational solutions to big data analysis and management (Schadt et al, 2010). Exploring big data sets provides opportunities for innovation and discoveries in the biological sciences. Review of ongoing tuberculosis control programmes highlighted the importance of prediction models. The objective of the chapter is to discuss the applications of prediction models and system biology in infection biology with reference to tuberculosis. The utility of big data resources in

prediction model development is also mentioned. Thereafter limitations, challenges, future research goals in prediction model development relevant to *M. tuberculosis* are described.

BACKGROUND

Tuberculosis primarily affects the lung and results in pulmonary tuberculosis. This also affects intestine, bone, joints, meninges, lymph nodes, skin and various tissues of the body causing extra pulmonary tuberculosis. This is called a disease of poverty. The incidence of new TB cases is not under control in parts of the globe where health systems are defective except relatively wealthy areas (Cobelens et al, 2012). This is either due to lack of funds and personnel or dysfunctional politics leading to the casual implementation of directly observed treatment (DOTS) programs. Resistance to any agent emerges rapidly. It is also possible in overt or covert monotherapy or noncompliance. For example, isoniazid monoresistance emerges rapidly. The risk of resistance to rifampin increases in the absence of isoniazid. This is because neither pyrazinamide nor ethambutol (nor streptomycin) is particularly effective in preventing resistance in companion drugs. After development of MDR tuberculosis, there is little potential to stop the rapid acquisition of resistance to the remaining agents. Further progression to pre-XDR and XDR tuberculosis is also possible with time. Transmission of MDR and XDR tuberculosis occurs, particularly in communities with a high incidence of HIV infection (Donald et al, 2009). Racial differences in susceptibility to infection by *M. tuberculosis* were published in 1990. They found that upon repeated tuberculin skin testing, blacks have about twice the relative risk of whites for infection. Role of vitamin D levels were reported and were found to be lower in blacks than whites. On this basis, blacks were said to be more prone to infection (Stead et al, 1990).

The limitations of the conventional methods for diagnosing tuberculosis have initiated multi-faceted research activities in this field throughout the world. Chromatographic methods may not be widely available in the developing countries. Molecular methods for diagnosis of tuberculosis have advantages of speed, sensitivity, and specificity. Adequate training of the manpower in molecular methods and prevention of laboratory-dependent contamination may help reduce false positive results (Tiwaria et al, 2007). Phage-based molecular methods also provide rapid results in susceptibility tests for anti-tubercular drugs. The diagnosis of tuberculosis continues to pose serious problems. This is mainly because of difficulties in differentiating between patients with active tuberculosis from those with healed lesions, normal *M. bovis* BCG (Bacillus Calmette Guerin) vaccinated individuals, and unvaccinated Manteux positives. In 1994, the Centers for Disease Control and Prevention (CDC) published recommendations for rapid diagnosis in laboratories. CDC proposed that smear results should be reported within 24 hr time period, detection and identification within 10–14 days and susceptibility within 15–30 days. It was mentioned that detection of *M. tuberculosis* through microscopy is difficult in specimens that contain fewer than 10^4 bacteria/mL. Hence, the culture method is taken with gold standard for diagnosing tuberculosis but it can take up to 6 weeks. Serological tests use various mycobacterial antigens and must be carefully interpreted (Garg et al, 2003). The MTB/RIF test is useful for sensitive detection of tuberculosis and rifampin resistance directly from untreated sputum in less than 2 hours. Xpert MTB/RIF [an automated molecular test for *M. tuberculosis* (MTB) and resistance to rifampin (RIF)] uses hemi-nested real-time polymerase chain-reaction (PCR) assay to amplify an MTB specific sequence of the *rpoB* gene. This gene is probed with molecular beacons for mutations within the rifampin-resistance determining region (Boehme et al, 2010). New multidisciplinary approaches are required to integrate the epidemiology with systems biology to eliminate TB (Comas et al, 2009). Also, integration of mathematical models with system biology data could help to study tuberculosis for immune system, infection state of individual and other complex biological processes (Gammack et al, 2005).

TB Control Programmes Worldwide

India established the National Tuberculosis Control Project (NTCP) 50 years ago (1962) and re-designed it as Revised NTCP (RNTCP) 19 years ago (1993). Vaccine efficacy of BCG was measured through a large clinical trial in Chingleput District (Tamil Nadu) under the TB Research Centre in 1968. BCG vaccination was found ineffective in TB control in 1979. Human immunodeficiency virus began spreading in India since 1984 with TB as the commonest opportunistic disease. In 1992, multi-drug resistance case in *M. tuberculosis* was also found to be prevalent. The World Health Organization declared TB as global emergency in 1993 but RNTCP was extended to the whole nation very slowly and took 13 years from inception. TB control also needs clear epidemiologic definition and measurable parameters for monitoring the level of control over time. They should include effective health education, strong public health, functional surveillance, sound public-private partnership, and more liberal financial support (John et al, 2013). Contact screening and chemoprophylaxis was recommended by India's Revised National Tuberculosis Control Programme (RNTCP) for asymptomatic children aged below 6 years. Trained health care workers and introduction of specific documentation such as isoniazid preventive therapy card (IPT card) and register improved the implementation of contact tracing and chemoprophylaxis for child contacts from 19% to 61% (Rekha et al, 2013).

The Tuberculosis Network European Trials group (TBNET) in this direction aims to promote clinical research in the field of tuberculosis in Europe through sharing and development of ideas and research protocols among the members of the network. TBNET members are spread throughout Europe including eastern European countries with a high burden of this disease. TBNET activities include three major areas such as 1) research, 2) training and capacity building, and 3) networking. Furthermore, two branches that focus their activities on tuberculosis in children and on diseases caused by non-tuberculous mycobacteria were recently established (Giehl et al, 2012). Tuberculosis (TB) remains a global public health problem in developing countries like Uganda. Results showed that previously treated TB, co-infection with HIV, cigarette smoking, and overcrowding were risk factors associated with TB. High medical related transport bills and drug resistance could undermine the usefulness of the current TB interventions and control measures (Muwonge et al, 2013). In addition to this, various other tuberculosis projects and consortium have been initiated throughout the world with the aim to combat with the drug resistant strains of *M. tuberculosis*. The details of ongoing TB projects worldwide and various TB databases are mentioned in Table 1 and Table 2.

PREDICTIVE COMPUTATIONAL MODELS ON TUBERCULOSIS

Computational models are useful to encode complex interactions among host and bacterial components. This helps in the understanding of pathogenesis and to identify the strategies to counter the disease. The *M. tuberculosis* host–pathogen interactome model with various nodes corresponding to host and pathogen molecules, cells, cellular states or processes are also important. Simulations help in predicting the tendency of the pathogen to persist under different conditions. We found various applications of TB prediction models in literature and classified them on the basis of their utility in tuberculosis research. Different types of computational models and their modeling tasks for biological problem are listed in Figure 1. Kind of biological data and big data issues is shown in Figure 2.

Diagnostic Models

Prediction models to identify patients with active TB was lacking due to the complexity of the

Figure 1. Types of computational models and different modeling tasks for biological system

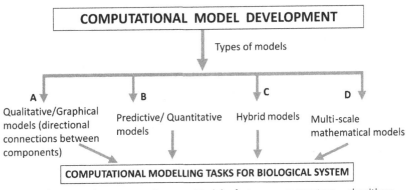

Table 1. List of ongoing projects and consortium for tuberculosis eradication worldwide

Name of Projects on TB	Application	Funding Agency and Country	Contact Details
TB-drugome	Structural proteome-wide drug-target network contains information of 274 drugs and 1730 proteins from *M.tb*. This was constructed by associating the putative ligand binding sites of the *M.tb* proteins with the known binding sites of approved drugs for which structural information was available.	TB-drugome is supported by National Institute of Health (NIH).	University of California, San Diego Prof. Philip E. Bourne (bourne@sdsc.edu)
PreDiCT-TB	To improve the predictive power of pre-clinical methods in order to speed up the delivery of new regimens effective against *M. tuberculosis*. To develop mathematical models based on PK-PD relationships and model improvements using novel technologies.	Project participants include GlaxoSmithKline, Spain Sanofi-Aventis Research and Development, France Janssen Infectious Diseases, Belgium and other universities/research organizations	Uppsala universitet, Uppsala, Sweden (www.uu.se/)
TBCDRC (Tuberculosis Clinical Diagnostics Research Consortium)	Interdisciplinary consortium of scientists, clinicians and supporting staff to provide data on diagnostics and TB management algorithms in endemic countries. To accelerate and improve the accuracy of TB diagnosis and the rapid detection of drug resistance.	TBCDRC project began in September 2009 (supported by NIAID) has four clinical sites: Uganda, South Africa, Brazil, South Korea and additional collaborators from USA, UK, Switzerland	Boston University (https://www.tbcdrc.org/home.aspx)
TBTC (Tuberculosis Trials Consortium)	TBTC is developing new TB treatment and prevention strategies and at present studying ultra short-course treatment for latent TB infection and started first clinical trial in multi-drug resistant TB. An expert data and safety monitoring board reviews active protocols and cooperative relationships with key manufacturers of TB drugs.	CDC (Center for Disease Control) funded project since 1998. First initiated for period 1999-2009 and current project started for 2010-2020. This project includes network of clinical sites worldwide, experts in tuberculosis treatment, prevention, experienced clinical coordinators and outreach workers at each of the funded sites.	A Data and Coordinating Center at the Centers for Disease Control and Prevention (CDC) in Atlanta. (www.cdc.gov/)
PanACEA (Pan-African Consortium for Evaluation of Anti-tuberculosis Antibiotics)	This is an African/European research collaboration to shorten and simplify the TB treatment.This was initiated for conducting standard phase IIa, IIb and phase III clinical trials for Moxifloxacin, Rifamycin and SQ109.	EDCTP (European and Developing Countries Clinical Trials Partnership) funded PanACEA in Dec 2007. Three projects under PanACEA are sponsored by UK, Germany and Netherlands.	16 European countries and 48 sub-Saharan African countries (http://www.edctp.org/)
Global Consortium for Drug-resistant TB Diagnostics (GCDD)	International collaboration of researchers, healthcare professionals and tuberculosis experts to reduce the time to detect XDRTB	Funded by NIH (National Institute of Health)	University of California at San Diego, USA (http://gcdd.ucsd.edu; http://nkatzir@ucsd.edu)

continued on following page

Table 1. Continued

Name of Projects on TB	Application	Funding Agency and Country	Contact Details
TB vaccine cluster consortium (TB-VAC)	To improve vaccines candidates issued from the TB Vaccine Cluster of the 5th frame work of the European Commission and to isolate and test them in Phase 1 clinical trials in Europe. To understand parameters important in protection and development of the disease To monitor need for adjuvant for an efficient vaccination and to understand both adaptive immunity and innate immunity.	Funded by European commission and involves 38 laboratories in Europe since 2000.	Dr Brigitte Gicquel Mycobacterial Genetics Unit, Institut Pasteur, France (www.tbethics.org/)
Revised National TB Control Programme (RNTCP)	For MDR prevention through sustained high-quality DOTS implantation, for rapid diagnosis of M/XDR TB, prevention, evaluation of extent of second line drug resistance and review of availability of second line anti-TB drugs in India.	Govt of India funded project since 1997.	Central TB Division Directorate General of Health Services Nirman Bhavan New Delhi - 110 011 India E-mail: ddgtb@rntcp.org (www.tbcindia.nic.in/)
EXPAND-TB (Expanding Access to New Diagnostics for TB) Project	To accelerate access to diagnostics for patients at risk of multidrug-resistant tuberculosis in 27 countries.	UNITAID funded project launched in 2009. This project is a collaboration between World Health Organization (WHO), the Global Laboratory Initiative (GLI), the Foundation for Innovative New Diagnostics (FIND) and the Stop TB Partnership Global Drug Facility (GDF)	World Health Organization (WHO) 20, avenue Appia CH-1211 Geneva 27 Switzerland E-mail: unitaid@who.int (www.unitaid.eu/)
TBXpert Project	To provide approximately 1.4 million Xpert MTB/RIF test cartridges and over 220 GeneXpert instruments for the rapid detection of TB and rifampicin resistance in 21 recipient countries in 2013-2015. The Xpert MTB/RIF assay, recommended by WHO (December 2010) useful for the simultaneous detection of TB and rifampicin resistance in under two hours. Furthermore, the sensitivity of Xpert MTB/RIF for detecting TB is significantly higher than that for microscopy and more useful in patients with HIV infection.	The USD 25.9 million TBXpert Project is funded by UNITAID and executed by the WHO Stop TB Department and the Stop TB Partnership. TBXpert Project partners include the Global Laboratory Initiative (GLI), TB REACH, the Global Drug Facility (GDF), the EXPAND-TB Project, Interactive Research and Development (IRD) and the African Society for Laboratory Medicine (ASLM).	World Health Organization (WHO) 20, avenue Appia CH-1211 Geneva 27 Switzerland E-mail: unitaid@who.int (www.unitaid.eu/)

Table 2. List of TB related databases

Name	Application	Website and Organisation/University
BioHealthBase	For rapid annotation using subsystem technology annotations for approximately 1,850 of the 2,000 complete bacterial genomes (including *M.tb*) currently available in PATRIC.	http://patricbrc.vbi.vt.edu/portal/portal/patric/IncumbentBRCs?page=bhb
The Collaborative Drug Discovery Tuberculosis Database	CDD comprises over 15 public datasets on *M.tb* specific datasets representing approx. 300,000 compounds derived from patents, literature and high throughput screening data shared by academic and pharmaceutical laboratories. This web-based database system also facilitates storing and sharing of private data.	www.collaborativedrug.com (CDD after funding from the Bill and Melinda Gates Foundation (BMGF) developed a unique community with over 20 pilot groups in the TB field. This includes groups in the EU funded New Medicines 4 Tuberculosis (NM4TB) initiative and groups funded by the BMGF Tuberculosis accelerator project).
GenoMycDB	Database is useful for the large-scale comparative analyses of completely sequenced mycobacterial genomes. It provides tools for functional classification and analysis of genome structure, organization and evolution.	http://157.86.176.108/~catanho/genomycdb/
Tbrowse	Useful for the integrative analysis of the TB genome across various online resources and datasets with over half a million data points and is a part of the open source drug discovery initiative of OSDD.	http://tbbrowse.osdd.net
TDR targets database	Computational assessment of target druggability and integration of large scale screening data with manually curated data to enable the assembly of candidate targets.	http://tdrtargets.org
Tuberculosis Drug Resistance Mutation Database	Database of mutations associated with TB drug resistance and the frequency of the most common mutations associated with resistance to specific drugs.	http://www.tbdreamdb.com/
TuberculList	Database provides a complete dataset of DNA and protein sequences derived from *M.tb* H37Rv and are linked to annotations and functional assignments through integration of genomic information.	http://genolist.pasteur.fr/TuberculList/help/about.html
The Tuberculosis Database	Genomic data of 28 annotated genomes and resources including several thousand microarray datasets from *in vitro* experiments on *M.tb* infected tissues. Researchers can deposit data prior to publication, browse gene detail pages, perform genome visualization and perform comparative analysis using the genome map tool, the genomes synteny map or operon map browser.	http://www.tbdb.org/
WebTB	Provides tools to search and browse the TB genome as well as summary pages on all known TB proteins. This includes the MTBreg database of proteins up- or down regulated in TB, top 100 persistence targets in TB and other additional tools.	www.webtb.org/
OSDD Chemical Database	Open molecule repository of all synthesized, extracted, semi-synthesized and virtual molecules. Well characterized molecules will be taken up by OSDD for screening antitubercular molecules and lead generation.	http://crdd.osdd.net/osddchem/and www.osdd.net

Figure 2. Kinds of biological data and big data issues

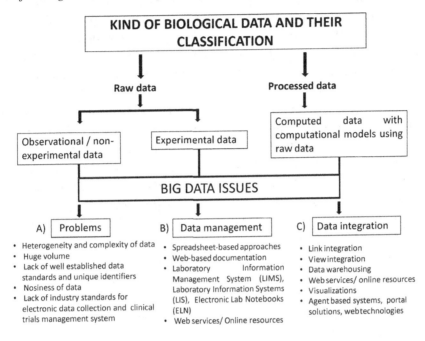

clinical and radiographic presentation. This was due to relatively small patient samples and poorly suited modeling techniques for the task. El-Solh et al (1997) introduced a classification tree to assist physicians regarding respiratory isolation for active pulmonary TB suspects. One limitation of this evaluation was the absence of the tuberculin skin test. In developing countries, the majority of these cases has been treated only on the basis of clinical and chest radiographic findings. Predictive models should be validated in the populations and these models must be validated and optimized in each setting in response to new diseases and shift in the pattern of natural disease processes or progression. It was mentioned as a cost-effective tool in a health care system with limited resources (Mello et al, 2006). This model achieved a high degree of sensitivity with low specificity. Neural networks are computational systems that process information in parallel with large numbers of simple units and are useful in tasks involving pattern recognition. This study is reported as the first to use a neural network for the diagnosis of active pulmonary TB (Mello et al, 2006).

Immune System Models

Mathematical models of *M. tuberculosis* infection were previously reported in humans and mice (Wigginton et al, 2001 and Sud et al, 2006). A mathematical model was developed for control of *M. tuberculosis* infection in the lungs of young (3 months) and aged (18 months) animals. This model included early participation of CD8+ T cells. These cells secrete IFN-γ in an antigen independent manner with an early resistance to infection. This leads to an initial reduction in the bacterial load within the lung. These models do not address the effect of increasing age on the development of tuberculosis disease. To focus on the effects of aging, this model includes only the cell populations and cytokines which play the most significant role in the control of an infection with *M. tuberculosis*. These parameters significantly change with increasing age. Additionally, boosting antigen presentation and T cell proliferation can decrease the *M. tuberculosis* burden in the lung (Friedman et al, 2008). Multiple immune factors control host responses to *M. tuberculosis* infection such as the formation of granulomas. TNF-alpha availability within a granuloma has been linked to play a critical role in immunity to *M. tuberculosis*. Processes which control TNF-α concentration and activities in a granuloma are still not clear. *In vivo* measurement of a TNF-α concentration gradient and activities within a granuloma are not experimentally feasible. Hence, a multiscale computational model was developed to include molecular, cellular and tissue scale events. This identifies the processes regulating TNF-α concentration and cellular behaviours. Finally, influences the outcome of infection within a granuloma. This model predicts the TNF-αR1 internalization kinetics to play a critical role in infection control within a granuloma. This also controls the clearance of bacteria, excessive inflammation, containment of bacteria within a stable granuloma, or uncontrolled growth of bacteria (Fallahi-Sichani et al, 2011; Fallahi-Sichani et al, 2013).

Drug Discovery Models

A pharmacokinetic (PBPK) model based on experimental data was developed to predict the absorption, distribution, metabolism, and excretion (ADME) of the second-line agent capreomycin. This is a cyclic peptide antibiotic belonging to the aminoglycoside antibiotics. This study estimated the various key pharmacokinetic parameter distributions and hypothesized a mechanism for capreomycin transport into the kidney. This is the first published PBPK model for an anti-tuberculosis drug. Using this model along with appropriate pharmacodynamic and toxicity data would help in optimizing drug regimens to treat MDR-TB (Reisfeld et al, 2012). The pharmaceutical company GlaxoSmithKline large-scale high throughput screen (HTS) data was used as input using computational approach to integrate the bioassay data, chemical properties and structural comparisons. They identified 139 targets alongside their respective hit compounds. This data was made accessible to the wider scientific community (Martinez-Jimenez et al, 2013). The TB-drugome (http://funsite.sdsc.edu/drugome/TB) is a computational resource in the development of safe and efficient anti-tubercular drugs (Kinnings et al, 2010). The TB community after extensive high-throughput screening efforts is still facing this challenge of optimizing data. This is important to move from a hit to a lead to a clinical candidate and finally a new drug (Ekins et al, 2011). Bayesian machine learning models are important for predicting compounds with activity against *M. tuberculosis*. This is based on publicly available large-scale HTS data from the Tuberculosis Antimicrobial Acquisition Coordinating Facility. A total of 124 actives including two families built around drug-like heterocyclic cores and several FDA-approved human kinase targeting drugs were reported against TB (Ekins et al, 2013).

Demographic Models

Demography also plays an important role in the transmission of TB infection. This is due to the fact that average rate of progression from infected (non-infectious) to active (infectious) TB is very slow. Two distinct demographic scenarios were studied. In the first study, exponential growth was observed over a long time scale. In the second study, exponential growth was observed over a short time scale (quasi-exponential growth). A stochastic Markov chain model was proposed to explore the impact of various geographic factors. Debanne et al (2000) also proposed a multivariate Markovian model to project the distribution of TB cases across the U.S.A by state, race and ethnic group. A contagious parameter was also used to define the average number of susceptible infected by an infectious case (Styblo, 1985; Styblo, 1991). The effect of HIV was considered as an exogenous input (Castillo-Chavez et al, 2004).

The autoregressive integrated moving average (ARIMA) model was first constructed with the data of tuberculosis report rate in Hubei province in China from Jan 2004 to Dec 2011. Data from

Jan 2012 to Jun 2012 were used to validate the model. Then the generalized regression neural network (GRNN)-ARIMA combination model was established based on the constructed ARIMA model. This hybrid model was found to be better than the traditional ARIMA model in the study to facilitate the allocation of health resources in China (Zhang et al, 2013). In another study, data of monthly TB incidence cases from January 2005 to December 2011 were obtained from the Ministry of Health, China. A seasonal autoregressive integrated moving average (SARIMA) model and a hybrid model which combined the SARIMA model and a generalized regression neural network model were used to fit the data from 2005 to 2010. Although both two models could reasonably forecast the incidence of TB, the hybrid model demonstrated better goodness-of-fit than the SARIMA model. The hybrid model showed better TB incidence forecasting than the SARIMA model. The seasonal trend of TB incidence in China differed from other countries (Cao et al, 2013).

Mathematical Prediction Models

A regression model consisting of a linear term and a non-linear term was proposed. In this model, the reversible jump Markov-chain-Monte-Carlo (MCMC) learning technique (Andrieu et al, 2001) was adopted to estimate the model order and the parameters. The proposed model achieved favorable prediction performance with sensitivity as compared with the Bayesian method (Geng et al, 2008). Differential equation (DE)-based models are useful for studying dynamics of cytokines and effector cells during the immune response to *M. tuberculosis*. These models are based on known interactions of immune cells in the lung during *M. tuberculosis* infection. Experimental data are used to estimate parameter values. Agent-based models (ABMs) are also known as individual based models. These are rule-based models and capture a variety of stochastic and discrete events

occurring in the immune system. An ABM has four components, 1) agents (e.g., immune cells and bacteria), 2) the environment where agents reside (e.g., a two-dimensional grid representing a section of lung tissue), 3) the rules that govern the dynamics of agents, including movements, actions, and interactions between agents as well as between agents and environment, and 4) timescales on which the rules are executed. ABMs are particularly useful for studying complex systems such as TB granulomas. First and second generation ABMs describes the immune response and mechanisms controlling the granuloma formation and function. Next-generation granuloma ABMs were developed in response to new biological data and indicated the importance of additional cell types, cytokines and chemokines (Fallahi-Sichani et al, 2013).

INTEGRATION OF SYSTEM BIOLOGY APPROACHES IN TB PREDICTION MODELS AND THEIR APPLICATIONS

The Tuberculosis Systems Biology Program is one of four centers established by the National Institute of Allergy and Infectious Diseases (NIAID) and this developed systems biology approaches to study infectious disease. This program will integrate experimental data and computationally model the molecular pathways of *M. tuberculosis* under conditions relevant to TB pathogenesis. This collaborative network will perform systematic profiling through molecular biology experiments such as ChIP-seq, transcriptomics, proteomics, glycomics, metabolomics, and lipidomics (Westerhoff et al, 2004). These data will be integrated into predictive computational models of the *M. tuberculosis* regulatory and metabolic networks. It was mentioned that all data and software developed in this project will be made publicly available. The TB Systems Biology Center (http://www.broadinstitute.org/annotation/tbsysbio) at

Stanford is using cell culture models along with a combination of biochemical and transcriptional profiling methods. This is done to characterize the state of the *M. tuberculosis* bacillus and the host at each stage of its infectious cycle and during transitions between stages. Incorporation of these data along with results of multi-dimensional assays would validate the status of DNA, RNA, proteins, lipids, and metabolites. Hence, there is a need of predictive models for the development of stage-specific therapeutics (Galagan et al, 2010).

A genome-scale metabolic model (GSMN-TB) of *M. tuberculosis* was constructed using 849 unique reactions and 739 metabolites along with 726 genes. This model was calibrated by growing *M. bovis* Bacille Calmette Guerin in continuous culture. Steady-state growth parameters were also measured. This model demonstrated the potential role of enzyme isocitrate lyase during the slow growth of mycobacteria. This hypothesis was also verified experimentally. The GSMN-TB model successfully simulated many of the growth properties of *M. tuberculosis*. This model examines the metabolic flexibility of bacteria along with prediction of the phenotype of mutants (Colijn et al, 2009; Beste et al, 2007). Computational approaches are applied using omics data for obtaining short-lists of possible targets for further experimental validation. Network analysis of the protein-protein interactome, a flux balance analysis of the reactome, experimentally derived phenotype essentiality data, sequence analyses and a structural assessment of targetability were incorporated in the study. This pipeline is expected to save enormous amounts of money, resources and time in the drug discovery process (Raman et al, 2008).

Metabolic coupling of *M. tuberculosis* to its host is first to its pathogenesis. Computational genome-scale metabolic models have shown utility in integrating omics as well as physiologic data for systemic and mechanistic analysis of metabolism. A cell-specific alveolar macrophage model (iAB-AMØ-1410) was constructed from the global human metabolic reconstruction, Recon 1. This model successfully predicted the experimentally verified ATP and nitric oxide production rates in macrophages. This model was then integrated with an *M. tuberculosis* H37Rv model (iNJ661), in order to build an integrated host–pathogen genome-scale reconstruction, iAB-AMØ-1410-Mt-661. Integrated host–pathogen network enables simulation of the metabolic changes during infection. Integrated host–pathogen reconstructions could help in understanding the biology and pathophysiology of infections (Bordbar et al, 2010). Investigation of the entire transcriptome of a cell during infection stage could provide a hint about the host-pathogen cross-talk. This is feasible using microarray technology which allows the simultaneous analysis of expression of thousand of genes. The interologs method predicts the interactions and the microarray data ensures that the interactors are present during infection (Rapanoel et al, 2013). High-throughput methods such as metagenomics, metabolomics and metaproteomics have been used to study the complex ecosystem residing in the mammalian gut. However, the metabolic interactions between a host and gut microbes have not yet been modeled using systems biology methods (Heinken et al, 2013). Due to the high complexity of biological data, it is difficult to separate cellular processes. A systems biology approach combining quantitative experimental data with dynamic mathematical modeling promises to yield deeper insights into these processes (Raue et al, 2013).

Current diagnostic and therapeutic approaches to medicine together with new technologies will enable a predictive and preventive medicine. This will lead to development of personalized medicine (Hood et al, 2004). This combination of patient data with systems medicine has led to a P4 medicine that is predictive, preventive, personalized, and participatory. It was stated that in coming 10 years each patient will be surrounded by a virtual cloud of billions of data points. P4 medicine will 1) improve health care, 2) reduce the cost of health care, and 3) stimulate innovation and new company creation. Institute for Systems Biology (ISB) in Seattle was established as a non-traditional institution with scientific collaboration across disciplines such as biologists and other scientists, along with technologists. This needs integration to utilize complex biological systems for predictive, preventive, personalized, and participatory (P4) medicine (Hood et al, 2013). The mathematical modeling of whole-body human systems, data analysis and modeling could contribute to the success of realizing the goal of individualized medicine. Systems biology will soon lead to better diagnosis and dynamic therapies of human disease than the present qualitative methodology in use (Weston et al, 2004). Computer simulations through integrating knowledge of organ and system-level responses will help prioritize targets and design clinical trials. These systems biology approaches would improve decision making in pharmaceutical development (Butcher et al, 2004). The availability of genome-scale sets of cloned open reading frames has facilitated proteome-scale data sets of protein–protein interactions to present interactome maps. These maps are useful resource in predicting the function(s) of thousands of genes (Cusick et al, 2005). Visualization is a key aspect of both the analysis and to understand the data. Challenges in visualization tool development includes in development of clear, meaningful and integrated visualizations with biological insight, without being effected by the intrinsic complexity of the data (Gehlenborg et al, 2010).

MAJOR COMPONENTS AND RESOURCES IN SYSTEM BIOLOGY

A system-level understanding of a biological system depends on four key properties: 1) System structures, 2) System dynamics, 3) The control method and 4) The design method. Systems Biology Workbench (SBW) is built on SBML. Application of systems biology research includes creating a detailed model of cell regulation, particular signal-transduction cascades and system-level insights into mechanisms of identified molecules in drug discovery. It was conceived that the U.S. Food and Drug Administration may also mandate simulation-based screening of therapeutic agents (Kitano, 2002). Advances in metabolomics and its integration into systems biology research is possible via combined expertise from biology, chemistry, instrumentation, computer science, physics, and mathematics branches (Marja et al, 2004). Systems Biology Graphical Notation (SBGN) is a visual language developed by a community of biochemists, modelers and computer scientists. SBGN consists of three complementary languages (process diagram, entity relationship diagram and activity flow diagram). SBGN will help in efficient and accurate representation, visualization, storage, exchange and reuse of information on all kinds of biological knowledge, from gene regulation, to metabolism and to cellular signaling (Novere et al, 2009). The Systems Biology Software Infrastructure (SBSI) facilitated the parameter-fitting process. SBSI is a modular software suite composed of three major components, 1) SBSI Numerics, a high-performance library containing parallelized algorithms for performing parameter fitting; 2) SBSI Dispatcher, a middleware application to track experiments and submit jobs to back-end servers; and 3) SBSI Visual, an extensible client application used to configure optimization experiments and view results (Adams et al, 2013). SBEToolbox (Systems Biology and Evolution Toolbox) is an open-source Matlab toolbox for biological network analysis. This toolbox takes a network file as input to calculate a variety of centralities and topological metrics. This finally clusters nodes into modules. This network is displayed using different graph layout algorithms. SBEGUI, a menu-driven graphical user interface (GUI) of SBEToolbox is useful for accessibility to various network and graph algorithms for programmers and non-programmers both (Konganti et al, 2013).

The model composition tool (Interface) within the PathCase-SB (PathCase Systems Biology) web portal helps users to compose systems biology models. Three tools support the model composition tool; (1) Model Simulation Interface (this generates a visual plot of the simulation according to user's input), (2) iModel Tool (for users to upload their own models to compose) and (3) SimCom Tool (for side by side comparison of models being composed in the same pathway) (Coskun et al, 2013). Understanding about protein and gene regulatory networks of biological systems is required for integration. This will improve drug development and will eventually lead to preventive drugs. These networks have key nodal points. The targeting of these nodes will allow one to avoid the disease potentials emerging from defective genes or pathological environmental stimuli. Computers are essential to this integration (Hegde et al, 2012).

SPECIFIC AREAS OF BIG DATA AND THEIR COMPUTATIONAL RESOURCES

Big data is applicable to various biological areas such as genomics, transcriptomics, proteomics, pharmacogenomics etc. Essential components/ requirements of big data are listed in Figure 3. Management of any project plan is a complex and dynamic process with interactions between multiple partners. Data flow between experimental scientists and computational experts is a critical success factor for the entire project. The data needs of the different partners are also diverse and need to be centrally coordinated. Based on this, a translational project such as PreDiCT-TB (Uppsala University, Sweden) was launched for the discovery and development of new TB drug combinations. Huge number of dynamic bioinformatic resources such as data and tools are available. This represents a big challenge for biologists due to major concerns for management and visualization. Bioinformaticians concerns the possibility of rap-

idly creating and executing *in-silico* experiments involving resources and activities spread over the WWW hyperspace. Physical distribution of data, semantic heterogeneity, co-existence of different computational paradigms and different invocation interfaces are important in data management such as OGSA for Grid nodes, SOAP for web services, Java RMI for Java objects and so on. *UBioLab* has been designed and developed as a prototype based on the above objectives. *UBioLab* is a guide for bioinformaticians and biologists to provide a flexible environment for visualizing, organizing and finding type of domain knowledge (Bartocci et al, 2012). Integration of heterogeneous and often distributed tools and datasets is a challenging task. However, a more reliable technique has been identified and proposed as the platform that would link together bioinformatics resources particularly web services. In the last decade the web services have spread wide in bioinformatics that handles biological datasets. However, due to high-throughput experimentation, a major concern is to handle large-scale data load. The data-partitioning strategy allows comparison with typical communication patterns for genomic sequence annotation. The results suggested that data-partitioning lowers resource demands of services with increase throughput. This allows executing *in-silico* experiments on genome-scale with standard SOAP web services and workflows (Sztromwasser et al, 2011). Data integration is needed to deal with the huge amounts of biological information now available and also performs data mining effectively. However, current data integration systems have some limitations such as the number of resources, their size and frequency of updates, their heterogeneity and distribution on the Internet. Integration is important to access network services through flexible and extensible data integration and analysis network tools. EXtensible Markup Language (XML), Web Services and Workflow Management Systems (WMS) can support the creation and operation of such systems. Many XML languages and web services

Figure 3. Essential requirements for big data analysis

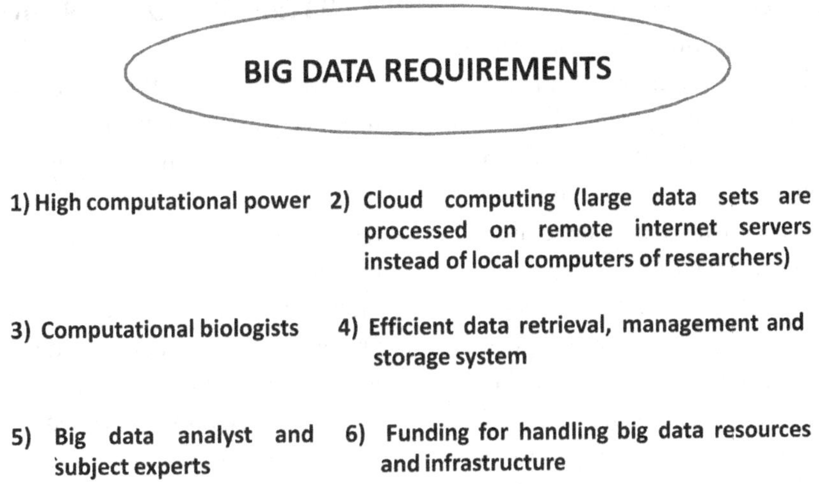

```
                ╭─────────────────────────────────╮
               ⟨     BIG DATA REQUIREMENTS          ⟩
                ╰─────────────────────────────────╯
```

1) High computational power   2) Cloud computing (large data sets are processed on remote internet servers instead of local computers of researchers)

3) Computational biologists   4) Efficient data retrieval, management and storage system

5) Big data analyst and subject experts   6) Funding for handling big data resources and infrastructure

for bioinformatics have already been designed and implemented with the systems and some WMS have been proposed recently (Romano, 2007).

Big datasets in a biological problem could help in finding patterns and relationships that would otherwise remain hidden. This is due to complete analysis of various factors in large datasets. There are significant advancements in high-throughput sequencing technologies and exponential expansion of biological datasets. Hence, bioinformatics faces difficulties in storage and analysis of huge amounts of biological data. The gap between sequencing throughput and computer capabilities in dealing with such big data is growing. With the latest technologies in science, biological data will accumulate at a much faster rate. Cloud computing utilizes multiple computers to provide convenient and on-demand access to hosted resources (e.g., computation, storage, applications, servers, network) through web Application Programming Interfaces (API). Due to its efficiency, it was believed that cloud computing is capable of transforming computing into a public utility and is more economical. Hadoop and its associated softwares are designed to handle load balancing among multiple nodes. Hadoop allows the distributed processing of large datasets across multiple computer nodes and supports big data scaling

(HDFS, HBase). MapReduce divides a computational program into many small sub-problems and distributes them on multiple computer nodes. HDFS (Hadoop Distributed File System) provides a file system that stores data on these nodes. The Electronic Medical Records and Genomics Consortium have enabled to manage and process big data relevant to health care of patients using hadoop system (Chute et al, 2013). In genomics, big data come from high-throughput sequencing with data analysis challenges. However, new technologies for genomics data analysis could help in data analysis (Ward et al, 2013).

Cloud computing bears a great promise in effectively addressing big data storage and analysis. Future efforts in building bioinformatics clouds involve developing a large variety of services from data storage, data acquisition, to data analysis. This would accordingly provide utility-supplied cloud computing delivered over the Internet. Bioinformatics clouds should integrate both data and software tools, equip with high-speed transfer technologies and other related technologies to help in big data transfer. This is possible, with suitable programming environment to help people develop customized pipelines for data analysis. This should be open and publicly accessible to the whole scientific community (Dai et al, 2012). Big data applications could help in monitoring countries or healthcare stakeholders in their plans to utilize big data to resolve healthcare issues. Big data projects undertaken by all leading countries government and healthcare industries have similar general common goals. Furthermore, for medical data shared across departmental boundaries, a top-down approach is needed to effectively manage and integrate big data. Finally, real-time analysis of in-motion big data should be made with protection of privacy and security (Jee et al, 2013). Freely available dynamic infectious disease risk maps would be valuable to a wide range of health professionals from policy makers to prioritize the limited resources to individual clinicians. One should never under estimate the value of risk maps in finding the extent of a public health problem. A comprehensive atlas of contemporary distributions would be beneficial in improving future assessments of the burden of disease (Hay et al, 2013). *M. tuberculosis* shows limited genomic diversity and makes the application of whole genome sequencing attractive for clinical and epidemiological investigation. However, an accurate knowledge of the rate of change in the genome over relevant timescales is required to find the transmission events. Deep sampling of a phylogenetic cluster allows the exclusion of possible transmission events. Hence, establishment of whole-genome databases will further enhance the possibility to compare samples to exclude or propose transmission (Bryant et al, 2013). Bioinformatics data is growing beyond the scope of a single computing architecture. Hence, to handle this accumulated large scale data, PoPLAR (Portal for Petascale Lifescience Applications and Research) portal presents the user with one location for data (inputs and results), easy organization of data into folders. This provides detailed history of all submitted jobs on web portal. Users can submit tasks online and notification of a job's completion is sent to the user via email. Different tools can be configured to run transparently on different computation resources and are made available to the user via the same interface (Rekapalli et al, 2013).

EMERGING CHALLENGES FOR SYSTEM BIOLOGY IN BIG DATA ERA

Our limited understanding of the various steps involved in biological processes as well as other details of the various physiological processes and mechanisms is a major challenge in prediction model development. Selection of appropriate model that considers different levels of biological hierarchy is very essential. Multi-scale integration presents a major challenge due to the diversity of modeling approaches that are available. Some models are rich in experimental detail, whereas others are extrapolators from a sparse database. The success of the models should be judged by their ability to provide a logical framework. Differences in the local microenvironment of the pathogen along with parameters when added into metabolic models could predict bacterial growth rates and susceptibility to drug and immune-mediated killing (Young et al, 2008). Computational system biology is playing an increasingly important role in contributions towards improving early diagnosis, designing patient-specific interventions, and accelerating the discovery of novel therapies. System biology information has been integrated to TB prediction models due to the advancement in high-throughput technologies and accumulation of huge amount of omics data of *M. tuberculosis*. Complete understanding about resistance mechanism in bacteria is lacking. A systems level analysis of the proteins involved will provide insights into the routes required for emergence of drug resistance. Integration of various model parameters into computational experiments in systems biology requires a high level of computational power. Simultaneously, the software needed to run the experiment must be usable by scientists with varying levels of computational expertise. Furthermore, our incomplete understanding of biological system is a major issue in designing efficient computational models for system biology studies.

CHALLENGES AND SOLUTIONS IN COMBINING BIG DATA AND SYSTEMS BIOLOGY

Data integration is both a challenge and an opportunity in big data for system biology. Biological systems cannot be understood by single-type of datasets as the system regulates at many levels. Hence, large heterogeneous datasets are required to investigate biological system (Gomez-Cabrero et al, 2014). Data exploitation component of data integration involves 3 steps; 1) use of prior knowledge and efficient storage system, 2) development of statistical methods for heterogeneous datasets, 3) tool development for data analysis (Gomez-Cabrero et al, 2014). Visual analytics (VA) tools are computational tools that integrate data analysis with interactive visualizations. This facilitates the performance of cognitive activities with big data analysis. However, their performance depends upon various factors such as integration of different sources of data, information processing steps and functional techniques (Ola et al, 2014). Ability to protect individual privacy in the era of big data has also become limited and there should be some legislative bodies to protect the data (Schadt et al, 2012). There is always a need for modifying the technology of data storage and transfer to ensure more rapid exchange of information (Trifonova et al, 2013).

The data management is problematic issue for biological and preclinical research due to enormous heterogeneity, complexity, huge volume and dependency of the data. Furthermore, the data generated via modern high-throughput methods lack well-established data standards and unique identifiers to allow easy mapping and data integration. There is constant need for new analytical tools but still the computational infrastructure continues to be underfunded. "Often in biology, a lot of money goes into generating data but a much smaller amount goes to analyzing it," said Nathan Price, associate director of the Institute

for Systems Biology in Seattle (http://www.wired.com/2013/10/big-data-biology/). Physicists have free access to university-sponsored supercomputers. However, most biologists don't have the right training to use them. Furthermore, the existing computers are not well suited for biological problems. "Very frequently, national-scale supercomputers, especially those set up for physics workflows, are not useful for life sciences," said Rob Knight, a microbiologist at the University of Colorado Boulder and the Howard Hughes Medical Institute. Rob Knight is involved in two projects viz. 1) the Earth Microbiome Project and 2) the Human Microbiome Project. Increased funding for computational resources and infrastructure would be beneficial for big data analysis. Systems biology is currently the most promising approaches to study biological problems in the big data era. Large amounts of funding are required for this highly interdisciplinary and collaborative study. This study requires proper sensitivity analysis to further explore the parameter space for useful variables on which system outputs are strongly dependent. Further investigation is also required in this area for continued development of multiscale and complex systems models. Parameter estimation techniques may be required for better parameter multiscale models.

FUTURE RESEARCH DIRECTIONS

Earlier prediction models were very primitive with minimal data sources but high throughput technologies have made much more advancement in studying complex biological processes. This has also showed deterministic to stochastic and empirical to theoretical parameter values using heterogeneous and multiple strains data. Although there is a remarkable progress in the development of prediction models of TB, still many interesting and challenging questions remain unanswered. Various factors such as immigration, race and ethnicity, genetics, sanitarium, global dynamics, time dependence and mean latent period were found to be important for accurate prediction models. In addition to this, knowledge about immune system and other biological pathways involved in host-pathogen interaction upon infection state is very important to develop accurate prediction models. According to an estimate by WHO, approx. 90% of the people infected with *M. tuberculosis* carry latent bacteria. These dormant bacteria get activated upon immune suppression. Hence, understanding the molecular mechanisms involved in the onset of latency or reactivation is very important. This is possible through system biology approaches integrating omics data of pathogen into mathematical models. Storage of big data obtained through high throughput technologies is also very important for future studies. This predictive modeling through utilization of the diversity of available data could help in identifying new potential-candidate molecules. This would promote development and identification of drugs that act on biological targets safely and effectively. Furthermore, patients in a clinical setting along with genetic information could help to target specific populations to develop personalized medicines and in search of potential vaccine candidates. This would enable clinical trials that are smaller, shorter, less expensive and more powerful. Data are captured electronically and their utilization at various stages is essential for drug discovery and clinical trials. This also includes contribution of scientific data from physicians and research organizations. Flow of data is very significant for the predictive analysis and model development.

CONCLUSION

Advanced high-throughput technology has led an enormous amount of biological data to researchers. Our understanding about human immune system and other physiological or biological processes could help us in designing various prediction models. To this part, big data storage is one issue but can be resolved by computational experts through development of storage resources. This data is valuable to computational biologists to develop prediction models. Advancement in understanding of biological processes and mechanisms in an organism has helped us in developing prediction models. Furthermore, integration of system biology also helped to understand the host-pathogen interactions during diseased state. Future applications of big data are in diverse areas of research. Prediction model development using big data with reference to tuberculosis infection has a lot of scope in future.

REFERENCES

Adams, R., Clark, A., Yamaguchi, A., Hanlon, N., Tsorman, N., & Ali, S. et al. (2013). SBSI: An extensible distributed software infrastructure for parameter estimation in systems biology. *Bioinformatics (Oxford, England)*, *29*(5), 664–665. doi:10.1093/bioinformatics/btt023 PMID:23329415

Adiamah, D. A., & Schwartz, J. M. (2012). Construction of a genome-scale kinetic model of *Mycobacterium tuberculosis* using generic rate equations. *Metabolites*, *2*(4), 382–397. doi:10.3390/metabo2030382 PMID:24957639

Andrieu, C., Freitas Nando, D., & Doucet, A. (2001). Robust full Bayesian learning for radial basis networks. *Neural Computation*, *13*(10), 2359–2407. doi:10.1162/089976601750541831 PMID:11571002

Bartocci, E., Cacciagrano, D., Berardini, M. R. D., Merelli, E., & Vito, L. (2012). UBioLab: A web laboratory for ubiquitous *in silico* experiments. *Journal of Integrative Bioinformatics*, *9*, 192. PMID:22773116

Beste, D. J. V., Hooper, T., Stewart, G., Bonde, B., Avignone-Rossa, C., & Bushell, M. E. et al. (2007). GSMN-TB: A web-based genome-scale network model of *Mycobacterium tuberculosis* metabolism. *Genome Biology*, 8(5), R89. doi:10.1186/gb-2007-8-5-r89 PMID:17521419

Boehme, C. C., Nabeta, P., Hillemann, D., Nicol, M. P., Shenai, S., & Krapp, F. et al. (2010). Rapid molecular detection of tuberculosis and rifampin resistance. *The New England Journal of Medicine*, 363(11), 1005–1015. doi:10.1056/NEJMoa0907847 PMID:20825313

Bordbar, A., Lewis, N. E., Schellenberger, J., Palsson, B. O., & Jamshidi, N. (2010). Insight into human alveolar macrophage and *M. tuberculosis* interactions via metabolic reconstructions. *Molecular Systems Biology*, 6, 422. doi:10.1038/msb.2010.68 PMID:20959820

Bryant, J. M., Schurch, A. C., Deutekom, H., Harris, S. R., Beer, J. L., & Jager, V. D. et al. (2013). Inferring patient to patient transmission of *Mycobacterium tuberculosis* from whole genome sequencing data. *BMC Infectious Diseases*, 13(1), 110. doi:10.1186/1471-2334-13-110 PMID:23446317

Butcher, E. C., Berg, E. L., & Kunkel, E. J. (2004). System biology in drug discovery. *Nature Biotechnology*, 22(10), 1253–1259. doi:10.1038/nbt1017 PMID:15470465

Calvert, J. (2013). Systems biology, big science and grand challenges. *Biosocieties*, 8(4), 466–479. doi:10.1057/biosoc.2013.27

Cao, S., Wang, F., Tam, W., Tse, L. A., Kim, J. H., Liu, J., & Lu, Z. (2013). A hybrid seasonal prediction model for tuberculosis incidence in China. *BMC Medical Informatics and Decision Making*, 13(1), 56. doi:10.1186/1472-6947-13-56 PMID:23638635

Castillo-Chavez, C., & Song, B. (2004). Dynamical models of tuberculosis and their applications. *Mathematical Biosciences and Engineering*, 1(2), 361–404. doi:10.3934/mbe.2004.1.361 PMID:20369977

Chute, C. G., Ullman-Cullere, M., Wood, G. M., Lin, S. M., He, M., & Pathak, J. (2013). Some experiences and opportunities for big data in translational research. *Genetics in Medicine*, 15(10), 802–809. doi:10.1038/gim.2013.121 PMID:24008998

Cobelens, F., Kampen, S., Ochodo, E., Atun, R., & Lienhardt, C. (2012). Research on implementation of interventions in tuberculosis control in low and middle income countries: A systematic review. *PLoS Medicine*, 9(12), e1001358. doi:10.1371/journal.pmed.1001358 PMID:23271959

Colijn, C., Brandes, A., Zucker, J., Lun, D. S., Weiner, B., & Farhat, M. R. et al. (2009). Interpreting expression data with metabolic flux models: Predicting *Mycobacterium tuberculosis* mycolic acid production. *PLoS Computational Biology*, 5(8), e1000489. doi:10.1371/journal.pcbi.1000489 PMID:19714220

Comas, I., & Gagneux, S. (2009). The past and future of tuberculosis research. *PLoS Pathogens*, 5(10), e1000600. doi:10.1371/journal.ppat.1000600 PMID:19855821

Coskun, S. A., Cicek, A. E., Lai, N., Dash, R. K., Ozsoyoglu, Z. M., & Ozsoyoglu, G. (2013). An online model composition tool for system biology models. *BMC Systems Biology*, 7(1), 88. doi:10.1186/1752-0509-7-88 PMID:24006914

Cusick, M. E., Klitgord, N., Vidal, M., & Hill, D. E. (2005). Interactome: Gateway into systems biology. *Human Molecular Genetics*, 14(suppl_2), R171–R181. doi:10.1093/hmg/ddi335 PMID:16162640

Dai, L., Gao, X., Guo, Y., Xiao, J., & Zhang, Z. (2012). Bioinformatics clouds for big data manipulation. *Biology Direct*, 7(1), 43. doi:10.1186/1745-6150-7-43 PMID:23190475

Debanne, A. M., Bielefeld, R. A., Cauthen, G. M., Daniel, T. M., & Rowland, D. Y. (2000). Multivariate Markovian modeling of tuberculosis: Forecasts for the United States. *Emerging Infectious Diseases*, 6(2), 148–157. doi:10.3201/eid0602.000207 PMID:10756148

Donald, P. R., & Helden, P. D. (2009). The global burden of tuberculosis – combating drug resistance in difficult times. *The New England Journal of Medicine*, 360(23), 2393–2395. doi:10.1056/NEJMp0903806 PMID:19494214

Ekins, S., Freundlich, J. S., Choi, I., Sarker, M., & Talcott, C. (2011). Computational databases, pathway and cheminformatics tools for tuberculosis drug discovery. *Trends in Microbiology*, 19(2), 65–74. doi:10.1016/j.tim.2010.10.005 PMID:21129975

Ekins, S., Reynolds, R. C., Franzblau, S. G., Wan, B., Freundlich, J. S., & Bunin, B. A. (2013). Enhancing hit identification in *Mycobacterium tuberculosis* drug discovery using validated dual-event Bayesian models. *PLoS ONE*, 8(5), e63240. doi:10.1371/journal.pone.0063240 PMID:23667592

El-Solh, A., Mylotte, J., Sherif, S., Serghani, J., & Grant, B. J. (1997). Validity of a decision tree for predicting active pulmonary tuberculosis. *American Journal of Respiratory and Critical Care Medicine*, 155(5), 1711–1716. doi:10.1164/ajrccm.155.5.9154881 PMID:9154881

Fallahi-Sichani, M., El-Kebir, M., Marino, S., Kirschner, D. E., & Linderman, J. J. (2011). Multi-scale computational modeling reveals a critical role for TNF receptor 1 dynamics in tuberculosis granuloma formation. *Journal of Immunolology*, 186(6), 3472–3483. doi:10.4049/jimmunol.1003299 PMID:21321109

Fallahi-Sichani, M., Marino, S., Flynn, J. L., Linderman, J. J., & Kirschner, D. E. (2013). A systems biology approach for understanding granuloma formation and function in tuberculosis. J. McFadden et al. (Eds.), Systems Biology of Tuberculosis (pp. 127-155), Springer.

Friedman, A., Turner, J., & Szomolay, B. (2008). A model on the influence of age on immunity to infection with *Mycobacterium tuberculosis*. *Experimental Gerontology*, 43(4), 275–285. doi:10.1016/j.exger.2007.12.004 PMID:18226868

Galagan, J. E., Sisk, P., Stolte, C., Weiner, B., Koehrsen, M., & Wymore, F. et al. (2010). TB database 2010: Overview and update. *Tuberculosis (Edinburgh, Scotland)*, 90(4), 225–235. doi:10.1016/j.tube.2010.03.010 PMID:20488753

Gammack, D., Ganguli, S., Marino, S., Segovia-Juarez, J., & Kirschner, D. E. (2005). Understanding the immune response in tuberculosis using different mathematical models and biological scales. *Multiscale Modeling & Simulation*, 3(2), 312–345. doi:10.1137/040603127

Garg, S. K., Tiwari, R. P., Tiwari, D., Singh, R., Malhotra, D., & Ramnani, V. K. et al. (2003). Diagnosis of tuberculosis: Available technologies, limitations, and possibilities. *Journal of Clinical Laboratory Analysis*, 17(5), 155–163. doi:10.1002/jcla.10086 PMID:12938143

Gehlenborg, N., O'Donoghue, S. I., Baliga, N. S., Goesmann, A., Hibbs, M. A., & Kitano, H. et al. (2010). Visualization of omics data for systems biology. *Nature Methods*, 7(3sSupplement), S56–S68. doi:10.1038/nmeth.1436 PMID:20195258

Geng, B., Zhou, X., Zhu, J., Hung, Y. S., & Wong, S. T. (2008). Comparison of reversible-jump Markov-chain-Monte-Carlo learning approach with other methods for missing enzyme identification. *Journal of Biomedical Informatics*, 41(2), 272–281. doi:10.1016/j.jbi.2007.09.002 PMID:17950040

Giehl, C., Lange, C., Duarte, R., Bothamley, G., Gerlach, C., & Cirillo, D. M. et al. (2012). TBNET-Collaborative research on tuberculosis in Europe. *European Journal of Microbiology and Immunology*, *2*(4), 264–274. doi:10.1556/EuJMI.2.2012.4.4 PMID:24265908

Gomez-Cabrero, D., Abugessaisa, I., Maier, D., Teschendorff, A., Merkenschlager, M., & Gisel, A. et al. (2014). Data integration in the era of omics: Current and future challenges. *BMC Systems Biology*, *8*(Suppl 2), I1. doi:10.1186/1752-0509-8-S2-I1 PMID:25032990

Hay, S. I., George, D. B., Moyes, C. L., & Brownstein, J. S. (2013). Big data opportunities for global infectious disease surveillance. *PLoS Medicine*, *10*(4), e1001413. doi:10.1371/journal.pmed.1001413 PMID:23565065

Hegde, S. R., Rajasingh, H., Das, C., Mande, S. S., & Mande, S. C. (2012). Understanding communication signals during Mycobacterial Latency through predicted genome-wide protein interactions and boolean modeling. *PLoS ONE*, *7*(3), e33893. doi:10.1371/journal.pone.0033893 PMID:22448278

Heinken, A., Sahoo, S., Fleming, R. M. T., & Thiele, I. (2013). Systems-level characterization of a host-microbe metabolic symbiosis in the mammalian gut. *Gut Microbes*, *4*(1), 28–40. doi:10.4161/gmic.22370 PMID:23022739

Hood, L. (2013). Systems biology and P4 medicine: Past, present, and future. *Rambam Maimonides Medical Journal*, *4*(2), e0012. doi:10.5041/RMMJ.10112 PMID:23908862

Hood, L., Heath, J. R., Phelps, M. E., & Lin, B. (2004). Systems biology and new technologies enable predictive and preventative medicine. *Science*, *306*(5696), 640–643. doi:10.1126/science.1104635 PMID:15499008

Jee, K., & Kim, G. H. (2013). Potentiality of big data in the medical sector: Focus on how to reshape the healthcare system. *Healthcare Informatics Research*, *19*(2), 79–85. doi:10.4258/hir.2013.19.2.79 PMID:23882412

John, T. J., Vashishtha, V. M., & John, S. M. (2013). 50 years of tuberculosis control in India: Progress, pitfalls and the way forward. *Indian Pediatrics*, *50*(1), 93–98. doi:10.1007/s13312-013-0021-4 PMID:23396780

Kinnings, S. L., Xie, L., Fung, K. H., Jackson, R. M., Xie, L., & Bourne, P. E. (2010). The *Mycobacterium tuberculosis* drugome and its polypharmacological implications. *PLoS Computational Biology*, *6*(11), e1000976. doi:10.1371/journal.pcbi.1000976 PMID:21079673

Kitano, H. (2002). Systems biology: A brief overview. *Science*, *295*(5560), 1662–1664. doi:10.1126/science.1069492 PMID:11872829

Konganti, K., Wang, G., Yang, E., & Cai, J. J. (2013). SBEToolbox: A Matlab toolbox for biological network analysis. *Evolutionary Bioinformatics*, *9*, 355. doi:10.4137/EBO.S12012 PMID:24027418

Marcotte, E. M., & Date, S. V. (2001). Exploiting big biology: Integrating large-scale biological data for function inference. *Briefings in Bioinformatics*, *2*(4), 363–374. doi:10.1093/bib/2.4.363 PMID:11808748

Marja, K., Caldentey, O., Inze, D., & Oresic, M. (2004). Connecting genes to metabolites by a systems biology approach. *Proceedings of the National Academy of Sciences of the United States of America*, *101*(27), 9949–9950. doi:10.1073/pnas.0403636101 PMID:15226495

Martinez-Jimenez, F., Papadatos, G., Yang, L., Wallace, I. M., Kumar, V., & Pieper, U. et al. (2013). Target prediction for an open access set of compounds active against *Mycobacterium tuberculosis. PLoS Computational Biology, 9*, e1003253. doi:10.1371/journal.pcbi.1003253 PMID:24098102

Marx, V. (2013). The big challenges of big data. *Nature, 498*(7453), 255–260. doi:10.1038/498255a PMID:23765498

Mello, F. C. Q., Bastos, L. G. V., Soares, S. L. M., Rezende, V. M. C., Conde, M. B., & Chaisson, R. E. et al. (2006). Predicting smear negative pulmonary tuberculosis with classification trees and logistic regression: A cross-sectional study. *BMC Public Health, 6*(1), 43. doi:10.1186/1471-2458-6-43 PMID:16504086

Muwonge, A., Malama, S., Johansen, T. B., Kankya, C., Biffa, D., & Ssengooba, W. et al. (2013). Molecular epidemiology, drug susceptibility and economic aspects of tuberculosis in Mubende district, Uganda. *PLoS ONE, 8*(5), e64745. doi:10.1371/journal.pone.0064745 PMID:23741382

Nachega, J. B., & Chaisson, R. E. (2003). Tuberculosis drug resistance: A global threat. *Clinical Infectious Diseases, 36*(Supplement 1), S24–S30. doi:10.1086/344657 PMID:12516027

Novere, N. L., Hucka, M., Mi, H., Moodie, S., Schreiber, F., & Sorokin, A. et al. (2009). The system biology graphical notation. *Nature Biotechnology, 27*(8), 735–741. doi:10.1038/nbt.1558 PMID:19668183

Ola, O., & Sedig, K. (2014). The challenge of big data in public health: An opportunity for visual analytics. *Online Journal of Public Health Informatics, 5*, e223. PMID:24678376

Raman, K., Yeturu, K., & Chandra, N. (2008). targetTB: A target identification pipeline for *Mycobacterium tuberculosis* through an interactome, reactome and genome-scale structural analysis. *BMC Systems Biology, 2*(1), 109. doi:10.1186/1752-0509-2-109 PMID:19099550

Rapanoel, H. A., Mazandu, G. K., & Mulder, N. J. (2013). Predicting and analyzing interactions between *Mycobacterium tuberculosis* and its human host. *PLoS ONE, 8*(7), e67472. doi:10.1371/journal.pone.0067472 PMID:23844013

Raue, A., Schilling, M., Bachmann, J., Matteson, A., Schelke, M., & Kaschek, D. et al. (2013). Lessons learned from quantitative dynamical modeling in systems biology. *PLoS ONE, 8*(9), e74335. doi:10.1371/journal.pone.0074335 PMID:24098642

Reisfeld, B., Metzler, C. P., Lyons, M. A., Mayeno, A. N., Brooks, E. J., & DeGroote, M. A. (2012). A physiologically based pharmacokinetic model for capreomycin. *Antimicrobial Agents and Chemotherapy, 56*(2), 926–934. doi:10.1128/AAC.05180-11 PMID:22143528

Rekapalli, B., Giblock, P., & Reardon, C. (2013). PoPLAR: Portal for petascale lifescience applications and research. *BMC Bioinformatics, 14*, S3. PMID:23902523

Rekha, B., Jagarajamma, K., Chandrasekaran, V., Wares, F., Sivanandham, R., & Swaminathan, S. (2013). Improving screening and chemoprophylaxis among child contacts in India's RNTCP: A pilot study. *The International Journal of Tuberculosis and Lung Disease, 17*(2), 163–168. doi:10.5588/ijtld.12.0415 PMID:23317950

Romano, P. (2007). Automation of *in-silico* data analysis processes through workflow management systems. *Briefings in Bioinformatics, 9*(1), 57–68. doi:10.1093/bib/bbm056 PMID:18056132

Schadt E. E. (2012). The challenging privacy landscape in the era of big data. *Molecular Systems Biology*, *8*, 612.

Schadt, E. E., Linderman, M. D., Sorenson, J., Lee, L., & Nolen, G. P. (2010). Computational solutions to large-scale data management and analysis. *Nature Reviews. Genetics*, *11*(9), 647–657. doi:10.1038/nrg2857 PMID:20717155

Sikri, K., & Tyagi, J. S. (2013). The evolution of Mycobacterium tuberculosis dormancy models. *Current Science*, *105*, 607–616.

Stead, W. W., Senner, J. W., Reddick, W. T., & Lofgren, J. P. (1990). Racial differences in susceptibility to infection by *Mycobacterium tuberculosis*. *The New England Journal of Medicine*, *322*(7), 422–427. doi:10.1056/NEJM199002153220702 PMID:2300105

Styblo, K. (1985). The relationship between the risk of tuberculosis infection and the risk of developing infectious tuberculosis. *Bulletin of the International Union Against Tuberculosis*, *60*, 117–119.

Styblo, K. (1991). *Epidemiology of tuberculosis, Selected Papers, 24*. The Hague: Royal Netherlands Tuberculosis Association.

Sud, D., Bigbee, C., Flynn, J. L., & Kirschner, D. E. (2006). Contribution of CD8+ T cells to control of *Mycobacterium tuberculosis* infection. *Journal of Immunology (Baltimore, MD.: 1950)*, *176*(7), 4296–4314. doi:10.4049/jimmunol.176.7.4296 PMID:16547267

Sztromwasser, P., Puntervoll, P., & Petersen, K. (2011). Data partitioning enables the use of standard SOAP web services in genome-scale workflows. *Journal of Integrative Bioinformatics*, *8*, 163. PMID:21788681

Tiwaria, R. P., Hattikudura, N. S., Bharmalb, R. N., Kartikeyanc, S., Deshmukhd, N. M., & Bisene, P. S. (2007). Modern approaches to a rapid diagnosis of tuberculosis: Promises and challenges ahead. *Tuberculosis (Edinburgh, Scotland)*, *87*(3), 193–201. doi:10.1016/j.tube.2006.07.005 PMID:17029964

Trifonova, O. P. L., Lin, V. A., Kolker, E. V., & Lisitsa, A. V. (2013). Big data in biology and medicine. *Acta Naturae*, *5*, 13–16. PMID:24303199

Ward, R. M., Schmieder, R., Highnam, G., & Mittelman, D. (2013). Big data challenges and opportunities in high-throughput sequencing. *Systems Biomedicine*, *1*(1), 29–34. doi:10.4161/sysb.24470

Westerhoff, H. V., & Palsson, B. O. (2004). The evolution of molecular biology into systems biology. *Nature Biotechnology*, *22*(10), 1249–1252. doi:10.1038/nbt1020 PMID:15470464

Weston, A. D., & Hood, L. (2004). Systems biology, proteomics and the future of health care: Toward predictive, preventative and personalized medicine. *Journal of Proteome Research*, *3*(2), 179–196. doi:10.1021/pr0499693 PMID:15113093

Wigginton, J. E., & Kirschner, D. E. (2001). A model to predict a cell-mediated immune regulatory mechanism during human infection with *Mycobacterium tuberculosis*. *Journal of Immunology (Baltimore, MD.: 1950)*, *166*(3), 1951–1967. doi:10.4049/jimmunol.166.3.1951 PMID:11160244

Wruck, W., Peuker, M., & Regenbrecht, C. R. A. (2012). Data management strategies for multinational large-scale systems biology projects. *Briefings in Bioinformatics*, *15*(1), 65–78. doi:10.1093/bib/bbs064 PMID:23047157

Young, D., Stark, J., & Kirschner, D. (2008). Systems biology of persistent infection: Tuberculosis as a case study. *Nature Reviews Systems Microbiology*, *6*(7), 520–528. doi:10.1038/nrmicro1919 PMID:18536727

Zhang, G., Huang, S., Duan, Q., Shu, W., Hou, Y., & Zhu, S. et al. (2013). Application of a hybrid model for predicting the incidence of tuberculosis in Hubei, China. *PLoS ONE*, *8*(11), e80969. doi:10.1371/journal.pone.0080969 PMID:24223232

ADDITIONAL READING

Afgan, E., Baker, D., Coraor, N., Goto, H., Paul, I. M., & Makova, K. D. et al. (2011). Harnessing cloud computing with Galaxy Cloud. *Nature Biotechnology*, *29*(11), 972–974. doi:10.1038/nbt.2028 PMID:22068528

Andersen, P., & Doherty, T. M. (2005). Opinion: The success and failure of BCG -implications for a novel tuberculosis vaccine. *Nature Reviews. Microbiology*, *3*(8), 656–662. doi:10.1038/nrmicro1211 PMID:16012514

Bailey, W. C., Gerald, L. B., Kimmerling, M. E., Redden, D., Brook, N., & Bruce, F. et al. (2002). Predictive model to identify positive tuberculosis skin tests results during contact investigations. *Journal of the American Medical Association*, *287*(8), 996–1002. doi:10.1001/jama.287.8.996 PMID:11866647

Bartocci, E., Cacciagrano, D., Cannata, N., Corradini, F., Merelli, E., Milanesi, L., & Romano, P. (2007). An agent-based multilayer architecture for bioinformatics grids. *IEEE Transactions on Nanobioscience*, *6*(2), 142–148. doi:10.1109/TNB.2007.897492 PMID:17695749

Bartocci, E., Corradini, F., Merelli, E., & Scortichini, L. (2007). BioWMS: A web-based Workflow Management System for bioinformatics. *BMC Bioinformatics*, *8*(Suppl 1), S2. doi:10.1186/1471-2105-8-S1-S2 PMID:17430564

Bhattacharya, S., & Mariani, T. J. (2013). Systems biology approaches to identify developmental bases for lung diseases. *Pediatric Research*, *73*(4-2), 514–522. doi:10.1038/pr.2013.7 PMID:23314295

Chen, H., Chiang, R. H., & Storey, V. C. (2012). Business intelligence and analytics: From big data to big impact. *Management Information Systems Quarterly*, *36*(4), 1165–1188.

Churchyard, G. J., Kaplan, G., Fallows, D., Wallis, R. S., Onyebujoh, P., & Rook, G. A. (2009). Advances in immunotherapy for tuberculosis treatment. *Clinics in Chest Medicine*, *30*(4), 769–782. doi:10.1016/j.ccm.2009.08.009 PMID:19925966

Fallahi-Sichani, M., Flynn, J. L., Linderman, J. J., & Kirschner, D. E. (2012). Differential risk of tuberculosis reactivation among anti-TNF therapies is due to drug binding kinetics and permeability. *Journal of Immunology (Baltimore, MD.: 1950)*, *188*(7), 3169–3178. doi:10.4049/jimmunol.1103298 PMID:22379032

Groves, P., Kayyali, B., Knott, D., & Van Kuiken, S. (2013). *The big data revolution in healthcare: accelerating value and innovation*. New York, NY: McKinsey Global Institute.

Haggart, C. R., Bartell, J. A., Saucerman, J. J., & Papin, J. A. (2011). Whole-genome metabolic network reconstruction and constraint-based modeling. *Methods in Enzymology*, *500*, 411–433. doi:10.1016/B978-0-12-385118-5.00021-9 PMID:21943909

Hoops, S., Sahle, S., Gauges, R., Lee, C., Pahle, J., & Simus, N. et al. (2006). COPASI – a COmplex PAthway SImulator. *Bioinformatics (Oxford, England)*, *22*(24), 3067–3074. doi:10.1093/bioinformatics/btl485 PMID:17032683

Hubner, K., Sahle, S., & Kummer, U. (2011). Applications and trends in systems biology in biochemistry. *The FEBS Journal, 278*(16), 2767–2857. doi:10.1111/j.1742-4658.2011.08217.x PMID:21707921

Kahn, S. D. (2011). On the future of genomic data. *Science, 331*(6018), 728–729. doi:10.1126/science.1197891 PMID:21311016

Lee, S., Wang, T. D., Hashmi, N., & Cummings, M. P. (2007). Bio-steer: A semantic web workflow tool for grid computing in the life sciences. *Future Generation Computer Systems, 23*(3), 497–509. doi:10.1016/j.future.2006.07.011

Office of Science and Technology Policy, Executive Office of the President of the United States. (2012). *The Obama administration unveils the "big data" initiative: announces $200 million in new R&D investments.* Washington, DC: Executive Office of the President.

Office of Science and Technology Policy, Executive Office of the President of the United States. (2012). *Big data across the federal government.* Washington, DC: Executive Office of the President.

Ohlhorst, F. J. (2013). *Big data analytics: turning big data into big money.* Hoboken, NJ: John Wiley & Sons.

Pena-Miller, R., Laehnemann, D., Jansen, G., Fuentes-Hernandez, A., Rosenstiel, P., Schulenburg, H., & Beardmore, R. (2013). When the most potent combination of antibiotics selects for the greatest bacterial load: The Smile-Frown transition. *PLoS Biology, 11*(4), e1001540. doi:10.1371/journal.pbio.1001540 PMID:23630452

Raman, K., & Chandra, N. (2008). *Mycobacterium tuberculosis* interactome analysis unravels potential pathways to drug resistance. *BMC Microbiology, 8*(1), 234. doi:10.1186/1471-2180-8-234 PMID:19105810

Sambarey, A., Prashanthi, K., & Chandra, N. (2013). Mining large-scale response networks reveals 'topmost activities' in *Mycobacterium tuberculosis* infection. *Scientific Reports, 3,* 2302. doi:10.1038/srep02302 PMID:23892477

Sarker, M., Talcott, C., & Galande, A. K. (2013). *In silico* systems biology approaches for the identification of antimicrobial targets. *Methods in Molecular Biology (Clifton, N.J.), 993,* 13–30. doi:10.1007/978-1-62703-342-8_2 PMID:23568461

Vashisht, R., Mondal, A. K., Jain, A., Shah, A., Vishnoi, P., & Priyadarshini, P. et al. (2012). Crowd sourcing a new paradigm for interactome driven drug target identification in *Mycobacterium tuberculosis. PLoS ONE, 7*(7), e39808. doi:10.1371/journal.pone.0039808 PMID:22808064

Wrzodek, C., Buchel, F., Drager, A., Ruff, M., & Zell, A. (2013). Precise generation of systems biology models from KEGG pathways. *BMC Systems Biology, 7*(1), 15. doi:10.1186/1752-0509-7-15 PMID:23433509

Zak, D. E., & Aderem, A. (2009). Systems biology of innate immunity. *Immunological Reviews, 227*(1), 264–282. doi:10.1111/j.1600-065X.2008.00721.x PMID:19120490

KEY TERMS AND DEFINITIONS

Cloud Computing: Cloud computing involves large number of computers to develop large variety of services from big data storage, data acquisition, to data analysis and making utility-supplied cloud computing delivered over the Internet.

Co-Targets: Proteins or receptors that reside in pathway adjacent to drug target.

Granuloma: A pathological condition during inflammatory process resulting in aggregates of immune cells in affected tissue(s).

High-Throughput Technology: Advanced experimental and computational tools and techniques that enable rapid acquisition of data.

Interactome: To analyze interactions between proteins and small molecules.

Mathematical Modeling: The process of developing mathematical models using mathematical concepts and equations.

Multi-Scale Models: Computational models that include representation of multiple spatial or temporal scales are defined as multi-scale models and are applied in studying complex biological phenomena.

System Biology: Study of complex interactions in biological processes through large-scale gene, protein and metabolite measurements ('omics') data.

Chapter 12
Bioinformatics–Driven Big Data Analytics in Microbial Research

Ratna Prabha
Indian Council of Agricultural Research, India

Anil Rai
Indian Council of Agricultural Research, India

D. P. Singh
Indian Council of Agricultural Research, India

ABSTRACT

With the advent of sophisticated and high-end molecular biological technologies, microbial research has observed tremendous boom. It has now become one of the most prominent sources for the generation of "big data." This is made possible due to huge data coming from the experimental platforms like whole genome sequencing projects, microarray technologies, mapping of Single Nucleotide Polymorphisms (SNP), proteomics, metabolomics, and phenomics programs. For analysis, interpretation, comparison, storage, archival, and utilization of this wealth of information, bioinformatics has emerged as a massive platform to solve the problems of data management in microbial research. In present chapter, the authors present an account of "big data" resources spread across the microbial domain of research, the efforts that are being made to generate "big data," computational resources facilitating analysis and interpretation, and future needs for huge biological data storage, interpretation, and management.

INTRODUCTION

Microorganisms are the oldest and most abundant life forms on the earth. Entwined with the remarkable power of natural selection, they successfully developed evolutionary aptitude to adapt diverse and often hostile environments. Because of their occurrence in normal to extreme environments, microbes can be seen as a living population with remarkable genotypic and phenotypic properties intrinsic to them. When explored and identified for their natural behavior, these organisms can act as prototype for molecular, biochemical and physiological manipulations rendering their direct or indirect benefits to crops and soils. The microbial biology is of great importance as it can represent functional trends of adaptation and evolution of the old and primitive organisms

DOI: 10.4018/978-1-4666-6611-5.ch012

that can mirror organisms in all kinds of natural ecosystems. Because of their primitive existence on the earth and the diverse behavior shown by them in diverse environmental conditions, these organisms are believed to possess unique genetic, molecular and biochemical mechanisms to cater their adaptation needs and address their evolutionary diversification (Keller & Zengler, 2004; Ouzounis, 2002). The journey of microorganisms parallel to the plants, animals and human being has led to their co-evolution in such a way that microbes are entwined with all kinds of biological systems. They have an associative biology which when deciphered, often leads to various levels of information about pathogenic, symbiotic and beneficial associations and the benefits associated with the function.

Microbial biology has many interesting lessons connecting the science to ecosystem function at basic to a very complex level. Molecular biology deals with the most fundamental aspect of biology and provides information about the internal functionalities of the organisms. The area basically finds its roots planted in the DNA which consists of all the genetic information pertaining to the creation, evolution and sustenance of life forms. Within the organisms, the information is usually encrypted in such a way that deciphering the same generates a large volume of data through many experimental platforms like whole genome sequencing projects, microarray technologies, mapping of single nucleotide polymorphisms (SNP), transcriptomics, proteomics, metabolomics, phenomics etc (Adnan, 2010; Fenstermacher, 2005; Waterman, 1995). For the management of the huge data and extraction of dynamic wealth of information from different experimental platforms, bioinformatics have come across the globe to solve the problems of biologists.

Microbial research in the present era is basically related to evolutionary diversification, phylogenetic lineages, identification and characterization, and adaptation of microbes in different extreme environmental conditions. Their interactions with biotic and abiotic entities including that with plants, microbes and other fauna, beneficial functions for plants, soil, environment and human being has led to explore the in-depth insights within the microbial genomes, proteomes and metabolomes (Goodman, 2002). During the past decades, the field of genomics has witnessed an explosion in huge data or 'big data' that of long strings of base pairs (A, T, G, C) which encode for all the genetic information required for life and sustainability of the organisms. Similar is true for –omics era in microbial research that has emerged as a major source of big data and need special and focused attention to bring out comprehensive, accurate and precise definitions of the life forms and their functions (Figure 1) (Casari et al., 1995).

In the present era of technological advancement, the microbial science is facing a phase of fast and dynamic data revolution. Since there is huge microbial diversity on the earth, the area is leading to the generation of large quantity of data on various aspects related to diverse microbial genomes and metagenomes, the impact on global climate change and genetic blueprints of microbes. Researchers are working to generate data, its refinement, analysis and visualization to make sense of the data to make it meaningful (McCulloch, 2013; Pearson & Lipman, 1988). Two decades back when the human whole genome sequencing project was taken up, it was thought to generate huge data (Watson, 1990). Now, in comparison to human genome, collection of the genomes of microbes within the human body and with other habitats like ocean, soil etc. has come-up rather more voluminous. The whole content of 3 billion base pairs with about 20,000 genes of human genome seems only a little part of the microbial genomes with a rough content of 100 billion base pairs and millions of genes that make up microbial world within the human body (Singer, 2013). Now, with the decipherization of many human genomes along with that of plants, animals and microbes, the public domain repertoire NCBI contains twenty petabytes of data (1 petabyte is

Figure 1. Experimentation aspects for big-data sources in microbial research

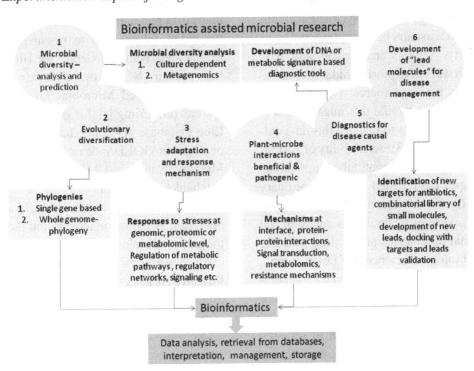

10^{15} bytes) containing genes, proteins and small molecules. This trend is even increasing at a very fast pace (Marx, 2013).

Advent of high-throughput –omics research, translated overall biology into big-data science. Earlier genomics and other –omics related research programs were majorly taken up by major research groups having major funding options. Since, the cost involved in the high-throughput sequencing technologies are decreasing by the time, biological laboratories with low budget are opting for whole genome sequencing projects on bacteria, actinobacteria, cyanobacteria and fungi (Metzke, 2010). Next generation DNA sequencing technologies has led to a revolution in the area of data generation at fast rate with low cost. Due to this reason, current phase may be termed as the age of "big biological data" to reflect sudden increase of existing information as a consequence of digital revolution. Nanotechnology and semiconductor based Next-Generation Sequencing (NGS) platforms are again generating

huge volume of biological data that reduce the cost and time for sequencing (Marx, 2013). This is again generating huge data sets in microbial research. Besides sequencing projects, various other projects on proteomics, transcriptomics as well as metabolomics are coming-up with huge volume of data on different aspects of microbial research (Kalisky & Quake, 2011; Kopke et al., 2005; Sogin et al., 2006). Biologists are now overburdened with massive datasets, challenges of data processing, refinement, handling and exchanging the information (Figure 1). This is why the development of cloud computing resources and grid computing networks with huge cluster computing environment running parallel to each other are now becoming popular in handling and storing big data sets coming out of microbial genomic and metagenomic projects.

Big data refers to large and complex compilation of data sets which are complicated in terms of their nature, origin, investigation, curation, analysis, interpretation and storage. Biologists are struggling hard to cope-up with the current scenario of data flow day by day. The enormous amount of data is usually being represented by its volume, variety, velocity and veracity and these are the key drivers in exploring hidden information from this big data source. Computational capacity required to handle this huge dataset is currently less sufficient to manage this data outcome (Wang et al., 2013). Availability of various sequencing platforms and continuous upgradation of technologies has resulted in an extraordinary explosion of genomic sequence data (O'Driscoll et al., 2013). Various technologies and high end computational approaches are dealing with big data sets of biological sciences (O'Driscoll et al., 2013). Research is now focused on data generation and interpretation where almost all aspect of life is united to derive conclusion from biological activities. A general representation of research areas in the field of microbial research is shown in Figure 1 to reflect a glimpse of data resources in microbial biology.

DEVELOPMENTS IN MICROBIAL RESEARCH FOR BIG DATA

Because of their very small and unseen structure, vast diversity, and long-track record of adaptation in extreme environments, microbes are unique in many aspects in making microbial research an excellent source of big data. Since last several decades, research on many aspects of the structural and functional exploration of microbes and their communities has helped in generating huge data although this was scattered, fragmented and spread across different laboratories all over the world. Major research programs generating data in microbial domain is presented in Figure 2. The outcome of such work has defined many direct and indirect implications of microbial world for the society, environment and agriculture but this data still need to be taken-up at one platform and need integration to derive more conclusive

benefits (Keller & Zengler, 2004). For microbes, many different databases are available to provide wealth of information to researchers working in this area. National Center for Biotechnology Information (NCBI) (http://www.ncbi.nlm.nih.gov/), Integrated Microbial Genomes (IMG) system (http://img.jgi.doe.gov/), Genomes On-Line Database (GOLD) (http://genomesonline.org/cgi-bin/GOLD/index.cgi), Comprehensive Microbial Resource (CMR) are the most important databanks in this area.

Microbes offer a small life cycle and ease of operation as model organisms and therefore, are the preferred biological source on which huge data can be generated to understand the biology of life. Researchers has generated huge data on different aspect of microbial life such as evolution biology, adaption mechanism in abiotic (cold, hot, saline, acidic, desert, chemical and heavy metal contamination etc.) condition, microbial pathogenicity and their biological control mechanisms, pest and disease control, metabolism of valuable enzymes, xenobiotics, antibiotics, secondary metabolites and other valuable products, bioenergy production, environmental remediation, biodegradation of contaminants, interactive and comparative biology (Ouzounis, 2002; Sugden & Pennisi, 2000). All these aspects were covered with single organism or single function or integrating multiple aspects. They usually involve omics research methodologies (genomics, transcriptomics, proteomics and metabolomics) to address biological functions and to define how organisms are working in a systems biological manner. Whole microbial genome and metagenome sequencing data has gained new heights due to NGS technologies and currently 2853 complete microbial genome sequences were stored with NCBI.

Microbial research has experienced technological developments since its inception. Single-cell microbiology is important due to functional advantages but newly emerged interest encompasses microbial community analysis in search of new species, new gene pool and metabolic diversity

Figure 2. Functional research sectors in microbial research to generate big data

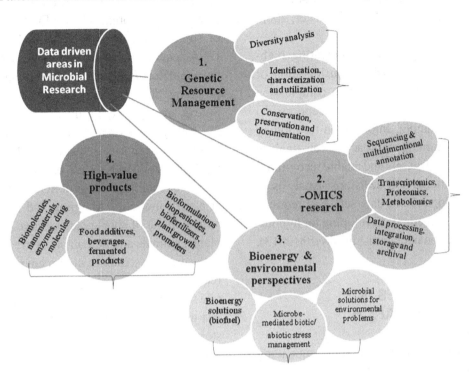

(Whitman *et al.* 1998). It is possible to isolate single cell, perform morphological identification and functional analysis along with genome sequencing. This has encouraged biologists to take up trait-specific and function-based challenges in microbes to connect it directly with the benefits (Kamagata and Tamaki 2005; Rappe and Giovannoni 2003). Before the genomic era, data on microbes were generated on microscopic and spectroscopic methods that enable localization, identification and functional characterization of cells in nature, detection of the uptake of labeled compounds, changes in cells due to environmental stimuli and interactions with biotic entities. Novel methods were adopted to generate multitude of fascinating observations holding great potential for testifying microbial ecological and evolutionary aspects in a number of natural and controlled conditions (Diéz *et al.* 2001; Kreft et al., 2013).

Similarly, the data on proteomics and metabolomics, RNA sequences, proteins and metabolite abundance, protein-protein interactions and gene expression are also of enormous importance. Other area is related to the developments in high-throughput computational capabilities and rapid advancements in softwares, tools, programs, databases etc. to analyze data. Even some high-throughput sequencing technologies are coupled with the computers which take care of data-generation processes of the instrument (DeLong, 2004; DeHaven et al, 2010; Griffn and Steinbeck, 2010; Thorvaldsdottir et al., 2013). Since such data is a heap of un-patterned information, customized computational tools and softwares can only make such complex data meaningful. Due to the significance of the data and requirement of computation in analyzing and processing big data for some useful information, these two entwined fields are now clubbed together and run in parallel with support from other branches of science like statistics, mathematics, physics, chemistry etc. Thus, the amalgamation and resourceful understanding of biological information science leads to the beginning of 'big data' and 'network biology' which continues as the newly emerging field (Jeong et al, 2000; Sharan & Ideker, 2006; Stelling, 2004).

Molecular biology is now generating high-throughput data that requires consideration of parameters like dimension reduction, compression and integration of data, visual perception and biological data mining. Information technology and machine learning approaches can analyze these large-scale data sets and enable recognition of complex patterns and decisions. Analysis of molecular-biological big data sets also requires strong statistical methods developing for hypothesis about functional relationships (Wirth, 2013).

BIG DATA SOURCES IN MICROBIAL RESEARCH

With the advent of massive genome sequencing projects on agriculturally, industrially or environmentally important prokaryotic and eukaryotic microorganisms, microbial molecular biology has become a heavily data-driven science. Complex, fast growing and interdependent research data has largely created the problems of data accumulation, analysis and sometimes misleading results due to inconsistence interpretations (Galagan et al., 2005). The biology-oriented computational approaches were required to enhance better understanding of biological systems as information processing systems. Microbial research is acquiring parallel strategies to accumulate large volume of data on a common integrated platform and analyze that data in terms of information to address essentiality in the biology and its functions.

Microbial Genomics

With increase in complete whole genome sequencing projects from 1000 microbial genomes in 2009 (Kyrpides, 2009) to 2853 till date (NCBI, Feb 2014) and more than 15000 ongoing projects (Table 1), the field of microbial genomics

has emerged as a great promise for the future research in microbial domain. Enormous amount of short sequence reads generated by the new DNA sequencing technologies necessitated the development of fast and accurately read alignment programs. Sequencing technologies like Illumina/Solexa are typically producing 50–200 million, 32–100 bp reads on a single run of the machine. In current scenario, sequencing platforms like GridION and MinION are proficient enough to give sequencing reads as long as ~100kb even at a very low cost. Mapping and alignment of large volume of short reads to large genomes of plants, animals and human poses great challenge to the existing sequence alignment programs and requires more efficient alignment tools for accurate short read mapping. In the coming time, this fast growing science will demand for more data storage and computational space, new methods and tools to interpret data and find out functionalities (Kisand and Lettieri, 2013). Comparative genomics compares genomes of different species to gain meaningful information, analyzes the relationship between genome structure, facilitates better understanding of function and describes evolutionary selection of the organisms or species (Fraser et al, 2002; Koser et al, 2012). Computational approaches to genome comparisons are gaining importance due to enormous amount of data and multiple kinds of analyses required in genome comparison studies. Similarly, whole genome comparison of multiple microbes at a time to point out similarities or differences will need high-end computation power to run continuous programs. Bioinformatics driven analysis is crucial for comparing biological functions that can result in functional biological discoveries (Edwards and Holt, 2013; Fraser et al, 2000; Kisand and Lettieri, 2013; Thorvaldsdottir et al., 2013).

Functional microbial genomics provides a much-needed effort on genome-wide studies on gene network and regulatory functions as well as the use of different methods and tools to address biological problems of the host (plant) and

Table 1. Worldwide big data resources on microbial genomics projects

S. No.	Organisms		Complete	Scaffolds or Contigs	SRA or Traces	Total
	Group	Sub-Group				
1.	Fungi	Ascomycetes	49	322	232	603
		Basidiomycetes	05	78	440	523
		Other	04	34	40	78
		Total	**58**	**434**	**712**	**1204**
2.	Microbes	Bacteria	2685	15398	2810	20893
		Archaea	168	167	03	338
		Total	**2853**	**15565**	**2813**	**21231**

(Source: NCBI Genome Database, Feb 2014)

pathogen (microbe), plant-microbe interaction or beneficial organisms (Nelson, 2003). Functional genomics facilitates assigning of the role of genes in microbial biological networks on the basis of genomic comparisons or inserting mutations in targeted genes. This highly data driven field involves high-throughput experimentations such as microarrays, mutation analysis, proteomics as well as metabolomics in consideration with statistics and computational analyses to conclude (Dondrup et al, 2002). Comparative genomics put efforts to understand the functional and evolutionary processes working on any genome by utilizing the information extracted through the signatures of selection. It deals with the exploration of both similarity and dissimilarity, not only in DNA sequence but also in proteins, RNA and regulatory regions of various organisms to provide better understanding on functions so that researchers could gain an insight of cellular functioning of microbial life (Strauss and Falkow, 1997; Suen et al, 2007; Fricke and Rasko, 2014). Structural genomics involves application of techniques like X-ray crystallography, Mass and NMR spectroscopy to identify entire structural component of particular molecules, generally proteins for which macromolecular structure can be analyzed using computational tools and theoretical predictions. Such efforts are extensively data generating and analysis can lead to a better understanding of microbial systems (Ko¨ser et al., 2012; Rondon et al, 2009; Thorvaldsdottir et al., 2013). In-depth study of genomics facilitated by array-based technologies has also generated large volume of data (Metzke, 2010).

Metagenomics

A deeper understanding on how microbial communities manage and support human, plant, soil, water and other habitats can be generated after customized data analysis. The understanding of how microbial population change with diseases will open new avenues for better treatment against diseases. Similarly, deciphering soil microbial population (above- and below-ground) could lead to new natural products like antibiotics and agrochemicals and could play critical role in developing crops that are rather tough towards natural stresses and more efficient. Custom large-scale sample processing of metagenomes which involves implementation of genome extractions and enable us to process multiple environmental samples at a time and to sequence them for annotation and analysis may be among the viable options for microbial community analysis.

Metagenomics is a much-needed microbiological application of genomics (Handelsman 2004) and with the availability of high-throughput, high-performance sequencers, it is now possible to take out DNA from any particular environmental sample (soil, water etc.) and perform sequencing (Handelsman 2004; Medini et al., 2008). Application of genomic technologies to characterize and analyze naturally occurring microbes is gaining wide acceptance as community genomics, environmental genomics, eco-genomics and microbial population genomics including metagenomics. Tremendous interest is seen in this area to explore both chemical and genetic diversity of different kind of habitats like water, air, forest, soil (both above- and below-ground), extreme habitats, sea, arctic's etc. The best example of environmental genomics is the Global Ocean Sampling Expedition Sorcerer II led by Craig Venter (Rusch et al., 2007). The samples collected on the sea from the ocean water were subjected to shotgun sequencing (i.e. breaking down all DNA present in the sample and get it sequenced by massively parallel sequencing effort) (Potters, 2010). Analysis of environmental genomics complexities are emerging at a very fast pace to identify structural and functional characteristics associated with the microbial communities in the natural ecological habitats (Simon & Daniel, 2011).

Huge data expected from various metagenomics projects has led to the bioprospecting of novel genes, alleles, proteins, biochemicals, antibiotics, enzymes, pharmaceuticals and agrochemical products. All such aspects from various agricultural and environmental habitats are again enormous in number and from the microbial population point of view, are ever dynamic and constantly changing. Thus, metagenomic analysis on the time-scale would again lead to the generation of huge voluminous data (Simon & Daniel, 2011).

Microbial Proteomics

The study of protein complement of the cell i.e. proteomics involves identification of a large number of proteins and solves complexities associated with their structure and function. Proteomics can provide insights into microbial biology. In com-bination with other tools like genetics, molecular biology, biochemistry and biophysics that usually depict cellular processes, this tool can be of great help in characterizing protein structures, functions and understanding novel methods for complex protein interactions (Yates & Washburn, 2000). This area is also becoming a prime source of big data in microbial research. Being associated with larger and complex datasets, proteomics requires advanced new data management capabilities, novel analysis algorithms, tools, interpretation and visualization techniques which enable management of large and heterogeneous data sets. In the last five years, algorithms for image analysis of two dimensional gels, peptide mass fingerprinting (PMF) and peptide fragmentation fingerprinting (PFF) have been developed and are widely used (Blueggel et al., 2004). Computational proteomics is a recently developing area covering computational approaches and databases used for the management, analysis and interpretation of the results of proteomics experiments (Wilkins et al., 1996).

The outcomes of proteomics data can directly be applied to various processes, developments and stages of economically important microbial cells and can be used for the selection and optimization of functions of the microbial strains for the industrial production of valuable metabolites, enzymes and antibiotics (Adrio and Demain, 2010; Barrios-Gonzalez et al, 2003; Gurung et al, 2013). It may be helpful in knowledge-discovery processes and can be applied on cell functions in response to the changes in production parameters, validation of down-streaming processing and outcome of products (Professor & Kovac, 2008). Complex and large volume of proteomic data on microbes and their host plants or animals may provide insights into their interaction behavior, recognition pattern, mechanisms to cause diseases etc. High-throughput proteomic data flow offers new challenges in data handling, reproducibility, tools interoperability and interconnections to fetch data generated at different high-throughput platforms.

Since data on functional proteomics are usually very complex, its proper handling is a challenge to researchers. Availability of open source data and tools like annotated spectral libraries can open new research opportunities to be exploited through the applications of computer science, machine learning techniques, statistics and signal processing techniques (Cannataro, 2008).

Microbial Metabolomics

Metabolomics is closely related with genomics and proteomics and deals with high throughput depiction of small molecule metabolites in the organisms in real time. When coupled with transcriptomic or proteomic data, metabolomics can provide a broader understanding of the biological system as a whole (Steuer & Junker, 2009). It is a rapidly increasing multi-disciplinary science which covers many different areas including targeted and unbiased chemical profiling under the conditions of biotic and abiotic stresses of plants, animals and microbes and provides prospective understanding on genotype-phenotype interactions. Metabolomics can define phenotypic functions of the microbes as a whole and genotype-environment relationships due to its direct linkup with the genotypic traits of the organisms (Fiehn, 2001).

Experiments in metabolomics usually involve generation and comparison of small molecule metabolites which is data integrative process. Plants and microbes are the richest source of natural products with majority of secondary metabolites that perform direct functions. In a complex sample mixture, we can identify myriad of metabolites that are qualitatively and quantitatively expressed and accumulated in different cellular states (e.g. disease, treatment exposure, stress conditions etc.) (DeHaven et al., 2010; Greef et al., 2006). Mass Spectrometer and Nuclear Magnetic Resonance (NMR) are the major analytical tools for metabolomic studies and since data quality is of high end, the area requires computational needs in the same way as with genomics, proteomics and transcriptomics (Garcia et al., 2008). Metabolomics is among the most prominent –omics areas next to genomics and proteomics. It is a cross-boundary field that strongly addresses chemistry and biology to answer biological questions with the help of analytical techniques and cheminformatics solutions (Allwood et al., 2008; Steinbeck et al., 2011).

Microbial metabolomics constitutes an integrated component of systems biology (Patti et al, 2012). Studying complete set of metabolites within a microorganism and monitoring the global outcome of interactions between its developmental processes and the environment in real time can potentially provide a more accurate state of physiological level of the cells (Mapelli et al., 2008). Recent metabolomic technologies and post-genomic developments ease the study and analysis of metabolome which reflects the real status metabolites within the organisms in any environmental conditions (Dudley et al, 2010; Winder et al., 2011). Such profiles are of great importance in microbial system as it can generate an understanding on changes in regulatory networks, chemical patterns as well as signature metabolites. Although, microbial metabolomics is a recently developing area, it will come up as extensively data driven science in the future (Roberts et al, 2012).

Bioinformatics is of absolute importance to metabolomics in managing data and information, screening and processing of raw analytical data, statistical analysis and data mining, integration of data and mathematical modeling of metabolic networks in such a way to represent systems biology approach. The quest for more sophisticated methods for data penetration in the metabolomics is creating pressure on scientists to develop more precise analytical equipments, procedures, protocols and methods with increased resolution, reproducibility, comprehensiveness, high speed and low noise to facilitate analytical assays and equipments (Shulaev, 2006).

Systems Biology

For a more profound understanding in the present microbial research, researchers are moving towards building comprehensive cellular map of microbial cells linked with accurately annotated genome sequence and gene expression to justify systems approach (Graham et al., 2007; Kirschner, 2005; Zhang et al., 2010). Systems biology is a holistic approach to define the data integration to explore the ways for the functional integration in biological systems (Lederberg & McCray, 2001). Genomics, transcriptomics, proteomics, metabolomics and other sub disciplines like lipidomics, antioxidomics or glycomics (dealing with, lipids, antioxidants and sugars, respectively), all facilitate such integration in biological system. The data from all these fields are now being analyzed and integrated by the researchers to define the whole biological system in terms of systems biology (Idekar et al., 2011; Potters, 2010).

MICROBIAL BIG DATA ANALYTICS: BIOINFORMATICS PERSPECTIVE

Computational advancements in molecular biology have led to the emergence of bioinformatics, an interdisciplinary discipline that addresses the specific needs of data acquisition, storage, analysis, integration and interpretation. In all fields of -omics research, bioinformatics finds a strong application. It gained real identity after DNA sequencing became a fundamental tool for molecular biologists and sequence data started to appear in significant volume. Bioinformatics have prime focus on uncovering functional traits in model organisms and regulatory systems in complete genome sequences. The area has facilitated researchers to analyze omics data in terms of microbial evolution, biodiversity, microbial interactions and adaptation strategies which remained poorly understood at molecular level for systematics research (Ouzounis, 2002). Methods

of bioinformatics are practiced worldwide to access various databases and to exchange information for comparison, confirmation, storage and analysis of biological data.

Introduction of biologically inspired computational research was much needed to enhance our understanding of biological systems for information processing and interpretation (Hogeweg, 2011; Singh et al., 2012). Bioinformatics driven approaches enabled researchers to work efficiently on microbial evolution, diversification, adaptation mechanisms, molecular taxonomy, community profiling of microbes, identification and characterization of unculturable organisms (metagenomics) (Rogozin et al., 2002; Singh et al., 2012). Therefore, incisive computing tools are required to allow the extraction of meaningful biological information from the raw data such as gene hunting, detection of epigenetic variants, genome sequencing and assembly, proteome analysis, gene expression data analysis and comparative genomics (Casari et al., 1995). Statistics and mathematical modeling arc integrated to connect data to systems biology and analysis of large amount of data to understand biology of unpatterned huge data sets. This usually helps in the prediction of the behavior of biological systems. Bioinformatics thus, covers the symbiotic relationship of computational approaches and tools in biological systems (genes and gene products) to fetch information about biological processes from research experiments. Since biological data sets are diverse in nature and generated under different conditions in different models, their integration at a common platform to make out real result is becoming almost inevitable (Bansal, 2005). Computers are now running parallel to biology in deciphering the systematic organizational structure, characters and functions. Computational skills based on the principles of logic and algorithms are able to decode the biological complex information and make it in a pattern to interpret and understand the functional complexities and finally stored for further use. This is why computation is the most important part of the post genomic era in analyzing complex biological information (Hogeweg, 2011).

As there is an exponential increase in biological data, there is an ever increasing need of tools, softwares, languages, infrastructure and techniques which can integrate and manage data and focus on analysis, modeling and prediction to result in useful information (Rhee et al., 2006). Along with these –omics fields, many newly emerging *-ome* components like interactome, epigenome, localizome and hormonome representing biological functionality have also been worked out to decipher biological functions and these areas are again data sources in biology (Rhee et al., 2006). Currently, foremost challenge with the bioinformatics is to assess and integrate complex biological data across the -omics platforms and link it to conventional genetics of plants, microbes or animals while using the genome, transcriptome, proteome and metabolome as a whole in the form of a phenome that will ultimately represent phenotype of the organism (Edwards & Batley, 2004; Mochida and Shinozaki, 2011). Other challenges faced by the bioinformatics community are the intelligent and efficient storage of huge amount of data and provide easy and reliable access to the data.

Due to its multiple features like volume (dimension), variety (organization), velocity (acquisition rate), veracity (tentative feature), variability (in information) and complexity (in interactions, origin), big data can be of tremendous value. This leads to the complexity of information extraction for biologists (Hopkins, 2011; Laney, 2001; Sribar, 2011). Extracting the meaningful information from massive biological data remains the primary challenge for bioinformatics and this is creating an unprecedented pressure on big data storage and analytics (Dai et al., 2012). Bioinformatics is currently facing problem not only in storage but also in the analysis of huge quantity of biological data at a time. There is continuous increase in gap between the output of sequencing technologies and computational capabilities for data process. Network analysis (or network biology) that al-

lows modeling of interactions among biological molecules can facilitate the management of large quantity of biological data. Concept of biomolecular network is now being used for understanding complex behavior and spatiotemporal interactions among cellular components within the cells (Wang et al., 2013). For such complex interactions, cloud computing can be put for the management and analysis of big data. Such a system did not require physical space at user's end or procurement of hardware and allows access of data and softwares from huge, off-site centers available to users on demand. One can create virtual spaces for data, software and results that anyone can access or can restrict the spaces using a firewall so that only a select group of collaborators can go through (Marx, 2013).

FUTURE RESEARCH DIRECTIONS

Extensive technological developments that are continuously taking place in the area of biological sciences, molecular biology, chemistry, biophysical sciences and agricultural sciences spurred by bioinformatics and computational biology are revolutionizing the science of biology. The promises, challenges and outcomes of this revolution are enormous and can only be looked upon over a wide span of time. As we know deeper and deeper into the basic biological mechanisms that drive the organism's progeny as well as their own biology, we learn more about how these processes are connected with the networks of genes, proteins and metabolites that regulate physiology and biochemistry of the organisms and affect agricultural productivity, address impact of climate change on crops, cause adaptations among organisms against stresses (biotic and abiotic), drive evolutionary mechanisms in microbes and other organisms, define pathogen interactions with host plants and animals, govern environmental processes including energy generation, help to develop next generation commercial crops, production of biofuels, management of global carbon and remediation of contaminated environmental resources.

The exponential growth in such sequence data generation can mirror the expansive needs of large-scale systems-based biological science coming up in future. However, to be useful to the researchers and end-user society, this progress must be paralleled by the advancements in the computational infrastructure, scaling up of our capabilities for processing, analyzing and interpreting extensive volume of samples for genomic and metagenomic characterization and capacity building in major areas of molecular biology and computation. Coming era should aim not only to develop custom large-scale sample-processing including the implementation of automated DNA/RNA extractions able to process multiple samples but to sequence, annotate, analyze, interpret and store big sequencing data for a definitive conclusion.

CONCLUSION

Among all the domains of life sciences, microbial molecular biology has now emerged as a major big data source that can facilitate solving out numerous informative and applicable challenges of the microorganisms and their environment. Researchers engaged in microbial research are generating huge data sets in terms of genomic, proteomic and metabolomic quality data on various subjects related to molecular mechanisms, taxonomy, evolutionary diversification, genetic blueprinting and global climatic effects on microbes. Biological information encrypted as large volume of data is being generated continuously through various highthroughput experimental platforms like genome sequencers, microarrays, MALDI-TOF, MS/MS, NMR, IR, X-ray crystallography and imaging tools like scanning electron and confocal laser microscopy. Such big data of large volume and complexity further complicates and create problems in terms of storage, exploration, investigation, curation and analysis. Biologists and computation

experts are together struggling hard to cope-up with the current scenario of data flow. Complex, wide-spread, rapidly growing and interdependent microbial research data accumulating from all across the world may become problems for data accumulation, analysis and sometimes misleading results may come due to inconsistent interpretations. Thus, the biology-oriented computational approaches were highly needed to improve better understanding of biological systems as information processing systems. Efficient computing tools are needed again to allow the extraction of biological information from the raw data and making sense of the data for future utilization.

ACKNOWLEDGMENT

Authors are thankful to National Agricultural Bioinformatics Grid project funded by National Agricultural Innovation Project (NAIP), Indian Council of Agricultural Research, India for financial support.

REFERENCES

Adnan, A. (2010). *Introduction to bioinformatics: Role of mathematics and technology*. Retrieved from biotecharticles.com

Adrio, J. L., & Demain, A. L. (2010). Recombinant organisms for production of industrial products. *Bioengineered Bugs, 1*(2), 116–131. doi:10.4161/bbug.1.2.10484 PMID:21326937

Allwood, J., Ellis, D., & Goodacre, R. (2008). Metabolomic technologies and their application to the study of plants and plant-host interactions. *Physiologia Plantarum, 132*(2), 117–135. PMID:18251855

Bansal, A. (2005). Bioinformatics in microbial biotechnology – a mini review. *Microbial Cell Factories, 4*(1), 19. doi:10.1186/1475-2859-4-19 PMID:15985162

Barrios-Gonzalez, J., Fernandez, F. J., & Tomasini, A. (2003). Microbial secondary metabolites production and strain improvement. *Indian Journal of Biotechnology*, 2(3), 322–333.

Blueggel, M., Chamrad, D., & Meyer, H. (2004). Bioinformatics in proteomics. *Current Pharmaceutical Biotechnology*, 5(1), 79–88. doi:10.2174/1389201043489648 PMID:14965211

Cannataro, M. (2008). Computational proteomics: Management and analysis of proteomics data. *Briefings in Bioinformatics*, 9(2), 97–101. doi:10.1093/bib/bbn011 PMID:18310104

Casari, G., Andrade, A., Bork, P., Boyle, J., Daruvar, A., & Ouzounis, C. et al. (1995). Challenging times for bioinformatics. *Nature*, 376(6542), 647–648. doi:10.1038/376647a0 PMID:7651513

Dai, L., Gao, X., Guo, Y., Xiao, J., & Zhang, Z. (2012). Bioinformatics clouds for big data manipulation. *Biology Direct*, 7(1), 43. doi:10.1186/1745-6150-7-43 PMID:23190475

DeHaven, C., Evans, A., Dai, H., & Lawton, K. (2010). Organization of GC/MS and LC/MS metabolomics data into chemical libraries. *Journal of Cheminformatics*, 2(1), 9. doi:10.1186/1758-2946-2-9 PMID:20955607

Delong, E. (2004). Microbial population genomics and ecology: The road ahead. *Environmental Microbiology*, 6(9), 875–878. doi:10.1111/j.1462-2920.2004.00668.x PMID:15305912

Díez, B., Pedrós-Alió, C., & Massana, R. (2001). Study of genetic diversity of eukaryotic picoplankton in different oceanic regions by small-subunit rRNA gene cloning and sequencing. *Applied and Environmental Microbiology*, 67(7), 2932–2941. doi:10.1128/AEM.67.7.2932-2941.2001 PMID:11425705

Dondrup, M., Albaum, S., Griebel, T., Henckel, K., Jünemann, S., & Kahlke, T. et al. (2002). Minimum information about a microarray experiment (MIAME) – towards standards for microarray data. *Nature Genetics*, 29, 365–371.

Dudley, E., Yousef, M., Wang, Y., & Griffiths, W. J. (2010). Targeted metabolomics and mass spectrometry. *Advances in Protein Chemistry and Structural Biology*, 80, 45–83. doi:10.1016/B978-0-12-381264-3.00002-3 PMID:21109217

Edwards, D., & Batley, J. (2004). Plant bioinformatics: From genome to phenome. *Trends in Biotechnology*, 22(5), 232–237. doi:10.1016/j.tibtech.2004.03.002 PMID:15109809

Edwards, D.J, & Holt, K.E. (2013). Beginner's guide to comparative bacterial genome analysis using next-generation sequence data. *Microbial Informatics and Experimentation*, 32.

Fenstermacher, D. (2005). Introduction to bioinformatics. *Journal of the American Society for Information Science and Technology*, 56(5), 440–446. doi:10.1002/asi.20133

Fiehn, O. (2001). Combining genomics, metabolome analysis, and biochemical modeling to understand metabolic networks. *Comparative and Functional Genomics*, 2(3), 155–168. doi:10.1002/cfg.82 PMID:18628911

Fraser, C. M., Eisen, J. A., Nelson, K. E., Paulsen, I. T., & Salzberg, S. L. (2002). The value of complete microbial genome sequencing (you get what you pay for). *Journal of Bacteriology*, 184(23), 6403–6405. doi:10.1128/JB.184.23.6403-6405.2002 PMID:12426324

Fraser, C. M., Eisen, J. A., & Salzberg, S. L. (2000). Microbial genome sequencing. *Nature*, 406(6797), 799–803. doi:10.1038/35021244 PMID:10963611

Fricke, W. F., & Rasko, D. A. (2014). Bacterial genome sequencing in the clinic: Bioinformatics challenges and solutions. *Nature Reviews. Genetics*, *15*(1), 49–55. doi:10.1038/nrg3624 PMID:24281148

Galagan, J., Henn, M., Ma, L., Cuomo, C., & Birren, B. (2005). Genomics of the fungal kingdom: Insights into eukaryotic biology. *Genome Research*, *15*(12), 1620–1631. doi:10.1101/gr.3767105 PMID:16339359

Garcia, D., Baidoo, E., Benke, P., Pingitore, F., Tang, Y., Villa, S., & Keasling, J. (2008). Separation and mass spectrometry in microbial metabolomics. *Current Opinion in Microbiology*, *11*(3), 233–239. doi:10.1016/j.mib.2008.04.002 PMID:18538626

Goodman, N. (2002). Biological data becomes computer literate: New advances in bioinformatics. *Current Opinion in Biotechnology*, *13*(1), 68–71. doi:10.1016/S0958-1669(02)00287-2 PMID:11849961

Graham, R., Graham, C., & McMullan, G. (2007). Microbial proteomics: A mass spectrometry primer for biologists. *Microbial Cell Factories*, *6*(1), 26. doi:10.1186/1475-2859-6-26 PMID:17697372

Greef, J., Hankemeier, T., & McBurney, N. (2006). Metabolomics-based systems biology and personalized medicine: Moving towards n = 1 clinical trials? *Pharmacogenomics*, *7*(7), 1087–1094. doi:10.2217/14622416.7.7.1087 PMID:17054418

Griffin, J. L., & Steinbeck, C. (2010). So what have data standards ever done for us? The view from metabolomics. *Genome Medicine*, *2*(6), 38. doi:10.1186/gm159 PMID:20587079

Gurung, N., Ray, S., Bose, S., & Rai, V. (2013). A broader view: Microbial enzymes and their relevance in industries, medicine, and beyond. *BioMed Research International*, *2013*, 329121. doi:10.1155/2013/329121 PMID:24106701

Handelsman, J. (2004). Metagenomics: Application of genomics to uncultured microorganisms. *Microbiology and Molecular Biology Reviews*, *68*(4), 669–685. doi:10.1128/MMBR.68.4.669-685.2004 PMID:15590779

Hogeweg, P. (2011). The roots of bioinformatics in theoretical biology. *PLoS Computational Biology*, *7*(3), e1002021–e1002021. doi:10.1371/journal.pcbi.1002021 PMID:21483479

Hopkins, B. (2011). *Blogging from the IBM big data symposium - Big is more than just big*. Link.

Idekar, T., Galitski, T., & Hood, L. (2001). A new approach to decoding life: Systems biology. *Annual Review of Genomics and Human Genetics*, *2*(1), 343–372. doi:10.1146/annurev.genom.2.1.343 PMID:11701654

Jeong, H., Tombor, B., Albert, R., Oltvai, N., & Barabási, L. (2000). The large-scale organization of metabolic networks. *Nature*, *407*(6804), 651–654. doi:10.1038/35036627 PMID:11034217

Kalisky, T., & Quake, S. (2011). Single-cell genomics. *Nature Methods*, *8*(4), 311–314. doi:10.1038/nmeth0411-311 PMID:21451520

Kamagata, Y., & Tamaki, H. (2005). Cultivation of uncultured fastidious microbes. *Microbes and Environments*, *20*(2), 85–91. doi:10.1264/jsme2.20.85

Keller, M., & Zengler, K. (2004). Tapping into microbial diversity. *Nature Reviews. Microbiology*, *2*(2), 141–150. doi:10.1038/nrmicro819 PMID:15040261

Kirschner, M. (2005). The meaning of systems biology. *Cell*, *121*(4), 503–504. doi:10.1016/j.cell.2005.05.005 PMID:15907462

Kisand, V., & Lettieri, T. (2013). Genome sequencing of bacteria: Sequencing, de novo assembly and rapid analysis using open source tools. *BMC Genomics*, *1*(14), 211. doi:10.1186/1471-2164-14-211 PMID:23547799

Ko¨pke, B., Wilms, R., Engelen, B., Cypionka, H., & Sass, H. (2005). Microbial diversity in coastal subsurface sediments: A cultivation approach using various electron acceptors and substrate gradients. *Applied and Environmental Microbiology*, *71*(12), 7819–7830. doi:10.1128/AEM.71.12.7819-7830.2005 PMID:16332756

Köser, C., Ellington, M., Cartwright, E., Gillespie, S., Brown, N., & Farrington, M. et al. (2012). Routine Use of Microbial Whole Genome Sequencing in Diagnostic and Public Health Microbiology. *PLoS Pathogens*, *8*(8), e1002824. doi:10.1371/journal.ppat.1002824 PMID:22876174

Kreft, J., Plugge, C., Grimm, V., Prats, C., Leveau, J., & Banitz, T. et al. (2013). Mighty small: Observing and modeling individual microbes becomes big science. *Proceedings of the National Academy of Sciences of the United States of America*, *110*(45), 18027–18028. doi:10.1073/pnas.1317472110 PMID:24194530

Kyrpides, N. (2009). Fifteen years of microbial genomics: Meeting the challenges and fulfilling the dream. *Nature Biotechnology*, *27*(7), 627–632. doi:10.1038/nbt.1552 PMID:19587669

Laney, D. (2001). *3-D data management: controlling data volume, velocity and variety*. Link.

Lederberg, J., & McCray, A. (2001). 'Ome Sweet' Omics–a genealogical treasury of words. *Scientist (Philadelphia, Pa.)*, *15*, 8.

Mapelli, V., Olsson, L., & Nielsen, J. (2008). Metabolic footprinting in microbiology: Methods and applications in functional genomics and biotechnology. *Trends in Biotechnology*, *26*(9), 490–497. doi:10.1016/j.tibtech.2008.05.008 PMID:18675480

Marx, V. (2013). Genomics in the clouds. *Nature Methods*, *10*(10), 941–945. doi:10.1038/nmeth.2654 PMID:24076987

McCulloch, E. (2013). Harnessing the power of big data in biological research. *Bioscience*, *63*(9), 715–716. doi:10.1093/bioscience/63.9.715

Medini, D., Serruto, D., Parkhill, J., Relman, D., Donati, C., & Moxon, R. et al. (2008). Microbiology in the post-genomic era. *Nature Reviews. Microbiology*, *6*, 419–430. PMID:18475305

Metzke, M. (2010). Sequencing technologies – the next generation. *Nature Reviews. Genetics*, *11*(1), 31–46. doi:10.1038/nrg2626 PMID:19997069

Mochida, K., & Shinozaki, K. (2011). Advances in omics and bioinformatics tools for systems analyses of plant functions. *Plant & Cell Physiology*, *52*(12), 2017–2038. doi:10.1093/pcp/pcr153 PMID:22156726

Nelson, K. (2003). The future of microbial genomics. *Environmental Microbiology*, *5*(12), 1223–1225. doi:10.1111/j.1462-2920.2003.00505.x PMID:14641569

O'Driscoll, A., Daugelaite, J., & Sleator, R. (2013). 'Big data', Hadoop and cloud computing in genomics. *Journal of Biomedical Informatics*, *46*(5), 774–781. doi:10.1016/j.jbi.2013.07.001 PMID:23872175

Ouzounis, C. (2002). Bioinformatics and the theoretical foundations of molecular biology. *Bioinformatics (Oxford, England)*, *18*(3), 377–378. doi:10.1093/bioinformatics/18.3.377 PMID:11934735

Patti, G. J., Yanes, O., & Siuzdak, G. (2012). Metabolomics: The apogee of the omics trilogy. *Nature Reviews. Molecular Cell Biology*, *13*(4), 263–269. doi:10.1038/nrm3314 PMID:22436749

Pearson, W., & Lipman, D. (1988). Improved tools for biological sequence comparison. *Proceedings of the National Academy of Sciences of the United States of America*, *85*(8), 2444–2448. doi:10.1073/pnas.85.8.2444 PMID:3162770

Potters, G. (2010). How the Human Genome Project Opened up the World of Microbes. *Nature Education, 3*(9), 34.

Professor, D., & Kovac, S. (2008). Application of proteomics in biotechnology: Microbial proteomics. *Biotechnology Journal, 3*(4), 496–509. doi:10.1002/biot.200700234 PMID:18320565

Rappé, M. S., & Giovannoni, S. J. (2003). The uncultured microbial majority. *Annual Review of Microbiology, 57*(1), 369–394. doi:10.1146/annurev.micro.57.030502.090759 PMID:14527284

Rhee, S., Dickerson, J., & Xu, D. (2006). Bioinformatics and its applications in plant biology. *Annual Review of Plant Biology, 57*(1), 335–360. doi:10.1146/annurev.arplant.56.032604.144103 PMID:16669765

Roberts, L.D., Souza, A.L., Gerszten, R.E., & Clish, C.B. (2012). Targeted metabolomics. *Current Protocols in Molecular Biology, 30*(2), 1-24.

Rogozin, I., Makarova, K., Natale, D., Spiridonov, A., Tatusov, R., & Wolf, Y. et al. (2002). Congruent evolution of different classes of non-coding DNA in prokaryotic genomes. *Nucleic Acids Research, 30*(19), 4264–4271. doi:10.1093/nar/gkf549 PMID:12364605

Rondon, M. R., Raffel, S. J., Goodman, R. M., & Handelsman, J. (1999). Toward functional genomics in bacteria: Analysis of gene expression in *Escherichia coli* from a bacterial artificial chromosome library of Bacillus cereus. *Proceedings of the National Academy of Sciences of the United States of America, 96*(11), 6451–6455. doi:10.1073/pnas.96.11.6451 PMID:10339608

Rusch, D., Halpern, A., Sutton, G., Heidelberg, K., Williamson, S., & Yooseph, S. et al. (2007). The Sorcerer II Global Ocean Sampling Expedition: Northwest Atlantic through Eastern Tropical Pacific. *PLoS Biology, 5*(3), e77. doi:10.1371/journal.pbio.0050077 PMID:17355176

Sharan, R., & Ideker, T. (2006). Modeling cellular machinery through biological network comparison. *Nature Biotechnology, 24*(4), 427–433. doi:10.1038/nbt1196 PMID:16601728

Shulaev, V. (2006). Metabolomics technology and bioinformatics. *Briefings in Bioinformatics, 7*(2), 128–139. doi:10.1093/bib/bbl012 PMID:16772266

Simon, C., & Daniel, R. (2011). Metagenomic analyses: Past and future trends [down-pointing small open triangle]. *Applied and Environmental Microbiology, 77*(4), 1153–1161. doi:10.1128/AEM.02345-10 PMID:21169428

Singer, E. (2013). Biology's big problem: There's too much data to handle. *Quanta Magazine.* Retrieved Jan 26, 2014 from http://www.wired.com/wiredscience/2013/10/big-data-biology/

Singh, D., Prabha, R., Rai, A., & Arora, D. (2012). Bioinformatics-assisted microbiological research: Tasks, developments and upcoming challenges. *American Journal of Bioinformatics, 1*(1).

Sogin, M., Morrison, H., Huber, J., Mark Welch, D., Huse, S., & Neal, P. et al. (2006). Microbial diversity in the deep sea and the underexplored ''rare biosphere''. *Proceedings of the National Academy of Sciences of the United States of America, 103*(32), 12115–12120. doi:10.1073/pnas.0605127103 PMID:16880384

Sribar, V. (2011). *'Big Data' is only the beginning of extreme information management.* Retrieved from https://www.gartner.com/doc/1622715/big-data-beginning-extreme-information

Steinbeck, C., Kuhn, S., Jayaseelan, K., & Moreno, P. (2011). Computational metabolomics – a field at the boundaries of cheminformatics and bioinformatics. *Journal of Cheminformatics, 3*(Suppl 1), 6.

Stelling, J. (2004). Mathematical models in microbial systems biology. *Current Opinion in Microbiology, 7*(5), 513–518. doi:10.1016/j.mib.2004.08.004 PMID:15451507

Steuer, R., & Junker, H. (2009). *Computational models of metabolism: stability and regulation in metabolic networks*. (A. Stuart, Ed.). John Wiley & Sons.

Strauss, E. J., & Falkow, S. (1997). Microbial pathogenesis: Genomics and beyond. *Science*, 276(5313), 707–712. doi:10.1126/science.276.5313.707 PMID:9115190

Suen, G., Arshinoff, B. I., Taylor, R. G., & Welch, R. D. (2007). Practical applications of bacterial functional genomics. *Biotechnology & Genetic Engineering Reviews*, 24(1), 213–242. doi:10.1080/02648725.2007.10648101 PMID:18059635

Sugden, A., & Pennisi, E. (2000). Diversity digitized. *Science*, 289, 2305–2305. PMID:11041798

Thorvaldsdóttir, H., Robinson, J., & Mesirov, J. (2013). Integrative Genomics Viewer (IGV): High-performance genomics data visualization and exploration. *Briefings in Bioinformatics*, 14(2), 178–192. doi:10.1093/bib/bbs017 PMID:22517427

Wang, Y., Zhang, X., & Chen, L. (2013). Computational systems biology in the big data era. *BMC Systems Biology*, 7(Suppl 2), S1. doi:10.1186/1752-0509-7-S2-S1 PMID:24564834

Waterman, M. (1995). Introduction to computational biology: maps, sequence and genomes. Chapman & Hall--CRC Press. ISBN 0 412 99391 0. doi:10.1007/978-1-4899-6846-3

Watson, J. (1990). The human genome project: Past, present, and future. *Science*, 248(4951), 44–49. doi:10.1126/science.2181665 PMID:2181665

Wilkins, M., Pasquali, C., Appel, R., Ou, K., Golaz, O., & Sanchez, J. et al. (1996). From proteins to proteomes: Large scale protein identification by two-dimensional electrophoresis and amino acid analysis. *Nature Biotechnology*, 14(1), 61–65. doi:10.1038/nbt0196-61 PMID:9636313

Winder, C., Dunn, W., & Goodacre, R. (2011). TARDIS-based microbial metabolomics: Time and relative differences in systems. *Trends in Microbiology*, 19(7), 315–322. doi:10.1016/j.tim.2011.05.004 PMID:21664817

Wirth, H. (n.d.). *Analysis of large-scale molecular biological data using self-organizing maps*. Available online: http://www.qucosa.de/fileadmin/data/qucosa/documents/10129/Dissertation%20Henry%20Wirth.pdf

Yates, J., & Washburn, M. (2000). Analysis of microbial proteome. *Current Opinion in Microbiology*, 3(3), 292–297. doi:10.1016/S1369-5274(00)00092-8 PMID:10851159

Zhang, W., Li, F., & Nie, L. (2010). Integrating multiple 'omics' analysis for microbial biology: Application and methodologies. *Microbiology*, 156(2), 287–301. doi:10.1099/mic.0.034793-0 PMID:19910409

ADDITIONAL READING

Edwards, D. J., & Holt, K. E. (2013). Beginner's guide to comparative bacterial genome analysis using next-generation sequence data. *Microbial Informatics and Experimentation*, 3(1), 2. doi:10.1186/2042-5783-3-2 PMID:23575213

Fraser, C. M., Eisen, J. A., Nelson, K. E., Paulsen, I. T., & Salzberg, S. L. (2002). The Value of Complete Microbial Genome Sequencing (You Get What You Pay For). *Journal of Bacteriology*, 184(23), 6403–6405. doi:10.1128/JB.184.23.6403-6405.2002 PMID:12426324

Fraser, C. M., Eisen, J. A., & Salzberg, S. L. (2000). Microbial genome sequencing. *Nature*, 406. PMID:10963611

Fricke, W. F., & Rasko, D. A. (2014). Bacterial genome sequencing in the clinic: Bioinformatic challenges and solutions. *Nature Reviews. Genetics*, *15*(1), 49–55. doi:10.1038/nrg3624 PMID:24281148

Human Microbiome Project: diversity of human microbes greater than previously predicted (http://www.sciencedaily.com/releases/2010/05/100520141214.htm)

Kisand, V., & Lettieri, T. (2013). Genome sequencing of bacteria: Sequencing, de novo assembly and rapid analysis using open source tools. *BMC Genomics*, *14*(1), 211. doi:10.1186/1471-2164-14-211 PMID:23547799

Ko¨ser, C. U., Ellington, M. J., Cartwright, E. J. P., Gillespie, S. H., Brown, N. M., & Farrington, M. et al. (2012). Routine use of microbial whole genome sequencing in diagnostic and public health microbiology. *PLoS Pathogens*, *8*(8), e1002824. doi:10.1371/journal.ppat.1002824 PMID:22876174

Nordberg, H., Cantor, M., Dusheyko, S., Hua, S., Poliakov, A., & Shabalov, I. ct al. (2014). The genome portal of the Department of Energy Joint Genome Institute: 2014 updates. *Nucleic Acids Research*, *42*(D1), D26–D31. doi:10.1093/nar/gkt1069 PMID:24225321

Suen, G., Arshinoff, B. I., Taylor, R. G., & Welch, R. D. (2007). Practical applications of bacterial functional genomics. *Biotechnology & Genetic Engineering Reviews*, *24*(1), 213–242. doi:10.1080/02648725.2007.10648101 PMID:18059635

Yang, L., Wei, G., Tang, K., Nardini, C., & Han, J. D. (2013). Understanding human diseases with high-throughput quantitative measurement and analysis of molecular signatures. *Sci China Life Sci.*, *56*(3), 213–219. doi:10.1007/s11427-013-4445-9 PMID:23526386

KEY TERMS AND DEFINITIONS

Antioxidomics: Study of antioxidants, their interactions and functions.

Big Data: Collection of large, complex and multifaceted datasets which are unable to process/analyze by on-hand data processing or data managing tools.

Bioinformatics: Utilizes different data-analytical and data-managements tools/technique to analyze and interpret data into meaningful manner.

Comparative Genomics: Study of similarity and dissimilarity of DNA, RNA or proteins and facilitates better understanding on cellular functioning.

Computational Biology: Field of biology which deals with the development of tools and techniques employed for analysis of biological data.

Functional Genomics: Study of function of genes in organisms, involves genome comparison and other techniques like mutation insertion for identification of function of specific genes.

Genomics: Study of entire gene complement and their interactions in any organism. Involves processes like sequencing, assembly, annotation and analysis to study structure, mapping, function and evolution of genomes.

Glycomics: Study of entire sugar complement (all glycan structures) in any specific cell.

Lipidomics: Study of entire lipid component in any biological sample.

Metabolomics: Quantification and analysis of small molecule metabolites of any biological sample.

Metagenomics: Study of DNA from any specific environmental conditions like soil, water etc. Enables to study those microbes which are unable to culture in laboratory conditions.

Molecular Biology: Deals with the study of macromolecules (e.g. nucleic acids, proteins) and provides information about molecular basis of biological functions.

Network Biology: Study of complex biological systems as computable networks which involves components (nodes) and edges (interactions) between them.

Next-generation sequencing: Next-generation sequencing (NGS) is high-throughput sequencing technologies for DNA and RNA. Involves 4 different technologies that is Illumina (Solexa), Roche (454), Ion torrent and Solid techniques.

Phenomics: Study of physical and biochemical traits of any organism i.e. its phenotype.

Proteomics: Study of entire protein complement of a cell.

Structural Genomics: Study of entire structure component of specific molecules. Involves computational tools, theoretical predictions and techniques like X-ray crystallography, Mass and NMR spectroscopy.

System Biology: Involves data integration for study of functional interconnections in biological system. Integrate all –omics sciences for this purpose.

Transcriptomics: Study of entire RNA complement of any cell at a specific time or condition.

Chapter 13
Perspectives on Data Integration in Human Complex Disease Analysis

Kristel Van Steen
University of Liége, Belgium & University of Liege, Belgium

Nuria Malats
Spanish National Cancer Research Centre (CNIO), Spain

ABSTRACT

The identification of causal or predictive variants/genes/mechanisms for disease-associated traits is characterized by "complex" networks of molecular phenotypes. Present technology and computer power allow building and processing large collections of these data types. However, the super-rapid data generation is counterweighted by a slow-pace for data integration methods development. Most currently available integrative analytic tools pertain to pairing omics data and focus on between-data source relationships, making strong assumptions about within-data source architectures. A limited number of initiatives exist aiming to find the most optimal ways to analyze multiple, possibly related, omics databases, and fully acknowledge the specific characteristics of each data type. A thorough understanding of the underlying assumptions of integrative methods is needed to draw sound conclusions afterwards. In this chapter, the authors discuss how the field of "integromics" has evolved and give pointers towards essential research developments in this context.

INTRODUCTION

DNA and RNA microarray technologies have made it possible to relate genome structure with gene expression patterns and physiological cell states. This paved the way towards a better understanding of tumor development, diseases progression, and drug response (Trevino, Falciani,

& Barrera-Saldana, 2007). Since their appearance, these technologies have been used to detect single nucleotide polymorphisms (SNPs) and other structural variations in the genome, such as copy number variations (CNVs) (Feuk, Carson, & Scherer, 2006; Macdonald, Ziman, Yuen, Feuk, & Scherer, 2014; Pang et al., 2010; Pang, Migita, Macdonald, Feuk, & Scherer, 2013), as

DOI: 10.4018/978-1-4666-6611-5.ch013

well as to examine changes involving all aspects of epigenetic interactions (Colyer, Armstrong, & Mills, 2012). Next Generation Sequencing (NGS) can also be used to identify novel mutations. In addition, NGS allows the identification of protein binding to chromatin, RNA quantification, and the investigation of spatial interactions, amongst others. Compared to micro-array experiments, sequencing-based experiments are more widely applicable, since they exhibit a potentially richer information content, but at the expense of higher analytical costs and the need for more sophisticated analytic tools and well-equipped IT-infrastructures to deal with the vast amounts of data they generate (Nekrutenko & Taylor, 2012).

Genome-wide association studies (GWAS) typically assay hundreds of thousands of SNPs in thousands of individuals (Johnson & O'Donnell, 2009). Such studies have reproducibly identified numerous SNP-trait associations, as are catalogued in the National Human Genome Research Institute (NHGRI) Catalog of Published Genome-Wide Association Studies (http://www.genome.gov/gwastudies) (Hindorff et al., 2009). The catalog includes over 1,500 curated publications of over 10,000 SNPs. With the bloom of analytic tools for gene-gene interaction analysis using SNPs (Van Steen, 2012), gene interaction studies are gradually being incorporated in the catalog as well (Welter et al., 2014). However, apart from gene-gene interactions, several other factors exist that makes GWAS less efficient, including compound or multiple phenotypes, genomic imprinting, gene-environment interactions. The latter type of interactions can be taken very broadly, realizing that intermediate phenotypes, such as gene or protein expression, DNA methylation or histone modification, also respond to variations in DNA, cascading into changes for the trait of interest. Clearly, independently carried out omics data analyses are unlikely to be sufficient to obtain a full comprehension of all the underlying principles that govern the functions of biological systems (Joyce & Palsson, 2006).

TAXONOMY

What "Integration" Is and Is Not

Data integration may mean different things in different contexts. In order to share scientific data and to analyze them as such, the available data sources need to be integrated via a uniform interface that accommodates different data types and/or data accessing from different remote locations. In this context, the term *data fusion* pops up. It refers to fusing records on the same entity into a single file, and involves putting measures in place to detect and remove erroneous or conflicting data (Wang et al., 2014). Several definitions of data fusion or data merging exist. Some of these definitions use "data integration" in their definition. However, although some data integration efforts will rely on data fusion processes, data fusion and data integration are not equivalent. In fact, new fusion techniques may appear as more complicated omics data integration tasks need to be accomplished. In line with our own viewpoints, and starting from mathematical formalisms, Oxley and Thorsen (Oxley & Thorsen, 2004) concluded that fusion can be defined as the process of optimally mapping several objects into a single object. In contrast, *integration* is the process of connecting systems (which may have fusion in them) into a larger system (Oxley & Thorsen, 2004).

A single data type omics analysis can be regarded as a comprehensive assessment of biochemical processes or interactions between molecules that belong to one specific layer of a cellular system. Examples of such layers are genomics, transcriptomic, proteomics and metabolomics. The data are characterized by their high-throughput. The analyses are often data-driven, but depending on the focus of the study (for instance, studying interactions between genetic variants or molecular interactions in cells) and/or the availability of sufficient IT infrastructure, these analyses may need to be hypothesis-driven rather than hypothesis-free. Obviously, a single omics study only provides limited information. For instance, the use of genomic information alone to obtain accurate predictions related to an individual's health can be improved by combining family history with an individual's SNP profile (Do, Hinds, Francke, & Eriksson, 2012). Genomic profiles can be complemented with proteomics information. This goes beyond interpreting gene expression levels in terms of protein levels. Note that the correlation between both can be as little as 40% depending on the system (Vogel & Marcotte, 2012). Hypothesizing that the observed fold change of proteomic targets may be associated with the dysregulation of their interacting partners at the level of mRNA, seeds of differentially expressed proteins can be used to improve the search for sub-networks of markers at the mRNA level (Nibbe, Koyuturk, & Chance, 2010). Exploiting the complementarity of different layers of cellular activity is starting to show its utility, both in terms of disease prediction and in better understanding disease mechanisms such as tumorigenesis (Nibbe et al., 2010).

Using the aforementioned definition of integration, omics integrative analyses surpass single omics analyses in that different cellular layers are connected into an "integrated system." This offers additional advantages above simply merging information that is independently derived from different layers. Fully exploiting the information that can be retrieved from studying relationships between data types is a major challenge in omics integration. One of the easiest measures for studying such relationships is correlation, being a measure of linear association. Steinfath and colleagues (Steinfath, Repsilber, Scholz, Walther, & Selbig, 2007) reviewed different methods of correlation analyses between omics, ranging from simple pairwise correlation to kernel canonical correlation. As the authors explain, several biases may hamper the analysis. Some of these biases relate to the way the data were generated (e.g., different experimental platforms) and the way the data were preprocessed (e.g. missing data handling). Adequately circumventing or handling such biases

becomes even more crucial in more complicated "integrative analyses."

In the next section, we summarize the components of a statistical data integration process, which includes data preprocessing.

FROM COMPONENTWISE TO GLOBAL STRATEGIES

First Attempts to Integrate Omics Data

An immediate generalization of classical SNP-disease trait GWAS, is to map the genetic architecture of intermediate molecular phenotypes, by using similar statistical approaches as when relating DNA variation to a disease trait. The classic example is an eQTL study which aims to discover the genetic variants that are associated with gene expression. Here, gene expression serves as an intermediate phenotype. These studies have proven their practical use, not in the least to assist in the interpretation of GWAS findings and to increase our understanding of gene regulatory processes (Nica & Dermitzakis, 2013). Interestingly, over 85% of the genetic variants identified as being associated with disease traits map outside the coding region of annotated genes (Pastinen, 2010). This raises questions about the importance of long-range control of gene expression in, for instance, cancer initiation or disease progression via eQTL analysis (van Heyningen & Bickmore, 2013). Given the small sample sizes of most eQTL studies, future meta-analyses are expected to reveal many more (small-effect) eQTLs, as a result of pooling studies and therefore increasing statistical power (Gaffney, 2013). However, although eQTL studies belong among the most popular multi-omics integrative approaches, a surprisingly small number of meta-eQTL analyses exist, which are either meta-analyze multi-center (Min et al., 2011) or multi-platform (Liang et al., 2013) eQTL data. This can in part be explained by the fact that also the genetics of gene expression appears to be complex and is modified by pleiotropy, gene-gene and gene-environment interactions (Skelly, Ronald, & Akey, 2009). Notably, the effects seen in eQTL mapping are often tissue specific. In effect, eQTLs may show opposite allelic directions when comparing different tissues in a common group of individuals (Fairfax et al., 2012; Fu et al., 2012). Several statistical frameworks exist to detect eQTLs in multiple tissues or cell types and several others, even more powerful ones, will emerge as more data become available. One such framework was developed by (Flutre, Wen, Pritchard, & Stephens, 2013) and explicitly models the potential for each eQTL to be active in some tissues and inactive in others. This increases the power to detect eQTLs that are present in more than one tissue, compared to a tissue-by-tissue analysis strategy. Omics integrative studies, such as eQTL studies, require the selection of adequate multiple-testing procedures, such as those based on bootstrap or permutation replicates. A resampling-based testing framework in eQTL studies could first involve carrying out a whole-genome scan for each resampled phenotype to find the maximum test statistic among all SNPs, and second selecting a threshold for the corrected *p*-values across all expression traits by controlling the false discovery rate (FDR) (X. Zhang, Huang, Sun, & Wang, 2012). Whether adopting a transcript-based or marker-based approach, or the more commonly used combined approach (i.e., simply testing all possible genotype-transcript combinations), dependencies between tests may exhibit different properties and classical FDR controlling methods may no longer be optimal (Kendziorski & Wang, 2006). Also the choice of association test may impact analysis results. When test assumptions are not met (for instance, when gene expression levels are non-normally distributed and ANOVA testing is used) even permutation based p-values may give rise to highly inflated type I errors (Szymczak, Igl, & Ziegler, 2009).

Another approach to integrate high-throughput functional data with genome-wide genotype data obtained from microarray- or sequence-based studies is to select SNPs that meet certain functional criteria. This can be carried out in a step-wise fashion, making use of several pieces of omics information (e.g., proteome or transcriptome) (Gamazon, Huang, Dolan, Cox, & Im, 2012). Such an "integrative" approach can be seen as a multi-stage filtering strategy, that narrows down the "alternative" search space during hypothesis testing for genotype-phenotype associations. Alternatively, eQTL weights are directly used in the genome-wide association analysis to improve its power, as in (Li et al., 2013).

Above, we have taken the example of eQTL studies to highlight main stream approaches to integrate collections of SNPs with gene expression data. Depending on the primary question of interest (e.g., finding relevant SNPs in relation to disease, finding gene transcripts that show different distributions for a SNP of interest, or discovering significant SNP-Transcript pairs) the method of choice will differ, assumptions underlying the validity of the method will differ, and care will need to be taken to select the most appropriate technique to adjust for multiple testing or to control false positives. Similar issues arise when linking epigenetic data to gene expression (van Eijk et al., 2012), or when associating the genome with epigenomes. Cataloging and interpreting genome-wide DNA methylation patterns of all human genes in all major tissues is one of the aims of the Human Epigenome Project (Eckhardt, Beck, Gut, & Berlin, 2004). Epigenetic changes do not alter the structure of the genes, but they may affect the way they are expressed. Advanced and sophisticated statistical efforts are required to fully understand how different environmental causes, and life-style factors (diet, stress exposures) relate to epigenetic changes and how these changes potentially affect for instance tumor suppressing genes that prevent cancer development. Reported strong associations between DNA methylation and smoking status at multiple sites across the genome (Elliott et al., 2014) and growing evidence that DNA methylation is important in regulating metabolic traits (Petersen et al., 2014) are only a few of several indications that "integrated analysis" of human complex traits ideally includes a variety of omics technologies that target different levels of cellular and micro/macro-environmental information.

Key Components of Statistical Data Integration

Omics data provide comprehensive descriptions of nearly all components and interactions within a cell (Joyce & Palsson, 2006). In contrast to single omics studies, integrated omics studies come with a set of unprecedented challenges. Some of these challenges have been reviewed for non-human species in general (Joyce & Palsson, 2006), and in animal biology (Quackenbush, 2006), for bacteria (De Keersmaecker, Thijs, Vanderleyden, & Marchal, 2006), plants (Fukushima, Kusano, Redestig, Arita, & Saito, 2009), or microbes (Zhang, Li, & Nie, 2010) in particular. Along with developments in the Human Variome Project (Cotton et al., 2009; Cotton et al., 2008; Cotton et al., 2007; Cotton & Macrae, 2010; Cotton, Vihinen, den Dunnen, Human Variome Project, & Standards, 2011; Kohonen-Corish, Smith, Robinson, & delegates of the 4th Biennial Meeting of the Human Variome Project, 2013; Oetting et al., 2013; Ring, Kwok, & Cotton, 2006), and the use of these developments towards improved mechanistic insights in complex diseases (Van Noorden, Ledford, & Mann, 2011), several authors have indicated the need for out-of-the-box thinking in complex disease studies. Human biology can be expected to be far more complex than non-human biology and hence it can be expected that the advantages of integrative efforts in model organisms will carry on to complex disease traits. Over the years, reviews and perspectives about integrating omics in human complex disease analysis have matured

from being rather general to more specific, displaying several possibilities and applied work. This maturation process is mainly due to the increasing accessibility to different collections of omics data (Baker, 2013; Choi & Pavelka, 2011; Hamid et al., 2009; Steinfath et al., 2007). Nevertheless, obtaining omics data on the same panel of individuals is a tough and expensive undertaking, but - we believe - will become the standard rather than the exception within the next decades. Therefore, gearing up the analytic methods to be able to deal with such data is essential and an investment that is worthwhile.

Any study that involves modeling and/or testing consists of components around a specific aspect of the study. Depending on the nature of the study, some of these components play a more prominent role than others or are more challenging than others. To successfully complete a sound integrated omics analysis, the following key steps are relevant:

1. The biological problem,
2. The data characterization,
3. Data preprocessing,
4. Integration analytics, including validation and replication procedures, and
5. Interpretation of results.

In the sequel, we give more details about the embodying of these modules in the context of omics integration studies. Clearly, modules 1-3 are important in selecting the data analytic techniques to successfully conduct step 4. Choices made for 1-4 impact the ability to interpret statistical findings (step 5). See Figure 1 for a graphical roadmap.

1. Understanding the Biological (Statistical) Problem

Traditional biological research questions have long been mainly hypothesis-driven. These days, vast amounts of data are generated in a hypothesis-free fashion. In such a scenario, data can be "mined,"

Figure 1. Building blocks of a data integration pipeline

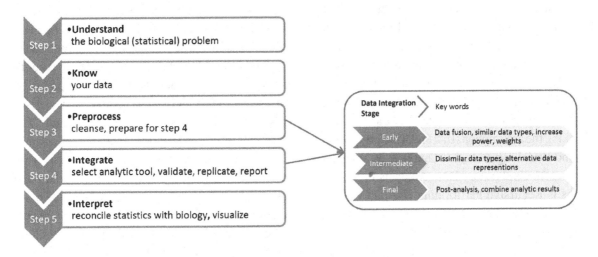

using a variety of computational and statistical (data mining) tools. The purpose of a hypothesis-free analysis may be to discover new knowledge, to formulate new hypotheses, or to answer a set of pre-specified questions. At the systems level, several biological questions can be formulated, hereby linking genomics to transcriptomics, proteomics, metabolomics, fluxomics, phenomics, or combinations thereof. For explicit examples, see for instance (Joyce & Palsson, 2006). Obviously, the nature of any integrated omics study will change depending on whether finding associations, predicting, or characterizing populations are the focus.

2. Identifying Characteristics of Data Types

Current "integrative" omics-analysis methods fall into two different categories: methods that involve merging similar data types (across studies) or methods that involve integrating dissimilar data types (across studies as well as within studies). In line with our definition of omics integration, the first category falls under "meta-analytics" rather than "integromics" and hence will not be considered in depth in this contribution. Here, we use the term "dissimilar data" whenever two

or more fundamentally different data sources are considered. For instance, the problem of developing a predictive model based on SNP and methylation data, as well as clinical data, clearly involves dissimilar data sources. Whether data are similar or dissimilar, the issue of quality and informativity is of great importance. Each data source is unavoidably subject to different levels of noise. Therefore, the concept of weighting data sources with quality and/or informativety scores should become an essential component of the framework.

In general, characterizing the available data at hand refers to exploring the potential information load of the data (e.g., within-data relationships), data quality and data-type specific noise patterns (e.g., related to employed technology or lab infrastructure and experimental protocols, systematic and random errors). In addition, it refers to understanding precision, accuracy (inversely related to error proneness), reliability and intrinsic properties that may be relevant for subsequent analytic choices (e.g., sample size and data format, "effective" data dimensionality). This step in the integrated analysis pipeline is as important as a classical Exploratory Data Analysis (EDA) in biostatistics. Naively, one could say that any method of looking at data that does not include formal statistical modeling or inference is part of EDA. In practice, EDA is a type of analysis that aims to provide insight into the main characteristics of the data. Examples include revealing underlying data (sub-)structure and identifying important (sets of) variables, detecting outlying observations and inconsistencies. EDA also covers checking the assumptions that underlie formal testing and modelling strategies. One well-established method for Exploratory Data Analysis in biostatistics is Recursive Partitioning (Strobl, Malley, & Tutz, 2009). The aim of recursive partitioning is to find homogeneous strata of individuals. In the context of omics integrated analyses, it may be highly relevant to identify subpopulations of homogeneous (similar) disease progression, or to find omics-driven subgroups of individuals within which the assignment to a treatment arm is similar (i.e., propensity stratification) or to find subpopulations within which the predictor-trait relationship is comparable (for instance, in drug-response studies) (Ciampi, Chang, Hogg, & McKinney, 1987).

3. Data Preprocessing

Genomic data are subject to different noises and errors, and a number of critical steps are required to preprocess raw measurements. Approaches for preprocessing vary depending on the type and nature of the data (e.g., arrays: background correction, normalization, quality assessment, which may differ from one platform to another). Several good resources exist that explain the technologies that generate the data and describe minimal standard operating procedures for data handling (e.g., Rodríguez-Ezpeleta, Hackenberg & Aransay, 2012; Mayer, 2011; Schneider & Orchard, 2011). Often these standards or checklists are omics-specific. Fortunately, several initiatives are emerging to further consolidate and harmonize standards (Field et al., 2009; Taylor et al., 2008), enhancing omics data sharing and integrative analyses.

When making inferences, two sources of uncertainty play a prominent role: statistical imprecision, which is caused by the stochastic character of the sampling process, and statistical ignorance, which is caused by the incompleteness or roughness of the data. Whereas statistical imprecision disappears with increasing sample size, statistical ignorance is persistent when the sample size becomes infinitely large (Molenberghs, Kenward, & Goetghebeur, 2001). Imputation as a missing data handling method may be well-studied and established in the context of genome-wide association studies (B. Howie, Fuchsberger, Stephens, Marchini, & Abecasis, 2012; B. Howie, Marchini, & Stephens, 2011; B. N. Howie, Donnelly, & Marchini, 2009; Marchini & Howie, 2008, 2010; Marchini, Howie, Myers, McVean, & Donnelly, 2007; Southam et al., 2011; Spencer, Su, Donnelly, & Marchini, 2009), but is less well studied (if at all) in omics integrated studies or interaction studies. This is a shortcoming, since completeness of data is frequently a requirement by data integration and interaction detection algorithms. Notably, imputation in Genome-Wide Association Interaction (GWAI) studies may increase allelic associations between SNPs. This may not only lead to so-called redundant SNPxSNP interactions but may also unnecessarily elevate the multiple testing burden (Van Steen, 2012). Genetic interactions themselves may be the subject of imputation strategies (Ulitsky, Krogan, & Shamir, 2009); little is known about optimal imputation strategies when different omics types are related, each exhibiting different degrees of missing data. Sensitivity analyses are needed to explore plausible departures from assumptions made by the missing data handling (Heraud-Bousquet, Larsen, Carpenter, Desenclos, & Le Strat, 2012).

In practice, data preprocessing can be performed at any step of the data integration process, most often at the beginning (see examples above) and prior to statistical analysis, where it may include checking assumptions of the analytic tool of choice and taking actions accordingly.

4. Integration Analytics

Following (Hamid et al., 2009), data from different sources can be fused or integrated at an early, intermediate or final stage. Whereas these authors describe early stage integration as merging data from different studies or experiments (to increase sample size and hence power), these authors refer to intermediate stage integration as transforming individual data sources to a common format or dimension to facilitate combining. An example of the latter includes computing similarity measures between individuals using genomics, epigenomics and transcriptomics data separately. The resulting three similarity matrices (with equal dimension, determined by the number of individuals for which all three data sources are available) can then easily be combined and submitted to an appropriate clustering algorithm to identify homogeneous subgroups of individuals in an integrated fashion. Meta-analytic approaches, enabling the aggregation of p-values or effect sizes across studies, would typically fall under final stage integration, according to (Hamid et al., 2009). Since meta-analysis involves (omics) data of the same type, we do not consider it to be part of a data integration strategy. See also Figure 1.

Note that attaching weights to data types prior to merging does not alter the general format nor does it change the main characteristics of the data. Also, this weighted merging of data is different from using one source of information to weight another. An example of the latter is to use information about eQTLs to weight genetic variants in GWA studies (L. Li et al., 2013). Another example is to use knowledge about inherent stratification among GWA SNPs as prior knowledge in subsequent variant-trait association or prediction analyses (Schork et al., 2013). In contrast, data transformation functions typically change the nature of the data. Hence care needs to be taken in interpreting results obtained from subsequent analyses. Examples of data transformations that change the original presentation of the data include those based on projections (e.g., principal components-based) and those based on kernel functions (Lanckriet, De Bie, Cristianini, Jordan, & Noble, 2004). As we will see later, principal components and similar methods are popular techniques in omics integrated analyses, since they help reducing the dimensionality of the original data. Note that feature selection methods (Saeys, Inza, & Larranaga, 2007), for instance those based on SNP functionality or possible deleterious effects, do not change the presentation of the data (P. H. Lee, Jung, & Shatkay, 2010; P. H. Lee & Shatkay, 2006, 2008a, 2008b, 2009). Although feature selection or variant prioritization methods may employ multiple omics data resources as well, they generally fall under genomic data fusion methods rather than omics data integration methods (Aerts et al., 2006; Schuierer, Tranchevent, Dengler, & Moreau, 2010; Sifrim et al., 2013; Tranchevent et al., 2008).

Clearly, guidelines are needed to promote transparent and accurate reporting of integrated analyses results. The EQUATOR Network (Enhancing the QUAlity and Transparency Of health Research) aims at providing such guidelines to enhance the value and reliability of resulting literature (Morris, 2008; Simera et al., 2010).

5. Interpretation

Interpretation is an important step in identifying characteristics of genetic, molecular and environmental attributes that influence a complex trait and in identifying relevant biological pathways. It usually involves consulting several external biological-related data bases. When doing so, care needs to be taken in how to condense the information derived from these sources. Indeed, biological-related data bases may differ in the way they assess and incorporate scoring systems to accumulate evidence, in the way they allow for uncertainty and redundancy, or in the way genetic variants are assigned to genes (for instance, due to different builds in time). Clearly, visual analytics will greatly enhance the interpretation of results from integrated analyses (Gribov et al., 2010), but is not sufficient to guarantee unquestionable interpretations.

Unambiguous interpretation is only possible when there are guidelines for the minimum information that should be reported about omics experiments and when these guidelines are actually adhered to (Brazma, 2009; Brazma et al., 2001; Deutsch et al., 2008; Deutsch et al., 2006). One popular set of guidelines is the so-called MIAME guidelines for microarray experiments. By analogy to these guidelines, checklists for more recent technologies have been developed as well. See for instance the MINSEQE initiative (http://www.mged.org/minseqe/), which provides and updates a checklist for Minimal Information about a high throughput SEQuencing Experiment, as well as deliverables from initiatives such as the EU COST Action BM1006 SEQAHEAD, an international network on Next Generation Sequencing Data Analysis. Integrated omics analyses not only deal with the cleansing process of each omics data type separately, but also impose some novel processes that specifically relate to data integration or integrative analytics. Guidelines regarding processes are underway.

Integration as a Multidisciplinary Approach

An omics *multidisciplinary approach* can be viewed as a strategy in which the initial problem is divided in data-specific subproblems and involves a fairly limited exchange of information between the omics-specific experts or omics-disciplines. The disperse pieces of information are combined or integrated in a limited way or at a later stage in the study. In contrast, a *trans-disciplinary approach* involves an active synergy between disciplines, to create a solution to the problem that otherwise could not have been found. Trans-disciplinary research requires cross-talk between disciplines and consequently a unified language that is accessible to all parties involved or a bridge between jargons and technical terminology. Currently, the omics integration analysis scene is marked by multidisciplinary and *interdisciplinary efforts*, where the latter refers to adopting discipline-specific perspectives in a joint effort to solve a common problem (Fawcett, 2013; Woods, 2007). Rather than giving a comprehensive review about methods and techniques for integrated research in human systems, we give a perspective on the positioning of these and on how they can be useful in future trans-disciplinary activities.

A first type of multidisciplinary study uses single omics data types to complement each discipline involved and to use this complementary view to address the research problem of interest. One of the advantages of such a study is the elimination of potential biases that arise from adhering to a single omics analysis. The integration is either performed by eye or by formal algorithms. The separate omics-specific studies may have equal weight and may be included in a fusion process. Alternatively, these studies can be used as input to enhance the analysis of other omics data. For example, In Similarity Network Fusion (SNF) networks of patients are constructed for each available omics data type and then efficiently fused into a single network. In practice, SNF fuses patient similarity networks that are obtained from each of their data types separately. These single networks are equivalent to classic patient-based similarity matrices. The networks are fused in a non-linear way, hereby iteratively updating each of the networks with the information from the other networks and making them more alike with each additional step. This is an example of what was called before "intermediate stage" integration, since the raw data are transformed into similarity measures between pairs of individuals prior to analysis (Wang et al., 2014). Gibbs et al. (Gibbs, Gralinski, Baric, & McWeeney, 2014) first built co-expression networks on transcript and peptide expression data separately (Langfelder et al., 2012; Langfelder & Horvath, 2008; Langfelder,

Zhang, & Horvath, 2008; A. Li & Horvath, 2007, 2009; Yip & Horvath, 2007) and second combined information from both networks in a bi-partite graph to obtain multi-omics signatures for disease. Complementary transcriptome and epigenome analysis, even though still performed on relatively small samples, may highlight novel candidate genes such as *ALDH1A3* for pancreatic cancer and may indicate a series of interesting avenues for follow-up that otherwise would not have reached the surface (Jia et al., 2013).

The second type of multidisciplinary study occurs when one data type is used to validate or support the findings of the other. Several studies have shown the utility of epigenetic features for interpreting GWAS results (Hardison, 2012). Expression QTL results can in turn be used to provide functional interpretation for findings from GWA studies (e.g., in pancreas cancer research (Wu et al., 2012) or (Chelala, Khan, & Lemoine, 2009; Dayem Ullah, Lemoine, & Chelala, 2012, 2013)). Using knowledge about the overlap between pairwise omics data sources (obtained via interdisciplinary or trans-disciplinary efforts), such as between genome, epigenome and transcriptome data panels, may increase the confidence in identified relationships with any of the omics data and the human complex trait under investigation.

A multidisciplinary approach also occurs in a third way, whenever external data base information is used, to either prioritize the focal points of analysis, or the enhance interpretation. One such data base, Gene Ontology, includes public ontologies to facilitate the mapping of gene products to their biological functions. In the context of multi-omics or integrated omics analysis, there is a need to accommodate several data types at once during this mapping process. Novel algorithms, such as the Multi-level ONtology Analysis (MONA) algorithm, provide promising alternatives to flexibly integrate different underlying regulatory motifs or ontologies (Sass, Buettner, Mueller, & Theis, 2013). Alternatively, manually curated and publicly available data are used to retrieve information about genomic data, pathways and molecular interactions, amongst others, to prioritize genes in relation to a disease phenotype (for instance, LYNX (Sulakhe et al., 2014)). Using biological information has turned rather useful in Genome-Wide Association Interaction (GWAI) studies. These studies suffer from being underpowered due to the large sample sizes needed to reach statistical significance (Van Steen, 2012). GWAI studies in particular benefit from integrating biological knowledge at all stages of the analysis protocol. Indeed, integration is not only helpful in selecting interesting interactive regions (hereby reducing the multiple testing burden) but it is also helpful in bridging the gap between statistical and biologically or clinically relevant interactions (facilitating interpretation) (Guserava, 2014). Real-life applications do not only suffer from replication issues but also from problems in interpreting the statistical findings (Ritchie, Van Steen, & Gusareva, 2014). Other within or between omics interaction studies are likely to suffer from the same growing pains as GWAIs.

Integration as an Interdisciplinary and Trans-Disciplinary Approach

Moving away from multidisciplinary research, towards interdisciplinary and trans-disciplinary research, data hierarchies and between data-type relationships, as well as synergetic interactions between different layers of cellular information, become more important. Ideally, the study of these aspects is made an integral part of the study. Note that the term *biologic interaction* (Rothman, 1974) is used to indicate deviation from additivity in risk differences for 2 causal risk factors. In contrast, in statistics, an *interaction* is merely used to indicate deviations from a model of additive multiple effects. These deviations might be expressed on different scales (e.g., linear or logarithmic), which would imply different definitions. Methods such as BRIDGE use penalized regressions and are based on the assumption that genes involved in disease with similar phenotypes share similar characteristics across multiple omics (Y. Chen, Wu, & Jiang, 2013). Non-parametric regression approaches relax some of the assumptions that are required by (semi-) parametric regression strategies in order to generate reliable results, and like penalized regressions, have shown their utility in large-scale screening efforts for statistical interactions. Alternatively, decision tree-based methods are used, such as recursive partitioning, random forests and logic regression (Chen et al., 2011; Malina, Ickstadt, Schwender, Posch, & Bogdan, 2014; Schwender & Ickstadt, 2008; Schwender & Ruczinski, 2010).

Especially in the absence of a trait of interest, there is a lot to be gained from pattern recognition approaches. These approaches extract patterns from the data as a whole, which are then used to solve the research question under investigation. Clustering algorithms belong to the oldest such approaches. They have been developed and applied in a variety of contexts. We believe that clustering ensembles (Strehl & Ghosh, 2003), combining multiple partitions of the given data into a single clustering solution of better quality, and related approaches (Avogadri & Valentini, 2009; Fodeh et al., 2013; E. Y. Kim, Hwang, & Ko, 2012; S. Y. Kim & Lee, 2007; Singh, Mukherjee, Peng, & Xu, 2010), are particularly interesting for integrated omics analyses. Whatever clustering method, scalability problems associated with large amounts of omics data and high dimensional data input spaces, are likely to emerge. To this regard, novel clustering algorithms for scalable clustering will need to be used (e.g., (Geraci, Leoncini, Montangero, Pellegrini, & Renda, 2009; Jin, Wong, & Leung, 2005; Milenova & Campos, 2002)). Other pattern recognition methods include Neural Networks. ATHENA (Holzinger, Dudek, Frase, Krauss, et al., 2013; Holzinger, Dudek, Frase, Pendergrass, & Ritchie, 2013; Turner, Dudek, & Ritchie, 2010) provides a tool to assist in feature prioritization, trait modelling and interpreting results. It was extended to be used as an integrative framework to identify interactions, not only within, but also between multi-levels of genomic data associated with traits of interest, using Grammatical Evolution Symbolic Regression (GESR) or Grammatical Evolution Neural Networks (Kim, Li, Dudek, & Ritchie, 2013). The use of evolutionary computation algorithms in relation to Neural Networks allows the optimization of inputs and the network architecture, apart from optimizing the weights assigned to edges connecting nodes, and is often more powerful than traditional Neural Network approaches (Motsinger-Reif, Dudek, Hahn, & Ritchie, 2008). Especially when including different layers of omics information in the architecture, more work is needed to investigate the effect on final results of unrecognized omics heterogeneity, different measurement scales and intrinsic (non-linear) relationships between features of the same data type.

Data becomes omics when nearly all information that can be retrieved from those data is covered. The huge amount of information does not become available effortless. Restriction imposed by IT-infrastructures or analytic methods may force the researcher to only focus on some very specific aspect of the data. It seems waste of money having to focus on narrow hypotheses and not exploiting the full complexity of the multiple, possibly related, omics collections. Obviously, the choice of hypothesis will affect the outcome of the analysis since we can only obtain answers to the questions we ask. If all nodes in a cellular layer are known though, together with their variability, a set of equations can be created that determine how the variability affects a disease outcome. By adjusting the variables and the order of the variables in the equations, a (structural equation) model of the system can be derived, giving rise to a causal network. Networks are graphical models consisting of nodes and edges connecting nodes. Knowledge about eQTLs that affect the variability of (parts of) a gene expression module is sufficient to initiate a causal network and hence to describe a causal mechanism to the trait under investigation. LIRNET implements a systematic approach to identify the loci that determine expression of a module (Lee et al., 2009). Genomics is increasingly being used to infer causal relationships between gene expression traits (e.g., (Aten, Fuller, Lusis, & Horvath, 2008; Liu, de la Fuente, & Hoeschele, 2008)). Unlike GENNs, structural equation modeling requires the a priori definition of the causal structure or architecture. Several such definitions can be proposed and formally compared (Rosa et al., 2011). For instance, (Schadt et al., 2005) adopted a likelihood-based causality model selection strategy to infer causal associations between gene expression and disease in an integrative genomics context.

Networks do not always need to be directed in order to derive useful information from them. Whether derived from statistical approaches (such as statistical epistasis networks (Hu, Andrew, Karagas, & Moore, 2013)) or from ensemble methods (such as GENIE3 (Huynh-Thu, Irrthum, Wehenkel, & Geurts, 2010)), investigating the network properties and relevant network measures will already identify key players that can be followed-up by ontology analyses. Examples of network measures include the number of edges involving a node (degree), the frequency of nodes of a particular degree (degree distribution) and the average shortest path between all node pairs (mean path length). One of the main challenges related to network integrative approaches is to adequately take into account hierarchies between networks representing different layers of cellular information (Sieberts & Schadt, 2007), and to formally compare integrated networks derived on different populations of individuals. Another challenge is to exploit or account for associated regulators (e.g., SNPs may be associated due to linkage disequilibrium; gene-expression intensity levels may be correlated due to gene co-expression) and to select the proper node representatives rather than arbitrary ones among a set of correlated features. Lastly, too large or too busy networks defeat

the purpose of network development. Hence, in order to facilitate visualization and interpretation, sub-modules of networks need to be identified. Several such approaches exist.

The reason why simply combining the available omics data is no option is that association results with the phenotypes of interest or clustering results of individuals using the combined data may be dominated by the largest, most variable omics data sets. A solution is to make the data types more comparable in size (i.e., number of variates, dispersity). This can be achieved by employing data reduction techniques or by summarizing data into representative components. Note that features selection is one such data reduction technique. Principal Components Analysis (PCA) is another, hereby changing the presentation of the data. Although the problem of domination still exists after data down-sizing, it will be less apparent. Despite this, the approach still requires defining appropriate weighting schemes to allow for different information loads and acknowledgment of differential degrees of sparseness, noise, measurement scales, etc.

In general, principal component analysis (PCA) enables the description of correlation patterns between numerical variables. In the light of data integration, and the development of a flexible approach that is applicable to different types of data, generalizations of PCA to accommodate qualitative variables and mixtures of qualitative and quantitative variables are required, as may be realized via optimal scaling (Costantini, Linting, & Porzio, 2010; Papadopoulos, 2010; Zhang & Block, 2009). In order to deal with outliers and differential noise, the utility of rank transforms and weighted ranks should be explored (Alonso & Roque, 2009). Canonical correlation analysis allows investigating many-to-many relationships. Canonical is the statistical term for analyzing latent variables (which are not directly observed) that represent multiple variables (which are directly observed). The method has been extended to analyze more than two sets simultaneously as generalized canonical analysis (GCA). To accommodate different measurement scales and high-dimensional intra-correlated data, generalized canonical analysis can be combined with optimal scaling, as before, and with sparsity (Parkhomenko, Tritchler, & Beyene, 2009; Waaijenborg & Zwinderman, 2009) and regularization criteria (Tenenhaus, Guillemot, Gidrol, & Frouin, 2010). The main challenge with components based approaches it to customize and implement appropriate algorithms that are able to accommodate high-dimensional data for which a substantial number of values may be missing (Raiko, Ilin, & Karhunen, 2008). Tool boxes such as mixOmics (available in R as a package) provide an outcome while allowing the application of PCA, Independent Principal Component Analysis (IPCA) (Yao, Coquery, & Le Cao, 2012), sparse Principal Component Analysis (sPCA) (Shen & Huang, 2008), and sparse Partial Least Squares Discriminant Analysis (sPLS-DA) (Le Cao, Boitard, & Besse, 2011) on a single omics data set. Co-regulated biological entities across 2 omics data types can be discovered via mixOmics as well via PLS (Le Cao, Martin, Robert-Granie, & Besse, 2009; Le Cao, Rossouw, Robert-Granie, & Besse, 2008) and regularized Canonical Correlation Analysis (rCCA) (González et al., 2009), and across >2 omics data types via for instance regularized Generalized CCA (rGCCA) (Tenenhaus & Tenenhaus, 2011). A generalization of PCA and an approach to combine and visualize multi-way omics data is Multiple Factor Analysis (MFA) (Escofier & Pagès, 1990). MFA is used to analyze a set of observations described by several groups of variables. For instance, group 1 may consist of genome-wide SNPs (represented by variates with maximal 3 categories), group 2 may consist of genome-wide methylation data (methylation is present or not), group 3 may represent transcriptome data (measured on a continuous scale). At the basis of an MFA lies a PCA in each group (omics data type). Each data set is subsequently normalized by dividing all its elements by the square root of the first eigenvalue obtained

from the data-specific PCA, prior to merging and subjecting the concatenated data to a global PCA. A Multiple Factor Analysis offers an integrated picture of observations and of the relationships between the groups of variables. Extra levels of data structure are accommodated in Hierarchical Multiple Factor Analysis (HMFA; hierarchy in the variates – for instance a group consisting of subgroup genome and epigenome data and a group consisting of subgroup transcriptome and proteome data) and in Dual Multiple Factor Analysis (DMFA; families of individuals) (Abdi, Williams, & Valentin, 2013).

Quite often kernel versions of data compression and de-noising algorithms exist (e.g., for Discriminant Analysis and PCA). In kernel-based methods, each data set is represented by a so-called kernel matrix, which essentially constitutes similarity measures between pairs of entities (genes, proteins, patients – same cancer type or not, etc.). The main challenge with these methods is to choose the right kernel for each data set and to appropriately combine the kernels from the different data sources to give a complete representation of the available data. A simple combination of kernels is to add, but possibly more optimal ways in the context of integrated omics analysis are to weight kernels by explicitly using information about data quality and informativeness. Also, kernel-based models often lack interpretability of the resulting model, due to the fact that the non-linear transformation of the input data is not explicitly known. For examples on kernel-based application in omics integration, see for instance (Daemen et al., 2009; De Bie, Tranchevent, van Oeffelen, & Moreau, 2007; Hamid et al., 2009).

FUTURE RESEARCH DIRECTIONS

Discussion

One of the major aims of molecular biology and medical science is to understand complex trait mechanisms. Microarray and Next Generation Sequencing technologies are helpful in that they provide the tools to generate the data from which knowledge about these mechanisms can be extracted. Although several statistical methods can be employed to derive patterns in data or to test for associations, the ultimate goal is to give a biological meaning to the observations. Understanding gene function (i.e., the aim of functional genomics) facilitates such a biological interpretation. Here, gene function can be viewed from different angles: biochemical, cellular, developmental or adaptive. For more details, we refer to (Bouchez & Hofte, 1998). Along the same lines, methods development and application in integromics have focused on functional genomics contexts, thus integrating genome-wide genetic data with data on the epigenome and transcriptome. Inspired by functional genomics practices, one popular definition for data integration emerged, namely one referring to the process of (statistical) data combination from several sources so as to provide a unified (integrated) view of the whole genome and to enable making large-scale statistical inferences (Lu, Xia, Paccanaro, Yu, & Gerstein, 2005). As indicated throughout this document, we prefer a more global definition of data integration (applied to omics data), not making explicit references to statistical, bioinformatics or particular computational tools (Oxley & Thorsen, 2004).

Biobanking efforts play a crucial role in advancing biomedical and translational research. The availability of tissue sample collections and cohorts around the globe are prerequisites for personalized medicine ("ESF Position Paper: European Biobanks and sample repositories – relevance to Personalised Medicine, 2011; Sarojini, Goy, Pecora, & Suh, 2012). Other data banks refer to data collections generated by specific projects such as the ENCODE Project, which aims to establish an ENCyclopedia Of DNA Elements (Consortium, 2004). One of the challenges is to connect the dispersed data collections world-wide and to facilitate accessing, viewing, and analyzing

them by creating the necessary infrastructures and by developing easy-to-use and well-documented tools, as well as by establishing a controlled vocabulary to enhance functional interpretation (Nakazato, Bono, & Takagi, 2011). In the context of integromics, several such efforts exist. We mention for instance GeneWeaver, a web-based software system that brings together a large data archive from diverse functional genomics data with a suite of combinatorial tools in an interactive environment (Jay & Chesler, 2014), and 3Omics, a web-based systems biology tool for analysis, integration and visualization of human transcriptomic, proteomic and metabolomic data (Kuo, Tian, & Tseng, 2013). "Big data" comes with several computational issues. Virtually all methods in integrated omics settings are hampered by small n (sample size, number of individuals) and large p (number of measurements, collected data features) problems and require adequate computational infrastructures. Advanced preprocessing and expressing the most computationally intensive part of the algorithm in terms of large matrix operations may overcome some of the computational burden (Shabalin, 2012).

The more data are collected, the higher the potential of them being incomplete in some sense. Unobserved or partially observed data points due to technical reasons or those associated with the individual's trait, erroneous measurements, etc., may seriously hamper the credibility of analytical results when not properly addressed. Missing data involves situations in which certain planned measurements are unobserved. The term incomplete data is generally used when measurements are observed but recorded on a rougher (coarser) scale; missing data can be seen as a particular aspect of coarsened data. Also measurements with error can be thought of as incomplete in that the true value, and hence the discrepancy between true and observed values, is unobserved (Van Steen, Laird, Markel, & Molenberghs, 2007). Incomplete data handling has a long tradition in biostatistics (e.g., (Hopke, Liu, & Rubin, 2001; Little et al., 2012;

Molenberghs et al., 2014; Rubin & 1976; Rubin, Witkiewitz, Andre, & Reilly, 2007)). In population genetics, far too often missing data are dealt with by removing individuals or allelic positions that are affected by them (Ferretti, Raineri, & Ramos-Onsins, 2012). Removing individuals or bases with missing alleles in NGS data would imply a huge loss of information and may actually bias the results when the data are not missing completely at random (Rubin & 6, 1976). Estimators and tests need to be developed such that missing data is adequately taken into account (see (Ferretti et al., 2012) for an example in population genetics). The issue of missing data in genetic association studies has primarily been discussed in the context of haplotype phase inference (Browning, 2008; Browning & Browning, 2007; Li & Li, 2008; Lin, Chakravarti, & Cutler, 2004; Stephens & Scheet, 2005) and genotype imputation for genome-wide association studies (Ellinghaus, Schreiber, Franke, & Nothnagel, 2009; Howie et al., 2012; Howie et al., 2011; Howie et al., 2009; Marchini & Howie, 2008, 2010; Marchini et al., 2007; Southam et al., 2011; Spencer et al., 2009). Integrated data analyses are particularly challenging (Nie, Wu, Culley, Scholten, & Zhang, 2007) and effectively handling incomplete data in those settings will require alternatives to classic and well-established incomplete data handling via statistical methods. Also, the optimality and feasibility of specific missing data handling approaches may depend on the chosen analytic tool to solve the research question of interest. See for instance (Marlin, 2008) for discussions on missing data handling in machine learning contexts. In omics analyses, imputation based on machine learning methods (e.g., k-nearest neighbour or self-organizing maps) are becoming increasingly popular (Jerez et al., 2010; Lakshminarayan, Harp, Goldman, & Samad, 1996; Richman, Trafalis, & Adrianto, 2009). These may actually outperform imputation methods based on statistical procedures (Jerez et al., 2010). Notably, the advantages of integrative analyses can be exploited to actually estimate

missing data, as was done in for instance (F. Li, Nie, Wu, Qiao, & Zhang, 2011).

Whether data for integration are similar or dissimilar, they are unavoidably subject to different levels of noise. Therefore, the concept of weighting data sources with quality and/or informativity scores or weighting features with a measure of confidence may become an essential component of the integrated analysis framework. Measurement error techniques frequently pop up in epidemiology and biostatistics (Apanasovich, Carroll, & Maity, 2009; Carroll, 1989; Carroll, Delaigle, & Hall, 2009; Carroll, Roeder, & Wasserman, 1999; Carroll & Stefanski, 1994; Clayton, 1994; Freedman, Fainberg, Kipnis, Midthune, & Carroll, 2004; Freedman, Midthune, Carroll, & Kipnis, 2008; Ma, Hart, Janicki, & Carroll, 2011; Wong, Day, Bashir, & Duffy, 1999; Wong, Day, & Wareham, 1999). They are increasingly being used in genetic epidemiology, where they can be combined to a growing body of analytic tools (Aschard et al., 2012) to investigate genome-wide gene-environment interactions (Lobach, Fan, & Carroll, 2010; Lobach, Mallick, & Carroll, 2011; Wong, Day, Luan, Chan, & Wareham, 2003; Wong, Day, Luan, & Wareham, 2004). Despite increased performance on genotyping accuracy, genotyping errors still exist. Also, diagnosis errors may invalidate genotype-phenotype association studies. Cooley et al. (Cooley, Clark, & Page, 2011) have shown that a percent sample size increase of approximately 40%-57% (respectively 19%-36%) is needed to restore power caused by a 1% genotype (respectively diagnosis) error, depending on whether the mode of inheritance is additive, dominant, recessive or multiplicative (Cooley, Clark, Folsom, & Page, 2010). Using different modes of inheritance usually involves different variable coding schemes. Little attention is given to selecting the most optimal coding scheme for variables included in an integrated omics analysis. Often genotypes are coded as 0, 1 and 2 and these allele counts are tested for an additive (dosage) effect with the normalized gene expression value.

Different measurement types lead to different measurement scales and hence scale-difference corrections need to be implemented.

Population stratification, defined as the presence of systematic differences in allele frequencies between subpopulations in a population, has several sources. One of these is genetic ancestry diversity. It is well-known that population stratification can confound the relationship between a genetic marker and disease. In the context of genome-wide association studies, several techniques exist to deal with the potential confounding effect of combining heterogeneous populations of different genetic ancestry (Bouaziz, Ambroise, & Guedj, 2011; L. Liu, Zhang, Liu, & Arendt, 2013; Price, Zaitlen, Reich, & Patterson, 2010; Sarasua, Collins, Williamson, Satten, & Allen, 2009). Population differences may also play some role in the magnitude and direction of eQTLs, although this seems to be a relatively rare occurrence (Stranger et al., 2012). Also, evidence exists that DNA methylation differences are present in distinct human populations (Heyn et al., 2013). More work is needed to investigate the extent of population stratification in different omics or inter-omics analyses and/or how several omics may contribute to understanding population stratification. These studies are currently limited, in part due to the unavailability of sufficiently large samples that have been typed for >2 omics. Multiple omics can also be used to identify subgroups of fairly homogeneous patient groups. Integromics profiles, rather than profiles based on genome-wide SNP data, are expected to give an improved characterization of a patient. Also these omics-driven patient substructures may confound a patient-control comparison study.

Lastly, replication and validation studies may give further credibility to results obtained from analytic tools (Konig, 2011). However, as the authors of (Konig, 2011) rightfully state, a replicated finding does not guarantee the finding to be true. Inversely, a non-replication may be due to a false negative or chance finding in the replication analysis. In integrated analysis studies, independent data for replication will virtually be non-existent, due to data heterogeneity. In GWA studies, it is expected that every significant result is validated in a second large cohort with genome-wide significance for the identified variants. The stringency becomes somewhat weaker when genome-wide gene-gene interaction studies are concerned. However, non-validated results may indicate different mechanisms playing a role in different subgroups of individuals and may actually trigger in-depth investigations about the influence of sample heterogeneity on the initial findings. In integromics, no clear definition exists for validation. In fact, validation seems to have different meanings depending on the omics subfield (Ioannidis & Khoury, 2011). A consensus approach for all omics and integromics is needed and first steps into that direction are emerging (Leek, Taub, & Rasgon, 2012). Even with such a consensus available, building and validating predictors for human complex traits in an integrated way will not be an easy task. There are many possible biases involved in such analyses that may decrease the reproducibility of results. Technical biases, associated with the experimental protocols that were used to generate the data, are probably among the easiest to remideate in the future. Alternatively, confidence is retrieved from experimental studies. Deliverables of working groups around the world (for instance, STATEGRA - http://stategra. eu/) that develop novel methods for experimental design in integrated omics studies and methods for experimental validation on integrated omics models, will be key and will complement parallel activities on statistical validation and replication protocols for integrated omics analyses.

"I Have a Dream ..."

Since 2005, GWAS using hundreds of thousands of SNPS have become popular strategies to unravel the genetic basis of a variety of human complex traits. The results of these studies are of little use when no reasonable interpretation can be given to them. Conservation across species is a popular proxy for important functionality (Himes et al., 2013; Wei et al., 2007; Y. Zhang et al., 2010). Interestingly, a recent study of Kindt and co-authors (Kindt, Navarro, Semple, & Haley, 2013) showed that only modest enrichment of trait-associated SNPs in conserved regions can be found. These authors furthermore showed that SNPs associated with a large number of annotation classes (including regulatory features, genic regions, patterns of histone modification) are more likely to be identified in genome-wide association screening as opposed to SNPs that cannot be annotated to any of the classes identified by the authors. The most influential functional annotations for trait-association status of genome-wide significant variants appeared to be annotations associated with chromatin state together with prior knowledge of the existence of a local eQTL. Over the last few years, several authors have indicated the limitations (apart from the advantages) of GWAS (Du, Xie, Chang, Han, & Cao, 2012; Riancho, 2012; Roukos, 2009; Tan, 2010). In general, findings from a GWAS, even in the presence of a functional interpretation, do not lend themselves to direct application to disease prevention or treatment of disease. A plausible reason is that there is more to learn about complex diseases than simply looking at collections of genomes via structural variations, such as SNPs. In reality, several omics data types exist (as we discussed before), including the exposome (Wild, 2005), the virome (Foxman & Iwasaki, 2011; Wylie, Weinstock, & Storch, 2012) and the microbiome (Clemente, Ursell, Parfrey, & Knight, 2012; Frick & Autenrieth, 2013) that all appear to have an alleged role in complex disease. In addition, several levels of resolution or granularity exist, from ecosystems, populations and organisms, over organs and tissues to cells and molecules. Hence, integration may involve a number of these levels, and/or the involvement of different omics data types as well as clinical or patient history data (Mardinoglu et al., 2013;

Mayer et al., 2011; Turinsky et al., 2008). These integrated analysis efforts may enhance drug target discovery (Penrod, Cowper-Sal-lari, & Moore, 2011) or substantially improve the clinical management of cancer and other complex diseases.

As biological complexity increases, the need to integrate increases as well. Pancreatic ductal adenocarcinoma (PDAC) provides a unique example of this concept. PDAC is the most common type of pancreatic cancer. It is a fatal orphan disease that, contrary to its low population incidence, has a high mortality rate worldwide. This is the unique cancer that did not improve its fatal prognosis over the last decades. The high mortality resulting from PDAC is mainly due to the difficulty in making early diagnosis, which is complicated by the absence of specific symptoms and biomarkers of early disease, as well as the aggressive nature of the disease. Incidence is slightly increasing in Westernized countries. Known environmental and genetic risk factors of PDAC explain only about 40% of all tumors. Unfortunately, primary prevention is not currently feasible because of the lack of knowledge of most factors contributing to PDAC complex etiological scenario. The difficulties in defining a high-risk population partly explain the unsuccessfully screening interventions conducted until present.

Among the different non-genetic factors reported to be associated with PDAC, smoking is the best established. About 30% of the disease is attributed to tobacco, with a reported odds ratio around 2 (Adami HO, 2002; Anderson, Mack, & Silverman, 2006; Fernandez, La Vecchia, D'Avanzo, Negri, & Franceschi, 1994). While the mechanisms tobacco impacts on pancreas carcinogenesis are not clearly identified, oxidative stress and chronic inflammation is the candidate pathway. Among the other, definitive and probable, factors associated with PDAC are type II diabetes, obesity, chronic pancreatitis, trace elements, blood group, and allergies/asthma (Amaral et al., 2012; Arslan et al., 2010; Huxley, Ansary-Moghaddam, Berrington de Gonzalez, Barzi, & Woodward,

2005; Lowenfels et al., 1993). Associations with PDAC risk are less clear for other environmental exposures such as infection with Helicobacter pylori, organochlorine pesticides, periodontitis, alcohol, coffee, some types of food, and passive exposure to cigarette smoke (Anderson et al., 2006; Michaud, Joshipura, Giovannucci, & Fuchs, 2007; Risch, 2012; Stolzenberg-Solomon et al., 2003). Again, inflammation seems to be the mechanism of action of most of these factors. While these exposures probably do not present individually in the population, epidemiological studies used to approach them though a "one-by-one basis" in the association and prediction studies; a too simplistic strategy when considering the reality. This fact, jointly with the knowledge of the presence of correlations among some of these factors, make of integration of data at the epidemiological level a must to mimic biology (upper part of Figure 2).

Regarding genetic risk, it is estimated that a 36% of PDAC cases may be attributable to hereditary factors (Lichtenstein et al., 2000). Having a family history of PDAC is associated with a 2- to

3-fold higher risk for tumour development and has an estimated attributable risk of about 10% (Fernandez et al., 1994). Germline alterations in BRCA1, BRCA2, PLAB2, APC, ATM, and SPINK explain low percentage of the familial aggregation of PDAC (Hahn et al., 2003; Jones et al., 2009; L. Li et al., 2009; Mocci et al., 2013; Real et al., 2002; Tischkowitz et al., 2009) the vast majority of familial pancreas cancer being of unknown causes. Genome-wide association studies allowed characterizing the low-penetrance genetic susceptibility of PDAC, the top variants being located in ABO, NR5A2, CLPTM1L, RNY1P8-MARK2P12, SLC1A1, BAI3, ARID1B, TFRC, DAB2, FAM19A5, NR, TFF1, and BACH1 (Amundadottir et al., 2009; G. M. Petersen et al., 2010; Wolpin et al., 2010; Wu et al., 2012). Interestingly, some of these genes are involved in inflammatory-related pathways (Wolpin et al., 2010). Altogether points to a polygenetic disease with several common and probably rare, variants of different penetrance, interacting among them and with non-genetic exposures contributing to PDAC

Figure 2. Chronic inflammation and pancreas cancer
As the complexity of disease underlying biological mechanisms increases so does the need to adopt an interdisciplinary or trans-disciplinary approach when disentangling disease risk factors.

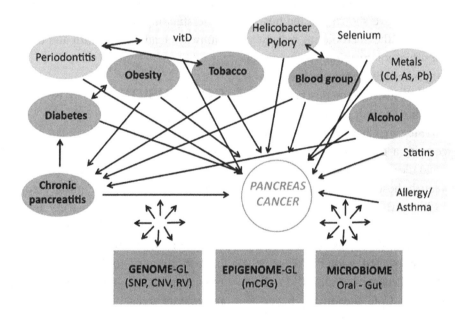

development. Therefore, a further characterization of the genomic component would provide valuable data to be integrated with that coming from epidemiological factors (Figure 2; bottom part).

The observations of an association between variations in the oral microbiome and both chronic pancreatitis and PDAC (Farrell et al., 2012) and between high levels of plasma antibodies against the periodontal pathogen Porphyromonas gingivalis and a higher risk of PDAC (Michaud et al., 2013), raise the potential role of microbiome and strengthen the inflammatory hypothesis in pancreatic carcinogenesis. In recent years, it has been shown that the microorganisms living in the human body interact with their host, playing an important role in its physiology. It has been reported that such interactions can affect important cellular processes like inflammation, immune defense, and metabolism, among others (Plottel & Blaser, 2011). Until recently, the study of the human microbiome through metagenomics was limited by technical problems and high costs. These types of studies are now more feasible, allowing the analysis of the interactions between hosts and the microbiome. However these associations could be masked by other factors. For example, it has been reported that non-genetic factors like diet and obesity can modify the microbiome. Similarly, studies in mice and human populations have shown that the host genotype has an effect on the microbiome, mainly by influencing microbial colonization. A previous study reported a high similarity in bacterial profiles between monozygotic twins, more modest between dizygotic twins, and showing little similarity among unrelated children (Stewart, Chadwick, & Murray, 2005). More recently, a cases-control study of Crohn´s disease and ulcerative colitis reported an association between the host genotype and shifts in microbial composition, which in turn was associated with disease phenotype (Frank et al., 2011).

Only one study has explored germline DNA epigenetic makers associated with PDAC at a whole-genome level (Pedersen et al., 2011). In an exploration of 1,505 CpG sites in 132 never-smoker PDAC patients and 60 never-smoker healthy controls as a training set and 240 PDAC cases and 240 matched controls as a test set, a prediction model with five CpG sites (IL10_P348, LCN2_P86, ZAP70_P220, AIM2_P624, TAL1_P817) provided moderate discriminative power. Interestingly, the authors also observed that methylation differences at certain CpG sites were partially attributable to genetic variation (Pedersen2011).

Altogether, these findings, along with the known complexity of PDAC development, make evident that a simple approach is not sufficient to characterize PDAC, which occur within a context of interaction between multiple genetic and non-genetic risk factors, chronic inflammation playing an important role. An integrative approach is fundamental to understand not only the epidemiologic, genomic, metagenomic, and epigenomic variation associated with PDAC, but also to understand how these factors interact among them to ultimately affect the development of the disease (inferior level of Figure 2). Data (epidemiological, *omics*, clinical, and pathological) integration is capital in this endeavour; also, hypotheses (candidate and exploratory strategies) and study designs (observational and experimental) "integration," will open new opportunities in understanding the determinants, risk factors and pathways leading to health and disease.

CONCLUSION

It leaves no doubt that there is a clear motive and opportunity for data integration. Notably, there is a conceptual difference between integrated analysis as in multidisciplinary approaches and integrated analysis as in truly interdisciplinary or even trans-disciplinary approaches. There is a future for all, yet the main challenge is to develop interdisciplinary methodologies and tools that require more than merely aggregating expertise in separate areas.

Currently, a lot of attention is given to (functional) annotation and pathway identification, and understanding the association between pairs of omics, or the integration of two omics data types to understand a(n) (intermediate) phenotypic response. Fewer attention is given to investigating to what extent multiple omics are able to characterize populations or patient groups (i.e., subphenotyping) and how to include such knowledge in classic analysis approaches with admixed or structured collections of individuals. Identifying and describing homogeneous strata will become increasingly important as integrated omics studies will need large sample sizes that can only be attained by joining forces over multiple centers and even multiple consortiums.

In this contribution, we have restricted attention to methods that can deal with individual-based information, keeping in mind that multiple data types will increasingly become available for the same set of individuals and that these data, undoubtedly, contain a wealth of information for improved personalized medicine (Shimokawa et al., 2010) and public health (Auffray et al., 2013). Of interest are methods that are flexible in integrating more than 2 dissimilar data sources, where measurements on different scales are easily accommodated. Ideally, hierarchies between data sources or non-linear relationships between data points are accounted for as well. So far, the application of integrative analytical methods has already enhanced functional interpretation and has led to a better understanding of biological mechanisms underlying complex disease traits. However, the adopted techniques are still too global to provide full functional explanations at a molecular level.

Given the increasing attention given to personalized medicine, and given the ongoing efforts to further improve data generation technologies, we expect to see a growing number of genomic, epigenomic, transcriptomic, proteomic and metobolomic data collections on the same panel of individuals. In theory, these and other omics collections will allow the analysis of between and within *omics* relationships at the background of an individual's exposome and microbiome, or making links to an individual's phenome. In practice, a series of challenges will need to be overcome. These challenges include protocol development for standardizing data generation and pre-processing or cleansing in integrative analysis contexts, development of computationally efficient analytic tools to extract knowledge from dissimilar data types to answer particular research questions, the establishment of validation and replication procedures, and tools to visualize results. Unprecedented opportunities lie ahead!

ACKNOWLEDGMENT

We acknowledge the participants of the COST Action BM1204 (http://www.cost.eu/domains_actions/bmbs/Actions/BM1204). In addition, the first author acknowledges support by the the Fonds de la Recherche Scientifique FNRS (Convention n° T.0180.13). The scientific responsibility rests with the authors.

REFERENCES

Abdi, H., Williams, L.J., & Valentin, D. (2013). Multiple factor analysis: Principal component analysis for multitable and multiblock data sets component analysis for multitable and multiblock data sets. *WIREs Comput. Stat.* doi: 10.1002/wics.124

Adami, H. O., Hunter, D., & Trichopoulos, D. (2002). *Textbook of Cancer Epidemiology*. New York: Oxford University Press.

Aerts, S., Lambrechts, D., Maity, S., Van Loo, P., Coessens, B., & De Smet, F. et al. (2006). Gene prioritization through genomic data fusion. *Nature Biotechnology*, 24(5), 537–544. doi:10.1038/nbt1203 PMID:16680138

Amaral, A. F., Porta, M., Silverman, D. T., Milne, R. L., Kogevinas, M., & Rothman, N. et al. (2012). Pancreatic cancer risk and levels of trace elements. *Gut*, *61*(11), 1583–1588. doi:10.1136/gutjnl-2011-301086 PMID:22184070

Amundadottir, L., Kraft, P., Stolzenberg-Solomon, R. Z., Fuchs, C. S., Petersen, G. M., & Arslan, A. A. et al. (2009). Genome-wide association study identifies variants in the ABO locus associated with susceptibility to pancreatic cancer. *Nature Genetics*, *41*(9), 986–990. doi:10.1038/ng.429 PMID:19648918

Anderson, K. E., Mack, T. M., & Silverman, D. T. (2006). Pancreatic cancer. In Textbook of Cancer Epidemiology (2nd ed., pp. 333-343). Oxford, UK: Oxford University Press.

Apanasovich, T. V., Carroll, R. J., & Maity, A. (2009). SIMEX and standard error estimation in semiparametric measurement error models. *Electron J Stat*, *3*(0), 318–348. doi:10.1214/08-EJS341 PMID:19609371

Arslan, A. A., Helzlsouer, K. J., Kooperberg, C., Shu, X. O., Steplowski, E., & Bueno-de-Mesquita, H. B. et al.Pancreatic Cancer Cohort, Consortium. (2010). Anthropometric measures, body mass index, and pancreatic cancer: A pooled analysis from the Pancreatic Cancer Cohort Consortium (PanScan). *Archives of Internal Medicine*, *170*(9), 791–802. doi:10.1001/archinternmed.2010.63 PMID:20458087

Aschard, H., Lutz, S., Maus, B., Duell, E. J., Fingerlin, T. E., & Chatterjee, N. et al. (2012). Challenges and opportunities in genome-wide environmental interaction (GWEI) studies. *Human Genetics*, *131*(10), 1591–1613. doi:10.1007/s00439-012-1192-0 PMID:22760307

Aten, J. E., Fuller, T. F., Lusis, A. J., & Horvath, S. (2008). Using genetic markers to orient the edges in quantitative trait networks: The NEO software. *BMC Systems Biology*, *2*(1), 34. doi:10.1186/1752-0509-2-34 PMID:18412962

Auffray, C., Caulfield, T., Khoury, M. J., Lupski, J. R., Schwab, M., & Veenstra, T. (2013). 2012 highlights in translational 'omics. *Genome Medicine*, *5*(1), 10. PMID:23369291

Avogadri, R., & Valentini, G. (2009). Fuzzy ensemble clustering based on random projections for DNA microarray data analysis. *Artificial Intelligence in Medicine*, *45*(2-3), 173–183. doi:10.1016/j.artmed.2008.07.014 PMID:18801650

Baker, M. (2013). Big biology: The 'omes puzzle. *Nature*, *494*(7438), 416–419. doi:10.1038/494416a PMID:23446398

Bouaziz, M., Ambroise, C., & Guedj, M. (2011). Accounting for population stratification in practice: A comparison of the main strategies dedicated to genome-wide association studies. *PLoS ONE*, *6*(12), e28845. doi:10.1371/journal.pone.0028845 PMID:22216125

Bouchez, D., & Hofte, H. (1998). Functional genomics in plants. *Plant Physiology*, *118*(3), 725–732. doi:10.1104/pp.118.3.725 PMID:9808716

Brazma, A. (2009). Minimum Information About a Microarray Experiment (MIAME)--successes, failures, challenges. *The Scientific World Journal*, *9*, 420–423. doi:10.1100/tsw.2009.57 PMID:19484163

Brazma, A., Hingamp, P., Quackenbush, J., Sherlock, G., Spellman, P., & Stoeckert, C. et al. (2001). Minimum information about a microarray experiment (MIAME)-toward standards for microarray data. *Nature Genetics*, *29*(4), 365–371. doi:10.1038/ng1201-365 PMID:11726920

Browning, S. R. (2008). Missing data imputation and haplotype phase inference for genome-wide association studies. *Human Genetics*, *124*(5), 439–450. doi:10.1007/s00439-008-0568-7 PMID:18850115

Browning, S. R., & Browning, B. L. (2007). Rapid and accurate haplotype phasing and missing-data inference for whole-genome association studies by use of localized haplotype clustering. *American Journal of Human Genetics*, *81*(5), 1084–1097. doi:10.1086/521987 PMID:17924348

Carroll, R. J. (1989). Covariance analysis in generalized linear measurement error models. *Statistics in Medicine*, *8*(9), 1075–1093. doi:10.1002/sim.4780080907 PMID:2678349

Carroll, R. J., Delaigle, A., & Hall, P. (2009). Nonparametric Prediction in Measurement Error Models. *Journal of the American Statistical Association*, *104*(487), 993–1014. doi:10.1198/jasa.2009.tm07543 PMID:20448838

Carroll, R. J., Roeder, K., & Wasserman, L. (1999). Flexible parametric measurement error models. *Biometrics*, *55*(1), 44–54. doi:10.1111/j.0006-341X.1999.00044.x PMID:11318178

Carroll, R. J., & Stefanski, L. A. (1994). Measurement error, instrumental variables and corrections for attenuation with applications to meta-analyses. *Statistics in Medicine*, *13*(12), 1265–1282. doi:10.1002/sim.4780131208 PMID:7973207

Chelala, C., Khan, A., & Lemoine, N. R. (2009). SNPnexus: A web database for functional annotation of newly discovered and public domain single nucleotide polymorphisms. *Bioinformatics (Oxford, England)*, *25*(5), 655–661. doi:10.1093/bioinformatics/btn653 PMID:19098027

Chen, C. C., Schwender, H., Keith, J., Nunkesser, R., Mengersen, K., & Macrossan, P. (2011). Methods for identifying SNP interactions: A review on variations of Logic Regression, Random Forest and Bayesian logistic regression. *IEEE/ACM Transactions on Computational Biology and Bioinformatics*, *8*(6), 1580–1591. doi:10.1109/TCBB.2011.46 PMID:21383421

Chen, Y., Wu, X., & Jiang, R. (2013). Integrating human omics data to prioritize candidate genes. *BMC Medical Genomics*, *6*(1), 57. doi:10.1186/1755-8794-6-57 PMID:24344781

Choi, H., & Pavelka, N. (2011). When one and one gives more than two: Challenges and opportunities of integrative omics. *Frontiers in Genetics*, *2*, 105. PMID:22303399

Ciampi, A., Chang, C., Hogg, S., & McKinney, S. (1987). Recursive partition: a versatile method for exploratory data analysis in biostatistics. In *Proceedings from Joshi Festschrift* (pp. 23–50). Amsterdam: North-Holland. doi:10.1007/978-94-009-4794-8_2

Clayton, D. (1994). Measurement error: Effects and remedies in nutritional epidemiology. *The Proceedings of the Nutrition Society*, *53*(1), 37–42. doi:10.1079/PNS19940007 PMID:8029234

Clemente, J. C., Ursell, L. K., Parfrey, L. W., & Knight, R. (2012). The impact of the gut microbiota on human health: An integrative view. *Cell*, *148*(6), 1258–1270. doi:10.1016/j.cell.2012.01.035 PMID:22424233

Colyer, H. A., Armstrong, R. N., & Mills, K. I. (2012). Microarray for epigenetic changes: Gene expression arrays. *Methods in Molecular Biology (Clifton, N.J.)*, *863*, 319–328. doi:10.1007/978-1-61779-612-8_20 PMID:22359303

Consortium, Encode Project. (2004). The ENCODE (ENCyclopedia Of DNA Elements) Project. *Science, 306*(5696), 636-640.

Cooley, P., Clark, R., Folsom, R., & Page, G. (2010). Genetic Inheritance and Genome Wide Association Statistical Test Performance. *J Proteomics Bioinform*, *3*, 330–334.

Cooley, P., Clark, R. F., & Page, G. (2011). The Influence of Errors Inherent in Genome Wide Association Studies (GWAS) in Relation To Single Gene Models. *J Proteomics Bioinform*, *4*, 138–144.

Costantini, P., Linting, M., & Porzio, G. C. (2010). Mining performance data through nonlinear PCA with optimal scaling. *Applied Stochastic Models in Business and Industry*, *26*(1), 85–101. doi:10.1002/asmb.771

Cotton, R. G., Al Aqeel, A. I., Al-Mulla, F., Carrera, P., Claustres, M., & Ekong, R. et al. (2009). Capturing all disease-causing mutations for clinical and research use: Toward an effortless system for the Human Variome Project. *Genetics in Medicine*, *11*(12), 843–849. doi:10.1097/GIM.0b013e3181c371c5 PMID:20010362

Cotton, R. G., Appelbe, W., Auerbach, A. D., Becker, K., Bodmer, W., & Boone, D. J. et al. (2007). Recommendations of the 2006 Human Variome Project meeting. *Nature Genetics*, *39*(4), 433–436. doi:10.1038/ng2024 PMID:17392799

Cotton, R. G., Auerbach, A. D., Axton, M., Barash, C. I., Berkovic, S. F., & Brookes, A. J. et al. (2008). GENETICS. The Human Variome Project. *Science*, *322*(5903), 861–862. doi:10.1126/science.1167363 PMID:18988827

Cotton, R. G., & Macrae, F. A. (2010). Reducing the burden of inherited disease: The Human Variome Project. *The Medical Journal of Australia*, *192*(11), 628–629. PMID:20528712

Cotton, R. G., Vihinen, M., & den Dunnen, J. T. (2011). Genetic tests need the Human Variome Project. *Genet Test Mol Biomarkers*, *15*(1-2), 3. doi:10.1089/gtmb.2010.1515 PMID:21275652

Daemen, A., Gevaert, O., Ojeda, F., Debucquoy, A., Suykens, J. A., & Sempoux, C. et al. (2009). A kernel-based integration of genome-wide data for clinical decision support. *Genome Medicine*, *1*(4), 39. doi:10.1186/gm39 PMID:19356222

Dayem Ullah, A. Z., Lemoine, N. R., & Chelala, C. (2012). SNPnexus: A web server for functional annotation of novel and publicly known genetic variants (2012 update). *Nucleic Acids Res, 40*(Web Server issue), W65-70.

Dayem Ullah, A. Z., Lemoine, N. R., & Chelala, C. (2013). A practical guide for the functional annotation of genetic variations using SNPnexus. *Briefings in Bioinformatics*, *14*(4), 437–447. doi:10.1093/bib/bbt004 PMID:23395730

De Bie, T., Tranchevent, L. C., van Oeffelen, L. M., & Moreau, Y. (2007). Kernel-based data fusion for gene prioritization. *Bioinformatics (Oxford, England)*, *23*(13), i125–i132. doi:10.1093/bioinformatics/btm187 PMID:17646288

De Keersmaecker, S. C., Thijs, I. M., Vanderleyden, J., & Marchal, K. (2006). Integration of omics data: How well does it work for bacteria? *Molecular Microbiology*, *62*(5), 1239–1250. doi:10.1111/j.1365-2958.2006.05453.x PMID:17040488

Deutsch, E. W., Ball, C. A., Berman, J. J., Bova, G. S., Brazma, A., & Bumgarner, R. E. et al. (2008). Minimum information specification for in situ hybridization and immunohistochemistry experiments (MISFISHIE). *Nature Biotechnology*, *26*(3), 305–312. doi:10.1038/nbt1391 PMID:18327244

Deutsch, E. W., Ball, C. A., Bova, G. S., Brazma, A., Bumgarner, R. E., & Campbell, D. et al. (2006). Development of the Minimum Information Specification for In Situ Hybridization and Immunohistochemistry Experiments (MISFISHIE). *OMICS: A Journal of Integrative Biology*, *10*(2), 205–208. doi:10.1089/omi.2006.10.205 PMID:16901227

Do, C. B., Hinds, D. A., Francke, U., & Eriksson, N. (2012). Comparison of family history and SNPs for predicting risk of complex disease. *PLOS Genetics*, *8*(10), e1002973. doi:10.1371/journal.pgen.1002973 PMID:23071447

Du, Y., Xie, J., Chang, W., Han, Y., & Cao, G. (2012). Genome-wide association studies: Inherent limitations and future challenges. *France Médecine*, *6*(4), 444–450. PMID:23124883

Eckhardt, F., Beck, S., Gut, I. G., & Berlin, K. (2004). Future potential of the Human Epigenome Project. *Expert Review of Molecular Diagnostics*, *4*(5), 609–618. doi:10.1586/14737159.4.5.609 PMID:15347255

Ellinghaus, D., Schreiber, S., Franke, A., & Nothnagel, M. (2009). Current software for genotype imputation. *Human Genomics*, *3*(4), 371–380. PMID:19706367

Elliott, H. R., Tillin, T., McArdle, W. L., Ho, K., Duggirala, A., & Frayling, T. M. et al. (2014). Differences in smoking associated DNA methylation patterns in South Asians and Europeans. *Clin Epigenetics*, *6*(1), 4. doi:10.1186/1868-7083-6-4 PMID:24485148

Escofier, B., & Pagès, J. (1990). Multiple factor analysis. *Computational Statistics & Data Analysis*, *18*(1), 121–140. doi:10.1016/0167-9473(94)90135-X

Fairfax, B. P., Makino, S., Radhakrishnan, J., Plant, K., Leslie, S., & Dilthey, A. et al. (2012). Genetics of gene expression in primary immune cells identifies cell type-specific master regulators and roles of HLA alleles. *Nature Genetics*, *44*(5), 502–510. doi:10.1038/ng.2205 PMID:22446964

Farrell, J. J., Zhang, L., Zhou, H., Chia, D., Elashoff, D., & Akin, D. et al. (2012). Variations of oral microbiota are associated with pancreatic diseases including pancreatic cancer. *Gut*, *61*(4), 582–588. doi:10.1136/gutjnl-2011-300784 PMID:21994333

Fawcett, J. (2013). Thoughts about multidisciplinary, interdisciplinary, and transdisciplinary research. *Nursing Science Quarterly*, *26*(4), 376–379. doi:10.1177/0894318413500408 PMID:24085679

Fernandez, E., La Vecchia, C., D'Avanzo, B., Negri, E., & Franceschi, S. (1994). Family history and the risk of liver, gallbladder, and pancreatic cancer. *Cancer Epidemiology, Biomarkers & Prevention*, *3*(3), 209–212. PMID:8019368

Ferretti, L., Raineri, E., & Ramos-Onsins, S. (2012). Neutrality tests for sequences with missing data. *Genetics*, *191*(4), 1397–1401. doi:10.1534/genetics.112.139949 PMID:22661328

Feuk, L., Carson, A. R., & Scherer, S. W. (2006). Structural variation in the human genome. *Nature Reviews. Genetics*, *7*(2), 85–97. doi:10.1038/nrg1767 PMID:16418744

Field, D., Sansone, S. A., Collis, A., Booth, T., Dukes, P., & Gregurick, S. K. et al. (2009). Megascience. 'Omics data sharing. *Science*, *326*(5950), 234–236. doi:10.1126/science.1180598 PMID:19815759

Flutre, T., Wen, X., Pritchard, J., & Stephens, M. (2013). A statistical framework for joint eQTL analysis in multiple tissues. *PLOS Genetics*, *9*(5), e1003486. doi:10.1371/journal.pgen.1003486 PMID:23671422

Fodeh, S. J., Brandt, C., Luong, T. B., Haddad, A., Schultz, M., Murphy, T., & Krauthammer, M. (2013). Complementary ensemble clustering of biomedical data. *Journal of Biomedical Informatics*, *46*(3), 436–443. doi:10.1016/j.jbi.2013.02.001 PMID:23454721

Foxman, E. F., & Iwasaki, A. (2011). Genome-virome interactions: Examining the role of common viral infections in complex disease. *Nature Reviews. Microbiology*, *9*(4), 254–264. doi:10.1038/nrmicro2541 PMID:21407242

Frank, D. N., Robertson, C. E., Hamm, C. M., Kpadeh, Z., Zhang, T., & Chen, H. et al. (2011). Disease phenotype and genotype are associated with shifts in intestinal-associated microbiota in inflammatory bowel diseases. *Inflammatory Bowel Diseases*, *17*(1), 179–184. doi:10.1002/ibd.21339 PMID:20839241

Freedman, L. S., Fainberg, V., Kipnis, V., Midthune, D., & Carroll, R. J. (2004). A new method for dealing with measurement error in explanatory variables of regression models. *Biometrics*, *60*(1), 172–181. doi:10.1111/j.0006-341X.2004.00164.x PMID:15032787

Freedman, L. S., Midthune, D., Carroll, R. J., & Kipnis, V. (2008). A comparison of regression calibration, moment reconstruction and imputation for adjusting for covariate measurement error in regression. *Statistics in Medicine*, *27*(25), 5195–5216. doi:10.1002/sim.3361 PMID:18680172

Frick, J. S., & Autenrieth, I. B. (2013). The gut microflora and its variety of roles in health and disease. *Current Topics in Microbiology and Immunology*, *358*, 273–289. doi:10.1007/82_2012_217 PMID:22476557

Fu, J., Wolfs, M. G., Deelen, P., Westra, H. J., Fehrmann, R. S., & Te Meerman, G. J. et al. (2012). Unraveling the regulatory mechanisms underlying tissue-dependent genetic variation of gene expression. *PLOS Genetics*, *8*(1), e1002431. doi:10.1371/journal.pgen.1002431 PMID:22275870

Fukushima, A., Kusano, M., Redestig, H., Arita, M., & Saito, K. (2009). Integrated omics approaches in plant systems biology. *Current Opinion in Chemical Biology*, *13*(5-6), 532–538. doi:10.1016/j.cbpa.2009.09.022 PMID:19837627

Gaffney, D. J. (2013). Global properties and functional complexity of human gene regulatory variation. *PLOS Genetics*, *9*(5), e1003501. doi:10.1371/journal.pgen.1003501 PMID:23737752

Gamazon, E. R., Huang, R. S., Dolan, M. E., Cox, N. J., & Im, H. K. (2012). Integrative genomics: Quantifying significance of phenotype-genotype relationships from multiple sources of high-throughput data. *Frontiers in Genetics*, *3*, 202. PMID:23755062

Geraci, F., Leoncini, M., Montangero, M., Pellegrini, M., & Renda, M. E. (2009). K-Boost: A scalable algorithm for high-quality clustering of microarray gene expression data. *Journal of Computational Biology*, *16*(6), 859–873. doi:10.1089/cmb.2008.0201 PMID:19522668

Gibbs, D. L., Gralinski, L., Baric, R. S., & McWeeney, S. K. (2014). Multi-omic network signatures of disease. *Frontiers in Genetics*, *4*, 309. doi:10.3389/fgene.2013.00309 PMID:24432028

González, I., Déjean, S., Martin, P. G. P., Goncalves, O., Besse, P., & Baccini, A. (2009). Highlighting relationships between heterogeneous biological data through graphical displays based on regularized canonical correlation analysis. *Journal of Biological System*, *17*(2), 173–199. doi:10.1142/S0218339009002831

Gribov, A., Sill, M., Luck, S., Rucker, F., Dohner, K., & Bullinger, L. et al. (2010). SEURAT: Visual analytics for the integrated analysis of microarray data. *BMC Medical Genomics*, *3*(1), 21. doi:10.1186/1755-8794-3-21 PMID:20525257

Gusareva, E. S., Carrasquillo, M. M., Bellenguez, C., Cuyvers, E., Colon, S., & Graff-Radford, N. R. et al. (2014). Genome-Wide Association Interaction Analysis for Alzheimer's Disease. *Neurobiology of Aging*, *35*(11), 2436–2443. doi:10.1016/j.neurobiolaging.2014.05.014 PMID:24958192

Hahn, S. A., Greenhalf, B., Ellis, I., Sina-Frey, M., Rieder, H., & Korte, B. et al. (2003). BRCA2 germline mutations in familial pancreatic carcinoma. *Journal of the National Cancer Institute*, *95*(3), 214–221. doi:10.1093/jnci/95.3.214 PMID:12569143

Hamid, J. S., Hu, P., Roslin, N. M., Ling, V., Greenwood, C. M., & Beyene, J. (2009). Data integration in genetics and genomics: Methods and challenges. *Human Genomics and Proteomics*, 2009. PMID:20948564

Hardison, R. C. (2012). Genome-wide epigenetic data facilitate understanding of disease susceptibility association studies. *The Journal of Biological Chemistry*, 287(37), 30932–30940. doi:10.1074/jbc.R112.352427 PMID:22952232

Heraud-Bousquet, V., Larsen, C., Carpenter, J., Desenclos, J. C., & Le Strat, Y. (2012). Practical considerations for sensitivity analysis after multiple imputation applied to epidemiological studies with incomplete data. *BMC Medical Research Methodology*, 12(1), 73. doi:10.1186/1471-2288-12-73 PMID:22681630

Heyn, H., Moran, S., Hernando-Herraez, I., Sayols, S., Gomez, A., & Sandoval, J. et al. (2013). DNA methylation contributes to natural human variation. *Genome Research*, 23(9), 1363–1372. doi:10.1101/gr.154187.112 PMID:23908385

Himes, B. E., Sheppard, K., Berndt, A., Leme, A. S., Myers, R. A., & Gignoux, C. R. et al. (2013). Integration of mouse and human genome-wide association data identifies KCNIP4 as an asthma gene. *PLoS ONE*, 8(2), e56179. doi:10.1371/journal.pone.0056179 PMID:23457522

Hindorff, L. A., Sethupathy, P., Junkins, H. A., Ramos, E. M., Mehta, J. P., Collins, F. S., & Manolio, T. A. (2009). Potential etiologic and functional implications of genome-wide association loci for human diseases and traits. *Proceedings of the National Academy of Sciences of the United States of America*, 106(23), 9362–9367. doi:10.1073/pnas.0903103106 PMID:19474294

Holzinger, E. R., Dudek, S. M., Frase, A. T., Krauss, R. M., Medina, M. W., & Ritchie, M. D. (2013). ATHENA: A tool for meta-dimensional analysis applied to genotypes and gene expression data to predict HDL cholesterol levels. *Pacific Symposium on Biocomputing. Pacific Symposium on Biocomputing*, 385–396. PMID:23424143

Holzinger, E. R., Dudek, S. M., Frase, A. T., Pendergrass, S. A., & Ritchie, M. D. (2014). ATHENA: The analysis tool for heritable and environmental network associations. *Bioinformatics (Oxford, England)*, 30(5), 698–705. doi:10.1093/bioinformatics/btt572 PMID:24149050

Hopke, P. K., Liu, C., & Rubin, D. B. (2001). Multiple imputation for multivariate data with missing and below-threshold measurements: Time-series concentrations of pollutants in the Arctic. *Biometrics*, 57(1), 22–33. doi:10.1111/j.0006-341X.2001.00022.x PMID:11252602

Howie, B., Fuchsberger, C., Stephens, M., Marchini, J., & Abecasis, G. R. (2012). Fast and accurate genotype imputation in genome-wide association studies through pre-phasing. *Nature Genetics*, 44(8), 955–959. doi:10.1038/ng.2354 PMID:22820512

Howie, B., Marchini, J., & Stephens, M. (2011). Genotype imputation with thousands of genomes. *G3 (Bethesda)*, 1(6), 457-470.

Howie, B. N., Donnelly, P., & Marchini, J. (2009). A flexible and accurate genotype imputation method for the next generation of genome-wide association studies. *PLOS Genetics*, 5(6), e1000529. doi:10.1371/journal.pgen.1000529 PMID:19543373

Hu, T., Andrew, A. S., Karagas, M. R., & Moore, J. H. (2013). Statistical epistasis networks reduce the computational complexity of searching three-locus genetic models. *Pacific Symposium on Biocomputing. Pacific Symposium on Biocomputing*, 397–408. PMID:23424144

Huxley, R., Ansary-Moghaddam, A., Berrington de Gonzalez, A., Barzi, F., & Woodward, M. (2005). Type-II diabetes and pancreatic cancer: A meta-analysis of 36 studies. *British Journal of Cancer*, *92*(11), 2076–2083. doi:10.1038/sj.bjc.6602619 PMID:15886696

Huynh-Thu, V. A., Irrthum, A., Wehenkel, L., & Geurts, P. (2010). Inferring regulatory networks from expression data using tree-based methods. *PLoS ONE*, *5*(9), e12776. doi:10.1371/journal.pone.0012776 PMID:20927193

Ioannidis, J. P., & Khoury, M. J. (2011). Improving validation practices in "omics" research. *Science*, *334*(6060), 1230–1232. doi:10.1126/science.1211811 PMID:22144616

Jay, J. J., & Chesler, E. J. (2014). Performing integrative functional genomics analysis in GeneWeaver.org. *Methods in Molecular Biology (Clifton, N.J.)*, *1101*, 13–29. doi:10.1007/978-1-62703-721-1_2 PMID:24233775

Jerez, J. M., Molina, I., Garcia-Laencina, P. J., Alba, E., Ribelles, N., Martin, M., & Franco, L. (2010). Missing data imputation using statistical and machine learning methods in a real breast cancer problem. *Artificial Intelligence in Medicine*, *50*(2), 105–115. doi:10.1016/j.artmed.2010.05.002 PMID:20638252

Jia, J., Parikh, H., Xiao, W., Hoskins, J. W., Pflicke, H., & Liu, X. et al. (2013). An integrated transcriptome and epigenome analysis identifies a novel candidate gene for pancreatic cancer. *BMC Medical Genomics*, *6*(1), 33. doi:10.1186/1755-8794-6-33 PMID:24053169

Jin, H., Wong, M. L., & Leung, K. S. (2005). Scalable model-based clustering for large databases based on data summarization. *IEEE Transactions on Pattern Analysis and Machine Intelligence*, *27*(11), 1710–1719. doi:10.1109/TPAMI.2005.226 PMID:16285371

Johnson, A. D., & O'Donnell, C. J. (2009). An open access database of genome-wide association results. *BMC Medical Genetics*, *10*(1), 6. doi:10.1186/1471-2350-10-6 PMID:19161620

Jones, S., Hruban, R. H., Kamiyama, M., Borges, M., Zhang, X., & Parsons, D. W. et al. (2009). Exomic sequencing identifies PALB2 as a pancreatic cancer susceptibility gene. *Science*, *324*(5924), 217. doi:10.1126/science.1171202 PMID:19264984

Joyce, A. R., & Palsson, B. O. (2006). The model organism as a system: Integrating 'omics' data sets. *Nature Reviews. Molecular Cell Biology*, *7*(3), 198–210. doi:10.1038/nrm1857 PMID:16496022

Kendziorski, C., & Wang, P. (2006). A review of statistical methods for expression quantitative trait loci mapping. *Mammalian Genome*, *17*(6), 509–517. doi:10.1007/s00335-005-0189-6 PMID:16783633

Kim, D., Li, R., Dudek, S. M., & Ritchie, M. D. (2013). ATHENA: Identifying interactions between different levels of genomic data associated with cancer clinical outcomes using grammatical evolution neural network. *BioData Min*, *6*(1), 23. doi:10.1186/1756-0381-6-23 PMID:24359638

Kim, E. Y., Hwang, D. U., & Ko, T. W. (2012). Multiscale ensemble clustering for finding modules in complex networks. *Physical Review E: Statistical, Nonlinear, and Soft Matter Physics*, *85*(2 Pt 2), 026119. doi:10.1103/PhysRevE.85.026119 PMID:22463291

Kim, S. Y., & Lee, J. W. (2007). Ensemble clustering method based on the resampling similarity measure for gene expression data. *Statistical Methods in Medical Research*, *16*(6), 539–564. doi:10.1177/0962280206071842 PMID:17698931

Kindt, A. S., Navarro, P., Semple, C. A., & Haley, C. S. (2013). The genomic signature of trait-associated variants. *BMC Genomics, 14*(1), 108. doi:10.1186/1471-2164-14-108 PMID:23418889

Kohonen-Corish, M. R., Smith, T. D., & Robinson, H. M. (2013). Beyond the genomics blueprint: The 4th Human Variome Project Meeting, UNESCO, Paris, 2012. *Genetics in Medicine, 15*(7), 507–512. doi:10.1038/gim.2012.174 PMID:23328891

Konig, I. R. (2011). Validation in genetic association studies. *Briefings in Bioinformatics, 12*(3), 253–258. doi:10.1093/bib/bbq074 PMID:21546448

Kuo, T. C., Tian, T. F., & Tseng, Y. J. (2013). 3Omics: A web-based systems biology tool for analysis, integration and visualization of human transcriptomic, proteomic and metabolomic data. *BMC Systems Biology, 7*(1), 64. doi:10.1186/1752-0509-7-64 PMID:23875761

Lakshminarayan, K., Harp, S. A., Goldman, R., & Samad, T. (1996). *Imputation of missing data using machine learning techniques.* In *Proceedings of the Second International Conference on Knowledge Discovery and Data Mining (KDD-96).* Portland, OR: KDD.

Lanckriet, G. R., De Bie, T., Cristianini, N., Jordan, M. I., & Noble, W. S. (2004). A statistical framework for genomic data fusion. *Bioinformatics (Oxford, England), 20*(16), 2626–2635. doi:10.1093/bioinformatics/bth294 PMID:15130933

Langfelder, P., Castellani, L. W., Zhou, Z., Paul, E., Davis, R., & Schadt, E. E. et al. (2012). A systems genetic analysis of high density lipoprotein metabolism and network preservation across mouse models. *Biochimica et Biophysica Acta, 1821*(3), 435–447. doi:10.1016/j.bbalip.2011.07.014 PMID:21807117

Langfelder, P., & Horvath, S. (2008). WGCNA: An R package for weighted correlation network analysis. *BMC Bioinformatics, 9*(1), 559. doi:10.1186/1471-2105-9-559 PMID:19114008

Langfelder, P., Zhang, B., & Horvath, S. (2008). Defining clusters from a hierarchical cluster tree: The Dynamic Tree Cut package for R. *Bioinformatics (Oxford, England), 24*(5), 719–720. doi:10.1093/bioinformatics/btm563 PMID:18024473

Le Cao, K. A., Boitard, S., & Besse, P. (2011). Sparse PLS discriminant analysis: Biologically relevant feature selection and graphical displays for multiclass problems. *BMC Bioinformatics, 12*(1), 253. doi:10.1186/1471-2105-12-253 PMID:21693065

Le Cao, K. A., Martin, P. G., Robert-Granie, C., & Besse, P. (2009). Sparse canonical methods for biological data integration: Application to a cross-platform study. *BMC Bioinformatics, 10*(1), 34. doi:10.1186/1471-2105-10-34 PMID:19171069

Le Cao, K. A., Rossouw, D., Robert-Granie, C., & Besse, P. (2008). A sparse PLS for variable selection when integrating omics data. *Statistical Applications in Genetics and Molecular Biology, 7*(1), 35. doi:10.2202/1544-6115.1390 PMID:19049491

Lee, P. H., Jung, J. Y., & Shatkay, H. (2010). Functionally informative tag SNP selection using a Pareto-optimal approach. *Advances in Experimental Medicine and Biology, 680,* 173–180. doi:10.1007/978-1-4419-5913-3_20 PMID:20865499

Lee, P. H., & Shatkay, H. (2006). BNTagger: Improved tagging SNP selection using Bayesian networks. *Bioinformatics (Oxford, England), 22*(14), e211–e219. doi:10.1093/bioinformatics/btl233 PMID:16873474

Lee, P. H., & Shatkay, H. (2008a). F-SNP: Computationally predicted functional SNPs for disease association studies. *Nucleic Acids Research*, 36(Database issue), D820–D824. PMID:17986460

Lee, P. H., & Shatkay, H. (2008b). Ranking single nucleotide polymorphisms by potential deleterious effects. *AMIA... Annual Symposium Proceedings/ AMIA Symposium. AMIA Symposium*, 667–671. PMID:18999314

Lee, P. H., & Shatkay, H. (2009). An integrative scoring system for ranking SNPs by their potential deleterious effects. *Bioinformatics (Oxford, England)*, 25(8), 1048–1055. doi:10.1093/bioinformatics/btp103 PMID:19228803

Lee, S. I., Dudley, A. M., Drubin, D., Silver, P. A., Krogan, N. J., Pe'er, D., & Koller, D. (2009). Learning a prior on regulatory potential from eQTL data. *PLOS Genetics*, 5(1), e1000358. doi:10.1371/journal.pgen.1000358 PMID:19180192

Leek, J. T., Taub, M. A., & Rasgon, J. L. (2012). A statistical approach to selecting and confirming validation targets in -omics experiments. *BMC Bioinformatics*, 13(1), 150. doi:10.1186/1471-2105-13-150 PMID:22738145

Li, A., & Horvath, S. (2007). Network neighborhood analysis with the multi-node topological overlap measure. *Bioinformatics (Oxford, England)*, 23(2), 222–231. doi:10.1093/bioinformatics/btl581 PMID:17110366

Li, A., & Horvath, S. (2009). Network module detection: Affinity search technique with the multi-node topological overlap measure. *BMC Research Notes*, 2(1), 142. doi:10.1186/1756-0500-2-142 PMID:19619323

Li, F., Nie, L., Wu, G., Qiao, J., & Zhang, W. (2011). Prediction and Characterization of Missing Proteomic Data in Desulfovibrio vulgaris. *Comparative and Functional Genomics*, 2011, 780973. doi:10.1155/2011/780973 PMID:21687592

Li, L., Fridley, B. L., Kalari, K., Jenkins, G., Batzler, A., Weinshilboum, R. M., & Wang, L. (2009). Gemcitabine and arabinosylcytosin pharmacogenomics: Genome-wide association and drug response biomarkers. *PLoS ONE*, 4(11), e7765. PMID:19898621

Li, L., Kabesch, M., Bouzigon, E., Demenais, F., Farrall, M., & Moffatt, M. F. et al. (2013). Using eQTL weights to improve power for genome-wide association studies: A genetic study of childhood asthma. *Frontiers in Genetics*, 4, 103. doi:10.3389/fgene.2013.00103 PMID:23755072

Li, X., & Li, J. (2008). Efficient haplotype inference from pedigrees with missing data using linear systems with disjoint-set data structures. *Computational Systems Bioinformatics/Life Sciences Society. Computational Systems Bioinformatics Conference*, 7, 297–308. PMID:19642289

Liang, L., Morar, N., Dixon, A. L., Lathrop, G. M., Abecasis, G. R., Moffatt, M. F., & Cookson, W. O. (2013). A cross-platform analysis of 14,177 expression quantitative trait loci derived from lymphoblastoid cell lines. *Genome Research*, 23(4), 716–726. doi:10.1101/gr.142521.112 PMID:23345460

Lichtenstein, P., Holm, N. V., Verkasalo, P. K., Iliadou, A., Kaprio, J., & Koskenvuo, M. et al. (2000). Environmental and heritable factors in the causation of cancer--analyses of cohorts of twins from Sweden, Denmark, and Finland. *The New England Journal of Medicine*, 343(2), 78–85. doi:10.1056/NEJM200007133430201 PMID:10891514

Lin, S., Chakravarti, A., & Cutler, D. J. (2004). Haplotype and missing data inference in nuclear families. *Genome Research*, 14(8), 1624–1632. doi:10.1101/gr.2204604 PMID:15256514

Little, R. J., D'Agostino, R., Cohen, M. L., Dickersin, K., Emerson, S. S., & Farrar, J. T. et al. (2012). The prevention and treatment of missing data in clinical trials. *The New England Journal of Medicine*, *367*(14), 1355–1360. doi:10.1056/NEJMsr1203730 PMID:23034025

Liu, B., de la Fuente, A., & Hoeschele, I. (2008). Gene network inference via structural equation modeling in genetical genomics experiments. *Genetics*, *178*(3), 1763–1776. doi:10.1534/genetics.107.080069 PMID:18245846

Liu, L., Zhang, D., Liu, H., & Arendt, C. (2013). Robust methods for population stratification in genome wide association studies. *BMC Bioinformatics*, *14*(1), 132. doi:10.1186/1471-2105-14-132 PMID:23601181

Lobach, I., Fan, R., & Carroll, R. J. (2010). Genotype-based association mapping of complex diseases: Gene-environment interactions with multiple genetic markers and measurement error in environmental exposures. *Genetic Epidemiology*, *34*(8), 792–802. doi:10.1002/gepi.20523 PMID:21031455

Lobach, I., Mallick, B., & Carroll, R. J. (2011). Semiparametric Bayesian analysis of gene-environment interactions with error in measurement of environmental covariates and missing genetic data. *Statistics and Its Interface*, *4*(3), 305–316. doi:10.4310/SII.2011.v4.n3.a5 PMID:21949562

Lowenfels, A. B., Maisonneuve, P., Cavallini, G., Ammann, R. W., Lankisch, P. G., & Andersen, J. R. et al. (1993). Pancreatitis and the risk of pancreatic cancer. International Pancreatitis Study Group. *The New England Journal of Medicine*, *328*(20), 1433–1437. doi:10.1056/NEJM199305203282001 PMID:8479461

Lu, L. J., Xia, Y., Paccanaro, A., Yu, H., & Gerstein, M. (2005). Assessing the limits of genomic data integration for predicting protein networks. *Genome Research*, *15*(7), 945–953. doi:10.1101/gr.3610305 PMID:15998909

Ma, Y., Hart, J. D., Janicki, R., & Carroll, R. J. (2011). Local and omnibus goodness-of-fit tests in classical measurement error models. *Journal of the Royal Statistical Society. Series B, Statistical Methodology*, *73*(1), 81–98. doi:10.1111/j.1467-9868.2010.00751.x PMID:21339886

Macdonald, J. R., Ziman, R., Yuen, R. K., Feuk, L., & Scherer, S. W. (2014). The Database of Genomic Variants: A curated collection of structural variation in the human genome. *Nucleic Acids Research*, *42*(1), D986–D992. doi:10.1093/nar/gkt958 PMID:24174537

Malina, M., Ickstadt, K., Schwender, H., Posch, M., & Bogdan, M. (2014). Detection of epistatic effects with logic regression and a classical linear regression model. *Statistical Applications in Genetics and Molecular Biology*, *13*(1), 83–104. doi:10.1515/sagmb-2013-0028 PMID:24413217

Marchini, J., & Howie, B. (2008). Comparing algorithms for genotype imputation. *American Journal of Human Genetics*, *83*(4), 535–539. doi:10.1016/j.ajhg.2008.09.007 PMID:18940314

Marchini, J., & Howie, B. (2010). Genotype imputation for genome-wide association studies. *Nature Reviews. Genetics*, *11*(7), 499–511. doi:10.1038/nrg2796 PMID:20517342

Marchini, J., Howie, B., Myers, S., McVean, G., & Donnelly, P. (2007). A new multipoint method for genome-wide association studies by imputation of genotypes. *Nature Genetics*, *39*(7), 906–913. doi:10.1038/ng2088 PMID:17572673

Mardinoglu, A., Agren, R., Kampf, C., Asplund, A., Nookaew, I., & Jacobson, P. et al. (2013). Integration of clinical data with a genome-scale metabolic model of the human adipocyte. *Molecular Systems Biology*, *9*(1), 649. doi:10.1038/msb.2013.5 PMID:23511207

Markos, A. I., Vozalis, M. G., & Margaritis, K. G. (2010). An Optimal Scaling Approach to Collaborative Filtering Using Categorical Principal Component Analysis and Neighborhood Formation. In *Proceedings of the 6th IFIP WG 12.5 International Conference*. AIAI. doi:10.1007/978-3-642-16239-8_6

Marlin, B. M. (2008). *Missing data problems in machine learning*. (Doctoral Thesis). University of Toronto, Toronto, Canada.

Mayer, B. (Ed.). (2011). Bioinformatics for Omics Data: Methods and Protocols (Vol. 719). New York: Springer Science + Business Media, LCC. doi:10.1007/978-1-61779-027-0

Mayer, G., Heinze, G., Mischak, H., Hellemons, M. E., Heerspink, H. J., & Bakker, S. J. et al. (2011). Omics-bioinformatics in the context of clinical data. *Methods in Molecular Biology (Clifton, N.J.)*, *719*, 479–497. doi:10.1007/978-1-61779-027-0_22 PMID:21370098

Michaud, D. S., Izard, J., Wilhelm-Benartzi, C. S., You, D. H., Grote, V. A., & Tjonneland, A. et al. (2013). Plasma antibodies to oral bacteria and risk of pancreatic cancer in a large European prospective cohort study. *Gut*, *62*(12), 1764–1770. doi:10.1136/gutjnl-2012-303006 PMID:22990306

Michaud, D. S., Joshipura, K., Giovannucci, E., & Fuchs, C. S. (2007). A prospective study of periodontal disease and pancreatic cancer in US male health professionals. *Journal of the National Cancer Institute*, *99*(2), 171–175. doi:10.1093/jnci/djk021 PMID:17228001

Milenova, B. L., & Campos, M. M. (2002). O-cluster: scalable clustering of large high dimensional data sets. In *Proceedings of the 2002 IEEE International Conference on Data Mining (ICDM 2002)*, (pp. 290-297). IEEE. doi:10.1109/ICDM.2002.1183915

Min, J. L., Taylor, J. M., Richards, J. B., Watts, T., Pettersson, F. H., & Broxholme, J. et al. (2011). The use of genome-wide eQTL associations in lymphoblastoid cell lines to identify novel genetic pathways involved in complex traits. *PLoS ONE*, *6*(7), e22070. doi:10.1371/journal.pone.0022070 PMID:21789213

Mocci, E., Milne, R. L., Mendez-Villamil, E. Y., Hopper, J. L., John, E. M., & Andrulis, I. L. et al. (2013). Risk of pancreatic cancer in breast cancer families from the breast cancer family registry. *Cancer Epidemiology, Biomarkers & Prevention*, *22*(5), 803–811. doi:10.1158/1055-9965.EPI-12-0195 PMID:23456555

Molenberghs, G., Kenward, M. G., Aerts, M., Verbeke, G., Tsiatis, A. A., Davidian, M., & Rizopoulos, D. (2014). On random sample size, ignorability, ancillarity, completeness, separability, and degeneracy: Sequential trials, random sample sizes, and missing data. *Statistical Methods in Medical Research*, *23*(1), 11–41. doi:10.1177/0962280212445801 PMID:22514029

Molenberghs, G., Kenward, M. G., & Goetghebeur, E. (2001). Sensitivity analysis for incomplete contingency tables: The Slovenian plebiscite case. *Applied Statistics*, *50*(1), 15–29. doi:10.1111/1467-9876.00217

Morris, C. (2008). The EQUATOR Network: Promoting the transparent and accurate reporting of research. *Developmental Medicine and Child Neurology*, *50*(10), 723. doi:10.1111/j.1469-8749.2008.03107.x PMID:18834380

Motsinger-Reif, A. A., Dudek, S. M., Hahn, L. W., & Ritchie, M. D. (2008). Comparison of approaches for machine-learning optimization of neural networks for detecting gene-gene interactions in genetic epidemiology. *Genetic Epidemiology*, *32*(4), 325–340. doi:10.1002/gepi.20307 PMID:18265411

Nakazato, T., Bono, H., & Takagi, T. (2011). Functional Interpretation of Omics Data by Profiling Genes and Diseases Using MeSH–Controlled Vocabulary. In *Advances in the Study of Genetic Disorders*. Available from: http://www.intechopen.com/books/advances-in-the-study-of-genetic-disorders/functional-interpretation-of-omics-data-by-profiling-genes-and-diseases-using-mesh-controlled-vocabu

Nekrutenko, A., & Taylor, J. (2012). Next-generation sequencing data interpretation: Enhancing reproducibility and accessibility. *Nature Reviews. Genetics*, *13*(9), 667–672. doi:10.1038/nrg3305 PMID:22898652

Nibbe, R. K., Koyuturk, M., & Chance, M. R. (2010). An integrative -omics approach to identify functional sub-networks in human colorectal cancer. *PLoS Computational Biology*, *6*(1), e1000639. doi:10.1371/journal.pcbi.1000639 PMID:20090827

Nica, A. C., & Dermitzakis, E. T. (2013). Expression quantitative trait loci: Present and future. *Philosophical Transactions of the Royal Society of London. Series B, Biological Sciences*, *368*(1620), 20120362. doi:10.1098/rstb.2012.0362 PMID:23650636

Nie, L., Wu, G., Culley, D. E., Scholten, J. C., & Zhang, W. (2007). Integrative analysis of transcriptomic and proteomic data: Challenges, solutions and applications. *Critical Reviews in Biotechnology*, *27*(2), 63–75. doi:10.1080/07388550701334212 PMID:17578703

Oetting, W. S., Robinson, P. N., Greenblatt, M. S., Cotton, R. G., Beck, T., & Carey, J. C. et al. (2013). Getting ready for the Human Phenome Project: The 2012 forum of the Human Variome Project. *Human Mutation*, *34*(4), 661–666. PMID:23401191

Oxley, M. E., & Thorsen, S. N. (2004). Fusion or integration: What's the difference? In *Proceedings of the 7th Int. Conf. Inform. Fusion*. (pp. 429-434). Academic Press.

Pang, A. W., MacDonald, J. R., Pinto, D., Wei, J., Rafiq, M. A., & Conrad, D. F. et al. (2010). Towards a comprehensive structural variation map of an individual human genome. *Genome Biology*, *11*(5), R52. doi:10.1186/gb-2010-11-5-r52 PMID:20482838

Pang, A. W., Migita, O., Macdonald, J. R., Feuk, L., & Scherer, S. W. (2013). Mechanisms of formation of structural variation in a fully sequenced human genome. *Human Mutation*, *34*(2), 345–354. doi:10.1002/humu.22240 PMID:23086744

Parkhomenko, E., Tritchler, D., & Beyene, J. (2009). Sparse canonical correlation analysis with application to genomic data integration. *Stat Appl Genet Mol Biol, 8*, Article 1.

Pastinen, T. (2010). Genome-wide allele-specific analysis: Insights into regulatory variation. *Nature Reviews. Genetics*, *11*(8), 533–538. doi:10.1038/nrg2815 PMID:20567245

Pedersen, K. S., Bamlet, W. R., Oberg, A. L., de Andrade, M., Matsumoto, M. E., & Tang, H. et al. (2011). Leukocyte DNA methylation signature differentiates pancreatic cancer patients from healthy controls. *PLoS ONE*, *6*(3), e18223. doi:10.1371/journal.pone.0018223 PMID:21455317

Penrod, N. M., Cowper-Sal-lari, R., & Moore, J. H. (2011). Systems genetics for drug target discovery. *Trends in Pharmacological Sciences*, *32*(10), 623–630. doi:10.1016/j.tips.2011.07.002 PMID:21862141

Petersen, A. K., Zeilinger, S., Kastenmuller, G., Romisch-Margl, W., Brugger, M., & Peters, A. et al. (2014). Epigenetics meets metabolomics: An epigenome-wide association study with blood serum metabolic traits. *Human Molecular Genetics*, *23*(2), 534–545. PMID:24014485

Petersen, G. M., Amundadottir, L., Fuchs, C. S., Kraft, P., Stolzenberg-Solomon, R. Z., & Jacobs, K. B. et al. (2010). A genome-wide association study identifies pancreatic cancer susceptibility loci on chromosomes 13q22.1, 1q32.1 and 5p15.33. *Nature Genetics*, *42*(3), 224–228. doi:10.1038/ng.522 PMID:20101243

Pinto da Costa, J. F., Alonso, H., & Roque, L. (2009). A weighted principal component analysis and its application to gene expression data. *IEEE/ACM Transactions on Computational Biology and Bioinformatics*, *8*(1), 246–252. doi:10.1109/TCBB.2009.61 PMID:21071812

Plottel, C. S., & Blaser, M. J. (2011). Microbiome and malignancy. *Cell Host & Microbe*, *10*(4), 324–335. doi:10.1016/j.chom.2011.10.003 PMID:22018233

ESF Position Paper (2011). *European Biobanks and sample repositories – Relevance to Personalised Medicine*. ESF.

Price, A. L., Zaitlen, N. A., Reich, D., & Patterson, N. (2010). New approaches to population stratification in genome-wide association studies. *Nature Reviews. Genetics*, *11*(7), 459–463. doi:10.1038/nrg2813 PMID:20548291

Quackenbush, J. (2006). From 'omes to biology. *Animal Genetics*, *37*(s1Suppl 1), 48–56. doi:10.1111/j.1365-2052.2006.01476.x PMID:16887002

Raiko, T., Ilin, A., & Karhunen, J. (2008). Principal component analysis for sparse high-dimensional data. *Neural Information Processing*, *4984*(Part I), 566–575. doi:10.1007/978-3-540-69158-7_59

Real, F. X., Malats, N., Lesca, G., Porta, M., Chopin, S., Lenoir, G. M., & Silinikova, O. (2002). Family history of cancer and germline BRCA2 mutations in sporadic exocrine pancreatic cancer. *Gut*, *50*(5), 653–657. doi:10.1136/gut.50.5.653 PMID:11950811

Riancho, J. A. (2012). Genome-wide association studies (GWAS) in complex diseases: Advantages and limitations. *Reumatol Clin*, *8*(2), 56–57. doi:10.1016/j.reuma.2011.07.005 PMID:22089059

Richman, M. B., Trafalis, T. B., & Adrianto, I. (2009). Missing Data Imputation Through Machine Learning Algorithms. In S. E. Haupt, A. Pasini, & C. Marzban (Eds.), *Artificial Intelligence Methods in Environment Science*. Berlin: Springer-Verlag. doi:10.1007/978-1-4020-9119-3_7

Ring, H. Z., Kwok, P. Y., & Cotton, R. G. (2006). Human Variome Project: An international collaboration to catalogue human genetic variation. *Pharmacogenomics*, *7*(7), 969–972. doi:10.2217/14622416.7.7.969 PMID:17054407

Risch, H. A. (2012). Pancreatic cancer: Helicobacter pylori colonization, N-nitrosamine exposures, and ABO blood group. *Molecular Carcinogenesis*, *51*(1), 109–118. doi:10.1002/mc.20826 PMID:22162235

Ritchie, M. D., Van Steen, K., & Gusareva, E. (2014, Manuscript submitted for publication). Dimensionality reduction in Genome-Wide Association Interaction Studies (GWAIS): Practical considerations. *Genome Medicine*.

Rodríguez-Ezpeleta, N., Hackenberg, M., & Aransay, A. M. (Eds.). (2012). Bioinformatics for High Throughput Sequencing. New York: Springer Science + Business Media, LLC. doi:10.1007/978-1-4614-0782-9

Rosa, G. J., Valente, B. D., de los Campos, G., Wu, X. L., Gianola, D., & Silva, M. A. (2011). Inferring causal phenotype networks using structural equation models. *Genetics, Selection, Evolution.*, *43*(1), 6. doi:10.1186/1297-9686-43-6 PMID:21310061

Rothman, K. J. (1974). Synergy and antagonism in cause-effect relationships. *American Journal of Epidemiology*, *99*(6), 385–388. PMID:4841816

Roukos, D. H. (2009). Personal genomics and genome-wide association studies: Novel discoveries but limitations for practical personalized medicine. *Annals of Surgical Oncology*, *16*(3), 772–773. doi:10.1245/s10434-008-0109-6 PMID:18726130

Rubin, D. B. (1976). Inference and missing data. *Biometrika*, *63*(3), 581–592. doi:10.1093/biomet/63.3.581

Rubin, L. H., Witkiewitz, K., Andre, J. S., & Reilly, S. (2007). Methods for Handling Missing Data in the Behavioral Neurosciences: Don't Throw the Baby Rat out with the Bath Water. *J Undergrad Neurosci Educ*, *5*(2), A71–A77. PMID:23493038

Saeys, Y., Inza, I., & Larranaga, P. (2007). A review of feature selection techniques in bioinformatics. *Bioinformatics (Oxford, England)*, *23*(19), 2507–2517. doi:10.1093/bioinformatics/btm344 PMID:17720704

Sarasua, S. M., Collins, J. S., Williamson, D. M., Satten, G. A., & Allen, A. S. (2009). Effect of population stratification on the identification of significant single-nucleotide polymorphisms in genome-wide association studies. *BMC Proc*, *3*(Suppl 7), S13.

Sarojini, S., Goy, A., Pecora, A., & Suh, K. S. (2012). Proactive Biobanking to Improve Research and Health Care. *J Tissue Sci Eng*, *3*(02), 116. doi:10.4172/2157-7552.1000116

Sass, S., Buettner, F., Mueller, N. S., & Theis, F. J. (2013). A modular framework for gene set analysis integrating multilevel omics data. *Nucleic Acids Research*, *41*(21), 9622–9633. doi:10.1093/nar/gkt752 PMID:23975194

Schadt, E. E., Lamb, J., Yang, X., Zhu, J., Edwards, S., & Guhathakurta, D. et al. (2005). An integrative genomics approach to infer causal associations between gene expression and disease. *Nature Genetics*, *37*(7), 710–717. doi:10.1038/ng1589 PMID:15965475

Schneider, M. V., & Orchard, S. (2011). Omics technologies, data and bioinformatics principles. *Methods in Molecular Biology (Clifton, N.J.)*, *719*, 3–30. doi:10.1007/978-1-61779-027-0_1 PMID:21370077

Schork, A. J., Thompson, W. K., Pham, P., Torkamani, A., Roddey, J. C., & Sullivan, P. F. et al. Tobacco and Genetics Consortium. (2013). All SNPs are not created equal: Genome-wide association studies reveal a consistent pattern of enrichment among functionally annotated SNPs. *PLOS Genetics*, *9*(4), e1003449. doi:10.1371/journal.pgen.1003449 PMID:23637621

Schuierer, S., Tranchevent, L. C., Dengler, U., & Moreau, Y. (2010). Large-scale benchmark of Endeavour using MetaCore maps. *Bioinformatics (Oxford, England)*, *26*(15), 1922–1923. doi:10.1093/bioinformatics/btq307 PMID:20538729

Schwender, H., & Ickstadt, K. (2008). Identification of SNP interactions using logic regression. *Biostatistics (Oxford, England)*, *9*(1), 187–198. doi:10.1093/biostatistics/kxm024 PMID:17578898

Schwender, H., & Ruczinski, I. (2010). Logic regression and its extensions. *Advances in Genetics*, *72*, 25–45. doi:10.1016/B978-0-12-380862-2.00002-3 PMID:21029847

Shabalin, A. A. (2012). Matrix eQTL: Ultra fast eQTL analysis via large matrix operations. *Bioinformatics (Oxford, England)*, *28*(10), 1353–1358. doi:10.1093/bioinformatics/bts163 PMID:22492648

Shen, H., & Huang, J. Z. (2008). Sparse principal component analysis via regularized low rank matrix approximation. *Journal of Multivariate Analysis*, *99*(6), 1015–1034. doi:10.1016/j.jmva.2007.06.007

Shimokawa, K., Mogushi, K., Shoji, S., Hiraishi, A., Ido, K., Mizushima, H., & Tanaka, H. (2010). iCOD: An integrated clinical omics database based on the systems-pathology view of disease. *BMC Genomics*, *11*(Suppl 4), S19. doi:10.1186/1471-2164-11-S4-S19 PMID:21143802

Sieberts, S. K., & Schadt, E. E. (2007). Moving toward a system genetics view of disease. *Mammalian Genome*, *18*(6-7), 389–401. doi:10.1007/s00335-007-9040-6 PMID:17653589

Sifrim, A., Popovic, D., Tranchevent, L. C., Ardeshirdavani, A., Sakai, R., & Konings, P. et al. (2013). eXtasy: Variant prioritization by genomic data fusion. *Nature Methods*, *10*(11), 1083–1084. doi:10.1038/nmeth.2656 PMID:24076761

Simera, I., Moher, D., Hirst, A., Hoey, J., Schulz, K. F., & Altman, D. G. (2010). Transparent and accurate reporting increases reliability, utility, and impact of your research: Reporting guidelines and the EQUATOR Network. *BMC Medicine*, *8*(1), 24. doi:10.1186/1741-7015-8-24 PMID:20420659

Singh, V., Mukherjee, L., Peng, J., & Xu, J. (2010). Ensemble Clustering using Semidefinite Programming with Applications. *Machine Learning*, *79*(1-2), 177–200. doi:10.1007/s10994-009-5158-y PMID:21927539

Skelly, D. A., Ronald, J., & Akey, J. M. (2009). Inherited variation in gene expression. *Annual Review of Genomics and Human Genetics*, *10*(1), 313–332. doi:10.1146/annurev-genom-082908-150121 PMID:19630563

Southam, L., Panoutsopoulou, K., Rayner, N. W., Chapman, K., Durrant, C., & Ferreira, T. et al. (2011). The effect of genome-wide association scan quality control on imputation outcome for common variants. *European Journal of Human Genetics*, *19*(5), 610–614. doi:10.1038/ejhg.2010.242 PMID:21267008

Spencer, C. C., Su, Z., Donnelly, P., & Marchini, J. (2009). Designing genome-wide association studies: Sample size, power, imputation, and the choice of genotyping chip. *PLOS Genetics*, *5*(5), e1000477. doi:10.1371/journal.pgen.1000477 PMID:19492015

Steinfath, M., Repsilber, D., Scholz, M., Walther, D., & Selbig, J. (2007). Integrated data analysis for genome-wide research. *EXS*, *97*, 309–329. doi:10.1007/978-3-7643-7439-6_13 PMID:17432273

Stephens, M., & Scheet, P. (2005). Accounting for decay of linkage disequilibrium in haplotype inference and missing-data imputation. *American Journal of Human Genetics*, *76*(3), 449–462. doi:10.1086/428594 PMID:15700229

Stewart, J. A., Chadwick, V. S., & Murray, A. (2005). Investigations into the influence of host genetics on the predominant eubacteria in the faecal microflora of children. *Journal of Medical Microbiology*, *54*(Pt 12), 1239–1242. doi:10.1099/jmm.0.46189-0 PMID:16278440

Stolzenberg-Solomon, R. Z., Dodd, K. W., Blaser, M. J., Virtamo, J., Taylor, P. R., & Albanes, D. (2003). Tooth loss, pancreatic cancer, and Helicobacter pylori. *The American Journal of Clinical Nutrition*, *78*(1), 176–181. PMID:12816788

Stranger, B. E., Montgomery, S. B., Dimas, A. S., Parts, L., Stegle, O., & Ingle, C. E. et al. (2012). Patterns of cis regulatory variation in diverse human populations. *PLOS Genetics*, *8*(4), e1002639. doi:10.1371/journal.pgen.1002639 PMID:22532805

Strehl, A., & Ghosh, J. (2003). Cluster ensembles --- a knowledge reuse framework for combining multiple partitions. *Journal of Machine Learning Research*, *3*, 583–617.

Strobl, C., Malley, J., & Tutz, G. (2009). An introduction to recursive partitioning: Rationale, application, and characteristics of classification and regression trees, bagging, and random forests. *Psychological Methods, 14*(4), 323–348. doi:10.1037/a0016973 PMID:19968396

Sulakhe, D., Balasubramanian, S., Xie, B., Feng, B., Taylor, A., & Wang, S. et al. (2014). Lynx: A database and knowledge extraction engine for integrative medicine. *Nucleic Acids Research, 42*(1), D1007–D1012. doi:10.1093/nar/gkt1166 PMID:24270788

Szymczak, S., Igl, B. W., & Ziegler, A. (2009). Detecting SNP-expression associations: A comparison of mutual information and median test with standard statistical approaches. *Statistics in Medicine, 28*(29), 3581–3596. doi:10.1002/sim.3695 PMID:19691035

Tan, E. K. (2010). Genome-wide association studies: Promises and pitfalls. *Annals of the Academy of Medicine, Singapore, 39*(2), 77–78. PMID:20237726

Taylor, C. F., Field, D., Sansone, S. A., Aerts, J., Apweiler, R., & Ashburner, M. et al. (2008). Promoting coherent minimum reporting guidelines for biological and biomedical investigations: The MIBBI project. *Nature Biotechnology, 26*(8), 889–896. doi:10.1038/nbt.1411 PMID:18688244

Tenenhaus, A., Guillemot, V., Gidrol, X., & Frouin, V. (2010). Gene association networks from microarray data using a regularized estimation of partial correlation based on PLS regression. *IEEE/ACM Transactions on Computational Biology and Bioinformatics, 7*(2), 251–262. doi:10.1109/TCBB.2008.87 PMID:20431145

Tenenhaus, A., & Tenenhaus, M. (2011). Regularized generalized canonical correlation analysis. *Psychometrika, 76*(2), 257–284. doi:10.1007/s11336-011-9206-8

Tischkowitz, M. D., Sabbaghian, N., Hamel, N., Borgida, A., Rosner, C., & Taherian, N. et al. (2009). Analysis of the gene coding for the BRCA2-interacting protein PALB2 in familial and sporadic pancreatic cancer. *Gastroenterology, 137*(3), 1183–1186. doi:10.1053/j.gastro.2009.06.055 PMID:19635604

Tranchevent, L. C., Barriot, R., Yu, S., Van Vooren, S., Van Loo, P., Coessens, B., De Moor, B., Aerts, S., & Moreau, Y. (2008). ENDEAVOUR update: A web resource for gene prioritization in multiple species. *Nucleic Acids Res, 36*(Web Server issue), W377-384.

Trevino, V., Falciani, F., & Barrera-Saldana, H. A. (2007). DNA microarrays: A powerful genomic tool for biomedical and clinical research. *Molecular Medicine (Cambridge, Mass.), 13*(9-10), 527–541. doi:10.2119/2006-00107.Trevino PMID:17660860

Turinsky, A. L., Fanea, E., Trinh, Q., Dong, X., Stromer, J. N., & Shu, X. et al. (2008). Integration of genomic and medical data into a 3D atlas of human anatomy. *Studies in Health Technology and Informatics, 132*, 526–531. PMID:18391362

Turner, S. D., Dudek, S. M., & Ritchie, M. D. (2010). ATHENA: A knowledge-based hybrid backpropagation-grammatical evolution neural network algorithm for discovering epistasis among quantitative trait Loci. *BioData Min, 3*(1), 5. doi:10.1186/1756-0381-3-5 PMID:20875103

Ulitsky, I., Krogan, N. J., & Shamir, R. (2009). Towards accurate imputation of quantitative genetic interactions. *Genome Biology, 10*(12), R140. doi:10.1186/gb-2009-10-12-r140 PMID:20003301

van Eijk, K. R., de Jong, S., Boks, M. P., Langeveld, T., Colas, F., & Veldink, J. H. et al. (2012). Genetic analysis of DNA methylation and gene expression levels in whole blood of healthy human subjects. *BMC Genomics, 13*(1), 636. doi:10.1186/1471-2164-13-636 PMID:23157493 van Heyningen, V., & Bickmore, W. (2013). Regulation from a distance: Long-range control of gene expression in development and disease. *Philosophical Transactions of the Royal Society of London. Series B, Biological Sciences, 368*(1620), 20120372. doi:10.1098/rstb.2012.0372 PMID:23650642

Van Noorden, R., Ledford, H., & Mann, A. (2011). New year, new science. *Nature, 469*(7328), 12. doi:10.1038/469012a PMID:21209635

Van Steen, K. (2012). Travelling the world of gene-gene interactions. *Briefings in Bioinformatics, 13*(1), 1–19. doi:10.1093/bib/bbr012 PMID:21441561

Van Steen, K., Laird, N. M., Markel, P., & Molenberghs, G. (2007). Approaches to handling incomplete data in family-based association testing. *Annals of Human Genetics, 71*(Pt 2), 141–151. doi:10.1111/j.1469-1809.2006.00325.x PMID:17096676

Vogel, C., & Marcotte, E. M. (2012). Insights into the regulation of protein abundance from proteomic and transcriptomic analyses. *Nature Reviews. Genetics, 13*(4), 227–232. PMID:22411467

Waaijenborg, S., & Zwinderman, A. H. (2009). Sparse canonical correlation analysis for identifying, connecting and completing gene-expression networks. *BMC Bioinformatics, 10*(1), 315. doi:10.1186/1471-2105-10-315 PMID:19785734

Wang, B., Mezlini, A. M., Demir, F., Fiume, M., Tu, Z., & Brudno, M. et al. (2014). Similarity network fusion for aggregating data types on a genomic scale. *Nature Methods*. PMID:24464287

Wei, T., Geiser, A. G., Qian, H. R., Su, C., Helvering, L. M., & Kulkarini, N. H. et al. (2007). DNA microarray data integration by ortholog gene analysis reveals potential molecular mechanisms of estrogen-dependent growth of human uterine fibroids. *BMC Women's Health, 7*(1), 5. doi:10.1186/1472-6874-7-5 PMID:17407572

Welter, D., Macarthur, J., Morales, J., Burdett, T., Hall, P., & Junkins, H. et al. (2014). The NHGRI GWAS Catalog, a curated resource of SNP-trait associations. *Nucleic Acids Research, 42*(1), D1001–D1006. doi:10.1093/nar/gkt1229 PMID:24316577

Wild, C. P. (2005). Complementing the genome with an "exposome": The outstanding challenge of environmental exposure measurement in molecular epidemiology. *Cancer Epidemiology, Biomarkers & Prevention, 14*(8), 1847–1850. doi:10.1158/1055-9965.EPI-05-0456 PMID:16103423

Wolpin, B. M., Kraft, P., Gross, M., Helzlsouer, K., Bueno-de-Mesquita, H. B., & Steplowski, E. et al. (2010). Pancreatic cancer risk and ABO blood group alleles: Results from the pancreatic cancer cohort consortium. *Cancer Research, 70*(3), 1015–1023. doi:10.1158/0008-5472.CAN-09-2993 PMID:20103627

Wong, M. Y., Day, N. E., Bashir, S. A., & Duffy, S. W. (1999). Measurement error in epidemiology: the design of validation studies I: univariate situation. *Statistics in Medicine, 18*(21), 2815–2829. doi:10.1002/(SICI)1097-0258(19991115)18:21<2815::AID-SIM280>3.0.CO;2-# PMID:10523744

Wong, M. Y., Day, N. E., Luan, J. A., Chan, K. P., & Wareham, N. J. (2003). The detection of gene-environment interaction for continuous traits: Should we deal with measurement error by bigger studies or better measurement? *International Journal of Epidemiology, 32*(1), 51–57. doi:10.1093/ije/dyg002 PMID:12690008

Wong, M. Y., Day, N. E., Luan, J. A., & Wareham, N. J. (2004). Estimation of magnitude in gene-environment interactions in the presence of measurement error. *Statistics in Medicine, 23*(6), 987–998. doi:10.1002/sim.1662 PMID:15027084

Wong, M. Y., Day, N. E., & Wareham, N. J. (1999). Measurement error in epidemiology: the design of validation studies II: bivariate situation. *Statistics in Medicine*, *18*(21), 2831–2845. doi:10.1002/(SICI)1097-0258(19991115)18:21<2831::AID-SIM282>3.0.CO;2-3 PMID:10523745

Woods, N. F. (2007). Multidisciplinary, Inter-disciplinary and Transdisciplinary Approaches to Women's Health Research: A View from the Seattle Midlife Women's Health Study. *Korean J Women Health Nurs*, *13*(4), 237–224.

Wu, C., Miao, X., Huang, L., Che, X., Jiang, G., & Yu, D. et al. (2011). Genome-wide association study identifies five loci associated with suscepti-bility to pancreatic cancer in Chinese populations. *Nature Genetics*, *44*(1), 62–66. doi:10.1038/ng.1020 PMID:22158540

Wylie, K. M., Weinstock, G. M., & Storch, G. A. (2012). Emerging view of the human virome. *Translational Research; the Journal of Labora-tory and Clinical Medicine*, *160*(4), 283–290. doi:10.1016/j.trsl.2012.03.006 PMID:22683423

Yao, F., Coquery, J., & Le Cao, K. A. (2012). Independent Principal Component Analysis for biologically meaningful dimension reduction of large biological data sets. *BMC Bioinformat-ics*, *13*(1), 24. doi:10.1186/1471-2105-13-24 PMID:22305354

Yip, A. M., & Horvath, S. (2007). Gene network in-terconnectedness and the generalized topological overlap measure. *BMC Bioinformatics*, *8*(1), 22. doi:10.1186/1471-2105-8-22 PMID:17250769

Zhang, G. Y., & Block, D. E. (2009). Integration of Data Mining Into a Nonlinear Experimental Design Approach for Improved Performance. *AIChE Journal. American Institute of Chemical Engineers*, *55*(11), 3017–3021. doi:10.1002/aic.11955

Zhang, W., Li, F., & Nie, L. (2010). Integrating multiple 'omics' analysis for microbial biology: Application and methodologies. *Microbiology*, *156*(Pt 2), 287–301. doi:10.1099/mic.0.034793-0 PMID:19910409

Zhang, X., Huang, S., Sun, W., & Wang, W. (2012). Rapid and robust resampling-based multiple-testing correction with application in a genome-wide expression quantitative trait loci study. *Genetics*, *190*(4), 1511–1520. doi:10.1534/genetics.111.137737 PMID:22298711

Zhang, Y., De, S., Garner, J. R., Smith, K., Wang, S. A., & Becker, K. G. (2010). Systematic analysis, comparison, and integration of disease based human genetic association data and mouse genetic phenotypic information. *BMC Medical Genomics*, *3*(1), 1. doi:10.1186/1755-8794-3-1 PMID:20092628

ADDITIONAL READING

Barabasi, A. L., Gulbahce, N., & Loscalzo, J. (2011). Network medicine: A network-based approach to human disease. *Nature Reviews. Genetics*, *12*(1), 56–68. doi:10.1038/nrg2918 PMID:21164525

Clevert, D.-A., Mayr, A., Mitterecker, A., Klam-bauer, G., Valsesia, A., & Forner, K. et al. (2013). Increasing the discovery power of -omics studies. *Systems Biomedicine*, *1*(2), 1–10. doi:10.4161/sysb.25774

Holmes, C., McDonald, F., Jones, M., Ozdemir, V., & Graham, J. E. (2010). Standardization and omics science: Technical and social dimen-sions are inseparable and demand symmetrical study. *OMICS: A Journal of Integrative Biology*, *14*(3), 327–332. doi:10.1089/omi.2010.0022 PMID:20455752

Milne, R., La Vecchia, C., Van Steen, K., Hahn, S., Buchholz, M., & Costello, E. et al. (2013). EU pancreas: An integrated european platform for pancreas cancer research--from basic science to clinical and public health interventions for a rare disease. *Public Health Genomics*, *16*(6), 305–312. doi:10.1159/000355937 PMID:24503591

Mitra, K., Carvunis, A.-R., Ramesh, S. K., & Ideker, T. (2013). Integrative approaches for finding modular structure in biological networks. *Nature Reviews. Genetics*, *14*(10), 719–732. doi:10.1038/nrg3552 PMID:24045689

KEY TERMS AND DEFINITIONS

Components-Based Analysis: One type of multivariate statistical technique that uses dependencies between variables or features of high-dimensional data to obtain a representation in lower-dimensional form, without loss of too much information. Examples include principal components analysis (maximizing the variance accounted for in the original data) or canonical correlation analysis (maximizing covariance accounted for by between-data relationships).

Data Fusion: Data fusion refers to the combination of multiple data sources to obtain improved data. Here, improved means more powerful (larger datasets) or of greater quality or detail.

Dimensionality Reduction: The transformation of high-dimensional data into a meaningful representation of reduced dimensions that is in accordance with the intrinsic holistic nature of the data. As the nature of the data changes by the transformation, obtaining a plausible interpretation of the reduced data remains a challenge.

Integrative Analysis: The use of techniques to connect separate units so as to obtain a holistic and more comprehensive view of the problem. An integrative analysis allows addressing questions that cannot be addressed by single unit analysis, neither by data fusion efforts.

Integromics: Currently, there is no consensus definition for integromics. The term is increasingly being used by the bioinformatics community, to refer to the integration of diverse types of omics data, possibly derived from different experimental platforms. It therefore encompasses both omics data fusion practices and integrated omics analyses.

Network Analysis: The name given to a particular set of techniques that involves defining nodes and edges to connect the nodes, and investigate the properties of the network or performing network inference. Properties of the network are often assessed by evaluating centrality measures (how important a node is) and graph-theoretic properties referring to the graphical representation of the network. Highly linked local regions in the networks (modules) are often targeted for subsequent association analysis with clinical trait variation.

Omics: The word omics refers to those fields of study in life sciences that end in the suffix *–omics*. The suffix is added whenever studies are indicated that are carried out on a large or genome-wide scale. Examples include genomics, epigenomics, transcriptomics, proteomics, interactomics, and metabolomics. No explicit definition exists of what is large, but –omics analyses usually require the availability of well-equipped IT infrastructures as well as computationally efficient algorithms.

Variable Selection: In contrast to dimensionality reduction, variable selection typically does not involve a data transformation and hence does not change the nature of the data. Variable selection refers to the choice of a subset of features based on criteria derived from statistics or prior biological knowledge.

Chapter 14
Current Study Designs, Methods, and Future Directions of Genetic Association Mapping

Jami Jackson
North Carolina State University, USA

Alison Motsinger-Reif
North Carolina State University, USA

ABSTRACT

Rapid progress in genotyping technologies, including the scaling up of assay technologies to genome-wide levels and next generation sequencing, has motivated a burst in methods development and application to detect genotype-phenotype associations in a wide array of diseases and other phenotypes. In this chapter, the authors review the study design and genotyping options that are used in association mapping, along with the appropriate methods to perform mapping within these study designs. The authors discuss both candidate gene and genome-wide studies, focused on DNA level variation. Quality control, genotyping technologies, and single-SNP and multiple-SNP analyses have facilitated the successes in identifying numerous loci influence disease risk. However, variants identified have generally explained only a small fraction of the heritable component of disease risk. The authors discuss emerging trends and future directions in performing analysis for rare variants to detect these variants that predict these traits with more complex etiologies.

INTRODUCTION

The identification and characterization of genetic risk factors that underlie diseases and other traits of clinical importance is a central goal of human genetics. While there are many study designs, technologies, and analytical tools to connect genotypic variation to such phenotype variation, association mapping has emerged as a commonly used suite of approaches to begin dissecting the etiology of complex traits in health related traits. Such association studies are performed to address a number of possible goals, typically related to either better understanding the biological process of a disease or trait or find variants that could serve as biomarkers to improve health care/long

DOI: 10.4018/978-1-4666-6611-5.ch014

term outcomes. In this chapter, we will review key concepts and choices in association studies that measure DNA sequence variations in order to identify genetic loci that influence a particular trait of interest. Most association mapping studies are able to find variants that are of relatively high frequency in the population, though recent studies are starting to interrogate less common, or even rare variants for association.

Unlike linkage studies that are commonly used for Mendelian traits using family based studies, association studies rely on linkage disequilibrium (LD) across the genome to associate phenotypes of interest to genetic loci. LD is a property of genetic variants that describes the degree to which an allele of one variant is inherited (correlated) with an allele of another variant within a population. LD is related to the idea of chromosomal linkage (where two markers on a chromosome are physically joined/inherited together across generations), but is a population level (not individual level) construct. Mutation and recombination with both break apart regions of the chromosome, and this linkage "decay" will build up across generations until eventually all alleles in the population are independent (in linkage equilibrium). There are a number of factors that influence the rate of decay of linkage in human populations, resulting in the fact that different human subpopulations have very different degrees and patterns of LD. An excellent review of LD, including a review of measures to quantify it, can be found in (Devlin & Risch, 1995; Reich et al., 2001).

LD is an important concept underlying association mapping, as it allows for association mapping without actually having to directly assay all variants in the genome (indirect association). Because variants are not statistically (or biologically) independent, a reasonable number of markers can contain a substantial amount of information about the variants across a region of the genome. As genotyping technology advances to allow more variants to be assayed, it cannot be assumed that significantly associated variants are the functional (causative) variant, but it is more likely that they are in LD with the true causal variant(s). This needs to be considered in the study design of an association mapping experiment, with follow up fine resolution mapping experiment and replication.

Traditionally, association mapping relies on the Common Disease Common Variant (CDCV) hypothesis. This hypothesis asserts that common, interacting disease variants are the underlying cause of common complex disease (perhaps with environmental factors as well). This hypothesis emerged from both population genetics theory, as well as some early initial success in associating variants with high allele frequencies to diseases such as Alzheimer's and Type II diabetes (Altshuler et al., 2000; Corder et al., 1993). There are a couple of key ramifications of this hypothesis for association mapping. First, if common variation influences disease, then the overall effect size (penetrance) of each of the common variants must be lower that that of the causal variants of rare disorders. This is due to the direct relationship between the allele frequency and the overall prevalence of disease. Second, if such common risk variants have small effect sizes, but the overall heritability (proportion of variation in the trait that is due to genetic variation) of a trait is high, then it follows that the trait etiology must be due to multiple common, low penetrant variants.

Such association analysis can be done at the level of a single locus test (evaluating a single locus) or, with developments in technology making high throughput (bid data) genotyping accessible, it is becoming common to test for associations at loci across the entire genome. In fact, such genome-wide association studies (GWASs) have successfully identified numerous genetic loci at which common variants influence disease risk. As of January 22, 2014, the National Human Genome Research Institute GWAS Catalog of GWAS publications has 1789 publications and

12331 associated Single Nucleotide Polymorphisms (SNPs) (Hindorff et al., 2014). These successes come from a range of study designs that we will review in the current chapter, along with emerging best practices in quality control and data processing.

While many of these positive results support the CDCV hypothesis for many traits, most studies have used relatively simple analytical tools that barely scratch the surface of the biological complexity understood for these traits. It is becoming clear that many important health traits are highly polygenic, and for many traits, a common disease rare variant hypothesis may be more appropriate. Many of the early genetic association tests involved single-SNP analysis, and now these tests are moving towards more statistically complex multiple-SNP analysis. It is also becoming clear that for many diseases and traits of interest, the complex relationship between genotype and phenotype, may ultimately prove to be inadequately described by simply summing the modest effects from several contributing SNPs (Culverhouse, Suarez, Lin, & Reich, 2002). Instead, the relationship may depend in a fundamental way on genetic etiologies that cannot be assayed on GWAS technologies without more complex analysis. For example, for many diseases, an important part of the genetic etiology may involve epistasis, the interaction between loci, and gene-environment interaction (Culverhouse et al., 2002). Rare variants of large effect may also explain a portion of the missing heritability, and statistical methods designed to jointly test both common and rare variants across genes are becoming increasingly popular.

The objective of this chapter is to review the study designs commonly used in association mapping, options for genotyping strategies, along with the analytical tools typically used to test for genotype/phenotype associations. We will focus most of the discussion on tests for association with common variants; though will briefly discuss emerging tools for uncommon/rare variants in the association analysis framework.

STUDY DESIGNS IN ASSOCIATION MAPPING

Sampling Designs

Two main types of sampling designs are used in association mapping: population-based and family-based. Population-based designs sample affected and unaffected unrelated individuals, while family-based designs sample affected and unaffected related individuals. Population-based designs are the most popular study designs and require fewer resources in terms of time and money than family-based designs. However, selection of participants is a key component in the validity of these designs because population-based designs can be subject to substantial biases and spurious associations (Pare & Henderson, 2013). Population-based designs have been found to be more powerful than family-based designs for localizing regions around common variants (Yang, Q. et al., 2007 and Hintsanen, P. et al., 2006), but family-based designs may be better positioned to detect the effect of very rare variants (Kazma, R. & Bailey, J. N., 2011). The main benefit of family-based designs is that, unlike population-based designs, they are not affected by population stratification bias and the data can be checked for genotyping errors through Mendelian inconsistencies (Kraft & Cox, 2008). When these study designs are conducted simultaneously, they may identify different variants (Zhang, X. et al., 2010).

Study Designs

Within the broad classification of population-based and family-based sampling approaches, there are a number of available study designs, each with their own advantages and disadvantages. These study designs include the following: cross-sectional, cohort, case-control, extreme values, triads and sibling pairs, case-parent-grandparent, general pedigrees, and case-only studies.

- Cross-sectional studies collect genotype and phenotype data across a random sample of the population in one specific point of time.
- Cohort studies collect genotype data, based on exposure status, of individuals that are disease-free and then follow them for disease incidence for a specific period of time.
- Case-control studies collect genotypes of individuals with the phenotype matched with individuals without the phenotype.
- Extreme values studies collect genotypes of individuals at the upper and lower extremes of the quantitative trait distribution.
- Triads and sibling paired collect genotypes of affected individuals and their parents or siblings.
- Case-parent-grandparent studies collect genotypes of affected individuals and their parents and grandparents.
- General pedigree studies collect genotype information of affected individuals and their related families.

- Case-only studies collect genotype information of only affected individuals.

Discussion

As always, there are benefits and limitations to each study design and these are described in Table 1. Which study design is optimal for interrogating a particular disease or trait of interest is dependent on a number of factors. The overall budget, sample availability, ease of phenotyping, etc. all play a role in optimizing the study design for a particular association mapping study.

As mentioned above, any of these study designs can be used in conjunction with any genotyping strategy – an investigator must match the appropriate analytical approach with the genotyping strategy and study design. Analysis methods commonly used for each of these study designs include: logistic regression, Chi-square tests, survival analysis, family-based association tests, and quantitative trait analysis. These and other analysis methods will be discussed further in the

Table 1. Advantages and disadvantages of commonly used study designs in association studies

Study Design	Benefits	Limitations	References
Cross-Sectional	Cost and time efficient; provides estimates of disease incidence; no loss to follow-up	Subject to bias if the disease is rare; causal inference is difficult	Levin (2006)
Cohort	Provides estimate of disease incidence; minimize information bias	Time-consuming and expensive; prone to selection bias and confounding	Welch (1998)
Case-Control	Ideal for rare diseases or long latency; No follow-up necessary; can study multiple exposures; can estimate relative risk	Needs careful selection of controls; subject to confounding; recall bias	Kestenbaum (2009)
Extreme Values	Reduced genotyping cost	Subject to biased estimates of genetic effects	Lin, Zeng, & Tang (2013)
Triads; Sibling Pairs	Robust to population stratification; can assess association and linkage simultaneously	More expensive than case-control design	Schwender et al. (2012)
Case-Parent-Grandparent	Robust to population stratification; can assess association and linkage simultaneously	Grandparents may not be available	Weinberg (2003)
General Pedigrees	Increased power from larger pedigrees; Robust to population stratification; can assess association and linkage simultaneously	Expensive; subject to missing individuals	Martin et al. (2000)
Case-Only	Inexpensive; Useful for detecting interactive effects	Subject to population stratification	Weinberg & Umbach (2000)

Table 2. A reference of association analysis methods commonly used in common study designs

Study Design	Analysis Method	References
Cross-Sectional	Logistic regression, Chi-square tests; linear regression; nonparametric	Zyriax, B-C. et al. (2013) Marson et al. (2014) Yu et al. (2014) Marinou et al. (2007)
Cohort	Survival analysis	Tan et al. (2006)
Case-Control	Logistic regression; Chi-square tests; nonparametric	Schaid et al. (2005) Clarke et al. (2011)
Extreme Values	Logistic regression; semi-parametric	Chen & Li (2011)
Triads; Sibling Pairs	Transmission/disequilibrium test; log-linear models	Starr, Hsu & Schwartz (2005) Troendle & Mills (2010)
Case-Parent-Grandparent	Log-linear models	Weinberg (2003)
General Pedigrees	Pedigree Disequilibrium Test (PDT); Family-based Association tests (FBAT); Quantitative Transmission/disequilibrium test (QTDT)	Wang et al. (2014) Ewens, Li, & Spielman (2008)
Case-Only	Logistic regression; linear regression	Hodgson et al. (2012) Suarez-Gestal et al. (2010)

single-SNP and multiple-SNP analysis sections. Table 2 lists the typical analysis methods used for these study designs.

CHOICES AND TRENDS IN GENOTYPING

As mentioned above, within any study design, a range of options exist for genotyping – from single variant testing through to genome-wide technologies that allow investigators to interrogate the whole genome for novel associations. Any genotyping approach can be used with any of the study designs described above, using appropriate hypothesis tests. Below, we discuss options for genotyping, focusing on DNA level variation, particularly single nucleotide polymorphisms (SNPs) and single nucleotide variants (SNVs). While there are a steadily increasing number of genotyping technologies available, the vast majority of association mapping in the last decade has relied on these markers, so they are the focus of the current chapter. SNPs and SNVs are single base-pair changes in the DNA sequence that occur

within the human genome. SNPs are the common terminology for common variants (often >5%), with SNVs referring to all variants, even those with less common or rare frequencies. SNPs are typically used as markers in association studies, relying on LD as mentioned above to have the SNP association serve as a proxy for functional/causal variants in the genome. For simplicity, we loosely use the term SNP throughout this chapter.

Candidate Gene Genotyping

Candidate gene genotyping has the longest history in genetic association studies. For candidate gene studies, a relatively small number of variants in candidate genes are evaluated. Candidate genes are chosen based on several sources of evidence. Genes may be selected as candidates based on expert biological knowledge (i.e. knowledge of the biochemical pathways that may be related to a disease based on animal models of disease, etc.). Candidates also might be selected on clinical knowledge of the disease. For example, information on the mechanism of action and metabolism of a drug for a drug response outcome might direct the selection of genes for genotyping. Candidate genes could also come from previous studies of the disease or trait, even if the biological or clinical relevance is unclear.

After candidate genes are selected based on any combination of such sources of evidence, the next step in a candidate gene study is the selection of variants within the gene to actually genotype. There are a variety of approaches for selecting variants, and different studies use specific combinations of these approaches. One approach is to select variants within genes based on potential functional significance. The function could be based on the SNPs association with gene expression (variants that are expression quantitative trait loci (eQTLs), on a nonsynonymous change in a protein coding region, or from the deepening annotation on gene function from projects like the Encyclopedia of DNA Elements (ENCODE) (Kuhn, Haussler, & Kent, 2013; Michaelson, Loguercio, & Beyer, 2009). Another commonly used approach for selecting variants within genes is to use linkage disequilibrium to select variant that cover the most information content across the gene. There are a number of tools to help select such "tag" SNPs that best cover the genome, including the TAGGER algorithm in Haploview (Barrett, Fry, Maller, & Daly, 2005; de Bakker et al., 2005). Such tools typically rely on reference populations (such as samples from the International Haplotype Map (HapMap) project) to pick SNPs that serve as good tags in the reference population that is appropriate for the population being evaluated in the planned candidate gene study (International HapMap et al., 2010). Another consideration in choosing variants in the candidate genes is the allele frequencies in the population being studied. Again, this information is typically derived from reference populations, and variants with frequencies high enough for good statistical power to perform association are selected.

Once both genes and variants are selected, candidate gene studies can involve 1-100,000 SNPs (J. Ragoussis, 2009). Broad ranges of technologies are available, as appropriate and cost effective for the scale of the study. For small-scale genotyping experiments (in terms of the number of SNPs), there are a wide variety of technologies available to assay SNPs. For larger scale candidate gene studies, microarray technologies are used to cheaply assay large numbers of SNPs.

The most commonly used genotyping technologies involve either allele discrimination or allele detection methods. All methods used for genotyping SNPs depend on PCR amplification of the genomic regions that span the SNPs before the actual genotyping reaction, and then use very different technologies for assaying variation. While an over generalization, there are a few broad categories of SNP genotyping approaches: hybridization-based methods, enzyme-based methods, and methods that rely on physical properties of DNA. In depth reviews of SNP genotyping technologies can be found in (Kim & Misra, 2007). For the purpose of the association analysis methods, the key outputs of any of the genotyping technologies are the SNP calls for individuals in the study – the two alleles at a particular genomic location. While some technologies can capture more complex genomic structure, most technologies assay bi-allelic SNPs. For biallelic SNPs, SNPs typically have two alleles, meaning within a population there are two commonly occurring base-pair possibilities for a SNP location, where the less common of the two is typically referred to as the minor allele.

For candidate gene studies, investigators have a wide range of options, from using assays like TaqMan for specific SNPs they are targeting, or creating custom chips working with major genotyping companies like Affymetrix (www.affymetrix.com) or Illumina (www.illumina.com) that will help create custom hybridization based SNP arrays with specific variants chosen for a candidate gene study. There are also a few available candidate gene chips available for specific applications. For example, for pharmacogenomics studies (where the traits of interest are drug response traits like toxicities, or measures of drug efficacy), both major genotyping companies Affymetrix (www.Affymetrix.com) and Illumina (www.illumina.com) offer candidate gene chips that cover variation in genes encoding for drug metabolism enzymes and drug transporters.

Genome-Wide Technologies

Genome-wide association studies (GWAS) have been made possible by advances in microarray chip technologies that can be used to genotype at least one million SNPs or more. While other technologies exist, there are two major platforms that are commonly used: Affymetrix Gene Chips, and Illumina's Infinium Beadchips. These two different companies use different assay technologies, and have also made different choices on how to select markers for the assays. Affymetrix assays are based on allelic discrimination by direct hybridization of genomic DNA to arrays containing locus- and allele- specific oligonucleotides that represent either perfect match (PM) or mismatch (MM) probes to each SNP. Illumina assays use a bead-based technology with longer DNA sequences to detect alleles that are slightly more expensive to produce but provide better specificity.

While these chips are called "genome-wide" none of them completely cover all common variation in the genome. As mentioned above, the two different technologies have used different approaches to select markers. The Illumina chips are more expensive to make but provide better specificity. Illumina has chosen to base the SNP selection strategy primarily on the HapMap project results and to supplement with genic and nonsynonymous SNPs plus assays for copy number variations (CNVs) regions, while Affymetrix selected SNPs based on distance-based coverage. There are also differences in the designs of specific chips based on the LD structure of different ethnicities. Researchers should consider these differences to select the genotyping technology that is best suited to the population or populations they are studying. A recent review of these two major

genotyping technologies and their advantages and disadvantages can be found in (Distefano & Taverna, 2011).

Such technologies produce "big data" that require the computational and programming infrastructure to manage this data. Below, we talk about the genotype calling and quality control procedures that are necessary to ensure that good data is being used for downstream analysis.

Next Generation Sequencing

Even as the genome-wide association chip technology improves, next generation sequencing technologies are rapidly changing the way that genetic variation can be assayed. For even larger sequence output, the great limitations of candidate gene and genome-wide association techniques were the need for gels or polymers used as separation media for the fluorescently labeled DNA fragments, the low number of samples which could be analyzed in parallel, and the difficulty of total automation of the sample preparation methods (Ansorge, 2009). Next generation sequencing (NGS) technologies overcomes the limited scalability of traditional sequencing techniques by removing the need for gels and allowing for millions of sequencing reactions to happen in parallel. There are a number of major technologies commercially available, and an ever-increasing number of technologies emerging. Some of the first include: 454 GenomeSequencer, Illumina Genome Analyzer, AB SOLiD, and HeliScope. The 454 GenomeSequencer uses pyrophosphate detection, Genome Analyzer uses sequencing-by-synthesis chemistry, AB SOLiD uses chemistry based on ligation, and HeliScope uses single-molecule DNA sequencing (Ansorge, 2009).

As the price of NGS decreases, it is more commonly being used for association analysis. While the focus of this chapter is more on GWAS chip technologies, it is important to introduce rapidly advancing technologies. The amount of data produced by NGS is even larger than the GWAS chip data, and requires even more computational overhead, even though the goals for mapping are unchanged. NGS is used to call variants in new ways, but the fundamental goals of mapping and the downstream analysis is unchanged – variants are tested for association with important health traits using the methods discussed below.

In such studies, variants are called from the reads that come off the sequencing technologies. Variants then must be called using a workflow that normally follows the following general workflow. First, filtering is performed on the set of NGS reads to remove sources of error/bias. Then reads are aligned to a reference genome. Next, using one of several potential algorithms, that are either based on a statistical model or some heuristics, the likelihood of variation at each locus is predicted. This prediction is based on the quality scores and allele counts of the aligned reads at that locus, and is filtered for quality before association analysis. A review on NGS and how variants are called using that data can be found in (Nielsen, Korneliussen, Albrechtsen, Li, & Wang, 2012).

Issues, Controversies, Problems

The requirement of a PCR amplification step to achieve sensitive and specific SNP genotyping is the main factor that limits the throughput of assays today. Although the main advantage of both the MassEXTEND and GOOD assays is that they avoid the labeling method, the MassEXTEND is an expensive instrument and the GOOD assay is a multi-step procedure (Syvanen, 2001). The main advantage of the Gene Chips are that they allow for very high probe density, but they also have very high failure rates (Syvanen, 2001). The DASH method has an inexpensive labeling method, but complex rules and the TaqMan assay is known for its simplicity, but the probes are expensive (Syvanen, 2001). The Invader assay avoids PCR amplification, but requires a large amount of DNA (Syvanen, 2001). Affymetrix and Infinium are the most widely use genotyping platforms for GWAS

and generally both have had comparable results. Two trends in GWA technologies are higher numbers of markers (Affymetrix) and multisample arrays (Illumina) (J. Ragoussis, 2009). In order to increase the speed and lower the cost associated with performing GWAS, new formats that enable the processing of 96 or even 384 samples in parallel and Affymetrix has already introduced a 96 plate format system (Gene Chip HT PM Array Plate) (J. Ragoussis, 2009). Next generation sequencing platforms provide high speed and throughput, in which genome sequencing projects that took several years with traditional sequencing methods can be completed in a matter of weeks. A limiting factor that remains is the high overall cost, even though compared with traditional sequencing methods, the cost per base is lower by several orders of magnitude (Ansorge, 2009). Another limiting factor is higher sequencing errors from next generation sequencing and the huge amount of data generated in the form of short reads from next generation sequencing that presents a challenge to software developers (Ansorge, 2009).

While genome-wide association studies have become more popular, there are still a number of advantages to candidate gene approaches that need to be considered. Candidate gene studies do have higher power than genome-wide studies of the same sample size, simply based on the lower multiple testing burden of such studies. Additionally, the results of candidate gene studies are often more readily interpreted than results from genome-wide studies. Because candidate genes and variants are chosen for potential functional significance and relevance for the disease or trait being studied, potential biological/clinical hypotheses of how the variants might influence the trait can more straight forward than genome-wide studies where annotation is less thorough. The large downside, of course, with candidate gene approaches is that the success of these studies is dependent on the selection of the correct candidates. Such studies are also limited in their ability to uncover "novel" biology in the association mapping.

In addition to choices in the actual genotyping technology used, the choice of the "scale" of genotyping introduces very different concerns with multiple comparisons from a statistical point of view. Multiple testing problems occur when one considers a number of statistical tests (for example across individual SNPs) simultaneously (Balding, 2006). False positive findings (incorrectly rejecting the null hypothesis) are more likely to occur when one considers the set as a whole, if no correction on the p-value cut-off for significance is performed. As the "scale" of genotyping increases, the number of hypothesis tests that are considered increases, and methods for correcting for multiple testing need to be used. Johnson et al. (2010) provides an excellent review on methods for correcting for multiple comparisons, especially in GWAS. An emerging standard for evidence of significance of a GWAS involving one million SNPs is generally considered to be $p < 5 \times 10^{-8}$ (Moskvina & Schmidt, 2008), which comes from assuming a 5% chance that a positive association occurs and is randomly divided by the total number of effective associations tested (the effective number of variants in the genome, accounting for the correlation between them). This improved Bonferroni correction grants statistical significance only to those SNPs with associated p-values less than 5×10^{-8}, or any other pre-determined standard for evidence of significance. This is considered to be a conservative approach to multiple testing since it aims to reduce the number of false positives but at a cost of potentially increases the number of false negatives. In fact, lower powered studies, (i.e. smaller sample sizes), can have inflated type II error rates under Bonferroni correction. Alternatively, depending on the context for the association analysis, it may be more desirable to focus on reducing the number of false negatives; in this case, the False Discovery Rate method can be applied (Moskvina & Schmidt, 2008). Finally, while traditional permutation testing is essentially a computationally intractable solution for multiple testing when dealing with millions of SNPs, there

have been efforts to adapt the method for GWAS data (Che, In Submission). For candidate gene studies, such extreme p-values would not need to be observed to declare results significant. This is an important issue in considering power – for a sample size, candidate gene studies will have much higher power to detect smaller genetic effects than GWAS studies.

Solutions and Recommendations

Users interested in applying SNP genotyping approaches face choices from a wide spectrum of commercially available systems. Selecting the most suitable system requires a clear definition of aims and understanding of the equipment. Systems capable of determining in one reaction hundreds of thousands of genotypes are appropriate for GWAS, whereas smaller numbers can be suitable for pharmacogenetic studies or in genetic tests (J. Ragoussis, 2006). Another factor to consider is the number of samples that need to be processed simultaneously. In some applications, it is important to determine the genotypes of 1-100 samples at a time in a cost-efficient way, whereas a candidate gene association study typically requires genotyping thousands of samples. GWAS are designed to detect weak effects and thus samples are frequently not representative of the population, while candidate gene studies generally require representative population-based samples (Teare, 2011). A huge gap in cost still exists between commercial genome-wide association platforms and custom SNP arrays. Overall cost savings could be achieved through the availability of validated assays for the largest proportion of the ~10 million SNPs in the human genome (J. Ragoussis, 2009). Next generation sequencing has novel applications in biology and medicine beyond traditional sequencing methods such as in personal genomics and analysis of RNA transcripts. Next generation sequencing techniques have already demonstrated the ability to detect cancer alleles with deep sequencing of genomic

DNA in cancerous tissues, which would have been very tedious for traditional sequencing techniques (Ansorge, 2009).

In addition to technological choices, choices in the "scale" of genotyping assay and study design need to carefully consider issues of power, largely driven by concerns with multiple testing. While it can be tempting to assay all variation, there are many cases where carefully thought through candidate gene approaches can be powerful and appropriate choices for a given phenotype.

QUALITY CONTROL

Genotype Calling

After genotyping the individuals, the alleles are represented as signal intensity data from the two allelic probes. With perfect data, all subjects with the same genotype would have identical signal intensities and there would only be three different signal intensity dots representing the three genotypes. However, many factors affect the signal intensity at the subject level, including DNA concentration and the hybridization process, so that signal intensities of all subjects for the three genotypes form three clusters instead (Ziegler, Konig, & Thompson, 2008). Genotype calling is the assignment of genotypes to individuals according to their signal intensities and is usually performed automatically by the platform's calling algorithms. Calling algorithms rely on clearly separated clusters to assign genotypes. If there are individuals that lie in the overlapping clusters, they are deemed missing by the algorithm, which leads to informative missingness (Weale, 2010). Informative missingness is a problem in GWAS because missing values are not randomly distributed and can lead to false positives and false negatives (Weale, 2010).

High accuracy of calling algorithms is necessary to avoid introducing errors in the association analyses. Inconsistencies between calling algo-

rithms can lead to variations in the associated SNPs (Hong et al., 2010a). Threshold parameters have to be set for calling algorithms. The threshold value determines whether a genotype is assigned or missing. For example, a study demonstrated that differences in threshold values affected the consistency of the Bayesian Robust Linear Model and Mahalanobis distance classifier (BRLMM) (Affymetrix, 2006) included in the Affymetrix software package and the inconsistency affected the number of significant associated SNPs (Hong et al., 2010b). Therefore, based on their study, when genotyping with the Affy500K and using the BLRMM calling algorithm, smaller and consistent thresholds should be used to make genotype calls for GWAS (Hong et al., 2010b). In addition, quality of the samples affects the calling algorithm. Low quality samples can be removed prior to genotype calling by reviewing the plots of the signal intensities for each SNP and looking for aberrations and genotypes that should be recalled in order to reduce genotyping error (Pluzhnikov et al., 2010).

Visual/manual inspection of all called SNPs across the genome would be an unrealistic task; it is crucial that some level of visualization is used in the quality control procedure. It is especially crucial that before significant findings (significant SNP-trait associations) are reported, that the genotype calls underlying those association are manually inspected.

Screening Variants and Samples

Even after taking measures to reduce the error rates of genotyping calls, additional standard quality control measures should be performed. These quality control measures can be divided into two areas: individual-level and SNP-level quality control steps. While each study may require slightly different QC approaches, there are a number of generally accepted guidelines for best practices, and a number of tools available to implement them. PLINK (http://pngu.mgh.

harvard.edu/purcell/plink/) is widely used to for quality control procedures (Purcell et al., 2007). Some of the best practices in QC filtering are outlined below.

Individual-Level Quality Control

- Genotype calling error rates should be assessed by reviewing a plot of missing genotype rates. Generally, individuals with greater than 3% missing genotypes should be removed (Ziegler, 2009).
- Gender checks should be performed using genotype data from the X-chromosome. Homozygosity rates can be calculated across all X-chromosome SNPs for each individual and compared to the expected rate or inbreeding coefficients can be calculated to determine the severity of the departure from Hardy-Weinberg equilibrium (Weale, 2010).
- Duplicates and relatedness among the individuals should be assessed. The metric, identity by state, IBS, is calculated for each pair of individuals based on the average frequency of alleles shared in common at the genotyped SNPs, and identity by descent, IBD, is estimated using genome-wide IBS data (Anderson et al., 2011). Typically, IBD > 0.1875 identifies related individuals and IBD > 0.98 identifies duplicates. (Anderson et al., 2011).
- Population stratification should be examined. Population stratification occurs when genotype differences are related to ethnic origin instead of disease (Cardon & Palmer, 2003). If the goal is to maintain a homogeneous study population, individuals from different ethnic backgrounds should be removed (Ziegler, 2009). Or if population substructure is to be included, researchers can analyze the data by stratifying it with the reported geographic location or ethnicity (Ziegler et al., 2008).

If population substructure is present and there is no geographical information about the subjects, adjustments can be made using genomic control (Devlin & Roeder, 1999), STRUCTURE (Pritchard, Stephens, & Donnelly, 2000), or EIGENSTRAT (Price et al., 2006). Genomic control can correct for population substructure by multiplying the Chi-square statistic by a factor of the inverse of the variance inflation factor, a factor that estimates over dispersion (Clayton et al., 2005). STRUCTURE can be used to infer population stratification and assign individuals to the ethnic groups (Pritchard et al., 2000). EIGENSTRAT uses principal components analysis (PCA) to infer the ethnicities, adjust genotypes and phenotypes by amounts attributable to ethnicity from the PCA, and then computes the final association statistics with the genotypes and phenotypes adjusted by ethnicity (Price et al., 2006).

- Heterozygosity rate should be examined. The heterozygosity rate is a measure of DNA sample quality. High heterozygosity rates indicate that the sample is contaminated while low heterozygosity rates indicate inbreeding (Anderson et al., 2010).

SNP-Level Quality Control

- Genotyping call rates for SNPs across all individuals should be assessed. SNPs with call rates that are less than 98% are generally removed (Ziegler, 2009).
- Deviations from the Hardy-Weinberg equilibrium (HWE), which assumes that there is a fixed relationship between allele and genotype frequencies, may point to quality problems in the genotyping (Ziegler et al., 2008). SNPs with HWE p-values < 0.0001 are usually removed (Ziegler, 2009). This filter for HWE should be used across the whole cohort if a quantitative trait or a co-

hort study is used, but should only be applied to the cases in a case/control study. This is because the sample selection violates assumptions for HWE, so disease associated SNPs would be removed by such a filter.

- Testing for significant differences in genotyping call rates between cases and controls should be completed. If cases and controls come from different sources, tests should be completed for significant differences in call rate and genetic frequencies (Anderson et al., 2011).

- SNPs with very low minor allele frequencies (MAF) are also typically removed (though, as we will discuss in later sections, this may not be applicable for rare variant analysis). Rare SNPs are typically removed for two reasons. First, genotype calling algorithms have difficulty calling SNPs with low MAF (Anderson et al., 2011). Second, studies are rarely powered to detect variants with low frequencies. Usually, SNPs with a MAF threshold smaller than 1-2% is removed, but studies with small sample size may need to set this threshold lower (Anderson et al., 2011).

Genotype Imputation

Genotype imputation is the process of using the observed genotypes at neighboring SNPs to predict the genotypes for the SNPs that were not directly assayed in the study. Genotype imputation can be used to replace missing SNPs that were removed during the quality control process or to add additional SNPs that were not directly genotyped for the study to try to increase coverage across the genome (Marchini et al., 2007). Additionally, genotype imputation is useful when combining genetic association studies for meta-analysis since there may be missing genotype data between studies (Marchini & Howie, 2010). Many genotyping platforms have multi-marker prediction

algorithms that tag certain SNPs in order to infer other SNPs that were not genotyped. The greatest boost in power for GWAS has been demonstrated for rare, untagged SNPs (Marchini et al., 2007). In addition, the accuracy of genotype imputation is improved with low-frequency variants when reference datasets from different populations are combined and it has been shown to be efficient with large sequence-based reference panels. (Howie, Marchini, & Stephens, 2011). Commonly used genotype imputation software includes IMPUTE2 (Howie, Donnelly, & Marchini, 2009), fastPHASE (Scheet & Stephens, 2006), BIMBAM (Servin & Stephens, 2007), MACH (Li et al., 2010), and BEAGLE (Browning & Browning, 2009). Other best practices in study design and QC could be the careful use of duplicates within and across plates to check for overall quality, and potential plate and batch effects.

Discussion

Implementing quality control is an integral part of genetic association studies and should be planned out in detail. Quality control procedures are designed to reduce the number of spurious associations, but there is some variation in filters that are applied between studies. In order to successfully implement a genetic association study and to adequately combine studies, proper experimental design and quality control records need to be maintained (Pluzhnikov et al., 2010). Additional quality control filters could be applied to family-based study designs. For example, a transmission test was developed to identify probands even after insufficient quality control filters (Fardo, Ionita-Laza, & Lange, 2009).

SINGLE-SNP ANALYSIS

Typically, regardless of the scale of genotyping (a single SNP candidate gene study or a GWAS), standard analysis involved testing for disease/trait association for a single SNP at a time. These associations analyses are done with pretty traditional statistical tests, relying on the quality control filtering stages to ensure compliance with parametric assumptions, or to indicate the need to switch to nonparametric tests. In the current section, we briefly review the commonly used tools for single-SNP analysis. Such analyses are typically repeated for all SNPs included in a study, with appropriate control for multiple comparisons applied to account for the genetic "scale" of the study. There are multiple examples of single-SNP analyses. Giaconni et al. (2014) studied two SNPs using linear regression models to test the association of each SNP with pro-inflammatory mediators, laboratory parameters, and zinc status. Yang et al. (2014) investigated three SNPs by testing the association between each SNP and risk for incident, sporadic colorectal adenomas using logistic regression. Four SNPs were examined by Shen et al. (2013) using Chi-square tests to test the association of each SNP with coronary artery disease and myocardial infarction in a case-control study design. Linear mixed effects models were used to analyze 22 SNPs by Hivert et al. (2008) by testing the association of each SNP with adiponectin levels and glycemic phenotypes. Single-SNP analyses must adjust for multiple testing by determining a p-value threshold for significance.

Regression Analysis

Linear regression and logistic regression are commonly used in population-based association studies. For quantitative traits, linear regression assumes a linear relationship between the mean value of the trait and the genotype. The trait is assumed to be approximately normally distributed for each genotype, with a common variance. If normality does not hold, a transformation such as log of the original trait values could be used have an approximately normal dataset. A typical linear regression model is:

$$E(Y) = \beta_0 + \beta_1 X + \beta_2 G$$

where Y is the dependent variable, X is the set of covariates, G is the set of genotypes of the SNP, and $\beta = (\beta_0, \beta_1, \beta_2)$ is the parameter vector (Bůžková, 2013).

Logistic regression is a variation of linear regression that fits a function with continuous or discrete independent variables and dichotomous dependent variables (Motsinger-Reif, Reif, Fanelli, & Ritchie, 2008). A typical logistic regression model is:

$$\text{logit}(\pi) = \log(\pi/(1 - \pi)) = \beta_0 + \beta_1 X + \beta_2 G$$

where π is the probability of disease risk, X is the set of covariates, G is the set of genotypes of the SNP, and $\beta = (\beta_0, \beta_1, \beta_2)$ is the parameter vector (Nick & Campbell, 2007).

Many standard statistical packages implement linear and logistic regression, including the PLINK software mentioned above that is commonly used.

Generalized Linear Models

Linear and logistic regression are a part of a larger group of models called generalized linear models. Two common linear models used in genetic association studies are log-linear models and mixed linear models. Log-linear models are used to model count data, such as the log of the expected counts of genotype combinations for mother, father, and offspring (Agopian & Mitchell, 2011). Mixed effects models separate genetic effects into random and fixed and are typically described as:

$$Y = X\beta + g + e$$

where, Y represents the outcome, X is the matrix of fixed effects that include the covariates and the SNP, g is the random genetic effect, and e is the random residual effect (Li & Zhu, 2013).

The majority of genetic association studies involving linear models report *p*-values using frequentist testing procedures such as likelihood ratio tests, Wald tests, and score tests. Bayesian approaches can be applied to linear models in order to utilize prior information and combine evidence from the data.

Standard statistical packages can fit linear models. Various packages that provide tools for Bayesian inference are included in software such as R, the open source statistical software (R Core Team, 2013).

Chi-Square Tests

Chi-square tests use contingency tables to test for independence of disease status and genotype status. The data for each SNP is represented in a contingency table of counts and association is determined using the Chi-square test of independence of the rows and columns of the contingency table. Chi-square tests have the power to detect gene–trait relationships, but can be less powerful than other methods that incorporate the assumed genetic trait model (Wang, 2012). Alternative methods such as Cochran-Armitage trend test can improve upon the Chi-square test by incorporating the assumed genetic model (Clarke et al., 2011). Chi-square tests are also highly sensitive to potential confounding population stratification (Wang, 2012). Chi-square tests can be implemented using standard statistical packages.

Survival Analysis

Survival analysis methods model the survivor function or hazard function as a function of genotype to assess genetic association with longevity. The Cox regression model has been commonly used for single-SNP analysis (Tan, Q. et al., 2006). Survival analysis methods can be implemented using standard statistical packages.

Semi-Parametric and Non-Parametric

Semi-parametric and non-parametric approaches do require distributional assumptions, such as normality. Semi-parametric approaches still generally incorporate a plausible model in the method, while non-parametric approaches do not incorporate models. Nonparametric methods used in genetic association studies include permutation tests and the Kruskal-Wallis test. Permutation tests determine statistical significance based on rearrangements of the labels of a genetic dataset (Efron & Tibshirani, 2007). The Kruskal-Wallis test is a robust method designed to detect the difference in the trait distributions of the genotypes, but can be suboptimal if the genetic model is dominant or recessive (Konietschke, Libiger, & Hothorn, 2012). The permutation tests and Kruskal-Wallis test can be readily conducted in R (R Core Team, 2013).

Family-Based Association Statistics

The simplest method of the family-based association methods is the transmission disequilibrium test (TDT), which uses parents who are heterozygous for an allele associated with disease and calculates the frequency that the allele is transmitted to offspring (Allison, 1997). TDT is resistant to confounding due to population stratification (Allison, 1997). TDT is a special case of family-based association tests (FBAT), which are non-parametric analysis tests for family data. Pedigree disequilibrium tests (PDT) test for departure of allele transmission to affected pedigree members from the null distribution (Martin et al., 2000). Quantitative transmission/disequilibrium test (QTDT) uses linkage disequilibrium tests based on the variance components of the genotypes and is protected from population stratification (Havill et al., 2005).

TDT can be implemented using Unphased (Dudbridge, 2008) or GeneHunter (Kruglyak & Lander, 1998). PDT can be implemented using the software PDT (Martin et al., 2000). FBAT can be implemented using the software FBAT (Laird, Horvath, & Xu, 2000). The software QTDT can be used for the QTDT (Abecasis, Cardon, & Cookson, 2000).

Discussion

One important point that needs to be considered when using any of these single SNP approaches is exactly how genotypes are encoded within these models. For methods like the generalized linear models, survival analysis, etc., SNPs could be entered into these models as a numeric value (such as 0,1, or 2 for the number of minor alleles), or dummy-encoding schemes could be used to force a categorical interpretation of the SNPs. These two different encodings correspond to two different genetic hypotheses – either an additive genetic effect or a genotypic effect (including dominant and recessive models). This choice of genotype encoding not only corresponds to different genetic assumptions, but this choice also has implications for the statistical power of a test, as the degrees of freedom for the test may change depending on the number of genotype-based groups that are observed. Understanding the differences in these modeling choices is important, and more details about these choices can be found in Lettre, Lange, & Hirschhorn (2007). While many investigators take different approaches and make different assumptions, a common practice for GWAS or large scale candidate gene studies is to examine additive models only, as the additive model has reasonable power to detect both additive and dominant effects (though very low power to detect recessive effects). If multiple genotype encodings are considered, it is important to correct for this with appropriate multiple testing control.

While the tests described above are often performed for a single SNP at a time, there are often several covariates included in these models (as mentioned briefly). It is important to highlight that the careful selection of covariates is very important for the success of these models. Covariates that are known to influence the trait or disease of interest should be included in the association model. Factors such as sex, age, study site, and other known clinical covariates are often candidates in human health application. Covariate adjustment reduces spurious associations due to sampling artifacts or biases in study design, but adjustment comes at the price of using additional degrees of freedom, which may impact statistical power. As mentioned above, measures of population substructure are also typically included to prevent issues with population substructure.

The usual statistical methods that are applied to the study designs mentioned in the previous section are listed in Table 2. While single-SNP analysis has resulting in many successes in association analysis, and will likely remain standard practice in most association analysis, there are many limitations that motivate additional analysis used in more recently developed methods. In general, single-SNP analysis can lead to increased computational burden compared to more advanced statistical approaches (Dai et al., 2013). Multiple testing is another issue, which can lead to inflated Type I error and reduced ability to detect small effects (Gao, Q. et al., 2011). Single-SNP analysis also ignores linkage disequilibrium and is not powered to detect rare variants (Kim et al., 2010). Single-SNP analyses have been found to be unable to detect the effect of ungenotyped SNPs and multi-SNP effects (Wu et al., 2013). Lastly, single-SNP analyses do not incorporate interactions in genetic association studies (Vermeulen et al., 2007). Multiple-SNP analyses have been developed to overcome many of these issues. Most of these single-SNP approaches discussed in this section can be expanded to include multiple SNPS.

MULTIPLE-SNP ANALYSIS

Unlike single-SNP analyses, which test SNPs one at a time, multiple-SNP analyses test a number of SNPs simultaneously in an association study. These approaches enhance single-SNP analyses and can help capture some of the missing heritability (Ehret et al., 2012). For example, Reimers et al. (2012) used logistic regression to test whether multiple alleles in a pathway were related to alcohol dependence. One of the first studies to use random forests to analyze a GWAS was conducted by Goldstein et al. (2010) and they found four new candidate genes associated with multiple sclerosis. Haplotype-based methods were used to determine whether multiple SNPs were associated with diabetic immunity (Aly et al., 2006).

In the current section, we briefly review some of the more popular methods for multiple-SNP analysis, pointing readers to references if they would like to learn more details of particular approaches.

Regression-Based Methods

The most frequently used regression methods for multiple-SNP analysis are generalized linear models, which include linear regression and logistic regression. A common statistical problem with these regression methods is variable selection, the process of deciding which variables to include in the model in order to retain the variables with the largest effect. Shrinkage regression methods have been developed for generalized linear models to address variable selection issues by using a penalty function that yields a sparse model with minimally biased estimators. Shrinkage methods include LASSO, ridge regression, boosting, NEG, MCP, and CAR scores.

- LASSO stands for Least Absolute Shrinkage and Selection Operator. LASSO shrinks some covariates and sets others to zero by minimizing the residual sum of squares subject to a constraint (Tibshirani, 1996). The LASSO method encourages

sparsity, but can lead to biased estimates (Ayers & Cordell, 2010).

- Ridge regression is a continuous process that also shrinks coefficients, but it does not shrink them to zero (Tibshirani, 1996). Ridge regression is also subject to bias (Ayers & Cordell, 2010).

- Boosting finds a highly accurate hypothesis by combining multiple weaker hypotheses using weights (Souza et al., 2010).

- NEG stands for Normal Exponential Gamma and it selects one SNP for each causal variant, indicating the number of underlying causal SNPs genotyped in the dataset (Hoggart et al., 2008).

- MCP stands for Minimax Concave Penalty and it uses the same rate of penalization as the LASSO when the covariates are near zero, but when the covariates are away from zero, it continuously relaxes the rate of penalization until it reaches a threshold (Ayers & Cordell, 2010). The MCP has less biased estimates of large covariates than LASSO because the covariate values that are above the threshold contribute equally to the total penalty (Ayers & Cordell, 2010).

- CAR scores, Correlation-Adjusted (marginal) correlation scores, do not rely on a penalty function and instead groups correlated covariates (Zuber & Strimmer, 2011). CAR scores have been shown to work as well as regression approaches including LASSO (Zuber & Strimmer, 2011).

LASSO, ridge regression, boosting, MCP, and CAR can be implemented in R (R Core Team, 2013). NEG can be implemented in the HLASSO software program (Hoggart et al., 2008). These approaches are successful for candidate gene studies, but are not readily computationally or statistically tractable for genome-wide association studies.

Machine Learning Methods

Machine learning approaches have gained popularity in genetic association studies due to their reduced reliance on model assumptions and their ability to detect interactions and non-linear effects. Machine learning approaches include kernel machines, decision trees, random forests, and support vector machines. Additionally, such approaches are computationally feasible for the "big data" of GWAS.

- Kernel machines use kernel functions, which are similarity metrics based on genotype values, to compare similarity in phenotypes between subjects with similarity in genotypes (Wu et al., 2013). The choice of the kernel can significantly impact power due to underlying trait differences (Wu et al., 2013).
- Decision trees are structures that iteratively divide the data into classifications. Decision trees have been found to be subject to noise and difficult to use when interpreting the value of an individual SNP within the tree (Guy, Santago, & Langefeld, 2012).
- Random forests builds a forest of unpruned classification and regression trees by repeatedly starting with a bootstrap sample of the data, selecting a random subset of all variables in the data, and finding a variable that best splits the data into groups (Goldstein, B. A. et al., 2010). Random forests make few model assumptions, have been shown to be accurate, and are robust to noise (Schwarz, König, & Ziegler, 2010).
- Support vector machines are learning algorithms that learn a classifier by mapping training samples into a high-dimensional space and finding an optimal hyper plane that separates them (Ban et al., 2010).

Kernel machines, decision trees, and random forests can be implemented in R (R Core Team, 2013). Support vector machines can be implemented using the SVM-light program (Joachims, 1999).

Haplotype-Based Methods

Haplotypes are believed to account for a large portion of human genetic variability. A haplotype is a combination of SNPs or other markers at adjacent locations on a chromosome that are inherited together. Haplotypes can correlate a gene with a phenotype without the need for single SNPs (Stephens et al., 2001). Since haplotypes are not observable, unphased genotypes have to be used to infer the haplotypes before testing can be done. There are multiple software programs that have been designed to infer haplotypes including the previously considered gold standard for unrelated individuals, Phase v2.1, which has been found to be slow in practice for large data sets (Stephens & Scheet, 2005). Testing methods for unrelated individuals include score statistics and regression methods, while testing for related individuals involve family-based association statistics (Liu, Zhang, & Zhao, 2008).

Epistasis and Gene-Environment Interactions

Epistasis is a general term used to describe any set of complex interactions among genetic loci and is believed to explain some of the underlying complexity of traits (Phillips, 2008). Gene-environment interactions are used to describe the effect between environmental exposures and genetic variants and their inclusion in statistical models may increase power to detect significant factors that influence complex traits (Winham & Biernacka, 2013). Four main search methods that are used for epistasis and gene-environment interactions are: exhaustive search, stochastic search, heuristic search, and stepwise approaches (Shang et al., 2011).

- Exhaustive search enumerates all M-locus interactions to identify the significant effects, but can be computationally burdensome for large datasets (Shang et al., 2011). Examples include multifactor dimensionality reduction (Ritchie et al., 2001), the backward genotype-trait association (Zheng, Wang, & Lo, 2006), tree-based epistasis association mapping (Zhang et al., 2010), and genome wide interaction search (Goudey et al., 2013).
- Stochastic search uses random chance to search for significant effects, but increased number of SNPs may reduce accuracy (Shang et al., 2011). Examples include random forests, Bayesian epistasis association mapping (Zhang & Liu, 2007), epistatic module detection (Tang et al., 2009), and an ensemble approached based on boosting (Li, Horstman, & Chen, 2011).
- Heuristic search relies on various techniques to increase speed and find significant effects, but they are not guaranteed to find globally optimal solutions (Shang et al., 2011). Approaches include a two-stage ant colony optimization algorithm (Wang et al., 2010), predictive rule inference (Wan et al., 2010), and cuckoo search epistasis (Aflakparast et al., 2014).

The feasibility of applying these methods to large-scale candidate gene or GWAS studies depends on the search method used. The exhaustive search approaches are not computationally feasible for higher order interactions on GWAS data, but are powerful for candidate gene studies. The other search techniques are computationally feasible for GWAS studies, but due to the incomplete search of the fitness landscape may miss some types of interactions. A review of some of the advantages and disadvantages of approaches for detecting interactions can be found in (McKinney, Reif, Ritchie, & Moore, 2006).

Discussion

While the results of multiple-SNP analyses are promising, there are some limitations. Multiple-SNP analyses require multiple degrees of freedom, which can lower the power of the test (Schaid et al., 2005). Many of the GWAS that search for interactions effects focus on pairwise interactions and have reduced ability to detect higher order interactions. In order to obtain computational efficiency, more recent studies are taking a stepwise approach to detect effects by first employing a filtering stage and then a search stage. BOOST, Boolean Operation-based Screening and Testing, first selects all pairs of SNPs that pass a specific threshold based on an approximate likelihood ratio statistic and then uses a likelihood ratio test to find significant pairs of SNPs (Wan et al., 2010). BOOST, however, is only designed for pairwise interactions. Screen and clean (SC) uses a lasso procedure to first filter the SNPs and then cleans the data using hypotheses testing to find significant interactions (Wu et al., 2010). SC considers all SNPs as main effects in the first step of the screening process, and then in the second step, it considers the candidate SNPs from the first step in addition to all pairwise interactions of the candidate SNPs (Wu et al., 2010). Leem et al. (2014) assessed epistasis using a *k*-means clustering filtering process combined with using mutual information theory to find significant interactions. All of these screening methods rely on filters that use statistical approaches, but biological filters, such as including pathway analysis, may be able to detect new complex interactions as well (Bush et al., 2011). With pathway analysis, genes, represented by multiple SNPs, are placed into biological pathways and the biological pathways are tested for association with the phenotype. However, the performance of statistical filters depends on the specific filter being used and the performance of biological filters relies on prior knowledge, which can be error-prone and incomplete (Sun et al., 2014). Therefore, biological and statistical filters may complement each other in studies to detect significant effects. In addition, newer methods are using genes as testing units instead of markers. Gene–gene interaction tests consist of tests for the interaction between two genes comprised of significant SNP interactions and have been found to detect novel interactions not seen in SNP-based tests (Oh et al., 2012 and Ma, Clark, & Keinan, 2013).

GWAS META-ANALYSIS

Meta-analysis of GWAS is becoming a common method for increasing the power to detect weak genotype effects, as more GWAS have been completed. A meta-analysis of GWAS involves combining and analyzing summary results from each of the studies. Since one GWAS may not be enough to detect significant effects, meta-analysis of GWAS are conducted to validate previously found associations and discover new findings. Two loci previously found in GWAS to be associated with Kawasaki disease were replicated in a GWAS replication and meta-analysis (Chang et al., 2013). In a GWAS replication and meta-analysis for IgA nephrology, four susceptibility loci to were replicated and two new alleles and an interaction effect were discovered (Kiryluk et al., 2012).

Statistical Methods

The statistical methods employed in meta-analysis studies are traditional statistical approaches. They include methods based on p-values and z-scores, fixed effects, random effects, and Bayesian approaches.

- The p-values approach is the easiest method and it combines p-values using Fisher's method, but it does not sufficiently account for differences between weights applied to the studies and differences in the directions of effects (Evangelou & Ioannidis, 2013). The z-score method is closely related to Fisher's approach, except that z-scores take into account the weights for the studies and the direction of effects (Begum et al., 2012).

- Fixed effects meta-analysis is a popular approach for synthesizing GWAS data and it assumes that genetic effects are the same across studies. The inverse variance weighting model is a widely used method that weights each study according to the inverse of its squared standard error (Evangelou & Ioannidis, 2013).

- Random effects meta-analysis assumes that genetic effects are different across studies. The most popular estimator of the between-study variance for the random effects approach is the DerSimonian and Laird estimator, which estimates the between-study variance using a non-iterative method of moments approach (Evangelou & Ioannidis, 2013). The DerSimonian and Laird estimator may give less robust results with small numbers, such as with rare variants (Evangelou & Ioannidis, 2013).

- Meta-analysis of GWAS involving Bayesian methods is still in its infancy due to the computational complexity. One study successfully applied Bayesian methods to a meta-analysis of candidate gene studies, but noted if the assumption of a common linkage disequilibrium (LD) structure across the studies is not valid, group-specific LD priors may increase computational time (Iorio et al., 2011).

METAL is widely used to implement methods based on p-values, z scores, and fixed effects

(Willer, Li, & Abecasis, 2010). PLINK (http://pngu.mgh.harvard.edu/purcell/plink/) is another popular software program that can implement a fixed effects and random effects meta-analysis (Purcell et al., 2007).

Discussion

Since there may be increased power in conducting a meta-analysis of GWAS, some groups have turned to conducting 'mega-analysis' of GWAS, which involves combining and analyzing raw data on individual patients from each of the studies. The idea is that a mega-analysis will yield better estimates than a meta-analysis since the analysis will have more detailed information. However, the process of obtaining the data on individual patients can be difficult and expensive. Lin & Zeng (2010) show that a meta-analysis is as efficient as a mega-analysis, provided that both analyses are performed under the same assumptions. Since meta-analysis has been useful in identifying main effects, the hope is that it will identify even more significant interaction effects. Sung et al. (2014) has shown that meta-analysis is effective for detecting interaction effects and that results for meta-analysis and mega-analysis are largely consistent for both main and interaction effects.

UNCOMMON AND RARE VARIANT ANALYSIS

Although GWAS are a powerful approach for detecting common variants, they are underpowered for detecting associations with rare variants (Li & Leal, 2008). Typically, uncommon variants are defined as variants with a minor allele frequency < 5% and rare variants are defined as variants with a minor allele frequency < 1%. Rare variants may be integral in determining the susceptibility for some complex diseases (Bodmer & Bonilla, 2008). There are multiple statistical methods that have been developed for rare variant analysis.

There are single-variant and multiple-variants analyses similar to the single-SNP and multiple-SNP analyses that were discussed in the previous sections. For single-variant analyses, these include Chi-square tests and regression models. Regression models and machine learning methods are also used for multiple-variant analyses. However, these traditional statistical methods may not be adequate for studying these uncommon and rare variants. In order to avoid multiple testing issues and multiple degrees of freedom while still taking into account the effects of these low frequency variants, collapsing methods have been developed. Collapsing methods combine information across multiple variant sites and include approaches that use weighted sums, model group heterogeneity, and model variant heterogeneity.

Weighted Sums

Methods involving weighted sums use the weighted sum of all rare variants in a region to test whether those variants are associated with disease. The popular methods include a group wise association test developed by Madsen & Browning (2009), a method developed by Morris & Zeggini (2010), and the combined multivariate and collapsing test (CMC) by Li & Leal (2008).

- The group wise association method group's variants based on function and weights each of the variants based on its frequency (Madsen & Browning, 2009). Each individual is assigned a score that is the sum of the weights of the variants and a permutation test that adjusts for the weights is used to test for excess variants in affected individuals (Madsen & Browning, 2009). With this test, common variants can be down-weighted and rare variants can be up-weighted.
- The method developed by Morris & Zeggini (2010) models the phenotype in a linear regression as a function of the ratio of the number of rare variants that have at

least one copy of a minor allele to the total number of rare variants. Likelihood ratio tests of association are conducted to detect the accumulation of rare variants to disease (Morris & Zeggini, 2010).

- The CMC test divides variants into groups, collapses the data within the groups, and applies a multivariate test to analyze the groups (Li & Leal, 2008). Rare and common variants could be grouped according to their allele frequency.

Group Heterogeneity

The methods that involve weighted sums have sufficient power if most of the variants have some effect and if the effects of the variants are either all protective or are all deleterious (Logsdon et al., 2014). However, if these assumptions are not valid, another group of tests have been developed to model the heterogeneity of effects among groups of variants. Popular methods included the c-alpha test developed by Neale et al. (2010) and the Sequence Kernel Association Test (SKAT) developed by Wu et al. (2011).

- The c-alpha test is used to test rare variants in cases and controls and compares the variance of the observed counts of the variants to the variance of the expected counts, assuming a binomial distribution (Neale et al., 2010). The assumption is that cases will have more variants associated with disease than controls. C-alpha is designed to detect the presence of a mixture of protective and deleterious variants (Neale et al., 2010).
- SKAT uses a multiple regression model to test for association between common and rare variants in a region and a dichotomous or continuous phenotype while adjusting for covariates (Wu et al., 2011). Unlike c-alpha, SKAT can account for confounders such as population stratification by using the covariates (Wu et al., 2011).

Variant Heterogeneity

Instead of assessing the effect of groups of variants, as in the previous methods, methods that involve variant heterogeneity use the data to model the effects of individual variants. Current methods include a step-wise selection model developed by Hoffman, Marini, & Witte (2010), CHARM (Cardin, Mefford, & Witte, 2012), and a variational Bayes discrete mixture test (Logsdon et al., 2014).

- The step-wise selection model selects the best combination of rare variants using the data by calculating a test statistic for each variant (Hoffman, Marini, & Witte, 2010).
- CHARM, Cross-Validated Hierarchical Aggregated Regression Method, uses a multiple logistic regression model with a hierarchical structure to jointly model the effect of each variant within a region (Cardin, Mefford, & Witte, 2012). CHARM uses a likelihood approach based on cross-validation to assess significance (Cardin, Mefford, & Witte, 2012).
- The variational Bayes discrete mixture test uses a discrete mixture model to model each rare variant effect and uses a likelihood ratio test for association (Logsdon et al., 2014).

Discussion

Methods for uncommon and rare variant analysis attempt to balance the low frequency signals of the uncommon and rare variants with the high frequency signals of the common variants. In general, these methods do not incorporate more sophisticated biological information such as pathway analysis. There is evidence that a pathway-based analysis of rare variants may identify significant variants missed in previous analyses (Hu et al., 2011). The developers of CHARM suggest that incorporating pathway analysis or models with functional sites such as nonsynonymous sites may improve the method (Cardin, Mefford, & Witte, 2012). However, one study found that the group wise association test performed better without the pathway analysis in terms of power (Peterson et al., 2010). In addition, rare variant analyses are being developed to analyze pedigree data (De et al., 2013) and family-based designs (Schaid et al., 2013), which are robust to population stratification. Different rare variants have been found for both population-based and family-based study designs, and therefore, both designs can complement each other for genetic association studies (Zhang et al., 2011). Lastly, meta-analysis of rare variants is poised to detect new variants in the future (Liu et al., 2014).

FUTURE DIRECTIONS

GWAS attempt to cover the entire genome, however their limitations are due primarily to their reliance on common variants. Two new sequencing methods, whole-genome sequencing and whole-exome sequencing, identify much more of the variation of the genome. Whole-genome sequencing sequences the entire genome. Whole-exome sequencing focuses on variants anywhere in the protein-coding portions of the genome (the "exome") that change the amino acid sequence of proteins. With this flood of data, rigorous attention needs to be paid to study design, quality control, and statistical methods. The similar statistical concerns exist with these sequencing-based genome associated studies, such as estimating genome-wide significance (Xu et al., 2014) and controlling for population stratification (Zhang, Shen, & Pan, 2013), but on a greater scale. These new sequencing methods are making the way for epigenetics, which characterize molecular mechanisms not associated with genetic variants, and transcriptomics (Schnabel et al., 2012). Epigenetics include studying DNA methylation, histone modification, noncoding RNA, and nucleosome positioning. Therefore,

methods with a systems biology approach need to be developed to better model the underlying biological architecture. Methods involving systems biology will attempt to capture the complexity of these biological networks using integrated statistical and mathematical models coupled with sophisticated computing.

CONCLUSION

Association mapping studies, and genome wide association studies specifically, have identified a wealth of novel disease associations with common variants. These insights have the potential to open new routes to novel treatments and personalized medicine. However, there is still missing heritability that could be explained by the inclusion of other factors such as rare variants, epistasis, and gene-environment interactions. These factors, combined with the deluge of data that is the result of advances in next-generation sequencing, will require advanced statistical methods that attempt to explain the additional heritability. Exploration of these novel loci will very likely uncover additional alleles, both common and rare, that will help pinpoint which gene(s) are responsible for the association to disease and provide predictive clinical and molecular tools that could be used for personalized medicine.

REFERENCES

Abecasis, G. R., Cardon, L. R., & Cookson, W. O. C. (2000). A General Test of Association for Quantitative Traits in Nuclear Families. *American Journal of Human Genetics*, *66*(1), 279–292. doi:10.1086/302698 PMID:10631157

Abecasis, G. R., Cherny, S. S., Cookson, W. O., & Cardon, L. R. (2002). Merlin–rapid analysis of dense genetic maps using sparse gene flow trees. *Nature Genetics*, *30*(1), 97–101. doi:10.1038/ng786 PMID:11731797

Affymetrix. (2006). *BRLMM: An improved genotype calling method for the GeneChip Human Mapping 500K Array Set* (Revision version 1.0). Affymetrix.

Aflakparast, M., Salimi, H., Gerami, A., Dubé, M.-P., Visweswaran, S., & Masoudi-Nejad, A. (2014). Cuckoo search epistasis: A new method for exploring significant genetic interactions. *Heredity*, *112*(6), 666–674. doi:10.1038/hdy.2014.4 PMID:24549111

Agopian, A., & Mitchell, L. E. (2011). MI-GWAS: A SAS platform for the analysis of inherited and maternal genetic effects in genome-wide association studies using log-linear models. *BMC Bioinformatics*, *12*(1), 117. doi:10.1186/1471-2105-12-117 PMID:21513519

Allison, D. B. (1997). Transmission-disequilibrium tests for quantitative traits. *American Journal of Human Genetics*, *60*(3), 676–690. PMID:9042929

Aly, T. A., Eller, E., Ide, A., Gowan, K., Babu, S. R., & Erlich, H. A. et al. (2006). Multi-SNP Analysis of MHC Region: Remarkable Conservation of HLA-A1-B8-DR3 Haplotype. *Diabetes*, *55*(5), 1265–1269. doi:10.2337/db05-1276 PMID:16644681

Anderson, C. A., Pettersson, F. H., Clarke, G. M., Cardon, L. R., Morris, A. P., & Zondervan, K. T. (2010). Data quality control in genetic case-control association studies. *Nature Protocols*, *5*(9), 1564–1573. doi:10.1038/nprot.2010.116 PMID:21085122

Ansorge, W. J. (2009). Next-generation DNA sequencing techniques. *New Biotechnology*, *25*(4), 195–203. doi:10.1016/j.nbt.2008.12.009 PMID:19429539

Ayers, K. L., & Cordell, H. J. (2010). SNP Selection in genome-wide and candidate gene studies via penalized logistic regression. *Genetic Epidemiology*, *34*(8), 879–891. doi:10.1002/gepi.20543 PMID:21104890

Bagos, P. G. (2013). Genetic model selection in genome-wide association studies: Robust methods and the use of meta-analysis. *Statistical Applications in Genetics and Molecular Biology*, *12*(3). doi:10.1515/sagmb-2012-0016 PMID:23629457

Balding, D. J. (2006). A tutorial on statistical methods for population association studies. *Nature Reviews. Genetics*, *7*(10), 781–791. doi:10.1038/nrg1916 PMID:16983374

Ban, H.-J., Heo, J. Y., Oh, K.-S., & Park, K.-J. (2010). Identification of Type 2 Diabetes-associated combination of SNPs using Support Vector Machine. *BMC Genetics*, *11*(1), 26. doi:10.1186/1471-2156-11-26 PMID:20416077

Begum, F., Ghosh, D., Tseng, G. C., & Feingold, E. (2012). Comprehensive literature review and statistical considerations for GWAS meta-analysis. *Nucleic Acids Research*, *40*(9), 3777–3784. doi:10.1093/nar/gkr1255 PMID:22241776

Bhagwat, V. M., & Ramachandran, B. V. (1975). Malathion A and B esterases of mouse liver-I. *Biochemical Pharmacology*, *24*(18), 1713–1717. doi:10.1016/0006-2952(75)90011-8 PMID:14

Bodmer, W., & Bonilla, C. (2008). Common and rare variants in multifactorial susceptibility to common diseases. *Nature Genetics*, *40*(6), 695–701. doi:10.1038/ng.f.136 PMID:18509313

Browning, B. L., & Browning, S. R. (2009). A Unified Approach to Genotype Imputation and Haplotype-Phase Inference for Large Data Sets of Trios and Unrelated Individuals. *American Journal of Human Genetics*, *84*(2), 210–223. doi:10.1016/j.ajhg.2009.01.005 PMID:19200528

Bůžková, P. (2013). Linear Regression in Genetic Association Studies. *PLoS ONE*, *8*(2), e56976. doi:10.1371/journal.pone.0056976 PMID:23437286

Cardin, N. J., Mefford, J. A., & Witte, J. S. (2012). Joint Association Testing of Common and Rare Genetic Variants Using Hierarchical Modeling: Joint Association Testing of Common and Rare Genetic Variants. *Genetic Epidemiology*, *36*(6), 642–651. doi:10.1002/gepi.21659 PMID:22807252

Cardon, L. R., & Palmer, L. J. (2003). Population stratification and spurious allelic association. *Lancet*, *361*(9357), 598–604. doi:10.1016/S0140-6736(03)12520-2 PMID:12598158

Chang, C.-J., Kuo, H.-C., Chang, J.-S., Lee, J.-K., Tsai, F.-J., & Khor, C. C. et al. (2013). Replication and Meta-Analysis of GWAS Identified Susceptibility Loci in Kawasaki Disease Confirm the Importance of B Lymphoid Tyrosine Kinase (BLK) in Disease Susceptibility. *PLoS ONE*, *8*(8), e72037. doi:10.1371/journal.pone.0072037 PMID:24023612

Che, R. J., Motsinger-Reif, A., & Brown, C. (In Submission). An adaptive permutation approach for genome-wide association study: Evaluation and recommendations for use. *BMC BioData Mining*.

Chen, H. Y., & Li, M. (2011). Improving power and robustness for detecting genetic association with extreme-value sampling design. *Genetic Epidemiology*, *35*(8), 823–830. doi:10.1002/gepi.20631 PMID:22006659

Clarke, G. M., Anderson, C. A., Pettersson, F. H., Cardon, L. R., Morris, A. P., & Zondervan, K. T. (2011). Basic statistical analysis in genetic case-control studies. *Nature Protocols*, *6*(2), 121–133. doi:10.1038/nprot.2010.182 PMID:21293453

Clayton, D. G., Walker, N. M., Smyth, D. J., Pask, R., Cooper, J. D., & Maier, L. M. et al. (2005). Population structure, differential bias and genomic control in a large-scale, case-control association study. *Nature Genetics*, *37*(11), 1243–1246. doi:10.1038/ng1653 PMID:16228001

Culverhouse, R., Suarez, B. K., Lin, J., & Reich, T. (2002). A Perspective on Epistasis: Limits of Models Displaying No Main Effect. *American Journal of Human Genetics*, *70*(2), 461–471. doi:10.1086/338759 PMID:11791213

Dai, H., Zhao, Y., Qian, C., Cai, M., Zhang, R., & Chu, M. et al. (2013). Weighted SNP Set Analysis in Genome-Wide Association Study. *PLoS ONE*, *8*(9), e75897. PMID:24098741

Dai, Y., Jiang, R., & Dong, J. (2012). Weighted selective collapsing strategy for detecting rare and common variants in genetic association study. *BMC Genetics*, *13*(1), 7. doi:10.1186/1471-2156-13-7 PMID:22309429

De, G., Yip, W.-K., Ionita-Laza, I., & Laird, N. (2013). Rare Variant Analysis for Family-Based Design. *PLoS ONE*, *8*(1), e48495. doi:10.1371/journal.pone.0048495 PMID:23341868

De Iorio, M., Newcombe, P. J., Tachmazidou, I., Verzilli, C. J., & Whittaker, J. C. (2011). Bayesian semiparametric meta-analysis for genetic association studies. *Genetic Epidemiology*, *35*(5), 333–340. doi:10.1002/gepi.20581 PMID:21400586

Devlin, B., & Roeder, K. (1999). Genomic Control for Association Studies. *Biometrics*, *55*(4), 997–1004. doi:10.1111/j.0006-341X.1999.00997.x PMID:11315092

Dudbridge, F. (2008). Likelihood-Based Association Analysis for Nuclear Families and Unrelated Subjects with Missing Genotype Data. *Human Heredity*, *66*(2), 87–98. doi:10.1159/000119108 PMID:18382088

Efron, B., & Tibshirani, R. (2007). On testing the significance of sets of genes. *The Annals of Applied Statistics*, *1*(1), 107–129. doi:10.1214/07-AOAS101

Ehret, G. B., Lamparter, D., Hoggart, C. J., Whittaker, J. C., Beckmann, J. S., & Kutalik, Z. (2012). A Multi-SNP Locus-Association Method Reveals a Substantial Fraction of the Missing Heritability. *American Journal of Human Genetics*, *91*(5), 863–871. doi:10.1016/j.ajhg.2012.09.013 PMID:23122585

Evangelou, E., & Ioannidis, J. P. A. (2013). Meta-analysis methods for genome-wide association studies and beyond. *Nature Reviews. Genetics*, *14*(6), 379–389. doi:10.1038/nrg3472 PMID:23657481

Ewens, W. J., Li, M., & Spielman, R. S. (2008). A Review of Family-Based Tests for Linkage Disequilibrium between a Quantitative Trait and a Genetic Marker. *PLOS Genetics*, *4*(9), e1000180. doi:10.1371/journal.pgen.1000180 PMID:18818728

Fardo, D. W., Ionita-Laza, I., & Lange, C. (2009). On Quality Control Measures in Genome-Wide Association Studies: A Test to Assess the Genotyping Quality of Individual Probands in Family-Based Association Studies and an Application to the HapMap Data. *PLOS Genetics*, *5*(7), e1000572. PMID:19629167

Fridley, B. L. (2009). Bayesian variable and model selection methods for genetic association studies. *Genetic Epidemiology*, *33*(1), 27–37. doi:10.1002/gepi.20353 PMID:18618760

Goddard, M. E., Wray, N. R., Verbyla, K., & Visscher, P. M. (2009). Estimating Effects and Making Predictions from Genome-Wide Marker Data. *Statistical Science*, *24*(4), 517–529. doi:10.1214/09-STS306

Goldstein, B. A., Hubbard, A. E., Cutler, A., & Barcellos, L. F. (2010). An application of Random Forests to a genome-wide association dataset: Methodological considerations & new findings. *BMC Genetics*, *11*(1), 49. doi:10.1186/1471-2156-11-49 PMID:20546594

Goudey, B., Rawlinson, D., Wang, Q., Shi, F., Ferra, H., & Campbell, R. M. et al. (2013). GWIS - model-free, fast and exhaustive search for epistatic interactions in case-control GWAS. *BMC Genomics*, *14*(Suppl 3), S10. doi:10.1186/1471-2164-14-S3-S10 PMID:23819779

Guy, R. T., Santago, P., & Langefeld, C. D. (2012). Bootstrap Aggregating of Alternating Decision Trees to Detect Sets of SNPs That Associate With Disease: Bagged ADTrees and Genetic Association. *Genetic Epidemiology*, *36*(2), 99–106. doi:10.1002/gepi.21608 PMID:22851473

Havill, L. M., Dyer, T. D., Richardson, D. K., Mahaney, M. C., & Blangero, J. (2005). The quantitative trait linkage disequilibrium test: A more powerful alternative to the quantitative transmission disequilibrium test for use in the absence of population stratification. *BMC Genetics*, *6*(Suppl 1), S91. doi:10.1186/1471-2156-6-S1-S91 PMID:16451707

Hayes, B. (2013). Overview of Statistical Methods for Genome-Wide Association Studies (GWAS). In C. Gondro, J. van der Werf, & B. Hayes (Eds.), *Genome-Wide Association Studies and Genomic Prediction* (Vol. 1019, pp. 149–169). Humana Press. doi:10.1007/978-1-62703-447-0_6

Hindorff, L. A., MacArthur, A., Morales, J., Junkins, H. A., Hall, P. A., Klemm, A. K., & Manolio, T. A. (2014). *Catalog of published genome-wide association studies*. National Human Research Genome Institute.

Hintsanen, P., Sevon, P., Onkamo, P., Eronen, L., & Toivonen, H. (2005). An empirical comparison of case-control and trio based study designs in high throughput association mapping. *Journal of Medical Genetics*, *43*(7), 617–624. doi:10.1136/jmg.2005.036020 PMID:16258007

Hivert, M.-F., Manning, A. K., McAteer, J. B., Florez, J. C., Dupuis, J., & Fox, C. S. et al. (2008). Common Variants in the Adiponectin Gene (ADIPOQ) Associated With Plasma Adiponectin Levels, Type 2 Diabetes, and Diabetes-Related Quantitative Traits: The Framingham Offspring Study. *Diabetes*, *57*(12), 3353–3359. doi:10.2337/db08-0700 PMID:18776141

Hodgson, E. M., Olshan, A. F., North, K. E., Poole, C. L., Zeng, D., & Tse, C.-K. et al. (2012). The case-only independence assumption: Associations between genetic polymorphisms and smoking among controls in two population-based studies. *International Journal of Molecular Epidemiology and Genetics*, *3*(4), 333–360. PMID:23205185

Hoffmann, T. J., Marini, N. J., & Witte, J. S. (2010). Comprehensive Approach to Analyzing Rare Genetic Variants. *PLoS ONE*, *5*(11), e13584. doi:10.1371/journal.pone.0013584 PMID:21072163

Hoggart, C. J., Whittaker, J. C., De Iorio, M., & Balding, D. J. (2008). Simultaneous Analysis of All SNPs in Genome-Wide and Re-Sequencing Association Studies. *PLOS Genetics*, *4*(7), e1000130. doi:10.1371/journal.pgen.1000130 PMID:18654633

Hong, H., Shi, L., Su, Z., Ge, W., Jones, W. D., & Czika, W. et al. (2010a). Assessing sources of inconsistencies in genotypes and their effects on genome-wide association studies with HapMap samples. *The Pharmacogenomics Journal*, *10*(4), 364–374. doi:10.1038/tpj.2010.24 PMID:20368714

Hong, H., Su, Z., Ge, W., Shi, L., Perkins, R., & Fang, H. et al. (2010b). Evaluating variations of genotype calling: A potential source of spurious associations in genome-wide association studies. *Journal of Genetics*, *89*(1), 55–64. doi:10.1007/s12041-010-0011-4 PMID:20505247

Horvath, S., Xu, X., & Laird, N. M. (2001). The family based association test method: Strategies for studying general genotypephenotype associations. *European Journal of Human Genetics*, *9*(4), 301–306. doi:10.1038/sj.ejhg.5200625 PMID:11313775

Howie, B., Marchini, J., Stephens, M., & Chakravarti, A. (2011). Genotype Imputation with Thousands of Genomes. *G3: Genes|Genomes|Genetics*, *1*(6), 457–470.

Howie, B. N., Donnelly, P., & Marchini, J. (2009). A Flexible and Accurate Genotype Imputation Method for the Next Generation of Genome-Wide Association Studies. *PLOS Genetics*, *5*(6), e1000529. doi:10.1371/journal.pgen.1000529 PMID:19543373

Hu, P., Xu, W., Cheng, L., Xing, X., & Paterson, A. D. (2011). Pathway-based joint effects analysis of rare genetic variants using Genetic Analysis Workshop 17 exon sequence data. *BMC Proceedings*, *5*(Suppl 9), S45.

Jackson, D., White, I. R., & Thompson, S. G. (2009). Extending DerSimonian and Laird's methodology to perform multivariate random effects meta-analyses. *Statistics in Medicine*, *29*(12), 1282–1297. doi:10.1002/sim.3602 PMID:19408255

Janssens, A. C. J. W., & van Duijn, C. M. (2008). Genome-based prediction of common diseases: Advances and prospects. *Human Molecular Genetics*, *17*(R2), R166–R173. doi:10.1093/hmg/ddn250 PMID:18852206

Joachims, T. (1999). Making large scale SVM learning practical. In B. Schölkopf, C. Burges, & A. Smola (Eds.), *Advances in Kernel Methods - Support Vector Learning*. Cambridge, USA: MIT Press.

Johnson, R. C., Nelson, G. W., Troyer, J. L., Lautenberger, J. A., Kessing, B. D., Winkler, C. A., & O'Brien, S. J. (2010). Accounting for multiple comparisons in a genome-wide association study (GWAS). *BMC Genomics*, *11*(1), 724. doi:10.1186/1471-2164-11-724 PMID:21176216

Kazma, R., & Bailey, J. N. (2011). Population-based and family-based designs to analyze rare variants in complex diseases. *Genetic Epidemiology*, *35*(S1), S41–S47. doi:10.1002/gepi.20648 PMID:22128057

Kestenbaum, B. (2009). Case-Control Studies. In *Epidemiology and Biostatistics* (pp. 45–57). Springer New York. doi:10.1007/978-0-387-88433-2_6

Kim, S., & Misra, A. (2007). SNP Genotyping: Technologies and Biomedical Applications. *Annual Review of Biomedical Engineering*, *9*(1), 289–320. doi:10.1146/annurev.bioeng.9.060906.152037 PMID:17391067

Kim, S., Morris, N. J., Won, S., & Elston, R. C. (2009). Single-marker and two-marker association tests for unphased case-control genotype data, with a power comparison. *Genetic Epidemiology*.

Kiryluk, K., Li, Y., Sanna-Cherchi, S., Rohanizadegan, M., Suzuki, H., & Eitner, F. et al. (2012). Geographic Differences in Genetic Susceptibility to IgA Nephropathy: GWAS Replication Study and Geospatial Risk Analysis. *PLOS Genetics*, *8*(6), e1002765. doi:10.1371/journal.pgen.1002765 PMID:22737082

Konietschke, F., Libiger, O., & Hothorn, L. A. (2012). Nonparametric Evaluation of Quantitative Traits in Population-Based Association Studies when the Genetic Model is Unknown. *PLoS ONE*, *7*(2), e31242. doi:10.1371/journal.pone.0031242 PMID:22363593

Kraft, P., & Cox, D. G. (2008). Study Designs for Genome-Wide Association Studies. In D. C. Rao & C. Gu (Ed.), Advances in genetics (Vol. 60, pp. 465–504). Academic Press.

Kruglyak, L., & Lander, E. S. (1998). Faster Multipoint Linkage Analysis Using Fourier Transforms. *Journal of Computational Biology*, *5*(1), 1–7. doi:10.1089/cmb.1998.5.1 PMID:9541867

Laird, N. M., Horvath, S., & Xu, X. (2000). Implementing a unified approach to family-based tests of association. *Genetic Epidemiology*, *19*(S1Suppl 1), S36–S42. doi:10.1002/1098-2272(2000)19:1+<::AID-GEPI6>3.0.CO;2-M PMID:11055368

Lanara, Z., Giannopoulou, E., Fullen, M., Kostantinopoulos, E., Nebel, J.-C., & Kalofonos, H. P. et al. (2013). Comparative study and meta-analysis of meta-analysis studies for the correlation of genomic markers with early cancer detection. *Human Genomics*, *7*(1), 14. doi:10.1186/1479-7364-7-14 PMID:23738773

Leem, S., Jeong, H., Lee, J., Wee, K., & Sohn, K.-A. (n.d.). Fast detection of high-order epistatic interactions in genome-wide association studies using information theoretic measure. [In Press]. *Computational Biology and Chemistry*. PMID:24581733

Lettre, G., Lange, C., & Hirschhorn, J. N. (2007). Genetic model testing and statistical power in population-based association studies of quantitative traits. *Genetic Epidemiology*, *31*(4), 358–362. doi:10.1002/gepi.20217 PMID:17352422

Levin, K. A. (2006). Study design III: Cross-sectional studies. *Evidence-Based Dentistry*, *7*(1), 24–25. doi:10.1038/sj.ebd.6400375 PMID:16557257

Lewis, C. M., & Knight, J. (2012). Introduction to Genetic Association Studies. *Cold Spring Harbor Protocols*, (3), 297–306.

Li, B., & Leal, S. M. (2008). Methods for Detecting Associations with Rare Variants for Common Diseases: Application to Analysis of Sequence Data. *American Journal of Human Genetics*, *83*(3), 311–321. doi:10.1016/j.ajhg.2008.06.024 PMID:18691683

Li, G., & Zhu, H. (2013). Genetic Studies: The Linear Mixed Models in Genome-wide Association Studies. *The Open Bioinformatics Journal*, *7*(Suppl 1), 27–33.

Li, J., Horstman, B., & Chen, Y. (2011). Detecting epistatic effects in association studies at a genomic level based on an ensemble approach. *Bioinformatics (Oxford, England)*, *27*(13), i222–i229. doi:10.1093/bioinformatics/btr227 PMID:21685074

Li, Y., Willer, C. J., Ding, J., Scheet, P., & Abecasis, G. R. (2010). MaCH: Using sequence and genotype data to estimate haplotypes and unobserved genotypes. *Genetic Epidemiology*, *34*(8), 816–834. doi:10.1002/gepi.20533 PMID:21058334

Lin, D. Y., & Zeng, D. (2009). Meta-analysis of genome-wide association studies: No efficiency gain in using individual participant data. *Genetic Epidemiology*, *34*(1), 60–66. PMID:19847795

Liu, N., Zhang, K., & Zhao, H. (2008). Haplotype-Association Analysis. In D. C. Rao & C. Gu (Ed.), Advances in genetics (Vol. 60, pp. 335–405). Academic Press.

Logsdon, B. A., Dai, J. Y., Auer, P. L., Johnsen, J. M., Ganesh, S. K., & Smith, N. L. et al. (2014). A Variational Bayes Discrete Mixture Test for Rare Variant Association. *Genetic Epidemiology*, *38*(1), 21–30. doi:10.1002/gepi.21772 PMID:24482836

Ma, L., Clark, A. G., & Keinan, A. (2013). Gene-Based Testing of Interactions in Association Studies of Quantitative Traits. *PLOS Genetics*, *9*(2), e1003321. doi:10.1371/journal.pgen.1003321 PMID:23468652

Marchini, J., & Howie, B. (2010). Genotype imputation for genome-wide association studies. *Nature Reviews. Genetics*, *11*(7), 499–511. doi:10.1038/nrg2796 PMID:20517342

Marchini, J., Howie, B., Myers, S., McVean, G., & Donnelly, P. (2007). A new multipoint method for genome-wide association studies by imputation of genotypes. *Nature Genetics*, *39*(7), 906–913. doi:10.1038/ng2088 PMID:17572673

Marinou, I., Healy, J., Mewar, D., Moore, D. J., Dickson, M. C., & Binks, M. H. et al. (2007). Association of interleukin-6 and interleukin-10 genotypes with radiographic damage in rheumatoid arthritis is dependent on autoantibody status. *Arthritis and Rheumatism*, *56*(8), 2549–2556. doi:10.1002/art.22814 PMID:17665434

Marson, F. A. de L., Bertuzzo, C., Ribeiro, A., & Ribeiro, J. (2014). Polymorphisms in the glutathione pathway modulate cystic fibrosis severity: A cross-sectional study. *BMC Medical Genetics*, *15*(1), 27. doi:10.1186/1471-2350-15-27 PMID:24593045

Martin, E., Monks, S., Warren, L., & Kaplan, N. (2000). A Test for Linkage and Association in General Pedigrees: The Pedigree Disequilibrium Test. *American Journal of Human Genetics*, *67*(1), 146–154. doi:10.1086/302957 PMID:10825280

Morris, A. P., & Zeggini, E. (2010). An evaluation of statistical approaches to rare variant analysis in genetic association studies. *Genetic Epidemiology*, *34*(2), 188–193. doi:10.1002/gepi.20450 PMID:19810025

Moskvina, V., & Schmidt, K. M. (2008). On multiple-testing correction in genome-wide association studies. *Genetic Epidemiology*, *32*(6), 567–573. doi:10.1002/gepi.20331 PMID:18425821

Motsinger-Reif, A. A., Reif, D. M., Fanelli, T. J., & Ritchie, M. D. (2008). A comparison of analytical methods for genetic association studies. *Genetic Epidemiology*, *32*(8), 767–778. doi:10.1002/gepi.20345 PMID:18561203

Nick, T., & Campbell, K. (2007). Logistic Regression. In W. Ambrosius (Ed.), *Topics in Biostatistics* (Vol. 404, pp. 273–301). Humana Press. doi:10.1007/978-1-59745-530-5_14

Oh, S., Lee, J., Kwon, M.-S., Weir, B., Ha, K., & Park, T. (2012). A novel method to identify high order gene-gene interactions in genome-wide association studies: Gene-based MDR. *BMC Bioinformatics*, *13*(Suppl 9), S5. doi:10.1186/1471-2105-13-S9-S5 PMID:22901090

Pare, G., & Henderson, M. A. (2013). Genome-Wide Association Studies (GWAS). In P. Sharma & J. F. Meschia (Eds.), *Stroke Genetics* (pp. 25–50). Springer London. doi:10.1007/978-0-85729-209-4_3

Petersen, A., Sitarik, A., Luedtke, A., Powers, S., Bekmetjev, A., & Tintle, N. L. (2011). Evaluating methods for combining rare variant data in pathway-based tests of genetic association. *BMC Proceedings, 5*(Suppl 9), S48.

Phillips, P. C. (2008). Epistasis – the essential role of gene interactions in the structure and evolution of genetic systems. *Nature Reviews. Genetics*, *9*(11), 855–867. doi:10.1038/nrg2452 PMID:18852697

Pluzhnikov, A., Below, J. E., Konkashbaev, A., Tikhomirov, A., Kistner-Griffin, E., & Roe, C. A. et al. (2010). Spoiling the Whole Bunch: Quality Control Aimed at Preserving the Integrity of High-Throughput Genotyping. *American Journal of Human Genetics*, *87*(1), 123–128. doi:10.1016/j.ajhg.2010.06.005 PMID:20598280

Price, A. L., Patterson, N. J., Plenge, R. M., Weinblatt, M. E., Shadick, N. A., & Reich, D. (2006). Principal components analysis corrects for stratification in genome-wide association studies. *Nature Genetics*, *38*(8), 904–909. doi:10.1038/ng1847 PMID:16862161

Pritchard, J. K., Stephens, M., & Donnelly, P. (2000). Inference of population structure using multilocus genotype data. *Genetics*, *155*(2), 945–959. PMID:10835412

Purcell, S., Neale, B., Todd-Brown, K., Thomas, L., Ferreira, M. A. R., & Bender, D. et al. (2007). PLINK: A Tool Set for Whole-Genome Association and Population-Based Linkage Analyses. *American Journal of Human Genetics*, *81*(3), 559–575. doi:10.1086/519795 PMID:17701901

R Core Team. (2013). R: A language and environment for statistical computing. In R Foundation for Statistical Computing. Vienna, Austria: Author.

Rabin, E. Z., & Weinberger, V. (1975). The isolation, purification, and properties of a ribonuclease from normal human urine. *Biochemical Medicine*, *14*(1), 1–11. doi:10.1016/0006-2944(75)90014-9 PMID:2164

Ragoussis, J. (2006). Genotyping technologies for all. *Drug Discovery Today. Technologies*, *3*(2), 115–122. doi:10.1016/j.ddtec.2006.06.013 PMID:24980397

Ragoussis, J. (2009). Genotyping Technologies for Genetic Research. *Annual Review of Genomics and Human Genetics*, *10*(1), 117–133. doi:10.1146/annurev-genom-082908-150116 PMID:19453250

Reimers, M. A., Riley, B. P., Kalsi, G., Kertes, D. A., & Kendler, K. S. (2012). Pathway based analysis of genotypes in relation to alcohol dependence. *The Pharmacogenomics Journal*, *12*(4), 342–348. doi:10.1038/tpj.2011.10 PMID:21468025

Ritchie, M. D., Hahn, L. W., Roodi, N., Bailey, L. R., Dupont, W. D., Parl, F. F., & Moore, J. H. (2001). Multifactor-Dimensionality Reduction Reveals High-Order Interactions among Estrogen-Metabolism Genes in Sporadic Breast Cancer. *American Journal of Human Genetics, 69*(1), 138–147. doi:10.1086/321276 PMID:11404819

Schaid, D., Mcdonnell, S., Hebbring, S., Cunningham, J., & Thibodeau, S. (2005). Nonparametric Tests of Association of Multiple Genes with Human Disease. *American Journal of Human Genetics, 76*(5), 780–793. doi:10.1086/429838 PMID:15786018

Schaid, D. J., McDonnell, S. K., Sinnwell, J. P., & Thibodeau, S. N. (2013). Multiple Genetic Variant Association Testing by Collapsing and Kernel Methods With Pedigree or Population Structured Data: Multiple Genetic Variant Association Testing. *Genetic Epidemiology, 37*(5), 409–418. doi:10.1002/gepi.21727 PMID:23650101

Scheet, P., & Stephens, M. (2006). A Fast and Flexible Statistical Model for Large-Scale Population Genotype Data: Applications to Inferring Missing Genotypes and Haplotypic Phase. *American Journal of Human Genetics, 78*(4), 629–644. doi:10.1086/502802 PMID:16532393

Schmoldt, A., Benthe, H. F., & Haberland, G. (1975). Digitoxin metabolism by rat liver microsomes. *Biochemical Pharmacology, 24*(17), 1639–1641. doi:10.1016/0006-2952(75)90094-5 PMID:10

Schnabel, R. B., Baccarelli, A., Lin, H., Ellinor, P. T., & Benjamin, E. J. (2012). Next Steps in Cardiovascular Disease Genomic Research--Sequencing, Epigenetics, and Transcriptomics. *Clinical Chemistry, 58*(1), 113–126. doi:10.1373/clinchem.2011.170423 PMID:22100807

Schwarz, D. F., Konig, I. R., & Ziegler, A. (2010). On safari to Random Jungle: A fast implementation of Random Forests for high-dimensional data. *Bioinformatics (Oxford, England), 26*(14), 1752–1758. doi:10.1093/bioinformatics/btq257 PMID:20505004

Schwender, H., Taub, M. A., Beaty, T. H., Marazita, M. L., & Ruczinski, I. (2012). Rapid Testing of SNPs and Gene-Environment Interactions in Case-Parent Trio Data Based on Exact Analytic Parameter Estimation. *Biometrics, 68*(3), 766–773. doi:10.1111/j.1541-0420.2011.01713.x PMID:22150644

Servin, B., & Stephens, M. (2007). Imputation-Based Analysis of Association Studies: Candidate Regions and Quantitative Traits. *PLOS Genetics, 3*(7), e114. doi:10.1371/journal.pgen.0030114 PMID:17676998

Shang, J., Zhang, J., Sun, Y., Liu, D., Ye, D., & Yin, Y. (2011). Performance analysis of novel methods for detecting epistasis. *BMC Bioinformatics, 12*(1), 475. doi:10.1186/1471-2105-12-475 PMID:22172045

Smith, R. J., & Bryant, R. G. (1975). Metal substitutions incarbonic anhydrase: A halide ion probe study. *Biochemical and Biophysical Research Communications, 66*(4), 1281–1286. doi:10.1016/0006-291X(75)90498-2 PMID:3

Souza, L., Pozo, A., da Rosa, J., & Neto, A. (2010). Applying correlation to enhance boosting technique using genetic programming as base learner. *Applied Intelligence, 33*(3), 291–301. doi:10.1007/s10489-009-0166-y

Starr, J. R., Hsu, L., & Schwartz, S. M. (2005). Assessing Maternal Genetic Associations: A Comparison of the Log-Linear Approach to Case-Parent Triad Data and a Case-Control Approach. *Epidemiology (Cambridge, Mass.), 16*(3), 294–303. doi:10.1097/01.ede.0000158223.98649.eb PMID:15824543

Stephens, J. C., Schneider, J. A., Tanguay, D. A., Choi, J., Acharya, T., & Stanley, S. E. et al. (2001). Haplotype Variation and Linkage Disequilibrium in 313 Human Genes. *Science*, *293*(5529), 489–493. doi:10.1126/science.1059431 PMID:11452081

Stephens, M., & Balding, D. J. (2009). Bayesian statistical methods for genetic association studies. *Nature Reviews. Genetics*, *10*(10), 681–690. doi:10.1038/nrg2615 PMID:19763151

Stephens, M., & Scheet, P. (2005). Accounting for Decay of Linkage Disequilibrium in Haplotype Inference and Missing-Data Imputation. *American Journal of Human Genetics*, *76*(3), 449–462. doi:10.1086/428594 PMID:15700229

Stranger, B. E., Stahl, E. A., & Raj, T. (2011). Progress and Promise of Genome-Wide Association Studies for Human Complex Trait Genetics. *Genetics*, *187*(2), 367–383. doi:10.1534/genetics.110.120907 PMID:21115973

Suarez-Gestal, M., Perez-Pampin, E., Calaza, M., Gomez-Reino, J. J., & Gonzalez, A. (2010). Lack of replication of genetic predictors for the rheumatoid arthritis response to anti-TNF treatments: A prospective case-only study. *Arthritis Research & Therapy*, *12*(2), R72. doi:10.1186/ar2990 PMID:20423481

Sun, X., Lu, Q., Mukheerjee, S., Crane, P. K., Elston, R., & Ritchie, M. D. (2014). Analysis pipeline for the epistasis search- statistical versus biological filtering. *Frontiers in Genetics*, *5*, 106. doi:10.3389/fgene.2014.00106 PMID:24817878

Sung, Y. J., Schwander, K., Arnett, D. K., Kardia, S. L. R., Rankinen, T., & Bouchard, C. et al. (2014). An Empirical Comparison of Meta-analysis and Mega-analysis of Individual Participant Data for Identifying Gene-Environment Interactions: Meta- and Mega-analyses of Interactions. *Genetic Epidemiology*, *38*(4), 369–378. doi:10.1002/gepi.21800 PMID:24719363

Syvänen, A.-C. (2001). Accessing genetic variation: Genotyping single nucleotide polymorphisms. *Nature Reviews. Genetics*, *2*(12), 930–942. doi:10.1038/35103535 PMID:11733746

Tan, Q. (2005). Genetic Association Analysis of Human Longevity in Cohort Studies of Elderly Subjects: An Example of the PON1 Gene in the Danish 1905 Birth Cohort. *Genetics*, *172*(3), 1821–1828. doi:10.1534/genetics.105.050914 PMID:16387878

Tang, W., Wu, X., Jiang, R., & Li, Y. (2009). Epistatic Module Detection for Case-Control Studies: A Bayesian Model with a Gibbs Sampling Strategy. *PLOS Genetics*, *5*(5), e1000464. doi:10.1371/journal.pgen.1000464 PMID:19412524

Teare, M. D. (2011). Candidate Gene Association Studies. In M. D. Teare (Ed.), *Genetic Epidemiology* (Vol. 713, pp. 105–117). Humana Press. doi:10.1007/978-1-60327-416-6_8

Tibshirani, R. (1996). Regression Shrinkage and Selection via the Lasso. *Journal of the Royal Statistical Society. Series B. Methodological*, *58*(1), 267–288.

Troendle, J. F., & Mills, J. L. (2010). Correction for Multiplicity in Genetic Association Studies of Triads: The Permutational TDT: The Permutational TDT. *Annals of Human Genetics*.

Vermeulen, S. H. H. M., Den Heijer, M., Sham, P., & Knight, J. (2007). Application of multi-locus analytical methods to identify interacting loci in case-control studies. *Annals of Human Genetics*, *71*(5), 689–700. doi:10.1111/j.1469-1809.2007.00360.x PMID:17425620

Wan, X., Yang, C., Yang, Q., Xue, H., Fan, X., Tang, N. L. S., & Yu, W. (2010). BOOST: A Fast Approach to Detecting Gene-Gene Interactions in Genome-wide Case-Control Studies. *American Journal of Human Genetics*, *87*(3), 325–340. doi:10.1016/j.ajhg.2010.07.021 PMID:20817139

Wan, X., Yang, C., Yang, Q., Xue, H., Tang, N. L. S., & Yu, W. (2010). Predictive rule inference for epistatic interaction detection in genome-wide association studies. *Bioinformatics (Oxford, England), 26*(1), 30–37. doi:10.1093/bioinformatics/btp622 PMID:19880365

Wang, K. (2012). Statistical tests of genetic association for case-control study designs. *Biostatistics (Oxford, England), 13*(4), 724–733. doi:10.1093/biostatistics/kxs002 PMID:22389176

Wang, S., van der Vaart, A., Xu, Q., Seneviratne, C., Pomerleau, O., & Pomerleau, C. et al. (2014). Significant associations of CHRNA2 and CHRNA6 with nicotine dependence in European American and African American populations. *Human Genetics, 133*(5), 575–586. doi:10.1007/s00439-013-1398-9 PMID:24253422

Wang, Y., Liu, X., Robbins, K., & Rekaya, R. (2010). AntEpiSeeker: Detecting epistatic interactions for case-control studies using a two-stage ant colony optimization algorithm. *BMC Research Notes, 3*(1), 117. doi:10.1186/1756-0500-3-117 PMID:20426808

Weale, M. (2010). Quality Control for Genome-Wide Association Studies. In M. R. Barnes & G. Breen (Eds.), *Genetic Variation* (Vol. 628, pp. 341–372). Humana Press. doi:10.1007/978-1-60327-367-1_19

Weich, S. (1998). The cohort study. *International Review of Psychiatry (Abingdon, England), 10*(4), 284–290. doi:10.1080/09540269874637 PMID:9657786

Weinberg, C. R. (2000). Choosing a Retrospective Design to Assess Joint Genetic and Environmental Contributions to Risk. *American Journal of Epidemiology, 152*(3), 197–203. doi:10.1093/aje/152.3.197 PMID:10933265

Weinberg, C. R. (2003). Studying Parents and Grandparents to Assess Genetic Contributions to Early-Onset Disease. *American Journal of Human Genetics, 72*(2), 438–447. doi:10.1086/346171 PMID:12533786

Willer, C. J., Li, Y., & Abecasis, G. R. (2010). METAL: Fast and efficient meta-analysis of genomewide association scans. *Bioinformatics (Oxford, England), 26*(17), 2190–2191. doi:10.1093/bioinformatics/btq340 PMID:20616382

Winham, S. J., & Biernacka, J. M. (2013). Gene-environment interactions in genome-wide association studies: Current approaches and new directions. *Journal of Child Psychology and Psychiatry, and Allied Disciplines, 54*(10), 1120–1134. doi:10.1111/jcpp.12114 PMID:23808649

Wu, J., Devlin, B., Ringquist, S., Trucco, M., & Roeder, K. (2010). Screen and clean: A tool for identifying interactions in genome-wide association studies. *Genetic Epidemiology, 34*(3), 275–285. PMID:20088021

Wu, M. C., Lee, S., Cai, T., Li, Y., Boehnke, M., & Lin, X. (2011). Rare-Variant Association Testing for Sequencing Data with the Sequence Kernel Association Test. *American Journal of Human Genetics, 89*(1), 82–93. doi:10.1016/j.ajhg.2011.05.029 PMID:21737059

Wu, M. C., Maity, A., Lee, S., Simmons, E. M., Harmon, Q. E., & Lin, X. et al. (2013). Kernel Machine SNP-Set Testing Under Multiple Candidate Kernels. *Genetic Epidemiology, 37*(3), 267–275. doi:10.1002/gepi.21715 PMID:23471868

Xu, C., Tachmazidou, I., Walter, K., Ciampi, A., Zeggini, E., & Greenwood, C. M. T. (2014). Estimating Genome-Wide Significance for Whole-Genome Sequencing Studies: Genome-Wide Significance for Rare Variants. *Genetic Epidemiology, 38*(4), 281–290. doi:10.1002/gepi.21797 PMID:24676807

Yang, Q., Kathiresan, S., Lin, J.-P., Tofler, G. H., & O'Donnell, C. J. (2007). Genome-wide association and linkage analyses of hemostatic factors and hematological phenotypes in the Framingham Heart Study. *BMC Medical Genetics*, *8*(Suppl 1), S12. doi:10.1186/1471-2350-8-S1-S12 PMID:17903294

Yu, B., Zheng, Y., Alexander, D., Morrison, A. C., Coresh, J., & Boerwinkle, E. (2014). Genetic Determinants Influencing Human Serum Metabolome among African Americans. *PLOS Genetics*, *10*(3), e1004212. doi:10.1371/journal.pgen.1004212 PMID:24625756

Zhang, X., He, H., Ding, L., Baye, T. M., Kurowski, B. G., & Martin, L. J. (2011). Family- and population-based designs identify different rare causal variants. *BMC Proceedings, 5*(Suppl 9), S36.

Zhang, X., Huang, S., Zou, F., & Wang, W. (2010). TEAM: Efficient two-locus epistasis tests in human genome-wide association study. *Bioinformatics (Oxford, England)*, *26*(12), i217–i227. doi:10.1093/bioinformatics/btq186 PMID:20529910

Zhang, Y., & Liu, J. S. (2007). Bayesian inference of epistatic interactions in case-control studies. *Nature Genetics*, *39*(9), 1167–1173. doi:10.1038/ng2110 PMID:17721534

Zhang, Y., Shen, X., & Pan, W. (2013). Adjusting for Population Stratification in a Fine Scale With Principal Components and Sequencing Data. *Genetic Epidemiology*, *37*(8), 787–801. doi:10.1002/gepi.21764 PMID:24123217

Zheng, T., Wang, H., & Lo, S.-H. (2006). Backward Genotype-Trait Association (BGTA)-Based Dissection of Complex Traits in Case-Control Designs. *Human Heredity*, *62*(4), 196–212. doi:10.1159/000096995 PMID:17114886

Ziegler, A. (2009). Genome-wide association studies: Quality control and population-based measures. *Genetic Epidemiology*, *33*(S1Suppl 1), S45–S50. doi:10.1002/gepi.20472 PMID:19924716

Ziegler, A., König, I. R., & Thompson, J. R. (2008). Biostatistical Aspects of Genome-Wide Association Studies. *Biometrical Journal. Biometrische Zeitschrift*, *50*(1), 8–28. doi:10.1002/bimj.200710398 PMID:18217698

Zuber, V., & Strimmer, K. (2011). High-Dimensional Regression and Variable Selection Using CAR Scores. *Statistical Applications in Genetics and Molecular Biology*, *10*(1), 1–27. doi:10.2202/1544-6115.1730

ADDITIONAL READING

Altshuler, D., Hirschhorn, J. N., Klannemark, M., Lindgren, C. M., Vohl, M. C., & Nemesh, J. et al. (2000). The common ppargamma pro12ala polymorphism is associated with decreased risk of type 2 diabetes. *Nature Genetics*, *26*(1), 76–80. doi:10.1038/79216 PMID:10973253

Altshuler, D. M., Gibbs, R. A., Peltonen, L., Altshuler, D. M., Gibbs, R. A., & Peltonen, L. et al.International HapMap. (2010). Integrating common and rare genetic variation in diverse human populations. *Nature*, *467*(7311), 52–58. doi:10.1038/nature09298 PMID:20811451

Ansorge, W. J. (2009). Next-generation DNA sequencing techniques. *New Biotechnology*, *25*(4), 195–203. doi:10.1016/j.nbt.2008.12.009 PMID:19429539

Balding, D. J. (2006). A tutorial on statistical methods for population association studies. *Nature Reviews. Genetics*, *7*(10), 781–791. doi:10.1038/nrg1916 PMID:16983374

Barrett, J. C., Fry, B., Maller, J., & Daly, M. J. (2005). Haploview: Analysis and visualization of ld and haplotype maps. *Bioinformatics (Oxford, England)*, *21*(2), 263–265. doi:10.1093/bioinformatics/bth457 PMID:15297300

Che, R.J., J.; Motsinger-Reif, A.; Brown, C. (In Submission). An adaptive permutation approach for genome-wide association study: Evaluation and recommendations for use. *BMC BioData Mining*.

Corder, E. H., Saunders, A. M., Strittmatter, W. J., Schmechel, D. E., Gaskell, P. C., & Small, G. W. et al. (1993). Gene dose of apolipoprotein e type 4 allele and the risk of alzheimer's disease in late onset families. *Science*, *261*(5123), 921–923. doi:10.1126/science.8346443 PMID:8346443

Culverhouse, R., Suarez, B. K., Lin, J., & Reich, T. (2002). A perspective on epistasis: Limits of models displaying no main effect. *American Journal of Human Genetics*, *70*(2), 461–471. doi:10.1086/338759 PMID:11791213

de Bakker, P. I., Yelensky, R., Pe'er, I., Gabriel, S. B., Daly, M. J., & Altshuler, D. (2005). Efficiency and power in genetic association studies. *Nature Genetics*, *37*(11), 1217–1223. doi:10.1038/ng1669 PMID:16244653

Devlin, B., & Risch, N. (1995). A comparison of linkage disequilibrium measures for fine-scale mapping. *Genomics*, *29*(2), 311–322. doi:10.1006/geno.1995.9003 PMID:8666377

Devlin, B., & Roeder, K. (1999). Genomic control for association studies. *Biometrics*, *55*(4), 997–1004. doi:10.1111/j.0006-341X.1999.00997.x PMID:11315092

Distefano, J. K., & Taverna, D. M. (2011). Technological issues and experimental design of gene association studies. *Methods in Molecular Biology (Clifton, N.J.)*, *700*, 3–16. doi:10.1007/978-1-61737-954-3_1 PMID:21204023

Evangelou, E., & Ioannidis, J. P. (2013). Meta-analysis methods for genome-wide association studies and beyond. *Nature Reviews. Genetics*, *14*(6), 379–389. doi:10.1038/nrg3472 PMID:23657481

Hindorff, L. A., MacArthur, J., Morales, J., Junkins, H. A., Hall, P. N., Klemm, A. K., & Manolio, T. A. (2014). Catalog of published genome-wide association studies. *National Human Research Genome Institute*. 2014, from http://www.genome.gov/gwastudies/index.cfm?pageid=26525384 - searchForm

Johnson, R. C., Nelson, G. W., Troyer, J. L., Lautenberger, J. A., Kessing, B. D., Winkler, C. A., & O'Brien, S. J. (2010). Accounting for multiple comparisons in a genome-wide association study (gwas). *BMC Genomics*, *11*(1), 724. doi:10.1186/1471-2164-11-724 PMID:21176216

Kim, S., & Misra, A. (2007). Snp genotyping: Technologies and biomedical applications. *Annual Review of Biomedical Engineering*, *9*(1), 289–320. doi:10.1146/annurev.bioeng.9.060906.152037 PMID:17391067

Kraft, P., & Cox, D. G. (2008). Study designs for genome-wide association studies. *Advances in Genetics*, *60*, 465–504. doi:10.1016/S0065-2660(07)00417-8 PMID:18358330

Kuhn, R. M., Haussler, D., & Kent, W. J. (2013). The ucsc genome browser and associated tools. *Briefings in Bioinformatics*, *14*(2), 144–161. doi:10.1093/bib/bbs038 PMID:22908213

Li, B., & Leal, S. M. (2008). Methods for detecting associations with rare variants for common diseases: Application to analysis of sequence data. *American Journal of Human Genetics*, *83*(3), 311–321. doi:10.1016/j.ajhg.2008.06.024 PMID:18691683

McKinney, B. A., Reif, D. M., Ritchie, M. D., & Moore, J. H. (2006). Machine learning for detecting gene-gene interactions: A review. *Applied Bioinformatics*, *5*(2), 77–88. doi:10.2165/00822942-200605020-00002 PMID:16722772

Michaelson, J. J., Loguercio, S., & Beyer, A. (2009). Detection and interpretation of expression quantitative trait loci (eqtl). *Methods (San Diego, Calif.)*, *48*(3), 265–276. doi:10.1016/j.ymeth.2009.03.004 PMID:19303049

Moskvina, V., & Schmidt, K. M. (2008). On multiple-testing correction in genome-wide association studies. *Genetic Epidemiology*, *32*(6), 567–573. doi:10.1002/gepi.20331 PMID:18425821

Motsinger-Reif, A. A., Reif, D. M., Fanelli, T. J., & Ritchie, M. D. (2008). A comparison of analytical methods for genetic association studies. *Genetic Epidemiology*, *32*(8), 767–778. doi:10.1002/gepi.20345 PMID:18561203

Nielsen, R., Korneliussen, T., Albrechtsen, A., Li, Y., & Wang, J. (2012). Snp calling, genotype calling, and sample allele frequency estimation from new-generation sequencing data. *PLoS ONE*, *7*(7), e37558. doi:10.1371/journal.pone.0037558 PMID:22911679

Pare, G., & Henderson, M. A. (2013). Genome-wide association studies (gwas). In P. Sharma & J. F. Meschia (Eds.), *Stroke genetics* (pp. 25–50). Springer London. doi:10.1007/978-0-85729-209-4_3

Price, A. L., Patterson, N. J., Plenge, R. M., Weinblatt, M. E., Shadick, N. A., & Reich, D. (2006). Principal components analysis corrects for stratification in genome-wide association studies. *Nature Genetics*, *38*(8), 904–909. doi:10.1038/ng1847 PMID:16862161

Pritchard, J. K., Stephens, M., & Donnelly, P. (2000). Inference of population structure using multilocus genotype data. *Genetics*, *155*(2), 945–959. PMID:10835412

Purcell, S., Neale, B., Todd-Brown, K., Thomas, L., Ferreira, M. A., & Bender, D. et al. (2007). Plink: A tool set for whole-genome association and population-based linkage analyses. *American Journal of Human Genetics*, *81*(3), 559–575. doi:10.1086/519795 PMID:17701901

Ragoussis, J. (2006). Genotyping technologies for all. *Drug Discovery Today. Technologies*, *3*(2), 115–122. doi:10.1016/j.ddtec.2006.06.013 PMID:24980397

Ragoussis, J. (2009). Genotyping technologies for genetic research. *Annual Review of Genomics and Human Genetics*, *10*(1), 117–133. doi:10.1146/annurev-genom-082908-150116 PMID:19453250

Reich, D. E., Cargill, M., Bolk, S., Ireland, J., Sabeti, P. C., & Richter, D. J. et al. (2001). Linkage disequilibrium in the human genome. *Nature*, *411*(6834), 199–204. doi:10.1038/35075590 PMID:11346797

Ritchie, M. D., Hahn, L. W., Roodi, N., Bailey, L. R., Dupont, W. D., Parl, F. F., & Moore, J. H. (2001). Multifactor-dimensionality reduction reveals high-order interactions among estrogen-metabolism genes in sporadic breast cancer. *American Journal of Human Genetics*, *69*(1), 138–147. doi:10.1086/321276 PMID:11404819

Syvanen, A. C. (2001). Accessing genetic variation: Genotyping single nucleotide polymorphisms. *Nature Reviews. Genetics*, *2*(12), 930–942. doi:10.1038/35103535 PMID:11733746

Teare, M. D. (2011). Candidate gene association studies. *Methods in Molecular Biology (Clifton, N.J.)*, *713*, 105–117. doi:10.1007/978-1-60327-416-6_8 PMID:21153614

Zhang, Y., & Liu, J. S. (2007). Bayesian inference of epistatic interactions in case-control studies. *Nature Genetics*, *39*(9), 1167–1173. doi:10.1038/ng2110 PMID:17721534

Ziegler, A., Konig, I. R., & Thompson, J. R. (2008). Biostatistical aspects of genome-wide association studies. *Biometrical Journal. Biometrische Zeitschrift*, *50*(1), 8–28. doi:10.1002/bimj.200710398 PMID:18217698

KEY TERMS AND DEFINITIONS

Case-Control Study: A commonly used association study design using unrelated individuals, werhe the frequency of alleles or genotypes is compared between the cases and controls. Cases are individuals that been carefully diagnosed with the disease or trait being studied. The controls are individuals who are either known to be unaffected, or who have been randomly selected from the population.

Family Based Association Studies: Association study using related individuals to avoid the potential confounding effects of population stratification.

Genetic Association: The occurrence, more often than can be readily explained by chance, of two or more traits in a population of individuals, of which at least one trait is known to be genetic.

Genome Wide Association Study: Examination of a large number of common genetic variants (typically over one million) in different individuals to see if any variant is statistically associated with a trait of interest, like a disease outcome or a drug response trait.

Genotype Quality Control: The process of performing statistical analysis to assess the quality of the genotype data, to avoid confounding and deal with missing data.

Single Nucleotide Polymorphim: A DNA sequence variation occurring when a single nucleotide – A, T, C or G – in the genome differs between individuals in a population or paired chromosomes.

Statistical Testing: A method of statistical inference using data from a scientific study. In statistics, a result is called statistically significant if it has been predicted as unlikely to have occurred by chance alone, according to a pre-determined threshold probability, the significance level.

Chapter 15
Personalized Disease Phenotypes from Massive OMICs Data

Hans Binder
University of Leipzig, Germany

Kathrin Lembcke
University of Leipzig, Germany

Lydia Hopp
University of Leipzig, Germany

Henry Wirth
University of Leipzig, Germany

ABSTRACT

Application of new high-throughput technologies in molecular medicine collects massive data for hundreds to thousands of persons in large cohort studies by characterizing the phenotype of each individual on a personalized basis. The chapter aims at increasing our understanding of disease genesis and progression and to improve diagnosis and treatment. New methods are needed to handle such "big data." Machine learning enables one to recognize and to visualize complex data patterns and to make decisions potentially relevant for diagnosis and treatment. The authors address these tasks by applying the method of self-organizing maps and present worked examples from different disease entities of the colon ranging from inflammation to cancer.

INTRODUCTION

Application of new high-throughput technologies in molecular medicine such as microarrays and next generation sequencing generates massive amounts of data for each individual patient studied. These methods enable to characterize the genotype and/or molecular phenotype on a personalized basis with the aim to increase our understanding of disease genesis and progression and, in final consequence, to improve diagnosis

and treatment options. New methods are needed to handle such 'big data' sets collected for hundreds to thousands of persons in large epidemiological cohort studies, e.g. to accomplish data mining and classification tasks with impact for diagnosis and therapy. From the perspective of bioinformatics and systems biomedicine, 'big data' challenge objectives such as data integration, dimension reduction, data compression and visual perception. To finally achieve a personalized therapy it is necessary to link genetic variations to molecular

DOI: 10.4018/978-1-4666-6611-5.ch015

disease phenotypes, to associate molecular with clinical data, to extract, to filter and to interpret bio-medical information and finally, to translate these discoveries into medical practice.

Machine learning represents one interesting option to tackle these tasks. Particularly, neural network algorithms such as self-organizing maps (SOMs) combine effective data processing and dimension reduction with strong visualization capabilities. These methods provide a suited basis to analyze large and complex data generated by modern bioanalytics.

The present contribution shortly describes the method of 'SOM portraying'. We demonstrate data compression capabilities which reduce the dimension of the relevant (in terms of functional information) data by several orders of magnitude. The strong visualization capabilities of the SOM approach are illustrated. They enable the comprehensive, intuitive and detailed analysis of 'big data' in molecular medicine by mapping them into phenotype and feature space. To illustrate the performance of the method we present a series of representative case studies from different disease entities and OMICs realms related to the human colon.

BACKGROUND

Big Data from High-Throughput Bioanalytics

Standard medical practice is moving from relatively ad-hoc and subjective decision making to so-called evidence-based healthcare which makes use of complex diagnosis technologies such as comprehensive laboratory analyses and powerful imaging techniques.

Powered by the progress in modern molecular biomedicine the number and granularity of accepted disease types and also the variety of related therapy options steeply increase. This trend is paralleled by increasing volume and complexity of data collected per patient in disease-related cohort studies and also in medical practice. Accordingly, the way of decision making in diagnosis changes, for example from evaluating a set of key laboratory markers to information mining in large and potentially 'big' data sets generated by high-throughput technologies. Moreover, the evaluation of currently collected data includes also their comparison with already accumulated knowledge and reference data which itself can constitute a 'big' data challenge.

As generally accepted, big data is characterized by the three (Beyer, 2011), and sometimes four 'V': big volume, big velocity, big variety and, also, big veracity referring usually to the scale of the data, the handling of streaming data, the manifold and complexity of different forms and values of data and to their uncertainty, respectively. For high-throughput data in molecular medicine these general criteria can be specified: Usually the number of single data items per sample measurement ranges from tens of thousands to several millions and even more depending on the type of data (e.g. proteomics measured by means of mass spectrometry or genomics measured by means of next generation sequencing) and on their level in the processing pipeline starting with raw data and ending with highly (information-) enriched data (see below). In this respect present- and next generation omics-technologies generate massive amounts of data. Velocity in terms of time needed to store and re-store the data and to process them in downstream analysis programs is an important point which however will not be addressed here. Variety is probably the most important aspect in omics-bioinformatics because the assignment of data to the patients on one hand and to relevant biological items such as genes on the other hand, and their covariance structure basically code the useful information which governs biological function. Biostatistics mainly addresses the veracity of biomedical molecular data with the main aim to optimize marker selection tasks by maximizing their significance in terms of sensitivity and specificity by taking into account the uncertainty inherent in the data. Recently more 'V' are added to be essential for big data such as 'variability' (variance in meaning), 'visualization', 'value', 'volatility' and 'validity' (Normandeu, 2013; van Rijmenam, 2013). 'Visualization' is a very important aspect because it makes big data comprehensible in a manner that is easy to understand and read. It is however a difficult but also extremely crucial challenge especially in personalized medicine because it can help medical doctors to evaluate big data based on visual perception without explicitly dealing with numbers.

'One of the biggest new ideas in computing is "big data".' ("The Big Data Conundrum: How to Define It?," 2013). Unfortunately the term 'big' invites quantification and thus overemphasis of the first 'V', synonymous for the volume (see ref. (Ward & Barker, 2013) for a detailed discussion). This makes a definition difficult and susceptible to misinterpretation. Recall that, despite the sudden interest in big data, the concept of the four 'V' is not really new and applies, at least partly, also to conventional data processing. 'Big' implies significance, complexity and challenge. In this sense 'big' can be understood as the challenge to data which are difficult to process using common management tools and/or data processing methods. Hence, 'Big Data can be actually very small and not all large data sets are really big' (Rindler, McLowry, & Hillard, 2013). For biomedical high-throughput data complexity and thus the variety 'V' and not size (usually annotated as 'massive' data) is often the most critical factor if one aims at finding and unlocking interesting patterns and associations to power the advance of stratified medicine.

Interestingly, other definitions link the term 'big' data with the technologies machine learning and artificial intelligence requiring significant compute power and focusing on the extraction of information from the data (Microsoft, 2013). However, machine learning and particularly, neural network algorithms such as self-organizing maps (SOMs) are relatively infrequently used in high-throughput bioanalytics possibly because involved bioinformaticians and statisticians are typically trained in 'classical' approaches for feature selection, class discovery and classification based on rigorous significance testing of single features. On the other hand, researchers with background in machine learning are often affiliated at engineering and technology departments and not or only peripherally involved into life science problems. Therefore machine learning and particularly SOM are still innovative methods in molecular biology and health science. In consequence application of the concept of SOM learning data transformation and visualization still requires explanation and adaptation. Moreover, the SOM algorithm accomplishes 'only' basal sorting and visualization tasks. It needs to be supplemented with add-ons for significance testing and marker extraction, visualization of biological properties inherent in the data and finally for information mining of the biological context to become an attractive application tool in life sciences.

Reducing the Dimensionality: Subtyping, Filtering, and Re-Weighting

Typical big data in molecular medicine comprises thousands to millions of 'single' features related to molecular items which are measured separately in dozens to thousands of patient-related samples. This data can describe the genotype of each individual if it contains heritable genomic information such as mutations or aberrations of the DNA. Other molecular technologies collect data about the molecular phenotype in terms of the abundance of proteins, messenger RNA (mRNA), micro RNA or metabolites. These molecular markers characterize structural and functional building blocks of the organism resulting from the transcription of heritable genomic information under the influence of environmental factors. In consequence the molecular phenotype of each individual is unique.

Formally each individual of the collective under study is represented by its own specific position in the N-dimensional space spanned by the entirety of these phenotypic features (see Figure 1a for illustration). Groups of individuals with similar phenotypes can be stratified into subtypes representing generalized phenotypes. They are characterized by subtype-related 'mean' feature values and also by the diversity of values of all individual members of the subtype which can be quantified using probabilistic measures such as frequency distributions and variance measures. The subtyping of large sample collectives into strata is a reasonable strategy in molecular diagnosis because it displays disease subtypes of different molecular origin. Appropriate subtyping is required to select features suited as classification markers with potential impact for diagnosis and therapy.

Usually the highly dimensional feature space is partly redundant because part of the features are covariant or simply uninformative with respect to the phenotypes, e.g., if they lack significant variability. Hence, handling of big data in molecular medicine requires first of all the reduction of dimensionality by removing or down-weighting redundant or uninformative data. This dimension reduction can be applied to the samples by clustering them into a reduced number of groups and using these generalized phenotypes in further analyses. Dimension reduction can be also applied to feature space either by removing uninformative features or by re-weighting the data via clustering.

A simple method for dimension reduction is filtering: It identifies uninformative features and removes them from data space. Note however, that filtering can be dangerous because it might also eliminate valuable information, for example, by removing noisy features which nevertheless carry important biological information. Hence, filtering is an optimization task with the requirement of removing virtually irrelevant data while preserving as much as possible information in the remaining part of the data. We have discussed this issue in terms of the antagonism between 'representativeness' and 'noisiness' of the filtered data where optimization aims at maximizing representativeness while minimizing noisiness (Wirth, Loeffler, von Bergen, & Binder, 2011).

Re-weighting is another option to reduce the dimensionality of the data. It can be achieved by clustering the features into appropriate groups where each of them is characterized by a representative meta-feature serving as prototype of the cluster. Further analyses can then be performed based on these prototypic data of reduced size. Each cluster can contain different numbers of single features represented by the respective prototype. Analyses based on prototypic data thus effectively alter the importance of the original data: Single features become effectively down-weighted if the clusters are large. Contrarily, they become effectively up-weighted if the clusters contain only a few single features. Hence, analysis on the level of prototypic data increases representativeness because highly redundant data are down-weighted while rare but important features become up-weighted (Wirth, Loeffler, von Bergen, & Binder, 2011). In general, reweighting is advantageous compared with filtering because no single feature is removed from the analysis. Instead the single data remain 'hidden' behind the prototypic features. Their values can be 're-accessed' and used for analyses if necessary.

ANALYZING AND VISUALIZING BIG OMICS DATA USING SELF ORGANIZING MAPS

SOM Portraying

A large number of clustering methods is available with different advantages and disadvantages depending mostly on the data type, the intrinsic structure of the data, their size but also on the performance and power of the respective algorithms. In this contribution we make use of the method of self organizing maps (SOM), a machine learning

Figure 1. SOM machine learning of patient-related 'big' data
a) Each sample occupies one position in n-dimensional feature space. Similar 'personal phenotypes' can be clustered into subtypes (dashed ellipses). b) SOM machine learning clusters the features into meta-features (see also Figure 3). They are transferred from a matrix-representation into a quadratic grid for 'portraying'. The values of the meta-features are visualized as 'profiles' (values of one selected meta-feature in all samples) or as 'personal portrait' (values of all meta-features in one selected sample) representing a colored image of the meta-feature landscape of a selected sample. c) The multitude of personal portraits included in the study are further analyzed to extract information about sample- and feature-diversity. The phenotype map allows the classification of 'personal' phenotypes into subtypes. The feature map clusters the features into spots modules (ellipses) where each of them comprises a list of single features. They can be associated with the phenotypes as illustrated by the bar plots quantifying the fraction of samples showing high feature values in the respective spot in their portrait. Spot-related profiles from opposite regions of the map are usually anticorrelated whereas adjacent spots are often correlated.

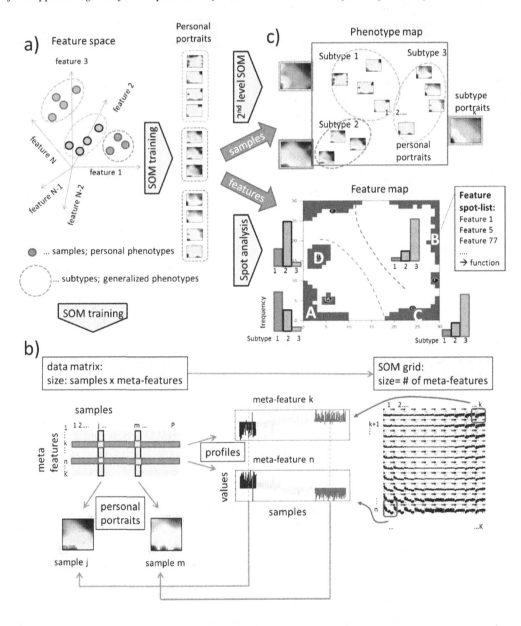

technology offering several advantages compared with alternative methods such as non-negative matrix factorization, K-means, hierarchical clustering or correlation clustering when applied to 'big' data in molecular medicine (Wirth, Loeffler, von Bergen, & Binder, 2011).

SOM is a supervised clustering method, i.e. it distributes the features under study over a pre-defined number of clusters called meta-features where features with similar values in all samples are clustered together. The value of each meta-feature serves as representative (prototypic value) for the respective cluster of single features. The meta-features are arranged in a quadratic grid called SOM space with the objective of visualizing their values separately for each sample (see Figure 1b). This 'data landscape' is obtained by coloring each pixel in the grid according to the value of the respective meta-feature using a suited color code. It is an important property of the SOM clustering that it 'self-organizes' meta-features with similar profiles together into neighboring pixels within the SOM space. Thus, after training of the data (see below) one obtains an individual mosaic image for each sample. Virtually it portrays the multidimensional data landscape in terms of a colored, blurry texture serving as molecular fingerprint of the respective patient-related sample. These images are therefore called molecular portraits. As a typical pattern they reveal often uniformly colored spot-like areas which represent clusters of co-variant meta-features with relatively high or low values in the respective sample. Further analysis of the spot patterns observed in the molecular portraits enables to identify such 'spot-' cluster of co-variant features. They can be interpreted as intrinsic modes of variability inherent in the data set. Importantly, clustering into spot modules is an unsupervised approach because their number is not defined by the user.

Hence, SOM portraying generates a pixelated mosaic image of the individual feature landscape of each sample where intrinsic modes of co-regulated features appear as colored spots.

As a rule of thumb, the number of pixels (i.e. of meta-features) must exceed the number of intrinsic modes by roughly a factor of $20 - 100$ to achieve a sufficient resolution which allows to detect all relevant modes. As a simple analogy one can compare SOM portraying with portraying objects on a television screen: TV also displays shapes as pixelated color image. For proper perception, the number of pixels used must largely exceed the number of relevant details.

In summary, SOM portraying combines a two-step compression of the original data with the intuitive imaging of its intrinsic structure. Both aspects will be discussed below.

SOM Training

SOM uses an iterative learning algorithm to cluster the data as described. It starts with appropriate initialization of the map space, followed by the training process to adjust the map space to the multivariate covariance structure of the input data, and it ends with the final mapping and visualization of the map space in terms of SOM portraits. The SOM training algorithm iteratively fits the meta-profiles to the profiles of the single features and, in parallel, assigns each single feature to the meta-feature of maximum similarity. Each iteration divides into three sub-steps: Firstly, one feature profile is selected as training vector. Secondly, the meta- profile of closest similarity (also called BMU – best matching unit) is determined using the Euclidean distance as criterion. Thirdly, the profile of the BMU and the profiles of its neighbors are adjusted to better resemble the selected training vector. The amount of adaption is downscaled with increasing distance to the BMU in the two-dimensional grid. With progressive number of iterations the algorithm settles down: the meta-profiles progressively cover the multitude of different profiles of input features, which, in turn, distribute among the meta-features available. SOM training is stopped after a few hundred thousand iterations ensuring convergence.

In consequence, the data space becomes segmented into clusters of single features mapped to each meta-feature after training. Each cluster is characterized by one meta-profile which is used for visualizing the feature's state at each condition studied (see above). For a detailed description of the SOM method we refer to the additional reading section and to (Wirth, von Bergen, & Binder, 2012).

Sampling and Visualizing the Feature and Phenotype Space

Our implementation of the SOM method enables to visually portray each sample in terms of a colored two-dimensional image (Wirth, Loeffler, von Bergen, & Binder, 2011; Wirth, von Bergen, & Binder, 2012). The portraits of a larger number of samples are analyzed in two principal ways (see Figure 1c):

Firstly, sample similarity analysis describes the feature space covered by the samples. We applied so-called second level SOM analysis to map the distribution of samples from the multidimensional feature space into two dimensions. The obtained phenotype map visualizes the distribution of personal portraits and allows to identify subtypes as clusters of samples with similar feature landscapes. The feature landscape of the generalized phenotypes can then be extracted as a mean image averaged over the personal portraits of each subtype.

Secondly, feature similarity analysis explicitly discovers the diversity of feature values in phenotype space. Features behaving similarly among the samples are clustered together into so-called spot modules in SOM analysis. They are called spots because these clusters appear as red or blue spot-like regions in the individual SOM portraits if the respective feature values are high or low, respectively. Each spot is represented by its prototypic meta-feature profile. Spot diversity analysis then provides statistical measures about the abundance of each of the spots in the different subtypes such as the respective frequency distribution. Moreover, the feature map summarizes the spot landscapes of the personal portraits into a master map which assigns the spots observed to the different subtypes. The feature map complements the phenotype map because it links sample diversity with feature diversity. Importantly, the different spot modules can be interpreted in terms of biological function using previous knowledge about the associated single features under reference conditions such as healthy and well defined diseased states (Wirth, von Bergen, & Binder, 2012).

Figure 2 shows an example illustrating phenotype and feature mapping: The underlying data are gene-related DNA-methylation data of colon cancer samples taken from 320 individuals collected in the TCGA (The Cancer Genome Atlas) project using the microarray technology (TCGA, 2012). These data estimate the methylation level of the promoter region of about 20,000 human genes in each individual sample. The phenotype map in Figure 2a reveals that the samples split clearly into the two gender-specific phenotypes 'men' and 'women' in vertical direction. In addition, four gender-independent methylator subtypes were identified (TCGA, 2012) which distribute mostly along the horizontal coordinate of the phenotype map. Visual inspection of the individual portraits indicates that the methylation landscapes decompose into two mutually independent subpatterns which are governed either by gender- or by methylator-phenotype-related traits. The former subpattern is dominated by spot 'X' assigned in part b of Figure 2. It contains 282 single genes in total where 268, i.e. virtually all of them are located on the sex-determining chromosome X (allosome). The respective genes are systematically hypermethylated in women (spot X becomes red) and hypomethylated in men (spot X becomes blue). The methylation profile of this spot is shown in panel c where the samples are ordered according to their methylator-phenotypes showing an almost perfect seperation of samples in a gender-specific manner. The scattered distribution

Figure 2. SOM analysis of gene-related dna-methylation data of a cohort of colon cancer samples taken from ref. (TCGA, 2012)

The data contain two mutually independent kinds of information about gender and cancer subtypes, respectively: (a) The phenotype map separates the samples in both a gender- and a cancer-specific way. It reveals four subtypes taken from the original publication (CH, CL, C3, C4; see below) which split into two gender-specific areas. (b) The methylation landscapes of selected samples show a gender-specific spot. It contains genes which are hypo-methylated in men and hyper-methylated in women. It is visible in the two-dimensional sample portraits as spot X colored in blue (men) or red (women). (c) The methylation profile of spot X strongly depends on the gender of the tumor patients but not on its subtype. In contrast, the methylation profile of spot A is subtype-specific but it virtually doesn't associate with the gender of the patients.

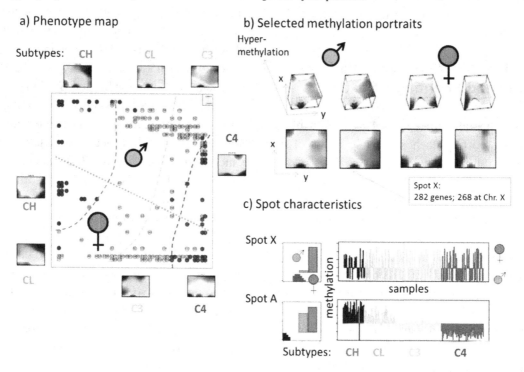

of high and low methylation values reflects the fact that men and women nearly equally distribute over the methylator phenotypes. In contrast, the methylation profile of another spot A strongly associates with the methylator subtypes. It contains genes associating with the methylator-phenotype.

Gender-specific hyper-methylation of genes on allosome X is well known as X chromosome inactivation (XCI) (Augui, Nora, & Heard, 2011). XCI is a dosage compensation effect leveling the expression of chromosome X genes in female cells. Recall that female cells contain the double set of X-chromosomes (XX) compared with male cells (XY). XCI silences part of the genes on the X chromosome in women by hyper-methylation of their promoter regions to prevent overexpression

compared with men. Gender-specific methylation thus considerably expands the phenotype space compared with that occupied by the cancer methylator subtypes solely. Since cancer subtyping studies are primarily interested in subtype-related characteristics it is desirable to confine phenotype space to that of the methylator subtypes. This can be simply achieved by removing the genes on chromosome X from the analysis. The obtained shrunken phenotype space is presented below in the examples section of this chapter.

Multi-Step Information Enrichment

The original set of high-dimensional data is presented in form of a matrix of dimension *samples x features*. Our SOM approach compresses the data in several consecutive steps which apply separately to the feature and sample dimensions (Figure 3): (i) SOM training collects similar profiles of single features into typically a few thousand micro clusters called meta-features, which reduces the number of features typically by one-to-two orders of magnitude compared with the original data. The meta-feature landscape of each sample is transformed into one mosaic image where each pixel is assigned to one meta-feature as described above. Further downstream analysis is based on these personal portraits and uses the underlying meta-feature data. (ii) The textures of the obtained SOM-portraits are decomposed into a few (typically about one dozen) spots representing clusters of concerted meta-features. The spot profiles can be understood as a sort of 'eigen-modes' characterizing the multitude of basal feature patterns inherent in the data. In other words, the spot-modules represent a natural choice of context-dependent patterns in complex data sets. Note that spot-clustering further compresses the data and reduces their volume by another one-to-two orders of magnitude compared with the preceding meta-feature level. (iii) Compression so far was applied to the feature dimension of the data. The last 'subtyping' step applies to the sample dimension using appropriate methods of class-discovery. The number of relevant classes is typically much smaller than the number of samples studied giving rise to further reduction of data size by at minimum one order of magnitude.

Taking together, this data compression pipeline reduces the volume of features used by up to six orders of magnitude. The main criterion for applying this pipeline requires that the relevant information content of the original data remains stored in the compressed data. Of course, the 'relevance' of information is related to the particular

Figure 3. SOM training of big data in molecular medicine is performed on two levels
(1) Feature space of the original items is compressed using 1st level SOM. It provides one mosaic image per sample (so-called sample or personal portrait). It allows to extract clusters of features as spot modules. (2) Sample space is 'scanned' using 2nd level SOM. It maps the sample portraits and allows to classify them into subtypes. Data compression using SOM clustering increases the information density of the data by several orders of magnitude.

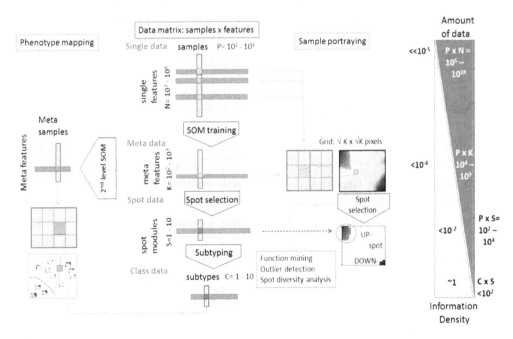

objective of the study. In the context discussed here, we focus on the main intrinsic structure of the data which decomposes into subtypes of similar samples on one hand and into related sets of features called spot-modules on the other hand.

Importantly, the dimension reduction of the data does not entail the loss of primary information in contrast to simple filtering which irretrievably removes part of the data as discussed above. Instead, the reduction of dimension is attained by re-weighting of primary information in the aggregation step. The whole set of single feature values remains virtually 'hidden' behind the meta-features. This primary information together with the respective annotations of the features can be extracted in later steps of analysis to interpret the observed SOM textures using concepts of biological function.

Second-level SOM analysis is applied for phenotype mapping as proposed by Guo et al. (Guo, Eichler, Feng, Ingber, & Huang, 2006) to visualize the similarity relations between the individual portraits. Second-level SOM analysis uses the personal portraits of all samples as input. It then clusters the samples and not the features as in first-level SOM analysis. Each tile of the second-level SOM mosaic characterizes the feature landscape of a representative meta-sample. The 2nd level SOM phenotype maps can be used for class discovery in the subtyping step.

Personalized Feature Landscapes

Each sample's feature landscape is described by the values of the meta-features in the respective column of the metadata matrix (see Figure 3). These values are arranged in the grid of the SOM map and visualized using an appropriate color gradient: Dark red usually reflects high meta-feature values; yellow and green tones indicate intermediate levels; and blue corresponds to low values. The resulting color patterns emerge as smooth textures owing to the self-organizing properties of the training algorithm as described

above. The obtained mosaic image visualizes the multidimensional feature landscape of the respective specimen. It thus provides a molecular portrait of each patient-related sample. Please note also that the assignment of the features to meta-features and therefore also their position in the map is identical in all sample portraits trained together. Hence, the coloring at a certain position in the map refers to the same features in all individual portraits. The invariant position of each feature in all portraits allows the direct comparison of its value between the maps.

Hence, visual inspection and intuitive interpretation play a central role in the initial steps of our portraying method. Figure 4 shows a few examples of characteristic types of feature landscapes observed frequently: The 'single peak'-type is characterized by a single peak protruding in an otherwise flat plain-like landscape. The peak contains single features with high values in the respective samples. The 'single-valley'-type represents the antagonistic landscape with a set of features with low values in the respective samples evident as a hole-like valley in an otherwise flat landscape. The 'peak-and-valley'-type shows a peak *and* a valley at the same time, often in opposite corners of the map. This type reflects two antagonistically-regulated sets of features, e.g. if one is high then the other one is low and vice versa. The 'multi-peak' and/or 'multi-valley' types reflect more complex landscapes which are characterized by the superposition of several modes forming a certain correlation network between the features. The 'rare single peak'-type shows essentially the same landscape as the 'single peak'-type discussed above. The peak however is observed in a relatively small fraction of samples and it is often located in the central part of the map. Moreover, valleys are not observed at the respective positions in any of the samples. Such patterns can be indicative for contaminations with another feature landscape which simply overlays with the first one. We found such patterns e.g. in expression studies of cancer samples which

Figure 4. Different types of feature landscapes reflect characteristic regulatory modes. Most of the landscapes are observed as mirror symmetric 'positive-negative' twins reflecting antagonistic modes.

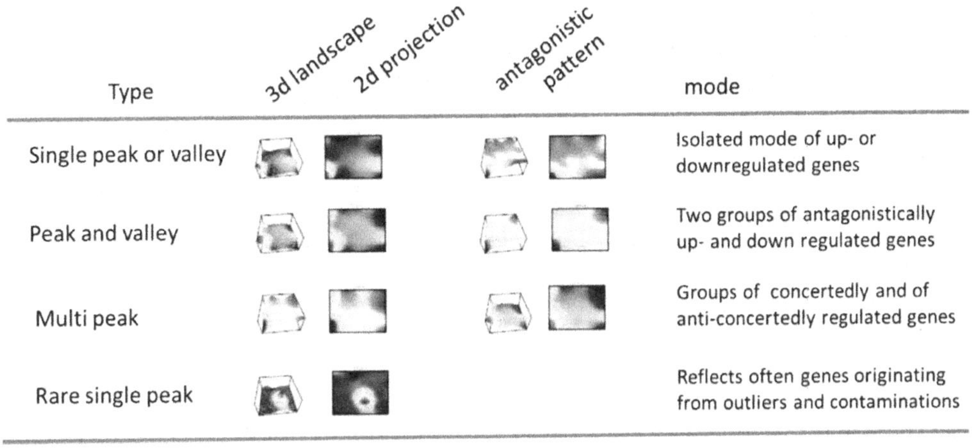

Type	3d landscape	2d projection	antagonistic pattern		mode
Single peak or valley					Isolated mode of up- or downregulated genes
Peak and valley					Two groups of antagonistically up- and down regulated genes
Multi peak					Groups of concertedly and of anti-concertedly regulated genes
Rare single peak					Reflects often genes originating from outliers and contaminations

are contaminated with healthy tissue (Hopp, Lembcke, Binder, & Wirth, 2013; Hopp, Wirth, Fasold, & Binder, 2013). We have shown that the landscapes allow identification and interpretation of outlier samples and thus to improve data quality. In summary, intuitive visualization of data landscapes using SOM portraits clearly promotes quality control and the discovery of the intrinsic covariance structure of the data.

Note that this image-based perception and decision making of multidimensional high-throughput data has something similar with conventional methods in pathology which evaluate and classify microscopic images of tissue sections using a set of key features taken from previous knowledge. Also these images represent surrogates of the underlying complex molecular patterns allowing precise diagnosis in many cases.

CASE STUDY: GENE EXPRESSION AND -METHYLATION PHENOTYPES OF THE HEALTHY AND DISEASED HUMAN COLON

For illustration of the SOM portraying method we selected a series of examples addressing the transcriptome and methylome of colon mucosa in

the healthy and diseased states. We demonstrate that different diseases and molecular parameters provide data of varying complexity. We also show that the information content of these large data sets can be easily extracted by means of SOM analysis. For direct comparison we use the same presentations of all examples.

Ulcerative Colitis Before and After Onset of Inflammation

Specimen were sampled by endoscopic mucosal biopsies from ulcerative colitis patients with and without microscopic signs of inflammation to investigate the effect of inflammation on gene expression (see (Olsen, Gerds, Seidelin, Csillag, Bjerrum et al., 2009) for details). We transformed the expression data of all samples into personal portraits grouped into the not-inflamed (Ni) and inflamed subtypes (If) (Figure 5a). The different textures of both subtypes clearly provide first indications of different gene activation patterns. Note that the whole data set comprises the expression levels of 22,000 genes measured in 24 samples, i.e. in total about half a million single items. The mean portraits were obtained by averaging all personal portraits of each subtype (Figure 5b). They reveal relatively simple landscapes of the

Figure 5. SOM portraying of gene expression landscapes of samples of inflamed and not-inflamed colon mucosa
(Data and sample assignments were taken from (Olsen, Gerds, Seidelin, Csillag, Bjerrum, et al., 2009)). See text.

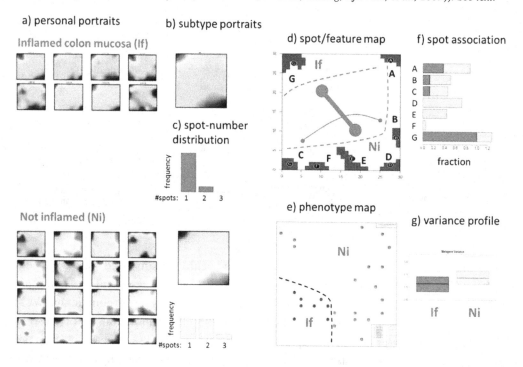

'peak and valley' type (see Figure 4) where two groups of genes are antagonistically up- or down-regulated in either of the subtypes. The minimum content of relevant information stored in the data is approximately one bit only.

More detailed inspection of the personal portraits and especially of that of the not-inflamed subtype reveals however a certain diversity of spot patterns. It is averaged out in the mean portraits (Figure 5b). Figure 5c estimates the diversity of spot patterns in each of the subtypes: It shows frequency histograms of the number of red overexpression spots observed in the personal portraits. Whereas the images of the inflamed cases mostly contain only one spot, lack of inflammation gives rise to at minimum one more spot in many of the personal portraits. However spots can appear at different positions. The spot/feature map in Figure 5d summarizes all relevant spots observed in any sample into one master map to provide an over-

view over all relevant expression modes. In total we identified seven spots denoted with capital letters A – G. The spot association histogram in Figure 5f depicts the faction of personal portraits of each subtype which show the respective spot. It consequently visualizes spot abundances. One sees that spot G is specific for the inflamed state: It is found in almost all inflamed samples. This result is in correspondence with the mean subtype portrait essentially showing this overexpression spot solely. In contrast, the remaining six spots are predominantly found in samples of the not-inflamed subtype however with different frequencies: The rarest one, spot F, is found only in one sample whereas the most frequent one D is found in 80% of the not-inflamed samples.

The information about spot-abundance allows to divide the feature map into areas which contain spots overexpressed in a certain subtype: The area of spots up-regulated in the inflamed state essentially restricts to the left upper corner of the map whereas the area of spots up-regulated in the not-inflamed state occupy a much larger area. This relation reflects the high heterogeneity of not-inflamed states compared with the relatively homogeneous landscapes of inflamed states. Interestingly, the phenotype map in Figure 5e transports essentially the same information: The inflamed samples occupy a relative small area in the map near the left-lower corner whereas the not-inflamed samples spread over a much larger area reflecting the larger diversity of their expression landscapes. Despite this heterogeneity, both inflamed and not-inflamed subtypes remain still separated without overlap of the respective areas. The variance profiles of the expression landscapes are given as boxplots in Figure 5g: Expression values are more variable in the not-inflamed samples. The dumbbell-like lines in the feature map Figure 5d connect anti-correlated spots: The strongest effect refers to spot-pairs identified as 'peak and valley'-like landscapes (spots G and D). Another pair of spots (B and C) however reveals a weaker anti-concerted mode appearing in the not-inflamed samples.

Finally, researchers are mostly interested in the biological meaning of the observed landscapes. Using gene set enrichment analysis we assign characteristic biological functions to the genes collected in the spot clusters (see ref. (Wirth, von Bergen, & Binder, 2012) for details). In the inflamed state genes related to processes like 'cell adhesion', 'chemokine activity' and 'blood coagulation' (spot G) become-up regulated whereas 'metabolism' and 'mitochondrion' (spot D) become down-regulated. In addition to these mostly expected results one finds that the diversity of not-inflamed states can be attributed to varying activities of processes related to 'transcription' (E), 'RNA-processing' (C), and 'cytosol' (B). The antagonism between spots C and B can be also attributed to the activity of the BCR-gene.

Colorectal Adenoma

The second example compares the expression landscapes of healthy colon mucosa (He) with that of colorectal adenoma (Ad), a precancerous lesion of colon mucosa. The original data set was taken from (Sabates-Bellver, Van der Flier, de Palo, Cattaneo, Maake et al., 2007) and comprises 32 samples of each class and 54,000 transcripts measured per sample. Figure 6 shows the characteristics for this data analogous to Figure 5. Both classes of samples were very similar with respect to the heterogeneity of their expression landscapes as estimated by the spot number distribution and variability of their expression landscapes. Accordingly both feature and phenotype maps divide into two nearly equal regions where each of them can be assigned to one of the subtypes. Importantly, these regions assigned to either healthy colon mucosa or adenoma are well separated without overlap. The mean subtype portraits are again of the 'peak-and-valley' type reflecting that the basal information content of this data is again one bit. Adenoma are characterized by up-regulation of processes like 'DNA-repair' and 'cell cycle' (spot E) and by down-regulation of 'T-cell activation' (A) and 'extracellular space' (B).

Methylator Phenotypes of Colorectal Cancer

Colorectal cancer (CRC) as most of other cancer entities has predominantly been considered a genetic disease. It is characterized by sequential accumulation of genetic alterations such as mutations and chromosomal instabilities leading to selective and progressive dysfunctions of genomic regulation. Epigenetic alterations however add an additional layer of complexity to the pathogenesis of CRC, and characterize a subgroup of CRC with a distinct etiology and prognosis (see, e.g. (van Engeland, Derks, Smits, Meijer, & Her-

Figure 6. SOM portraying of gene expression landscapes of healthy colon mucosa and of colorectal adenoma

(Data and sample assignments were taken from (Sabates-Bellver, Van der Flier, de Palo, Cattaneo, Maake, et al., 2007)). Only 30 samples portraits per subtype are shown. See text.

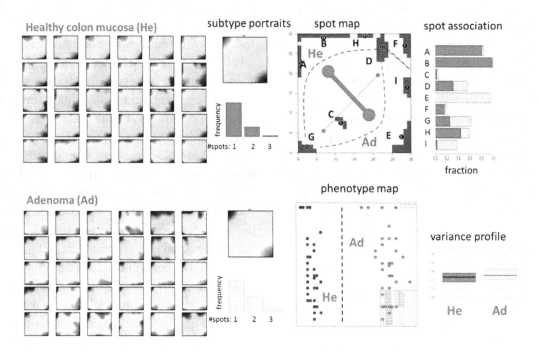

man, 2011)). The most extensively characterized epigenetic alteration in CRC is hypermethylation, which occurs at CpG dinucleotide dense regions, called CpG islands, present at the 5' region of approximately 60% of the genes. Most CpG islands lack methylation in normal colon mucosa, independent of the transcriptional status of the gene. Hypermethylation of promoter CpG islands however has been observed for numerous tumor suppressor- and DNA repair-genes with consequences for gene activity equivalent to mutations.

The recognition that a distinct subset of colorectal adenomas and CRCs display significantly more promoter methylation than others has led to the introduction of the concept of CpG island methylator phenotype (CIMP) (Toyota, Ahuja, Ohe-Toyota, Herman, Baylin et al., 1999). The existence of four different CIMP subtypes, each with specific molecular characteristics, has recently been postulated based on high-throughput methylation data (TCGA, 2012). This data is presented

above using methylation values of genes taken from all chromosomes including chromosome X (Figure 2). The same data set was again analyzed considering however only genes located on autosomes (Figure 7). The phenotype map obtained clearly distinguishes the four different methylator subtypes without the gender-specific split seen in Figure 2. The data set comprises 235 samples where only randomly selected examples from each subtype are shown in Figure 7 as portraits. The mean portraits of two subtypes (CIMP_high (CH) and to a less degree CIMP_low (CL)) are of the 'single-peak' types. The red peak-spot contains about 1,000 single genes strongly hypermethylated in these CIMP subtypes. The personal CIMP-portraits are relatively homogeneous showing mostly only this single peak. The landscapes of the other two subtypes, 'cluster 3' (C3) and 'cluster 4' (C4), are characterized by a broader spot number distribution reflecting a more heterogeneous diversity of methylation landscapes.

Figure 7. SOM portraying of gene promoter methylation data of colorectal cancer
(Data and assignment of the samples to the four methylator phenotypes were taken from (TCGA, 2012)).

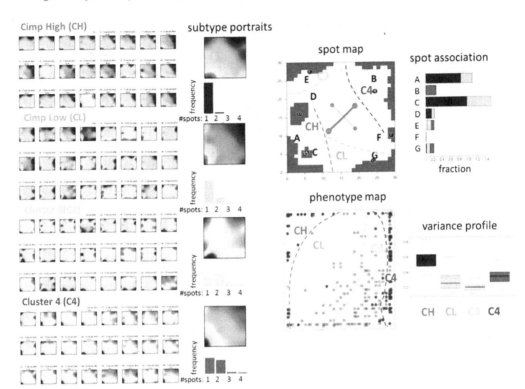

The mean subtype portraits of C3 and partly of C4 can be attributed to the 'multi-peak'-type revealing a more complex substructure of three to four groups of differentially methylated genes. The respective peak landscapes of the C3 and partly of the C4 types are however more smooth compared with the steeper landscapes of the CIMP high subtypes (see the variance profile in Figure 7). In consequence a smaller number of peaks is detected in C3 and C4 (see spot associations in Figure 7). Note however that the basal information content of the data is multivariate and splits into two-to four different modes.

The spot hyper-methylated in the CIMP subtypes (spot A) contains a high number of genes related to 'nervous systems function and development' whereas the spot hyper-methylated in C4 (spot B) enriches genes related to 'DNA transcription' and 'cell division'.

The Expression Landscape of Colorectal Cancer is Governed by Its Methylator Phenotype

Expression of hyper-methylated DNA is silenced via recruitment and binding of methyl-CpG binding proteins and associated co-repressors such as HDACs, which create a repressive chromatin structure. Hence, methylation is expected to modulate the gene expression landscapes of CRC. Expression data of the CRC-cases analyzed in the previous subsection are available and analyzed using our SOM portraying pipeline (Figure 8). Interestingly, the expression portraits of the subtypes clearly reveal an anti-matching characteristics when compared with the respective methylation landscapes. For example, the strong red hyper-methylation peak in the methylation landscapes of the CIMP subtypes is paralleled by a sharp ex-

Figure 8. SOM portraying of gene expression data of colorectal cancer
Samples and assignment of the samples were taken from (TCGA, 2012).

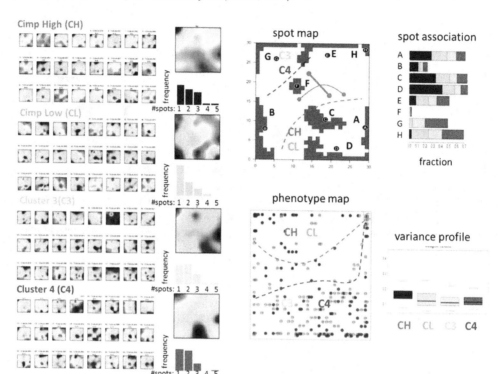

pression minimum in their expression landscapes whereas the hypo-methylation minimum of the C3 and C4 subtypes is paralleled by an expression peak in the expression landscapes (compare with Figure 7). This result reflects the basal inhibitory effect of methylation on expression, namely that increased promoter methylation reduces the expression level of the respective gene and vice versa. Note that the position of the maxima and minima in both types of maps disagrees because both SOM are trained independently giving rise to different distributions of the genes in the maps.

Note also that the phenotype and feature maps of the expression data clearly reflect the grouping of samples into methylator subtypes. In other words, the expression landscapes are clearly affected by the underlying methylation landscapes which govern activity of many genes. The variance profile of expression landscapes reflect this gene-dosis effect: large methylation changes in the CIMP_H subtype are associated with large

changes of the expression level. The gene expression landscapes are however affected also by other factors than DNA methylation. For example, many genes up-regulated in the CIMP-subtypes (spot D) can be attributed to immune function and inflammation which constitute cancer hallmarks activated by other mechanisms than methylation.

FUTURE RESEARCH DIRECTIONS

Portraying the Epigenome

Growing recognition of the importance of epigenetic processes in development and disease has fueled an insatiable thirst for new technologies to detect epigenetic modifications on a genome wide scale. The complex nature of epigenetic modifications and their manifold places many demands on analytical tools and data management. This comprises DNA-methylation and the variety of different histone modifications and their combinatorial patterns. We recently developed a method that combines global epigenome segmentation with SOM machine learning (Steiner, Hopp, Wirth, Galle, Binder et al., 2012). It provides intuitive maps of epigenetic patterns across multiple levels of organization, e.g. of the co-occurrence of different epigenetic marks in different cell types. Another recent application analyzes complex epigenome data using SOM mapping ("An integrated encyclopedia of DNA elements in the human genome," 2012).

OMICs Integration and Association

Our examples address applications of the portraying method to single OMICs realms such as transcriptome and methylome. There is however increasing need in the emerging field of joint analysis of disparate OMIC data from genomics, transcriptomics, proteomics, etc. in order to better understand key biological processes on the systems level, and particularly, to extract associations and causalities between different OMICs levels, e.g. between mutations and gene activity. Our examples demonstrate that expression and methylation landscapes of colon cancer samples strongly affect each other. Fist attempts are made to combine mRNA and miRNA expression levels using SOM machine learning (Çakir, Wirth, Hopp, & Binder, 2014; Wirth, Çakir, Hopp, & Binder, 2014). Recently a multi-OMICs clustering framework using hidden variables was proposed (Mo, Wang, Seshan, Olshen, Schultz et al., 2013). Further conceptual and methodological developments of these tools are needed for the integration of various data types across the multiple levels of OMICs-organization.

Towards Personalized Medicine

Traditional clinical diagnosis focuses on the individual patient's clinical signs and symptoms. Decreasing costs and increasing technological prospects of modern molecular bioanalytics open the perspective for applying also high-throughput bioanalytics for diagnostic and prognostic tasks: Laboratory technologies however need to be complemented with suited data mining and imaging tools. Here, SOM portraying constitutes one option for an individual view of complex data as one requirement of personalized diagnostics.

CONCLUSION

Gathering and maintaining large collections of data is one thing, but extracting useful information from these collections is often more challenging. Big Data not only changes the tools one can use for predictive analytics, it also changes our way of thinking about knowledge extraction and interpretation. Ironically, availability of more data at present can lead to fewer options in constructing predictive models, because tools allow for processing large datasets in a reasonable amount of time are often not available. Machine learning constitutes a clever alternative to overcome those problems at the edge of statistics, computer science and emerging applications in systems biomedicine.

SOM machine learning enables recognizing complex patterns in large-scale data generated by high-throughput omics technologies. The method allows portraying molecular phenotypes by generating individualized, easy to interpret images of the particular phenotypic data landscape in combination with phenotype and feature mappings and other analysis options. SOM machine learning reduces dimension of big data and enriches their information content using the concept of stepwise data compression in feature space (single features, meta-features, spot-modules) and the concept of subtyping in sample space.

In future healthcare every patient will be represented by a large dossier of data including massive data from omics diagnostics. Personal portraying of these data as feature landscapes and their projection into phenotype and feature maps previously 'learned' from large collectives of patients would provide one way to evaluate quantitatively the risk for the respective patient. Image-based, reductionist machine learning methods thus provide one interesting perspective how to deal with massive molecular omics data in future diagnostics of complex diseases.

ACKNOWLEDGMENT

H.W., K.L. and L.H. were supported by the Federal Ministry of Education and Research (BMBF), project grant Nos. FKZ 031 6065 (HNPCC-SYS) and FKZ 031 6166 (MMML-MYC-SYS), and by the European Regional Development Fund (ERDF) within the PhD groups 'Systems Medicine' and 'Cancer Microenvironment and Metastasis'.

REFERENCES

An Integrated Encyclopedia of DNA Elements in the Human Genome. (2012). *Nature, 489*(7414), 57-74.

Augui, S., Nora, E. P., & Heard, E. (2011). Regulation of X-chromosome inactivation by the X-inactivation centre. *Nat Rev Genet, 12*(6), 429-442.

Beyer, M. (2011). *Gartner Says Solving 'Big Data' Challenge Involves More Than Just Managing Volumes of Data.* Gartner. Retrieved from http://www.gartner.com/newsroom/id/1731916

Çakir, M., Wirth, H., Hopp, L., & Binder, H. (2014). MicroRNA Expression Landscapes in Stem Cells, Tissues, and Cancer. In M. Yousef & J. Allmer (Eds.), *miRNomics: MicroRNA Biology and Computational Analysis* (Vol. 1107, pp. 279–302). New York: Humana Press.

Guo, Y., Eichler, G. S., Feng, Y., Ingber, D. E., & Huang, S. (2006). Towards a Holistic, Yet Gene-Centered Analysis of Gene Expression Profiles: A Case Study of Human Lung Cancers. *Journal of Biomedicine & Biotechnology, 2006*, 69141. doi:10.1155/JBB/2006/69141 PMID:17489018

Hopp, L., Lembcke, K., Binder, H., & Wirth, H. (2013). Portraying the Expression Landscapes of B-Cell Lymphoma- Intuitive Detection of Outlier Samples and of Molecular Subtypes. *Biology, 2*(4), 1411–1437. doi:10.3390/biology2041411 PMID:24833231

Hopp, L., Wirth, H., Fasold, M., & Binder, H. (2013). Portraying the expression landscapes of cancer subtypes: A glioblastoma multiforme and prostate cancer case study. *Systems Biomedicine, 1*(2). doi:10.4161/sysb.25897

Microsoft. (2013). *The Big Bang: How the Big Data Explosion Is Changing the World.* Microsoft UK Enterprise Insights Blog. Retrieved from http://blogs.msdn.com/b/microsoftenterpriseinsight/archive/2013/04/15/big-bang-how-the-big-data-explosion-is-changing-the-world.aspx

Mo, Q., Wang, S., Seshan, V. E., Olshen, A. B., Schultz, N., & Sander, C. et al. (2013). Pattern discovery and cancer gene identification in integrated cancer genomic data. *Proceedings of the National Academy of Sciences of the United States of America, 110*(11), 4245–4250. doi:10.1073/pnas.1208949110 PMID:23431203

Normandeu, K. (2013). *Beyond Volume, Variety and Velocity is the Issue of Big Data Veracity.* Inside Big Data. Retrieved from http://insidebigdata.com/2013/09/12/beyond-volume-variety-velocity-issue-big-data-veracity/

Olsen, J., Gerds, T. A., Seidelin, J. B., Csillag, C., Bjerrum, J. T., Troelsen, J. T., & Nielsen, O. H. (2009). Diagnosis of ulcerative colitis before onset of inflammation by multivariate modeling of genome-wide gene expression data. *Inflammatory Bowel Diseases, 15*(7), 1032-1038. Doi: .10.1002/ibd.20879

Rindler, A., McLowry, S., & Hillard, R. (2013). *Big Data Definition*. MIKE2.0, the open source methodology for Information Development. Retrieved from http://mike2.openmethodology.org/wiki/Big_Data_Definition

Sabates-Bellver, J., Van der Flier, L. G., de Palo, M., Cattaneo, E., Maake, C., & Rehrauer, H. et al. (2007). Transcriptome Profile of Human Colorectal Adenomas. *Molecular Cancer Research, 5*(12), 1263–1275. doi:10.1158/1541-7786.MCR-07-0267 PMID:18171984

Steiner, L., Hopp, L., Wirth, H., Galle, J., Binder, H., Prohaska, S. J., & Rohlf, T. (2012). A Global Genome Segmentation Method for Exploration of Epigenetic Patterns. *PLOS one, 7*(10), e46811.

TCGA. (2012). Comprehensive molecular characterization of human colon and rectal cancer. *Nature, 487*(7407), 330-337.

The Big Data Conundrum: How to Define It? (2013). *MIT Technology Review*. Retrieved from http://www.technologyreview.com/view/519851/the-big-data-conundrum-how-to-define-it/

Toyota, M., Ahuja, N., Ohe-Toyota, M., Herman, J. G., Baylin, S. B., & Issa, J.-P. J. (1999). CpG island methylator phenotype in colorectal cancer. *Proceedings of the National Academy of Sciences of the United States of America, 96*(15), 8681–8686. doi:10.1073/pnas.96.15.8681 PMID:10411935

van Engeland, M., Derks, S., Smits, K. M., Meijer, G. A., & Herman, J. G. (2011). Colorectal Cancer Epigenetics: Complex Simplicity. *Journal of Clinical Oncology, 29*(10), 1382–1391. doi:10.1200/JCO.2010.28.2319 PMID:21220596

van Rijmenam, M. (2013). *Why The 3V's Are Not Sufficient To Describe Big Data*. Big data startup. Retrieved from http://www.bigdata-startups.com/3vs-sufficient-describe-big-data/

Ward, J. S., & Barker, A. (2013). *Undefined By Data: A Survey of Big Data Definitions*. eprint arXiv:1309.5821.

Wirth, H., Çakir, M., Hopp, L., & Binder, H. (2014). Analysis of MicroRNA Expression Using Machine Learning. *Methods in Molecular Biology (Clifton, N.J.), 1107*, 257–278. doi:10.1007/978-1-62703-748-8_16 PMID:24272443

Wirth, H., Loeffler, M., von Bergen, M., & Binder, H. (2011). Expression cartography of human tissues using self organizing maps. *BMC Bioinformatics, 12*(1), 306. doi:10.1186/1471-2105-12-306 PMID:21794127

Wirth, H., von Bergen, M., & Binder, H. (2012). Mining SOM expression portraits: Feature selection and integrating concepts of molecular function. *BioData Mining, 5*, 18.

ADDITIONAL READING

Brunet, J.-P., Tamayo, P., Golub, T. R., & Mesirov, J. P. (2004). Metagenes and molecular pattern discovery using matrix factorization. *Proceedings of the National Academy of Sciences of the United States of America, 101*(12), 4164–4169. doi:10.1073/pnas.0308531101 PMID:15016911

Esteller, M. (2007). Cancer epigenomics: DNA methylomes and histone-modification maps. *Nat Rev Genet, 8*(4), 286-298.

Kim, P. M., & Tidor, B. (2003). Subsystem Identification Through Dimensionality Reduction of Large-Scale Gene Expression Data. *Genome Research, 13*(7), 1706–1718. doi:10.1101/gr.903503 PMID:12840046

Kohonen, T. (1982). Self-organized formation of topologically correct feature maps. *Biological Cybernetics, 43*(1), 59-69.

McAfee, A., & Brynjolfsson, E. (2012). Big Data: The Management Revolution. *Harvard Business Review*. PMID:23074865

Saeys, Y., Inza, I., & Larrañaga, P. (2007). A review of feature selection techniques in bioinformatics. *Bioinformatics (Oxford, England), 23*(19), 2507–2517. doi:10.1093/bioinformatics/btm344 PMID:17720704

KEY TERMS AND DEFINITIONS

Chromosome: An elementary unit of packed DNA in the cell nucleus. It represents a single piece of coiled DNA containing many genes, regulatory elements and other nucleotide sequences but also DNA-bound proteins, which serve to package the DNA and control its functions. Chromosomal DNA encodes organism's genetic information. Chromosomes appear as autosomes equally found in males and females as well or as allosomes (sex chromosomes) found either only in males (Y-chromosome) or in different quantities in males (one X-chromosome) and females (two X-chromosomes). Humans contain 22 autosomes and one allosome.

DNA-Methylation: Substitutes hydrogens at the DNA-nucleotides cytosine or adenine by methyl groups. This chemical modification strongly affects the structure of the DNA and, as a consequence, the expression of the associated genes.

Gene: The molecular unit of heredity of an organism. Its structural basis is some region of deoxyribonucleic acids (DNA) that code for a polypeptide or for an RNA chain that has a function in the organism.

Gene Expression: The process by which information from certain functional regions of the DNA defined as genes is transcribed into RNA-products which can be further used in the synthesis of functional products. These products can be proteins (in this case the RNA-product is messenger RNA) or non-protein coding functional RNA.

Genotype: The entirety of hereditary information coded in the genes of an organism.

Feature: An observable characterizing the genotype and/or phenotype of an organism.

Omics: A useful concept in biology aiming at the collective characterization and quantification of pools of biological molecules that translate into the structure, dynamics and function of an organism. Accordingly 'genomics' deals with the entirety of an organism's hereditary information coded in its DNA (also called genome); 'transcriptomics' deals with the entirety of RNA transcribed from the DNA (transcriptome), 'proteomics' deals with the entirety of proteins translated from the mRNA (proteome) and 'epigenomics' addresses factors and mechanisms affecting the accessibility of genomic information by modifications of its structure, e.g. via DNA-methylation or chemical modifications of the histones serving as DNA-packing proteins (epigenome).

Phenotype: The entirety of an organism's observable characteristics resulting from both, the expression of the genes and environmental factors. The molecular phenotype consequently comprises the entirety of molecular building blocks providing the basis of organism's structure and function.

Section 3
Issues and Concerns in the Big Data Era

Chapter 16
Intellectual Property Protection for Synthetic Biology, Including Bioinformatics and Computational Intelligence

Matthew K. Knabel
Fernandez & Associates, LLP, USA

Katherine Doering
Fernandez & Associates, LLP, USA & JD Candidate, University of Nebraska, USA

Dennis S. Fernandez
Fernandez & Associates, LLP, USA

ABSTRACT

Since the completion of the Human Genome Project, biologists have shifted their efforts from understanding biology to modifying it. Synthetic biology is a rapidly growing interdisciplinary field that includes developing and manufacturing synthetic nucleotide sequences, systems, genomes, and medical devices. Gaining patent protection represents an imperative and significant tool for business development in synthetic biology. Without IP protection, investors most likely will not commit necessary resources for progress. While there have been many important breakthroughs in biotechnology, recent case law rulings and legislative statutes have created obstacles for inventors to gain patent protection of novel synthetic biology inventions. These issues cause hesitation in license agreements and postpone creation of synthetic biology start-up companies. Nevertheless, inventors still can gain patent protection in many branches of synthetic biology. This chapter examines the issues, controversies, and problems associated with patent protection in synthetic biology. It then gives solutions, recommendations, and future directions for the field.

INTRODUCTION

Synthetic biology is an emerging field that combines the disciplines of biology, engineering, and computer science. It encompasses parts (or genes), pathways (or multiple genes), genomes, devices, and systems (Rabinow, 2009). In the past 15 years, advances made in bioinformatics and computational intelligence have led to its quick expansion and success. Specifically, developing

DOI: 10.4018/978-1-4666-6611-5.ch016

new algorithms and statistics to assess relationships among members of large data sets, reading large nucleotide or protein sequences, and utilizing tools for efficient access to and management of healthcare have allowed for researchers and healthcare professionals to expand diagnostic and treatment options related to synthetic biology. For example, researchers at SUNY at Buffalo recently teamed up with IBM to identify efficiently patients with genetic variations associated with a higher risk of multiple sclerosis (Ramanathan, 2012). SUNY researchers have been able to reduce the time to conduct the analysis from 27.2 hours to less than 12 minutes (Ramanathan, 2012).

Because of the exponential increase, venture capitalists and business professionals have invested significant time and money into this field. Patent protection represents one important aspect of business development and success in synthetic biology. However, due not only to the diversity of involved arts but also to recent Supreme Court and Federal Circuit rulings, intellectual property protection in synthetic biology is a complex, yet poorly researched, topic. This chapter will discuss an overview of synthetic biology and provide evidence for recent successes in the field. It will then discuss recent legal cases that affect this industry. Finally, this chapter will include recommendations on how to patent synthetic biology successfully based on recent legislation and case law.

BACKGROUND

Synthetic biology is a unique way to study life that combines the arts of life science, engineering, and computer science to promote human health and preserve the environment. Since the completion of the Human Genome Project in 2001, the scientific field has learned the function of many gene products. These advances have led to assembly of biological parts, such as DNA, plasmids, promoters, and translational units, into registries. Most notably, the International Genetically Engineered

Machine (iGEM) Foundation (https://www.igem.org), which developed out of Massachusetts Institute of Technology, has cataloged the Registry of Standard Biological Parts which supports this goal by indexing biological components and offering assembly services to construct new parts, devices, and systems (Trafton, 2011).

A patent in the United States is an exclusive property right that protects inventions, including any process, machine, manufacture, or composition of matter, or any improvement thereof, that is novel, useful, and non-obvious (http://www.uspto.gov/patents/resources/general_info_concerning_patents.jsp). For a period of 20 years (depending on the type of patent), an inventor and/or assignee has a monopoly over making, using, licensing, or selling the invented property in exchange for full disclosure of the invention. This process promotes economic growth and progress by disclosing knowledge to both individuals skilled in that particular field and laypersons who are interested in the process or invention. Patent protection in synthetic biology has increased rapidly in the past 25 years. In 1990, only 13 patents associated with technologies in synthetic biology were filed. Since then, there has been a 600% increase worldwide in the number of filed patents (van Doren, 2013). Activity in the United States is the most dynamic, as the number of patents filed has increased by over 400%.

Interest in understanding the function of each gene product has grown rapidly since the completion of the Human Genome Project. (Venter, 2001) To expedite this process, researchers have invested time and effort into identifying gene sequencing methods that are more affordable. To this effort, one company that specializes in DNA sequencing, Illumina, Inc., has reported a machine that would decrease the cost of sequencing an entire genome from $3 billion in 2001 to only $1000 today (Young, 2014; http://www.illumina.com/systems/hiseq-x-sequencing-system.ilmn). This low cost will aid researchers not only in understanding gene product function, but also to identify changes as small as a single base pairing that results in structural or functional consequences. As gene expression and localized functions are identified and cataloged, the field is shifting drastically from understanding nature to modifying it. In 2010, J. Craig Venter's research group assembled a bacterial genome that led to the first self-replicating, synthetic bacterial cell (Gibson, 2010). This breakthrough allows for later modifications of this genomic scaffolding that could be used in bioenergy, biomedical research, and healthcare.

Synthetic biology has attracted many other disciplines because of its potential medical, industrial and commercial applications (Jain, 2012). The number of synthetic biology patent applications, as a result, are increasing at a much more rapid rate compared to all applications (Figure 1). Implantable medical devices carrying the ability

to detect endogenous biological materials utilize wireless and semiconductor technology (Kakaday, 2009). Large sequencing data sets are analyzed using advanced algorithms. Computer models predict nucleotide and protein folding patterns that allow scientists to predict and understand their function (Mullins, 2012). Industrially and politically, there is a huge push to create biofuels that utilize eco-friendly hydrogen and ethanol. Because of the multi-discipline approach to synthetic biology, confusion can arise when dealing with patent protection, especially as new laws and case rulings change the face of patent prosecution and litigation. This chapter will examine the issues, controversies and problems associated with patent protection in synthetic biology. It then will give solutions, recommendations, and future directions for the field.

Figure 1. All new applications received at the uspto each year versus new applications with the search term "synthetic biology" received at the uspto each year

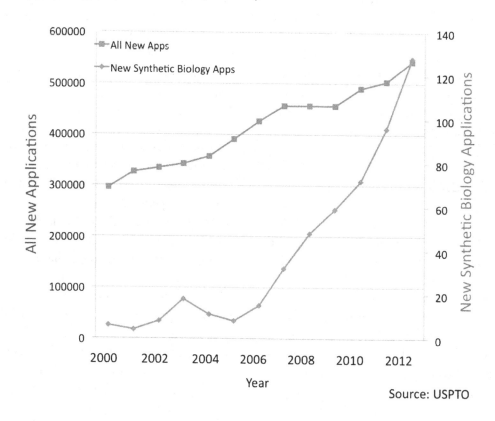

Source: USPTO

ISSUES, CONTROVERSIES, AND PROBLEMS OF IP PROTECTION OF SYNTHETIC BIOLOGY

An art as diverse and rapidly developing as synthetic biology causes many individuals inside and outside of the field to question and take issue with many aspects, such as the marketing, licensing, and patentability of the methods, techniques, and technologies relating to synthetic DNA sequences. Some view existing intellectual property (IP) law as insufficient to protect rapidly developing biotechnologies (Saukshmya, 2010). The main challenge is providing a framework to encourage investment without stifling research or restricting benefits. These challenges create obstacles for inventors seeking patent protection (van den Belt, 2013). Moreover tension between investors and public interest groups like the BioBricks Foundation (http://biobricks.org), which promote using freely available standardized biological parts that are safe, ethical, cost-effective and publicly accessible, impede IP progress.

Importantly, political views on IP practices dealing with synthetic biology are uncertain. After three public meetings in 2011, the Presidential Commission for the Study of Bioethical Issues took a subtle and somewhat non-committal stance on synthetic biology. They advocated an ongoing process of prudent vigilance that carefully monitors, identifies, and mitigates potential and realized harms over time (Dias, 2013; De Rosa-Joynt, 2013). The Commission offered no specific opinion on the effectiveness of current intellectual property practices and policies in synthetic biology (Viers, 2011). With no clear, relevant guidelines, venture capitalists, investors, and start-ups were left to interpret the existing laws and cases. Most cases and laws relevant to this topic interpret 35 U.S.C. §101 (patentability), §102 (patentability and novelty), §103 (obviousness), and §112 (written description, best mode and enablement) (http://www.uspto.gov/web/offices/pac/mpep/mpep-9015-appx-l.pdf).

Patent statutes have no specific provision relating to the field of synthetic biology. Section 101, Congress' only clue as to what constitutes patentable subject matter, states only that anyone that invents or discovers "any new and useful process, machine, manufacture, or composition of matter, or any new and useful improvement thereof" can obtain a patent (http://www.uspto.gov/web/offices/pac/mpep/mpep-9015-appx-l.html). As discussed in detail below, the Federal Circuit and the Supreme Court have issued rulings over the past 35 years that have laid the groundwork in intellectual property protection of synthetic biology inventions. Specifically, many rulings over the past five years by these two judiciary groups have given inventors and assignees more clarity as to what is patentable. While the field will continue to evolve over the next decade, it is important for venture capitalists and investors to understand key legal rulings that affect how intellectual property law is currently practiced.

Prior to 1980, there was a major gap in IP protection for biological materials, including the field of synthetic biology. There was a general feeling in the realm of law that living creatures, and any components of living creatures, were not patentable as they are a "work of nature" (See *Funk Bros. Seed Co. v. Kalo Inoculant Co.*, 333 U.S. 127, 130 (1948)). Things considered to be "manifestations of laws of nature" were to remain "free to all men and reserved exclusively to none" (*Id.*).

In 1980, the Supreme Court ruled that genetically engineered microorganisms are patentable subject matter by affirming *Diamond v. Chakrabarty,* which remains to this day a landmark holding regarding subject matter patentability. Ananda Chakrabarty, a genetic engineer for General Electric, modified the genome of a previously-known bacterium, creating a new organism now called *Pseudomonas putida* (Chakrabarty, 1975). Eventually, genetic modification made the bacterium capable of breaking down crude oil, which promised to have important implications for environmental science, especially the clean-up of oil spills. The USPTO had initially issued a §101 rejection, claiming that Chakrabarty was trying to gain patent protection on a living organism. The USPTO held to the contemporary idea that laws of nature and physical phenomena could not be patented, as there is no inventive step (See *Diamond v. Chakrabarty*, 447 U.S. 303, 309 (1980)). The Supreme Court, however, ruled in favor of Chakrabarty, saying that the bacterium only existed by virtue of Chakrabarty's scientific intervention and was therefore not a law of nature or naturally occurring physical phenomena (See *Diamond v. Chakrabarty*, 447 U.S. at 309-310). This opened the door for allowing the patenting of genetically modified organisms. Perhaps, most importantly, the Court acknowledged that living organisms and components thereof were not automatically barred from patentability. Such a precedent served as the foundation of IP policy for synthetic biology.

Some individuals have qualms over the idea of patenting genetically modified organisms, especially those that are multicellular. In 1987, when the USPTO granted a patent to Harvard's famous "OncoMouse," a mouse genetically engineered to have an increased susceptibility to cancer, many were uncomfortable with the implications (Seide, 1995). The OncoMouse patent writer was careful to specify that the inventors were only claiming *non-human* transgenic mammals, an important clarification to make to avoid moral and ethical concerns (U.S. Patent 4,736,866). For other countries, such as Canada, however, the OncoMouse was a bridge too far, and the Supreme Court of Canada rejected the patent on the grounds that higher life forms were not patentable (Idris, 2006). Patents for genetically modified organisms such as the OncoMouse set an important precedent for all scientific fields, including synthetic biology. The United States appears willing to weigh important issues, such as public health and safety, against minimal ethical concerns that stifles

the patentability of multicellular organisms in other countries ("Bioethics and Patent Law: The Case of the Oncomouse." http://www.wipo.int/wipo_magazine/en/2006/03/article_0006.html.

An area of patentable subject matter that has strong implications for synthetic biology is that which involves computers. Given the amount of data that must be processed by biologists and with burgeoning fields such as systems biology, patenting computer software will be integral to the discipline. Computer patents have been an area of much judicial modification over the recent decades. Originally, the Supreme Court limited computer patents. In *Gottschalk v. Benson*, the Court held that the claimed computer program, which was essentially an algorithmic computer code, was unpatentable as an abstract idea (See *Gottschalk v. Benson*, 409 U.S. 63 (1972)). As computers became more prevalent and integral to society, the Supreme Court began to shift their views, clarifying that their previous holdings should not be interpreted to mean that subject matter becomes unpatentable because "it uses a mathematical formula, computer program, or digital computer" (See *Diamond v. Diehr*, 450 U.S. 175, 187 (1981)). Even when a law of nature or mathematical formula is combined with a known structure or process, it may still be patentable (*Id.*).

The ability to patent a "process" has been around for many years and in a realm such as synthetic biology, where data collection is paramount, it is important to understand the limitations of patenting a process. In the last five years, two other landmark cases, *Bilski v. Kappos* and *Mayo Medical Laboratories, et al. v. Prometheus Laboratories, Inc.*, clarified some of these limitations. In *Bilski*, the Supreme Court's holding regarding the patentability of risk hedging showed some leniency in what processes are patent-eligible. In the subsequent case, *In re Bilski*, the Court affirmed §100(b)'s definition of a process as a "process, art, or method, and includes a new use of a known process, machine, manufacture, composition of matter, or material." These holdings allow biotechnology and bioinformatics inventions and processes to remain patentable. The Supreme Court's ruling in *Bilski* also claimed that the machine-or-transformation test is not the ultimate test of patentability, placing importance on the commonly accepted exceptions to §101 patentable subject matter: laws of nature, physical phenomena, and abstract ideas. In *Mayo*, the court upheld these exceptions when the patentees sought protection of a "method" that involved a human decision whether to change dosage of a drug. The Court found that the patent was invalid because it was merely describing the underlying law of nature, and thus was unpatentable under §101.

Generally, simply discovering a relevant piece of DNA is not enough to obtain a patent, which the Supreme Court upheld in *Association for Molecular Pathology v. Myriad Genetics, Inc.* (133 S.Ct. 2107, 2116 (2013)). The Supreme Court held that the claimed isolated genomic DNA (specifically the breast cancer genes, BRCA1 and BRCA2) is not patentable because it is identical to what is found in nature (Id.)). The *Myriad* Court distinguished the patentable microorganism in *Diamond v. Chakrabarty*. In *Chakrabarty*, the bacterium was new, with different characteristics than those found in nature due to additional plasmids. However, most importantly to those businesses that deal with synthetic biology, the Supreme Court took a different approach to patentability with synthetic genes. Keeping in line with *Chakrabarty*, complementary DNA (cDNA) and other synthesized sequences are currently patentable because they are not naturally occurring, potentially increasing interest in synthetic biology (See *Association for Molecular Pathology v. Myriad Genetics, Inc.*, 133 S.Ct. at 2119). Since naturally occurring DNA cannot be patented, research laboratories and universities may benefit from the use of artificial sequences, which can receive patent protection as long as it fulfills all other requirements of a valid patent.

Recently, the Supreme Court debated whether patent holders could enforce their patent rights on the products of self-replicating technologies after an authorized sale in *Bowman v. Monsanto, Co.*, 657 F.3d 1341 (2011). Generally, legal sale of an invention extinguishes a patent holder's further rights of exclusion in a process known as "exhaustion." The decision in *Bowman v. Monsanto, Co.*, which was affirmed unanimously by the Federal Circuit, favored Monsanto and concluded that farmers need the patent owner's permission to plant and harvest a protected product. In other words, even though farmers purchased the original, patented seeds to plant, they could not use seeds from the second generation for further harvests without the patent holder's permission. While the Court examined seeds from genetically modified plants, this ruling could impact the commercial development of useful products and constructive applications of synthetic biology.

In September 2011, President Obama signed into law the Leahy-Smith America Invents Act (AIA), which includes some of the most significant changes to U.S. patent law in the last 50 years (See Press Secretary Release, http://www.whitehouse.gov/the-press-office/2011/09/16/president-obama-signs-america-invents-act-over-hauling-patent-system-stim). Most significant of these changes is the transition to a first-inventor-to-file patent system from a first-to-invent patent system. Irrespective of who the first inventor is, the inventor who files the application first gets priority in the race for patent protection. This system effectively brings the United States in line with the rest of the world and reduces a layer of complexity that American inventors encountered in dealing with the U.S. system and those abroad. This system also encourages inventors to file an application for patent sooner rather than later in order to unambiguously lock in their priority date. Additionally, §102(b) has been amended such that while it preserves the grace period given between a disclosure and when a patent application must be filed, it puts a serious burden on the small inventor to make an expeditious public disclosure. While record keeping is still important, disclosure history is now more essential than proof of conception and reduction to practice.

New legal precedent and legislation represent only one component that venture capitalists and investors need to consider when seeking protection for synthetic biology inventions. Synthetic biologists often combine multiple 'parts' from many different disciplines. With many different parts or genes contributing to one particular system or genome, an inventor may be more vulnerable to prior art rejections (on the grounds that the patent is not novel) and infringement suit. Arti Rai, a synthetic biology-focused intellectual property expert from the Duke University School of Law, cautions that patents covering synthetic biology "parts" could create protection blocks because of transaction cost heavy patent thickets and patent trolls (Kumar, 2007).

Patenting synthetic biology intellectual property potentially includes combining ideas from multiple disciplines. With this in mind, an inventor may encounter infringement suits based on any and all relevant patents. To expedite this process, the AIA includes a novel process, post-grant review, which allows the non-patent holder to petition for a review of the patentability of one or more claims in a patent on any ground that can be raised under 35 U.S.C. §282(b)(2) or (3) relating to invalidity (such as novelty, obviousness, written description, indefiniteness, but not best mode) (http://www. uspto.gov/aia_implementation/bpai.jsp). A post-grant review may be instituted upon a showing that at least one challenged claim is, more likely than not, unpatentable. If the proceedings are instituted and not dismissed, a final determination by the Board will be issued within one year which can be extended for good cause by an additional six months.

ADDRESSING THE ISSUES: SOLUTIONS AND RECOMMENDATIONS OF IP PROTECTION OF SYNTHETIC BIOLOGY

Although recent legal holdings and laws have in some ways limited the possibility of patent protection in synthetic biology, researchers should continue to pursue protection for their inventions. Understanding the updated patent system and utilizing the following recommendations based on recent case law will increase the likelihood that protection is awarded. As its patent portfolio is developed, a company's value will no doubt increase. The remainder of this chapter will discuss a series of recommendations for venture capitalists and investors when seeking IP protection on synthetic biology inventions.

Importantly, careful steps must be taken during patent prosecution. Since synthetic biology combines multiple arts, prior art from different disciplines could lead to rejection of submitted applications, increasing the importance of thorough prior art research. Therefore, collaborations among patent attorneys, agents, and technical specialists are vital, especially when drafting requires specialized knowledge of different arts. It is important that engineers and scientists with different areas of expertise work together so that the invention is described using the best mode, with a detailed written description, and proper enablement. Patent protection in synthetic biology necessitates experts of varying backgrounds to cooperate to overcome many §112 rejections.

Having experts from diverse backgrounds describe the invention in detail will allow for examiners to understand its novelty and which will result in fewer §103 rejections. The 2007 Supreme Court's holding in *KSR International Co. v. Teleflex, Inc. et al.* tightened regulations of "obviousness" to the point that the mere suggestion by an individual in the field to combine prior art can be grounds for patent rejection due to non-obviousness. However, the USPTO Board of Appeals and Interferences has not seen an increase in the percentage of §103 rejections based on the *KSR* standard. With this in mind, responses to examiner rejections and appeals to the Board could be argued in favor of patent issuance.

Although many different arts and prior inventions are combined to produce a synthetic biology method, machine, manufacture, or composition of matter, inventors should be optimistic about gaining patent protection. Those pursuing infringement suits need to prove that the new invention utilizes what is already protected. Recently, the Supreme Court examined a case involving licensing implantable cardiac simulator patents. In *Medtronic, Inc. v. Mirowski Family Ventures, LLC*, the Court reversed the Federal Circuit's decision, saying that the burden of proof remains on the patentee when the issues are infringement and declaratory judgments. This victory by Medtronic is a positive

step for synthetic biology investors, as it will now be up to the patent holder to prove infringement.

Many companies, like DNA2.0, are choosing not to patent their DNA 'parts.' (Ledford, 2013, www.DNA20.com). Instead, they prefer open access to molecular components that will allow for combinatorial inventions in the future. Many compare it to the early days of software engineers, where the genetic code is similar to the programming language. If others choose this path, venture capitalists and investors could avoid costly patent thickets, licensing nightmares, and potential litigation when investing in new inventions.

After gaining patent protection, companies need to identify technologies that are most likely to lead to financial success. Separating different technologies into "utilize," "likely not to utilize," or "will not utilize" categories allows companies to determine how to create a business plan which may include expanding new products or protecting existing products (Figure 2).

Figure 2. Recommended patent prosecution procedure

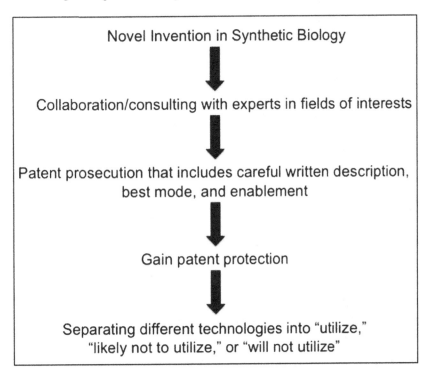

387

FUTURE DIRECTIONS

We are in the midst of a potentially lucrative period to gain patent protection for inventions in synthetic biology. Advances in research and better understanding of gene products have shifted the thinking from simply understanding biology to manipulating it. In the next few decades, continued progress and evolution of technology will continue to expand on the usable parts and gene systems that are available for new inventions.

Thus far, the Supreme Court has been cautious to include synthetic biology technology among living things that are unpatentable based on §101 rejections. However, the field needs to monitor developments of congressional rulings, as well as any Supreme Court and Federal Circuit decisions that would overturn patentability of synthetic DNA and proteins. Given that the Supreme Court recently deemed genomic DNA unpatentable, it is possible that there may be an eventual shift to reject or invalidate synthetic DNA patents.

The goal of synthetic biology development remains focused on improved healthcare efficacy with reduced costs in big data analysis. Data collection in fields such as next generation sequencing and new genome development are becoming an integral part of patient care, and it will allow caregivers to determine efficiently the course of treatment. Similarly, as we enter the era or personalized medicine, algorithms from big data analysis will predict the effectiveness of a time course of drug treatment.

CONCLUSION

We are currently in an exciting period of development for synthetic biology. Although new laws and judicial holdings continue to change the field, IP protection in synthetic biology is as important as it is for any other scientific field. Over the next few decades, synthetic biology will continue to grow as methods, techniques, technologies and DNA sequences continue to evolve. The field has the potential to generate vast amounts of patents and licenses while contributing to the benefit of public health and environmental protection. Those planning to invest in synthetic biology should seek patent protection initially.

REFERENCES

Chakrabarty, A. M., Mylroie, J. R., Friello, D. A., & Vacca, J. G. (1975). Transformation of Pseudomonas putida and Escherichia coli with plasmid-linked drug-resistance factor DNA. *Proceedings of the National Academy of Sciences of the United States of America, 72*(9), 3647–3651. doi:10.1073/pnas.72.9.3647 PMID:1103151

De Rosa-Joynt, B. M. (2013). *Comments on New and emerging issues relating to the conservation and sustainable use of biodiversity*. Retrieved January 29, 2014, from http://www.cbd.int/doc/emerging-issues/US-reviewcomments-SBImpacts-2013-09-en.pdf

Dias, B. F. S. (2013). *New and emerging issues relating to the conservation and sustainable use of biodiversity*. Retrieved January 29, 2014, from http://www.cbd.int/doc/notifications/2013/ntf-2013-018-emerging-issues-en.pdf

Gibson, D. G., Glass, J. I., Lartigue, C., Noskov, V. N., Chuang, R., & Algire, M. A. et al. (2010). Creation of a Bacterial Cell Controlled by a Chemically Synthesized Genome. *Science, 329*(5987), 52–56. doi:10.1126/science.1190719 PMID:20488990

Idris, K. (2006). Bioethics and Patent Law: The Case of the Oncomouse. *WIPO Magazine*. Retrieved January 29, 2014, from http://www.wipo.int/wipo_magazine/en/2006/03/article_0006.html

Jain, K. K. (2012). Synthetic Biology and Personalized Medicine. *Medical Principles and Practice*, *22*(3), 209–219. doi:10.1159/000341794 PMID:22907209

Kakaday, T., Hewitt, A. W., Voelcker, N. H., Li, J. S., & Craig, J. E. (2009). Advances in telemetric continuous intraocular pressure assessment. *The British Journal of Ophthalmology*, *93*(8), 992–996. doi:10.1136/bjo.2008.144261 PMID:19244268

Kumar, S., & Rai, A. (2007). Synthetic Biology: The Intellectual Property Puzzle. *Texas Law Review*, *85*, 1745.

Ledford, H. (2013). Bioengineers look beyond patents. *Nature*, *499*(7456), 16–17. doi:10.1038/499016a PMID:23823774

Mullins, J. G. (2012). Structural modeling pipelines in next generation sequencing projects. *Advances in Protein Chemistry and Structural Biology*, *89*, 117–167. doi:10.1016/B978-0-12-394287-6.00005-7 PMID:23046884

Rabinow, P., & Bennett, G. (2009). Synthetic biology: Ethical ramifications 2009. *Systems and Synthetic Biology*, *3*(1-4), 99–108. doi:10.1007/s11693-009-9042-7 PMID:19816805

Ramanathan, M., et al. (2012). *IBM: Large Gene interaction Analytics at University at Buffalo, SUNY*. Retrieved from http://public.dhe.ibm.com/common/ssi/ecm/en/imc14675usen/IMC14675USEN.PDF

Saukshmya, T., & Chugh, A. (2010). Intellectual property rights in synthetic biology: An anti-thesis to open access to research? *Systems and Synthetic Biology*, *4*(4), 241–245. doi:10.1007/s11693-011-9067-6 PMID:22132050

Seide, R., & Smith, F. (1995). Intellectual property protection and biotechnology. *New York State Bar Journal*, *67*, 52–58.

Trafton, A. (2011). Rewiring Cells. *MIT Technology Review*. Retrieved January 29, 2014, from http://www.technologyreview.com/article/423703/rewiring-cells/

van den Belt, H. (2013). Synthetic biology, patenting, health and global justice. *Systems and Synthetic Biology*, *7*(3), 87–98. doi:10.1007/s11693-012-9098-7 PMID:24432146

van Doren, D., Koenigstein, S., & Reiss, T. (2013). The development of synthetic biology: A patent analysis. *Systems and Synthetic Biology*, *7*(4), 209–220. doi:10.1007/s11693-013-9121-7 PMID:24255694

Venter, J. C., Adams, M. D., Myers, E. W., Li, P. W., & Mural, R. J. et al. (2001). The Sequence of the Human Genome. *Science*, *291*(5507), 1304–1351. doi:10.1126/science.1058040 PMID:11181995

Viers, H. (2011). *Synthetic Biology and Beyond: Commission's Goal: keep the dialogue going*. Retrieved January 29, 2014, from http://blog.bioethics.gov/2011/02/08/synthetic-biology-and-beyond-commissions-goal-keep-the-dialogue-going/

Young, S. (2014). Does Illumina have the first $1000 genome? *MIT Technology Review*. Retrieved January 29, 2014 from http://www.technologyreview.com/news/523601/does-illumina-have-the-first-1000-genome/

ADDITIONAL READING

Baker, M. (2011). Synthetic genomes: The next step for the synthetic genome. *Nature*, *473*(7347), 403–408, 405–408. doi:10.1038/473403a PMID:21593873

Bohannon, J. (2011). The life hacker. *Science*, *333*(6047), 1236–1237. doi:10.1126/science.333.6047.1236 PMID:21885768

Church, G., & Regis, E. (2012). *Regenesis*. New York, NY: Basic Books.

Dobson, A. W., & Evans, J. P. (2012). Gene patents in the US - focusing on what really matters. *Genome Biology*, *13*(6), 161. doi:10.1186/gb4027 PMID:22748211

Elowitz, M. B., & Leibler, S. (2000). A synthetic oscillatory network of transcriptional regulators. *Nature*, *403*(6767), 335–338. doi:10.1038/35002125 PMID:10659856

Endy, D. (2005). Foundations for Engineering Biology. *Nature*, *438*(7067), 449–453. doi:10.1038/nature04342 PMID:16306983

Freemont, P. S., & Kitney, R. I. (2012). *Synthetic Biology – A Primer*. Singapore: World Scientific Publishing. doi:10.1142/p837

Fu, P., & Panke, S. (2009). Systems Biology and Synthetic Biology. Singapore: Wiley-AIChE.

Gardner, T. S., Cantor, C. R., & Collins, J. J. (2000). Construction of a genetic toggle switch in Escherichia coli. *Nature*, *403*(6767), 339–342. doi:10.1038/35002131 PMID:10659857

Gimpel, J. A., Specht, E. A., Georgianna, D. R., & Mayfield, S. P. (2013). Advances in microalgae engineering and synthetic biology applications for biofuel production. *Current Opinion in Chemical Biology*, *17*(3), 489–495. doi:10.1016/j.cbpa.2013.03.038 PMID:23684717

Hemphill, T. A. (2012). The biotechnology sector and US gene patents: Legal challenges to intellectual property rights and the impact on basic research and development. *Science & Public Policy*, *39*(6), 815–826. doi:10.1093/scipol/scs051

Jain, A., Bhatia, P., & Chugh, A. (2012). Microbial synthetic biology for human therapeutics. *Systems and Synthetic Biology*, *6*(1-2), 9–22. doi:10.1007/s11693-012-9092-0 PMID:23730360

Jefferson, O. A., Kollhofer, D., Ehrich, T. H. E., & Jefferson, R. A. (2013). Transparency tools in gene patenting for informing policy and practice. *Nature Biotechnology*, *31*(12), 1086–1093. doi:10.1038/nbt.2755 PMID:24316644

Kampf, M. M., & Weber, W. (2010). Synthetic biology in the analysis and engineering of signaling processes. *Integrative Biology*, *2*(1), 12–24. doi:10.1039/b913490e PMID:20473408

Khalil, A. S., & Collins, J. J. (2010). Synthetic biology: Applications come of age. *Nature Reviews. Genetics*, *11*(5), 367–379. doi:10.1038/nrg2775 PMID:20395970

Kohl, L. J., & Endy, D. (2013). A survey of enabling technologies in synthetic biology. *Journal of Biological Engineering*, *7*(1), 13. doi:10.1186/1754-1611-7-13 PMID:23663447

Lee, B. R., Cho, S., Song, Y., Kim, S. C., & Cho, B. K. (2013). Emerging tools for synthetic genome design. *Molecules and Cells*, *35*(5), 359–370. doi:10.1007/s10059-013-0127-5 PMID:23708771

Lee, S. J., Lee, S. J., & Lee, D. W. (2013). Design and development of synthetic microbial platform cells for bioenergy. *Frontiers in Microbiology*, *4*, 92. doi:10.3389/fmicb.2013.00092 PMID:23626588

Mooallem, J. (2010). Do-It-Yourself Genetic Engineering. *New York Times Sunday Magazine*. Retrieved from http://www.nytimes.com/2010/02/14/magazine/14Biology-t.html?pagewanted=all

Paradise, J., & Fitzpatrick, E. (2012). Synthetic Biology: Does Re-Writing Nature Require Re-Writing Regulation? *Penn State Law Review*, *117*, 1.

Rimmer, M., & McLennan, A. (2012). *Intellectual Property and Emerging Technologies: The New Biology*. Cheltenham, UK: Edward Elgar Publishing. doi:10.4337/9781781001189

Ro, D. K., Paradise, E. M., Ouellet, M., Fisher, K. J., Newman, K. L., & Ndungu, J. M. et al. (2006). Production of the antimalarial drug precursor artemisinic acid in engineered yeast. *Nature*, *440*(7086), 940–943. doi:10.1038/nature04640 PMID:16612385

Singh, V. (2014). Recent advancements in synthetic biology: Current status and challenges. *Gene*, *535*(1), 1–11. doi:10.1016/j.gene.2013.11.025 PMID:24269673

So, D., & Joly, Y. (2013). Commercial Opportunities and Ethical Pitfalls in Personalized Medicine: A Myriad of Reasons to Revisit the Myriad Genetics Saga. *Current Pharmacogenomics and Personalized Medicine*, *11*(2), 98–109. doi:10.2174/1875692111311020003 PMID:23885284

Stephanopoulos, G. (2012). Synthetic biology and metabolic engineering. *ACS Synthetic Biology*, *1*(11), 514–525. doi:10.1021/sb300094q PMID:23656228

Wang, Y. H., Wei, K. Y., & Smolke, C. D. (2013). Synthetic biology: Advancing the design of diverse genetic systems. *Chemical and Biomolecular Engineering Annual Reviews*, *4*(1), 69–102. doi:10.1146/annurev-chembio-eng-061312-103351 PMID:23413816

Wen, M., Bond-Watts, B. B., & Chang, M. C. (2013). Production of advanced biofuels in engineered *E. coli*. *Current Opinion in Chemical Biology*, *17*(3), 472–479. doi:10.1016/j.cbpa.2013.03.034 PMID:23659832

KEY TERMS AND DEFINITIONS

America Invents Act: A federal law passed in September, 2011, that changed the landscape of United States Patent Law. Most importantly, it changed the rights in the US from first-to-invent to first-to-file. This statute represents the biggest change in patent law in over 50 years.

Association for Molecular Pathology, et al. v. Myriad Genetics, Inc., et al: A case presided over by the Supreme Court. It was decided in June, 2012, that naturally occurring genes could not be patented. Myriad held a number of patents for BRCA1 and BRCA2, two genes that are mutated in many breast cancer patients. This ruling, however, did not prevent complementary DNA (cDNA) or synthetic genes from patentability.

Bioinformatics: An interdisciplinary branch of life sciences that utilizes computer science, mathematics and bioengineering to organize, process and interpret complex data sets and sequences. It often includes complex algorithms, soft computing and simulation to understand biological processes.

Minimal Genome: A genome that contains only essential genes such that cell physiology, normal homeostasis and division can occur.

Patent: An exclusive property right that protects inventions, including any process, machine, manufacture, or composition of matter, or any improvement thereof, that is novel, useful, and non-obvious. It gives the patent owner the right to inhibit someone from making, use, offer for sale or sell an invention.

Patent Thickets: An intertwining array of patents that an inventor or entrepreneur will encounter that consists of patent rights that may overlap with a novel item that one wishes to commercialize. Thickets often impede development of a novel product.

Synthetic Biology: A branch of life science that combines the disciplines of biology, engineering, and computer science. It encompasses genes, genomes, devices, and systems.

Synthetic Genome: A genome that is made from custom designed nucleotide sequences and is sufficient for replication. In 2010, Gibson et al created the first synthetic yeast genome using 25 overlapping DNA fragments.

Chapter 17

Clinical Data Linkages in Spinal Cord Injuries (SCI) in Australia:
What Are the Concerns?

Jane Moon
University of Melbourne, Australia

Mary P. Galea
University of Melbourne, Australia

Megan Bohensky
Royal Melbourne Hospital, Australia

ABSTRACT

Clinical data linkage amongst patients with Spinal Cord Injury (SCI) is a challenge, as the Australian Health System is fragmented and there is lack of coordination between multiple data custodians at the state and federal levels, private and public hospitals, and acute and allied health sectors. This is particularly problematic in chronic conditions such as SCI, where multiple data custodians collect data on patients over long periods of time. The author presents findings based on interviews with a range of data custodians for SCI categorized as clinical, statutory, and financial data custodians. It is found that data are kept in different silos, which are not coordinated, hence duplication exists and patient information that exists on many different databases is inconsistently updated. This chapter describes the importance of Clinical Data Linkage for healthcare in predicting disease trajectories for SCI and discusses how administrative and clinical data are collected and stored and some of the challenges in linking these datasets.

INTRODUCTION

Clinical Data Linkage (CDL) is a statistical tool which allows linking of different datasets kept in different locations that relate to the same individual (Christen, 2013). This method has been powerful in population health in identifying risk factors and evaluating preventative measures and treatments for various diseases.

Medical conditions such as spinal cord injuries (SCI) require high intervention over extended periods of time, and items of medical information

DOI: 10.4018/978-1-4666-6611-5.ch017

are not always current, reliable and available to the appropriate person throughout the life span of the person with SCI (NISU, 2013).

Often patients have frequent visits to hospitals and doctors due to associated secondary conditions (Dryden et al., 2004; Norton, 2010). Many SCI patients undergo lengthy rehabilitation and are heavily reliant on medical interventions (Norman et al., 2010; Norton, 2010; Wyndaele & Wyndaele, 2006) and may be dependent on social welfare. It is not uncommon for patients to move from one hospital to another, not necessarily confined to one geographic area. Recent trends have shown there has been an increase in mobility to different states, which makes it difficult to gather information about such patients into one comprehensive information source (ABS, 2011; AIHW, 2012).

There is a range of data in addition to the main clinical condition. These include associated information such as pathology reports, radiology and pharmaceutical information. In addition, there is a large amount of administrative information collected and stored by a range of data custodians. All data custodians have vested interests in collection of the data, and the items of clinical information are kept in silos (Moon, 2014).

This chapter has three aims: firstly, to describe the current state of clinical data linkage in Australia and compare it to best practices in other countries, secondly, to present the best possible solution to link multiple heterogeneous data sources from various custodians and lastly, to discuss the challenges involved in effective linkage.

BACKGROUND

What is Clinical Data Linkage?

'Clinical Data Linkage (CDL)' or 'Record linkage' are terms used interchangeably to describe the process of bringing together two or more records relating to the same individual or entity (e.g. family). A good example occurs in the health field where cross-referencing of different health information sources occurs. The art of record linkage can be quite challenging if there are multiple data custodians involved and if the infrastructure of the health system is heterogeneous. A theory of record linkage goes back to 1969 when Fellegi and Sunter introduced mathematical algorithms to link two or more sets of data that belonged to the same entities (Fellegi & Sunter, 1969). There have been other methods of record linkage based on vector methods and decision trees but no method has surpassed the Fellegi and Sunter model (Christen, 2013).

CDL is needed because individual identifiers (e.g. an individual driver's license number, health identifier number, hospital patient number) are unique in different settings and may not be able to connect different services (Christen, 2012; Christen & Churches, 2006). CDL allows information from multiple sources to be joined together to produce richer data sets for research purposes and has wide applicability in public health and epidemiological research.

In SCI, linkage has been used by researchers in predicting mortality after traumatic SCI (Hagen, Lie, Rekand, Gilhus, & Gronning, 2010), survival after the injury (O'Connor, 2005), looking for patterns of morbidity and rehospitalisation after SCI and incidences and patterns (Middleton, Lim, Taylor, Soden, & Rutkowski, 2004),

The following section will explore how data linkage is applied internationally and locally with respect to co-ordination of disparate datasets, and in particular its practical application to making available health information for patient conditions with high medical intervention, e.g. for chronic diseases.

Best Practices of CDL

Many countries have attempted various stages of data linkage. Some have had success and others have not, due to incomplete linkage (Ardolino, Sleat, & Willett, 2012). The following section describes some of the best practice examples of comprehensive data systems.

Canada

The British Columbia Linked Health Database was established in 1996 and covers datasets on the medical services plan, PharmaCare, hospital separations, continuing care, birth registrations, death registrations, records of mental health episodes, workers compensation board and the British Columbia Cancer agency cancer incidence file (BCLHD, 2014).

The Population Health Research Data Repository housed in the Manitoba Centre for Health Policy, holds a complete collection of health, social, education, justice, registries, and database support files. The project started in 1970 and holds the data repository of the residents; these are then linkable with a scrambled identifier which is unique to a family (not the individual) (PHRDR, 2014).

UK

The Oxford Record Linkage Study (ORLS) started in 1963 as a joint project between the National Health Service and Oxford University. It began with linked death and hospitalization data in the Oxford Region, comprising 2.5 million residents. Since 1998, deaths and hospitalisation data from all of England have been linked (Goldacre, 2011). The Oxford Group continues to do English national linkage with funding from National Institute for Health Research on a variety of national projects such as examination of hospital and mortality data (NHIS, 2014).

Scotland has a strong track record for performing linkage for research purposes owing to routinely collected and well-maintained national administrative health data sets, with the emergence of the Scottish record linkage system and organi-

zations like the Information Services Division of NHS National Services Scotland, which hold permanently linked patient-based databases centrally (SWDLF, 2012). An example of the coordinated and well-integrated service in Scotland is child protection services, where child protection officers share files with schools or police so that the three services can be integrated to protect the child. Another example is local General Practitioners (GPs) sharing patients' symptoms and diagnoses with hospitals to improve coordination of services throughout the national health services (FARS, 2013; Garrison & Smith, 2010).

USA

The Rochester Epidemiology Project started in 1966 and links all medical records of residents living in Olmsted County, Minnesota in a single research database (REP, 2014). Records are tracked using a computerized bar coding system. The data available electronically include demographic characteristics, medical diagnostic codes, surgical procedure codes and death information. The system covers residents of all ages and both sexes, regardless of socio-economic status, ethnicity or insurance status (St Sauver et al., 2012).

Another example of a well-coordinated system in the US is the system for monitoring road traffic injuries, where four data systems are linked: the General Estimates System, the Fatality Analysis Reporting System, the Crashworthiness Data System and the Crash Injury Research Estimates System. These are all integrated and available to decision and policy makers at the national level. (FARS, 2013; Garrison & Smith, 2010).

Australia

The Population Health Research Network (PHRN) is the center for national data linkage in Australia, funded through the National Collaborative Research Infrastructure Strategy (NCRIS, 2013). Its objective is to build a national infrastructure that supports linkage of population datasets for health and disease surveillance, so that policy makers and providers can respond effectively to the changing needs of the population (PHRN, 2013).

As can be seen in Figure 1, there are six linkage centres in Australia. At a state level, the Western Australia Data Linkage Service (WADLS) leads data linkage in Australia and is the only state that links the entire population to a central system (WADLS, 2013b). In Victoria, there is the Victorian Data Linkage (VDL) program, supported by the Victorian Government (VDL, 2013), however, this has a limited role in that this work is mostly used for research and not all collected materials are linked on site. The Australian Capital Territory and New South Wales have similar approaches to connect health information with the FEBRL (Freely Extensible Biomedical Record Linkage) project, which is supposed to provide large-scale, high performance data linkage (Christen, 2012; Christen, Churches, & Hegland, 2004; Christen, Willmore, & Churches, 2006).

Western Australia has been coordinating data linkage since 1970, with the involvement of four departments: Department of Health, the University of Western Australia, Curtin University and the Telethon Institute for Child Health Research. Since the introduction of the program WADLS (Western Australia Data Linkage Service) in 1995, all health related information about residents of WA is linked to provide valuable information. It comprises complete information rather than small blocks of information. This linked information is used for (WADLS, 2013a):

- Population based health services research and policy development
- Investigation of potential projects, (i.e. testing hypotheses and pilot studies)
- As a capture-recapture tool, to improve the quality of datasets
- Follow-up and comparison of different treatment regimes.

Figure 1. Linkage centres in Australia

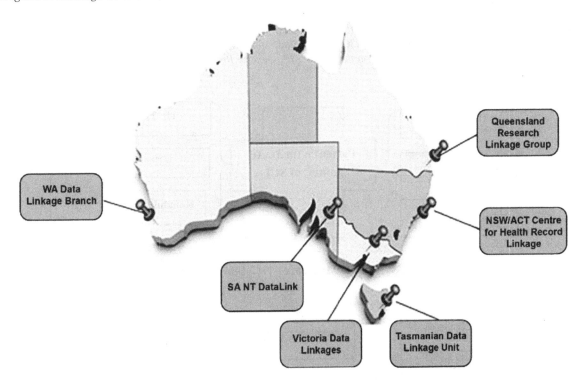

Other uses of CDL in Australia have included an examination of trends in colorectal and lung cancer (Goldsbury, Armstrong, Simonella, Armstrong, & O'Connell, 2012), dental research (Slack-Smith, 2012), trends of smokers using primary health (Jorm, Shepherd, Rogers, & Blyth, 2012), recording of births in New South Wales (Lam, 2011), investigating the cause of acute lower respiratory infection hospitalization in children (Moore et al., 2012) and the epidemiology of oral health in Western Australia (Slack-Smith, 2012).

CHALLENGES WITH LINKING SCI DATA AND RECOMMENDATIONS

There are many challenges with linking SCI data in Australia and this is explored in the following section.

Multiple-Data Custodians

Each data custodians will have necessary information from their record keeping, but it is not easy to access all the information necessary for one particular person. This is because data custodians are independent and do not communicate and the individual patient data sets are collected to fulfil their own purposes. The heterogeneous data custodians of SCI are shown in Figure 2, where they can be classified as clinical, statutory and financial custodians (Moon, 2014).

In Figure 2, each health provider has one complete file about an individual and they are not linked. Providers such as hospital administrators, financial administrators, and statutory administrators have their own information that is not shared. Clinical information is held in both in public and private sectors. Patients may visit Pharmacies and GP practices at various geographic locations over their life span of an average of 40 years, and these resources will hold much valuable clinical information. Data concerning rehabilitation, including from allied health professionals as well as from social welfare support agencies, are also not linked but could potentially be helpful in clinical decisions.

Figure 2. Clinical information flow: Multiple data custodians
VAED: Victorian Admitted Episode Datasets; ASCIR: Australian Spinal Cord Injury Register; VSTORM: Victorian State Trauma Outcomes Registry; HITH: Hospitals in the homes; GP: General Practitioners; TAC: Trafic Accident Commission Data Exist in Silos.

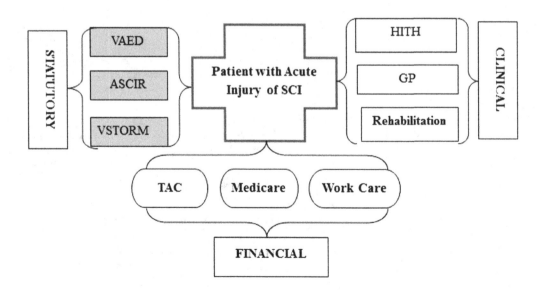

Data Duplication and Inconsistencies

Problems exist when providers duplicate patient data in unlinked systems without regular updating, i.e. when a patient's history, rehabilitation, drug chart or allergy information is stored in an autonomous database and is not updated into a single database automatically. It presents huge problems when a patient's details are updated in one system and not another.

Lack of standardization of information makes it difficult to merge databases between hospitals. In Victoria, prior to trauma centres being established, all patients with SCI were taken to specialist spinal services at the Austin Hospital and surgery to stabilize the spine was performed there. However, when the trauma centres were established, most patients with SCI were taken to one of those centres first and had their surgery there, and then they were transferred for ongoing care and rehabilitation.

Trying to track down patient histories from one hospital to another is a challenge as they come under different unique identifiers. Not all health administrators are trained in the same way and not all are aware of the standardized coding scheme that is used at major hospitals in Victoria (ICD, 2013). Many patients spend a long period in rehabilitation where there is limited health information services, making it difficult to merge datasets with major hospitals (Moon, 2014).

Data Linkage Methods

Another important aspect of CDL is that the method selected for data linkage depends on the types of datasets involved. There are two main techniques used in clinical data linkage: deterministic and probabilistic linkage. A combination of both techniques has been used in various projects, the linkage variables will depend on the datasets being used.

Deterministic Data Linkage

Deterministic data linkage involves matching variables with exact agreement. In this, a high degree of certainty is required. This method requires exact spelling of surnames or Medicare number or driver's license numbers. A Unique Identifier or combination of identifier is needed. This method is robust if there is a unique national identifier that is well coded (Christen, 2012; Karmel et al., 2010).

Probabilistic Data Linkage

Probabilistic record linkage involves linking two (or more) files based on the probabilities of agreement and disagreement between ranges of matched variables. Probabilistic matching allows for variation in reported characteristics by deriving a measure of similarity across variables used to identify matches, called the match weight. The weight indicates the importance of the variables.

The match weight is used to decide whether a comparison between records of two datasets is accepted (high weight) or rejected (low weight) as a match, or link. If no Unique Identifier is available, then probabilistic linkage techniques are preferred (Christen, 2012; Li & Shen, 2013).

Probabilistic record linkage has been shown to be more flexible than deterministic record linkage in a simulation study (Méray, Reitsma, Ravelli, & Bonsel, 2007; Tromp, Méray, Ravelli, Reitsma, & Bonsel, 2008; Tromp, Ravelli, Bonsel, Hasman, & Reitsma, 2008). Marquez et al. used a clustering technique, which is a use of standardised data formatting based on lexicon-based tokenization and probabilistic hidden Markov models ((Márquez, Chirlaque, & C. Navarro, 2008).

Data Quality

The success of CDL relies on the quality of the datasets. Understanding data linkage methods is essential for any clinical data linkage project as different techniques have different limitations. Choosing the correct linkage method is important and will depend on an understanding of datasets. How data are collected and in what format datasets are stored will also determine the appropriate data linkage method.

For instance, some data sets from hospitals might be unstructured in that there may have duplications and redundancies. Hence analysis without the pre-processing of data will yield incorrect results and could lead to incorrect predictions. This process is called 'data cleansing' in a generic sense or 'normalization' in technical terms (El-Sofany, Ghaleb, & El-Seoud, 2010). The process of normalization depends on how the data are collected. The data cleansing or normalization process should eliminate duplication and improve accuracy thereby improving efficiency.

Efficient Linkage

Because patients from three trauma centres in Victoria move from one site to another, it is not easy to obtain a comprehensive picture of a patient history. A better coordinated and efficient method is required to understand the full picture. The results of CDL can provide valuable information about causes of disease, early intervention and treatments, and effective management of diseases, and can be used to educate clinicians and the wider community.

Accurate Linkage

The probability matching techniques underpinning record linkage bring together records on a patient using key identifying information on each record. The accuracy of probabilistic record linkage is variable. Many researchers report varying degrees of success in using the probabilistic approach. Da Silveira and Artman report from their systematic review that accuracy ranged from 74% to 98%

(Silveira & Artmann, 2009) and Jebamani et al from Manitoba in Canada reported a 99% match on gender, a 70% match on surname, a 94% match on given name, and a 96% match on birth year (Jebamani, Burchill, & Martens, 2005). Bohensky et al. reported that readers must watch out for false negative and positives when reading reports (Bohensky et al., 2010).

Privacy and Ethics

Currently the PHRN has stringent policies and guidelines for researchers about when data can be released and how they can be used (PHRN, 2013) after ethics clearance certifying that it meets Human Research Ethics Committee guidelines (HREC, 2013). All of the datasets within the PHRN are linked through key identifiers. The individual information is not released to researchers but the information is provided as a record ID with Linkage ID and is strictly accessed only by authorized persons. The regular updates sent from various data custodians are done using statistical probability methods (PHRN, 2013).

FUTURE RESEARCH DIRECTIONS

The benefits of clinical data linkage have been widely recognized by the government and researchers in Australia. Two initiatives have commenced to improve from current system:

SCI Registry

At a state level, a prospective study has been commenced to capture clinical details of all cases of SCI in spinal units. This will provide valuable epidemiological information about patients with SCI (AustinHealth, 2014).

The Australian Spinal Cord Injury Register is a national database established by the Australian Institute of Health and Welfare in 1995, and is managed by National Institute of Surveillance Unit (NISU) at Flinders University. The rationale for this registry is to produce annual epidemiological information on the incidence of SCI in Australia (NISU, 2013).

Personally Controlled Electronic Health Record - PCEHR

The Australian government initiative NEHTA (National E-Health Transition Authority) has implemented the Personally Controlled Electronic Health Record (PCEHR) in July, 2012. The government claims that a PCEHR can provide:

- Summaries of patients' health information;
- Secure access for patients and healthcare providers to their e-health records;
- Rigorous governance and oversight to maintain privacy (NEHTA, 2013).
- National Authentications Services Health (NASH) will issue digital certificates and tokens to health providers to enable them to navigate through patient data.

While this may be a valuable start to collating information for SCI patients, developers of the PCEHR need to be aware of the problems that this particular condition presents and the data required for successful treatment i.e. privacy (da Silva et al., 2012; Exeter, Rodgers, & Sabel, 2013).

Currently, the Australian PCEHR is in its infancy; it only links patients' visits to doctors via Medicare for adults. It does not provide diagnoses or results of the patient treatment. For children younger than 18 years, it provides vaccination records which can be very helpful (NEHTA, 2013). It has the potential to include medical diagnosis, pathology results and pharmacy results to support both clinicians and patients for better for services.

CONCLUSION

The chapter described the importance of Clinical Data Linkage for healthcare in predicting disease trajectories for chronic diseases, using SCI as an example. Best practices of effective health information systems worldwide such as WADLS, ORLS, Manitoba, British Colombia and the Rochester Epidemiology Project are excellent models.

The results of CDL can provide valuable information about causes of disease, early intervention and treatments, and effective management of diseases, and can be used to educate clinicians and the wider community (Glasson & Hussain, 2008). In addition to linking clinical data, the issues of security (avoiding hacking), privacy and ethics must be considered, to ensure that patients' privacy is not compromised and that data are utilized ethically.

Various Australian national initiatives, including the national registry of SCI and the PCEHR provide potential solutions to some of the barriers to CDL in the future.

REFERENCES

ABS. (2011). *Australian Social Trends, Online @ home*. Commonwealth of Australia.

AIHW. (2012). *Australia's health 2012. Australia's health no. 13. Cat. no. AUS 156*. Canberra: AIHW.

Ardolino, A., Sleat, G., & Willett, K. (2012). Outcome measurements in major trauma–Results of a consensus meeting. *Injury. Int. J. Care Injured, 43*(10), 1662–1666. doi:10.1016/j.injury.2012.05.008 PMID:22695320

AustinHealth. (2014). *Austin Health*. Retrieved 6th Nov, 2013, from www.austin.org.au

BCLHD. (2014). *British Columbia Linked Health Database*. Retrieved 12th Jan, 2014, from https://www.popdata.bc.ca/datalinkage

Bohensky, M. A., Jolley, D., Sundararajan, V., Evans, S., Pilcher, D. V., Scott, I., & Brand, C. A. (2010). Data linkage: A powerful research tool with potential problems. *BMC Health Services Research*, *10*(1), 346–346. doi:10.1186/1472-6963-10-346 PMID:21176171

Christen, P. (2012). Data matching [electronic resource]: Concepts and techniques for record linkage, entity resolution, and duplicate detection. Berlin: Springer.

Christen, P. (2013). *Data Matching*. Heidelberg, Germany: Springer.

Christen, P., & Churches, T. (2006). *Secure health data linkage and geocoding: Current approaches and research directions*. Paper presented at the National e-Health Privacy and Security Symposium. New York, NY.

Christen, P., Churches, T., & Hegland, M. (2004). *Febrl - A parallel open source data linkage system*. Sydney: Springer. doi:10.1007/978-3-540-24775-3_75

Christen, P., Willmore, A., & Churches, T. (2006). *A probabilistic geocoding system utilising a parcel based address file*. Cairns: Springer.

da Silva, M. E., Coeli, C. M., Ventura, M., Palacios, M., Magnanini, M. M., Camargo, T. M., & Camargo, K. R. Jr. (2012). Informed consent for record linkage: A systematic review. *Journal of Medical Ethics*, *38*(10), 639–642. doi:10.1136/medethics-2011-100208 PMID:22403083

Dryden, D., Saunders, L., Rowe, B., May, L., Yiannakoulias, N., & Svenson, L. et al. (2004). Utilization of health services following spinal cord injury: A 6-year follow-up study. *Spinal Cord*, *42*(9), 513–525. doi:10.1038/sj.sc.3101629 PMID:15249928

El-Sofany, F. H., Ghaleb, F. M. F., & El-Seoud, A. S. (2010). The Impact of XML Databases Normalization on Design and Usability of Internet Applications. [Article]. *International Journal of Advanced Corporate Learning*, *3*(2), 4–13. doi:10.3991/ijac.v3i2.1265

Exeter, D. J., Rodgers, S., & Sabel, C. E. (2013). "Whose data is it anyway?" The implications of putting small area-level health and social data online. *Health Policy (Amsterdam)*, (0). doi:10.1016/j.healthpol.2013.07.012 PMID:23932285

FARS. (2013). *Fatality analysis reporting system (FARS): National Highway Traffic Safety Administration*. Retrieved 6th April, 2013, from http://www-fars.nhtsa.dot.gov/Main/index.aspx

Fellegi, P. I., & Sunter, B. A. (1969). A theory for record linkage. *Journal of the American Statistical Association*, *64*(328), 1183–1210. doi:10.1080/01621459.1969.10501049

Garrison, G. H., & Smith, L. J. (2010). Is Fatality-Free Travel on North Carolina's Streets and Highways Feasible? It's Time to Think the Unthinkable. *North Carolina Medical Journal*, *71*(6), 561–564. PMID:21500671

Glasson, E. J., & Hussain, R. (2008). Linked data: Opportunities and challenges in disability research. [Article]. *Journal of Intellectual & Developmental Disability*, *33*(4), 285–291. doi:10.1080/13668250802441409 PMID:19039688

Goldacre, M. (2011). *EuroREACH expert panel meeting*. EuroREACH.

Goldsbury, E. D., Armstrong, K., Simonella, L., Armstrong, K. B., & O'Connell, L. D. (2012). Using administrative health data to describe colorectal and lung cancer care in New South Wales, Australia: A validation study. *BMC Health Services Research*, *12*(1), 387. doi:10.1186/1472-6963-12-387 PMID:23140341

Hagen, E. M., Lie, S. A., Rekand, T., Gilhus, N. E., & Gronning, M. (2010). Mortality after traumatic spinal cord injury: 50 years of follow-up. *Journal of Neurology, Neurosurgery, and Psychiatry, 81*(4), 368–373. doi:10.1136/jnnp.2009.178798 PMID:19726408

HREC. (2013). *Human Research Reseach Committee*. Retrieved 5th June, 2013, from http://www. nhmrc.gov.au/health-ethics/human-research-ethics-committees-hrecs/human-research-ethics-committees-hrecs

ICD. (2013). *International Classification of Diseases*. Retrieved 4th July, 2013, from http://www. who.int/classifications/icd/en/

Jebamani, L. S., Burchill, C. A., & Martens, P. J. (2005). Using Data Linkage to Identify First Nations Manitobans. *Canadian Journal of Public Health, 96*, S28–S32. PMID:15686150

Jorm, R. L., Shepherd, C. L., Rogers, D. K., & Blyth, M. F. (2012). Smoking and use of primary care services: Findings from a population-based cohort study linked with administrative claims data. *BMC Health Services Research, 12*(1), 263–263. doi:10.1186/1472-6963-12-263 PMID:22900643

Karmel, R., Anderson, P., Gibson, D., Peut, A., Duckett, S., & Wells, Y. (2010). Empirical aspects of record linkage across multiple data sets using statistical linkage keys: The experience of the PIAC cohort study. [Article]. *BMC Health Services Research, 10*(1), 41–53. doi:10.1186/1472-6963-10-41 PMID:20167118

Lam, M. K. (2011). How good is New South Wales admitted patient data collection in recording births? *Health Information Management Journal, 40*(3), 12–19. PMID:22006432

Li, X., & Shen, C. (2013). Linkage of patient records from disparate sources. *Statistical Methods in Medical Research, 22*(1), 31–38. doi:10.1177/0962280211403600 PMID:21665896

Márquez, M., Chirlaque, D. M., & Navarro, C., C. (2008). DataLink Record Linkage Software Applied to the Cancer Registry of Murcia, Spain. *Methods of Information in Medicine, 47*, 448–453. doi:10.3414/ME0529 PMID:18852919

Méray, N., Reitsma, B. J., Ravelli, C. J. A., & Bonsel, J. G. (2007). Probabilistic record linkage is a valid and transparent tool to combine databases without a patient identification number. *Journal of Clinical Epidemiology, 60*(9), 883.e881–883.e811. doi:10.1016/j.jclinepi.2006.11.021 PMID:17689804

Middleton, J., Lim, K., Taylor, L., Soden, R., & Rutkowski, S. (2004). Patterns of morbidity and rehospitalisation following spinal cord injury. *Spinal Cord, 42*(6), 359–367. doi:10.1038/sj.sc.3101601 PMID:15007376

Moon, J., Hart, K. G., & Nunn, A. (2014). An eJourney through the Life Cycle of Spinal Cord Injury. In M. Khosrow-Pour (Ed.), *Encyclopedia of Information Science and Technology* (3rd ed.). Hershey, PA: IGI. doi:10.4018/978-1-4666-5888-2.ch325

Moore, H. C., de Klerk, N., Keil, A. D., Smith, D. W., Blyth, C. C., Richmond, P., & Lehmann, D. (2012). Use of data linkage to investigate the aetiology of acute lower respiratory infection hospitalisations in children. *Journal of Paediatrics and Child Health, 48*(6), 520–528. doi:10.1111/j.1440-1754.2011.02229.x PMID:22077532

NCRIS. (2013). *National Collaborative Research Infrastructure Strategy*. Retrieved from http://ncris.innovation.gov.au/Pages/default.aspx

NEHTA. (2013). *NEHTA – National E-Health Transition Authority*. Retrieved 18th, March, 2013, from http://www.nehta.gov.au/

NHIS. (2014). *National Institute for Health Research*. Retrieved 11th Jan, 2014, from http://www. nihr.ac.uk/systems/Pages/default.aspx

NISU. (2013). *Research Centre for Injury Studies*. Flinders University Adelaide, Australia. Retrieved 2nd of Feb, 2013, from http://www.nisu.flinders. edu.au/

Norman, C., Benter, L. J., MacDonald, J., Dunn, M., Dunne, S., & Siu, B. et al. (2010). Questions that individuals with spinal cord injury have regarding their chronic pain: A qualitative study. *Disability and Rehabilitation, 32*(2), 114–124. doi:10.3109/09638280903033248 PMID:19817663

Norton, L. (2010). Spinal cord injury, Australia 2007-2008. Canberra, Australia: Academic Press.

O'Connor, J. P. (2005). Survival After Spinal Cord Injury in Australia. *Archives of Physical Medicine and Rehabilitation, 86*(1), 37–47. doi:10.1016/ S0003-9993(04)00396-X PMID:15640987

PHRDR. (2014). *Population Health Research Data Repository*. Retrieved 14th Jan, 2014, from http://www.umanitoba.ca/faculties/medicine/ units/community_health_sciences/departmental_units/mchp/resources/repository/index.html

PHRN. (2013). *Population Health Research Network*. Retrieved 12th of June, 2012, from http:// www.phrn.org.au

REP. (2014). *Rochester Epidemiology Project*. Retrieved 12th Dec, 2013, from http://www. rochesterproject.org/

Silveira, D. P., & Artmann, E. (2009). Accuracy of probabilistic record linkage applied to health databases: Systematic review. *Revista de Saude Publica, 43*(5), 875–882. doi:10.1590/S0034-89102009005000060 PMID:19784456

Slack-Smith, L. (2012). How population-level data linkage might impact on dental research. *Community Dentistry and Oral Epidemiology, 40*, 90–94. doi:10.1111/j.1600-0528.2012.00726.x PMID:22998311

St Sauver, J. L., Grossardt, B. R., Yawn, B. P., Melton, L. J., Pankratz, J. J., Brue, S. M., & Rocca, W. A. (2012). Data resource profile: The Rochester Epidemiology Project (REP) medical records-linkage system. *International Journal of Epidemiology, 41*(6), 1614–1624. doi:10.1093/ ije/dys195 PMID:23159830

SWDLF. (2012). *A Scotland-wide Data Linkage Framework for Statistics and Research Consultation Paper on the Aims and Guiding Principles*. St. Andrews: Scottish Government. Retrieved from http://www.scotland.gov.uk/Resource/0039/00390444.pdf

Tromp, M., Méray, N., Ravelli, C. J. A., Reitsma, B. J., & Bonsel, J. G. (2008). Ignoring Dependency between Linking Variables and Its Impact on the Outcome of Probabilistic Record Linkage Studies. *Journal of the American Medical Informatics Association, 15*(5), 654–660. doi:10.1197/jamia. M2265 PMID:18579842

Tromp, M., Ravelli, C. A., Bonsel, J. G., Hasman, A., & Reitsma, B. J. (2008). Original Article: Results from simulated data sets: probabilistic record linkage outperforms deterministic record linkage. [Article]. *Journal of Clinical Epidemiology, 64*(5), 565–572. doi:10.1016/j.jclinepi.2010.05.008 PMID:20952162

VDL. (2013). *Victorian Data Linkages*. Retrieved 12th Feb, 2013, from http://www.health.vic.gov. au/vdl/

WADLS. (2013a). *Western Australia Data Linkage System*. Retrieved 12th Feb, 2013, from http:// www.datalinkage-wa.org/

WADLS. (2013b). *Western Australia Data Linkage System*. Retrieved 7th July, 2013, from http:// www.datalinkage-wa.org/

Wyndaele, M., & Wyndaele, J. J. (2006). Incidence, prevalence and epidemiology of spinal cord injury: What learns a worldwide literature survey? *Spinal Cord, 44*(9), 523–529. doi:10.1038/ sj.sc.3101893 PMID:16389270

ADDITIONAL READING

Alberto, C.-P., & Sabrina, S. (2012). Improving data quality using a cross layer protocol in wireless sensor networks. [Article]. *Computer Networks*. doi:10.1016/j.comnet.2012.08.001

Banfield, M., Gardner, K., McRae, I., Gillespie, J., Wells, R., & Yen, L. (2013). Unlocking information for coordination of care in Australia: A qualitative study of information continuity in four primary health care models. *BMC Family Practice*, *14*(1), 1–11. doi:10.1186/1471-2296-14-34 PMID:23497291

Chini, F., Pezzotti, P., Orzella, L., Borgia, P., & Guasticchi, G. (2011). Can we use the pharmacy data to estimate the prevalence of chronic conditions? a comparison of multiple data sources. *BMC Public Health*, *11*(1), 688. doi:10.1186/1471-2458-11-688 PMID:21892946

DePasquale, M. J., Freeman, K., Amin, M. M., Park, S. H., Rivers, S., & Hopkins, R. et al. (2012). Efficient linking of birth certificate and newborn screening databases for laboratory investigation of congenital cytomegalovirus infection and preterm birth: Florida, 2008. *Maternal and Child Health Journal*, *16*(2), 486–494. doi:10.1007/s10995-010-0740-2 PMID:21203810

Exeter, D. J., Rodgers, S., & Sabel, C. E. (2013). "Whose data is it anyway?" The implications of putting small area-level health and social data online. *Health Policy (Amsterdam)*, (0). doi:10.1016/j.healthpol.2013.07.012 PMID:23932285

Fouad, M. N., Lee, J. Y., Catalano, P. J., Vogt, T. M., Yousuf Zafar, S., & West, D. W. et al. (2013). Enrollment of Patients With Lung and Colorectal Cancers Onto Clinical Trials. [Article]. *Journal of Oncology Practice*, *9*(2), e40–e47. doi:10.1200/JOP.2012.000598 PMID:23814523

Hopf, Y. M., Bond, C., Francis, J., Haughney, J., & Helms, P. J. (2013). Views of healthcare professionals to linkage of routinely collected healthcare data: A systematic literature review. *Journal of the American Medical Informatics Association*. doi:10.1136/amiajnl-2012-001575 PMID:23715802

Hurdle, J. F., Haroldsen, S. C., Hammer, A., Spigle, C., Fraser, A. M., Mineau, G. P., & Courdy, S. J. (2013). Identifying clinical/translational research cohorts: Ascertainment via querying an integrated multi-source database. *Journal of the American Medical Informatics Association*, *20*(1), 164–171. doi:10.1136/amiajnl-2012-001050 PMID:23059733

Jebamani, L. S., Burchill, C. A., & Martens, P. J. (2005). Using Data Linkage to Identify First Nations Manitobans. *Canadian Journal of Public Health*, *96*, S28–S32. PMID:15686150

Juan F Orueta1, Roberto Nuño-Solinis2†, Maider Mateos2†, Itziar Vergara3,4,5†, Gonzalo Grandes6†, & Esnaola7†, a. S. (2012). Monitoring the prevalence of chronic conditions: which data should we use? *Orueta et al. BMC Health Services Research 12*, 365.

Laborde, D. V., Griffin, J. A., Smalley, H. K., Keskinocak, P., & Mathew, G. (2011). A framework for assessing patient crossover and health information exchange value. *Journal of the American Medical Informatics Association*, *18*(5), 698–703. doi:10.1136/amiajnl-2011-000140 PMID:21705458

Li, X., & Shen, C. (2013). Linkage of patient records from disparate sources. *Statistical Methods in Medical Research*, *22*(1), 31–38. doi:10.1177/0962280211403600 PMID:21665896

Márquez, M., Chirlaque, D. M., & Navarro, C., C. (2008). DataLink Record Linkage Software Applied to the Cancer Registry of Murcia, Spain. *Methods of Information in Medicine*, *47*, 448–453. doi:10.3414/ME0529 PMID:18852919

Newgard, C., Malveau, S., Staudenmayer, K., Wang, N. E., Hsia, R. Y., & Mann, N. C. et al. (2012). Evaluating the Use of Existing Data Sources, Probabilistic Linkage, and Multiple Imputation to Build Population-based Injury Databases Across Phases of Trauma Care. *Academic Emergency Medicine*, *19*(4), 469–480. doi:10.1111/j.1553-2712.2012.01324.x PMID:22506952

Patel, V. N., Dhopeshwarkar, R. V., Edwards, A., Barron, Y., Likourezos, A., & Burd, L. et al. (2011). Low-income, ethnically diverse consumers' perspective on health information exchange and personal health records. *Informatics for Health & Social Care*, *36*(4), 233–252. doi:10.3109/17538157.2011.554930 PMID:21851182

Patel, V. N., Dhopeshwarkar, R. V., Edwards, A., Barrón, Y., Sparenborg, J., & Kaushal, R. (2012). Consumer support for health information exchange and personal health records: A regional health information organization survey. *Journal of Medical Systems*, *36*(3), 1043–1052. doi:10.1007/s10916-010-9566-0 PMID:20703633

Rocca, W. A., Yawn, B. P., St Sauver, J. L., Grossardt, B. R., & Melton, L. J. (2012). History of the Rochester Epidemiology Project: Half a Century of Medical Records Linkage in a US Population. *Mayo Clinic Proceedings*, *87*(12), 1202–1213. doi:10.1016/j.mayocp.2012.08.012 PMID:23199802

Sebastian Coleman, L. (2013). *Measuring data quality for ongoing improvement: a data quality assessment framework Measuring Data Quality for Ongoing Improvement.*

Silveira, D. P., & Artmann, E. (2009). Accuracy of probabilistic record linkage applied to health databases: Systematic review. *Revista de Saude Publica*, *43*(5), 875–882. doi:10.1590/S0034-89102009005000060 PMID:19784456

Smailyte, G., Jasilionis, D., Ambrozaitiene, D., & Stankuniene, V. (2012). Educational inequalities in cancer incidence and mortality in Lithuania: A record linkage study. *Cancer Epidemiology*, *36*(5), e279–e283. doi:10.1016/j.canep.2012.05.009 PMID:22705124

Smith, T. C., Vachino, M. E., John, A., Wu, C. Y., Obremski, C. D., & Higa-Smith, K. (2011). *Modeling the Federal User Identity, Credential, and Access Management (ICAM) decision space to facilitate secure information sharing* (p. 56). IEEE Operations Center.

St Sauver, J. L., Grossardt, B. R., Yawn, B. P., Melton, L. J., Pankratz, J. J., Brue, S. M., & Rocca, W. A. (2012). Data resource profile: The Rochester Epidemiology Project (REP) medical records-linkage system. *International Journal of Epidemiology*, *41*(6), 1614–1624. doi:10.1093/ije/dys195 PMID:23159830

Sun, S., Austin, T., & Kalra, D. (2012). A data types profile suitable for use with ISO EN 13606. *Journal of Medical Systems*, *36*(6), 3621–3635. doi:10.1007/s10916-012-9837-z PMID:22399066

Taylor, L. K., Bentley, J., Hunt, J., Madden, R., McKeown, S., Brandt, P., & Baker, D. (2012). Enhanced reporting of deaths among Aboriginal and Torres Strait Islander peoples using linked administrative health datasets. *BMC Medical Research Methodology*, *12*(1), 91–91. doi:10.1186/1471-2288-12-91 PMID:22747900

Vu, T., Day, L., & Finch, C. F. (2012). Linked versus unlinked hospital discharge data on hip fractures for estimating incidence and comorbidity profiles. *BMC Medical Research Methodology*, *12*(1), 113–113. doi:10.1186/1471-2288-12-113 PMID:22853324

Whitelaw, F. G., Nevin, S. L., Taylor, R. J., & Watt, A. H. (1996). Morbidity and prescribing patterns for the midldle-aged population of Scotland. *The British Journal of General Practice*, (Dec): 707–714. PMID:8995849

KEY TERMS AND DEFINITIONS

AIHW: Australian Institute of Health and Welfare.

ASCIR: Australian Spinal Cord Injury Register.

CDL: Clinical Data Linkage.

DL: Data Linkage.

HITH: Hospitals in the homes.

NASH: National Authentications Services Health.

NEHTA: National eHealth Transition Authority.

NISU: National Institute of Surveillance Unit.

NT: Northern Territory.

ORLS: Oxford Record Linkage Study.

PCEHR: Personally Controlled Electronic Health Record.

PHRN: Population Health Research Network.

SA: South Australia.

SCI: Spinal Cord Injury.

TAC: Traffic Accident Committee.

VDL: Victorian Data Linkage.

VSTORM: Victorian State Trauma Outcome Registry.

WA: Western Australia.

WADLS: Western Australian Data Linkage Service.

Chapter 18
The Benefits of Big Data Analytics in the Healthcare Sector:
What Are They and Who Benefits?

Andrea Darrel
University of Southern Queensland, Australia

Timothy Hardie
Lakehead University, Canada

Margee Hume
University of Southern Queensland, Australia

Jeffery Soar
University of Southern Queensland, Australia

ABSTRACT

The benefits of big data analytics in the healthcare sector are assumed to be substantial, and early proponents have been very enthusiastic (Chen, Chiang, & Storey, 2012), but little research has been carried out to confirm just what those benefits are, and to whom they accrue (Bollier, 2010). This chapter presents an overview of existing literature that demonstrates quantifiable, measurable benefits of big data analytics, confirmed by researchers across a variety of healthcare disciplines. The chapter examines aspects of clinical operations in healthcare including Cost Effectiveness Research (CER), Clinical Decision Support Systems (CDS), Remote Patient Monitoring (RPM), Personalized Medicine (PM), as well as several public health initiatives. This examination is in the context of searching for the benefits described resulting from the deployment of big data analytics. Results indicate the principle benefits are delivered in terms of improved outcomes for patients and lower costs for healthcare providers.

INTRODUCTION

Biomedical informatics is the science of information applied to medicine and is "distinct from related fields like computer science, statistics and biomedicine, which have different objects of study"(Bernstam, Smith, & Johnson, 2010).

Biomedical informatics incorporates a "core set of methodologies for managing data, information and knowledge" (Sarkar, 2010) with the goal of "improving the quality and safety of healthcare while reducing the costs" (Hersh, 2009).

Advances in biomedical informatics have been proceeding at an astonishing pace, with some no-

DOI: 10.4018/978-1-4666-6611-5.ch018

table successes and some equally notable setbacks. The following chapter offers a comprehensive review of what benefits, and what drawbacks, current research into the application of big data analytics to healthcare and biomedical engineering have revealed, in an effort to guide further research and to understand more clearly what benefits arise where big data intersects with healthcare, and to whom those benefits accrue.

According to a McKinsey report (2011) on the potential financial savings to be harvested from big data analytics, healthcare is particularly rich in opportunity. Clinical operations, payment and pricing, R&D, public health and new business models all have the potential to benefit from the analysis of large sets of data. Preliminary investigation reveals that there have been many documented, quantified gains that accumulate to improve physician performance, provide better guidance for treatment, dramatically improve patient outcomes and significantly lower costs for hospitals, insurers and co-payees.

The looming demographic shift in the United States and other developed nations portends health care costs that will consume a significant portion of national budgets in the years to come, and delivering better health care to more people for less cost will be a critical policy issue (Ahern, Smith, Topol, Mack, & Fitzgerald, 2013; Bloom, Börsch-Supan, McGee, & Seike, 2012; Morton & Weng, 2013; Vogeli et al., 2007).

BACKGROUND

What is Big Data?

In general, we can define big data as pools of information so large that conventional analytical techniques cannot make sense of them (Bertot, Jaeger, & Grimes, 2010). In a very real sense, the definition is a moving target. As our capacity to store information increases and techniques to analyze that data continue to develop and improve,

the amounts of data that constitute big are similarly changing (see Figure 1). Since launching the National Archives and Records Administration in 2005 (Sproull & Eisenberg, 2005), the amount of information in the form of archival records the US government is managing has grown from 17 terabytes (TB) to 142 TB as of 2012, representing over 7 billion electronic artifacts, a number that is projected to continue to grow (Reed, Murray, & Jacobson, 2013).

Two important characteristics distinguish big data from ordinary data:

1. The efficacy of standard analytical techniques
2. The dynamic nature of the analysis.

Figure 1. Virtual storage terms and definitions

1 bit = binary digit

8 bits = 1 byte

1024 bytes = 1 kilobyte

1024 kilobytes = 1 megabyte

1024 megabytes = 1 gigabyte

1024 gigabytes = terabyte

1024 terabytes = 1 petabyte

1024 petabytes = 1 exabyte

1024 exabytes = 1 zettabyte

1024 zettabytes = 1 yottabyte

1024 yottabytes = 1 brontobyte

1024 brontobytes = 1 geopbyte

Big data is any dataset that "exceeds the processing capabilities of conventional database systems" (Gupta, Gupta, & Mohania, 2012), and big data is analyzed and processed in real time, allowing human decision makers to use the data to guide their behaviour as the analysis is unfolding.

To illustrate the analytical complexity of "big data," consider the following: credit card companies routinely collect transaction information on millions of customers, amounting to very large datasets (Steffes, Murthi & Rao, 2011). That data can be mined using traditional analytical techniques to detect spending patterns and predict future transactions, information that is packaged and sold to direct marketing firms, who target products and services based on those spending patterns (Bult & Wansbeek, 1995). While the dataset being used is very large, the analytical techniques use straightforward estimation and inference calculations on a static dataset that is not being updated as the analysis proceeds. The dataset in this instance is simply "data."

If the exact same dataset consists of information that is changing at the time of analysis and the analytical techniques consist of advanced algorithms that mine the data without human supervision or prompting after initial installation, it becomes "big data." The dataset of spending patterns can now allow banks to detect fraudulent use of credit cards as it happens, through the use of algorithms that use associative learning rules to classify transactions into different risk categories. Field applications have demonstrated that these real time programs allow banks to detect 95% of fraudulent card use as it occurs (Ogwueleka, 2011; Rani, Kumar, Mohan, & Shankar, 2011).

Neural network and artificial intelligence algorithms running behind standard bank software can potentially detect the use of a credit card and then combine that information with other data sources such geolocation information and social media to offer services or discounts tailored to specific customers. Banks have not been eager to embrace the use of social media in their marketing

efforts, but the capability to do so exists, and is continuing to grow (Mitic, 2012).

That may seem far-fetched, but when Hurricane Sandy struck the Atlantic coast of the United States in 2012, the Federal Emergency Management Agency (FEMA) created an innovative partnership with private companies and other federal agencies that used Twitter hashtags, Instagram photos, geo-tagged photos from the Civil Air Patrol (CAP) and sensor data from the National Oceanic and Atmospheric Administration (NOAA) to target areas in need of supplies, and kept a pulse on how the community was responding to disaster relief efforts, all assisted by the advanced algorithms of big data analytics (Mapcite, 2013).

When it comes to healthcare, the opportunity for big data to deliver tangible benefits is very real, and healthcare in particular is embracing the potential of big data analytics.

Exploring the existing literature, Jourdan (2008) found five areas of research that were of interest to investigators:

1. **Artificial Intelligence:** Algorithms and applications that address classification, prediction, web mining, and machine learning.
2. **Benefits:** How businesses have used data warehousing, data mining, and/or enterprise wide BI systems to achieve some measurable financial benefit.
3. **Decision:** Using data modeling, decision-making and decision modeling to improve overall decision making.
4. **Implementation:** Using data warehousing, data mining, customer relationship management (CRM), enterprise resource planning (ERP), knowledge management systems (KMS), and eBusiness projects to address project management issues.
5. **Strategy:** How to apply BI tools and technologies.

After analyzing 167 papers in the BI literature area, Jourdan (2008) comes to the conclusion that

Strategy is the most discussed topic (59 papers), followed by Artificial Intelligence (37 papers) and discussions surrounding Implementation (35 papers). Using BI to improve Decision-Making is of less interest (26 papers) and the accrued Benefits of BI is the least studied area (10 papers). Jourdan (2008) theorizes that one of the difficulties faced by researchers trying to identify the specific benefits is quantifying exactly how the use of big data results in an advantage to the firm.

At the end of this chapter, readers should have a clear understanding of what big data is and why it is important, why healthcare practitioners and various other stakeholders pursue big data analytics, what benefits have been shown to arise from those initiatives, how those benefits are defined, and what the future could look like as more and more data becomes available for analysis.

MAIN FOCUS OF THE CHAPTER

Issues, Controversies, Problems

When businesses use big data to enhance their competitiveness, both the process and the product are often referred to as "business intelligence." The process concerns the methods that businesses use to collect and analyze information that is of value to them. The product is the information that allows businesses to predict how "competitors, suppliers, customers, technologies, acquisitions, markets, products and services, and the general business environment" are likely to respond to various stimuli (Vedder, 1999).

For both private and public organizations, a benefit can be defined as anything that enhances the organization's ability to carry out its mission, or in other words, to enhance competitive advantage. A competitive advantage is achieved when outcomes (whether in terms of profits or attaining goals) consistently exceed the average within a defined industry (Porter, 2008). Porter defines two basic types of benefits that can enhance an organization's competitive advantage: cost advantage and differentiation advantage.

A *cost advantage* arises when an organization can deliver the same products or services as competitors at a lower cost, and a *differentiation advantage* arises when an organization can deliver products or services with benefits that exceed those of the competition. For the purposes of this chapter, in recognition of the fact that healthcare organizations and firms can be motivated by a profit incentive, but are not necessarily, benefits are defined in Table 1.

For many nationalized health care systems, market forces are not material in determining costs, but this does not reduce the pressures on these systems to deliver maximum value for taxpayer money. A looming demographic crisis and a rapidly aging population has exerted tremendous pressure on many national health systems to address the costs of delivering services (Meijer,

Table 1. Cost advantages of big data applied to healthcare

Cost Advantages	Applied to Healthcare Using Big Data
Lower Costs	Activities that allow healthcare organizations to provide the same products or services at a lower cost than previously achieved
Improved Productivity	Activities that allow healthcare organizations to deliver their products or services in a more efficient or effective way than previously achieved
Increased Market Share	Activities that allow healthcare organizations to capture a greater share of the market or to identify new markets
Price Premium	Activities that allow healthcare organizations to charge more for products or services
Limiting Liability	Activities that allow healthcare organizations to limit their exposure to liability claims

Wouterse, Polder, & Koopmanschap, 2013). A primary driver for developing and deploying advanced analytics is to reduce the costs of delivering healthcare products and services, and many big data applications are successful in achieving significant savings.

Improved productivity in the field of healthcare includes delivering products and services more efficiently, which may or may not result in a cost advantage. A major aspect of productivity is reduced morbidity and negative health outcomes for patients, which is a social good in and of itself, with the added advantage of cost savings when complications leading to death are prevented from occurring in the first place, saving both the patient's life and the expense of treating the complication.

Increasing market share through capturing market share from competitors or by identifying new markets takes two distinct forms in the healthcare sector. The healthcare organizations primarily interested in capturing increased market share are pharmaceutical companies and medical device and equipment manufacturers (Costa, 2013), although private hospitals have also used big data analytics to draw more insured patients to highly rated hospitals and surgeons (Marjoua, Butler, & Bozic, 2012). When healthcare providers identify and reach underserved populations of patients, particularly vulnerable patients, they are in effect discovering new markets for products and services.

The ability to charge a price premium comes into effect in the healthcare sector as physician payment models shift from fee-for-service plans, which reward volume, to performance-based pricing plans, which reward outcomes. Physicians achieve a price premium for their services when they are able to produce the best patient outcomes or achieve cost controls. Physicians working with terminal patients in particular are rewarded when they are able to achieve costs controls while still affording maximal care to patients, and a failure to replace fee-for-service payment plans reduces physician's willingness to use best-practices and

standard protocols identified through big data analytics (Neumann, Palmer, Nadler, Fang, & Ubel, 2010; Timbie, Fox, Van Busum, & Schneider, 2012).

Performance based pricing plans allow physicians to test the cost efficacy of new treatment regimens, supported by big data analytics. Value-based pricing (VBP) models in Sweden identified Acomplia as a potentially effective treatment for obesity related diabetes, and a set reimbursement plan was put into place, contingent upon outcomes, allowing physicians to either switch treatment or continue at substantially reduced costs, in effect delivering a price premium (Persson, Willis, & Odegaard, 2010).

Limiting liability is a concern for many healthcare practitioners, and the use of big data specifically generates significant benefits in the pharmaceutical silo of the healthcare sector. The use of big data in designing clinical trials, analyzing and aggregating trial results and monitoring the efficacy of approved treatments is greatly assisted by the advanced analytics of big data.

Estimates about the cost of bringing new drugs to market vary widely, with some pharmaceutical companies estimating their costs in the low range of $90 million and others reporting an upper limit of $880 million, an almost tenfold difference in estimated costs. Systematic reviews of cost reporting reveal that there are no gold standards of reporting in this area, and all drug development cost claims should be subject to reasonable audit and disclosure criteria (Morgan, Grootendorst, Lexchin, Cunningham, & Greyson, 2011). What is more well-known is the cost of getting it wrong. When drug companies introduce products that are subsequently shown to be harmful, they are held to liability claims that are significantly in excess of even the highest estimates of development costs. In 2012, GlaxoSmithKline (GSK) was ordered to pay a $3 billion dollar settlement for promoting two products for off-label use that were later shown to have harmful side effects. Since 2009, the US government has collected more than $11 billion dollars in liability claims against pharmaceutical companies (Outterson, 2012). Pharmaceutical and insurance companies are thus highly motivated to reduce their liability and big data plays a big role in their ability to do that.

Unsurprisingly, the majority of benefits arising from the use of big data analytics in the health care sector relate to reducing costs and improving productivity.

Big data is demonstrably effective at achieving some of those savings across a number of fields. In the following section, we will examine the use of big data to lower costs and improve productivity, as it applies to:

- Cost Effectiveness Research (CER)
- Clinical Decision Support Systems (CDS)
- Transparency
- Remote Patient Monitoring (RPM)
- Public Health Administration (PHA)
- Personalized Medicine (PM).

Methodology

Potentially relevant articles were identified using keyword searches and then divided into two categories: those that appeared relevant based on abstract and title, and those that appeared relevant but required careful review as the abstract and title provided insufficient information. Full text retrievals were carried out for articles with titles and abstracts that appeared relevant, which were then evaluated for the following criteria:

- Use of large datasets
- Use of advanced analytics
- Use of dynamic data.

Articles that did not meet the criteria were excluded from analysis. The same procedure was deployed for articles that appeared relevant but contained insufficient information in the title

and abstract alone. After the first section on comparative effectiveness research was conducted, the parameters for publication dates were tightened, as evidence demonstrated that virtually no use of big data analytics could be detected prior to 2009. A second reviewer confirmed article relevance and verified the application of exclusion/inclusion criteria (see Figure 2).

CLINICAL OPERATIONS

Clinical operations in healthcare are all the actions that relate to the patient bedside, including diagnosing and monitoring the course of disease or trauma or other injury, and all observations and treatments administered, many of which are now collected in the form of digital records. Electronic Health Records (EHR) have the potential "for establishing new patient-stratification principles and for revealing unknown disease correlations" (Jensen, Jensen, & Brunak, 2012). Advances in medical genomics brings the possibility of personalized medicine based on a specific patient's gene sequence closer to fruition, and while there are challenges in integrating genomic data into EHR, advanced data analytics present a "promising means of disseminating genetic testing into diverse care settings (Kho et al., 2013).

Clinical operations represent a fertile ground for the use of big data to lower the costs of delivering medical services and products and to improve outcomes for patients. Specific clinical operations that have successfully deployed big data to achieve measurable, quantifiable benefits:

1. Cost Effectiveness Research (CER)
2. Clinical Decision Support (CDS) software systems
3. Transparency
4. Remote Patient Monitoring (RPM)
5. Personalized Medicine (PM).

Figure 2. Flow chart of results from the literature

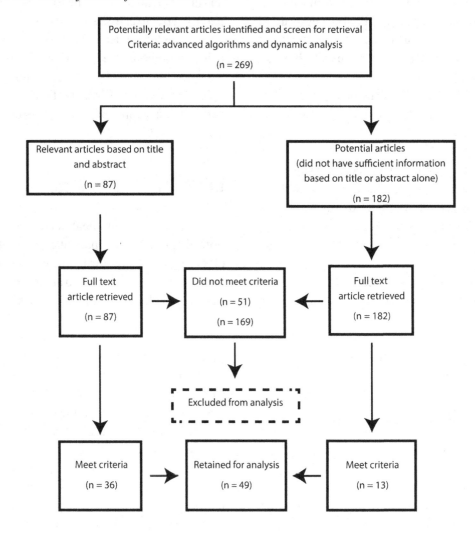

Cost Effectiveness Research (CER)

Cost Effectiveness Research (CER) is based on the idea that healthcare resource allocation decisions can be guided by considering the costs of a particular treatment in relation to the expected benefits. The basic principles of CER are as follows:

- The ratio of net health-care costs to net health benefits provides an index by which priorities may be set.
- Quality-of-life concerns, including both adverse and beneficial effects of therapy,

may be incorporated in the calculation of health benefits as adjustments to life expectancy.

- The timing of future benefits and costs may be accounted for by the appropriate use of discounting.
- Current decisions must inevitably be based on imperfect information, but sensitivity analysis can increase the level of confidence.
- Analyses should be adaptable to the needs of various health-care decision makers, including planners, administrators and providers (Weinstein & Stason, 1977).

CER considers not just financial costs, but also a broader societal perspective that accounts for "benefits, harms and costs to all parties," including patients, care providers, insurers and auxiliary product and service providers (Russell, Gold, Siegel, Daniels, & Weinstein, 1996). CER is not intended to limit or restrict access to treatments or medicines, but rather "to provide healthcare decision makers, and patients and their personal physicians with more and potentially better information to help choose the best intervention, and thereby facilitate the best possible patient outcomes" (Siegel et al., 2012).

When the analytical tools of big data are applied to CER, the emphasis is on "the generation and synthesis of evidence that compares the benefits and harms of alternative methods to prevent, diagnose, treat and monitor a clinical condition or to improve the delivery of care" (Gandjour, 2011). Early advocates for CER and big data analytics predicted that "better information will result in better health outcomes and more effective use of resources" (Sox & Greenfield, 2009). CER has been promoted as an essential aspect of health care reform, given its potential to "prevent blunt incentives from inadvertently harming patients and to foster intelligent changes that can improve both the efficiency and the quality of care" (Mushlin & Ghomrawi, 2010).

The vast majority of published work in the realm of CER either uses static data and traditional analytic techniques, disqualifying it from consideration as an example of big data, or theorizes only probable outcomes (Avorn & Fischer, 2010; Chalkidou et al., 2009; Fischer & Avorn, 2004). For example, a standard decision tree-analysis on the cost effectiveness of a particular vaccination strategy was conducted on 180 000 infants in the Netherlands (Rozenbaum et al., 2010), which is undeniably a very large sample size, but the analytical techniques were of a standard variety and the data was static during analysis.

Existing evidence shows a promising confirmation of the predicted benefits of CER. The following table summarizes literature that confirms at least one benefit of big data analytics in the area of CER per publication (see Table 2).

While the macro justification for CRE is aimed at lowering costs of delivering medical services (Orszag & Emanuel, 2010), at the practitioner level, the emphasis remains on patient health and improving outcomes with cost savings only a secondary benefit, an initiative described as "goal-oriented patient care" (Reuben & Tinetti, 2012) across a wide variety of medical specialities. The following table illustrates the journals that published at least one article on CER, demonstrating how widespread the adoption of CER is across medical disciplines.

Clinical Decision Support Systems (CDS)

Clinical Decision Support Systems (CDS) are software programs that anticipate probable outcomes of particular treatment strategies by comparing the proposed treatment to previous patient outcomes. The software mines digital patient records and offers therapeutic suggestions and recommendations for the current patient based on what tended to work for previous patients presenting the same symptoms (Berner, 2007). These suggestions are offered at the time a decision about a particular therapy or regimen occurs, thereby meeting the two criteria for big data: large datasets are considered and the analysis happens in real time as the decisions are made.

CDS systems are primarily designed to address quality issues by providing practitioners with guidelines that have been proven to work in the past (Romano & Stafford, 2011). They are not intended to replace the judgement of individual practitioners faced with unique patients, but rather meant to act in a support capacity by revealing probable outcomes based on previous applications (Trowbridge & Weingarten, 2001). For maximum efficacy, CDS systems need to:

Table 2. Demonstrated benefits of CER

Citation	Benefit	Summary of Findings
(Kremers et al., 2011)	Lower costs, improved productivity through better patient outcomes	Medical records generated by different healthcare providers over many years to specific individuals are linked in a single database that enables long term, population based planning for rheumatic disease treatment in a constantly changing population
(Abernethy et al., 2010)	Lower costs, improved productivity through better patient outcomes	An insurance provider serving more than 8 million patients maintains a database of patient records and 300 standard treatment protocols for cancer and analyzes best treatment options in real time, providing patients and doctors with best option suggestions at the time of treatment
(F Akram, J H Kim, & K N Choi, 2013)	Improved productivity through better detection of malignancies	Digital mammograms are pre-processed using advanced algorithms, removing digital obstacles such as labels, scanning and taping artifacts and physical obstacles such as pectoral muscles for use in CAD programs that alert radiologists to problems as files are examined
(S Ayyachamy & M Vasuki, 2013)	Lower costs through appropriate treatment regimens and improved productivity through better patient outcomes	Content Based Medical Image Retrieval (CBMIR) extracts stored images from a database using a variety of transforms (Fourier, discrete cosine, etc) and analyzes their visual content to assist both physicians and CAD programs in recognition, diagnosis, and treatment of lesions under consideration
(Du, 2010)	Improved productivity through elimination of unnecessary imaging analysis	The use of unsupervised data mining algorithms to detect microscopic cell abnormalities in digital images containing large numbers of cells, to help guide medical imaging choices.
(Prasad, Zimmermann, Prabhu, & Pai, 2010)	Lower costs through reduction of false positive identifications for breast cancer	Automatic classification of breast cancer tissue stains into positive or negative through the use of image analysis algorithms that draw on a large set of images collected in a university database
(Z. Chen et al., 2013)	Lower costs through elimination of unnecessary treatment and improved productivity through better patient outcomes	Replacing binary models of toxicity in cancer trials with an algorithm that detects and analyzes toxicity continuously calculating next dose levels from existing data
(Lacson et al., 2012)	Improved productivity through enhanced patient safety by alerting all caregivers of critical diagnostic results	Automated retrieval of radiology reports that cite critical imaging findings to enhance communication of critical results between caregivers
(Su, Wang, Jiao, & Guo, 2011)	Improved productivity through better and faster detection of breast cancer	Automatic detection and classification of breast tumors in ultrasonic imaging without any manual intervention using a self-organizing neural network that detects areas of interest by analyzing pixel textures and other digital morphologies
(Skounakis et al., 2010)	Lower costs and improved productivity through accurate and early detection of cancer	An open access interactive platform for 3D tomographic datasets that combines manual and semi-automatic segmentation techniques with integrated correction tools to identify tumors, and that can be adapted by different caregivers to plan treatments accordingly

1. Provide decision support automatically as part of clinician workflow.
2. Deliver decision support at the time and location of decision making.
3. Provide actionable recommendations.
4. Use a computer to generate the decision support, without requiring clinician initiative (Kawamoto, Houlihan, Balas, & Lobach, 2005).

CDS system efficiency has a built in requirement for big data analytics, since the maximum productivity and efficacy of these systems are effected when the analysis takes place in real time, at the time and location of the decision making (Wright et al., 2009). The use of CDS systems is by far the most explored topic in big data analytics and clinical operations, likely due to the fact that many of these systems operate in conjunction with computerized Physician Order Entry (POE) systems, which have been in place since the late 1990s (Bates, 1998; Bates et al., 1999). Most of these early POE systems were aimed at preventing medication errors which are both costly and lead to negative patient outcomes. The dataset consists of pharmaceutical compound characteristics and counter-indications, potential over-dosages and under-dosages based on unique patient records that generate alerts for the prescribing physician at the time the order is entered.

The central benefit described in the literature relates to improved productivity through better patient outcomes, but by eliminating inadequate treatments which can lead to complications, and superfluous treatments which can lead to unnecessary costs, they also provide a lower costs benefit. When a busy emergency room used a CDS system that assessed patients and then alerted nursing staff to prompt patients to consider seasonal influenza vaccinations, they were able to capture market share from private physicians and realize a profit from the additional vaccinations (Venkat et al., 2010). Even so, the principle motivator was to increase the uptake in vaccinations rates, and the financial benefit was of secondary consideration.

Unlike CER, which is very often prompted by a desire to reduce the costs of delivering high quality healthcare, CDS systems are almost uniformly designed to achieve higher productivity through better outcomes for patients (Moxey et al., 2010). Bright et al. (2012) compared 148 different CDS randomized trials and found that while patient outcomes were improved, there was little evidence to support a claim for consistent economic savings.

While a significant percentage of the articles returned after a keyword search for CDS do describe benefits, many of them do not meet the criteria for inclusion in the study, because the datasets they describe are historical and the analysis is static (Eppenga et al., 2012; Krasowski & Penrod, 2012; Scharnweber et al., 2013).

The papers in Table 3 describe CDS systems using big data analytics to improve productivity and reduce costs.

Transparency

The issues of transparency and the application of big data analytics fall into four broad categories:

1. Sharing of clinical trials data
2. Sharing of patient information between healthcare providers
3. Sharing of information between patients and healthcare providers
4. Evaluating healthcare organizations and providers for effectiveness.

Pharmaceutical companies and other healthcare service providers and researchers within the private sector have tended to see clinical trials data as commercially proprietary information and have resisted the call to register and reveal the results of clinical trials, despite evidence that some firms have engaged in data suppression, misrepresentation and manipulation (Bian & Wu, 2010). In a particularly egregious example of data suppression, GlaxoSmithKline (GSK) was sued for suppressing reports of suicidal thinking, leading to physician over-prescription, especially amongst children, for a popular antidepressant (Sibbald, 2004), prompting New York State Attorney to demand that GSK develop and maintain an online clinical trials registry that includes information about safety, efficacy, side effects, methodologies

Table 3. Demonstrated benefits of CDS

Citation	Benefit	Summary of Findings
(Bates et al., 1999)	Improved productivity through appropriate dosing and avoidance of errors, and lower costs through avoidance of complications and over-prescription of potentially costly treatments	An 86% decrease in medication errors following the implementation of computerized physician order entry (POE). Upon entering the order, the computer generated appropriate does and frequencies, displayed relevant laboratory data, screening orders for allergy and drug interactions, assisting physicians in making the best orders for individual patients
(Robbins et al., 2012)	Improved productivity through better patient outcomes	Automatically generated computer alerts to inform both patients and care-givers of virologic failure and 11 over other abnormal lab results for patients with HIV, facilitating appointment rescheduling and repeated lab testing
(Kozel, 2012)	Improved productivity through better patient outcomes and lower costs through avoidance of serious complications	Automated protocols for newborns added to electronic records to automatically detect risk factors for hypoglycemia, reducing nursing errors in detecting those factors from 21% to 5%.
(Seidling et al., 2010)	Lower costs through avoidance of over-prescribing costly medications and improved productivity through better patient outcomes by avoiding toxic drug doses	An algorithm extracting relevant patient information and comparing that information with upper dose limits for various compounds instantly alerts physicians at the time a drug order is entered that upper limits may be compromised specific to individual patients
(Venkat et al., 2010)	Capturing market share by offering seasonal influenza vaccines in ER departments	Patients presenting at emergency rooms are entered into a EHR system, which evaluates their suitability for seasonal flu vaccinations and then prompts nursing staff to offer it, resulting in greater uptake of flu shots at a profit for the ER
(Haut, Lau, Kraenzlin, & et al., 2012)	Improved productivity through better patient outcomes	An evidence based algorithm identifies patient risk stratification levels and recommends appropriate treatment regimens for venous thromboembolism in trauma patients
(Bressan, James, & McGregor, 2012)	Improved productivity through better neonatal patient outcomes	The Artemis System for monitoring neonatal patients for signs of infection is optimized to include data streams from infusion pumps, EEG monitors and cerebral oxygenation monitors assisting care providers with decision making during critical prematurity
(Verberne et al., 2012)	Improved productivity through better colorectal cancer patient outcomes	An intelligent algorithm monitors lab results for colorectal cancer patients automatically issuing letters to patients to attend follow up appointments, scheduling appointments urgently when lab results indicate
(Raja et al., 2012)	Lower costs through the elimination of unnecessary imaging	Historical patient records were mined to create a CDS system that assists physicians in determining if current emergency room patients require computed tomographic (CT) pulmonary angiography for the diagnosis of pulmonary embolism
(McLachlan, Wells, Furness, Jackson, & Kerr, 2010)	Improved productivity through better patient outcomes, particularly for ethnic and low-income patients	CDS deployed to address care disparities arising from patient's ethnic or socioeconomic status in cardiovascular risk management post myocardial infarction. The use of EHR and automatic detection of risk factors enhanced care for patients who might otherwise have received inadequate care
(Ongenae, Dhaene, De Turck, Benoit, & Decruyenaere, 2010)	Improved productivity through better patient outcomes by early detection of sepsis in an ICU unit	Machine Learning Techniques augment the medical time series collected for a specific patient in the ICU and then calculates the probability the patient is septic
(Mariotti, Gentilini, & Dapor, 2013)	Improved productivity through the efficient use of specialists.	Patients waiting to see orthopaedic and ENT specialists were grouped according to explicit clinical indicators and on clinical priorities and appointments were automatically generated, resulting in enhanced agreement between primary and specialist providers.

continued on following page

Table 3. Continued

Citation	Benefit	Summary of Findings
(Cho, Park, Kim, Lee, & Bates, 2013)	Improved productivity through the prevention of pressure ulcers in critically ill patients.	A predictive decision model embedded within an EHR prompted staff in an ICU to take preventative measures to present pressure ulcers in vulnerable patients, reducing the prevalence of pressure ulcers by tenfold.
(Smith, Murphy, et al., 2013)	Improved productivity through improved follow-up for patients returning abnormal cancer related test results	Automated, system wide tracking of cancer-related abnormal test results lacking follow-up documentation generated context specific prompts to care providers
(Graven, Allen, Smith, & MacDonald, 2013)	Improved productivity through reduced mortality rates	The entire country of Belize experienced reduced mortality rates in eight disease management algorithm domains that used automated alerts to coordinate care
(Ip et al., 2012)	Improved productivity through improved screening of PAP tests for patients at the Mayo Clinic.	50 000 PAP results were examined to develop a CDS to identify abnormal test results, which was then combined with screening and management guidelines, generating alerts for care providers.
(Suganthi & Madheswaran, 2012)	Improved productivity through improved detection of malignant breast tumors	Neural networks and a multi-objective genetic algorithm are deployed to detect malignant tumors using texture and shape features extracted from mammograms, automatically advising clinicians of potential breast cancers.

and early terminations, but this requirement was not extended to all other drug companies.

By 2008, the World Medical Association revised the Declaration of Helsinki to include the requirement that "every clinical trial must be registered in a publicly accessible database before the recruitment of the first subject" (WorldMedicalAssociation, 2013). The main purpose of trial registration is to reduce or eliminate publication and reporting bias, whereby only positive and commercially valuable results are released, to provide reliable evidence for decision making, protecting public health and reducing liability for healthcare providers (Krleža-Jerić & Lemmens, 2009). The creation of these large, publicly available databases immediately opens the possibility for big data analytics to mine the data for relationships and correlations that may not be easily detected by any other means.

The benefits of transparency in clinical trials data relate primarily to improved productivity through improved outcomes for patients and reduced costs through the elimination of collecting new data when sufficient data already exists, and by increasing the probability that the trial will reach conclusion.

Gotzsche (2011) identifies four specific benefits of mandatory data sharing:

1. Better results through harm reduction,
2. Reduced incentive to cheat when results can be confirmed independently,
3. Improved efficiency by eliminating the need to collect data where sufficient data exists,
4. Meta-analyses based on published summary data would be much more reliable.

Gotzsche notes a potential harm that can arise from data sharing – that anyone with an agenda "could selectively interpret the data in a way that furthers this agenda (p.6), but suggests that making data widely available would allow those agendas to be challenged as easily as they can be asserted.

Much of the current literature on the benefits of transparency in the sharing of clinical trial data remains speculative, but almost all literature specifically identifies the potential for big data analytics to deliver both lower costs and improved productivity (Mello et al., 2013). Mello identifies nine specific benefits of sharing clinical trial data and the principal beneficiaries which are analyzed in Table 4.

Table 4. Potential benefits of sharing clinical trial data

Benefit	Primary Beneficiaries				
	Public or Patients	Research Participants	Scientific Community	Regulators	Trial Sponsors
Encourage accurate characterization of the benefits and risks of drugs in research reports, improving public confidence in clinical research and pharmaceuticals	x		x	x	x
Improving surveillance of drug safety and effectiveness	x		x	x	
Facilitate secondary analysis of clinical trial data to explore new scientific questions	x		x		x
Speed innovation	x		x		x
Enable patients and advocacy groups to learn more about their specific medical problems	x				
Ensure that research participants are not exposed to unnecessary risks		x	x		
Ensure that research subjects' participation advances science		x	x		
Achieve operational efficiencies in conducting clinical trials			x		x
Inform strategic decisions about potential avenues of research and development			x		x

The following papers confirm at least one of the benefits identified by Mello and Gotzsche, delivered through the use of advanced algorithms analyzing dynamic data in real time. While much literature exists describing the benefits of open clinical trials, only those specifically describing the use of big data analytics are included in the analysis. Large sample sizes are insufficient for inclusion if the data is not analyzed using advanced algorithms that offer correctives or other information at the time of the trial. For example a study of over 5000 patients randomly prescribed medication to treat diabetes was not included because the analysis used traditional proportional hazards regressions to evaluate historical data that was not changing at the time of analysis (Ginsberg et al., 2010). In contrast, a study of over 20 000 clinical trials conducted at Pfizer was used to create a database of historical controls in the area of pain management, allowing future pain control trials to partially reduce their need to subject some trial participants to a placebo arm by automatically displaying the results from previous studies when new trials are initiated (Desai, Bowen, Danielson, Allam, & Cantor, 2013). While double-blind, randomized trials remain the preferred methodology for clinical trial research (Avins, Cherkin, Sherman, Goldberg, & Pressman, 2012), the reality is that participants do not like being part of the placebo group and will often drop out of a study if they feel that is the case, seriously compromising the research (Llewellyn-Thomas, McGreal, Thiel, Fine, & Erlichman, 1991). The creation of an historical controls database, containing the data from placebo groups allows researchers to reduce the number of patients receiving placebos while maintaining the integrity of the trial.

The scarcity of literature in the area is likely the result of the fact that despite strenuous calls to do so, most trial results are simply not reported. Huser & Cimino (2013) found that of 8907 trials registered at ClinicalTrials.gov, only 9.2% reported results by both registry and publication. For the cited examples, the principle benefit realized was improved productivity through appropriately selecting trial participants based on combined results from previous trials and other data sources (see Table 5).

Remote Patient Monitoring (RPM)

Remote Patient Monitoring (RPM) is an aspect of telemedicine that requires the use of big data analytics almost by definition. Defined broadly, telemedicine "is the use of electronic information and communications technologies to provide and

support health care when distance separates the participants" (Field & Grigsby, 2002). Historically, telemedicine used video and land based communications to deliver health services to remote populations (see Table 6).

A very early project involving NASA, the Tohono O'odham Indian Nation, the Lockheed Missile and Space Company, the Indian Health Service and the Department of Health, Education and Welfare demonstrated "the feasibility of a consortium of public and private partners working together to provide medical care to remote populations via telecommunication" as early as

Table 5. Demonstrated benefits applied to transparency

Citation	Benefit	Summary of Findings
(Fenstermacher, Wenham, Rollison, & Dalton, 2011)	Improved productivity through better outcomes for cancer patients and lower costs by identifying clinical trial participants	Over 100 000 patients records are continuously updated and monitored for participation in appropriate cancer clinical trials
(Li et al., 2013)	Improved productivity by increasing clinical trial participants leading to better drug development	Automating clinical trial eligibility by recognizing medication attributes using natural language processing
(Desai et al., 2013)	Improved productivity through better outcomes for patients in pain therapeutic area and lower costs by increasing the likelihood that clinical trial participants will continue trial by reducing randomization factor	20 000 Pfizer trials were mined to examine effects on placebo subjects and used to create a historical placebo group database to supplement distribution calculations for future placebo groups
(Fraccaro, Dentone, Fenoglio, & Giacomini, 2013)	Improved productivity through the creation of patient cohorts for enrollment in clinical trials in the areas of HIV and eye diseases	A web-based Clinical Data Management System captures patient information from EHRs and allows simultaneous sharing of the information for multicenter research, automatically generating patient cohorts specific to each center
(Ginn, Alexander, Edelstein, Abedi, & Wixon, 2013)	Improved productivity through sharing of results from gene therapy trials across the internet	A searchable database records the results from all gene therapy trials around the world, accessible on the internet to all future researchers

Table 6. Telehealth definitions

	Definition
Telehealthcare	The use of any information technology to provide healthcare at a distance
Telemedicine	The use of electronic information and telecommunication technologies to support long distance health care, patient and professional health care, patient and professional health related education, public health and health administration
Telemonitoring	Monitoring patients who are not at the same location as the health care provider
Remote Patient Monitoring	The use of technology to enable monitoring of patients outside of conventional clinical settings

the 1970s (Freiburger, Holcomb, & Piper, 2007). These early telemedicine initiatives did not require the use of advanced data analytics, but rapid advances in both communications and medical technology have made RPM considerably more complex than simple videoconferencing.

RPM involves continuous monitoring of the "physiological status of patients using heterogeneous sensors such as blood pressure, weight, blood glucose, and/or physical activity sensors in order to shift medical services from hospital and clinical settings to an in-home monitoring scenario" (Lan et al., 2012). The principal rationale behind early RPM systems is to improve the delivery of health care services for better patient outcomes, especially when those patients were underserved (Shea et al., 2006). Using a variety of sensors and wireless technology to monitor "multiple biological and environmental signals simultaneously, the RPM system can also provide alarms/alerts for the patient or the caregiver in real time so that the patient gets assistance in a timely manner when an acute event occurs" (Joshi, Moradshahi, & Goubran, 2013).

While improved outcomes for patients are still an important feature of RPM, the benefits of big data analytics in this area related primarily to reduced costs (Baker, Johnson, Macaulay, & Birnbaum, 2011; Cryer, Shannon, Van Amsterdam, & Leff, 2012; Klersy et al., 2011). When the data generated by RPM is processed using an analytics engine that provides "intelligent back-end processing and machine learning algorithms," the rate of false negatives falls dramatically as opposed to conventional RPM (Lee et al., 2013). This means that rates of readmission for any particular condition declines, as the advanced algorithms of big data analytics are far better at detecting which patients require readmission than human interpreters, who tend to be risk adverse and recommend readmission if there is any doubt in their minds (Radhakrishnan, Jacelon, & Roche, 2012). Despite the quantifiable benefits both in terms of reduced patient morbidity and lower

costs, less than half of eligible patients are enrolled in RPM programs for implantable cardioverter-defibrillators, indicating that the area of RPM is likely to continue to experience significant growth (Akar et al., 2013).

While most of the articles describe the benefits of remote and automated monitoring of implantable devices, which are more effective in detecting adverse cardiac events than clinical evaluations (Guédon-Moreau, Mabo, & Kacet, 2013), another interesting application involves the use of Interactive Voice-Response Systems (IVR) for the management of chronic diseases (Piette, 2000). Patients suffering from mental health issues (Baer et al., 1995; González, Costello, La Tourette, Joyce, & Valenzuela, 1997; Kobak et al., 1997), diabetes (Mahoney, Tennstedt, Friedman, & Heeren, 1999; Piette & Mah, 1997; Piette, McPhee, Weinberger, Mah, & Kraemer, 1999), heart failure (Patel & Babbs, 1992), drug and alcohol addictions (Alemi et al., 1994; Perrine, Mundt, Searles, & Lester, 1995), lower back pain (Millard & Carver, 1999) and patients undergoing outpatient chemotherapy (Christ & Siegel, 1990) were all monitored using IVR which was consistently more effective, or at least *as* effective as a traditional clinical assessment at identifying patients requiring clinical follow-ups. The use of software and automated telephone inquiry systems result in dramatically lower costs as routine follow-ups with human caregivers are targeted at those patients who require additional attention. IVR technology that includes big data analytics results in health care providers receiving alerts as the software analyzes the responses to questions, allowing the "clinical team to intervene sooner when a patient's symptoms worsen" (Rich, Howe, Larson, & Chuang, 2013). The potential to deliver IVR and provide caregivers with real time analytics is a topic of considerable interest, but the true potential of combining IVR data with other data sources to alert patients and/or providers has yet to be realized (Willig et al., 2013). See Table 7 for potential future applications.

Table 7. Future applications

Technology	Potential Medical Applications
High frequency electromagnetic wave sensors (microwaves)	• Detect changes in heart and respiratory rates by measuring vibrations on the body surface • Detect changes in sympathovagal balance as a measurement of stress • Low power Doppler radar to detect respiratory rates in newborns, alerting caregivers when no movement is detected
Frequency modulated continuous wave radar	• Detection of physical orientation of bodies • Monitoring nighttime movements of patients with dementia, which is associated with increased rates of injury • Monitoring vital signs through evaluation of signal echoes
Infrared thermography	Rapid detection of infectious disease in airports and other areas when large numbers of people congregate
Global positioning systems	Enable rapid response to cardiac events through the use of wearable ECG monitors that continuously convey data via smartphones

(Jose & Jingle, 2013; Suzuki & Matsui, 2012)

Table 8. Demonstrated benefits of RPM

Citation	Benefit	Summary of Findings
(Varma & Michalski, 2013)	Lower costs by preventing readmission following heart implants	Patients monitored remotely were automatically alerted to follow-up appointments at regular intervals post-implant, resulting in better adherence to follow-up protocols and better detection of adverse events
(Abraham, 2013)	Lower costs by preventing readmission following heart implants	Patients monitored remotely were alerted to adverse events using a pulmonary artery pressure measurement system which automatically detects the onset of heart failure permitting intervention before more serious events that require hospitalization occur
(Mabo et al., 2012)	Lower costs by preventing readmission following implantation of a pacemaker	Data collected from pacemakers automatically transmits to a data service center for analysis and alerts are sent to health care providers when adverse advents are detected, permitting interventions to take place before more serious complications arise
(Varma, Pavri, Stambler, & Michalski, 2013)	Lower costs through same day detection of implantable cardioverter –defibrillator malfunction	ICD devices continuously monitored for malfunction and alerts automatically generated when malfunctions were detected, allowing repairs to be made before adverse events occurred undetected
(Zanaboni et al., 2013)	Lower costs through reduced hospital admissions	Patients with implantable cardiac devices monitored remotely had lower hospital admission rates in all studies examined
(Kosse, Brands, Bauer, Hortobagyi, & Lamoth, 2013)	Lower costs through the detection of preventable falls among elderly patients	Intelligent alarms monitor physical parameters and alert caregivers to changes that indicate a potential fall, reducing falls by 77% with minimal false alarms
(Pecchia, Melillo, & Bracale, 2011)	Lower costs through the early detection of problematic heart arrhythmias	Historical ECG records were mined to create classification rules for arrhythmias and patients with implantable heart devices were monitored for adverse signals which triggered automatic alerts to health care providers
(Amir, Wolf, Rappaport, & Abraham, 2012)	Lower costs through early detection of pulmonary congestion leading to heart failure	Remote detection of pulmonary congestion using dielectric senor technology
(Arasaratnam et al., 2012)	Lower costs through appropriate dosage	Automated, remote site dose monitoring for patients undergoing cardiac catheterization provides consistent optimal dosage instructions automatically to remote clinics

Table 8 describes several different areas in which RPM and the use of big data analytics resulted in lower costs by avoiding costly readmissions. Articles that described RPM through the use of telephone or video communications were not included, and only those articles that referenced RPM through the use of big data analytics and real time alerts/alarms were considered, which is not to say that RPM through more traditional, static communications is not of value. Medicare patients with heart failure who were monitored via video and land based telephone lines experienced fewer hospitalization events and subsequently lower costs accrued to the hospitals (Pekmezaris et al., 2012). A meta-analysis of all RPM strategies for patients with heart failure demonstrates that either continuous device monitoring with a Human-to-Machine (HM) interface or structured telephone support with Human-to-Human (HH) interaction reduces mortality rates, but RPM with HM interaction is more cost effective (Pandor et al., 2013).

Personalized Medicine (PM)

Personalized Medicine (PM) uses "modern imaging and exploratory technologies to disclose genomic, proteomic and epigenetic information peculiar to each patient, in the effort to individualize prognosis and therapeutic care" (Nicolaidis, 2013). Big data in biomedicine is "driven by the single premise of one day having personalized medicine programs that will...establish the causal genetic factors that could help manage the golden triangle of treatment: the right target, the right chemistry, the right patient" (see Figure 3) (Costa, 2013).

Ten years after the completion of the Human Genome Project, progress towards the goal of PM has stalled, largely because the science is harder than expected and because economic incentives are not aligned to invest in diagnostics (Lester, 2009; Towse, Ossa, Veenstra, Carlson, & Garrison, 2013).

While PM makes use of large sets of data stored digitally, not all PM is based on analytics that qualify as "big data." Some of the obstacles to reaching the full potential inherent in big data and PM include:

- Lack of an appropriate computational infrastructure and architecture to generate, maintain, transfer and analyze large data sets,
- Integrating that data with *omics* data and other data sets, such as imaging and patient clinical records,
- Managing the costs associated with generating, storing and analyzing data,
- Difficulties in transferring data from one location to another (usually done by mailing external hard drives),
- Maintaining the security and privacy of the data (Costa, 2013).

Personalized medicine represents the clinical area that originally showed the most promise in terms of deploying big data analytics, but has proven to be the most difficult to implement. Specific barriers to implementation:

Figure 3. The golden triangle

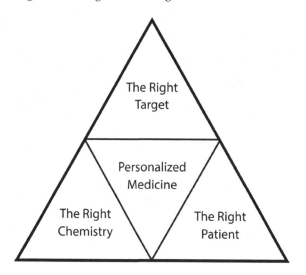

- **Scientific Challenges:** Including identifying clinically significant genetic markers, limiting off-target effects of gene therapy, and conducting clinical trials to identify genetic variants associated with a particular drug response.
- **Regulatory Challenges:** Including defined regulatory pathways for coordinated approval of co-developed diagnostics and therapies, the development of risk-based reviews to assess validity and utility, and ensuring data transparency.
- **Commercialization Challenges:** Including creating downstream market opportunities and enticing private sector participants to explore how new understandings of genes, proteins and pathways can lead to new and better drug targets, accelerating and sharing the costs of preclinical development phases, and formalizing partnerships between private and public sector organizations.
- **Data Challenges:** Including the development of tissue banks containing specimens along with information linking them to clinical outcomes, sufficient processing power to retain and analyze massive sets of information, and enhanced ability to share and move data between sites.
- **Translational Challenges:** Including the development of a standard ontology and evaluation tools, such as biomarkers and assays, the inclusion of pharmacogenomics information in drug labelling, standardizing the accuracy of diagnostic tests and clarifying the processes manufacturers must follow regarding claims about how treatments, and diagnostics work (Hamburg & Collins, 2010).

Despite these limitations, researchers and technology developers continue to explore opportunities to realize the promise of big data and personalized medicine. The New York Genome Center (NYGC) and IBM announced an initiative to use IBM's Watson cognitive system to deliver personalized treatment options for aggressive genetic cancers like glioblastoma, a type of brain cancer that kills 13 000 people each year in the United States. Waston is a "new class of software, services and apps that think, improve by learning, and discover answers and insights to complex questions from massive amounts of Big Data" (NYGC, 2014). Dr. R. Kravitz (2014) notes that personalized medicine in terms of phenotypes and patient preferences offers ample opportunities to deliver patient specific treatment options without necessarily relying on genomic data.

Public Health Administration (PHA)

According to the World Health Organization (WHO), public health refers to all organized measures (whether public or private) to prevent disease, promote health, and prolong life among the population as a whole. Its activities aim to provide conditions in which people can be healthy and focus on entire populations, not on individual patients or diseases. Thus, public health is concerned with the total system and not only the eradication of a particular disease. The three main public health functions are:

1. The assessment and monitoring of the health of communities and populations at risk to identify health problems and priorities.
2. The formulation of public policies designed to solve identified local and national health problems and priorities.
3. To assure that all populations have access to appropriate and cost-effective care, including health promotion and disease prevention services.

Public health initiatives include:

- Vaccination and control of infectious diseases,

- Motor vehicle safety,
- Safer workplaces,
- Safer and healthier foods,
- Safe drinking water,
- Healthier mothers, babies and families,
- Decline in deaths from preventable illnesses such as heart disease, diabetes and cancer (Bonita, Beaglehole, & Kjellstrom, 2006).

Public health providers have been using very large, novel sources of data since 1999, making this section of healthcare one of the earliest adopters of huge datasets to prompt actions in very close to real time. These early initiatives do not meet both criteria for big data analytics, however, as the methods used to analyze the data were not automated, did not use advanced mining algorithms or any kind of machine learning and analyzed static data that was not changing at the time of analysis.

Epidemiology, a subset of public health is defined as the "study of all health and disease" (Morris, 1975), although in more colloquial uses it refers to the study of infectious disease outbreaks, specifically. Digital epidemiology, e-epidemiology and Tele-epidemiology all refer to the use of novel data sources to track infectious disease.

Traditionally, epidemiology has been based on data collected by public health agencies through health personnel in hospitals, doctors offices and out in the field (Salathe, Freifeld, Mekaru, Tomasulo, & Brownstein, 2013). The use of data generated by weather, satellite and ocean technologies created advanced opportunities to detect and respond to infectious disease outbreaks, but digital epidemiology in this form still used standard analytics on static data.

The French National Space Agency (CNES) has carried out several Tele-epidemiology projects that have allowed public health officials to detect infectious disease outbreaks almost as soon they happen.

Some early successes in Tele-epidemiology include:

- **S2E Guyana:** Dengue fever in Guyana.
- **EMERCASE:** Rift Valley fever in Senegal and Southern Mauritania.
- **S2E Argos:** Tropical diseases in Niger and Burkina Faso.
- **S2E Migrating:** Aavian flu in the Camargue area of France, a joint project with the National Institute for Health and Medical Research (INSERM).
- **MATE:** Dengue fever in Argentina, a joint project with the Argentinean Spatial Agency (CONAE).
- **BIBO:** Avian flu, a joint project with the Chinese Space Agency (CRESDA).
- **VIBRIO:** Cholera in the Mediterranean. (Marechal, Ribeiro, Lafaye, & Güell, 2008).

The prime driver for these initiatives is to create or amplify the effects of Early Warning Systems (EWS) to prevent the spread of disease (Thomson & Connor, 2001), which delivers two key benefits:

1. Improved productivity through a dramatic reduction in mortality and morbidity rates.
2. Lower costs through avoidance of economic impact of wide-spread infectious disease.

Public health care providers tend to be driven by the need to improve productivity and reduce the suffering and mortality associated with infectious disease outbreaks. "At its core, public health is concerned with promoting and protecting the health of populations" (Childress et al., 2002). Policy makers, in comparison, tend to be concerned with the economic impact of large scale disease outbreaks, and the impact can be significant. The aggregate annual economic cost of a dengue fever outbreak in Puerto Rico was estimated to be $46 million, and the weighted average cost of treatment per case is $3 078, representing 19% of the per capita GDP ($16 300 in 2010). Who pays these costs?

- 36% paid by government
- 40% incurred by households
- 18% incurred by insurance
- 6% incurred by employers. (Halasa, Shepard, & Zeng, 2012)

Both benefits tend to accrue together in the case of public health administration, and which benefit is stressed depends on whether the perspective of policy or provider is emphasized. In almost every case, both reduced morbidity and mortality and avoidance of costs occurs in tandem.

There are four specific ways that digital data can be used to study infectious disease dynamics:

1. Early detection of outbreaks
2. Continuous monitoring of disease levels
3. Assessment of health related behaviours relevant to disease control
4. Additional method for analyzing the period before an outbreak. (Salathe et al., 2013)

The opportunity for big data in public health administration is to capture data from novel sources such as social media, mobile telecommunications and the Internet to automatically detect opportunities to enhance public health and create alerts that notify relevant personnel at the moment the opportunity is detected.

Google Flu is an excellent example of how a machine algorithm can detect an outbreak of influenza long before health care personnel, by compiling a list of flu-related search words and tracking their entry into the search engine by geographic location (Olson, Konty, Paladini, Viboud, & Simonsen, 2013). Google Flu is not without flaws, and can often miss outbreaks (Olson, 2013), but as the search engine grows increasingly experienced, its abilities will improve. Combining the search engine with results from

retail pharmacies, tracking both over the counter and prescription medicine orders for flu-related symptoms (Patwardhan & Bilkovski, 2012) or emergency room visits for flu-like symptoms (Dugas et al., 2012) increases the predictive efficacy of Google Flu. When the search engine data is further refined through the use of control engineering mathematical models that measure probabilistic dependence between latent state variables, and observed measurements generated by the search engine, the predictive power of the enterprise to detect influenza outbreaks increases (Dukic, Lopes, & Polson, 2012).

The majority of the scholarly literature is concerned with developing the architecture to effectively initiate digital epidemiology that can generate alerts in real time, but little of this has been tested in the field to date. In a review of influenza syndromic surveillance in emergency rooms, none of the 58 studies reviewed made use of big data analytics (Hiller, Stoneking, Min, & Rhodes, 2013), although several stressed the potential big data might offer (Kass-Hout et al., 2012; Painter, Eaton, & Lober, 2013)

Researchers at Johns Hopkins have demonstrated that by mining over 2 billion tweets, Twitter can effectively be used to extract public health information regarding a variety of ailments and conditions, but that demonstration has not yet led to implementation of a Twitter based symptom surveillance program (Paul & Dredze, 2012). See Table 9 for a summary of public health and social media potential.

In a similar vein, researchers were able to illustrate and model individual behaviors using social media data that are capable of predicting depression *before* onset by exploring language, emotion, style, egonetworks and user engagement to predict depressive episodes. The research found that depressive individuals demonstrated the following characteristics:

- Lowered social activity
- Greater negative emotions

Table 9. Public health and social media potential

How to Use Twitter to Track Conditions Using Most Likely Words							
	Allergies	**Insomnia**	**Obesity**	**Injuries**	**Respiratory**	**Dental**	**Aches/Pains**
General	allergies nose eyes allergy allergic	sleep asleep fell awake hours	blood weight eat healthy fat	knee leg right ankle shoulder	throat stop better voice hurts	"ow" teeth tooth wisdom dentist	body needs neck hurts head
Symptoms	sneezing coughing cold nose runny	insomnia fall burning pain falling	pressure weight loss blood high	pain sore arthritis limping neck	cough coughing cold sneeze sneezing	pain toothache sore infection tooth	aches pain sore muscle aching
Treatments	medicine benadryl Claritin zyrtec drops	sleeping pills caffeine Tylenol pill	diet exercise dieting insulin exercising	surgery brace crutches physical therapy	medicine antibiotics codeine vitamin Tylenol	braces pain relief muscle surgery	massage exercise massages bath hot

(Paul & Dredze, 2012)

- High self-attentional focus
- Increased relational and medicinal concerns
- Heightened expression of religious thoughts
- Usually belonged to highly clustered, close-knit networks
- Highly embedded with their audiences. (De Choudhury, Gamon, Counts, & Horvitz, 2013)

In theory, the observation of the above characteristics could trigger an alert to both the individual and a mental health care provider, but at the moment, the opportunity exists only in theory.

An interesting drawback to the use of internet or social media based data sources has to do with signal amplification. In 2011, a team of researchers discovered a link between the use of pravastatin in combination with paroxetine and hyperglycemia, which they confirmed by mining search engines for those specific keywords and related terms. Subsequent media attention to the relationship resulted in many more people searching for those terms, amplifying the signal power and suggesting, incorrectly, that more people were experiencing problems than was actually the case. "Search data are very sensitive to media, marketing and viral social influence ... if there are murmurs there is a dangerous drug, people on the drug will look it up. They may not have the problem, they are just worried" (Kuehn, 2013). It's an on-going issue that architects and designers are attempting to address (Diaz-Aviles, Stewart, Velasco, Denecke, & Nejdl, 2012).

In the area of traffic management, much of the deployment of big data analytics is concerned with military surveying and mapping (Tang & Yuwen, 2013) or military logistics management (tracking personnel and equipment) (Becker et al., 2013). Additionally, most of the literature is concerned with developing the algorithms and architecture necessary to realize the potential benefits, but there have also been some notable successes at using data to improve public safety on the transportation network, both on the ground and in the air (see Table 10) which shows papers describing the actual deployment of big data analytics in the area of public health administration, and the benefits accrued.

Table 10. Demonstrated benefits in the area of public health

Citation	Benefits Described	Summary of Findings
(Takeshi, Makoto, & Yutaka, 2010)	Improved productivity through quick notification and lower costs by alerting citizens to an earthquake in progress	Earthquakes greater than 3 on the seismic scale are detected through the continuous monitoring of Twitter and users in the area of the earthquake are notified that a quake is in progress allowing them to take protective actions
(Schmidt, 2012)	Improved productivity through quick notification and lower costs by alerting citizens to an outbreak in progress	Development of a iPhone application (HealthMap) that mines news websites, government alerts, eyewitness accounts and other data sources for reports of disease outbreaks and then delivers maps directly to users via mobile phones to alert them at the time an outbreak is detected
(Diaz-Aviles et al., 2012)	Improved productivity through quick notification and effective tracking of transmissions and lower costs by alerting citizens to an outbreak in progress	Twitter carefully monitored during an outbreak of *Enterohemorrhagic Escherichia coli* in Germany triggering alarms well before more established systems detected a problem, and effectively tracking transmission patterns
(Chunara, Andrews, & Brownstein, 2012)	Improved productivity through quick notification and effective use of resources and lower costs by alerting citizens to safe water sources and treatment centers before the cholera became serious	Creation of maps (using Health Map) that transmit real time data via mobile phones showing confirmed cases, location of hospitals, treatment centers, safe water installations and water points to combat the cholera epidemic after the 2010 earthquake in Haiti
(Larson et al., 2013)	Improved productivity through instant awareness of vaccine concerns in a specific location and lower costs through avoidance of preventable disease outbreaks	Real time monitoring of negative public opinions about vaccines over social media using Health Maps to allow immunization programs to tailor programs for greater uptake
(Gerz, Tafferner, Park, & Keis, 2012)	Lower costs through better prediction of weather conditions and improved productivity through enhanced safety	Algorithms combine radar, satellite and surface station data to detect snow fall and icing conditions at airports, and report weather conditions in real time, automatically alerting ground crews to changing or dangerous conditions
(Ovide, 2012)	Improved productivity through faster detection of traffic flow problems	Millions of cellphone and GPS signals are combined with car speed information, weather data and sports schedules to detect interruptions in traffic in Woodbridge, N.J., alerting traffic control personnel of problems

FUTURE RESEARCH DIRECTIONS

This chapter organized the relevant literature into six distinct sections: Cost Effectiveness Research (CER), Clinical Decision Support Systems (CDS), Transparency, Remote Patient Monitoring (RPM), Personalized Medicine (PM), and Public Health Administration (PHA). Of the six areas investigated, CDS shows the most use of big data analytics, likely a result of the ability of algorithms to build on the vast data sources about drug regimes captured by automated physician order entry systems. CER has also has some notable successes, again building on the cached data sources maintained by pharmaceutical companies and insurance pro-

viders. Public health, with ample data sources to draw on has been successful in implementing some innovative big data strategies. RPM is just beginning to realize the potential in having advanced, learning algorithms monitor patients with both implantable and wearable devices, which both alert caregivers to potential problems (including device malfunction) and dramatically reduce re-hospitalization rates by detecting problems at the earliest stages.

The biggest setbacks have occurred in the area of PM, where the sequencing of the human genome originally held such promise. The actual practice of genomic medicine has turned out to be vastly technically complex, and requires huge tissue and bio-banks to mine for information. As the technical and infrastructure problems are addressed, the potential for big data will become increasingly easier to harness.

CONCLUSION

In the healthcare sector of the economy, the application of big data analytics is motivated by the dual incentives to reduce the costs of delivering healthcare services and products while improving the ability of healthcare providers to enhance patient outcomes. While costs pressures are significant, there is little evidence that cost alone motivates practitioners to embrace the opportunities and benefits of advanced analytics (Mueller & Szczesny, 2013; Smith, Saunders, Stuckhardt, & McGinnis, 2013; Tuckson, Newcomer, & De Sa, 2013). The benefits of big data accrue primarily to patients in terms of reduced morbidity and mortality rates, more effective and targeted treatments and better monitoring of chronic conditions, and to health services providers who are able to deliver more effective treatments and services while using healthcare resources more efficiently.

The two principle benefits tend to occur in tandem. In the case of RPM, reducing the costs of monitoring patients was a primary driver, but outcomes for patients were almost always improved as well.

Pharmaceutical companies and medical equipment providers are motivated to realize the benefits of capturing additional market share (Gagnon, 2013) and limiting liability (Jones, 2013), but the adoption of particular pharmaceutical regimes or specific equipment in the field is motivated by the initial two benefits of lowering costs while improving patient outcomes.

Table 11 summarizes the findings in each section analyzed.

Most of applications of big data analytics are in nascent stages of adoption. This is particularly true for personalized medicine, but efforts to create the large datasets and tissue banks necessary to realize the full potential of big data are underway, including efforts to communicate the vital importance of these datasets to both patients and practitioners alike. "The critical value of tissue bank samples, bioinformatics, and EMR in the early stages of the biomarker discovery process for personalized medicine is often overlooked," according to Suh et. al. (2013) but that is slowly changing as the benefits of big data analytics accrue and become clear to all stakeholders.

The way forward will require that certain challenges, some very specific to healthcare, be tackled:

Table 11. Summary of findings

Area of Inquiry	Benefit Observed	Primary Beneficiary
Cost Effectiveness Research	Lower costs Improved productivity	Healthcare providers Patients
Clinical Decision Support	Improved productivity Lower costs Increased market share	Patients Healthcare providers Health care providers
Transparency	Improved productivity	Patients
Remote Patient Monitoring	Lower costs	Healthcare providers
Public Health	Improved productivity Lower costs	Patients and the general public Transportation providers
Personalized Medicine	Improved productivity	Patients

- Continual technical advances to store and efficiently access the rapidly expanding amount of data
- Ensuring patient privacy and security
- Collecting good data that is accurate and relatively complete
- Aligning economic incentives to encourage the development of diagnostics. (Adler-Milstein et al., 2013)

Big data is poised to reshape the way we live, work, and think. A worldview built on the importance of causation is being challenged by a preponderance of correlations. The possession of knowledge, which once meant an understanding of the past, is coming to mean an ability to predict the future. The challenges posed by big data will not be easy to resolve. Rather, they are simply the next step in the timeless debate over how to best understand the world. (Cukier & Mayer-Schoenberger, 2013).

REFERENCES

Adler-Milstein, J., Jha, A. K., Caballero, A. E., Davidson, J., Elmi, A., & Gavin, J. et al. (2013). Healthcare's "Big Data" Challenge. *The American Journal of Managed Care*, *19*(7), 537–538. PMID:23919417

Ahern, D. K., Smith, J. M., Topol, E. J., Mack, J. F., & Fitzgerald, M. (2013). Addressing the cost crisis in Health Care. *American Journal of Preventive Medicine*, *44*(1).

Akar, J. G., Bao, H., Jones, P., Wang, Y., Chaudhry, S. I., & Varosy, P. et al. (2013). Use of Remote Monitoring of Newly Implanted Cardioverter-Defibrillators: Insights From the Patient Related Determinants of ICD Remote Monitoring (PREDICT RM) Study. *Circulation*, *128*(22), 2372–2383. doi:10.1161/CIRCULATIONAHA.113.002481 PMID:24043302

Alemi, F., Stephens, R., Parran, T., Llorens, S., Bhatt, P., Ghadiri, A., & Eisenstein, E. (1994). Automated Monitoring of Outcomes Application to Treatment of Drug Abuse. *Medical Decision Making*, *14*(2), 180–187. doi:10.1177/0272989X9401400211 PMID:8028471

Avins, A. L., Cherkin, D. C., Sherman, K. J., Goldberg, H., & Pressman, A. (2012). Should we reconsider the routine use of placebo controls in clinical research? *Trials*, *13*(1), 44. doi:10.1186/1745-6215-13-44 PMID:22540350

Avorn, J., & Fischer, M. (2010). 'Bench to behavior': Translating comparative effectiveness research into improved clinical practice. *Health Affairs*, *29*(10), 1891–1900. doi:10.1377/hlthaff.2010.0696 PMID:20921491

Baer, L., Jacobs, D. G., Cukor, P., O'Laughlen, J., Coyle, J. T., & Magruder, K. M. (1995). Automated telephone screening survey for depression. *Journal of the American Medical Association*, *273*(24), 1943–1944. doi:10.1001/jama.1995.03520480063041 PMID:7783305

Baker, L. C., Johnson, S. J., Macaulay, D., & Birnbaum, H. (2011). Integrated telehealth and care management program for Medicare beneficiaries with chronic disease linked to savings. *Health Affairs*, *30*(9), 1689–1697. doi:10.1377/hlthaff.2011.0216 PMID:21900660

Bates, D. W. (1998). Effect of Computerized Physician Order Entry and a Team Intervention on Prevention of Serious Medication Errors. *Journal of the American Medical Association*, *280*(15), 1311. doi:10.1001/jama.280.15.1311 PMID:9794308

Bates, D. W., Teich, J. M., Lee, J., Seger, D., Kuperman, G. J., & Ma'Luf, N. et al. (1999). The impact of computerized physician order entry on medication error prevention. *Journal of the American Medical Informatics Association*, *6*(4), 313–321. doi:10.1136/jamia.1999.00660313 PMID:10428004

Becker, D., King, T. D., McMullen, B., Lalis, L. D., Bloom, D., Obaidi, A., & Fickitt, D. (2013). Big Data Quality Case Study Preliminary Findings. Bedford, MA: National Security Engineering Center.

Berner, E. S. (2007). *Clinical Decision Support Systems*. Springer Science+Business Media, LLC.

Bernstam, E. V., Smith, J. W., & Johnson, T. R. (2010). What is biomedical informatics? *Journal of Biomedical Informatics*, *43*(1), 104–110. doi:10.1016/j.jbi.2009.08.006 PMID:19683067

Bertot, J. C., Jaeger, P. T., & Grimes, J. M. (2010). Using ICTs to create a culture of transparency: E-government and social media as openness and anti-corruption tools for societies. *Government Information Quarterly*, *27*(3), 264–271. doi:10.1016/j.giq.2010.03.001

Bian, Z.-X., & Wu, T.-X. (2010). Commentary Legislation for trial registration and data transparency. *Trials*, *11*(64).

Bloom, D. E., Börsch-Supan, A., McGee, P., & Seike, A. (2012). Population Ageing: Macro Challenges and Policy Responses. *Global Population Ageing: Peril or Promise?*, 35.

Bollier, D. (2010). *The Promise and Peril of Big Data*. Paper presented at the Eighteenth Annual Aspen Institute Roundtable on Information Technology. Washington, DC. Retrieved from http://creativecommons.org/licenses/by-nc/3.0/us/

Bonita, R., Beaglehole, R., & Kjellstrom, T. (2006). *Basic Epidemiology*. Geneva, Switzerland: World Health Organization.

Bright, T. J., Wong, A., Dhurjati, R., Bristow, E., Bastian, L., & Coeytaux, R. R. et al. (2012). Effect of clinical decision-support systems: A systematic review. *Annals of Internal Medicine*, *157*(1), 29–43. doi:10.7326/0003-4819-157-1-201207030-00450 PMID:22751758

Bult, J. R., & Wansbeek, T. (1995). Optimal Selection for Direct Mail. *Marketing Science*, *14*(4), 378–394. doi:10.1287/mksc.14.4.378

Chalkidou, K., Tunis, S., Lopert, R., Rochaix, L., Sawicki, P. T., Nasser, M., & Xerri, B. (2009). Comparative effectiveness research and evidence-based health policy: Experience from four countries. *The Milbank Quarterly*, *87*(2), 339–367. doi:10.1111/j.1468-0009.2009.00560.x PMID:19523121

Chen, H., Chiang, R. H. L., & Storey, V. C. (2012). Business Intelligence and Analytics: From Big Data to Big Impact. *Management Information Systems Quarterly*, *36*(4), 1165–1188.

Childress, J. F., Faden, R. R., Gaare, R. D., Gostin, L. O., Kahn, J., & Bonnie, R. J. et al. (2002). Public Health Ethics: Mapping the Terrain. *Law. Medical Ethics (Burlington, Mass.)*, *30*(2), 170–178. doi:10.1111/j.1748-720X.2002.tb00384.x PMID:12066595

Christ, G., & Siegel, K. (1990). Monitoring quality-of-life needs of cancer patients. *Cancer*, *65*(S3), 760–765. doi:10.1002/1097-0142(19900201)65:3+<760::AID-CNCR2820651321>3.0.CO;2-F PMID:2302653

Costa, F. F. (2013). Big data in biomedicine. *Drug Discovery Today*. doi:10.1016/j.drudis.2013.10.012

Cryer, L., Shannon, S. B., Van Amsterdam, M., & Leff, B. (2012). Costs for 'hospital at home' patients were 19 percent lower, with equal or better outcomes compared to similar inpatients. *Health Affairs*, *31*(6), 1237–1243. doi:10.1377/hlthaff.2011.1132 PMID:22665835

Cukier, K., & Mayer-Schoenberger, V. (2013). The Rise of Big Data. *Foreign Affairs*, *92*(3), 27–40.

De Choudhury, M., Gamon, M., Counts, S., & Horvitz, E. (2013). *Predicting Depression via Social Media*. Redmond, WA: Microsoft.

Desai, J. R., Bowen, E. A., Danielson, M. M., Allam, R. R., & Cantor, M. N. (2013). Creation and implementation of a historical controls database from randomized clinical trials. *Journal of the American Medical Informatics Association, 20*(e1), e162–e168. doi:10.1136/amiajnl-2012-001257 PMID:23449762

Diaz-Aviles, E., Stewart, A., Velasco, E., Denecke, K., & Nejdl, W. (2012). *Epidemic Intelligence for the Crowd, by the Crowd.* Paper presented at the ICWSM. New York, NY.

Dugas, A. F., Hsieh, Y. H., Levin, S. R., Pines, J. M., Mareiniss, D. P., & Mohareb, A. et al. (2012). Google Flu Trends: Correlation with emergency department influenza rates and crowding metrics. *Clinical Infectious Diseases, 54*(4), 463–469. doi:10.1093/cid/cir883 PMID:22230244

Dukic, V., Lopes, H. F., & Polson, N. G. (2012). Tracking epidemics with google flu trends data and a state-space SEIR model. *Journal of the American Statistical Association, 107*(500), 1410–1426. doi:10.1080/01621459.2012.713876

Eppenga, W. L., Derijks, H. J., Conemans, J. M., Hermens, W. A., Wensing, M., & De Smet, P. A. (2012). Comparison of a basic and an advanced pharmacotherapy-related clinical decision support system in a hospital care setting in the Netherlands. *Journal of the American Medical Association, 19*(1), 66–71. doi:10.1136/amiajnl-2011-000360 PMID:21890873

Field, M. J., & Grigsby, J. (2002). Telemedicine and remote patient monitoring. *Journal of the American Medical Association, 288*(4), 423–425. doi:10.1001/jama.288.4.423 PMID:12132953

Fischer, M. A., & Avorn, J. (2004). Economic implications of evidence-based prescribing for hypertension: Can better care cost less? *Journal of the American Medical Association, 291*(15), 1850–1856. doi:10.1001/jama.291.15.1850 PMID:15100203

Freiburger, G., Holcomb, M., & Piper, D. (2007). The STARPAHC collection: Part of an archive of the history of telemedicine. *Journal of Telemedicine and Telecare, 13*(5), 221–223. doi:10.1258/135763307781458949 PMID:17697507

Gagnon, J. P. (2013). The research manufacturing pharmaceutical industry. In M. I. Smith, A. I. Vertheimer, & J. E. Fincham (Eds.), *Pharmacy and the US Healthcare System* (p. 215). London: Pharmaceutical Press.

Gandjour, A. (2011). Prioritizing Comparative Effectiveness Research. *PharmacoEconomics, 29*(7), 555–561. PMID:21534639

Ginsberg, H. N., Elam, M. B., Lovato, L. C., Crouse, J. R. III, Leiter, L. A., & Linz, P. et al. (2010). Effects of combination lipid therapy in type 2 diabetes mellitus. *The New England Journal of Medicine, 362*(17), 1563–1574. doi:10.1056/NEJMoa1001282 PMID:20228404

González, G. M., Costello, C. R., La Tourette, T. R., Joyce, L. K., & Valenzuela, M. (1997). Bilingual telephone-assisted computerized speech-recognition assessment: Is a voice-activated computer program a culturally and linguistically appropriate tool for screening depression in English and Spanish? *Cultural Diversity and Mental Health, 3*(2), 93–111. doi:10.1037/1099-9809.3.2.93 PMID:9231537

Gøtzsche, P. C. (2011). Why we need easy access to all data from all clinical trials and how to accomplish it. *Trials, 12*(1), 249. doi:10.1186/1745-6215-12-249 PMID:22112900

Guédon-Moreau, L., Mabo, P., & Kacet, S. (2013). Current clinical evidence for remote patient management. *Europace, 15*(suppl 1), i6–i10. doi:10.1093/europace/eut119 PMID:23737234

Gupta, R., Gupta, H., & Mohania, M. (2012). Cloud Computing and Big Data Analytics: What Is New from Databases Perspective? In S. Srinivasa & V. Bhatnagar (Eds.), *Big Data Analytics* (Vol. 7678, pp. 42–61). Springer. doi:10.1007/978-3-642-35542-4_5

Halasa, Y. A., Shepard, D. S., & Zeng, W. (2012). Economic cost of dengue in Puerto Rico. *The American Journal of Tropical Medicine and Hygiene, 86*(5), 745–752. doi:10.4269/ajtmh.2012.11-0784 PMID:22556069

Hamburg, M. A., & Collins, F. S. (2010). The path to personalized medicine. *The New England Journal of Medicine, 363*(4), 301–304. doi:10.1056/NEJMp1006304 PMID:20551152

Hersh, W. (2009). A stimulus to define informatics and health information technology. *BMC Medical Informatics and Decision Making, 9*(1), 24. doi:10.1186/1472-6947-9-24 PMID:19445665

Hiller, K. M., Stoneking, L., Min, A., & Rhodes, S. M. (2013). Syndromic Surveillance for Influenza in the Emergency Department–A Systematic Review. *PLoS ONE, 8*(9), e73832. doi:10.1371/journal.pone.0073832 PMID:24058494

Huser, V., & Cimino, J. J. (2013). Linking ClinicalTrials. gov and PubMed to Track Results of Interventional Human Clinical Trials. *PLoS ONE, 8*(7), e68409. doi:10.1371/journal.pone.0068409 PMID:23874614

Jensen, P. B., Jensen, L. J., & Brunak, S. (2012). Mining electronic health records: Towards better research applications and clinical care. *Nature Reviews. Genetics, 13*(6), 395–405. doi:10.1038/nrg3208 PMID:22549152

Jones, R. M. (2013). *A New World Order: The Expansion of Executive Corporate Liability in the Life Sciences Industry.* Student Scholarship, Paper 250.

Jose, J., & Jingle, I. B. J. (2013). Remote Heart Monitoring and Diagnosis Service Platform via Wearable ECG Monitor. *International Journal of Science, Engineering and Technology Research, 2*(5), 1095–1099.

Joshi, V., Moradshahi, P., & Goubran, R. (2013). *Operating system performance measurements for remote patient monitoring applications.* Paper presented at the Medical Measurements and Applications Proceedings (MeMeA). New York, NY.

Jourdan, Z., Rainer, R. K., & Marshall, T. E. (2008). Business Intelligence: An Analysis of the Literature. *Information Systems Management, 25*(2), 121–131. doi:10.1080/10580530801941512

Kass-Hout, T. A., Xu, Z., McMurray, P., Park, S., Buckeridge, D. L., & Brownstein, J. S. et al. (2012). Application of change point analysis to daily influenza-like illness emergency department visits. *Journal of the American Medical Informatics Association, 19*(6), 1075–1081. doi:10.1136/amiajnl-2011-000793 PMID:22759619

Kawamoto, K., Houlihan, C. A., Balas, E. A., & Lobach, D. F. (2005). Improving clinical practice using clinical decision support systems: A systematic review of trials to identify features critical to success. *British Medical Journal, 330*(7494), 765. doi:10.1136/bmj.38398.500764.8F PMID:15767266

Kho, A. N., Rasmussen, L. V., Connolly, J. J., Peissig, P. L., Starren, J., Hakonarson, H., & Hayes, M. G. (2013). Practical challenges in integrating genomic data into the electronic health record. *Genetics in Medicine, 15*(10), 772–778. doi:10.1038/gim.2013.131 PMID:24071798

Klersy, C., De Silvestri, A., Gabutti, G., Raisaro, A., Curti, M., Regoli, F., & Auricchio, A. (2011). Economic impact of remote patient monitoring: An integrated economic model derived from a meta-analysis of randomized controlled trials in heart failure. *European Journal of Heart Failure, 13*(4), 450–459. doi:10.1093/eurjhf/hfq232 PMID:21193439

Kobak, K. A., Dottl, S. L., Greist, J. H., Jefferson, J. W., Burroughs, D., & Mantle, J. M. et al. (1997). A computer-administered telephone interview to identify mental disorders. *Journal of the American Medical Association, 278*(11), 905–910. doi:10.1001/jama.1997.03550110043034 PMID:9302242

Krasowski, M. D., & Penrod, L. E. (2012). Clinical decision support of therapeutic drug monitoring of phenytoin: Measured versus adjusted phenytoin plasma concentrations. *BMC Medical Informatics and Decision Making, 12*(1), 7. doi:10.1186/1472-6947-12-7 PMID:22333264

Kravitz, R. L. (2014). Personalized Medicine Without the "Omics." *Journal of General Internal Medicine, 29*(4), 551–551. doi:10.1007/s11606-014-2789-x PMID:24504920

Krleža-Jerić, K., & Lemmens, T. (2009). 7th revision of the Declaration of Helsinki: Good news for the transparency of clinical trials. *Croatian Medical Journal, 50*(2), 105–110. doi:10.3325/cmj.2009.50.105 PMID:19399942

Kuehn, B. M. (2013). Scientists mine web search data to identify epidemics and adverse events. *Journal of the American Medical Association, 309*(18), 1883–1884. doi:10.1001/jama.2013.4015 PMID:23652502

Lan, M., Samy, L., Alshurafa, N., Suh, M.-K., Ghasemzadeh, H., Macabasco-O'Connell, A., & Sarrafzadeh, M. (2012). *WANDA: an end-to-end remote health monitoring and analytics system for heart failure patients.* Paper presented at the Conference on Wireless Health. New York, NY. doi:10.1145/2448096.2448105

Lee, S. I., Ghasemzadeh, H., Mortazavi, B., Lan, M., Alshurafa, N., Ong, M., & Sarrafzadeh, M. (2013). *Remote Patient Monitoring: What Impact Can Data Analytics Have on Cost?* Paper presented at the Wireless Health '13. Baltimore, MD. doi:10.1145/2534088.2534108

Lester, D. S. (2009). Will personalized medicine help in 'transforming' the business of healthcare? *Personalized Medicine, 6*(5), 555–565. doi:10.2217/pme.09.31

Llewellyn-Thomas, H. A., McGreal, M. J., Thiel, E. C., Fine, S., & Erlichman, C. (1991). Patients' willingness to enter clinical trials: Measuring the association with perceived benefit and preference for decision participation. *Social Science & Medicine, 32*(1), 35–42. doi:10.1016/0277-9536(91)90124-U PMID:2008619

Mahoney, D., Tennstedt, S., Friedman, R., & Heeren, T. (1999). An automated telephone system for monitoring the functional status of community-residing elders. *The Gerontologist, 39*(2), 229–234. doi:10.1093/geront/39.2.229 PMID:10224719

Manyika, J. Chui, M., Brown, B., Bughin J., Dobbs, R. Roxburgh, C. and Byers, A.H. (2011). *Big Data: The Next Frontier for Innovation, Competition and Productivity.* San Fransisco: McKinsey Global Institute.

Mapcite. (2013). *How Emergency Managers Can Benefit from Big Data.* Retrieved 23/10/13, 2013, from http://www.mapcite.com/posts/2013/july/how-emergency-managers-can-benefit-from-big-data.aspx

Marechal, F., Ribeiro, N., Lafaye, M., & Güell, A. (2008). Satellite imaging and vector-borne diseases: The approach of the French National Space Agency (CNES). *Geospatial Health, 3*(1), 1–5. PMID:19021103

Marjoua, Y., Butler, C. A., & Bozic, K. J. (2012). Public Reporting of Cost and Quality Information in Orthopaedics. *Clinical Orthopaedics and Related Research, 470*(4), 1017–1026. doi:10.1007/s11999-011-2077-6 PMID:21952744

Meijer, C., Wouterse, B., Polder, J., & Koopman-schap, M. (2013). The effect of population aging on health expenditure growth: A critical review. *European Journal of Ageing*, 1–9. doi:10.1007/s10433-013-0280-x

Mello, M. M., Francer, J. K., Wilenzick, M., Teden, P., Bierer, B. E., & Barnes, M. (2013). Preparing for responsible sharing of clinical trial data. *The New England Journal of Medicine*. PMID:24144394

Millard, R. W., & Carver, J. R. (1999). Cross-sectional comparison of live and interactive voice recognition administration of the SF-12 health status survey. *The American Journal of Managed Care*, 5(2), 153. PMID:10346511

Mitic, M., & Kapoulas, A. (2012). Understanding the role of social media in bank marketing. *Marketing Intelligence & Planning*, 30(7), 668–686. doi:10.1108/02634501211273797

Morgan, S., Grootendorst, P., Lexchin, J., Cunningham, C., & Greyson, D. (2011). The cost of drug development: A systematic review. *Health Policy (Amsterdam)*, 100(1), 4–17. doi:10.1016/j.healthpol.2010.12.002 PMID:21256615

Morris, J. N. (1975). *Uses of Epidemiology*. Edinburgh, UK: Churchill Livingstone.

Morton, L. W., & Weng, C.-Y. (2013). Health and Healthcare Among the Rural Aging. In N. Glasgow & E. H. Berry (Eds.), Rural Aging in 21st Century America (Vol. 7, pp. 179-194). Springer Netherlands. doi:10.1007/978-94-007-5567-3_10

Moxey, A., Robertson, J., Newby, D., Hains, I., Williamson, M., & Pearson, S.-A. (2010). Computerized clinical decision support for prescribing: Provision does not guarantee uptake. *Journal of the American Medical Informatics Association*, 17(1), 25–33. doi:10.1197/jamia.M3170 PMID:20064798

Mueller, S., & Szczesny, A. (2013). *Cost Pressure, Rationalization, Specialization and the Quality of Health Care*. Social Sciences Research Network.

Mushlin, A. I., & Ghomrawi, H. (2010). Health Care Reform and the Need for Comparative-Effectiveness Research. *The New England Journal of Medicine*, 362(3), e6. doi:10.1056/NEJMp0912651 PMID:20054035

Neumann, P. J., Palmer, J. A., Nadler, E., Fang, C.-H., & Ubel, P. (2010). Cancer Therapy Costs Influence Treatment: A National Survey Of Oncologists. *Health Affairs*, 29(1), 196–202. doi:10.1377/hlthaff.2009.0077 PMID:20048377

Nicolaidis, S. (2013). Personalized medicine in neurosurgery. *Metabolism*, 62, S45–S48. doi:10.1016/j.metabol.2012.08.022

NYGC. (2014). *The New York Genome Center and IBM Watson Group Announce Collaboration to Advance Genomic Medicine*. Retrieved April 17, 2014, 2014, from http://www.nygenome.org/news/new-york-genome-center-ibm-watson-group-announce-collaboration-advance-genomic-medicine/

Ogwueleka, F. N. (2011). Data Mining Application in Credit Card Fraud Detection System. *Journal of Engineering Science and Technology*, 6(3), 311–322.

Olson, D. R. (2013). *How Accurate Is Google Flu Trends? A Comparative Study of Internet Search Data and Public Health Syndromic Surveillance for Monitoring Seasonal and Pandemic Influenza, 2003-2013*. Paper presented at the 2013 CSTE Annual Conference. New York, NY.

Olson, D. R., Konty, K. J., Paladini, M., Viboud, C., & Simonsen, L. (2013). Reassessing Google Flu Trends Data for Detection of Seasonal and Pandemic Influenza: A Comparative Epidemiological Study at Three Geographic Scales. *PLoS Computational Biology*, 9(10), e1003256. doi:10.1371/journal.pcbi.1003256 PMID:24146603

Orszag, P. R., & Emanuel, E. J. (2010). Health care reform and cost control. *The New England Journal of Medicine*, *363*(7), 601–603. doi:10.1056/NEJMp1006571 PMID:20554975

Outterson, K. (2012). Punishing Health Care Fraud–Is the GSK Settlement Sufficient? *The New England Journal of Medicine*, *367*(12), 1082–1085. doi:10.1056/NEJMp1209249 PMID:22970920

Painter, I., Eaton, J., & Lober, B. (2013). Using Change Point Detection for Monitoring the Quality of Aggregate Data. *Online Journal of Public Health Informatics*, *5*(1). doi:10.5210/ojphi.v5i1.4597

Pandor, A., Gomersall, T., Stevens, J. W., Wang, J., Al-Mohammad, A., & Bakhai, A. et al. (2013). Remote monitoring after recent hospital discharge in patients with heart failure: A systematic review and network meta-analysis. *Heart (British Cardiac Society)*, *99*(23), 1717–1726. doi:10.1136/heartjnl-2013-303811 PMID:23680885

Patel, U. H., & Babbs, C. F. (1992). A computer-based, automated, telephonic system to monitor patient progress in the home setting. *Journal of Medical Systems*, *16*(2-3), 101–112. doi:10.1007/BF00996591 PMID:1402436

Patwardhan, A., & Bilkovski, R. (2012). Comparison: Flu Prescription Sales Data from a Retail Pharmacy in the US with Google Flu Trends and US ILINet (CDC) Data as Flu Activity Indicator. *PLoS ONE*, *7*(8), e43611. doi:10.1371/journal.pone.0043611 PMID:22952719

Paul, M. J., & Dredze, M. (2012). A model for mining public health topics from Twitter. *Health*, *11*, 16–16.

Pekmezaris, R., Mitzner, I., Pecinka, K. R., Nouryan, C. N., Lesser, M. L., & Siegel, M. et al. (2012). The impact of remote patient monitoring (telehealth) upon Medicare beneficiaries with heart failure. *Telemedicine Journal and e-Health*, *18*(2), 101–108. doi:10.1089/tmj.2011.0095 PMID:22283360

Perrine, M. W., Mundt, J. C., Searles, J. S., & Lester, L. S. (1995). Validation of daily self-reported alcohol consumption using interactive voice response (IVR) technology. *Journal of Studies on Alcohol and Drugs*, *56*(5), 487. PMID:7475027

Persson, U., Willis, M., & Odegaard, K. (2010). A case study of ex ante, value-based price and reimbursement decision-making: TLV and rimonabant in Sweden. *The European Journal of Health Economics*, *11*(2), 195–203. doi:10.1007/s10198-009-0166-1 PMID:19639352

Piette, J. D. (2000). Interactive voice response systems in the diagnosis and management of chronic disease. *The American Journal of Managed Care*, *6*(7), 817–827. PMID:11067378

Piette, J. D., & Mah, C. A. (1997). The feasibility of automated voice messaging as an adjunct to diabetes outpatient care. *Diabetes Care*, *20*(1), 15–21. doi:10.2337/diacare.20.1.15 PMID:9028687

Piette, J. D., McPhee, S. J., Weinberger, M., Mah, C. A., & Kraemer, F. B. (1999). Use of automated telephone disease management calls in an ethnically diverse sample of low-income patients with diabetes. *Diabetes Care*, *22*(8), 1302–1309. doi:10.2337/diacare.22.8.1302 PMID:10480775

Porter, M. E. (2008). *Competitive advantage: Creating and sustaining superior performance*. Simon and Schuster.

Radhakrishnan, K., Jacelon, C., & Roche, J. (2012). Perceptions on the Use of Telehealth by Homecare Nurses and Patients With Heart Failure: A Mixed Method Study. *Home Health Care Management & Practice*, 24(4), 175–181. doi:10.1177/1084822311428335

Rani, J. K., Kumar, S. P., Mohan, U. R., & Shankar, C. U. (2011). Credit Card Fraud Detection Analysis. *International Journal of Computer Trends and Technology*, 2(1), 24–27.

Reed, J., Murray, K., & Jacobson, M. (2013). Digitization Standards at the National Archives and Records Administration. *Archiving Conference*, 2013(1), 211-215.

Reuben, D. B., & Tinetti, M. E. (2012). Goal-oriented patient care--an alternative health outcomes paradigm. *The New England Journal of Medicine*, 366(9), 777–779. doi:10.1056/NEJMp1113631 PMID:22375966

Rich, J., Howe, J., Larson, L., & Chuang, C. (2013). Implementing Interactive Voice Recognition Technology to Activate Vulnerable Patients. *Journal of the International Society for Telemedicine and eHealth*, 1(1), 3-11.

Romano, M. J., & Stafford, R. S. (2011). Electronic health records and clinical decision support systems: Impact on national ambulatory care quality. *Archives of Internal Medicine*, 171(10), 897–903. doi:10.1001/archinternmed.2010.527 PMID:21263077

Rozenbaum, M. H., Sanders, E. A. M., van Hoek, A. J., Jansen, A. G. S. C., van der Ende, A., & van den Dobbelsteen, G. et al. (2010). Cost effectiveness of pneumococcal vaccination among Dutch infants: Economic analysis of the seven valent pneumococcal conjugated vaccine and forecast for the 10 valent and 13 valent vaccines. *BMJ (Clinical Research Ed.)*, 340(1), c2509. doi:10.1136/bmj.c2509 PMID:20519267

Russell, L. B., Gold, M. R., Siegel, J. E., Daniels, N., & Weinstein, M. C. (1996). THe role of cost-effectiveness analysis in health and medicine. *Journal of the American Medical Association*, 276(14), 1172–1177. doi:10.1001/jama.1996:03540140060028 PMID:8827972

Salathe, M., Freifeld, C. C., Mekaru, S. R., Tomasulo, A. F., & Brownstein, J. S. (2013). Influenza A (H7N9) and the importance of digital epidemiology. *The New England Journal of Medicine*, 369(5), 401–404. doi:10.1056/NEJMp1307752 PMID:23822655

Sarkar, I. N. (2010). Biomedical informatics and translational medicine. *Journal of Translational Medicine*, 8(22), 12. PMID:20187952

Scharnweber, C., Lau, B. D., Mollenkopf, N., Thiemann, D. R., Veltri, M. A., & Lehmann, C. U. (2013). Evaluation of medication dose alerts in pediatric inpatients. *International Journal of Medical Informatics*, 82(8), 676–683. doi:10.1016/j.ijmedinf.2013.04.002 PMID:23643148

Shea, S., Weinstock, R. S., Starren, J., Teresi, J., Palmas, W., & Field, L. et al. (2006). A randomized trial comparing telemedicine case management with usual care in older, ethnically diverse, medically underserved patients with diabetes mellitus. *Journal of the American Medical Informatics Association*, 13(1), 40–51. doi:10.1197/jamia.M1917 PMID:16221935

Sibbald, B. (2004). Legal action against GSK over SSRI data. *Canadian Medical Association Journal, 171*(1), 23-23a.

Siegel, J. P., Rosenthal, N., Buto, K., Lilienfeld, S., Thomas, A., & Odenthal, S. (2012). Comparative Effectiveness Research in the Regulatory Setting. *Pharmaceutical Medicine*, 26(1), 5–11. doi:10.1007/BF03256887

Smith, M., Saunders, R., Stuckhardt, L., & McGinnis, J. M. (2013). *Best care at lower cost: the path to continuously learning health care in America.* National Academies Press.

Sox, H. C., & Greenfield, S. (2009). Comparative Effectiveness Research: A Report From the Institute of Medicine. *Annals of Internal Medicine, 151*(3), 203–205. doi:10.7326/0003-4819-151-3-200908040-00125 PMID:19567618

Sproull, R. F., & Eisenberg, J. (2005). Building an electronic records archive at the National Archives and Records Administration recommendations for a long-term strategy (p. xii). Retrieved from http://ezproxy.usq.edu.au/login?url=http://site.ebrary.com/lib/unisouthernqld/Doc?id=10082366

Suh, K. S., Sarojini, S., Youssif, M., Nalley, K., Milinovikj, N., & Elloumi, F. et al. (2013). Tissue banking, bioinformatics, and electronic medical records: The front-end requirements for personalized medicine. *Journal of Oncology, 368751.* doi:10.1155/2013/368751 PMID:23818899

Suzuki, S., & Matsui, T. (2012). *Remote sensing for medical and health care applications.* Remote Sensing-Applications. doi:10.5772/36924

Tang, L., & Yuwen, J. (2013). *The Study on Digital Traffic Service System and Key Technologies of Location Based Service.* Paper presented at the 2013 the International Conference on Remote Sensing, Environment and Transportation Engineering (RSETE 2013). New York, NY. doi:10.2991/rsete.2013.148

Thomson, M. C., & Connor, S. J. (2001). The development of Malaria Early Warning Systems for Africa. *Trends in Parasitology, 17*(9), 438–445. doi:10.1016/S1471-4922(01)02077-3 PMID:11530356

Timbie, J. W., Fox, D. S., Van Busum, K., & Schneider, E. C. (2012). Five Reasons That Many Comparative Effectiveness Studies Fail To Change Patient Care And Clinical Practice. *Health Affairs, 31*(10), 2168–2175. doi:10.1377/hlthaff.2012.0150 PMID:23048092

Towse, A., Ossa, D., Veenstra, D., Carlson, J., & Garrison, L. (2013). Understanding the Economic Value of Molecular Diagnostic Tests: Case Studies and Lessons Learned. *Journal of Personalized Medicine, 3*(4), 288–305. doi:10.3390/jpm3040288

Trowbridge, R., & Weingarten, S. (2001). Clinical decision support systems. *Making health care safer: A critical analysis of patient safety practices. Evidence Report/technology Assessment*, 43.

Tuckson, R. V., Newcomer, L., & De Sa, J. M. (2013). Accessing genomic medicine: Affordability, diffusion, and disparities. *Journal of the American Medical Association, 309*(14), 1469–1470. doi:10.1001/jama.2013.1468 PMID:23571584

Vedder, R. G., Vanecek, M. T., Guynes, C. S., & Cappel, J. J. (1999). CEO and CIO perspectives on competitive intelligence. *Communications of the ACM, 42*(8), 108–116. doi:10.1145/310930.310982

Venkat, A., Chan-Tompkins, N. H., Hegde, G. G., Chuirazzi, D. M., Hunter, R., & Szczesiul, J. M. (2010). Feasibility of integrating a clinical decision support tool into an existing computerized physician order entry system to increase seasonal influenza vaccination in the emergency department. *Vaccine, 28*(37), 6058–6064. doi:10.1016/j.vaccine.2010.06.090 PMID:20620167

Vogeli, C., Shields, A. E., Lee, T. A., Gibson, T. B., Marder, W. D., Weiss, K. B., & Blumenthal, D. (2007). Multiple Chronic Conditions: Prevalence, Health Consequences, and Implications for Quality, Care Management, and Costs. *Journal of General Internal Medicine, 22*(3), 391–395. doi:10.1007/s11606-007-0322-1 PMID:18026807

Weinstein, M. C., & Stason, W. B. (1977). Foundations of cost-effectiveness analysis for health and medical practices. *The New England Journal of Medicine, 296*(13), 716–721. doi:10.1056/NEJM197703312961304 PMID:402576

Willig, J. H., Krawitz, M., Panjamapirom, A., Ray, M. N., Nevin, C. R., & English, T. M. et al. (2013). Closing the Feedback Loop: An Interactive Voice Response System to Provide Follow-up and Feedback in Primary Care Settings. *Journal of Medical Systems*, *37*(2), 1–9. doi:10.1007/s10916-012-9905-4 PMID:23340825

WorldMedicalAssociation. (2013). World Medical Association declaration of Helsinki: Ethical principles for medical research involving human subjects. *Journal of the American Medical Association*.

Wright, A., Sittig, D. F., Ash, J. S., Sharma, S., Pang, J. E., & Middleton, B. (2009). Clinical Decision Support Capabilities of Commercially-available Clinical Information Systems. *Journal of the American Medical Informatics Association*, *16*(5), 637–644. doi:10.1197/jamia.M3111 PMID:19567796

KEY TERMS AND DEFINITIONS

Artificial Intelligence: Algorithms and applications that address classification, prediction, web mining and machine learning.

Big Data: Pools of information so large that conventional analytical techniques cannot make sense of them. Requires use of dynamic data that is changing at the time of analysis, advanced algorithms and very large datasets.

Biomedical Informatics: The science of information applied to medicine.

Business Intelligence: The use of data to enhance competitiveness.

Clinical Decision Support Systems: Software programs that anticipate probable outcomes of particular treatment strategies by comparing the proposed treatment to previous patient outcomes.

Clinical Operations: All the actions that relate to the patient bedside, including diagnosing and monitoring the course of disease or trauma or other injury, and all observations and treatments administered.

Competitive Advantage: Anything that enhances an organization's ability to carry out its mission.

Cost Advantage: Arises when an organization can deliver the same products or services as competitors at a lower cost.

Cost Effectiveness Research: Healthcare resource allocation guided by considering the costs of a particular treatment in relation to the expected benefits.

Differentiation Advantage: Arises when an organization can deliver products or services with benefits that exceed those of the competition.

Electronic Health Record: A digital copy of a patient's health record.

Epigenetics: The study of heritable changes in gene activity which are not caused by changes in the DNA sequence.

Genomics: A discipline in genetics that applies recombinant DNA, DNA sequencing methods and bioinformatics to sequence, assemble, and analyze the structure and function of genomes (the complete set of DNA within a single organism).

Improved Productivity: Delivering products and services more efficiently, which may or may not result in a cost advantage.

Metabolomics: The study of the unique chemical fingerprints that specific cellular processes leave behind.

Personalized Medicine: The use of modern imaging and exploratory technologies to disclose genomic, proteomic and epigenetic information peculiar to each patient, in the effort to individualize prognosis and therapeutic care.

Price Premium: The ability to charge a higher price for a product or service that has greater perceived value than competing products or services.

Proteomics: The study of the function and structure of the complete set of proteins produced or modified by an organism or system.

Public Health Administration: All organized measures (whether public or private) to prevent disease, promote health, and prolong life among the population as a whole.

Remote Patient Monitoring: Continuous monitoring of the physiological status of patients using heterogeneous sensors such as blood pressure, weight, blood glucose, and/or physical activity sensors in order to shift medical services from hospital and clinical settings to an in-home monitoring scenario.

Transparency: Sharing of information between healthcare providers, patients and other health care organizations.

Tele-Epidemiology: The study of human and animal epidemics, the spread of which is closely tied to environmental factors. By combining data from various earth-orbiting satellites, hydrology data and clinical data from humans and animals, outbreaks of infectious disease can be predicted with accuracy.

Compilation of References

Abdi, H., Williams, L.J., & Valentin, D. (2013). Multiple factor analysis: Principal component analysis for multitable and multiblock data sets component analysis for multitable and multiblock data sets. *WIREs Comput Stat.* doi: 10.1002/wics.124

Abecasis, G. R., Altshuler, D., Auton, A., Brooks, L. D., Durbin, R. M., Gibbs, R. A., & McVean, G. A. (2010). A map of human genome variation from population-scale sequencing. *Nature, 467*(7319), 1061–1073. doi:10.1038/nature09534 PMID:20981092

Abecasis, G. R., Cardon, L. R., & Cookson, W. O. C. (2000). A General Test of Association for Quantitative Traits in Nuclear Families. *American Journal of Human Genetics, 66*(1), 279–292. doi:10.1086/302698 PMID:10631157

Abecasis, G. R., Cherny, S. S., Cookson, W. O., & Cardon, L. R. (2002). Merlin—rapid analysis of dense genetic maps using sparse gene flow trees. *Nature Genetics, 30*(1), 97–101. doi:10.1038/ng786 PMID:11731797

Abeel, T., Helleputte, T., Van de Peer, Y., Dupont, P., & Saeys, Y. (2010). Robust biomarker identification for cancer diagnosis with ensemble feature selection methods. *Bioinformatics (Oxford, England), 26*(3), 392–398. doi:10.1093/bioinformatics/btp630 PMID:19942583

ABS. (2011). *Australian Social Trends, Online @home.* Commonwealth of Australia.

Adami, H. O., Hunter, D., & Trichopoulos, D. (2002). *Textbook of Cancer Epidemiology.* New York: Oxford University Press.

Adams, R., Clark, A., Yamaguchi, A., Hanlon, N., Tsorman, N., & Ali, S. et al. (2013). SBSI: An extensible distributed software infrastructure for parameter estimation in systems biology. *Bioinformatics (Oxford, England), 29*(5), 664–665. doi:10.1093/bioinformatics/btt023 PMID:23329415

Adiamah, D. A., & Schwartz, J. M. (2012). Construction of a genome-scale kinetic model of *Mycobacterium tuberculosis* using generic rate equations. *Metabolites, 2*(4), 382–397. doi:10.3390/metabo2030382 PMID:24957639

Adler-Milstein, J., Jha, A. K., Caballero, A. E., Davidson, J., Elmi, A., & Gavin, J. et al. (2013). Healthcare's "Big Data" Challenge. *The American Journal of Managed Care, 19*(7), 537–538. PMID:23919417

Adnan, A. (2010). *Introduction to bioinformatics: Role of mathematics and technology.* Retrieved from biotecharticles.com

Adrio, J. L., & Demain, A. L. (2010). Recombinant organisms for production of industrial products. *Bioengineered Bugs, 1*(2), 116–131. doi:10.4161/bbug.1.2.10484 PMID:21326937

Aerts, S., Haeussler, M., van Vooren, S., Griffith, O. L., Hulpiau, P., & Jones, S. J. et al. (2008). Text-mining assisted regulatory annotation. *Genome Biology, 9*(2), R31. doi:10.1186/gb-2008-9-2-r31 PMID:18271954

Aerts, S., Lambrechts, D., Maity, S., Van Loo, P., Coessens, B., & De Smet, F. et al. (2006). Gene prioritization through genomic data fusion. *Nature Biotechnology, 24*(5), 537–544. doi:10.1038/nbt1203 PMID:16680138

Affymetrix. (2006). *BRLMM: An improved genotype calling method for the GeneChip Human Mapping 500K Array Set* (Revision version 1.0). Affymetrix.

Aflakparast, M., Salimi, H., Gerami, A., Dubé, M.-P., Visweswaran, S., & Masoudi-Nejad, A. (2014). Cuckoo search epistasis: A new method for exploring significant genetic interactions. *Heredity*, *112*(6), 666–674. doi:10.1038/hdy.2014.4 PMID:24549111

Agopian, A., & Mitchell, L. E. (2011). MI-GWAS: A SAS platform for the analysis of inherited and maternal genetic effects in genome-wide association studies using log-linear models. *BMC Bioinformatics*, *12*(1), 117. doi:10.1186/1471-2105-12-117 PMID:21513519

Agranat, L., Raitskin, O., Sperling, J., & Sperling, R. (2008). The editing enzyme ADAR1 and the mRNA surveillance protein hUpf1 interact in the cell nucleus. *Proceedings of the National Academy of Sciences of the United States of America*, *105*(13), 5028–5033. doi:10.1073/pnas.0710576105 PMID:18362360

Ahern, D. K., Smith, J. M., Topol, E. J., Mack, J. F., & Fitzgerald, M. (2013). Addressing the cost crisis in Health Care. *American Journal of Preventive Medicine*, *44*(1).

AIHW. (2012). *Australia's health 2012. Australia's health no. 13. Cat. no. AUS 156*. Canberra: AIHW.

Akar, J. G., Bao, H., Jones, P., Wang, Y., Chaudhry, S. I., & Varosy, P. et al. (2013). Use of Remote Monitoring of Newly Implanted Cardioverter-Defibrillators: Insights From the Patient Related Determinants of ICD Remote Monitoring (PREDICT RM) Study. *Circulation*, *128*(22), 2372–2383. doi:10.1161/CIRCULATIONAHA.113.002481 PMID:24043302

Alaiya, A., Al-Mohanna, M., & Linder, S. (2005). Clinical cancer proteomics: Promises and pitfalls. *Journal of Proteome Research*, *4*(4), 1213–1222. doi:10.1021/pr050149f PMID:16083271

Alemi, F., Stephens, R., Parran, T., Llorens, S., Bhatt, P., Ghadiri, A., & Eisenstein, E. (1994). Automated Monitoring of Outcomes Application to Treatment of Drug Abuse. *Medical Decision Making*, *14*(2), 180–187. doi:10.1177/0272989X9401400211 PMID:8028471

Allal, A. S., Kähne, T., Reverdin, A. K., Lippert, H., Schlegel, W., & Reymond, M.-A. (2004). Radioresistance-related proteins in rectal cancer. *Proteomics*, *4*(8), 2261–2269. doi:10.1002/pmic.200300854 PMID:15274120

Allison, D. B. (1997). Transmission-disequilibrium tests for quantitative traits. *American Journal of Human Genetics*, *60*(3), 676–690. PMID:9042929

Allwood, J., Ellis, D., & Goodacre, R. (2008). Metabolomic technologies and their application to the study of plants and plant-host interactions. *Physiologia Plantarum*, *132*(2), 117–135. PMID:18251855

Al-Mubaid, H., & Singh, R. K. (2010). A text-mining technique for extracting gene-disease associations from the biomedical literature. *International Journal of Bioinformatics Research and Applications*, *6*(3), 270–286. doi:10.1504/IJBRA.2010.034075 PMID:20615835

Almufti, R., Wilbaux, M., Oza, A., Henin, E., Freyer, G., & Tod, M. et al. (2014). A critical review of the analytical approaches for circulating tumor biomarker kinetics during treatment. *Annals of Oncology*, *25*(1), 41–56. doi:10.1093/annonc/mdt382 PMID:24356619

Alon, U. (2007). *An introduction to systems biology: design principles of biological circuits*. Boca Raton, FL: Chapman & Hall/CRC.

Alsner, J., Andreassen, C. N., & Overgaard, J. (2008). Genetic markers for prediction of normal tissue toxicity after radiotherapy. *Seminars in Radiation Oncology*, *18*(2), 126–135. doi:10.1016/j.semradonc.2007.10.004 PMID:18314067

Altshuler, D. M., Gibbs, R. A., Peltonen, L., Dermitzakis, E., Schaffner, S. F., & Yu, F. L. et al. (2010). Integrating common and rare genetic variation in diverse human populations. *Nature*, *467*(7311), 52–58. doi:10.1038/nature09298 PMID:20811451

Aly, T. A., Eller, E., Ide, A., Gowan, K., Babu, S. R., & Erlich, H. A. et al. (2006). Multi-SNP Analysis of MHC Region: Remarkable Conservation of HLA-A1-B8-DR3 Haplotype. *Diabetes*, *55*(5), 1265–1269. doi:10.2337/db05-1276 PMID:16644681

Amaral, A. F., Porta, M., Silverman, D. T., Milne, R. L., Kogevinas, M., & Rothman, N. et al. (2012). Pancreatic cancer risk and levels of trace elements. *Gut*, *61*(11), 1583–1588. doi:10.1136/gutjnl-2011-301086 PMID:22184070

Amir, B.-D., & Zohar, Y. (1999). Clustering gene expression patterns. In *Proceedings of the third annual international conference on Computational molecular biology*. ACM.

Amundadottir, L., Kraft, P., Stolzenberg-Solomon, R. Z., Fuchs, C. S., Petersen, G. M., & Arslan, A. A. et al. (2009). Genome-wide association study identifies variants in the ABO locus associated with susceptibility to pancreatic cancer. *Nature Genetics*, *41*(9), 986–990. doi:10.1038/ng.429 PMID:19648918

An Integrated Encyclopedia of DNA Elements in the Human Genome. (2012). *Nature, 489*(7414), 57-74.

Anderson, K. E., Mack, T. M., & Silverman, D. T. (2006). Pancreatic cancer. In Textbook of Cancer Epidemiology (2nd ed., pp. 333-343). Oxford, UK: Oxford University Press.

Anderson, C. A., Pettersson, F. H., Clarke, G. M., Cardon, L. R., Morris, A. P., & Zondervan, K. T. (2010). Data quality control in genetic case-control association studies. *Nature Protocols*, *5*(9), 1564–1573. doi:10.1038/nprot.2010.116 PMID:21085122

Andreassen, C. N., & Alsner, J. (2009). Genetic variants and normal tissue toxicity after radiotherapy: A systematic review. *Radiotherapy and Oncology*, *92*(3), 299–309. doi:10.1016/j.radonc.2009.06.015 PMID:19683821

Andrieu, C., Freitas Nando, D., & Doucet, A. (2001). Robust full Bayesian learning for radial basis networks. *Neural Computation*, *13*(10), 2359–2407. doi:10.1162/089976601750541831 PMID:11571002

Ansorge, W. J. (2009). Next-generation DNA sequencing techniques. *New Biotechnology*, *25*(4), 195–203. doi:10.1016/j.nbt.2008.12.009 PMID:19429539

Apanasovich, T. V., Carroll, R. J., & Maity, A. (2009). SIMEX and standard error estimation in semiparametric measurement error models. *Electron J Stat*, *3*(0), 318–348. doi:10.1214/08-EJS341 PMID:19609371

Ardolino, A., Sleat, G., & Willett, K. (2012). Outcome measurements in major trauma—Results of a consensus meeting. *Injury. Int. J. Care Injured*, *43*(10), 1662–1666. doi:10.1016/j.injury.2012.05.008 PMID:22695320

Arnold, P., Erb, I., Pachkov, M., Molina, N., & Nimwegen, E. (2012). MotEvo: Integrated Bayesian probabilistic methods for inferring regulatory sites and motifs on multiple alignments of DNA sequences. *Bioinformatics (Oxford, England)*, *28*(4), 487–494. doi:10.1093/bioinformatics/btr695 PMID:22334039

Arslan, A. A., Helzlsouer, K. J., Kooperberg, C., Shu, X. O., Steplowski, E., & Bueno-de-Mesquita, H. B. et al. Pancreatic Cancer Cohort, Consortium. (2010). Anthropometric measures, body mass index, and pancreatic cancer: A pooled analysis from the Pancreatic Cancer Cohort Consortium (PanScan). *Archives of Internal Medicine*, *170*(9), 791–802. doi:10.1001/archinternmed.2010.63 PMID:20458087

Aschard, H., Lutz, S., Maus, B., Duell, E. J., Fingerlin, T. E., & Chatterjee, N. et al. (2012). Challenges and opportunities in genome-wide environmental interaction (GWEI) studies. *Human Genetics*, *131*(10), 1591–1613. doi:10.1007/s00439-012-1192-0 PMID:22760307

Ashburner, M., Ball, C. A., Blake, J. A., Botstein, D., Butler, H., & Cherry, J. M. et al. (2000). Gene ontology: Tool for the unification of biology. The Gene Ontology Consortium. *Nature Genetics*, *25*(1), 25–29. doi:10.1038/75556 PMID:10802651

Asmann, Y. W., Klee, E. W., Thompson, E. A., Perez, E. A., Middha, S., & Oberg, A. L. et al. (2009). 3' tag digital gene expression profiling of human brain and universal reference RNA using Illumina Genome Analyzer. *BMC Genomics*, *10*(1), 531. doi:10.1186/1471-2164-10-531 PMID:19917133

Association, T. G. (2010). Risk Management: Research on Risk Managemant, Assessment and Prevention. *Geneva Association Information Newsletter, 47*. Retrieved January, 2014, from http://aws.amazon.com/glacier/pricing/

Aten, J. E., Fuller, T. F., Lusis, A. J., & Horvath, S. (2008). Using genetic markers to orient the edges in quantitative trait networks: The NEO software. *BMC Systems Biology*, *2*(1), 34. doi:10.1186/1752-0509-2-34 PMID:18412962

Auffray, C., Caulfield, T., Khoury, M. J., Lupski, J. R., Schwab, M., & Veenstra, T. (2013). 2012 highlights in translational 'omics. *Genome Medicine*, *5*(1), 10. PMID:23369291

Augui, S., Nora, E. P., & Heard, E. (2011). Regulation of X-chromosome inactivation by the X-inactivation centre. *Nat Rev Genet, 12*(6), 429-442.

AustinHealth. (2014). *Austin Health*. Retrieved 6th Nov, 2013, from www.austin.org.au

Avins, A. L., Cherkin, D. C., Sherman, K. J., Goldberg, H., & Pressman, A. (2012). Should we reconsider the routine use of placebo controls in clinical research? *Trials*, *13*(1), 44. doi:10.1186/1745-6215-13-44 PMID:22540350

Avogadri, R., & Valentini, G. (2009). Fuzzy ensemble clustering based on random projections for DNA microarray data analysis. *Artificial Intelligence in Medicine*, *45*(2-3), 173–183. doi:10.1016/j.artmed.2008.07.014 PMID:18801650

Avorn, J., & Fischer, M. (2010). 'Bench to behavior': Translating comparative effectiveness research into improved clinical practice. *Health Affairs*, *29*(10), 1891–1900. doi:10.1377/hlthaff.2010.0696 PMID:20921491

Ayers, K. L., & Cordell, H. J. (2010). SNP Selection in genome-wide and candidate gene studies via penalized logistic regression. *Genetic Epidemiology*, *34*(8), 879–891. doi:10.1002/gepi.20543 PMID:21104890

Baer, L., Jacobs, D. G., Cukor, P., O'Laughlen, J., Coyle, J. T., & Magruder, K. M. (1995). Automated telephone screening survey for depression. *Journal of the American Medical Association*, *273*(24), 1943–1944. doi:10.1001/jama.1995.03520480063041 PMID:7783305

Bagos, P. G. (2013). Genetic model selection in genome-wide association studies: Robust methods and the use of meta-analysis. *Statistical Applications in Genetics and Molecular Biology*, *12*(3). doi:10.1515/sagmb-2012-0016 PMID:23629457

Bailey, T., & Elkan, C. (1994). Fitting a mixture model by expectation maximization to discovery motifs in biopolymers. In *Proc. 2nd. Intl. Conf. on Intell. Sys. for Mol. Bio.*, (pp. 28-36). Academic Press.

Bairoch, A., & Apweiler, R. (2000). The SWISS-PROT protein sequence database and its supplement TrEMBL in 2000. *Nucleic Acids Research*, *28*(1), 45–48. doi:10.1093/nar/28.1.45 PMID:10592178

Baker, L. C., Johnson, S. J., Macaulay, D., & Birnbaum, H. (2011). Integrated telehealth and care management program for Medicare beneficiaries with chronic disease linked to savings. *Health Affairs*, *30*(9), 1689–1697. doi:10.1377/hlthaff.2011.0216 PMID:21900660

Baker, M. (2013). Big biology: The 'omes puzzle. *Nature*, *494*(7438), 416–419. doi:10.1038/494416a PMID:23446398

Baker, W., van den Broek, A., Camon, E., Hingamp, P., Sterk, P., Stoesser, G., & Tuli, M. A. (2000). The EMBL Nucleotide Sequence Database. *Nucleic Acids Research*, *28*(1), 19–23. doi:10.1093/nar/28.1.19 PMID:10592171

Balding, D. J. (2006). A tutorial on statistical methods for population association studies. *Nature Reviews. Genetics*, *7*(10), 781–791. doi:10.1038/nrg1916 PMID:16983374

Ballestar, E. (Ed.). (2011). *Epigenetic contributions in autoimmune disease*. Heidelberg, Germany: Springer. doi:10.1007/978-1-4419-8216-2

Ban, H.-J., Heo, J. Y., Oh, K.-S., & Park, K.-J. (2010). Identification of Type 2 Diabetes-associated combination of SNPs using Support Vector Machine. *BMC Genetics*, *11*(1), 26. doi:10.1186/1471-2156-11-26 PMID:20416077

Bansal, A. (2005). Bioinformatics in microbial biotechnology – a mini review. *Microbial Cell Factories*, *4*(1), 19. doi:10.1186/1475-2859-4-19 PMID:15985162

Barker, W. C., Garavelli, J. S., Huang, H. Z., McGarvey, P. B., Orcutt, B. C., & Srinivasarao, G. Y. et al. (2000). The Protein Information Resource (PIR). *Nucleic Acids Research*, *28*(1), 41–44. doi:10.1093/nar/28.1.41 PMID:10592177

Barreiro, L. B., Laval, G., Quach, H., Patin, E., & Quintana-Murci, L. (2008). Natural selection has driven population differentiation in modern humans. *Nature Genetics*, *40*(3), 340–345. doi:10.1038/ng.78 PMID:18246066

Barrios-Gonzalez, J., Fernandez, F. J., & Tomasini, A. (2003). Microbial secondary metabolites production and strain improvement. *Indian Journal of Biotechnology*, 2(3), 322–333.

Barry, W. T., Nobel, A. B., & Wright, F. A. (2005). Significance analysis of functional categories in gene expression studies: A structured permutation approach. *Bioinformatics (Oxford, England)*, 21(9), 1943–1949. doi:10.1093/bioinformatics/bti260 PMID:15647293

Bartocci, E., Cacciagrano, D., Berardini, M. R. D., Merelli, E., & Vito, L. (2012). UBioLab: A web laboratory for ubiquitous *in silico* experiments. *Journal of Integrative Bioinformatics*, 9, 192. PMID:22773116

Batagelj, V., & Mrvar, A. (1998). Pajek – Program for Large Network Analysis. *Connections*, 21, 47–57.

Bateman, A., Birney, E., Durbin, R., Eddy, S. R., Howe, K. L., & Sonnhammer, E. L. L. (2000). The Pfam protein families database. *Nucleic Acids Research*, 28(1), 263–266. doi:10.1093/nar/28.1.263 PMID:10592242

Bates, D. W. (1998). Effect of Computerized Physician Order Entry and a Team Intervention on Prevention of Serious Medication Errors. *Journal of the American Medical Association*, 280(15), 1311. doi:10.1001/jama.280.15.1311 PMID:9794308

Bates, D. W., Teich, J. M., Lee, J., Seger, D., Kuperman, G. J., & Ma'Luf, N. et al. (1999). The impact of computerized physician order entry on medication error prevention. *Journal of the American Medical Informatics Association*, 6(4), 313–321. doi:10.1136/jamia.1999.00660313 PMID:10428004

Bauer-Mehren, A., Rautschka, M., Sanz, F., & Furlong, L. I. (2010). DisGeNET: A Cytoscape plugin to visualize, integrate, search and analyze gene-disease networks. *Bioinformatics (Oxford, England)*, 26(22), 2924–2926. doi:10.1093/bioinformatics/btq538 PMID:20861032

Baumann, M., Hölscher, T., & Begg, A. C. (2003). Towards genetic prediction of radiation responses: ESTRO's GENEPI project. *Radiotherapy and Oncology*, 69(2), 121–125. doi:10.1016/j.radonc.2003.08.006 PMID:14643948

Baylin, S. B., Esteller, M., Rountree, M. R., Bachman, K. E., Schuebel, K., & Herman, J. G. (2001). Aberrant patterns of DNA methylation, chromatin formation and gene expression in cancer. *Human Molecular Genetics*, 10(7), 687–692. doi:10.1093/hmg/10.7.687 PMID:11257100

BCLHD. (2014). *British Columbia Linked Health Database*. Retrieved 12th Jan, 2014, from https://www.popdata.bc.ca/datalinkage

Becker, D., King, T. D., McMullen, B., Lalis, L. D., Bloom, D., Obaidi, A., & Fickitt, D. (2013). Big Data Quality Case Study Preliminary Findings. Bedford, MA: National Security Engineering Center.

Begum, F., Ghosh, D., Tseng, G. C., & Feingold, E. (2012). Comprehensive literature review and statistical considerations for GWAS meta-analysis. *Nucleic Acids Research*, 40(9), 3777–3784. doi:10.1093/nar/gkr1255 PMID:22241776

Belfield, E. et al. (2014). *Microarray-based optimization to detect genomic deletion mutations*. Genomics Data.

Benson, D. A., Karsch-Mizrachi, I., Lipman, D. J., Ostell, J., Rapp, B. A., & Wheeler, D. L. (2000). GenBank. *Nucleic Acids Research*, 28(1), 15–18. doi:10.1093/nar/28.1.15 PMID:10592170

Bentzen, S. M. (2008). From cellular to high-throughput predictive assays in radiation oncology: Challenges and opportunities. *Seminars in Radiation Oncology*, 18(2), 75–88. doi:10.1016/j.semradonc.2007.10.003 PMID:18314062

Bentzen, S. M., Constine, L. S., Deasy, J. O., Eisbruch, A., Jackson, A., & Marks, L. B. et al. (2010). Quantitative Analyses of Normal Tissue Effects in the Clinic (QUANTEC): An introduction to the scientific issues. *International Journal of Radiation Oncology, Biology, Physics*, 76(3Suppl), S3–S9. doi:10.1016/j.ijrobp.2009.09.040 PMID:20171515

Berner, E. S. (2007). *Clinical Decision Support Systems*. Springer Science+ Business Media, LLC.

Bernstam, E. V., Smith, J. W., & Johnson, T. R. (2010). What is biomedical informatics? *Journal of Biomedical Informatics*, 43(1), 104–110. doi:10.1016/j.jbi.2009.08.006 PMID:19683067

Bernstein, B. E., Birney, E., Dunham, I., Green, E. D., Gunter, C., & Snyder, M. (2012). An integrated encyclopedia of DNA elements in the human genome. *Nature*, *489*(7414), 57–74. doi:10.1038/nature11247 PMID:22955616

Bertot, J. C., Jaeger, P. T., & Grimes, J. M. (2010). Using ICTs to create a culture of transparency: E-government and social media as openness and anti-corruption tools for societies. *Government Information Quarterly*, *27*(3), 264–271. doi:10.1016/j.giq.2010.03.001

Beste, D. J. V., Hooper, T., Stewart, G., Bonde, B., Avignone-Rossa, C., & Bushell, M. E. et al. (2007). GSMN-TB: A web-based genome-scale network model of *Mycobacterium tuberculosis* metabolism. *Genome Biology*, *8*(5), R89. doi:10.1186/gb-2007-8-5-r89 PMID:17521419

Beyer, M. (2011). *Gartner Says Solving 'Big Data' Challenge Involves More Than Just Managing Volumes of Data*. Gartner. Retrieved from http://www.gartner.com/newsroom/id/1731916

Bezdek, J. (1973). Cluster validity with fuzzy sets. *J. Cybernet*, *3*(3), 58–73. doi:10.1080/01969727308546047

Bezdek, J. (1981). *Pattern Recognition with Fuzzy Objective Function Algorithms*. New York: Plenum. doi:10.1007/978-1-4757-0450-1

Bhagwat, V. M., & Ramachandran, B. V. (1975). Malathion A and B esterases of mouse liver-I. *Biochemical Pharmacology*, *24*(18), 1713–1717. doi:10.1016/0006-2952(75)90011-8 PMID:14

Bian, Z.-X., & Wu, T.-X. (2010). Commentary Legislation for trial registration and data transparency. *Trials*, *11*(64).

Blanco, A. I., Chao, K. S., El Naqa, I., Franklin, G. E., Zakarian, K., Vicic, M., & Deasy, J. O. (2005). Dose-volume modeling of salivary function in patients with head-and-neck cancer receiving radiotherapy. *International Journal of Radiation Oncology, Biology, Physics*, *62*(4), 1055–1069. doi:10.1016/j.ijrobp.2004.12.076 PMID:15990009

Bleik, S., Mishra, M., Huan, J., & Song, M. (2013). Text Categorization of Biomedical Data Sets Using Graph Kernels and a Controlled Vocabulary. *IEEE/ACM Transactions on Computational Biology and Bioinformatics*, *10*(5), 1211–1217. doi:10.1109/TCBB.2013.16 PMID:24384709

Bloom, D. E., Börsch-Supan, A., McGee, P., & Seike, A. (2012). Population Ageing: Macro Challenges and Policy Responses. *Global Population Ageing: Peril or Promise?*, 35.

Blueggel, M., Chamrad, D., & Meyer, H. (2004). Bioinformatics in proteomics. *Current Pharmaceutical Biotechnology*, *5*(1), 79–88. doi:10.2174/1389201043489648 PMID:14965211

Bodmer, W., & Bonilla, C. (2008). Common and rare variants in multifactorial susceptibility to common diseases. *Nature Genetics*, *40*(6), 695–701. doi:10.1038/ng.f.136 PMID:18509313

Boehme, C. C., Nabeta, P., Hillemann, D., Nicol, M. P., Shenai, S., & Krapp, F. et al. (2010). Rapid molecular detection of tuberculosis and rifampin resistance. *The New England Journal of Medicine*, *363*(11), 1005–1015. doi:10.1056/NEJMoa0907847 PMID:20825313

Bohensky, M. A., Jolley, D., Sundararajan, V., Evans, S., Pilcher, D. V., Scott, I., & Brand, C. A. (2010). Data linkage: A powerful research tool with potential problems. *BMC Health Services Research*, *10*(1), 346–346. doi:10.1186/1472-6963-10-346 PMID:21176171

Boissonneault, V., Plante, I., Rivest, S., & Provost, P. (2009). MicroRNA-298 and microRNA-328 regulate expression of mouse beta-amyloid precursor protein-converting enzyme 1. *The Journal of Biological Chemistry*, *284*(4), 1971–1981. doi:10.1074/jbc.M807530200 PMID:18986979

Bollier, D. (2010). *The Promise and Peril of Big Data*. Paper presented at the Eighteenth Annual Aspen Institute Roundtable on Information Technology. Washington, DC. Retrieved from http://creativecommons.org/licenses/by-nc/3.0/us/

Bonita, R., Beaglehole, R., & Kjellstrom, T. (2006). *Basic Epidemiology*. Geneva, Switzerland: World Health Organization.

Bordbar, A., Lewis, N. E., Schellenberger, J., Palsson, B. O., & Jamshidi, N. (2010). Insight into human alveolar macrophage and *M. tuberculosis* interactions via metabolic reconstructions. *Molecular Systems Biology*, *6*, 422. doi:10.1038/msb.2010.68 PMID:20959820

Botstein, D., & Risch, N. (2003). Discovering genotypes underlying human phenotypes: Past successes for mendelian disease, future approaches for complex disease. *Nature Genetics*, *33*(3sSuppl), 228–237. doi:10.1038/ng1090 PMID:12610532

Bouaziz, M., Ambroise, C., & Guedj, M. (2011). Accounting for population stratification in practice: A comparison of the main strategies dedicated to genome-wide association studies. *PLoS ONE*, *6*(12), e28845. doi:10.1371/journal.pone.0028845 PMID:22216125

Bouchez, D., & Hofte, H. (1998). Functional genomics in plants. *Plant Physiology*, *118*(3), 725–732. doi:10.1104/pp.118.3.725 PMID:9808716

Bozdogan, H. (1987). Model selection and Akaike's Information Criterion (AIC): The general theory and its analytical extensions. *Psychometrika*, *52*(3), 345–370. doi:10.1007/BF02294361

Bradley, J. D., Hope, A., El Naqa, I., Apte, A., Lindsay, P. E., Bosch, W., . . . Deasy, J. O. (2007). A nomogram to predict radiation pneumonitis, derived from a combined analysis of RTOG 9311 and institutional data. *Int J Radiat Oncol Biol Phys*, *69*(4), 985-992. doi: 10.1016/j.ijrobp.2007.04.077

Bradley, J., Deasy, J. O., Bentzen, S., & El-Naqa, I. (2004). Dosimetric correlates for acute esophagitis in patients treated with radiotherapy for lung carcinoma.[pii]. *International Journal of Radiation Oncology, Biology, Physics*, *58*(4), 1106–1113. doi:10.1016/j.ijrobp.2003.09.080 PMID:15001251

Bray, N. J., Buckland, P. R., Owen, M. J., & O'Donovan, M. C. (2003). Cis-acting variation in the expression of a high proportion of genes in human brain. *Human Genetics*, *113*(2), 149–153. doi:10.1007/s00439-003-0956-y PMID:12728311

Brazma, A. (2009). Minimum Information About a Microarray Experiment (MIAME)--successes, failures, challenges. *TheScientificWorldJournal*, *9*, 420–423. doi:10.1100/tsw.2009.57 PMID:19484163

Brazma, A., Hingamp, P., Quackenbush, J., Sherlock, G., Spellman, P., & Stoeckert, C. et al. (2001). Minimum information about a microarray experiment (MIAME)-toward standards for microarray data. *Nature Genetics*, *29*(4), 365–371. doi:10.1038/ng1201-365 PMID:11726920

Brenner, S., Johnson, M., Bridgham, J., Golda, G., Lloyd, D. H., Johnson, D., & Corcoran, K. (2000). Gene expression analysis by massively parallel signature sequencing (MPSS) on microbead arrays. *Nature Biotechnology*, *18*(6), 630–634. doi:10.1038/76469 PMID:10835600

Bright, T. J., Wong, A., Dhurjati, R., Bristow, E., Bastian, L., & Coeytaux, R. R. et al. (2012). Effect of clinical decision-support systems: A systematic review. *Annals of Internal Medicine*, *157*(1), 29–43. doi:10.7326/0003-4819-157-1-201207030-00450 PMID:22751758

Brohee, S., & van Helden, J. (2006). Evaluation of clustering algorithms for protein-protein interaction networks. *BMC Bioinformatics*, *7*(1), 488. doi:10.1186/1471-2105-7-488 PMID:17087821

Browning, B. L., & Browning, S. R. (2009). A Unified Approach to Genotype Imputation and Haplotype-Phase Inference for Large Data Sets of Trios and Unrelated Individuals. *American Journal of Human Genetics*, *84*(2), 210–223. doi:10.1016/j.ajhg.2009.01.005 PMID:19200528

Browning, S. R. (2008). Missing data imputation and haplotype phase inference for genome-wide association studies. *Human Genetics*, *124*(5), 439–450. doi:10.1007/s00439-008-0568-7 PMID:18850115

Browning, S. R., & Browning, B. L. (2007). Rapid and accurate haplotype phasing and missing-data inference for whole-genome association studies by use of localized haplotype clustering. *American Journal of Human Genetics*, *81*(5), 1084–1097. doi:10.1086/521987 PMID:17924348

Brown, M. P., Grundy, W. N., Lin, D., Cristianini, N., Sugnet, C. W., Furey, T. S., & Haussler, D. (2000). Knowledge-based analysis of microarray gene expression data by using support vector machines. *Proceedings of the National Academy of Sciences of the United States of America*, *97*(1), 262–267. doi:10.1073/pnas.97.1.262 PMID:10618406

Bryant, J. M., Schurch, A. C., Deutekom, H., Harris, S. R., Beer, J. L., & Jager, V. D. et al. (2013). Inferring patient to patient transmission of *Mycobacterium tuberculosis* from whole genome sequencing data. *BMC Infectious Diseases*, *13*(1), 110. doi:10.1186/1471-2334-13-110 PMID:23446317

Bult, J. R., & Wansbeek, T. (1995). Optimal Selection for Direct Mail. *Marketing Science, 14*(4), 378–394. doi:10.1287/mksc.14.4.378

Burnet, N. G., Elliott, R. M., Dunning, A., & West, C. M. L. (2006). Radiosensitivity, Radiogenomics and RAPPER. *Clinical Oncology, 18*(7), 525–528. doi:10.1016/j.clon.2006.05.007 PMID:16969982

Bussink, J., Kaanders, J. H. A. M., van der Graaf, W. T. A., & Oyen, W. J. G. (2011). PET-CT for radiotherapy treatment planning and response monitoring in solid tumors. *Nat Rev Clin Oncol, 8*(4), 233–242. doi:10.1038/nrclinonc.2010.218 PMID:21263464

Butcher, E. C., Berg, E. L., & Kunkel, E. J. (2004). System biology in drug discovery. *Nature Biotechnology, 22*(10), 1253–1259. doi:10.1038/nbt1017 PMID:15470465

Bůžková, P. (2013). Linear Regression in Genetic Association Studies. *PLoS ONE, 8*(2), e56976. doi:10.1371/journal.pone.0056976 PMID:23437286

Cabili, M. N., Trapnell, C., Goff, L., Koziol, M., Tazon-Vega, B., Regev, A., & Rinn, J. L. (2011). Integrative annotation of human large intergenic noncoding RNAs reveals global properties and specific subclasses. *Genes & Development, 25*(18), 1915–1927. doi:10.1101/gad.17446611 PMID:21890647

Cairo, A. (2013). *The functional art: an introduction to information graphics and visualization.* Academic Press.

Çakir, M., Wirth, H., Hopp, L., & Binder, H. (2014). MicroRNA Expression Landscapes in Stem Cells, Tissues, and Cancer. In M. Yousef & J. Allmer (Eds.), *miRNomics: MicroRNA Biology and Computational Analysis* (Vol. 1107, pp. 279–302). New York: Humana Press.

California Institute of Technology, Washington University of St. Louis & The Wellcome Trust Sanger Institute. (2013). *Mission Statement.* Retrieved Jan. 10, 2014, from WormBase: Nematode Information Resource: https://www.wormbase.org/about#0--10

Calvert, J. (2013). Systems biology, big science and grand challenges. *Biosocieties, 8*(4), 466–479. doi:10.1057/biosoc.2013.27

Cannataro, M. (2008). Computational proteomics: Management and analysis of proteomics data. *Briefings in Bioinformatics, 9*(2), 97–101. doi:10.1093/bib/bbn011 PMID:18310104

Cao, L. J., Chua, K. S., Chong, W. K., Lee, H. P., & Gu, Q. M. (2003). A comparison of PCA, KPCA and ICA for dimensionality reduction in support vector machine. *Neurocomputing, 55*(1&2), 321–336.

Cao, S., Wang, F., Tam, W., Tse, L. A., Kim, J. H., Liu, J., & Lu, Z. (2013). A hybrid seasonal prediction model for tuberculosis incidence in China. *BMC Medical Informatics and Decision Making, 13*(1), 56. doi:10.1186/1472-6947-13-56 PMID:23638635

Cardin, N. J., Mefford, J. A., & Witte, J. S. (2012). Joint Association Testing of Common and Rare Genetic Variants Using Hierarchical Modeling: Joint Association Testing of Common and Rare Genetic Variants. *Genetic Epidemiology, 36*(6), 642–651. doi:10.1002/gepi.21659 PMID:22807252

Cardon, L. R., & Palmer, L. J. (2003). Population stratification and spurious allelic association. *Lancet, 361*(9357), 598–604. doi:10.1016/S0140-6736(03)12520-2 PMID:12598158

Carroll, R. J. (1989). Covariance analysis in generalized linear measurement error models. *Statistics in Medicine, 8*(9), 1075–1093. doi:10.1002/sim.4780080907 PMID:2678349

Carroll, R. J., Delaigle, A., & Hall, P. (2009). Nonparametric Prediction in Measurement Error Models. *Journal of the American Statistical Association, 104*(487), 993–1014. doi:10.1198/jasa.2009.tm07543 PMID:20448838

Carroll, R. J., Roeder, K., & Wasserman, L. (1999). Flexible parametric measurement error models. *Biometrics, 55*(1), 44–54. doi:10.1111/j.0006-341X.1999.00044.x PMID:11318178

Carroll, R. J., & Stefanski, L. A. (1994). Measurement error, instrumental variables and corrections for attenuation with applications to meta-analyses. *Statistics in Medicine, 13*(12), 1265–1282. doi:10.1002/sim.4780131208 PMID:7973207

Carthew, R. W., & Sontheimer, E. J. (2009). Origins and Mechanisms of miRNAs and siRNAs. *Cell, 136*(4), 642–655. doi:10.1016/j.cell.2009.01.035 PMID:19239886

Casari, G., Andrade, A., Bork, P., Boyle, J., Daruvar, A., & Ouzounis, C. et al. (1995). Challenging times for bioinformatics. *Nature, 376*(6542), 647–648. doi:10.1038/376647a0 PMID:7651513

Caspi, R., Altman, T., Billington, R., Dreher, K., Foerster, H., & Fulcher, C. A. et al. (2014). The MetaCyc database of metabolic pathways and enzymes and the BioCyc collection of Pathway/Genome Databases. *Nucleic Acids Research, 42*(1), D459–D471. doi:10.1093/nar/gkt1103 PMID:24225315

Castillo-Chavez, C., & Song, B. (2004). Dynamical models of tuberculosis and their applications. *Mathematical Biosciences and Engineering, 1*(2), 361–404. doi:10.3934/mbe.2004.1.361 PMID:20369977

Center for Disease Control. (2013, August 16). *HIV, STD, & Teen Pregnancy Prevention.* Retrieved Jan. 17, 2014, from CDC - Sexual Risk Behavior: http://www.cdc.gov/HealthyYouth/sexualbehaviors/

Center for Disease Control. (2013, July 11). *CDC - Transmission Risk.* Retrieved Jan. 14, 2014, from CDC - HIV and the Law: http://www.cdc.gov/hiv/policies/law/risk.html

Chakrabarty, A. M., Mylroic, J. R., Friello, D. A., & Vacca, J. G. (1975). Transformation of Pseudomonas putida and Escherichia coli with plasmid-linked drug-resistance factor DNA. *Proceedings of the National Academy of Sciences of the United States of America, 72*(9), 3647–3651. doi:10.1073/pnas.72.9.3647 PMID:1103151

Chalkidou, K., Tunis, S., Lopert, R., Rochaix, L., Sawicki, P. T., Nasser, M., & Xerri, B. (2009). Comparative effectiveness research and evidence-based health policy: Experience from four countries. *The Milbank Quarterly, 87*(2), 339–367. doi:10.1111/j.1468-0009.2009.00560.x PMID:19523121

Chang, C.-J., Kuo, H.-C., Chang, J.-S., Lee, J.-K., Tsai, F.-J., & Khor, C. C. et al. (2013). Replication and Meta-Analysis of GWAS Identified Susceptibility Loci in Kawasaki Disease Confirm the Importance of B Lymphoid Tyrosine Kinase (BLK) in Disease Susceptibility. *PLoS ONE, 8*(8), e72037. doi:10.1371/journal.pone.0072037 PMID:24023612

Chan, M., Liaw, C. S., Ji, S. M., Tan, H. H., Wong, C. Y., & Thike, A. A. et al. (2013). Identification of circulating microRNA signatures for breast cancer detection. *Clinical Cancer Research, 19*(16), 4477–4487. doi:10.1158/1078-0432.CCR-12-3401 PMID:23797906

Chaudhuri, R. R., Yu, L., Kanji, A., Perkins, T. T., Gardner, P. P., & Choudhary, J. et al. (2011). Quantitative RNA-seq analysis of the Campylobacter jejuni transcriptome. *Microbiology, 157*(Pt 10), 2922–2932. doi:10.1099/mic.0.050278-0 PMID:21816880

Che, R. J., Motsinger-Reif, A., & Brown, C. (In Submission). An adaptive permutation approach for genome-wide association study: Evaluation and recommendations for use. *BMC BioData Mining.*

Chelala, C., Khan, A., & Lemoine, N. R. (2009). SNPnexus: A web database for functional annotation of newly discovered and public domain single nucleotide polymorphisms. *Bioinformatics (Oxford, England), 25*(5), 655–661. doi:10.1093/bioinformatics/btn653 PMID:19098027

Chen, C. C., Schwender, H., Keith, J., Nunkesser, R., Mengersen, K., & Macrossan, P. (2011). Methods for identifying SNP interactions: A review on variations of Logic Regression, Random Forest and Bayesian logistic regression. *IEEE/ACM Transactions on Computational Biology and Bioinformatics, 8*(6), 1580–1591. doi:10.1109/TCBB.2011.46 PMID:21383421

Chen, G., Wang, C., & Shi, T. (2011). Overview of available methods for diverse RNA-Seq data analyses. *Sci China Life Sci, 54*(12), 1121–1128. doi:10.1007/s11427-011-4255-x PMID:22227904

Chen, H. Y., & Li, M. (2011). Improving power and robustness for detecting genetic association with extreme-value sampling design. *Genetic Epidemiology, 35*(8), 823–830. doi:10.1002/gepi.20631 PMID:22006659

Chen, H., Chiang, R. H. L., & Storey, V. C. (2012). Business Intelligence and Analytics: From Big Data to Big Impact. *Management Information Systems Quarterly, 36*(4), 1165–1188.

Chen, H., & Sharp, B. M. (2004). Content-rich biological network constructed by mining PubMed abstracts. *BMC Bioinformatics, 5*(1), 147. doi:10.1186/1471-2105-5-147 PMID:15473905

Chen, J., & Greider, C. W. (2005). Functional analysis of the pseudoknot structure in human telomerase RNA. *Proceedings of the National Academy of Sciences of the United States of America, 102*(23), 8080–8085. doi:10.1073/pnas.0502259102 PMID:15849264

Chen, X., Zen, K., & Zhang, C. Y. (2013). Reply to Lack of detectable oral bioavailability of plant microRNAs after feeding in mice. *Nature Biotechnology, 31*(11), 967–969. doi:10.1038/nbt.2741 PMID:24213764

Chen, Y., Wu, X., & Jiang, R. (2013). Integrating human omics data to prioritize candidate genes. *BMC Medical Genomics, 6*(1), 57. doi:10.1186/1755-8794-6-57 PMID:24344781

Childress, J. F., Faden, R. R., Gaare, R. D., Gostin, L. O., Kahn, J., & Bonnie, R. J. et al. (2002). Public Health Ethics: Mapping the Terrain. *Law. Medical Ethics (Burlington, Mass.), 30*(2), 170–178. doi:10.1111/j.1748-720X.2002.tb00384.x PMID:12066595

Choi, H., & Pavelka, N. (2011). When one and one gives more than two: Challenges and opportunities of integrative omics. *Frontiers in Genetics, 2*, 105. PMID:22303399

Cho, S., & Yoo, S. (2006). Fuzzy Bayesian validation for cluster analysis of yeast cell-cycle data. *Pattern Recognition, 39*(12), 2405–2414. doi:10.1016/j.patcog.2005.12.007

Christen, P. (2012). Data matching [electronic resource]: Concepts and techniques for record linkage, entity resolution, and duplicate detection. Berlin: Springer.

Christen, P., & Churches, T. (2006). *Secure health data linkage and geocoding: Current approaches and research directions.* Paper presented at the National e-Health Privacy and Security Symposium. New York, NY.

Christen, P., Willmore, A., & Churches, T. (2006). *A probabilistic geocoding system utilising a parcel based address file.* Cairns: Springer.

Christen, P. (2013). *Data Matching.* Heidelberg, Germany: Springer.

Christen, P., Churches, T., & Hegland, M. (2004). *Febrl - A parallel open source data linkage system.* Sydney: Springer. doi:10.1007/978-3-540-24775-3_75

Christensen, R. (2011). *Bayesian ideas and data analysis: an introduction for scientists and statisticians.* Boca Raton, FL: CRC Press.

Christ, G., & Siegel, K. (1990). Monitoring quality-of-life needs of cancer patients. *Cancer, 65*(S3), 760–765. doi:10.1002/1097-0142(19900201)65:3+<760::AID-CNCR2820651321>3.0.CO;2-F PMID:2302653

Chun, H. W., Tsuruoka, Y., Kim, J. D., Shiba, R., Nagata, N., Hishiki, T., & Tsujii, J. (2006). Extraction of gene-disease relations from Medline using domain dictionaries and machine learning. *Pacific Symposium on Biocomputing*, 4-15. doi:10.1142/9789812701626_0002

Chu, S., DeRisi, J., Eisen, M., Mulholland, J., Botstein, D., Brown, P., & Herskowitz, I. (1998). The transcriptional program of sporulation in budding yeast. *Science, 282*(5389), 699–705. doi:10.1126/science.282.5389.699 PMID:9784122

Chu, S., Keerthi, S., Ong, C. J., & Ghahramani, Z. (2006). Bayesian Support Vector Machines for Feature Ranking and Selection. In I. Guyon & A. Elisseeff (Eds.), *Feature Extraction: Studies in Fuzziness and Soft Computing* (Vol. 207, pp. 403–418). Berlin: Springer. doi:10.1007/978-3-540-35488-8_19

Chute, C. G., Ullman-Cullere, M., Wood, G. M., Lin, S. M., He, M., & Pathak, J. (2013). Some experiences and opportunities for big data in translational research. *Genetics in Medicine, 15*(10), 802–809. doi:10.1038/gim.2013.121 PMID:24008998

Chu, Y., & Corey, D. R. (2012). RNA sequencing: Platform selection, experimental design, and data interpretation. *Nucleic Acid Ther, 22*(4), 271–274. doi:10.1089/nat.2012.0367 PMID:22830413

Ciampi, A., Chang, C., Hogg, S., & McKinney, S. (1987). Recursive partition: a versatile method for exploratory data analysis in biostatistics. In *Proceedings from Joshi Festschrift* (pp. 23–50). Amsterdam: North-Holland. doi:10.1007/978-94-009-4794-8_2

Cibulskis, K., Lawrence, M. S., Carter, S. L., Sivachenko, A., Jaffe, D., & Sougnez, C. et al. (2013). Sensitive detection of somatic point mutations in impure and heterogeneous cancer samples. *Nature Biotechnology, 31*(3), 213–219. doi:10.1038/nbt.2514 PMID:23396013

Clancy, S. (2008). DNA Transcription. *Nature Education, 1*(1), 41.

Clarke, G. M., Anderson, C. A., Pettersson, F. H., Cardon, L. R., Morris, A. P., & Zondervan, K. T. (2011). Basic statistical analysis in genetic case-control studies. *Nature Protocols, 6*(2), 121–133. doi:10.1038/nprot.2010.182 PMID:21293453

Clarke, J., Wu, H. C., Jayasinghe, L., Patel, A., Reid, S., & Bayley, H. (2009). Continuous base identification for single-molecule nanopore DNA sequencing. *Nature Nanotechnology, 4*(4), 265–270. doi:10.1038/nnano.2009.12 PMID:19350039

Clayton, D. (1994). Measurement error: Effects and remedies in nutritional epidemiology. *The Proceedings of the Nutrition Society, 53*(1), 37–42. doi:10.1079/PNS19940007 PMID:8029234

Clayton, D. G., Walker, N. M., Smyth, D. J., Pask, R., Cooper, J. D., & Maier, L. M. et al. (2005). Population structure, differential bias and genomic control in a large-scale, case-control association study. *Nature Genetics, 37*(11), 1243–1246. doi:10.1038/ng1653 PMID:16228001

Clemente, J. C., Ursell, L. K., Parfrey, L. W., & Knight, R. (2012). The impact of the gut microbiota on human health: An integrative view. *Cell, 148*(6), 1258–1270. doi:10.1016/j.cell.2012.01.035 PMID:22424233

Cloonan, N., Forrest, A. R., Kolle, G., Gardiner, B. B., Faulkner, G. J., & Brown, M. K. et al. (2008). Stem cell transcriptome profiling via massive-scale mRNA sequencing. *Nature Methods, 5*(7), 613–619. doi:10.1038/nmeth.1223 PMID:18516046

Cobelens, F., Kampen, S., Ochodo, E., Atun, R., & Lienhardt, C. (2012). Research on implementation of interventions in tuberculosis control in low and middle income countries: A systematic review. *PLoS Medicine, 9*(12), e1001358. doi:10.1371/journal.pmed.1001358 PMID:23271959

Cohan, K. B., Christianse, T., Baumgartner, W. A., Jr., Verspoor, K., & Hunter, L. E. (2011). Fast and simple semantic class assignment for biomedical text. In *Proceedings of Workshop on Biomedical Natural Language Processing*, (pp. 38-45). Academic Press.

Cohen, R. (2012). *Gartner Announces 2012 Magic Quadrant for Cloud Infrastructure as a Service*. Retrieved from http://www.forbes.com/sites/reuvencohen/2012/10/22/gartner-announces-2012-magic-quadrant-for-cloud-infrastructure-as-a-service/

Cohen, A. M., & Hersh, W. R. (2005). A survey of current work in biomedical text mining. *Briefings in Bioinformatics, 6*(1), 57–71. doi:10.1093/bib/6.1.57 PMID:15826357

Cole, C., Sobala, A., Lu, C., Thatcher, S. R., Bowman, A., & Brown, J. W. et al. (2009). Filtering of deep sequencing data reveals the existence of abundant Dicer-dependent small RNAs derived from tRNAs. *RNA (New York, N.Y.), 15*(12), 2147–2160. doi:10.1261/rna.1738409 PMID:19850906

Colijn, C., Brandes, A., Zucker, J., Lun, D. S., Weiner, B., & Farhat, M. R. et al. (2009). Interpreting expression data with metabolic flux models: Predicting *Mycobacterium tuberculosis* mycolic acid production. *PLoS Computational Biology, 5*(8), e1000489. doi:10.1371/journal.pcbi.1000489 PMID:19714220

Colyer, H. A., Armstrong, R. N., & Mills, K. I. (2012). Microarray for epigenetic changes: Gene expression arrays. *Methods in Molecular Biology (Clifton, N.J.), 863*, 319–328. doi:10.1007/978-1-61779-612-8_20 PMID:22359303

Comas, I., & Gagneux, S. (2009). The past and future of tuberculosis research. *PLoS Pathogens, 5*(10), e1000600. doi:10.1371/journal.ppat.1000600 PMID:19855821

Community, G. (2014). *1000 Genomes Statistics*. Retrieved from http://www.1000genomes.org/category/statistics

Conceptual Fundamentals. (2014). *Conceptual Fundamentals of Effective Data Visualization Systems*. Retrieved January 9, 2014, from http://www.panopticon.com/White-Papers D3.js

Condeelis, J., & Weissleder, R. (2010). In vivo imaging in cancer. *Cold Spring Harb Perspect Biol, 2*(12), a003848. doi: 10.1101/cshperspect.a003848

Consortium, Encode Project. (2004). The ENCODE (ENCyclopedia Of DNA Elements) Project. *Science, 306*(5696), 636-640.

Consortium, M. (2006). The MicroArray Quality Control (MAQC) project shows inter- and intraplatform reproducibility of gene expression measurements. *Nature Biotechnology*, *24*(9), 1151–1161. doi:10.1038/nbt1239 PMID:16964229

Cooley, P., Clark, R. F., & Page, G. (2011). The Influence of Errors Inherent in Genome Wide Association Studies (GWAS) in Relation To Single Gene Models. *J Proteomics Bioinform*, *4*, 138–144.

Cooley, P., Clark, R., Folsom, R., & Page, G. (2010). Genetic Inheritance and Genome Wide Association Statistical Test Performance. *J Proteomics Bioinform*, *3*, 330–334.

Coskun, S. A., Cicek, A. E., Lai, N., Dash, R. K., Ozsoyoglu, Z. M., & Ozsoyoglu, G. (2013). An online model composition tool for system biology models. *BMC Systems Biology*, *7*(1), 88. doi:10.1186/1752-0509-7-88 PMID:24006914

Costa, F. F. (2013). Big data in biomedicine. *Drug Discovery Today*. doi:10.1016/j.drudis.2013.10.012

Costantini, P., Linting, M., & Porzio, G. C. (2010). Mining performance data through nonlinear PCA with optimal scaling. *Applied Stochastic Models in Business and Industry*, *26*(1), 85–101. doi:10.1002/asmb.771

Cotton, R. G., Al Aqeel, A. I., Al-Mulla, F., Carrera, P., Claustres, M., & Ekong, R. et al. (2009). Capturing all disease-causing mutations for clinical and research use: Toward an effortless system for the Human Variome Project. *Genetics in Medicine*, *11*(12), 843–849. doi:10.1097/GIM.0b013e3181c371c5 PMID:20010362

Cotton, R. G., Appelbe, W., Auerbach, A. D., Becker, K., Bodmer, W., & Boone, D. J. et al. (2007). Recommendations of the 2006 Human Variome Project meeting. *Nature Genetics*, *39*(4), 433–436. doi:10.1038/ng2024 PMID:17392799

Cotton, R. G., Auerbach, A. D., Axton, M., Barash, C. I., Berkovic, S. F., & Brookes, A. J. et al. (2008). GENETICS. The Human Variome Project. *Science*, *322*(5903), 861–862. doi:10.1126/science.1167363 PMID:18988827

Cotton, R. G., & Macrae, F. A. (2010). Reducing the burden of inherited disease: The Human Variome Project. *The Medical Journal of Australia*, *192*(11), 628–629. PMID:20528712

Cotton, R. G., Vihinen, M., & den Dunnen, J. T. (2011). Genetic tests need the Human Variome Project. *Genet Test Mol Biomarkers*, *15*(1-2), 3. doi:10.1089/gtmb.2010.1515 PMID:21275652

Couto, F. M., Silva, M. J., Lee, V., Dimmer, E., Camon, E., & Apweiler, R. et al. (2006). GOAnnotator: Linking protein GO annotations to evidence text. *Journal of Biomedical Discovery and Collaboration*, *1*(1), 19. doi:10.1186/1747-5333-1-19 PMID:17181854

Cowper-Sallari, R., Cole, M. D., Karagas, M. R., Lupien, M., & Moore, J. H. (2011). Layers of epistasis: genome-wide regulatory networks and network approaches to genome-wide association studies. *Wiley Interdiscip Rev Syst Biol Med*, *3*(5), 513-526. doi: 10.1002/wsbm.132

Cryer, L., Shannon, S. B., Van Amsterdam, M., & Leff, B. (2012). Costs for 'hospital at home' patients were 19 percent lower, with equal or better outcomes compared to similar inpatients. *Health Affairs*, *31*(6), 1237–1243. doi:10.1377/hlthaff.2011.1132 PMID:22665835

Cukier, K., & Mayer-Schoenberger, V. (2013). The Rise of Big Data. *Foreign Affairs*, *92*(3), 27–40.

Culverhouse, R., Suarez, B. K., Lin, J., & Reich, T. (2002). A Perspective on Epistasis: Limits of Models Displaying No Main Effect. *American Journal of Human Genetics*, *70*(2), 461–471. doi:10.1086/338759 PMID:11791213

Cusick, M. E., Klitgord, N., Vidal, M., & Hill, D. E. (2005). Interactome: Gateway into systems biology. *Human Molecular Genetics*, *14*(suppl_2), R171–R181. doi:10.1093/hmg/ddi335 PMID:16162640

Czarnecki, J., Nobeli, I., Smith, A. M., & Shepherd, A. J. (2012). A text-mining system for extracting metabolic reactions from full-text articles. *BMC Bioinformatics*, *13*(1), 172. doi:10.1186/1471-2105-13-172 PMID:22823282

da Silva, M. E., Coeli, C. M., Ventura, M., Palacios, M., Magnanini, M. M., Camargo, T. M., & Camargo, K. R. Jr. (2012). Informed consent for record linkage: A systematic review. *Journal of Medical Ethics*, *38*(10), 639–642. doi:10.1136/medethics-2011-100208 PMID:22403083

Daemen, A., Gevaert, O., Ojeda, F., Debucquoy, A., Suykens, J. A., & Sempoux, C. et al. (2009). A kernel-based integration of genome-wide data for clinical decision support. *Genome Medicine*, *1*(4), 39. doi:10.1186/gm39 PMID:19356222

Dahiya, A., Gavin, M., Luo, R., & Dean, D. (2000). Role of the LXCXE Binding Site in Rb Function. *Molecular and Cellular Biology*, *20*(18), 6799–6805. doi:10.1128/MCB.20.18.6799-6805.2000 PMID:10958676

Dai, H., Zhao, Y., Qian, C., Cai, M., Zhang, R., & Chu, M. et al. (2013). Weighted SNP Set Analysis in Genome-Wide Association Study. *PLoS ONE*, *8*(9), e75897. PMID:24098741

Dai, L., Gao, X., Guo, Y., Xiao, J., & Zhang, Z. (2012). Bioinformatics clouds for big data manipulation. *Biology Direct*, *7*(1), 43. doi:10.1186/1745-6150-7-43 PMID:23190475

Dai, Y., Jiang, R., & Dong, J. (2012). Weighted selective collapsing strategy for detecting rare and common variants in genetic association study. *BMC Genetics*, *13*(1), 7. doi:10.1186/1471-2156-13-7 PMID:22309429

Data Visualization. (2014). *Data Visualization: 7 Considerations for Visualization Deployment*. Retrieved January 10, 2014, from http://www.sas.com/en_us/whitepapers/iia-data-visualization-7-considerations-for-deployment-106892.html

Dayem Ullah, A. Z., Lemoine, N. R., & Chelala, C. (2012). SNPnexus: A web server for functional annotation of novel and publicly known genetic variants (2012 update). *Nucleic Acids Res, 40*(Web Server issue), W65-70.

Dayem Ullah, A. Z., Lemoine, N. R., & Chelala, C. (2013). A practical guide for the functional annotation of genetic variations using SNPnexus. *Briefings in Bioinformatics*, *14*(4), 437–447. doi:10.1093/bib/bbt004 PMID:23395730

De Backer, S., Naud, A., & Scheunders, P. (1998). Nonlinear dimensionality reduction techniques for unsupervised feature extraction. *Pattern Recognition Letters*, *19*(8), 711–720. doi:10.1016/S0167-8655(98)00049-X

De Bie, T., Tranchevent, L. C., van Oeffelen, L. M., & Moreau, Y. (2007). Kernel-based data fusion for gene prioritization. *Bioinformatics (Oxford, England)*, *23*(13), i125–i132. doi:10.1093/bioinformatics/btm187 PMID:17646288

De Choudhury, M., Gamon, M., Counts, S., & Horvitz, E. (2013). *Predicting Depression via Social Media*. Redmond, WA: Microsoft.

De Iorio, M., Newcombe, P. J., Tachmazidou, I., Verzilli, C. J., & Whittaker, J. C. (2011). Bayesian semiparametric meta-analysis for genetic association studies. *Genetic Epidemiology*, *35*(5), 333–340. doi:10.1002/gepi.20581 PMID:21400586

De Keersmaecker, S. C., Thijs, I. M., Vanderleyden, J., & Marchal, K. (2006). Integration of omics data: How well does it work for bacteria? *Molecular Microbiology*, *62*(5), 1239–1250. doi:10.1111/j.1365-2958.2006.05453.x PMID:17040488

de Oliveira, J. V., & Pedrycz, W. (Eds.). (2007). *Advances in Fuzzy Clustering and its Applications*. John Wiley & Sons Ltd. doi:10.1002/9780470061190

de Paula Careta, F., & Paneto, G. G. (2012). Recent patents on High-Throughput Single Nucleotide Polymorphism (SNP) genotyping methods. *Recent Patents on DNA & Gene Sequences*, *6*(2), 122–126. doi:10.2174/187221512801327370 PMID:22670603

De Rosa-Joynt, B. M. (2013). *Comments on New and emerging issues relating to the conservation and sustainable use of biodiversity*. Retrieved January 29, 2014, from http://www.cbd.int/doc/emerging-issues/US-reviewcomments-SBImpacts-2013-09-en.pdf

Dean, G. H., Zheng, H., Tewari, J., Huang, J., Young, D. S., & Hwang, Y. T. et al. (2007). The *Arabidopsis MUM2* Gene Encodes a β-Galactosidase Required for the Production of Seed Coat Mucilage with Correct Hydration Properties. *The Plant Cell*, *19*(12), 4007–4021. doi:10.1105/tpc.107.050609 PMID:18165329

Deasy, J. O., Bentzen, S. r. M., Jackson, A., Ten Haken, R. K., Yorke, E. D., Constine, L. S., . . . Marks, L. B. (2010). Improving Normal Tissue Complication Probability Models: The Need to Adopt a ‚ÄúData-Pooling‚Äù Culture. *International Journal of Radiation Oncology*Biology*Physics, 76*(3, Supplement), S151-S154. doi:10.1016/j.ijrobp.2009.06.094

Deasy, J. O., & El Naqa, I. (2008). Image-based modeling of normal tissue complication probability for radiation therapy. *Cancer Treatment and Research*, *139*, 215–256. doi:10.1007/978-0-387-36744-6_11 PMID:18236719

Debanne, A. M., Bielefeld, R. A., Cauthen, G. M., Daniel, T. M., & Rowland, D. Y. (2000). Multivariate Markovian modeling of tuberculosis: Forecasts for the United States. *Emerging Infectious Diseases*, *6*(2), 148–157. doi:10.3201/eid0602.000207 PMID:10756148

De, G., Yip, W.-K., Ionita-Laza, I., & Laird, N. (2013). Rare Variant Analysis for Family-Based Design. *PLoS ONE*, *8*(1), e48495. doi:10.1371/journal.pone.0048495 PMID:23341868

Degner, J. F., Marioni, J. C., Pai, A. A., Pickrell, J. K., Nkadori, E., Gilad, Y., & Pritchard, J. K. (2009). Effect of read-mapping biases on detecting allele-specific expression from RNA-sequencing data. *Bioinformatics (Oxford, England)*, *25*(24), 3207–3212. doi:10.1093/bioinformatics/btp579 PMID:19808877

DeHaven, C., Evans, A., Dai, H., & Lawton, K. (2010). Organization of GC/MS and LC/MS metabolomics data into chemical libraries. *Journal of Cheminformatics*, *2*(1), 9. doi:10.1186/1758-2946-2-9 PMID:20955607

Delong, E. (2004). Microbial population genomics and ecology: The road ahead. *Environmental Microbiology*, *6*(9), 875–878. doi:10.1111/j.1462-2920.2004.00668.x PMID:15305912

DeLuca, D. S., Levin, J. Z., Sivachenko, A., Fennell, T., Nazaire, M. D., & Williams, C. et al. (2012). RNA-SeQC: RNA-seq metrics for quality control and process optimization. *Bioinformatics (Oxford, England)*, *28*(11), 1530–1532. doi:10.1093/bioinformatics/bts196 PMID:22539670

Dembélé, D., & Kastner, P. (2003). Fuzzy C-Means for Clustering Microarray Data. *Bioinformatics (Oxford, England)*, *19*(8), 973–980. doi:10.1093/bioinformatics/btg119 PMID:12761060

Dempster, A. P., Laird, N. M., & Rubin, D. B. (1977). Maximum Likelihood from Incomplete Data via the EM Algorithm. *Journal of the Royal Statistical Society. Series A (General)*, *39*(1), 1–38.

Department of Health Services. (2014). *Respiratory virus surveillance report for the week ending January 4, 2014*. Department of Health Services.

DePristo, M. A., Banks, E., Poplin, R., Garimella, K. V., Maguire, J. R., & Hartl, C. et al. (2011). A framework for variation discovery and genotyping using next-generation DNA sequencing data. *Nature Genetics*, *43*(5), 491–498. doi:10.1038/ng.806 PMID:21478889

Desai, J. R., Bowen, E. A., Danielson, M. M., Allam, R. R., & Cantor, M. N. (2013). Creation and implementation of a historical controls database from randomized clinical trials. *Journal of the American Medical Informatics Association*, *20*(e1), e162–e168. doi:10.1136/amiajnl-2012-001257 PMID:23449762

Deutsch, E. W., Ball, C. A., Berman, J. J., Bova, G. S., Brazma, A., & Bumgarner, R. E. et al. (2008). Minimum information specification for in situ hybridization and immunohistochemistry experiments (MISFISHIE). *Nature Biotechnology*, *26*(3), 305–312. doi:10.1038/nbt1391 PMID:18327244

Deutsch, E. W., Ball, C. A., Bova, G. S., Brazma, A., Bumgarner, R. E., & Campbell, D. et al. (2006). Development of the Minimum Information Specification for In Situ Hybridization and Immunohistochemistry Experiments (MISFISHIE). *OMICS: A Journal of Integrative Biology*, *10*(2), 205–208. doi:10.1089/omi.2006.10.205 PMID:16901227

Devlin, B., & Roeder, K. (1999). Genomic Control for Association Studies. *Biometrics*, *55*(4), 997–1004. doi:10.1111/j.0006-341X.1999.00997.x PMID:11315092

Di Camillo, B., Toffolo, G., & Cobelli, C. (2009). A gene network simulator to assess reverse engineering algorithms. *Annals of the New York Academy of Sciences*, *1158*(1), 125–142. doi:10.1111/j.1749-6632.2008.03756.x PMID:19348638

Dias, B. F. S. (2013). *New and emerging issues relating to the conservation and sustainable use of biodiversity*. Retrieved January 29, 2014, from http://www.cbd.int/doc/notifications/2013/ntf-2013-018-emerging-issues-en.pdf

Diaz-Aviles, E., Stewart, A., Velasco, E., Denecke, K., & Nejdl, W. (2012). *Epidemic Intelligence for the Crowd, by the Crowd*. Paper presented at the ICWSM. New York, NY.

Diaz-Uriarte, R., & Alvarez de Andres, S. (2006). Gene selection and classification of microarray data using random forest. *BMC Bioinformatics*, *7*(1), 3. doi:10.1186/1471-2105-7-3 PMID:16398926

Dickinson, B., Zhang, Y., Petrick, J. S., Heck, G., Ivashuta, S., & Marshall, W. S. (2013). Lack of detectable oral bioavailability of plant microRNAs after feeding in mice. *Nature Biotechnology*, *31*(11), 965–967. doi:10.1038/nbt.2737 PMID:24213763

Díez, B., Pedrós-Alió, C., & Massana, R. (2001). Study of genetic diversity of eukaryotic picoplankton in different oceanic regions by small-subunit rRNA gene cloning and sequencing. *Applied and Environmental Microbiology*, *67*(7), 2932–2941. doi:10.1128/AEM.67.7.2932-2941.2001 PMID:11425705

Djebali, S., Davis, C. A., Merkel, A., Dobin, A., Lassmann, T., & Mortazavi, A. et al. (2012). Landscape of transcription in human cells. *Nature*, *489*(7414), 101–108. doi:10.1038/nature11233 PMID:22955620

Do, C. B., Hinds, D. A., Francke, U., & Eriksson, N. (2012). Comparison of family history and SNPs for predicting risk of complex disease. *PLOS Genetics*, *8*(10), e1002973. doi:10.1371/journal.pgen.1002973 PMID:23071447

Doms, A., & Schroeder, M. (2005). GoPubMed: exploring PubMed with the Gene Ontology. *Nucleic Acids Research*, *33*(Web Server issue), W783-786. doi:10.1093/nar/gki470

Donald, P. R., & Helden, P. D. (2009). The global burden of tuberculosis — combating drug resistance in difficult times. *The New England Journal of Medicine*, *360*(23), 2393–2395. doi:10.1056/NEJMp0903806 PMID:19494214

Dondrup, M., Albaum, S., Griebel, T., Henckel, K., Jünemann, S., & Kahlke, T. et al. (2002). Minimum information about a microarray experiment (MIAME) – towards standards for microarray data. *Nature Genetics*, *29*, 365–371.

Dong, L., Luo, M., Wang, F., Zhang, J., Li, T., & Yu, J. (2013). TUMIR: An experimentally supported database of microRNA deregulation in various cancers. *Journal of Clinical Bioinformatics*, *3*(1), 7. doi:10.1186/2043-9113-3-7 PMID:23594715

Drake, J. W., Charlesworth, B., Charlesworth, D., & Crow, J. F. (1998). Rates of spontaneous mutation. *Genetics*, *148*(4), 1667–1686. PMID:9560386

Dryden, D., Saunders, L., Rowe, B., May, L., Yiannakoulias, N., & Svenson, L. et al. (2004). Utilization of health services following spinal cord injury: A 6-year follow-up study. *Spinal Cord*, *42*(9), 513–525. doi:10.1038/sj.sc.3101629 PMID:15249928

Dudbridge, F. (2008). Likelihood-Based Association Analysis for Nuclear Families and Unrelated Subjects with Missing Genotype Data. *Human Heredity*, *66*(2), 87–98. doi:10.1159/000119108 PMID:18382088

Dudley, E., Yousef, M., Wang, Y., & Griffiths, W. J. (2010). Targeted metabolomics and mass spectrometry. *Advances in Protein Chemistry and Structural Biology*, *80*, 45–83. doi:10.1016/B978-0-12-381264-3.00002-3 PMID:21109217

Dugas, A. F., Hsieh, Y. H., Levin, S. R., Pines, J. M., Mareiniss, D. P., & Mohareb, A. et al. (2012). Google Flu Trends: Correlation with emergency department influenza rates and crowding metrics. *Clinical Infectious Diseases*, *54*(4), 463–469. doi:10.1093/cid/cir883 PMID:22230244

Duitama, J., Srivastava, P., & Mandoiu, I. (2012). Towards accurate detection and genotyping of expressed variants from whole transcriptome sequencing data. *BMC Genomics*, *13*(Suppl 2), S6. doi:10.1186/1471-2164-13-S2-S6 PMID:22537301

Dukic, V., Lopes, H. F., & Polson, N. G. (2012). Tracking epidemics with google flu trends data and a state-space SEIR model. *Journal of the American Statistical Association*, *107*(500), 1410–1426. doi:10.1080/01621459.2012.713876

Dunn, W. B., Broadhurst, D. I., Atherton, H. J., Goodacre, R., & Griffin, J. L. (2011). Systems level studies of mammalian metabolomes: The roles of mass spectrometry and nuclear magnetic resonance spectroscopy. *Chemical Society Reviews*, *40*(1), 387–426. doi:10.1039/b906712b PMID:20717559

Du, Y., Xie, J., Chang, W., Han, Y., & Cao, G. (2012). Genome-wide association studies: Inherent limitations and future challenges. *France Médecine*, *6*(4), 444–450. PMID:23124883

Dweep, H., Sticht, C., Pandey, P., & Gretz, N. (2011). miRWalk--database: Prediction of possible miRNA binding sites by "walking" the genes of three genomes. *Journal of Biomedical Informatics*, 44(5), 839–847. doi:10.1016/j.jbi.2011.05.002 PMID:21605702

Eberle, M. A., Stone, J., Galver, L., Hansen, M., Tsan, C., & Seagale, D. (2011). A new whole-genome genotyping array of almost 4.5 million SNPs based on data from the 1000 Genomes Project. In *Proceedings of 12th International Congress of Human Genetics (ICHG)*. ICHG.

Eckhardt, F., Beck, S., Gut, I. G., & Berlin, K. (2004). Future potential of the Human Epigenome Project. *Expert Review of Molecular Diagnostics*, 4(5), 609–618. doi:10.1586/14737159.4.5.609 PMID:15347255

Eddy, S., & Durbin, R. (1994). RNA sequence analysis using covariance models. *Nucleic Acids Research*, 22(11), 2079–2088. doi:10.1093/nar/22.11.2079 PMID:8029015

Edgren, H., Murumagi, A., Kangaspeska, S., Nicorici, D., Hongisto, V., Kleivi, K., & Kallioniemi, O. (2011). Identification of fusion genes in breast cancer by paired-end RNA-sequencing. *Genome Biology*, 12(1), R6. doi:10.1186/gb-2011-12-1-r6 PMID:21247443

Editorial, N. (2004). Making data dreams come true. *Nature*, 428(6980), 239–239. doi:10.1038/428239b PMID:15029154

Edwards, D.J, & Holt, K.E. (2013). Beginner's guide to comparative bacterial genome analysis using next-generation sequence data. *Microbial Informatics and Experimentation*, 32.

Edwards, D., & Batley, J. (2004). Plant bioinformatics: From genome to phenome. *Trends in Biotechnology*, 22(5), 232–237. doi:10.1016/j.tibtech.2004.03.002 PMID:15109809

Efron, B., & Tibshirani, R. (2007). On testing the significance of sets of genes. *The Annals of Applied Statistics*, 1(1), 107–129. doi:10.1214/07-AOAS101

Ehret, G. B., Lamparter, D., Hoggart, C. J., Whittaker, J. C., Beckmann, J. S., & Kutalik, Z. (2012). A Multi-SNP Locus-Association Method Reveals a Substantial Fraction of the Missing Heritability. *American Journal of Human Genetics*, 91(5), 863–871. doi:10.1016/j.ajhg.2012.09.013 PMID:23122585

Eisen, M., Spellman, P., Brown, P., & Botstein, D. (1998). Cluster analysis and display of genome-wide expression patterns. *Proceedings of the National Academy of Sciences of the United States of America*, 95(25), 14863–14868. doi:10.1073/pnas.95.25.14863 PMID:9843981

Ekins, S., Freundlich, J. S., Choi, I., Sarker, M., & Talcott, C. (2011). Computational databases, pathway and cheminformatics tools for tuberculosis drug discovery. *Trends in Microbiology*, 19(2), 65–74. doi:10.1016/j.tim.2010.10.005 PMID:21129975

Ekins, S., Reynolds, R. C., Franzblau, S. G., Wan, B., Freundlich, J. S., & Bunin, B. A. (2013). Enhancing hit identification in *Mycobacterium tuberculosis* drug discovery using validated dual-event Bayesian models. *PLoS ONE*, 8(5), e63240. doi:10.1371/journal.pone.0063240 PMID:23667592

El Naqa, I. (2012). Machine learning methods for predicting tumor response in lung cancer. *Wiley Interdisciplinary Reviews: Data Mining and Knowledge Discovery*, 2(2), 173–181. doi:10.1002/widm.1047

El Naqa, I. (2013). Outcomes Modeling. In G. Starkschall & C. Siochi (Eds.), *Informatics in Radiation Oncology* (pp. 257–275). Boca Raton, FL: CRC Press, Taylor and Francis.

El Naqa, I., Bradley, J. D., Lindsay, P. E., Blanco, A. I., Vicic, M., Hope, A. J., & Deasy, J. O. (2006). Multivariable modeling of radiotherapy outcomes including dose-volume and clinical factors. *International Journal of Radiation Oncology, Biology, Physics*, 64(4), 1275–1286. doi:10.1016/j.ijrobp.2005.11.022 PMID:16504765

El Naqa, I., Bradley, J., Lindsay, P. E., Hope, A., & Deasy, J. O. (2009). Predicting Radiotherapy Outcomes using Statistical Learning Techniques. *Physics in Medicine and Biology*, 54(18), S9–S30. doi:10.1088/0031-9155/54/18/S02 PMID:19687564

El Naqa, I., Craft, J., Oh, J., & Deasy, J. (2011). Biomarkers for Early Radiation Response for Adaptive Radiation Therapy. In X. A. Li (Ed.), *Adaptive Radiation Therapy* (pp. 53–68). Boca Baton, FL: Taylor & Francis.

El Naqa, I., Deasy, J. O., Mu, Y., Huang, E., Hope, A. J., & Lindsay, P. E. et al. (2010). Datamining approaches for modeling tumor control probability. *Acta Oncologica (Stockholm, Sweden)*, 49(8), 1363–1373. doi:10.3109/02841861003649224 PMID:20192878

El Naqa, I., Grigsby, P., Apte, A., Kidd, E., Donnelly, E., & Khullar, D. et al. (2009). Exploring feature-based approaches in PET images for predicting cancer treatment outcomes. *Pattern Recognition, 42*(6), 1162–1171. doi:10.1016/j.patcog.2008.08.011 PMID:20161266

El Naqa, I., Pater, P., & Seuntjens, J. (2012). Monte Carlo role in radiobiological modelling of radiotherapy outcomes. *Physics in Medicine and Biology, 57*(11), R75–R97. doi:10.1088/0031-9155/57/11/R75 PMID:22571871

El Naqa, I., Suneja, G., Lindsay, P. E., Hope, A. J., Alaly, J. R., & Vicic, M. et al. (2006). Dose response explorer: An integrated open-source tool for exploring and modelling radiotherapy dose-volume outcome relationships. *Physics in Medicine and Biology, 51*(22), 5719–5735. doi:10.1088/0031-9155/51/22/001 PMID:17068361

El Naqa, I., & Yang, Y. (2014). The Role of Content-Based Image Retrieval in Mammography CAD. In K. Suzuki (Ed.), *Computational Intelligence in Biomedical Imaging* (pp. 33–53). Springer New York. doi:10.1007/978-1-4614-7245-2_2

Ellinghaus, D., Schreiber, S., Franke, A., & Nothnagel, M. (2009). Current software for genotype imputation. *Human Genomics, 3*(4), 371–380. PMID:19706367

Elliott, H. R., Tillin, T., McArdle, W. L., Ho, K., Duggirala, A., & Frayling, T. M. et al. (2014). Differences in smoking associated DNA methylation patterns in South Asians and Europeans. *Clin Epigenetics, 6*(1), 4. doi:10.1186/1868-7083-6-4 PMID:24485148

El-Sofany, F. H., Ghaleb, F. M. F., & El-Seoud, A. S. (2010). The Impact of XML Databases Normalization on Design and Usability of Internet Applications.[Article]. *International Journal of Advanced Corporate Learning, 3*(2), 4–13. doi:10.3991/ijac.v3i2.1265

El-Solh, A., Mylotte, J., Sherif, S., Serghani, J., & Grant, B. J. (1997). Validity of a decision tree for predicting active pulmonary tuberculosis. *American Journal of Respiratory and Critical Care Medicine, 155*(5), 1711–1716. doi:10.1164/ajrccm.155.5.9154881 PMID:9154881

Enright, A. J. (2002). An efficient algorithm for large-scale detection of protein families. *Nucleic Acids Research, 30*(7), 1575–1584. doi:10.1093/nar/30.7.1575 PMID:11917018

Eppenga, W. L., Derijks, H. J., Conemans, J. M., Hermens, W. A., Wensing, M., & De Smet, P. A. (2012). Comparison of a basic and an advanced pharmacotherapy-related clinical decision support system in a hospital care setting in the Netherlands. *Journal of the American Medical Association, 19*(1), 66–71. doi:10.1136/amiajnl-2011-000360 PMID:21890873

Erichsen, H. C., & Chanock, S. J. (2004). SNPs in cancer research and treatment. *British Journal of Cancer, 90*(4), 747–751. doi:10.1038/sj.bjc.6601574 PMID:14970847

Eschrich, S., Zhang, H., Zhao, H., Boulware, D., Lee, J.-H., Bloom, G., & Torres-Roca, J. F. (2009). Systems Biology Modeling of the Radiation Sensitivity Network: A Biomarker Discovery Platform. *International Journal of Radiation Oncology*Biology*Physics, 75*(2), 497–505.

Escofier, B., & Pagès, J. (1990). Multiple factor analysis. *Computational Statistics & Data Analysis, 18*(1), 121–140. doi:10.1016/0167-9473(94)90135-X

ESF Position Paper (2011). *European Biobanks and sample repositories – Relevance to Personalised Medicine*. ESF.

European Bioinformatics Institute & Wellcome Trust Sanger Institute. (2013, December). *About the Ensembl Project*. Retrieved Jan. 10, 2014, from Ensembl Genome Browser: http://useast.enscmbl.org/info/about/index.html

European Molecular Biology Laboratory. (2014). *EMBL History*. Retrieved Jan. 10, 2014, from EMBL Heidelberg - The European Molecular Biology Laboratory: http://www.embl.de/aboutus/general_information/history/

Evangelou, E., & Ioannidis, J. P. A. (2013). Meta-analysis methods for genome-wide association studies and beyond. *Nature Reviews. Genetics, 14*(6), 379–389. doi:10.1038/nrg3472 PMID:23657481

Ewens, W. J., Li, M., & Spielman, R. S. (2008). A Review of Family-Based Tests for Linkage Disequilibrium between a Quantitative Trait and a Genetic Marker. *PLOS Genetics, 4*(9), e1000180. doi:10.1371/journal.pgen.1000180 PMID:18818728

Exeter, D. J., Rodgers, S., & Sabel, C. E. (2013). "Whose data is it anyway?" The implications of putting small area-level health and social data online. *Health Policy (Amsterdam)*, (0). doi:10.1016/j.healthpol.2013.07.012 PMID:23932285

Fairfax, B. P., Makino, S., Radhakrishnan, J., Plant, K., Leslie, S., & Dilthey, A. et al. (2012). Genetics of gene expression in primary immune cells identifies cell type-specific master regulators and roles of HLA alleles. *Nature Genetics*, 44(5), 502–510. doi:10.1038/ng.2205 PMID:22446964

Fallahi-Sichani, M., Marino, S., Flynn, J. L., Linderman, J. J., & Kirschner, D. E. (2013). A systems biology approach for understanding granuloma formation and function in tuberculosis. J. McFadden et al. (Eds.), Systems Biology of Tuberculosis (pp. 127-155), Springer.

Fallahi-Sichani, M., El-Kebir, M., Marino, S., Kirschner, D. E., & Linderman, J. J. (2011). Multi-scale computational modeling reveals a critical role for TNF receptor 1 dynamics in tuberculosis granuloma formation. *Journal of Immunolology*, 186(6), 3472–3483. doi:10.4049/jimmunol.1003299 PMID:21321109

Fardo, D. W., Ionita-Laza, I., & Lange, C. (2009). On Quality Control Measures in Genome-Wide Association Studies: A Test to Assess the Genotyping Quality of Individual Probands in Family-Based Association Studies and an Application to the HapMap Data. *PLOS Genetics*, 5(7), e1000572. PMID:19629167

Farrell, J. J., Zhang, L., Zhou, H., Chia, D., Elashoff, D., & Akin, D. et al. (2012). Variations of oral microbiota are associated with pancreatic diseases including pancreatic cancer. *Gut*, 61(4), 582–588. doi:10.1136/gutjnl-2011-300784 PMID:21994333

FARS. (2013). *Fatality analysis reporting system (FARS): National Highway Traffic Safety Administration.* Retrieved 6th April, 2013, from http://www-fars.nhtsa.dot.gov/Main/index.aspx

Fawcett, J. (2013). Thoughts about multidisciplinary, interdisciplinary, and transdisciplinary research. *Nursing Science Quarterly*, 26(4), 376–379. doi:10.1177/0894318413500408 PMID:24085679

Fazendeiro, P., & de Oliveira, J. V. (2008). A fuzzy clustering algorithm with a variable focal point. In *Proceedings of IEEE International Conference on Fuzzy Systems*, (pp. 1049-1056). IEEE. doi:10.1109/FUZZY.2008.4630499

Fazendeiro, P., & de Oliveira, J. V. (2014). Observer Biased Fuzzy Clustering. *IEEE Transactions on Fuzzy Systems*, 1. doi:10.1109/TFUZZ.2014.2306434

Feinendegen, L., Hahnfeldt, P., Schadt, E. E., Stumpf, M., & Voit, E. O. (2008). Systems biology and its potential role in radiobiology. *Radiation and Environmental Biophysics*, 47(1), 5–23. doi:10.1007/s00411-007-0146-8 PMID:18087710

Fellegi, P. I., & Sunter, B. A. (1969). A theory for record linkage. *Journal of the American Statistical Association*, 64(328), 1183–1210. doi:10.1080/01621459.1969.10501049

Fenstermacher, D. (2005). Introduction to bioinformatics. *Journal of the American Society for Information Science and Technology*, 56(5), 440–446. doi:10.1002/asi.20133

Fernandez, E., La Vecchia, C., D'Avanzo, B., Negri, E., & Franceschi, S. (1994). Family history and the risk of liver, gallbladder, and pancreatic cancer. *Cancer Epidemiology, Biomarkers & Prevention*, 3(3), 209–212. PMID:8019368

Ferretti, L., Raineri, E., & Ramos-Onsins, S. (2012). Neutrality tests for sequences with missing data. *Genetics*, 191(4), 1397–1401. doi:10.1534/genetics.112.139949 PMID:22661328

Feuk, L., Carson, A. R., & Scherer, S. W. (2006). Structural variation in the human genome. *Nature Reviews. Genetics*, 7(2), 85–97. doi:10.1038/nrg1767 PMID:16418744

Few, S., & Perceptual, E. (2007). Data Visualization: Past, Present, and Future. Academic Press.

Fichtlscherer, S., Zeiher, A. M., Dimmeler, S., & Sessa, W. C. (2011). Circulating microRNAs: Biomarkers or mediators of cardiovascular diseases? *Arteriosclerosis, Thrombosis, and Vascular Biology*, 31(11), 2383–2390. doi:10.1161/ATVBAHA.111.226696 PMID:22011751

Fiehn, O. (2001). Combining genomics, metabolome analysis, and biochemical modeling to understand metabolic networks. *Comparative and Functional Genomics*, 2(3), 155–168. doi:10.1002/cfg.82 PMID:18628911

Field, D., Sansone, S. A., Collis, A., Booth, T., Dukes, P., & Gregurick, S. K. et al. (2009). Megascience. 'Omics data sharing. *Science*, 326(5950), 234–236. doi:10.1126/science.1180598 PMID:19815759

Field, M. J., & Grigsby, J. (2002). Telemedicine and remote patient monitoring. *Journal of the American Medical Association*, 288(4), 423–425. doi:10.1001/jama.288.4.423 PMID:12132953

Filipowicz, W., Bhattacharyya, S. N., & Sonenberg, N. (2008). Mechanisms of post-transcriptional regulation by microRNAs: Are the answers in sight? *Nature Reviews. Genetics*, *9*(2), 102–114. doi:10.1038/nrg2290 PMID:18197166

Finak, G., Bertos, N., Pepin, F., Sadekova, S., Souleimanova, M., & Zhao, H. et al. (2008). Stromal gene expression predicts clinical outcome in breast cancer. *Nature Medicine*, *14*(5), 518–527. doi:10.1038/nm1764 PMID:18438415

Fischer, M. A., & Avorn, J. (2004). Economic implications of evidence-based prescribing for hypertension: Can better care cost less? *Journal of the American Medical Association*, *291*(15), 1850–1856. doi:10.1001/jama.291.15.1850 PMID:15100203

Fleischmann, R., & Adams, M., White, O., Clayton. (1995). Whole genome random sequencing and assembly of Hoemophilus influenzae. *Rd. Sci.*, *269*(5223), 496–512. PMID:7542800

Flutre, T., Wen, X., Pritchard, J., & Stephens, M. (2013). A statistical framework for joint eQTL analysis in multiple tissues. *PLOS Genetics*, *9*(5), e1003486. doi:10.1371/journal.pgen.1003486 PMID:23671422

Fodeh, S. J., Brandt, C., Luong, T. B., Haddad, A., Schultz, M., Murphy, T., & Krauthammer, M. (2013). Complementary ensemble clustering of biomedical data. *Journal of Biomedical Informatics*, *46*(3), 436–443. doi:10.1016/j.jbi.2013.02.001 PMID:23454721

Fodor, S., Rava, R. P., Huang, X. C., Pease, A. C., Holmes, C. P., & Adams, C. L. (1993). Multiplexed biochemical assays with biological chips. *Nature*, *364*(6437), 555–556. doi:10.1038/364555a0 PMID:7687751

Foxman, E. F., & Iwasaki, A. (2011). Genome-virome interactions: Examining the role of common viral infections in complex disease. *Nature Reviews. Microbiology*, *9*(4), 254–264. doi:10.1038/nrmicro2541 PMID:21407242

Frank, D. N., Robertson, C. E., Hamm, C. M., Kpadeh, Z., Zhang, T., & Chen, H. et al. (2011). Disease phenotype and genotype are associated with shifts in intestinal-associated microbiota in inflammatory bowel diseases. *Inflammatory Bowel Diseases*, *17*(1), 179–184. doi:10.1002/ibd.21339 PMID:20839241

Fraser, C. M., Eisen, J. A., Nelson, K. E., Paulsen, I. T., & Salzberg, S. L. (2002). The value of complete microbial genome sequencing (you get what you pay for). *Journal of Bacteriology*, *184*(23), 6403–6405. doi:10.1128/JB.184.23.6403-6405.2002 PMID:12426324

Fraser, C. M., Eisen, J. A., & Salzberg, S. L. (2000). Microbial genome sequencing. *Nature*, *406*(6797), 799–803. doi:10.1038/35021244 PMID:10963611

Freedman, L. S., Fainberg, V., Kipnis, V., Midthune, D., & Carroll, R. J. (2004). A new method for dealing with measurement error in explanatory variables of regression models. *Biometrics*, *60*(1), 172–181. doi:10.1111/j.0006-341X.2004.00164.x PMID:15032787

Freedman, L. S., Midthune, D., Carroll, R. J., & Kipnis, V. (2008). A comparison of regression calibration, moment reconstruction and imputation for adjusting for covariate measurement error in regression. *Statistics in Medicine*, *27*(25), 5195–5216. doi:10.1002/sim.3361 PMID:18680172

Freeman, T. C., Goldovsky, L., Brosch, M., van Dongen, S., Maziere, P., & Grocock, R. J. et al. (2007). Construction, visualisation, and clustering of transcription networks from microarray expression data. *PLoS Computational Biology*, *3*(10), 2032–2042. doi:10.1371/journal.pcbi.0030206 PMID:17967053

Freiburger, G., Holcomb, M., & Piper, D. (2007). The STARPAHC collection: Part of an archive of the history of telemedicine. *Journal of Telemedicine and Telecare*, *13*(5), 221–223. doi:10.1258/135763307781458949 PMID:17697507

Fricke, W. F., & Rasko, D. A. (2014). Bacterial genome sequencing in the clinic: Bioinformatics challenges and solutions. *Nature Reviews. Genetics*, *15*(1), 49–55. doi:10.1038/nrg3624 PMID:24281148

Frick, J. S., & Autenrieth, I. B. (2013). The gut microflora and its variety of roles in health and disease. *Current Topics in Microbiology and Immunology*, *358*, 273–289. doi:10.1007/82_2012_217 PMID:22476557

Fridley, B. L. (2009). Bayesian variable and model selection methods for genetic association studies. *Genetic Epidemiology*, *33*(1), 27–37. doi:10.1002/gepi.20353 PMID:18618760

Friedman, A., Turner, J., & Szomolay, B. (2008). A model on the influence of age on immunity to infection with *Mycobacterium tuberculosis*. *Experimental Gerontology*, *43*(4), 275–285. doi:10.1016/j.exger.2007.12.004 PMID:18226868

Friendly, M. (2008). A Brief History of Data Visualization. In *Handbook of Data Visualization* (pp. 15–56). Springer. doi:10.1007/978-3-540-33037-0_2

Friendly, M., & Daniel, J. D. (2008). *Milestones in the history of thematic cartography, statistical graphics, and data visualization. Seeing Science*. Today American Association for the Advancement of Science.

Frifth, M., Hansen, U., Spouge, J., & Weng, Z. (2003). Finding functional sequence elements by multiple local alignment. *Nucleic Acids Research*, *32*(1), 189–200. doi:10.1093/nar/gkh169 PMID:14704356

Frifth, M., Saunders, N., Kobe, B., & Bailey, T. (2008). Discoverying Sequence Motifs with Arbitrary Insertions and Deletions. *PLoS Computational Biology*, *4*(5), e1000071. doi:10.1371/journal.pcbi.1000071 PMID:18437229

Frijters, R., van Vugt, M., Smeets, R., van Schaik, R., de Vlieg, J., & Alkema, W. (2010). Literature mining for the discovery of hidden connections between drugs, genes and diseases. *PLoS Computational Biology*, *6*(9), e1000943. doi:10.1371/journal.pcbi.1000943 PMID:20885778

Fu, J., Wolfs, M. G., Deelen, P., Westra, H. J., Fehrmann, R. S., & Te Meerman, G. J. et al. (2012). Unraveling the regulatory mechanisms underlying tissue-dependent genetic variation of gene expression. *PLOS Genetics*, *8*(1), e1002431. doi:10.1371/journal.pgen.1002431 PMID:22275870

Fukushima, A., Kusano, M., Redestig, H., Arita, M., & Saito, K. (2009). Integrated omics approaches in plant systems biology. *Current Opinion in Chemical Biology*, *13*(5-6), 532–538. doi:10.1016/j.cbpa.2009.09.022 PMID:19837627

Fusaro, V. A., Patil, P., Gafni, E., Wall, D. P., & Tonellato, P. J. (2011). Biomedical cloud computing with Amazon Web Services. *PLoS Computational Biology*, *7*(8), e1002147. doi:10.1371/journal.pcbi.1002147 PMID:21901085

Fusioncharts. (2014). *FusionCharts - JavaScript Charts for the Grown-Ups*. Retrieved January 12, 2014, from http://www.fusioncharts.com/

Futschik, M., & Carlisle, B. (2005). Noise-robust Soft Clustering of Gene Expression Time-course Data. *Journal of Bioinformatics and Computational Biology*, *3*(04), 965–988. doi:10.1142/S0219720005001375 PMID:16078370

Futschik, M., & Kasabov, N. (2002). Fuzzy clustering of gene expression data. In *Proceedings of the 2002 IEEE International Conference on Fuzzy Systems*, (pp. 414-419). IEEE.

Fu, Y., Frith, M. C., Haverty, P. M., & Weng, Z. (2004). MotifViz: An analysis and visualization tool for motif discovery. *Nucleic Acids Research*, *32*(suppl 2), 420–423. doi:10.1093/nar/gkh426 PMID:15215422

Gaffney, D. J. (2013). Global properties and functional complexity of human gene regulatory variation. *PLOS Genetics*, *9*(5), e1003501. doi:10.1371/journal.pgen.1003501 PMID:23737752

Gagnon, J. P. (2013). The research manufacturing pharmaceutical industry. In M. I. Smith, A. I. Vertheimer, & J. E. Fincham (Eds.), *Pharmacy and the US Healthcare System* (p. 215). London: Pharmaceutical Press.

Galagan, J. E., Sisk, P., Stolte, C., Weiner, B., Koehrsen, M., & Wymore, F. et al. (2010). TB database 2010: Overview and update. *Tuberculosis (Edinburgh, Scotland)*, *90*(4), 225–235. doi:10.1016/j.tube.2010.03.010 PMID:20488753

Galagan, J., Henn, M., Ma, L., Cuomo, C., & Birren, B. (2005). Genomics of the fungal kingdom: Insights into eukaryotic biology. *Genome Research*, *15*(12), 1620–1631. doi:10.1101/gr.3767105 PMID:16339359

Gamazon, E. R., Huang, R. S., Dolan, M. E., Cox, N. J., & Im, H. K. (2012). Integrative genomics: Quantifying significance of phenotype-genotype relationships from multiple sources of high-throughput data. *Frontiers in Genetics*, *3*, 202. PMID:23755062

Gammack, D., Ganguli, S., Marino, S., Segovia-Juarez, J., & Kirschner, D. E. (2005). Understanding the immune response in tuberculosis using different mathematical models and biological scales. *Multiscale Modeling & Simulation*, *3*(2), 312–345. doi:10.1137/040603127

Gandjour, A. (2011). Prioritizing Comparative Effectiveness Research. *PharmacoEconomics*, *29*(7), 555–561. PMID:21534639

Garcia, D., Baidoo, E., Benke, P., Pingitore, F., Tang, Y., Villa, S., & Keasling, J. (2008). Separation and mass spectrometry in microbial metabolomics. *Current Opinion in Microbiology, 11*(3), 233–239. doi:10.1016/j.mib.2008.04.002 PMID:18538626

Garg, S. K., Tiwari, R. P., Tiwari, D., Singh, R., Malhotra, D., & Ramnani, V. K. et al. (2003). Diagnosis of tuberculosis: Available technologies, limitations, and possibilities. *Journal of Clinical Laboratory Analysis, 17*(5), 155–163. doi:10.1002/jcla.10086 PMID:12938143

Garrison, G. H., & Smith, L. J. (2010). Is Fatality-Free Travel on North Carolina's Streets and Highways Feasible? It's Time to Think the Unthinkable. *North Carolina Medical Journal, 71*(6), 561–564. PMID:21500671

Garten, Y., Tatonetti, N. P., & Altman, R. B. (2010). Improving the prediction of pharmacogenes using text-derived drug-gene relationships. In *Proceedings of Pacific Symposium on Biocomputing*, (pp. 305-314). Academic Press.

Gehlenborg, N., O'Donoghue, S. I., Baliga, N. S., Goesmann, A., Hibbs, M. A., & Kitano, H. et al. (2010). Visualization of omics data for systems biology. *Nature Methods, 7*(3sSupplement), S56–S68. doi:10.1038/nmeth.1436 PMID:20195258

Geman, S., & Geman, D. (1984). Stochastic Relaxation, Gibbs Distributions, and the Bayesian Restoration of Images. *IEEE Transactions on Pattern Analysis and Machine Intelligence, 6*(6), 721–741. doi:10.1109/TPAMI.1984.4767596 PMID:22499653

Geng, B., Zhou, X., Zhu, J., Hung, Y. S., & Wong, S. T. (2008). Comparison of reversible-jump Markov-chain-Monte-Carlo learning approach with other methods for missing enzyme identification. *Journal of Biomedical Informatics, 41*(2), 272–281. doi:10.1016/j.jbi.2007.09.002 PMID:17950040

George, C. T., Ghosh, D., & Feingold, E. (2012). Comprehensive literature review and statistical considerations for microarray meta-analysis. *Nucleic Acids Research, 40*(9), 3785–3799. doi:10.1093/nar/gkr1265 PMID:22262733

Geraci, F., Leoncini, M., Montangero, M., Pellegrini, M., & Renda, M. E. (2009). K-Boost: A scalable algorithm for high-quality clustering of microarray gene expression data. *Journal of Computational Biology, 16*(6), 859–873. doi:10.1089/cmb.2008.0201 PMID:19522668

Ghouila, A., Yahia, S. B., Malouche, D., Jmel, H., Laouini, D., Guerfali, F. Z., & Abdelhak, S. (2009). Application of multi-SOM clustering approach to macrophage gene expression analysis. *Infection, Genetics and Evolution, 9*(3), 328–336. doi:10.1016/j.meegid.2008.09.009 PMID:18992849

Gibbs, D. L., Gralinski, L., Baric, R. S., & McWeeney, S. K. (2014). Multi-omic network signatures of disease. *Frontiers in Genetics, 4*, 309. doi:10.3389/fgene.2013.00309 PMID:24432028

Gibson, D. G., Glass, J. I., Lartigue, C., Noskov, V. N., Chuang, R., & Algire, M. A. et al. (2010). Creation of a Bacterial Cell Controlled by a Chemically Synthesized Genome. *Science, 329*(5987), 52–56. doi:10.1126/science.1190719 PMID:20488990

Giehl, C., Lange, C., Duarte, R., Bothamley, G., Gerlach, C., & Cirillo, D. M. et al. (2012). TBNET-Collaborative research on tuberculosis in Europe. *European Journal of Microbiology and Immunology, 2*(4), 264–274. doi:10.1556/EuJMI.2.2012.4.4 PMID:24265908

Ginsberg, H. N., Elam, M. B., Lovato, L. C., Crouse, J. R. III, Leiter, L. A., & Linz, P. et al. (2010). Effects of combination lipid therapy in type 2 diabetes mellitus. *The New England Journal of Medicine, 362*(17), 1563–1574. doi:10.1056/NEJMoa1001282 PMID:20228404

Girosi, F., Jones, M., & Poggio, T. (1995). Regularization Theory and Neural Networks Architectures. *Neural Computation, 7*(2), 219–269. doi:10.1162/neco.1995.7.2.219

Glasson, E. J., & Hussain, R. (2008). Linked data: Opportunities and challenges in disability research. [Article]. *Journal of Intellectual & Developmental Disability, 33*(4), 285–291. doi:10.1080/13668250802441409 PMID:19039688

Goddard, M. E., Wray, N. R., Verbyla, K., & Visscher, P. M. (2009). Estimating Effects and Making Predictions from Genome-Wide Marker Data. *Statistical Science*, *24*(4), 517–529. doi:10.1214/09-STS306

Goldacre, M. (2011). *EuroREACH expert panel meeting*. EuroREACH.

Goldsbury, E. D., Armstrong, K., Simonella, L., Armstrong, K. B., & O'Connell, L. D. (2012). Using administrative health data to describe colorectal and lung cancer care in New South Wales, Australia: A validation study. *BMC Health Services Research*, *12*(1), 387. doi:10.1186/1472-6963-12-387 PMID:23140341

Goldstein, B. A., Hubbard, A. E., Cutler, A., & Barcellos, L. F. (2010). An application of Random Forests to a genome-wide association dataset: Methodological considerations & new findings. *BMC Genetics*, *11*(1), 49. doi:10.1186/1471-2156-11-49 PMID:20546594

Gomez-Cabrero, D., Abugessaisa, I., Maier, D., Teschendorff, A., Merkenschlager, M., & Gisel, A. et al. (2014). Data integration in the era of omics: Current and future challenges. *BMC Systems Biology*, *8*(Suppl 2), I1. doi:10.1186/1752-0509-8-S2-I1 PMID:25032990

González, G. M., Costello, C. R., La Tourette, T. R., Joyce, L. K., & Valenzuela, M. (1997). Bilingual telephone-assisted computerized speech-recognition assessment: Is a voice-activated computer program a culturally and linguistically appropriate tool for screening depression in English and Spanish? *Cultural Diversity and Mental Health*, *3*(2), 93–111. doi:10.1037/1099-9809.3.2.93 PMID:9231537

González, I., Déjean, S., Martin, P. G. P., Goncalves, O., Besse, P., & Baccini, A. (2009). Highlighting relationships between heterogeneous biological data through graphical displays based on regularized canonical correlation analysis. *Journal of Biological System*, *17*(2), 173–199. doi:10.1142/S0218339009002831

Goodman, N. (2002). Biological data becomes computer literate: New advances in bioinformatics. *Current Opinion in Biotechnology*, *13*(1), 68–71. doi:10.1016/S0958-1669(02)00287-2 PMID:11849961

Google Charts. (2014). *Google Charts — Google Developers*. Retrieved January 13, 2014, from https://developers.google.com/chart/

Gottfrid, D. (2007). *Self-Service, Prorated Supercomputing Fun!* Retrieved January, 2014, from http://open.blogs.nytimes.com/2007/11/01/self-service-prorated-super-computing-fun/?_php=true&_type=blogs&_r=0

Gøtzsche, P. C. (2011). Why we need easy access to all data from all clinical trials and how to accomplish it. *Trials*, *12*(1), 249. doi:10.1186/1745-6215-12-249 PMID:22112900

Goudey, B., Rawlinson, D., Wang, Q., Shi, F., Ferra, H., & Campbell, R. M. et al. (2013). GWIS - model-free, fast and exhaustive search for epistatic interactions in case-control GWAS. *BMC Genomics*, *14*(Suppl 3), S10. doi:10.1186/1471-2164-14-S3-S10 PMID:23819779

Graham, R., Graham, C., & McMullan, G. (2007). Microbial proteomics: A mass spectrometry primer for biologists. *Microbial Cell Factories*, *6*(1), 26. doi:10.1186/1475-2859-6-26 PMID:17697372

Graux, C., Cools, J., Melotte, C., Quentmeier, H., Ferrando, A., Levine, R., & Hagemeijer, A. (2004). Fusion of NUP214 to ABL1 on amplified episomes in T-cell acute lymphoblastic leukemia. *Nature Genetics*, *36*(10), 1084–1089. doi:10.1038/ng1425 PMID:15361874

Greef, J., Hankemeier, T., & McBurney, N. (2006). Metabolomics-based systems biology and personalized medicine: Moving towards n = 1 clinical trials? *Pharmacogenomics*, *7*(7), 1087–1094. doi:10.2217/14622416.7.7.1087 PMID:17054418

Greenman, C. D., Bignell, G., Butler, A., Edkins, S., Hinton, J., Beare, D., & Stratton, M. R. (2010). PICNIC: An algorithm to predict absolute allelic copy number variation with microarray cancer data. *Biostatistics (Oxford, England)*, *11*(1), 164–175. doi:10.1093/biostatistics/kxp045 PMID:19837654

Gregg, C., Zhang, J., Weissbourd, B., Luo, S., Schroth, G. P., Haig, D., & Dulac, C. (2010). High-resolution analysis of parent-of-origin allelic expression in the mouse brain. *Science*, *329*(5992), 643–648. doi:10.1126/science.1190830 PMID:20616232

Gribov, A., Sill, M., Luck, S., Rucker, F., Dohner, K., & Bullinger, L. et al. (2010). SEURAT: Visual analytics for the integrated analysis of microarray data. *BMC Medical Genomics*, *3*(1), 21. doi:10.1186/1755-8794-3-21 PMID:20525257

Griffin, J. L., & Steinbeck, C. (2010). So what have data standards ever done for us? The view from metabolomics. *Genome Medicine*, *2*(6), 38. doi:10.1186/gm159 PMID:20587079

Grimson, A., Farh, K. K., Johnston, W. K., Garrett-Engele, P., Lim, L. P., & Bartel, D. P. (2007). MicroRNA targeting specificity in mammals: Determinants beyond seed pairing. *Molecular Cell*, *27*(1), 91–105. doi:10.1016/j.molcel.2007.06.017 PMID:17612493

Group, B. D. W. (2001). Biomarkers and surrogate endpoints: preferred definitions and conceptual framework. *Clin Pharmacol Ther, 69*(3), 89-95. doi: 10.1067/mcp.2001.113989

Grunberg-Manago, M., Ortiz, P. J., & Ochoa, S. (1956). Enzymic synthesis of polynucleotides I. polynucleotide phosphorylase of Azotobacter vinelandii. *Biochimica et Biophysica Acta*, *20*, 269–285. doi:10.1016/0006-3002(56)90286-4 PMID:13315374

Guédon-Moreau, L., Mabo, P., & Kacet, S. (2013). Current clinical evidence for remote patient management. *Europace*, *15*(suppl 1), i6–i10. doi:10.1093/europace/eut119 PMID:23737234

Gulliford, S. L., Webb, S., Rowbottom, C. G., Corne, D. W., & Dearnaley, D. P. (2004). Use of artificial neural networks to predict biological outcomes for patients receiving radical radiotherapy of the prostate. *Radiotherapy and Oncology*, *71*(1), 3–12. doi:10.1016/j.radonc.2003.03.001 PMID:15066290

Guo, Y., Sheng, Q., Li, C., Samuels, D. C., & Shyr, Y. (2013). *RNA Somatic Mutation Caller (RSMC): Identifying somatic mutation using RNAseq data*. Retrieved from https://github.com/shengqh/rsmc/wiki

Guo, Y., Eichler, G. S., Feng, Y., Ingber, D. E., & Huang, S. (2006). Towards a Holistic, Yet Gene-Centered Analysis of Gene Expression Profiles: A Case Study of Human Lung Cancers. *Journal of Biomedicine & Biotechnology*, *2006*, 69141. doi:10.1155/JBB/2006/69141 PMID:17489018

Guo, Y., Li, C. I., Ye, F., & Shyr, Y. (2013). Evaluation of read count based RNAseq analysis methods. *BMC Genomics*, *14*(Suppl 8), S2. doi:10.1186/1471-2164-14-S8-S2 PMID:24564449

Guo, Y., Li, J., Li, C. I., Shyr, Y., & Samuels, D. C. (2013). MitoSeek: Extracting mitochondria information and performing high-throughput mitochondria sequencing analysis. *Bioinformatics (Oxford, England)*, *29*(9), 1210–1211. doi:10.1093/bioinformatics/btt118 PMID:23471301

Guo, Y., Long, J., He, J., Li, C. I., Cai, Q., & Shu, X. O. et al. (2012). Exome sequencing generates high quality data in non-target regions. *BMC Genomics*, *13*(1), 194. doi:10.1186/1471-2164-13-194 PMID:22607156

Guo, Y., Samuels, D. C., Li, J., Clark, T., Li, C. I., & Shyr, Y. (2013). Evaluation of allele frequency estimation using pooled sequencing data simulation. *TheScientificWorldJournal*, *895496*. doi:10.1155/2013/895496 PMID:23476151

Guo, Y., Sheng, Q., Li, J., Ye, F., Samuels, D. C., & Shyr, Y. (2013). Large Scale Comparison of Gene Expression Levels by Microarrays and RNAseq Using TCGA Data. *PLoS ONE*, *8*(8), e71462. doi:10.1371/journal.pone.0071462 PMID:23977046

Guo, Y., Ye, F., Sheng, Q., Clark, T., & Samuels, D. C. (2013). Three-stage quality control strategies for DNA re-sequencing data. *Briefings in Bioinformatics*. doi:10.1093/bib/bbt069 PMID:24067931

Gupta, R., Gupta, H., & Mohania, M. (2012). Cloud Computing and Big Data Analytics: What Is New from Databases Perspective? In S. Srinivasa & V. Bhatnagar (Eds.), *Big Data Analytics* (Vol. 7678, pp. 42–61). Springer. doi:10.1007/978-3-642-35542-4_5

Gurung, N., Ray, S., Bose, S., & Rai, V. (2013). A broader view: Microbial enzymes and their relevance in industries, medicine, and beyond. *BioMed Research International*, *2013*, 329121. doi:10.1155/2013/329121 PMID:24106701

Gusareva, E. S., Carrasquillo, M. M., Bellenguez, C., Cuyvers, E., Colon, S., & Graff-Radford, N. R. et al. (2014). Genome-Wide Association Interaction Analysis for Alzheimer's Disease. *Neurobiology of Aging*, *35*(11), 2436–2443. doi:10.1016/j.neurobiolaging.2014.05.014 PMID:24958192

Guy, R. T., Santago, P., & Langefeld, C. D. (2012). Bootstrap Aggregating of Alternating Decision Trees to Detect Sets of SNPs That Associate With Disease: Bagged ADTrees and Genetic Association. *Genetic Epidemiology*, *36*(2), 99–106. doi:10.1002/gepi.21608 PMID:22851473

Gyon, I., & Elisseeff, A. (2003). An Introduction to Variable and Feature Selection. *Journal of Machine Learning Research*, *3*, 1157–1182.

Haeussler, M., Gerner, M., & Bergman, C. M. (2011). Annotating genes and genomes with DNA sequences extracted from biomedical articles. *Bioinformatics (Oxford, England)*, *27*(7), 980–986. doi:10.1093/bioinformatics/btr043 PMID:21325301

Hagen, E. M., Lie, S. A., Rekand, T., Gilhus, N. E., & Gronning, M. (2010). Mortality after traumatic spinal cord injury: 50 years of follow-up. *Journal of Neurology, Neurosurgery, and Psychiatry*, *81*(4), 368–373. doi:10.1136/jnnp.2009.178798 PMID:19726408

Hahn, S. A., Greenhalf, B., Ellis, I., Sina-Frey, M., Rieder, H., & Korte, B. et al. (2003). BRCA2 germline mutations in familial pancreatic carcinoma. *Journal of the National Cancer Institute*, *95*(3), 214–221. doi:10.1093/jnci/95.3.214 PMID:12569143

Halasa, Y. A., Shepard, D. S., & Zeng, W. (2012). Economic cost of dengue in Puerto Rico. *The American Journal of Tropical Medicine and Hygiene*, *86*(5), 745–752. doi:10.4269/ajtmh.2012.11-0784 PMID:22556069

Hall, E. J., & Giaccia, A. J. (2006). *Radiobiology for the radiologist* (6th ed.). Philadelphia: Lippincott Williams & Wilkins.

Halperin, E. C., Perez, C. A., & Brady, L. W. (2008). *Perez and Brady's principles and practice of radiation oncology* (5th ed.). Philadelphia: Wolters Kluwer Health/Lippincott Williams & Wilkins.

Hamburg, M. A., & Collins, F. S. (2010). The path to personalized medicine. *The New England Journal of Medicine*, *363*(4), 301–304. doi:10.1056/NEJMp1006304 PMID:20551152

Hamid, J. S., Hu, P., Roslin, N. M., Ling, V., Greenwood, C. M., & Beyene, J. (2009). Data integration in genetics and genomics: Methods and challenges. *Human Genomics and Proteomics*, 2009. PMID:20948564

Handelsman, J. (2004). Metagenomics: Application of genomics to uncultured microorganisms. *Microbiology and Molecular Biology Reviews*, *68*(4), 669–685. doi:10.1128/MMBR.68.4.669-685.2004 PMID:15590779

Hardison, R. C. (2012). Genome-wide epigenetic data facilitate understanding of disease susceptibility association studies. *The Journal of Biological Chemistry*, *287*(37), 30932–30940. doi:10.1074/jbc.R112.352427 PMID:22952232

Hastie, T., Tibshirani, R., & Friedman, J. H. (2001). *The elements of statistical learning: data mining, inference, and prediction: with 200 full-color illustrations*. New York: Springer.

Havill, L. M., Dyer, T. D., Richardson, D. K., Mahaney, M. C., & Blangero, J. (2005). The quantitative trait linkage disequilibrium test: A more powerful alternative to the quantitative transmission disequilibrium test for use in the absence of population stratification. *BMC Genetics*, *6*(Suppl 1), S91. doi:10.1186/1471-2156-6-S1-S91 PMID:16451707

Hayes, B. (2013). Overview of Statistical Methods for Genome-Wide Association Studies (GWAS). In C. Gondro, J. van der Werf, & B. Hayes (Eds.), *Genome-Wide Association Studies and Genomic Prediction* (Vol. 1019, pp. 149–169). Humana Press. doi:10.1007/978-1-62703-447-0_6

Hay, S. I., George, D. B., Moyes, C. L., & Brownstein, J. S. (2013). Big data opportunities for global infectious disease surveillance. *PLoS Medicine*, *10*(4), e1001413. doi:10.1371/journal.pmed.1001413 PMID:23565065

Heap, G. A., Yang, J. H., Downes, K., Healy, B. C., Hunt, K. A., & Bockett, N. et al. (2010). Genome-wide analysis of allelic expression imbalance in human primary cells by high-throughput transcriptome resequencing. *Human Molecular Genetics*, *19*(1), 122–134. doi:10.1093/hmg/ddp473 PMID:19825846

Hegde, S. R., Rajasingh, H., Das, C., Mande, S. S., & Mande, S. C. (2012). Understanding communication signals during Mycobacterial Latency through predicted genome-wide protein interactions and boolean modeling. *PLoS ONE*, *7*(3), e33893. doi:10.1371/journal.pone.0033893 PMID:22448278

Heinken, A., Sahoo, S., Fleming, R. M. T., & Thiele, I. (2013). Systems-level characterization of a host-microbe metabolic symbiosis in the mammalian gut. *Gut Microbes*, *4*(1), 28–40. doi:10.4161/gmic.22370 PMID:23022739

Heraud-Bousquet, V., Larsen, C., Carpenter, J., Desenclos, J. C., & Le Strat, Y. (2012). Practical considerations for sensitivity analysis after multiple imputation applied to epidemiological studies with incomplete data. *BMC Medical Research Methodology*, *12*(1), 73. doi:10.1186/1471-2288-12-73 PMID:22681630

Hersh, W. (2009). A stimulus to define informatics and health information technology. *BMC Medical Informatics and Decision Making*, *9*(1), 24. doi:10.1186/1472-6947-9-24 PMID:19445665

Heyde, C. C., Crepel, P., Fienberg, S. E., Seneta, E., Gani, J. (2013). *Statisticians of the Centuries* (2001 edition.). New York: Springer.

Heyn, H., Moran, S., Hernando-Herraez, I., Sayols, S., Gomez, A., & Sandoval, J. et al. (2013). DNA methylation contributes to natural human variation. *Genome Research*, *23*(9), 1363–1372. doi:10.1101/gr.154187.112 PMID:23908385

Hiller, K. M., Stoneking, L., Min, A., & Rhodes, S. M. (2013). Syndromic Surveillance for Influenza in the Emergency Department–A Systematic Review. *PLoS ONE*, *8*(9), e73832. doi:10.1371/journal.pone.0073832 PMID:24058494

Himes, B. E., Sheppard, K., Berndt, A., Leme, A. S., Myers, R. A., & Gignoux, C. R. et al. (2013). Integration of mouse and human genome-wide association data identifies KCNIP4 as an asthma gene. *PLoS ONE*, *8*(2), e56179. doi:10.1371/journal.pone.0056179 PMID:23457522

Hindorff, L. A., MacArthur, A., Morales, J., Junkins, H. A., Hall, P. A., Klemm, A. K., & Manolio, T. A. (2014). *Catalog of published genome-wide association studies*. National Human Research Genome Institute.

Hindorff, L. A., Sethupathy, P., Junkins, H. A., Ramos, E. M., Mehta, J. P., Collins, F. S., & Manolio, T. A. (2009). Potential etiologic and functional implications of genome-wide association loci for human diseases and traits. *Proceedings of the National Academy of Sciences of the United States of America*, *106*(23), 9362–9367. doi:10.1073/pnas.0903103106 PMID:19474294

Hintsanen, P., Sevon, P., Onkamo, P., Eronen, L., & Toivonen, H. (2005). An empirical comparison of case-control and trio based study designs in high throughput association mapping. *Journal of Medical Genetics*, *43*(7), 617–624. doi:10.1136/jmg.2005.036020 PMID:16258007

Hivert, M.-F., Manning, A. K., McAteer, J. B., Florez, J. C., Dupuis, J., & Fox, C. S. et al. (2008). Common Variants in the Adiponectin Gene (ADIPOQ) Associated With Plasma Adiponectin Levels, Type 2 Diabetes, and Diabetes-Related Quantitative Traits: The Framingham Offspring Study. *Diabetes*, *57*(12), 3353–3359. doi:10.2337/db08-0700 PMID:18776141

Ho, A. Y., Atencio, D. P., Peters, S., Stock, R. G., Formenti, S. C., Cesaretti, J. A., . . . Rosenstein, B. S. (2006). Genetic Predictors of Adverse Radiotherapy Effects: The Gene-PARE project. *International Journal of Radiation Oncology*Biology*Physics*, *65*(3), 646-655.

Hodgson, E. M., Olshan, A. F., North, K. E., Poole, C. L., Zeng, D., & Tse, C.-K. et al. (2012). The case-only independence assumption: Associations between genetic polymorphisms and smoking among controls in two population-based studies. *International Journal of Molecular Epidemiology and Genetics*, *3*(4), 333–360. PMID:23205185

Hoffmann, T. J., Marini, N. J., & Witte, J. S. (2010). Comprehensive Approach to Analyzing Rare Genetic Variants. *PLoS ONE*, *5*(11), e13584. doi:10.1371/journal.pone.0013584 PMID:21072163

Hogeweg, P. (2011). The roots of bioinformatics in theoretical biology. *PLoS Computational Biology*, *7*(3), e1002021–e1002021. doi:10.1371/journal.pcbi.1002021 PMID:21483479

Hoggart, C. J., Whittaker, J. C., De Iorio, M., & Balding, D. J. (2008). Simultaneous Analysis of All SNPs in Genome-Wide and Re-Sequencing Association Studies. *PLOS Genetics*, *4*(7), e1000130. doi:10.1371/journal.pgen.1000130 PMID:18654633

Holzinger, A., Simonic, K. M., & Yildirim, P. (2012). Disease-disease relationships for rheumatic diseases: Web-based biomedical textmining and knowledge discovery to assist medical decision making. In *Proceedings of International Conference on Computer Software and Applications (COMPSAC)*, (pp. 573-580). Izmir: IEEE. doi:10.1109/COMPSAC.2012.77

Holzinger, E. R., Dudek, S. M., Frase, A. T., Krauss, R. M., Medina, M. W., & Ritchie, M. D. (2013). ATHENA: A tool for meta-dimensional analysis applied to genotypes and gene expression data to predict HDL cholesterol levels. *Pacific Symposium on Biocomputing. Pacific Symposium on Biocomputing*, 385–396. PMID:23424143

Holzinger, E. R., Dudek, S. M., Frase, A. T., Pendergrass, S. A., & Ritchie, M. D. (2014). ATHENA: The analysis tool for heritable and environmental network associations. *Bioinformatics (Oxford, England)*, 30(5), 698–705. doi:10.1093/bioinformatics/btt572 PMID:24149050

Hong, D., Rhie, A., Park, S. S., Lee, J., Ju, Y. S., & Kim, S. et al. (2012). FX: An RNA-Seq analysis tool on the cloud. *Bioinformatics (Oxford, England)*, 28(5), 721–723. doi:10.1093/bioinformatics/bts023 PMID:22257667

Hong, H., Shi, L., Su, Z., Ge, W., Jones, W. D., & Czika, W. et al. (2010a). Assessing sources of inconsistencies in genotypes and their effects on genome-wide association studies with HapMap samples. *The Pharmacogenomics Journal*, 10(4), 364–374. doi:10.1038/tpj.2010.24 PMID:20368714

Hong, H., Su, Z., Ge, W., Shi, L., Perkins, R., & Fang, H. et al. (2010b). Evaluating variations of genotype calling: A potential source of spurious associations in genome-wide association studies. *Journal of Genetics*, 89(1), 55–64. doi:10.1007/s12041-010-0011-4 PMID:20505247

Hood, L. (2013). Systems biology and P4 medicine: Past, present, and future. *Rambam Maimonides Medical Journal*, 4(2), e0012. doi:10.5041/RMMJ.10112 PMID:23908862

Hood, L., Heath, J. R., Phelps, M. E., & Lin, B. (2004). Systems biology and new technologies enable predictive and preventative medicine. *Science*, 306(5696), 640–643. doi:10.1126/science.1104635 PMID:15499008

Hooper, S. D., & Bork, P. (2005). Medusa: A simple tool for interaction graph analysis. *Bioinformatics (Oxford, England)*, 21(24), 4432–4433. doi:10.1093/bioinformatics/bti696 PMID:16188923

Hope, A. J., Lindsay, P. E., El Naqa, I., Alaly, J. R., Vicic, M., Bradley, J. D., & Deasy, J. O. (2006). Modeling radiation pneumonitis risk with clinical, dosimetric, and spatial parameters. *Int J Radiat Oncol Biol Phys, 65*(1), 112-124. doi: 10.1016/j.ijrobp.2005.11.046

Hope, A. J., Lindsay, P. E., El Naqa, I., Bradley, J. D., Vicic, M., & Deasy, J. O. (2005). *Clinical, Dosimetric, and Location-Related Factors to Predict Local Control in Non-Small Cell Lung Cancer.* Paper presented at the ASTRO 47th Annual Meeting. Denver, CO. doi:10.1016/j.ijrobp.2005.07.394

Hopke, P. K., Liu, C., & Rubin, D. B. (2001). Multiple imputation for multivariate data with missing and below-threshold measurements: Time-series concentrations of pollutants in the Arctic. *Biometrics*, 57(1), 22–33. doi:10.1111/j.0006-341X.2001.00022.x PMID:11252602

Hopkins, B. (2011). *Blogging from the IBM big data symposium - Big is more than just big.* Link.

Hopp, L., Lembcke, K., Binder, H., & Wirth, H. (2013). Portraying the Expression Landscapes of B-Cell Lymphoma- Intuitive Detection of Outlier Samples and of Molecular Subtypes. *Biology*, 2(4), 1411–1437. doi:10.3390/biology2041411 PMID:24833231

Hopp, L., Wirth, H., Fasold, M., & Binder, H. (2013). Portraying the expression landscapes of cancer subtypes: A glioblastoma multiforme and prostate cancer case study. *Systems Biomedicine*, 1(2). doi:10.4161/sysb.25897

Hoque, M., Ji, Z., Zheng, D., Luo, W., Li, W., & You, B. et al. (2013). Analysis of alternative cleavage and polyadenylation by 3' region extraction and deep sequencing. *Nature Methods*, 10(2), 133–139. doi:10.1038/nmeth.2288 PMID:23241633

Horvath, S., Xu, X., & Laird, N. M. (2001). The family based association test method: Strategies for studying general genotypephenotype associations. *European Journal of Human Genetics*, 9(4), 301–306. doi:10.1038/sj.ejhg.5200625 PMID:11313775

Howie, B., Marchini, J., Stephens, M., & Chakravarti, A. (2011). Genotype Imputation with Thousands of Genomes. *G3: Genes|Genomes|Genetics, 1*(6), 457–470.

Howie, B. N., Donnelly, P., & Marchini, J. (2009). A flexible and accurate genotype imputation method for the next generation of genome-wide association studies. *PLOS Genetics*, 5(6), e1000529. doi:10.1371/journal.pgen.1000529 PMID:19543373

Howie, B., Fuchsberger, C., Stephens, M., Marchini, J., & Abecasis, G. R. (2012). Fast and accurate genotype imputation in genome-wide association studies through prephasing. *Nature Genetics*, *44*(8), 955–959. doi:10.1038/ng.2354 PMID:22820512

HREC. (2013). *Human Research Reseach Committee*. Retrieved 5th June, 2013, from http://www.nhmrc.gov.au/health-ethics/human-research-ethics-committees-hrecs/human-research-ethics-committees-hrecs

Hsu, S. D., Lin, F. M., Wu, W. Y., Liang, C., Huang, W. C., & Chan, W. L. et al. (2011). miRTarBase: A database curates experimentally validated microRNA-target interactions. *Nucleic Acids Research*, *39*(Database issue), D163–D169. doi:10.1093/nar/gkq1107 PMID:21071411

Hu, P., Xu, W., Cheng, L., Xing, X., & Paterson, A. D. (2011). Pathway-based joint effects analysis of rare genetic variants using Genetic Analysis Workshop 17 exon sequence data. *BMC Proceedings, 5*(Suppl 9), S45.

Hu, X., Macdonald, D. M., Huettner, P. C., Feng, Z., El Naqa, I. M., Schwarz, J. K., . . . Wang, X. (2009). A miR-200 microRNA cluster as prognostic marker in advanced ovarian cancer. *Gynecol Oncol, 114*(3), 457-464. doi:10.1016/j.ygyno.2009.05.022

Huang, E. X., Bradley, J. D., Naqa, I. E., Hope, A. J., Lindsay, P. E., Bosch, W. R., . . . Deasy, J. O. (2011). Modeling the Risk of Radiation-Induced Acute Esophagitis for Combined Washington University and RTOG Trial 93-11 Lung Cancer Patients. *Int J Radiat Oncol Biol Phys*. doi: 10.1016/j.ijrobp.2011.02.052

Huang, D. W., Sherman, B. T., & Lempicki, R. A. (2009). Systematic and integrative analysis of large gene lists using DAVID bioinformatics resources. *Nature Protocols*, *4*(1), 44–57. doi:10.1038/nprot.2008.211 PMID:19131956

Huang, E. X., Hope, A. J., Lindsay, P. E., Trovo, M., El Naqa, I., Deasy, J. O., & Bradley, J. D. (2011). Heart irradiation as a risk factor for radiation pneumonitis. *Acta Oncologica (Stockholm, Sweden)*, *50*(1), 51–60. doi:10.3109/0284186X.2010.521192 PMID:20874426

Huang, N., Shah, P. K., & Li, C. (2012). Lessons from a decade of integrating cancer copy number alterations with gene expression profiles. *Briefings in Bioinformatics*, *13*(3), 305–316. doi:10.1093/bib/bbr056 PMID:21949216

Hu, J., Ge, H., Newman, M., & Liu, K. (2012). OSA: A fast and accurate alignment tool for RNA-Seq. *Bioinformatics (Oxford, England)*, *28*(14), 1933–1934. doi:10.1093/bioinformatics/bts294 PMID:22592379

Huser, V., & Cimino, J. J. (2013). Linking ClinicalTrials.gov and PubMed to Track Results of Interventional Human Clinical Trials. *PLoS ONE*, *8*(7), e68409. doi:10.1371/journal.pone.0068409 PMID:23874614

Hu, T., Andrew, A. S., Karagas, M. R., & Moore, J. H. (2013). Statistical epistasis networks reduce the computational complexity of searching three-locus genetic models. *Pacific Symposium on Biocomputing. Pacific Symposium on Biocomputing*, 397–408. PMID:23424144

Huttenhower, C. et al. (2007). Nearest neighbor networks: Clustering expression data based on gene neighborhoods. *BMC Bioinformatics*, *8*(250), 1–13. PMID:17626636

Huxley, R., Ansary-Moghaddam, A., Berrington de Gonzalez, A., Barzi, F., & Woodward, M. (2005). Type-II diabetes and pancreatic cancer: A meta-analysis of 36 studies. *British Journal of Cancer*, *92*(11), 2076–2083. doi:10.1038/sj.bjc.6602619 PMID:15886696

Huynh-Thu, V. A., Irrthum, A., Wehenkel, L., & Geurts, P. (2010). Inferring regulatory networks from expression data using tree-based methods. *PLoS ONE*, *5*(9), e12776. doi:10.1371/journal.pone.0012776 PMID:20927193

IAEA. (2002). *Predictive assays and their role in selection of radiation as the therapeutic modality*. IAEA.

IBM. (n.d.a). *The Four V's of Big Data*. Retrieved January, 2013, from http://www.ibmbigdatahub.com/infographic/four-vs-big-data

IBM. (n.d.b). *What is big data?* Retrieved January, 2013, from http://www-01.ibm.com/software/data/bigdata/what-is-big-data.html

ICD. (2013). *International Classification of Diseases*. Retrieved 4th July, 2013, from http://www.who.int/classifications/icd/en/

Idekar, T., Galitski, T., & Hood, L. (2001). A new approach to decoding life: Systems biology. *Annual Review of Genomics and Human Genetics*, *2*(1), 343–372. doi:10.1146/annurev.genom.2.1.343 PMID:11701654

Ideker, T., Thorsson, V., Ranish, J. A., Christmas, R., Buhler, J., & Eng, J. K. et al. (2001). Integrated genomic and proteomic analyses of a systematically perturbed metabolic network. *Science*, *292*(5518), 929–934. doi:10.1126/science.292.5518.929 PMID:11340206

Idris, K. (2006). Bioethics and Patent Law: The Case of the Oncomouse. *WIPO Magazine*. Retrieved January 29, 2014, from http://www.wipo.int/wipo_magazine/en/2006/03/article_0006.html

Illumina. (n.d.). Retrieved from http://www.illumina.com/

Ioannidis, J. P., & Khoury, M. J. (2011). Improving validation practices in "omics" research. *Science*, *334*(6060), 1230–1232. doi:10.1126/science.1211811 PMID:22144616

Iragne, F., Nikolski, M., Mathieu, B., Auber, D., & Sherman, D. (2005). ProViz: Protein interaction visualization and exploration. *Bioinformatics (Oxford, England)*, *21*(2), 272–274. doi:10.1093/bioinformatics/bth494 PMID:15347570

Ishida, S., Umeyama, H., Iwadate, M., & Taguchi, Y.-h. (in press). Bioinformatic Screening of Autoimmune Disease Genes and Protein Structure Prediction with FAMS for Drug Discovery. *Protein Pept Lett*. Retrieved from http://www.benthamscience.com/journal/index.php?journalID=ppl

Iwakawa, M., Noda, S., Yamada, S., Yamamoto, N., Miyazawa, Y., & Yamazaki, H. et al. (2006). Analysis of non-genetic risk factors for adverse skin reactions to radiotherapy among 284 Breast Cancer patients. *Breast Cancer (Tokyo, Japan)*, *13*(3), 300–307. doi:10.2325/jbcs.13.300 PMID:16929125

Jackson, A., Marks, L. B., Bentzen, S. M., Eisbruch, A., Yorke, E. D., Ten Haken, R. K., . . . Deasy, J. O. (2010). The lessons of QUANTEC: recommendations for reporting and gathering data on dose-volume dependencies of treatment outcome. *Int J Radiat Oncol Biol Phys, 76*(3 Suppl), S155-160. doi: 10.1016/j.ijrobp.2009.08.074

Jackson, D., White, I. R., & Thompson, S. G. (2009). Extending DerSimonian and Laird's methodology to perform multivariate random effects meta-analyses. *Statistics in Medicine*, *29*(12), 1282–1297. doi:10.1002/sim.3602 PMID:19408255

Jacob, F., Perrin, D., Sanchez, C., & Monod, J. (1960). L'opéeron: Groupe de gènes à expression coordonnée par un opérateur. *Compt. Rend.*, 1727-1729.

Jain, K. K. (2007). Cancer biomarkers: Current issues and future directions. *Current Opinion in Molecular Therapeutics*, *9*(6), 563–571. PMID:18041667

Jain, K. K. (2012). Synthetic Biology and Personalized Medicine. *Medical Principles and Practice*, *22*(3), 209–219. doi:10.1159/000341794 PMID:22907209

Janssens, A. C. J. W., & van Duijn, C. M. (2008). Genome-based prediction of common diseases: Advances and prospects. *Human Molecular Genetics*, *17*(R2), R166–R173. doi:10.1093/hmg/ddn250 PMID:18852206

Javierre, B. M., Fernandez, A. F., Richter, J., Al-Shahrour, F., Martin-Subero, J. I., & Rodriguez-Ubreva, J. et al. (2010). Changes in the pattern of DNA methylation associate with twin discordance in systemic lupus erythematosus. *Genome Research*, *20*(2), 170–179. doi:10.1101/gr.100289.109 PMID:20028698

Jay, J. J., & Chesler, E. J. (2014). Performing integrative functional genomics analysis in GeneWeaver.org. *Methods in Molecular Biology (Clifton, N.J.)*, *1101*, 13–29. doi:10.1007/978-1-62703-721-1_2 PMID:24233775

Jebamani, L. S., Burchill, C. A., & Martens, P. J. (2005). Using Data Linkage to Identify First Nations Manitobans. *Canadian Journal of Public Health*, *96*, S28–S32. PMID:15686150

Jee, K., & Kim, G. H. (2013). Potentiality of big data in the medical sector: Focus on how to reshape the healthcare system. *Healthcare Informatics Research*, *19*(2), 79–85. doi:10.4258/hir.2013.19.2.79 PMID:23882412

Jeffries, M. A., Dozmorov, M., Tang, Y., Merrill, J. T., Wren, J. D., & Sawalha, A. H. (2011). Genomewide DNA methylation patterns in CD4+ T cells from patients with systemic lupus erythematosus. *Epigenetics*, *6*(5), 593–601. doi:10.4161/epi.6.5.15374 PMID:21436623

Jensen, P. B., Jensen, L. J., & Brunak, S. (2012). Mining electronic health records: Towards better research applications and clinical care. *Nature Reviews. Genetics*, *13*(6), 395–405. doi:10.1038/nrg3208 PMID:22549152

Jeong, H., Tombor, B., Albert, R., Oltvai, N., & Barabási, L. (2000). The large-scale organization of metabolic networks. *Nature, 407*(6804), 651–654. doi:10.1038/35036627 PMID:11034217

Jerez, J. M., Molina, I., Garcia-Laencina, P. J., Alba, E., Ribelles, N., Martin, M., & Franco, L. (2010). Missing data imputation using statistical and machine learning methods in a real breast cancer problem. *Artificial Intelligence in Medicine, 50*(2), 105–115. doi:10.1016/j.artmed.2010.05.002 PMID:20638252

Jia, J., Parikh, H., Xiao, W., Hoskins, J. W., Pflicke, H., & Liu, X. et al. (2013). An integrated transcriptome and epigenome analysis identifies a novel candidate gene for pancreatic cancer. *BMC Medical Genomics, 6*(1), 33. doi:10.1186/1755-8794-6-33 PMID:24053169

Jiang, D., Tang, C., & Zhang, A. (2004). Cluster analysis for gene expression data: A survey. *IEEE Transactions on Knowledge and Data Engineering, 16*(11), 1370–1386. doi:10.1109/TKDE.2004.68

Jiang, Q., Wang, Y., Hao, Y., Juan, L., Teng, M., & Zhang, X. et al. (2009). miR2Disease: A manually curated database for microRNA deregulation in human disease. *Nucleic Acids Research, 37*(Database issue), D98–D104. doi:10.1093/nar/gkn714 PMID:18927107

Jimenez-Rodriguez, L. O., Arzuaga-Cruz, E., & Velez-Reyes, M. (2007). Unsupervised Linear Feature-Extraction Methods and Their Effects in the Classification of High-Dimensional Data. *Geoscience and Remote Sensing, 45*(2), 469–483. doi:10.1109/TGRS.2006.885412

Jin, H., Wong, M. L., & Leung, K. S. (2005). Scalable model-based clustering for large databases based on data summarization. *IEEE Transactions on Pattern Analysis and Machine Intelligence, 27*(11), 1710–1719. doi:10.1109/TPAMI.2005.226 PMID:16285371

Joachims, T. (1999). Making large scale SVM learning practical. In B. Schölkopf, C. Burges, & A. Smola (Eds.), *Advances in Kernel Methods - Support Vector Learning.* Cambridge, USA: MIT Press.

Johansson, B., Mertens, F., & Mitelman, F. (1996). Primary vs. secondary neoplasia-associated chromosomal abnormalities-balanced rearrangements vs. genomic imbalances? *Genes, Chromosomes & Cancer, 16*(3), 155–163. doi:10.1002/(SICI)1098-2264(199607)16:3<155::AID-GCC1>3.0.CO;2-Y PMID:8814447

Johnson, A. D., & O'Donnell, C. J. (2009). An open access database of genome-wide association results. *BMC Medical Genetics, 10*(1), 6. doi:10.1186/1471-2350-10-6 PMID:19161620

Johnson, R. C., Nelson, G. W., Troyer, J. L., Lautenberger, J. A., Kessing, B. D., Winkler, C. A., & O'Brien, S. J. (2010). Accounting for multiple comparisons in a genome-wide association study (GWAS). *BMC Genomics, 11*(1), 724. doi:10.1186/1471-2164-11-724 PMID:21176216

John, T. J., Vashishtha, V. M., & John, S. M. (2013). 50 years of tuberculosis control in India: Progress, pitfalls and the way forward. *Indian Pediatrics, 50*(1), 93–98. doi:10.1007/s13312-013-0021-4 PMID:23396780

Joiner, M., & Kogel, A. d. (2009). *Basic clinical radiobiology* (4th ed.). London: Hodder Arnold.

Jones, R. M. (2013). *A New World Order: The Expansion of Executive Corporate Liability in the Life Sciences Industry.* Student Scholarship, Paper 250.

Jones, S., Hruban, R. H., Kamiyama, M., Borges, M., Zhang, X., & Parsons, D. W. et al. (2009). Exomic sequencing identifies PALB2 as a pancreatic cancer susceptibility gene. *Science, 324*(5924), 217. doi:10.1126/science.1171202 PMID:19264984

Jonnalagadda, S., & Srinivasan, R. (2009). NIFTI: An evolutionary approach for finding number of clusters in microarray data. *BMC Bioinformatics, 10*(1), 40. doi:10.1186/1471-2105-10-40 PMID:19178750

Jorm, R. L., Shepherd, C. L., Rogers, D. K., & Blyth, M. F. (2012). Smoking and use of primary care services: Findings from a population-based cohort study linked with administrative claims data. *BMC Health Services Research, 12*(1), 263–263. doi:10.1186/1472-6963-12-263 PMID:22900643

Jose, J., & Jingle, I. B. J. (2013). Remote Heart Monitoring and Diagnosis Service Platform via Wearable ECG Monitor. *International Journal of Science, Engineering and Technology Research, 2*(5), 1095–1099.

Joshi, V., Moradshahi, P., & Goubran, R. (2013). *Operating system performance measurements for remote patient monitoring applications.* Paper presented at the Medical Measurements and Applications Proceedings (MeMeA). New York, NY.

Jourdan, Z., Rainer, R. K., & Marshall, T. E. (2008). Business Intelligence: An Analysis of the Literature. *Information Systems Management*, 25(2), 121–131. doi:10.1080/10580530801941512

Joyce, A. R., & Palsson, B. O. (2006). The model organism as a system: Integrating 'omics' data sets. *Nature Reviews. Molecular Cell Biology*, 7(3), 198–210. doi:10.1038/nrm1857 PMID:16496022

Kakaday, T., Hewitt, A. W., Voelcker, N. H., Li, J. S., & Craig, J. E. (2009). Advances in telemetric continuous intraocular pressure assessment. *The British Journal of Ophthalmology*, 93(8), 992–996. doi:10.1136/bjo.2008.144261 PMID:19244268

Kalisky, T., & Quake, S. (2011). Single-cell genomics. *Nature Methods*, 8(4), 311–314. doi:10.1038/nmeth0411-311 PMID:21451520

Kalyana-Sundaram, S., Kumar-Sinha, C., Shankar, S., Robinson, D. R., Wu, Y. M., & Cao, X. et al. (2012). Expressed pseudogenes in the transcriptional landscape of human cancers. *Cell*, 149(7), 1622–1634. doi:10.1016/j.cell.2012.04.041 PMID:22726445

Kamagata, Y., & Tamaki, H. (2005). Cultivation of uncultured fastidious microbes. *Microbes and Environments*, 20(2), 85–91. doi:10.1264/jsme2.20.85

Kanehisa, M., Goto, S., Sato, Y., Kawashima, M., Furumichi, M., & Tanabe, M. (2014). Data, information, knowledge and principle: Back to metabolism in KEGG. *Nucleic Acids Research*, 42(1), D199–D205. doi:10.1093/nar/gkt1076 PMID:24214961

Karmel, R., Anderson, P., Gibson, D., Peut, A., Duckett, S., & Wells, Y. (2010). Empirical aspects of record linkage across multiple data sets using statistical linkage keys: The experience of the PIAC cohort study. [Article]. *BMC Health Services Research*, 10(1), 41–53. doi:10.1186/1472-6963-10-41 PMID:20167118

Kasianowicz, J. J., Brandin, E., Branton, D., & Deamer, D. W. (1996). Characterization of individual polynucleotide molecules using a membrane channel. *Proceedings of the National Academy of Sciences of the United States of America*, 93(24), 13770–13773. doi:10.1073/pnas.93.24.13770 PMID:8943010

Kass-Hout, T. A., Xu, Z., McMurray, P., Park, S., Buckeridge, D. L., & Brownstein, J. S. et al. (2012). Application of change point analysis to daily influenza-like illness emergency department visits. *Journal of the American Medical Informatics Association*, 19(6), 1075–1081. doi:10.1136/amiajnl-2011-000793 PMID:22759619

Kawaji, H., Nakamura, M., Takahashi, Y., Sandelin, A., Katayama, S., & Fukuda, S. et al. (2008). Hidden layers of human small RNAs. *BMC Genomics*, 9(1), 157. doi:10.1186/1471-2164-9-157 PMID:18402656

Kawamoto, K., Houlihan, C. A., Balas, E. A., & Lobach, D. F. (2005). Improving clinical practice using clinical decision support systems: A systematic review of trials to identify features critical to success. *British Medical Journal*, 330(7494), 765. doi:10.1136/bmj.38398.500764.8F PMID:15767266

Kazma, R., & Bailey, J. N. (2011). Population-based and family-based designs to analyze rare variants in complex diseases. *Genetic Epidemiology*, 35(S1), S41–S47. doi:10.1002/gepi.20648 PMID:22128057

Kearney, L., & Horsley, S. W. (2005). Molecular cytogenetics in haematological malignancy: Current technology and future prospects. *Chromosoma*, 114(4), 286–294. doi:10.1007/s00412-005-0002-z PMID:16003502

Keilwagen, J., Grau, J., Paonov, I. A., Posch, S., Strickert, M., & Große, I. (2011). Dispom: A discriminitive de-novo discovery tool based on the JStacs library. *PLOS Comput. Bio., 7*(2).

Keller, A., Leidinger, P., Bauer, A., Elsharawy, A., Haas, J., & Backes, C. et al. (2011). Toward the blood-borne miRNome of human diseases. *Nature Methods*, 8(10), 841–843. doi:10.1038/nmeth.1682 PMID:21892151

Keller, M., & Zengler, K. (2004). Tapping into microbial diversity. *Nature Reviews. Microbiology*, 2(2), 141–150. doi:10.1038/nrmicro819 PMID:15040261

Kemper, B., Matsuzaki, T., Matsuoka, Y., Tsuruoka, Y., Kitano, H., Ananiadou, S., & Tsujii, J. (2010). PathText: A text mining integrator for biological pathway visualizations. *Bioinformatics (Oxford, England)*, 26(12), i374–i381. doi:10.1093/bioinformatics/btq221 PMID:20529930

Kendziorski, C., & Wang, P. (2006). A review of statistical methods for expression quantitative trait loci mapping. *Mammalian Genome, 17*(6), 509–517. doi:10.1007/s00335-005-0189-6 PMID:16783633

Kerns, S. L., Ostrer, H., Stock, R., Li, W., Moore, J., Pearlman, A., . . . Rosenstein, B. S. (2010). Genome-wide association study to identify single nucleotide polymorphisms (SNPs) associated with the development of erectile dysfunction in African-American men after radiotherapy for prostate cancer. *Int J Radiat Oncol Biol Phys, 78*(5), 1292-1300. doi: 10.1016/j.ijrobp.2010.07.036

Kerns, S. L., Stock, R., Stone, N., Buckstein, M., Shao, Y., Campbell, C., . . . Rosenstein, B. S. (n.d.). A 2-Stage Genome-Wide Association Study to Identify Single Nucleotide Polymorphisms Associated With Development of Erectile Dysfunction Following Radiation†Therapy for Prostate Cancer. *International Journal of Radiation Oncology*Biology*Physics, (0).

Kerr, G., Ruskin, H. J., Crane, M., & Doolan, P. (2008). Techniques for clustering gene expression data. *Computers in Biology and Medicine, 38*(3), 283–293. doi:10.1016/j.compbiomed.2007.11.001 PMID:18061589

Kerr, M. K., Martin, M., & Churchill, G. A. (2000). Analysis of variance for gene expression microarray data. [Comparative Study]. *Journal of Computational Biology, 7*(6), 819–837. doi:10.1089/10665270050514954 PMID:11382364

Kestenbaum, B. (2009). Case-Control Studies. In *Epidemiology and Biostatistics* (pp. 45–57). Springer New York. doi:10.1007/978-0-387-88433-2_6

Khan, F. M. (2007). *Treatment planning in radiation oncology* (2nd ed.). Philadelphia: Lippincott Williams & Wilkins.

Khatri, P., Sirota, M., & Butte, A. J. (2012). Ten Years of Pathway Analysis: Current Approaches and Outstanding Challenges. *PLoS Comput Biol, 8*(2). doi: 10.1371/journal.pcbi.1002375

Khatri, P., Draghici, S., Tarca, A. L., Hassan, S. S., & Romero, R. (2007). A system biology approach for the steady-state analysis of gene signaling networks. *Progress in Pattern Recognition, Image Analysis and Applications. Proceedings, 4756*, 32–41.

Kho, A. N., Rasmussen, L. V., Connolly, J. J., Peissig, P. L., Starren, J., Hakonarson, H., & Hayes, M. G. (2013). Practical challenges in integrating genomic data into the electronic health record. *Genetics in Medicine, 15*(10), 772–778. doi:10.1038/gim.2013.131 PMID:24071798

Khoury, J. D., Tannir, N. M., Williams, M. D., Chen, Y., Yao, H., & Zhang, J. et al. (2013). Landscape of DNA Virus Associations across Human Malignant Cancers: Analysis of 3,775 Cases Using RNA-Seq. *Journal of Virology, 87*(16), 8916–8926. doi:10.1128/JVI.00340-13 PMID:23740984

Kidd, E. A., El Naqa, I., Siegel, B. A., Dehdashti, F., & Grigsby, P. W. (2012). FDG-PET-based prognostic nomograms for locally advanced cervical cancer. *Gynecol Oncol, 127*(1), 136-140. doi: 10.1016/j.ygyno.2012.06.027

Kim, S., Morris, N. J., Won, S., & Elston, R. C. (2009). Single-marker and two-marker association tests for unphased case-control genotype data, with a power comparison. *Genetic Epidemiology*.

Kim, D., Li, R., Dudek, S. M., & Ritchie, M. D. (2013). ATHENA: Identifying interactions between different levels of genomic data associated with cancer clinical outcomes using grammatical evolution neural network. *BioData Min, 6*(1), 23. doi:10.1186/1756-0381-6-23 PMID:24359638

Kim, D., Pertea, G., Trapnell, C., Pimentel, H., Kelley, R., & Salzberg, S. L. (2013). TopHat2: Accurate alignment of transcriptomes in the presence of insertions, deletions and gene fusions. *Genome Biology, 14*(4), R36. doi:10.1186/gb-2013-14-4-r36 PMID:23618408

Kim, D.-W., Lee, K.-Y., Lee, K., & Lee, D. (2006). Towards clustering of incomplete microarray data without the use of imputation. *Bioinformatics (Oxford, England), 23*(1), 107–113. doi:10.1093/bioinformatics/btl555 PMID:17077099

Kim, E. Y., Hwang, D. U., & Ko, T. W. (2012). Multiscale ensemble clustering for finding modules in complex networks. *Physical Review E: Statistical, Nonlinear, and Soft Matter Physics, 85*(2 Pt 2), 026119. doi:10.1103/PhysRevE.85.026119 PMID:22463291

Kim, J., Cole, J., & Pramanik, S. (1996). Alignment of possible secondary structures in multiple RNA sequences using simulated annealing. *Computer Applications in the Biosciences, 12*(4), 259–267. PMID:8902352

Kim, S. Y., & Lee, J. W. (2007). Ensemble clustering method based on the resampling similarity measure for gene expression data. *Statistical Methods in Medical Research, 16*(6), 539–564. doi:10.1177/0962280206071842 PMID:17698931

Kim, S., Kwon, D., Shin, S. Y., & Wilbur, W. J. (2012). PIE the search: Searching PubMed literature for protein interaction information. *Bioinformatics (Oxford, England), 28*(4), 597–598. doi:10.1093/bioinformatics/btr702 PMID:22199390

Kim, S., & Misra, A. (2007). SNP Genotyping: Technologies and Biomedical Applications. *Annual Review of Biomedical Engineering, 9*(1), 289–320. doi:10.1146/annurev.bioeng.9.060906.152037 PMID:17391067

Kindt, A. S., Navarro, P., Semple, C. A., & Haley, C. S. (2013). The genomic signature of trait-associated variants. *BMC Genomics, 14*(1), 108. doi:10.1186/1471-2164-14-108 PMID:23418889

Kinnings, S. L., Xie, L., Fung, K. H., Jackson, R. M., Xie, L., & Bourne, P. E. (2010). The *Mycobacterium tuberculosis* drugome and its polypharmacological implications. *PLoS Computational Biology, 6*(11), e1000976. doi:10.1371/journal.pcbi.1000976 PMID:21079673

Kinoshita, R., Iwadate, M., Umeyama, H., & Taguchi, Y.-. (2014). Genes associated with genotype-specific DNA methylation in squamous cell carcinoma as candidate drug targets. *BMC Systems Biology, 8*(S1), S4. doi:10.1186/1752-0509-8-S1-S4 PMID:24565165

Kirschner, M. (2005). The meaning of systems biology. *Cell, 121*(4), 503–504. doi:10.1016/j.cell.2005.05.005 PMID:15907462

Kiryluk, K., Li, Y., Sanna-Cherchi, S., Rohanizadegan, M., Suzuki, H., & Eitner, F. et al. (2012). Geographic Differences in Genetic Susceptibility to IgA Nephropathy: GWAS Replication Study and Geospatial Risk Analysis. *PLOS Genetics, 8*(6), e1002765. doi:10.1371/journal.pgen.1002765 PMID:22737082

Kisand, V., & Lettieri, T. (2013). Genome sequencing of bacteria: Sequencing, de novo assembly and rapid analysis using open source tools. *BMC Genomics, 1*(14), 211. doi:10.1186/1471-2164-14-211 PMID:23547799

Kitano, H. (2002). Systems biology: A brief overview. *Science, 295*(5560), 1662–1664. doi:10.1126/science.1069492 PMID:11872829

Klersy, C., De Silvestri, A., Gabutti, G., Raisaro, A., Curti, M., Regoli, F., & Auricchio, A. (2011). Economic impact of remote patient monitoring: An integrated economic model derived from a meta-analysis of randomized controlled trials in heart failure. *European Journal of Heart Failure, 13*(4), 450–459. doi:10.1093/eurjhf/hfq232 PMID:21193439

Klopp, A. H., Jhingran, A., Ramdas, L., Story, M. D., Broadus, R. R., & Lu, K. H. et al. (2008). Gene expression changes in cervical squamous cell carcinoma after initiation of chemoradiation and correlation with clinical outcome. *International Journal of Radiation Oncology, Biology, Physics, 71*(1), 226–236. doi:10.1016/j.ijrobp.2007.10.068 PMID:18406887

Ko¨pke, B., Wilms, R., Engelen, B., Cypionka, H., & Sass, H. (2005). Microbial diversity in coastal subsurface sediments: A cultivation approach using various electron acceptors and substrate gradients. *Applied and Environmental Microbiology, 71*(12), 7819–7830. doi:10.1128/AEM.71.12.7819-7830.2005 PMID:16332756

Kobak, K. A., Dottl, S. L., Greist, J. H., Jefferson, J. W., Burroughs, D., & Mantle, J. M. et al. (1997). A computer-administered telephone interview to identify mental disorders. *Journal of the American Medical Association, 278*(11), 905–910. doi:10.1001/jama.1997.03550110043034 PMID:9302242

Koboldt, D. C., Zhang, Q., Larson, D. E., Shen, D., McLellan, M. D., & Lin, L. et al. (2012). VarScan 2: Somatic mutation and copy number alteration discovery in cancer by exome sequencing. *Genome Research, 22*(3), 568–576. doi:10.1101/gr.129684.111 PMID:22300766

Kodzius, R., Kojima, M., Nishiyori, H., Nakamura, M., Fukuda, S., & Tagami, M. et al. (2006). CAGE: Cap analysis of gene expression. *Nature Methods, 3*(3), 211–222. doi:10.1038/nmeth0306-211 PMID:16489339

Koff, D. A., & Shulman, H. (2006). An overview of digital compression of medical images: Can we use lossy image compression in radiology? *Canadian Association of Radiologists Journal, 57*(4), 211–217. PMID:17128888

Kohonen-Corish, M. R., Smith, T. D., & Robinson, H. M. (2013). Beyond the genomics blueprint: The 4th Human Variome Project Meeting, UNESCO, Paris, 2012. *Genetics in Medicine, 15*(7), 507–512. doi:10.1038/gim.2012.174 PMID:23328891

Kolen, J., & Hutcheson, T. (2002). Reducing the time complexity of the fuzzy c-means algorithm. *IEEE Transactions on Fuzzy Systems, 10*(2), 263–267. doi:10.1109/91.995126

Konganti, K., Wang, G., Yang, E., & Cai, J. J. (2013). SBEToolbox: A Matlab toolbox for biological network analysis. *Evolutionary Bioinformatics, 9*, 355. doi:10.4137/EBO.S12012 PMID:24027418

Konietschke, F., Libiger, O., & Hothorn, L. A. (2012). Nonparametric Evaluation of Quantitative Traits in Population-Based Association Studies when the Genetic Model is Unknown. *PLoS ONE, 7*(2), e31242. doi:10.1371/journal.pone.0031242 PMID:22363593

Konig, I. R. (2011). Validation in genetic association studies. *Briefings in Bioinformatics, 12*(3), 253–258. doi:10.1093/bib/bbq074 PMID:21546448

Korn, J. M., Kuruvilla, F. G., McCarroll, S. A., Wysoker, A., Nemesh, J., & Cawley, S. et al. (2008). Integrated genotype calling and association analysis of SNPs, common copy number polymorphisms and rare CNVs. *Nature Genetics, 40*(10), 1253–1260. doi:10.1038/ng.237 PMID:18776909

Kosaka, N. (Ed.). (2013). *Circulating microRNAs*. Heidelberg, Germany: Springer. doi:10.1007/978-1-62703-453-1

Köser, C., Ellington, M., Cartwright, E., Gillespie, S., Brown, N., & Farrington, M. et al. (2012). Routine Use of Microbial Whole Genome Sequencing in Diagnostic and Public Health Microbiology. *PLoS Pathogens, 8*(8), e1002824. doi:10.1371/journal.ppat.1002824 PMID:22876174

Kostic, A. D., Ojesina, A. I., Pedamallu, C. S., Jung, J., Verhaak, R. G., Getz, G., & Meyerson, M. (2011). PathSeq: Software to identify or discover microbes by deep sequencing of human tissue. *Nature Biotechnology, 29*(5), 393–396. doi:10.1038/nbt.1868 PMID:21552235

Koturbash, I., Zemp, F. J., Pogribny, I., & Kovalchuk, O. (2011). Small molecules with big effects: The role of the microRNAome in cancer and carcinogenesis. *Mutation Research, 722*(2), 94–105. doi:10.1016/j.mrgentox.2010.05.006 PMID:20472093

Kozomara, A., & Griffiths, S. J. (2014). miRBase: Annotating high confidence microRNAs using deep sequencing data. *Nucleic Acids Research, 42*(D1), D68–D73. doi:10.1093/nar/gkt1181 PMID:24275495

Kraft, P., & Cox, D. G. (2008). Study Designs for Genome-Wide Association Studies. In D. C. Rao & C. Gu (Ed.), Advances in genetics (Vol. 60, pp. 465–504). Academic Press.

Krallinger, M., Leitner, F., Vazquez, M., Salgado, D., Marcelle, C., & Tyers, M. et al. (2012). How to link ontologies and protein-protein interactions to literature: Text-mining approaches and the BioCreative experience. *Database (Oxford), 2012*(0), bas017. doi:10.1093/database/bas017 PMID:22438567

Krämer, A., Green, J., Pollard, J., & Tugendreich, S. (2013). Causal Analysis Approaches in Ingenuity Pathway Analysis (IPA). *Bioinformatics (Oxford, England)*.

Krasowski, M. D., & Penrod, L. E. (2012). Clinical decision support of therapeutic drug monitoring of phenytoin: Measured versus adjusted phenytoin plasma concentrations. *BMC Medical Informatics and Decision Making, 12*(1), 7. doi:10.1186/1472-6947-12-7 PMID:22333264

Kravitz, R. L. (2014). Personalized Medicine Without the "Omics". *Journal of General Internal Medicine, 29*(4), 551–551. doi:10.1007/s11606-014-2789-x PMID:24504920

Kreft, J., Plugge, C., Grimm, V., Prats, C., Leveau, J., & Banitz, T. et al. (2013). Mighty small: Observing and modeling individual microbes becomes big science. *Proceedings of the National Academy of Sciences of the United States of America, 110*(45), 18027–18028. doi:10.1073/pnas.1317472110 PMID:24194530

Krishna, R., Kelleher, K., & Stahlberg, E. (2007). Patient confidentiality in the research use of clinical medical databases. *American Journal of Public Health, 97*(4), 654–658. doi:10.2105/AJPH.2006.090902 PMID:17329644

Krleža-Jerić, K., & Lemmens, T. (2009). 7th revision of the Declaration of Helsinki: Good news for the transparency of clinical trials. *Croatian Medical Journal, 50*(2), 105–110. doi:10.3325/cmj.2009.50.105 PMID:19399942

Kruglyak, L., & Lander, E. S. (1998). Faster Multipoint Linkage Analysis Using Fourier Transforms. *Journal of Computational Biology, 5*(1), 1–7. doi:10.1089/cmb.1998.5.1 PMID:9541867

Kuehn, B. M. (2013). Scientists mine web search data to identify epidemics and adverse events. *Journal of the American Medical Association, 309*(18), 1883–1884. doi:10.1001/jama.2013.4015 PMID:23652502

Kuhn, D. E., Martin, M. M., Feldman, D. S., Terry, A. V. Jr, Nuovo, G. J., & Elton, T. S. (2008). Experimental Validation of miRNA Targets. *Methods (San Diego, Calif.), 44*(1), 47–54. doi:10.1016/j.ymeth.2007.09.005 PMID:18158132

Kumar, V., Gu, Y., Basu, S., Berglund, A., Eschrich, S. A., Schabath, M. B., . . . Gillies, R. J. (2012). Radiomics: the process and the challenges. *Magn Reson Imaging, 30*(9), 1234-1248. doi: 10.1016/j.mri.2012.06.010

Kumar, S., & Rai, A. (2007). Synthetic Biology: The Intellectual Property Puzzle. *Texas Law Review, 85*, 1745.

Kuo, T. C., Tian, T. F., & Tseng, Y. J. (2013). 3Omics: A web-based systems biology tool for analysis, integration and visualization of human transcriptomic, proteomic and metabolomic data. *BMC Systems Biology, 7*(1), 64. doi:10.1186/1752-0509-7-64 PMID:23875761

Kyrpides, N. (2009). Fifteen years of microbial genomics: Meeting the challenges and fulfilling the dream. *Nature Biotechnology, 27*(7), 627–632. doi:10.1038/nbt.1552 PMID:19587669

LaFramboise, T. (2009). Single nucleotide polymorphism arrays: A decade of biological, computational and technological advances. *Nucleic Acids Research, 37*(13), 4181–4193. doi:10.1093/nar/gkp552 PMID:19570852

Laird, N. M., Horvath, S., & Xu, X. (2000). Implementing a unified approach to family-based tests of association. *Genetic Epidemiology, 19*(S1Suppl 1), S36–S42. doi:10.1002/1098-2272(2000)19:1+<::AID-GEPI6>3.0.CO;2-M PMID:11055368

Lakshminarayan, K., Harp, S. A., Goldman, R., & Samad, T. (1996). *Imputation of missing data using machine learning techniques.* In *Proceedings of the Second International Conference on Knowledge Discovery and Data Mining (KDD-96).* Portland, OR: KDD.

Lambin, P., Rios-Velazquez, E., Leijenaar, R., Carvalho, S., van Stiphout, R. G., Granton, P., . . . Aerts, H. J. (2012). Radiomics: extracting more information from medical images using advanced feature analysis. *Eur J Cancer, 48*(4), 441-446. doi: 10.1016/j.ejca.2011.11.036

Lambin, P., Roelofs, E., Reymen, B., Velazquez, E. R., Buijsen, J., & Zegers, C. M. L. et al. (2013). ‚ÄòRapid Learning health care in oncology‚Äô ‚Äì An approach towards decision support systems enabling customised radiotherapy‚Äô. *Radiotherapy and Oncology, 109*(1), 159–164. doi:10.1016/j.radonc.2013.07.007 PMID:23993399

Lam, M. K. (2011). How good is New South Wales admitted patient data collection in recording births? *Health Information Management Journal, 40*(3), 12–19. PMID:22006432

Lan, M., Samy, L., Alshurafa, N., Suh, M.-K., Ghasemzadeh, H., Macabasco-O'Connell, A., & Sarrafzadeh, M. (2012). *WANDA: an end-to-end remote health monitoring and analytics system for heart failure patients.* Paper presented at the Conference on Wireless Health. New York, NY. doi:10.1145/2448096.2448105

Lanara, Z., Giannopoulou, E., Fullen, M., Kostantinopoulos, E., Nebel, J.-C., & Kalofonos, H. P. et al. (2013). Comparative study and meta-analysis of meta-analysis studies for the correlation of genomic markers with early cancer detection. *Human Genomics, 7*(1), 14. doi:10.1186/1479-7364-7-14 PMID:23738773

Lanckriet, G. R., De Bie, T., Cristianini, N., Jordan, M. I., & Noble, W. S. (2004). A statistical framework for genomic data fusion. *Bioinformatics (Oxford, England), 20*(16), 2626–2635. doi:10.1093/bioinformatics/bth294 PMID:15130933

Laney, D. (2001). *3-D data management: controlling data volume, velocity and variety.* Link.

Langfelder, P., Castellani, L. W., Zhou, Z., Paul, E., Davis, R., & Schadt, E. E. et al. (2012). A systems genetic analysis of high density lipoprotein metabolism and network preservation across mouse models. *Biochimica et Biophysica Acta, 1821*(3), 435–447. doi:10.1016/j.bbalip.2011.07.014 PMID:21807117

Langfelder, P., & Horvath, S. (2008). WGCNA: An R package for weighted correlation network analysis. *BMC Bioinformatics, 9*(1), 559. doi:10.1186/1471-2105-9-559 PMID:19114008

Langfelder, P., Zhang, B., & Horvath, S. (2008). Defining clusters from a hierarchical cluster tree: The Dynamic Tree Cut package for R. *Bioinformatics (Oxford, England), 24*(5), 719–720. doi:10.1093/bioinformatics/btm563 PMID:18024473

Lashkari, D. A., DeRisi, J. L., McCusker, J. H., Namath, A. F., Gentile, C., Hwang, S. Y., & Davis, R. W. (1997). Yeast microarrays for genome wide parallel genetic and gene expression analysis. *Proceedings of the National Academy of Sciences of the United States of America, 94*(24), 13057–13062. doi:10.1073/pnas.94.24.13057 PMID:9371799

Lawrence, C. A., Boguski, M., Liu, J., Neuwald, A., & Wooten, J. (1993). Detecting subtle sequence signals: A Gibbs sampling strategy for multiple alignment. *Science, 262*(5131), 208–214. doi:10.1126/science.8211139 PMID:8211139

Le Cao, K. A., Boitard, S., & Besse, P. (2011). Sparse PLS discriminant analysis: Biologically relevant feature selection and graphical displays for multiclass problems. *BMC Bioinformatics, 12*(1), 253. doi:10.1186/1471-2105-12-253 PMID:21693065

Le Cao, K. A., Martin, P. G., Robert-Granie, C., & Besse, P. (2009). Sparse canonical methods for biological data integration: Application to a cross-platform study. *BMC Bioinformatics, 10*(1), 34. doi:10.1186/1471-2105-10-34 PMID:19171069

Le Cao, K. A., Rossouw, D., Robert-Granie, C., & Besse, P. (2008). A sparse PLS for variable selection when integrating omics data. *Statistical Applications in Genetics and Molecular Biology, 7*(1), 35. doi:10.2202/1544-6115.1390 PMID:19049491

Lederberg, J., & McCray, A. (2001). 'Ome Sweet' Omics—a genealogical treasury of words. *Scientist (Philadelphia, Pa.), 15*, 8.

Ledford, H. (2013). Bioengineers look beyond patents. *Nature, 499*(7456), 16–17. doi:10.1038/499016a PMID:23823774

Lee, S. I., Ghasemzadeh, H., Mortazavi, B., Lan, M., Alshurafa, N., Ong, M., & Sarrafzadeh, M. (2013). *Remote Patient Monitoring: What Impact Can Data Analytics Have on Cost?* Paper presented at the Wireless Health '13. Baltimore, MD. doi:10.1145/2534088.2534108

Lee, C. T., Risom, T., & Strauss, W. M. (2007). Evolutionary conservation of microRNA regulatory circuits: An examination of microRNA gene complexity and conserved microRNA-target interactions through metazoan phylogeny. *DNA and Cell Biology, 26*(4), 209–218. doi:10.1089/dna.2006.0545 PMID:17465887

Leek, J. T., Taub, M. A., & Rasgon, J. L. (2012). A statistical approach to selecting and confirming validation targets in -omics experiments. *BMC Bioinformatics, 13*(1), 150. doi:10.1186/1471-2105-13-150 PMID:22738145

Leem, S., Jeong, H., Lee, J., Wee, K., & Sohn, K.-A. (n.d.). Fast detection of high-order epistatic interactions in genome-wide association studies using information theoretic measure.[In Press]. *Computational Biology and Chemistry.* PMID:24581733

Lee, P. H., Jung, J. Y., & Shatkay, H. (2010). Functionally informative tag SNP selection using a Pareto-optimal approach. *Advances in Experimental Medicine and Biology, 680*, 173–180. doi:10.1007/978-1-4419-5913-3_20 PMID:20865499

Lee, P. H., & Shatkay, H. (2006). BNTagger: Improved tagging SNP selection using Bayesian networks. *Bioinformatics (Oxford, England), 22*(14), e211–e219. doi:10.1093/bioinformatics/btl233 PMID:16873474

Lee, P. H., & Shatkay, H. (2008a). F-SNP: Computationally predicted functional SNPs for disease association studies. *Nucleic Acids Research, 36*(Database issue), D820–D824. PMID:17986460

Lee, P. H., & Shatkay, H. (2008b). Ranking single nucleotide polymorphisms by potential deleterious effects. *AMIA ... Annual Symposium Proceedings / AMIA Symposium. AMIA Symposium*, 667–671. PMID:18999314

Lee, P. H., & Shatkay, H. (2009). An integrative scoring system for ranking SNPs by their potential deleterious effects. *Bioinformatics (Oxford, England)*, 25(8), 1048–1055. doi:10.1093/bioinformatics/btp103 PMID:19228803

Lee, S. I., Dudley, A. M., Drubin, D., Silver, P. A., Krogan, N. J., Pe'er, D., & Koller, D. (2009). Learning a prior on regulatory potential from eQTL data. *PLOS Genetics*, 5(1), e1000358. doi:10.1371/journal.pgen.1000358 PMID:19180192

Lee, Y. S., Shibata, Y., Malhotra, A., & Dutta, A. (2009). A novel class of small RNAs: tRNA-derived RNA fragments (tRFs). *Genes & Development*, 23(22), 2639–2649. doi:10.1101/gad.1837609 PMID:19933153

LeFever, L. (2013). *The art of explanation: making your ideas, products, and services easier to understand.* Hoboken, NJ: John Wiley & Sons.

Lehnert, S. (2008). *Biomolecular action of ionizing radiation.* New York: Taylor & Francis.

Leidinger, P., Backes, C., Deutscher, S., Schmitt, K., Mueller, S. C., & Frese, K. et al. (2013). A blood based 12-miRNA signature of Alzheimer disease patients. *Genome Biology*, 14(7), R78. doi:10.1186/gb-2013-14-7-r78 PMID:23895045

Lein, E., Hawrylycz, M. J., Ao, N., Ayres, M., Bensinger, A., & Bernard, A. et al. (2007). Genome-wide atlas of gene expression in the adult mouse brain. *Nature*, 445(7124), 168–176. doi:10.1038/nature05453 PMID:17151600

Leong, L., Toombs, D., Gill, B., Petri, G., & Haynes, T. (2013). *Magic Quadrant for Cloud Infrastructure as a Service.* Retrieved from http://www.gartner.com/technology/reprints.do?id=1-1IMDMZ5&ct=130819&st=sb

Lester, D. S. (2009). Will personalized medicine help in 'transforming' the business of healthcare? *Personalized Medicine*, 6(5), 555–565. doi:10.2217/pme.09.31

Lettre, G., Lange, C., & Hirschhorn, J. N. (2007). Genetic model testing and statistical power in population-based association studies of quantitative traits. *Genetic Epidemiology*, 31(4), 358–362. doi:10.1002/gepi.20217 PMID:17352422

Levegrun, S., Jackson, A., Zelefsky, M. J., Skwarchuk, M. W., Venkatraman, E. S., & Schlegel, W. et al. (2001). Fitting tumor control probability models to biopsy outcome after three-dimensional conformal radiation therapy of prostate cancer: Pitfalls in deducing radiobiologic parameters for tumors from clinical data. *International Journal of Radiation Oncology, Biology, Physics*, 51(4), 1064–1080. doi:10.1016/S0360-3016(01)01731-X PMID:11704332

Levine, M., & Tjian, R. (2003). Transcription regulation and animal diversity. *Nature*, 424(6945), 147–151. doi:10.1038/nature01763 PMID:12853946

Levin, K. A. (2006). Study design III: Cross-sectional studies. *Evidence-Based Dentistry*, 7(1), 24–25. doi:10.1038/sj.ebd.6400375 PMID:16557257

Lewis, C. M., & Knight, J. (2012). Introduction to Genetic Association Studies. *Cold Spring Harbor Protocols*, (3), 297–306.

Li, G., & Zhu, H. (2013). Genetic Studies: The Linear Mixed Models in Genome-wide Association Studies. *The Open Bioinformatics Journal, 7*(Suppl 1), 27–33.

Li, A., & Horvath, S. (2007). Network neighborhood analysis with the multi-node topological overlap measure. *Bioinformatics (Oxford, England)*, 23(2), 222–231. doi:10.1093/bioinformatics/btl581 PMID:17110366

Li, A., & Horvath, S. (2009). Network module detection: Affinity search technique with the multi-node topological overlap measure. *BMC Research Notes*, 2(1), 142. doi:10.1186/1756-0500-2-142 PMID:19619323

Liang, L., Morar, N., Dixon, A. L., Lathrop, G. M., Abecasis, G. R., Moffatt, M. F., & Cookson, W. O. (2013). A cross-platform analysis of 14,177 expression quantitative trait loci derived from lymphoblastoid cell lines. *Genome Research*, 23(4), 716–726. doi:10.1101/gr.142521.112 PMID:23345460

Liao, J. Y., Ma, L. M., Guo, Y. H., Zhang, Y. C., Zhou, H., & Shao, P. et al. (2010). Deep sequencing of human nuclear and cytoplasmic small RNAs reveals an unexpectedly complex subcellular distribution of miRNAs and tRNA 3' trailers. *PLoS ONE*, *5*(5), e10563. doi:10.1371/journal.pone.0010563 PMID:20498841

Li, B., & Leal, S. M. (2008). Methods for Detecting Associations with Rare Variants for Common Diseases: Application to Analysis of Sequence Data. *American Journal of Human Genetics*, *83*(3), 311–321. doi:10.1016/j.ajhg.2008.06.024 PMID:18691683

Lichtenstein, P., Holm, N. V., Verkasalo, P. K., Iliadou, A., Kaprio, J., & Koskenvuo, M. et al. (2000). Environmental and heritable factors in the causation of cancer--analyses of cohorts of twins from Sweden, Denmark, and Finland. *The New England Journal of Medicine*, *343*(2), 78–85. doi:10.1056/NEJM200007133430201 PMID:10891514

Liebowitz, J. (2013). *Big data and business analytics*. Boca Raton, FL: CRC Press. doi:10.1201/b14700

Liew, A., Yan, H., & Wu, S. (2003). A novel OPTOC-based clustering algorithm for gene expression data analysis. In *Information, Communications and Signal Processing, 2003 and Fourth Pacific Rim Conference on Multimedia: Proceedings of the 2003 Joint Conference of the Fourth International Conference on*, (vol. 3, pp. 1427 1431). Academic Press.

Li, F., Nie, L., Wu, G., Qiao, J., & Zhang, W. (2011). Prediction and Characterization of Missing Proteomic Data in Desulfovibrio vulgaris. *Comparative and Functional Genomics*, *2011*, 780973. doi:10.1155/2011/780973 PMID:21687592

Li, J. W., Wan, R., Yu, C. S., Co, N. N., Wong, N., & Chan, T. F. (2013). ViralFusionSeq: Accurately discover viral integration events and reconstruct fusion transcripts at single-base resolution. *Bioinformatics (Oxford, England)*, *29*(5), 649–651. doi:10.1093/bioinformatics/btt011 PMID:23314323

Li, J., Horstman, B., & Chen, Y. (2011). Detecting epistatic effects in association studies at a genomic level based on an ensemble approach. *Bioinformatics (Oxford, England)*, *27*(13), i222–i229. doi:10.1093/bioinformatics/btr227 PMID:21685074

Li, L., Fridley, B. L., Kalari, K., Jenkins, G., Batzler, A., Weinshilboum, R. M., & Wang, L. (2009). Gemcitabine and arabinosylcytosin pharmacogenomics: Genome-wide association and drug response biomarkers. *PLoS ONE*, *4*(11), e7765. PMID:19898621

Li, L., Kabesch, M., Bouzigon, E., Demenais, F., Farrall, M., & Moffatt, M. F. et al. (2013). Using eQTL weights to improve power for genome-wide association studies: A genetic study of childhood asthma. *Frontiers in Genetics*, *4*, 103. doi:10.3389/fgene.2013.00103 PMID:23755072

Lin, D. Y., & Zeng, D. (2009). Meta-analysis of genome-wide association studies: No efficiency gain in using individual participant data. *Genetic Epidemiology*, *34*(1), 60–66. PMID:19847795

Lin, S., Chakravarti, A., & Cutler, D. J. (2004). Haplotype and missing data inference in nuclear families. *Genome Research*, *14*(8), 1624–1632. doi:10.1101/gr.2204604 PMID:15256514

Lipshutz, R., Fodor, S. P. A., Gingeras, T. R., & Lockhart, D. J. (2000). High density synthesis oligonucleotide arrays. *Nature Genetics*, *21*(Supplement), 20–24. doi:10.1038/4447 PMID:9915496

Little, R. J., D'Agostino, R., Cohen, M. L., Dickersin, K., Emerson, S. S., & Farrar, J. T. et al. (2012). The prevention and treatment of missing data in clinical trials. *The New England Journal of Medicine*, *367*(14), 1355–1360. doi:10.1056/NEJMsr1203730 PMID:23034025

Liu, N., Zhang, K., & Zhao, H. (2008). Haplotype-Association Analysis. In D. C. Rao & C. Gu (Ed.), Advances in genetics (Vol. 60, pp. 335–405). Academic Press.

Liu, B., de la Fuente, A., & Hoeschele, I. (2008). Gene network inference via structural equation modeling in genetical genomics experiments. *Genetics*, *178*(3), 1763–1776. doi:10.1534/genetics.107.080069 PMID:18245846

Liu, H., Christiansen, T., Baumgartner, W. A. Jr, & Verspoor, K. (2012). BioLemmatizer: A lemmatization tool for morphological processing of biomedical text. *Journal of Biomedical Semantics*, *3*(1), 3. doi:10.1186/2041-1480-3-3 PMID:22464129

Liu, H., Jin, T., Liao, R., Wan, L., Xu, B., Zhou, S., & Guan, J. (2012). miRFANs: An integrated database for Arabidopsis thaliana microRNA function annotations. *BMC Plant Biology*, *12*(1), 68. doi:10.1186/1471-2229-12-68 PMID:22583976

Liu, J. S. (1994). The Collapsed Gibbs Sampler in Bayesian Computations with Applications to a Gene Regulation Problem. *Journal of the American Statistical Association*, *89*(427), 958–966. doi:10.1080/01621459.1994.10476829

Liu, L., Li, Y., Li, S., Hu, N., He, Y., Pong, R., & Law, M. (2012). Comparison of next-generation sequencing systems. *Journal of Biomedicine & Biotechnology*, *251364*. doi:10.1155/2012/251364 PMID:22829749

Liu, L., Zhang, D., Liu, H., & Arendt, C. (2013). Robust methods for population stratification in genome wide association studies. *BMC Bioinformatics*, *14*(1), 132. doi:10.1186/1471-2105-14-132 PMID:23601181

Liu, Y., Aryee, M. J., Padyukov, L., Fallin, M. D., Hesselberg, E., & Runarsson, A. et al. (2013). Epigenome-wide association data implicate DNA methylation as an intermediary of genetic risk in rheumatoid arthritis. *Nature Biotechnology*, *31*(2), 142–147. doi:10.1038/nbt.2487 PMID:23334450

Liu, Y., Navathe, S. B., Civera, J., Dasigi, V., Ram, A., Ciliax, B. J., & Dingledine, R. (2005). Text mining biomedical literature for discovering gene-to-gene relationships: A comparative study of algorithms. *IEEE/ACM Transactions on Computational Biology and Bioinformatics*, *2*(1), 62–76. doi:10.1109/TCBB.2005.14 PMID:17044165

Li, X., & Li, J. (2008). Efficient haplotype inference from pedigrees with missing data using linear systems with disjoint-set data structures. *Computational Systems Bioinformatics / Life Sciences Society. Computational Systems Bioinformatics Conference*, *7*, 297–308. PMID:19642289

Li, X., & Shen, C. (2013). Linkage of patient records from disparate sources. *Statistical Methods in Medical Research*, *22*(1), 31–38. doi:10.1177/0962280211403600 PMID:21665896

Li, Y., Willer, C. J., Ding, J., Scheet, P., & Abecasis, G. R. (2010). MaCH: Using sequence and genotype data to estimate haplotypes and unobserved genotypes. *Genetic Epidemiology*, *34*(8), 816–834. doi:10.1002/gepi.20533 PMID:21058334

Llewellyn-Thomas, H. A., McGreal, M. J., Thiel, E. C., Fine, S., & Erlichman, C. (1991). Patients' willingness to enter clinical trials: Measuring the association with perceived benefit and preference for decision participation. *Social Science & Medicine*, *32*(1), 35–42. doi:10.1016/0277-9536(91)90124-U PMID:2008619

Lobach, I., Fan, R., & Carroll, R. J. (2010). Genotype-based association mapping of complex diseases: Gene-environment interactions with multiple genetic markers and measurement error in environmental exposures. *Genetic Epidemiology*, *34*(8), 792–802. doi:10.1002/gepi.20523 PMID:21031455

Lobach, I., Mallick, B., & Carroll, R. J. (2011). Semi-parametric Bayesian analysis of gene-environment interactions with error in measurement of environmental covariates and missing genetic data. *Statistics and Its Interface*, *4*(3), 305–316. doi:10.4310/SII.2011.v4.n3.a5 PMID:21949562

Logemann, E., Birkenbihl, R. P., Rawat, V., Schneeberger, K., Schmelzer, E., & Somssich, I. E. (2013). Functional dissection of the PROPEP2 and PROPEP3 promoters reveals the importance of WRKY factors in mediating microbe-associated molecular pattern-induced expression. *The New Phytologist*, *198*(4), 1165–1177. doi:10.1111/nph.12233 PMID:23496690

Logsdon, B. A., Dai, J. Y., Auer, P. L., Johnsen, J. M., Ganesh, S. K., & Smith, N. L. et al. (2014). A Variational Bayes Discrete Mixture Test for Rare Variant Association. *Genetic Epidemiology*, *38*(1), 21–30. doi:10.1002/gepi.21772 PMID:24482836

Lohr, S. (2013). *The Origins of 'Big Data': An Etymological Detective Story*. Retrieved January, 2014, from http://bits.blogs.nytimes.com/2013/02/01/the-origins-of-big-data-an-etymological-detective-story

Long, M. (2000). A new function evolved from gene fusion. *Genome Research*, *10*(11), 1655–1657. doi:10.1101/gr.165700 PMID:11076848

Looney, C. (2002). Interactive clustering and merging with a new fuzzy expected value. *Pattern Recognition*, *35*(11), 2413–2423. doi:10.1016/S0031-3203(01)00213-8

Lowenfels, A. B., Maisonneuve, P., Cavallini, G., Ammann, R. W., Lankisch, P. G., & Andersen, J. R. et al. (1993). Pancreatitis and the risk of pancreatic cancer. International Pancreatitis Study Group. *The New England Journal of Medicine*, *328*(20), 1433–1437. doi:10.1056/NEJM199305203282001 PMID:8479461

LTC-AB. (n.d.). Retrieved from http://www.lifetechnologies.com/de/de/home/brands/applied-biosystems.html

Lu, J. J., & Brady, L. W. (2011). *Decision making in radiation oncology*. Heidelberg, Germany: Springer.

Lukashin, A., & Fuchs, R. (2001). Analysis of temporal gene expression profiles: clustering by simulated annealing and determining the optimal number of clusters. *Bioinformatics*. doi: / 17.5.405.10.1093/bioinformatics

Lu, L. J., Xia, Y., Paccanaro, A., Yu, H., & Gerstein, M. (2005). Assessing the limits of genomic data integration for predicting protein networks. *Genome Research*, *15*(7), 945–953. doi:10.1101/gr.3610305 PMID:15998909

Macdonald, J. R., Ziman, R., Yuen, R. K., Feuk, L., & Scherer, S. W. (2014). The Database of Genomic Variants: A curated collection of structural variation in the human genome. *Nucleic Acids Research*, *42*(1), D986–D992. doi:10.1093/nar/gkt958 PMID:24174537

Maclellan, S. A., Lawson, J., Baik, J., Guillaud, M., Poh, C. F., & Garnis, C. (2012). Differential expression of miRNAs in the serum of patients with high-risk oral lesions. *Cancer Med*, *1*(2), 268–274. doi:10.1002/cam4.17 PMID:23342275

Mahoney, D., Tennstedt, S., Friedman, R., & Heeren, T. (1999). An automated telephone system for monitoring the functional status of community-residing elders. *The Gerontologist*, *39*(2), 229–234. doi:10.1093/geront/39.2.229 PMID:10224719

Ma, L., Clark, A. G., & Keinan, A. (2013). Gene-Based Testing of Interactions in Association Studies of Quantitative Traits. *PLOS Genetics*, *9*(2), e1003321. doi:10.1371/journal.pgen.1003321 PMID:23468652

Malina, M., Ickstadt, K., Schwender, H., Posch, M., & Bogdan, M. (2014). Detection of epistatic effects with logic regression and a classical linear regression model. *Statistical Applications in Genetics and Molecular Biology*, *13*(1), 83–104. doi:10.1515/sagmb-2013-0028 PMID:24413217

Many Eyes. (2014). *Many Eyes*. Retrieved January 13, 2014, from http://www-958.ibm.com/software/analytics/manyeyes/

Manyika, J. Chui, M., Brown, B., Bughin J., Dobbs, R. Roxburgh, C. and Byers, A.H. (2011). *Big Data: The Next Frontier for Innovation, Competition and Productivity*. San Fransisco: McKinsey Global Institute.

Mapcite. (2013). *How Emergency Managers Can Benefit from Big Data*. Retrieved 23/10/13, 2013, from http://www.mapcite.com/posts/2013/july/how-emergency-managers-can-benefit-from-big-data.aspx

Mapelli, V., Olsson, L., & Nielsen, J. (2008). Metabolic footprinting in microbiology: Methods and applications in functional genomics and biotechnology. *Trends in Biotechnology*, *26*(9), 490–497. doi:10.1016/j.tibtech.2008.05.008 PMID:18675480

Marchini, J., & Howie, B. (2008). Comparing algorithms for genotype imputation. *American Journal of Human Genetics*, *83*(4), 535–539. doi:10.1016/j.ajhg.2008.09.007 PMID:18940314

Marchini, J., & Howie, B. (2010). Genotype imputation for genome-wide association studies. *Nature Reviews. Genetics*, *11*(7), 499–511. doi:10.1038/nrg2796 PMID:20517342

Marchini, J., Howie, B., Myers, S., McVean, G., & Donnelly, P. (2007). A new multipoint method for genome-wide association studies by imputation of genotypes. *Nature Genetics*, *39*(7), 906–913. doi:10.1038/ng2088 PMID:17572673

Marcotte, E. M., & Date, S. V. (2001). Exploiting big biology: Integrating large-scale biological data for function inference. *Briefings in Bioinformatics, 2*(4), 363–374. doi:10.1093/bib/2.4.363 PMID:11808748

Mardinoglu, A., Agren, R., Kampf, C., Asplund, A., Nookaew, I., & Jacobson, P. et al. (2013). Integration of clinical data with a genome-scale metabolic model of the human adipocyte. *Molecular Systems Biology, 9*(1), 649. doi:10.1038/msb.2013.5 PMID:23511207

Marechal, F., Ribeiro, N., Lafaye, M., & Güell, A. (2008). Satellite imaging and vector-borne diseases: The approach of the French National Space Agency (CNES). *Geospatial Health, 3*(1), 1–5. PMID:19021103

Margolin, A. A., Nemenman, I., Basso, K., Wiggins, C., Stolovitzky, G., Dalla Favera, R., & Califano, A. (2006). ARACNE: An algorithm for the reconstruction of gene regulatory networks in a mammalian cellular context. *BMC Bioinformatics, 7*. doi: Artn S7

Margolin, A. A., Wang, K., Lim, W. K., Kustagi, M., Nemenman, I., & Califano, A. (2006). Reverse engineering cellular networks. *Nature Protocols, 1*(2), 663–672. doi:10.1038/nprot.2006.106 PMID:17406294

Mariño-Ramírez, L., Sheetlin, S., Landsman, D., & Spouge, J. (2005). Alignments anchored on genomic landmarks can aid in the identification of regulatory elements. *Bioinformatics, 21*(suppl 1), i440-i448.

Marinou, I., Healy, J., Mewar, D., Moore, D. J., Dickson, M. C., & Binks, M. H. et al. (2007). Association of interleukin-6 and interleukin-10 genotypes with radiographic damage in rheumatoid arthritis is dependent on autoantibody status. *Arthritis and Rheumatism, 56*(8), 2549–2556. doi:10.1002/art.22814 PMID:17665434

Marioni, J. C., Mason, C. E., Mane, S. M., Stephens, M., & Gilad, Y. (2008). RNA-seq: An assessment of technical reproducibility and comparison with gene expression arrays. *Genome Research, 18*(9), 1509–1517. doi:10.1101/gr.079558.108 PMID:18550803

Marja, K., Caldentey, O., Inze, D., & Oresic, M. (2004). Connecting genes to metabolites by a systems biology approach. *Proceedings of the National Academy of Sciences of the United States of America, 101*(27), 9949–9950. doi:10.1073/pnas.0403636101 PMID:15226495

Marjoua, Y., Butler, C. A., & Bozic, K. J. (2012). Public Reporting of Cost and Quality Information in Orthopaedics. *Clinical Orthopaedics and Related Research, 470*(4), 1017–1026. doi:10.1007/s11999-011-2077-6 PMID:21952744

Markos, A. I., Vozalis, M. G., & Margaritis, K. G. (2010). An Optimal Scaling Approach to Collaborative Filtering Using Categorical Principal Component Analysis and Neighborhood Formation. In *Proceedings of the 6th IFIP WG 12.5 International Conference*. AIAI. doi:10.1007/978-3-642-16239-8_6

Marks, L. B. (2002). Dosimetric predictors of radiation-induced lung injury. *International Journal of Radiation Oncology, Biology, Physics, 54*(2), 313–316. doi:10.1016/S0360-3016(02)02928-0 PMID:12243802

Marlin, B. M. (2008). *Missing data problems in machine learning*. (Doctoral Thesis). University of Toronto, Toronto, Canada.

Márquez, M., Chirlaque, D. M., & Navarro, C., C. (2008). DataLink Record Linkage Software Applied to the Cancer Registry of Murcia, Spain. *Methods of Information in Medicine, 47*, 448–453. doi:10.3414/ME0529 PMID:18852919

Marson, F. A. de L., Bertuzzo, C., Ribeiro, A., & Ribeiro, J. (2014). Polymorphisms in the glutathione pathway modulate cystic fibrosis severity: A cross-sectional study. *BMC Medical Genetics, 15*(1), 27. doi:10.1186/1471-2350-15-27 PMID:24593045

Martens-Uzunova, E. S., Olvedy, M., & Jenster, G. (2012). Beyond microRNA – Novel RNAs derived from small non-coding RNA and their implication in cancer. *Cancer Letters*, (0). doi:10.1016/j.canlet.2012.11.058 PMID:23376637

Martin, E., Monks, S., Warren, L., & Kaplan, N. (2000). A Test for Linkage and Association in General Pedigrees: The Pedigree Disequilibrium Test. *American Journal of Human Genetics, 67*(1), 146–154. doi:10.1086/302957 PMID:10825280

Martinez-Jimenez, F., Papadatos, G., Yang, L., Wallace, I. M., Kumar, V., & Pieper, U. et al. (2013). Target prediction for an open access set of compounds active against *Mycobacterium tuberculosis*. *PLoS Computational Biology, 9*, e1003253. doi:10.1371/journal.pcbi.1003253 PMID:24098102

Marx, V. (2013). Genomics in the clouds. *Nature Methods*, *10*(10), 941–945. doi:10.1038/nmeth.2654 PMID:24076987

Marx, V. (2013). The big challenges of big data. *Nature*, *498*(7453), 255–260. doi:10.1038/498255a PMID:23765498

Mashey, J. R. (1998). *Big Data ... and the Next Wave of InfraStress*. Paper presented at the SGI. New York, NY.

Ma, Y., Hart, J. D., Janicki, R., & Carroll, R. J. (2011). Local and omnibus goodness-of-fit tests in classical measurement error models. *Journal of the Royal Statistical Society. Series B, Statistical Methodology*, *73*(1), 81–98. doi:10.1111/j.1467-9868.2010.00751.x PMID:21339886

Mayer, B. (Ed.). (2011). Bioinformatics for Omics Data: Methods and Protocols (Vol. 719). New York: Springer Science + Business Media, LCC. doi:10.1007/978-1-61779-027-0

Mayer, G., Heinze, G., Mischak, H., Hellemons, M. E., Heerspink, H. J., & Bakker, S. J. et al. (2011). Omics-bioinformatics in the context of clinical data. *Methods in Molecular Biology (Clifton, N.J.)*, *719*, 479–497. doi:10.1007/978-1-61779-027-0_22 PMID:21370098

Mayeux, R. (2004). Biomarkers: Potential uses and limitations. *NeuroRx*, *1*(2), 182–188. doi:10.1602/neurorx.1.2.182 PMID:15717018

McCarroll, S. A., Kuruvilla, F. G., Korn, J. M., Cawley, S., Nemesh, J., Wysoker, A., & Altshuler, D. (2008). Integrated detection and population-genetic analysis of SNPs and copy number variation. *Nature Genetics*, *40*(10), 1166–1174. doi:10.1038/ng.238 PMID:18776908

McCoy, C. E. (2011). The role of miRNAs in cytokine signaling. *Frontiers in Bioscience (Landmark Edition)*, *16*(1), 2161–2171. doi:10.2741/3845 PMID:21622168

McCulloch, E. (2013). Harnessing the power of big data in biological research. *Bioscience*, *63*(9), 715–716. doi:10.1093/bioscience/63.9.715

McDonald, D., Su, H., Xu, J., Tseng, C.-J., Chen, H., & Leroy, G. (2005). Gene Pathway Text Mining and Visualization. In H. Chen, S. Fuller, C. Friedman, & W. Hersh (Eds.), *Medical Informatics* (Vol. 8, pp. 519–546). Springer. doi:10.1007/0-387-25739-X_18

McDonald, R., & Pereira, F. (2005). Identifying gene and protein mentions in text using conditional random fields. *BMC Bioinformatics*, *6*(Suppl 1), S6. doi:10.1186/1471-2105-6-S1-S6 PMID:15960840

McNutt, T. (2013). *Analytic database for personalized and evidence-based radiation oncology*. Paper presented at the ICCR. Melbourne, Australia.

McPherson, A., Hormozdiari, F., Zayed, A., Giuliany, R., Ha, G., Sun, M. G., & Shah, S. P. (2011). deFuse: An algorithm for gene fusion discovery in tumor RNA-Seq data. *PLoS Computational Biology*, *7*(5), e1001138. doi:10.1371/journal.pcbi.1001138 PMID:21625565

Meaburn, K. J., Misteli, T., & Soutoglou, E. (2007). Spatial genome organization in the formation of chromosomal translocations.[Review]. *Seminars in Cancer Biology*, *17*(1), 80–90. doi:10.1016/j.semcancer.2006.10.008 PMID:17137790

Medini, D., Serruto, D., Parkhill, J., Relman, D., Donati, C., & Moxon, R. et al. (2008). Microbiology in the post-genomic era. *Nature Reviews. Microbiology*, *6*, 419–430. PMID:18475305

Meijer, C., Wouterse, B., Polder, J., & Koopmanschap, M. (2013). The effect of population aging on health expenditure growth: A critical review. *European Journal of Ageing*, 1–9. doi:10.1007/s10433-013-0280-x

Mello, F. C. Q., Bastos, L. G. V., Soares, S. L. M., Rezende, V. M. C., Conde, M. B., & Chaisson, R. E. et al. (2006). Predicting smear negative pulmonary tuberculosis with classification trees and logistic regression: A cross-sectional study. *BMC Public Health*, *6*(1), 43. doi:10.1186/1471-2458-6-43 PMID:16504086

Mello, M. M., Francer, J. K., Wilenzick, M., Teden, P., Bierer, B. E., & Barnes, M. (2013). Preparing for responsible sharing of clinical trial data. *The New England Journal of Medicine*. PMID:24144394

Méray, N., Reitsma, B. J., Ravelli, C. J. A., & Bonsel, J. G. (2007). Probabilistic record linkage is a valid and transparent tool to combine databases without a patient identification number. *Journal of Clinical Epidemiology*, *60*(9), 883.e881–883.e811. doi:10.1016/j.jclinepi.2006.11.021 PMID:17689804

Metropolis, N., Rosenbluth, A. W., Rosenbluth, M. N., Teller, A. H., & Teller, E. (1953). Equation of state calculations by fast computing machines. *The Journal of Chemical Physics*, 1807–1813.

Metzke, M. (2010). Sequencing technologies – the next generation. *Nature Reviews. Genetics*, *11*(1), 31–46. doi:10.1038/nrg2626 PMID:19997069

Mewes, H. W., Frishman, D., Gruber, C., Geier, B., Haase, D., & Kaps, A. et al. (2000). MIPS: A database for genomes and protein sequences. *Nucleic Acids Research*, *28*(1), 37–40. doi:10.1093/nar/28.1.37 PMID:10592176

Michaud, D. S., Izard, J., Wilhelm-Benartzi, C. S., You, D. H., Grote, V. A., & Tjonneland, A. et al. (2013). Plasma antibodies to oral bacteria and risk of pancreatic cancer in a large European prospective cohort study. *Gut*, *62*(12), 1764–1770. doi:10.1136/gutjnl-2012-303006 PMID:22990306

Michaud, D. S., Joshipura, K., Giovannucci, E., & Fuchs, C. S. (2007). A prospective study of periodontal disease and pancreatic cancer in US male health professionals. *Journal of the National Cancer Institute*, *99*(2), 171–175. doi:10.1093/jnci/djk021 PMID:17228001

Microsoft Excel. (2014). *Microsoft Excel*. Retrieved January 12, 2014, from http://office.microsoft.com/en-us/excel/

Microsoft. (2013). *The Big Bang: How the Big Data Explosion Is Changing the World*. Microsoft UK Enterprise Insights Blog. Retrieved from http://blogs.msdn.com/b/microsoftenterpriseinsight/archive/2013/04/15/big-bang-how-the-big-data-explosion-is-changing-the-world.aspx

Microsoft. (n.d.). *Maximum capacity specifications for SQL server*. Retrieved from http://technet.microsoft.com/en-us/library/ms143432(v=sql.110).aspx

Middleton, J., Lim, K., Taylor, L., Soden, R., & Rutkowski, S. (2004). Patterns of morbidity and rehospitalisation following spinal cord injury. *Spinal Cord*, *42*(6), 359–367. doi:10.1038/sj.sc.3101601 PMID:15007376

Mi, H., Dong, Q., Muruganujan, A., Gaudet, P., Lewis, S., & Thomas, P. D. (2010). PANTHER version 7: Improved phylogenetic trees, orthologs and collaboration with the Gene Ontology Consortium. *Nucleic Acids Research*, *38*(Database issue), D204–D210. doi:10.1093/nar/gkp1019 PMID:20015972

Milenova, B. L., & Campos, M. M. (2002). O-cluster: scalable clustering of large high dimensional data sets. In *Proceedings of the 2002 IEEE International Conference on Data Mining (ICDM 2002)*, (pp. 290-297). IEEE. doi:10.1109/ICDM.2002.1183915

Millard, R. W., & Carver, J. R. (1999). Cross-sectional comparison of live and interactive voice recognition administration of the SF-12 health status survey. *The American Journal of Managed Care*, *5*(2), 153. PMID:10346511

Miller, A. C., Obholzer, N. D., Shah, A. N., Megason, S. G., & Moens, C. B. (2013). RNA-seq-based mapping and candidate identification of mutations from forward genetic screens. *Genome Research*, *23*(4), 679–686. doi:10.1101/gr.147322.112 PMID:23299976

Min, J. L., Taylor, J. M., Richards, J. B., Watts, T., Pettersson, F. H., & Broxholme, J. et al. (2011). The use of genome-wide eQTL associations in lymphoblastoid cell lines to identify novel genetic pathways involved in complex traits. *PLoS ONE*, *6*(7), e22070. doi:10.1371/journal.pone.0022070 PMID:21789213

Mitelman, F., Johansson, B., & Mertens, F. (2007). The impact of translocations and gene fusions on cancer causation. *Nature Reviews. Cancer*, *7*(4), 233–245. doi:10.1038/nrc2091 PMID:17361217

Mitic, M., & Kapoulas, A. (2012). Understanding the role of social media in bank marketing. *Marketing Intelligence & Planning*, *30*(7), 668–686. doi:10.1108/02634501211273797

Mocci, E., Milne, R. L., Mendez-Villamil, E. Y., Hopper, J. L., John, E. M., & Andrulis, I. L. et al. (2013). Risk of pancreatic cancer in breast cancer families from the breast cancer family registry. *Cancer Epidemiology, Biomarkers & Prevention*, *22*(5), 803–811. doi:10.1158/1055-9965.EPI-12-0195 PMID:23456555

Mochida, K., & Shinozaki, K. (2011). Advances in omics and bioinformatics tools for systems analyses of plant functions. *Plant & Cell Physiology*, *52*(12), 2017–2038. doi:10.1093/pcp/pcr153 PMID:22156726

Moissenko, V., Deasy, J. O., & Van Dyk, J. (2005). Radiobiological Modeling for Treatment Planning. In J. Van Dyk (Ed.), *The Modern Technology of Radiation Oncology: A Compendium for Medical Physicists and Radiation Oncologists* (Vol. 2, pp. 185–220). Madison, WI: Medical Physics Publishing.

Molenberghs, G., Kenward, M. G., Aerts, M., Verbeke, G., Tsiatis, A. A., Davidian, M., & Rizopoulos, D. (2014). On random sample size, ignorability, ancillarity, completeness, separability, and degeneracy: Sequential trials, random sample sizes, and missing data. *Statistical Methods in Medical Research*, *23*(1), 11–41. doi:10.1177/0962280212445801 PMID:22514029

Molenberghs, G., Kenward, M. G., & Goetghebeur, E. (2001). Sensitivity analysis for incomplete contingency tables: The Slovenian plebiscite case. *Applied Statistics*, *50*(1), 15–29. doi:10.1111/1467-9876.00217

Moon, J., Hart, K. G., & Nunn, A. (2014). An eJourney through the Life Cycle of Spinal Cord Injury. In M. Khosrow-Pour (Ed.), *Encyclopedia of Information Science and Technology* (3rd ed.). Hershey, PA: IGI. doi:10.4018/978-1-4666-5888-2.ch325

Moore, H. C., de Klerk, N., Keil, A. D., Smith, D. W., Blyth, C. C., Richmond, P., & Lehmann, D. (2012). Use of data linkage to investigate the aetiology of acute lower respiratory infection hospitalisations in children. *Journal of Paediatrics and Child Health*, *48*(6), 520–528. doi:10.1111/j.1440-1754.2011.02229.x PMID:22077532

Mo, Q., Wang, S., Seshan, V. E., Olshen, A. B., Schultz, N., & Sander, C. et al. (2013). Pattern discovery and cancer gene identification in integrated cancer genomic data. *Proceedings of the National Academy of Sciences of the United States of America*, *110*(11), 4245–4250. doi:10.1073/pnas.1208949110 PMID:23431203

Morgan, S., Grootendorst, P., Lexchin, J., Cunningham, C., & Greyson, D. (2011). The cost of drug development: A systematic review. *Health Policy (Amsterdam)*, *100*(1), 4–17. doi:10.1016/j.healthpol.2010.12.002 PMID:21256615

Morris, A. P., & Zeggini, E. (2010). An evaluation of statistical approaches to rare variant analysis in genetic association studies. *Genetic Epidemiology*, *34*(2), 188–193. doi:10.1002/gepi.20450 PMID:19810025

Morris, C. (2008). The EQUATOR Network: Promoting the transparent and accurate reporting of research. *Developmental Medicine and Child Neurology*, *50*(10), 723. doi:10.1111/j.1469-8749.2008.03107.x PMID:18834380

Morris, J. N. (1975). *Uses of Epidemiology*. Edinburgh, UK: Churchill Livingstone.

Morton, L. W., & Weng, C.-Y. (2013). Health and Healthcare Among the Rural Aging. In N. Glasgow & E. H. Berry (Eds.), Rural Aging in 21st Century America (Vol. 7, pp. 179-194). Springer Netherlands. doi:10.1007/978-94-007-5567-3_10

Moskvina, V., & Schmidt, K. M. (2008). On multiple-testing correction in genome-wide association studies. *Genetic Epidemiology*, *32*(6), 567–573. doi:10.1002/gepi.20331 PMID:18425821

Motsinger-Reif, A. A., Dudek, S. M., Hahn, L. W., & Ritchie, M. D. (2008). Comparison of approaches for machine-learning optimization of neural networks for detecting gene-gene interactions in genetic epidemiology. *Genetic Epidemiology*, *32*(4), 325–340. doi:10.1002/gepi.20307 PMID:18265411

Motsinger-Reif, A. A., Reif, D. M., Fanelli, T. J., & Ritchie, M. D. (2008). A comparison of analytical methods for genetic association studies. *Genetic Epidemiology*, *32*(8), 767–778. doi:10.1002/gepi.20345 PMID:18561203

Moxey, A., Robertson, J., Newby, D., Hains, I., Williamson, M., & Pearson, S.-A. (2010). Computerized clinical decision support for prescribing: Provision does not guarantee uptake. *Journal of the American Medical Informatics Association*, *17*(1), 25–33. doi:10.1197/jamia. M3170 PMID:20064798

Mueller, S., & Szczesny, A. (2013). *Cost Pressure, Rationalization, Specialization and the Quality of Health Care*. Social Sciences Research Network.

Müller, H., & Röder, T. (2004). *Der Experimentator Microarrays* (Vol. 1). München: Spektrum Akademischer Verlag, Elsevier GmbH.

Mullins, J. G. (2012). Structural modeling pipelines in next generation sequencing projects. *Advances in Protein Chemistry and Structural Biology*, *89*, 117–167. doi:10.1016/B978-0-12-394287-6.00005-7 PMID:23046884

Munley, M. T., Lo, J. Y., Sibley, G. S., Bentel, G. C., Anscher, M. S., & Marks, L. B. (1999). A neural network to predict symptomatic lung injury. *Physics in Medicine and Biology*, *44*(9), 2241–2249. doi:10.1088/0031-9155/44/9/311 PMID:10495118

Murakami, Y., Toyoda, H., Tanahashi, T., Tanaka, J., Kumada, T., & Yoshioka, Y. et al. (2012). Comprehensive miRNA expression analysis in peripheral blood can diagnose liver disease. *PLoS ONE*, *7*(10), e48366. doi:10.1371/journal.pone.0048366 PMID:23152743

Murray, B. S., Choe, S. E., Woods, M., Ryan, T. E., & Liu, W. (2010). An in silico analysis of microRNAs: Mining the miRNAome. *Molecular BioSystems*, *6*(10), 1853–1862. doi:10.1039/c003961f PMID:20539892

Mushlin, A. I., & Ghomrawi, H. (2010). Health Care Reform and the Need for Comparative-Effectiveness Research. *The New England Journal of Medicine*, *362*(3), e6. doi:10.1056/NEJMp0912651 PMID:20054035

Muwonge, A., Malama, S., Johansen, T. B., Kankya, C., Biffa, D., & Ssengooba, W. et al. (2013). Molecular epidemiology, drug susceptibility and economic aspects of tuberculosis in Mubende district, Uganda. *PLoS ONE*, *8*(5), e64745. doi:10.1371/journal.pone.0064745 PMID:23741382

MySQL. D.10.3. limits on table size. (n.d.). Retrieved from http://dev.mysql.com/doc/refman/5.7/en/table-size-limit.html

Nachega, J. B., & Chaisson, R. E. (2003). Tuberculosis drug resistance: A global threat. *Clinical Infectious Diseases*, *36*(Supplement 1), S24–S30. doi:10.1086/344657 PMID:12516027

Nagaraj, N. S. (2009). Evolving 'omics' technologies for diagnostics of head and neck cancer. *Brief Funct Genomic Proteomic, 8*(1), 49-59. doi: 10.1093/bfgp/elp004

Nakazato, T., Bono, H., & Takagi, T. (2011). Functional Interpretation of Omics Data by Profiling Genes and Diseases Using MeSH–Controlled Vocabulary. In *Advances in the Study of Genetic Disorders.* Available from: http://www.intechopen.com/books/advances-in-the-study-of-genetic-disorders/functional-interpretation-of-omics-data-by-profiling-genes-and-diseases-using-mesh-controlled-vocabu

Nakazato, T., Bono, H., Matsuda, H., & Takagi, T. (2009). Gendoo: functional profiling of gene and disease features using MeSH vocabulary. *Nucleic Acids Res, 37*(Web Server), W166–169.

National Center for Biotechnology Information. (2004, May 21). *Programs and Activities.* Retrieved Jan. 10, 2014, from National Center for Biotechnology Information: http://www.ncbi.nlm.nih.gov/About/glance/programs.html

Nawrocki, E. P., & Eddy, S. (2013). Infernal 1.1: 100-fold faster RNA homology searches. *Bioinformatics (Oxford, England)*, *29*(22), 2933–2935. doi:10.1093/bioinformatics/btt509 PMID:24008419

NCRIS. (2013). *National Collaborative Research Infrastructure Strategy.* Retrieved from http://ncris.innovation.gov.au/Pages/default.aspx

NEHTA. (2013). *NEHTA – National E-Health Transition Authority.* Retrieved 18th, March, 2013, from http://www.nehta.gov.au/

Nekrutenko, A., & Taylor, J. (2012). Next-generation sequencing data interpretation: Enhancing reproducibility and accessibility. *Nature Reviews. Genetics*, *13*(9), 667–672. doi:10.1038/nrg3305 PMID:22898652

Nelson, K. (2003). The future of microbial genomics. *Environmental Microbiology*, *5*(12), 1223–1225. doi:10.1111/j.1462-2920.2003.00505.x PMID:14641569

Neumann, P. J., Palmer, J. A., Nadler, E., Fang, C.-H., & Ubel, P. (2010). Cancer Therapy Costs Influence Treatment: A National Survey Of Oncologists. *Health Affairs*, *29*(1), 196–202. doi:10.1377/hlthaff.2009.0077 PMID:20048377

Newbold, K., Partridge, M., Cook, G., Sohaib, S. A., Charles-Edwards, E., & Rhys-Evans, P. et al. (2006). Advanced imaging applied to radiotherapy planning in head and neck cancer: A clinical review. *The British Journal of Radiology*, *79*(943), 554–561. doi:10.1259/bjr/48822193 PMID:16823059

NHIS. (2014). *National Institute for Health Research.* Retrieved 11th Jan, 2014, from http://www.nihr.ac.uk/systems/Pages/default.aspx

Nibbe, R. K., Koyuturk, M., & Chance, M. R. (2010). An integrative -omics approach to identify functional sub-networks in human colorectal cancer. *PLoS Computational Biology*, *6*(1), e1000639. doi:10.1371/journal.pcbi.1000639 PMID:20090827

Nica, A. C., & Dermitzakis, E. T. (2013). Expression quantitative trait loci: Present and future. *Philosophical Transactions of the Royal Society of London. Series B, Biological Sciences, 368*(1620), 20120362. doi:10.1098/rstb.2012.0362 PMID:23650636

Nick, T., & Campbell, K. (2007). Logistic Regression. In W. Ambrosius (Ed.), *Topics in Biostatistics* (Vol. 404, pp. 273–301). Humana Press. doi:10.1007/978-1-59745-530-5_14

Nicolaidis, S. (2013). Personalized medicine in neurosurgery. *Metabolism, 62*, S45–S48. doi:10.1016/j.metabol.2012.08.022

Nie, L., Wu, G., Culley, D. E., Scholten, J. C., & Zhang, W. (2007). Integrative analysis of transcriptomic and proteomic data: Challenges, solutions and applications. *Critical Reviews in Biotechnology, 27*(2), 63–75. doi:10.1080/07388550701334212 PMID:17578703

Nikitin, A., Egorov, S., Daraselia, N., & Mazo, I. (2003). Pathway studio—the analysis and navigation of molecular networks. *Bioinformatics (Oxford, England), 19*(16), 2155–2157. doi:10.1093/bioinformatics/btg290 PMID:14594725

Nikjoo, H., Uehara, S., Emfietzoglou, D., & Cucinotta, F. A. (2006). Track-structure codes in radiation research. *Radiation Measurements, 41*(9-10), 1052–1074. doi:10.1016/j.radmeas.2006.02.001

NISU. (2013). *Research Centre for Injury Studies*. Flinders University Adelaide, Australia. Retrieved 2nd of Feb, 2013, from http://www.nisu.flinders.edu.au/

Norman, C., Benter, L. J., MacDonald, J., Dunn, M., Dunne, S., & Siu, B. et al. (2010). Questions that individuals with spinal cord injury have regarding their chronic pain: A qualitative study. *Disability and Rehabilitation, 32*(2), 114–124. doi:10.3109/09638280903033248 PMID:19817663

Normandeu, K. (2013). *Beyond Volume, Variety and Velocity is the Issue of Big Data Veracity*. Inside Big Data. Retrieved from http://inside-bigdata.com/2013/09/12/beyond-volume-variety-velocity-issue-big-data-veracity/

Norton, L. (2010). Spinal cord injury, Australia 2007-2008. Canberra, Australia: Academic Press.

Notredame, C., O'Brien, E., & Higgins, D. (1997). RAGA: RNA sequence alignment by genetic algorithm. *Nucleic Acids Research, 25*(22), 4570–4580. doi:10.1093/nar/25.22.4570 PMID:9358168

Novere, N. L., Hucka, M., Mi, H., Moodie, S., Schreiber, F., & Sorokin, A. et al. (2009). The system biology graphical notation. *Nature Biotechnology, 27*(8), 735–741. doi:10.1038/nbt.1558 PMID:19668183

Nuyten, D. S., & van de Vijver, M. J. (2008). Using microarray analysis as a prognostic and predictive tool in oncology: Focus on breast cancer and normal tissue toxicity. *Seminars in Radiation Oncology, 18*(2), 105–114. doi:10.1016/j.semradonc.2007.10.007 PMID:18314065

NYGC. (2014). *The New York Genome Center and IBM Watson Group Announce Collaboration to Advance Genomic Medicine*. Retrieved April 17, 2014, 2014, from http://www.nygenome.org/news/new-york-genome-center-ibm-watson-group-announce-collaboration-advance-genomic-medicine/

Nylund, L., Satokari, R., Nikkilä, J., Rajilić-Stojanović, M., Kalliomäki, M., & Isolauri, E. et al. (2013). Microarray analysis reveals marked intestinal microbiota aberrancy in infants having eczema compared to healthy children in at-risk for atopic disease. *BMC Microbiology, 13*(1), 12. doi:10.1186/1471-2180-13-12 PMID:23339708

O'Connor, J. P. (2005). Survival After Spinal Cord Injury in Australia. *Archives of Physical Medicine and Rehabilitation, 86*(1), 37–47. doi:10.1016/S0003-9993(04)00396-X PMID:15640987

O'Driscoll, A., Daugelaite, J., & Sleator, R. (2013). 'Big data', Hadoop and cloud computing in genomics. *Journal of Biomedical Informatics, 46*(5), 774–781. doi:10.1016/j.jbi.2013.07.001 PMID:23872175

Oetting, W. S., Robinson, P. N., Greenblatt, M. S., Cotton, R. G., Beck, T., & Carey, J. C. et al. (2013). Getting ready for the Human Phenome Project: The 2012 forum of the Human Variome Project. *Human Mutation, 34*(4), 661–666. PMID:23401191

Ofir, M., Hacohen, D., & Ginsberg, D. (2011). MiR-15 and miR-16 are direct transcriptional targets of E2F1 that limit E2F-induced proliferation by targeting cyclin E. *Molecular Cancer Research, 9*(4), 440–447. doi:10.1158/1541-7786.MCR-10-0344 PMID:21454377

Ogawa, K., Murayama, S., & Mori, M. (2007). Predicting the tumor response to radiotherapy using microarray analysis[Review]. *Oncology Reports*, *18*(5), 1243–1248. PMID:17914580

Ogwueleka, F. N. (2011). Data Mining Application in Credit Card Fraud Detection System. *Journal of Engineering Science and Technology*, *6*(3), 311–322.

Oh, J. H., & El Naqa, I. (2009). *Bayesian network learning for detecting reliable interactions of dose-volume related parameters in radiation pneumonitis*. Paper presented at the International Conference on Machine Learning and Applications (ICMLA). Miami, FL. doi:10.1109/ICMLA.2009.122

Oh, J. H., Craft, J., Al Lozi, R., Vaidya, M., Meng, Y., Deasy, J. O., ... El Naqa, I. (2011). A Bayesian network approach for modeling local failure in lung cancer. *Phys Med Biol, 56*(6), 1635-1651. doi: 10.1088/0031-9155/56/6/008

Oh, J. H., Craft, J. M., Townsend, R. R., Deasy, J. O., Bradley, J. D., & El Naqa, I. (2011). A Bioinformatics Approach for Biomarker Identification in Radiation-Induced Lung Inflammation from Limited Proteomics Data. *Journal of Proteome Research*, *10*(3), 1406–1415. doi:10.1021/pr101226q PMID:21226504

Oh, S., Lee, J., Kwon, M.-S., Weir, B., Ha, K., & Park, T. (2012). A novel method to identify high order gene-gene interactions in genome-wide association studies: Gene-based MDR. *BMC Bioinformatics*, *13*(Suppl 9), S5. doi:10.1186/1471-2105-13-S9-S5 PMID:22901090

Okazaki, N., & Ananiadou, S. (2006). Building an abbreviation dictionary using a term recognition approach. *Bioinformatics (Oxford, England)*, *22*(24), 3089–3095. doi:10.1093/bioinformatics/btl534 PMID:17050571

Okazaki, N., Ananiadou, S., & Tsujii, J. (2010). Building a high-quality sense inventory for improved abbreviation disambiguation. *Bioinformatics (Oxford, England)*, *26*(9), 1246–1253. doi:10.1093/bioinformatics/btq129 PMID:20360059

Ola, O., & Sedig, K. (2014). The challenge of big data in public health: An opportunity for visual analytics. *Online Journal of Public Health Informatics*, *5*, e223. PMID:24678376

Olsen, J., Gerds, T. A., Seidelin, J. B., Csillag, C., Bjerrum, J. T., Troelsen, J. T., & Nielsen, O. H. (2009). Diagnosis of ulcerative colitis before onset of inflammation by multivariate modeling of genome-wide gene expression data. *Inflammatory Bowel Diseases, 15*(7), 1032-1038. Doi: .10.1002/ibd.20879

Olson, D. R. (2013). *How Accurate Is Google Flu Trends? A Comparative Study of Internet Search Data and Public Health Syndromic Surveillance for Monitoring Seasonal and Pandemic Influenza, 2003-2013*. Paper presented at the 2013 CSTE Annual Conference. New York, NY.

Olson, D. R., Konty, K. J., Paladini, M., Viboud, C., & Simonsen, L. (2013). Reassessing Google Flu Trends Data for Detection of Seasonal and Pandemic Influenza: A Comparative Epidemiological Study at Three Geographic Scales. *PLoS Computational Biology*, *9*(10), e1003256. doi:10.1371/journal.pcbi.1003256 PMID:24146603

O'Neill, M., & Ryan, C. (2001). Grammatical evolution. *IEEE Transactions on Evolutionary Computation*, *5*(4), 349–358. doi:10.1109/4235.942529

Orszag, P. R., & Emanuel, E. J. (2010). Health care reform and cost control. *The New England Journal of Medicine*, *363*(7), 601–603. doi:10.1056/NEJMp1006571 PMID:20554975

Outterson, K. (2012). Punishing Health Care Fraud—Is the GSK Settlement Sufficient? *The New England Journal of Medicine*, *367*(12), 1082–1085. doi:10.1056/NEJMp1209249 PMID:22970920

Ouzounis, C. (2002). Bioinformatics and the theoretical foundations of molecular biology. *Bioinformatics (Oxford, England)*, *18*(3), 377–378. doi:10.1093/bioinformatics/18.3.377 PMID:11934735

Oxley, M. E., & Thorsen, S. N. (2004). Fusion or integration: What's the difference? In *Proceedings of the 7th Int. Conf. Inform. Fusion*. (pp. 429-434). Academic Press.

Ozgur, A., Vu, T., Erkan, G., & Radev, D. R. (2008). Identifying gene-disease associations using centrality on a literature mined gene-interaction network. *Bioinformatics (Oxford, England)*, *24*(13), i277–i285. doi:10.1093/bioinformatics/btn182 PMID:18586725

Ozsolak, F., Kapranov, P., Foissac, S., Kim, S. W., Fishilevich, E., & Monaghan, A. P. et al. (2010). Comprehensive polyadenylation site maps in yeast and human reveal pervasive alternative polyadenylation. *Cell, 143*(6), 1018–1029. doi:10.1016/j.cell.2010.11.020 PMID:21145465

Ozsolak, F., & Milos, P. M. (2011). RNA sequencing: Advances, challenges and opportunities. *Nature Reviews. Genetics, 12*(2), 87–98. doi:10.1038/nrg2934 PMID:21191423

Painter, I., Eaton, J., & Lober, B. (2013). Using Change Point Detection for Monitoring the Quality of Aggregate Data. *Online Journal of Public Health Informatics, 5*(1). doi:10.5210/ojphi.v5i1.4597

Palaniswamy, S. K., James, S., Sun, H., Lamb, R. S., Davuluri, R. V., & Grotewold, E. (2006). AGRIS and AtRegNet: A platform to link cis-regulatory elements and transcription factors into regulatory networks. *Plant Physiology, 140*(3), 818–829. doi:10.1104/pp.105.072280 PMID:16524982

Pandor, A., Gomersall, T., Stevens, J. W., Wang, J., Al-Mohammad, A., & Bakhai, A. et al. (2013). Remote monitoring after recent hospital discharge in patients with heart failure: A systematic review and network meta-analysis. *Heart (British Cardiac Society), 99*(23), 1717–1726. doi:10.1136/heartjnl-2013-303811 PMID:23680885

Pang, A. W., MacDonald, J. R., Pinto, D., Wei, J., Rafiq, M. A., & Conrad, D. F. et al. (2010). Towards a comprehensive structural variation map of an individual human genome. *Genome Biology, 11*(5), R52. doi:10.1186/gb-2010-11-5-r52 PMID:20482838

Pang, A. W., Migita, O., Macdonald, J. R., Feuk, L., & Scherer, S. W. (2013). Mechanisms of formation of structural variation in a fully sequenced human genome. *Human Mutation, 34*(2), 345–354. doi:10.1002/humu.22240 PMID:23086744

Papadopoulos, G. L., Alexiou, P., Maragkakis, M., Reczko, M., & Hatzigeorgiou, A. G. (2009). DIANAmirPath: Integrating human and mouse microRNAs in pathways. *Bioinformatics (Oxford, England), 25*(15), 1991–1993. doi:10.1093/bioinformatics/btp299 PMID:19435746

Papadopoulos, G. L., Reczko, M., Simossis, V. A., Sethupathy, P., & Hatzigeorgiou, A. G. (2009). The database of experimentally supported targets: A functional update of TarBase. *Nucleic Acids Research, 37*(Database issue), D155–D158. doi:10.1093/nar/gkn809 PMID:18957447

Pare, G., & Henderson, M. A. (2013). Genome-Wide Association Studies (GWAS). In P. Sharma & J. F. Meschia (Eds.), *Stroke Genetics* (pp. 25–50). Springer London. doi:10.1007/978-0-85729-209-4_3

Parkhomenko, E., Tritchler, D., & Beyene, J. (2009). Sparse canonical correlation analysis with application to genomic data integration. *Stat Appl Genet Mol Biol, 8*, Article 1.

Pastinen, T. (2010). Genome-wide allele-specific analysis: Insights into regulatory variation. *Nature Reviews. Genetics, 11*(8), 533–538. doi:10.1038/nrg2815 PMID:20567245

Patel, U. H., & Babbs, C. F. (1992). A computer-based, automated, telephonic system to monitor patient progress in the home setting. *Journal of Medical Systems, 16*(2-3), 101–112. doi:10.1007/BF00996591 PMID:1402436

Patti, G. J., Yanes, O., & Siuzdak, G. (2012). Metabolomics: The apogee of the omics trilogy. *Nature Reviews. Molecular Cell Biology, 13*(4), 263–269. doi:10.1038/nrm3314 PMID:22436749

Patwardhan, A., & Bilkovski, R. (2012). Comparison: Flu Prescription Sales Data from a Retail Pharmacy in the US with Google Flu Trends and US ILINet (CDC) Data as Flu Activity Indicator. *PLoS ONE, 7*(8), e43611. doi:10.1371/journal.pone.0043611 PMID:22952719

Paul, M. J., & Dredze, M. (2012). A model for mining public health topics from Twitter. *Health, 11*, 16–16.

Pearson, W., & Lipman, D. (1988). Improved tools for biological sequence comparison. *Proceedings of the National Academy of Sciences of the United States of America, 85*(8), 2444–2448. doi:10.1073/pnas.85.8.2444 PMID:3162770

Pedersen, K. S., Bamlet, W. R., Oberg, A. L., de Andrade, M., Matsumoto, M. E., & Tang, H. et al. (2011). Leukocyte DNA methylation signature differentiates pancreatic cancer patients from healthy controls. *PLoS ONE, 6*(3), e18223. doi:10.1371/journal.pone.0018223 PMID:21455317

Pekmezaris, R., Mitzner, I., Pecinka, K. R., Nouryan, C. N., Lesser, M. L., & Siegel, M. et al. (2012). The impact of remote patient monitoring (telehealth) upon Medicare beneficiaries with heart failure. *Telemedicine Journal and e-Health*, *18*(2), 101–108. doi:10.1089/tmj.2011.0095 PMID:22283360

Penrod, N. M., Cowper-Sal-lari, R., & Moore, J. H. (2011). Systems genetics for drug target discovery. *Trends in Pharmacological Sciences*, *32*(10), 623–630. doi:10.1016/j.tips.2011.07.002 PMID:21862141

Perrine, M. W., Mundt, J. C., Searles, J. S., & Lester, L. S. (1995). Validation of daily self-reported alcohol consumption using interactive voice response (IVR) technology. *Journal of Studies on Alcohol and Drugs*, *56*(5), 487. PMID:7475027

Persson, U., Willis, M., & Odegaard, K. (2010). A case study of ex ante, value-based price and reimbursement decision-making: TLV and rimonabant in Sweden. *The European Journal of Health Economics*, *11*(2), 195–203. doi:10.1007/s10198-009-0166-1 PMID:19639352

Petersen, A., Sitarik, A., Luedtke, A., Powers, S., Bekmetjev, A., & Tintle, N. L. (2011). Evaluating methods for combining rare variant data in pathway-based tests of genetic association. *BMC Proceedings, 5*(Suppl 9), S48.

Petersen, A. K., Zeilinger, S., Kastenmuller, G., Romisch-Margl, W., Brugger, M., & Peters, A. et al. (2014). Epigenetics meets metabolomics: An epigenome-wide association study with blood serum metabolic traits. *Human Molecular Genetics*, *23*(2), 534–545. PMID:24014485

Petersen, G. M., Amundadottir, L., Fuchs, C. S., Kraft, P., Stolzenberg-Solomon, R. Z., & Jacobs, K. B. et al. (2010). A genome-wide association study identifies pancreatic cancer susceptibility loci on chromosomes 13q22.1, 1q32.1 and 5p15.33. *Nature Genetics*, *42*(3), 224–228. doi:10.1038/ng.522 PMID:20101243

Phillips, P. C. (2008). Epistasis — the essential role of gene interactions in the structure and evolution of genetic systems. *Nature Reviews. Genetics*, *9*(11), 855–867. doi:10.1038/nrg2452 PMID:18852697

PHRDR. (2014). *Population Health Research Data Repository*. Retrieved 14th Jan, 2014, from http://www.umanitoba.ca/faculties/medicine/units/community_health_sciences/departmental_units/mchp/resources/repository/index.html

PHRN. (2013). *Population Health Research Network*. Retrieved 12th of June, 2012, from http://www.phrn.org.au

Picardi, E., & Pesole, G. (2012). Mitochondrial genomes gleaned from human whole-exome sequencing. *Nature Methods*, *9*(6), 523–524. doi:10.1038/nmeth.2029 PMID:22669646

Picardi, E., & Pesole, G. (2013). REDItools: High-throughput RNA editing detection made easy. *Bioinformatics (Oxford, England)*, *29*(14), 1813–1814. doi:10.1093/bioinformatics/btt287 PMID:23742983

Piet, D., Frederik De, K., Vincent, V., Sigrid, S., Robert, H., & Sandra, N. (2008). Diffusion-Weighted Magnetic Resonance Imaging to Evaluate Major Salivary Gland Function Before and After Radiotherapy. *International Journal of Radiation Oncology, Biology, Physics*.

Piette, J. D. (2000). Interactive voice response systems in the diagnosis and management of chronic disease. *The American Journal of Managed Care*, *6*(7), 817–827. PMID:11067378

Piette, J. D., & Mah, C. A. (1997). The feasibility of automated voice messaging as an adjunct to diabetes outpatient care. *Diabetes Care*, *20*(1), 15–21. doi:10.2337/diacare.20.1.15 PMID:9028687

Piette, J. D., McPhee, S. J., Weinberger, M., Mah, C. A., & Kraemer, F. B. (1999). Use of automated telephone disease management calls in an ethnically diverse sample of low-income patients with diabetes. *Diabetes Care*, *22*(8), 1302–1309. doi:10.2337/diacare.22.8.1302 PMID:10480775

Pillot, M., Baroux, C., Vazquez, M. A., Autran, D., Leblanc, O., & Vielle-Calzada, J. P. et al. (2010). Embryo and Endosperm Inherit Distinct Chromatin and Transcriptional States from the Female Gametes *Arabidopsis*. *The Plant Cell*, *22*(2), 307–320. doi:10.1105/tpc.109.071647 PMID:20139161

Pinkel, D., & Albertson, D. G. (2005). Comparative genomic hybridization. *Annual Review of Genomics and Human Genetics*, 6(1), 331–354. doi:10.1146/annurev.genom.6.080604.162140 PMID:16124865

Pinkel, D., Segraves, R., Sudar, D., Clark, S., Poole, I., Kowbel, D., & Albertson, D. G. (1998). High resolution analysis of DNA copy number variation using comparative genomic hybridization to microarrays. *Nature Genetics*, 20(2), 207–211. doi:10.1038/2524 PMID:9771718

Pinto da Costa, J. F., Alonso, H., & Roque, L. (2009). A weighted principal component analysis and its application to gene expression data. *IEEE/ACM Transactions on Computational Biology and Bioinformatics*, 8(1), 246–252. doi:10.1109/TCBB.2009.61 PMID:21071812

Pirim, H., Ekşioğlu, B., Perkins, A. D., & Yüceer, Ç. (2012). Clustering of high throughput gene expression data. *Computers & Operations Research*, 39(12), 3046–3061. doi:10.1016/j.cor.2012.03.008 PMID:23144527

Piskol, R., Ramaswami, G., & Li, J. B. (2013). Reliable Identification of Genomic Variants from RNA-Seq Data. *American Journal of Human Genetics*, 93(4), 641–651. doi:10.1016/j.ajhg.2013.08.008 PMID:24075185

Plottel, C. S., & Blaser, M. J. (2011). Microbiome and malignancy. *Cell Host & Microbe*, 10(4), 324–335. doi:10.1016/j.chom.2011.10.003 PMID:22018233

Pluzhnikov, A., Below, J. E., Konkashbaev, A., Tikhomirov, A., Kistner-Griffin, E., & Roe, C. A. et al. (2010). Spoiling the Whole Bunch: Quality Control Aimed at Preserving the Integrity of High-Throughput Genotyping. *American Journal of Human Genetics*, 87(1), 123–128. doi:10.1016/j.ajhg.2010.06.005 PMID:20598280

Porter, M. E. (2008). *Competitive advantage: Creating and sustaining superior performance*. Simon and Schuster.

Potters, G. (2010). How the Human Genome Project Opened up the World of Microbes. *Nature Education*, 3(9), 34.

PowerPivot. (2014). *PowerPivot | Microsoft BI*. Retrieved January 12, 2014, from http://www.microsoft.com/en-us/bi/powerpivot.aspx

Prasad, S., & Bruce, L. M. (2008). Overcoming the Small Sample Size Problem in Hyperspectral Classification and Detection Tasks. In *Geoscience and Remote Sensing Symposium:* Vol.5. *IGARSS 2008* (pp. V381-V384) IEEE International. doi:10.1109/IGARSS.2008.4780108

Pribnow, D. (1975). Nucleotide sequence of an RNA polymerase binding site at an early T7 promoter. *Proceedings of the National Academy of Sciences of the United States of America*, 72(3), 785–788. doi:10.1073/pnas.72.3.784 PMID:1093168

Price, A. L., Patterson, N. J., Plenge, R. M., Weinblatt, M. E., Shadick, N. A., & Reich, D. (2006). Principal components analysis corrects for stratification in genome-wide association studies. *Nature Genetics*, 38(8), 904–909. doi:10.1038/ng1847 PMID:16862161

Price, A. L., Zaitlen, N. A., Reich, D., & Patterson, N. (2010). New approaches to population stratification in genome-wide association studies. *Nature Reviews. Genetics*, 11(7), 459–463. doi:10.1038/nrg2813 PMID:20548291

Prifti, E., Zucker, J.-D., Clement, K., & Henegar, C. (2008). FunNet: An integrative tool for exploring transcriptional interactions. *Bioinformatics (Oxford, England)*, 24(22), 2636–2638. doi:10.1093/bioinformatics/btn492 PMID:18799481

Priness, I., Maimon, O., & Ben-Gal, I. (2007). Evaluation of gene-expression clustering via mutual information distance measure. *BMC Bioinformatics*, 8(1), 111. doi:10.1186/1471-2105-8-111 PMID:17397530

Pritchard, J. K., Stephens, M., & Donnelly, P. (2000). Inference of population structure using multilocus genotype data. *Genetics*, 155(2), 945–959. PMID:10835412

Professor, D., & Kovac, S. (2008). Application of proteomics in biotechnology: Microbial proteomics. *Biotechnology Journal*, 3(4), 496–509. doi:10.1002/biot.200700234 PMID:18320565

Provart, N. & Zhu, T. (2003). A Browser-based Functional Classification SuperViewer for Arabidopsis Genomics. In *Currents in Computational Molecular Biology*, (pp. 271-272). Academic Press.

Provost, F., & Fawcett, T. (2013). Data Science and its Relationship to Big Data and Data-Driven Decision Making. *Big Data*, *1*(1), 51–59. doi:10.1089/big.2013.1508

Pruitt, K. D., Tatusova, T., & Maglott, D. R. (2005, January1). NCBI Reference Sequence (RefSeq): A curated non-redundant sequence database of genomes, transcripts and proteins. *Nucleic Acids Research*, *33*, D501–D504. doi:10.1093/nar/gki025 PMID:15608248

Purcell, S., Neale, B., Todd-Brown, K., Thomas, L., Ferreira, M. A. R., & Bender, D. et al. (2007). PLINK: A Tool Set for Whole-Genome Association and Population-Based Linkage Analyses. *American Journal of Human Genetics*, *81*(3), 559–575. doi:10.1086/519795 PMID:17701901

Pu, S., Vlasblom, J., Emili, A., Greenblatt, J., & Wodak, S. J. (2007). Identifying functional modules in the physical interactome of *Saccharomyces cerevisiae*. *Proteomics*, *7*(6), 944–960. doi:10.1002/pmic.200600636 PMID:17370254

Pustejovsky, J., Castano, J., Cochran, B., Kotecki, M., & Morrell, M. (2001). Automatic extraction of acronym-meaning pairs from MEDLINE databases. *Studies in Health Technology and Informatics*, *84*(Pt 1), 371–375. PMID:11604766

Putri, S. P., Yamamoto, S., Tsugawa, H., & Fukusaki, E. (2013). Current metabolomics: Technological advances. *Journal of Bioscience and Bioengineering*, *116*(1), 9–16. doi:10.1016/j.jbiosc.2013.01.004 PMID:23466298

Pyysalo, S., Salakoshi, T., Aubin, S., & Nazarenko, A. (2006). Lexical adaptation of link grammar to the biomedical sublanguage: A comparative evaluation of three approaches. *BMC Bioinformatics*, *7*(Suppl 3), S2. doi:10.1186/1471-2105-7-S3-S2 PMID:17134475

Qiu, W., He, W., Wang, X., & Lazarus, R. (2008). A marginal mixture model for selecting differentially expressed genes across two types of tissue samples. *The International Journal of Biostatistics*, *4*(1), 20. doi:10.2202/1557-4679.1093 PMID:20231912

Quackenbush, J. (2006). From 'omes to biology. *Animal Genetics*, *37*(s1Suppl 1), 48–56. doi:10.1111/j.1365-2052.2006.01476.x PMID:16887002

R Core Team. (2013). R: A language and environment for statistical computing. In R Foundation for Statistical Computing. Vienna, Austria: Author.

R Project. (2014). *The R Project for Statistical Computing*. Retrieved January 12, 2014, from http://www.r-project.org/

Rabin, E. Z., & Weinberger, V. (1975). The isolation, purification, and properties of a ribonuclease from normal human urine. *Biochemical Medicine*, *14*(1), 1–11. doi:10.1016/0006-2944(75)90014-9 PMID:2164

Rabinow, P., & Bennett, G. (2009). Synthetic biology: Ethical ramifications 2009. *Systems and Synthetic Biology*, *3*(1-4), 99–108. doi:10.1007/s11693-009-9042-7 PMID:19816805

Radhakrishnan, K., Jacelon, C., & Roche, J. (2012). Perceptions on the Use of Telehealth by Homecare Nurses and Patients With Heart Failure: A Mixed Method Study. *Home Health Care Management & Practice*, *24*(4), 175–181. doi:10.1177/1084822311428335

Ragoussis, J. (2006). Genotyping technologies for all. *Drug Discovery Today. Technologies*, *3*(2), 115–122. doi:10.1016/j.ddtec.2006.06.013 PMID:24980397

Ragoussis, J. (2009). Genotyping Technologies for Genetic Research. *Annual Review of Genomics and Human Genetics*, *10*(1), 117–133. doi:10.1146/annurev-genom-082908-150116 PMID:19453250

Raiko, T., Ilin, A., & Karhunen, J. (2008). Principal component analysis for sparse high-dimensional data. *Neural Information Processing*, *4984*(Part I), 566–575. doi:10.1007/978-3-540-69158-7_59

Rajagopalan, H., & Lengauer, C. (2004). Aneuploidy and cancer. *Nature*, *432*(7015), 338–341. doi:10.1038/nature03099 PMID:15549096

Ramanan, V. K., Shen, L., Moore, J. H., & Saykin, A. J. (2012). Pathway analysis of genomic data: Concepts, methods, and prospects for future development. *Trends in Genetics*, *28*(7), 323–332. doi:10.1016/j.tig.2012.03.004 PMID:22480918

Ramanathan, M., et al. (2012). *IBM: Large Gene interaction Analytics at University at Buffalo, SUNY*. Retrieved from http://public.dhe.ibm.com/common/ssi/ecm/en/imc14675usen/IMC14675USEN.PDF

Raman, K., Yeturu, K., & Chandra, N. (2008). targetTB: A target identification pipeline for *Mycobacterium tuberculosis* through an interactome, reactome and genome-scale structural analysis. *BMC Systems Biology, 2*(1), 109. doi:10.1186/1752-0509-2-109 PMID:19099550

Ramaswami, G., Zhang, R., Piskol, R., Keegan, L. P., Deng, P., O'Connell, M. A., & Li, J. B. (2013). Identifying RNA editing sites using RNA sequencing data alone. *Nature Methods, 10*(2), 128–132. doi:10.1038/nmeth.2330 PMID:23291724

Rani, J. K., Kumar, S. P., Mohan, U. R., & Shankar, C. U. (2011). Credit Card Fraud Detection Analysis. *International Journal of Computer Trends and Technology, 2*(1), 24–27.

Rapanoel, H. A., Mazandu, G. K., & Mulder, N. J. (2013). Predicting and analyzing interactions between *Mycobacterium tuberculosis* and its human host. *PLoS ONE, 8*(7), e67472. doi:10.1371/journal.pone.0067472 PMID:23844013

Rapin, N., Hoor, I., Lund, O., & Nielsen, M. (2010). The MHC Motif Viewer: A Visualization Tool for the MHC Binding Motifs. *Current Protocols in Immunology, 18*(17). doi:10.1002/0471142735.im1817s88 PMID:20143317

Rappé, M. S., & Giovannoni, S. J. (2003). The uncultured microbial majority. *Annual Review of Microbiology, 57*(1), 369–394. doi:10.1146/annurev.micro.57.030502.090759 PMID:14527284

Raue, A., Schilling, M., Bachmann, J., Matteson, A., Schelke, M., & Kaschek, D. et al. (2013). Lessons learned from quantitative dynamical modeling in systems biology. *PLoS ONE, 8*(9), e74335. doi:10.1371/journal.pone.0074335 PMID:24098642

Real, F. X., Malats, N., Lesca, G., Porta, M., Chopin, S., Lenoir, G. M., & Silinikova, O. (2002). Family history of cancer and germline BRCA2 mutations in sporadic exocrine pancreatic cancer. *Gut, 50*(5), 653–657. doi:10.1136/gut.50.5.653 PMID:11950811

Rebholz-Schuhmann, D., Oellrich, A., & Hoehndorf, R. (2012). Text-mining solutions for biomedical research: Enabling integrative biology. *Nature Reviews. Genetics, 13*(12), 829–839. doi:10.1038/nrg3337 PMID:23150036

Redhead, E., & Bailey, T. (2007). Discriminative motif discovery in DNA and protein sequences using the DEME algorithm. *BMC Bioinformatics, 8*(1), 385–404. doi:10.1186/1471-2105-8-385 PMID:17937785

Reed, J., Murray, K., & Jacobson, M. (2013). Digitization Standards at the National Archives and Records Administration. *Archiving Conference, 2013*(1), 211–215.

Reference Genome Group of the Gene Ontology. (2009). The Gene Ontology's Reference Genome Project: A unified framework for functional annotation across species. *PLoS Computational Biology, 5*(7), e1000431. doi:10.1371/journal.pcbi.1000431 PMID:19578431

Reimand, J., Arak, T., & Vilo, J. (2011). g:Profiler -- a web server for functional interpretation of gene lists (2011 update). *Nucleic Acids Research, 39*(suppl), W307–W315. doi:10.1093/nar/gkr378 PMID:21646343

Reimers, M. A., Riley, B. P., Kalsi, G., Kertes, D. A., & Kendler, K. S. (2012). Pathway based analysis of genotypes in relation to alcohol dependence. *The Pharmacogenomics Journal, 12*(4), 342–348. doi:10.1038/tpj.2011.10 PMID:21468025

Reinartz, J., Bruyns, E., Lin, J. Z., Burcham, T., Brenner, S., Bowen, B., & Woychik, R. (2002). Massively parallel signature sequencing (MPSS) as a tool for in-depth quantitative gene expression profiling in all organisms. [Review]. *Briefings in Functional Genomics & Proteomics, 1*(1), 95–104. doi:10.1093/bfgp/1.1.95 PMID:15251069

Reisfeld, B., Metzler, C. P., Lyons, M. A., Mayeno, A. N., Brooks, E. J., & DeGroote, M. A. (2012). A physiologically based pharmacokinetic model for capreomycin. *Antimicrobial Agents and Chemotherapy, 56*(2), 926–934. doi:10.1128/AAC.05180-11 PMID:22143528

Rekapalli, B., Giblock, P., & Reardon, C. (2013). PoPLAR: Portal for petascale lifescience applications and research. *BMC Bioinformatics, 14*, S3. PMID:23902523

Rekha, B., Jagarajamma, K., Chandrasekaran, V., Wares, F., Sivanandham, R., & Swaminathan, S. (2013). Improving screening and chemoprophylaxis among child contacts in India's RNTCP: A pilot study. *The International Journal of Tuberculosis and Lung Disease*, *17*(2), 163–168. doi:10.5588/ijtld.12.0415 PMID:23317950

REP. (2014). *Rochester Epidemiology Project*. Retrieved 12th Dec, 2013, from http://www.rochesterproject.org/

Reuben, D. B., & Tinetti, M. E. (2012). Goal-oriented patient care--an alternative health outcomes paradigm. *The New England Journal of Medicine*, *366*(9), 777–779. doi:10.1056/NEJMp1113631 PMID:22375966

Rhee, S. Y., Beavis, W., Berardini, T. Z., Chen, G., Dixon, D., & Doyle, A. (2003). The Arabidopsis Information Resource (TAIR): A model organism database providing a centralized, curated gateway to Arabidopsis biology, research materials and community. *Nucleic Acids Research*, *31*(1), 224–228. doi:10.1093/nar/gkg076 PMID:12519987

Rhee, S., Dickerson, J., & Xu, D. (2006). Bioinformatics and its applications in plant biology. *Annual Review of Plant Biology*, *57*(1), 335–360. doi:10.1146/annurev.arplant.56.032604.144103 PMID:16669765

Riancho, J. A. (2012). Genome-wide association studies (GWAS) in complex diseases: Advantages and limitations. *Reumatol Clin*, *8*(2), 56–57. doi:10.1016/j.reuma.2011.07.005 PMID:22089059

Rich, J., Howe, J., Larson, L., & Chuang, C. (2013). Implementing Interactive Voice Recognition Technology to Activate Vulnerable Patients. *Journal of the International Society for Telemedicine and eHealth, 1*(1), 3-11.

Richards, A. et al. (2008). A comparison of four clustering methods for brain expression microarray data. *BMC Bioinformatics*, *9*(490), 1–17. PMID:19032745

Richman, M. B., Trafalis, T. B., & Adrianto, I. (2009). Missing Data Imputation Through Machine Learning Algorithms. In S. E. Haupt, A. Pasini, & C. Marzban (Eds.), *Artificial Intelligence Methods in Environment Science*. Berlin: Springer-Verlag. doi:10.1007/978-1-4020-9119-3_7

Rifton, L. P., Goldberg, M. L., Karp, R. W., & Hogness, D. (1978). The organization of the histone genes in Drosiphila melanogaster. *Cold Spring Harbor Symposia on Quantitative Biology*, *42*(2), 1047–1051. PMID:98262

Riggs, E., Wain, K. E., Riethmaier, D., Smith-Packard, B., Faucett, W. A., & Hoppman, N. et al. (2014). Chromosomal microarray impacts clinical management. *Clinical Genetics*, *85*(2), 147–153. doi:10.1111/cge.12107 PMID:23347240

Rindler, A., McLowry, S., & Hillard, R. (2013). *Big Data Definition*. MIKE2.0, the open source methodology for Information Development. Retrieved from http://mike2.openmethodology.org/wiki/Big_Data_Definition

Ring, H. Z., Kwok, P. Y., & Cotton, R. G. (2006). Human Variome Project: An international collaboration to catalogue human genetic variation. *Pharmacogenomics*, *7*(7), 969–972. doi:10.2217/14622416.7.7.969 PMID:17054407

Risch, H. A. (2012). Pancreatic cancer: Helicobacter pylori colonization, N-nitrosamine exposures, and ABO blood group. *Molecular Carcinogenesis*, *51*(1), 109–118. doi:10.1002/mc.20826 PMID:22162235

Risch, N. J. (2000). Searching for genetic determinants in the new millennium. *Nature*, *405*(6788), 847–856. doi:10.1038/35015718 PMID:10866211

Ritchie, M. D., Hahn, L. W., Roodi, N., Bailey, L. R., Dupont, W. D., Parl, F. F., & Moore, J. H. (2001). Multifactor-Dimensionality Reduction Reveals High-Order Interactions among Estrogen-Metabolism Genes in Sporadic Breast Cancer. *American Journal of Human Genetics*, *69*(1), 138–147. doi:10.1086/321276 PMID:11404819

Ritchie, M. D., Van Steen, K., & Gusareva, E. (2014, Manuscript submitted for publication). Dimensionality reduction in Genome-Wide Association Interaction Studies (GWAIS): Practical considerations. *Genome Medicine*.

Ritz, A., Paris, P. L., Ittmann, M. M., Collins, C., & Raphael, B. J. (2011). Detection of recurrent rearrangement breakpoints from copy number data. *BMC Bioinformatics*, *12*(1), 114. doi:10.1186/1471-2105-12-114 PMID:21510904

Roberts, L.D., Souza, A.L., Gerszten, R.E., & Clish, C.B. (2012). Targeted metabolomics. *Current Protocols in Molecular Biology, 30*(2), 1-24.

Rodríguez-Ezpeleta, N., Hackenberg, M., & Aransay, A. M. (Eds.). (2012). Bioinformatics for High Throughput Sequencing. New York: Springer Science + Business Media, LLC. doi:10.1007/978-1-4614-0782-9

Roelofs, E., Dekker, A., Meldolesi, E., van Stiphout, R. G. P. M., Valentini, V., & Lambin, P. (2014). International data-sharing for radiotherapy research: An open-source based infrastructure for multicentric clinical data mining. *Radiotherapy and Oncology, 110*(2), 370–374. doi:10.1016/j.radonc.2013.11.001 PMID:24309199

Roelofs, E., Persoon, L., Nijsten, S., Wiessler, W., Dekker, A., & Lambin, P. (2013). Benefits of a clinical data warehouse with data mining tools to collect data for a radiotherapy trial. *Radiotherapy and Oncology, 108*(1), 174–179. doi:10.1016/j.radonc.2012.09.019 PMID:23394741

Rogozin, I., Makarova, K., Natale, D., Spiridonov, A., Tatusov, R., & Wolf, Y. et al. (2002). Congruent evolution of different classes of non-coding DNA in prokaryotic genomes. *Nucleic Acids Research, 30*(19), 4264–4271. doi:10.1093/nar/gkf549 PMID:12364605

Roix, J. J., McQueen, P. G., Munson, P. J., Parada, L. A., & Misteli, T. (2003). Spatial proximity of translocation-prone gene loci in human lymphomas.[Comparative Study]. *Nature Genetics, 34*(3), 287–291. doi:10.1038/ng1177 PMID:12808455

Romano, M. J., & Stafford, R. S. (2011). Electronic health records and clinical decision support systems: Impact on national ambulatory care quality. *Archives of Internal Medicine, 171*(10), 897–903. doi:10.1001/archinternmed.2010.527 PMID:21263077

Romano, P. (2007). Automation of *in-silico* data analysis processes through workflow management systems. *Briefings in Bioinformatics, 9*(1), 57–68. doi:10.1093/bib/bbm056 PMID:18056132

Romero, R., Iglesias, E. L., Borrajo, L., & Marey, C. M. R. (2011). Using Dictionaries for Biomedical Text Classification. In M. Rocha, J. C. Rodríguez, F. Fdez-Riverola, & A. Valencia (Eds.), *Proceedings of International Conference on Practical Applications of Computational Biology & Bioinformatics* (PACBB 2011), (pp. 365-372). Springer. doi:10.1007/978-3-642-19914-1_47

Rommer, A., Steinleitner, K., Hackl, H., Schneckenleithner, C., Engelmann, M., & Scheideler, M. et al. (2013). Overexpression of primary microRNA 221/222 in acute myeloid leukemia. *BMC Cancer, 13*(1), 364. doi:10.1186/1471-2407-13-364 PMID:23895238

Rondon, M. R., Raffel, S. J., Goodman, R. M., & Handelsman, J. (1999). Toward functional genomics in bacteria: Analysis of gene expression in *Escherichia coli* from a bacterial artificial chromosome library of Bacillus cereus. *Proceedings of the National Academy of Sciences of the United States of America, 96*(11), 6451–6455. doi:10.1073/pnas.96.11.6451 PMID:10339608

Rosa, G. J., Valente, B. D., de los Campos, G., Wu, X. L., Gianola, D., & Silva, M. A. (2011). Inferring causal phenotype networks using structural equation models. *Genetics, Selection, Evolution., 43*(1), 6. doi:10.1186/1297-9686-43-6 PMID:21310061

Rossini, A., Tierney, L., & Li, N. (2003). *Simple Parallel Statistical Computing in R*. The Berkeley Electronic Press.

Rothman, K. J. (1974). Synergy and antagonism in cause-effect relationships. *American Journal of Epidemiology, 99*(6), 385–388. PMID:4841816

Roukos, D. H. (2009). Personal genomics and genome-wide association studies: Novel discoveries but limitations for practical personalized medicine. *Annals of Surgical Oncology, 16*(3), 772–773. doi:10.1245/s10434-008-0109-6 PMID:18726130

Rozenbaum, M. H., Sanders, E. A. M., van Hoek, A. J., Jansen, A. G. S. C., van der Ende, A., & van den Dobbelsteen, G. et al. (2010). Cost effectiveness of pneumococcal vaccination among Dutch infants: Economic analysis of the seven valent pneumococcal conjugated vaccine and forecast for the 10 valent and 13 valent vaccines. *BMJ (Clinical Research Ed.), 340*(1), c2509. doi:10.1136/bmj.c2509 PMID:20519267

Rozowsky, J., Abyzov, A., Wang, J., Alves, P., Raha, D., & Harmanci, A. et al. (2011). AlleleSeq: Analysis of allele-specific expression and binding in a network framework. *Molecular Systems Biology*, *7*(1), 522. doi:10.1038/msb.2011.54 PMID:21811232

Rubin, D. B. (1976). Inference and missing data. *Biometrika*, *63*(3), 581–592. doi:10.1093/biomet/63.3.581

Rubin, L. H., Witkiewitz, K., Andre, J. S., & Reilly, S. (2007). Methods for Handling Missing Data in the Behavioral Neurosciences: Don't Throw the Baby Rat out with the Bath Water. *J Undergrad Neurosci Educ*, *5*(2), A71–A77. PMID:23493038

Ruepp, A., Kowarsch, A., Schmidl, D., Buggenthin, F., Brauner, B., & Dunger, I. et al. (2010). PhenomiR: A knowledgebase for microRNA expression in diseases and biological processes. *Genome Biology*, *11*(1), R6. doi:10.1186/gb-2010-11-1-r6 PMID:20089154

Rusch, D., Halpern, A., Sutton, G., Heidelberg, K., Williamson, S., & Yooseph, S. et al. (2007). The Sorcerer II Global Ocean Sampling Expedition: Northwest Atlantic through Eastern Tropical Pacific. *PLoS Biology*, *5*(3), e77. doi:10.1371/journal.pbio.0050077 PMID:17355176

Russell, L. B., Gold, M. R., Siegel, J. E., Daniels, N., & Weinstein, M. C. (1996). THe role of cost-effectiveness analysis in health and medicine. *Journal of the American Medical Association*, *276*(14), 1172–1177. doi:10.1001/jama.1996.03540140060028 PMID:8827972

Sabates-Bellver, J., Van der Flier, L. G., de Palo, M., Cattaneo, E., Maake, C., & Rehrauer, H. et al. (2007). Transcriptome Profile of Human Colorectal Adenomas. *Molecular Cancer Research*, *5*(12), 1263–1275. doi:10.1158/1541-7786.MCR-07-0267 PMID:18171984

Saeys, Y., Inza, I., & Larranaga, P. (2007). A review of feature selection techniques in bioinformatics. *Bioinformatics (Oxford, England)*, *23*(19), 2507–2517. doi:10.1093/bioinformatics/btm344 PMID:17720704

Salathe, M., Freifeld, C. C., Mekaru, S. R., Tomasulo, A. F., & Brownstein, J. S. (2013). Influenza A (H7N9) and the importance of digital epidemiology. *The New England Journal of Medicine*, *369*(5), 401–404. doi:10.1056/NEJMp1307752 PMID:23822655

Samuels, D. C., Han, L., Li, J., Quanghu, S., Clark, T. A., Shyr, Y., & Guo, Y. (2013). Finding the lost treasures in exome sequencing data. *Trends in Genetics*, *29*(10), 593–599. doi:10.1016/j.tig.2013.07.006 PMID:23972387

Sandelin, A., Alkema, W., Engröm, P., Wasserman, W. W., & Lenhard, B. (2004). JASPAR: An open-access database for eukaryotic transcription factory binding profiles. *Nucleic Acids Research*, *32*(suppl 1), 91–94. doi:10.1093/nar/gkh012

Sanger, F., & Coulson, A. R. (1975). A rapid method for determining sequences in DNA by primed synthesis with DNA polymerase. *Journal of Molecular Biology*, *94*(3), 441–448. doi:10.1016/0022-2836(75)90213-2 PMID:1100841

Sanmann, J. N., Pickering, D. L., Stevens, J. M., & Sanger, W. G. (2013). Microarray Studies in Pediatric T-Cell Acute Lymphoblastic Leukemia/Lymphoma: A Report of Four Cases. *Cancer Genetics*, *206*(5), 213. doi:10.1016/j.cancergen.2013.05.010

Sarajlić, A., & Pržulj, N. (2014). Survey of Network-Based Approaches to Research of Cardiovascular Diseases. *BioMed Research International*, 10.

Sarasua, S. M., Collins, J. S., Williamson, D. M., Satten, G. A., & Allen, A. S. (2009). Effect of population stratification on the identification of significant single-nucleotide polymorphisms in genome-wide association studies. *BMC Proc, 3*(Suppl 7), S13.

Sarkar, I. N. (2010). Biomedical informatics and translational medicine. *Journal of Translational Medicine*, *8*(22), 12. PMID:20187952

Sarojini, S., Goy, A., Pecora, A., & Suh, K. S. (2012). Proactive Biobanking to Improve Research and Health Care. *J Tissue Sci Eng*, *3*(02), 116. doi:10.4172/2157-7552.1000116

SAS. (2014). *Business Analytics and Business Intelligence Software | SAS*. Retrieved January 12, 2014, from http://www.sas.com/en_us/home.html

Sasaki, Y., Tsuruoka, Y., McNaught, J., & Ananiadou, S. (2008). How to make the most of NE dictionaries in statistical NER. *BMC Bioinformatics*, *9*(Suppl 11), S5. doi:10.1186/1471-2105-9-S11-S5 PMID:19025691

Sass, S., Buettner, F., Mueller, N. S., & Theis, F. J. (2013). A modular framework for gene set analysis integrating multilevel omics data. *Nucleic Acids Research, 41*(21), 9622–9633. doi:10.1093/nar/gkt752 PMID:23975194

Saukshmya, T., & Chugh, A. (2010). Intellectual property rights in synthetic biology: An anti-thesis to open access to research? *Systems and Synthetic Biology, 4*(4), 241–245. doi:10.1007/s11693-011-9067-6 PMID:22132050

Schacker, T., Collier, A., Hughes, J., Shea, T., & Corey, L. (1996). Clinical and epidemiologic features of primary HIV infection. *Annals of Internal Medicine, 125*(4), 257–264. doi:10.7326/0003-4819-125-4-199608150-00001 PMID:8678387

Schadt E. E. (2012). The challenging privacy landscape in the era of big data. *Molecular Systems Biology, 8,* 612.

Schadt, E. E., Lamb, J., Yang, X., Zhu, J., Edwards, S., & Guhathakurta, D. et al. (2005). An integrative genomics approach to infer causal associations between gene expression and disease. *Nature Genetics, 37*(7), 710–717. doi:10.1038/ng1589 PMID:15965475

Schadt, E. E., Linderman, M. D., Sorenson, J., Lee, L., & Nolen, G. P. (2010). Computational solutions to large-scale data management and analysis. *Nature Reviews. Genetics, 11*(9), 647–657. doi:10.1038/nrg2857 PMID:20717155

Schafer, J., & Strimmer, K. (2005). *Learning Large-Scale Graphical Gaussian Models from Genomic Data.* Paper presented at the AIP Conference. New York, NY. doi:10.1063/1.1985393

Schaid, D. J., McDonnell, S. K., Sinnwell, J. P., & Thibodeau, S. N. (2013). Multiple Genetic Variant Association Testing by Collapsing and Kernel Methods With Pedigree or Population Structured Data: Multiple Genetic Variant Association Testing. *Genetic Epidemiology, 37*(5), 409–418. doi:10.1002/gepi.21727 PMID:23650101

Schaid, D., Mcdonnell, S., Hebbring, S., Cunningham, J., & Thibodeau, S. (2005). Nonparametric Tests of Association of Multiple Genes with Human Disease. *American Journal of Human Genetics, 76*(5), 780–793. doi:10.1086/429838 PMID:15786018

Scharnweber, C., Lau, B. D., Mollenkopf, N., Thiemann, D. R., Veltri, M. A., & Lehmann, C. U. (2013). Evaluation of medication dose alerts in pediatric inpatients. *International Journal of Medical Informatics, 82*(8), 676–683. doi:10.1016/j.ijmedinf.2013.04.002 PMID:23643148

Scheet, P., & Stephens, M. (2006). A Fast and Flexible Statistical Model for Large-Scale Population Genotype Data: Applications to Inferring Missing Genotypes and Haplotypic Phase. *American Journal of Human Genetics, 78*(4), 629–644. doi:10.1086/502802 PMID:16532393

Scheider, T. D., & Stephens, R. M. (1990). Sequence Logos: A New Way to Display Consensus Sequences. *Nucleic Acids Research, 18*(20), 6097–6100. doi:10.1093/nar/18.20.6097 PMID:2172928

Schena, M. et al. (1996a). Genome analysis with gene expression microarray. *Bioessaya, 18*(5), 427–431. doi:10.1002/bies.950180513 PMID:8639166

Schena, M., Shalon, D., Davis, R. W., & Brown, P. O. (1995). Quantitative Monitoring of Gene Expression Patterns with a Complementary DNA Microarray. *Science, 270*(5235), 467–470. doi:10.1126/science.270.5235.467 PMID:7569999

Schena, M., Shalon, D., Heller, R., Chai, A., Brown, P. O., & Davis, R. W. (1996b). Parallel human genome analysis: Microarray-based expression monitoring of 1000 genes. *Proceedings of the National Academy of Sciences of the United States of America, 93*(20), 10614–10616. doi:10.1073/pnas.93.20.10614 PMID:8855227

Schmoldt, A., Benthe, H. F., & Haberland, G. (1975). Digitoxin metabolism by rat liver microsomes. *Biochemical Pharmacology, 24*(17), 1639–1641. doi:10.1016/0006-2952(75)90094-5 PMID:10

Schnabel, R. B., Baccarelli, A., Lin, H., Ellinor, P. T., & Benjamin, E. J. (2012). Next Steps in Cardiovascular Disease Genomic Research--Sequencing, Epigenetics, and Transcriptomics. *Clinical Chemistry, 58*(1), 113–126. doi:10.1373/clinchem.2011.170423 PMID:22100807

Schneider, M. V., & Orchard, S. (2011). Omics technologies, data and bioinformatics principles. *Methods in Molecular Biology (Clifton, N.J.), 719,* 3–30. doi:10.1007/978-1-61779-027-0_1 PMID:21370077

Scholkopf, B. (2001). In T. K. Leen, T. G. Dietterich, & V. Tresp (Eds.), *The kernel trick for distances* (pp. 301–307). Advances in neural information processing systems. MIT Press.

Schork, A. J., Thompson, W. K., Pham, P., Torkamani, A., Roddey, J. C., & Sullivan, P. F. et al.Tobacco and Genetics Consortium. (2013). All SNPs are not created equal: Genome-wide association studies reveal a consistent pattern of enrichment among functionally annotated SNPs. *PLOS Genetics*, *9*(4), e1003449. doi:10.1371/journal.pgen.1003449 PMID:23637621

Schuierer, S., Tranchevent, L. C., Dengler, U., & Moreau, Y. (2010). Large-scale benchmark of Endeavour using MetaCore maps. *Bioinformatics (Oxford, England)*, *26*(15), 1922–1923. doi:10.1093/bioinformatics/btq307 PMID:20538729

Schuler, G., Altschul, S., & Lipman, D. (1991). A workbench for multiple alignment construction and analysis. *Proteins*, *9*(3), 180–190. doi:10.1002/prot.340090304 PMID:2006136

Schwarz, D. F., Konig, I. R., & Ziegler, A. (2010). On safari to Random Jungle: A fast implementation of Random Forests for high-dimensional data. *Bioinformatics (Oxford, England)*, *26*(14), 1752–1758. doi:10.1093/bioinformatics/btq257 PMID:20505004

Schwender, H., & Ickstadt, K. (2008). Identification of SNP interactions using logic regression. *Biostatistics (Oxford, England)*, *9*(1), 187–198. doi:10.1093/biostatistics/kxm024 PMID:17578898

Schwender, H., & Ruczinski, I. (2010). Logic regression and its extensions. *Advances in Genetics*, *72*, 25–45. doi:10.1016/B978-0-12-380862-2.00002-3 PMID:21029847

Schwender, H., Taub, M. A., Beaty, T. H., Marazita, M. L., & Ruczinski, I. (2012). Rapid Testing of SNPs and Gene-Environment Interactions in Case-Parent Trio Data Based on Exact Analytic Parameter Estimation. *Biometrics*, *68*(3), 766–773. doi:10.1111/j.1541-0420.2011.01713.x PMID:22150644

Seide, R., & Smith, F. (1995). Intellectual property protection and biotechnology. *New York State Bar Journal*, *67*, 52–58.

Servin, B., & Stephens, M. (2007). Imputation-Based Analysis of Association Studies: Candidate Regions and Quantitative Traits. *PLOS Genetics*, *3*(7), e114. doi:10.1371/journal.pgen.0030114 PMID:17676998

Sethupathy, P., Corda, B., & Hatzigeorgiou, A. G. (2006). TarBase: A comprehensive database of experimentally supported animal microRNA targets. *RNA (New York, N.Y.)*, *12*(2), 192–197. doi:10.1261/rna.2239606 PMID:16373484

Shabalin, A. A. (2012). Matrix eQTL: Ultra fast eQTL analysis via large matrix operations. *Bioinformatics (Oxford, England)*, *28*(10), 1353–1358. doi:10.1093/bioinformatics/bts163 PMID:22492648

Shahi, P., Loukianiouk, S., Bohne-Lang, A., Kenzelmann, M., Kuffer, S., & Maertens, S. et al. (2006). Argonaute--a database for gene regulation by mammalian microRNAs. *Nucleic Acids Research*, *34*(Database issue), D115–D118. doi:10.1093/nar/gkj093 PMID:16381827

Shang, J., Zhang, J., Sun, Y., Liu, D., Ye, D., & Yin, Y. (2011). Performance analysis of novel methods for detecting epistasis. *BMC Bioinformatics*, *12*(1), 475. doi:10.1186/1471-2105-12-475 PMID:22172045

Shannon, P., Markiel, A., Ozier, O., Baliga, N. S., Wang, J. T., & Ramage, D. et al. (2003). Cytoscape: A software environment for integrated models of biomolecular interaction networks. *Genome Research*, *13*(11), 2498–2504. doi:10.1101/gr.1239303 PMID:14597658

Sharan, R., & Ideker, T. (2006). Modeling cellular machinery through biological network comparison. *Nature Biotechnology*, *24*(4), 427–433. doi:10.1038/nbt1196 PMID:16601728

Shea, S., Weinstock, R. S., Starren, J., Teresi, J., Palmas, W., & Field, L. et al. (2006). A randomized trial comparing telemedicine case management with usual care in older, ethnically diverse, medically underserved patients with diabetes mellitus. *Journal of the American Medical Informatics Association*, *13*(1), 40–51. doi:10.1197/jamia.M1917 PMID:16221935

Shen, H., & Huang, J. Z. (2008). Sparse principal component analysis via regularized low rank matrix approximation. *Journal of Multivariate Analysis*, *99*(6), 1015–1034. doi:10.1016/j.jmva.2007.06.007

Shen, J., Wang, A., Wang, Q., Gurvich, I., Siegel, A. B., Remotti, H., & Santella, R. M. (2013). Exploration of Genome-wide Circulating MicroRNA in Hepatocellular Carcinoma (HCC): MiR-483-5p as a Potential Biomarker. *Cancer Epidemiology, Biomarkers & Prevention, 22*(12), 2364–2373. doi:10.1158/1055-9965.EPI-13-0237 PMID:24127413

Shida, K. (2006). GibbsST: A Gibbs sampling method for motif discovery with enhanced resistance to local optima. *BMC Bioinformatics, 7*(1), 486–504. doi:10.1186/1471-2105-7-486 PMID:17083740

Shi, L., Campbell, G., Jones, W. D., Campagne, F., Wen, Z., & Walker, S. J. et al. (2010). The MicroArray Quality Control (MAQC)-II study of common practices for the development and validation of microarray-based predictive models. *Nature Biotechnology, 28*(8), 827–838. doi:10.1038/nbt.1665 PMID:20676074

Shimokawa, K., Mogushi, K., Shoji, S., Hiraishi, A., Ido, K., Mizushima, H., & Tanaka, H. (2010). iCOD: An integrated clinical omics database based on the systems-pathology view of disease. *BMC Genomics, 11*(Suppl 4), S19. doi:10.1186/1471-2164-11-S4-S19 PMID:21143802

Shirdel, E. A., Xie, W., Mak, T. W., & Jurisica, I. (2011). NAViGaTing the micronome--using multiple microRNA prediction databases to identify signalling pathway-associated microRNAs. *PLoS ONE, 6*(2), e17429. doi:10.1371/journal.pone.0017429 PMID:21364759

Shivade, C., Raghavan, P., Fosler-Lussier, E., Embi, P. J., Elhadad, N., Johnson, S. B., & Lai, A. M. (2013). A review of approaches to identifying patient phenotype cohorts using electronic health records. *Journal of the American Medical Informatics Association*. doi:10.1136/amiajnl-2013-001935 PMID:24201027

Shojaie, A., & Michailidis, G. (2009). Analysis of Gene Sets Based on the Underlying Regulatory Network. *Journal of Computational Biology, 16*(3), 407–426. doi:10.1089/cmb.2008.0081 PMID:19254181

Shulaev, V. (2006). Metabolomics technology and bioinformatics. *Briefings in Bioinformatics, 7*(2), 128–139. doi:10.1093/bib/bbl012 PMID:16772266

Sibbald, B. (2004). Legal action against GSK over SSRI data. *Canadian Medical Association Journal, 171*(1), 23-23a.

Siddharthan, R., Siggia, E., & van Nimwegen, E. (2005). PhyloGibbs: A Gibbs Sampling Motif Finder That Incorporates Phylogeny. *PLoS Computational Biology, 1*(7), e67. doi:10.1371/journal.pcbi.0010067 PMID:16477324

Sieberts, S. K., & Schadt, E. E. (2007). Moving toward a system genetics view of disease. *Mammalian Genome, 18*(6-7), 389–401. doi:10.1007/s00335-007-9040-6 PMID:17653589

Siegel, J. P., Rosenthal, N., Buto, K., Lilienfeld, S., Thomas, A., & Odenthal, S. (2012). Comparative Effectiveness Research in the Regulatory Setting. *Pharmaceutical Medicine, 26*(1), 5–11. doi:10.1007/BF03256887

Siegel, R., Ma, J., Zou, Z., & Jemal, A. (2014). Cancer statistics, 2014. *CA: a Cancer Journal for Clinicians, 64*(1), 9–29. doi:10.3322/caac.21208 PMID:24399786

Siegel, R., Naishadham, D., & Jemal, A. (2013). Cancer statistics, 2013. *CA: a Cancer Journal for Clinicians, 63*(1), 11–30. doi:10.3322/caac.21166 PMID:23335087

Sifrim, A., Popovic, D., Tranchevent, L. C., Ardeshirdavani, A., Sakai, R., & Konings, P. et al. (2013). eXtasy: Variant prioritization by genomic data fusion. *Nature Methods, 10*(11), 1083–1084. doi:10.1038/nmeth.2656 PMID:24076761

Sigrist, C., de Castro, E., Cerutti, L., Cuche, B., Hulo, N., & Bridge, A. et al. (2013). New and continuing developments at PROSITE. *Nucleic Acids Research, 41*(D1), D344–D337. doi:10.1093/nar/gks1067 PMID:23161676

Sikri, K., & Tyagi, J. S. (2013). The evolution of Mycobacterium tuberculosis dormancy models. *Current Science, 105*, 607–616.

Silveira, D. P., & Artmann, E. (2009). Accuracy of probabilistic record linkage applied to health databases: Systematic review. *Revista de Saude Publica, 43*(5), 875–882. doi:10.1590/S0034-89102009005000060 PMID:19784456

Simera, I., Moher, D., Hirst, A., Hoey, J., Schulz, K. F., & Altman, D. G. (2010). Transparent and accurate reporting increases reliability, utility, and impact of your research: Reporting guidelines and the EQUATOR Network. *BMC Medicine, 8*(1), 24. doi:10.1186/1741-7015-8-24 PMID:20420659

Simon, C., & Daniel, R. (2011). Metagenomic analyses: Past and future trends[down-pointing small open triangle]. *Applied and Environmental Microbiology, 77*(4), 1153–1161. doi:10.1128/AEM.02345-10 PMID:21169428

Simon, R. (2008). Microarray-based expression profiling and informatics. *Current Opinion in Biotechnology, 19*(1), 26–29. doi:10.1016/j.copbio.2007.10.008 PMID:18053704

Simon, R. (2009). Analysis of DNA microarray expression data. *Best Practice & Research. Clinical Haematology, 22*(2), 271–282. doi:10.1016/j.beha.2009.07.001 PMID:19698933

Singer, E. (2013). Biology's big problem: There's too much data to handle. *Quanta Magazine*. Retrieved Jan 26, 2014 from http://www.wired.com/wiredscience/2013/10/big-data-biology/

Singh, D., Prabha, R., Rai, A., & Arora, D. (2012). Bioinformatics-assisted microbiological research: Tasks, developments and upcoming challenges. *American Journal of Bioinformatics, 1*(1).

Singh, V., Mukherjee, L., Peng, J., & Xu, J. (2010). Ensemble Clustering using Semidefinite Programming with Applications. *Machine Learning, 79*(1-2), 177–200. doi:10.1007/s10994-009-5158-y PMID:21927539

Sisense. (2014). *Business Intelligence Software - SiSense Prism*. Retrieved January 12, 2014, from http://www.sisense.com/

Skelly, D. A., Ronald, J., & Akey, J. M. (2009). Inherited variation in gene expression. *Annual Review of Genomics and Human Genetics, 10*(1), 313–332. doi:10.1146/annurev-genom-082908-150121 PMID:19630563

Slack-Smith, L. (2012). How population-level data linkage might impact on dental research. *Community Dentistry and Oral Epidemiology, 40*, 90–94. doi:10.1111/j.1600-0528.2012.00726.x PMID:22998311

Sleater, D. D., & Temperley, D. (1991). Parsing English with a link grammar. *Tech Rep CMU-CS-91-196*

Smith, A., Sumazin, P., & Zhang, M. (2004). Identifying tissue-selective transcription factor binding sites in vertebrate promoters. *Proceedings of the National Academy of Sciences of the United States of America, 102*(5), 1560–1565. doi:10.1073/pnas.0406123102 PMID:15668401

Smith, M., Saunders, R., Stuckhardt, L., & McGinnis, J. M. (2013). *Best care at lower cost: the path to continuously learning health care in America*. National Academies Press.

Smith, R. J., & Bryant, R. G. (1975). Metal substitutions incarbonic anhydrase: A halide ion probe study. *Biochemical and Biophysical Research Communications, 66*(4), 1281–1286. doi:10.1016/0006-291X(75)90498-2 PMID:3

Sogin, M., Morrison, H., Huber, J., Mark Welch, D., Huse, S., & Neal, P. et al. (2006). Microbial diversity in the deep sea and the underexplored ''rare biosphere''. *Proceedings of the National Academy of Sciences of the United States of America, 103*(32), 12115–12120. doi:10.1073/pnas.0605127103 PMID:16880384

Somogyi, R., & Wen, X. et al. (1995). Developmental kinetics of GAD familym RNAs parallel neurogenesis in the rat spinal cord. *The Journal of Neuroscience, 15*, 2575–2591. PMID:7722616

Soowhan, H., Lee, I., & Pedrycz, W. (2009). Modified fuzzy c-means and Bayesian equalizer for nonlinear blind channel. *Applied Soft Computing, 9*(3), 1090–1096. doi:10.1016/j.asoc.2009.02.006

Southam, L., Panoutsopoulou, K., Rayner, N. W., Chapman, K., Durrant, C., & Ferreira, T. et al. (2011). The effect of genome-wide association scan quality control on imputation outcome for common variants. *European Journal of Human Genetics, 19*(5), 610–614. doi:10.1038/ejhg.2010.242 PMID:21267008

Souza, L., Pozo, A., da Rosa, J., & Neto, A. (2010). Applying correlation to enhance boosting technique using genetic programming as base learner. *Applied Intelligence, 33*(3), 291–301. doi:10.1007/s10489-009-0166-y

Sox, H. C., & Greenfield, S. (2009). Comparative Effectiveness Research: A Report From the Institute of Medicine. *Annals of Internal Medicine, 151*(3), 203–205. doi:10.7326/0003-4819-151-3-200908040-00125 PMID:19567618

Sparkman, O. D. (2000). *Mass spectrometry desk reference* (1st ed.). Pittsburgh, Pa.: Global View Pub.

Spencer, C. C., Su, Z., Donnelly, P., & Marchini, J. (2009). Designing genome-wide association studies: Sample size, power, imputation, and the choice of genotyping chip. *PLOS Genetics, 5*(5), e1000477. doi:10.1371/journal.pgen.1000477 PMID:19492015

Spotfire. (2014). *TIBCO Spotfire - Business Intelligence Analytics Software & Data Visualization*. Retrieved January 12, 2014, from http://spotfire.tibco.com/

Spratlin, J. L., Serkova, N. J., & Eckhardt, S. G. (2009). Clinical applications of metabolomics in oncology: a review. *Clin Cancer Res, 15*(2), 431-440. doi: 10.1158/1078-0432.CCR-08-1059

Sproull, R. F., & Eisenberg, J. (2005). Building an electronic records archive at the National Archives and Records Administration recommendations for a long-term strategy (p. xii). Retrieved from http://ezproxy.usq.edu.au/login?url=http://site.ebrary.com/lib/unisouthernqld/Doc?id=10082366

SPSS. (2014). *IBM SPSS software*. Retrieved January 12, 2014, from http://www-01.ibm.com/software/analytics/spss/

Sribar, V. (2011). *'Big Data' is only the beginning of extreme information management*. Retrieved from https://www.gartner.com/doc/1622715/big-data-beginning-extreme-information

St Sauver, J. L., Grossardt, B. R., Yawn, B. P., Melton, L. J., Pankratz, J. J., Brue, S. M., & Rocca, W. A. (2012). Data resource profile: The Rochester Epidemiology Project (REP) medical records-linkage system. *International Journal of Epidemiology, 41*(6), 1614–1624. doi:10.1093/ije/dys195 PMID:23159830

Starr, J. R., Hsu, L., & Schwartz, S. M. (2005). Assessing Maternal Genetic Associations: A Comparison of the Log-Linear Approach to Case-Parent Triad Data and a Case-Control Approach. *Epidemiology (Cambridge, Mass.), 16*(3), 294–303. doi:10.1097/01.ede.0000158223.98649.eb PMID:15824543

Stata. (2014). *Stata | Data Analysis and Statistical Software*. Retrieved January 27, 2014, from http://www.stata.com/

Stead, W. W., Senner, J. W., Reddick, W. T., & Lofgren, J. P. (1990). Racial differences in susceptibility to infection by *Mycobacterium tuberculosis. The New England Journal of Medicine, 322*(7), 422–427. doi:10.1056/NEJM199002153220702 PMID:2300105

Steel, G. G. (2002). Basic clinical radiobiology (3rd ed.). London: Oxford University Press.

Stefani, G., & Slack, F. J. (2008). Small non-coding RNAs in animal development. *Nature Reviews. Molecular Cell Biology, 9*(3), 219–230. doi:10.1038/nrm2347 PMID:18270516

Steinbeck, C., Kuhn, S., Jayaseelan, K., & Moreno, P. (2011). Computational metabolomics – a field at the boundaries of cheminformatics and bioinformatics. *Journal of Cheminformatics, 3*(Suppl 1), 6.

Steiner, L., Hopp, L., Wirth, H., Galle, J., Binder, H., Prohaska, S. J., & Rohlf, T. (2012). A Global Genome Segmentation Method for Exploration of Epigenetic Patterns. *PLOS one, 7*(10), e46811.

Steinfath, M., Repsilber, D., Scholz, M., Walther, D., & Selbig, J. (2007). Integrated data analysis for genome-wide research. *EXS, 97*, 309–329. doi:10.1007/978-3-7643-7439-6_13 PMID:17432273

Stelling, J. (2004). Mathematical models in microbial systems biology. *Current Opinion in Microbiology, 7*(5), 513–518. doi:10.1016/j.mib.2004.08.004 PMID:15451507

Stephens, J. C., Schneider, J. A., Tanguay, D. A., Choi, J., Acharya, T., & Stanley, S. E. et al. (2001). Haplotype Variation and Linkage Disequilibrium in 313 Human Genes. *Science, 293*(5529), 489–493. doi:10.1126/science.1059431 PMID:11452081

Stephens, M., & Balding, D. J. (2009). Bayesian statistical methods for genetic association studies. *Nature Reviews. Genetics*, *10*(10), 681–690. doi:10.1038/nrg2615 PMID:19763151

Stephens, M., & Scheet, P. (2005). Accounting for decay of linkage disequilibrium in haplotype inference and missing-data imputation. *American Journal of Human Genetics*, *76*(3), 449–462. doi:10.1086/428594 PMID:15700229

Steuer, R., & Junker, H. (2009). *Computational models of metabolism: stability and regulation in metabolic networks*. (A. Stuart, Ed.). John Wiley & Sons.

Stevenson, K. R., Coolon, J. D., & Wittkopp, P. J. (2013). Sources of bias in measures of allele-specific expression derived from RNA-seq data aligned to a single reference genome. *BMC Genomics*, *14*(1), 536. doi:10.1186/1471-2164-14-536 PMID:23919664

Stewart, J. A., Chadwick, V. S., & Murray, A. (2005). Investigations into the influence of host genetics on the predominant eubacteria in the faecal microflora of children. *Journal of Medical Microbiology*, *54*(Pt 12), 1239–1242. doi:10.1099/jmm.0.46189-0 PMID:16278440

Stolzenberg-Solomon, R. Z., Dodd, K. W., Blaser, M. J., Virtamo, J., Taylor, P. R., & Albanes, D. (2003). Tooth loss, pancreatic cancer, and Helicobacter pylori. *The American Journal of Clinical Nutrition*, *78*(1), 176–181. PMID:12816788

Strachan, T., & Read, A. P. (2005). *Molekulare Humangenetik*. Academic Press.

Stranger, B. E., Montgomery, S. B., Dimas, A. S., Parts, L., Stegle, O., & Ingle, C. E. et al. (2012). Patterns of cis regulatory variation in diverse human populations. *PLOS Genetics*, *8*(4), e1002639. doi:10.1371/journal.pgen.1002639 PMID:22532805

Stranger, B. E., Stahl, E. A., & Raj, T. (2011). Progress and Promise of Genome-Wide Association Studies for Human Complex Trait Genetics. *Genetics*, *187*(2), 367–383. doi:10.1534/genetics.110.120907 PMID:21115973

Stratton, M. R., Campbell, P. J., & Futreal, P. A. (2009). The cancer genome. *Nature*, *458*(7239), 719–724. doi:10.1038/nature07943 PMID:19360079

Strauss, E. J., & Falkow, S. (1997). Microbial pathogenesis: Genomics and beyond. *Science*, *276*(5313), 707–712. doi:10.1126/science.276.5313.707 PMID:9115190

Strehl, A., & Ghosh, J. (2003). Cluster ensembles --- a knowledge reuse framework for combining multiple partitions. *Journal of Machine Learning Research*, *3*, 583–617.

Strintzis, M. G. (1998). A review of compression methods for medical images in PACS. *International Journal of Medical Informatics*, *52*(1-3), 159–165. doi:10.1016/S1386-5056(98)00135-X PMID:9848413

Strobl, C., Malley, J., & Tutz, G. (2009). An introduction to recursive partitioning: Rationale, application, and characteristics of classification and regression trees, bagging, and random forests. *Psychological Methods*, *14*(4), 323–348. doi:10.1037/a0016973 PMID:19968396

Styblo, K. (1985). The relationship between the risk of tuberculosis infection and the risk of developing infectious tuberculosis. *Bulletin of the International Union Against Tuberculosis*, *60*, 117–119.

Styblo, K. (1991). *Epidemiology of tuberculosis, Selected Papers, 24*. The Hague: Royal Netherlands Tuberculosis Association.

Suarez-Gestal, M., Perez-Pampin, E., Calaza, M., Gomez-Reino, J. J., & Gonzalez, A. (2010). Lack of replication of genetic predictors for the rheumatoid arthritis response to anti-TNF treatments: A prospective case-only study. *Arthritis Research & Therapy*, *12*(2), R72. doi:10.1186/ar2990 PMID:20423481

Subramanian, A., Tamayo, P., Mootha, V. K., Mukherjee, S., Ebert, B. L., & Gillette, M. A. et al. (2005). Gene set enrichment analysis: A knowledge-based approach for interpreting genome-wide expression profiles. *Proceedings of the National Academy of Sciences of the United States of America*, *102*(43), 15545–15550. doi:10.1073/pnas.0506580102 PMID:16199517

Sud, D., Bigbee, C., Flynn, J. L., & Kirschner, D. E. (2006). Contribution of CD8+ T cells to control of *Mycobacterium tuberculosis* infection. *Journal of Immunology (Baltimore, MD.: 1950)*, *176*(7), 4296–4314. doi:10.4049/jimmunol.176.7.4296 PMID:16547267

Suen, G., Arshinoff, B. I., Taylor, R. G., & Welch, R. D. (2007). Practical applications of bacterial functional genomics. *Biotechnology & Genetic Engineering Reviews*, *24*(1), 213–242. doi:10.1080/02648725.2007.10648101 PMID:18059635

Sugar, C., & James, G. (2003). Finding the number of clusters in a data set, an information theoretic approach. *Journal of the American Statistical Association*, *98*(463), 750–763. doi:10.1198/016214503000000666

Sugden, A., & Pennisi, E. (2000). Diversity digitized. *Science*, *289*, 2305–2305. PMID:11041798

Suh, K. S., Sarojini, S., Youssif, M., Nalley, K., Milinovikj, N., & Elloumi, F. et al. (2013). Tissue banking, bioinformatics, and electronic medical records: The front-end requirements for personalized medicine. *Journal of Oncology*, *368751*. doi:10.1155/2013/368751 PMID:23818899

Sulakhe, D., Balasubramanian, S., Xie, B., Feng, B., Taylor, A., & Wang, S. et al. (2014). Lynx: A database and knowledge extraction engine for integrative medicine. *Nucleic Acids Research*, *42*(1), D1007–D1012. doi:10.1093/nar/gkt1166 PMID:24270788

Sullivan, R., Peppercorn, J., Sikora, K., Zalcberg, J., Meropol, N. J., & Amir, E. et al. (2011). Delivering affordable cancer care in high-income countries. *The Lancet Oncology*, *12*(10), 933–980. doi:10.1016/S1470-2045(11)70141-3 PMID:21958503

Su, M., Miftena, M., Whiddon, C., Sun, X., Light, K., & Marks, L. (2005). An artificial neural network for predicting the incidence of radiation pneumonitis. *Medical Physics*, *32*(2), 318–325. doi:10.1118/1.1835611 PMID:15789575

Sung, Y. J., Schwander, K., Arnett, D. K., Kardia, S. L. R., Rankinen, T., & Bouchard, C. et al. (2014). An Empirical Comparison of Meta-analysis and Mega-analysis of Individual Participant Data for Identifying Gene-Environment Interactions: Meta- and Mega-analyses of Interactions. *Genetic Epidemiology*, *38*(4), 369–378. doi:10.1002/gepi.21800 PMID:24719363

Sun, W. (2012). A statistical framework for eQTL mapping using RNA-seq data. *Biometrics*, *68*(1), 1–11. doi:10.1111/j.1541-0420.2011.01654.x PMID:21838806

Sun, X., Lu, Q., Mukheerjee, S., Crane, P. K., Elston, R., & Ritchie, M. D. (2014). Analysis pipeline for the epistasis search- statistical versus biological filtering. *Frontiers in Genetics*, *5*, 106. doi:10.3389/fgene.2014.00106 PMID:24817878

Sun, Y., Fu, Y., Li, Y., & Xu, A. (2012). Genome-wide alternative polyadenylation in animals: Insights from high-throughput technologies. *Journal of Molecular Cell Biology*, *4*(6), 352–361. doi:10.1093/jmcb/mjs041 PMID:23099521

Suzuki, S., & Matsui, T. (2012). *Remote sensing for medical and health care applications*. Remote Sensing-Applications. doi:10.5772/36924

Suzuki, S., Tenjin, T., Shibuya, T., & Tanaka, S. (1997). Chromosome 17 copy numbers and incidence of p 53 gene deletion in gastric cancer cells. Dual color fluorescence in situ hybridization analysis. *Nippon Ika Daigaku Zasshi*, *64*(1), 22–29. PMID:9119949

Svensson, J. P., Stalpers, L. J., Esveldt-van Lange, R. E., Franken, N. A., Haveman, J., Klein, B., . . . Giphart-Gassler, M. (2006). Analysis of gene expression using gene sets discriminates cancer patients with and without late radiation toxicity. *PLoS Med*, *3*(10), e422. doi: 10.1371/journal.pmed.0030422

SWDLF. (2012). *A Scotland-wide Data Linkage Framework for Statistics and Research Consultation Paper on the Aims and Guiding Principles*. St. Andrews: Scottish Government. Retrieved from http://www.scotland.gov.uk/Resource/0039/00390444.pdf

Syvänen, A.-C. (2001). Accessing genetic variation: Genotyping single nucleotide polymorphisms. *Nature Reviews. Genetics*, *2*(12), 930–942. doi:10.1038/35103535 PMID:11733746

Szczesniak, M. W., Deorowicz, S., Gapski, J., Kaczynski, L., & Makalowska, I. (2012). miRNEST database: An integrative approach in microRNA search and annotation. *Nucleic Acids Research*, *40*(Database issue), D198–D204. doi:10.1093/nar/gkr1159 PMID:22135287

Sztromwasser, P., Puntervoll, P., & Petersen, K. (2011). Data partitioning enables the use of standard SOAP web services in genome-scale workflows. *Journal of Integrative Bioinformatics*, *8*, 163. PMID:21788681

Szymczak, S., Igl, B. W., & Ziegler, A. (2009). Detecting SNP-expression associations: A comparison of mutual information and median test with standard statistical approaches. *Statistics in Medicine*, *28*(29), 3581–3596. doi:10.1002/sim.3695 PMID:19691035

Tableau. (2014). *Business Intelligence and Analytics | Tableau Software*. Retrieved January 12, 2014, from http://www.tableausoftware.com/

Taguchi, Y.-h., & Okamoto, A. (2012). Principal Component Analysis for Bacterial Proteomic Analysis. In T. Shibata, H. Kashima, J. Sese, & S. Ahmad. (Eds.), *Pattern Recognition in Bioinformatics:7th IAPR International Conference, PRIB 2012* (pp. 441–452). Berlin: Springer. doi:10.1007/978-3-642-34123-6_13

Taguchi, Y.-, & Murakami, Y. (2013). Principal component analysis based feature extraction approach to identify circulating microRNA biomarkers. *PLoS ONE*, *8*(6), e66714. doi:10.1371/journal.pone.0066714 PMID:23874370

Tamayo, P., Slonim, D., Mesirov, J., Zhu, Q., Kitareewan, S., & Dmitrovsky, E. et al. (1999). Interpreting patterns of gene expression with self-organizing maps: Methods and application to hematopoietic differentiation. *Proceedings of the National Academy of Sciences of the United States of America*, *96*(6), 2907–2912. doi:10.1073/pnas.96.6.2907 PMID:10077610

Tam, O. H., Aravin, A. A., Stein, P., Girard, A., Murchison, E. P., & Cheloufi, S. et al. (2008). Pseudogene-derived small interfering RNAs regulate gene expression in mouse oocytes. *Nature*, *453*(7194), 534–538. doi:10.1038/nature06904 PMID:18404147

Tan, E. K. (2010). Genome-wide association studies: Promises and pitfalls. *Annals of the Academy of Medicine, Singapore*, *39*(2), 77–78. PMID:20237726

Tang, L., & Yuwen, J. (2013). *The Study on Digital Traffic Service System and Key Technologies of Location Based Service*. Paper presented at the 2013 the International Conference on Remote Sensing, Environment and Transportation Engineering (RSETE 2013). New York, NY. doi:10.2991/rsete.2013.148

Tang, K. W., Alaei-Mahabadi, B., Samuelsson, T., Lindh, M., & Larsson, E. (2013). The landscape of viral expression and host gene fusion and adaptation in human cancer. *Nature Communications*, *4*, 2513. doi:10.1038/ncomms3513 PMID:24085110

Tang, W., Wu, X., Jiang, R., & Li, Y. (2009). Epistatic Module Detection for Case-Control Studies: A Bayesian Model with a Gibbs Sampling Strategy. *PLOS Genetics*, *5*(5), e1000464. doi:10.1371/journal.pgen.1000464 PMID:19412524

Tan, Q. (2005). Genetic Association Analysis of Human Longevity in Cohort Studies of Elderly Subjects: An Example of the PON1 Gene in the Danish 1905 Birth Cohort. *Genetics*, *172*(3), 1821–1828. doi:10.1534/genetics.105.050914 PMID:16387878

Tarca, A. L., Romero, R., & Draghici, S. (2006). Analysis of microarray experiments of gene expression profiling. *American Journal of Obstetrics and Gynecology*, *195*(2), 373–388. doi:10.1016/j.ajog.2006.07.001 PMID:16890548

Tateno, Y., Miyazaki, S., Ota, M., Sugawara, H., & Gojobori, T. (2000). DNA Data Bank of Japan (DDBJ) in collaboration with mass sequencing teams. *Nucleic Acids Research*, *28*(1), 24–26. doi:10.1093/nar/28.1.24 PMID:10592172

Tavazoie, S., Hughes, J., Campbell, M., Cho, R., & Church, G. (1999). Systematic determination of genetic network architecture. *Nature Genetics*, *22*(3), 281–285. doi:10.1038/10343 PMID:10391217

Taylor, C. F., Field, D., Sansone, S. A., Aerts, J., Apweiler, R., & Ashburner, M. et al. (2008). Promoting coherent minimum reporting guidelines for biological and biomedical investigations: The MIBBI project. *Nature Biotechnology*, *26*(8), 889–896. doi:10.1038/nbt.1411 PMID:18688244

TCGA. (2012). Comprehensive molecular characterization of human colon and rectal cancer. *Nature, 487*(7407), 330-337.

Teare, M. D. (2011). Candidate Gene Association Studies. In M. D. Teare (Ed.), *Genetic Epidemiology* (Vol. 713, pp. 105–117). Humana Press. doi:10.1007/978-1-60327-416-6_8

Tenenhaus, A., Guillemot, V., Gidrol, X., & Frouin, V. (2010). Gene association networks from microarray data using a regularized estimation of partial correlation based on PLS regression. *IEEE/ACM Transactions on Computational Biology and Bioinformatics*, *7*(2), 251–262. doi:10.1109/TCBB.2008.87 PMID:20431145

Tenenhaus, A., & Tenenhaus, M. (2011). Regularized generalized canonical correlation analysis. *Psychometrika, 76*(2), 257–284. doi:10.1007/s11336-011-9206-8

The Big Data Conundrum: How to Define It? (2013). *MIT Technology Review.* Retrieved from http://www.technologyreview.com/view/519851/the-big-data-conundrum-how-to-define-it/

Theisen, A. (2008). Microarray-based Comparative Genomic Hybridization (aCGH). *Nature Education, 1.*

Thieme, S., & Groth, P. (2013). Genome Fusion Detection: A novel method to detect fusion genes from SNP-array data. *Bioinformatics (Oxford, England), 29*(6), 671–677. doi:10.1093/bioinformatics/btt028 PMID:23341502

Thierry-Mieg, D., & Thierry-Mieg, J. (2006). AceView: A comprehensive cDNA-supported gene and transcripts annotation. *Genome Biology, 7*(Suppl 1), S12–S14. doi:10.1186/gb-2006-7-s1-s12 PMID:16925834

Thomas-Chollier, M., Herrmann, C., Defrance, M., Sand, O., Thieffry, D., & Helden, J. (2012). RSAT peak-motifs: Motif-analysis in full-size ChIP-seq datasets. *Nucleic Acids Research, 40*(4), e31. doi:10.1093/nar/gkr1104 PMID:22156162

Thomas, P. D., Campbell, M. J., Kejariwal, A., Mi, H., Karlak, B., & Daverman, R. et al. (2003). PANTHER: A library of protein families and subfamilies indexed by function. *Genome Research, 13*(9), 2129–2141. doi:10.1101/gr.772403 PMID:12952881

Thomas, S., & Bonchev, D. (2010). A survey of current software for network analysis in molecular biology. *Human Genomics, 4*(5), 353–360. doi:10.1186/1479-7364-4-5-353 PMID:20650822

Thompson, D. M., & Parker, R. (2009). Stressing out over tRNA cleavage. *Cell, 138*(2), 215–219. doi:10.1016/j.cell.2009.07.001 PMID:19632169

Thompson, W., Rouchka, E., & Lawrence, C. (2003). Gibbs Recursive Sampler: Finding transcription factor binding sites. *Nucleic Acids Research, 31*(13), 3580–3585. doi:10.1093/nar/gkg608 PMID:12824370

Thomson, M. C., & Connor, S. J. (2001). The development of Malaria Early Warning Systems for Africa. *Trends in Parasitology, 17*(9), 438–445. doi:10.1016/S1471-4922(01)02077-3 PMID:11530356

Thorvaldsdóttir, H., Robinson, J., & Mesirov, J. (2013). Integrative Genomics Viewer (IGV): High-performance genomics data visualization and exploration. *Briefings in Bioinformatics, 14*(2), 178–192. doi:10.1093/bib/bbs017 PMID:22517427

Tian, B., & Manley, J. L. (2013). Alternative cleavage and polyadenylation: The long and short of it. *Trends in Biochemical Sciences, 38*(6), 312–320. doi:10.1016/j.tibs.2013.03.005 PMID:23632313

Tibshirani, R. (1996). Regression shrinkage and selection via the lasso. *Journal of the Royal Statistical Society. Series B. Methodological, 58*(1), 267–288.

Timbie, J. W., Fox, D. S., Van Busum, K., & Schneider, E. C. (2012). Five Reasons That Many Comparative Effectiveness Studies Fail To Change Patient Care And Clinical Practice. *Health Affairs, 31*(10), 2168–2175. doi:10.1377/hlthaff.2012.0150 PMID:23048092

Tischkowitz, M. D., Sabbaghian, N., Hamel, N., Borgida, A., Rosner, C., & Taherian, N. et al. (2009). Analysis of the gene coding for the BRCA2-interacting protein PALB2 in familial and sporadic pancreatic cancer. *Gastroenterology, 137*(3), 1183–1186. doi:10.1053/j.gastro.2009.06.055 PMID:19635604

Tiwaria, R. P., Hattikudura, N. S., Bharmalb, R. N., Kartikeyanc, S., Deshmukhd, N. M., & Bisene, P. S. (2007). Modern approaches to a rapid diagnosis of tuberculosis: Promises and challenges ahead. *Tuberculosis (Edinburgh, Scotland), 87*(3), 193–201. doi:10.1016/j.tube.2006.07.005 PMID:17029964

Tomatis, S., Rancati, T., Fiorino, C., Vavassori, V., Fellin, G., & Cagna, E. et al. (2012). Late rectal bleeding after 3D-CRT for prostate cancer: Development of a neural-network-based predictive model. *Physics in Medicine and Biology, 57*(5), 1399–1412. doi:10.1088/0031-9155/57/5/1399 PMID:22349550

Tomlins, S. A., Rhodes, D. R., Perner, S., Dhanasekaran, S. M., Mehra, R., Sun, X. W., & Chinnaiyan, A. M. (2005). Recurrent fusion of TMPRSS2 and ETS transcription factor genes in prostate cancer. *Science, 310*(5748), 644–648. doi:10.1126/science.1117679 PMID:16254181

Tonner, P., Srinivasasainagendra, V., Zhang, S., & Zhi, D. (2012). Detecting transcription of ribosomal protein pseudogenes in diverse human tissues from RNA-seq data. *BMC Genomics, 13*(1), 412. doi:10.1186/1471-2164-13-412 PMID:22908858

Torii, M., Hu, Z., Wu, C. H., & Liu, H. (2009). BioTagger-GM: A gene/protein name recognition system. *Journal of the American Medical Informatics Association, 16*(2), 247–255. doi:10.1197/jamia.M2844 PMID:19074302

Towse, A., Ossa, D., Veenstra, D., Carlson, J., & Garrison, L. (2013). Understanding the Economic Value of Molecular Diagnostic Tests: Case Studies and Lessons Learned. *Journal of Personalized Medicine, 3*(4), 288–305. doi:10.3390/jpm3040288

Toyota, M., Ahuja, N., Ohe-Toyota, M., Herman, J. G., Baylin, S. B., & Issa, J.-P. J. (1999). CpG island methylator phenotype in colorectal cancer. *Proceedings of the National Academy of Sciences of the United States of America, 96*(15), 8681–8686. doi:10.1073/pnas.96.15.8681 PMID:10411935

Trafton, A. (2011). Rewiring Cells. *MIT Technology Review*. Retrieved January 29, 2014, from http://www.technologyreview.com/article/423703/rewiring-cells/

Tranchevent, L. C., Barriot, R., Yu, S., Van Vooren, S., Van Loo, P., Coessens, B., De Moor, B., Aerts, S., & Moreau, Y. (2008). ENDEAVOUR update: A web resource for gene prioritization in multiple species. *Nucleic Acids Res, 36*(Web Server issue), W377-384.

Trevino, V., Falciani, F., & Barrera-Saldana, H. A. (2007). DNA microarrays: A powerful genomic tool for biomedical and clinical research. *Molecular Medicine (Cambridge, Mass.), 13*(9-10), 527–541. doi:10.2119/2006-00107.Trevino PMID:17660860

Trifonova, O. P. L., Lin, V. A., Kolker, E. V., & Lisitsa, A. V. (2013). Big data in biology and medicine. *Acta Naturae, 5*, 13–16. PMID:24303199

Troendle, J. F., & Mills, J. L. (2010). Correction for Multiplicity in Genetic Association Studies of Triads: The Permutational TDT: The Permutational TDT. *Annals of Human Genetics.*

Tromp, M., Méray, N., Ravelli, C. J. A., Reitsma, B. J., & Bonsel, J. G. (2008). Ignoring Dependency between Linking Variables and Its Impact on the Outcome of Probabilistic Record Linkage Studies. *Journal of the American Medical Informatics Association, 15*(5), 654–660. doi:10.1197/jamia.M2265 PMID:18579842

Tromp, M., Ravelli, C. A., Bonsel, J. G., Hasman, A., & Reitsma, B. J. (2008). Original Article: Results from simulated data sets: probabilistic record linkage outperforms deterministic record linkage.[Article]. *Journal of Clinical Epidemiology, 64*(5), 565–572. doi:10.1016/j.jclinepi.2010.05.008 PMID:20952162

Trowbridge, R., & Weingarten, S. (2001). Clinical decision support systems. *Making health care safer: A critical analysis of patient safety practices. Evidence Report/technology Assessment*, 43.

Trutschl, M., Kilgore, P., Cvek, U., & Scott, R. (2014). Scalable Genome-Wide Discovery and Presentation of Motifs. In *Proceedings of 6th Int. Conf. on Bioinf. and Bio. Comp.* Las Vegas, NV: International Society for Computers and their Applications.

Tucker, S. L., Cheung, R., Dong, L., Liu, H. H., Thames, H. D., & Huang, E. H. et al. (2004). Dose-volume response analyses of late rectal bleeding after radiotherapy for prostate cancer. *International Journal of Radiation Oncology, Biology, Physics, 59*(2), 353–365. doi:10.1016/j.ijrobp.2003.12.033 PMID:15145148

Tuckson, R. V., Newcomer, L., & De Sa, J. M. (2013). Accessing genomic medicine: Affordability, diffusion, and disparities. *Journal of the American Medical Association, 309*(14), 1469–1470. doi:10.1001/jama.2013.1468 PMID:23571584

Tufte, E. R. (2001). *The Visual Display of Quantitative Information* (2nd ed.). Cheshire, CT: Graphics Pr.

Turinsky, A. L., Fanea, E., Trinh, Q., Dong, X., Stromer, J. N., & Shu, X. et al. (2008). Integration of genomic and medical data into a 3D atlas of human anatomy. *Studies in Health Technology and Informatics, 132*, 526–531. PMID:18391362

Turner, S. D., Dudek, S. M., & Ritchie, M. D. (2010). ATHENA: A knowledge-based hybrid backpropagation-grammatical evolution neural network algorithm for discovering epistasis among quantitative trait Loci. *BioData Min, 3*(1), 5. doi:10.1186/1756-0381-3-5 PMID:20875103

Tusher, V. G., Tibshirani, R., & Chu, G. (2001). Significance analysis of microarrays applied to the ionizing radiation response. *Proceedings of the National Academy of Sciences of the United States of America, 98*(9), 5116–5121. doi:10.1073/pnas.091062498 PMID:11309499

Tutarel, O., Dangwal, S., Bretthauer, J., Westhoff-Bleck, M., Roentgen, P., & Anker, S. D. et al. (2013). Circulating miR-423_5p fails as a biomarker for systemic ventricular function in adults after atrial repair for transposition of the great arteries. *International Journal of Cardiology, 167*(1), 63–66. doi:10.1016/j.ijcard.2011.11.082 PMID:22188991

Twyman, R. M. (2004). *Principles of proteomics*. New York: BIOS Scientific Publishers.

Tyburski, J. B., Patterson, A. D., Krausz, K. W., Slavik, J., Fornace, A. J., Jr., Gonzalez, F. J., & Idle, J. R. (2008). Radiation metabolomics. 1. Identification of minimally invasive urine biomarkers for gamma-radiation exposure in mice. *Radiat Res, 170*(1), 1-14. doi:10.1667/RR1265.1

Tyndall, M. W., Patrick, D., Spittal, P., Li, K., O'Shaughnessy, M. V., & Schechter, T. (2002). Risky sexual behaviours among injection drugs users with high HIV prevalence: Implications for STD control. *Sexually Transmitted Infections, 78*(suppl. 1), i170–i175. doi:10.1136/sti.78.suppl_1.i170 PMID:12083439

Ulitsky, I., Krogan, N. J., & Shamir, R. (2009). Towards accurate imputation of quantitative genetic interactions. *Genome Biology, 10*(12), R140. doi:10.1186/gb-2009-10-12-r140 PMID:20003301

UniProt Consortium. (2014). *About UniProt*. Retrieved Jan. 10, 2014, from UniProtKB: http://www.uniprot.org/help/about

Uzuner, O., South, B. R., Shen, S., & DuVall, S. L. (2011). 2010 i2b2/VA challenge on concepts, assertions, and relations in clinical text. *Journal of the American Medical Informatics Association, 18*(5), 552–556. doi:10.1136/amiajnl-2011-000203 PMID:21685143

Vaidya, M., Creach, K. M., Frye, J., Dehdashti, F., Bradley, J. D., & El Naqa, I. (2012). Combined PET/CT image characteristics for radiotherapy tumor response in lung cancer. *Radiother Oncol, 102*(2), 239-245. doi:10.1016/j.radonc.2011.10.014

van Berkum, N. L., Lieberman-Aiden, E., Williams, L., Imakaev, M., Gnirke, A., Mirny, L. A., & Lander, E. S. (2010). Hi-C: A method to study the three-dimensional architecture of genomes. *Journal of Visualized Experiments*, (39). doi:10.3791/1869 PMID:20461051

van den Belt, H. (2013). Synthetic biology, patenting, health and global justice. *Systems and Synthetic Biology, 7*(3), 87–98. doi:10.1007/s11693-012-9098-7 PMID:24432146

van Doren, D., Koenigstein, S., & Reiss, T. (2013). The development of synthetic biology: A patent analysis. *Systems and Synthetic Biology, 7*(4), 209–220. doi:10.1007/s11693-013-9121-7 PMID:24255694

van Eijk, K. R., de Jong, S., Boks, M. P., Langeveld, T., Colas, F., & Veldink, J. H. et al. (2012). Genetic analysis of DNA methylation and gene expression levels in whole blood of healthy human subjects. *BMC Genomics, 13*(1), 636. doi:10.1186/1471-2164-13-636 PMID:23157493

van Engeland, M., Derks, S., Smits, K. M., Meijer, G. A., & Herman, J. G. (2011). Colorectal Cancer Epigenetics: Complex Simplicity. *Journal of Clinical Oncology, 29*(10), 1382–1391. doi:10.1200/JCO.2010.28.2319 PMID:21220596

van Heyningen, V., & Bickmore, W. (2013). Regulation from a distance: Long-range control of gene expression in development and disease. *Philosophical Transactions of the Royal Society of London. Series B, Biological Sciences, 368*(1620), 20120372. doi:10.1098/rstb.2012.0372 PMID:23650642

Van Noorden, R., Ledford, H., & Mann, A. (2011). New year, new science. *Nature, 469*(7328), 12. doi:10.1038/469012a PMID:21209635

van Rijmenam, M. (2013). *Why The 3V's Are Not Sufficient To Describe Big Data*. Big data startup. Retrieved from http://www.bigdata-startups.com/3vs-sufficient-describe-big-data/

Van Steen, K. (2012). Travelling the world of gene-gene interactions. *Briefings in Bioinformatics*, *13*(1), 1–19. doi:10.1093/bib/bbr012 PMID:21441561

Van Steen, K., Laird, N. M., Markel, P., & Molenberghs, G. (2007). Approaches to handling incomplete data in family-based association testing. *Annals of Human Genetics*, *71*(Pt 2), 141–151. doi:10.1111/j.1469-1809.2006.00325.x PMID:17096676

Vapnik, V. (1998). *Statistical Learning Theory*. New York: Wiley.

Varshavsky, R., Gottlieb, A., Horn, D., & Linial, M. (2007). Unsupervised feature selection under perturbations: Meeting the challenges of biological data. *Bioinformatics (Oxford, England)*, *23*(24), 3343–3349. doi:10.1093/bioinformatics/btm528 PMID:17989091

VDL. (2013). *Victorian Data Linkages*. Retrieved 12th Feb, 2013, from http://www.health.vic.gov.au/vdl/

Vedder, R. G., Vanecek, M. T., Guynes, C. S., & Cappel, J. J. (1999). CEO and CIO perspectives on competitive intelligence. *Communications of the ACM*, *42*(8), 108–116. doi:10.1145/310930.310982

Velculescu, V. E., Zhang, L., Vogelstein, B., & Kinzler, K. W. (1995). Serial analysis of gene expression. *Science*, *270*(5235), 484–487. doi:10.1126/science.270.5235.484 PMID:7570003

Velculescu, V., Zhang, L., Zhou, W., Vogelstein, J., Basrai, M. A., & Bassett, D. E. Jr et al. (1997). Characterization of the yeast transcriptome. *Cell*, *88*(2), 243–251. doi:10.1016/S0092-8674(00)81845-0 PMID:9008165

Venkat, A., Chan-Tompkins, N. H., Hegde, G. G., Chuirazzi, D. M., Hunter, R., & Szczesiul, J. M. (2010). Feasibility of integrating a clinical decision support tool into an existing computerized physician order entry system to increase seasonal influenza vaccination in the emergency department. *Vaccine*, *28*(37), 6058–6064. doi:10.1016/j.vaccine.2010.06.090 PMID:20620167

Venter, J. C., Adams, M. D., Myers, E. W., Li, P. W., & Mural, R. J. et al. (2001). The Sequence of the Human Genome. *Science*, *291*(5507), 1304–1351. doi:10.1126/science.1058040 PMID:11181995

Vergoulis, T., Vlachos, I. S., Alexiou, P., Georgakilas, G., Maragkakis, M., & Reczko, M. et al. (2012). TarBase 6.0: Capturing the exponential growth of miRNA targets with experimental support. *Nucleic Acids Research*, *40*(Database issue), D222–D229. doi:10.1093/nar/gkr1161 PMID:22135297

Vermeulen, S. H. H. M., Den Heijer, M., Sham, P., & Knight, J. (2007). Application of multi-locus analytical methods to identify interacting loci in case-control studies. *Annals of Human Genetics*, *71*(5), 689–700. doi:10.1111/j.1469-1809.2007.00360.x PMID:17425620

Veuthey, A. L., Bridge, A., Gobeill, J., Ruch, P., McEntyre, J. R., Bougueleret, L., & Xenarios, I. (2013). Application of text-mining for updating protein post-translational modification annotation in UniProtKB. *BMC Bioinformatics*, *14*(1), 104. doi:10.1186/1471-2105-14-104 PMID:23517090

Viers, H. (2011). *Synthetic Biology and Beyond: Commission's Goal: keep the dialogue going*. Retrieved January 29, 2014, from http://blog.bioethics.gov/2011/02/08/synthetic-biology-and-beyond-commissions-goal-keep-the-dialogue-going/

Viswanathan, G. A., Seto, J., Patil, S., Nudelman, G., & Sealfon, S. C. (2008). Getting Started in Biological Pathway Construction and Analysis. *PLoS Computational Biology*, *4*(2), e16. doi:10.1371/journal.pcbi.0040016 PMID:18463709

Vogel, C., & Marcotte, E. M. (2012). Insights into the regulation of protein abundance from proteomic and transcriptomic analyses. *Nature Reviews. Genetics*, *13*(4), 227–232. PMID:22411467

Vogeli, C., Shields, A. E., Lee, T. A., Gibson, T. B., Marder, W. D., Weiss, K. B., & Blumenthal, D. (2007). Multiple Chronic Conditions: Prevalence, Health Consequences, and Implications for Quality, Care Management, and Costs. *Journal of General Internal Medicine*, *22*(3), 391–395. doi:10.1007/s11606-007-0322-1 PMID:18026807

Waaijenborg, S., & Zwinderman, A. H. (2009). Sparse canonical correlation analysis for identifying, connecting and completing gene-expression networks. *BMC Bioinformatics*, *10*(1), 315. doi:10.1186/1471-2105-10-315 PMID:19785734

WADLS. (2013a). *Western Australia Data Linkage System*. Retrieved 12th Feb, 2013, from http://www.datalinkage-wa.org/

Wang, X., & El Naqa, I. M. (2008). Prediction of both conserved and nonconserved microRNA targets in animals. *Bioinformatics, 24*(3), 325-332. doi: 10.1093/bioinformatics/btm595

Wang, B., Mezlini, A. M., Demir, F., Fiume, M., Tu, Z., & Brudno, M. et al. (2014). Similarity network fusion for aggregating data types on a genomic scale. *Nature Methods*. PMID:24464287

Wang, K. (2012). Statistical tests of genetic association for case-control study designs. *Biostatistics (Oxford, England), 13*(4), 724–733. doi:10.1093/biostatistics/kxs002 PMID:22389176

Wang, K., Li, H., Yuan, Y., Etheridge, A., Zhou, Y., & Huang, D. et al. (2012). The complex exogenous RNA spectra in human plasma: An interface with human gut biota? *PLoS ONE, 7*(12), e51009. doi:10.1371/journal.pone.0051009 PMID:23251414

Wang, L., Zhang, B., Wolfinger, R. D., & Chen, X. (2008). An Integrated Approach for the Analysis of Biological Pathways using Mixed Models. *PLOS Genetics, 4*(7), e1000115. doi:10.1371/journal.pgen.1000115 PMID:18852846

Wang, Q., Jia, P., & Zhao, Z. (2013). VirusFinder: Software for efficient and accurate detection of viruses and their integration sites in host genomes through next generation sequencing data. *PLoS ONE, 8*(5), e64465. doi:10.1371/journal.pone.0064465 PMID:23717618

Wang, S., van der Vaart, A., Xu, Q., Seneviratne, C., Pomerleau, O., & Pomerleau, C. et al. (2014). Significant associations of CHRNA2 and CHRNA6 with nicotine dependence in European American and African American populations. *Human Genetics, 133*(5), 575–586. doi:10.1007/s00439-013-1398-9 PMID:24253422

Wang, T., Li, M., Guan, J., Li, P., Wang, H., & Guo, Y. et al. (2011). MicroRNAs miR-27a and miR-143 Regulate Porcine Adipocyte Lipid Metabolism. *International Journal of Molecular Sciences, 12*(11), 7950–7959. doi:10.3390/ijms12117950 PMID:22174642

Wang, Y., Liu, X., Robbins, K., & Rekaya, R. (2010). AntEpiSeeker: Detecting epistatic interactions for case-control studies using a two-stage ant colony optimization algorithm. *BMC Research Notes, 3*(1), 117. doi:10.1186/1756-0500-3-117 PMID:20426808

Wang, Y., Tetko, I. V., Hall, M. A., Frank, E., Facius, A., Mayer, K. F., & Mewes, H. W. (2005). Gene selection from microarray data for cancer classification–a machine learning approach. *Computational Biology and Chemistry, 29*(1), 37–46. doi:10.1016/j.compbiolchem.2004.11.001 PMID:15680584

Wang, Y., Zhang, X., & Chen, L. (2013). Computational systems biology in the big data era. *BMC Systems Biology, 7*(Suppl 2), S1. doi:10.1186/1752-0509-7-S2-S1 PMID:24564834

Wang, Z., Gerstein, M., & Snyder, M. (2009). RNA-Seq: A revolutionary tool for transcriptomics. *Nature Reviews. Genetics, 10*(1), 57–63. doi:10.1038/nrg2484 PMID:19015660

Wan, X., Yang, C., Yang, Q., Xue, H., Fan, X., Tang, N. L. S., & Yu, W. (2010). BOOST: A Fast Approach to Detecting Gene-Gene Interactions in Genome-wide Case-Control Studies. *American Journal of Human Genetics, 87*(3), 325–340. doi:10.1016/j.ajhg.2010.07.021 PMID:20817139

Wan, X., Yang, C., Yang, Q., Xue, H., Tang, N. L. S., & Yu, W. (2010). Predictive rule inference for epistatic interaction detection in genome-wide association studies. *Bioinformatics (Oxford, England), 26*(1), 30–37. doi:10.1093/bioinformatics/btp622 PMID:19880365

Ward, J. S., & Barker, A. (2013). *Undefined By Data: A Survey of Big Data Definitions*. eprint arXiv:1309.5821.

Ward, M. O., Grinstein, G., Keim, D. (2010). *Interactive Data Visualization: Foundations, Techniques, and Applications*. Natick, MA: A K Peters/CRC Press.

Ward, R. M., Schmieder, R., Highnam, G., & Mittelman, D. (2013). Big data challenges and opportunities in high-throughput sequencing. *Systems Biomedicine, 1*(1), 29–34. doi:10.4161/sysb.24470

Watanabe, T., Totoki, Y., Toyoda, A., Kaneda, M., Kuramochi-Miyagawa, S., & Obata, Y. et al. (2008). Endogenous siRNAs from naturally formed dsRNAs regulate transcripts in mouse oocytes. *Nature, 453*(7194), 539–543. doi:10.1038/nature06908 PMID:18404146

Waterman, M. (1995). Introduction to computational biology: maps, sequence and genomes. Chapman & Hall--CRC Press. ISBN 0 412 99391 0. doi:10.1007/978-1-4899-6846-3

Watkins, K., Metzger, B. A., Woody, G., & McLellan, A. T. (1992). High-Risk Sexual Behaviors of Intravenous Drug Users In- and Out-of-Treatment: Implications for the Spread of HIV Infection. *The American Journal of Drug and Alcohol Abuse, 18*(4), 389–398. doi:10.3109/00952999209051037 PMID:1449121

Watson, J. (1990). The human genome project: Past, present, and future. *Science, 248*(4951), 44–49. doi:10.1126/science.2181665 PMID:2181665

Weale, M. (2010). Quality Control for Genome-Wide Association Studies. In M. R. Barnes & G. Breen (Eds.), *Genetic Variation* (Vol. 628, pp. 341–372). Humana Press. doi:10.1007/978-1-60327-367-1_19

Webb, S. (2001). *The physics of three-dimensional radiation therapy: conformal radiotherapy, radiosurgery, and treatment planning.* Bristol, UK: Institute of Physics Pub.

Weich, S. (1998). The cohort study. *International Review of Psychiatry (Abingdon, England), 10*(4), 284–290. doi:10.1080/09540269874637 PMID:9657786

Weinberg, C. R. (2000). Choosing a Retrospective Design to Assess Joint Genetic and Environmental Contributions to Risk. *American Journal of Epidemiology, 152*(3), 197–203. doi:10.1093/aje/152.3.197 PMID:10933265

Weinberg, C. R. (2003). Studying Parents and Grandparents to Assess Genetic Contributions to Early-Onset Disease. *American Journal of Human Genetics, 72*(2), 438–447. doi:10.1086/346171 PMID:12533786

Weinstein, M. C., & Stason, W. B. (1977). Foundations of cost-effectiveness analysis for health and medical practices. *The New England Journal of Medicine, 296*(13), 716–721. doi:10.1056/NEJM197703312961304 PMID:402576

Wei, T., Geiser, A. G., Qian, H. R., Su, C., Helvering, L. M., & Kulkarini, N. H. et al. (2007). DNA microarray data integration by ortholog gene analysis reveals potential molecular mechanisms of estrogen-dependent growth of human uterine fibroids. *BMC Women's Health, 7*(1), 5. doi:10.1186/1472-6874-7-5 PMID:17407572

Welter, D., Macarthur, J., Morales, J., Burdett, T., Hall, P., & Junkins, H. et al. (2014). The NHGRI GWAS Catalog, a curated resource of SNP-trait associations. *Nucleic Acids Research, 42*(1), D1001–D1006. doi:10.1093/nar/gkt1229 PMID:24316577

Werner, T., Motyka, V., Laucou, V., Smets, R., Onckelen, H. V., & Schmülling, T. (2003). Cytokinin-Deficient Transgenic Arabidopsis Plants Show Multiple Developmental Alterations Indicating Opposite Functions of Cytokinins in the Regulation of Shoot and Root Meristem Activity. *The Plant Cell, 15*(11), 2532–2550. doi:10.1105/tpc.014928 PMID:14555694

West, C., & Rosenstein, B. S. (2010). Establishment of a Radiogenomics Consortium. *International Journal of Radiation Oncology*Biology*Physics, 76*(5), 1295-1296. doi:10.1016/j.ijrobp.2009.12.017

West, C. M. (1995). Invited review: Intrinsic radiosensitivity as a predictor of patient response to radiotherapy. *The British Journal of Radiology, 68*(812), 827–837. doi:10.1259/0007-1285-68-812-827 PMID:7551778

West, C. M. L., Elliott, R. M., & Burnet, N. G. (2007). The Genomics Revolution and Radiotherapy. *Clinical Oncology, 19*(6), 470–480. doi:10.1016/j.clon.2007.02.016 PMID:17419040

Westerhoff, H. V., & Palsson, B. O. (2004). The evolution of molecular biology into systems biology. *Nature Biotechnology, 22*(10), 1249–1252. doi:10.1038/nbt1020 PMID:15470464

Weston, A. D., & Hood, L. (2004). Systems biology, proteomics and the future of health care: Toward predictive, preventative and personalized medicine. *Journal of Proteome Research, 3*(2), 179–196. doi:10.1021/pr0499693 PMID:15113093

Wiegers, T. C., Davis, A. P., Cohen, K. B., Hirschman, L., & Mattingly, C. J. (2009). Text mining and manual curation of chemical-gene-disease networks for the comparative toxicogenomics database (CTD). *BMC Bioinformatics*, *10*(1), 326. doi:10.1186/1471-2105-10-326 PMID:19814812

Wigginton, J. E., & Kirschner, D. E. (2001). A model to predict a cell-mediated immune regulatory mechanism during human infection with *Mycobacterium tuberculosis. Journal of Immunology (Baltimore, MD.: 1950)*, *166*(3), 1951–1967. doi:10.4049/jimmunol.166.3.1951 PMID:11160244

Wild, C. P. (2005). Complementing the genome with an "exposome": The outstanding challenge of environmental exposure measurement in molecular epidemiology. *Cancer Epidemiology, Biomarkers & Prevention*, *14*(8), 1847–1850. doi:10.1158/1055-9965.EPI-05-0456 PMID:16103423

Wilkins, M., Pasquali, C., Appel, R., Ou, K., Golaz, O., & Sanchez, J. et al. (1996). From proteins to proteomes: Large scale protein identification by two-dimensional electrophoresis and amino acid analysis. *Nature Biotechnology*, *14*(1), 61–65. doi:10.1038/nbt0196-61 PMID:9636313

Willer, C. J., Li, Y., & Abecasis, G. R. (2010). METAL: Fast and efficient meta-analysis of genomewide association scans. *Bioinformatics (Oxford, England)*, *26*(17), 2190–2191. doi:10.1093/bioinformatics/btq340 PMID:20616382

Willig, J. H., Krawitz, M., Panjamapirom, A., Ray, M. N., Nevin, C. R., & English, T. M. et al. (2013). Closing the Feedback Loop: An Interactive Voice Response System to Provide Follow-up and Feedback in Primary Care Settings. *Journal of Medical Systems*, *37*(2), 1–9. doi:10.1007/s10916-012-9905-4 PMID:23340825

Willmann, J. K., van Bruggen, N., Dinkelborg, L. M., & Gambhir, S. S. (2008). Molecular imaging in drug development. *Nat Rev Drug Discov, 7*(7), 591-607. doi:10.1038/nrd2290

Winder, C., Dunn, W., & Goodacre, R. (2011). TARDIS-based microbial metabolomics: Time and relative differences in systems. *Trends in Microbiology*, *19*(7), 315–322. doi:10.1016/j.tim.2011.05.004 PMID:21664817

Winham, S. J., & Biernacka, J. M. (2013). Gene-environment interactions in genome-wide association studies: Current approaches and new directions. *Journal of Child Psychology and Psychiatry, and Allied Disciplines, 54*(10), 1120–1134. doi:10.1111/jcpp.12114 PMID:23808649

Wirth, H. (n.d.). *Analysis of large-scale molecular biological data using self-organizing maps.* Available online: http://www.qucosa.de/fileadmin/data/qucosa/documents/10129/Dissertation%20Henry%20Wirth.pdf

Wirth, H., von Bergen, M., & Binder, H. (2012). Mining SOM expression portraits: Feature selection and integrating concepts of molecular function. *BioData Mining, 5,* 18.

Wirth, H., Çakir, M., Hopp, L., & Binder, H. (2014). Analysis of MicroRNA Expression Using Machine Learning. *Methods in Molecular Biology (Clifton, N.J.)*, *1107*, 257–278. doi:10.1007/978-1-62703-748-8_16 PMID:24272443

Wirth, H., Loeffler, M., von Bergen, M., & Binder, H. (2011). Expression cartography of human tissues using self organizing maps. *BMC Bioinformatics*, *12*(1), 306. doi:10.1186/1471-2105-12-306 PMID:21794127

Wittmann, A. (2012). *When To Pick Up Cloud As A Tool.* Retrieved January, 2014, from http://www.informationweek.com/it-leadership/when-to-pick-up-cloud-as-a-tool/d/d-id/1103313

Wolberg, W. (1991). *Wisconsin Breast Cancer Database.* University of Wisconsin Hospitals Madison. Retrieved from http://archive.ics.uci.edu/ml/machine-learning-databases/breast-cancer-wisconsin/breast-cancer-wisconsin.names

Wolpin, B. M., Kraft, P., Gross, M., Helzlsouer, K., Bueno-de-Mesquita, H. B., & Steplowski, E. et al. (2010). Pancreatic cancer risk and ABO blood group alleles: Results from the pancreatic cancer cohort consortium. *Cancer Research*, *70*(3), 1015–1023. doi:10.1158/0008-5472.CAN-09-2993 PMID:20103627

Wong, M. Y., Day, N. E., Bashir, S. A., & Duffy, S. W. (1999). Measurement error in epidemiology: the design of validation studies I: univariate situation. *Statistics in Medicine*, *18*(21), 2815–2829. doi:10.1002/(SICI)1097-0258(19991115)18:21<2815::AID-SIM280>3.0.CO;2-# PMID:10523744

Wong, M. Y., Day, N. E., Luan, J. A., Chan, K. P., & Wareham, N. J. (2003). The detection of gene-environment interaction for continuous traits: Should we deal with measurement error by bigger studies or better measurement? *International Journal of Epidemiology*, *32*(1), 51–57. doi:10.1093/ije/dyg002 PMID:12690008

Wong, M. Y., Day, N. E., Luan, J. A., & Wareham, N. J. (2004). Estimation of magnitude in gene-environment interactions in the presence of measurement error. *Statistics in Medicine*, *23*(6), 987–998. doi:10.1002/sim.1662 PMID:15027084

Wong, M. Y., Day, N. E., & Wareham, N. J. (1999). Measurement error in epidemiology: the design of validation studies II: bivariate situation. *Statistics in Medicine*, *18*(21), 2831–2845. doi:10.1002/(SICI)1097-0258(19991115)18:21<2831::AID-SIM282>3.0.CO;2-3 PMID:10523745

Woods, N. F. (2007). Multidisciplinary, Interdisciplinary and Transdisciplinary Approaches to Women's Health Research: A View from the Seattle Midlife Women's Health Study. *Korean J Women Health Nurs*, *13*(4), 237–224.

WorldMedicalAssociation. (2013). World Medical Association declaration of Helsinki: Ethical principles for medical research involving human subjects. *Journal of the American Medical Association*.

Wouters, B. G. (2008). Proteomics: Methodologies and Applications in Oncology. *Seminars in Radiation Oncology*, *18*(2), 115–125. doi:10.1016/j.semradonc.2007.10.008 PMID:18314066

Wright, A., Sittig, D. F., Ash, J. S., Sharma, S., Pang, J. E., & Middleton, B. (2009). Clinical Decision Support Capabilities of Commercially-available Clinical Information Systems. *Journal of the American Medical Informatics Association*, *16*(5), 637–644. doi:10.1197/jamia.M3111 PMID:19567796

Wruck, W., Peuker, M., & Regenbrecht, C. R. A. (2012). Data management strategies for multinational large-scale systems biology projects. *Briefings in Bioinformatics*, *15*(1), 65–78. doi:10.1093/bib/bbs064 PMID:23047157

Wu, C., Miao, X., Huang, L., Che, X., Jiang, G., & Yu, D. et al. (2011). Genome-wide association study identifies five loci associated with susceptibility to pancreatic cancer in Chinese populations. *Nature Genetics*, *44*(1), 62–66. doi:10.1038/ng.1020 PMID:22158540

Wu, J., Devlin, B., Ringquist, S., Trucco, M., & Roeder, K. (2010). Screen and clean: A tool for identifying interactions in genome-wide association studies. *Genetic Epidemiology*, *34*(3), 275–285. PMID:20088021

Wu, M. C., Lee, S., Cai, T., Li, Y., Boehnke, M., & Lin, X. (2011). Rare-Variant Association Testing for Sequencing Data with the Sequence Kernel Association Test. *American Journal of Human Genetics*, *89*(1), 82–93. doi:10.1016/j.ajhg.2011.05.029 PMID:21737059

Wu, M. C., Maity, A., Lee, S., Simmons, E. M., Harmon, Q. E., & Lin, X. et al. (2013). Kernel Machine SNP-Set Testing Under Multiple Candidate Kernels. *Genetic Epidemiology*, *37*(3), 267–275. doi:10.1002/gepi.21715 PMID:23471868

Wylie, K. M., Weinstock, G. M., & Storch, G. A. (2012). Emerging view of the human virome. *Translational Research; the Journal of Laboratory and Clinical Medicine*, *160*(4), 283–290. doi:10.1016/j.trsl.2012.03.006 PMID:22683423

Wyndaele, M., & Wyndaele, J. J. (2006). Incidence, prevalence and epidemiology of spinal cord injury: What learns a worldwide literature survey? *Spinal Cord*, *44*(9), 523–529. doi:10.1038/sj.sc.3101893 PMID:16389270

Xiao, F., Zuo, Z., Cai, G., Kang, S., Gao, X., & Li, T. (2009). miRecords: An integrated resource for microRNA-target interactions. *Nucleic Acids Research*, *37*(Database issue), D105–D110. doi:10.1093/nar/gkn851 PMID:18996891

Xie, B., Ding, Q., Han, H., & Wu, D. (2013). miRCancer: A microRNA-cancer association database constructed by text mining on literature. *Bioinformatics (Oxford, England)*, *29*(5), 638–644. doi:10.1093/bioinformatics/btt014 PMID:23325619

Xie, X., & Beni, G. (1991). A validity measure for fuzzy clustering. *IEEE Transactions on* Pattern Analysis and Machine Intelligence, *13*, 841–847.

Xu, C., Tachmazidou, I., Walter, K., Ciampi, A., Zeggini, E., & Greenwood, C. M. T. (2014). Estimating Genome-Wide Significance for Whole-Genome Sequencing Studies: Genome-Wide Significance for Rare Variants. *Genetic Epidemiology*, 38(4), 281–290. doi:10.1002/gepi.21797 PMID:24676807

Yamaguchi, Y., Huffaker, A., Bryan, A. C., Tax, F. E., & Ryan, C. A. (2010). PEPR2 Is a Second Receptor for the Pep1 and Pep2 Peptides and Contributes to Defense Responses in *Arabidopsis*. *The Plant Cell*, 22(2), 508–522. doi:10.1105/tpc.109.068874 PMID:20179141

Yamamoto, K., Kudo, T., Konagaya, A., & Matsumoto, Y. (2004). Use of morphological analysis in protein name recognition. *Journal of Biomedical Informatics*, 37(6), 471–482. doi:10.1016/j.jbi.2004.08.001 PMID:15542020

Yang, H. H., Hu, N., Wang, C., Ding, T., Dunn, B. K., & Goldstein, A. M. et al. (2010). Influence of genetic background and tissue types on global DNA methylation patterns. *PLoS ONE*, 5(2), e9355. doi:10.1371/journal.pone.0009355 PMID:20186319

Yang, H., Spasic, I., Keane, J. A., & Nenadic, G. (2009). A text mining approach to the prediction of disease status from clinical discharge summaries. *Journal of the American Medical Informatics Association*, 16(4), 596–600. doi:10.1197/jamia.M3096 PMID:19390098

Yang, Q., Kathiresan, S., Lin, J.-P., Tofler, G. H., & O'Donnell, C. J. (2007). Genome-wide association and linkage analyses of hemostatic factors and hematological phenotypes in the Framingham Heart Study. *BMC Medical Genetics*, 8(Suppl 1), S12. doi:10.1186/1471-2350-8-S1-S12 PMID:17903294

Yang, X., Cao, A., & Song, Q. (2006). A New Cluster Validity for Data Clustering. *Neural Processing Letters*, 23(3), 325–344. doi:10.1007/s11063-006-9005-x

Yang, Z., Ren, F., Liu, C., He, S., Sun, G., & Gao, Q. et al. (2010). dbDEMC: A database of differentially expressed miRNAs in human cancers. *BMC Genomics*, 11(Suppl 4), 55. doi:10.1186/1471-2164-11-S4-S5 PMID:21143814

Yanpeng, L., Honfei, L., & Zhihao, Y. (2007). Two Approaches for Biomedical Text Classification. In *Proceedings of International Conference on Bioinformatics and Biomedical Engineering*, (pp. 310-313). IEEE.

Yan, Q. (2005). Biomedical informatics methods in pharmacogenomics. *Methods in Molecular Medicine*, 108, 459–486. PMID:16028700

Yao, F., Coquery, J., & Le Cao, K. A. (2012). Independent Principal Component Analysis for biologically meaningful dimension reduction of large biological data sets. *BMC Bioinformatics*, 13(1), 24. doi:10.1186/1471-2105-13-24 PMID:22305354

Yao, Z., Weinberg, Z., & Ruzzo, W. L. (2006). CMfinder - a covariance model based RNA motif finding algorithm. *Bioinformatics (Oxford, England)*, 22(4), 445–452. doi:10.1093/bioinformatics/btk008 PMID:16357030

Yates, J., & Washburn, M. (2000). Analysis of microbial proteome. *Current Opinion in Microbiology*, 3(3), 292–297. doi:10.1016/S1369-5274(00)00092-8 PMID:10851159

Yau, N. (2013). *Data points visualization that means something*. Hoboken, NJ: Wiley.

Yeung, K., Fraley, C., Murua, A., Raftery, A., & Ruzzo, W. (2001). Model-based clustering and data transformations for gene expression data. *Bioinformatics (Oxford, England)*, 17(10), 977–987. doi:10.1093/bioinformatics/17.10.977 PMID:11673243

Yip, A. M., & Horvath, S. (2007). Gene network interconnectedness and the generalized topological overlap measure. *BMC Bioinformatics*, 8(1), 22. doi:10.1186/1471-2105-8-22 PMID:17250769

Yoon, K., Lee, S., Han, T. S., Moon, S. Y., Yun, S. M., & Kong, S. H. et al. (2013). Comprehensive genome- and transcriptome-wide analyses of mutations associated with microsatellite instability in Korean gastric cancers. *Genome Research*, 23(7), 1109–1117. doi:10.1101/gr.145706.112 PMID:23737375

Young, S. (2014). Does Illumina have the first $1000 genome? *MIT Technology Review*. Retrieved January 29, 2014 from http://www.technologyreview.com/news/523601/does-illumina-have-the-first-1000-genome/

Young, D., Stark, J., & Kirschner, D. (2008). Systems biology of persistent infection: Tuberculosis as a case study. *Nature Reviews Systems Microbiology*, 6(7), 520–528. doi:10.1038/nrmicro1919 PMID:18536727

Yu, B., Zheng, Y., Alexander, D., Morrison, A. C., Coresh, J., & Boerwinkle, E. (2014). Genetic Determinants Influencing Human Serum Metabolome among African Americans. *PLOS Genetics*, *10*(3), e1004212. doi:10.1371/journal.pgen.1004212 PMID:24625756

Yu, J., Mani, R. S., Cao, Q., Brenner, C. J., Cao, X., Wang, X., & Chinnaiyan, A. M. (2010). An integrated network of androgen receptor, polycomb, and TMPRSS2-ERG gene fusions in prostate cancer progression. *Cancer Cell*, *17*(5), 443–454. doi:10.1016/j.ccr.2010.03.018 PMID:20478527

Yu, S. L., Chen, H. Y., Chang, G. C., Chen, C. Y., Chen, H. W., & Singh, S. et al. (2008). MicroRNA signature predicts survival and relapse in lung cancer. *Cancer Cell*, *13*(1), 48–57. doi:10.1016/j.ccr.2007.12.008 PMID:18167339

Zaidi, H., & El Naqa, I. (2010). PET-guided delineation of radiation therapy treatment volumes: A survey of image segmentation techniques. *European Journal of Nuclear Medicine and Molecular Imaging*, *37*(11), 2165–2187. doi:10.1007/s00259-010-1423-3 PMID:20336455

Zhang, B., & Horvath, S. (2005). A general framework for weighted gene co-expression network analysis. *Statistical Applications in Genetics and Molecular Biology, 4*.

Zhang, X., He, H., Ding, L., Baye, T. M., Kurowski, B. G., & Martin, L. J. (2011). Family- and population-based designs identify different rare causal variants. *BMC Proceedings*, *5*(Suppl 9), S36.

Zhang, G. Y., & Block, D. E. (2009). Integration of Data Mining Into a Nonlinear Experimental Design Approach for Improved Performance. *AIChE Journal. American Institute of Chemical Engineers*, *55*(11), 3017–3021. doi:10.1002/aic.11955

Zhang, G., Huang, S., Duan, Q., Shu, W., Hou, Y., & Zhu, S. et al. (2013). Application of a hybrid model for predicting the incidence of tuberculosis in Hubei, China. *PLoS ONE*, *8*(11), e80969. doi:10.1371/journal.pone.0080969 PMID:24223232

Zhang, W., Li, F., & Nie, L. (2010). Integrating multiple 'omics' analysis for microbial biology: Application and methodologies. *Microbiology*, *156*(2), 287–301. doi:10.1099/mic.0.034793-0 PMID:19910409

Zhang, X., Huang, S., Sun, W., & Wang, W. (2012). Rapid and robust resampling-based multiple-testing correction with application in a genome-wide expression quantitative trait loci study. *Genetics*, *190*(4), 1511–1520. doi:10.1534/genetics.111.137737 PMID:22298711

Zhang, X., Huang, S., Zou, F., & Wang, W. (2010). TEAM: Efficient two-locus epistasis tests in human genome-wide association study. *Bioinformatics (Oxford, England)*, *26*(12), i217–i227. doi:10.1093/bioinformatics/btq186 PMID:20529910

Zhang, Y., De, S., Garner, J. R., Smith, K., Wang, S. A., & Becker, K. G. (2010). Systematic analysis, comparison, and integration of disease based human genetic association data and mouse genetic phenotypic information. *BMC Medical Genomics*, *3*(1), 1. doi:10.1186/1755-8794-3-1 PMID:20092628

Zhang, Y., & Liu, J. S. (2007). Bayesian inference of epistatic interactions in case-control studies. *Nature Genetics*, *39*(9), 1167–1173. doi:10.1038/ng2110 PMID:17721534

Zhang, Y., Shen, X., & Pan, W. (2013). Adjusting for Population Stratification in a Fine Scale With Principal Components and Sequencing Data. *Genetic Epidemiology*, *37*(8), 787–801. doi:10.1002/gepi.21764 PMID:24123217

Zheng, T., Wang, H., & Lo, S.-H. (2006). Backward Genotype-Trait Association (BGTA)-Based Dissection of Complex Traits in Case-Control Designs. *Human Heredity*, *62*(4), 196–212. doi:10.1159/000096995 PMID:17114886

Zheng, X., Pan, C., Diao, Y., You, Y., Yang, C., & Hu, Z. (2013). Development of microsatellite markers by transcriptome sequencing in two species of Amorphophallus (Araceae). *BMC Genomics*, *14*(1), 490. doi:10.1186/1471-2164-14-490 PMID:23870214

Zhou, W., Torvik, V. I., & Smalheiser, N. R. (2006). ADAM: Another database of abbreviations in MEDLINE. *Bioinformatics (Oxford, England)*, *22*(22), 2813–2818. doi:10.1093/bioinformatics/btl480 PMID:16982707

Zhu, H. J., Bogdanov, M. B., Boyle, S. H., Matson, W., Sharma, S., Matson, S., . . . Network, Pharmacometabolomics Res. (2013). Pharmacometabolomics of Response to Sertraline and to Placebo in Major Depressive Disorder - Possible Role for Methoxyindole Pathway. *Plos One, 8*(7).

Zhu, H., Pei, H.-, Zeng, S., Chen, J., Shen, L.-, & Zhong, M.- et al. (2009). Profiling Protein Markers Associated with the Sensitivity to Concurrent Chemoradiotherapy in Human Cervical Carcinoma. *Journal of Proteome Research*, *8*(8), 3969–3976. doi:10.1021/pr900287a PMID:19507834

Ziegler, A. (2009). Genome-wide association studies: Quality control and population-based measures. *Genetic Epidemiology*, *33*(S1Suppl 1), S45–S50. doi:10.1002/gepi.20472 PMID:19924716

Ziegler, A., König, I. R., & Thompson, J. R. (2008). Biostatistical Aspects of Genome-Wide Association Studies. *Biometrical Journal. Biometrische Zeitschrift*, *50*(1), 8–28. doi:10.1002/bimj.200710398 PMID:18217698

Zuber, V., & Strimmer, K. (2011). High-Dimensional Regression and Variable Selection Using CAR Scores. *Statistical Applications in Genetics and Molecular Biology*, *10*(1), 1–27. doi:10.2202/1544-6115.1730

About the Contributors

Baoying Wang is an associate professor in Waynesburg University. She received her PhD degree in Computer Science from North Dakota State University, Master's degree from Minnesota State University of St. Cloud, and Bachelor's degree from Beijing University of Science and Technology. Her research interests include data mining, data warehouse, bioinformatics, parallel computing. She is a member of ACM, ISCA, and SIGMOD. As professional activities, she serves as a reviewer and/or a committee member of many international conferences and journals.

Ruowang Li is pursuing a PhD in Bioinformatics and Genomics at the Pennsylvania State University, University Park, Pennsylvania, USA. He was fascinated by the complexity of the molecular biology, so he studied Biology and Computer Science at Worcester Polytechnic Institute, Worcester, Massachusetts, USA, from 2007 to 2011. His has been developing and applying computational methods to identify the molecular factors affecting individuals' chemotherapeutic drug responses as well as cancer patients' survival status. He is currently a National Science Foundation graduate fellow in the laboratory of Dr. Marylyn Ritchie.

William Perrizo is a Professor of Computer Science at North Dakota State University. He holds a PhD degree from the University of Minnesota, a Master's degree from the University of Wisconsin, and a Bachelor's degree from St. John's University. He has been a Research Scientist at the IBM Advanced Business Systems Division and the U.S. Air Force Electronic Systems Division. His areas of expertise are Data Mining, Knowledge Discovery, Database Systems, Distributed Database Systems, High Speed Computer and Communications Networks, Precision Agriculture, and Bioinformatics. He is a member of ISCA, ACM, IEEE, IAAA, and AAAS.

* * *

Anamika Basu is an Assistant Professor in Dept. of Biochemistry of Gurudas College in Kolkata from the year 2004. She is currently pursuing her research work in the fields of genetics, molecular docking, phylogenetics, plant biology, embryogenesis, bioinformatics, and computational biology. She obtained her MTech degree in Biotechnology from Jadavpur University and MSc degree in Biochemistry from Kalyani University. She teaches Bioinformatics, Genetics, and other subjects in graduate level. She is a co-author of one book chapter and four conference papers. Her research interests include Computational Biology, Bioinformatics, Molecular Modelling, Data Mining, Metabolomics, Proteomics, Molecular Biology, and Plant Biology.

Hans Binder is a Biophysicist by training and worked for many years on biomembranes using computer simulations and optical spectroscopy. Later, his interests changed to bioinformatics where he developed sophisticated calibration methods for microarray expression data using physico-chemical models. Presently, his group at the Interdisciplinary Centre for Bioinformatics of the University of Leipzig is involved in numerous studies discovering the molecular background of complex diseases such as cancer using data-driven mining and hypothesis-driven modeling approaches with the special focus on gene-regulatory mechanisms caused by genetic and epigenetic dysfunctions. For these applications, he, together with his coworkers, develops methods of class discovery, feature selection, and function mining for high-dimensional omics data using machine learning and particularly self-organizing maps. These methods are applied to different cancer entities such as glioma, lymphoma, colon cancer, and melanoma, and also to different kinds of civilization diseases such as adipositas.

Christine Birdwell received her Bachelor of Arts in Chemistry from the University of North Texas in 2009 and joined the graduate program at LSUHSC-Shreveport in 2010. The focus of her research has been on the consequences of Epstein-Barr Virus (EBV) modulation of the host epigenome in epithelial cells, which can lead to a more tumorigenic phenotype even in the absence of viral gene expression. Her work has primarily focused on two members of the Wnt signaling pathway that were identified as having epigenetic modifications and being upregulated in EBV infected and EBV-negative transiently infected cells and their role in the invasive phenotype observed. By identifying markers of past EBV infection that are epigenetically maintained and are involved in a tumorigenic phenotype, they can provide potential therapeutics for EBV-associated carcinomas as well as carcinomas that are EBV-negative but have hallmarks of past EBV infection.

Margot Bjoring completed her undergraduate studies at Rice University in Houston, TX, in 2009, receiving a BA in Linguistics (Cognitive Sciences). Her academic and work experience includes cognitive linguistics, syntax parsing for improving search engines, typography, and graphic design and editing. She currently works as a technical editor and writer for the Center for Quantitative Sciences at the Vanderbilt University Medical Center in Nashville, TN.

Megan Bohensky is an experienced post-doctoral researcher based in Melbourne, Australia. Megan holds academic positions at Monash University and the University of Melbourne, which are two of the top-ranked universities for medicine and public health in Australia. As a health services researcher specialising in the use of existing data, Megan's work concentrates on the evaluation of health outcomes and the application of evidence-based, cost-effective healthcare. Megan has published over 30 peer-reviewed journal articles and numerous government and industry reports in this area and presented her work at conferences in Australia and internationally. Dr. Bohensky holds a PhD from Monash University, a Master's of Public Health specialising in epidemiology and biostatistics from the University of Melbourne, and a Bachelor's degree in Psychology from Stanford University.

Urska Cvek is a Professor of Computer Science and Abe Sadoff Distinguished Chair in Bioinformatics at LSUS at the Louisiana State University in Shreveport, Louisiana. She received a Bachelor's of Economics and Marketing degree from University of Ljubljana, Slovenia, and MBA and ScD degrees in Computer Science from the University of Massachusetts Lowell. She is a faculty member of the Bioinformatics Core for the Center for Molecular and Tumor Virology (CMTV) and the Bioinformatics, Biostatistics, and Computational Biology Core for the Louisiana Biomedical Research Network. Dr. Cvek has actively pursued research in the field of bioinformatics and computational biology with an emphasis on the utilization of visual and analytical tools to biomedical data sets, and she brings unique multidisciplinary expertise and insight. Her work has been funded by the National Institutes of Health, National Science Foundation, and Louisiana Board of Regents. She frequently serves on international conference program committees and is a reviewer for a number of publications.

Andrea Darrel is currently a PhD candidate in the School of Management and Enterprise at the University of Southern Queensland. With a background teaching business studies in China, she is involved in a program of research spanning big data, analytics, and applications for entrepreneurs around the world.

José Valente de Oliveira received the PhD (1996), MSc (1992), and the "Licenciado" degrees in Electrical and Computer Engineering (1988), all from the IST, Technical University of Lisbon. Currently, he is an Assistant Professor at the Faculty of Science and Technology of the University of Algarve with research interests in interdisciplinary areas of computational intelligence and machine learning. José Valente de Oliveira is an Associated Editor of the *Journal of Intelligent & Fuzzy Systems*, IOS Press, and co-editor of the books *Advances in Fuzzy Clustering and Its Applications*, Wiley 2007; and *Human-Computer Interaction: The Agency Perspective*, Springer, 2012. He was a visiting Faculty at University of Alberta (2005), Universidade Nacional de Timor Loro Sae (2005), Carnegie Mellon University (2012), and Universidade Federal do Ceará (2013).

Qin Ding is an Associate Professor in the Department of Computer Science at East Carolina University. She received her BS and MEng in Computer Science from Nanjing University in 1988 and 1991, respectively, and PhD in Computer Science from North Dakota State University in 2002. Her research interests include data mining, database, and bioinformatics. She has published more than 50 refereed articles in those areas, some of which have been highly cited by her peers. Before joining East Carolina University, she was an Assistant Professor in Computer Science at Pennsylvania State University in Harrisburg. She has served as reviewer for journals and program committee member for multiple international conferences in computer science.

Katherine Doering is entering her final year of study at the University of Nebraska College of Law in Lincoln, Nebraska, relocating from St. Louis, Missouri. Prior to law school, she studied Biological Anthropology at the University of Missouri in Columbia and went on to receive a Master's of Education in Curriculum and Instruction in Secondary Science Education. She taught high school biology for a few years before deciding to pursue a career in intellectual property law, with a focus on patent litigation. Katherine is a member of Moot Court and Phi Alpha Delta, as well as numerous other school clubs and organizations.

Issam El Naqa received his BSc (1992) and MSc (1995) in Electrical and Communication Engineering from the University of Jordan, Jordan, and was awarded a first place young investigator award for his MSc work. He worked as a software engineer at the Computer Engineering Bureau (CEB), Jordan, 1995-1996. He was awarded a DAAD scholarship to Germany, where he was a visiting scholar at the

RWTH Aachen, 1996-1998. He completed his PhD (2002) in Electrical and Computer Engineering from Illinois Institute of Technology, Chicago, IL, USA, receiving highest academic distinction award for his PhD work. He completed an MA (2007) in Biology Science from Washington University in St. Louis, St. Louis, MO, USA, where he was pursuing a post-doctoral fellowship in medical physics and was subsequently hired as a Instructor (2005-2007) and then an Assistant Professor (2007-2010) at the departments of Radiation Oncology and the division of Biomedical and Biological Sciences and was an adjunct faculty at the department of Electrical Engineering. He is currently an Associate Professor at McGill University Health Centre/Medical Physics Unit and associate member of at the departments of Physics, Biomedical Engineering, and Experimental Medicine. He is certified Medical Physicist by the American Board of Radiology. He is a recognized expert in the fields of image processing, bioinformatics, computational radiobiology, and treatment outcomes modeling, and has published extensively in these areas. He is an acting member of several academic and professional societies, which include IEEE, AAPM, ASTRO, ESTRO, and COMP, and participates in their meetings and serves in their task groups. His research has been funded by several federal and private grants and serves as a peer reviewer and associate editor for several leading international journals in his areas of expertise. He is currently a designated FRSQ and CIHR scholar.

Paulo Fazendeiro holds a PhD in Computer Science and Engineering (University of Beira Interior, Portugal). Currently, he is an Assistant Professor and course director of the Bioengineering BSc at the Informatics Department of the University of Beira Interior. His research interests encompass Bioinformatics, Computational Intelligence and Granular Computing including the application of fuzzy set theory and fuzzy systems, evolutionary algorithms, multi-objective optimization and clustering techniques. Dr. Fazendeiro is member of the Pattern and Image Analysis group of the Instituto de Telecomunicações (Portuguese Telecommunications Institute) and he is also a collaborator of the Laboratory of Informatics, Systems, and Parallelism.

Dennis S. Fernandez, Managing Partner Fernandez & Associates, LLP, has over 20 years of experience in Silicon Valley and High-Tech Industry, as a patent prosecutor and intellectual property litigator, a venture capitalist, and an engineering manager. He specializes in developing offensive and defensive patent strategies for start-up electronics, software and biotech companies, and their investors. Dennis serves as strategic advisor to leading venture capital firms, including Sevin Rosen, Venrock, Charles River Ventures, and Walden International. Representative clients include Marvell Technology, SiRF Technology, Ayala Corporation, Stanford University, and Northwestern University, as well as various start-up companies acquired by Cisco, Broadcom, Ciena, and Cadence Design Systems. He also serves on the Editorial Board of the *Nanotechnology Law & Business Journal*, the Board of Directors of the Association of Patent Law Firms, and the Science and Technology Advisory Council. Previously, Dennis served on a consultancy with the United Nations Development Programme on Asian economic development. Dennis is also an inventor of several U.S. and international patents in the areas of digital television, sensor networks, and bioinformatics. He has an Electrical Engineering degree from Northwestern University, a law degree from Suffolk University Law School, and is a Registered U.S. Patent Attorney.

Mary Galea is Professorial Fellow in the Department of Medicine (Royal Melbourne Hospital) at the University of Melbourne. She was previously Foundation Professor of Clinical Physiotherapy at the University of Melbourne and Director of the Rehabilitation Sciences Research Centre at Austin Health.

She is a physiotherapist and neuroscientist whose research program includes both laboratory-based and clinical projects with the overall theme of control of voluntary movement by the brain, and factors that promote recovery following nervous system damage. Professor Galea is currently the lead investigator on a large multi-site program of research, SCIPA (Spinal cord injury and physical activity), investigating the effects of exercise after spinal cord injury.

Philip Groth has a Master's degree in Bioinformatics and a PhD in Computer Science from the Humboldt-University of Berlin. After working on yield prediction in genetically modified plants for two years, he assumed a position as research scientist in the Oncology department of Bayer Pharma AG in Berlin. In 2013, he assumed a position as IT Business Partner at Bayer Pharma AG, coordinating IT project portfolio for Oncology and Genomics. He lives in Berlin, Germany, with his wife and two children and in his spare time enjoys sailing and horseback riding.

Yan Guo is an assistant professor at the Department of Cancer Biology, Vanderbilt University. He is currently serving as the Technical Director of Bioinformatics for Vanderbilt Technologies for Advanced Genomics Analysis and Research Design (VANGARD). He received his PhD in Computer Science with a focus on Bioinformatics from the University of South Carolina. His research focus is development of bioinformatics methodology and analysis approaches for high dimensional genomic data, currently, primarily on next generation sequencing analysis and interpretation.

Leng Han received his BS degree in Biotechnology from Wuhan University, Hubei, China, in 2005, and he then obtained his PhD degree in genetics from Kunming Institute of Zoology, Chinese Academy of Sciences, Kunming, China, in 2010. He then conducted research as a Postdoc Fellow at Stanford University, Stanford, CA. He currently works at MD Anderson Cancer Center, Houston, TX, USA. His research interests focus on interpretation of the mechanism of complex diseases, including cancer and cardiovascular diseases, through high-throughput technologies, such as Next-Generation Sequencing (NGS) and microarray.

Timothy T. Hardie is an Associate Professor of Management and Organizational Theory at the Faculty of Business Administration, at Lakehead University's Thunder Bay, Ontario (Canada) campus. Professor Hardie's research focuses on the management and organizational issues surrounding success in service delivery (including data management). Both qualitative and quantitative research themes have included international educational service delivery, the theory behind knowledge flow and organizational size, as well as work on the professional management of international service businesses. His work has been published in the *International Journal of Management in Education*, the *Journal of Intellectual Capital*, the *International Journal of Organisational Behaviour*, the *Journal of Comparative International Management*, the *International Journal of Teaching and Case Studies*, and the *Journal of Knowledge Management*.

Heng Bee Hoon has been the director of Health Services and Outcomes Research (HSOR), National Healthcare Group, Singapore, since its establishment in 2005. Under her guidance, HSOR has rapidly grown into a department providing the best available evidence for decision-making and knowledge translation, building capacity and advancing knowledge in health services research. She leads a multidisciplinary research team including evaluation research, medical informatics, heath economics, and operations research. One of her recent projects is leading HSOR providing critical support to population health management of National Healthcare Group and beyond using multiple innovative techniques such as big data analytics and interactive visualization.

Lydia Hopp studied Biomathematics. Afterwards, she started working as a PhD student in the group of Hans Binder at the Interdisciplinary Centre for Bioinformatics, Leipzig University. She is interested in transcriptional regulation and dysfunction in disease and ageing driven by epigenetic factors. Therefore, a method for integrating different omics data using machine learning is being set up.

Margee Hume specialises in service experience mapping and innovation and IT service management. Her focus is on sustainable work communities research. She is the Campus Academic Coordinator for Research Development at Springfield Campus USQ and is a leader on the Collaborative Research Network: Digital futures. She is a member of the Australian Centre for Sustainable Business Development and the Australian Digital Futures Institute.

Mitsuo Iwadate was born in 1973. He has received BS, MS, and PhD in Biotechnology in 1995, 1997, and 2000, respectively, from Tokyo University of Agriculture and Technology. Then he became Research Associate and Assistant Professor in Department of Biomolecular Design, School of Pharmaceutical Science, Kitasato University, in 2000 and 2003, respectively. Then he moved to Department of Biological Sciences at Chuo University in 2008. His major research interest is computational inference of protein tertiary structure.

Jami Jackson is currently a PhD student in Statistics at NC State University and a recipient of the National Science Foundation Graduate Research Fellowship. She was previously funded by the NCSU Biostatistics Training in the Omics Era training grant 5T32GM081057. She is a graduate of Columbia University with a bachelor's degree in Psychology and a concentration in the Pre-Medical Sciences. She worked at Memorial Sloan-Kettering Cancer Center for five years in clinical research and decided to pursue her PhD in Statistics after being exposed to the diverse biostatistical challenges in healthcare. She is currently a member of the Eastern North American Region (ENAR) Council for Emerging and New Statisticians to help ENAR better serve students and recent graduates. She is interested in statistical genetics research and big data problems.

Amandeep Kaur Kahlon, PhD Research Associate, Biotechnology Division, Central Institute of Medicinal and Aromatic Plants (Council of Scientific and Industrial Research), did her BSc (Zoology, Botany, and Chemistry) at University of Delhi, New Delhi, in 2001 and MSc in Toxicology at Jamia Hamdard University, New Delhi, in 2004. Afterwards, she joined Department of Medicine, AIIMS, New Delhi in 2004 and worked as Junior Research Fellow on "Efficacy and Safety of Mw Vaccine on Pulmonary Tuberculosis Patients." Thereafter, she joined JNU PhD programme of CSIR-CIMAP, Lucknow, Uttar Pradesh in 2007 and was awarded with a doctorate degree in 2013 from Jawaharlal Nehru University, New Delhi. She worked under the supervision of Dr. Ashok Sharma on "Molecular Interaction Studies of Antibacterial Phytomolecules against Human Pathogen *Staphylococcus Aureus*" through bioinformatics and molecular biology approaches. Her areas of interest include Drug Discovery,

Structural Biology, Human Pathogens, Gene Regulation, Immunomodulation, and Infection Biology (host-pathogen interaction). She has more than 6 years of experience in microbiology and bioinformatics. At present, she is working as Research Associate at CSIR-CIMAP, Lucknow, Uttar Pradesh, India, on prediction models of *Mycobacterium tuberculosis* through bioinformatics approaches.

Phillip C. S. R. Kilgore is a native Louisianan holding a BS in Computer Science (LSU Shreveport, 2008) and an MS in Computer Systems Technology (LSU-S, 2012). His research interests include high-performance computing, machine learning, human-computer interaction, information visualization, and bioinformatics. He was first involved in scientific research as part of an undergraduate research program sponsored by LSU-S; since then, he has published on resolving point-occlusion in high-dimensional data visualization with self-organizing maps, a panoramic range slider control, and a framework for high-throughput motif elicitation. His Master's thesis, "Optimization of iNNfovis Algorithms via Concurrent Programming," addresses the simulation of self-organizing maps as applied to classical visualization techniques in a distributed computational environment. He is presently employed as a research scientist for the Louisiana Biomedical Research Network at LSU Shreveport's Computer Science Department.

Matthew Knabel, PhD, joined Fernandez & Associates, LLP, as an IP Intern in 2013. There, he helped to expand the firm's utility patent portfolio by drafting new patent applications. He also aided with Reply Briefs to the USPTO and PTAB. A Registered Patent Agent, Dr. Knabel earned his undergraduate degree in Biology from the Johns Hopkins University and his PhD in Human Genetics & Molecular Biology from the Johns Hopkins University School of Medicine. Dr. Knabel's Doctoral thesis focused on molecular and therapeutic approaches to understand dysregulation of microRNAs in liver fibrosis. He is currently a Patent Analyst at Landon IP, Inc., where he examines novelty, patentability, and industrial applicability of life science PCT Applications.

Kathrin Lembcke studied Mathematics. Afterwards, she started working as a PhD student in the group of Hans Binder at the Interdisciplinary Centre for Bioinformatics, Leipzig University. She is interested in machine learning and methods of classification and discrimination particularly in high dimension data.

Ninte Malats is head of the Genetic and Molecular Epidemiology Group at the Spanish National Cancer Research Centre (CNIO), since September 2007. She was one of the first scientists working in genetic and molecular epidemiology in Spain by coordinating a national multicentre project on the molecular epidemiology of pancreatic cancer. She was Visiting Scientist at the International Agency for Research on Cancer (IARC-WHO) in Lyon, France, where she trained until 1998 in Genetic Epidemiology. Before moving to CNIO, Dr. Malats was a Scientist at the CREAL-IMIM, Barcelona, leading and participating in national and international competitively funded projects. She also coordinated the Spanish research network on bladder cancer. At present, she leads large multidisciplinary and international case-control studies integrating scientific interests and data to identify factors involved in bladder and pancreatic cancer development and progression. Dr. Malats is also chair of the COST Action EU-Pancreas.

Ravi Mathur is currently a PhD student in Bioinformatics working on novel algorithms for pathway analysis. Furthermore, he has worked on projects comprising the development of novel processes for evolutionary algorithms and discovering database information. He received Master's and Bachelor's degrees in Biomedical Engineering and Bioengineering, respectively, from Binghamton University. As a Master's student, he worked on Data Mining research using evolutionary algorithms for classification problems. He has published several peer-reviewed papers and has given presentations at national conferences. He is interested in further developing the software available for pathway analysis including inferring pathways using data. Furthermore, he is interested in exploring analysis methods that combine data from different technologies together.

Jane Moon is an honorary associate with RMIT, teaches Haematology, Health Informatics, and Laboratory Management to both undergraduate and postgraduate students. She also works as a medical laboratory scientist at the Austin Health, a teaching hospital to the University of Melbourne. She has a diverse background of immunology, linguistics, and an international MBA. She has a degree in medical science (Immunology), and a Master of Arts (Linguistics) from the University of Melbourne; graduate diploma in Education, graduate diploma in Health Administration and Business Studies and a MBA from LaTrobe University, as well as a graduate certificate in European business studies from ESC-Rouen, France, and a postgraduate diploma in Immunology, and a graduate diploma in Computer Science, Master of Information Management Systems from Monash University, Australia. She is a member of the Australian Institute of Medical Science. She is a PhD candidate at the Department of Medicine, University of Melbourne; her project involves "developing a conceptual model for patients' with chronic diseases for a better health outcome." She has a keen interest in health informatics, impact of ICT on health management and self-efficacy.

Alison Motsinger-Reif is an Associate Professor in the Bioinformatics Research Center and the Department of Statistics at North Carolina State University. The primary goal of her research is the development of computational methods to detect genetic risk factors of common, complex traits in human populations. As the field of human genetics increasingly accepts a complex model of phcnotypic development that involves many genetic and environment factors, it is increasingly important to develop analytical strategies that incorporates this complexity. Data collected from different physiological compartments that represent biological flux across time and space (such as genetic, proteomic, and environmental data) will need to be incorporated to gain a fuller understanding of the biological mechanism underlying complex phenotypes. Her research is focused on the development of and application of methods to detect such complex predictive models in high-throughput "-omics" data.

Yoshiki Murakami is an associate professor of Medical Science at Graduate School of Medicine, Osaka City University, Osaka, Japan. He majored in Medical Science at the Kanazawa University, Ishikawa, Japan, in 1992, and attended Graduate School of Medicine, Kyoto Prefectural University, Kyoto, as an exchange student, and received a PhD in Medical Science from the Department of Pathology at Kyoto Prefectural University of Medicine in 1999. He has studied at French National Institute of Health and Medical Science (INSERM) as research scientist for two years. His research interests include Hepatology and Virology (Hepatitis B Virus and Hepatitis C Virus), as well as clinical application of bioinformatics.

Akira Okamoto is an associate professor in Aichi University of Education and is teaching Microbiology, Immunology, and Nutrition in the course of School Health Sciences. He majored in Bacteriology at Nagoya University Graduate School of Medicine, and received his PhD in 2011. His research focused on genomics and proteomics of bacteria associated with infectious diseases, including group A streptococci, pneumococci, *Staphylococcus aureus*, foodborne pathogen *Bacillus cereus*, and *Legionella pneumophila*. Another interests of his recent works involved hygiene education in school child age. He won an award for "Development of High-Throughput Screening Strategy of Antigens" from a division of Biological Mass Spectrometry, The Mass Spectrometry Society of Japan in 2008.

Ratna Prabha post-graduated in Bioinformatics from Banasthali University, Rajasthan, India. She is pursuing her PhD from Mewar University, Rajasthan, in Bioinformatics on "Whole Genome Approach to Study Cyanobacterial Evolutionary Diversification and Adaptations to Environments." Ms. Prabha is associated with "National Agricultural Bioinformatics Grid (NABG)" project of Indian Council of Agricultural Research (ICAR), India. She has developed various databases and published 11 research papers in international journals and 2 book chapters to her credit. Her current research interest lies in database development, codon usage pattern analysis, whole genome phylogeny, pan-genome analysis, and comparative analysis of prokaryotic genomes, especially cyanobacteria.

Anil Rai is a Principal Scientist for Computer Applications and Head, Center for Agricultural Bioinformatics (CABin) at Indian Agricultural Statistical Research Institute, India. Dr. Rai did his PhD in Agricultural Statistics from Indian Agricultural Research Institute, India. He has more than 20 years of experience of research/teaching/training in the field of sample surveys and computer applications. Dr. Rai has been principal investigator and organizer of 35 consultancy projects, trainings, and workshops, author of 30 project reports and technical manuals in different areas including crop science and production statistics, and has more than 100 publications to his credit.

Gerhard Reuter worked ten years as a network architect and head of an international security team for Bayer. In addition to Firewalls and Proxy Servers, he also focused on Intrusion Prevention Systems and the secure connection of partner companies via virtual private networks. In 2011, he joined the R&D IT team of Bayer as an Engineer and Architect for providing virtualized applications to healthcare researchers. In parallel Gerhard contributed his knowledge of network designs and IT security to optimize the first cloud-based genomic pipelines using the Amazon Cloud (AWS). Gerhard Reuter was born in 1962, lives in Leverkusen, is married with children, and spends his leisure time soaring (motor-) gliders, reading, and jogging.

Anasua Sarkar has completed her PhD work on Bioinformatics in Jadavpur University, Kolkata, India. She was also awarded EMMA-EPU fellowship, 2011, to pursue her research work at LaBRI, University Bordeaux1, France. She is presently an Assistant Professor in IT Department, Government College of Engineering and Leather Technology, Kolkata since 2007. She has published 10 original research papers in peer-reviewed journals. She is also a co-author in 8 book chapters and 17 conference papers. She is also reviewer in *Journal of Parallel and Distributed Computing* (JPDC), Elsevier, and IEEE SMCC-C. She is also a Student Member, ISCB, 2010-2011, SMIEEE in 2014, member CSTA, ACM Chapter, ACM IGUCCS and IAENG. She has worked with INRIA MAGNOME group for 18 months in France for the expansion of Genolevures database for inclusion of PISO and ARAD species. Her research interests include Proteomics, Phylogenetics, Computational Biology, Pattern Recognition, Data Mining, Bioinformatics, and Embedded and Parallel Systems.

Rona S. Scott is currently an Assistant Professor of Microbiology and Immunology at the Louisiana State University Health Sciences Center in Shreveport, Louisiana. She obtained her Bachelor's of Science from the Pennsylvania State University and her PhD from the Department of Biochemistry at the University of North Carolina at Chapel Hill. Her research interests over the last 14 years have been to understand how Epstein-Barr Virus-induced epigenetic alterations lead to virally associated cancer. Her work has been funded by an NIH COBRE grant, an award from the Department of Defense Breast research program, an NIH RO1 grant, and the Louisiana Board of Regents. She is the Director of the Genomics/DNA Array Core for the Center of Molecular and Tumor Virology (CMTV) and scientific advisor for genomics at LSUHSC-S. She uses bioinformatics to analyze the big data generated from microarrays and next-generation sequencing in her research.

Ashok Sharma, PhD, Chief Scientist and Head, Biotechnology Division, Central Institute of Medicinal and Aromatic Plants (Council of Scientific and Industrial Research), is Professor of Biological Sciences in AcSIR (Academy of Scientific and Innovative Research), CSIR, and Adjunct Professor, JNU, New Delhi, for CIMAP-JNU PhD programme. He is also Coordinator of Bioinformatics Centre at CSIR-CIMAP, Lucknow, Uttar Pradesh, India. His research interests includes bioinformatics and computational biology of medicinal and aromatic plants, bioprospection of phytomolecules in infectious diseases and metabolic diseases for human health, metabolic pathway elucidation and modulation, analysis of regulatory elements, DNA barcoding of plants, microRNA, phytoremediation. He has published more than 70 research and review papers, 10 books, and book chapters.

Dhananjaya P. Singh is a Senior Scientist (Biotechnology) with National Bureau of Agriculturally Important Microorganisms, Indian Council of Agricultural Research, India, at Maunath Bhanjan, India. He did his Master's degree at G. B. Pant University of Agriculture & Technology, Pantnagar, India, and PhD in Biotechnology from Banaras Hindu University, India. Research interests of Dr. Singh lie in bioprospecting of metabolites, microbe-mediated stress management in plants, metabolomics-driven search for small molecules, and bioinformatics. He is running National Agricultural Bioinformatics Grid (microbial domain) of ICAR. He has 60 research papers, 1 edited book, 17 book chapters, 15 reviews, and 1 Indian Patent to his credit.

Jeffrey Soar holds a Personal Chair in Human Centred Technology in the School of Management and Enterprise at the University of Southern Queensland. Prof Soar entered academia in 2001 following a career in senior executive roles in healthcare and public safety organisations in Australia and New Zealand. He is a researcher in informatics for ageing and independent living; in 2007, he founded the Queensland Smart Home Initiative that attracted grants and industry support for demonstrator smart homes. His research has translated into national policy in Australia and New Zealand; through international agencies, he developed and implemented information strategy for developing nations.

Y-H. Taguchi was born in 1961. He has received his BS in Applied Physics, MS and Dr Sci in Physics from Tokyo Institute of Technology, Japan, in 1984, 1986, and 1988, respectively. From 1988 to 1997, he was an assistant professor in Tokyo Institute of Technology. Then he moved to Chuo University as an associate professor in 1997. He has been a full professor there from 2006 to the present. His research interests include bioinformatics and nonlinear science.

Kiok-Liang Teow obtained his basic degree in Electrical Engineering, and Master's degree in Industrial & Systems Engineering, both from National University of Singapore. He started his career on operations research with the Ministry of Defence, then joined Defence Science & Technology Agency, and is now with National Healthcare Group (Health Services & Outcomes Research) since 2005. His current work includes analysing healthcare data and providing recommendation. The domain of work includes but not limited to emergency department, inpatient and outpatient. He also conducts training and publishes a few papers. He was the principal investigator for a Health Services Research Competitive Research Grant awarded by Ministry of Health (2012-2013). More recently, he works with his colleagues on analysing large data sets. His research interests are in various operations research methods and data analytics.

Sebastian Thieme studied Bioinformatics at the Free University of Berlin from 2006 to 2012. During his Master's studies, he worked as a student assistant at the Max Planck Institute for Molecular Genetics. He contributed to different projects like the phylogeny of multi-domain proteins and massive parallel RNA-sequencing resulting in two publications. At the end of his Master's studies, he worked as a freelance docent in the field of sequence analysis at a consulting company for advanced trainings in Berlin. Later, he got an internship at Bayer HealthCare Pharmaceuticals, which was extended for his Master's Thesis. He developed a novel algorithm for the identification of Fusion proteins in tumor samples, based on the statistical evaluation of CN data, which was published in Bioinformatics. In 2012, he started his PhD in the department of theoretical biophysics at the Humboldt-University zu Berlin, where he works in the field of signal transduction networks complexity.

Marjan Trutschl is Professor of Computer Science at the Louisiana State University in Shreveport, Louisiana. He received his Bachelor of Science and Doctor of Science degrees from Louisiana State University and University of Massachusetts Lowell, respectfully. Dr. Trutschl is the Director of the Bioinformatics Core at the Center for Molecular and Tumor Virology, and serves as a scientific advisor for bioinformatics at Louisiana Health Sciences Center in Shreveport. He has worked on numerous interdisciplinary projects over the past 20 years, most of them in collaboration with the life science community. His projects are funded by the National Institutes of Health, Department of Defense, National Science Foundation, and Louisiana Board of Regents. His main interest is the application of bioinformatics and high-performance computing to large data generated by next-generation sequencing. He is actively pursuing research in the field and is a member of program and organization committees for international conferences and symposia as well as review panels for scientific journals.

Hideaki Umeyama was born in 1944. He has received BS in Pharmaceutical Department of Tokyo University, MS and PhD in the graduate school of Pharmaceutical Department of Tokyo University in 1968, 1970, and 1973, respectively. He has moved to Kitasato University as an assistant professor. Then he became a full professor there in 1988. He has become an honorary professor of Kitasato University in 2010. In the same year, he got the Pharmaceutical Society Prize of Japan. And he has moved to Chuo University as a joint research member. His research interests include bioinformatics, molecular mechanics, and quantum chemistry.

Kristel Van Steen is an associate professor in bioinformatics at the Montefiore Institute of the University of Liartment of Neurobiology & Anatomy. Under the mentoring of Dr. Veronica Tom, her research unit at the GIGA-R (Belgium). She is an honorary professor at the Catholic University of Leuven and the University of Ghent (Belgium). She was a research fellow at the European Organisation for Research and Treatment of Cancer (EORTC, Belgium) and was for two years a post-doctoral research fellow at the Harvard School of Public Health (Boston, USA). Kristel Van Steen received her first PhD in exact sciences (mathematics) at the University of Ghent (Belgium) in 1996 and her second PhD in biomedical sciences (statistical genetics) at Hasselt University/Maastricht University in 2005. Her research interests cover a wide area, from the field of mathematics over biostatistics, towards statistical genetics and bioinformatics (e.g., GxG and GxE interactions, omics-integrated analysis).

Henry Wirth studied Computer Science with specialization in Artificial Intelligence. He was afterwards awarded with a scholarship from Helmholtz scientific society and worked as Doctoral student in the Hans Binder group at the Interdisciplinary Centre for Bioinformatics, Leipzig University. During his graduation, he developed and implemented analytic software tools for intuitive yet comprehensive analysis of large-scale molecular-biological data. After achieving his PhD, he is now working as research fellow at the Centre for Bioinformatics, continuing methodical research and algorithmic development mainly but not solely in the field of cancer transcriptomics.

Di Wu received her BS in Biotechnology from Sichuan University in 2007 and her PhD from East Carolina University, Department of Physiology in 2012. Her research focused on understanding the molecular mechanisms that regulate nerve regenerative responses after injuries. Her thesis studied the functional significance of miRNA pathway in peripheral nerve regeneration following sciatic nerve injury under the direction of Dr. Alexander Murashov. Now a post-doctoral researcher, she works in Drexel University College of Medicine at the Department of Neurobiology & Anatomy. Under the mentoring of Dr. Veronica Tom, her current study is to device combinatory strategies that will tackle different impediments to adult axon regrowth and result in robust nerve regeneration after spinal cord injury.

Boya Xie is a software development engineer at Microsoft in Seattle, Washington. She received her Master's degree in Computer Science from East Carolina University where she discovered her interests in bioinformatics. After graduation, she moved to New York City and worked in investment banking as IT analyst for two year. Albeit the fun living and working experience in New York, Ms. Xie decided to move to Seattle and work at Microsoft to be closer to the most advanced technologies. The miRCancer project was initiated by Ms. Xie as her Master's thesis project, and she has been researching on text mining methods to discover microRNA profiles in human cancers ever since. Besides spending significant spare time in miRCancer project, she also loves kayaking, camping, playing table tennis, and practicing Taiji.

Shilin Zhao received his PhD at 2012 in Shanghai Institutes for Biological Sciences, Chinese Academy of Sciences and now is a research fellow of the Center for Quantitative Sciences at Vanderbilt University. He has comprehensive backgrounds in bioinformatics and proteomics. And his research interest includes development of the next generation sequencing methods and integration analysis for the omics data.

Zhu Zhecheng holds his bachelor and Master's degrees in Information Engineering, Shanghai Jiao Tong University and PhD degree in Industrial and Systems Engineering from National University of Singapore. He joined Health Services and Outcomes Research, National Healthcare Group in 2008 as Operations Research Specialist. His research areas include applied optimization, discrete event simulation, and data visualization, etc. He has extensive project experience in demand projection, capacity planning, patient flow analysis, what-if scenario analysis, and so on. One of his recent projects is supporting population health management of National Healthcare Group in patient profiling, risk group clustering, network connection analysis using techniques such as interactive visualization and geographical information system.

Index